EXPOSITION OF JOHN

An Exposition
of the
Gospel According to

John

In Which
The Sense of the Sacred Text is Given;
Doctrinal and Practical Truths
are Set in a Plain and Easy Light;
Difficult Passages Explained;
Seeming Contradictions Reconciled;
And Whatever is Material in the Various Readings,
and the Several Oriental Versions, is Observed;
The Whole Illustrated with Notes Taken from the
Most Ancient Jewish Writings.

By John Gill

The Newport Commentary Series

The Publication of this book is made
possible through the shared vision of the

Grace Baptist Church, Lebanon, Missouri

This 2003 edition set in 10 point
New Century Schoolbook was
reproduced unabridged utilizing both the
second, corrected edition
(London: George Keith, 1774),
and the third edition
(London: Mathews and Leigh, 1809).

Particular Baptist Press

2766 W. Farm Road 178
Springfield, Missouri 65810

First Printing

Cataloging data:

Gill, John, 1697-1771

Originally Published in volumes one and two of
An Exposition of the New Testament, 3 Vols.
(London: Aaron Ward, 1746-1748)

• Bible Commentaries
• Baptist Doctrinal Works
• Particular Baptists - Great Britain
• Regular Baptists - United States

ISBN 1-888514-21-3

Printed in the United States of America

Contents

Acknowledgments

The publishers extend their thankfulness under God to pastor Don Preusch and the congregation of the Grace Baptist Church in Lebanon, Missouri for their shared vision and support in making the publication of this book possible.

The editor would also like to express his heartfelt gratitude to his friend and pastor Gary Long for the labor of love expended in the Lord's service in the typesetting and formatting of this volume.

We also again appreciate the assistance of pastor Don Fortner of the Grace Baptist Church of Danville, Kentucky for aiding us in supplying the Greek and Hebrew words used in the text.

Illustrations

"Friends of this valuable author:"

Recovering the truth of how the founders of the General Missionary (or Triennial) Convention of Regular Baptists in America viewed the beginnings of the modern missionary movement and the theology of John Gill.

When the General Missionary Convention convened its first triennial session at Philadelphia in May of 1817, Richard Furman, as president of the Convention, in delivering the opening address, expressed his "sentiments of the most ardent gratitude to the God of mercy," at the rising interest shown in the work of the new convention since its formation in 1814. He also included the following remarks on a query still lingering in the minds of the assembled delegates:

> If it be asked, why have missionary efforts been so long deferred? We might answer by asking, why was the Reformation delayed so long? Or, why was not the idea of Bible Institutions, or Sunday schools, and of Tract societies, earlier conceived and brought into efficiency? The truth seems to lie in this single consideration. 'To every thing there is a season, and a time to every purpose under the sun.' Sometimes for reasons which infinite wisdom approves and eternal rectitude will vindicate, the hand of God is hidden in his bosom—while, at other seasons, it is revealed. We have lived to see the period when 'the Lord has made bare his holy arm in the eyes of all the nations;' when minor exhibitions of mercy lose their importance in a glory that excelleth. 'It is a light thing,' saith the Lord, 'that thou shouldest be my servant, to raise up the tribes of Jacob and to preserve the restored of Israel; I will also give thee for a light to the Gentiles, that thou mayest be my salvation to the ends of the earth.'[1]

---

[1] *Proceedings of the General Convention of the Baptist Denomination in the United States at Their First Triennial Meeting, Held in Philadelphia, from the 7th to the 14th of May, 1817* (Philadelphia: Anderson & Meehan, 1817), 127. The last Scripture reference is to Christ, in Isaiah 49:6. "The General Missionary Convention of the Baptist Denomination in the United States of America for Foreign Missions" was formed on May 18, 1814, by 33 delegates from eleven states, 26 of whom were ministers. Due to the distance of travel, the sessions were held every three years, and so the body became popularly known as the "Triennial Convention." This was the American counterpart of the Particular Baptist Missionary Society in England.

Furman's answer in reference to Ecclesiastes 3:1 and God's own timetable in bringing about His purposes could not have been more appropriate. For as it was, this concerted effort in behalf of foreign mission work [2] which began among the Regular Baptists in America in the early years of the nineteenth century, was itself a direct result of the leading of God in what had only recently been brought to fruition in England with the formation of the Particular Baptist Missionary Society in 1792. Through the instrumentality of William Carey, the Christian imperative of taking the gospel "unto all the world" and "making disciples of all nations," [3] was reasserted.

These early Baptists saw no incompatibility whatsoever between their firm belief in the Doctrine of Sovereign grace and worldwide missionary endeavor. Modern historians however, have sought to impose a disjunction between the faith and practice of these early Baptists. For example, in his biography of one of the founders of the Particular Baptist Missionary Society, Samuel Pearce (1766-1799), S. Pearce Carey attempts to explain away his subject's doctrinal convictions, assuring the reader that there was "nothing striking in Pearce's confession of his Faith," that it "followed the formal manner of the time," and was "his least individual document," adding:

> The fact is he was preacher and hymnist rather than abstruse and dogmatic theologian. Needless to say, no Baptist preacher now would announce the staple message of his ministry in any such phrases. Much water has flowed beneath the bridge since 1790. What modern student would make bold to affirm: 'I believe that before the world began God did of His own free and sovereign purpose and grace choose a certain number of the human race unto everlasting salvation, making provision

---

[2] Baptists on both sides of the Atlantic had already been engaged in domestic missionary labors for some time. At the formation of the Massachusetts Baptist Missionary Society on April 29, 1802, the constitution of the society in article VI read: "The object of the Society shall be to furnish occasional preaching, and to promote the knowledge of evangelistic truth in the new settlements within these United States; *or further if circumstances should render it proper*" (emphasis mine). W. H. Eaton, *Historical Sketch of the Massachusetts Baptist Missionary Society and Convention, 1802-1902* (Boston: Mass. Baptist Convention, 1903), 9.

[3] This is the literal meaning of "teach all nations" in Matthew 28:19. While recognizing that the Moravians and others had not only preceded but in some ways influenced Carey, it was mainly through the establishment of the Particular Baptist Missionary Society in England and its resulting mission to India, that the interest in foreign missions among the mainline denominations was aroused. We respectfully dissent from the view of historians such as L. C. Barnes in his *Two Thousand Years of Missions Before Carey* (1902), and uphold the earlier consensus of our forefathers that the Jesuit spread of Roman Catholicism did not constitute a gospel witness.

for this display of His mercy in perfect harmony with the justice of His character, in the covenant of grace.[4]

S. Pearce Carey was not of the same doctrinal stamp as either his namesake Samuel Pearce, nor his great-grandfather, William Carey. In the mission statement drawn up by Carey and his associates at Serampore, India are found the following opening statements:

> The *Redeemer*, in planting us in the heathen nation, rather than in any other, has imposed upon us the cultivation of peculiar qualifications. We are firmly persuaded that Paul might plant and Apollos water, in vain, in any part of the world, did not God give the increase. We are sure that only those who are ordained to eternal life will believe, and that God alone can add to the church such as shall be saved. Nevertheless we cannot but observe with admiration that Paul, the great champion for the glorious doctrines of free and sovereign grace, was the most conspicuous for his personal zeal in the work of persuading men to be reconciled to God. In this respect he is a noble example for our imitation.[5]

It was John Ryland, Jr. who later wrote, "I believe that God himself infused into the mind of Carey that solicitude for the salvation of the heathen which

---

[4] S. Pearce Carey, *Samuel Pearce, A. M., the Baptist Brainerd* (London: The Carey Press, 1913), 96-97. Carey further stated, "Yet probably Pearce meant little more than could have been accepted by Robert Hall [Jr.], for whom, as we have seen, the milk of Calvinism was turning sour." We, on the other hand, will choose to take Pearce at his word, and that he meant what he wrote.

[5] "*Form of Agreement* respecting the *great principles* upon which the Brethren of the mission at Serampore think it is their duty to act in the work of instructing the Heathen, agreed upon at a meeting of the Brethren at Serampore, on Monday, October 7, 1805," in *Periodical Accounts Relative to the Baptist Missionary Society*, III, 199, first paragraph. The Scriptures referred to in this statement are from Acts 13:48, Acts 2:47, and 2 Cor. 5:11, 20. This testimony of the Calvinistic principles on which the Serampore mission was founded is omitted in all of the standard biographies of Carey, but is cited in full in Appendix A of the work by the Dutch Reformed minister Aalbertinus H. Oussoren, *William Carey, Especially His Missionary Principles* (Leiden, Netherlands: A. W. Sijthoff's Uitgeversmaatschappij, 1945), 274-284, English text. In Oussoren's transcription the word *sottish* is erroneously shown as *Scottish* on page 275.

cannot be fairly traced to any other source."[6]

Ryland's statement accords perfectly with Furman's conclusion that the newly awakened interest in foreign missionary endeavor could be traced to "this single consideration," that the "season" and "time" of the Lord's appointing had come. As the Psalmist wrote concerning Zion, God's people, "the time to favor her, yea, *the set time*" had come.[7]

As alluded to earlier, this "set time" which originated in England had its successive parallel in America, with Samuel Pearce urging the American Baptists to form their own missionary society in a letter to William Rogers in 1794.[8] And the unmistakable hand of Providence eventually led men associated with the Philadelphia Association to form the General Missionary Convention in 1814.[9] William R. Williams later recalled that:

> American Baptists had purposed to continue as they had begun, to aid their English brethren by collections raised here and transmitted thither. But God, in his gracious arrangements, raised up Adoniram Judson, a man of high endowments, rare energy, and true piety. He left our shores a Paedobaptist, studied the Bible, and on reaching Serampore was a convert to our views of the ordinances and church. Without further resources from the Paedobaptist body before sustaining him, he was advised to apply to the English Baptists. But God put it into the hearts of him and his fellow-missionary and convert, Luther Rice, to appeal to the American churches. Our own body found themselves suddenly called to a work which they had not planned. It was like Paul's Macedonian voyage, a Providence beckoning and

---

[6] As F. W. Boreham said of Carey, "The map of the world hung in his room, but it only hung in his room because it already hung in his heart." *A Bunch of Everlastings, or Texts That Made History* (New York: The Abingdon Press, 1920), 163-164.

[7] Psalm 102:13; emphasis mine.

[8] Andrew Fuller, compiler, *Memoirs of the Late Rev. Samuel Pearce, A. M.* (Boston: Manning & Loring, 1801), 54. William Rogers was a co-pastor along with Thomas Ustick and Morgan Edwards of the First Baptist Church of Philadelphia. He was also the moderator of the annual session of the Philadelphia Association in 1794, where the motion was made that "all donations for the propagation of the Gospel among the Hindoos, in the East Indies, be forwarded to him." A. D. Gillette, *Minutes of the Philadelphia Baptist Association, 1707-1807* (Philadelphia: A.B.P.S., 1851; Tricentennial Edition by Particular Baptist Press, Springfield, MO, 2002), 298, 303.

[9] It was fitting that the Convention was formed by delegates meeting at the First Baptist Church of Philadelphia, with William Rogers as one of the delegates.

leading the blind by a way which they for themselves had not known.[10]

When William Gammell wrote his history of the work of the General Missionary (or Triennial) Convention, he gave the following summary of the events leading up to its organization:

> The establishment of Mr. and Mrs. Judson in Burmah and the enlistment of the American Baptists in the support of their mission, it has been often observed, were brought about by a train of events of the most remarkable and providential character. No human wisdom or foresight selected the field in which were to be put forth their earliest labors, and no spontaneous charity furnished the means which were to constitute their support. The honor of commencing the missions of the American Baptists, let it be confessed, is to be ascribed rather to the divine Head of the Church, than to any leading movement or agency of the denomination itself. The way was prepared and the field was opened by God alone, and it only remained for true-hearted men to enter in and prosecute the noble work to which they had thus been summoned.
>
>   *   *   *   *   *
>
> Immediately after Messrs. Judson and Rice had avowed their change of sentiments respecting baptism, and had received the rite according to its apostolic form at the hands of Rev. Mr. Ward, they communicated the fact to the Secretary of the American Board of Commissioners, and at the same time stated, that should a missionary society be formed by the Baptists, they were ready to place themselves under its direction in the prosecution of their labors. They also wrote to Rev. Dr. Baldwin, stating the same general facts, and urging the importance of forming a Baptist Missionary Society. The same views were also strongly urged by Dr. Carey and the other missionaries at Serampore. These letters were received at Boston in February, 1813. The intelligence which they contained spread with electric rapidity, and imparted to the spirit of benevolence and the sense of Christian obligation a depth and fervor such as they before had never experienced. Immediately on the receipt of the letter of Mr. Judson, a meeting of several of the leading ministers of Massachusetts

---

[10] William R. Williams, *Lectures on Baptist History* (Philadelphia: A.B.P.S., 1877), 302-303.

was convened at the house of Dr. Baldwin, in Boston, in order to consider the new attitude in which these events had placed the churches. But one sentiment of deep and fervent thankfulness filled the minds of all who were present. The indications of Providence were too plain to be mistaken, and the clergymen who were thus assembled proceeded immediately to form the "Baptist Society for Propagating the Gospel in India and other Foreign Parts." The society was so organized as to admit of its cooperating with any other societies that might be formed for the same purpose in other sections of the country, and one of the articles of its constitution plainly pointed to the organization of a General Convention, composed of delegates from societies in every part of the Union. The formation of this society was the first movement that sprang from the new events in the East, and, though apparently local in its character, is undoubtedly to be regarded as the germ of the Triennial Convention of a later period, which for so long a time managed the missions of the American Baptists.[11]

Other authorities could also be cited, but these will suffice within the brief context of this introduction to propose to the reader that the prevailing consensus among the Regular Baptists in America during the years in which the General Missionary (or Triennial) Convention was established, and in the years preceding the Civil War, was that God, in His own set time, had again called His people to actively pursue a worldwide gospel outreach.[12]

The descriptive words used in the above quotations from Baptists of that day—of God's purpose being "revealed," of finding themselves "suddenly called to a work which they had not planned" by "a Providence beckoning and leading the blind by a way which they for themselves had not known," through a "train of events of the most remarkable and providential character," in which "the indications of Providence were too plain to be mistaken," contrast markedly with the later historical perspective that the modern missionary

---

[11] William Gammell, *A History of American Baptist Missions* (Boston: Gould, Kendall and Lincoln, 1849), 8, 14-15. It might surprise the reader to know that there are over three times the number of Baptist believers in Burma (Myanmar) today as there are in England. See Albert W. Wardin, ed., *Baptists Around the World, A Comprehensive Handbook* (Nashville, TN: Broadman & Holman, 1995), Appendix II, 473-474.

[12] Those who would readily acknowledge that God had prepared the world for the reception of the gospel in ancient times through the institution of the Greek language throughout the Roman Empire often overlook its parallel in the establishment of the British overseas empire which greatly facilitated the spread of the gospel through missionary activity.

movement was a direct result of the Particular Baptists in England becoming freed from "a hard and barren hyper-Calvinism," as stated in the following:

> During the eighteenth century the Particular Baptists made little progress. In opposition to the current Socinianism a hard and barren hyper-Calvinism was developed, in accordance with which evangelistic effort is an impertinence. Through the influence of the evangelical revival of the middle of the eighteenth century the Calvinism of John Gill and John Brine gradually gave way to the more benignant teaching of Andrew Fuller and Robert Hall, and the great missionary movement inaugurated by William Carey became a possibility.[13]

Though this view is now for the most part the standard interpretation given in our Baptist histories, it was not so in the years prior to and during the existence of the Triennial Convention, 1814-1844. At that time, American Baptists viewed the ushering in of the modern missionary movement singularly in terms of God's providence, with no mention at all that being "freed" from "hyper-Calvinism" was even a contributing factor.[14] This is due to the fact that these missionary Regular Baptists in America were Calvinists themselves, who for the most part not only approved of Gill's theology but endorsed it, as will be seen later. And as seen in the above citation from Newman, in order to support this later view the inevitable comparisons begin to be made between the Particular Baptists before Carey, and those both contemporary with and after him. While the historical inquiry itself can be very beneficial, it all too often proceeds on a premise we believe is fundamentally flawed. To compare the originators of the Baptist Missionary

---

[13] A. H. Newman, *A History of the Baptist Churches in the United States* (New York: The Christian Literature Co., 1894), 55. It is not surprising that this view prevails in virtually all of the standard Baptist histories since the latter half of the nineteenth century, when Arminian theological views were ascendant.

[14] See: *Brief Narrative of the Baptist Mission in India* (Boston, 1811); William Staughton, *The Baptist Mission in India: Containing a Narrative of its Rise, Progress, and Present Condition* (Phila., 1811); David Benedict, *A General History of the Baptist Denomination* (Boston, 1813), Vol. 1, pp. 234-246; Ira M. Allen, *The United States Baptist Annual Register and Almanac* (Phila., 1833), and *The Triennial Register, No. 2, 1836* (Phila., 1836); Baron Stow, *History of American Baptist Missions* (Boston, 1835);and William Gammell, *A History of American Baptist Missions* (Boston, 1849). This is not to say that there were no aberrant forms of Calvinistic theology in existence in the eighteenth and nineteenth centuries, just as there are today, but rather to point out the significant difference in the historical and theological perspectives before and after the mid-nineteenth century.

Society and their successors, to those who preceded them, by commending the former for their evangelistic zeal while in retrospect condemning the latter for their perceived lack thereof, is to commit a historical injustice. John Gill, John Brine, Benjamin Wallin, and others of their contemporaries usually singled out for such criticism, were all deceased years before Carey presented his plan to evangelize the heathen at the meeting of the Northampton Baptist Association in 1786,[15] and even before the famous "Prayer Call of 1784."[16] It is often overlooked that it was owing, under God, to William Carey's persistence that even his friends, including Andrew Fuller, and their contemporaries, were finally persuaded of the feasibility of the mission to India:

> Indeed, [Carey] laid the burden of his soul on all his brother ministers, especially on those of his own age, as likeliest to listen. 'They mostly regarded it,' says Fuller, 'as a wild impracticable scheme, and gave him no encouragement. Yet he would not give it up, but talked with us *one by one*, till he had made some impression.' Like the Ancient Mariner, 'he held them with his will.' Fuller was as little custom-bound as any, yet even he was tempted to say, ' If the Lord should make windows in heaven, could such a thing be?'[17]

And as Fuller also wrote:

> The other ministers...had been *compelled to think* of the subject by his repeatedly advancing it, and they became desirous of it, if it could be accomplished; but feeling the difficulty of setting out in an unbeaten path, their minds revolted at the idea of attempting it. It seemed to them something too great, and too much like grasping at an object utterly beyond their reach.[18]

The truth of the matter was, that regardless of one's theological persuasion,

---

[15] Carey was born in 1761. Brine died in 1765, Gill in 1771 and Wallin in 1782.

[16] See Ernest A. Payne, *The Prayer Call of 1784* (London: Baptist Layman's Missionary Movement, 1941).

[17] S. Pearce Carey, *William Carey, D. D., Fellow of Linnaean Society* (New York: George H. Doran Co., 1923), 52.

[18] As cited in Frank Deaville Walker, *William Carey: Missionary Pioneer and Statesman* (Chicago: Moody Press [preface 1925]), 63.

the idea of establishing a gospel mission in a country such as India or Burma was an altogether new and radical concept to Christians among all the mainline denominations in the eighteenth century.[19] If the principal cause by which the modern missionary movement "became a possibility" can be attributed to the overcoming of a doctrinally unfavorable climate among the Particular Baptists in England, then what hindrance can be said to have kept Dan Taylor's "New Connexion" of General Baptists from leading out in foreign missionary work at their inception in 1770?[20] Or, for that matter, any other denominational body?[21]

 Gill, Brine, Wallin and others must be viewed in the light of their own times. To do otherwise would be to indict generations of godly Christians who lived and died in the faith before Carey.[22] For did they not also desire the gospel to extend to all the earth? Certainly they did, as their own writings will attest.[23]

 It is true that during this same period under consideration, the early to mid-nineteenth century, there were some Baptists in Great Britain and America who were critical of Gill's theology. One of the most oft-repeated criticisms of Gill and his works is that made by the English Baptist Robert Hall, Jr., the source of which was originally related by his biographer Dr. Olinthus Gregory, from some "conversational remarks" he recorded from Hall, as seen in the following:

---

[19] Even though the command to take the gospel into all the world had a prior and clear biblical mandate, it had been neglected for centuries amid all the religious turmoil in Europe.

[20] With no disrespect to Dan Taylor, but following the lead of our doctrinal critics, would we assign as the cause of this lack of initative "a hard and barren" *hyper-Arminianism*?

[21] The Anglicans and the Wesleyan Methodists each had formed a mission society prior to the B. M. S., but both along former patterns, and not with the same conception as Carey.

[22] For example, did taking the gospel to India ever occur to John Bunyan? And are the volumes of the writings of John Owen filled with an earnest desire to begin missionary endeavor on foreign fields?

[23] "Go cheerfully through your work," Gill wrote, "find much pleasure in it, and with great satisfaction see the Gospel spread, souls converted, Satan's kingdom weakened, and the interest of your Redeemer thrive and flourish; than which nothing can more contribute to complete the joy of the ministers of Christ"—comments on John 16:24. Many other citations could be given, but for a few examples see his comments in his *Expositions* on Prov. 11:30; Mark 16:16; John 3:30, 5:36, 6:33 and 10:16; 1 Cor. 9:22; and 2 Cor. 10:16.

He [Hall, Jr.] did not like Dr. Gill as an author. When Mr. Christmas Evans was in Bristol, he was talking to Mr. Hall about the Welch language, which he said was very copious and expressive. 'How I wish, Mr. Hall, that Dr. Gill's works had been written in Welch.'—[to which Hall replied,] 'I wish they had, sir; I wish they had, with all my heart, for then I should never have read them. They are a continent of mud, sir.'[24]

What is not as commonly known is that Hall also spoke disparagingly of another great Calvinistic theologian, John Owen.[25] And this is not surprising that Hall would have had such a distaste for the writings of both Gill and Owen, given his doctrinal persuasion, for as he declared, "I believe firmly in general redemption; I often preach it."[26] What is surprising is that Hall would inconsistently remain within a communion to whose doctrinal confession he could not subscribe.[27] We therefore would not consider Hall a competent judge of either Gill or Owen, or any other Calvinistic author.[28] In his own time Hall was primarily known as an eloquent orator, though today for the most part, as an English historian observed years ago, "Hall's sermons now lie unopened

---

[24] Olinthus Gregory, ed., *The Works of the Rev. Robert Hall, A. M.* (New York: Harper & Brothers, 1838), III: 82. Hall, Jr.'s "continent of mud" reference to Gill has been erroneously attributed to C. H. Spurgeon twice in Lewis Drummond's *Spurgeon: Prince of Preachers* (Grand Rapids, MI: Kregel Publications, 1992), 64, 182.

[25] Ibid., 78-79. Hall stated that one could find Owen's ideas "buried" in his works "amid a heap of rubbish." See also George Redford and John A. James, editors, *The Autobiography of William Jay* (Carlisle, PA: Banner of Truth Trust, 1974 reprint of the 1854 edition), 124, 382.

[26] Ibid., 76.

[27] Hall stayed within Particular Baptist circles despite his general atonement beliefs. Even his biographer and compiler Dr. Gregory conceded that Hall's views on the atonement, "seemed to me, at the time, to be encumbered with considerable difficulties," while remarking that Hall's comments concerning Owen were "ludicrous but characteristic observations." (Ibid., 79).

[28] And so agrees a late nineteenth century assessment of Hall: "He held Arminian views of the atonement, and in a measure of some of the other doctrines of grace, and he spoke scornfully of the works of Dr. Gill, a writer who knew immensely more of the languages and teachings of the Bible than himself; he believed that unbaptized persons might come to the Lord's table. He had other peculiarities of doctrine as unscriptural as those just named." William Cathcart, ed., *The Baptist Encyclopedia* (Phila.: Louis H. Everts, 1881), I: 489-490.

on library shelves."[29]

It was rightly stated by a Swiss poet that, "Truth is the secret of eloquence,"[30] and far from being a thing to be apologized for, the works of John Gill have long been esteemed for the consistent clarity in which the author sets forth the truth of God's Word.

This brings us back to where we began this essay, to the meeting of the General Missionary Convention in Philadelphia in May of 1817, where following the opening address by Richard Furman, reports of the activities of the board of the Convention and its missionaries were read, and then the following in a list of resolutions was adopted:

> Resolved, unanimously, That the Convention earnestly recommend to the churches throughout our country, to UNITE IN THE GENERAL CONCERT PRAYER MEETING, on the *first Monday of every month*, for the purpose of imploring the blessing of Almighty God on missionary efforts.[31]

The resolution was followed shortly after by the reading of a letter presented to Richard Furman by Philadelphia printer William W. Woodward, as we read in the Convention minutes:

> A letter from Mr. W. W. Woodward, addressed to the President, was read as follows: 'Permit me, for the information of the members from various parts of America to inform you, that I am progressing with the extensive Commentary of the Rev. Dr. Gill on the Old and New Testaments. The whole of the New Testament has been some time since published in three volumes, and the first volume of the Old Testament has been ready for some time past. Volume 2d of the Old Testament is printed as far as 600 pages, and is expected to be completed in June or July. The other volumes will, with Divine permission, progress until the whole is completed. My expenses are very heavy, and call for the smiles and approba-

---

[29] A. C. Underwood, *A History of the English Baptists* (London: The Carey Kingsgate Press, 1947), 169. Unfortunately this is true of many other early Baptist authors as well, but the point is made to demonstrate that while the works of both Gill and Owen have been reprinted numerous times in the past century, those of Hall have not.

[30] Henri-Frédéric Amiel, "Journal," as cited in John Bartlett, ed., *Familiar Quotations* (London: MacMillan and Co., 1937), 1073.

[31] *Proceedings of the General Convention of the Baptist Denomination in the United States at their First Triennial Meeting*, op cit., 133-134.

tion of the friends of this valuable author. If I can be favoured with the good wishes of your honourable body for my success, I shall feel myself under lasting obligations. May the Lord crown your exertions to promote his glory and the welfare of souls, with his divine benediction.

Your affectionate friend and servant,

W. W. WOODWARD.[32]

Whereupon the following decision was recorded:

> Resolved, unanimously, That this Convention appreciate highly the works of Dr. Gill, and consider the specimens already produced by Mr. Woodward, of the faithfulness and excellency of the execution of the work, and the heavy expense incurred in the publication, as deserving peculiar regard. They earnestly renew their recommendation that the Exposition be generally patronized by the churches and friends of religion throughout the Union.[33]

As can be plainly seen, contrary to the revisionist views of later historians, these missionary Regular Baptists, far from viewing Gill's works as "hyper-Calvinistic," on the contrary expressed "unanimously" that they appreciated "highly the works of Dr. Gill," earnestly renewing their recommendation that his *Exposition of the Old and New Testaments* "be generally patronized by the churches and friends of religion throughout the Union." To demonstrate that this was no idle motion on the part of the Convention in aiding William Woodward in his worthy project, twenty-three of the thirty-three original founding delegates of the Convention underwrote the reprinting of Gill's work through subscriptions.[34] When one bears in mind that the money given in

---

[32] Ibid., 134. The Philadelphia Association had previously resolved "to support the publishing of the work to the utmost," at their annual meeting on Oct. 8, 1807. A. D. Gillette, *Minutes of the Philadelphia Baptist Association*, 439. The Charleston Association likewise expressed their approbation of the same at their session in 1809, and the Massachusetts Baptist Missionary Society gave its "recommendation" to Woodward's undertaking in their publication as well. See *The Massachusetts Baptist Missionary Magazine* Vol. II, No. 12, December, 1810, 376-377.

[33] Ibid.

[34] This information was derived by comparing the names of the constituting delegates of the General Missionary Convention listed in William Gammell's *History of American Baptist Missions* (1849), p. 18, with the "Subscriber's Names" in the back of Volume III of John Gill's *Exposition of the New Testament* (Phila.: William W. Woodward, 1811), n.p. Northern Baptists will be interested in knowing that Jonathan Going, a founder

these subscriptions could have been placed instead in the general fund for missionary work, the importance they attached to the publication becomes obvious.

From the beginning of their foreign missionary endeavors, the Regular Baptists in America—the doctrinal heirs of their Particular Baptist forefathers, viewed the onset of their foreign missionary activities as an event singularly ordained by God's providence and their Calvinistic theology as no hindrance at all to their evangelism. Here, as we have just read, we see them "imploring the blessing of Almighty God on missionary efforts," while at the same time giving their hearty endorsement to the first American printing of John Gill's *Exposition of the Old and New Testaments.*

"What is more honourable," wrote Gill, "than to be the servant of the most high God, and to be employed in such service as his, as to show unto men the way of salvation? Than to be ambassadors of Christ, and stand in his stead, and beseech men to be reconciled to God? To be stewards of the mysteries of Christ, and of the manifold grace of God?"[35]

We trust that under God's blessing, this new edition of John Gill's *Exposition of the Gospel According to John* will prove to be, as it was to our forefathers in the faith, a wellspring of doctrinal truth to all those actively engaged in the spread of the gospel.

Terry Wolever
October 20, 2003

For we can do nothing against the truth,
but for the truth - 2 Corinthians 13:8

---

of the American Baptist Home Mission Society in 1832, and Stephen Gano of Providence, R. I. were among the subscribers. Southern subscribers included not only Richard Furman, but William B. Johnson, the first President of the Southern Baptist Convention, and Jesse Mercer. What a contrast between today's American Baptist leaders and such prominent men of our denomination of the past in regards to Gill's theology!

[35] John Gill, *The Work of a Gospel Minister Recommended to Consideration* (London: George Keith, 1764; reprinted by the Baptist Standard Bearer, Paris, AR, 2002), 16.

Portrait of John Gill as he appeared at the age of 51 years in 1748. This likeness, drawn by Mr. Highmore, Jr. and engraved by G. Vertue, was printed as a frontispiece to the third volume of *An Expostion of the New Testament* (London: Aaron Ward, 1748). Reflecting on the life of Gill many years later, John Rippon wrote that, "Notwithstanding his exalted attainments and usefulness, he was *meek*, *humble*, and of a *sympathizing* spirit. His strong affections discovered themselves on various occasions; especially on the hearing of any remarkable success attending the Gospel, either in private families, in particular churches, in the colonies of America, or elsewhere." *A Brief Memoir of the Life and Writings of the Late Rev. John Gill, D. D.* (London: J. Bennett, 1838; reprinted Harrisonburg, VA: Gano Books, 1992), 129.

Some helps to the Reader

This *Exposition of the Gospel According to John* was originally presented in the form of sermons delivered by John Gill to his London congregation, and then published in Volumes One and Two of the three-volume set entitled, *An Exposition of the New Testament* (London: Aaron Ward, 1746-1748).

As was true of many of his predecessors such as John Bunyan, Gill wrote *scripturally*, that is, he often incorporated scriptural phrases and terminology in his sentences, and in most cases without citing the references. Gill rightly assumed that Christian people should be familiar enough with their Bibles to follow his reasoning. But this manner of writing served another purpose as well, and that was to induce his hearers and readers to think biblically—in biblical language. We have taken the liberty in this present edition to italicize most of these Scriptural references and have inserted the passages thus cited in brackets. All such additions to the text or footnotes made by the editor are thus bracketed, or otherwise indicated.

After Gill passed away in 1771, "A New Edition, Corrected," was issued by his son-in-law George Keith in 1774. In carefully comparing Keith's edition with the later edition produced by Mathews and Leigh in 1809,[36] a number of differences became apparent. In the Mathews and Leigh edition, there are numerous abridgments and other wording changes made to Gill's comments, while the citations from the Jewish authors have been expanded in many cases. Though the omitted words do not compromise the integrity of Gill's commentary on the Gospel of John, nevertheless I thought it best to restore the complete text of Gill's comments using the Keith edition. And since the extended citations of the Jewish writings gave a clearer contextual application, we chose to retain this feature from the Mathews and Leigh edition.

As in our previous commentary on Romans, Gill's references to the Apocrypha have been cited in full. This, along with another valuable suggestion—to include Gill's numerous references to his notes in the earlier Gospels and elsewhere as endnotes, have greatly aided making this present commentary a self-contained work. A bracketed number in bold thus: **[22]**, will help the reader to locate the appropriate note placed in New Testament chronological order at the back of this volume.

It will be noticed that throughout his *Exposition*, Gill will often use the context to call the reader's attention to a proof of the Deity of the Lord Jesus Christ. This was due to the fact that at the time in which this commentary

---

[1] The Mathews and Leigh edition has been the most commonly reproduced set due to the fact that the earlier, eighteenth century edition by Keith contains the archaic ligatures of the period (the s's that look like f's, etc.) which were done away with in the early years of the nineteenth century.

was written there was a rising tide of Unitarian sentiment in England, which found expression in two forms—Arianism and Socinianism. These heretical views assail in one way or another the orthodox Christian view of the Trinitarian nature of the Godhead, as revealed to us in God's Word. Arianism has been revived of late in the "Jehovah's Witness" teachings, while Unitarianism in various other forms is also still very much a part of the religious landscape. Therefore Gill's arguments for the Deity of Christ in this connection are a relevant today as when they were first penned.

The text of this *Exposition* has been essentially preserved as originally published, with only minor grammatical changes. These include conforming the spelling to current American usage, changing certain past tense expressions such as "has bore" to the past perfect tense of "has borne," and changing phrases such as "cannot you" to "can you not," none of which alter the meaning of the text of this commentary as Gill wrote it.

The "R." as in "R. Abraham ben David" stands for "Rabbi." The term "Gloss" means an explanation or interpretation of the text.

Lastly, the abbreviation &c. is a former way of writing *etc.*, or *et cetera*, which is Latin phrase comparable to our saying "and so forth."

For years now I have wanted to produce some new editions of Gill's *Exposition* in a modern, easier to read format. It is through the help of likeminded friends that this dream has now, with this volume, and the preceding one on Romans, become a reality. May the Lord bless the effort for His Kingdom's sake.

T. W.

Preface

The sacred books, of which the following work is an exposition, are of equal authority with the oracles of God, the writings of the Old Testament; being, as they, divinely inspired; and are profitable to the same ends and purposes, of *doctrine, reproof, correction*, and *instruction in righteousness* [2 *Tim. 3:16*]: they contain things of the greatest moment and importance to the spiritual and eternal welfare of men, to the honor and interest of the great Redeemer, and to the glory of God; and therefore should be most carefully perused, most diligently searched into, and, as much as in us lies, should be studiously, distinctly, and rightly explained, and which is attempted in this performance.

The *four evangelists* have recorded every thing material, relating to the great Author and Institutor of the Christian religion, the sum and substance of the Gospel, our Lord Jesus Christ: they give us an account of His harbinger and forerunner, John the Baptist; of His parents, His wonderful conception and birth, with several amazing circumstances belonging thereunto; they describe His qualifications for His important office, His mien and deportment, His dress and diet, His conduct and conversation, His preaching and baptism, His success and His followers, His imprisonment and death; and point at several prophecies as fulfilled in Him: but above all, they are chiefly concerned with Christ Himself. They declare Him to be the Son of God, and the Son of man; they shew His descent as man, to be from the kings of Judah, and from the ancient patriarchs Abraham, Isaac, and Jacob; yea, they trace it to the first man, Adam; they tell us who His real mother, and supposed father were; of what family they were, and where they lived; what their characters, worldly circumstances, and business of life [were]; they speak of His miraculous conception, through the power of the Holy Ghost, and of the time and place of His birth; and of what went before, or followed after, necessary to be known; they record some things done in His infancy, and childhood; they give us an account of His baptism, and of His entrance on His public ministry; they have written down His sermons to His disciples, and the multitude; His several discourses with the Jews, chief priests, Scribes, Pharisees, and Sadducees; His parables, proverbial sayings, and pity sentences; they make mention of various surprising miracles wrought by Him, which were proofs of His Deity, divine mission, and Messiahship; they inform us of the names and number of His apostles, whom He sent forth to preach in His name; and they relate His fatiguing journeys which He took, to do good to the bodies and souls of men, by healing diseases, and preaching the Gospel; as also the temptations of Satan He was exercised with, in the wilderness; the reproaches and insults of men, He endured; His sufferings and death, with all the circumstances attending it; and likewise His resurrection from the dead, and ascension to heaven: and the whole is a complete history of the life of Christ, for what one evangelist omits, another relates; and all is done with the utmost impartiality, simplicity, and truth; and there is an entire harmony and agreement between the sacred historians; for though there are some things, in which at first sight they may seem to contradict each other, these will admit of a fair reconciliation, and which is observed in the following exposition.

Now to have a true knowledge, and right understanding of books of so much concern as these are, must be desirable to all, who have a just value for them, and esteem of them; but *who is sufficient for these things?* [2 Cor. 2:16]. It is certain, that the Holy Spirit, who has dictated the sacred Scriptures, and inspired holy men of God to write them, is the best interpreter of them; and He does lead and guide His people, more or less, into the truths contained in them; His assistance is therefore in the first place to be implored, and without it, nothing of this kind is to be attempted: to compare *spiritual things with spiritual* [1 Cor. 2:13], or in other words, to compare Scripture with itself; the more obscure and difficult parts of it, with those that are more plain and clear, must be of considerable service, for the better understanding them: and to observe the analogy of faith, the agreement of truth with itself, and of one truth with another; *the form of sound words* [2 Tim. 1:13], the summary of Gospel truths, to be collected out of the sacred writings, with which the sense of every passage must agree, is of exceeding great use in this affair; to which may be added, the gracious experience that the man of God has in himself, of the truth, power, influence, and weight of the Word of God upon his own soul; for next to the Scriptures themselves, in general, it should be considered, whether such an interpretation of a particular passage, is agreeable to the common experience of the saints, and to a man's own: a competent knowledge of the languages, in which the Scriptures are written, cannot fail of being very helpful in the study of them, in many instances; and indeed, all arts and sciences, liberal or mechanical, yea, every thing within the compass of knowledge, natural, moral, and civil, contribute more or less unto, and assist in the understanding of the books of the New Testament; and among the many helps, and several means which should be, and are made use of for such a purpose, a knowledge of the affairs of the Jews, of their rites and ceremonies, of their laws, usages, customs, and traditions, as they were in and about the times of Christ and His apostles, is not the most inconsiderable; which will appear, if it be observed,

That our Lord Jesus Christ, whose life is written by the four evangelists, was a Jew Himself; He was born of Jewish parents, in the land of Judea; He was brought up in the Jewish religion; He conformed to their laws, rites, and customs, throughout the whole of His life, which were lawful to conform unto; He was sent to the people of the Jews, as a prophet, and to them only; to them he delivered His sermons, with them He frequently discoursed, and among them He wrought His miracles; in short, among them He lived and died. Now it can not be thought, but that He should speak in the dialect of that nation, should express Himself in words and phrases, which were in common use; and refer to various things, and allude to rites and customs in practice among them; wherefore the knowledge of their phraseology, or way of speaking, of their usages and customs, must be of singular use, for the understanding of many things said by Christ, which are recorded in the four evangelists: let it also be further observed,

That all the apostles of Christ, and all the writers of the New Testament, were Jews; they were educated in the Jewish religion; they preached to the Jews only, in the times of Christ; and first to them, after their commission was enlarged to preach to the Gentiles; and the first churches, even among the Gentiles, greatly consisted of Jews, to whom the Epistles were written, as the Epistles themselves shew. Now can it be imagined, but that notwithstanding divine inspiration, and though they wrote in the Greek language, they would retain the idioms and forms of speech, to which they had been used; and that they would allude to rites and customs, they had been observant of, and the people also to whom they wrote? Had the books of the New Testament been written by Englishmen, though inspired by the Holy Ghost, doubtless there would have appeared many Anglicisms in them, as it is notorious enough there are in them [an] abundance of Hebraisms; and that they would have referred to the rites and customs of their own nation, as these have done: wherefore the knowledge of the Jewish language and customs, must be of service for the better understanding of various things, to be met with in the writings of these men: to which may be added,

That Judaism, properly so called, as it was a peculiar religion, and distinct from Christianity, though not contrary to it, was in being, and in full force, in Christ's time, though near its end, and was abolished in the times of the apostles, and Christianity was established by them: now it is not reasonable to believe, that an affair of this nature should be transacted, that there should be an abrogation of Jewish rites and ceremonies, and a setting up of Gospel ordinances, which were to continue to the end of time, that in the disputes with the Jews upon this subject, and the account that is given of this matter, there should be no references and expressions, which the knowledge of Jewish affairs can give us light into.

Being convinced by these considerations many years ago, I set about the reading of the most ancient writings of the Jews I could come at, in order to satisfy myself of the truth of these things, and the better to understand the New Testament; and though this has been attended with great difficulty, fatigue, and labor, and may have hindered the pursuit of other useful studies, I cannot say I repent of it. The method I took at first, and which I all along followed, was to write down in an *Adversaria*, or notebook, what occurred in reading, which I thought might be of any service, to give light to any passage in the New Testament, and which I put against that passage: in a course of time this book began to swell, which put me on thoughts of making these notes public; which I sometimes inclined to do in one way, and sometimes in another; but at length determined to do with them as I have done, in the following work. The writings I have chiefly read with this view, are the

Targums, or Chaldee paraphrases of the Old Testament; the *Mishnah*, or the Jews' oral law; the two *Talmuds*, Jerusalem and Babylonian; the *Rabbot*, or mystical expositions of the ancient doctors of the Jewish synagogue; the book of *Zohar*, with others of a later date, and less note.

Some may think I have made too much use of Jewish authorities in the following *Exposition*; my concern is, that I have made no more use of them; and that my reading and observations have not furnished me with more materials of this kind, which I am very well satisfied might be obtained from them; for which reason I should have chosen to deferred the publication of it, hoping I might be able, by such means, to give further light to some passages of Scripture; and only the importunity of my friends, and the consideration of the uncertainty of life, have prevailed upon me to let it go into the world as it is. I have used all diligence, both from my own reading, and from the observations of others, to make it as perfect in this way as I could; and from none have I had so much help and assistance as from the great Dr. Lightfoot, who has broken the ice for me, and pointed out the way in which I should proceed, as Wagenseil observes. On consulting my *Adversaria*, and comparing my notes with what the doctor has observed, I found some things taken notice of which he has published; and indeed, it can hardly be thought it should be otherwise in reading the same writings, and with the same view; but I have not thought proper to drop them on that account, but have rather chosen to make use of others produced by him, unobserved by me, in order to make this work as complete as I could, and which lovers of Hebrew learning will thank me for; though the reader will not be able to observe scarce any thing but what is either corrected, improved, or confirmed. And as for those who may not have a taste for these things, I hope they will find without them a satisfactory exposition of the sacred text; and I may further observe, that citations of this sort will not appear so frequently and largely in the other parts of the work, as in the first volume. It is very possible, that my fondness for this kind of literature may have betrayed me into some weaknesses, which I hope will be overlooked. And no doubt but there are mistakes made by me in this sort of learning itself, which men of candor and ingenuity, especially such who know the difficulty and intricacy of such studies, will not bear hard upon me for, but gently correct. Some of my readers may be offended with some things they may meet within the citations out of Jewish writings, not being used to such reading; and this is an infelicity that attends testimonies produced out of both heathenish and Jewish authors, that there is often something not pleasing and grateful to Christian ears; I have, as much as I could, pared off what might not be so agreeable; but sometimes it has been necessary to recite more than is eligible, in order to finish the sentence, and complete the sense; and the reader should observe, that he is not further to regard the citation, than as it concerns that for which it is made the phraseology, history, rite, or custom referred unto.

As for the Oriental versions I have chiefly made us of in this work, they are those that are published in the London Polyglott Bible; and I have, for the most part, followed the translations of them in it, choosing rather that my readers should trust to the labors of those learned men concerned in that work, than to that little knowledge and skill I have in those languages. The various readings of the text I have not entered into a critical examination of; I have only selected some of the most material ones, which differ most from the commonly received reading, or agree with the Vulgate Latin and eastern versions, or furnish out of a useful observation. Nor need the reader be uneasy, lest the authority of the Scripture should be weakened, and become doubtful by these different readings: for as a learned man of our own nation has observed, "it is an invincible reason for the Scriptures' part, that other escapes should be so purposely and infinitely let pass, and yet no saving or substantial part at all scarce moved out of its place. To say the truth, these varieties of readings in a few bye-places do the same office to the main Scripture, as the variations of the compass to the whole magnet of the earth; the mariner knows so much the better for these how to steer his course."[37]

I have nothing more to observe, only that I have here and there taken notice of the more material objections of the Jews to the writings of the New Testament, and have given a short answer to them; and the rather, as they may partly serve to remove their prejudices against them, and partly to confirm Christians in them; so likewise to obviate the exceptions of deists, who join with them in them, and make use of the same, and improve them to the same purpose.

As to my religious principles from which I am denominated by men, they are pretty much known in the world by the writings I have already published, and my notes on the several parts of Scripture will be found to correspond with them. I have studied consistency with the truth, and with myself; and I hope nothing will appear contradictory to the form of sound words, and the analogy of faith, or be *yea and nay*,[38] but harmonious, uniform and all of a piece.

And now I do, in the most sincere and grateful manner, give thanks to God for that measure of health and strength of body; and for all the gifts and graces of His Spirit afforded me, by which I have been enabled to go through this arduous work thus far, and would be depending upon Him for fresh supplies of grace and strength for the publication of the whole. I most freely acknowledge, that all I have of nature, literature, and grace, I have from Him, from who *every good and perfect gift* comes; I have nothing but what I have received: nor would I glory as though I had received it not: and if I have written any thing contrary to the divine perfections, or what may reflect any dishonor on the dear name of Jesus, or be any way injurious to the truth, as it is in Him, or be detrimental to the interest of pure and undefiled religion,

---

[1] J. Gregory's *Preface* to his works.

[2] See 2 Cor. 1:19.

I do most humbly entreat forgiveness at the hands of God; I am sure I have not written any thing of this kind knowingly, and on purpose. To conclude, I do most earnestly desire and implore the blessing of God upon these labors of mine, that they might be useful to many in reading them, that their minds may be enlightened, their faith may be established, their knowledge of divine things may be increased, and God may be glorified.

John Gill
London, 1745.[39]

---

[3] Abridged from Gill's *Preface* to his *Exposition of the New Testament* (London: George Keith, 1809), I: iii-xxiv. The date is taken from John Rippon, *A Brief Memoir of the Life and Writings of the late Rev. John Gill, D. D.* (London: J. Bennett, 1838), 58-59.

THE GOSPEL OF JOHN

INTRODUCTION TO JOHN

The author of this Gospel is John, the son of Zebedee and Salome, the brother of James the greater; he outlived the rest of the disciples, and wrote this Gospel after the other evangelists; and in it many things are recorded, which are not in the other Gospels; [such] as various discourses of Christ, and miracles done by Him; several incidents in His life, and circumstances that attended His sufferings and death.

The occasion of it is generally thought to be the errors of Ebion and Cerinthus, who denied the divinity of Christ, asserted He was a mere man, and that He did not exist before His incarnation; and the design of it is to confute them. And it is easy to observe, that he begins his Gospel with the divinity of Christ; asserts Him to be God, and proves Him to be truly and properly so, by the works of creation, which were wrought by Him, as well as shows that He was really man.

Clemens[1] calls this Gospel of John, πνευματικον ευαγγελιον, *a spiritual Gospel*, as indeed it is; consisting of the spiritual discourses of our Lord, on various occasions, both at the beginning, and in the course of His ministry, and especially a little before His sufferings and death. And the same writer observes, that John, the last of the evangelists, considering that in the other Gospels were declared the things relating to the body of Christ, that is, to Him, as He was after the flesh; to His genealogy and birth as man; to what was done to Him, or by Him, in His infancy; to His baptism, temptations, journeys, &c., at the request of His familiar friends, and moved by the Spirit of God, composed this Gospel.

Moreover, it is observed by some,[2] that the other three evangelists only record what was done by Christ, in one year after John the Baptist was cast into prison, as appears from *Matt. 4:12; Mark 1:14; Luke 3:20.* Wherefore John, at the entreaty of his friends, put these things into his Gospel, which were done or said by Christ, before John was cast into prison. He was called very early by Christ, though young; and was with Him throughout the whole of His ministry, and was an eye and ear witness of what he here relates, and his testimony is to be received. He was the beloved disciple, he leaned on the bosom of Jesus, and had great intimacy with Him; and might be privy to some things, which others were not acquainted with. And though he was a Galilean, and an unlearned man, *Acts 4:13,* yet being endowed with the extraordinary gifts of the Spirit, he was abundantly qualified to write this book: for what

---

[1] Apud Euseb. Eccl. Hist. l. 6. c. 14.

[2] Ibid. l. 3. c. 24.

1

some ancient writers[3] say of him, that he was a priest, and wore a plate, that is, of gold upon his forehead, cannot be true, since he was not of the tribe of Levi; and besides, only the high priest wore that upon his miter; unless they mean, as seems most likely, that he was a Christian bishop. Perhaps the mistake may arise from John the Baptist, who was of the priestly order, and is called by some Jewish writers,[4] John the high priest.

When and where this Gospel was written, is not certain; some say in[5] Asia, after he had written his *Revelation* in Patmos; and others say particularly, that it was written at Ephesus. The title of it in the Syriac version, signifies as much, which runs thus:

"The holy Gospel, the preaching of John, which he spoke and published in Greek at Ephesus."

And to the same purpose is the title of it in the Persic version:

"The Gospel of John, one of the twelve apostles, which was spoken in the city of Ephesus, in the Greek-Roman tongue."

Verse. 1. **In the beginning was the Word,** &c. That this is said not of the written Word, but of the essential Word of God, the Lord Jesus Christ, is clear, from all that is said from hence, to *verse 14,* as that this *Word was in the beginning*, was with God, and is God; from the creation of all things being ascribed to Him, and His being said to be *the life and light of men*; from His coming into the world, and usage in it; from His bestowing the privilege of adoption on believers; and from His incarnation; and also there is a particular application of all this to Christ, *verses 15-18*. And likewise from what this evangelist elsewhere says of Him, when he calls Him *the Word of life*, and places Him between the Father and the Holy Ghost; and speaks of the record of the Word of God, and the testimony of Jesus, as the same thing; and represents Him as a warrior and conqueror, *1 John 1:1-2;* and *5:7; Rev. 1:2, 9;* and *19:11-16.*

Moreover this appears to be spoken of Christ, from what other inspired writers have said of Him, under the same character; as the Evangelist Luke, *chapter 1:2*, the Apostle Paul, *Acts 20:32; Heb. 4:12,* and the Apostle Peter, *2 Pet. 3:5.* And who is called *the Word*, not as man; for as man He was not in the

---

[3] Polycrates in ib. l. 3. c. 31. & l. 5. c. 24. & Hieron. Catalog. Script. Eccles. fol. 96. sect. 55.

[4] Ganz Tzemach David, par. 1. fol. 25. 2.

[5] Hieron. Prolog. Evang. Joannis.

beginning with God, but became so in the fulness of time; nor is the man God; besides, as such, He is a creature, and not the Creator, nor is He the life and light of men; moreover, He was the Word, before He was man, and therefore not as such: nor can any part of the human nature be so called; not the flesh, for *the Word was made flesh*; nor His human soul, for self-subsistence, Deity, eternity, and the creation of all things, can never be ascribed to that; but He is the Word as the Son of God, as is evident from what is here attributed to Him, and from the Word being said to be so, as in *verses 14,18*; and from those places, where *the Word* is explained by *the Son*, compare *1 John 5:5,7; Matt. 28:19.* And [He] is so called from His nature, being begotten of the Father; for as the Word, whether silent or expressed, is the birth of the mind, the image of it, equal to it, and distinct from it; so Christ is *the only begotten of the Father, the express image of his person* [*Heb. 1:3*], in all things equal to Him, and a distinct person from Him: and He may be so called, from some action, or actions, said of Him, or ascribed to Him; as that He spoke for, and on the behalf of the elect of God, in the eternal council and covenant of grace and peace; and spoke all things out of nothing, in creation; for with regard to those words so often mentioned in the history of the creation, *and God said*, may *Jehovah* the Son be called *the Word*; also He was spoken of as the promised Messiah, throughout the whole Old Testament dispensation; and is the interpreter of His Father's mind, as He was in Eden's garden, as well as in the days of His flesh; and now speaks in heaven for the saints.

The phrase, מימרא דיי, *the Word of the Lord*, so frequently used by the Targumists, is well known: and it is to be observed, that the same things which John here says of the Word, they say likewise, as will be observed on the several clauses; from whence it is more likely, that John should take this phrase, since the paraphrases of Onkelos and Jonathan ben Uzziel were written before his time, than that he should borrow it from the writings of Plato, or his followers, as some have thought; with whose philosophy, Ebion and Cerinthus are said to be acquainted; wherefore John, the more easily to gain upon them, uses this phrase, when that of the Son of God would have been disagreeable to them. That there is some likeness between the Evangelist John and Plato in their sentiments concerning the Word, will not be denied. Amelius,[6] a Platonic philosopher, who lived after the times of John, manifestly refers to these words of his, in agreement with his master's doctrine; his words are these:

> "and this was truly *Logos*, or the Word, by whom always existing, the things that are made, were made, as also Heraclitus thought; and who, likewise that Barbarian (meaning the Evangelist John) reckons, was in the order and dignity of the beginning, constituted with God, and

---

[6]   Apud Euseb. Prepar. Evangel. l. 11. c. 19.

was God, by whom all things are entirely made; in whom, whatsoever is made, lives, and has life, and being; and who illapsed [*or* flowed] into bodies, and was clothed with flesh, and appeared a man; so notwithstanding, that he showed forth the majesty of his nature; and after his dissolution, he was again deified, and was God, as he was before he descended into a body, flesh and man. "

In which words it is easy to observe plain traces of what the evangelist says in the first four verses, and in the fourteenth verse of this chapter; yet it is much more probable, that Plato had his notion of the *Logos,* or Word, out of the writings of the Old Testament, than that John should take this phrase, or what he says concerning the Word, from him; since it is a matter of fact not disputed, that Plato went into Egypt to get knowledge. Not only Clemens Alexandrinus, a Christian writer says, that he was a philosopher of the Hebrews,[7] and understood prophecy,[8] and stirred up the fire of the Hebrew philosophy;[9] but it is affirmed by heathen writers, that he went into Egypt to learn of the priests,[10] and to understand the rites of the prophets;[11] and Aristobulus, a Jew, affirms,[12] he studied their law; and Numenius, a Pythagoric philosopher,[13] charges him with stealing what he wrote, concerning God and the world, out of the books of Moses; and used to say to him, "What is Plato, but Moses *Atticising*? or Moses speaking *Greek*?" And Eusebius,[14] an ancient Christian writer, points at the very places from whence Plato took his hints. Wherefore it is more probable, that the evangelist received this phrase of the Word, as a divine person, from the Targums, where there is such frequent mention made of it; or however, there is a very great agreement between what he and these ancient writings of the Jews say of the Word, as will be hereafter shown. Moreover, the phrase is frequently used in

---

[7] Stromat. l. 1. p. 274.

[8] Ibid. p. 303.

[9] Ibid. Paedagog. l. 2. c. 1. p. 150.

[10] Valer. Maxim. l. 8. c. 7.

[11] Apuleius de Dogmate Platonis, l. 1. in Principio.

[12] Apud. Euseb. Prepar. Evangel. l. 13. c. 12.

[13] Hesych. Miles. de Philosophis. p. 50.

[14] Prepar. Evangel. l. 11. c. 9.

like manner, in the writings of Philo the Jew; from whence it is manifest, that the name was well known to the Jews, and may be the reason of the evangelist's using it.

This Word, he says, *was in the beginning*; by which is meant, not the Father of Christ; for He is never called the beginning, but the Son only; and was He, He must be such a beginning as is without one; nor can He be said to be so, with respect to the Son or Spirit, who are as eternal as Himself; only with respect to the creatures, of whom He is the author and efficient cause: Christ is indeed in the Father, and the Father in Him, but this cannot be meant here; nor is the beginning of the Gospel of Christ, by the preaching of John the Baptist, intended here: John's ministry was an evangelical one, and the Gospel was more clearly preached by him, and after him by Christ and His apostles, than before; but it did not then begin; it was preached before by the angel to the shepherds, at the birth of Christ; and before that, by the prophets under the former dispensation, as by Isaiah, and others; it was preached before unto Abraham, and to our first parents, in the garden of Eden; nor did Christ begin to be, when John began to preach; for John's preaching and baptism were for the manifestation of Him: yea, Christ existed as man, before John began to preach; and though He was born after him as man, yet as the Word and Son of God, He existed before John was born; He was in being in the times of the prophets, which were before John; and in the times of Moses, and before Abraham, and in the days of Noah: but by *the beginning* is here meant, the beginning of the world, or the creation of all things; and which is expressive of the eternity of Christ, He was in the beginning, as the Maker of all creatures, and therefore must be before them all.

And it is to be observed, that it is said of Him, that in the beginning He *was*; not *made*, as the heavens and earth, and the things in them were; nor was He merely in the purpose and predestination of God, but really existed as a divine person, as He did from all eternity; as appears from His being set up in office from everlasting; from all the elect being chosen in Him, and given to Him before the foundation of the world [*Eph. 1:3-5*; *John 6:37* and *17:1-2*]; from the covenant of grace, which is from eternity, being made with Him; and from the blessings and promises of grace, being as early put into His hands; and from His nature as God, and His relation to His Father. So Philo the Jew often calls the *Logos,* or Word, the eternal Word, the most ancient Word, and more ancient than any thing that is made.[15] The eternity of the Messiah is acknowledged by the ancient Jews: *Micah 5:2* is a full proof of it; which by

---

[15]   De Leg. Alleg. l. 2. p. 93. de Plant. Noe, p. 217. de Migrat. Abraham, p. 389. de Profugis, p. 466. quis. rer. divin. Haeres. p. 509.

them[16] is thus paraphrased:

> "Out of thee, before me, shall come forth the Messiah, that he may exercise dominion over Israel; whose name is said from eternity, from the days of old."

Jarchi upon it only mentions *Psa. 72:17*, which is rendered by the Targum on the place, *before the sun his name was prepared*; it may be translated, *before the sun his name was Yinnon*; that is, the Son, namely the Son of God; and Aben Ezra interprets it, יקרא בן, *he shall be called the son*; and to this agrees what the Talmudists say,[17] that the name of the Messiah was before the world was created; in proof of which they produce the same passage;

and the Word was with God; not with men or angels; for He was before either of these; but with God, not essentially, but personally considered; with God His Father: not in the Socinian sense, that He was only known to Him, and to no other before the ministry of John the Baptist; for He was known and spoken of by the angel Gabriel before; and was known to Mary and to Joseph; and to Zacharias and Elisabeth; to the shepherds, and to the wise men; to Simeon and Anna, who saw Him in the temple; and to the prophets and patriarchs in all ages, from the beginning of the world: but this phrase denotes the existence of the Word with the Father, His relation and nearness to Him, His equality with Him, and particularly the distinction of His person from Him, as well as His eternal being with Him; for He was always with Him, and is, and ever will be: He was with Him in the council and covenant of grace, and in the creation of the universe, and is with Him in the providential government of the world; He was with Him as the Word and Son of God in heaven, while He, as man, was here on earth; and He is now with Him, and ever will be. And as John here speaks of the Word, as a distinct person from God the Father, so do the Targums, or Chaldee paraphrases; *Psa. 110:1*, *The Lord said to my Lord*, is rendered, *the Lord said to his Word*; where He is manifestly distinguished from *Jehovah*, that speaks to Him; and in *Hos. 1:7*, the Lord promises to *have mercy on the house of Judah*, and *save them by the Lord their God*. The Targum is, *I will redeem them by the Word of the Lord their God*; where the Word of the Lord, who is spoken of as a Redeemer and Savior, is distinguished from the Lord, who promises to save by Him. This distinction of *Jehovah* and His *Word*, may be observed in multitudes of places, in the Chaldee paraphrases, and in the writings of Philo the Jew; and this phrase, of *the word* being *with God*, is in the Targums expressed by, מן קדם מימר, *the word from before the Lord*, or *which is before the Lord*; being always

---

[16]   Targum Jon. in loc.

[17]   T. Bab. Pesachim, fol. 54. 1. & Nedarim, fol. 39. 2. Pirke Eliezer, c. 3.

in His presence, and the angel of it; so Onkelos paraphrases *Gen. 31:22, And the Word from before the Lord, came to Laban*, &c. and *Ex. 20:19* thus, *And let not the Word from before the Lord speak with us, lest we die*; for so it is read in the King of Spain's Bible; and Wisdom, which is the same with the Word of God, is said to be *by Him*, or *with Him*, in *Prov. 8:30*, agreeably to which John here speaks. John makes use of the word God, rather than Father, because the Word is commonly called the Word of God, and because of what follows;

and the Word was God; not *made* a God, as He is said hereafter to be *made flesh*; nor constituted or appointed a God, or a God by office; but truly and properly God, in the highest sense of the word, as appears from the names by which He is called; as *Jehovah*, God; our, your, their, and my God; God with us; the mighty God; God over all; the great God; the living God; the true God; and eternal life; and from His perfections, and the whole fulness of the Godhead that dwells in Him, as independence, eternity, immutability, omnipresence, omniscience, and omnipotence; and from His works of creation and providence, His miracles, the work of redemption, His forgiving sins, the resurrection of Himself and others from the dead, and the administration of the last judgment; and from the worship given Him, as prayer to Him, faith in Him, and the performance of baptism in His name. Nor is it any objection to the proper Deity of Christ, that the article is here wanting; since when the Word is applied to the Father, it is not always used, and even in this chapter, *verses 6,13,18*, and which shows, that the word *God*, is not the subject, but the predicate of this proposition, as we render it: so the Jews often use the Word of the Lord for *Jehovah*, and call Him God. Thus the words in *Gen. 28:20-21*, are paraphrased by Onkelos:

"if *the Word of the Lord* will be my help, and will keep me, &c. then *the Word of the Lord* shall be, לי לאלהא, *my God*;"

again, *Lev. 26:12* is paraphrased by the Targum ascribed to Jonathan ben Uzziel, thus:

"I will cause the glory of my Shekinah to dwell among you, and *my Word* shall be *your God*, the Redeemer."

Once more, *Deut. 26:17* is rendered by the Jerusalem Targum after this manner:

"Ye have made *the Word of the Lord* king over you this day, that he may be your God."

And this is frequent with Philo the Jew, who says, the name of God is His Word, and calls Him, *My Lord, the divine Word*; and affirms, that the most ancient Word is God.[18]

---

[18] De Allegor. l. 2. p. 99, 101. & de Somniis, p. 599.

Verse 2. **The same was in the beginning with God**. This is a repetition of what is before said, and is made to show the importance of the truths before delivered; namely, the eternity of Christ, His distinct personality, and proper Deity; and that the phrase, *in the beginning*, is to be joined to each of the above sentences; and so proves, not only His eternal existence, but His eternal existence with the Father, and also His eternal Deity; and is also made to carry on the thread of the discourse concerning the Word, and not God the Father; and to express, not only His coexistence in nature, but His co-operation in the works of creation next mentioned.

Verse 3. **All things were made by him**, &c. Which is a proof at once of all that is said before; as that He was in the beginning; and that He was with God the Father in the beginning; and that He was God; otherwise all things could not have been made by Him, had either of these been untrue: which is to be understood, not of the new creation; for this would be a restraining *all* things to a *few* persons only; nor is it any where said, that all things are new made, but made; and it is false, that all were converted, that have been converted by the ministry of Christ, as man: all men are not renewed, regenerated, nor reformed; and the greater part of those that were renewed, were renewed before Christ existed, as man; and therefore could not be renewed by Him, as such: though indeed, could this sense be established, it would not answer the end for which it is coined; namely, to destroy the proof of Christ's Deity, and of His existence before His incarnation; for in all ages, from the beginning of the world, some have been renewed; and the new creation is a work of God, and of almighty power, equally with the old; for who can create spiritual light, infuse a principle of spiritual life, take away the heart of stone, and give a heart of flesh, or produce faith, but God? Regeneration is denied to be of man, and is always ascribed to God; nor would Christ's being the author of the new creation, be any contradiction to His being the author of the old creation, which is intended here: by *all things*, are meant the heaven, and all its created inhabitants, the airy, starry, and third heavens, and the earth, and all therein; the sea, and every thing that is in that: and the Word, or Son of God, is the efficient cause of all these, not a bare instrument of the formation of them; for the preposition *by* does not always denote an instrument, but sometimes an efficient, as in *1 Cor. 1:9; 2 Cor. 1:1; Gal. 1:1*, and so here, though not to the exclusion of the Father, and of the Spirit:

and without him was not any thing made that was made: in which may be observed the conjunct operation of the Word, or Son, with the Father, and Spirit, in creation; and the extent of His concern in it to every thing that is made; for without Him there was not one single thing in the whole compass of the creation made; and the limitation of it to things that are made; and so excludes the increated [*or* uncreated] being—Father, Son, and Spirit; and sin

8

also, which is not a principle made by God, and which has no efficient, but a deficient cause. So the Jews ascribe the creation of all things to the Word. The Targumists attribute the creation of man, in particular, to the Word of God: it is said in *Gen. 1:27*, *God created man in his own image*; the Jerusalem Targum of it is,

"And the word of the Lord created man in his likeness."

And *Gen. 3:22, and the Lord God said, Behold the man is become as one of us*, the same Targum paraphrases thus:

"And the Word of the Lord God said, Behold the man whom I have created, is the only one in the world."

Also in the same writings, the creation of all things in general is ascribed to the Word: the passage in *Deut. 33:27, The eternal God is thy refuge, and underneath are the everlasting arms*, is paraphrased by Onkelos,

"The eternal God is a habitation, by whose Word the world was made."

In *Isa. 48:13*, it is said, *Mine hand also hath laid the foundation of the earth.* The Targum of Jonathan ben Uzziel on it is,

"Yea, by my Word I have founded the earth:"

which agrees with what is said in *Heb. 11:3; 2 Pet. 3:5,7.* And the same says Philo the Jew, who not only calls Him the archetype, and exemplar of the world, but the *power* that made it: he often ascribes the creation of the heavens, and the earth unto Him, and likewise the creation of man after whose image, he says, he was made.[19] The Ethiopic version adds, at the end of this verse, *and also that which is made is for himself.*

Verse 4. **In him was life**, &c. The Persic version reads in the plural number, *lives.* There was life in the Word with respect to Himself; a divine life, the same with the life of the Father and of the Spirit; and is in Him, not by gift, nor by derivation or communication; but originally, and independently, and from all eternity: indeed He lived before His incarnation as Mediator, and Redeemer. Job knew Him in his time, as his living Redeemer; but this regards Him as the Word and living God, and distinguishes Him from the written word, and shows that He is not a mere idea in the divine mind, but a truly divine person: and there was life in Christ the Word, with respect to others; the fountain of natural life is in Him, He is the efficient cause, and preserver of it; whether vegetative, animal, or rational; and proves Him to be truly God, and that He existed before His incarnation; since creatures, who have received such a life from Him, did: and spiritual life was also in Him; all His elect are dead in trespasses and sins, and cannot quicken themselves. Christ has procured life for them, and gives it to them, and implants it in them; a life of

---

[19]   De Mundi Opificio, p. 4, 5, 31, 32. De Alleg. l. 1. p. 44. De Sacrificiis Abel & Cain, p. 131. De Profugis, p. 464. & de Monarch. p. 823.

sanctification is from Him; and a life of justification is upon Him, and of faith is by Him; all the comforts of a spiritual life, and all things appertaining to it, are from Him, and He maintains, and preserves it. Eternal life is in Him, and with Him; not the purpose of it only, nor the promise of it barely, but the gift of it itself; which was granted in consequence of His asking it, and which He had by way of stipulation; and hence has a right and power to bestow it: now, this being in Him, proves Him to be the true God, and shows us where life is to be had, and the safety and security of it:

and the life was the light of men; the life which was in, and by the Word, was, with respect to men, a life of light, or a life attended with light: by which is meant, not a mere visive faculty, receptive of the sun's light, but rational knowledge and understanding; for when Christ, the Word, breathed into man *the breath of life,* and he *became a living soul [Gen. 2:7],* He filled him with rational light and knowledge. Adam had a knowledge of God; of His being, and perfections; of the persons in the Trinity; of his relation to God, dependence on Him, and obligation to Him; of His mind and will; and knew what it was to have communion with Him. He knew much of himself, and of all the creatures; this knowledge was natural and perfect in its kind, but losable; and different from that which saints now have of God, through Christ the Mediator; and since this natural light was from Christ the Word, as a Creator, He must be the eternal God. The Socinians are not willing to allow this sense, but say that Christ is the *light of men*, by preaching the heavenly doctrine, and by the example of His holy life; but hereby He did not enlighten every man that cometh into the world; the greatest part of men before the preaching and example of Christ, sat in darkness; and the greatest part of the Jews remained in darkness, notwithstanding His preaching and example; and the patriarchs that were enlightened under the former dispensation, were not enlightened this way: it will be owned, that all spiritual and supernatural light, which any of the sons of men have had, since the fall, was from Christ, from whom they had their spiritual life; even all spiritual light in conversion, and all after-degrees of light; through Him they enjoyed the light of God's countenance, and had the light of joy and gladness here, and of glory hereafter.

Verse. 5. **And the light shineth in darkness**, &c. Which, through sin, came upon the minds of men; who are naturally in the dark about the nature and perfections of God; about sin, and the consequences of it; about Christ, and salvation by Him; about the Spirit of God, and His work upon the soul; and about the Scriptures of truth, and the doctrines of the Gospel. Man was created a knowing creature, but not content with his knowledge, sinned, and was banished from the presence of God, the fountain of light; which brought a darkness on him and his posterity, and which is increased in them by personal iniquity, and in which Satan, the god of this world, has a hand; and sometimes they are left to judicial blindness, and which issues in total darkness, if grace prevents not: now amidst this darkness there were some remains of the light of nature, with respect to the being of God, which shines in the works of creation and providence; and to the worship of God, though very dimly; and to the knowledge of moral good and evil:

and the darkness comprehended it not; or *perceived it not*, as the Syriac version renders it. By the light of nature, and the remains of it, men could not come to any clear and distinct knowledge of the above things; and much less to any knowledge of the true way of salvation: unless, rather by the light should be meant the light of the Messiah, or of the Gospel, shining in the figures, types, and shadows of the law, and in the prophecies and promises of the Old Testament: and yet, such was the darkness upon the minds of men, that they could not very distinctly apprehend it, and much less fully comprehend it, so that there was need of a fresh and fuller revelation; an account of which follows.

Verse. 6. **There was a man sent from God,** &c. John the Baptist: he was not the *Logos*, or Word; nor was he an angel, but a man; yet an extraordinary one, in his conception of a barren woman, and in being born when both parents were stricken in years; and while he was in the womb, he leaped for joy at the salutation of Mary; and as soon as born was filled with the Holy Ghost; and when he was grown up, and appeared in public, it was in an uncommon manner: his dress and his diet were both out of the common way; and his temper and spirit were that of Elias the prophet; and as for his work and office, it was very peculiar; he was the forerunner of Christ, and the first administrator of the new ordinance of baptism, and the greatest of all the prophets. This person had his mission from God, both to preach and baptize:

whose name *was* John; the name given him by the angel before his conception, and by his mother Elisabeth, after her neighbors and cousins had given him another; and which was confirmed by his father Zacharias, when deaf and dumb: it signifies *grace*, or *gracious*; and a gracious man he was; he was very acceptable to his parents; a man that had the grace of God in him, and great gifts of grace bestowed on him; he was a preacher of the doctrines of grace; and his ministry was very grateful to many.

Verse 7. **The same came for a witness**, &c. The end of his being sent, and the design of his coming were,

to bear witness of the Light: by which is meant, not the light of nature, or reason; nor the light of the Gospel: but Christ Himself, the author of light— natural, spiritual, and eternal. This was one of the names of the Messiah with the Jews; of whom they say,[20] נהירא שמו, *light is his name*; as it is said in *Dan. 2:22, and the light dwelleth with him*; on which they have[21] elsewhere this gloss, *This is the King Messiah*; and so they interpret *Psa. 43:3* of Him.[22] Philo the Jew often speaks of the *Logos*, or Word, as light, and calls Him the intelligible light; the universal light, the most perfect light; represents Him as full of divine light; and says, He is called the sun.[23] Now John came to bear a testimony to Him, as he did; of which an account is given in this chapter very largely, and elsewhere; as that he testified of His existence before His incarnation; of His being with the Father, and in His bosom; of His Deity and divine Sonship; of His being the Messiah; of the fulness of grace that was in Him; of His incarnation and satisfaction; of His descent from heaven; and of His relation to His church, as in *chapter 1:15,16,18,23,27,29, 30,34,36;* and in *chapter 3:29,31;* the end of which witness was,

that all *men* through him might believe; that is, that the Jews, to whom he preached, might, through his testimony, believe that Jesus was the Light, and true Messiah; for these words are to be taken in a limited sense, and not to be extended to every individual of mankind; since millions were dead before John began his testimony, and multitudes then in being, and since, whom it never reached: nor can it design more than the Jews, to whom alone he bore witness of Christ; and the faith which he taught, and required by his testimony, was an assent unto Him as the Messiah. Though the preaching of the Gospel is a means of true spiritual faith in Christ; and doubtless it was so to many, as preached by John: it points out the object of faith, and encourages souls to believe in Christ; and hence, Gospel ministers are instruments by whom ethers believe; and *faith comes by hearing, and hearing by the word of God*; and then is a considerable end of the Gospel ministry answered.

Verse 8. **He was not that Light**, &c. He was a light; he was the forerunner of the Sun of Righteousness, the *phosphorus* of the Gospel day; he had great light in him; he knew that the Messiah was ready to come, and declared it; and upon His baptism he knew Him personally, and signified Him to others: he had great light into the person and work of Christ; and into the way of salvation by Him, and remission of sins through Him; into the doctrines of

---

[20] Echa Rabbati, fol. 50. 2.

[21] Bereshit Rabba, fol. 1. 3.

[22] Jarchi in ibid.

[23] De Mundi Opificio, p. 6. De Allegor. l. 2. p. 80. & de Somniis, p. 576, 578.

faith in Christ, and of evangelical repentance towards God; and into the abolition of the legal Mosaic and Jewish dispensation; and was an instrument of giving light to others; yea, he *was a burning and shining light* [5:35], in whose light the Jews rejoiced, at least for a season: but then he was not *that Light*, the Word and Wisdom of God; that increated [*or* uncreated] Light that dwelt with Him from all eternity; nor that which was the Light of men, from the creation; nor that Light which was of old promised to the saints and patriarchs of the Old Testament, and shone in the ordinances and predictions of that state; nor that fountain and giver of light, of every sort, to men; not that Light in which *is no darkness* [*1 John 1:5*], and always shines; not that true Light, or Sun of Righteousness, the Messiah, or *that lightens every man that comes into the world*:

but *was sent* to bear witness of that Light; which is repeated, to distinguish him from *that Light*; to show what he was sent for, and that he acted according to his mission; and to express the honorableness to his work.

Verse 9. **That was the true Light**, &c. Christ is that Light, that famous and excellent Light, the fountain of all light to all creatures; that gave light to the dark earth at first, and spoke light out of darkness; that light of all men in the earth, and of all the angels in heaven, and of all the saints below, and of all the glorified ones above: He is the *true* Light, in distinction from *typical* lights; the *Urim* of the former dispensation; the candlestick, with the lamps of it; the pillar of fire which directed the Israelites by night in the wilderness; and from all the typical light there was in the institutions and sacrifices of the law; and in opposition to the law itself, which the Jews[24] magnify, and cry up as *the light*, saying, *There is no light but the law*; and in opposition to all false lights, as priests, diviners, and soothsayers among the Gentiles, Scribes, and Pharisees, and the learned Rabbins among the Jews, so much boasted of as the lights of the world; and to all false Christs and prophets that have risen, or shall rise, in the world:

which lighteth every man that cometh into the world. The sense is, either that every man that is enlightened in a spiritual manner, is enlightened by Him, which is true of Christ, as the Son of God, existing from the beginning: but not in the Socinian sense, as if they were enlightened by His human ministry and example; for the Old Testament saints were not enlightened by his preaching; and many were enlightened by the ministry of John the Baptist; and multitudes afterwards, through the ministry of the apostles; and very few, comparatively, were enlightened under the ministry

---

[24] T. Bava Bathra, fol. 4. 1.

of Christ; and none we read of, in this sense, enlightened by Him, when, and as soon as they came into the world: or, the meaning is, that He is *that Light* which lighteth all sorts of men; which is true in a spiritual sense. Some connect the phrase, *that cometh into the world*, not with *every man*, but with the *true Light*; and the Arabic version so reads, and joins it to the following verse; but this reading is not so natural, and the order of the words requires the common reading; nor is the difficulty removed hereby; for still it is every man that is enlightened. It is best therefore to understand these words of the light of nature, and reason, which Christ, as the Word, and Creator and Light of men, gives to every man that is born into the world; and which serves to detect the Quakers' notion of the *light within*, which every man has, and is no other than the light of a natural conscience; and shows how much men, even natural men, are obliged to Christ, and how great a person He is, and how deserving of praise, honor, and glory. The phrase, *every man that cometh into the world*, is Jewish, and often to be met with in Rabbinical writings, and signifies all men that are born into the world; the instances are almost innumerable; take one or two: on those words in *Job 25:3, On whom doth not his light arise?* it is asked,[25] Who is he that cometh,

> "באי עולם מכל, *of all that come into the world*; and says, the sun hath not lightened me by day, nor hath the moon lightened me by night? Thou enlightenest those above, and those below, and *all that come into the world*."

Again, God is introduced thus speaking:[26]

> "I am the God, לכל באי עולם, *of all that come into the world*; and I have not united my name, but to the people of Israel."

Once more,[27]

> "Moses, our master, from the mouth of power (that is, God; see *Matt. 26:64*), commanded to oblige, את כל באי העולם, *all that come into the world*, to receive the commandments which were commanded the sons of Noah."

Verse 10. **He was in the world**, &c. This is to be understood, not of His incarnation; for the word *was* denotes past existence in the world, even all the

---

[25] Vajikra Rabba, sect. 31. fol. 171. 4.

[26] Midrash Ruth, c. l. v. 1. fol. 27. 3.

[27] Maimon. Hilch. Melakim. c. 8. sect. 10. Vid. Mishna Roshhashana, c.l. sect. 2. T. Hieros. Sanhedrin, fol. 25. 4. & 26. 3. Sepher Bahir apud Zohar in Gen. fol. 30. 3. Tzeror Hammor, fol. 21. 2. & 22. 3. & 24. 3. & 27. 2. Caphtor, fol. 56. 1. Jarchi in Exod. 15. 2.

time past from the creation of the world; and the *world* intends the world in general, as opposed to Judea, and the people of the Jews in the next verse; besides, the incarnation of the Word is spoken of in *verse 14* as a new and distinct thing from this: but of His being in the world when first made, and since, by His essence, by which He fills the whole world; and by His power, upholding and preserving it; and by His providence, ordering and managing all the affairs of it, and influencing and governing all things in it: He was in it as the light and life of it, giving natural life and light to creatures in it, and filling it, and them, with various blessings of goodness; and He was in the promise and type before, as well as after the Jews were distinguished from other nations, as His peculiar people; and He was frequently visible in the world, in a human form, before His incarnation, as in Eden's garden to our first parents, to Abraham, Jacob, Manoah and his wife, and others:

and the world was made by him. So Philo the Jew often ascribes the making of the world to the *Logos*, or Word, as before observed on *verse 3*, and this regards the whole universe, and all created beings in it, and therefore cannot design the new creation. Besides, if all men in the world were anew created by Christ, they would know Him; for a considerable branch of the new creation lies in knowledge; whereas, in the very next clause it is asserted, that *the world knew him not*; and they would also love Him, and obey Him, which the generality of the world do not; they would appear to be in Him, and so not be condemned by Him, as multitudes will. To understand this of the old creation, best suits the context, and proves the Deity of Christ, and His pre-existence, as the Word and Son of God, to His incarnation;

and the world knew him not; that is, the inhabitants of the world knew Him not as their Creator, nor did they acknowledge the mercies they received from Him; nor did they worship, serve, and obey Him; or love and fear Him; nor did they, the greater part of them, know Him as the Messiah, Mediator, Savior, and Redeemer. There was, at first, a general knowledge of Christ throughout the world among all the sons of Adam, after the first promise of Him; and which, for a while, continued; but this, in process of time, being neglected and slighted, it was forgot, and utterly lost, as to the greater part of mankind; for the Gentiles, for many hundreds of years, as they knew not the true God, so they were without Christ, without any notion of the Messiah; and this their ignorance, as it was first their sin, became their punishment.

Verse 11. **He came unto his own,** &c. Not all the world, who are His own by right of creation; for these, His own, are opposed to the world, and distinguished from them; and His coming to them designs some particular favor, which is not vouchsafed to all: nor yet are the elect of God intended; though they are Christ's own, in a very special sense; they are His by His own choice, by His Father's gift, by His own purchase, and through the conquest of His grace, and are the objects of His special love; and for their sake He came in the flesh, and to them He comes in a spiritual way, and to them will He appear a second time at the last day unto salvation: but they cannot be meant, because when He comes to them they receive Him; whereas these did not, as the next clause affirms: but by *his own* are meant the whole body of the Jewish nation; so called, because they were chosen by the Lord above all people; had distinguishing favors bestowed upon them, as the adoption, the covenants, the promises, the giving of the law, and the service of God; and had the Shekinah, and the symbol of the divine presence in a remarkable manner among them; and the promise of the Messiah was in a particular manner made to them; and indeed, He was to be born of them, so that they were His kindred, His people, and His own nation: and this His coming to them is to be understood not of His incarnation; though when He came in the flesh, as He came of them, so He came to them, particularly being *sent to the lost sheep of the house of Israel* [*Matt. 15:24*], and was rejected by them as the Messiah; yet His incarnation is afterwards spoken of in *verse 14* as a new and distinct thing from this; and to understand it of some coming of His before His incarnation, best suits with the context, and the design of the evangelist. Now Christ, the Word, came to the Jews before His incarnation, not only in types, personal and real, and in promises and prophecies, and in the Word and ordinances, but in person; as to Moses in the bush, and gave orders to deliver the children of Israel out of Egypt: He came and redeemed them Himself with a mighty hand, and a stretched-out arm; in His love and pity he led them through the Red Sea as on dry ground; and through the wilderness in a pillar of cloud by day, and a pillar of fire by night; and He appeared to them at Mount Sinai, who gave unto them the lively oracles of God:

and his own received him not. They did not believe in Him, nor obey His voice; they rebelled against Him, and tempted Him often, particularly *at Massah and Meribah*; they provoked Him to anger, and vexed and grieved His Holy Spirit, as they afterwards slighted and despised His Gospel by the prophets. Of this nonreception of the Word by the Jews, and their punishment for it, the Targumist on *Hos. 9:17* thus speaks:

"my God will remove them far away, because, לא קבילו למימריה, *they receive not his Word*; and they shall wander among the people."

And so they treated this same *Logos*, or Word of God, when He *was made flesh, and dwelt among them*. Somewhat remarkable is the following discourse of some Jews among themselves:[28]

"When the Word of God comes, who is his messenger, we shall honor him. Says R. Saul, Did not the prophets come, and we slew them, and

---

[28] Ben Arama in Gen. 47:4. apud Galatin. de Arcan. Cathol. Verse l. 3. c. 5.

shed their blood? (compare this with *Matt. 23:30,31,37*). How therefore now, נקבל מדברו, *shall we receive his word?* or wherefore shall we believe? Says R. Samuel, the Levite, to him, because he will heal them, and deliver them from their destructions; and because of these signs we shall believe him, and honor him."
But they did not.

Verse 12. **But as many as received him**, &c. This is explained, in the latter part of the text, by *believing* in His name; for faith is the receiving Him as the Word, and Son of God, as the Messiah, Savior, and Redeemer; a receiving grace out of His fulness, and every blessing from Him, as a justifying righteousness, pardon of sin, and an inheritance among them that are sanctified; for though the generality rejected Him, there were some few that received Him:

to them gave he power to become the sons of God; as such were very early called, in distinction from the children of men, or of the world; see *Gen. 6:2,4*. To be the sons of God is a very special favor, a great blessing, and high honor: saints indeed are not in so high a sense the sons of God, as Christ is; nor in so low a sense, as angels and men in common are; nor in such sense as civil magistrates; nor merely by profession of religion; much less by natural descent; but by adopting grace: and in this, Christ, the Word, has a concern, as all the three divine persons have. The Father predestinated men to the adoption of children, secures this blessing for them in the covenant of His grace, and puts them among the children, and assigns them a goodly heritage: the Spirit, and who is therefore called *the Spirit of adoption*, discovers and applies this blessing to them, and *witnesses to their spirits that they are the children of God [Rom. 8:15-16]*: and Christ, the Word, or Son of God, not only espoused their persons, and in time assumed their nature, and by the redemption of them opened a way for their reception of the adoption of children; but actually bestows upon them the *power*, as it is here called, of *becoming the sons of God*: by which is meant, not a power of free will to make themselves the sons of God, if they will make use of it; but it signifies the honor and dignity conferred on such persons: so Nonnus calls it, *the heavenly honor*; as indeed, what can be a greater? It is more honorable than to be a son or daughter of the greatest potentate on earth: and it is expressive of its being a privilege; for so it is an undeserved and distinguishing one, and is attended with many other privileges; for such are of God's household and family, and are provided for by Him; have liberty of access unto Him; are Christ's free men, and are heirs to an incorruptible inheritance. This is a privilege that excels all others, even justification and remission of sins; and is an everlasting one: and it also intends the open right which believers have unto this privilege, and their claim of it: hence it follows,

17

even **to them that believe in his name;** that is, in Himself, in Christ, the Word: the phrase is explanative of the former part of the verse, and is a descriptive and manifestative character of the sons of God; for though the elect of God, by virtue of electing grace, and the covenant of grace, are the children of God before faith; and were so considered in the gift of them to Christ, and when He came into the world to gather them together, and save them; and so, antecedent to the Spirit of God being sent down into their hearts, to make this known to them; yet no man can know His adoption, nor enjoy the comfort of it, or claim his interest in it, until he believes.

Verse 13. **Which were born, not of blood**, &c. Or *bloods*, in the plural number. The birth, here spoken of, is regeneration, expressed by a being born again, or from above; by a being quickened by the Spirit and grace of God; by Christ being formed in men; and by a partaking of the divine nature; and by being made new creatures, as all that believe in the name of Christ are; and which is the evidence of their being the sons of God: and now this is owing not to blood, or bloods; not to the blood of circumcision; nor of the passover, which the Jews had a high opinion of, and ascribe life and salvation to, and to which notion this may be opposed: so their commentators[29] on *Ezek. 16:6*, where the word *live* is twice used, observe on the first *live*, by the blood of the passover, on the second *live*, by the blood of circumcision; but, alas! these contribute nothing to the life of the new creature: nor is regeneration owing to the blood of ancestors, to natural descent, as from Abraham, which the Jews valued themselves upon; for sin, and not grace, is conveyed by natural generation: all men are of one blood, and that is tainted with sin, and therefore can never have any influence on regeneration; no blood is to be valued, or any one upon it, but *the blood of Christ, which cleanses from all sin [1 John 1:7]*;

nor of the will of the flesh; man's free will, which is carnal and corrupt, is enmity to God, and impotent to every thing that is spiritually good [see *1 Cor. 2:14*]: regeneration is ascribed to another will and power, even to the will and power of God [see *James 1:18*], and denied of this:

nor of the will of man: of the best of men, as Abraham, David, and others; who, though ever so willing and desirous that their children, relations, friends, and servants, should be born again, be partakers of the grace of God, and live in His sight, yet cannot effect any thing of this kind: all that they can do, is to pray for them, give advice, and bring them under the means of grace; but all is ineffectual without a divine energy. So with the Jews, אִישׁ, *a man*, signifies a great man, in opposition to *Adam*, or *Enosh*, which signify a mean

---

[29] Jarchi & Kimchi in loc. Shemot Rabba, sect. 19. fol. 103. 2. & 104. 4. & Mattanot Cehuna in Vajikra Rabba, sect. 23. fol. 164. 2. Zohar in Lev. fol. 39. 2.

[that is, lacking distinction or of a lowly regard], weak, frail man; and our translators have observed this distinction in *Isa. 2:9, and the mean man* (Adam) *boweth down, and the great man* (Ish) *humbleth himself.* On which Jarchi has this note, *Adam boweth down*, that is, little men; *and a man humbleth himself*, that is, princes and mighty men, men of power: and so Kimchi on *Psa. 4:2, O ye sons of men*, observes, that the Psalmist calls them the sons of men, with respect to the great men of Israel; for there were with Absalom the sons of great men. Though sometimes the Jews say,[30]

"Adam is greater than any of the names of men, as Geber, Enosh, Ish."

But now our evangelist observes, let a man be ever so great, or good, or eminent for gifts and grace, he cannot communicate grace to another, or to whom he will; none are born again of any such will:

but of God. Of God, the Father of Christ, who begets to *a lively hope* [*1 Pet. 1:3*]; and of the Son, who quickens *whom he will* [*John 5:21*]; and of the grace of the Spirit, to whom regeneration is generally ascribed.

Verse 14. **And the Word was made flesh**, &c. The same Word, of whom so many things are said in the preceding verses; and is no other than the Son of God, or second person in the Trinity; for neither the Father, nor the Holy Ghost, were made flesh, as is here said of the Word, but the Son only: and *flesh* here signifies, not a part of the body, nor the whole body only, but the whole human nature, consisting of a true body, and a reasonable soul; and is so called, to denote the frailty of it, being encompassed with infirmities, though not sinful; and to show, that it was a real human nature, and not a phantom, or appearance, that He assumed. And when He is said to be *made* flesh, this was not done by the change of one nature into another, the divine into the human, or the Word into a man; but by the assumption of the human nature, the Word taking it into personal union with Himself; whereby the natures are not altered; Christ remained what He was, and became what He was not; nor are they confounded and blended together, and so make a third nature; nor are they separated and divided, so as to constitute two persons, a divine person, and a human person; but are so united as to be but one person; and this is such a union as can never be dissolved, and is the foundation of the virtue and efficacy of all Christ's works and actions, as Mediator:

and dwelt among us; or *tabernacled among us*; in allusion to the tabernacle, which was a type of Christ's human nature: the model of the tabernacle was of God, and not of man; it was coarse without, but full of holy things within; here God dwelt, granted His presence, and His glory was seen; here the

---

[30] Zohar in Lev. fol. 20. 2.

sacrifices were brought, offered, and accepted. So the human nature of Christ was of God's pitching, and not man's; and though it looked mean [or lowly] without, the fulness of the Godhead dwelt in it, as well as a fulness of grace and truth; in the face of Christ the glory of God is seen, and through Him, even the veil of His flesh, saints have access unto Him, and enjoy His presence; and by Him their spiritual sacrifices become acceptable to God: or this is observed, in allusion to the feast of tabernacles, when the Jews dwelt in booths, in remembrance of their manner of living in the wilderness: the feast of tabernacles was typical of Christ, and of His tabernacling in our nature. Solomon's temple, which was also a type of Christ, was dedicated at the time of that feast; and it seems probable, that our Lord was born at that time; for as He suffered at the time of the passover, which had respect unto Him, and the pouring forth of the Spirit was on the very day of Pentecost, which that prefigured; so it is highly probable, that Christ was born at the time of the feast of tabernacles, which pointed out His dwelling among us; and is therefore very pertinently hinted at, when mention is here made of His incarnation. However, reference is manifestly had to the Shekinah, and the glory of it, in the tabernacle and temple; and almost the very word is here used. The Targumists sometimes speak of the Shekinah of the Word dwelling among the Israelites: so Onkelos in *Num. 11:20*, where the Israelites are threatened with flesh, till they loathe it; because, says the paraphrast,

"Ye have loathed *the Word of the Lord*, whose Shekinah dwelleth among you."

Jonathan ben Uzziel, on the same place, expresses it thus:

"because ye have loathed the Word of the Lord, the glory of whose Shekinah dwelleth among you."

And it follows here,

(and we beheld his glory; the glory of His divine nature, which is essential to Him, and underived, is equal to the Father's glory, is transcendent to all creatures, and is ineffable, and incomprehensible; some breakings forth of which there were in His incarnate state, and which were observed by the evangelist, and his companions; who, in various instances saw plainly, that Christ was possessed of divine perfections, such as omniscience and omnipotence; since He knew the thoughts of the heart, and could do the things He did: His Father declared Him to be His beloved Son; and the miracles He wrought, and the doctrines He taught, manifested forth His glory. And not only there were some beams of His glory at His transfiguration, which were seen by the apostles, among which the Evangelist John was one, and to which he may have here a particular reference; but even at His apprehension and death, and especially at His resurrection from the dead. The Jews speak of the glory of the Messiah to be seen in the world to come. They say,[31]

"If a man is worthy of the world to come (that is, the times of the Messiah), he shall *see the glory* of the King Messiah."

And of Moses, they say,[32]

"There was (or will be) no generation like that in which he lived, until the generation in which the King Messiah comes, which shall *behold the glory* of the holy, blessed God, as he."

This our evangelist, and the other disciples of Christ have seen:

the glory as of the only begotten of the Father); a glory becoming Him, suitable to Him as such; the very real glory of the Son of God; for the *as,* here, is not a note of similitude, but of certainty, as in *Matt. 14:5; Psa. 2:8*; and the Word is here called, *the only begotten of the Father*; which cannot be said of Christ, as man; for as such, He was not *begotten* at all: nor on the account of His resurrection from the dead; for so He could not be called the *only begotten*, since there are others that have been, and millions that will be raised from the dead, besides Him: nor by reason of adoption; for if *adopted*, then not begotten; these two are inconsistent. Besides, He could not be called the only begotten, in this sense, because there are many adopted sons, even all the elect of God: nor by virtue of His office, as magistrates are called the sons of God; for then He would be so only in a figurative and metaphorical sense, and not properly; whereas He is called God's own Son, the Son of the same nature with Him; and, as here, *the only begotten of the Father*, begotten by Him in the same nature, in a way inconceivable and inexpressible by us:

full of grace and truth. That is, He dwelt among men, and appeared to have a fulness of each of these: for this clause is not to be joined with the glory of the only begotten, as if this was a branch of that; but regards Him as incarnate, and in His office, as Mediator; who, as such, was full of *grace;* the Spirit, and the gifts of the Spirit; of all the blessings of grace, of justifying, pardoning, adopting, sanctifying, and persevering grace; of all the promises of grace; of all light, life, strength, comfort, peace, and joy: and also of *truth*, of all Gospel truths; and as He had the truth, the sum, and substance of all the types and prophecies concerning Him in Him; and as He fulfilled all His own engagements, and His Father's promises; and as possessed of sincerity towards men, and faithfulness and integrity to God.

---

[31] Gloss. in T. Bab. Beracot, fol. 58. 1.

[32] Zohar in Lev. fol. 9. 4.

21

Verse 15. **John bare witness of him**, &c. Which was his office and business, for which purpose he was sent, *verses 6-8,*

and cried; this agrees with his work and office, according to the prophecy of him in *Isa. 40:3,* and with the time of his ministry, the year of Jubilee; and with the nature of his ministry, which was clear, open, and public; and performed with vigor, and in a powerful manner; with much assurance and certainty, with boldness and intrepidity, and with great zeal and fervency, and in an evangelical way; for it was such a cry as debased the creature, and exalted Christ:

saying, This was he, of whom I spake; when he first entered upon his ministry and baptism, before he saw Christ, or baptized Him; see *Matt. 3:11;*

He that cometh after me; for Christ came into the world after John; He was born six months after him; He came after him to be baptized by him, and attended on his ministry; and came later into the public ministry than he did;

is preferred before me; by God the Father, in setting Him up as Mediator; constituting Him the Head of the church; causing a fulness of grace to dwell in Him; appointing Him the Savior of His people; and ordaining Him Judge of quick and dead. And by the prophets, who spake much of Him, and sparingly of John; and of Him as the Messiah and Savior, and of John only as His harbinger: and by John himself, who represents Him as coming from above, and as above all; and himself as of the earth, earthly: and by all Gospel ministers, and every true believer; and good reason there is for it:

for he was before me; which cannot be meant of honor and dignity; for this is expressed before; and it would be proving one thing by the same; nor of his birth, as man: for John in that sense was before Him, being born before Him; besides, being born before another, is no proof of superior worth; others were born before John, whom he yet excelled: but of His eternal existence, as the Word, and Son of God, who was before John, or any of the prophets; before Abraham, and Noah, and Adam, or any creature whatever. The Arabic and Persic versions read, *for he was more ancient than me*; being from everlasting, *from the beginning, or ever the earth was.*

Verse 16. **And of his fulness have all we received**, &c. These are the words, not of John the Baptist, but of the evangelist, carrying on his account of Christ, after he had inserted the testimony of the Baptist, in connection with *verse 14*, where He is said to be *full of grace and truth*; and which fulness is here intended; for the fulness of the Godhead in Him is incommunicable; and the fulness of His fitness, and ability for His office, as Mediator, was for Himself; but His fulness of grace and truth is dispensatory, and is in Him, on purpose to be communicated unto others: and *of it*, the evangelist says, *have* *all we received*; not all mankind, though they all receive natural light and life from Him; nor merely all the prophets of the Old Testament, though they had their gifts and grace from Him, who then was, as now, the Head of the church; nor only all the apostles of Christ, though these may be principally intended; but all believers, who, though they have not all the same measure of grace, nor the same gifts, yet all have *received* something: nor is there any reason for discouragement, envy, or reproach. Faith is the hand which receives Christ, and grace from Him; and the act of *receiving*, being expressed in the past tense, seems to regard, first conversion, when faith is first wrought, and along with it abundance of grace is received; for a believer has nothing but what is given him [see *John 3:27* and *1 Cor. 4:7*], and what he has, is in a way of receiving; so that there is no room for boasting, but great reason for thankfulness, and much encouragement to apply to Christ for more grace, which is the thing received, as follows:

and grace for grace. According to the different senses of the preposition αντι, different interpretations are given of this passage; as that signifies a substitution of a person, or thing, in the room of another, the sense is thought to be, the Gospel, instead of the law; or the grace of the present dispensation, instead of the grace of the former dispensation; grace, different from the former grace, as Nonnus expresses it. If it designs the original, and moving cause, the meaning is, grace is for the sake of grace; for there is no other cause of electing, justifying, pardoning, adopting, and regenerating grace, and even eternal life, but the grace, or free favor of God; and the one is the reason why the other is received: if it signifies the end, or final cause, then it is explained in this way; the disciples received the grace of apostleship, or gifts of grace, in order to preach the Gospel of the grace of God, and for the implanting and increasing grace in men; and grace also, in this life, is received in order to the perfection of grace, or glory, in the other: if it denotes the measure and proportion of a thing, as one thing is answerable to another, then it may be interpreted after this manner; the saints receive grace from the fulness of Christ, according, or answerable to the grace that is in Him; or according to the measure of the gift of Christ, and in proportion to the place, station, and office they bear in the church. Some think the phrase only designs the freeness of grace, and the free and liberal manner in which it is distributed, and received; along with which, I also think, the abundance of it, at first conversion, with all after supplies, is intended; and that *grace for grace*, is the same with grace *upon* grace, heaps of grace; and that the phraseology is the same with this Jewish one,[33] טיבו על ההוא טיבו, *goodness upon that goodness*, an additional goodness; so here, grace upon grace, an abundance of it, an addi-

---

[33] Zohar in Exod. fol. 45. 1.

tion to it, and an increase of it: so חדו על חדו ,[34] *joy upon joy*, is an abundance of joy, a large measure of it; and *holiness upon holiness*,[35] abundance of it.

Verse 17. **For the law was given by Moses**, &c. Both *moral* and *ceremonial*. The *moral* law was given to Adam, in innocence, which having been broken, and almost lost out of the minds and memories of men, was given by Moses, in a new edition of it, in writing; and points out what is man's duty, both to God and men; discovers sin, accuses of it, convicts of it, and condemns for it; nor could it give strength to perform its demands; nor does it give the least hint of forgiveness; nor will it admit of repentance: and hence is opposed to *grace*; though it was a benefit to men, being in its own nature good and useful in its effects. The *ceremonial* law pointed out the pollution of human nature, the guilt and punishment of sin; was a type and shadow of deliverance by Christ, but could not give the grace it shadowed; and therefore is opposed both to *grace* and *truth*. Now both these were given by Moses to the people of the Jews, not as the maker, but the minister of them: it was God who appointed each of these laws, and ordained them in the hand of the mediator, Moses; who received them from Him, by the disposition of angels, and delivered them to the people of Israel: and a very high office this was he was put into, and a very great honor was conferred upon him; but Jesus Christ is a far greater person, and in a higher office:

but **grace and truth came by Jesus Christ**: by *grace and truth*, is meant the Gospel, in opposition to the Law; which is called *grace*, because it is a declaration of the love and grace of God to men; it ascribes salvation, in all the parts of it, to the free grace and favor of God; and is the means of implanting and increasing grace in the hearts of men. And *truth*, not only because it contains truth, and nothing but truth, it coming from the God of truth; and the substance of it being Christ, who is the truth; and being revealed, applied, and led into by the Spirit of truth; but because it is the truth of the types, and the substance of the shadows of the law: or these two may mean distinct things; *grace* may design all the blessings of grace which are in Christ, and come by Him; and *truth*, the promises, and the fulfilment of them, which *are all yea, and amen, in Christ*: and when these are said to be by Him, the meaning is, not that they are by Him as an instrument, but as the author of them; for Christ is the author of the Gospel, and the fulfiller of the promises, and the giver of *all grace*; which shows the superior excellency of Christ to Moses, and to all men, and even to angels also.

---

[34] Ibid. in Lev. fol. 28. 1. & in Num. fol. 69. 2. & 71. 2.

[35] Ibid. fol. 40. 3. & in Num. fol. 61. 1.

Verse 18. **No man hath seen God at any time**, &c. That is, God the Father, whose voice was never heard, nor His shape seen by angels or men; for though Jacob, Moses, the elders of Israel, Manoah and his wife, are said to *see* God, and Job expected to see Him with his bodily eyes, and the saints *will see Him as He is* [*1 John 3:2*], in which will lie their great happiness; yet all seems to be understood of the second person, who frequently appeared to the Old Testament saints in a human form; and will be seen by the saints in heaven, in His real human nature; or of God in and by Him: for the essence of God is invisible, and not to be seen with the eyes of the body; nor indeed with the eyes of the understanding, so as to comprehend it; nor immediately, but through and by certain means: God is seen in the works of creation and providence, in the promises, and in His ordinances; but above all, in Christ, *the brightness of His glory, and the express image of His person* [*Heb. 1:3*]. This may chiefly intend here, man's not knowing any thing of God in a spiritual and saving way, but in and by Christ; since it follows,

the only begotten Son; the Word that was with God in the beginning. The Jerusalem Targum on *Gen. 3:22* says almost the same of the Word of the Lord, as here, where it introduces Him saying,

"The Word of the Lord God said, Lo, the man whom I created, the only one in my world, even as I am, יחיד, *the only one* (or, as the word is sometimes rendered, *the only begotten*), in the highest heavens."

And to the same purpose the Targum of Jonathan, and also Jarchi, on the same place. The Syriac version here renders it, *the only begotten, God which is in the bosom of the Father*; clearly showing, that He is the only begotten, as He is God: the phrase,

which is in the bosom of the Father, denotes unity of nature and essence in the Father and Son; their distinct personality; strong love, and affection between them; the Son's acquaintance with His Father's secrets; His being at that time, as the Son of God, in the bosom of His Father, when here on earth as the Son of man; and which qualified Him to make the declaration of Him:

he hath declared *him*. The Persic and Ethiopic versions further add, *to us*; He has clearly and fully declared His nature, perfections, purposes, promises, counsels, covenant, word, and works; His thoughts and schemes of grace; His love and favor to the sons of men; His mind and will concerning the salvation of His people: He has made, and delivered a fuller revelation of these things, than ever was yet; and to which no other revelation in the present state of things will be added. Somewhat like this the Jews[36] say of the Messiah:

"There is none that can declare the name of his Father, and that knows

---

[36] R. Moses Haddarsan in Psa. 85:11. apud Galatin. de Arcan, Cathol. verse l. 8. c. 2.

him; but this is hid from the eyes of the multitude, until he comes, ויגידהו, and he shall declare him."

He is come, and has declared Him: so Philo speaks of the *Logos*, or Word, as the interpreter of the mind of God, and a teacher of men.[37]

Verse 19. **And this is the record of John**, &c. The evangelist proceeds to give a large, and full account of the testimony John the Baptist bore to Christ, which he had hinted at before, and had signified was his work, and office, and the end of his being sent:

when the Jews sent priests and Levites from Jerusalem to ask him, Who art thou? The Jews that sent were the great Sanhedrin that sat at Jerusalem, whose business it was to inquire into, examine, and try prophets, whether true or false,[38] and John appearing as a prophet, and being so esteemed by the people, they deputed messengers to him to interrogate him, and know who he was. The persons sent were very likely of their own body, since priests and Levites were in that council. For it is said,[39]

> "They do not constitute, or appoint in the Sanhedrin but priests, Levites, and Israelites, who have their genealogies...And it is commanded, that there should be in the great Sanhedrin priests and Levites, as it is said, *Deut. 17:9, and thou shalt come unto the priests, the Levites*, &c. and if they are not to be found, though they are all Israelites (not of the tribe of Levi), it is right."

Such a Sanhedrin is a lawful one; but priests and Levites, if such could be found, that had proper qualifications, were to be admitted in the first place. A message from so august an assembly, at so great a distance (for Jordan was a day's journey distant from Jerusalem;[40] according to Josephus,[41] it was 210 furlongs, or 26 miles and a quarter), and by the hands of persons of such character and figure, was doing John a great deal of honor, and serves to make his testimony of Christ the more public and remarkable; and it also shows what a noise John's ministry and baptism made among the Jews, that it even reached Jerusalem, and the great council of the nation; and likewise

---

[37] De nominum mutat. p. 1047.

[38] Mishna Sanhedrin, c. 1. sect. 5.

[39] Maimon. Hilch. Sanhedrin, c. 2. sect. 1, 2.

[40] Mishna Maaser Sheni, c. 5. sect. 2. Juchasin, fol. 65. 2. Jarchi in Isa. 24:16.

[41] De Bello Jud. [The Jewish War], l. 5. c. 4.

the question put to him, which by John's answer seems to intimate as if it was thought he was the Messiah, shows the opinion that was entertained of him, and even the Sanhedrin might not be without thoughts this way: and the question they put by their messengers might not be, as some have thought, to ensnare John, nor out of disrespect to Jesus, who, as yet, was not made manifest; but might be in good earnest, having from many circumstances reason to think there might be something in the people's opinion of him; since, though the government was not wholly departed from Judah, yet they could not but observe it was going away apace, an Idumean having been upon the throne for some years, placed there by the Roman senate; and now the government was divided among his sons by the same order. Daniel's weeks, they could not but see, were just accomplishing; and besides, from the uncommon appearance John made, the austerity of his life; the doctrine of remission of sins he preached, and the new ordinance of baptism he administered, they might be ready to conclude he was the person.

Verse 20. **And he confessed, and denied not**, &c. He freely, and without any reserve, declared, and in the plainest and strongest terms professed to the messengers, before all the people, that he was not the Messiah; nor did he retract his confession, or draw in his words again, or drop any thing that looked doubtful or suspicious;

but confessed, I am not the Christ: he stood to it, and insisted on it, that he was not that illustrious person; nor had they any reason to entertain such an opinion of him; nor would he have them do so; they might assure themselves he was not Christ.

Verse 21. **And they asked him, What then? Art thou Elias?** &c. *Elijah, the prophet; the Tishbite,* as Nonnus in his paraphrase expresses it, *who was translated, soul and body, to heaven*: the Jews had a notion that that prophet would come in person a little before the coming of the Messiah; see the note on *Matt. 17:10* **[25]**. Wherefore these messengers inquire, that since he had so fully satisfied them that he was not the Messiah, that he would as ingenuously answer to this question, if he was Elias, or not:

And he saith, I am not. That is, he was not Elijah the prophet that lived in Ahab's time, and was called the Tishbite; for John's answer is to the intention of their question, and their own meaning in it, and is no contradiction to what Christ says of him, *Matt. 11:14, that he was the Elias that was to come*; for he was the person meant by Him in *Mal. 4:5*, though not in the sense the Jews understood it; nor is it any contradiction to what the angel said to Zacharias, *Luke 1:17*; for he does not say that John should come in the body, but *in the power and spirit of Elias*; see the note on *Matt. 11:14* **[16]**.

Art thou that prophet? Jeremiah, whom some of the Jews[42] have thought to be the prophet Moses spoke of in *Deut. 18:15,* and expected that he would appear about the times of the Messiah; see *Matt. 16:14;* or any one of the ancient prophets risen from the dead, which they also had a notion of, *Luke 9:8,19*; or, as it may be rendered, *Art thou a prophet?* for prophecy had long ceased with them:

And he answered, No. He was not Jeremiah, nor any one of the old prophets risen from the dead, nor a prophet in the sense they meant: he was not like one of the prophets of the Old Testament; he was *a prophet, and more than a prophet*, as Christ says, *Matt. 11:9*; yet not such a prophet as they were; his prophesying lay not so much in predicting future events, as in pointing out Christ, and preaching the doctrine of the remission of sins by Him.

Verse 22. **Then said they unto him, Who art thou?** &c. Since, as yet, he had only answered in negatives, who he was not, that he was not *the Christ*, nor *Elias*, nor *that prophet*; they desire he would give them a positive account who he was:

that we may give answer to them that sent us; that their labor might not be in vain; that they might not come so far for nothing, without knowing who he was; and that they might be capable of giving an account of him to the Sanhedrin:

What sayest thou of thyself? They insisted on it, that he would openly and honestly declare who he was, and what was his office and business; that from his own mouth, and not from the opinion and conjectures of others, they might represent him in a true light to those who had deputed them on this errand.

Verse 23. **He said, I *am* the voice of one crying in the wilderness**, &c. These words are cited by the other evangelists, and applied to John the Baptist; but then they are only to be considered as their citation, and as an application of them to him by them: but here they are used by John himself, who both expresses them, and interprets them of himself; and in which he was undoubtedly under the infallible direction of the blessed Spirit; and which confirms the sense of the evangelists, who apply the words to him. The Jews give a different interpretation of the words; though one of their celebrated commentators[43] owns, that the comforts spoken of in the preceding verses are

---

[42] Baal Hatturim in Deut. 18:15. Tzeror Hammor, fol. 127. 4. & 143. 4. Siphre in Jarchi in Jer. 1:5.

[43] Kimchi in Isa. 40:1.

what will be in the days of the King Messiah: one of them[44] interprets, *the voice*, of the Holy Ghost; and so far it may be true, as John was filled with the Holy Ghost, and he spake by Him in his ministry: and another,[45] of the resurrection of the dead, or the voice that will be heard then, which will be the voice of the archangel: though another of them[46] better explains it by, הם המבשרים, *they are they that bring glad tidings*, or *good news*; such are Gospel preachers; only it should have been in the singular number: for the text speaks but of one voice; of one person crying; and of John the Baptist, who brought the good news, and glad tidings, that the Messiah was coming, yea, that He was already come, and that *the kingdom of heaven was at hand.* The Hebrew writers generally understand the passage, of the return of the Jews from the Babylonish captivity, and of removing all obstructions in their way to Jerusalem; to which sense the Targum on the place inclines, which paraphrases it thus:

"the voice of him that crieth in the wilderness, Prepare the way before the people of the Lord, make in the plain, paths before the congregation of our God."

But not the people of the Lord, but the Lord Himself, and not the congregation of God, but God Himself is intended; whose ways were to be prepared and made plain, even the King Messiah; which was to be done, and was done by His forerunner John the Baptist, who, with great modesty, expresses Himself in the language of this Scripture, as being a prophecy of Him: he was a *voice*, but not a mere voice; nor was his ministry a mere voice of words, as the law was, but it was the sweet voice of the Gospel, proclaiming the coming of the Messiah; encouraging men to believe in Him; calling them to evangelical repentance, and publishing remission of sins in the name of Christ, and pointing Him out as the Lamb of God, which takes away the sin of the world: this voice was *crying;* it was not a still small voice, it was a very loud one; John lifted up his voice like a trumpet; he delivered himself with great zeal and fervency; and it was *in the wilderness* where this voice was heard, in the wilderness of Judea, as in *Matt. 3:1,* where Jesus came preaching. The Ethiopic version renders the words, *I am the voice of one that goes about in the wilderness*; that is, in the several towns and villages which were in the wilderness, to whom John went and preached the Gospel. The Persic version reads, *I am the voice and cry which cometh out of the wilderness*; referring to the place where he was before he entered on his public ministry, and from

---

[44] Jarchi in Isa. 40:3.

[45] Zohar in Gen. fol. 70. 4.

[46] Aben Ezra in Isa. ibid.

whence he came; for he *was in the deserts till the day of his showing unto Israel, Luke 1:80.* The words this voice cried were,

Make straight the way of the Lord; he called upon persons to reform their ways, and walk in the way of the Lord, to repent of their sins, believe in Christ, and submit to the ordinance of baptism. The Ethiopic version reads, *the way of God*; and such was the person he came to prepare the way for, even the Son of God, and who is truly and properly God,

as said the prophet Esaias, in *Isa. 40:3;* see the note on *Matt. 3:3* **[2]**.

Verse 24. **And they which were sent were of the Pharisees.** Who were the straitest sect of religion among the Jews; were very zealous of the traditions of the elders, and professed an expectation of the Messiah; and were famous in the nation for their knowledge and learning, as well as for their devotion and sanctity: and many of them were in the Sanhedrin, as appears from *chapter 3:1; Acts 23:6;* see the note on *Matt. 3:7* **[3]**.

Verse 25. **And they asked him, and said unto him**, &c. They put a question, by saying to him,

Why baptizest thou then, if thou be not that Christ, nor Elias, neither that prophet? Since he denied that he was the Messiah, or Elias that was to come before the Messiah, according to the expectation of the Jews, or *that* prophet, or *a* prophet, they demand by what authority he introduced a new rite and ordinance among them, which they had never been used to; for though there were divers washings or baptisms among them, enjoined by the law of Moses in certain cases, and others which obtained by tradition, as the immersion of themselves after they had been at market, and of cups, pots, brazen vessels, and tables, yet nothing of this kind that John administered: and as for the baptism of proselytes, it seems to be of a later date than this, and had no manner of likeness to it. The ordinance John administered was such, as they apprehended that no one ought to practice, unless he was the Messiah, or His forerunner, or some eminent prophet; they insist upon it therefore, that since he denied he was either of these, that he would show his credentials, and what commission he had from God to baptize; or they suggest he was liable to be called to an account by their Sanhedrin, and be condemned as a false prophet, or an innovator in religious affairs. From hence it appears, that the Jews expected that baptism would be administered in the times of the Messiah and His forerunner; but from whence they had this notion, it is not easy to say, whether from *Zech. 13:1*, as Grotius, or from *Ezek. 36:25*, as Lightfoot; nor do they speak contemptibly of it, but rather consider it as a very solemn affair, to be performed only by great personages: and this may teach modern ones to think and speak more respectfully of this ordinance than they do, who have given themselves great liberties, and have treated it with much contempt and virulence; calling it by the names of uncleanness, abomination, filthy water, and a devoting of persons to Satan.[47] Likewise, it is clear from hence, that they expected that this ordinance would be first administered by some person of very great note, either some very famous prophet, as Elias, whom they looked for before the coming of the Messiah, or else the Messiah Himself, and not by a common teacher, or any ordinary person; wherefore this rite, as performed by John, could have no likeness with any thing that was in common use among them: besides, it was expressly done in the name of the Messiah, *Acts 19:5;* therefore they conclude He, or His forerunner, must be come; and that John must be one, or other of them, otherwise, why did he administer it? And it is also evident from hence, that no such practice had obtained before among them, or they would not have been alarmed at it, as they were; nor would they have troubled themselves to have sent after John, and inquire of him who he was, that should practice in this manner.

Verse 26. **John answered them, saying, I baptize with water,** &c. Or *in water*, so the Vulgate Latin, and all the Oriental versions render it. The sense of the answer is, that he indeed baptized persons in water, which was all that he could do, or pretended to do; and he owned, that this was a new rite, and that he was the administrator of a new ordinance; but he suggests, as may be supplied from *Matt. 3:11*, that there was one at hand, and even now among them, *that should baptize*, and so it is read in one of Stephens's copies here, *in the Holy Ghost, and in fire*; and it was by His authority, by a commission he had received from Him, that he baptized in water; and that His speedy manifestation and appearance as the Messiah, which would be confirmed by His power of baptizing in the Holy Ghost, and by His ministry and miracles, would be a sufficient vindication of his conduct, and support him in his administration of water baptism:

but there standeth one among you; or *hath stood*, as the Vulgate Latin version renders it; referring, not to His being among them at twelve years of age, but a few days ago when He came to John to be baptized, and was baptized by him; for from *verse 29* it is plain He was not now, or *today*, as Nonnus expresses it, standing in the midst of them. The Ethiopic version renders it, *there is one about to stand among you*, as He did the next day: though the meaning of the phrase may only be, that He was then in being, and dwelt somewhere among them, and not that He was personally present at that time:

---

[47] Vet. Nizzachon, p. 56, 62, 64, 70, 74, 77, 148, 191, 193.

whom ye know not; neither from whence He is, nor who He is, or what is His work and office; neither the dignity of His person, nor the end of His coming into the world, nor the nature of His business in it.

Verse 27. **He it is, who coming after me**, &c. Both into the world, and into the ministry of the Word; for John was before Christ, in both these respects, though greatly behind Him in others, and therefore he adds,

is **preferred before me**: being not only of a more excellent nature, the Son of God, and of a higher extract, the Lord from heaven; but in a higher office, and having greater gifts, and the Spirit of God without measure on Him; and also being more followed by the people; for John decreased, but He increased: or rather the words may be rendered, *who was before me*; being the eternal Son of God, *whose goings forth were of old, from everlasting* [*Micah 5:2*]; who *was set up from everlasting, from the beginning, or ever the earth was* [*Prov. 8:23*]; the firstborn, or first bringer forth of every creature; and therefore must be before all things, which are created by Him; see the note on *verse 15;*

whose shoe's latchet I am not worthy to unloose; which was one of the meanest [*or* lowliest]; services done by a servant to his master; see the note on *Matt. 3:11* **[4]**.

Verse 28. **These things were done in Bethabara**, &c. That is, this testimony was borne by John; and this discourse passed between him and the Pharisees, at the place here mentioned; which was a passage over Jordan, where much people walked to go on the other side,

beyond Jordan; and **where** also **John was baptizing**; which brought a great concourse of people together: so that this witness was borne in a very public manner, and before a large number; and it is to this that Christ refers, in *chapter 5:33*, for this was so well known, that there was no hiding or denying it. The place where this conversation passed, is in the Vulgate Latin, and all the Eastern versions; and in the Alexandrian copy, and many other copies, and so in Nonnus, called Bethany; but as De Dieu observes, Bethany was not beyond Jordan, nor in the wilderness of Judea, but near to Jerusalem, about two miles distant from it; nor was it situated by waters convenient for baptizing, unless they went to the brook Kidron, which indeed was not far from it: but it is clear from the history, that John was not so near Jerusalem; nor did that brook, which might be forded over, continues the same learned author, seem fit and proper enough, "mergendis baptizandorum corporibus," *for plunging the bodies of those that were to be baptized*; wherefore he rightly concludes, that either this reading is an error, or there was another Bethany near Jordan: Bethabara signifies, *the house of passage*, and is thought to be the place where the Israelites passed over Jordan, to go into the land of

Canaan, *Josh. 3:16-17*. And which, as it must be a very convenient place for the administration of baptism by immersion, used by John, so it was very significant of the use of this ordinance; which is, as it were, the passage, or entrance, into the Gospel church state; for persons ought first to be baptized, and then be admitted into a Gospel church, according to the example of the primitive Christians, *Acts 2:41*. But whether there was a place of this name, where the Israelites went over Jordan, is not certain; and if there was, it does not seem so likely to be the place here designed, since that was right over against Jericho; whereas this seems to be rather farther off, and over against Galilee: there were several passages of Jordan, *Judges 12:5-6*. There was a bridge over it, between the lake of Samochon and Gennesaret, now called *Jacob's bridge*, where Jacob is supposed to have wrestled with the angel, and to have met with his brother Esau; and there was another over it at Chammath, near Tiberias, and in other places: and it might be at one of these passages, by which they went over into Galilee, that John pitched upon to continue preaching and baptizing at; partly because of the number of people that went over, to whom he had the opportunity of preaching; and partly, for the sake of baptizing those who became proper subjects of that ordinance, through his ministry. Some have thought, that this place is the same with *Bethbarah*, in *Judges 7:24*, which was either in the tribe of Ephraim, or of Manasseh, and not far from the parts where this place must be, but was on this side Jordan; and so Beza says the words should be rendered; and those who came to John at Jordan, are not said to pass over that river: others are of opinion, that *Bethabara* is the same with *Betharabah, Josh. 15:6, 61*, since this is called *Bethabara* by the Septuagint, in *Josh. 18:22*. However, be it what place soever, and wheresoever, it was no doubt very proper for John's purpose; and therefore he chose it, and for a while continued at it. And here, says Jerome,[48]

"To this day many of the brethren, that is, of the number of believers, desiring there to be born again, are baptized in the vital stream;"

such veneration had they for the place where John first baptized. Origen says,[49] that in his time it was said,

"that Bethabara was shown by the banks of Jordan, where they report John baptized."

Verse 29. **The next day John seeth Jesus coming unto him**, &c. Not to be baptized, for He had been baptized before by him. This seems to have been after Christ had been forty days in the wilderness, from whence He now

---

[48]   De Locis Hebraicis, fol. 89. L.

[49]   Comment in Joannem, tom. 8. p. 131.

returned, and came to attend on John's ministry; both to do honor to him, and that he might be made manifest by Him; and this was the day after John had borne such a testimony concerning Him, to the priests and Levites; and which Christ the omniscient God, knew full well, and therefore came at this season, when the minds of the people were prepared by John's testimony, to expect and receive Him. One part of the work of Elias, which the Jews assign unto him, and the precise time of his doing it, exactly agree with this account of John the Baptist; they say[50] that,

> "His work is to bring to them (the Israelites) the good news of the coming of the Redeemer; and this shall be, יום אחד, *one day*, before the coming of the Messiah; and this is that which is written, *Behold I will send you Elijah the prophet, before the coming of the great and dreadful day of the Lord, Mal. 4:5.*"

For John, the day before Christ came to him, had signified to the priests and Levites, that the Messiah was already come; and now on the day following, seeing Him, pointed as with his finger to Him,

and saith, Behold the Lamb of God, which taketh away the sin of the world: he calls him a *lamb*, either with respect to any lamb in common, for His harmlessness and innocence; for His meekness and humility; for His patience; and for His usefulness, both for food and clothing, in a spiritual sense; as well as for His being to be a sacrifice for the sins of His people: or else with respect to the lambs that were offered in sacrifice, under the legal dispensation; and that either to the passover lamb, or rather to the lambs of the daily sacrifice, that were offered morning and evening; since the account of them best agrees with what is said of this Lamb of God, who was slain in type, in the morning of the world, or *from the foundation of the world [Rev. 13:8]*; and actually in the evening of the world, or in the end of it; and who has a continued virtue to take away the sins of His people, from the begin-ning, to the end of the world; and their sins, both of the day and night, or which are committed every day: for as they are daily committed, there is need of the daily application of the blood and sacrifice of Christ, to remove them; or of continual looking unto Him by faith, whose blood has a continual virtue, to cleanse from all sin. The Jewish doctors say[51] that,

> "The morning daily sacrifice, made atonement for the iniquities done in the night; and the evening sacrifice, made atonement for the iniquities that were by day:"

and in various things they were typical of Christ, as that they were lambs of

---

[50] R. Abraham ben David in Mishna Ediot, c. 8. sect. 7.

[51] R. Menachem, fol. 115. apud Ainsworth, in Exod. 29:39.

the first year, which may denote the weakness of the human nature of Christ, which had all the sinless infirmities of it; they were also without spot, signifying the purity of Christ's human nature, who was holy and harmless, a lamb without spot and blemish; these were offered as a sacrifice, and for the children of Israel only, as Christ has given Himself an offering and a sacrifice to God, both in soul and body, for the sins of the mystical Israel of God, the Israel whom God has chosen for Himself, whether Jews or Gentiles; for Christ is the propitiation for the sins of both: and these were offered daily, morning and evening; and though Christ was but once offered, otherwise He must have often suffered; yet as He has *by one offering*, put away sin for ever [see *Heb. 10:12,14*], so there is a perpetual virtue in His sacrifice to take it away, and there is a constant application of it for that purpose. To which may be added, that these lambs were offered with fine flour, oil and wine, for a sweet savor to the Lord; denoting the acceptableness of the sacrifice of Christ to His Father, to whom it is *for a sweet smelling savor, Eph. 5:2*. And Christ is styled *the Lamb of God*, in allusion to the same, whom the Cabalistic Jews[52] call the secret of the mystery, and כבשי רחמנא, *the Lambs of God*; because God has a special property in Him; He is His own Son; and because He is of His providing and appointing, as a sacrifice for sin, and is acceptable to Him as such; and to distinguish Him from all other lambs; and to give Him the preference, since He does that which they could not do, *taketh away the sin of the world*. By the *sin of the world*, is not meant the sin, or sins of every individual person in the world; for some die in their sins, and their sins go beforehand to judgment, and they go into everlasting punishment for them; which could not be, if Christ took them away: rather, the sin which is common to the whole world, namely, original sin; but then it must be observed, that this is not the only sin Christ takes away; for He also takes away actual sins; and the Arabic and Ethiopic versions read in the plural, *the sins of the world*; and also that this He takes away only with respect to the elect; wherefore they are the persons intended by *the world*, as in *chapter 6:33, 51*, whose sin, or sins, Christ takes away: and a peculiar regard seems to be had to the elect among the Gentiles, who are called *the world*, in distinction from the Jews, as in *chapter 3:16; 1 John 2:2*; and the rather, since the lambs of the daily sacrifice, to which the allusion is, were only offered for the sins of the Jews: but John here signifies, that the Lamb of God he pointed at, and which was the antitype of these lambs, not only took away the sins of God's people among the Jews, but the sins of such of them also as were among the Gentiles; and this seems to me to be the true sense of the passage. The phrase *taking away sin*, signifies a taking it up, as Christ did; He took it voluntarily upon Himself, and became responsible to divine justice for it; and also a bearing and carry-

---

[52] Raya Mehimna, in Zohar in Lev. fol. 33. 2.

ing it, for taking it upon Himself, He bore it *in His own body on the tree* [*1 Pet. 2:24*], and carried it away, as the scapegoat did under the law; and so likewise a taking it quite away: Christ has removed it as far as the east is from the west, out of sight, so as never to be seen any more; He has destroyed, abolished, and made an utter end of it: and this is expressed in the present tense, *taketh away*, to denote the continued virtue of Christ's sacrifice to take away sin, and the constant efficacy of His blood to cleanse from it, and the daily application of it to the consciences of His people; and which is owing to the dignity of His person, as the Son of God; and to His continual and powerful mediation and intercession. This must be a great relief to minds afflicted with the continual ebullitions of sin, which is taken away by the Lamb of God, as fast as it rises; and who, for that purpose, are called to *behold*, and wonder at, the love and grace of Christ in taking up, bearing, and taking away sin; and to look to Him by faith continually for everlasting salvation; and love Him, and give Him the honor of it, and glorify Him for it.

Verse 30. **This is he, of whom it is said**, &c. Either the day before, as in *verse 27*, or some time before that, *verse 15*, when he first began to baptize, even before Christ came to be baptized by him, and before he personally knew Him; see *Matt. 3:11,13*;

After me cometh a man; not a mere man, but the man God's fellow: and this is said, not because he was now a grown man, or to show the truth of His human nature; but seems to be a common Hebraism, and is all one as if it had been said, *after me cometh one*, or a certain person: for the sense of this phrase, and what follows, see the note on *verse 15*.

Verse 31. **And I knew him not**, &c. Ομμασιν, *by sight*, as Nonnus paraphrases it; personally he had never seen Him, nor had had any conversation and familiarity with Him; for though they were related to each other, yet lived at such a distance, as not to know one another, or have a correspondence with each other: John was in the deserts, *until the day of his showing unto Israel* [*Luke 1:80*]; and Christ dwelt with His parents at Nazareth, in a very mean [*or* lowly] and obscure manner, till He came from thence to Jordan to John, to be baptized by him; and which was the first interview they had: and this was so ordered by Providence, as also this is said by John, lest it should be thought, that the testimony he bore to Jesus, and the high commendation he gave of Him, arose from the relation between them; or from a confederacy and compact they had entered into:

but that he should be made manifest to Israel; who had been for many years hid in Galilee, an obscure part of the world: and though He had been known to Joseph and Mary, and to Zacharias and Elisabeth, and to Simeon and Anna; yet He was not made manifest to the people of Israel in common; nor did they know that the Messiah was come, but that He might be known:

therefore am I come baptizing with water; or *in water*, as before: for by administering this new ordinance, the people were naturally put upon inquiry after the Messiah, whether come, and where He was, since such a new rite was introduced; and besides, John, when he baptized any, exhorted them to believe on Him which should come after him, that is, on Christ Jesus; and moreover, by Christ's coming to his baptism, he came to have a personal knowledge of Him himself, and so was capable of pointing Him out, and making Him manifest to others, as he did.

Verse 32. **And John bare record**, &c. The same day that he said the above things, and at the same time:

saying, I saw the Spirit; that is, of God, as is said in *Matt. 3:16*, and which Nonnus here expresses; and the Ethiopic version reads, *the Holy Ghost*,

descending from heaven like a dove; at the time of His baptism; see the note on *Matt. 3:16* **[5]**.

and it abode upon him; for some time; so long as that John had a full sight of it, and so was capable of giving a perfect account of it, and bearing a certain and distinct testimony to it.

Verse 33. **And I knew him not**, &c. That is, before He came to be baptized by him; when it was secretly suggested to him who He was, and the following signal was given him, to confirm Him in it:

but he that sent me to baptize with water; or *in water*; that is, God; for John's mission was from God, as in *verse 6*, and his baptism from heaven; he had a divine warrant and commission for what he did:

the same said unto me; either by an articulate voice, or by a divine impulse on his mind, or by the revelation of the Spirit:

Upon whom thou shalt see the Spirit descending, and remaining on him, the same is he which baptizeth with the Holy Ghost; that is, the Messiah; see the notes on *Matt. 3:11, 16* **[4, 5]**.

Verse 34. **And I saw**, &c. The Spirit descending from heaven as a dove, and lighting upon Jesus, and remaining some time on Him; this he saw with his bodily eyes:

and bare record; at the same time, before all the people that were with him when he baptized Jesus:

that this is the Son of God; the natural, essential, and eternal Son of God; who being sent in the fulness of time, had assumed a human nature, in which He became subject to all ordinances, and had the Spirit without measure bestowed on Him; and which was an evidence who He was, and of what He came about.

Verse 35. **Again the next day after**, &c. The third day from the priests and Levites having been with John, to know who he was. The Syriac, Arabic, and Persic versions, leave out the word *again*:

John stood, and two of his disciples; one of these was Andrew, Simon Peter's brother, as appears from *verse 40*, and very likely the other was the Evangelist John, the writer of this Gospel, who always chooses to conceal himself. John the Baptist stood, and these disciples by him, in some certain place near Jordan, where he was preaching and baptizing.

Verse 36. **And looking upon Jesus as he walked**, &c. Walked, either by them, or as He was going from them to His lodgings; it being toward the close of the day, when John had finished his work for that day, and the people were departing home: John fixed his eyes intently on Christ, with great pleasure and delight, and pointing at Him,

he saith, Behold the Lamb of God; as in *verse 29*, where it is added, *which taketh away the sin of the world*; and which the Ethiopic version subjoins here.

Verse 37. **And the two disciples heard him speak,** &c. Speak the above words, and took notice of them; faith in Christ came by hearing them; they reached their hearts, and they found their affections, and the desires of their souls, to be after Christ:

and they followed Jesus; left their master, and went after Him, in order to get some acquaintance with Him, and receive some instructions from Him.

Verse 38. **Then Jesus turned, and saw them following**, &c. That is, *following him*, as the Vulgate Latin, and all the Oriental versions add: He saw by their walk, and by their countenances, that they were following Him; and which He knew before He turned Himself. He knew what John had said, and what an effect it had upon these disciples, and what was working in their hearts, and how desirous they were of coming up to Him, and conversing with Him; and therefore He turned Himself, that they might have an opportunity of speaking to Him; or rather, in order to speak to them first, as He did:

and saith unto them, What seek ye? This He said, not as ignorant of whom, and what they were seeking, and desirous of; but to encourage them to speak to Him, which, through fear and bashfulness, they might be backward to do; and therefore, He who *will not break the bruised reed, nor quench the smoking flax [Isa. 42:3; Matt. 12:20]*, but cherishes and encourages the first motions of grace, begins first with them, and treats them in a free and familiar manner; thereby to animate and engage them to use freedom with Him, and which end was answered:

They said unto him, Rabbi; a title which now began to be in much use with the Jews, and which they gave to their celebrated doctors; and these disciples of John, observing how magnificently their master spoke of Jesus, in great reverence to Him, addressed Him under this character; see the note on *Matt. 23:7* **[32]**;

(which is to say, being interpreted, Master). These are the words of the evangelist, interpreting the word *Rabbi*, and not of the disciples, and are left out in the Syriac and Persic versions, who, for *Rabbi*, read *our master*, or *our Rabbi*; being said by both the disciples, or by one in the name of both, putting the following question:

where dwellest thou? Signifying, that that was not a proper place, in the public way, to enter into a conversation with Him, and acquaint Him with what they were desirous of; but should be glad to know where He lodged, that they might wait upon Him there, either then, or on the morrow, or at any convenient time.

Verse 39. **He saith unto them, Come and see**, &c. He gave them an invitation to go along with Him directly, and see with their own eyes where He dwelt, and there and then converse with Him, and at any other time; to which they had a hearty welcome:

They came and saw where he dwelt; they accepted of the invitation, and went along with Him immediately, and saw, and took notice of the place where He had lodgings, that they might know it, and find it another time; which, Dr. Lightfoot conjectures, was at Capernaum, which is very probable; since that was His own city, where he paid tribute, where He frequently resorted, and was on the banks of Jordan, near the lake of Gennesaret; and these disciples were Galileans:

and abode with him that day; the remaining part of the day, which they spent in delightful conversation with Him; by which they knew that He was the Messiah; at least they were better instructed in this matter, and more confirmed in it. The Arabic version renders it, *they remained with him that his own day*; and Dr. Lightfoot thinks the next day is meant, and that it was the sabbath day, which they kept with Him in private devotion and conference:

for it was about the tenth hour; which, according to the Roman way of reckoning, must be ten o'clock in the morning; so that there was a considerable part of the day before them; but according to the Jewish way of reckoning, who reckon twelve hours to a day, it must be four o'clock in the afternoon, when there were but two hours to night: and this being about the time when the lamb of the daily sacrifice of the evening was offered up, very seasonably did John point out unto them at this time, Christ the Lamb of God, the antitype of that sacrifice; for the daily evening sacrifice was slain at eight and a half, and was offered at nine and a half,[53] or between the ninth and tenth hours of the day. The Ethiopic version renders it, *they remained with him that day unto the tenth hour.*

Verse 40. **One of the two which heard John *speak***, &c. Speak the above things, concerning Jesus being the Lamb of God:

and followed him; that is, *Jesus*, as the Syriac and Arabic versions read; and the Persic version, *Christ*: and the Ethiopic version, *the Lord Jesus*; for not John, but Jesus they followed:

was Andrew, Simon Peter's brother: see *Matt. 4:18*; the other, as before observed, might be the writer of this Gospel.

Verse 41. **He first findeth his own brother Simon**, &c. Findeth him, either before the other disciple, or before he found any other person: after he and the other disciple departed from Christ, being affected with the grace bestowed upon him, and his heart warm with the conversation he had had with Him, and transported with joy at finding the Messiah, goes in all haste in search of his relations, friends, and acquaintance, to communicate what he had seen and heard, in order to bring them to the knowledge of the same; for such is the nature of grace, it is very communicative, and those that have it, are very desirous that all others should be partakers of it: and the first person he lighted on was Simon, who was afterwards called *Peter*, who was his own brother; not a brother-in-law, but his own brother, by father and mother's side, and so dear unto him by the ties of nature and blood:

and saith unto him; with all eagerness imaginable, and in a rapture of joy:

We have found the Messias; I, and a fellow disciple have had the Messiah, so often foretold by the prophets, and so long expected by our fathers, pointed out to us; and we have followed Him, and have had conversation with Him, and are well assured He is that illustrious person:

---

[53] Mishna Pesachim, c. 5. sect. 1.

which is, being interpreted, the Christ; which, as in *verse 38*, are the words of the evangelist, and not Andrew, and are therefore left out in the Syriac version; the word *Messiah* needing no interpretation in that language, and which was the language in which Andrew spoke. This name, *Messiah*, was well known among the Jews, for that great person who was promised, and they expected would come, as a Savior and Redeemer; though it is not very often mentioned in the books of the Old Testament, chiefly in the following places, *Psa. 2:2; 18:50; 89:39,51; Dan. 9:25-26*; but is very much used in the Chaldee paraphrases: Elias Levita[54] says, he found it in more than fifty verses; and Buxtorf[55] has added others to them, and the word appears in seventy-one places, which he takes notice of, and are worthy of regard; for they show the sense of the ancient synagogue, concerning the passages of the Old Testament, respecting the Messiah. This Hebrew word is interpreted by the Greek word, *Christ*; and both signify *anointed,* and well agree with the person to whom they belong, to which there is an allusion in *Song of Sol. 1:3, thy name is as ointment poured forth.* He is so called, because He was anointed from everlasting, to be Prophet, Priest, and King; see *Psa. 2:6* and *89:20; Prov. 8:22-23*; and He was *anointed* as man, *with the oil of gladness*, with the graces of the Spirit, without measure, *Psa. 45:7; Acts 10:38.* And it is from Him the saints receive the anointing, or grace in measure; and are from Him called *Christians*, and are really anointed ones; see *1 John 2:27; Acts 11:26; 2 Cor. 1:21*; hence it is a name precious to the saints, and savory to them. These words were delivered by Andrew, in a very exulting strain, expressing great joy; as indeed what can be greater joy to a sensible soul, than to find Christ? Which, in a spiritual sense, is to have a clear sight of Him by faith, to go unto Him, and lay hold on Him, as the only Savior and Redeemer: who is to be found in the Scriptures of truth, which testify of Him; in the promises of grace, which are full of Him; and in the Gospel, of which He is the sum and substance; and in the ordinances of it, where He shows Himself; for He is not to be found by the light of nature, or by carnal reason, nor by the law of Moses, but by means of the Gospel, and the Spirit of God attending that, as a Spirit of wisdom and revelation, in the knowledge of Him: and happy are those souls that find Christ under His direction; for they find life, spiritual and eternal, in Him; a justifying righteousness; free and full pardon of their sins; spiritual food for their souls; and peace, comfort, joy, and rest, and eternal glory. Wherefore this must needs be matter of joy unto them, since such a finding is a rich one, a pearl of great price, riches durable and unsearchable; and which a man that has found, would not part with for all the

---

[54] Prefat ad Methurgeman, & in voce מְשִׁח.

[55] Lexicon Talmud p. 1268.

41

world; but parts with all he has for it; and is what can never be lost again; and particularly to two sorts of persons, finding Christ must give a peculiar pleasure, and an inexpressible joy; to such as are under a sense of sin and damnation, and to such who have been under desertion. The phrase of *finding* a person, twice used in this text, and hereafter in some following verses, is frequent in Talmudic and Rabbinic writings; as,

"He went, אשכחיה לרב, *and found him with Rab.*"[56]

Verse 42. **And he brought him to Jesus**, &c. That is, Andrew brought his brother Simon to Jesus; he persuaded him to go along with him, and showed him where He was; which discovered great zeal for Christ, being desirous of gaining souls unto Him; and great affection to his brother, being heartily concerned that he might know Christ, as well as himself; nor did he choose that he should take up with the bare account that he gave of Him, but would have him go to Him in person, that he might be personally acquainted with Him, and instructed by Him: and this also shows the readiness and willingness of Simon, to see and hear Christ himself, and not sit down contented with the bare relation his brother gave: no doubt he found his heart stirred up within him, and the desires of his soul going after Christ; and therefore he at once rose up and went with Andrew to Him; and thus one person may be the means of bringing another to Christ: and it may be observed, that Peter was not the first of the apostles that was called by Christ, or first knew Him; Andrew was before him, and the means of bringing him into an acquaintance with Christ; had it been the reverse, the Papists would have improved it in favor of Peter, as the prince of the apostles. This clause is omitted in the Persic version.

And when Jesus beheld him; as he was coming, or come to Him: He had beheld him before in the glass of His Father's purposes and decrees; He had viewed him in His blood, and said unto him, *live*; and he now looked upon Him with a look of love, of complacency and delight:

he said, Thou art Simon, the son of Jona; thy name is Simon, and thy father's name is Jona: He knew both their names, though He might have never seen their faces, nor heard of them before: this He said to give Simon a testimony of His omniscience; and which, no doubt, must strike him at once. Simon, or Simeon, was a common name among the Jews, being the name of one of the twelve patriarchs; see the note on *Matt. 10:2* **[11]**; and so likewise was Jona, being the name of a prophet of theirs; see the note on *Matt. 16:17* **[24]**; and inasmuch as the prophet Jonah was of Geth Hephar in Zebulun, which was in Galilee; see the note on *chapter 7:52*; this might be a common

---

[56] T. Bab. Sabbat, fol. 108. 1. Zohar in Lev. fol. 15. 3.

name among the Galileans; so that there seems no reason why it should be thought to be the same with *John*, as the Ethiopic version reads it, and by way of interrogation, *Art thou not Simon the son of John?*

Thou shall be called Cephas, which is, by interpretation, A stone; or *Peter* as it should rather be rendered; and as it is in the Vulgate Latin, and Ethiopic versions; and as *Cepha,* or *Cephas*, in the Syriac and Chaldee languages signifies a *stone*, or *rock*,[57] so does *Peter* in Greek: hence, the Syriac version here gives no interpretation of the word. Christ not only calls Simon by his present name, at first sight of him, but tells him what his future name should be; and which imports, not only that he should be a lively stone in the spiritual building, the church, but should have a considerable hand in that work, and abide firm and steadfast to Christ and His interest, notwithstanding his fall; and continue constant and immoveable until death, as he did. The Jews also, in their writings, call him *Simeon Kepha*.[58]

Verse 43. **The day following**, &c. Not the day after John had pointed out Christ, as the Lamb of God to two of his disciples; but the day after Simon had been with Him, being brought by Andrew:

Jesus would go forth into Galilee; from whence He came to Jordan, to John, to be baptized by him; and which being done, and His temptations in the wilderness over, it was His will, resolution, and determination, to return to Galilee, the place of His education and conversation, till this time; and therefore chose to begin His ministry and miracles there, both to give honor to it, and to fulfil a prophecy in *Isa. 9:1-2*; and besides this, He had doubtless another end in going thither, which was, to call some other disciples that dwelt there:

and findeth Philip; as He was going to Galilee, or rather, when in it; not by hap or chance; but knowing where he was, as *the Shepherd and Bishop of souls* [*1 Pet. 2:25*], looked him up and found him out, and called him by His grace, to be a disciple of His; see the note on *Matt. 10:3* **[12]**;

and saith unto him, Follow me; leave thy friends, thy calling, and business, and become a disciple of mine: and such power went along with these words, that he at once left all, and followed Christ; as the other disciples, Peter, and Andrew, James, and John, and Matthew did, as is recorded of them, though not of this; but the following history makes it appear he did.

---

[57] Vid. Targum in Psal. 40:3. & Prov. 17:8. T. Bab. Ceritot, fol. 6. 1. & Gloss. in ibid. Tzeror Hammor, fol. 63. 2.

[58] Toldos Jesu, p. 20-23.

Verse 44. **Now Philip was of Bethsaida,** &c. A town on the lake of Gennesaret, afterwards made a city by Philip the tetrarch, and called *Julias,* after the name of Caesar's daughter.[59] It was a fishing town, and had its name from thence; and the disciples that were of it, were of this business:

the city of Andrew and Peter; or *Simon*, as read the Syriac and Persic versions: three apostles were called out of this place, as mean and wicked as it was; see *Matt. 11:21*; which was no small honor to it. It is a saying of the Jews[60] that,

"A man's place (his native place) does not honor him, but a man honors his place."

This was the case here.

Verse 45. **Philip findeth Nathanael,** &c. Who was of Cana of Galilee, *chapter 21:2*; and where, it is very likely, Philip found him, since we quickly read of Jesus and His disciples being there. This man is thought by some to be the same with *Bartholomew*; and so he is called *Bartholomew*, in a Syriac dictionary;[61] and the rather, since he and Philip are always mentioned together in the account of the apostles, *Matt. 10:3; Mark 3:18; Luke 6:14.* And certain it is, from the above mentioned place, that Nathanael was among the apostles after our Lord's resurrection; and it is highly probable was one of them: his name might be *Nathanael bar Tholmai,* the son of Tholmai, Ptolomy, or Tholomew. It is the same name with *Nethaneel*, and which is read *Nathanael,* as here, in [the Apocrypha] 1 Esdras 9:22:

"And of the sons of Phaisur; Elionas, Massias Israel, and Nathanael, and Ocidelus and Talsas;"

and by the Septuagint on *1 Chron. 2:14; 15:24; 24:6* and *26:4; 2 Chron. 35:9; Ezra 10:22; Neh. 12:36*; and signifies *one given of God*; and is the same with *Theodore* in Greek, and *Adeodatus* in Latin. A doctor of this name, R. Nathaniel, is mentioned in the Jewish writings;[62]

and saith unto him, We have found him of whom Moses, in the law, and the prophets, did write. He does not say, that he, and Andrew, and Simon, had found the Messiah; though he designs Him by this circumlocution: Nathanael being, as is generally thought, a person well versed in the

---

[59] Joseph. Antiqu. [Antiquities of the Jews] l. 18. c. 3.

[60] T. Bab. Taanith, fol. 21. 2.

[61] Bar Bahlul apud Castell Lex. Polyglott. col. 2437.

[62] Pirke Eliezer, c. 48.

law and the prophets, and so would at once know who Philip meant: for Moses, in the law, or *Pentateuch*, in the five books written by him, frequently speaks of the Messiah as *the seed of the woman, that should break the serpent's head;* as *the seed of Abraham, in whom all nations should be blessed*; and as *the Shiloh, to whom the gathering of the people should be*; and as *the great prophet, like to himself, God would raise up among the children of Israel, to whom they were to hearken*: and as for the prophets, they wrote of His birth of a virgin; of the place of His birth, Bethlehem; of His sufferings, and the glory that should follow; of His resurrection from the dead, His ascension to heaven, and session at the right hand of God; and of many things relating to His person, and office, and work. And Philip having given this general account of Him, proceeds to name Him particularly; and affirms Him to be,

Jesus of Nazareth, the son of Joseph; that His name was *Jesus*, which signifies a Savior; and answers to the promises, and prophecies, and character of Him in the Old Testament; that He was *of Nazareth*, a place not above three hours walk from Cana, as Adrichomius says, where Philip and Nathanael were. Nazareth was the place where Christ had lived almost all His days hitherto, and therefore is said to be of it; though Bethlehem was the place of His birth, which Philip might not as yet know; as Capernaum afterwards was His city, or the more usual place of His residence: and that He was *the son of Joseph*; this Philip says, according to the common opinion of people; for He was supposed to be *the son of Joseph*, he having married His mother Mary.

Verse 46. **And Nathanael said unto him**, &c. Nathanael taking notice of, and laying hold on what Philip said, that He was of Nazareth, which at once stumbled, and prejudiced him against Jesus being the Messiah; knowing very well that Bethlehem was to be the place of His birth, said,

Can there any good thing come out of Nazareth? The whole country of Galilee was had in contempt with the Jews; but Nazareth was so mean [*or*, of low regard] a place, that it seems it was even despised by its neighbors, by the Galileans themselves; for Nathanael was a Galilean, that said these words. It was so miserable a place, that he could hardly think that any sort of good thing, even any worldly good thing, could come from thence; and it was so wicked, as appears from their murderous designs upon our Lord, that he thought no good man could arise from thence; and still less, any prophet, any person of great note; and still least of all, that that good thing, or person, *the Messiah*, should spring from it: so that his objection and prejudice proceeded not only upon the oracle in *Micah 5:2*, which points out Bethlehem as the birthplace of the Messiah, but also upon the wickedness, and meanness, and obscurity of Nazareth.

Philip saith unto him, Come and see; who though he might not be master of this point, and knew not how to solve this difficulty, and remove this prejudice from Nathanael's mind, he yet persuades him to go with him to Jesus; who, he doubted not, would give him full satisfaction in this, and all other points; and then it would most clearly appear to him, as it had done to Philip, that He was the true Messiah. The phrase, חזי תא, *come, see*, is often used in the book of Zohar;[63] so it is, and likewise, בא וראה, *come and see*, in the Talmudic writings.[64]

Verse 47. **Jesus saw Nathanael coming to him**, &c. For notwithstanding his prejudices, he was a man of so much uprightness and honesty, that he thought Philip's request was very reasonable; and that it was but right and fair, that he should see and hear, and judge for himself, whether the person Philip spoke of was the Messiah, or not; and therefore he came along with him; and as he was coming, Jesus saw him, who knew all that had passed between him and Philip:

and saith of him; to those that were standing by him, and in the hearing of Nathanael,

Behold an Israelite indeed! A son of Israel, as the Syriac and Persic versions read; a true son of Jacob; an honest, plain-hearted man, like him; one that was an Israelite at heart; inwardly so; not one *after the flesh* only, but *after the Spirit*; see *Rom. 2:28-29; 1 Cor. 10:18*; and which was a rare thing at that time; and therefore a note of admiration is prefixed to it; for *all were not Israel, that were of Israel [Rom. 9:6];* and indeed but a very few then: and so, בן ישראל, *a son of Israel*, and, ישראל גמור, *a perfect Israelite*, are[65] said of such who have a due regard to the articles of the Jewish faith, though not even of the seed of Israel. It is added,

in whom there is no guile. Not that he was without sin; nor is this said of him; nor was he in such sense without guile, as Christ Himself was; but guile was not a governing principle in him: the course of his life and conversation was with great integrity and uprightness, and without any prevailing hypocrisy and deceit, either to God or men. This Christ said, to show how much such

---

[63] In Gen. fol. 13. 1. & 14. 3. & 16. 1, 2. & in Exod. fol. 83. 4. & passim.

[64] T. Bab. Taanith, fol. 8. 1. & 23. 2. & 24. 1. Kiddushin, fol. 20. 1. & 33. 1. & Sota, fol. 5. 1, 2. & passim.

[65] Addareth Eliahu apud Trigland. de Sect. Karaeorum, c. 10. p. 175, 176.

a character is approved by Him; and that He knew the secrets of men's hearts, and the inward frames of their minds.

Verse 48. **Nathanael saith unto him, Whence knowest thou me?** &c. This he said as one surprised that He, who was a stranger to him, should hit upon his general character, and describe the internal state and frame of his soul. This was more surprising to him, than if He had called him by his name *Nathanael*, as He did Simon; or had said what was the place of his abode, Cana of Galilee; since this ordinarily was only to be had from a long and familiar acquaintance and conversation. By Nathanael's reply, it looks as if he had no doubt or fear about the character Christ gave him; but rather, that he believed it, as every good man must be conscious to himself of his own integrity; only it was amazing to him, how He should know it.

Jesus answered and said unto him; in order to satisfy him, how He could know this inward temper of his mind, and to give him some undeniable proofs of His omniscience, which He Himself must acknowledge, being such as none but an all-seeing eye could discover:

Before that Philip called thee, when thou wast under the fig tree, I saw thee; in which words Christ gives two instances of His omniscience; the one is, that He knew Philip had called him; He was privy to all that passed between them, though they were alone, and the conversation was had in the most private manner. Christ knew what an account Philip had given of Him, and what objection Nathanael had made; and what an invitation Philip had given him to go along with him to Christ, and judge for himself; which is here meant by *calling* him, and with which he complied: and the other is, that He *saw him under the fig tree* before that: he was sitting under it, as men in those countries used to do; see *Micah 4:4*, where he might be reading the Scriptures, and meditating upon them; and if, as some observe, he was reading, and thinking upon Jacob's dream, concerning the ladder which reached from earth to heaven, and on which *he saw the angels of God ascending and descending*, the words of Christ in *verse 51* must strike him with fresh surprise, and give him another convincing proof of His omniscience: or he might be praying here in secret, and so acted a different part from the generality of religious men of that nation, who chose to pray *in the synagogues, and corners of the streets, that they might be seen [Matt. 6:5]*; and likewise proved him to be what Christ had said of him, a true and rare Israelite, without guile and hypocrisy, which were so visible and prevailing among others. It was usual with the doctors to read, and study in the law, under fig trees, and sometimes, though rarely, to pray there. It is said,[66]

---

[66] T. Hieros. Beracot, fol. 5. 3. Vid. Shirhashirim Rabba, fol. 16. 4.

"R. Jacob, and his companions, were *sitting,* studying in the law, תאינה תחות חדא, *under a certain fig tree.*"

And the rule they give about praying, on, or under one, is thus:[67]

"He that prays on the top of an olive tree, or on the top of a *fig tree*, or on any other trees, must come down, and *pray below.*"

It is said of Nathanael, in the Syriac dictionary,[68] that his mother hid him under a fig tree, when the infants were slain, that is, at Bethlehem; which, if it could be depended upon, must be to Nathanael a surprising, and undeniable proof of the Deity of Christ, and of His being the true Messiah; since, at that time, he was an infant of days himself, and was the person Herod was seeking to destroy, as the Messiah, and king of the Jews.

Verse 49. **Nathanael answered and saith unto him**, &c. Being fully convinced of His omniscience by these instances:

Rabbi; that is, Master, as it is interpreted in *verse 38*, and is not here, because it is there:

thou art the Son of God; not by creation, for this would be to say no more of Him, than may be said of every man; nor by adoption, for in that sense Nathanael himself was a son of God, and many others; nor on account of His wonderful incarnation, which, it is very likely, at this time Nathanael knew nothing of; nor by reason of His resurrection from the dead, which, as yet, was not; and still less might be known by His person: nor because of His office, as Mediator, for this is expressed in the next clause; but by nature, as being of the same essence, and possessed of the same perfections God is; and of which he was convinced by the instances He gave of His omniscience; for it was from hence, and no other consideration, that he concludes Him to be *the Son of God*: wherefore this phrase must be understood of Him, not as Mediator, but as a divine person; as the natural, essential, and eternal Son of God; and who is truly and properly God: he adds,

thou art the King of Israel; having in view, no doubt, the passage in *Psa. 2:6-7,* where the characters of Son of God and King of Zion, meet in the same person: not *King of Israel*, in a literal sense; though He was the Son of David, and a descendant of his in a right line, and was of the royal line, and had a legal right to the throne of Israel; and Nathanael might have a view to this, being tinctured with the common national prejudice, that the Messiah would be a temporal prince: but His kingdom is *not of this world* [*John 18:36*]; nor

---

[67] Ibid. col. 1. & T. Bab. Beracot, fol. 16. 1.

[68] Bar Bahluli apud Castell. Lexic. Polyglott. col. 2437.

with observation; but is spiritual; and He is a King over Israel in a spiritual sense, even of saints, whether Jews or Gentiles: whom He conquers by His power, and rules in their hearts by His Spirit and grace; and protects, and defends them from all their enemies.

Verse 50. **Jesus answered and said unto him**, &c. Not as reproving him for his faith, as if he was too credulous, and too easily gave into the belief of Christ, as the Son of God and true Messiah, upon these single expressions of His; but as approving of it, and surprised at it:

because I said unto thee, I saw thee under the fig tree, believest thou? Some read the words, not by way of interrogation, but as an assertion; *thou believest*, or *hast believed*, as the Vulgate Latin, Arabic, and Persic versions:

thou shalt see greater things than these. Meaning, that he should have larger discoveries of His person, and perfections, and should see things done by Him, much more surprising than any thing he had seen yet; referring to the miracles of raising the dead, casting out devils, and healing all manner of diseases.

Verse 51. **And he saith unto him, Verily, verily, I say unto you**, &c. Not only to Nathanael, but to the rest of the disciples that were then with Him; and to show Himself to be the *Amen*, and faithful witness, as well as more strongly to asseverate what He was about to say, He doubles the expression, *verily, verily,*

Hereafter you shall see heaven open; either in a literal sense, as it had been at His baptism; or, in a mystical sense, that there should be a clearer manifestation of heavenly truths made by His ministry; and that the way into the holiest of all should be made more manifest; and a more familiar intercourse be opened between God and His people; and also between angels and saints:

and the angels of God ascending and descending upon the Son of man; or *to the Son of man*, as the Syriac, Arabic, and Ethiopic versions render it; meaning, Himself in human nature; the second Adam, and seed of the woman; and is expressive both of the truth, and infirmity of that nature. Reference may here be had to the ladder Jacob dreamed of, in *Gen. 28:12*, which was a representation of Christ, in His person, as God-man; who, as God, was in heaven, while He, as man, was on earth; and in His office, as Mediator between God and man, making peace between them both; and in the ministration of angels to Him in person, and to His body the church. And it is observable, that some of the Jewish writers[69] understand the ascent, and descent of the angels, in *Genesis [28:12]*, as aforesaid, to be not upon the ladder, but upon Jacob; which makes the phrase there still more agreeable to this; and so they render עליו, in *Gen. 28:13*, not *above it*, but *above him*. Or the sense is, that there would be immediately made such clearer discoveries of His person and grace, by His ministry, and such miracles would be wrought by Him in confirmation of it, that it would look as if heaven was open, and the angels of God were continually going to and fro, and bringing fresh messages, and performing miraculous operations; as if the whole host of them were constantly employed in such services: and this the rather seems to be the sense, since the next account we have, is of the beginning of Christ's miracles to manifest forth His glory in Cana of Galilee, where Nathanael lived; and since the word, rendered *hereafter*, signifies, *from henceforward*; or, as the Persic version renders it, *from this hour*; though the word is left out in the Vulgate Latin and Ethiopic versions.

CHAPTER 2

Verse 1. **And the third day there was a marriage,** &c. Either the third day from the second testimony borne by John the Baptist concerning Christ, and from the call of Simon Peter, which seem to be of the same date; see *chapter 1:35,36,42,43*; or from Christ's coming into Galilee; or from the conversation He had with Nathanael; from either of which the date is taken, it matters not; the first is as agreeable and plain as any. There is much dispute, and many rules with the Jews about the times, and days of marriage:

> "A virgin (they say,[1]) marries on the fourth day (of the week), and a widow on the fifth, because the Sanhedrin sit in the cities twice in the week, on the second, and on the fifth days; so that if there is any

---

[69] Bereshit Rabba, sect. 68. fol. 61. 2. & sect. 69. fol. 61. 3, 4.

[1] Mishna Cetubot, c. 1. sect. 1.

dispute about virginity, he (the husband) may come betimes to the Sanhedrin."

This was a law that obtained since the times of Ezra; for it is said,[2]

"before the order of Ezra, a woman might be married on any day;"

but in after times, feast days, and sabbath days, were particularly excepted. One of their canons is,[3]

"they do not marry women on a feast day, neither virgins, nor widows."

The reason of it was, that they might not mix one joy with another; and lest a man should leave the joy of the feast, for the joy of his wife. The account Maimonides[4] gives of these several things is this:

"It is lawful to espouse on any common day, even on the ninth of Ab, whether in the day, or in the night; but they do not marry wives neither on the evening of the sabbath, nor on the first of the week: the decree is, lest the sabbath should be profaned by preparing the feast; for the bridegroom is employed about the feast: and there is no need to say, that it is unlawful to marry a wife on the sabbath day; and even on the common day of a feast they do not marry wives, as we have explained; because they do not mix one joy with another, as it is said in *Gen. 29:27, fulfil her week, and we will give thee this also*: but on the rest of the days it is lawful to marry a wife, any day a man pleases; for he must be employed in the marriage feast three days before the marriage. A place in which the Sanhedrin do not sit, but on the second and fifth days only, a virgin is married on the fourth day; that if there is any objection to her virginity, he (her husband) may come betimes to the Sanhedrin: and it is a custom of the wise men, that he that marries one that has been married, he may marry her on the fifth day, that so he may rejoice with her on the fifth day, and on the evening of the sabbath (that is, the sixth), and on the sabbath day, and may go forth to his work on the first day."

But elsewhere it is said[5] that,

"now they are used to marry on the sixth day of the week."

Yea,[6] that,

---

[2] T. Bab. Cetubot, fol. 3. 1.

[3] Mishna Moed Katon, c. 1. sect. 7. & T. Bab. Moed Katon, fol. 8. 2. & 18. 2.

[4] Hachot Ishot, c. 10. sect. 14, 15.

[5] Piske Toseph. Cetubot, art. 6.

[6] Ibid. art. 28.

"it is lawful to marry, and to make the feast on the sabbath day."
But whether this marriage was of a virgin, or a widow, cannot be known; nor with certainty can it be said on what day of the week it was. If that day was a sabbath day on which the disciples abode with Christ, as Dr. Lightfoot conjectures, then it must be on the first day that Christ went into Galilee, and found Philip, and conversed with Nathanael; and if this third day is reckoned from John's second testimony, it must be on a Tuesday, the third day of the week; but if from Christ's going into Galilee, then it must be on a Wednesday, the fourth day of the week, the day fixed by the Jewish canon for the marriage of a virgin. This marriage was,

in Cana of Galilee. The Syriac and Persic versions, read, in *Kotne, a city of Galilee*; and which, in the Jewish map, is called קטנא בגליל, *Katna in Galilee*, and is placed in the tribe of Zebulun, which was in Galilee, and not far from Nazareth; and bids fair to be the same place with this; though it is more generally thought,[7] that Cana in the tribe of Asher, mentioned in *Josh. 19:28*, which was also in Galilee, is here meant; and is so called to distinguish it from another *Kanah*, in the tribe of Ephraim, *Josh. 16:8* and *17:9*. Josephus[8] speaks of a town or village of Galilee, called *Cana*, which was a day's march from it to Tiberias, and seems to be the same place: and another Jewish writer[9] says,

"to me it appears that *Cepher Chanania*, is *Cepher Cana*; or the village of Cana, as is clear in Mishna Sheviith, c. 9. sect. 1, for there is the beginning of lower Galilee,"

which also accords with this. Now in the case of marriage, there was some difference between Judea and Galilee, and certain rules were laid down relating thereunto: and it is said,[10]

"There are three countries, for the celebration of marriages; Judea, the country beyond Jordan, and Galilee;"

that is, that were obliged to marry among themselves; so that if any one married a wife out of any of these countries, she was not obliged to go along with him from one country to another:[11] hence it follows,

"They do not bring them out from city to city (that is, oblige them to go with them from city to city), nor from town to town; but in the same

---

[7] Jerome de Locis Hebraicis, fol. 90. B.

[8] In vita sua.

[9] Juchasin, fol. 57. 2.

[10] Mishna Cetubot, c. 13. sect. 10. T. Hieros. Cetubot, fol. 36. 2.

[11] Bartenora in ibid.

country they bring them out from city to city, and from town to town."
And it is elsewhere observed[12] that,

"In Judea, at first, they joined the bridegroom and bride together an
hour before they went into the bride chamber, that so his heart might
be lifted up in her; but in Galilee they did not do so. In Judea, at first,
they appointed for them two companions, one for him, and another for
her, that they might minister to, or wait on the bridegroom and bride,
when they went into the bride chamber; but in Galilee they did not do
so. In Judea, at first, the companions slept in the house where the
bridegroom and bride slept; but in Galilee they did not do so."

Next we have an account of the persons that were present at this marriage:

and the mother of Jesus was there; who seems to have been a principal
person at this wedding, and was very officious; when wine was wanted, she
signified it to her son, and ordered the servants to do whatever He bid them;
and since she, and Jesus, and His brethren, were all here, it looks as if it was
a relation of her's that was now married; and since these brethren were the
kinsmen of Christ: Simon, Judas, and Joses, the sons of Cleophas or Alphaeus,
whose wife was sister to the mother of our Lord; and since one of them, to
distinguish him from Simon Peter, is called *Simon the Canaanite*, or an
inhabitant of Cana, as some have thought; hence it is conjectured by Dr.
Lightfoot, that Alphaeus had an house in Cana, and that his family dwelt
there, and that it was for one of his family that this marriage feast was made;
see *chapter 2:2,3,5,12* and *19:25; Matt. 13:55* and *10:4*. Joseph, the husband
of Mary, perhaps, was now dead, since no mention is made of him here, nor
any where else, as alive, after Christ had entered on His public ministry.

Verse 2. **And both Jesus was called**, &c. Or invited, as being a relation,
according to the flesh:

and his disciples, to the marriage. Who were bidden on His account; and
they seem to be these, Andrew, and the other disciple [John] that followed
Jesus, and Simon Peter, and Philip, and Nathanael, who was of this place: and
accordingly they all went to it. Christ, and His five disciples, made six of the
ten, which were always necessary to be present at the benediction of
bridegrooms; for so runs the canon:[13]

"They do not bless the blessing of bridegrooms, but with ten principal
and free men; and the bridegroom may be one of the number."

---

[12]   T. Bab. Cetubot, fol. 12. 1.

[13]   Maimon. Hilch. Ishot, c. 10. sect. 5. Pirke Eliezer, c. 19. Shirhashirim Rabba, fol.
9. 3.

To attend a wedding, was reckoned, with the Jews, an act of beneficence and kindness.[14] Our Lord, being at this wedding, was acting like Himself, and His general character of being free, affable, and courteous; who accepted of every invitation, and refused not to be at any entertainment, made by whom it would, or on whatever occasion. And particularly in this instance, it shows His humility in not disdaining His poor relations, but giving them His company at such a time; as also it was bearing a testimony to the institution of marriage, as honorable; and teaches us to rejoice with them that rejoice: and as this was at the first of Christ's ministry and miracles, it is likely it might give the occasion of that calumny cast on Him in *Matt.11:19*. The disciples of Christ followed the example of their master. According to the Jewish canons,[15] a disciple of a wise man might not partake of any feast, but what was according to the commandment, as the feast of espousals, and of marriage; and such a feast was this, which Christ and His disciples were at; and so was not to be condemned for it, according to their own maxims.

Verse 3. **And when they wanted wine**, &c. Or *wine was wanting*; not through the intemperance of the guests, rather through the poverty of the family, who were not able to provide very largely; and it may be by reason of a larger number of guests than were expected; however, so it was ordered by Divine Providence, that there might be an opportunity for Christ to manifest forth His glory:

the mother of Jesus saith unto him, They have no wine. Being concerned for the family, lest they should be put to shame and disgrace, and the entertainment should not proceed with becoming credit and honor; and knowing the power of Christ to help in this time of necessity, she modestly moves it to Him, perhaps by a whisper, sitting next [to] Him; or, it may be, might call Him out, and just drop the hint; being well persuaded of His power, as she might; not from any miracles wrought by Him in her family for the support of it, when in distress; for as Christ wrought no miracle, in the time of His public ministry, for the support of Himself or His disciples, but for others, it is not likely He should do it for His family in private life; but from the wonderful things told her by the angel that brought the news of her conception, and by the shepherds, and by Simeon and Anna, which she had laid up in her heart; and from His being the Messiah, who, according to the general belief of the nation, was to work miracles; and particularly from the last words of the preceding chapter; see the note there [*verse 50*]: for she might

---

[14] Maimon in Mishna Peah, c. 1. sect. 1

[15] T. Bab. Pesachim, fol. 49. 1. & Maimon. Hilchot Deyot, c. 5. sect. 2.

be present at the delivery of them; and therefore might hope that as this was the first opportunity that offered after, that He would display His power in supplying the family with wine in this time of exigence.

Verse 4. **Jesus saith unto her, Woman**, &c. Calling her *woman*, as it was no ways contrary to her being a virgin, *Gal. 4:4*, so it was no mark of disrespect; it being a usual way of speaking with the Jews, when they showed the greatest respect to the person spoken to; and was used by our Lord when He addressed His mother with the greatest tenderness, and strongest affection, *chapter 19:26*. The Jews frequently object this passage to us Christians: one of their writers forms his objection in this manner:[16]

"They (the Christians) say, the mother of Jesus is never called a woman in their law; but here her son himself calls her a woman."

Another puts it thus:[17]

"It is their (the Christians) belief, that Mary, even after she brought forth Jesus, was a virgin; but if she was, as they say, why does not her son call her by the name of virgin? But he calls her a woman, which signifies one known by man, as appears from *chapter 4:2* and *8:10*."

To which may be replied, that the mother of Jesus is never called a *woman* in the New Testament, is not said by us Christians: it is certain she is so called, both here, and elsewhere; but then this is no contradiction to her being a virgin; one, and the same person, may be a virgin, and a woman: the damsel, Abraham's servant was sent to take for a wife for his son Isaac, is called a *woman*, though a virgin that had never known any man, *Gen. 24:5,8,14, 16,43,44*. Besides, we do not think ourselves obliged to maintain the perpetual virginity of Mary, the mother of our Lord; it is enough that she was a virgin when she conceived, and when she brought forth her firstborn: and as the Jews endeavor to take an advantage of this against the character of Mary, the Papists are very solicitous about the manner in which these words are said, lest they should be thought to contain a reproof, which they cannot bear she should be judged worthy of; or suggest any thing to her dishonor, whom they magnify as equal to her son: but certain it is, that the following words,

what have I to do with thee? show resentment and reproof. Some render the words, *what is it to thee and me?* and give this as the sense: What concern is this of ours? What business have we with it? Let them look to it who are

---

[16] Vet. Nizzachon, p. 222.

[17] R. Isaac Chizzuk Emuna, par. 2. c. 42. p. 433.

the principal in the feast, and have the management of it. The Jew [18] objects to this sense of the words, but gives a very weak reason for it:

"But I say (says he), Who should be concerned but the master of the feast? And he was the master of the feast:"

whereas it is a clear case that He was one of the guests, one that was *invited*, *verse 2*, and that there was a governor or ruler of the feast, who might be more properly called the master of it than Jesus, *verses 8, 10*. However, since Christ afterwards did concern Himself in it, it looks as if this was not His meaning. Others render it to the sense we do, *what have I with thee?* as the Ethiopic version; or *what business hast thou with me?* as the Persic version; and is the same with, מה לי ולך, *what have I to do with thee?* used in *1 Kings 17:18* and *2 Kings 3:13*, where the Septuagint uses the same phrase as here; and such a way of speaking is common with Jewish writers: [19] hereby signifying, that though, as man, and a son of hers, He had been subject to her, in which He had set an example of obedience to parents; yet as God, He had a Father in heaven, whose business He came to do; and in that, and in His office, as Mediator, she had nothing to do with Him; nor was He to be directed by her in that work; or to be told, or the least hint given when a miracle should be wrought by Him in confirmation of His mission and doctrine. Moreover, He adds,

mine hour is not yet come. Meaning not the hour of His sufferings and death, in which sense He sometimes uses this phrase; as if the hint was, that it was not proper for Him to work miracles as yet, lest it should provoke His enemies to seek His life before His time; but rather the time of His public ministry and miracles, which were to go together, and the one to be a proof of the other; though it seems to have a particular regard to the following miracle, the time of doing that was *not yet come*; the proper juncture, when, all fit circumstances meeting together, it would be both the more useful, and the more illustrious: or His meaning is, that His time of doing miracles in public was not yet; and therefore, though He was willing to do this miracle, yet He chose to do it in the most private manner; so that only a few, and not the principal persons at the feast, should know it: wherefore the reproof was not so much on the account of the motion itself, as the unseasonableness of it; and so His mother took it.

Verse 5. **His mother said unto the servants**, &c. She took the reproof in good part, and by the words He said, and the manner in which He spoke them,

---

[18] Vet. Nizzachon, p. 223.

[19] Vid. Kimchi in Psa. 2:12. Bechinat Olam, p. 70.

or by the looks He gave, and the gestures He might use, she hoped, and even believed, that the thing she moved for would be done; and therefore went immediately to the servants, and gave them the following instructions:

Whatsoever he saith unto you, do *it*; punctually observe and obey His orders in every circumstance.

Verse 6. **And there were set six waterpots of stone**, &c. To distinguish them from other vessels made of different matter: for the Jews had,

"vessels made of dust, and the dung of beasts, כלי אבנים, *vessels of stone*, vessels of earth, vessels made of shells, vessels of niter, vessels made of the bones and skins of fishes."[20]

And as these vessels were very likely for washing of hands, such were used for that purpose: their rule is,[21]

"they may put water for the hands in all sorts of vessels; in vessels of dung, *in stone vessels*, and in vessels of earth."

At a wedding were set vessels of various sizes to wash hands and feet in; there was one vessel called משיכלא, which the gloss says was a large pitcher, or basin, out of which the whole company washed their hands and their feet; and there was another called משיכלתא, which was a lesser, and a beautiful basin, which was set alone for the more honorable persons, as for the bride, and for any gentlewoman,[22] and such might be these six stone jars, or pots:

after the manner of the purifying of the Jews; or *for the purifying of the Jews*, as the Syriac, Arabic, and Persic versions render it; that is, for the washing of them, their hands and feet, and their vessels, pots and cups, according to the traditions of the elders; see *Mark 7:2-4*:

containing two or three firkins apiece. The Ethiopic version reads, *some held two measures, and some three*; how large the *metreta*, or *measure* was, which we render a *firkin*, is not certain; it is most likely it answered to the Hebrew *bath*, which was a common measure of liquids with the Jews, and held four gallons and a half, or more; see the note on *Luke 16:6* **[53]**; so that such of these vessels, that held two of these measures, contained nine gallons, and such as held three of them, thirteen gallons and a half; and six of these contained a large quantity of wine, one with another: and which makes the following miracle the greater; and shows the liberality of Christ the more, in

---

[20] Mishna Celim, c. 10. sect. 1. & Maimon. & Bartenora in ibid.

[21] Mishna Yadaim, c. 1. sect. 2.

[22] Gloss in T. Bab. Sabbat, fol. 77. 2.

providing for the following days of the feast, for a marriage was kept seven days,[23] and for the family, some time after it was over.

Verse 7. **Jesus saith unto them**, &c. To the servants that waited at the feast,

Fill the waterpots with water. The Ethiopic version adds, *to their brims*, as they did. Christ chose the waterpots, and not the vessel, or vessels, or bottles, now empty, out of which they had drank their wine; that it might not be said that there was any left therein, which gave color and flavor to the water: and He ordered them to be filled *with water* by the servants, that they might take notice, and be witnesses, that that, and nothing else, was put into them; and up to the brims, so that they could not he capable of having any other liquor infused into them:

And they filled them up to the brim; strictly observing the orders of Christ, and the instructions of His mother.

Verse 8. **And he saith unto them, Draw out now**, &c. As soon as ever the vessels were filled with water, without any more delay, He ordered the servants to draw out of those larger, into lesser vessels; He does not say what, water or wine:

and bear unto the governor of the feast. Who either had the ordering and management of the feast, and the command of the whole affair; hence the Ethiopic version calls him, *the master of the waiters*, or *servants*: or he was the chief guest, as the word seems to import, who sat, or rather lay, on the chief couch at the table; and so a proper person to begin with, and put the cup round: or else he might be doctor or chaplain: for such a one was necessary at a marriage; since there were six or seven benedictions to be pronounced; and particularly a blessing was said over the cup of wine; for if there was any wine, a cup of it was brought and he blessed over it first, and ordered every thing concerning the cup: and this made up seven blessings at such a time;[24] and therefore was a very fit person to bear the wine to first:

and they bare *it*. The servants [see *Heb. 10:12,14*] having drawn out of the stone vessels, by cocks, into smaller ones, carried the liquor, as they were ordered, to the above person.

Verse 9. **When the ruler of the feast had tasted the water**, &c. The Persic version reads, *tasted of the wine*, and adds, what is not in the text, *it was of a*

---

[23] Maimon. Hilchot Ishot, c. 10. sect. 12, 13.

[24] Maimon. Hilchot Ishot, c. 10. sect. 3, 4.

very grateful flavor: but the sense is, he tasted of that which was before water, but now,

was made wine; not in such sense as the Papists pretend that the bread and wine, in the Lord's supper, are transubstantiated into the body and blood of Christ by the consecration of the priest; after which they appear to have the same properties of bread and wine as before; but this water, that was turned into wine, ceased to be what it was before, and became what it was not: it had no more the properties, the color, and taste of water, but of wine; of which the whole company were judges:

and knew not whence it was; from whence it came, where it was had, nor any thing of the miracle that was wrought, and therefore was a proper person to have it put into his hands first; since it cannot be thought he should say what he does in the following verse, from any compact with Christ, or in favor of Him:

(but the servants which drew the water knew); they knew from whence they had it, out of the water pots; and they knew that they filled them with water; and that that liquor, which the ruler of the feast had in his hands, and commended as most excellent wine, was drawn out of them; and that there was no juggle, nor deceit in the case: and, upon tasting of it,

the governor of the feast called the bridegroom. To him out of the place where he sat, and which might not be far from him,

Verse 10. **And saith unto him**, &c. And saith the following words; expressing the common custom used at feasts:

Every man at the beginning doth set forth good wine; that is, it is usual with men, when they make entertainments, first to give the guests the best, the most generous, and strongest bodied wine; as being most suitable for them, and they being then better able to bear it, and it being most for the credit of the maker of the feast:

and when men have well drunk; not to excess, but freely, so as that they are exhilarated; and their spirits cheerful, but their brains not intoxicated: so the word, as answering to the Hebrew word שכר, is used by the Septuagint in *Gen. 43:34* and *Song of Sol. 5:1*,

then that which is worse; not bad wine, but τον ελασσω, *that which is lesser*; a weaker bodied wine, that is lowered, and of less strength, and not so intoxicating, and which is fittest for the guests. So Martial[25] advises Sextilianus, after he had drank the tenth cup, not to drink the best wine, but to ask his host for wine of Laletania, which was a weaker and lower sort of wine;

but **thou hast kept the good wine until now**; which shows he knew nothing of the miracle wrought. And as the bridegroom here did, in the apprehension of the ruler of the feast, at this his marriage, so does the Lord, the husband of the church, in the marriage feast of the Gospel; and so He will do at the marriage supper of the lamb. The Gospel, which may be compared to wine for its purity, pleasant taste, and generous effects, in reviving drooping spirits, refreshing weary persons, and comforting distressed minds, as also for its antiquity, was published before the coming of Christ, in the times of Adam, Noah, Abraham, Moses, David, and the prophets, but in a lower and weaker way; *at sundry times*, here a little, and there a little, by piecemeals, as it were; *and in divers manners* [*Heb. 1:1*], by promises, prophecies, types, shadows, and sacrifices; and was attended with much darkness and bondage: but under the Gospel dispensation, which is compared to a marriage feast, it is more fully dispensed, more clearly published, and more freely ministered. The whole of it is delivered, and with open face beheld; and saints are made free by it; it is set in the strongest and clearest light; the best wine is reserved till now; God has *provided some better thing for us, Heb. 11:40.* And so with respect to the future state of the saints, their best things are kept for them till last. They have many good things now; as the Gospel, Gospel ordinances, the blessings and promises of grace, the love of God shed abroad in their hearts, the presence of God, and communion with Christ, at least at times; all which are *better than wine*: but then there is an alloy to these; they are lowered by other things, as the corruptions of the heart, the temptations of Satan, the hidings of God's face, and a variety of afflictions; but they shall have their good and best things hereafter, and drink new wine in Christ's Father's kingdom, without any thing to lower and weaken it. They will have full joys, and never fading pleasures, and shall be without sin and sorrow; no more deserted, nor afflicted, and shall be out of the reach of Satan's temptations, and with Christ for evermore. Happy are they that are called to the marriage supper of the Lamb!

Verse 11. **This beginning of miracles,** &c. This miracle of turning water into wine, was the first miracle Christ ever wrought, either in public or private; for

---

[25] A Caupone tibi faex Laletana petatur Si plus quam decies, Sextiliane, bibis. L. 1. Ep. 25.

as for what miracles He is said to do in His infancy, there is no reason to give credit to them: and this,

did Jesus in Cana of Galilee; not that this was the only one He did in that place; He afterwards working another there, namely, the cure of a nobleman's son, *chapter 4:46,54*; but the first miracle He did any where, and it was in this place; and which the Syriac and Persic versions again call *Kotne of Galilee*; see the note on *verse 1;*

and manifested forth his glory; the glory of His Deity and divine Sonship, which was hid by His assumption of human nature, but broke forth and showed itself in His miraculous operations, and particularly in this:

and his disciples believed on him. The above five disciples; see *verse 2*; whom He had called, and who were with Him at this marriage, and were made acquainted with this miracle: and though they believed in Him before, and had declared, and professed Him to be the Messiah Moses and the prophets spoke of, and the Son of God, and King of Israel; yet they were, by this miracle, more and more confirmed in the faith of these things: besides, others might be made His disciples at this time, and be hereby brought to believe in Him.

Verse 12. **After this he went down to Capernaum**, &c. After He had been at Cana, and at the wedding there, after He had wrought the miracle of turning water into wine; and after He had manifested forth the glory of His Deity thereby, and had confirmed the faith of His disciples, He departed from thence, and went lower into the country of Galilee, to Capernaum, a city near the sea of Tiberias; and which, from henceforward, He made the more usual place of His residence, and whither He frequently resorted, and therefore it is called His city, *Matt. 9:1*. This refers not to the same journey recorded in *Matt. 4:12-13*, for that was after John was cast into prison, whereas this was before; see *chapter 3:24*. The company that went with Him, are as follow,

he, and his mother; who had been with Him at Cana, and was a principal guest at the wedding: and she now returning home, He accompanies her, to see her to her own habitation; or to settle her in Capernaum, while He went about discharging His public ministry;

and his brethren; or near kinsmen according to the flesh, the sons of Alphaeus, or Cleophas, and Mary, sister to the mother of our Lord; whose names were James, Joses, Simon, and Judas, three of which afterwards became His apostles;

and his disciples: as many as He had yet called, which were Andrew, and the disciple [John] that followed Jesus with him, and Simon Peter, and Philip, and Nathanael,

and they continued there not many days; not because of the impenitence, unbelief, and wickedness of the place, but for the reason following.

Verse 13. **And the Jews' passover was at hand**, &c. That feast of the passover, which was kept on the fourteenth day of Nisan, in commemoration of the Lord's passing over and by the houses of the Israelites, when He slew the firstborn in Egypt: and it is called the Jews' passover, because they only were obliged to keep it; nor was it obligatory upon the Gentiles; and, besides, was now abolished when John wrote this Gospel, though still retained by the Jews. And moreover, John was now among the Gentiles, and for whose sake he penned this Gospel; and therefore so distinguishes this feast, which was typical of the Christian passover, or of *Christ our passover* that *is sacrificed for us* [*1 Cor. 5:7*]. This was the *first* passover after Christ's baptism, which is generally thought to have been about half a year before; though so much time cannot be made out from the scriptural account; for from His baptism, to His return out of the wilderness to John, were forty days; and from thence, to His coming to Cana, four or five days more; and perhaps He might be seven days in Cana; for so long a wedding was usually kept; and His stay at Capernaum was but a few days; all which do not amount to above eight or nine weeks at most. The *second* passover after this, is, by some, thought to be the feast mentioned in *chapter 5:1*; and the *third* in *chapter 6:4*; and the *fourth* and last, at which He suffered, in *chapter 18:28*. The Evangelist John is the only writer that gives an account of the passovers after Christ entered on His public ministry, by which is known the duration of it, which is generally thought to be about three years and a half. *Three years and a half*, the Jews say,[26] *the Shekinah sat upon the Mount of Olives, expecting that the Israelites would repent, but they did not*; and this seems to be the term of time for disciples to learn of their masters: it is said,[27]

> "One came from Athens to Jerusalem, and he served *three years and a half* to learn the doctrine of wisdom, and he learned it not."

And Jesus went up to Jerusalem; not alone, but His disciples with Him, as appears from *verse 17*, to keep the passover, as He had been wont to do, and as the law required; and He being *under the law* [*Gal. 4:4*], as a son of Abraham, and the surety of His people, it became Him *to fulfil all right-eousness* [*Matt. 3:15*], ceremonial as well as moral, and which He strictly

---

[26] Praefat. Echa Rabbati, fol. 40. 4.

[27] Echa Rabbati, fol. 44. 4.

observed. He is said to go *up to Jerusalem*, because that stood on higher ground than the low lands of Galilee, and was the only place where the passover might be kept; see *Deut. 16:2*.

Verse 14. **And found in the temple**, &c. Not in the holy place itself, nor in the court of the priests, where the sacrifices were offered, nor in the court of the women, nor in the court of the Israelites, where the people worshiped; but in the court of the Gentiles, or the outward court, even all that space of ground which was between the wall which divided the whole from common ground, and the buildings of the temple, and which was open to the air; for the whole sacred enclosure, or all within the wall, went by the name of the temple. Into this all strangers might come; and the passover now being at hand, here were:

those that sold oxen, and sheep, and doves: the oxen, or bullocks, were for the *Chagigah*, or feast kept on the second day of the passover; see the note on *chapter 18:28*; and the sheep, or *lambs*, as the Persic version reads, for the passover supper; and the doves were for the offerings of the poorer sort of lying-in women[*that is*, those who had recently given birth]: with these they were supplied from the Mount of Olives. It is said,[28]

"There were two cedar trees on the Mount of Olives, and under one of them were four shops of them that sold things for purification; and out of one of them they brought forty bushels of young doves every month: and out of them the Israelites had enough for the nests, or the offerings of turtle doves;"

see the note on *Matt. 21:12* **[29]**;

and the changers of money sitting. Who changed foreign money into the current coin of the Jews, strangers coming, at this feast, from several parts of the world; and sometimes there was need of changing shekels into half shekels, which, at certain times, were paid for the ransom of Israelites; see the note on the place above mentioned.

Verse 15. **And when he had made a scourge of small cords**, &c. That is, *Jesus*, as the Persic version expresses it. This scourge might be made either of thongs cut out of the hides of beasts slain in sacrifice; or of the cords, with which the owners of the cattle had brought them to this place; or with which they had fastened them in it. And it seems to be made, and used, not so much for force and terror, as to intimate, that these persons, the violators of the holy place, deserved the scourge of divine wrath and punishment; as well as to show the miraculous power of Christ in driving such a number of men before

---

[28] Echa Rabbati, fol. 52. 4.

Him, with so small and insignificant a weapon; for the phrase is diminutive. The reason given by Dr. Lightfoot, and others, why Christ made use of a whip, or scourge, rather than a staff, is, because it was contrary to a Jewish canon [29] to go *into the mountain of the house*, or temple, with a staff in the hand; and yet *the man of the mountain of the house*, or the master of it, who used to go about every ward with torches burning before him, if he found a Levite asleep in his ward,[30] struck him, במקלו, *with his staff*, and had power to burn his clothes.

He drove them all out of the temple; that is, He drove out *the men*, as the Persic version reads; the merchants, the sellers of oxen, sheep, and doves, and the money changers:

and the sheep, and the oxen likewise; the Persic version adds, *doves*; but these are after mentioned:

and poured out the changers money; off of the tables, or out of the boxes, or dishes, or drawers, or purses, in which it was put:

and overthrew the tables; at which they sat, and on which they told [*or* counted]their money.

Verse 16. **And said unto them that sold doves**, &c. For as these were kept in coups, or cages, they could not be driven as the sheep and oxen, nor could they be let out, and fly, without loss to the owners: and therefore Christ said to them,

Take these things hence; not only the doves, but the pens, coups, or cages, in which they were, and both together:

make not my Father's house an house of merchandise. So He calls the temple, which was built as a house for God, and where He took up His residence; where were the symbols of His presence; where His worship was kept, and sacrifices offered to Him: and He asserts God, whose house this was, to be His Father, and Himself to be His Son, as none of the prophets that went before Him did; and in such sense as neither men nor angels are; and which carries in it a reason why He was so much concerned for the honor of God, and so much resented the profanation of His house, because He was His Father. A like action with this, done by Christ at another time, is recorded in *Matt. 21:12-13.* This was at the beginning of His ministry, that at the close of it, in which He expressed Himself with more warmth and severity than here: here

---

[29] Mishna Beracot, c. 9. sect. 5.

[30] Mishna Middot, c. 1. sect. 2.

He only charges them with making His Father's house *a house of merchandise*, but there with making it *a den of thieves*; since they had not only slighted and despised His first reproof, but had returned to their evil ways, and might grow more wicked and audacious. This instance of Christ, now coming into the temple as a public minister, and which was the first time of His entrance into it, after He had taken this character, was a further accomplishment of *Mal. 3:1*, for He now went into it, as the Lord and proprietor of it; and which this action of His, in driving out the merchants with their cattle, shows; and was a surprising instance of His divine power; and is equal to other miracles of His: that a single person, a stranger, one of no power and authority in the government, unassisted and unarmed, with only a scourge of small cords, should carry such awe and majesty with Him, and inject such terror into, and drive such a number of men before Him, who were selling things for religious uses, and were supported in it by the priests and Sanhedrin of the nation.

Verse 17. **And his disciples remembered that it was written,** &c. Written in *Psa. 69:9,* which Psalm belongs to the Messiah, as is manifest from the citations out of it in the New Testament, and the application of them to Christ, as in *chapter 15:25* and *19:28; Rom. 15:3*, compared with *Psa. 69:4, 9, 21.* Christ is represented in it, as suffering for the sins of His people; for He Himself was innocent; and was hated without a cause; but having the sins of His people imputed to Him, He made satisfaction for them, and so restored what He took not away. His sufferings are spoken of in it as very great; and from it we learn, that they are fitly called, by Himself, *a baptism*, which He desired *to be baptized with, Luke 12:50*, since the waters are said to come into His soul, and He to be in deep waters, where the floods overflowed Him; so that He was as one immersed in them. It is not only prophesied of Him in it, that He should be the object of the scorn and contempt of the Jewish nation, and be rejected by them, and treated with the utmost indignity, and loaded with reproaches; but it foretold, that they should give Him *gall to eat*, and *vinegar to drink*, which were literally fulfilled in Him: and even the Jews themselves seem to be under some conviction, that the Psalm has respect to Him; for Aben Ezra, a noted commentator of theirs, on the last words of the Psalm, has this note:

"The sense is, they and their children shall inherit it in the days of David, or in the days of the Messiah."

It appears from hence, that the disciples of Christ were acquainted with the sacred writings, and had diligently read them, and searched into them, and had made them their study; and upon this wonderful action of Christ, called to mind, and reflected upon the following passage of Scripture, which they judged very proper and pertinent to Him:

the zeal of thine house hath eaten me up. This passage, so far as it is cited, agrees exactly, word for word, with the original text in *Psa. 69:9*, wherefore it is very strange that Surenhusius[31] should remark a difference, and give himself a good deal of trouble to reconcile it: he observes, that in the Hebrew text, it is read, קנאת יהוה, *the zeal of the Lord*, in the third person; whereas it is there, קנאת ביתך, *the zeal of thine house*, as here, in the second person. Indeed, the word כי, *for*, is left out, as he remarks, there being no need of it in the citation; the evangelist only historically relating the accommodation of it to Christ, by the disciples; whereas in the original text, the words contain a reason of the reproach and shame which Christ endured, and was put to by the Jews on account of His zeal for the house, honor, and worship of God; and the latter part of the text is not produced at all, being not for the present purpose, though very applicable to Christ; and is cited, and applied to Him by the apostle, in *Rom. 15:3*. Such was Christ's regard to His Father's house, and which was typical of the church of God; and such His concern for His honor, ordinances, and worship, that when He saw the merchandise that was carried on in the temple, His zeal, which was a true and hearty affection for God, and was according to knowledge, was stirred up in Him, and to such a degree, that it was like a consuming fire within Him, that ate up His spirits; so that He could not forbear giving it vent, and expressing it in the manner He did, by driving those traders out of it. Phinehas and Elias were in their zeal, as well as other things, types of Christ; and in the Spirit and power of the latter he came; and Christ not only expressed a zeal for the house of God, the place of religious worship, but for the church and people of God, whose salvation He most earnestly desired, and most zealously pursued: He showed His strong, and affectionate regard to it, by His suretyship engagements for them, by His assumption of their nature, by His ardent desire to accomplish it, and by His voluntary and cheerful submission to death on account of it. And such was His zeal for it, that it ate Him up, it inflamed His spirit and affections, consumed His time and strength, and, at last, His life. And He also showed a zeal for the discipline of God's house, by His severe reflections on human traditions; by asserting the spirituality of worship; by commanding a strict regard to divine institutions; and by sharply inveighing against the sins of professors of religion. And He discovered a warm zeal for the truths of the Gospel, by a lively and powerful preaching of them; by His constancy and assiduity in it; by the many fatiguing journeys He took for that purpose; by the dangers He exposed Himself to by it; and by the care He took to free the Gospel from prejudice and calumnies: and it becomes us, in imitation of our great Master, to be zealous for His truths and ordinances, and

---

[31] Biblos Katallages, p. 347.

for the discipline of His house, and not to bear with either the erroneous principles, or the bad practices of wicked men.

Verse 18. **Then answered the Jews, and said unto him,** &c. They did not lay hands on Him, or offer any violence to Him; they did not, as the inhabitants of Nazareth did, thrust Him out, and lead Him to a precipice, to cast Him down headlong; nor did they now take up stones to stone Him, as they afterwards did, when He asserted His Deity: and it is surprising, that they did not rise up and destroy Him at once, a single man, unarmed, and without assistance, having so highly provoked them; the restraint upon them must be His almighty power: nor do they deny what He suggested, that they had made His Father's house a house of merchandise; nor do they offer to vindicate their profanation of the temple, or object to the purging of it; only demand a proof of His right to do it: and which demand was made, not by the common people, or by the sellers of oxen, sheep, and doves, and the money changers, who were driven out, and had not spirit to rally; but by the chief priests and elders, the Sanhedrin of the nation, who had the care and government of the temple, and under whose authority the above persons acted; and whose gain and worldly interest were promoted hereby, as a like demand was afterwards made by the same persons; see *Matt. 21:23*:

What sign shewest thou unto us, seeing that thou doest these things? They argued, that either He did these things of Himself, by His own authority, and then they must be deemed rash and unjustifiable; or He did it by the authority of others: they knew it was not by theirs, who were the great council of the nation, from whom He should have had His instructions and orders, if He acted by human authority; and if He pretended to a divine authority, as they supposed He did, then they insisted upon a sign or miracle to be wrought, to prove that God was His Father, as He suggested; and that He was the proprietor and owner of the temple, and had a right to purge it, as He had done; see *1 Cor. 1:22*.

Verse 19. **Jesus answered and said unto them**, &c. Jesus answered them in a dark and enigmatical way, yet very properly and pertinently; since it was with respect to the temple, and His power over it, and right to purge it, that a sign was required of Him:

Destroy this temple; pointing, as it were, with His finger to His body; for of that He spake, as appears from *verse 21*; the dissolution of which, by death He means, the separation of His soul from His body, though not of either from His divine person: and it is to be understood, not as a command, or a grant, or as an exhortation and advice to them to kill His body; but rather as a prophecy of what they would do; or as putting the case, that should they, as He knew they would, destroy His body, then, says He, as a sign of having a power to do what I have done,

in three days I will raise it up; by which He would appear to be *the Son of God with power [Rom. 1:4]*, that had power of laying down His life, and taking it up again; and is the very sign, namely, His resurrection from the dead on the third day, He gives the Jews, when they sought one of Him at another time, and upon another occasion.

Verse 20. **Then said the Jews**, &c. *The Jews said unto him*, as read the Syriac, Arabic, Persic, and Ethiopic versions:

Forty and six years was this temple in building; which cannot be understood of the temple as built by Solomon, for that was but seven years in building, *1 Kings 6:37-38*. But rather of the temple, as built by Zorobabel, commonly called the second temple, and might be more properly said to be *this temple*; the calculations of this made by learned men, are various and endless to recite. Daniel's seven weeks, or forty-nine days, which are so many years, can have nothing to do with this account; since they regard not the building of the temple, but the city of Jerusalem; though from the second year of Cyrus, in which the temple began to be built, to the thirty-second of Darius exclusive, was just forty-six years; Cyrus reigning three years, Artaxerxes Ahasuerus fourteen years, and Artaxerxes Darius thirty-two; but their account is more likely, which begins at the first of Artaxerxes Longimanus, who reigned forty years, and ends in the sixth year of Darius, his successor, in which year the temple was finished, *Ezra 6:15*. But to me it seems rather, that Herod's temple, or the temple as rebuilt, or repaired by Herod, is here meant; and which the Jews call, בניין הורודוס, *the building of Herod*;[32] and say of it that,

"he who has not seen Herod's building, never saw a beautiful building."
And this, according to Josephus,[33] was begun in the *eighteenth* year of his reign, in the *thirty-fifth* of which Christ was born, who was now *thirty* years of age: so that reckoning either the eighteenth year of Herod, or the thirtieth of Christ, the present year exclusively, just forty-six years had run out, since the rebuilding or reparations were first begun; and which were not yet finished; for some years after this, the above writer observes,[34] the temple was finished, even in the times of Nero and Agrippa: and agreeable to this, the

---

[32] T. Bab. Bava Bathra, fol. 4. 1.

[33] Antiqu. Jud. l. 15. c. 14.

[34] Antiqu. Jud. l. 20. c. 8.

words may be rendered, *forty-six years has this temple been building*; and which still adds more force to the following reasoning of the Jews:

and wilt thou rear it up in three days? The thing is impossible and impracticable; it is madness to the last degree to talk at this rate: thus from the length of time which had run out from Herod's first beginning to repair and beautify the temple, till now, and yet not finished, they argue the absurdity of His pretending to raise up such a fabric, should it be demolished, in three days time; they understanding Him either ignorantly or wilfully, to speak of the material temple, when His sense was otherwise, as appears from the words of the evangelist, in the next verse. The Jew[35] objects to this account, of the temple being forty-six years in building; he observes that,

> "According to the sense of the Nazarenes, this was the building of King Herod, that it was in the time of Jesus; and the whole time of his reign were but seven and thirty years, as is manifest from the book of Joseph ben Gorion, cap. 65. Besides, that which Herod built, was built in eight years, as is evident from the same author, cap. 55, wherefore the number of forty-six years, in the words of the writer (the evangelist), is a palpable error."

To which may be replied, that admitting there is an error in this number, it is not the error of the evangelist, but of the Jews, whose words the evangelist relates; and supposing this was a mistake of theirs, either ignorantly or wilfully made, to aggravate the absurdity and impossibility of Christ's rebuilding the temple; and that even the evangelist knew it to be a mistake; yet he acts the most faithful and upright part, in repeating the words of the Jews as they delivered them; and it lies upon the Jew to prove, that these words were not said by them, or that it is not credible that they should: that this was the building of Herod which is here referred to, and that he reigned but thirty-seven years, will be granted; but this is no objection to its being forty-six years in building, since in this account it is not said that it was forty-six years in building by Herod; the sense is only, that such a number of years had passed, since it was first begun to be built by him. As for what Joseph ben Gorion says, of its being built by him in the space of eight years, it is not to be depended upon, since he is not the true Josephus, that wrote the history of the Jews, and is to be corrected by the genuine historian; and from what has been before observed, from the time which, according to the true Josephus, this building was begun, to this present year of Christ, when this discourse was had, were just forty-six years; and admitting, that the main of the building was finished in eight years time, yet additions were continually made to it, so that it was not finished entirely, until many years after.

---

[35] R. Isaac Chizzuk Emuna, par. 2. c. 43. p. 434.

Verse 21. **But he spake of the temple of his body.** Which body was the antitype of the material temple; and might well be called so, since the bodies of the saints are called *temples, 1 Cor. 3:16-17* and *6:19; 2 Cor. 6:16*; and the human nature of Christ is called a *tabernacle, Heb. 8:2*; and He himself, in prophecy, is said to be למקדש, *for a sanctuary*, or temple, *Isa. 8:14*; and that because *the fulness of the Godhead* dwelt in Him bodily, the train of the divine perfections *filled the temple* of His human nature, *Col. 2:9; Isa. 6:1.* And because here, as in the temple, God grants His presence, and communes with His saints, accepts of their prayers and praises, and all their spiritual sacrifices, through Him; Him who is the oracle, the true *Urim* and *Thummim*, by whom He delivers His whole mind and will to His people.

Verse 22. **When therefore he was risen from the dead**, &c. Which resurrection was three years after this:

his disciples remembered that he had said this unto them; either to the Jews, or to them the disciples; though the phrase *to them*, is not in the Vulgate Latin, nor in any of the Oriental versions. The disciples themselves were very dull of understanding the doctrine of Christ's resurrection; and so they continued, notwithstanding He gave them afterwards very full hints of it, until He was actually risen; and then they called to mind these words of His, with others that dropped from Him upon the same subject:

and they believed the Scripture; that spoke of His resurrection, *Psa. 16:10*, and on the third day, *Hos. 6:2:*

and the word which Jesus had said; concerning His rising again the third day, at this time, and at others, as in *Matt. 16:21; 17:23* and *20:19*; and they believed His word equally with the Scripture, it agreeing to it, and being founded on it.

Verse 23. **Now when he was in Jerusalem at the passover**, &c. He went to Jerusalem in order to keep the passover, that being at hand, and now come; see *verse 13*;

in the feast *day*; either on the day the *Chagigah* was eaten, which was sometimes emphatically called *the feast*, as in *Num. 28:16-17, And in the fourteenth day of the first month,* is *the passover of the Lord; and in the fifteenth day of this month,* is *the feast*; the passover lamb was eaten on the fourteenth day of the month *Nisan*, and the *Chagigah* was on the fifteenth; in the former only a lamb was eaten, in the other, cattle out of the herds; hence mention is made both of flocks and herds, for the keeping the passover, *Deut. 16:2.* Jarchi's note upon the place is, that the herds were for the *Chagigah*, with which the Talmud[36] agrees; and Jonathan ben Uzziel paraphrases the words thus,

"And ye shall slay the passover before the Lord your God, between the evenings, and the sheep and oxen on the morrow, in that very day, for the joy of the feast;"

for it was observed with great joy and mirth: and the rather this is here meant, since the *Chagigah* is not only called *the feast*, but this here is distinguished from the passover, as that is in the passage above cited, *Num. 28:16-17*. For the passover here, seems to be the general name for the whole seven days of the festival; and the feast, to be the particular feast of the first day of it, which was the fifteenth; to which may be added, that on this day all the males made their appearance in court,[37] and so was a very proper time for Christ to work His miracles in, when there were so many spectators: though it may design the whole time of the feast, all the seven days of unleavened bread; during which time Christ was at Jerusalem, and wrought miracles, which had the following effect:

many believed in his name; that He was some great prophet, or *the* prophet, or the Messiah; they gave a historical assent unto Him as such, at least for that time:

when they saw the miracles which he did; for as miracles, according to the prophecies of the Old Testament, were to be performed by the Messiah, such as giving sight to the blind, causing the deaf to hear, the dumb to speak, and the lame to walk, *Isa. 35:5-6*, so they were expected by the ancient Jews, that they would be wrought by Him, when He came; wherefore these Jews, seeing such like wonderful things wrought by Jesus, they concluded He must be the Messiah: though the modern ones, in order to shift off the evidence of Jesus being the Messiah, from His miracles, deny that miracles are the characteristic of the Messiah, or will be performed by Him; at least, that there is no necessity of them to prove Him to be the person. What miracles these were, which were now wrought by Christ, are not recorded by this, or any other evangelist; see *chapter 20:30*. However, being surprised at the marvelous things He did, and upon the evidence of these extraordinary works, there were many that concluded He must be come from God; among these it seems as if Nicodemus was one; see *chapter 3:2*. [A] great part of these, at least some of them, were only nominal and temporary believers, who were not to be confided in as true disciples, and hearty followers of Christ; and who

---

[36] Pesachim, fol. 70. 2.

[37] Maimonides Hilchot Chagigah, c. 1. sect. 1.

continued not long in the same mind and profession, as appears by what follows.

Verse 24. **But Jesus did not commit himself unto them**, &c. The sense according to some of the ancients is, that He did not *commit* the whole of the Gospel to them; He did not make known to them all His mind and will; this He only did to the twelve apostles, His special disciples and friends; nor was the time come, that He would make known, or have made known, the things concerning His person, office, obedience, sufferings, death, and resurrection from the dead: but rather the meaning is, that He did not trust Himself with these persons, who believed in Him on the foot [*or* basis] of His miracles; He did not take them into the number of His associates; He did not admit them to intimacy with Him; nor did He freely converse with them, or make any long stay among them; but soon withdrew Himself from hence, and went into other parts of Judea, and into Galilee:

because he knew all *men*; good and bad: all openly profane sinners, and all their actions; not only their more public ones, but those that are done in the dark, and which are the most secretly devised, and leveled against the saints; and He so knew them, as to bring them into judgment: and all good men, true believers; He knows their persons, as they are his Father's choice, His gift of them to Him, His own purchase, and as called by His grace; and so as to distinguish them at the last day, and give up the full account of every one of them to His Father: He knows the worst of them, the sin that dwells in them, their daily infirmities, their secret personal sins; their family sins, both of omission and commission; and their church sins, or which are committed in the house of God; and takes notice of them, so as to resent them, and chastise them for them; He knows the best of them, their graces, their faith, hope, love, patience, humility, self-denial, &c. He knows their good works, and all their weaknesses and their wants: and He knows all nominal professors, on what foot [*or* basis] they take up their profession, and what trust they place in it; He can distinguish between grace and mere profession, and discern the secret lusts which such indulge, and the spring and progress of their apostasy: He knew all these men, that upon seeing His miracles, professed at this time to believe in Him; He knew the hypocrisy and dissimulation of some of them; and He knew the notions they had of a temporal Messiah, and the temporal views they had in believing in Him; and their design to set Him up as a temporal prince, as some afterwards would have done: He knew the flashy affections of others, who were like John's hearers, that were pleased for a while; He knew what sort of faith it was they believed in Him with, that it would not hold long, nor they continue with Him; for He knew not only all persons, but παντα, *all things*, as some copies read here; see *chapter 21:17.*

Verse 25. **And needed not that any should testify of man**, &c. Testify of this or the other man, that he was a good or a bad man; He needed no proofs to be made, or testimonies borne, or evidence given of men's characters and actions; He was of quick understanding, and could distinguish at once between a wicked man and a good man; and so had the characteristic which the Jews require of the Messiah; for they rejected Bar Cozba from being the Messiah, and slew him, because *he could not smell*, referring to *Isa. 11:3*, or discern a bad man from a good man,[38] but this Jesus could do, without any external evidence:

for he knew what was in man. Which none but the spirit of a man can know; his inward thoughts, the secrets of the heart; thus Christ knew the thoughts of the Scribes and Pharisees, *Matt. 9:4*, being *a discerner of the thoughts, and intents of the heart, Heb. 4:12*. This Apollonius Tyaneus, the ape [*or* copier] of Christ, ascribed to himself;[39] but is what is peculiar to God; and Christ, being God, knows all that is in man; that there is no good in him naturally, nothing but what comes from His Father, is imparted by Himself, or implanted by His Spirit; He knows the wickedness there is in man, that his heart is *deceitful* and *desperately wicked* [*Jer. 17:9*], and full of all manner of iniquities; He knows in what condition all the powers and faculties of the souls of men are; what their affections are set upon, on earthly or heavenly things; whether there is any light in their understandings, or not; whether their wills are subdued and resigned to the will of God, or not; whether their minds and consciences are defiled, or their hearts are *sprinkled from an evil conscience* [*Heb. 10:22*]; in short, whether the internal good work of grace is begun upon their souls, or not; and He knows the secret springs of all actions, good and bad; all which prove His true and proper Deity, and show Him to be a suitable Savior of sinners, and qualify Him to be the Judge of the whole earth.

---

[38]   T. Bab. Sanhedrin, fol. 93. 2.

[39]   Philostrat. Vit. Apollonii, l. 1. c. 13.

CHAPTER 3

Verse 1. **There was a man of the Pharisees**, &c. The Syriac version adds, *there*; that is, at Jerusalem; and who was among those that believed in the name of Christ, upon seeing the miracles He did at the feast of the passover, in that place. This man was not a common and ordinary man, but a man of note and eminence, of dignity and figure; and who was of the sect of the Pharisees, which was the strictest sect for religion and holiness among the Jews; and which, as corrupt as it was, was also the soundest; as having not only a regard to a Messiah, and to all the writings of the Old Testament, but also believed the doctrines of angels and spirits, and the resurrection of the dead, which the Sadducees denied; but yet they were implacable enemies of Christ; and therefore it is the more to be wondered at, that such a one should come to Him, and desire a conversation with Him:

named Nicodemus; frequent mention is made of נקדימון בן גוריון, *Nicodemon ben Gorion*, the brother of Josephus ben Gorion,[1] the writer of the Wars and Antiquities of the Jews; and there are some things which make it probable, that he was the same with this Nicodemus; for the Nicodemon the Jews speak so much of, lived in this age; as appears, not only from his being the brother of Josephus, but also from his being contemporary with R. Jochanan ben Zaccai, who lived in this time, and until the destruction of the temple; since these two are said[2] to be together at a feast, made for the circumcision of a child. Moreover, he is represented as very rich, and is said to be one of the three rich men in Jerusalem,[3] and who was able to have maintained מדינה, *a city ten years*;[4] and they speak of his daughter, as exceeding rich: they say, that she had for her dowry a thousand thousand golden denarii, or pence; and that her bed was strewed with (that is, the furniture of it cost) twelve thousand golden denarii; and that a Tyrian golden denarius was spent upon her every week, for a certain kind of soup,[5] and the wise men decreed her four

---

[1] Ganz Tzemach David, par. 1. fol. 25. 1. Shalshalet Hakabala, fol. 19. 1.

[2] Pirke Eliezer, c. 2. & Juchasin, fol. 23. 2.

[3] T. Bab. Gittin, fol. 56. 1.

[4] Midrash Kohelet, fol. 75. 4.

[5] Abot R. Nathan, c. 6. fol. 3. 2.

hundred golden denarii, for a box of spices every day;[6] and it is elsewhere[7] said, five hundred: and this our Nicodemus was very rich, as appears from his liberality at the funeral of our Lord, *chapter 19:39*. Moreover, the Nicodemon of the Jews, is said to be a counselor[8] in Jerusalem; and so was this, as seems evident from *chapter 7:32,50,51;* and it may be further observed,[9] that the right name of Nicodemon, was *Boni;*[10] now Boni elsewhere,[11] is said to be one of the disciples of Jesus, as Nicodemus was secretly, and perhaps at, and after His death openly, as his associate Joseph of Arimathea was; to which may be added, the extreme poverty that his daughter is by them said to be reduced unto; for they report, that R. Jochanan ben Zaccai saw her gathering barley corns from under the horses' hoofs in Aco;[12] or as it is elsewhere said, out of the dung of the beasts of the Arabians; when she asked alms of him, and he inquired of her, what was become of her father's substance. Now to this low estate, the family of our Nicodemus might be reduced through the persecution of the Christians by the Jews. The name is Greek, as at this time many Greek names were in use among the Jews, and signifies the same as Nicolas; but the Jews give an etymology of it, agreeable to the Hebrew language; and say, that he was so called, because the sun, נקדה, *shone out for his sake*: the occasion and reason of it, they tell us, were this,[13] Nicodemon, upon want of water at one of the feasts, agreed with a certain man for twelve wells of water, to be returned on such a day, or pay twelve talents of silver; the day being come, the man demanded the water, or the money; Nicodemon went and prayed, and a plentiful rain fell, and filled the wells with water; but meeting the man, he insisted on it that the day was past, the sun being set, and therefore required the money; Nicodemon went and prayed again, and the sun shone out; and they add,

---

[6] T. Bab. Cetubot, fol. 66. 2.

[7] Echa Rabbati, fol. 49. 2.

[8] Echa Rabbati, fol. 46. 3. Midrash Kohelet, fol. 75. 1.

[9] T. Bab. Taanith, fol. 20. 1.

[10] T. Bab. Sanhedrin, fol. 43. 1.

[11] Echa Rabbati, fol. 49. 3.

[12] T. Bab. Cetubot, fol. 66. 2.

[13] T. Bab. Taanith, fol. 20. 1.

THE GOSPEL OF JOHN

"that there are three persons for whom the sun נקדמה, *was prevented*, detained, or hindered in its course (a word nearer his name than the former), Moses, and Joshua, and Nicodemon ben Gorion;"

for the two former they produce Scripture, and for the latter tradition: hence it is elsewhere said,[14]

"that as the sun stood still for Joshua, so it stood still for Moses, and for Nicodemon ben Gorion."

But to proceed with the account of our Nicodemus, he was,

a ruler of the Jews; not a civil magistrate; for the civil government was now in the hands of the Romans; but an ecclesiastical ruler; he was a member of the Sanhedrin, which consisted of the doctors, or wise men, and priests, Levites, and elders of the people; and so was a dignified person, and as afterwards called, *a master in Israel*.

Verse 2. **The same came to Jesus by night**, &c. Came by night, through fear of the Jews; of being reproached, or turned out of his place by them; or through shame, that such a doctor as he was, should be known to go to Jesus of Nazareth to be instructed by Him; or lest he should offend any of his brethren of the Sanhedrin. Though some things may be said in favor of this conduct of Nicodemus; for since Christ would not trust Himself with those that believed in Him upon seeing His miracles, *chapter 2:23-24*, among whom Nicodemus seems to be; or would not admit them into His company, and enter into a free conversation with Him; it was necessary, that if he would have any discourse with Him, that he should take this method; and if it was the same night, in which he had seen His miracles in the day, as is probable, he took the first opportunity he could, and which shows great readiness and respect; add to which, that it was very common with the Jewish doctors, to meet and converse together, and study the law in the night.

"R. Aba rose, בפלגות ליליא, *in the middle of the night*, and the rest of the companions, to study in the law." [15]

And it is often[16] said of R. Simeon ben Jochai, and Eleazar his son,

"that they sat in the night and labored in the law;"

and it was reckoned very commendable so to do, and highly pleasing to God:

---

[14] T. Bab. Avoda Zara, fol. 25. 1.

[15] Zohar in Exod. fol. 84. 1.

[16] Ibid. fol. 88. 2. in Lev. fol. 5. 3, 4. & 10. 1. & passim.

it is said,[17]

> "Whoever studies in the law in the night, the holy blessed God draws
> a thread of mercy upon him in the day:"

and likewise[18] that,

> "Every one that studies in the law in the night, the Shekinah is over
> against him."

But it seems, the Babylonian Jews did not study in the law in the night:[19] it might seem a needless question to ask, whether Nicodemus came alone, or not, were it not that according to the Jewish canon,[20] a scholar might not go out in the night alone, because of suspicion:

and said unto him, Rabbi; a title which now greatly obtained among the Jewish doctors, and of which they were very fond; see the note on *Matt. 23:7* [32]. It comes from a word, which signifies *great* and *large*; and was used by them, to suggest the large compass, and great plenty of knowledge they would be thought to have had; and best becomes and suits with our Lord Jesus Christ, in whom *all the treasures of wisdom and knowledge* are [*Col. 2:3*]. Salutations among the Jews, were forbidden in the night;[21]

> "Says R. Jochanan, it is forbidden a man to salute his neighbor in the
> night, lest it should be a demon:"

but here was no such danger; nor was this salutation made in the street, and in the dark, which the canon seems to respect:

we know that thou art a teacher come from God; the Jews expected the Messiah as a *teacher*, which they might learn from many prophecies, as from *Isa. 2:2-3; 48:17* and *61:1*. Upon the first of which, and on that passage in it, *he will teach us of his ways*, a noted commentator[22] of theirs has this remark:

> "המורה, *the teacher*, he is the King Messiah."

---

17   T. Bab. Chagiga, fol. 12. 2. Avoda Zara, fol. 3. 2. Maimon. Hilch. Talmud Tora, c. 3. sect. 13.

18   T. Bab. Tamid. fol. 32. 2.

19   T. Bab. Taanith, fol. 9. 2.

20   T. Bab. Cholin, fol. 91. 1. Piske Tosephot Pesach. art. 12. & Maimon. Hilch. Deyot. c. 5. sect. 9.

21   T. Bab. Sanhedrin, fol. 44. 1. & Megilla, fol. 3. 1. & Piske Tosephot Megilla, art. 4. & in Yebamot, art. 238.

22   R. David Kimchi in loc.

And the Targum, on *Joel 2:23*, paraphrases the words thus:

"O ye children of Zion, rejoice and be glad in the Word of the Lord your God, for he will return, ית מלפכון, *your teacher* to you."

And Nicodemus acknowledges Jesus as such; and as one that did not come, or was sent by men, as their doctors were; nor did He come of Himself, as false teachers did; but He came *from God*, and had His mission and commission from Him: and this was a known case, a clear point, not only to himself, but to many of the Jews; and even to some of his brethren, the members of the Sanhedrin; who, upon hearing of, and seeing the miracles done by Christ, might meet and converse freely together about Him; and give their sentiments of Him; and might then agree pretty much in this at that time, that He was at least a prophet, and some extraordinary *teacher*, whom God had sent among them; and Nicodemus coming directly from them, repeats his own *sense* and theirs, supported by the following reason:

for no man can do these miracles that thou doest, except God be with him: referring to the miracles He had done at the passover in Jerusalem, very lately; see *chapter 2:23*. And which, though they are not particularly mentioned, may be concluded to be such, as the dispossessing of devils, the curing of all manner of diseases by a word, or touch, from what He at other times, and elsewhere did. Miracles were expected by the Jews to be wrought by the Messiah, and many believed in Jesus on this account; see *chapter 6:14* and *7:31*; though the modern Jews deny it to be necessary, that miracles should be done by the Messiah;[23] but Nicodemus and other Jews thought otherwise, and considered the miracles of Christ, as such as could never be done by man, nor without the presence and power of God; and concluded that He was with God, and God with Him, and was the true Immanuel, who is *God with us*.

Verse 3. **Jesus answered and said unto him**, &c. Not to any express question put by Nicodemus; unless it can be thought that a question of this kind might be asked, What is *the kingdom of God*, so much spoken of in thy ministry? And what is requisite to the seeing and enjoying of it? though not recorded by the evangelist; but rather to the words of Nicodemus, concluding from His miracles, that He was the Messiah; and that the kingdom of God was now approaching, or the world to come, the Jews so much speak of; and in which all Israel, according to their notion, were to have a part;[24] and which notion, our Lord in the following words seems to oppose:

---

[23] Maimonides Hilchot Melachim, c. 11. sect. 3.

[24] Mishna Sanhedrin, c. 11. sect. 1.

Verily, verily, I say unto thee, Except a man be born again, he cannot see the kingdom of God; Nicodemus, according to the general sense of the nation, thought that when the Messiah came, and His kingdom was set up, they should all share in it, without any more ado; they being the descendants of Abraham, and having him for their father: but Christ assures him, that he must be *born again*; in distinction from, and opposition to his first birth by nature; in which he was vile, polluted, carnal, and corrupt, being conceived *in sin*, and *shapen in iniquity* [*Psa. 51:5*], and was *a transgressor from the womb* [*Isa. 48:8*], and *by nature* a child *of wrath* [*Eph. 2:3*]; and in opposition to his descent from Abraham, or being born of him, and of his seed; for this would be of no avail to him in this case, nor give him any right to the privileges and ordinances of the kingdom of God, or the Gospel dispensation; see *Matt. 3:9*; as also to birth by proselytism; for the Jews have a frequent saying[25] that,

"One that is made a proselyte, כקטון שנולד דמי, *is like a child new born*:" which they understand, not in a spiritual, but in a civil sense; such being free from all natural and civil relations, and from all obligations to parents, masters,[26] &c. And by this phrase our Lord signifies, that no man, either as a man, or as a son of Abraham, or as a proselyte to the Jewish religion, can have any true knowledge of, or right unto, the enjoyment of *the kingdom of God*, unless he is *born again*; or regenerated, and quickened by the Spirit of God; renewed in the spirit of his mind; has Christ formed in his heart; becomes a partaker of the divine nature; and in all respects *a new creature*; and another in heart, in principle, in practice, and conversation; or unless he be *born from above*, as the word is rendered in *verse 31*; that is, by a supernatural power, having the heavenly image instamped on him; and being called with a heavenly calling, even with *the high calling of God in Christ Jesus* [*Phil. 3:14*]: if this is not the case, a man can have no true knowledge of the kingdom of the Messiah, which is not a temporal and carnal one; it is not of this world, nor does it come with observation; nor can he have any right to the ordinances of it, which are of a spiritual nature; and much less can he be thought to have any true notions, or to be possessed of the kingdom of grace, which lies in *righteousness, peace, and joy in the Holy Ghost* [*Rom. 14:17*]; or to have either a meetness for, or a right unto the kingdom of glory: though by the following words it seems, that the word is rightly rendered *again,* or a *second time*, as it is by Nonnus.

Verse 4. **Nicodemus saith unto him**, &c. Understanding Him of a natural birth, to be repeated, says,

---

[25] T. Bab. Yebamot, fol. 22. 1. 48. 2. 62. 1. & 97. 2.

[26] Vid. Maimon. Issure Bia, c. 14. sect. 11. & Eduth, c. 13. sect. 2.

How can a man be born when he is old? As it seems by this, he himself now was:

can he enter the second time into his mother's womb, and be born? The Ethiopic version adds, *again*; and the Arabic version, *and then be born*; this he urges, as absurd, impracticable, and impossible; and which shows him to have been as yet a natural man, who could not receive nor discern spiritual things [see *1 Cor. 2:2-14*].

Verse 5. **Jesus answered, Verily, verily, I say unto thee**, &c. Jesus, explaining somewhat more clearly what He had before said, answered,

Except a man be born of water and *of* the Spirit: these are, מלות שנות, *two words*, which express the same thing, as Kimchi observes in many places in his commentaries, and signify the grace of the Spirit of God. The Vulgate Latin and Ethiopic versions read, *the Holy Spirit*, and so Nonnus; and who doubtless is intended: by *water*, is not meant material water, or baptismal water; for water baptism is never expressed by water only, without some additional word, which shows, that the ordinance of water baptism is intended: nor has baptism any regenerating influence in it; a person may be baptized, as Simon Magus was, and yet not *born again*; and it is so far from having any such virtue, that a person ought to be born again, before he is admitted to that ordinance; and though submission to it is necessary, in order to a person's entrance into a Gospel church state, yet it is not necessary to the kingdom of heaven, or to eternal life and salvation: such a mistaken sense of this text, seems to have given the first birth and rise to infant baptism in the African churches; who taking the words in this bad sense, concluded their children must be baptized, or they could not be saved; whereas by *water* is meant, in a figurative and metaphorical sense, the grace of God, as it is elsewhere; see *Ezek. 36:25; John 4:14;* which is the moving cause of this new birth, and according to which God begets men again to *a lively hope* [*1 Pet. 1:3*], and that by which it is effected; for it is by the grace of God, and not by the power of man's free will, that any are regenerated, or made new creatures: and if Nicodemus was an officer in the temple, that took care to provide water at the feasts, as Dr. Lightfoot hints, and as it should seem Nicodemon ben Gorion was, by the story before related of him; see the note on *verse 1*; very pertinently does our Lord make mention of water, it being His own element: regeneration is sometimes ascribed to God the Father, as in *1 Pet. 1:3; James 1:18*; and sometimes to the Son, *1 John 2:29;* and here to the Spirit, as in *Titus 3:5*, who convinces of sin, sanctifies, renews, works faith, and every other grace; begins and carries on the work of grace, unto perfection; and unless a man has this work of His wrought on his soul,

he cannot enter into the kingdom of God; as he will never understand divine and spiritual things, so he can have no right to Gospel ordinances, or things appertaining to the kingdom of God; nor can he be thought to have passed from death to life, and to have entered into an open state of grace, and the kingdom of it; or that living and dying so, he shall ever enter into the kingdom of heaven; for unless a man is regenerated, he is not born heir apparent to it; and without internal holiness, shall not enter into it, enjoy it, or see God.

Verse 6. **That which is born of the flesh is flesh**, &c. Man by his natural birth, and as he is born according to the flesh, of his natural parents, is a mere natural man; that is, he is carnal and corrupt, and cannot discern spiritual things; nor can he as such, enter into, and inherit the kingdom of God; see *1 Cor. 2:14* and *15:50*. And therefore there is a necessity of his being born again, or of the grace of the Spirit, and of his becoming a spiritual man; and if he was to be, or could be born again of the flesh, or ever so many times enter into his mother's womb, and be born, was it possible, he would still be but a natural and a carnal man, and so unfit for the kingdom of God. By *flesh* here, is not meant the fleshy part of man, the body, as generated of another fleshy substance; for this is no other than what may be said of brutes; and besides, if this was the sense, *spirit*, in the next clause, must mean the soul, whereas one soul is not generated from another: but by flesh is designed, the nature of man; not merely as weak and frail, but as unclean and corrupt, through sin; and which being propagated by natural generation from sinful men, cannot be otherwise; for *who can bring a clean thing out of an unclean? not one, Job 14:4.* And though the soul of man is of a spiritual nature, and remains a spirit, notwithstanding the pollution of sin; yet it being defiled with the flesh, and altogether under the power and influence of the lusts of the flesh, it may well be said to be carnal or fleshly: hence *flesh*, as it stands opposed to *spirit*, signifies the corruption of nature, *Gal. 5:17;* and such who are in a state of unregeneracy, are said to be *after the flesh*, and *in the flesh*, and even the mind itself is said to be *carnal, Rom. 8:5-8;*

and that which is born of the Spirit, is spirit: a man that is regenerated by the Spirit of God, and the efficacy of His grace, is a spiritual man; he can discern and judge all things of a spiritual nature; he is a fit person to be admitted to spiritual ordinances and privileges; and appears to be in the spiritual kingdom of Christ; and has a right to the world of blessed spirits above; and when his body is raised a spiritual body, will be admitted in soul, body, and spirit, into the joy of his Lord. *Spirit* in the first part of this clause, signifies the Holy Spirit of God, the author of regeneration and sanctification; whence that work is called the *sanctification of the Spirit*, and the *renewing of the Holy Ghost, 1 Pet. 1:2; Titus 3:5.* And *spirit*, in the latter part, intends the internal work of grace upon the soul, from whence a man is denominated a spiritual man; and as a child bears the same name with its parent, so this is called by the same, as the author and efficient cause of it; and besides, it is of a spiritual nature itself, and exerts itself in spiritual acts and exercises, and directs to, and engages in spiritual things; and has its seat also in the spirit, or soul of man.

Verse 7. **Marvel not that I said unto thee,** &c., For Nicodemus marveled, and was quite astonished at this doctrine of the new birth; it was altogether new to him, and unheard of by him; nor could he understand, nor conceive in what manner it could be:

Ye must be born again; in *four* of Beza's copies, it is read *we*; but as Christ was not begotten in a carnal way, or descended not from Adam in the ordinary way of generation, He was not carnal and corrupt, nor in the least tainted with sin; and so stood in no need of regeneration; wherefore such a reading must be rejected. There is a necessity of the regeneration of those, who are the *chosen* of God, and the *redeemed* of the Lamb; and of them only can the words be understood; for as for others, they neither can, nor will, nor must be born again: but the people of God *must*; partly because it is the will of God; it is His purpose and resolution, that they shall be regenerated; He has chosen them, *through sanctification of the Spirit*, unto salvation by Christ [*2 Thess. 2:13*]: this is the way and method of saving sinners He has fixed upon, namely, not to save them by works of righteousness, but by grace, and according to His abundant mercy, *through the washing of regeneration*, and the *renewing of the Holy Ghost* [*Titus 3:5*]: and partly, because of the case and condition of men, which requires it; for whereas the chosen people of God, are *predestinated to the adoption of children* [*Eph. 1:5*], and are taken into the family of God, and are heirs to an inheritance, it is necessary they should have a nature, temper, and disposition of mind, suitable to the inheritance they are to enjoy; which they have not in their natural estate, and which is conveyed to them in regeneration. Besides, their carnal minds are enmity to God, and it is necessary that they should be friendly to Him, which cannot be without regeneration; nor can they, till they are born again, please God, or do those things which are pleasing to Him: to which may be added, which Christ has before suggested, and which shows the necessity of it, that without it, *no man can* either see, or *enter into the kingdom of God*. To take off the surprise of Nicodemus, our Lord instances in a common natural case, and to which this affair of regeneration may be compared, and by it illustrated.

Verse 8. **The wind bloweth where it listeth,** &c. And always will, for ought any mortal can say, or do to the contrary: and so the Spirit of God is a free agent in regeneration; He works how, and where, and when He pleases; He acts freely in the first operation of His grace on the heart, and in all after influences of it; as well as in the donation of His gifts to men, for different purposes; see *1 Cor. 12:11*; and this grace of the Spirit in regeneration, like *the wind*, is powerful and irresistible; it carries all before it; there is no withstanding it; it throws down Satan's strongholds, demolishes the fortifications of sin; the whole posse of hell, and the corruptions of a man's heart, are not a match for it; when the Spirit works, who can let?

and thou hearest the sound thereof, but canst not tell whence it cometh, and whither it goeth; as the wind, though its sound is heard, and its force felt, it cannot be seen; nor is it known certainly, from whence it comes, and where are the treasures [*or* source] of it; from whence it begins, and where it ends: so is the grace of the Spirit of God in regeneration to a natural man; it is imperceptible, indiscernible, and unaccountable by him, *1 Cor. 2:14*;

so is every one that is born of the Spirit: he is regenerated by *grace*, which is as free and sovereign, as powerful and irresistible, and as secret and imperceptible, as the wind is: and seeing so ordinary a thing as the blowing of the wind, is of such a nature, and so little to be accounted for; regeneration by the Spirit of God, who is comparable to the wind, and whose name so signifies, need not be thought so marvelous and astonishing, though the natural man discerns it not, and cannot account for it. The beauty and propriety of this simile will more appear by observing, that the same Hebrew word, רוח, is used both for the *wind*, and for the *Holy Spirit* of God; it is used for the *wind*, in *Gen. 3:8* and *8:1; 1 Kings 19:11; Eccl. 1:6*, and in other places; and for the Spirit of God, in *Gen. 1:2* and *6:3; Job 33:4*, and elsewhere: and so likewise the Greek word πνευμα, is used for them both, for the *wind* in this place, and often for the *Holy Ghost*. And it may be observed, that the Holy Spirit, because of His powerful, comfortable, and quickening influences, is compared to the wind, especially to the *south wind*, in some passages of the Old Testament, which Christ might have in view, *Song of Sol. 4:16; Zech. 9:14*. What our Lord here says, concerning the wind, is confirmed by all experience, and philosophical observations; the rise of winds, from whence they come, and whither they go, cannot be ascertained; the treasures of them are only with God, and known to Him; see *Eccl. 11:5*.

Verse 9. **Nicodemus answered and said unto him,** &c. Nicodemus remaining still as ignorant as ever, though Christ had explained the phrase *born again*, at which he stumbled, by a being *born of water and of the Spirit*, or of the grace of the Spirit of God; and had illustrated this by the free, powerful, and invisible blowing of the wind, said,

How can these things be? The Arabic version reads, *how can this be?* referring either to the last thing said, that a man's being born of the Spirit, is like the blowing of the wind; or to the explanation of the first expression, that a man should be born of water, and of the Spirit; or to the first assertion itself, that a man should be born again; which notwithstanding the explanation and illustration, seemed as impossible, and as impracticable as ever; or rather to them all, and so the Persic version reads, *how can all these things be?*

Verse 10. **Jesus answered and said unto him**, &c. Jesus answered, upbraiding him with his continued and invincible ignorance, which was aggravated by his dignified character:

Art thou a master in Israel? Or *of Israel*, as all the Oriental versions render it, as it literally may be rendered. He was one of the חכמי ישראל, *wise men*, or *doctors of Israel*,[27] so often mentioned by the Jews. One of the Jewish doctors was answered, by a boy, just in such language as is here used; who, not understanding the direction he gave him about the way into the city, said to him, אתה הוא חכם של ישראל, *art thou he, a doctor*, or *master of Israel? Did not I say to thee so?* &c.[28] He was not a common teacher; not a teacher of babes, nor a teacher in their synagogues, or in their *Midrashim*, or divinity schools, but in their great Sanhedrin; and the article before the word used will admit it to be rendered, *that master*, doctor, or teacher; that famous, and most excellent one, who was talked of all over Jerusalem and Judea, as a surpassing one: and now, though he was not only an Israelite, with whom were the laws, statutes, judgments, and oracles of God, the writings of Moses, and the prophets; but a teacher of Israelites, and in the highest class of teachers, and of the greatest fame among them, yet was he ignorant of the first and most important things in religion:

and knowest not these things? Which were so plainly to be suggested in the sacred writings, with which he was, or ought to have been conversant: for the same things Christ had been speaking of, are there expressed by a circumcision of the heart; by a birth, a nation's being born at once; by sanctification; by the grace of God, signified under the metaphor of water; and by quickening persons, comparable to dry bones, through the wind blowing, and breathing into them, *Deut. 30:6; Isa. 49:21 and 66:8; Ezek. 36:25 and 37:9-10.*

---

[27] Derech Eretz, fol. 18. 1.

[28] Echa Rabbati, fol. 44. 4.

Verse 11. **Verily, verily, I say unto thee, we speak that we do know**, &c. Meaning by *we*, either Himself, and John the Baptist His forerunner, who preached the same doctrine of regeneration, internal sanctification, and evangelical repentance, as well as outward reformation, as necessary to an entrance into the kingdom of heaven, or the Gospel dispensation, He declared was just at hand; or His disciples with Himself, who were now with Him, and whom He had called to preach the same truths He Himself did; or the prophets of the Old Testament, who agreed with Him in these things; or the Father that was with Him, and never left Him alone, and the Holy Spirit that was upon Him, by whom He was anointed to preach these things, and who spoke them in Him: or else He may use the plural number of Himself alone, as being one in authority, and speaking with it, as He sometimes did, *Mark 4:30*; and the rather this seems to be the sense, since He immediately, in the next verse, speaks in the singular number, *if I have told you earthly things*, &c. Now Christ must needs thoroughly and certainly know what He spoke, since He was not only the omniscient God, but, as Mediator, had all the treasures of wisdom and knowledge in Him, and the Spirit of wisdom and knowledge rested on Him:

and testify that we have seen; and therefore ought to have been received as a credible witness, as He was a faithful one; since *seeing* and *knowing* are qualifications in a witness, *Lev. 5:1*; and though these were eminently in Christ, the generality of the Jews gave no credit to His testimony:

and ye received not our witness; which was an aggravation of their sin and unbelief; see *verse 32.*

Verse 12. **If I have told you earthly things**, &c. Not that the doctrines He delivered were earthly ones; for He was not of the earth, but from heaven, and above all, and so spake not of the earth, but of heaven, *verse 31*; and this doctrine of regeneration was a heavenly doctrine; and the thing itself required supernatural power, and grace from above: but either they were the more easy doctrines of the Gospel; or were delivered in a plain and easy style, and illustrated by similes taken from earthly things, as from human birth, from the water, and from the wind:

and ye believe not; that is, believe not those things; ye do not receive them, nor give credit to them; or *me*, as the Ethiopic Version adds, who relate them on the best evidence, having fully known, and clearly seen them:

how shall ye believe; give credit to me, or receive my testimony:

if I tell you *of* heavenly things? Of the more sublime doctrines of the Gospel, such as the descent of the Messiah from heaven; the union of the two natures, human and divine, in Him; His being the only begotten Son of God;

His crucifixion and death, signified by the lifting up of the serpent on a pole in the wilderness; and the wonderful love of God to the Gentile world, in giving Christ to, and for them; and the salvation, and eternal happiness of all that believe in Him, whether they be Jews or Gentiles; and these delivered in language suitable to them, with figures, or natural similes, which help the understanding, and convey ideas of things more easily to it.

Verse 13. **And no man hath ascended up to heaven,** &c. Though Enoch and Elias had ascended thither, yet not by their own power, nor in the sense our Lord designs; whose meaning is, that no man had, or could go up to heaven, to bring from thence the knowledge of divine and heavenly things; in which sense the phrase is used in *Deut. 30:12; Rom. 10:6*; and which may be illustrated by *John 1:18*. Wherefore inasmuch as Nicodemus had acknowledged Christ to be *a teacher come from God*, our Lord would have him know, that He was the only teacher of heavenly things, as being the only person that had been in heaven, and in the bosom of the Father; and therefore if he, and the rest of the Jews, did not receive instructions from Him, they must for ever remain ignorant; for there never had been, nor was, nor could be, any mere man that could go up to heaven and learn the mysteries of God, and of the kingdom of heaven, and return and instruct men in them:

but he that came down from heaven; meaning Himself, who is *the Lord from heaven* [*1 Cor. 15:47*], and came from thence to do the will of God, by preaching the Gospel, working miracles, obeying the law, and suffering death in the room of His people, and thereby obtaining eternal redemption for them. Not that He brought down from heaven with Him either the whole of His human nature, or a part of it; either a human soul, or a human body; nor did He descend locally, by change of place, He being God omnipresent, infinite and immense, but by assumption of the human nature into union with His divine person:

even **the Son of man which is in heaven**. At the same time He was then on earth: not that He was in heaven in His human nature, and as He was the Son of man; but in His divine nature, as He was the Son of God; see *chapter 1:18*; though this is predicated of His person, as denominated from the human nature, which was proper to Him only in His divine nature; for such is omnipresence, or to be in heaven and earth at the same time: just as, on the other hand, God is said to purchase the church with His blood, and the Lord of glory is said to be crucified, *Acts 20:28; 1 Cor. 2:8;* where those things are spoken of Christ, as denominated from His divine nature, which were proper only to His human nature; and is what divines call a communication of idioms or properties; and which will serve as a key to open all such passages of Scripture. And now as a proof of our Lord's having been in heaven, and of His being *a teacher come from God*, and such a one as never was, or can be, He opens and explains a type respecting Himself, in the following verse.

Verse 14. **And as Moses lifted up the serpent in the wilderness,** &c. The history referred to is in *Num. 21:8*. There is, in many things, an agreement between this serpent, and Jesus Christ: as in the *matter* of it, it was a brazen serpent; it was made not of gold, nor of silver, but of brass, the meaner metal, and was a very unlikely means, of itself, to heal the Israelites; and might be despised by many. This may denote the meanness [*that is*, the lowliness and humbleness], of Christ in His human nature, in His birth and parentage, and place of education and converse [*or* social interaction]; and especially in His crucifixion and death: and which, to an eye of carnal sense and reason, seemed a very improbable means of saving sinners; and therefore were to some *a stumbling block*, and to others *foolishness* [*1 Cor. 1:23*]: though on the other hand, as brass is a shining metal, and might be chosen for the serpent in the wilderness to be made of, that by the luster of it the eyes of the Israelites might be attracted and directed to it, who were at the greatest distance in the camp; so it may be expressive of the glory of Christ, as the only begotten of the Father, and who is the *brightness of His Father's glory* [*Heb. 1:3*]; and which is the great attractive, motive, and inducement to engage souls to look unto Him, and believe in Him, *Isa. 45:22*; and whereas brass is both a strong and durable metal, it may signify the strength of Christ, who is the mighty God, and mighty to save; and His duration, as a Savior, being *the same today, yesterday, and for ever* [*Heb. 13:8*]. Likewise, the comparison between the serpent Moses lifted up, and Christ, may be observed in the *form* of it. The brazen serpent had the form of a serpent, but not the poison and venomous nature of one; so Christ was sent, *in the likeness of sinful flesh* [*Rom. 8:3*], and was *found in fashion as a man* [*Phil. 2:8*], as a sinful man, but was without sin, and was perfectly holy; and yet being in this form, was made both sin and a curse, that He might redeem His people both from sin, and from the curse of the law, by dying a death which denominated Him accursed; of which the serpent was an emblem. Besides, this serpent was a fiery one; at least it looked like one of the fiery serpents, being of brass, which shone as though it burned in a furnace; and may be an emblem both of Christ's Father's wrath, which was poured out like fire upon Him, and of His love to His people, which was like burning fire, the coals whereof gave a most vehement flame. Moreover, this serpent Moses made, and was ordered to make, was but *one*, though the fiery serpents, with which the Israelites were bitten, were many; so there is but one Mediator between God and man; but one Savior, in whom alone is salvation, and in no other, even Jesus Christ. To which may be added the *situation* in which this serpent was put: it was set by Moses on a pole; it was lifted up on high, that every one in the camp of Israel might see it; and may point out the ascension of Christ into heaven, and His exaltation at God's right hand there, as some think; or His being set up in the ministry of the Word, and held forth and exalted there as the only Savior of lost sinners; or rather His crucifixion, which is sometimes expressed by a lifting up, *chapter 8:28* and *12:32*. Once more, there is an agreement in the effect that followed upon the lifting up of the serpent; and which was the design of it, namely, the healing of such Israelites as were bitten by the fiery serpents, who looked to this: for as the Israelites were bitten by fiery serpents, with the poison of which they were infected, and were in danger of death, and to many of them their bitings were mortal; so men are poisoned with the venom of the old serpent the devil, by which they are subjected to a corporeal death, and are brought under a spiritual, or moral death, and are liable to an eternal one. And as these bitings were such as Moses could not cure, so the wounds of sin, through the old serpent, are such as cannot be healed by the law, moral or ceremonial, or by obedience to either. And as they were the Israelites who were convinced of their sin, and acknowledged it, and had a cure by looking to the brazen serpent; so such whom the Spirit of God convinces of sin, and to whom He gives the seeing eye of faith, these, through seeing the Son, and looking to Jesus, as crucified and slain, receive healing by His stripes and wounds. And as those, who were ever so much bit and poisoned by the fiery serpents, or were at ever so great a distance from the pole, or had the weakest eye, yet if they could but discern the serpent on the pole, though it only appeared as a shining piece of brass, had a cure: so the greatest of sinners, and who are afar off from God, and all that is good, and who have faith but as a grain of mustard seed, or but glimmering view of Christ, of His glory, fulness, and suitableness, shall be saved by Him. To add no more, this was done *in the wilderness*: which may signify this world, Christ's coming into it, His crucifixion in it, and His going without the camp, bearing our reproach, or suffering without the gates of Jerusalem. It is certain, that the Jews had a notion that the brazen serpent was symbolical and figurative: Philo the Jew makes it to be a symbol of fortitude and temperance, [29] and the author of the apocryphal book of Wisdom, [30] calls it *a sign of salvation*. They thought there was something mysterious in it: hence they say, [31]

"In four places it is said, *Make thee*, &c. In three places it is explained, namely, *Gen. 6:14; Num. 10:2; Josh. 5:2*; and one is not explained, *Num. 21:8, make thee a fiery serpent*, לך אֵ פירשׂ, *is not explained*."

---

[29] De Agricult. p. 202. & Allegor. l. 3. p. 1101-1104

[30] Chapter 16. v. 6.

[31] T. Hieros. Roshhashanah, fol. 59. 1.

And elsewhere[32] they ask,

> "And could the serpent kill, or make alive? But at the time that Israel
> looked up, and served with their hearts their Father which is in
> heaven, they were healed; but if not, they were brought low."

So that the look was not merely to the brazen serpent, but to God in heaven;
yea, to the Word of God, His essential *Logos*, as say the Targumists on *Num.
21:9*. The Jerusalem Targum paraphrases the words thus:

> "And Moses made a serpent of brass, and put it upon a high place, and
> whoever was bitten by the serpents, and lift up his face in prayer to his
> Father which is in heaven, and looked upon the serpent of brass, lived."

And Jonathan ben Uzziel paraphrases them thus:

> "And Moses made a serpent of brass, and put it on a high place; and it
> was, when a serpent had bitten any man, and he looked to the serpent
> of brass, *and directed his heart*, דיי מימרא לשום, *to the name of the
> Word of the Lord*, he lived."

And this healing they understand not only of bodily healing, but of the healing
of the soul: for they observe[33] that,

> "As soon as they said, *We have sinned*, immediately their iniquity was
> expiated; and they had the good news brought them *of the healing of
> the soul*, as it is written, *Make thee a seraph*; and he does not say a
> serpent; and this is it: *And it shall come to pass, that every one that is
> bitten, when he looketh upon it, shall live*, רפואת הנפש, *through the
> healing of the soul*."

Yea, they compare the Messiah to a serpent; for so the Targum on *Isa. 14:29*,
paraphrases that passage:

> "The Messiah shall come forth from Jesse's children's children; and his
> works shall be among you as a *flying serpent*."

And who else can be designed by the *other serpent of life*,[34] and the *holy
serpent*[35] they speak of, in opposition to the evil serpent that seduced Eve? And
it is well known, that נחש, *a serpent*, and משיח, *Messiah*, are numerically, or
by gematry, the same; a way of interpretation and explanation often in use
with the Jews. Now, as this serpent was lifted up on a pole on high, that every
one that was bitten with the fiery serpent might look to it, and be healed:

---

[32] Mishna Roshhashanah, c. 3. sect. 3.

[33] Tzeror Hammor, fol. 123. 2.

[34] Zohar in Gen. fol. 36. 2.

[35] Tikkune Zohar in Jetzira, p. 134.

even so must the Son of man be lifted up; upon the cross, and die: the crucifixion and death of Christ were necessary, and must be, because of the decrees and purposes of God, by which He was foreordained thereunto, and by which *determinate counsel* He was delivered, taken, crucified, and slain [*Acts 2:22-23*]; and because of His own engagements as a surety, laying Himself under obligations in the council and covenant of peace, to suffer, and die, in the room of His people; and because of the prophecies in the Old Testament, and His own predictions, that so it should be; as also, that the antitype might answer the type; and particularly, that He might be a suitable object of faith for wounded sinners, sensible of sin, to look unto.

Verse 15. **That whosoever believeth in him**, &c. Whether Jew or Gentile, a greater, or a lesser sinner, and of whatsoever state and condition, age or sex; and though ever so weak a believer, provided his faith is of the right kind: not a historical or temporary one, a mere assent to the truth of things respecting His person, office, and work; but such a faith, by which a soul sees a glory, fulness, and suitableness in Him as a Savior; goes to Him, ventures on Him, commits itself to Him, lays hold on Him, and receives Him, leans and relies upon Him, and trusts in Him, and lives upon Him; and which is the faith of God's elect; a gift of His grace, and the operation of His Spirit; and which works by love, and is attended with the fruits of righteousness. Now the end of Christ's crucifixion and death is, that such a one,

should not perish; though he is in a lost and perishing condition in Adam, and by nature, and sees himself to be so, and comes to Christ as such; and though his frames and comforts are perishing, and he sometimes fears he shall be utterly lost; and though he is subject to slips and falls, and great spiritual decays; and shall perish, as to the outward man, by death; yet he shall never perish eternally, or be punished with everlasting destruction, as the wicked will:

but have eternal life; not by his works, but as the gift of God: and which he that truly believes has already in the covenant of grace, in Christ his head, in faith and hope; and has the earnest and pledge of it, the Spirit of God; and the beginning of it, which is the knowledge of God in Christ; and shall hereafter possess it fully, and in person, to all eternity: even a life of perfect holiness and knowledge; a life of never ending pleasure; a life free from all the sorrows, distresses, and imperfections of the present; and which will always continue.

Verse 16. **For God so loved the world**, &c. The Persic version reads *men*: but not every man in the world is here meant, or all the individuals of human nature; for all are not the objects of God's special love, which is here designed, as appears from the instance and evidence of it, the gift of His Son: nor is

Christ God's gift to every one; for to whomsoever He gives His Son, He gives all things freely with Him [see *Rom. 8:32*]; which is not the case of every man. Nor is human nature here intended, in opposition to, and distinction from, the angelic nature; for though God has shown a regard to fallen men, and not to fallen angels, and has provided a Savior for the one, and not for the other; and Christ has assumed the nature of men, and not angels; yet not for the sake of all men, but the spiritual seed of Abraham; and besides, it will not be easily proved, that human nature is ever called *the world*: nor is the whole body of the chosen ones, as consisting of Jews and Gentiles, here designed; for though these are called *the world, chapter 6:33,51*; and are the objects of God's special love, and to them Christ is given, and they are brought to believe in Him, and shall never perish, but shall be saved with an everlasting salvation; yet rather the Gentiles particularly, and God's elect among them, are meant; who are often called *the world*, and *the whole world*, and *the nations of the world*, as distinct from the Jews; see *Rom. 11:12,15; 1 John 2:2; Luke 12:30*, compared with *Matt. 6:32*. The Jews had the same distinction we have now, *the church* and *the world*; the former they took to themselves, and the latter they gave to all the nations around. Hence we often meet with this distinction, *Israel*, and *the nations of the world*; on those words,

> "*Let them bring forth their witness*, that they may be justified, *Isa. 43:9*; (say[36] the doctors) these are *Israel*; or *Let them hear and say it is truth*, these are *the nations of the world*."

And again,[37]

> "The holy, blessed God said to Israel, when I judge *Israel*, I do not judge them as *the nations of the world*."

And so in a multitude of places: and it should be observed, that our Lord was now discoursing with a Jewish Rabbi, and that He is opposing a commonly received notion of theirs, that when the Messiah came, the Gentiles should have no benefit or advantage by Him, only the Israelites; so far should they be from it, that, according to their sense, the most dreadful judgments, calamities, and curses, should befall them; yea, hell and eternal damnation.

> "There is a place (they say,[38]) the name of which is *Hadrach, Zech. 9:1*. This is the King Messiah, who is, חד ודרך, *sharp and tender*; sharp to *the nations*, and tender to *Israel*."

---

[36] T. Bab. Avoda Zara, fol. 2. 1.

[37] Ibid. fol. 4. 1. Vid. T. Bab. Sanhedrin, fol. 91. 2. & Bereshit Rabba, fol. 11. 3.

[38] Shirhashirim Rabba, fol. 24. 1. Jarchi & Kimchi in Zech. 9:1.

And so of the *sun of righteousness*, in *Mal. 4:2*, they say,[39]
> "There is healing for the Israelites in it: but the idolatrous nations
> shall be burnt by it."

And that,[40]
> "there is mercy for Israel, but judgment for the rest of the nations."

And on those words in *Isa. 21:12, the morning cometh, and also the night*, they observe,[41]
> "The morning is for the righteous, and the night for the wicked; the
> morning is for *Israel*, and the night for *the nations of the world*."

And again,[42]
> "In the time to come (the times of the Messiah), the holy, blessed God
> will bring *darkness* upon *the nations*, and will enlighten *Israel*, as it is
> said, *Isa. 60:2*."

Once more,[43]
> "In the time to come, the holy, blessed God will bring the nations of the
> world, and will cast them into the midst of hell under the Israelites, as
> it is said, *Isa. 43:3*."

To which may be added that denunciation of theirs,[44]
> "Woe to *the nations of the world*, who perish, and they know not that
> they perish: in the time that the sanctuary was standing, the altar
> atoned for them; but now, who shall atone for them?"

Now, in opposition to such a notion, our Lord addresses this Jew; and it is as if He had said, You Rabbins say, that when the Messiah comes, only the Israelites, the peculiar favorites of God, shall share in the blessings that come by, and with Him; and that the Gentiles shall reap no advantage by Him, being hated of God, and rejected of Him: but I tell you, God has so loved the Gentiles, as well as the Jews,

that he gave his only begotten Son; to, and for them, as well as for the Jews; to be a covenant of the people, the Gentiles, the Savior of them, and a sacrifice for them; a gift which is a sufficient evidence of His love to them; it

---

[39] Zohar in Gen. fol. 112. 2.

[40] Zohar in Exod. fol. 15. 1, 2.

[41] T. Hieros. Taaniot, fol. 64. 1.

[42] Shemot Rabba, sect. 14. fol. 99. 4.

[43] Ibid. sect. 11. fol. 98. 3.

[44] T. Bab. Succa, fol. 55. 2.

being a large and comprehensive one, an irreversible and unspeakable one; no other than His own Son by nature, of the same essence, perfections, and glory with Him; begotten by Him in a way inconceivable and inexpressible by mortals; and His only begotten one; the object of His love and delight, and in whom He is ever well pleased; and yet, such is His love to the Gentiles, as well as Jews, that He has given Him, in human nature, up, into the hands of men, and of justice, and to death itself:

that whosoever believeth in him, whether Jew or Gentile,

should not perish, but have everlasting life; see the note on the preceding verse.

Verse 17. **For God sent not his Son into the world**, &c. God did send His Son into the world in the likeness of sinful flesh, being made of a woman, and made under the law; and which is an instance of His great love, and not of any disrespect to His Son, or of any inequality between them: but then this was not,

to condemn the world; even any part of it, or any in it: not the Gentiles, as the Jews thought He would; for though God had suffered them to walk in their own ways, and had winked at, or overlooked the times of their ignorance [*Acts 17:30*], and had sent no prophet unto them, nor made any revelation of His will, or any discovery of His special grace unto them; yet He sent His Son now, not to destroy them for their idolatry and wickedness, but to be the Savior of them: nor the Jews; for as impenitent and unbelieving, and as wicked as they were, He did not accuse them to the Father, nor judge and condemn them; He was to come again in power and great glory, when He would take vengeance on them, and cause wrath to come upon them to the uttermost, for their disbelief and rejection of Him; but this was not His business now: nor the wicked of the world in general; to judge, and condemn them, will be His work, when He comes a second time, in the day God has appointed *to judge the world in righteousness* [*Acts 17:31*]:

but, the end of His mission, and first coming is,

that the world through him might be saved; even the world of the elect in general, whom God determined to save, and has chosen, to obtain salvation by Jesus Christ [*I Thess. 5:9; 2 Thess. 2:13-14; 2 Tim. 2:10*], and has appointed Christ to be the salvation of; and who being sent, came into the world to seek and save them; and His chosen people among the Gentiles in particular: wherefore He is said to be God's *salvation to the ends of the earth*: and all the ends of the earth are called upon to look unto Him, and be saved by Him, *Isa. 49:6* and *45:22*.

Verse 18. **He that believeth on him is not condemned**, &c. Whether Jew or Gentile, because a believer is openly in Christ; and there is *no condemnation* to those that are in Him [*Rom. 8:1*]: and though the sentence of death passed upon all in Adam, and *judgment came upon all men to condemnation* in him [*Rom 5:18*]; yet this sentence being executed on Christ, the surety of His people, who has been condemned to death, and has suffered it in their stead, His death is a security to them from all condemnation; and they are delivered by Him from the curse and condemnation of the law: and having in conversion openly passed from death to life, they shall never enter into condemnation; and this is the happy case of every one that believes in Christ:

but he that believeth not is condemned already. The Persic version renders it, *from the beginning*; he remains under the sentence of condemnation, passed in Adam upon him; the law accuses him, and pronounces him guilty before God; he is under the curse of it, and it is a ministration of condemnation and death to him; nor has he any thing to secure him from its charge, curse, and condemnation: this must be understood of one that is a final unbeliever, or that lives and dies in a state of impenitence, and unbelief:

because he hath not believed in the name of the only begotten Son of God; whom God has sent to be the Savior of lost sinners, and to deliver them from *wrath to come* [*1 Thess. 1:10*]; and there is no other name but His, whereby men can *be saved* [*Acts 4:12*]; so that those who do not believe in Him, must be damned.

Verse 19. **And this is the condemnation**, &c. The condemnation of him that believes not in Christ; that is, this is the matter and cause of his condemnation, and by which it is aggravated, and appears to be just:

that light is come into the world: by which is meant, not natural or corporeal light; though natural darkness is, by some, preferred to this, being more convenient for their evil works; as by thieves, murderers, and adulterers: nor is the light of nature designed, with which every man is enlightened that comes into the world; which, though but a dim light, might be of more use and service than it is; and is often rejected and rebelled against by wicked men; and which will be the condemnation of the heathen world: but rather, the light of divine revelation, both in the law of God, and Gospel of Christ, especially the latter, is here intended; and which, though so great a favor to fallen men, is despised, and denied by the sons of darkness: though it may be best of all to understand it of Christ Himself, *the light of the world*, and who is come a light into it; see *chapter 8:12* and *12:46*; who may be called *light*, because He has set revelation in its clearest and fullest light; He has declared the whole mind and will of God concerning the affair of divine worship, and the business of salvation: *grace and truth* are come by Him; the doctrines of grace, and the truths of the Gospel, are most clearly brought to light by Him; the types and shadows of the law are removed; and the promises and the prophecies of the Old Testament, are most largely expounded by Him, and most perfectly fulfilled in Him: and besides, He is the author and giver of the light of grace, by which men see themselves to be what they are, lost and undone sinners; and see Him to be the only able, willing, suitable, sufficient, and complete Savior: and He it is that now gives the saints the glimpse of glory they have, and will be the light of the new Jerusalem, and the everlasting light of His people hereafter. He, by His incarnation, may be said to *come into the world* in general, which was made by Him, as God; and as He was in it, as man; though He was not known by it as the God-man, Mediator, and Messiah: and particularly He came into the Jewish world, where He was born, brought up, conversed, lived, and died; and into the Gentile world, by the ministry of His apostles, whom He *sent* into all the world, to *preach the Gospel to every creature* [*Mark 16:15*], and spread the glorious light of it in every place:

and men loved darkness rather than light: the Jews, the greater part of them, preferred the darkness of the ceremonial law, and the Mosaic dispensation, and even the traditions of their elders, before the clear Gospel revelation made by Christ Jesus; and the Gentiles also, for the most part, chose rather to continue in their heathenish ignorance and idolatry, and to walk in their own ways, and in the vanity of their minds, than to embrace Christ and His Gospel, and submit to His ordinances and appointments; and the generality of men, to this day, love their natural darkness, and choose to walk in it, and to have fellowship with the works of darkness, and delight in the company of the children of darkness, rather than follow Christ, the Light of the world, receive His Gospel, and walk in His ways, in fellowship with His saints: the reason of all this is,

because their deeds were evil; which they chose not to relinquish; and Christ, His Gospel and ordinances, are contrary to them; for the doctrine of the grace of God, which has appeared, and shone out in great luster and splendor, in the world, teaches men to deny *ungodliness and worldly lusts* [*Titus 2:2*]; and therefore it is hated and rejected by men.

Verse 20. **For every one that doeth evil, hateth the light**, &c. Every man, the series of whose life and conversation is evil, hates Christ and His Gospel, because they make manifest his evil deeds, convict him of them, and rebuke him for them:

neither cometh to the light; to hear Christ preach, or preached; to attend on the Gospel ministration and means of grace:

lest his deeds should be reproved; or discovered, and made manifest, and he be brought to shame, and laid under blame, and advised to part with them, which he cares not to do; see *Eph 5:11-13*.

Verse 21. **But he that doeth truth**, &c. That doeth that which is true, right and good: *he whose work is just*, as the Ethiopic version renders it; or, *he that does that which is right*, so the Persic; that which is according to the will of God, and from a principle of love to Him, and with a view to His glory:

cometh to the light; to Christ, and to His Word, and ordinances:

that his deeds may be made manifest; being brought to the light, to the test and standard, whether they are right, or wrong; and that it may appear,

that they are wrought in God; or *by God*; by His assistance, and gracious influence, without which men can do nothing; for it is God that works in them *both to will and to do* [*Phil. 2:13*]: or, *according to God*, as others render it; according to the will of God, both for matter and manner: or *for God*, as the Ethiopic version renders it; for the glory of God, which ought to be the aim and end of every action. The Persic version reads the whole thus, *that the work which is between God and him may be known*; that such deeds may be discovered, which are only known to God and himself.

Verse 22. **After these things**, &c. After Christ's coming to Jerusalem, at the feast of the passover, with His disciples, and driving the buyers and sellers from the temple, and doing the miracles He did there, upon which many believed on Him; and after the long discourse He had with Nicodemus, concerning regeneration, and other things:

came Jesus and his disciples into the land of Judea; or *into Judea, the country*, having been in Jerusalem, the city part or chief city in Judea; so that the country is distinguished from, and opposed to the city. And thus, a countryman, and a Jerusalemite, or citizen of Jerusalem, are distinguished, [45]

> "If, הקרתני, *a countryman* (one that lives in the country any where in the land of Israel out of Jerusalem[46]), receives a field, מירושלמי, *from a man of Jerusalem*, the second tithes belong to the Jerusalemite; but the wise men say, the countryman may bring them up, and eat them at Jerusalem."

Or, it may be, because that Jerusalem was part of it in the tribe of Benjamin, and the other in the tribe of Judah; therefore, when Christ and His disciples

---

[45] Mishna Demai, c. 6. sect. 4.

[46] Maimon. & Bartenora in ibid.

left Jerusalem, they might more properly be said to come into the land of Judea. Indeed, it is commonly said by the Jews,[47] that Jerusalem was not divided among the tribes, and that it did not belong to any tribe; and if so, then with greater propriety still might Christ be said to come into the land of Judea, when He departed from Jerusalem; unless it should be thought, that He went into Galilee, and after that came into the land of Judea; so Nonnus:

and there he tarried with them: with His disciples, as Nonnus; and with the inhabitants of those parts: He made a longer stay here than at Jerusalem, having more work to do here, and being more delighted with the plainness and simplicity of the country people; or *he conversed with them*, as the Syriac version renders it; He exercised, and employed Himself among them, as the Greek word used signifies: He went about from village to village, doing good, healing diseases, and preaching the Gospel, which was made useful to many:

and baptized; not He Himself, but His disciples, by His orders, and in His name; see *chapter 4:2*; whereby He gave fresh countenance and sanction to the ordinance of water baptism, administering it to others, as well as submitting to it Himself.

Verse 23. **And John also was baptizing in Ænon**, &c. The Syriac and Persic versions call it *Ain*, or *In-yon*, the *fountain of the dove*; and the Arabic version reads it, *the fountain of Nun*: and whether it was a town, or river, it seems to have its name from a fountain near it, or that itself was one, where was an abundance of water, as the text shows. There is a city of this name in the Septuagint version of *Josh. 15:61*, and mention is made of *Hazer Enon* in *Num. 34:9; Ezek. 47:17*, but neither of them seem to be the same with this; but be it where, and what it will, it was,

near to Salim; and where that was, is as difficult to know as the other. Some take it to be *Shalem*, a city of Shechem, mentioned in *Gen. 33:18*, but that is not the same name with this; and besides was in Samaria; and indeed, is by some there thought not to be the proper name of any place. Others are of opinion, that it is the same with *Shalim* in *1 Sam. 9:4*, though it seems rather to be the place which Arias Montanus calls,[48] "Salim juxta torrentem," *Salim by the brook*; and which he places in the tribe of Issachar: and might be so called, either because it was near this Ænon, and may be the brook or river intended, by which it was; or because it was not far from the place where the two rivers, Jabbok and Jordan, met; and so the Jewish maps place near

---

[47] T. Bab. Yoma, fol. 12. 1, & Megilla, fol. 26. 1.

[48] Antiqu. Jud. l. 2. c. 3.

Jordan, in the tribe of Manasseh, bordering on the tribe of Issachar, a *Shalem*, and by it Ain-yon. And the Septuagint, in *Josh. 19:22,* mention *Salim by the sea,* as in the tribe of Issachar. There is a passage in the Talmud,[49] which, whether it has any regard to this Ænon, and Salim, I leave to be considered:

> "The wine of Ogedoth, why is it forbidden? Because of the village Pegesh; and that of Borgetha, because of the Saracene palace; and of Ain-Cushith, because of the village Salem."

Nonnus here calls Ænon, *a place of deep waters*; and Salim he reads *Salem*; and so some copies. Ænon, where John baptized, according to Jerome,[50] was eight miles from Scythopolis, to the south, and was near Salim and Jordan; and he makes Salim to be at the same distance from Scythopolis. However, John was baptizing in these parts, at the same time that Christ was teaching and baptizing: he did not leave off on that account. This was the work he was sent to do, and which he continued in as long as he had his liberty; and he chose this place,

because there was much water there; or *many waters*; not little purling streams, and rivulets; but, as Nonnus renders it, *abundance of water*; or *a multitude* of it, as in the Arabic version; see *Rev. 1:15* and *17:1, 15; 19:6; Song of Sol. 8:7* and the Septuagint in *Psa. 77:19* and *Psa. 107:23*; and what was sufficient to immerse the whole body in, as Calvin, Aretius, Piscator, and Grotius, on the place, observe; and which was agreeable not only to the practice of the Jews, who used dipping in their baptisms and purifications, as Musculus and Lightfoot assert, but to John's method and practice elsewhere:

and they came, and were baptized. The Ethiopic version renders it, *they came to him*, that is, to John, *and he baptized them*; as the Persic version adds, *there*, in Ænon, near Salim, in the much water there. It may be understood of the people coming both to John and Christ, and of their being baptized by them; though it seems rather to be said of John; and so Nonnus paraphrases it.

Verse 24. **For John was not yet cast into prison**. As he afterwards was by Herod, for the sake of Herodias, because he reproved Herod for taking her to be his wife, when she was wife to his brother Philip; see *Matt. 14:3-4*; and this circumstance shows, that these things were done before that journey of Christ into Galilee, mentioned in *Matt. 4:12-13*.

---

[49] T. Hieros. Avoda Zara, fol. 44. 4.

[50] De locis Hebraicis fol. 89. C. & fol, 94. F.

Verse 25. **Then there arose a question**, &c. A dispute, or controversy, occasioned by the baptism of John and Christ:

between *some* **of John's disciples, and the Jews**. The Syriac and Persic versions read, *between one of John's disciples, and a certain Jew*; and Nonnus renders it, *with a Hebrew man*; and so the Alexandrian manuscript; many others read, *with a Jew*: the contention between them was,

about purifying; either about the ceremonial purifications, and ablutions commanded in the law of Moses; or concerning the various washings of persons, and vessels, according to the traditions of the elders, which the Jews in common were very tenacious of; and which they thought were brought into neglect and contempt, by the baptism of John: and this seems to have been occasioned by the baptism of Christ; which the Jew might improve against the disciple of John, and urge, that since another, besides his master, had set up baptizing, who could tell which was rightest and safest to follow? and therefore it would have been much better, if no such rite at all had been used by any, but that the purifications required by the law of Moses, and by their elders, had been strictly and solely attended to.

Verse 26. **And they came unto John**, &c. The Persic version reads, *he came unto John*; that disciple that had the controversy with the Jew about purifying, who not knowing well how to answer him, and which might be the case of more, applied to John:

and said unto him, Rabbi; or *Master*; or, *our Master*; as the Syriac and Persic versions read, which was a title of great respect and reverence and much in use in those times; see the notes on *Matt. 23:7, 8* **[32, 33]**. The Arabic version joins this word to the following clause, and applies it to Christ, rendering it thus, *the master that was with thee beyond Jordan*; which is making them to speak more honorably of Christ than they intended; for though they speak very respectfully to John, yet with much disdain and neglect of Christ; not so much as mentioning His name, or using any term of honor or respect; only saying,

he that was with thee beyond Jordan; namely, at Bethabara; who came from Galilee to Jordan unto John, to be baptized by him, and who was baptized by him; and for some little time continued with him, and attended on his ministry; and as they thought, was a disciple of John's:

to whom thou bearest witness; that He was before him, and to be preferred unto him; and that He was the Lamb of God, and even the Son of God; suggesting, that by this testimony of his, Christ had gained all the credit and reputation He had; and that therefore he had done a wrong thing in enlarging so much in the praise, and commendation of Him:

behold the same baptizeth; takes upon Him to administer the ordinance of baptism; at least gives orders to administer it; which John's disciples thought was the proper, and peculiar business of their master; and therefore speak of this as an intrusion into his office, and an entering into his province; and an assuming that which only belonged to him: and what gave still more uneasiness, and increased the complaint, was,

and all *men* **come to him**; that is, *many*, as the Syriac and Persic versions render it, even more than came to John; see *chapter 4:1*. Multitudes from all parts flocked to hear Christ preach, and great numbers were made disciples by Him, and then baptized. That He should baptize, gave them great offense; and that He was so followed, raised their envy; and His being so near to John, might add to their uneasiness. It is a rule with the Jews that,

> "it is not lawful for a disciple to teach the constitutions, or sentences of the law, before his master; but must be twelve miles distant from him, as the camp of Israel."

And they say that,

> "A disciple that teaches before, or in the presence of his master, is guilty of death."[51]

Verse 27. **John answered and said**, &c. The Syriac and Arabic versions add, *to them*; the answer being made to the disciples of John, who came to him with their complaint:

a man can receive nothing; the Syriac and Persic versions add, *of his own will*: some understand this of Christ, as man, who did not take upon Him the character of the Messiah, nor the office of a Mediator, nor the honor of it, of Himself; and who received the gifts and graces of the Spirit of God without measure, and had His success in His work from above: and indeed, it is true of both Christ, and John; for as Christ, so John received his office, and honor, as the harbinger and forerunner of Christ, and all his gifts qualifying him for it, and his success in it, not of himself, but of God: and since therefore the superior office, and honor, and usefulness of the one above the other, were according to the sovereign will of God, there was no room for complaint, murmuring, and envy; but there ought to be contentment and pleasure in the wise disposition of things by God. Yea, this is true of every man, who has nothing of his own; and whatever he has in nature, providence and grace, is a gift to him; and all he enjoys is in a way of receiving: nor can he receive it,

except it be given him from heaven; from God who dwells there; see the note on *Matt. 21:25* **[31]**; who is the author and donor of every gift, temporal,

---

[51] T. Hieros. Sheviith, fol. 37. 3.

spiritual, and eternal; particularly he cannot perceive and discern spiritual things, nor receive Gospel truths; as it appeared to John his disciples could not, unless spiritual light is given from above; and such a favor is bestowed, as to know the mysteries of the kingdom of heaven: and therefore, for every office, whether of a superior, or inferior kind, and for every degree of honor, and for whatsoever blessing and gift, whether for soul or body, for time, or for eternity, men ought to be thankful, and not glory in them, as though they had not received them [*1 Cor. 4:7*]; nor is there any reason to murmur against God, or envy one another, as these disciples did.

Verse 28. **Ye yourselves bear me witness,** &c. They witnessed in what they now said, and referred to, in describing Christ, as He to whom John bore witness; and he appeals to them for what he said in their presence, and before all the people, in that testimony:

that I said, I am not the Christ; see *chapter 1:19-20*; wherefore, if He, who is the Christ, is now come, and teaches, and baptizes, and has the greatest number of followers, it is not to be wondered at; and much less to be envied; but rather to be rejoiced at. For John, by repeating what he had before said, that he was not the Christ, suggests, that Jesus was; and therefore was superior to him in office, honor, and usefulness, who was only His harbinger and forerunner, as follows:

but I am sent before him; to prepare His way, to make straight His paths, to proclaim His coming and kingdom being at hand; and that the expectations of men may be raised, and they may be ready to receive Him when come: and hereby the end of John's office and ministry had its accomplishment. The Ethiopic version adds, *to preach him*.

Verse 29. **He that hath the bride**, &c. By whom particular persons seem here to be meant, who were called, converted, and brought to Christ, and were made His disciples, and baptized, and so were openly espoused unto Him; though sometimes it designs a particular church of Christ, and even the whole *general assembly and church of the firstborn*, whose names are *written in heaven* [*Heb. 12:23*]; all the elect of God, whether among Jews, or Gentiles; see *2 Cor. 11:2; Rev. 21:2,9*. These Christ has in a conjugal relation; and He came, and comes to have them after this manner: He saw them in His Father's purposes, and decrees, in all the glory He meant to bring them to; and loved them, and desired them of His Father, as His spouse, who gave them to Him, as such; and He betrothed them to Himself for ever; and in time He sends His ministering servants with His Gospel, to engage and betroth them to Him; and, by the power of His grace, He makes them willing to give up themselves to Him [see *Psa. 110:3*]; which is the open espousal of them; and at the last day, when the number of the elect are completed, the marriage of the Lamb will be publicly solemnized, and a marriage supper will be made; and all that are called and ready, will enter into the marriage chamber, and share in the joys and pleasures of that day. Thus by virtue of the Father's gift, Christ has them now as His own property, as His portion, His jewels, His bride, and wife; and by, and through His great love to them, He has them not only in His arms, from whence they can never be plucked; but in His heart, where they are set as a seal; and by virtue of this love, they are united to Him, become one with Him, are members of His body, flesh, and bones; and are one spirit with Him, and nothing can be able to separate them [see *Rom. 8:35-39*]; and He will have them all with Him to all eternity, to be where He is, and behold His glory: and now, *He that has the bride*, in this sense,

is the bridegroom; and such is Christ; see *Matt. 9:15* and *25:1*; and He acts and behaves as such; He loves the saints, as a bridegroom loves his bride, with a love prior to theirs: with a love of complacency and delight, which is single, chaste, and inviolable; free, and sovereign, wonderful, unchangeable, and from everlasting to everlasting. He sympathizes with them in all their adversities, and afflictions; He nourishes, and cherishes them, and provides every thing for them, for food, and clothing, for refreshment and protection; and interests them in all He has: and an amazing instance of grace this is, that such who are no better than others, children of wrath by nature; exceeding great sinners, guilty, and filthy; bankrupts, and beggars on the dunghill; and yet are taken into so near a relation to Him; who is in the form of God, and equal to Him, *the brightness of His glory, and the express image of His person* [*Heb. 1:3*], the Son of God, in whom all the fulness of the Godhead dwells; the King of kings, and Lord of lords. And this being the case, John suggests, that by these persons following Christ, and giving up themselves to Him, it appeared that He was the bridegroom; and to whom should they betake themselves but to Him? Nor did it become him, or any other, to seek to draw them from Him; nor should any envy His enjoyment of them, since they were His in so peculiar a sense, and in so near a relation:

but the friend of the bridegroom; meaning himself: and such is every true minister of the Gospel; he is a lover of Christ, a friend to His interest, and seeks by all means to promote it, and to bring souls unto Him. The allusion is to a custom among the Jews, who, at their marriages, used to have persons both on the side of the bride, and of the bridegroom, as companions that attended each, and were called their *friends*; see *Judges 14:20*. Such a one is called by the Rabbins, שׁוֹשְׁבִין; and this word is interpreted by אוֹהֵב, *a lover*, or *friend*, the same as here; and by רֵעוֹ, *his* (the bridegroom's) *friend* in the time of his marriage.[52] There were two of these, one for the bride, and another for the bridegroom; for so it is said,[53]

> "Formerly they appointed two שושבינין, *friends*, one for him (the bridegroom), and one for her (the bride), that they might minister to the bridegroom, and do all things at their entrance into the marriage chamber. —And formerly, these friends slept where the bridegroom and bride slept."

And so as John is here represented as the friend of Christ, the bridegroom of the church, the Jews speak of Moses as *the friend of God, the bridegroom of the people of Israel*. So one of their writers,[54] having delivered a parable concerning *a certain king going into a far country, and leaving his espoused wife with his maidservants, who raising an evil report on her, his friend tore in pieces the matrimonial contract*, thus applies it:

> "The king, this is the holy, blessed God; the maidens, these are the mixed multitude; and השושבין, *the friend*, this is Moses; and the spouse of the holy, blessed God is Israel."

The Jews say,[55] that Michael and Gabriel were the שושבינן, *bridal friends* to the first Adam;

which standeth; the phrase may be seen in the above parable of the Jewish writer[56] referred to, עמד שושבינה, *his friend standeth*. This was the posture of servants, and is fitly applied to John, who was the harbinger of Christ, and judged himself unworthy to bear His shoes; and well agrees with the ministers of the Gospel, who *stand* before Christ, wait upon Him, and minister in His name, and are the servants of the churches for His sake:

and heareth him; hearkens to His words; observes, and obeys them; hears His voice, so as to understand it, and distinguish it from another's; and hears it with delight and pleasure, as every true friend of Christ does His Gospel, which is His voice, and is a joyful sound; and so,

rejoiceth greatly because of the bridegroom's voice: such a one rejoices at the sight of His person, and in communion with Him; he rejoices at the

---

[52] Mishna Sanhedrin, c. 3. sect. 5. & Bartenora in ibid.

[53] T. Bab. Cetubot, fol. 12. 1.

[54] Jarchi in Exod. 34:1. Vid. Shemot Rabba, sect. 46. fol. 142. 2.

[55] Bereshit Rabba, sect. 8. fol. 8. 2.

[56] Jarchi in ibid.

sound of His voice; and is delighted to hear Him in the ministry of the Word, calling to one and to another, to come unto Him, and causing them to believe in Him, and give up themselves to Him:

this my joy therefore is fulfilled; in Christ, He being come in person, and His voice heard in the land of Judea, and multitudes of souls flocking to Him, who, believing in Him, were baptized; than which, nothing could be a greater pleasure to John, or to any Gospel minister. This was the accomplishment and perfection of his joy, which carried it to its utmost height: this was what he wished for; and now he had the desire of his heart. It was usual for the friend of the bridegroom to carry provisions with him, and eat and drink with the bridegroom, and rejoice with him; and this rejoicing was mutual. Hence those words,

"Give me שׁוֹשְׁבִינִי, *my friend*, that I may rejoice with him:"
the gloss upon it is,

"and eat at his marriage, even as he also rejoiced, and ate at my marriage."[57]

To this rejoicing the allusion is here.

Verse 30. **He must increase**, &c. Not in stature of body, or in wisdom and understanding of mind, as man, He being come to maturity in these things already; but in fame, credit, and reputation among men; as He afterwards did in the land of Judea, by reason of His miracles and doctrines; and after that among the Gentiles, through the publication of His Gospel; and will more and more in the latter day, when He, and He alone, shall be exalted: and *He must increase* in the ministry of His Word, which was published by Him and His disciples throughout all the cities of Israel; and which, after His resurrection and ascension, grew and increased mightily, notwithstanding the opposition made unto it both by their civil and ecclesiastical rulers; and which, by the means of His apostles, was spread throughout the Gentile world, and will hereafter cover the earth, as the waters do the sea: and also in His kingdom and interest, which at first were very small, like a grain of mustard seed, or like a little stone cut out of the mountain without hands; but in process of time grew exceedingly, and will, ere long, fill the face of the whole earth; for *the kingdoms of this world* will become *the kingdoms of our Lord, and of His Christ [Rev. 11:15]*; and His dominion shall be *from sea to sea, and from the river to the ends of the earth [Psa. 72:8]*; and of the increase of it *there shall be no end [Isa. 9:7]*. And so likewise in the number of His followers, which at first were but a few in Judea only, but afterwards greatly increased, and especially among the Gentiles; and will be very numerous in the latter day glory, when

---

[57] T. Bab. Bava Bathra, fol. 144. 2. & 145. 1.

the nation of the Jews will *be born at once*, and the fulness and forces of the Gentiles are brought in: [So the author interprets *Isaiah 66:8* with *Romans 11:25-26, q.v. - Editor*]

but I *must* decrease; as he did in his esteem among the people; see *John 5:35;* and in his work and office, which were now come to an end, Christ, whose forerunner he was, being come; and quickly after this he was put into prison, and there put to death.

Verse 31. **He that cometh from above**, &c. Meaning Christ; not that He brought His human nature with Him from heaven, or that that is of a celestial kind; but He came from heaven in His divine person, not by change of place, He being God immense and infinite, but by assumption of the human nature; which He took upon Him, in order to do in it His Father's will, and the work of our salvation:

is above all; above John, before whom He was preferred, for He was before him; above the prophets of the Old Testament, and even above Moses, the chief of them; yea, above all the angels in heaven, being God *over all, blessed for ever* [*Rom. 9:5*]: wherefore all glory is to be given Him; no honor is to be envied Him, or detracted from Him;

he that is of the earth; as John was, and all mankind are, being descended from Adam, who was made of the dust of the earth; and who dwell in houses of clay, and in earthly tabernacles, which are at last to be resolved into their original dust:

is earthly; of an earthly nature, frame, temper, and disposition; see *verse 6*. Men naturally mind earthly things; and it is owing to the Spirit and grace of God, if they mind and savor spiritual things, or have their affections set on things above, or their conversation in heaven; and even such, at times, find that their souls cleave unto the dust, and are hankering after the things of the earth:

and speaketh of the earth; of earthly things, as in *verse 12*; and indeed of heavenly things in an earthly manner, in a low way, and by similes and comparisons taken from the things of the earth; not being able to speak of celestial things as they are in their own nature, and in that sublime way the subject requires: but,

he that cometh from heaven is above all: men and angels, in the dignity of His person; and all prophets and teachers, in the excellency of His doctrine, and manner of delivering it: and therefore it is not to be wondered at that He should be followed as He is; but rather it should seem marvelous, that He has no more followers than He has; see [in the Aprocrypha] 2 Esdras 4:21:

"For like as the ground is given unto the wood, and the sea to his floods: even so they that dwell upon the earth may understand nothing but that which is upon the earth: and he that dwelleth above the heavens may only understand the things that are above the height of the heavens."

Verse 32. **And what he hath seen and heard**, &c. Seen and heard of the Father, of His mind and will, of His purposes and promises, of His love, grace, and mercy, in the council and covenant of peace, lying in His bosom, and being privy to all His secrets. The phrases express the clear and perfect knowledge Christ has of all truths and doctrines; He having all the treasures of wisdom and knowledge in Him;

that he testifieth; fully, freely, and faithfully; withholds nothing, but declares the whole counsel of God; and is deservedly called *the faithful witness, Rev. 1:5;*

and no man receiveth his testimony; though it was the testimony of God, which is greater than that of man; yet few, and which were next to none at all, gave any heed or credit to it; few or none among the Jews, or among the disciples of John, or even among those that followed Christ. John, and his disciples, widely differed; they thought that all men came to Christ, and believed in Him; and John thought few or none, in comparison of the numbers he could have wished, did: and indeed, no one person can receive the testimony of Christ, and believe in Him, unless it be given him from above, by the grace of God [see *John 3:27; 1 Cor. 2:14; Phil. 1:29*]: for the natural man receives not divine and spiritual things; see *verse 11.*

Verse 33. **He that hath received his testimony**, &c. For there was here and there one that received it, who believed in Him as the Messiah, and embraced His Gospel, and submitted to His ordinances, and truly and sincerely followed Him: and for the encouragement of such, it is said,

hath set to his seal that God is true; faithful in fulfilling the promises He has made concerning the Messiah, and His coming: he firmly believes that God is true to every word of His, and will make good every promise; and this he seals, ratifies, and confirms by his embracing the testimony of Christ; whereas, on the contrary, *he that believeth not* makes God a liar, than which, nothing can be more reproachful to Him, *1 John 5:10*. The Jews have a saying,[58] that *the seal of the blessed God is truth*. The Arabic version renders it, *he is already sealed, because God is true*; and the Ethiopic version, *God*

---

[58] T. Hieros. Sanhedrin, fol. 18. 1. & T. Bab. Sanhedrin, fol. 64. 1. & Yoma, fol. 69. 2.

hath sealed him, because he is true; namely, with His Holy Spirit; see *2 Cor. 1:22; Eph. 1:13* and *4:30.*

Verse 34. **For he whom God hath sent**, &c. Still meaning Christ, who was *sent* in human nature, in the likeness of sinful flesh, in the fulness of time; to be the Savior of the world, of that which was lost, of the chief of sinners; and to preach the glad tidings of the Gospel, which is more especially here designed; and for which He was abundantly qualified by the Spirit of God, with which He was anointed:

speaketh the words of God; the words which God gave unto Him; the doctrines of grace; the Word of truth; the Word of faith; the Word of righteousness; the Word of reconciliation; the words of salvation and eternal life; the whole mind and will of God; and whatever He spoke were as true as the oracles of God, and were such.

for God giveth not the Spirit by measure *unto him*, as He did to the prophets of the Old Testament, and to the apostles of the New; and to the ordinary ministers of the Word, who have gifts differing one from another; to one is given one gift of the Spirit; and to another, another gift, as the Spirit pleaseth; and to everyone is given grace, or gifts of grace, *according to the measure of the gift of Christ, Eph. 4:7.* To which agrees what the Jews say[59] of the Holy Spirit, and His gifts:

"Says R. Joden bar R. Simeon, Even the waters which descend from above are not given, but במדה, *in measure.*—Says R. Acha, Even the Holy Spirit, which dwells upon the prophets, does not dwell, but במשקל, *in weight.*"

But the Lord Jesus has every gift of the Spirit, and the fulness of grace in Him: He is anointed *with the oil of gladness*, with the Holy Ghost above His fellows [*Heb. 1:9*]; and has an immeasurable unction of the Holy One; which, like the precious oil poured on Aaron, descends from Him to the members of His body.

Verse 35. **The Father loveth the Son**, &c. There is such a relation as that of Father and Son subsisting between the first and second persons in the Trinity; which is not by constitution and appointment: or arbitrary, arising from, and depending on the will of the first, but is natural and necessary; the second person being begotten by the first, and is of the same nature, and equally a divine person: and which relation is the foundation of the distinction of their persons; and which existed from all eternity, and coexisted with their being and essence; and is what no other stand in, angels or men, in such sense

---

[59] Vajikra Rabba, sect. 15. fol. 157. 3.

as the second person does; and is not to be conceived of, expressed and explained by us: and from this relation arises love; hence, the Son of the Father is His dear Son, the Son of His love; as He must needs be, since He is of the same nature, has the same perfections He has, and is the *brightness of His glory, and the express image of His person*: and hence He continues to love Him in every form and appearance of His; in every office He sustains; in every state and condition into which He comes: He delighted in Him as His elect, as chosen and appointed by Him to be the Savior of His people; He took pleasure in Him as the surety of them, and when He saw Him engaging as such, and declaring it was His heart to do His will, and work out their salvation; He loved Him when He appeared in human nature, in the form of a servant; and in His state of humiliation, more than once He declared, by a voice from heaven, that He was His beloved Son, and particularly at His baptism: and indeed, as in that, so in every thing else, He always did the things that pleased Him; He loved Him when He laid down His life for the sheep: when He was bruised, and His soul made an offering for sin; He loved Him when on the cross, and even when He hid His face from Him; when He lay in the grave He left Him not, nor would He suffer Him to see corruption; He raised Him from the dead, and gave Him glory; exalted Him, and received Him into heaven with a welcome; and placed Him at His right hand; and now looks with pleasure upon Him, upon His person, His sacrifice, blood, and right-eousness: and this love is a love of complacency and delight, and is from everlasting to everlasting; the evidence of which follows,

and hath given all things into his hand; or *by his hand*; as the doctrines of the Gospel, the gifts of the Spirit, grace, and glory: or rather, *into his hand*; with which He, being the Son of God, a divine person, is fit to be entrusted, which otherwise He would not be: παντα, *all,* includes *all persons*; all the angels, the good angels which are chosen in Him, and He is the head of; and by whom they are confirmed in the state they are: and who are at His command and beck, and minister to Him and His. The evil angels, though they have broken away from God, and rebelled against Him, yet are, in some sense, in the hands of Christ, and under His power: as appears by His dispossessing them from the bodies of men on earth, His spoiling them on the cross, and triumphing over them in His ascension to heaven, and by His binding Satan a thousand years. All men are given to Him; the elect, in a special sense, as His bride and spouse, as His children, and as His sheep; hence, He died for them, and effectually calls them, and brings them to Himself; and they shall never perish, or be plucked out of His hands, but shall have eternal life. And wicked men are, in a sense, given to Him; their wrath He restrains, and makes it to praise Him; He rules them with a rod of iron, and breaks them in pieces as a potter's vessel. And *all things* also are *given into His hand*; all temporal things, the things of nature and providence; the light of nature, and all the gifts and attainments of it; all the good things of the world, and which are wisdom's left hand blessings; and Christ disposes of them to His people in mercy, and as covenant ones: all spiritual things are in His hands; all the gifts of the Spirit, and the fulness of all grace — sanctifying, justifying, pardoning, adopting, and persevering grace; all the promises and blessings of the covenant; the government of the church, and the judgment of the world; all power, both in heaven and in earth; the salvation of the elect, and their eternal inheritance, happiness, and glory. For all which, no creature, angels or men, are fit, only the Son of God.

Verse 36. **He that believeth on the Son**, &c. The Son, who is a proper object of faith and trust; which, if He was not truly and properly God, He would not be: and this is to be understood not of any sort of faith, a temporary, or a historical one; but of that which is the faith of God's elect, the gift of God, and the operation of His Spirit; by which a man sees the Son, goes unto Him, ventures and relies upon Him, and commits himself to Him, and expects life and salvation from Him; and who shall not be ashamed and confounded; for such a one,

hath everlasting life; he has it in Christ his Head, in whom he believes; he has a right unto it through the justifying righteousness of Christ, and a meetness for it by His grace; he has it in faith and hope; he has the beginning of it in the knowledge of Christ, and communion with Him; he has some foretastes of it in his present experience; and he has the earnest and pledge of it in his heart, even the blessed Spirit, who works him up for this selfsame thing:

and he that believeth not the Son; that does not believe Christ to be the Son of God, or Jesus to be the Messiah; or rejects Him as the Savior; who lives and dies in a state of impenitence and unbelief:

shall not see life; eternal life; he shall not enter into it, and enjoy it; he shall die the second death. Very remarkable are the following words of the Jews[60] concerning the Messiah, whom they call the *latter Redeemer*:

"Whosoever believes in him *shall live*; but he that believes not in him shall go to the nations of the world, and they shall kill him."

But the wrath of God abideth on him; as the sentence of wrath, of condemnation, and death, and the curse of the law, were pronounced upon him in Adam, as on all mankind, it continues, and will continue, and will never be reversed, but will be executed on him, he not being redeemed from it, as his final unbelief shows; and as he was *by nature* a child of wrath [*Eph.*

---

[60] Midrash Ruth, fol. 33. 2.

2:3], as others, he remains such; and as *the wrath of God is revealed from heaven against all ungodliness and unrighteousness of men [Rom. 1:18]*, it comes upon the children of disobedience, and remains there; it hangs over their heads, and lights upon them, and they will be filled with a dreadful sense of it to all eternity. The Syriac and Arabic versions render it, *shall abide upon him;* so some copies.

CHAPTER 4

Verse 1. **When therefore our Lord knew**, &c. Or *Jesus*, as some copies, as the Vulgate Latin, Syriac, Arabic, and Persic versions read; who is Lord of all, Lord of lords, the one and only Lord of saints: and who knew all things as God; every man, and what is in man; who would believe in Him, and who [would] not, and who would betray Him; He knew His adversaries, what they thought, said, or did; what was told them, and how it operated in them; and what were the secret motions of their hearts, and their most private counsels and designs; for this is not merely to be understood of His knowledge as man, which He might have by private intelligence from others; though what is here said might be true also in this sense:

how the Pharisees; the inveterate and implacable enemies of Christ, and particularly those that dwelt at Jerusalem, and were of the great Sanhedrin, or council of the nation:

had heard; either by their spies, which they constantly kept about Christ; or by John's disciples, who, through envy, might apply to the Sanhedrin to put a stop to, or check upon, the baptism and ministry of Christ; or by common fame:

that Jesus made and baptized more disciples than John; see *chapter 3:26.* The method Christ took was, He first made men disciples, and then baptized them; and the same He directed His apostles to, saying, *go and teach,* or *disciple all nations, baptizing them, &c.[Matt. 28:19].* And this should be a rule of conduct to us, to baptize only such who appear to have been made the disciples of Christ: now a disciple of Christ, is one that has learned of Christ, and has learned Christ; the way of life, righteousness, and salvation by Him; who is a believer in Him; who has seen a beauty, glory, fulness, and suitableness in Him, as a Savior; and is come to Him, and has ventured on Him, and trusted in Him; and who has been taught to deny himself, sinful self, and righteous self; to part with his sins, and to renounce his own righteousness, and all dependence on it, for justification before God; and who has been made willing to leave and forsake all worldly things and advantages, and to bear all reproaches, indignities, and persecutions, for Christ's sake: and such who are Christ's disciples in this sense, are the only proper persons to be baptized; these are they that ought to put on this badge, and wear Christ's livery: nor can baptism be of any use to any others; for such only are baptized into Him, and into His death, and partake of the saving benefits of it; for *whatsoever is not of faith, is sin* [*Rom. 14:23*]; and *without faith* also, *it is impossible to please God* [*Heb. 11:6*].

Verse 2. (**Though Jesus himself baptized not**, &c. And therefore as Nonnus observes, it was a false report that was made to the Pharisees; at least in part, so far as concerns the act of baptizing: though it may be this is observed, not so much to show the falsehood of that report, as to correct what is said of Christ's baptizing; lest it should be understood as if He baptized in His own person; whereas He did not, that not so well comporting with His greatness and majesty: wherefore *the King did not baptize in water*, as Nonnus expresses it, but left that for His disciples and servants to do; He had other and greater work to perform, as to preach the Gospel, and work miracles, heal diseases, cast out devils, &c. And besides, had another sort of baptism, of a more excellent nature, to administer, namely, the baptism of the Spirit [see *John 1:33; 1 Cor. 12:13*]; and since water baptism is administered in His name, as well as in the name of the Father and of the Spirit, it does not seem that it would have been administered with that propriety by Himself, in His own name; add to which, as is also observed by others, it might have occasioned contentions and disputes among the baptized, had some been baptized by Christ, and others by His disciples; the one valuing themselves on that account above the others. The Persic version indeed suggests, as if both Christ and His disciples baptized, rendering the words thus, *Jesus was not alone who baptized, but the disciples also baptized*: whereas the truth of the matter is, that Christ did not baptize in water at all:

but his disciples); they baptized in His name, and by His orders, such who were first made disciples by Him.

Verse 3. **He left Judaea,** &c. Where He had been for some time: at the feast of the passover He went up to Jerusalem, and after a short stay there, He came into the country part of Judea, where He tarried longer; and in both about the space of eight months; for it was now but four months to harvest, which began at the passover; see *chapter 2:13, 3:22* and *4:35.* And now, upon the Pharisees being made acquainted with His success in these parts, He leaves them; not through fear of them, but because He would not irritate and provoke them, and stir up their malice and envy against Him, which might put them upon measures to seek to take away His life; whereas His time was not yet come, and He had other work to do elsewhere:

and departed again into Galilee; where He had spent the greatest part of His time, in private life; from whence He came to Jordan unto John to be baptized by him; and after that went thither again, where He wrought His first miracle: and now having been in Judea some time, He removes to Galilee again; and of this journey of His thither, after the imprisonment of John, an account is given, in *Matt. 4:12-13.* The Persic version leaves out the word *again,* and so do the Alexandrian copy, and many copies; but is by others retained, and very justly.

Verse 4. **And he must needs go through Samaria**. Not through the city, but the country of Samaria; for the way to Galilee from Judea, lay through the midst of Samaria; nor was there any other way, without going a great way about; see *Luke 9:51-52* and *17:11*; and which is also confirmed by Josephus;[1] and this accounts for His going through Samaria, consistently with His forbidding His apostles going in the way of the Gentiles, or into any of the cities of the Samaritans; since here was a necessity for it, or otherwise He Himself would not have gone, where He forbid His disciples to go; though the prohibition may be understood, not of barely going into a Samaritan city; for it was lawful for them, notwithstanding that, to go into one of them, as appears from *verse 8* and *Luke 9:52*; but of going to preach there, *Matt. 10:5-7.* And besides this necessity, there was another thing that lay upon Him, and obliged Him to take this tour, and that is, the calling and conversion of a certain woman, and other Samaritans, whom the Father had given to Him, and He was to redeem by His blood; and the time of whose effectual vocation [or calling] was now come; and therefore He must needs go this way, and at this particular time. The Arabic and Persic versions represent it, as a purpose and determination in His mind to go this way.

---

[1] Antiqu. Jud. 1.20. c 5. & in vita sua, p. 1019.

Verse 5. **Then cometh he to a city of Samaria, which is called Sychar**, &c. Now called Neapolis,[2] the same with *Sichem*, or *Shechem*, as appears from its situation,

near to the parcel of ground that Jacob gave to his son Joseph; see *Gen. 33:18-19* and *48:22; Josh. 24:32*; and is either the same, only its termination is changed from *em* into *ar*, as *Achan* into *Achar*, *1 Chron. 2:7*. Or it is a new name that was given it, and by which it went in the time of Christ; and might be so called, either from סוכר, *Socher*, which signifies a grave; because here, Joseph and the rest of the patriarchs were buried, *Josh. 24:32; Acts 7:16*. Or rather, it was a name of reproach, and so called, from שכר, *drunken*; since the Ephraimites, the posterity of Joseph, which dwelt in these parts, were infamous for their sin of drunkenness; see *Isa. 28:1*. Hence *Sychar Sichem*, is *drunken Sichem*; or with respect to *Shekar*, a lie; as an idol is, and so may point at the idolatry of the Samaritans: and Reland[3] thinks some regard was had in this name to *Heb. 2:18*, where a molten image is called *morah shekar*, and *morah* is a name given to *Shechem*[4]: mention is made in the Talmud,[5] of a place called סיכרא, *Sichra*. The *parcel of ground*, or of a *field*, as in *Gen. 33:19* and *Josh. 24:32*, is in the Persic version, called *a vineyard*; and so Nonnus renders it, *a field planted with vines*; and which may serve to confirm the above conjecture, concerning *Sychar* being a nickname.

Verse 6. **Now Jacob's well was there**, &c. A well so called, either because it was dug by him; or because he and his family made use of it when in those parts, as in *verse 12*; though no mention is made of it elsewhere, unless any reference is had to it in the blessing of Joseph, to whom this place belonged, *Gen. 49:22*, as Dr. Lightfoot thinks, or in *Deut. 33:28*, as Grotius suggests. In the Talmud[6] there is mention made, of עין סוכר, *the fountain of Sochar*; and may not improperly be rendered, *the well of Sychar*: but whether the same with this, is not certain; that appears to be a great way from Jerusalem, as this also was, even forty miles:

---

[2]   Hieron. Epitaph. Paulae, tom. I. fol. 59. & R. Benjamin Itin. p. 38.

[3]   Dissert. De Monte Tarizzim, Sect. 9. p. 141.

[4]   T. Bab. Sotah, fol. 33.2.

[5]   T. Bava Metzia, fo. 42.1 & 83.1 & Cholin, fol. 94.2.

[6]   T. Hieros. Shekalim, fol. 48. 4. T. Bab. Bava Kama, fol. 82. 2. & Menachot, fol. 64. 2. & Gloss. in Sanhedrin, fol. 11. 2.

Jesus therefore being wearied with his journey; having traveled on foot from Judea thither; and He having a body like to ours, subject to weariness, and which proves the truth and reality of it, was greatly fatigued; having very probably traveled all that morning, if not a day, or days before:

sat thus on the well; or by it; by the side of it, upon the brink of it, as Nonnus paraphrases it, upon the bare ground. The Syriac, Arabic, and Persic versions, leave out *thus*; and the Ethiopic version reads it, *there*; but it is rightly retained, and is emphatical; and signifies, that He sat like a weary person, glad to set Himself down any where; and not caring how, or where, He sat to rest His weary limbs:

and it was about the sixth hour; about twelve o'clock at noon. The Ethiopic version adds by way of explanation, *and it was then noon*; and all the Oriental versions omit ωσει, *about*; rendering it, *it was the sixth hour*: and now Christ had been traveling all the morning, and it was a time of day to take some refreshment, which as yet He had not, the disciples being gone to buy food; and a time of day also, when the sun, if out, and has any strength, beats with its greatest vehemence; and all which considered, it is no wonder that He should be weary, faint, and thirsty.

Verse 7. **There cometh a woman of Samaria**, &c. A woman *out of Samaria*; not out of the city of Samaria, but out of the country of Samaria; out of Sychar, a city of Samaria: her coming was not by chance, but by the providence of God, and agreeable to His purpose, who orders all things according to the counsel of His will [*Eph. 1:11*]. And it is an amazing instance of grace, that a woman, a Samaritan woman, a lewd and infamous one, should be a chosen vessel of salvation, should be the object of divine favor, and be effectually called by the grace of God; when so many wise, learned, and religious men in Judea, were passed by! And not only so, but she was the happy means of conveying the knowledge of the Savior to many of her neighbors: she came, indeed,

to draw water; for her present temporal use and service; she little thought of meeting at Jacob's well with Christ, the fountain of gardens, and well of living water; she came for natural water, having no notion of water in a spiritual sense: or of carrying back with her the water of life, even a well of it, springing up to everlasting life.

Jesus saith unto her, give me to drink; that is, water to drink, out of the pot or pitcher she brought with her, for He was athirst; which is another proof of the truth of His human nature, and of His taking it with the sinless infirmities of it: though indeed this request was made to introduce a discourse with the woman, He having a more violent thirst, and a stronger desire, after the welfare of her immortal soul.

114

Verse 8. (**For his disciples were gone away**, &c. This action of theirs is related, not so much to give a reason why Christ asked the woman for water, because His disciples were not present to minister to Him; but rather to show, that Christ took the opportunity, in their absence, to converse with her; partly to avoid the scandal and offense they might take at His conversation with her, being a Samaritan; as it appears to have been astonishing to them, when they found Him talking with her, *verse 27.* And partly, that He might not put the woman to shame and blushing before them all; He chooses to tell her of the sins of her former life, in a private way. The disciples were gone,

unto the city: to the city Sychar, which was hard by; and their business there was,

to buy meat): for though it is said, in the following verse, that the Jews have no dealings with the Samaritans; yet this is not to be understood in the strictest sense; for they had dealings with them in some respects, as will be seen hereafter; particularly their food, eatables, and drinkables, were lawful to be bought of them, and used. It is said by R. Juda bar Pazi, in the name of R. Ame,[7]

"A roasted egg of the Cuthites (or Samaritans), lo, this is lawful: says R. Jacob bar Acha, in the name of R. Lazar, the boiled victuals of the Cuthites (Samaritans), lo, these are free; this he says concerning boiled food, because it is not their custom to put wine and vinegar into it;"

for these were forbidden: hence it is often said[8] that,

"The unleavened bread of the Cuthites (or Samaritans), is lawful, and that a man is allowed the use of it at the passover"

And there was a time when their wine was lawful; for one of their canons runs thus,[9]

"He that buys wine of the Cuthites (Samaritans), says, the Two logs that I shall separate, lo, they are first fruits, &c."

It is indeed said in one place, by R. Eliezer,[10]

"that he that eats the bread of the Cuthites (or Samaritans), is as if he eats swine's flesh; to whom (who reported this) says (R. Akiba), Be silent, I will not tell you what R. Eliezer thinks concerning it."

---

[7] T. Hieros. Avoda Zara, fol. 44. 4.

[8] T. Bab. Gittin, fol. 10. 1. & Cholin, fol. 4. 1. & Kiddushin, fol. 76. 1.

[9] Mishna Demai, c. 7. sect. 4. Vid. Bartenora in ibid.

[10] Mishna Sheviith, c. 8. sect. 10. Pirke Eliezer, c. 38.

Upon which the commentators observe,[11] that this is not to be understood strictly; because he that eats bread of the Samaritans, does not deserve stripes according to the law, but according to the constitutions of the wise men; but these, Christ and His disciples had no regard to.

Verse 9. **Then saith the woman of Samaria unto him**, &c. She said, in a scoffing, jeering way,

how is it, that thou being a Jew; which she might know, by His language and His dress:

askest drink of me, which am a woman of Samaria? Not that the waters of Samaria were unlawful for a Jew to drink of; for as,

"the land of the Cuthites (or Samaritans), was pure, or clean, so, מקותיה, *their collections of water*, and their habitations, and their ways were clean,"[12]

and might be used; but because the Jews used no familiarity with the Samaritans, nor would they receive any courtesy or kindness from them, as follows:

for the Jews have no dealings with the Samaritans. Some take these to be the words of the evangelist, commenting upon, and explaining the words of the woman; but they seem rather to be her own words, giving a reason why she returned such an answer; and which must be understood, not in the strictest sense, as if they had no dealings at all with them: indeed in some things they had no dealings with them, and at some certain times; hence that discourse of the Samaritans with a Jewish Rabbi:[13]

"The Cuthites (or Samaritans) inquired of R. Abhu, Your fathers, היו מסתפקין, *used to deal with us* (or minister to us, or supply us with necessaries), wherefore do not ye deal with us? (or take a supply from us?); He replied unto them, Your fathers did not corrupt their works, you have corrupted your works."

They might not use their wine and vinegar, nor admit them to their tables. They say of a man,[14]

"Because the Cuthites (or Samaritans) ate at his table, it was the

---

[11] Maimonides & Bartenora in Mishna ibid.

[12] T. Hieros. Avoda Zara, fol. 44. 4.

[13] Ibid.

[14] T. Bab. Sanhedrin, fol. 104. 1.

reason why his children went into captivity—and further add, That whoever invites a Cuthite (or Samaritan) into his house, and ministers to him, is the cause of captivity to his children."

And they forbid a man to enter into partnership with a Cuthite (or Samaritan[15]): and particularly,

"three days before the feasts of idolaters (for such they reckoned the Samaritans, as well as others), it is forbidden to have any commerce with them, to borrow of them, or lend to them, &c."[16]

But then at other times, and in other respects, they had dealings with them; they might go into their cities and buy food of them, as the disciples did, *verse 8*; they might send their wheat to a Samaritan miller, to be ground;[17] and as it appears from the above citations, their houses and habitations were clean, and might be lodged in, with which compare *Luke 9:52*; the poor of the Samaritans were maintained with the poor of Israel;[18] wherefore the sense is, as Dr. Lightfoot observes, that the Jews refused to receive the least favor or kindness at the hand of a Samaritan; and therefore the woman might justly wonder, that Christ should ask so small a favor of her, as a little water. The reason of this distance and aversion, was religion; and so the Ethiopic version, rather paraphrasing than translating, renders the words, *the Jews do not agree in religion, nor do they communicate with the Samaritans, nor mix together*: and this was of long standing, and had been occasioned and increased by various incidents. For when the ten tribes revolted in Jeroboam's time, the calves were set up in Dan and Bethel, in order to draw off the people from worship at Jerusalem, which gave great umbrage to the tribes of Judah and Benjamin; and when the ten tribes were carried away captive by the king of Assyria, he planted the cities of Samaria with colonies in their room, consisting of heathenish and idolatrous persons, brought from Babylon, and other places; to whom he sent a priest, to instruct them in the manner of the God of the land; but with these instructions, they still retained their idols, and their idolatrous practices; see *2 Kings 17:24-41*; which must render them odious to the Jews: and these were the principal adversaries of the Jews, after their return from captivity; and discouraged them, and weakened their hands, in the building of the second temple. But what latest, and most of all had fixed this aversion and enmity, was this: Manasseh, brother to Jaddua the

---

[15] T. Bab. Becorot, fol. 7. 2. Piske Toseph. ibid. art. 4. & in Megilla, art. 102.

[16] Mishna Avoda Zara, c. 1. sect. 1.

[17] Mishna Demai, c. 3. sect. 4.

[18] Piske Tosephot Yoma, art. 63.

high priest, having married Sanballat's daughter, governor of Samaria, was for it removed from the priesthood; who applying to his father-in-law, he proposed building for him a temple on Mount Gerizim, and making him a high priest; for which he obtained leave of Alexander the Great, and accordingly built one, and made his son-in-law high priest; which drew a great many profligate Jews over to him, who mixing with the Samaritans, set up a worship, religion, and priesthood, in distinction from the Jews; and this was ever after, a matter of contention and quarrel between these people, and the reason why they would have no dealings with them.

Verse 10. **Jesus answered and said unto her**, &c. In a very serious manner, in a different way from hers:

if thou knewest the gift of God; meaning, not the Holy Spirit with His gifts and graces, as some think, but Himself; for the following clause is explanatory of it;

and who it is that saith to thee, give me to drink; and Christ is also spoken of in the Old Testament, as *the gift of God, Isa. 9:6;* and He had lately spoken of Himself as such, *John 3:16*; and He is, by way of eminency, *the gift of God*; which is comprehensive of all others, is exceeding large, and very suitable to the wants and cases of men; and is irrevocable, unchangeable, and unspeakable: for He is God's gift, as He is His own and only begotten Son; and He is given for a covenant to the people, with all the promises and blessings of it; and as a head, both of eminence and influence; and to be a Savior of them, and a sacrifice for their sins; and as *the Bread of life*, for them to feed and live upon; of which gift, men are naturally ignorant, as this woman was: they know not the dignity of His person; nor the nature and usefulness of His offices; nor the way of peace, righteousness, and salvation by Him; nor do they see any amiableness, or loveliness in Him; and whatever notional knowledge some natural men may have of Him, they know Him not spiritually and experimentally, or as the gift of God to them:

thou wouldst have asked of him; a favor and benefit; for such who truly know Christ, the worth and value of Him, and their need of Him, will apply to Him for grace, as they have encouragement to do; since all grace is treasured up in Him, and He gives it freely, and upbraideth not; and souls are invited to ask it of Him, and take it freely; nor is it to be had anywhere else: but knowledge of Christ, is absolutely necessary to asking any thing of Him; for till He is known, He will not be applied to; but when He is made known to any, in His fulness and suitableness, they will have recourse to Him, and ask grace and mercy of Him; and which is freely had: the Vulgate Latin very wrongly adds, *perhaps;* reading it, *perhaps thou wouldst have asked*; whereas our Lord's meaning is, that she would certainly have asked:

and he would have given thee living water; pardoning and justifying grace, every branch of sanctifying grace, and all the supplies of it; so called, because His grace quickens sinners dead in sin, and dead in law, and in their own apprehensions; and causes them to live in themselves, and before God; and because it refreshes and comforts, revives and cheers, and is like rivers of water in a dry land; and because it maintains and supports spiritual life in their souls; and it ever abides, and continues, and springs up unto everlasting life: for the allusion is to spring water, that bubbles up in a fountain, and is ever running; for such water the Jews call *living water*; see *Gen. 26:19*; where in the Hebrew text it is *living water*; which we, and also the Chaldee paraphrase, render *springing water*. So living waters with them, are said to be always flowing, and never cease.[19]

Verse 11. **The woman saith unto him, Sir**, &c. Which was a usual way in those countries of addressing men, and especially strangers; and expresses no uncommon respect to Christ, of whose dignity and greatness she was entirely ignorant, and at whom she was now scoffing; for so the following words are to be understood:

thou hast nothing to draw with; no pail, or bucket, or rope to let it down with, as Nonnus adds; for it seems, there was no bucket, or vessel, fastened at the well for common use, but everyone brought one with them, when they came to draw: though it is strange there was not one; since, according to common usage, and even of the Jews,[20]

"a public well had, קול, *a bucket*, or pitcher; but a private well had no bucket:"

and the well is deep; that which is now called Jacob's well, is by some said to be forty cubits deep, and by others thirty-five yards:

from whence then hast thou that living water? This she said in a sneering, scoffing manner: she reasoned with Him, either that He must have it out of this well; but that could not be, since He had no vessel to draw with, and the well was so deep, that He could not come at the water without one; or He must have it from some neighboring spring; upon which she scoffs at Him in the following manner.

Verse 12. **Art thou greater than our father Jacob**, &c. Art thou a person of greater worth and character than he, who was content to drink of this

---

[19] Bartenora in Mishna Negaim, c. 14. sect. 1.

[20] T. Hieros. Erubin, fol. 20. 2.

water; or wiser and more knowing than he, who could find out no better fountain of water in all these parts? She calls Jacob the father of them, according to the common notion and boasting of those people, when it served their turn; otherwise they were not the descendants of Jacob; for after the ten tribes were carried away captive by the king of Assyria, he placed in their room, in the cities of Samaria, men from Babylon, Cuthah, Ava, Hamath, and Sepharvaim; heathenish and idolatrous people: see *2 Kings 17:24*. And from these, the then Samaritans sprung; only upon Sanballat's building a temple on Mount Gerizim, for Manasseh his son-in-law, when put away from the priesthood by the Jews for his marriage of his daughter, several wicked persons of the like sort came out of Judea, and joined themselves to the Samaritans: and such a mixed medley of people were they at this time, though they boasted of Jacob as their father, as this woman did; and so to this day, they draw their genealogy from Abraham, Isaac, and Jacob; and particularly call Joseph their father, and say, From whence are we, but from the tribe of Joseph the just, from Ephraim?[21] as they formerly did:[22]

"R. Meir saw a Samaritan, he said to him, From whence comest thou? (that is, from what family); he answered, From the (tribe) of Joseph;"

which gave us the well; Jacob gave it indeed to Joseph and his posterity, along with the parcel of ground in which it was; see *verse 5*; but not to this mixed company:

and drank thereof himself, and his children, and his cattle? Which shows both the goodness and plenty of the water: though our Lord had spoken of *living water*, this woman understood Him of no other water, but *spring water*; called living water, from its motion, because it is continually springing up, bubbling, and ever running. So carnal persons, when they hear of spiritual things under earthly metaphors, think of nothing but carnal things; as Nicodemus, when Christ talked of being born again; and the Jews at Capernaum, when He discoursed concerning eating His flesh, and drinking His blood; for spiritual things are neither known nor received by the natural man.

Verse 13. **Jesus answered and said unto her**, &c. In a mild and gentle manner, patiently bearing all her scoffs and flouts, and continuing to instruct and inform her concerning this living water, showing the preferableness of it to all others:

---

[21] Epist. Samar. ad Scaliger. in Antiqu. Eccl. Oriental. p. 123, 124, 126.

[22] Bereshit Rabba, sect. 94. fol. 82. 1.

whosoever drinketh of this water; meaning in that well called Jacob's well, or any other common water:

shall thirst again; as this woman had often done, and would again, as she herself knew, *verse 15*, and as Jesus did, who very likely afterwards drank of it, *chapter 19:28*. For though water allays heat, quenches thirst, and refreshes and revives the spirits for a while, yet, in process of time, natural heat increases, and thirst returns, and there is a necessity of drinking water again.

Verse 14. **But whosoever drinketh of the water that I shall give him**, &c. Meaning, the Spirit and His grace; see *chapter 7:38-39*; and which He more than once speaks of, as His gift here, and in the context: of which, whoever truly partakes,

shall never thirst; either after sinful lusts and pleasures, and his former vicious way of living, which he now disrelishes: not but there are desires and lustings after carnal things in regenerate persons, as there were lustings in the Israelites after the onions, garlic, and flesh pots in Egypt, when they were come out from thence; yet these are not so strong, prevalent, and predominant; they are checked and restrained by the grace of God; so that they do not hanker after sin as they did, nor *drink up iniquity like water [Job 15:16]*, or commit sin with greediness, as before: or else it means thirsting after the grace of God; thirsty persons are invited to *take* and drink of *the water of life freely* [Rev. 22:17], and are pronounced blessed; and it is promised, that they shall be filled, or satisfied; yet not so in this life, that they shall never thirst after or desire more; for as they need more grace, and it is promised them, they thirst after it, and desire it; and the more they taste and partake of it, the more they desire it: but the sense is, either as some read the words, *they shall not thirst for ever*; though they may for a time, and be in a distressed condition for want of a supply of it, yet they shall not always; God will open rivers and fountains for them, and give drink to His people, His chosen; and in the other state, they shall hunger and thirst no more; for the Lamb shall lead them to fountains of living waters: or rather, they shall never thirst, so as to be like the thirsty and parched earth, dried up, and have no moisture in them; for however this may seem sometimes to be their case, God will, and does, pour out water and floods upon them; yea, that grace which is infused into their souls, is an abundant and an abiding principle, which will preserve them from languishing, so as to perish:

but the water that I shall give him, shall be in him a well of water; which denotes the plenty of it; for the grace of God, given at conversion, is exceeding abundant, it superabounds all the aboundings of sin; it comes in large flows into the hearts of regenerate persons, and flows out of them, as rivers of living water: and which also abides, for it continues,

springing up into everlasting life. It is a seed which remains, an immortal and never dying principle; it is inseparably connected with eternal life; it is the beginning of it, and it issues in it; whoever has grace, shall have glory; and whoever are called, sanctified, justified, and pardoned, shall be glorified [see *Rom. 8:28-30*]: such is the nature, influence, and use of this living water, in Christ's gift: the words of the law are, in the Targum on *Song of Sol. 4:15*, compared to a well of living water.

Verse 15. **The woman saith unto him, Sir**, &c. See the note on *verse 11*:

give me this water, that I thirst not: the Syriac and Persic versions add, *again:*

neither come hither: the Ethiopic version adds here, *again:*

to draw. This she said also, in the same sneering and scoffing way, as her talking of not thirsting and coming thither to draw water, shows; and it is as if she had said, "Pray give me some of this fine water you talk of, that I may never thirst again; and so have no occasion to be at all this fatigue and trouble, to come daily to this well for water": though some think, that she now spoke seriously, having some little knowledge of what our Lord meant by *living water*, but with a mixture of much ignorance, and that she heartily desired it; but the reason she gives, shows the contrary.

Verse 16. **Jesus saith unto her**, &c. Observing that she continued an ignorant scoffer at Him, and His words, determined to take another method with her; and convince her, that He was not a common and ordinary person she was conversing with, as she took Him to be; and that also He knew what a sinner she was, and what a vicious course of life she had lived; so that she might see that she stood in need of Him, as the gift of God, and Savior of men; and of the grace He had been speaking of, under the notion of living water: saying to her,

go, call thy husband, and come hither; go directly from hence to the city of Sychar, and call thy husband, and come back hither along with him again. This Christ said, not to have him come to teach and instruct him, and as if he would more readily and easily understand Him, and that he might be, with her, a partaker of the same grace; but to bring on some further conversation, by which she would understand that He knew her state and condition, and what a course of life she now lived, and so bring her under a conviction of her sin and danger, and need of Him and His grace.

Verse 17. **The woman answered and said, I have no husband**, &c. Which was a truth she would not have spoken at another time and place, or to any of her neighbors; but Christ being a stranger, and no odium incurring upon her by it; and this serving a purpose to excuse her going to call him, she declares the truth of the matter:

Jesus said unto her, thou hast well said, I have no husband; this is the truth, it is really fact, and is the true state of the case, between thee and him who goes for thy husband.

Verse 18. **For thou hast had five husbands**, &c. She either had had five husbands lawfully, and had buried one after another; and which was no crime, and might be: the Sadducees proposed a case to Christ, in which a woman is said to have had seven husbands successively, in a lawful manner, *Matt. 22:25-28*; or rather, she had had so many, and had been divorced from every one of them for adultery; for no other cause, it should seem, did the Samaritans divorce; seeing that they only received the law of Moses, and rejected, at least many of, the traditions of the elders; and since they are particularly said,[23]
"not to be expert in the law of marriages and divorces."
And the rather this may seem to be the case, as Dr. Lightfoot observes; since these husbands are mentioned, as well as he with whom she lived in an adulterous manner; and which suggests, that she had not lived honestly with them:

and he whom thou now hast is not thy husband; that is, *not thy lawful husband*, as the Persic version reads, and Nonnus paraphrases; being not married to him at all, though they cohabited as man and wife, when there was no such relation between them:

in that saidst thou truly; or that which is truth: thus Christ the omniscient God, who knew her full well, and the whole of her past infamous conversation [*or* conduct], and her present lewd and wicked way of living, exposes all unto her.

Verse 19. **The woman saith unto him, Sir**, &c. With another countenance, and a different air and gesture, with another accent and tone of speech, dropping her scoffs and jeers:

I perceive that thou art a prophet; such a one as Samuel was, who could tell Saul what was in his heart, and that his father's asses were found, and

---

[23]   T. Bab. Kiddushin, fol 76. 1.

where they were, *1 Sam. 9:19-20*; and as Elisha, whose heart went with his servant Gehazi, when Naaman turned to him to meet him, and give him presents; and who could tell, ere the king's messenger came to him, that the son of a murderer had sent to take away his head, *2 Kings 5:26* and *6:32*. And such a prophet, that had such a spirit of discerning, this woman took Christ to be; and who indeed is greater than a prophet, and is the omniscient God; who knows all men's hearts, thoughts, words, and actions, and needs not that any should testify of them to Him; for He knows what is in them, and done by them [see *chapter 2:25*]; and can tell them all that ever they did, as He did this woman, *verse 29*. Now in order either to shift off the discourse from this subject, which touched her to the quick; or else being truly sensible of her sin, and willing to reform, and for the future to worship God in the place and manner He had directed, she addressed Christ in the following words.

Verse 20. **Our fathers worshiped in this mountain**, &c. In Mount Gerizim, which was just by, and within sight; so that the woman could point to it; it was so near to Shechem, or Sychar, that Jotham's voice was heard from the top of it thither, *Judges 9:6-7*. By the *fathers*, this woman claims as theirs, are meant, not the immediate ancestors of the Samaritans, or those only of some few generations past; but the patriarchs Abraham, Isaac, and Jacob, whose descendants they would be thought to be; and they improved every instance of their worshiping in these parts, in favor of this mountain, being a sacred place. And Abraham did indeed build an altar to the Lord, in the plain of Moreh, *Gen. 12:6-7*; and which the Jews themselves own,[24] is the same with Sichem; but their tradition, which Theophylact reports, that Isaac was offered upon the Mount of Gerizim, is entirely false. Jacob, it is true, came to Shalem, a city of Shechem; and upon this very spot of ground, the parcel of a field he bought of the children of Hammor, and gave to his son Joseph, he built an altar, and called it *El-elohe-Israel*, *Gen. 33:18-20*. And also upon this very mountain, the tribe of Joseph, with others, stood, when they were come over Jordan, and blessed the people; all which circumstances, the Samaritans failed not to make use of in vindication of themselves, and their worship in this mountain; and which this woman might be acquainted with, and might refer unto: but as for any temple, or place of worship on this mount, there was none till of late years, even after the second temple was built. The occasion of it, as Josephus relates,[25] was this: Manasseh, brother to Jaddua the high

---

[24] Mishna Sota, c. 7. sect. 5. T. Bab. Sota, fol. 33. 2.

[25] Antiqu. l. 12. c. 1. Vid. Juchasin, fol. 14. 2.

priest, having married Nicasso, daughter of Sanballat, governor of Samaria, was on that account driven from the priesthood; he fled to his father-in-law, and related the case to him, expressing great love to his daughter, and yet a regard to his office; upon which Sanballat proposed to build him a temple on Mount Gerizim, for which he did not doubt of obtaining leave of Darius the Persian monarch, and to make him a high priest. Darius being overcome by Alexander the Great, Sanballat made his court to him, and petitioned him for the building of this temple, who granted him his request; and accordingly he built one, and Manasseh became the high priest; and many of the profligate Jews, that had married strange wives, or violated the sabbath, or had eaten forbidden meat, came over and joined him. This temple, we are told,[26] was built about forty years after the second temple at Jerusalem; and stood two hundred years, and then was destroyed by Jochanan, the son of Simeon, the son of Mattathiah, who was called Hyrcanus, and so says Josephus.[27] It might now be rebuilt: however, this did not put a stop to worship in this place, about which there were great contentions, between the Jews and the Samaritans; of which we have some instances, in the writings of the former. It is said[28] that,

"R. Jonathan went to pray in Jerusalem, and passed by that mountain (the gloss says, Mount Gerizim), and a certain Samaritan saw him, and said to him, Whither art thou going? He replied, that he was going to pray at Jerusalem; he said to him, Is it not better for thee to pray in this blessed mountain, and not in that dunghill house? He replied, why is it blessed? He answered, Because it was not overflowed by the waters of the flood. The thing was hid from the eyes of R. Jonathan, and he could not return an answer."

This story is told elsewhere,[29] with a little variation, and more plainly as to the place, thus:

"It happened to R. Jonathan, that he went to Neapolis of the Cuthites, or Samaritans (that is, to Sichem, for Sichem is now called Naplous), and he was riding upon an ass, and a herdsman with him; a certain Samaritan joined himself to them: when they came to Mount Gerizim, the Samaritan said to R. Jonathan, How came it to pass that we are come to this holy mountain? R. Jonathan replied, Whence comes it to

---

[26] Juchasin, fol. 14. 2. & 15. 1.

[27] Antiqu. l. 13. c. 17

[28] Bereshit Rabba, sect. 32. fol. 27. 4. & Shirhashirim Rabba, fol. 16. 3.

[29] Debarim Rabba, sect. 3. fol. 238. 2.

be holy? The Samaritan answered him, Because it was not hurt by the waters of the flood."

Much the same story is told of R. Ishmael bar R. Jose.[30] It is to be observed in this account, that the Samaritans call this mountain the *holy* mountain, they imagined there was something sacred in it; and the *blessed* mountain, or the mountain of blessing; no doubt, because the blessings were pronounced upon it; though a very poor reason is given by them in the above passages. And they not only urged the above instances of the worship or the patriarchs at, or about this place, which this woman refers to; but even falsified a passage in the Pentateuch, as is generally thought, in favor of this mount; for in *Deut. 27:4*, instead of Mount Ebal, in the Samaritan Pentateuch Mount Gerizim is inserted. So stood the case on one side of the question; on the other hand, the Jews pleaded for the temple at Jerusalem:

and ye say, that in Jerusalem is the place where men ought to worship; that is, in the temple there; who urged, and very rightly, that God had chosen that place to put His name, and fix His worship there; and had ordered them to come thither and bring their offerings and sacrifices, and to keep their passover and other feasts; see *Deut. 12:5-6* and *16:2; 2 Chron. 9:12.* This was built by Solomon, according to the command and direction of God, some hundreds of years before Mount Gerizim was made use of for religious worship; and they had not only these things to plead, but also the worship which was here given to God in this place before the temple was built upon it, which they failed not to do. So the Targumist on *2 Chron. 3:1* enlarges on this head:

"And Solomon began to build the sanctuary of the Lord in Jerusalem, on Mount Moriah, in the place where Abraham worshiped and prayed in the name of the Lord: הוא אתר ארע פולחנא, *this place is the land of worship*; for there all generations worshiped before the Lord; and there Abraham offered up his son Isaac for a burnt offering, and the Word of the Lord delivered him, and a ram was appointed in his stead; there Jacob prayed when he fled from Esau his brother; there the angel of the Lord appeared to David, when he disposed the sacrifice in the place he bought of Ornan, in the floor of Ornan the Jebusite."

And since, now there were so many things to be said on each side of the question, this woman desires, that seeing Christ was a prophet, He would be pleased to give her His sense of the matter, and inform her which was the right place of worship.

---

[30] Bereshit Rabba, sect. 81. fol. 71. 1.

Verse 21. **Jesus saith unto her, woman, believe me**, &c. Believe me in what I am now going to say, since you own me to be a prophet:

the hour cometh; the time is at hand; it is very near; it is just coming:

when ye shall neither in this mountain, nor yet at Jerusalem, worship the Father. That is, God, whom the Jews, and so the Samaritans, knew under the character of the Father of all men, as the Creator and preserver of them; for not God as the Father of Christ, or of the saints by adopting grace, is here intended, which this ignorant woman at least had no knowledge of. And the reason of our Lord's speaking after this manner, signifying, that she need not trouble herself about the place of worship, was, partly, because in a little time Jerusalem, and the temple in it, would be destroyed, and *not one stone left upon another* [*Matt. 24:2*]; and that Samaria, and this mountain of Gerizim, with whatsoever edifice might be upon it, would be laid desolate, so that neither of them would continue long to be places of religious worship; and partly, because all distinction of places in religion would entirely cease; and one place would be as lawful, and as proper to worship in, as another; and men should lift up holy hands, and pray, and offer up spiritual sacrifices in every place, even *from the rising of the sun, to the going down of the same, Mal. 1:11.*

Verse 22. **Ye worship ye know not what**, &c. However, as to her question, He more directly replies by condemning the Samaritans, and their ignorance in worship, and by approving the Jews; and so manifestly gives the preference to the Jews, not only with respect to the place, and object of worship, but with respect to knowledge and salvation. As for the Samaritans, He suggests, that they were ignorant, not only of the true object of worship, but knew not what they themselves worshiped; or, at least, were not agreed in it. The original inhabitants of those parts, from whence these Samaritans sprung, were idolatrous heathens, placed by the king of Assyria in the room of the ten tribes he carried away captive; and these feared not the Lord, for they *knew not the manner of the God of the land* [*2 Kings 17:26*]: wherefore lions were sent among them, which slew many of them; upon which the king of Assyria ordered a priest to be sent to instruct them: but notwithstanding this, they had every one gods of their own, some one, and some another; and so served divers graven images, they and their children, and their children's children, to the time of the writer of the Book of Kings; see *2 Kings 17:24-41.* And though after Manasseh, and other Jews were come among them, and they had received the law of Moses, they might have some knowledge of the true God, yet they glorified Him not as God; and though they might in words profess Him, yet in works they denied Him; and even after this they are very highly charged by the Jews with idolatrous practices on this mount. Sometimes they

127

say[31] the Cuthites, or Samaritans, worshiped fire; and at other times, and which chiefly prevails with them, they assert,[32] that their wise men, upon searching, found that they worshiped the image of a dove on Mount Gerizim; and sometimes they say,[33] they worshiped the idols, the strange gods, or *Teraphim*, which Jacob hid under the oak in Sichem; which last, if true, may serve to illustrate these words of Christ, that they worshiped *they knew not what*, since they worshiped idols hid in the mount.

"R. Ishmael bar Jose, they say,[34] went to Neapolis (Sichem, called Naplous), the Cuthites, or Samaritans came to him (to persuade him to worship with them in their mountain); he said unto them, I will show you that ye do not *worship at this mountain*, but *the images which are hid under it*; for it is written, *Gen. 35:4, and Jacob hid them under the oak which was by Shechem.*"

And elsewhere[35] it is reported of the same Rabbi, that he went to Jerusalem to pray, as before related on *verse 20*, and after what passed between him, and the Samaritan he met with at Mount Gerizim, before mentioned, he added:

"and said to him, I will tell you what ye are like, (ye are like) to a dog that lusts after carrion; so because ye know the idols are hid under it (the mountain), as it is written, *Gen. 35:4, and Jacob hid them*, therefore ye lust after it. They said, This man knows that idols are hid here, and perhaps he will take them away; and they consulted together to kill him. He arose, and made his escape in the night."

But this was not the case of the Jews:

we know what we worship; Christ puts Himself among them, for He was a Jew, as the woman took Him to be; and, as man, was a worshiper of God: He feared, loved, and obeyed God; He trusted in Him, and prayed unto Him; though, as God, He was the object of worship Himself: and the true worshipers among the Jews, of which sort Christ was, knew God, whom they worshiped, spiritually and savingly; and the generality of that people had right notions of the God of Israel, having the oracles, and service of God, and being instructed out of Moses and the prophets:

---

[31] T. Bab. Taanith, fol. 5. 2

[32] Maimon. in Mishna Beracot, c. 8. sect. 8. & Bartenora in ibid. c. 7. sect. 1. & in Nidda, c. 4. sect. 1.

[33] Shalshelet Hakkabala, fol. 15. 2.

[34] T. Hieros. Avoda Zara, fol. 44. 4.

[35] Bereshit Rabba, sect. 81. fol. 71. 1.

for salvation is of the Jews. The promises of salvation, and of a Savior, were made to them, when the Gentiles were strangers to them; the means of salvation, and of the knowledge of it, as the Word, statutes, and ordinances, were enjoyed by them, when others were ignorant of them; and the Messiah, who is sometimes styled *Salvation*, see *Gen. 49:18; Psa. 14:7; Luke 2:30*, was not only prophesied of in their books, and promised unto them, but came of them, as well as to them; and the number of the saved ones had been for many hundreds of years, and still was among them; the line of election ran among them, and few among the Gentiles were called and saved, as yet.

Verse 23. **But the hour cometh, and now is, when the true worshipers**, &c. The true worshipers of the true God, and who worship in a right manner, whether Jews or Samaritans, or of whatsoever nation:

shall worship the Father; the one true God, the Father of spirits, and of all flesh living:

in spirit; in opposition to all carnal conceptions of Him, as if He was a corporeal being, or circumscribed in some certain place, dwelling in temples made with hands, or was to be worshiped with men's hands; and in distinction from the carnal worship of the Jews, which lay greatly in the observation of carnal ordinances: and this shows, they should not worship with their bodies only, for *bodily exercise profiteth little [1 Tim. 4:8]*; but with their souls or spirits, with their whole hearts engaged therein; and by, and under the influence and assistance of the Spirit of God, without whom men cannot perform worship, neither prayer, praise, preaching, or hearing, aright:

and in truth; in opposition to hypocrisy, with true hearts, in the singleness, sincerity, and integrity of their souls; and in distinction from Jewish ceremonies, which were only shadows, and had not the truth and substance of things in them; and according to the Word of truth, the Gospel of salvation; and in Christ, who is the truth, the true tabernacle, in, and through whom access is had to God, prayer is made to Him, and every part of religious worship with acceptance: so Enoch is said, פלח בקושטא, *to worship in truth*, before the Lord, in the Targums of Jonathan and Jerusalem, in *Gen. 5:24*. And it may be that the worship of all the three persons in the Godhead, as more distinctly performed under the Gospel dispensation, is here intended: for the words may be thus read, *shall worship the Father, with the Spirit, and with the truth*; so the preposition εν is rendered in *Eph. 6:2*, and elsewhere; and then the sense is, they shall *worship the Father*; the first person in the Trinity, who is the Father of Christ, His only begotten Son, and together and equally with Him *the Spirit*; the holy Spirit, as the Ethiopic version reads; and Nonnus calls it the divine Spirit: and the rather He may be thought to be intended, since it follows in *verse 24*, *the Spirit is God*; for so the words lie in the Greek text; and are so rendered in the Vulgate Latin, Syriac, and Ethiopic versions; and therefore is the proper object of religious worship; whose temples the saints are, with whom they have communion, to whom they pray, and in whose name they are baptized: and also together *with the truth*; with Christ *the way, the truth, and the life* [*chapter 14:6*]; who is *the true God, and eternal life* [*1 John 5:20*]; and who is equally to be worshiped as the Father and Spirit, as He is by the angels in heaven, and by the saints on earth; who pray unto Him, trust in Him, and are also baptized in His name, as in the name of the other two persons: and the rather this may be thought to be the sense, since Christ is speaking, not of the manner, but of the object of worship, in the preceding verse:

for the Father seeketh such to worship him; it being agreeable to Him to be worshiped in the manner as above related; and His desire is, that the Son and Spirit should be honored equally as Himself; and such worshipers He has found, having made them such, both among the Jews and Gentiles; and such only are acceptable to Him; see *Phil. 3:3*.

Verse 24. **God *is* a Spirit**, &c. Or *the Spirit is God*; a divine person, possessed of all divine perfections, as appears from His names, works, and worship, ascribed unto Him; see the note on the preceding verse; though the Arabic and Persic versions, and others, read as we do, *God is a Spirit*; that is, God—Father, Son, and Holy Ghost: for taking the words in this light, not one of the persons is to be understood exclusive of the other; for this description, or definition, agrees with each of them, and they are all the object of worship, and to be worshiped in a true and spiritual manner. *God is a Spirit*, and not a body or a corporeal substance: the nature and essence of God is like a spirit, simple and uncompounded, not made up of parts; nor is it divisible; nor does it admit of any change and alteration. God, as a spirit, is immaterial, immortal, invisible, and an intelligent, willing, and active being; but differs from other spirits, in that He is an uncreated one, an immense and infinite Spirit, and an eternal one, which has neither beginning nor end. He is therefore *a Spirit* by way of eminency, as well as effectively, He being the author and former of all spirits: whatever excellence is in them, must be ascribed to God in the highest manner; and whatever is imperfect in them, must be removed from Him:

and they that worship him; worship is due to Him on account of His nature and perfections, both internal and external; with both the bodies and souls of men; and both private and public; in the closet, in the family, and in the church of God; as prayer, praise, attendance on the Word and ordinances:

must worship *him* in spirit and in truth; in the true and spiritual manner before described, which is suitable to His nature, and agreeable to His will.

Verse 25. **The woman saith unto him**, &c. The woman not knowing well what to say to these things Christ had been discoursing about, as the place, object, and manner of worship; and being undetermined in her judgment of them, by what He had said, was willing to refer them to the Messiah's coming; of which she and the Samaritans had some knowledge.

I know that Messias cometh, which is called Christ: the last clause, *which is called Christ*, are not the words of the woman explaining the Hebrew word *Messiah*; for as, on the one hand, she did not understand Greek, so, on the other, she could not think that the person she was conversing with, who she knew was a Jew, needed that word to be explained to Him; but they are the words of the evangelist, interpreting the Hebrew word *Messiah*, by the Greek word *Christ*, in which language he wrote: hence this clause is left out in the Syriac version, as unnecessary to a Syriac reader, not needing the word to be explained to Him. The Arabic and Ethiopic versions, and some copies, read in the plural number, *we know that Messias cometh*; the knowledge of the coming of the Messiah was not peculiar to this woman, but was common to all the Samaritans; for as they received the five books of Moses, they might learn from thence, that a divine and excellent person was to come, who is called the seed of the woman, that should bruise the serpent's head [*Gen. 3:15*]; *Shiloh*, to whom the gathering of the people should be [*Gen. 49:10*]; and a prophet like unto Moses [*Deut. 18:15-19* with *34:10*]: and though the word *Messiah* is not found in those books, yet, as it was usual with the Jews to call the same person by this name, they might easily take it from them, and make use of it; and they not only knew that there was a Messiah to come, and expected Him, but that He was coming, just ready to come; and this they might conclude, not only from the general expectation of the Jewish nation about this time, but from *Gen. 49:10*. And it is certain, that the Samaritans to this day do expect a Messiah, though they know not His name, unless it be הַשָּׁהֵב; the meaning of which they do not understand:[36] to me it seems to be an abbreviation of הַשָּׁהְבָא, or הוּא אֲשֶׁר הַבָּא, *he that is to come*; by which circumlocution the Jews understand the Messiah; see *Matt. 11:3*; and to which this Samaritan woman seems to have some respect:

when he is come he will tell us all things. The whole mind and will of God; all things relating to the worship of God, and to the salvation of men. This the Samaritans might conclude from His general character, as *a prophet like unto Moses*, to whom men were to hearken, *Deut. 18:15*; and from a common prevailing notion among the Jews, that the times of the Messiah would be times of great knowledge, founded on several prophecies, as *Isa. 2:3*

---

[36] 1 Epist. Samar. ad Scaliger, in Antiq. Eccl. Oriental, p. 125.

and *11:2, 9; Jer. 31:34*; and which they sometimes express in the following manner:[37]

> "In the days of the Messiah, even the little children in the world shall find out the hidden things of wisdom, and know in it the ends and computations (of times), and at that time he shall be made manifest unto all."

And again,[38]

> "Says R. Judah, The holy, blessed God will reveal the deep mysteries of the law in the times of the King Messiah; for *the earth shall be filled with the knowledge of the Lord*, &c. And it is written, *they shall not teach every man his brother*, &c."

And elsewhere,[39]

> "The whole world shall be filled with the words of the Messiah, and with the words of the law, and with the words of the commandments; and these things shall extend to the isles afar off; to many people, the uncircumcised in heart, and the uncircumcised in flesh; and they shall deal in the secrets of the law.—And there shall be no business in the world, but to know the Lord only; wherefore the Israelites shall be exceeding wise, and know secret things, and comprehend the knowledge of their Creator, as much as is possible for a man to do, as it is said, *the earth shall be filled with the knowledge of the Lord*, &c."

Accordingly, the Messiah is come, who lay in the bosom of the Father, and has made known all things to His disciples, He hath heard of Him; He has declared Him to them—His love, grace, and mercy. God has spoken all He has to say that appertains to His own worship, and the salvation of the children of men by His Son Jesus Christ.

Verse 26. **Jesus saith unto her**, &c. Upon her making mention of the Messiah, of His coming, and of His work, He took the opportunity of making Himself known unto her:

I that speak unto thee am *he*; the Messiah; see *Isa. 52:6*. This is a wonderful instance of the grace of Christ to this woman, that He should make Himself known in so clear and plain a manner, to so mean [*or* lowly] a person, and so infamous a creature as she had been: we never find that He ever made so clear a discovery of Himself, in such express terms, to any, as to her, unless

---

[37] Zohar in Gen. fol. 74. 1.

[38] Zohar in Lev. 10:1.

[39] Maimonides Hilchot Melachim, c. 11. sect. 4. & 12. 5.

it were to His immediate disciples; and these He would sometimes charge not to tell who He was.

Verse 27. **And upon this came his disciples**, &c. Just as He was saying the above words, and making Himself known in this full manner, His disciples, who had been into the city to buy food, came up to them:

and marveled that he talked with the woman; or with a woman; for, according to the Jewish canons, it was not judged decent, right, and proper, nor indeed lawful, to enter into a conversation, or hold any long discourse with a woman. Their rule is this,

> "Do not multiply discourse with a woman; with his wife they say; much less with his neighbor's wife: hence the wise men say, At whatsoever time a man multiplies discourse with a woman, he is the cause of evil to himself, and ceases from the words of the law, and at last shall go down into hell."[40]

And especially this was thought to be very unseemly in any public place, as in an inn, or in the street: hence that direction,[41]

> "Let not a man talk with a woman in the streets, even with his wife; and there is no need to say, with another man's wife."

And particularly it was thought very unbecoming a religious man, a doctor, or scholar, or a disciple of a wise man, so to do. This is one of the six things which are a reproach to a scholar, *to talk with a woman in the street.*[42] And it is even said,[43]

> "Let him not talk with a woman in the street, though she is his wife, or his sister, or his daughter."

And besides, the disciples might marvel, not only that He talked with a woman, but that He should talk with that woman, who was a Samaritan; since the Jews had no familiar conversation with Samaritans, men or women: and the woman was as much astonished that Christ should have any thing to say to her, and especially to ask a favor of her; for though they might, and did converse in a way of trade and business, yet did they not multiply discourse, or enter into a free conversation with one another: and it may be, that the disciples might overhear what He said to the woman, just as they came up; so

---

[40] Pirke Abot, c. 1. sect. 5. Abot R. Nathan, c. 7. fol. 3. 3. & Derech Eretz, fol. 17. 3.

[41] Bemidbar Rabba, sect 10. fol. 200. 2.

[42] T. Bab. Beracot, fol. 43. 2.

[43] Maimonides Hilchot Dayot, c. 5. sect. 7.

that their astonishment was not merely at His talking with a woman, and with a Samaritan woman, but at what He said unto her, that He should so plainly tell her that He was the Messiah, when He so strictly charged them to tell no man.

Yet no man said; no, not Peter, as Nonnus observes, who was bold and forward to put and ask questions:

What seekest thou? Or inquirest of her about? Is it food, or drink, or what?

or, Why talkest thou with her? when it is not customary, seemly, and lawful. It may be considered, whether or not these two questions may not relate, separately, the one to the woman, the other to Christ; as, the first, *What seekest thou?* to the woman; and the sense be, that no man said to her, What do you want with our master? What are you inquiring about of Him? What would you have of Him? Or what do you seek for from Him? and the latter, *Why talkest thou with her?* peculiarly to Christ. The Arabic, Persic, and Ethiopic versions, and Beza's ancient copy indeed read, *no man said to him*; which confines both the questions to Christ. Now this shows the reverence the disciples had for Christ, and the great opinion they entertained of Him, that whatever He did was well, and wisely done; though it might seem strange to them, and they could not account for it. However, they did not think that He, who was their Lord and master, was accountable to them for what He did; and they doubted not but He had good reasons for His conduct.

Verse 28. **The woman then left her waterpot**, &c. She then left her pail or pot she brought with her to the well to draw water in: this she left, for either Christ or His disciples to make use of; or rather, through haste and forgetfulness, her mind being greatly impressed, and her thoughts much taken up with what Christ had said to her, and ran to acquaint others with it. So the disciples left their nets, their business, their friends, and all for Christ; and so the saints are brought to quit their earthly and worldly things for the sake of Christ and His Gospel. The Ethiopic version renders it, *she left her disputation*: she left off discoursing with Christ upon the disciples coming to Him.

And went her way into the city: the city of Sychar, to inform her friends, relations, and neighbors what she had met with. So Andrew and Philip, when they had found Christ themselves, acquaint others with it, and bring them to Him; so Levi, the publican, being called himself by Christ, makes a feast for Christ, and invites many publicans and sinners to sit down with Him, that they might know Him as well as himself; so the Apostle Paul, when converted, expresses a great concern for his *brethren* and *kinsmen according to the flesh*

[*Rom. 9:3*]; and such is the nature of true grace, that those that have it, would have others partakers of it likewise:

and saith to the men; the Ethiopic version adds, *of her house;* no doubt the men of the place in general are meant; not only those of her family, but the inhabitants of the city. The Syriac version leaves out the words, *to the men.* The Jews will not allow the Cuthites, or Samaritans, to be called *men*; this they peculiarly ascribe to priests, Levites, and Israelites.[44]

Verse 29. **Come, see a man**, &c. Come and see an uncommon, an extra-ordinary man, a prophet, and, who Himself says, He is the Messiah, who is now at Jacob's well; come, go along with me, and see Him, and converse with Him, and judge for yourselves, who, and what He is: she does not say, *go and see*; for she proposed to go along with them herself, that she might have more conversation with Him, and knowledge of Him, and grace from Him: so such that have *tasted that the Lord is gracious* [*1 Pet. 2:3*], desire more grace from Him, and communion with Him;

which told me all things that ever I did: the more remarkable things that had been done by her in the whole series of her life and conversation; referring more especially to the account He had given her of her having had five husbands, and what the man was she now lived with; when, no doubt, all the transactions of her life were laid before her, and she had, at once, a view of all her iniquities; when her sins stared her in the face, and her conscience was filled with guilt and remorse, and her soul with shame and confusion; and so it is when Christ, by His Spirit, convinces *of sin, of righteousness, and of judgment* [see *chapter 16:8*]:

is not this the Christ? that was to come, has been promised and prophesied of, and we have expected, who is of quick understanding, and even God omniscient; surely this must be He, as He Himself says He is.

Verse 30. **Then they went out of the city**, &c. *The men*, as the Syriac version expresses it; the inhabitants of Sychar left their business, and came out of the city:

and came unto him; to Christ, to see Him, and converse with Him, that they might know who He was: for though the woman had been a woman of ill fame, yet such was the account that she gave of Christ, and such power went along with her words; that what with the strangeness of the relation, and the curiosity with which they were led, and chiefly through the efficacy of divine

---

[44] T. Bab. Yebamot, fol. 61. 1. & Tosephot in ibid.

grace, at least in many of them, they were moved to regard what she said, and to follow her directions and solicitations.

Verse 31. **In the mean while**, &c. While the woman was gone into the city, and had acquainted the inhabitants, that such a wonderful person was at Jacob's well, and invited them to come and see Him:

his disciples prayed him, saying, Master, eat. For they perceived a disinclination in Him to food; and they knew that He was weary with His journey, and that it was the time of day, and high time, that He had had some food; and therefore out of great respect to Him, and in concern for His health and welfare, they entreated Him that He would take some food: so far was Christ from indulging His sensual appetite; and so little reason had the Scribes and Pharisees to traduce Him as a winebibber and glutton [*Luke 7:34*].

Verse 32. **But he said unto them**, &c. That is, *Jesus*, as the Persic, or, *the Lord Jesus*, as the Ethiopic versions express it:

I have meat to eat that ye know not of. Meaning the conversion of the Samaritan woman, and of other Samaritans, who were flocking in great numbers to Him, which He knew, though His disciples did not; and the harvest of souls He had a prospect of, see *verse 35*, was as meat unto Him, delightful and refreshing; and His mind and thoughts were so taken up with these things, that He had no inclination to any corporeal food.

Verse 33. **Therefore said the disciples one to another**, &c. They said privately, among themselves, though in His hearing; at least He knew what they said by His answer;

hath any man; or any one, any angel from heaven, or any of the inhabitants of the city, or any man or woman, or this woman they had found Him talking with:

brought him *ought* to eat? For they thought of nothing else but bodily food; just as when He cautioned them against the leaven of the Sadducees and Pharisees, they imagined He said it, because they had taken no bread; whereas He meant the doctrine of these persons. So dull of understanding in spiritual things were the disciples themselves, that it is not so much to be wondered at that the Samaritan woman, while in her carnal state, when Christ spoke of living water, should understand Him of material water, or spring water.

Verse 34. **Jesus saith unto them,** &c. To His disciples:

my meat is to do the will of him that sent me; the Ethiopic version reads, *of my Father that sent me*; and who is undoubtedly intended. Now as food is pleasant, and delightful, and refreshing to the body of man, so doing the will of God was as delightful and refreshing to the soul of Christ: He took as much pleasure in it, as a hungry man does in eating and drinking. One part of the will of God was to assume human nature; this He had done, and with delight and pleasure. Another part of it was to fulfil the law; and this was in His heart, and was His delight, and He was now doing it. And another branch of it was to suffer and die in the room and stead of His people; and as disagreeable as this was in itself to the human nature, yet He cheerfully agreed to it; and was sometimes, as it were, impatient till it was accomplished; and He voluntarily became obedient to it: no man could with greater eagerness fall to eating, when hungry, than Christ went about His Father's will and work, even that which was most ungrateful to Him, as man.

and to finish his work. One part of which was to preach the Gospel, and for which He was anointed and sent; and which He did with great assiduity and constancy. And another part of it was the conversion of sinners by it, whom He was sent to call, and with whom He delighted to be; and was the work He was now about, and took great pleasure in, as the text expresses. And beside these, miracles were works His Father gave Him to finish; such as healing diseases, and dispossessing of devils, and which He went about doing continually, with great delight. But the chief work of all is, that of the redemption and salvation of His chosen ones: this was a work His Father called Him to, and sent Him into this world to perform, which He gave unto Him, and Christ accepted of, and agreed to do; and though it was a very toilsome and laborious one, there being a righteous law to be fulfilled, justice to be satisfied, the sins of all His people to bear, as well as the wrath of God, and the curse of the law, and numerous enemies to grapple with, and an accursed death to undergo; yet with pleasure He performed this: for the joy of doing His Father's will, accomplishing His counsels and covenant, and His own engagements, and procuring the salvation of His people, He endured the cross patiently, and despised the shame of it. The whole of the will and work of God was done by Him, just as the Lord commanded it; exactly, according to the pattern given Him, with all faithfulness and integrity; with the most consummate wisdom and prudence; with all application, diligence, and constancy, and so as to finish it, and that without the help of any other; and in such a manner that nothing can be added to it to make it more perfect, or that it can be undone again by men or devils: and that the doing and finishing of this were His meat, or as delightful and refreshing to Him as meat is to the body, appears from His ready and cheerful engaging in it in eternity; from His early and industrious entrance on it in time; from His constancy in it when He had begun, insomuch that nothing could deter Him from it; nor did He sink and fail under it, nor left it till He had finished it.

Verse 35. **Say not ye, there are yet four months**, &c. Our Lord had been in Jerusalem and Judea about eight months from the last passover, and there remained four more to the next passover:

and *then* cometh harvest? Barley harvest, which began at that time. Now as the passover was in the middle of the month Nisan, which was about the latter end of our March; reckoning four months back from thence shows, that it was about the latter end of our November, or beginning of December, that Christ was in Samaria, and at Jacob's well. Some think, that this does not refer to the then present time, as if there were so many months from thence to the next harvest; but to a common way of speaking, that there were four months from seedtime to harvest; during which time there was a comfortable hope, and longing expectation of it: but this will, by no means, agree either with the wheat or barley harvest. The wheat was sown before this time, and the barley a good while after.

"Half Tisri, Marcheshvan, and half Chisleu, were, זרע, *seed's time*"[45]
The earliest they sowed their wheat was in Tisri, which answers to our September and October; that is, to half one, and half the other. The month of Marcheshvan, which answers to October and November, was the principal month for sowing it:[46] hence that paraphrase on *Eccl. 11:2*:

"Give a good part of thy seed to thy field in Tisri, and do not refrain from sowing even in Chisleu."

As for the barley, that was sown in the months of Shebet and Adar, and usually in the latter;[47] the former of which answers to January and February, and the latter to February and March. And we read[48] of their sowing seventy days before the passover, which was within six weeks of the beginning of barley harvest.

Behold, I say unto you, Lift up your eyes, and look on the fields: pointing to the lands which lay near the city of Sychar:

---

[45] T. Bab. Bava Metzia, fol. 106. 2.

[46] Gloss in T. Bab. Roshhashana, fol. 16. 1.

[47] Gloss in Bava Metzia & in Roshhashana ibid.

[48] Mishna Menachot, c. 8. sect. 2.

for they are white already to harvest. Alluding to the corn fields, which, when ripe, and near harvest, look white. Hence we read[49] of, שדה הלבן, *the white field*, which the Jews say is a field sown with wheat or barley, and so called to distinguish it from a field planted with trees; though it may be rather, that it is so called from its white look when ripe. So the three Targums paraphrase *Gen. 49:12*:

> "His hills (his valleys, or fields, as Onkelos) יחוורן, *are white* with corn, and flocks of sheep."

Christ here speaks not literally; for the fields could not be white at such a distance from harvest; but spiritually, of a harvest of souls; and has regard to the large number of Samaritans that were just now coming out of the city, and were within sight, and covered the adjacent fields: and these He calls upon His disciples to lift up their eyes and behold; and suggests to them, that it was not a time for eating and drinking, but for working, since here was such a number of souls to be gathered in: and thus, as from corporeal food he proceeded to treat of spiritual food; so from a literal harvest He goes on to speak of a spiritual one, and encourages His disciples to labor in it, by the following arguments.

Verse 36. **And he that reapeth receiveth wages**, &c. Angels are sometimes called *reapers*, and so are ministers of the Gospel here. The work and ministry of the apostles are here expressed by *reaping*: for as in reaping, when the corn is ripe, the sickle is put in, and the corn is cut down, and laid to the ground, and then bound in sheaves, and gathered into the barn; so when things are ripe in providence, and God's set time is come to convert any of His people, He makes use of His ministers for cutting them down, laying low the loftiness and haughtiness of man, stripping him of all his goodliness, and taking him off of a dependence on his own righteousness and works, and for the gathering them into His churches, which is done with a great deal of joy and pleasure. And such as are so employed, and in this way made useful, shall *receive wages*; shall not only be taken care of in providence, and have a sufficient and comfortable maintenance, the laborer being *worthy of his hire* [*Luke 10:7*]; but shall have pleasure, delight, and satisfaction in their work, that being blessed for the good of souls, and the glory of Christ, and they having the presence of God in it; and also shall hereafter receive the crown of righteousness, when they have finished their course, and *shall shine* like *the stars for ever and ever* [*Dan. 12:3*].

And gathereth fruit unto life eternal: by *fruit* are meant sinners converted and turned from the error of their ways; which are the fruit of a Gospel

---

[49]   Mishna Sheviith, c. 2. sect. 1. & Moed Katon, c. 1. sect. 4.

ministry, of the efficacy and power of divine grace accompanying it; see *chapter 15:16*; and these are *gathered* by the preaching of the Gospel, out from among the rest of mankind, unto Christ, the *Shiloh*, or peacemaker, and into His churches; and remain, abide, and persevere to the end; that grace, which is implanted in their souls, being *a well of living water, springing up to everlasting life*; so that they are at last gathered into Christ's garner, into heaven, where they shall live with Him for ever:

that both he that soweth, and he that reapeth, may rejoice together. The sowers are the prophets of the Old Testament, who sowed that seed in their prophecies, which sprung up in Gospel times, and laid the foundation therein of the great success of the apostles of Christ in preaching the Word; for they so clearly described the Messiah, and pointed out Christ, His offices, and His work, in so distinct a manner, that when He was come He was readily known, and cheerfully embraced; they greatly facilitated the work of the apostles, who had nothing to do but to preach Christ, as come in the flesh: and hence they reaped and gathered a vast harvest of souls every where. John the Baptist also was one that *sowed*; he prepared the way of the Lord, and made straight His paths: and our Lord Himself was *a sower*, that *went forth to sow*, and who sowed good seed in the field; all which succeeded well, and were ripening apace for a general harvest, which began on the day of Pentecost, after our Lord's ascension to heaven. This was in Judea; and in the Gentile world there was a sowing in providence, which contributed to make the work of the disciples more easy there, and to bring on, in time, a large harvest. The books of the Old Testament were translated into the Greek language; and the Jews were scattered in the several parts of the world; and the Greek tongue, in which the New Testament was to be written, was every where generally spoken; and these providences were ripening apace to bring on a great work there. And now, as before observed, the apostles were the reapers; they were remarkably successful in the gathering in of souls, even more than the prophets, than John the Baptist, or Christ Himself; never was such a harvest of souls, either in Judea, or in the Gentile world, before or since; of which the conversion of these Samaritans was a pledge or earnest. Now when the whole harvest is gathered in, at the end of the world, all these will rejoice together, the patriarchs and prophets, the forerunner of Christ, and Christ Himself, and all His apostles and ministers; the different parts they have had in this work all concurring and agreeing together, and issuing in the glory of God, and the good of souls.

Verse 37. **And herein is that saying true**, &c. This verifies that proverbial expression so much in use, and which may be applied to different persons and cases:

one soweth, and another reapeth. The prophets sowed, and the apostles reaped.

Verse 38. **I sent you to reap**, &c. To preach the Gospel, and gather in souls by your ministry; referring to the mission of them in *Matt. 10:6-7*:

that whereon ye bestowed no labor; being sent to the Jews, who had the writings of the prophets, and were versed in them; and had learned from them that the Messiah was to come, and were now in general expectation of Him; so that they had nothing more to do, than to declare to those persons who were cultivated by the prophets, and were like to ground ready tilled and manured to their hands, that the Messiah was come, and the kingdom of heaven was at hand;

other men labored; the prophets, and John the Baptist:

and ye are entered into their labors. To finish the work they had begun, and which was almost done beforehand.

Verse 39. **And many of the Samaritans of that city**, &c. Many of the inhabitants of Sychar, which was a city of Samaria;

believed on him; that He was the true Messiah as He had told the woman He was; and she put it to them whether He was or not: before they saw Him, or had any conversation with Him themselves, they believed in Him; see *chapter 20:29*;

for the saying of the woman which testified, he told me all that ever I did. The account she gave was so plain, and honest, and disinterested, that they could not but give credit to it; and since the person was an utter stranger to her, and yet had laid before her the whole series of her past life and conversation, they concluded He could be no other than the Messiah, who should tell all things; and being of quick understanding or smell [that is, discernment], was able to disclose the secrets of men.

Verse 40. **So when the Samaritans were come unto him**, &c. The Ethiopic version reads, *all the Samaritans*; they came to Him at Jacob's well, upon the woman's solicitations, and the account she gave of this extraordinary person. And after they had conversed with Him, and heard Him themselves, they were taken with His divine discourses, and being thoroughly persuaded that He was the Messiah,

they besought him that he would tarry with them; they were not like the Gergesenes, who besought Him *to depart out of their coasts* [*Mark 5:17*] as soon He was in them: but these men were delighted with His company; and, notwithstanding His being a Jew, desired a conversation with Him, and entreated that He would go along with them to their city, and stay with them:

and he abode there two days; He went with them to Sychar. He would not deny their request, lest they should be discouraged; and yet would not make any long stay with them, that He might give no umbrage to the Jews; though it is very likely from this short stay in Samaria, they afterwards reproached Him as a *Samaritan, chapter 8:48*. Our Lord's direction to His disciples not to enter into any of the cities of the Samaritans, was not a rule to Himself, or binding upon Him, and was only a rule to them *pro tempore* [or for the time being].

Verse 41. **And many more believed**, &c. The Vulgate Latin, and all the Oriental versions add, *on him*: when He was come into the city, and had preached to the inhabitants in general, a larger multitude than before believed in Him as the Messiah, and professed Him, and became followers of Him:

because of his own word; which came to them, not in word only, but in power, and was *the power of God unto salvation* to them [*Rom. 1:16*]; and was received by them, not as the word of man, but as the Word of God; and it wrought effectually in them, and was a hammer to break their rocky hearts in pieces, and to bring them into subjection to Himself, His Gospel and ordinances: whether His Word or doctrine was accompanied with miracles, is not certain; this shows, that their faith in Him was founded on His own Word, which fell with great weight upon them. It seems to have an emphasis laid upon it, His *own* Word, in distinction from the woman's saying.

Verse 42. **And said unto the woman**, &c. It appears that the woman kept hearing Christ, attending on Him, and conversing with Him; for having tasted of His grace, she could not leave Him:

now we believe, not because of thy saying; not on account of that only: it should seem that these were the same persons that believed upon her word, before they went out of the city; and who, when come to Christ, invited Him into it; and now, having heard His excellent discourses, were confirmed in the faith of Him:

for we have heard *him* ourselves; not only externally, with their bodily ears, but internally, having ears given them to hear, so as to understand what He said [see *Prov. 20:12* with *Matt. 13:13-16* and *Rom. 10:17*]; to mix it with faith, and receive it in love [*Heb. 4:2; 2 Thess. 2:10*]; to feel the power of it in their hearts, and taste the sweetness of it, and be nourished by it; and so as to distinguish His voice from another's, as Christ's true sheep are capable of doing:

and know that this is indeed the Christ; the true Messiah, and not a false one; the Messiah spoken of by Moses, whose books the Samaritans received, as *the seed of the woman*, the Shiloh, and prophet like to Moses; the Christ of God, who is anointed to be prophet priest, and King. The Vulgate Latin and Ethiopic versions leave out the word *Christ,* and only read what follows,

the Savior of the world. They knew Him to be the Savior, He who was spoken of as such; for His work, *to bruise* the serpent's head, implies it, and His name *Shiloh* imports as much: and besides, He is called by Jacob *God's salvation, Gen. 49:18.* God appointed Him as a Savior; He sent Him, and He came as such, and is become the author of salvation; and His name is called *Jesus*, on this account [see *Matt. 1:21*]: and a great Savior He is; both able and willing; and He is suitable to the case of sinners; and is a complete, and an only one: and these Samaritans knew Him to be *the Savior of the world*; not of every individual person in it, for all are not saved by Him; nor of the Jewish world, for many of them died in their sins; but of the Gentiles, in distinction from the Jews; see *chapter 3:16; 1 John 2:2*; even of all God's elect, whether among Jews or Gentiles; of all that believe in Him, of whatsoever nation, and in whatsoever state and condition: so that their knowledge of Him, and faith in Him, were beyond that of the Jews, who looked upon the Messiah only as a Savior of their nation; and that the Gentiles would have no manner of benefit and advantage by Him: though the Jews[50] do call the angel in *Ex. 23:20,* פרוקא דעלמא, *the Savior*, or *Redeemer of the world*. And this the Samaritans might know from the writings of Moses, as from *Gen. 22:18* and *49:10*. Their present knowledge of Christ was not a mere notional, speculative, and general one, but was special, spiritual, and saving, which they had from the Spirit of wisdom and revelation in the knowledge of Christ; they approved of Him as their Savior; they trusted in Him as such; they had an experimental acquaintance with Him, and practically owned Him; and which they attained to by hearing Him.

Verse 43. **Now after two days he departed thence**, &c. When he had stayed two days at Sychar, conversing with, and discoursing to the Samaritans, which were the means of the conversion of many of them; He departed out of that country, and passed on His way:

and went into Galilee. As He first intended; see *verse 3*.

---

[50]   Zohar in Gen. fol. 124. 4.

Verse 44. **For Jesus himself testified**, &c. See *Matt. 13:57;*

that a prophet hath no honor in his own country. All the Oriental versions read, *in his own city*; that is, Nazareth: for these words must not be understood as a reason why Christ left Judea, and went into Galilee, because He had no honor in Judea, in which was Bethlehem, the place of His nativity; but are a reason why, when He came into Galilee, He did not go to Nazareth, His own city, where He was educated, and had been brought up, and had lived the greatest part of His life, because they treated Him with great disrespect and contempt; see the note on *Matt. 13:57* **[19]**.

Verse 45. **Then when he was come into Galilee**, &c. Was come into that part of Galilee in which Cana lay, as appears by what follows:

the Galileans received him; willingly, readily, and cheerfully, with much delight and pleasure, and with marks of great esteem and respect: they received Him into their houses, and entertained Him, and provided for Him and His disciples:

having seen all the things that he did at Jerusalem, at the feast: of the passover; the miracles He wrought there, see *chapter 2:23*;

for they also went unto the feast. As well as Jesus and His disciples. They kept the feast of the passover, and went yearly to Jerusalem on that account: so Josephus speaks of the Galileans going to the Jewish festivals at Jerusalem, when he says:[51]

"It was the custom, or usual with the Galileans, when they went to the
holy city at the festivals, to go through the country of the Samaritans;"
which was the way that Christ now came from thence to them.

Verse 46. **So Jesus came again unto Cana of Galilee**, &c. To Cana where He had been once before; see *chapter 2:1-2*. The Syriac version here, as there, calls it *Kotne of Galilee*; and the Persic version, *Catneh of Galilee*:

where he made the water wine. See *chapter 2:9,11*;

And there was a certain nobleman; the Vulgate Latin renders it, *a petty king*; the Arabic version, and Nonnus, call him, *a royal man*; and the Syriac version renders it, *a king's servant*; with which agrees the Ethiopic, calling him *a minister, a steward, the king's domestic*. The Persic version makes it to be his name, reading it, *there was a great man, whose name was Abdolmelic*, which signifies *a king's servant*: from the whole, he seems to be one that

---

[51] Antiqu. Jud. l. 20. c. 5.

belonged to the palace of Herod Antipas, and was one of his courtiers; who, though he was but tetrarch of Galilee, yet is sometimes called *a king*, *Mark 6:14*;

whose son was sick at Capernaum. Some versions, as the Syriac, Arabic, and Persic, read the phrase, *in Capernaum*, with the former clause, *there was a nobleman in Capernaum*: and others, as we do with this; and both may be true; for he might be an inhabitant of Capernaum, and his house be there where his son lay sick. Some think this nobleman was either Chuza, Herod's steward, *Luke 8:3*, or Manaen, who had been brought up with Herod, *Acts 13:1*.

Verse 47. **When he heard that Jesus was come out of Judea**, &c. For the fame of Christ, for His doctrine and miracles, was spread every where; so that it was known, and talked of, in most places, where He was and what course He was steering: and this nobleman understanding that He had left Judea, and was come,

into Galilee; and having inquired in what part of Galilee He was,

he went unto him; though it was many miles from Capernaum, where Jesus was, at least a day's journey; since, when the servants met their master, the child had been healed at one o'clock the day before; see *verse 52*. Some reckon it about fifteen miles, but one would think it should be more:

and besought him, that he would come down; for Capernaum, though it was built on a hill, lay lower down in the country of Galilee than Cana did, near the sea of Tiberias: a like way of speaking is used in *chapter 2:12*;

and heal his son; the nobleman believed that Christ had power to do it, by what he had heard concerning Him, but thought His corporeal presence was absolutely necessary to it:

for he was at the point of death. Or *would die*: he was very near it; there was no likelihood of his recovery; the physicians had given him over; and when he left him, he seemed to be near his death, and must die for any human help that could be obtained, or natural means that could be used.

Verse 48. **Then said Jesus unto him**, &c. With some degree of roughness in His speech, and severity in His countenance, in a way of reproof for his unbelief, as if He could not heal his son without going down to Capernaum along with him:

except ye see signs and wonders ye will not believe. This was the cast of the Jews every where, both in Judea and Galilee; they required signs and miracles to be wrought, in confirmation of Christ's being the Messiah, and which indeed was but right; and Christ did perform them for that purpose. But their sin of unbelief lay in this, that they wanted still more and more signs; they could not be contented with what they had seen, but required more, being sluggish and backward to believe. Our Lord seems to say this chiefly for the sake of the Galileans that were about Him; who, though they might be acquainted with His former miracles, when among them, of turning water into wine, and had seen His wondrous works at the feast at Jerusalem, yet were very desirous of seeing more, and perhaps very pressing for this cure.

Verse 49. **The nobleman saith unto him, Sir**, &c. Notwithstanding this reproof, and seeming denial, the nobleman presses Him again, and addressing Him in a handsome and courteous manner, importunately entreats Him, saying,

come down ere my son die. Here was faith with a mixture of unbelief; he believed that Christ was able to heal his son, but he still thought that His going down with him was necessary; that He must be corporeally present, and must lay His hands on him, or touch him, or speak, and command the distemper off, or something of this kind, and which must be done before he died; for otherwise, should he die first, all hope was then gone; he had no notion of Christ being able to raise him from the dead.

Verse 50. **Jesus saith unto him, go thy way**, &c. Go, return home in peace, be not over-much troubled and distressed about this matter; leave it with me, I will take care of it; all will be well: so the Persic version reads, *be not anxious, and go thy way*; do not be solicitous for my presence, or urge me to go with thee; depart alone, there is no necessity for my being upon the spot:

thy son liveth; he is now recovered of his disease, and is well, and in perfect health, and lives, and will live:

and the man believed the word that Jesus had spoken to him; such power went along with the words of Christ, as not only cured the son at that distance, who lay at the point of death, but also the father of his unbelief; and he no more insisted on His going down with him, but firmly believed that his son was alive, and well, as Christ had said he was:

and he went his way. He took his leave of Christ, and set out for Capernaum; very probably, not the same day, it being now in the afternoon of the day; but the next morning, as it should seem from what follows.

Verse 51. **And as he was now going down**, &c. As he was going down from Cana to Capernaum, the day after he had been with Christ:

his servants met him, and told *him*, saying, Thy son liveth. As soon as this cure was wrought, though it was not known in the family how, and by whom it was done, immediately some of the servants were dispatched to carry the news to their master, that his sorrow might be removed; and he give himself no further trouble in seeking for a cure: these meeting him on the road, with an air of pleasure, at once address him with the joyful news, that his son was thoroughly recovered of his disorder, and was alive, and well; news which he was acquainted with, and believed before; though it must give him an additional pleasure to have it confirmed.

Verse 52. **Then inquired he of them the hour**, &c. He did not at all hesitate about the truth of it, or was in any surprise upon it; but, that he might compare things together, he asked the exact time,

when he began to amend; or grow better; for he seemed to think, that his recovery might be gradual, and not all at once, as it was:

and they said unto him, Yesterday at the seventh hour; which was one o'clock in the afternoon:

the fever left him. Entirely, and at once, so that he was perfectly well immediately.

Verse 53. **So the father knew that *it was* at the same hour**, &c. He had precisely observed what time of day it was in which he conversed with Jesus; and particularly,

in that which Jesus said to him, Thy son liveth. When He told him his son was alive and well, and when he took his leave of Him; and by comparing the account of his servants, with that, found all things entirely agreed, and that the cure was wrought exactly at the time that Jesus spoke the words:

and himself believed, and his whole house. When he came home, he related the whole affair to his family, and he and they all believed that Jesus was the Messiah, and became His disciples and followers. If this nobleman was Chuza, Herod's steward, we have an account of his wife, whose name was Joanna, that she followed Christ, and ministered to Him of her substance, with other women, *Luke 8:3*. There is a story told by the Jews, and which seems somewhat like to this:[52]

> "It is reported concerning R. Chanina ben Dosa, that when he prayed for the sick, he used to say, יֵח הֶז, *This liveth, and this dies*. It was said to him, Whence knowest thou this? He replied, If my prayer be ready

---

[52] Mishna Beracot, c. 5. sect. 5.

in my mouth, I know that he is accepted (of God, that is, the sick man for whom he prayed); but if not, I know that he will be snatched away (by the disease)."

Upon which the Gemarists give the following relation:[53]

"It happened that the son of Rabban Gamaliel (the Apostle Paul's master) was sick, he sent two disciples to R. Chanina ben Dosa, to ask mercy for him. When he saw them, he went up to a chamber, and sought mercy for him; and when he came down, he said unto them, לכו שחלצתו חמה, *Go your way, for the fever has left him.* They said unto him, Art thou a prophet? He replied, I am not a prophet, nor the son of a prophet; but so I have received, that if my prayer is ready in my mouth, I know that he is accepted; and if not, I know that he shall be snatched away; and they sat and wrote, and observed *the very hour.* And when they came to Rabban Gamaliel, he said unto them, This service ye have not been wanting in, nor abounded in; but so the thing was, that in that hour the fever left him, and he asked of us water to drink."

Which story perhaps is told, to vie with this miracle of Christ, and to obscure the glory of it.

Verse 54. This *is* again the second miracle *that* Jesus did, &c. That is, the second He did in that place, in Cana of Galilee; for otherwise, in Jerusalem and Judea, He had done many miracles, between the former and this; see *chapters 2:23* and *3:2*; and so the following words explain it:

when he was come out of Judea into Galilee. This was the first He wrought, after His coming out of Judea into Galilee, this time, and was the second that He wrought in Cana of Galilee; see *chapter 2:11.*

CHAPTER 5

Verse 1. **After this there was a feast of the Jews**, &c. After Christ had been in Samaria, which was four months ago, *chapter 4:35*; and had been in Galilee for that time, and had cured the nobleman's son, and had done other

---

[53] T. Bab. Beracot, fol. 34. 2.

mighty works, the time came on for one of the three festivals of the Jews; either the feast of Pentecost, as some think; or, as others, the feast of Tabernacles; or rather, the feast of the Passover, so called, in *chapter 4:45,* since John is very particular in giving an account of the several passovers in Christ's ministry:

and Jesus went up to Jerusalem. According to the law of God, which obliged all the males to appear there at that time; and to show His compliance with it, and obedience to it, whom it became to fulfil all righteousness; and this He did also, that He might have an opportunity of discoursing, and doing His miracles before all the people, which came at this time from the several parts of the land.

Verse 2. **Now there is at Jerusalem by the sheep *market***, &c. The word *market* is not in the text, and of such a market, no account is given in the Scripture, nor in the Jewish writings; and besides, in our Lord's time, sheep and oxen were sold in the temple; rather therefore this signifies, the *sheep-gate*, of which mention is made, in *Neh. 3:1,32* and *12:39,* through which the sheep were brought into the city, to the temple:

a pool; the Vulgate Latin and Ethiopic versions read, *there is at Jerusalem a sheep pool*; and so it is interpreted in the Arabic version; and Jerome calls it *the cattle pool.*[1] The Targumist on *Jer. 31:39,* speaks of a pool called עגלה בריכה, *the calf,* or *heifer pool,* as Dr. Lightfoot renders it; though the translations of it, both in the London Polyglott, and in the King of Spain's Bible, interpret it *the round pool.* This pool of Bethesda, is thought by some to be the same which the Jews call *the great pool* in Jerusalem; they say,[2]

"between Hebron and Jerusalem, is the fountain Etham, from whence the waters come by way of pipes, unto *the great pool*, which is in Jerusalem."

And R. Benjamin[3] speaks of a pool, which is to be seen to this day, where the ancients slew their sacrifices, and all the Jews write their names on the wall. And some think it was so called, because the sheep that were offered in sacrifice, were there washed; which must be either before, or after they were slain; not before, for it was not required, that what was to be slain for sacrifice, should be washed first; and afterwards, only the entrails of a beast were washed; and for this there was a particular place in the temple, called

---

[1]   De Locis Hebraicis, p. 89. L. Tom. III.

[2]   Cippi Hebraici, p. 10.

[3]   Itinerar. p. 43.

לשכת המדיחין, *the washing room*; where, they say,[4] they washed the inwards of the holy sacrifices. This pool here therefore, seems rather, as Dr. Lightfoot observes, to have been a bath for unclean persons; and having this miraculous virtue, hereafter spoken of, diseased persons, only at certain times, had recourse to it. The Syriac and Persic versions call it, *a place of a baptistery*; and both leave out the clause, *by the sheep market*, or *gate*. It is not easy to say where and what it was:

which is called in the Hebrew tongue, Bethesda; which signifies, according to the Syriac, Arabic, and Persic versions, *a house of mercy*, or *grace*, or *goodness*; because many miserable objects here received mercy, and a cure. Hegesippus[5] speaks of a Bethesda, which Cestius the Roman general entered into, and burnt; and which, according to him, seems to be without Jerusalem, and so not the place here spoken of; and besides, this is called a *pool*, though the buildings about it doubtless went by the same name. The Vulgate Latin and Ethiopic versions read *Bethsaida*, very wrongly; and it is called by Tertullian[6] the pool of *Bethsaida*. The Hebrew tongue here mentioned is הנהר כתב של עבר, *the language of those beyond the river*,[7] that is, the river Euphrates; which is the Chaldee language, as distinct from the Assyrian language, which is called the holy and blessed language; the former is what the Cuthites, or Samaritans used; the latter, that in which the book of the law was written.[8]

having five porches. Or cloistered walks, which were very convenient for the diseased which lay here for a cure, so Nonnus. Athanasius[9] speaks of the pool itself, as in being, though the buildings round about lay in ruins in his time; and[10] Daviler observes, there are still remaining five arches of the

---

[4] Mishna Middot, c. 5. sect. 2. Maimon. Beth Habbechira, c. 5. sect. 17.

[5] De Excidio, l. 2. c. 15.

[6] Adv. Judaeos, c. 13.

[7] De Semente, p. 845. Tom. I.

[8] In Chambers' Dictionary, in the word *Piscina*.

[9] Vid. Gloss. in T. Bab. Sabbat, fol. 115. 1. Megilla, fol. 18. 2. & Sanhedrin, fol. 21. 2.

[10] Maimon. & Bartenora in Mishna Yadaim, c. 4. sect. 5. Vid. Gloss. in T. Bab. Megilla, fol. 8. 2.

portico, and part of the basin. Now this place may be an emblem of the means of grace, the ministry of the Word, and ordinances: the house of God, where the Gospel is preached, may be called a *Bethesda*, a house of mercy; since here the free, sovereign, rich, and abundant grace and mercy of God, through Christ, is proclaimed, as the ground and foundation of a sinner's hope; the mercy of God, as it is displayed in the covenant of grace, in the mission of Christ, and redemption by Him, in regeneration, and in the forgiveness of sin, and indeed, in the whole of salvation, from first to last, is here held forth for the relief of distressed mind. And this Bethesda being a pool, some of the ancients have thought it was an emblem of, and prefigured the ordinance of baptism; and that the miraculous virtue in it, was put into it to give honor and credit to that ordinance, shortly to be administered: but as that is not the means of regeneration and conversion, or of a cure or cleansing, but pre-requires them; rather it might be a symbol of the fountain of Christ's blood, opened for polluted sinners to wash in, and which cleanses from all sin, and cures all diseases; and this is opened in the house of mercy, and by the ministry of the Word: or rather, best of all, the Gospel itself, and the ministration of it, may be signified; which is sometimes compared to waters, and a fountain of them; see *Isa. 55:1; Zech. 14:8; Joel 3:18*. And whereas this pool was in Jerusalem, and that so often designs the church of Christ under the Gospel dispensation, it may fitly represent the ministry of the Word there: and it being near the sheep market, or gate, or a sheep pool, may not be without its significancy; and may lead us to observe, that near where Christ's sheep are, which the Father has given Him, and He has died for, and must bring in, He fixes His Word and ordinances, in order to gather them in: and inasmuch as there were five porches, or cloistered walks, leading unto, or adjoining to this place, it has been thought by some of the ancients, that the law, as lying in the five books of Moses, may be intended by them; for under the law, and under a work of it, men are, before they come into the light, and liberty, and comfort of the Gospel; and as the people which lay in these porches received no cure there, so there is no relief, peace, joy, life, and salvation, by the law of works.

Verse 3. **In these lay a great multitude of impotent folk**, &c. In these lay many sick and weak persons; who were an emblem of men under the law of works, and in a state of unregeneracy; who are enfeebled by sin, and are impotent and unable to do any thing of themselves; as to keep the law of God, to which they have neither will nor power, and to atone for the transgressions of it; nor to redeem themselves from the curse of the law; nor to begin and carry on a work of grace upon their souls; nor to do any thing that is spiritually good; no, not to think a good thought, or to do a good action, as is required:

of blind; these also may represent men in a state of nature, who are ignorant of, and blind to every thing that is spiritual; as to the true knowledge of God in Christ, the way of salvation by Him, the plague of their own hearts, and the exceeding sinfulness of sin; to the Spirit of God, and His work upon the soul; and to the truths of the Gospel, in the power of them:

halt, or *lame*; this word sometimes is used of persons in suspense about religious things, hesitating concerning them, halting *between two opinions* [*1 Kings 18:21*]; and sometimes designs the infirmities of the saints, and their faltering in religious exercises; and here may be expressive, in a figurative way, of the incapacity of natural men, to go or walk of themselves; as to come to Christ for grace and life, which no man can do, except the Father draw him [*chapter 6:44*]; or to walk by faith in Him: it is added,

withered; one limb or another of them dried up: their arms or legs were withered, and their sinews shrunk, and were without radical moisture, or the free use of the animal spirits; and may point out carnal persons, such as are sensual, not having the Spirit, destitute of the grace of God, without faith, hope, love, knowledge, and the fear of God; without God, Christ, and the Spirit; and in a lifeless, helpless, hopeless, and perishing condition:

waiting for the moving of the water. Hereafter mentioned: and so it is in providence, and a wonderful thing it is, that the hearts of so many unregenerate persons should be inclined to attend upon the outward means of grace, and should be waiting at Wisdom's gates, and watching at the posts of her door [see *Prov. 8:34*].

Verse 4. **For an angel went down at a certain season into the pool**, &c. This angel is not to be understood of a messenger sent from the Sanhedrin, or by the priests, as Dr. Hammond thinks; who has a strange conceit, that this pool was used for the washing of the entrails of the sacrifices; and which at the passover being very numerous, the water in it mixed with the blood of the entrails, was possessed of an healing virtue; and which being stirred by a messenger sent from the Sanhedrin for that purpose, whoever went in directly received a cure: but this angel was *an angel of the Lord*, as the Vulgate Latin, and two of Beza's copies read; and so the Ethiopic version reads, *an angel of God*; who either in a visible form came down from heaven, and went into the pool; the Ethiopic version very wrongly renders it, *was washed in the pool;* or it was concluded by the people, from the unusual agitation of the water, and the miraculous virtue which ensued upon it, that an angel did descend into it; and this was not at all times, but at a certain time; either once a year, as Tertullian thought, at the time of the feast of the passover, or every sabbath, as this was now the sabbath day; or it may be there was no fixed period for it, but at some times and seasons in the year so it was, which kept the people continually waiting for it:

and troubled the water. Agitated and moved it to and fro, caused it to swell and rise, to bubble and boil up, and to roll about, and be as in a ferment. The Jews have a notion of spirits troubling waters; they speak of a certain fountain where a spirit resided, and an evil spirit attempted to come in his room; upon which a contest arose, and they saw, ערבובייא דמייא, *the waters troubled*, and thick drops of blood upon them.[11] The Syriac[12] writers have a tradition that,

"Because the body of Isaiah the prophet was hid in Siloah, therefore an angel descended and moved the waters."

Whosoever then first after the troubling of the waters stepped in was made whole of whatsoever disease he had. From whence it seems, that only one person at a season received a cure, by going in first into the water, so Tertullian thought.[13] The Jews ascribe a healing virtue to the well of Miriam; they say,

"A certain ulcerous person went to dip himself in the sea of Tiberias, and it happened at that time, that the well of Miriam flowed, and he washed, ואיתסי, *and was healed*."[14]

Now this angel may represent a minister of the Gospel, for such are called *angels, Rev. 1:20*; being called of God, and sent by Him with messages of grace to the sons of men; and the preaching of the Gospel by such, may be aptly signified by the troubling of the waters, as it is by the shaking of heaven, earth, and sea; see *Hag. 2:6-7*, compared with *Heb. 12:25-26;* especially when attended with the Spirit of God, who moved upon the face of the waters in the first creation; and who, in and by the ministry of the Word, troubles the minds of men, and while the prophet prophesies, causes a shaking among the dry bones, which is done at certain seasons; for as there are certain seasons for the preaching of the Gospel, so there is more especially a fixed, settled, and appointed one, for the conversion of God's elect; who are called according to purpose [*Rom. 8:28*], and at the time the Lord has appointed [*1Thess. 5:9*]: and whoever now, upon the preaching of the Gospel, are enabled to step forth and come to Christ, and believe in Him, are cured of all their soul maladies and

---

[11]   Vajikra Rabba, sect. 24. fol. 165. 2.

[12]   Vid. Hackspan. Interpr. Errabund. sect. 20.

[13]   De Baptismo, c. 5.

[14]   Midrash Kohelet, fol. 71. 4.

diseases, be they what they will; all their iniquities are pardoned, their persons justified, and they are saved in Christ, with an everlasting salvation: and as this cure was not owing to any natural virtue in the water, nor even to the angel's troubling it, but to a supernatural power; so the conversion of a sinner is not owing to ministers, and to the Word and ordinances as administered by them, but to the superior power of the grace of God; and which is exerted in His time, and on whom He pleases.

Verse 5. **And a certain man was there**, &c. A man was at Bethesda's pool, in one of the five porches, or cloisters, that belonged to it:

which had an infirmity thirty and eight years. What his infirmity was, is not said; he was one of the weak, or impotent folk, for so he is called, *verse 7.* Some think his distemper was the palsy, and though he had had this infirmity so many years, it is not certain that he had waited so long in this place for a cure; though it may be, for that he had attended some time, is clear from *verse 7.* Nor indeed can it be known how long there had been such a preternatural motion in this pool, and such a miraculous virtue in the water; some have thought, that it began at the repairing of the sheep gate by Eliashib, in Nehemiah's time; so Tremellius and Junius, on *Neh. 3:1;* and others have thought, that it had been some few years before the birth of Christ, and about the time that this man was first taken with his disorder. Tertullian says,[15] that there was in Judea a medicinal lake, before Christ's time; and that the pool of Bethsaida (it should be *Bethesda*) was useful in curing the diseases of the Israelites; but ceased from yielding any benefit, when the name of the Lord was blasphemed by them, through their rage and fury, and continuance in it;[16] but in what year it began, and the precise time it ceased, he says not. The Persic version here adds, *and was reduced to such a state that he could not move.*

Verse 6. **When Jesus saw him lie, and knew that he had been now a long time, *in that case*,** &c. Jesus knew he had been long in a helpless condition, and now lay in that sad case, or *in his disease*, as the Ethiopic version supplies; even seven years before Christ was born; which is a proof of His omniscience. The words may be literally rendered, as they are in the Vulgate Latin and Syriac versions, *that he had had much time*; or as the Arabic version, *that he had had many years*; that is, had lived many years, and was now an old man; he had his disorder eight and thirty years, and

---

[15] De Anima, c. 50.

[16] Adv. Judaeos, c. 13.

154

which seems from *verse 14* to have arisen from some sin of his, from a vicious course of living, perhaps intemperance; so that he might be a middle-aged man, when this distemper first seized him, and therefore must be now stricken in years:

he saith unto him, Wilt thou be made whole? Which question is put, not as if it was a doubt whether he was desirous of it, or not; for to what purpose did he lie and wait there else? but partly to raise in the man an expectation of a cure, and attention in the people to it: and it may be His sense and meaning is, Wilt thou be made whole on this day, which was the sabbath; or hast thou faith that thou shalt be made whole in this way, or by me?

Verse 7. **The impotent man answered him, Sir**, &c. To say, Sir, was a common and courteous way of speaking, much in use with the Jews, especially to strangers. The Syriac, Arabic, and Persic versions read, *Yea Lord*, which is a direct answer to the question:

I have no man; the Ethiopic version reads, *men*; he had no servant, so Nonnus, or servants, to wait upon him, and take him up in their arms, and carry him into the pool; he was a poor man, and such God is pleased to choose and call by His grace:

when the water is troubled, to put me into the pool; that is, as soon as it is troubled by the angel, to put him in first before any other; for it was the first man only that had a cure this way:

but while I am coming; in a slow way, by the help of his crutches, or in the best manner he could:

another steppeth down before me. Not so much disordered, but more active and nimble: so among those that wait on the ministry of the Word, some are sooner in Christ, or earlier called by His grace, than others; some lie here a long time, and see one and another come to Christ, believe in Him, profess His name, and are received into the church; and they still left in an uncalled and unconverted estate.

Verse 8. **Jesus saith to him, rise**, &c. Jesus said, Arise from thy bed, or couch, on which he lay in one of the porches: and,

take up thy bed and walk. These words were spoken by the same power as those to Lazarus, which called him out of his grave; as appears from the effect they had upon the man, who was in himself impotent, weak, and helpless.

Verse 9. **And immediately the man was made whole**, &c. As soon as ever the words were spoken by Christ, such power went with them, as restored the man to perfect health; and he finding himself to be quite well, rose up directly:

and took up his bed and walked; which may be expressive of a sinner's rising from the bed of sin, and taking up the cross, or carrying the body of sin and death with him; and walking by faith in Christ, as he has received Him:

and on the same day was the sabbath. Which is remarked, for the sake of what follows.

Verse 10. **The Jews therefore said unto him that was cured**, &c. The Jews, when they saw him, either at the place, or as he walked through the streets, with his bed on his back, said,

It is the sabbath day: Do you not know it? Surely you forget yourself, or you would never be guilty of such an action as this;

it is not lawful for thee to carry *thy* bed. It was forbidden by the law, to carry any burden on the sabbath day; see *Neh. 13:15,19* and *Jer. 17:22*; for,
"carrying out and bringing in any thing, from one place to another, is said[17] to be work, and one of the principal works;"
and therefore forbidden by the law, which says, *Thou shall not do any work*; and one of the traditions of the elders is this,[18]
"Whoever carries any thing out (that is, on the sabbath day), whether in his right hand, or in his left, in his bosom, or כתיפו על, *on his shoulder*, is guilty; for so carried the Kohathites."
And particularly it is said[19] that,
"He that rolls up a bed of the brasiers or tinkers (that is, on the sabbath day) is bound to a sin offering;"
which was a fold up bed, such as tinkers, and those that went from city to city to work, had; and who carried their beds with them, as the gloss observes; and were so far from being lawful to be carried by them on the sabbath, that they might not fold them up.

Verse 11. **He answered them**, &c. That is, the impotent man, who was now made whole, replied to the Jews:

---

[17] Maimon. Hilchot Sabbat, c. 12. sect. 8.

[18] Mishna Sabbat, c. 10. sect. 3.

[19] T. Bab. Sabbat, fol. 47. 1. & 138. 1.

he that made me whole, the same said unto me, take up thy bed and walk. Intimating, that He that had such divine power, as to make him whole, had power to dispense with the sabbath, and such an action on it; and that His word was warrant and authority sufficient to support Him in what He did; for He that had wrought this cure for him, he concluded must be from God; was at least a great prophet, and to be hearkened to and obeyed, in one thing as well as another.

Verse 12. **Then asked they him,** &c. Suspecting who had made him whole, and gave him this order:

What man is that which said unto thee, Take up thy bed and walk? They take no notice of the cure, being unwilling to give any glory to Christ, and still less to spread it; but chose rather that it should be obscured, hid, and unobserved; but they laid hold on that which they thought might be improved to His reproach and scandal; and they call Him a man, as supposing Him to be a mere man, and a wicked man too, for giving orders to transgress a tradition of the elders, though no mere man could work such a cure as this was. And so the Jews since, though they cannot find fault with the cure, which they put an *if* upon, yet are highly displeased with the order to take up his bed and carry it:

"If (say they,[20]) he wrought a cure, lo, that is good, but why did he bid him take up his bed?"
The answer may be, "To show that he was cured."

Verse 13. **And he that was healed, wist not who it was**, &c. The impotent man had never seen, and perhaps had never heard of Christ before, and so knew Him not; and besides, Christ gave him no opportunity of conversing with Him, or so much as to ask Him who He was:

for Jesus had conveyed himself away; had slidden [or slipped] away, as soon as ever He had wrought the miracle:

a multitude being in *that* place. Or *from the multitude that were in* that *place*; not that He hid Himself among them, and there remained undiscovered; but He passed through them, and went His way to the temple, where He found the man He had healed, as in the following verse.

Verse 14. **Afterward Jesus findeth him in the temple**, &c. Perhaps Jesus found him there on the same day; for as soon as he had been at home, and laid down his bed, it is very likely he went directly to the temple, there to show

---

[20] Vet. Nizzachon, p. 207.

himself, attend the worship of the place, and return thanks to God for the great mercy bestowed on him:

and said unto him, Behold thou art made whole; cured of the disease that had troubled him so many years; and a wonderful cure it was. Well may a *behold* be prefixed; though this is here not only a note of admiration, but of attention, to what He was about to say to him. Sin is a disease, which is original, natural, and hereditary to men; it is an epidemical one, all are affected with it, and all the powers and faculties of the soul; and it is a nauseous and loathsome one; and what is mortal and incurable in itself, and only to be cured by the great physician, Jesus Christ: God's elect are attended with it as others, and being made sensible thereof, they come to Christ for a cure, and receive one, as this man did, to whom He said,

sin no more; intimating, that as all diseases of the body spring from sin, so had his; and that the time past of his life should suffice, for a course of sinning; and that the mercy he had received, laid him under an obligation to guard against it, to which there would still be a proneness in him. Nor did our Lord imagine, that he could hereafter live without sin, but that he should not indulge himself in it, and give up himself unto it, and live in it. So all the diseases of the soul arise from sin; and when a person is converted, he ought not to walk as others do, or as he himself has done: and though there is a propensity to sin and backslide from God after conversion, yet the grace of God teaches men to deny sin, and to live righteously; and though it cannot be thought that they should be, and act without sin, yet it becomes them not to live in sin, or go on in a course of it, as heretofore:

lest a worse thing come unto thee. For God could send a worse disease, or a sorer affliction, than He had yet done; a heavier punishment, either in this world, or that to come. And apply this to a good man, a converted man, one called by grace, and cured by Christ, and a worse thing through sin may come unto him than a bodily disorder, namely, the hidings of God's face [*e.g. Psa. 30:7*]; for as His presence is life, His absence is death, to such persons; and as for such who only make a profession of religion, and are externally reformed only, such, if they sin and fall away, their *latter end is worse than the beginning* [2 Pet. 2:20].

Verse 15. **The man departed**, &c. From Christ, and from the temple, not through displeasure, or as resenting what was said to him, but as highly delighted that he had found his kind benefactor and physician; and went either to Bethesda, where the miracle was wrought, and where a multitude of people were, and where he might expect to find some of the persons that had questioned him about carrying his bed, and who it was that bid him do it;

or rather to the Sanhedrin; see *verse 33* [following] compared with *chapter 1:19*;

and told the Jews; the members of that great council, the chief priests, scribes, and elders, whose business it was to judge of a prophet, and of any one that should set up for the Messiah:

that it was Jesus; of Nazareth, of whom so much talk was about His doctrines and miracles, and who was thought to be the Messiah:

which had made him whole. This he did, not out of any ill will to Christ, or with any bad design upon Him, to impeach and accuse Him as a violator of the sabbath, for what He had said and done to him; for this would have been most ungrateful, and even barbarous, brutish, and diabolical; but with a good intention, that Jesus might have the glory of the cure, and that others of his fellow creatures in distress might know where, and from whom to have relief; and chiefly that the Sanhedrin might be induced hereby to believe that Jesus was the Messiah, and to declare and patronize Him as such: and that his end was good, is clear from this, that he does not say it was Jesus that bid him take up his bed and walk, which was what the Jews cavilled at, not caring to hear of the cure; but that made him whole: he observes the miracle to them with a grateful spirit, to the honor of his physician, and that He might be thought to be what He really was.

Verse 16. **And therefore did the Jews persecute Jesus**, &c. Persecuted Him with their tongues, reproaching and reviling Him, as a sabbath-breaker, a destroyer of the law, and a sinful wicked man:

and sought to slay him; either in a violent way, by setting the *zealots*, a sort of ruffians under the pretense of religion, upon Him; or rather in a judicial way, summoning him before the Sanhedrin, in order to condemn Him to death for the breach of the sabbath, which by the law of Moses was punishable with death:

because he had done these things on the sabbath day. Because He had cured the man of his disease, under which he had labored eight and thirty years, and had ordered him to take up his bed, and walk home with it on his back on the sabbath day. This drew upon Him their resentment, to such a degree, that they not only persecuted Him with their tongues, but sought to take away His life. Nothing would satisfy them but His blood.

Verse 17. **But Jesus answered them**, &c. Being convened before them, and charged by them with the violation of the sabbath, He vindicated Himself in the following manner, saying;

my Father worketh hitherto: He who is my Father, not by creation, or adoption, but by nature, though He ended all His work on the seventh day, and rested from what He had done; yet He did not cease from working at all, but has continued to work ever since, on sabbath days, as well as on other days; in upholding and governing the world, in continuing the species of beings, and all creatures in their being; in providing for them, and in dispensing the bounties of His providence to them; in causing His sun to shine, and showers of rain to descend on the earth; and in taking care of, and protecting even the meanest [or lowliest] of His creatures: and much more men; and still more His own people:

and I work. Or, *also I work*; as the Syriac and Arabic versions read; that is, in conjunction with Him, as a coefficient cause in the works of providence, in the government of the world, in upholding all things in it, in bearing up the pillars of the earth [*1 Sam. 2:8; Psa. 75:3*], in holding things together, and sustaining all creatures: or, I also work in imitation of Him, in doing good both to the bodies and souls of men on the sabbath day, being the Lord of it: I do but what my Father does, and therefore, as He is not to be blamed for His works on that day, as none will say He is, no more am I. So Philo the Jew says,[21]

"God never ceases to work; but as it is the property of fire to burn, and of snow to cool, so of God to work."

And what most men call Fortune, He calls the divine *Logos*, or Word, to whom He ascribes all the affairs of providence.[22]

Verse 18. **Therefore the Jews sought the more to kill him**, &c. The Jews were therefore the more desirous to take away His life, and were more bent and resolute upon it, and studied all ways and means how to bring it about;

because he had not only broken the sabbath; as they imagined; for He had not really broken it: and if they had known what that means, that God *will have mercy, and not sacrifice* [*Matt. 9:13*], they would have been convinced that He had not broken it by this act of mercy to a poor distressed object:

but said also that God was his Father; His own Father, His proper Father, His Father by nature, and that He was His own Son by nature; and this they gathered from His calling Him *my Father*, and assuming a cooperation with Him in His divine works:

---

[21] Leg. Allegor. l. 1. p. 41.

[22] Quod Deus sit Immutab. p. 318.

making himself to be equal with God. To be of the same nature, and have the same perfections, and do the same works; for by saying that God was His Father, and so that He was the Son of God, a phrase, which, with them, signified a divine person, as they might learn from *Psa. 2:7,12*; and by ascribing the same operations to Himself as to His Father, they rightly understood Him, that He asserted His equality with Him; for had He intended no more, and had they imagined that He intended no more by calling God His Father, than that He was so by creation, as He is to all men, or by adoption, as He was to the Jews, they would not have been so angry with Him; for the phrase, in this sense, they used themselves: but they understood Him otherwise, as asserting His proper deity, and perfect equality with the Father; and therefore to the charge of sabbath-breaking, they added that of blasphemy, and on account of both, sought to put him to death; for, according to their canons, both the sabbath-breaker and the blasphemer were to be stoned.[23]

Verse 19. **Then answered Jesus, and said unto them**, &c. They charged Him with blasphemy for calling God His Father, and making Himself equal to Him: and His answer is so far from denying the thing, or observing any mistake, or misrepresentation of His words, that He allows the whole, and vindicates Himself in so saying:

Verily verily, I say unto you; nothing is more certain; it may be depended on as truth; I who am truth itself, the *Amen*, and faithful witness, aver it with the greatest assurance:

The Son can do nothing of himself; or He does do nothing of Himself, nor will He do any thing of Himself; that is, He neither does, nor will, nor can do any thing alone or separate from His Father, or in which He is not concerned; not any thing without His knowledge and consent, or contrary to His will: He does every thing in conjunction with Him; with the same power, having the same will, being of the same nature, and equal to each other: for these words do not design any weakness in the Son, or want [*or* lack] of power in Him to do any thing of Himself; that is, by His own power: for He has by His word of power spoken all things out of nothing, and by the same upholds all things [*Heb. 1:3*]; He has Himself borne the sins of His people, and by Himself purged them away, and has raised Himself from the dead; but they express His perfection, that He does nothing, and can do nothing of Himself, in opposition to His Father, and in contradiction to His will. As Satan speaks of his own; and evil men, alienated from God, act of themselves, and do that which is contrary to the nature and will of God; but the Son cannot do so, being of the

---

[23] Mishna Sanhedrin, c. 7. sect. 4.

same nature with God, and therefore never acts separate from Him, or contrary to Him, but always cooperates and acts with Him, and therefore is never to be blamed for what He does. The Syriac, Arabic, and Persic versions render it, *the Son cannot do any thing of his own will*; so Nonnus; as separate from, or contrary to His Father's will, but always in agreement with it, they being one in nature, and so in will and work. He does nothing therefore,

but what he seeth the Father do; not that He sees the Father actually do a work, and then He does one after Him, as the creation of the world, the assumption of human nature, and redemption of man, or any particular miracle, as if upon observing one done, He did the like; but that He being brought up with Him, and lying in His bosom [*chapter 1:18*], was privy to the whole plan of His works, and saw in His nature and infinite mind, and in His vast counsels, purposes, and designs, all that He was doing, or would do, and so did the same, or acted agreeably to them; and which still shows and proves their unity of nature, and perfect equality, since there was nothing in the Father's mind but was known to the Son, seen, and observed, and acted up to by Him. So Philo the Jew[24] says of the,

> "Father's most ancient Son, whom he otherwise calls *the firstborn*; that being begotten, he imitates the Father, and *seeing*, or *looking to his exemplars and archetypes*, forms species;"

that is, being conversant with the original and eternal ideas of things in the divine mind, acts according to them, which He could not do if He was not of the same nature with, and equal to His Father. Moreover, the Son sees what the Father does by cooperating with Him, and so does no other than what He sees the Father do, in conjunction with Him: to which may be added, that the phrase shows, that the Son does nothing but in wisdom, and with knowledge; and that as the Father, so He does all things after the counsel of His will:

for whatsoever things he doeth, these also doeth the Son likewise. The Son does the selfsame works as the Father does, such as the works of creation and providence, the government both of the church, and of the world; and He does these things in like manner, with the same power, and by the same authority His Father does, and which proves Him to be equal with Him; the very thing the Jews understood Him to have asserted, and which they charged Him with: and this He strongly maintained. The Syriac version reads, *for the things which the Father does, the same also does the Son*; and the Persic version, *whatsoever God has done, the Son also does like unto it*.

Verse 20. **For the Father loveth the Son**, &c. As being His Son, His image, *the brightness of His glory, and the express image of His person* [*Heb. 1:3*]; as

---

[24] De Confus. Ling. p. 329.

being of the same nature, and having the same perfections, and so equal to Him; see the note on *chapter 3:35;*

and showeth him all things that himself doeth; not as if He was ignorant of them, since He lies in the bosom of His Father [*chapter 1:18*], is *the wisdom of God* [*1 Cor. 1:24*], is the omniscient God, that knows all things; not only all things in men, but all things in God, even the deep things of God: but this is said of the Father, as consulting with Him, communicating His designs to Him, as His equal; doing nothing without Him, as He never did in the works of nature, or of grace: He drew the plan of peace, reconciliation, and salvation in Him; He made the worlds by Him; and He does nothing in the government of the world without Him; and indeed He shows Him all things He does, by doing all things; and by Him He shows Himself, and His works, to men:

and he will show him greater works than these; or He will do greater works by Him than these: either than the works of creation; namely, the redemption of the elect, the justification of their persons by His righteousness, and pardon of their sins through His blood, and the regeneration and conversion of them by His Spirit and grace; either of which is a greater work than the making of the world: or greater than He has done under the Old Testament dispensation; than the redeeming of Israel out of Egypt, leading them through the wilderness, and settling them in the land of Canaan; giving them the law, the statutes, and ordinances of God, and working miracles among them: for the redemption of God's people, by Christ, from sin, Satan, the world, the law, death, and hell, the publishing of the Gospel, the effusion of the Spirit, and setting up of the Gospel dispensation, are greater works than these; and more and greater miracles were wrought by Christ than by Moses, or any prophet under the former dispensation. Though rather the sense is, that greater miracles would be shown, and done by Christ, than these He had now done, in curing a man of his disorder, who had had it eight and thirty years, and bidding him take up his bed and walk; such as raising Jairus's daughter to life, when dead, and the widow of Nain's son, when he was carrying to the grave, and Lazarus, when he had been dead four days:

that ye may marvel. This was not properly the end of these greater works shown to, and done by Christ, which were to prove His divine Sonship, His proper deity, His true Messiahship, to confirm the faith of His followers in Him, and for the glory of God; but this eventually followed upon them: some wondered at them, and believed in Him; and others were amazed at them, and confounded by them.

Verse 21. **For as the Father raiseth up the dead, and quickeneth *them*,** &c. Which may be understood either spiritually, of raising dead sinners from the death of sin, to a life of grace and holiness; and the rather, because it is expressed in the present tense *raiseth*, and not *hath raised*; or naturally, of raising those that are dead in a corporeal sense, and quickening them, as the widow of Sarepta's son by Elijah, and the Shunamite's son by Elisha:

even so the Son quickeneth whom he will. Both in a spiritual sense, being *the resurrection and the life* [*chapter 11:25*], or the author of the resurrection from a moral death to a spiritual life, whose voice, in the Gospel, the dead in sin hear and live; and in a natural sense, as in the above instances of Jairus's daughter, the widow of Nain's son, and Lazarus; and in the general resurrection, when at His voice, and word of power, all that are in their graves shall come forth, some to everlasting life, and some to everlasting damnation [see *verse 28*]; and all this as He wills: He quickens, in a spiritual sense, whom He pleases, even as many as the Father has given Him [see *chapter 6:37*]; and He will raise up to everlasting life, at the last day, whom He pleases, even as many as were made His care and charge, whom He has redeemed by His blood, and called by His grace. Now as the quickening of the dead is an act of almighty power, and this being exercised by the Son in a sovereign way, as is by His Father, it shows His proper Deity, and full equality with the Father. The resurrection of the dead is here expressed by *quickening,* as it frequently is by the Jews, who often speak of, תחיית המתים, *the quickening the dead*, for the resurrection; so the Targumist on *Zech. 3:8, In the quickening of the dead*, אחיינך, *I will quicken thee*; see the Jerusalem Targum on *Gen. 19:26* and *25:34.*

Verse 22. **For the Father judgeth no man**, &c. That is, He judgeth none without the Son; which is another proof of their equality: for that He does judge is certain; He is the Judge of the whole earth; He is God that judgeth in the earth, or governs the world with His Son, who works together in the affairs of providence: He judged and condemned the old world, but not without His Son, who by His Spirit, or in His divine nature, went and preached to the spirits now in prison, then disobedient in the times of Noah [*1Pet. 3:19-20*]; He judged and condemned Sodom and Gomorrah, but not without the Son; for Jehovah the Son rained, from Jehovah the Father, fire and brimstone upon those cities, and consumed them [see *Gen. 18:1-33* and *19:21, 24-25*]; He judged the people of Israel, and often chastised them for their sins, but not without His Son; the *angel of His presence* that went before them [see *Ex. 14:19; 23:20, 23; 32:34*; and *33:2; Isa. 63:9*]; He judges all men, and justifies and acquits whom He pleases, but not without His Son; but through His justifying righteousness, which He imputes to them; in doing which He appears to be a just judge, and to do right; and *He will judge the world in righteousness* at the last day by His Son, *whom He has ordained* [*Acts 17:31*]; so as the Son does nothing without the Father, the Father does nothing without the Son, which shows perfect equality. The Jews had an officer in their Sanhedrin, whom they called "Ab Beth Din," or *the father of the house of* *judgment*, to whom belonged the trying of causes, and of judging and determining them. Hence the Targumist on *Song of Sol. 7:4* says,

"ואב בית דינא, *and the father of the house of judgment*, who judgeth thy

judgments, or determines thy causes, is mighty over thy people, &c."
Whether there may not be some allusion here to this officer, I leave to be considered:

but hath committed all judgment to the Son. As the judgment, or government of His church and people, especially under the Gospel dispensation; and which He exercises by giving ordinances peculiar to it, such as baptism and the Lord's supper; and by enacting laws, and prescribing rules for the discipline of His house, over which He is as a Son; and by appointing proper officers under Him, over His churches, to administer these ordinances, and see that these laws are put in execution, which He qualifies them for, by bestowing proper gifts upon them; and He exercises this judgment, by protecting and defending His people from all their enemies, so that they dwell safely under His government: as also the general judgment of the world at the last day is committed to Him; which affair will be managed by Christ, the Son of God, when He comes a second time; He will then raise the dead, *that everyone may receive for the things done in his body*, whether good or evil [*2 Cor. 5:10*]; He will gather all nations before Him, and all shall stand before His judgment seat, both great and small; He will separate one from another, the sheep from the goats, and set the one on His right hand, and the other on His left; He will bring every work into judgment, with every secret thing, and show Himself to be the searcher of the hearts, and the trier of the reins of the children of men, and will pass a most righteous and decisive sentence upon all. Now for such a trust, and such a work as this, whether the particular government of the church, or the general judgment of the world, He would not be fit, was He not God equal with the Father; the thing He had suggested, and which He supports and maintains in this vindication of Himself.

Verse 23. **That all *men* should honor the Son**, &c. This honor is the end of all judgment to the Son, the exercise of all authority and power being committed to Him; namely, that He might have the honor given Him by men that is due unto Him:

even as they honor the Father. That the same honor and glory may be given to the one, as to the other; which must never have been done was He not equal with Him, since He gives not His glory to another, *Isa. 42:8* and *48:11*. Indeed, all men do not honor the Father as they should; the Gentiles, who had some knowledge of God, *glorified Him not as God* [*Rom. 1:21*]; and the Jews, who had an external revelation of the one, true, and living God, which other nations had not, yet were greatly deficient in honoring Him, which made Him complain, and say, *If then I be a Father, where is mine honor? Mal. 1:6*. And

Christians, who are favored with a clearer revelation still of the Father of Christ, are much wanting [or lacking] in giving Him His due glory; but in common He is honored, though in an imperfect manner; nor is there so much danger of the Father's losing His honor, as of the Son's losing His; the reason is this, though the Son is in the form of God, and equal with Him, yet by taking upon Him *the form of a servant*, by becoming man, He has veiled the glory of His divine person, and *made himself of no reputation* [*Phil. 2:7*]; and by reason of this was reckoned by many, or most, as a mere man: wherefore, by agreement, that judgment, power, and authority, which equally belonged to the Father, and the Son, the exercise of it is put visibly and openly into the Son's hands, that He might have His due honor and glory from all men, whether they will or not: from true believers in Him He has it willingly, by their ascribing Deity to Him, by putting their trust in Him, by attributing the whole of their salvation to Him, and the glory of it, and by worshiping Him: and He will be honored by all men at the last day; they will be obliged to do it; for all judgment being committed to Him, and He being Judge of all, *every knee shall bow* to Him, and *every tongue shall confess* that He *is Lord*, to His own glory, and to the glory of God the Father; see *Isa. 45:23; Phil. 2:10-11*.

He that honoreth not the Son; that denies His divine Sonship, or His proper Deity; that detracts from the dignity of His person or office; that shows no regard to Him in point of salvation, or of obedience:

honoreth not the Father which hath sent him. They are so the same in nature and perfections, in power, will, affections, and operations; and their interests and honors are so involved together, that whatever dishonor is done to one, reflects on the other: and indeed, whatever is done in a way of disrespect to the Son, as incarnate, and in his office capacity, highly reflects on His Father, that sent Him in the fulness of time, in human nature, to obtain eternal redemption for His people [*Gal. 4:4-6*], according to a rule often expressed by the Jews, *A man's messenger is as himself*; see the note on *Matt. 10:40* **[15]**.

Verse 24. **Verily verily, I say unto you**, &c. Who am *the Amen, the faithful and true witness* [*Rev. 3:14*]:

He that heareth my word; by which is meant the Gospel, and is so called, both because it is spoken by Christ, and first began to be spoken by Him; and because He is spoken of in it; His person, office, and work, peace, pardon, righteousness, life, and salvation by Him, being the sum and substance of it: and by *hearing* it, is meant, not a bare external hearing it; for so it may be heard, and not understood; and it may be understood in a notional and speculative way, and yet the consequences hereafter mentioned may not follow: but an internal hearing it is here designed, so as to understand it spiritually, or to have an experimental knowledge of it; so as to approve of it, love, and like it; to distinguish it from that which is not His doctrine, and to feel the power of it on the heart, and yield the obedience of faith unto it: for faith in Christ Himself, the sum and substance of the Word of the Gospel, is hereby expressed; to which is joined faith in God His Father, they being equally the object of it; and which is introduced as a further proof of the equality in nature which is between them; see *chapter 14:1*;

and believeth on him that sent me; He does not say that believes on me, which might have been expected from Him; but that believes on Him that sent me, that is, on the Father; for as he that rejects Christ, and receives not His words, rejects and receives not Him that sent Him; so he that hears Christ's words, and receives Him, and believes in Him, receives and believes in Him that sent Him; and the same effects and consequences follow upon the one as on the other, upon hearing the Word of Christ, as upon believing on the Father of Christ; and which is no inconsiderable proof of their perfect equality: for such a person that hears the one, and believes on the other,

hath everlasting life; not only in the purpose of God, and in the covenant of His grace, and in the hands of Christ, and in faith and hope; but he has a right unto it, and a claim of it, according to the declaration of the Gospel; and besides, has the principle of it in himself, the grace of God, which springs up into, is the beginning of, and issues in eternal life; he also has a meetness for it, and has the pledge and earnest of it, the Spirit of God, and shall certainly enjoy it:

and shall not come into condemnation; neither for original sin, though *judgment* has passed *upon all men unto condemnation* for it [*Rom. 5:18*]; nor for actual sins and transgressions; for though everyone deserves condemnation, yet were there as many sentences of condemnation issued out as sins committed, not one of them could be executed on such who are in Christ Jesus, as he that believes in Him is openly and manifestatively in Him: the reason is, because the death of Christ is a security against all condemnation; and whoever believes in Him shall not be condemned, but saved; and though he may come into judgment, yet not into condemnation: he shall stand in judgment, and be acquitted by the righteousness of Christ, which he, by faith, receives as his justifying righteousness;

but is passed from death unto life. Both from a moral death to a spiritual life, being quickened, who before was *dead in trespasses and sins* [*Eph. 2:1*]; and from under a sentence of condemnation, and eternal death, which, as a descendant of Adam, and according to the tenor of the law of works, he was subject to, to an open state of justification, according to the tenor of the covenant of grace; the righteousness of Christ being revealed to him, and

167

received by faith, and the sentence of justification passed upon his conscience by the Spirit; so that he who before, in his own apprehension, was a dead man in a law sense, is now alive to God, and secure from the second death, and being hurt by it.

Verse 25. **Verily, verily, I say unto you**, &c. He says, with the same asseveration as before, and for the further illustration and confirmation of the same thing, occasioned by the last clause of the preceding verse, as well as improving upon the argument in *verse 21*, for His equality with the Father, which He is still pursuing:

The hour is coming, and now is, when the dead shall hear the voice of the Son of God, and they that hear shall live. Which may be understood either of a corporeal resurrection, and of some particular instances of it, which should shortly be; and of some persons who would be in the state of the dead, and to whom the voice of Christ would be attended with such power as to cause them to hear and live; as did Jairus's daughter upon his saying, "Talitha Cumi," *damsel arise*; and the widow of Nain's son, upon His saying, *Young man arise*; and Lazarus, upon His calling to him, *Lazarus, come forth*; and which is a full proof of His being equal to God that quickens the dead: or rather, this is to be understood of a spiritual resurrection, and the rather, because this sense best agrees with the foregoing verse; and a corporeal resurrection is expressed in somewhat different words, and seems to be distinguished from this in *verses 28-29*. And besides, the hour, or time of the resurrection of the above particular persons, was not strictly come; nor could they, with propriety, be said to be *dead*; to which may be added, that the phrase, *they that hear shall live*, and none but them, best agrees with this sense: so then by the *dead* are meant such who are dead in trespasses and sins; who are separated from God, *alienated from the life of God* [*Eph. 4:18*], and in whom the image of God is defaced; who are dead in all the powers and faculties of their souls, to that which is spiritually good; and are without spiritual breath, sense, feeling, and motion. And by *the voice* of Christ is intended His Gospel, which is a voice of love, grace, and mercy, of life and liberty, of peace, pardon, righteousness, and salvation by Him; and which being attended with His power, is the means of quickening dead sinners; who may be said to *hear* it, when it comes not in word only, but in power, and works effectually in them; and is spirit and life [see *chapter 6:63*], and *the power of God unto salvation* to them [*Rom. 1:16*], when they receive it, understand, believe, and obey it: and such persons *shall live*; comfortably, pleasantly, and delightfully, a life of faith on Christ, a life of communion with Him, and shall live eternally with Him hereafter.

Verse 26. **For as the Father hath life in himself,** &c. As He is the living God, the fountain of life, and is the author of life to all living creatures; or rather has eternal life in His mind, His heart, His counsel, and His covenant, and in His hands, for all His chosen ones, which seems to be the peculiar sense here:

so hath he given to the Son to have life in himself; He hath not only made the purpose of it in Him, and given the promise of it to Him; but even eternal life itself He has put into His hands, and secured it in Him for them, *1 John 5:11*, to give it to as many as He has given Him: and He does give it to all His sheep, so that not one of them shall perish; which shows that He and His Father are one, though not in person, yet as in affection, will, and power, so in nature and essence. The Son has *life in himself*, essentially, originally, and inderivatively as the Father has, being equally the living God, the fountain of life, and donor of it, as He; and therefore this is not a life which He gives, or communicates to Him; but eternal life is what the one gives, and the other receives, according to the economy of salvation settled between them: and hence it is, that all that hear Christ's voice spiritually shall live eternally; for these words are a reason of the former, and confirm the truth of them, as well as show the equality of the Son with the Father, in that He is equal to such a trust, as to have eternal life committed to Him.

Verse 27. **And hath given him authority to execute judgment also,** &c. Both in His church and kingdom, in the present state of things, and at the last day, when all shall stand before His judgment seat: and that,

because he is the Son of man. Truly and properly man; because, though He was in the form of God, and equal to Him, yet became man, and was in the form of a servant [see *Phil. 2:5-11*]: and so reads the Ethiopic version, *because the Son of God is the Son of man*; and therefore the authority of executing judgment, according to the council and covenant of peace, is committed to Him; or that men might have a visible judge, or be judged by one in their own nature: agreeably the Persic version renders it, *because the Son himself is he who judges the sons of men*; or rather, because He is that *Son of man* spoken of in prophecy, especially in *Dan. 7:13*; by whom is meant the *Messiah*, as the Jews themselves allow,[25] and who was not a mere man, but the man God's fellow; and so being both omniscient and omnipotent, was equal to such a work, which otherwise He would not have been; see the note on *verse 22*. The Syriac version joins this clause to the beginning of the next verse, and reads it thus, *because he is the Son of man, marvel not at this*; let this be no

---

[25] Zohar in Gen. fol. 85. 4. Bemidbar Rabba, sect. 13. fol. 209. 4. Jarchi & Saadiah Gaon in Dan. 7:13. & R. Jeshuah in Aben Ezra in ibid.

obstruction to your faith of His quickening the dead, and having authority to execute judgment on all; since, though the Son of man, He is not a mere man, but God *over all* [*Rom. 9:5*], as what is next ascribed to Him manifestly shows.

Verse 28. **Marvel not at this**, &c. Either at the cure of the man that had been diseased thirty and eight years, as some think; or at the Son of God being also the Son of man, as the Syriac version suggests; or rather at the dead hearing the voice of the Son of God, and living upon it; and at His having authority to execute judgment upon all, to govern and defend His own church and people, and in the last day acquit them, and to take vengeance on His and their enemies, both now and hereafter:

for the hour is coming, in which all that are in their graves shall hear his voice; this respects the general resurrection; for there will be a resurrection *both of the just and unjust* [*Acts 24:15*], of all that are in their graves; and though all that are dead are not in graves, or interred in the earth, as some are in the sea &c.; yet, because the greater part are in *graves*, this phrase is chosen to express the universality of the resurrection: and this is also a proof of the resurrection of the same body; for what else are in the graves, but bodies? And what else can come forth from them, but the same bodies? And the time is hastening on when these bodies shall be quickened, and *hear* the *voice* of the Son of God; which whether the same with the voice of the archangel in *1 Thess. 4:16*; and whether an articulate voice, or a violent clap of thunder, which is the voice of God [*e.g. Psa. 77:18* and *104:7*], or only the exertion of Christ's mighty power is intended, is not easy to determine, and may be needless to inquire. Certain it is, that this voice of Christ will be attended with almighty power, as the effect following upon it will show. The Jews observe[26] that,

> "There are three things which do not come into the world but *by voices;* there is the voice of a living creature, as it is written, *Gen. 3:16, in sorrow thou shalt bring forth children*, and as it is written, *Gen. 30:22, and God hearkened to her*; and there is the voice of rains, as it is written, *1 Kings 18:4, for there is a voice of abundance of rain*, and it is written, *Psa. 29:3, the voice of the Lord is upon the waters*; and קול תחיית המתים, *there is the voice of the resurrection of the dead*, as it is written, *Isa. 40:3, the voice of him that crieth in the wilderness;*"

but that was the voice of John the Baptist. It will be the voice of the Son of God that will quicken and raise the dead.

Verse 29. **And shall come forth**, &c. Out of their graves, as Lazarus came

---

[26] Zohar in Gen. fol. 70. 4.

forth from his at the word of command, and as the bodies of the saints did after the resurrection of Christ, when their graves were opened:

they that have done good; which none of Adam's posterity naturally do, or can do of themselves: such are designed here who *believe* in Christ, which to do *is the work of God* [*chapter 6:29*], and the greatest and best of works; and without which *it is impossible to please God* in any [*Heb. 11:6*]; and indeed, *whatever is not of faith is sin* [*Rom. 14:23*], and cannot be a *good* work: a good work is that which is done according to the will of God, from love to Him, in faith, and with a view to His glory; and those that do such works shall come forth,

unto the resurrection of life; that is, unto everlasting life, glory, and happiness; this is the first and better resurrection; and those that have part in it, over them the second death shall have no power. All shall rise to life, to an immortal life, so as never to die more; yet only good men shall rise to enjoy a happy and glorious life; which will lie in communion with God, angels, and saints, and in conformity to Christ, and in the everlasting vision of Him:

and they that have done evil; who give up themselves to work wickedness; whose continual employment, and the business, series, and course of whose lives it is to commit sin; who are slaves unto it, and vassals of it, and are properly *workers of iniquity* [*e.g. Psa. 5:5; Prov. 10:29*]; otherwise there is no man but what does that which is evil, and that daily: these shall come forth,

unto the resurrection of damnation. That is, to everlasting damnation, shame, and reproach; they shall be condemned by the Judge of the whole earth [*Gen. 18:25*], and shall be pronounced cursed; and shall be ordered to go into everlasting fire, and shall go into everlasting punishment; which will be a punishment both of loss and sense: they will lose, or be deprived of, the presence of God, and feel His wrath in their consciences. All will rise, but with a difference; *the dead in Christ will rise first* [*1 Thess. 4:16; 1 Cor. 15:23*], in the morning of the resurrection, in the beginning of the thousand years, and therefore are here mentioned first; the rest, the wicked, will not rise until the evening of that day, till the thousand years are ended, and therefore are spoken of last. The former will rise by virtue of union to Christ, the other by His power, and both at hearing His voice; the saints will rise with bodies glorious, powerful, and spiritual; and wicked men, though with bodies immortal, yet vile and dishonorable: the one will rise to a life of joy and happiness that will last for ever, and which will be properly *life*; the other, though they will rise and live for ever, yet in misery and woe, and which will be the second, or eternal *death* [see *Rev. chapter 20*]; see a like distinction in *Dan. 12:2*, to which there seems to be some reference here. And He at whose voice all this shall be, must be equal to God.

171

Verse 30. **I can of mine own self do nothing,** &c. This is the conclusion of the matter, the winding up of the several arguments concerning the Son's equality to the Father, and the application of the whole to Christ. He had before been chiefly speaking of the Son, in relation to the Father, as if He was a third person; but now He applies what He had said of the Son to Himself: and it is as if He had said, I am the Son that can do nothing separate from the Father, and contrary to His will, but do all things in conjunction with Him; who sees all that He does, by being in Him, and cooperating with Him, and do the selfsame. I am the Son to whom the Father shows, and by whom He does, all He does; and to whom He will show, and by whom He will do, as a coefficient with Him, greater works than what, as yet, He has done: I am the Son that quickens whom He pleases, and to whom all judgment is committed, and have the same honor the Father has: I am He that quickens dead sinners now, and will raise all the dead at the last day; and have authority to execute judgment on all mankind: and,

as I hear, I judge; not as He hears men, or, according to the evidence men will give one of another; for it is denied of Him that He will proceed in judgment in this manner, *Isa. 11:3,* but as He hears His Father; for being in His bosom, and one with Him, as He sees, and knows all He does, His whole plan of operations, and acts according to them; so He hears, knows, and is perfectly acquainted with all His counsels, purposes, and rules of judgment, and never deviates from them. *Hearing* here signifies perfect knowledge, and understanding of a cause; and so it is used in the Jewish writings, in matters of difficulty, that come before a court of judicature:[27]

> "There were three courts of judicature; one that sat at the gate of the mountain of the house; and one that sat at the gate of the court; and another that sat in the paved chamber: they go (first) to that which is at the gate of the mountain of the house, and say, so have I expounded, and so have the companions expounded; so have I taught, and so have the companions (or colleagues) taught: אם שמעו, *if they hear,* they say (that is, as one of their commentators explains it,[28] if they know the law, and hear, or understand the sense of the law; in such a case they declare what they know); if not, they go to them that are at the gate of the court, and say (as before).—And, *if they hear,* they tell them; but if not, they go to the great Sanhedrin in the paved chamber, from whence goes forth the law to all Israel."

Christ was now before the great Sanhedrin, and speaks to them in their own

---

[27] Mishna Sanhedrin, c. 10. sect. 2.

[28] Maimon. in ibid.

language, and as a superior judge to them:

and my judgment is just; in the administration of the affairs of His church, which are done in the strictest justice; *just and true are all His ways*, as *King of saints* [*Rev. 15:3*]; and in the execution of the last judgment, which will be in righteousness and truth; the judgment He passes must be right, since it is according to that perfect knowledge He has of His Father's will, which is an infallible rule of judgment:

because I seek not mine own will, but the will of the Father which hath sent me. That is, He did not seek to gratify His own will, as distinct from His Father's, or in opposition to it; for He had no private end to answer, or separate interest, or advantage to pursue; and seeing therefore He acted according to His Father's will, and not His own, as contrary to that; His judgment must be just, and the sentence He passes right; since the will of God is indisputably such. The Vulgate Latin, and all the Oriental versions, the Alexandrian copy, and two of Beza's copies, leave out the word *Father,* without altering or hurting the sense at all.

Verse 31. **If I bear witness of myself**, &c. Which it was not allowed any man to do; nor indeed is it proper that a man should be a witness in his own cause: and, according to the Jewish canons, a man might not be a witness for his wife, because she was reckoned as himself.

> "A husband is not to be believed in bearing witness for his wife, that had been carried captive, that she is not defiled, שאין אדם מעיד לעצמו, *for no man bears witness of himself.* "[29]

So likewise they say,[30]

> "A city that is subdued by an army, all the priestesses (or priests' daughters) that are found in it are rejected (from the priesthood, as defiled); but if they have witnesses, whether a servant, or a handmaid, lo, they are to be believed; but no man is to be believed for himself: says R. Zechariah ben Hakatzah, by this habitation (swearing by the temple) her hand was not removed from my hand, from the time the Gentiles entered Jerusalem, till they went out: they replied to him, *no man bears witness of himself.*"

Christ reasons here upon their own principles, and according to their sense of things, that should He bear witness of Himself; then, says He,

---

[29] Maimonides Issure Bia, c. 18. sect. 19.

[30] Mishna Cetubot, c. 2. sect. 9. T. Bab. Cetubot, fol. 27. 2. Juchasin, fol. 56. 1.

my witness is not true, לא נאמן, *not to be believed*, or admitted as an authentic testimony: and so the Ethiopic version renders it, *is not credible*; not valid in law, or in such a court of judicature in which Christ now was; for, as according to the Jewish law, no man was admitted a witness for himself, so neither was any thing established by a single testimony, but *by the mouth of two or three witnesses, Deut. 19:15*. Christ's meaning is, that His testimony alone, His single witness, how true soever it was, would stand for nothing in their court; and therefore He would not insist upon it, but drop it; for *true* here, is not opposed to that which is *false,* but to that which is not valid in law. Christ's testimony was true in itself; nor could it be any other, it coming from Him, who is truth itself, *the Amen*, and *faithful witness* [*Rev. 3:14*]; but being considered as a human testimony, and in His own cause, was not to be admitted as sufficient; and this He allows. From arguments, proving His equality with the Father, He passes to testimonies; and without making use of His own, He had enough to produce, and which were valid and authentic, and are as follow.

Verse 32. **There is another that beareth witness of me**, &c. Meaning not His Father, who is another, and a distinct person, from Him, as the Spirit is *another comforter* [*chapter 14:16*]; and both distinct testifiers from Him, as well as of Him. This is indeed the sense of some interpreters; but the Father is particularly mentioned in *verse 37*; and the thread of the discourse, and the climax, or gradation, here used, show, that it is to be understood of *another man*, as Nonnus paraphrases it; of John the Baptist, who is spoken of by name in the next verse, as a witness; and then a greater than he, the works of Christ, and then the Father:

and I know that the witness, which he witnesseth of me, is true. For John was now alive, though in prison, and continued to bear a testimony to Christ; and therefore He speaks of him as now bearing witness of Him, and abiding by that which he had borne; and Christ knew not only that what he testified of Him was true in itself, but that his testimony was a valid and authentic testimony, with the generality of the Jews; who held John to be a prophet, and looked upon him as a man of great probity and integrity, and whose word was to be taken: nor indeed could the Sanhedrin, before whom Christ now was, object to his character, nor to him as a witness; nor ought they, since they themselves had so judged of him, as appears by their message to him, which Christ next fails not to take notice of.

Verse 33. **Ye sent unto John**, &c. The Sanhedrin at Jerusalem made a deputation of priests and Levites to him, to know who he was, whether the Messiah, or Elias, or that prophet, *John 1:19*. Now had they not looked upon him, from what they knew of him, or from the character they had of him, as

174

a faithful witness, they would never have shown him so much respect, and have been at so much pains and charge, as to send such a body of men so far unto him, as from Jerusalem to beyond Jordan; which circumstance our Lord improves in favor of this evidence He produces:

and he bare witness unto the truth. To Christ, who is the Truth itself; and to the truth of His person, and office; to His dignity, and eternity, as being before him, though coming after him; and to His divine Sonship, the thing now in debate, declaring, that He was the Son of God; and to His office, as Mediator, pointing to Him as the Lamb of God, who, by His blood and sacrifice, takes away the sins of men. The Ethiopic version reads by way of interrogation, *Did you not send unto John?* &c.

Verse 34. **But I receive not testimony from man**, &c. He stood in no need of a human testimony, nor did He rest the truth of His Deity and divine Sonship thereon: He had other, and greater testimonies to produce; as He needed not that any man should testify of man to Him, He had no need that any man should testify of Him; and if the testimony of men was received, as this of John could not well be objected to, the testimony of God is greater, and which He had; and therefore should not have mentioned John's for his own sake:

but these things I say, that ye might be saved. That is, He produced this testimony of John, who was a person of so great a character among them, that they might be induced by it to believe in Him as the Messiah; and so be saved from that ruin and destruction, that would come upon their nation, city, and temple, for their rejection and disbelief of Him.

Verse 35. **He was a burning and a shining light**, &c. He *was not that Light*, the famous Light, the *Messiah*, the Sun of righteousness; yet he was the *phosphorus,* the forerunner of that Light, and was himself a very great one: he had much light himself into the person and office of the Messiah; in the doctrines of faith in Christ, and repentance towards God; in the Gospel dispensation, and in the abolition of the Mosaic economy; and gave great light to others, in the business of salvation, and remission of sins, and was the means of guiding the feet of many in the way of peace. His light of pure doctrine, and of a holy and exemplary conversation [or conduct], shone very visibly, and brightly before men; and he burned with strong love and affection for Christ, and the souls of men; and with flaming zeal for the honor of God, and true religion, and against all sin and profaneness, which he was a faithful reprover of, and for which he lost his life. It was common with the Jews to call their doctors, who were famous for their knowledge and holiness of life, *lights,* *burning lights*, and *shining lights*; or in words which amount to the same. So

175

R. Simeon ben Jochai is often called in the book of Zohar, בוצינא קדישא, *the holy light*; and particularly it is said of him,[31]

> "R. Simeon, כבוצינא דשרגא דאדליק, is as *the lamp of light which burns above*, and *burns* below; and by the light which burns below all the children of the world are enlightened: woe to the world, when the light below ascends to the light above."

So R. Abhu is called בוצינא דנהורא, *the lamp of light*:[32] and it is[33] said of Shuah, Judah's father-in-law, that he was בוצינא דאתרא, *the light of the place*; that is, where he lived. The gloss on the place says, *he was a man of note in the city, and enlightened their eyes*; and it is very frequent with them still, when they are praising any of their doctors, to say of him, he was הגדול , *a great light*, who enlightened the eyes of Israel, and in whose light the people walked;[34] so among the philosophers, Xenophon, and Plato, are called "duo lumina,"[35] *two lights*; see the note on *Matt. 5:14* **[8]**;

and ye were willing for a season, or *for an hour*,

to rejoice in his light. Or *to glory in it*, or *boast of* it, as the Syriac and Persic versions render it. When John first appeared among them, they were fond, and even proud of him; they gloried in him, that a man of such uncommon endowments, and of such exemplary holiness, was raised up among them; and hoped that he was the Messiah, or Elias, that was to come before Him; and pleased themselves, that times of great outward honor and prosperity were hastening on: wherefore they flocked about him, and many of the Pharisees and Sadducees attended his ministry, and would have been baptized by him; but when they found that he was not the Messiah, nor Elias, nor that prophet, but bore a testimony to Jesus of Nazareth, that He was the Messiah; and ran counter to their notions of a temporal kingdom, and of birth privileges, and their own righteousness; and threatened them with ruin and destruction, both in this world, and that which is to come, in case of their impenitence and unbelief; they grew sick of him, and said he had a devil, and rejected the counsel of God he declared, and despised his baptism. Such was

---

[31] Zohar in Exod. fol. 79. 1.

[32] T. Bab. Cetubot, fol. 17. 1.

[33] Bereshit Rabba, sect. 85. fol. 74. 4. & Mattanot Cehunah in ibid.

[34] Vid. R. David Ganz. Tzemach David, par. 1. fol. 38. 1. 41. 1. 44. 2. 45. 1. 46. 2. & 47. 1.

[35] A. Gell. Noct. Attic. l. 14. c. 3.

their fickleness and inconstancy, which Christ here tacitly charges them with. They were like the stony ground hearers, and like some of the Apostle Paul's admirers among the Galatians, who at first could have plucked out their eyes for him, but afterwards became his enemies for telling them the truth [*Gal. 4:16*].

Verse 36. **But I have greater witness than** *that* **of John**, &c. The Vulgate Latin, and Ethiopic versions read, *greater than John*, but wrongly; for the testimonies of Christ's works, and of His Father, are not compared with John himself, but with his testimony; and the sense is, that Christ had *a greater witness than* the witness *of John*; and so it is expressed in the Persic version: and His meaning is, that He had no need to insist upon John's testimony; He had other, and greater witnesses to produce:

for the works which the Father hath given me to finish; such as the preaching of the Gospel, the fulfilling of the law, and the redemption of His people; all which were appointed by His Father, and given Him to do, and which He completely finished. The whole Gospel came, and was published by Jesus Christ, and the law was entirely fulfilled by Him; and the work of man's salvation was finished by Him, and these bear witness to the truth of His Deity, and divine Sonship; for none but the Son of God could have done these things. The Ethiopic version reads in the singular number, *this work which my Father hath given me,* &c., and if it was a single work that is referred to, the work of redemption bids fair to be it. But, these works include not only what Christ did on earth, in His state of humiliation, but what He has done since, and will do; which His Father has given Him to finish, and He has finished, or will finish them; such as the resurrection of Himself from the dead, the effusion of the gifts and graces of the Spirit, the spreading and succeeding His Gospel in the world, the conversion of His redeemed ones, the gathering in the fulness of the Gentiles, and the conversion of the Jews, the destruction of antichrist, the resurrection of all the dead, and the judgment of the whole world. Though more especially His miracles are here intended, and which, and not His mediatorial works, were demonstrations and proofs to men of His divine Sonship; see *Matt. 14:33* and *27:54;*

the same works that I do, bear witness of me, that the Father hath sent me. And that He was in the Father, and the Father in Him; or that they were one in nature, and equal in power and glory, *John 10:30-37* and *14:11*.

Verse 37. **And the Father himself, which hath sent me**, &c. Not only the works He gave Him to do, and which He did, but He Himself in person:

hath borne witness of me; not only in the writings of Moses, and the prophecies of the Old Testament, but by an audible, articulate voice from

177

heaven, at the time of Christ's baptism, *Matt. 3:17;* which was a full testimony of the Sonship of Christ, and of the Father's well-pleasedness in Him; and which was repeated at His transfiguration on the mount, *Matt. 17:5;* and the Sonship of Christ is the grand thing which the three that bear record in heaven, the Father, the Word, and the Holy Ghost, testify of, *1 John 5:7;*

ye have neither heard his voice at any time, nor seen his shape. For the voices that were heard, and the forms that were seen under the Old Testament dispensation, from the first of this kind in Eden's garden, to the incarnation of Christ, which are ascribed to God, or to a divine person, were either by the ministry of angels, or they were voices uttered by the Son of God, or forms assumed by Him, who often appeared in a human form, as a prelude of His incarnation; so that it was unusual, and wonderful, and remarkable, that the Father should bear a testimony to the Sonship of Christ by a voice from heaven; and which therefore ought to be attended to, and received as a sufficient and valid testimony.

Verse 38. **And ye have not his word abiding in you,** &c. Which some understand of Christ Himself, the *Logos,* or Word: who, though He was now with them, being made flesh, and dwelling among them, yet would not long continue with them: though rather this designs the written Word, or the Scriptures of truth; and especially that part of them, which contains prophecies concerning the Messiah, which did not dwell in them richly, nor they dwell in their meditations on them, as was requisite. Or rather, it may intend that Word of God expressed in the testimony He bore to the Sonship of Christ at His baptism, by a voice from heaven, which made no lasting impression upon the minds and hearts of the Jews that heard it; as appears by what follows:

for whom he hath sent, him ye believe not. Meaning Himself; for if they had had either a due regard to the sacred oracles, or to that voice from heaven at His baptism, they would have received and embraced Him as the Messiah, and sent of God, and not have disbelieved and rejected Him, as now they did.

Verse 39. **Search the Scriptures**, &c. The writings of Moses and the prophets, which were of divine inspiration and authority, and are often appealed unto by Christ and His apostles, for the truth of what they delivered; and were the standard of faith, and the test of doctrines; and therefore to be *searched* diligently into, for finding divine knowledge, and improvement in it, and for the trial of doctrines. The words may be rendered in the indicative, as an assertion, *Ye do search the Scriptures.* The Jews had the sacred oracles committed to them, and these they read, not only their kings, princes, and judges, but the common people, who brought up their children to the reading of them, and instructed them in them: and besides this, these writings were read, and expounded publicly in their synagogues every sabbath day; and at this time especially these records were examined, and particularly those of them which respected the Messiah, since there was now a general expectation of Him: and certain it is, that the chief priests, Scribes, and elders, or the Sanhedrin, were very much versed in the Scriptures, and could readily refer to those which concerned the Messiah; see an instance of this in *Matt. 2:4-6*;

for in them ye think ye have eternal life; not the doctrine of eternal life, nor the promises of it, nor the way to it; though all these are contained in them, and pointed out by them: for though *life and immortality* are brought *to light* by the Gospel [*2 Tim. 1:10*], and the promise of eternal life belongs to the covenant of grace, and the way of life and righteousness by Christ is manifested without the law, and not by it; yet there is much of the Gospel, and an exhibition of the covenant of grace, and its promises, and Christ, the way of life, is directed to typically by the tree of life, and the brazen serpent, and other things in those writings. But the meaning here is, that they imagined, by having these writings in their hands, and by their reading them, and hearing them expounded every sabbath day, they should obtain and inherit everlasting life: hence they call[36] the law eternal life, and say[37] concerning the reading of it that,

"He that begins to read in the book of the law is obliged to bless after this manner: blessed be he that has chosen us above all nations, and hath given us his law.—And he that finishes blesses after him in this manner: blessed is he who hath given us his law, the law of truth, and has planted *eternal life* in the midst of us."

This was an opinion of theirs: so the Persic version reads, *for such is your opinion*; and though this was a very vain one, yet it shows what a very high opinion they had of the Scriptures: and now to these our Lord appeals as witnesses for Him, and against which they could not object, upon their own principles:

and they are they which testify of me. As they do of His proper Deity and divine Sonship, calling Him *Jehovah*, God, the mighty God, and the Son of God; and of His offices as Prophet, Priest, and King; and of His incarnation of a virgin; and of the tribe, family, and place of His birth; of the miracles which He should work; of the treatment He should meet with from men; of His sufferings and death; of the circumstances leading on to them, and attending them; as His riding on an ass into Jerusalem, the betraying Him by one of His

---

[36] Zohar in Gen. fol. 100. 3.

[37] Maimon. in Mishna Megilla, c. 4. sect. 1.

familiar acquaintance, the selling Him for thirty pieces of silver, the spitting upon and scourging Him, giving Him gall for His meat, and vinegar for His drink, and parting His garments, and casting lots for His vesture; and the crucifixion of Him, and that between two thieves; and of His burial, resurrection from the dead, ascension to heaven, and session at the right hand of God, and of His future coming to judgment.

Verse 40. **And ye will not come to me,** &c. Which is to be understood, not of a corporeal coming to Him; for many of the Jews did come to Him in this sense; some for one thing, and some for another; some for the loaves, that they might eat and be filled; some to see His miracles, and others to partake of the benefit of them; some to hear Him preach, and others to catch and cavil at what they could: nor is bare coming to hear Christ preached, or an outward attendance on, and submission to His ordinances, such a coming to Him as is here designed; for with these eternal life is not connected: *bodily exercise* profiteth not in this way [see *1 Tim. 4:8*]; but a spiritual coming to Christ, or a coming to Him by faith is here meant; in which sense the phrase is frequently used in this Gospel, especially in the next chapter; see *verses 35,37,44,45,65*; and those who come aright to Christ, come to Him as the alone, able, suitable, and sufficient Savior; and in themselves as sinners, and ready to perish; and as such they are received by Him with a welcome. But these men did not see themselves as such; nor did they see any need they had of coming to Christ; for they thought they had eternal life elsewhere: and such were their ignorance of themselves and Christ; and such their prejudices against Him; and such the depravity, perverseness, and stubbornness of their wills, that they had no inclination, desire, and will to come to Christ, any more than power; which is an argument against, and not for the free will of man, unless it be to that which is evil: and this perverseness of their wills to come to Christ, when revealed in the external ministry of the Word, was blameworthy in them, since this was not owing to any decree of God, but to the corruption and vitiosity of nature; which being blameworthy in them, that which follows upon it must be so too; and it was the greater aggravation of their sin, that they had the Scriptures which testified of Christ, and pointed at Him as the way of life, and yet would not come to Him for it:

that ye might have life. That is, eternal life, as is expressed in the foregoing verse, and is so read here in Beza's old copy, in the Syriac, Arabic, and Persic versions. This is in Christ, not only the purpose and promise of it, but that itself: He has the disposal of it, gives the right unto it, and a meetness for it, with all the comforts arising from it, and all the promises and blessings relating to it; and all that come to Christ by faith, may, and shall have it: this is the will of the Father, the end of His giving of Christ, and of His mission and coming into the world, and is inseparably connected with believing in Him.

Verse 41. **I receive not honor from men.** Not but that honor from men was due to Christ; and it becomes all men to honor Him, as they do the Father; and He does receive honor, and glory, and blessing, from His saints, by their praying to Him, praising Him, believing in Him, and serving Him; but His sense is, that in asserting His equality with the Father, and in producing the testimonies He did, in proof of it, His view was not to obtain honor and applause among men, but to vindicate Himself, and glorify His Father: nor did He say what He had just now said, about men's coming to Him, with any such intention, to gather a party to Him, to set up Himself as a temporal king, in great pomp and splendor, and receive worldly homage and honor from men, as His subjects; for His kingdom was not of this world, and coming and subjection to Him, were things of a spiritual nature.

Verse 42. **But I know you**, &c. Being the omniscient God, He knew not only their persons, but their hearts, the thoughts of their hearts; what was in them, and what was wanting in them: particularly,

that ye have not the love of God in you. And which is not in any man's heart naturally; for the carnal mind is enmity to God; and men by nature are haters of Him, and enemies in their minds to Him, till this grace, which is a fruit of the Spirit, is implanted in them in regeneration: love to God, is one of the weightier matters of the law the Jews passed over; without which, all the actions of men signify nothing: this they made great pretensions to, and would have had it thought, that it was from love to God that they sought to kill Jesus for His violation of the sabbath, and making Himself equal with God; but it was not from a delight in the sabbath, or from love to the Lord of it, but out of ill will to Christ, that they expressed such dissembled piety and false zeal: they were lovers of themselves, and not God; they were covetous men, and loved the world, and the things in it, which is inconsistent with the love of the Father; and besides, if they had loved Him, they would have loved Him that was begotten of Him, and not sought to have killed Him.

Verse 43. **I am come in my Father's name,** &c. In my Father's power and authority; by His consent, with His will, and according to a covenant with Him: Christ came not of Himself, of His own accord, by a separate power and will of His own, but was called, and sent, and came by mutual agreement; and brought His credentials with Him, doing the works and miracles which His Father gave Him to finish:

and ye receive me not; notwithstanding this, they rejected Him as the Messiah, and would not receive Him as such; yea, traduced Him as an impostor, and a deceiver:

181

if another shall come in his own name; which some understand of Simon Magus, others of antichrist; rather the false Christs are intended, of whom our Lord speaks in *Matt. 24:24*, who would rise up of themselves, and not be able to give any proof of their mission; or do any thing which might entitle them to the character of the Messiah, or Christ, a name they would take to themselves: and so the Ethiopic version reads, *if another shall come in my name*; saying he is Christ, or the Messiah:

him ye will receive. As thousands of them did receive Barchocab, the false Christ, who rose up some years after in Adrian's time; and even some of their greatest Rabbins, as particularly the famous R. Akiba, who was his armor-bearer: and it is easy to observe, that though they were so backward to receive, and so much prejudiced against the true Messiah, they were always forward enough to embrace a false one; and indeed to follow any, that set up himself for a temporal deliverer of them; as the instances of Theudas, and Judas of Galilee, with others, show; see *Acts 5:36-37*. And the true reason why they rejected Christ was, because He did not appear in outward pomp and glory, nor set up a temporal kingdom, or give out that He would deliver them from the Roman yoke.

Verse 44. **How can ye believe, which receive honor one of another?** &c. As the Scribes and Pharisees did, who were ambitious of honor and respect from one another, as well as from the common people; doing all they did to be seen of men, and to gain applause among them: choosing the uppermost rooms at feasts, and chief places in the synagogues, and delighting in the pompous title of *Rabbi, Rabbi*; and were in expectation of the temporal kingdom of the Messiah, when they hoped to be advanced to places of great honor and profit: and all this was a hindrance to them from believing in Christ, who appeared in such an abject form, and made so mean [*or* lowly] a figure; whose doctrine was so unsuitable to their carnal minds, and whose followers were so poor and contemptible; and besides, it was made a law among them, that those who professed Him to be the Messiah, should be cast out of the synagogue: hence many who were convinced that He was the Messiah, durst not confess Him, lest they should lose their honor and respect among men, which they preferred to the praise of God:

and seek not the honor that *cometh* from God only. Or *from the only God*, as the Vulgate Latin; or *from the one God*, as the Syriac, Arabic, and Persic versions render it: the honor that comes from Him is, that of being born of Him; of being a son or daughter of His, having that *new name* [*Isa. 62:2; Rev. 3:12*], which is better than that of sons and daughters of the greatest princes on earth; of being made *all glorious within*, and clothed with *gold of Ophir*, with *raiment of needlework* [*Psa. 45:9-15*], with *the robe of righteous-*

ness, and *garments of salvation* [*Isa. 61:10*]; of being *translated* into the spiritual kingdom of Christ [*Col. 1:13*], and made *kings and priests unto God* by Him [*Rev. 1:6*]; of being set on the same throne with Christ, having on a crown of life and righteousness, and enjoying a kingdom and glory; being *heirs of God, and joint heirs with Christ* [*Rom. 8:17*]; which honor all the saints have, or shall have, and which these men cared not for.

Verse 45. **Do not think that I will accuse you to the Father**, &c. Think not that I accuse you to *God the Father*, as the Ethiopic version reads. The Syriac and Persic versions read by way of interrogation, *Do ye think that I will?* &c. Christ is no accuser of men; no, not of the worst of men; see *John 8:10-11*; He came not into the world to bring charges against men and condemn them, but to save them; to be an accuser is not agreeable to His characters of a Surety, a Savior, an Advocate, and Judge: there were enough to accuse these persons of; as their perverseness and stubbornness, in not coming to Christ for life; their want [*or* lack] of love to God; their rejection of Him, though He came in His Father's name; their reception of another, that should come in his own name; their taking honor one of another, and not seeking the true spiritual and eternal honor, which God gives; but though He hints these things to them, He would not have them think that He accused them thereof to the Father: the Jews have a notion, that when the Messiah comes, there will be accusations lodged against their doctors and wise men.[38]

"R. Zeira says, that R. Jeremiah bar Aba said, That in the generation in which the son of David shall come, there will be בתלמידי חכמים קטוגוריא, *accusations against the disciples of the wise men*."

And one of their writers[39] thus interprets *Dan. 12:1:*

"and at that time *shall Michael stand up*; he shall be as silent as a dumb man, when he shall see the holy blessed God contending with him, and saying, How shall I destroy a nation so great as this, for the sake of Israel? *And there shall be a time of trouble* in the family above, and there shall be *accusations* against the disciples of the wise men."

However, there was no need for Christ to accuse them; for as it follows,

there is *one* that accuseth you, *even* Moses, in whom ye trust. By whom is meant, not Moses personally; for when on earth, he was a mediator between God and the people of Israel, and an intercessor for them; and since he has been in heaven, as *the dead know not any thing* [*Eccl. 9:5*], he knew nothing of their affairs; and when he was on the mount with Christ, his discourse with

---

[38] T. Bab. Cetubot, fol. 112. 2.

[39] Jarchi in Dan 12:1. Vid. Abkath Rocel, par. 2. p. 265.

Him turned upon another subject: but either the writings of Moses, as in *Luke 16:29,31*and *24:27*; or the doctrine of Moses, as *1 Cor. 10:2; John 9:28*; or rather the law of Moses, *Matt. 22:24; Mark 7:10; Acts 6:11* and *21:21.* And in this the Jews trusted; they rested in it, and made their boast of it; and expected eternal life and salvation on account of their having it, and through their hearing it read every sabbath day, and by their obedience to it: and now sin being a transgression of the law, this same law brings charges against them, and accuses them of the breach of the several precepts of it, and pronounces them guilty before God; it curses and passes a sentence of condemnation on them, and according to it, will they perish eternally, without an interest in Christ; for their own righteousness by the law of works, will be of no avail to them; the law in which they trust for life, will rise up in judgment, and be a swift witness against them: so the Jews sometimes speak of the law, as witnessing against the people of Israel.[40]

Verse 46. **For had ye believed Moses**, &c. The doctrine of Moses, and what he says in his writings:

ye would have believed me; for there is an agreement between Moses and Christ; *Christ is the end of the law* of Moses [*Rom. 10:4*], and in Him is the accomplishment of his writings:

for he wrote of me. In the books written by him, Christ is spoken of, as the seed of the woman, that should bruise the serpent's head [*Gen. 3:15*]; as the seed of Abraham, in whom all nations of the earth should be blessed [*Gen. 12:1-3* with *Gal. 3:16; Heb. 2:16*]; as the Shiloh, to whom the gathering of the people should be [*Gen. 49:10*]; and as that Prophet, who should be like unto himself, to whom the people of Israel should hearken [*Deut. 18:15-19*]; and he wrote many things typically of Christ. And indeed, the whole Mosaic economy was typical of Christ, as the epistle to the Hebrews shows: and therefore disbelieving Christ, was disbelieving Moses; who therefore would be an accuser of them, and a witness against them.

Verse 47. **But if ye believe not his writings**, &c. They believed them to be his writings, and that they were the Word of God, and yet did not believe the things contained in them, respecting Christ; or did not see, and could not believe that they belonged unto, and were applicable to Jesus of Nazareth; and therefore it could not be supposed they would give credit to him, or his words:

---

[40] Prefat. Echa Rabbati, fol. 40. 1.

how shall ye believe my words? Not that Moses was greater than Christ, or rather to be credited than He: Moses indeed was faithful, but Christ was worthy of more honor and credit than he was; Moses was but a servant, but Christ was a Son in His own house: but this is said with respect to the Jews, with whom Moses was in great veneration and esteem; and it was more likely they should regard what he should say, than what Jesus of Nazareth should, whom they despised.

CHAPTER 6

Verse 1. **After these things,** &c. After Christ's curing the man at Bethesda's pool, and the vindication of Himself for doing it on the sabbath day, and for asserting His equality with God; near a year *after these things*: for these were done at the feast of the passover, and now it was near another; and what is related here, was after the death of John the Baptist, and when the disciples had returned from preaching in the several cities and towns where Christ afterwards went, and had given an account of their success; see *Matt. 14:12-13; Mark 6:30-31; Luke 9:10*. Quickly after the passover was ended, Christ departed from Jerusalem, and went into Galilee, and preached in the several cities and towns in those parts, and wrought many miracles: and after these things, in process of time,

Jesus went over the sea of Galilee; the same with the *lake of Gennesaret, Luke 5:1*;

which is *the sea* of Tiberias. And is frequently so called by the Jewish writers,[1] who often make use of, של ימה טבריה, *the sea of Tiberias*; and as one of the seven seas; and by other writers, it is called *the lake of Tiberias;*[2] Pliny, who calls it *the lake of Genesara,*[3] says,

---

[1] T. Bab. Bava Kama, fol. 81. 2. & Bava Bathra, fol. 74. 2. Becorot, fol. 55. 1. Megilla, fol. 5. 2. & 6. 1. Moed. Katon, fol. 18. 2. & T. Hieros. Kilaim, fol. 32. 3. & Erubin, fol. 25. 2.

[2] Solin, c. 48. Pausan. l. 5. p. 298.

[3] Liber 5. c. 15.

"It was sixteen miles long, and six broad, and was beset with very pleasant towns; on the east were Julias and Hippo, and on the south Tariches, by which name some call the lake, and on the west Tiberias, wholesome for the hot waters."

And these are the waters which the Jews call, דימוסין דטבריא, or, חמי, *the hot baths of Tiberias*;[4] and from the city of Tiberias built by Herod, and called so in honor of Tiberius Caesar, the sea took its name.

Verse 2. **And a great multitude followed him**, &c. They followed Him from several cities and towns in Galilee, where He had been preaching and working miracles:

because they saw his miracles which he did on them that were diseased. So that it was not for the sake of His doctrine, or for the good of their souls, they followed Him; but either to gratify their curiosity in seeing His miracles, or to be healed in their bodies, as others had been.

Verse 3. **And Jesus went up into a mountain**, &c. Jesus went up into a desert place near Bethsaida, *Luke 9:10;*

and there he sat with his disciples. Partly for security from the cruelty of Herod, having just heard of the beheading of John; and partly for privacy, that He might have some conversation alone with His disciples, upon their return from off their journey; as also for the sake of rest and refreshment; and according to the custom of the Jewish doctors, which now prevailed, see the note on *Matt. 5:1* [**7**], He *sat* with His disciples, in order to teach and instruct them.

Verse 4. **And the passover, a feast of the Jews, was nigh.** This was the third passover, since our Lord's baptism, and entrance on His public ministry; see *chapter 2:13 and 5:1*. Whether Christ went up to this feast is not certain; some think He did not; but from what is said in *chapter 7:1*, it looks as if He did: how nigh it was to the feast, cannot well be said. Thirty days before the feast, they began to talk about it; and especially in the last fifteen days, they made preparations for it, as being at hand;[5] and if there was now so long a time to it, there was time enough for Jesus to go to it.

---

[4] T. Hieros. Peah, fol. 21. 2. & Sheviith, fol. 38. 4. Kiddushin, fol. 61. 1. R. Benj. Itinerar. p. 53.

[5] T. Bab. Pesach. fol. 6. 1. Maimonides & Bartenora in Mishna Shekalim, c. 3. sect. 1.

Verse 5. **When Jesus then lifted up *his* eyes,** &c. Being before engaged in close conversation with His disciples, and looking wistly and intently on them, while He was discoursing with them:

and saw a great company come unto him; who came on foot, over the bridge at Chammath, from Capernaum, and other cities of Galilee:

he saith unto Philip; He directed His discourse to him particularly, because he was of Bethsaida, near to which place Christ now was, and therefore might be best able to answer the following question:

Whence shall we buy bread, that these may eat? This, according to the other evangelists, must be said after Christ came from the mountain, and the people were come to Him, and He had received them kindly, and had instructed them about the kingdom of God, and had healed the diseased among them, and expressed great compassion for them; and after the disciples had desired Him to dismiss them, that they might go to the adjacent towns and provide food for themselves; which Christ would not admit of, and declared it unnecessary, and then put this question, with the following view.

Verse 6. **And this he said to prove him,** &c. Or, *tempting him*, trying his faith, and not only his, but that of the rest of the disciples; not as ignorant of it Himself, but in order to discover it to him and them, and to prepare them for the following miracle; and that it might appear the more illustrious and marvelous:

for he himself knew what he would do. Christ had determined to work a miracle, and feed the large number of people that were with Him, with that small provision they had among them; and being God omniscient, He knew that He was able to do it, and that He was determined to do it, and it would be done; but He was willing first to try the faith of His apostles.

Verse 7. **Philip answered him**, &c. Very quick and short, and in a carnal and unbelieving way:

Two hundred pennyworth of bread is not sufficient for them; two hundred pence, or Roman *denarii*, which may be here meant, amount to six pounds five shillings of our money; and this sum is mentioned, because it might be the whole stock that was in the bag, or that Christ and His disciples had; or because this was a round sum, much in use among the Jews; see the note on *Mark 6:37* [41]. Or this may be said by Philip, to show how impracticable it was to provide for such a company; that supposing they had two hundred pence to lay out in this way, though where should they have that, he suggests? Yet if they had it, as much bread as that would purchase would not be sufficient:

that everyone of them might take a little. It would be so far from giving them a meal, or proper refreshment, that every one could not have a small bit to taste of, or in the least to stay or blunt his appetite. A penny with the Jews, would buy as much bread as would serve ten men; so that two hundred pence, would buy bread enough for two thousand men; but here were three thousand more, besides women and children, who could not have been provided for with such a sum of money.

Verse 8. **One of his disciples, Andrew, Simon Peter's brother,** &c. Who also, and his brother Peter, were of Bethsaida, as well as Philip, and was a disciple of Christ's; he hearing what Christ said to Philip, and what answer he returned,

saith unto him; to Christ, with but little more faith than Philip, if any:

Verse 9. **There is a lad here,** &c. Who either belonged to Christ and His disciples, and was employed to carry their provisions for them; which, if so, shows how meanly [*or* humbly] Christ and His disciples lived; or he belonged to some in the multitude; or rather, he came here to sell what he had gotten:

which hath five barley loaves; the land of Canaan was a land of barley, as well as wheat, *Deut. 8:8*; this sort of grain grew there in plenty, and was in much use; the Jews had a barley harvest, *Ruth 1:22*, which was at the time of the passover; for on the second day after the passover, the sheaf of the first fruits was waved before the Lord, which was of barley. Hence the Targumist on the place just cited, paraphrases it thus:

"They came to Bethlehem in the beginning of the passover, and on the day the children of Israel began to reap the sheaf of the wave offering, which was of barley."

And it was now about the time of the passover, as appears from *verse 4*; and had it been quite the time, and the barley sheaf had been waved, it might have been thought that these loaves were made of the new barley; but though barley was in use for bread among the Jews, as is evident, from the mention that is made of barley loaves and cakes, *2 Kings 4:42; Judges 7:13*; yet it was bread of the coarsest sort, and what the meaner [*or* lower, poorer] sort of people ate; see *Ezek. 4:12*. Yea, barley was used for food for horses and dromedaries, *1 Kings 4:28*; and since therefore these loaves were, if not designed for the use of Christ and His twelve apostles, yet for some of His followers, and which they all ate of; it is an instance of the meanness [*or* lowliness] and poverty of them: but however, they had better bread than this, even *the bread of life*, which is afterwards largely treated of in this chapter, which some of them at least ate of; and as our countryman Mr. Dod used to say,

"Brown bread and the Gospel are good fare."

And it may be further observed, that the number of these loaves were but few; there were but *five* of them, for *five thousand* persons; and these do not seem to be very large ones, since one lad was able to carry them; and indeed, these loaves were no other than cakes, in which form they used to be made:

and two small fishes; there were but *two*, and these *small*; it is amazing, that five thousand persons should every one have something of them, and enough. These fishes seem to be what the Jews[6] call, מונינ, and which the gloss interprets *small fishes*: and by the word which is used of them, they seem to be salted, or pickled fishes, and such it is very probable these were; Nonnus calls them, ιχθυας οπταλεους, *fishes which were broiled*, or perhaps dried in the sun; see *Luke 24:42;*

but what are they among so many? Every one cannot possibly have a taste, much less any refreshment, still less a meal.

Verse 10. **And Jesus said, Make the men sit down**, &c. The Syriac version reads, *all the men*; and the Persic version, *all the people*: men, women, and children. Christ, without reproving His disciples for their unbelief, ordered them directly to place the people upon the ground, and seat them in rows by hundreds and by fifties, in a rank and company, as persons about to take a meal:

Now there was much grass in the place. At the bottom of the mountain; and it was green, as one of the evangelists observes, it being the spring of the year, and was very commodious to sit down upon:

So the men sat down, in number about five thousand. Besides women and children, *Matt. 14:21*, so that there was but one loaf for more than a thousand persons.

Verse 11. **And Jesus took the loaves**, &c. Into His hands, as also the fishes, in order to feed the multitude with them:

and when he had given thanks; for them, and blessed them, or implored a blessing on them, that they might be nourishing to the bodies of men, as was his usual manner, and which is an example to us;

---

[6] T. Bab. Cetubot, fol. 60. 2. & Sanhedrin, fol. 49. 1.

he distributed to the disciples, and the disciples to them that were set down. The Vulgate Latin, and all the Oriental versions, only read, *he distributed to them that were set down*: but it was not by His own hands, but by means of the disciples, who received from Him, and gave it to them; so that the sense is the same:

and likewise of the fishes, as much as they would. That is, they had as much, both of the bread and of the fishes, distributed to them, and which they took and ate, as they chose. In some printed copies it is read, *as much as he would*, and so the Persic version; that is, as much as Jesus would; but the former is the true reading, and makes the miracle more illustrious.

Verse 12. **When they were filled**, &c. When they had not only eaten, but had made a full meal, and were thoroughly satisfied, having eaten as much as they could, or chose to eat:

he said unto his disciples, Gather up the fragments that remain, that nothing be lost. This He said, partly that the truth, reality, and greatness of the miracle might be clearly discerned; and partly, to teach frugality, that in the midst of abundance, care be taken that nothing be lost of the good things which God gives; and which may be useful to other persons, or to them at another time.

Verse 13. **Therefore they gathered *them* together**, &c. The several broken bits of bread, which lay about upon the grass, which the people had left, after they had been sufficiently refreshed:

and filled twelve baskets; every disciple had a basket filled:

with the fragments of the five barley loaves; and it may be of the fishes also:

which remained over and above unto them that had eaten. Such a marvelous increase was there, through the power of Christ going along with them; insomuch that they multiplied to such a degree, either in the hands of the distributors, or of the eaters.

Verse 14. **Then those men**, &c. The five thousand men, who had been fed with the loaves and fishes:

when they had seen the miracle that Jesus did; in feeding so many of them with so small a quantity of food; in multiplying the provision in such a prodigious manner, that after they had eaten to the full, so many baskets of fragments were taken up:

said, This is of a truth that prophet that should come into the world. Meaning that Prophet that Moses spoke of in *Deut. 18:15*; for the ancient Jews understood this passage of the Messiah, though the modern ones apply it to others; see the note on *Acts 3:22* **[59]**. And these men concluded that Jesus was *that prophet*, or the true Messiah, from the miracle He wrought; in which He appeared, not only to be *like to Moses* [see *Deut. 34:10-12*], but greater than he.

Verse 15. **When Jesus therefore perceived,** &c. When Jesus *perceived*, as being the omniscient God, who knew their hearts, and the secret thoughts and purposes of them; or, as man, understood by their words and gestures:

that they would come and take him by force, and make him a king; that they had *determined*, as the Arabic version renders it; or *had it in their mind*, as the Persic; to gather about Him as one man, and seize Him in a violent manner, whether He would or not; and proclaim Him the King Messiah; place Him at the head of them, to deliver the nation from the Roman yoke, and set up a temporal kingdom, in which they might hope for great secular advantages: and they might the rather be induced to take such a step, since by this miracle, they could not doubt of His being able to support such an army of men, and to succeed in the enterprise; for He that could do this, what was it He could not do? But,

he departed again into a mountain, himself alone. He left the company directly, upon this resolution of theirs, and even took not His disciples with Him, who were in the same way of thinking about a temporal kingdom as the people, and might encourage them in this undertaking. The mountain Christ went into, very probably, was the same He went up to before; the reasons of His departure, were to prevent the attempt; to show that His kingdom was not of this world; to teach His followers to forsake the honors and riches of this world for His sake, and to let them know, that those who sought only for a temporal redeemer, were unworthy of His presence. And also He went away alone, for the sake of secret retirement, and private prayer; and it may be, chiefly, that He prayed that God would open the minds of these men, and particularly the disciples; that they might be convinced of their mistaken notions of Him as a temporal prince: some copies add, *and he prayed there*; the Syriac, Ethiopic, and Persic versions leave out the word *again*; and the latter, contrary to all others, renders it, *Christ departed from the mountain alone*.

Verse 16. **And when even was *now* come**, &c. The last of the evenings, when night was coming on; for the first of the evenings took place before they sat down to eat, when the above miracle was wrought; see *Matt. 14:15,23*;

his disciples went down unto the sea; of Galilee, or Tiberias, to the sea side; and this was by the order, and even constraint of Christ, who would have them go before Him, that He might be clear of the multitude, and have an opportunity for solitary prayer, *Matt. 14:22* **[20]** and *Mark 6:45* **[42]**; see the notes there.

Verse 17. **And entered into a ship**, &c. The ship in which they came, and was waiting for them; or into another:

and went over the sea towards Capernaum. Steered their course from Bethsaida, where they took shipping, over the sea of Galilee; at least over one part of it, a creek or bay of it, as they intended, towards the city of Capernaum, which lay over against Bethsaida:

And it was now dark; quite night, which made their voyage more uncomfortable, especially as it afterwards was tempestuous: but the worst of all was,

and Jesus was not come to them. As they expected, and therefore were obliged to set sail and go without Him.

Verse 18. **And the sea arose**, &c. Swelled, and was tumultuous and raging; the waves mounted up, and tossed the ship to and fro:

by reason of a great wind that blew. Which agitated the waters of the sea, and lifted up the waves; which storm seems to have arose after they had set sail, and were got into the midst of the sea.

Verse 19. **So when they had rowed,** &c. For the wind being contrary, they could not make use of their sails, but betook themselves to their oars, and by that means got,

about five and twenty or thirty furlongs; which were three or four miles, or little more than a league; no further had they got, though they had been rowing from the time it was dark, to the fourth watch, which was after three o'clock in the morning; all this while they had been tossed in the sea;

they saw Jesus walking on the sea; see the notes on *Matt. 14:25-26* and *29* **[21, 23]**.

And drawing nigh unto the ship; though Mark says, He *would have passed by them* [*Mark 6:48*]; that is, He seemed as if He would, but His intention was to come to them, and save them from perishing, as He did:

and they were afraid. That He was a spirit, some nocturnal apparition, or demon, in a human form; see the note on *Matt. 14:26* **[21]**.

192

Verse 20. **But he saith to them, it is I, be not afraid**. See the note on *Matt. 14:27* **[22]**.

Verse 21. **Then they willingly received him into the ship**, &c. When they knew who He was; and especially He was the more welcome, as they were in distress; and He able, as they well knew, to help them:

and immediately the ship was at the land whither they went. Which was done, as Nonnus observes, by a divine motion; for not only the wind ceased, but another miracle was wrought; the ship was in an instant at the place whither they intended to go.

Verse 22. **The day following**, &c. The day after that in which the miracle of feeding five thousand men with five loaves and two fishes was done, the morning after the disciples had had such a bad voyage:

when the people which stood on the other side of the sea; from that in which the disciples now were, being landed at Capernaum; that is, they stood on that side, or shore, where they took shipping, near Bethsaida and Tiberias: here, after they were dismissed by Christ, they stood all night, waiting for boats to carry them over; or rather, knowing that Christ was not gone with His disciples, they continued, hoping to meet with Him in the morning, and enjoy some more advantage by Him: for they,

saw that there was none other boat there, save that one whereinto his disciples were entered, and that Jesus went not with his disciples into the boat, but that his disciples were gone away alone; from whence they concluded, that since there was only that boat, and Jesus did not go into it, but that the disciples went off without Him, that He must be therefore somewhere on shore, and not far off, and they hoped to find Him in the morning; wherefore it was very surprising to them, when they found Him at Capernaum, when, and how He got there.

Verse 23. **(Howbeit there came other boats from Tiberias**, &c. Tiberias was a city by the sea side, built by Herod, and so called in honor of Tiberius Caesar; though the Jews give a different etymology of it; they say, it is the same with *Rakkath, Josh. 19:35*, and that it was a fortified place from the days of Joshua, and that on one side, ימה חומתה, *the sea was its wall;*[7] and so Jonathan the Targumist on *Deut. 3:17* says, that *Tiberias was near the sea of salt*. This place became famous for many of the wise men that lived here; here

---

[7]   T. Bab. Megilla, fol. 5. 2. & Hieros. Megilla, fol. 70. 1.

was a famous university, and here the Mishna and Jerusalem Talmud were written; and here the Sanhedrin sat, after it removed from Jerusalem:

nigh unto the place where they did eat bread; where the day before they had been fed in so miraculous a manner: the meaning is, either that Tiberias was near to the place where the miracle was wrought, or the boats from Tiberias came near to that place, and both were true; so that these men that were waiting by the seaside, had an opportunity of going over in these boats in quest of Christ, to whom they were now become greatly attached, by feeding them in so wonderful a manner:

after that the Lord had given thanks); which clause is added to show, that the multiplication of the bread, and the refreshment the men had by it, were owing to the power of Christ, and His blessing it; though this is wanting in Beza's most ancient copy, and in some others.

Verse 24. **When the people therefore saw that Jesus was not there**, &c. At the seaside, at the usual place of taking boat; and having reason to think He was not on that side of the lake, but was gone from thence:

neither his disciples; when they found that there were neither of them there, but both were all gone, and considering that it was to no purpose for them to stay there:

they also took shipping, and came to Capernaum, seeking for Jesus. They might observe, that the disciples steered their course towards this place; and they knew that it was a place of general resort with Christ and His disciples; therefore they took boat, and came directly thither, and sought for Him in the synagogue, it being on a day in which the people used to go thither; and where Christ, as often as he had opportunity, attended.

Verse 25. **And when they had found him on the other side of the sea**, &c. At Capernaum, and in the synagogue there; see *verse 59*.

They said unto him, Rabbi; or *master*, a name now much in use with the Jewish doctors, and by which they delighted to be called; and these men being convinced by the miracle, that Christ was that prophet that should come, honor Him with this title, saying,

when camest thou hither? Since He did not go with His disciples, and there was no other boat that went off the night before, but that in which they went; and they came over in the first that came out that morning, and He did not come in any of them; and therefore it was amazing to them, both when and how He came, since they could not devise how He should get there by shipping, and also how He should so soon get there afoot.

Verse 26. **Jesus answered them and said**, &c. Not by replying to their question, or giving a direct answer to that, which He could have done, by telling them that He walked upon the water, and found His disciples in great distress, and delivered them, and came early that morning with them to the land of Gennesaret, and so to Capernaum; but not willing to gratify their curiosity, and knowing from what principles, and with what views they sought after Him, and followed Him; and willing to let them know that He knew them, being the searcher of hearts, and to reprove them therefore, thus addressed them:

Verily, verily, I say unto you; this is a certain truth, and was full well known to Christ, and what their own consciences must attest:

Ye seek me not because ye saw the miracles; of feeding so large a number with so small a quantity of food, and of healing them that needed it, *Luke 9:11.* Not but that they did regard the miracles of Christ, and concluded from thence He must be that prophet that was to come, and were for taking Him by force, and proclaiming Him king; but then they had a greater respect to their own worldly interest, and their carnal appetites, than to these, as follows:

but because ye did eat of the loaves, and were filled. They regarded their own bellies more than the honor and glory of Christ, and even than the good of their immortal souls, and the spiritual and eternal salvation of them: and it is to be feared that this is the case of too many who make a profession of religion; their view being their own worldly advantages, and not the spiritual and everlasting good of their souls, and the real interest of a Redeemer: hence the following advice.

Verse 27. **Labor not for the meat which perisheth**, &c. Meaning either food for the body, which is perishing; its virtue is perishing; man cannot live by it alone, nor does it last long; its substance is perishing; it is received into the stomach, and there digested; it goes into the belly, and is cast out into the draft; and that which it supports, for a while, is perishing; and both the one, and the other, shall be destroyed; *even meats for the belly, and the belly for meats [1 Cor. 6:13].* Now, though it becomes men to work for their bread, to provide it for themselves and families; yet they should not be anxiously solicitous about it, or labor only for that, and prefer it to spiritual food. Or else food for the mind is meant, and that either in a sensual way, as sinful lusts and pleasures, the honors of this world, and the riches of it; which are sweet morsels, though bread of deceit to carnal minds, and which they labor hard for: or, in a religious way, as superstition, will worship, external works of righteousness, in order to please God, and obtain eternal life and salvation; which to labor for in such a way, is to *spend money for that which is not bread,* and *labor for that which profiteth not* [*Isa. 55:2*]; and in each of these ways were these Jews laboring for perishing food, from which Christ dissuades them:

but for that meat which endureth unto everlasting life; either the grace of Christ, which, as meat, is quickening and refreshing, strengthening and supporting, and which causes nourishment and growth, and by virtue of which work is done; and this springs up unto everlasting life, and is inseparably connected with it; and particularly the blessings of grace, such as sanctification, adoption, pardon, and justification: or the Gospel, and the ordinances of it, which are refreshing, and strengthening, and by which the saints are nourished up unto everlasting life; or rather the flesh of Christ, eaten in a spiritual sense, by faith, of which Christ so largely discourses in the following part of the chapter:

which the Son of man shall give unto you; meaning either everlasting life, which is in Christ's gift, and is a free grace gift of His; or else the meat which endures unto it: for though it is to be labored for, not so as to prepare it, or to purchase it, but by asking for it in prayer, and by attending on ordinances, and exercising faith on Christ; yet it is His gift, and He gives it freely; grace, and the blessings of it, are freely given by Him, and so are the Gospel and its ordinances; and also His own flesh, which is first given by Him, by way of sacrifice, in the room and stead of His people, and for the life of them, *verse 51*; and then it is given unto them to feed upon spiritually by faith, and which is here designed:

for him hath God the Father sealed. Designated and appointed to be the Savior and Redeemer of His people, and has sent, authorized, and commissioned Him as such; and has made Him known, and approved of Him, by the descent of the Spirit on Him, and by a voice from heaven, declaring Him His beloved Son; and has confirmed Him to be the Messiah by the miraculous works He gave Him to finish; for all which several uses seals are, as to distinguish one thing from another, to render any thing authentic, to point it out, or to confirm it.

Verse 28. **Then said they unto him**, &c. Understanding by what He said, that they must labor and work, though not for perishing food, yet for durable food; and, as they imagined, in order to obtain eternal life by working:

what shall we do that we might work the works of God? Such as are agreeable to His will, acceptable to Him, and well pleasing in His sight: they seem to intimate, as if they desired to know whether there were any other works of this kind, than what Moses had directed them to, or than they had done; and if there were, they suggest they would gladly do them: for this was

196

the general cast and complexion of these people; they were seeking for righteousness, and life, not by faith, but, as it were, by the works of the law.

Verse 29. **Jesus answered and said unto them, This is the work of God,** &c. This is the main and principal work, and which is well pleasing in His sight; and without which it is impossible to please Him; and without which no work whatever is a good work; and this is of the operation of God, which He Himself works in men; it is not of themselves, it is the pure gift of God:

that ye believe on him whom he hath sent. There are other works which are well pleasing to God, when rightly performed; but faith is the chief work, and others are only acceptable when done in the faith of Christ. This, as a principle, is purely God's work; as it is an act, or as it is exercised under the influence of divine grace, it is man's act: *that ye believe*; the object of it is Christ, as sent by the Father, as the Mediator between God and men, as appointed by Him to be the Savior and Redeemer; and believing in Christ, is believing in God that sent Him. The Jews reduce all the six hundred and thirteen precepts of the law, for so many they say there are, to this one, *the just shall live by his faith*, *Hab. 2:4.*[8]

Verse 30. **They said therefore unto him**, &c. Seeing He proposed believing in Him as the grand work of God to be done, and what is most acceptable in His sight:

What sign showest thou then, that we may see and believe thee? The people of the Jews were always requiring signs and wonders, and when they had one and another shown them, they still sought for more, and were never satisfied; see *Matt. 12:39* and *16:1*. These men had lately seen various signs and miracles of Christ, as healing the sick, and feeding five thousand of them, and more, with five loaves and two fishes; and though for the time present, these had some influence upon them, and they were ready to believe He was that prophet; yet now, at least some of them, begin to retract, and signify, that unless some other, and greater signs were shown, they should not believe in Him as the Messiah:

what dost thou work? More than others, or Moses? They seem to make light of the miracle of the loaves, or at least require some greater sign and miracle, to engage their belief in Him as the Messiah; and as they were lovers of their bellies, and expected dainties in the times of the Messiah, they seem to move for, and desire miracles of that kind to be wrought; and which sense the following words confirm.

---

[8] T. Bab. Maccot, fol. 23. 2. & 24. 1.

Verse 31. **Our fathers did eat manna in the wilderness**, &c. Which was a sort of food prepared by angels in the air, and rained down from thence about the tents of the Israelites; it was *a small round thing, as small as the hoar frost on the ground* [*Ex. 16:14*]; it was like *a coriander seed*, and the color of it was *the color of bdellium* [*Num. 11:7*]: it was so called, either from מנה, *to prepare*, because it was prepared, and gotten ready for the Israelites; or from the first words that were spoken upon sight of it, מן הו, *What is it?* For they knew not what it was: and this the Jewish fathers fed upon all the while they were in the wilderness, till they came to Canaan's land, and they only; it was food peculiar to them: *our fathers did eat manna*; and so the Jews[9] observe on those words in *Ex. 16:35*:

> "And the children of Israel did eat manna forty years; the children of Israel, ולא אחרא, *and not another*. And the children of Israel saw, and said, *What is it?* and not the rest of the mixed multitude."

Now these Jews object this miracle to Christ, and intimate, that He indeed had fed five thousand of them with barley loaves, and fishes, for one meal; but their fathers in the times of Moses, to the number of six hundred thousand, and more, were fed, and that with manna, very sweet and delightful food, and for the space of forty years; even all the while they were in the wilderness: and therefore, unless He wrought as great a miracle, or a greater than this, and that of the like kind, they should not think fit to relinquish Moses, and follow Him; and in proof of what they said, they produce Scripture:

as it is written, in *Psa. 78:24-25*, or rather in *Ex. 16:15*; and perhaps both places may be respected:

He gave them bread from heaven to eat. They leave out the word *Lord*, being willing it should be understood of Moses, to whom they ascribed it, as appears from the following words of Christ, who denies that Moses gave it; and they add the phrase *from heaven*, to set forth the excellent nature of it, which is taken from *Ex. 16:4*, where the manna, as here, is called *bread from heaven*.

Verse 32. **Then Jesus said unto them, Verily, verily, I say unto you**, &c. It is truth, and may be depended on, whether it will be believed or not:

Moses gave you not that bread from heaven; in which Christ denies that that bread, or manna, did come from heaven; that is, from the highest heavens, only from the air, and was not such celestial bread he after speaks of, and which came down from the heaven of heavens: and moreover, He denies that Moses gave them that bread; it was the Lord that gave them it, as

---

[9] Zohar in Exod. fol. 75. 2.

is expressly said in the passage referred to in the above citation. Moses had no hand in it; he did not so much as pray for it, much less procure it, or prepare it: it was promised and prepared by God, and rained by Him, and who directed to the gathering and use of it. This stands opposed to a notion of the Jews, that the manna was given by means of Moses, for his sake, and on account of his merits: for they say,[10]

"There arose up three good providers, or pastors for Israel, and they are these, Moses, and Aaron, and Miriam; and three good gifts were given by their means, and they are these, the *well*, the *cloud*, and the *manna*; the well by the merits of Miriam; the pillar of cloud by the merits of Aaron; מן בזכות משה, *the manna, by the merits of Moses*."

This our Lord denies; and then affirms,

but my Father giveth you the true bread from heaven. He not only gave the manna to the Jewish fathers, and not Moses; but He also gives that *bread* which the manna was typical of, by which He means Himself; who may be compared to *bread*, because of the original of it, or the matter of it, of which it is made, wheat; He is called a *corn of wheat*, *John 12:24*; and from its preparation for food, being threshed, and winnowed, and ground, and kneaded, and baked; all which may express the sufferings and death of Christ, by which He becomes fit food for faith; and from its being the main part of human sustenance, and from its nourishing and strengthening nature, and from its being a means of maintaining and supporting life: and He may be called the *true bread*, because He is the truth and substance of the types of Him; the unleavened bread, eaten at the passover, was typical of Him, as He was free from sin in nature and life; and from all error in doctrine; and so was the showbread a type of His intercession, and set forth the continuance of it, its efficacy and acceptance, of which the priests only shared; and so were the meat offerings in the sacrifices, which were offered up day by day; and particularly the manna, the bread from heaven, the Jews were now speaking of: Christ was the truth of that type; that was but shadowy bread, Christ is the *true* bread, or the antitype of it in its name; whether it be derived from *manah*, "to prepare," Christ being the bread of life, and salvation of God, prepared in the council and covenant of grace, and by His sufferings and death before the face of all people; or from the words *man hu*, "What is it?" Christ being as little known by carnal men, as the manna was at first to the Israelites: and in its nature, kind, form, and quality; it was round in form, which might be expressive of the perfections of Christ, and particularly His eternity, being without beginning or end; it was white in color, which may denote the purity and innocence of Him; it was sweet in taste, as He, His

---

[10] T. Bab. Taanith, fol. 9. 1. Seder Olam Rabba, p. 28.

fruits, His Word, and ordinances, are sweet to them that are born again; it was small in quantity, which may set forth the meanness [*or* lowliness] of Christ in His state of humiliation: it was also typical of Christ in its usefulness; it was sufficient to supply a great multitude, and that for many years, as the fulness of grace in Christ is sufficient for the whole family in heaven and in earth, in time and to all eternity: the Israelites all shared in it, and had all an equal portion of it; so all the people of God have an interest in Christ, and equally participate of the blessings of His grace, and shall enjoy the same eternal life and glory by Him: one has neither more nor less than another; Christ is all in all, and made alike all things to them: and He may be called the *bread from heaven*, because He came from thence, not by change of place, but by assumption of nature, even from the highest heavens, the third heaven, from whence the manna came not: He is *the Lord from heaven*, and is such bread as has a virtue and tendency in it to nourish men for heaven, and is truly of a heavenly nature: and this is Christ's Father's gift, and is of pure grace, without any consideration of works and merits in men. Philo the Jew says,[11]

"The heavenly food of the soul, which is called *manna*, the divine Word distributes alike to all that ask."

Verse 33. **For the bread of God is he which cometh down from heaven**, &c. Cometh down in the way and manner just now mentioned: and which clearly points out Christ Himself, who may be called *the bread of God*; to distinguish Him from common bread, and to show the excellency of Him, and that He is of God's providing and giving, and which He would have His children feed upon:

and giveth life unto the world. A spiritual life, which He is the author, supporter, and maintainer of; and eternal life, which He gives a right unto and meetness for, and nourishes up unto; and this not to a few only, or to the Israelites only, but to the Gentiles also, and even to the whole world of God's elect: not indeed to every individual in the world, for all are not quickened now, nor shall inherit eternal life hereafter; but to all the people of God, in all parts of the world, and in all ages of time; of such extensive virtue and efficacy is Christ, *the bread of God*, in which He appears greatly superior to that manna the Jews instance in.

Verse 34. **Then said they unto him**, &c. At least some of them:

Lord, evermore give us this bread. That is so divine and heavenly, and has such a quickening virtue in it. These words are said by them either

---

[11] Quis rer. divin. haeres. p. 507.

seriously, and to be understood of bread for their bodies, of which they imagined Christ was speaking; and so sprung from ignorance of His sense; and from sensuality in them, who followed Him for the loaves; and from a covetous disposition, being desirous of being supplied with such excellent food without charge; and from idleness, to save labor and pains in working for it; and from a vain desire of the continuance of this earthly life, being willing to live for ever, and therefore would have this bread evermore; and from a gross opinion of plenty and delicacy of corporeal food in the times of the Messiah; see the note on *Luke 14:15* [**52**]; or else these words are spoken ironically, by way of derision, as if there was no such bread; and if there was, that Christ could not give it. However, the words may be improved, when considered as a petition coming from, and suitable to, a sensible and enlightened soul: for such who are sensible of their famishing condition by nature, and of their need of Christ, the bread of life, and whose taste is changed, and have tasted how good this bread is, will earnestly desire always to be supplied with it, and to live upon it; for nothing is more grateful to them, and more nourishing and satisfying to their souls; they are never weary of it; it is always new and delightful to them, and they always stand in need of it, and wait in the use of means and ordinances for it: and this has always an abiding, lasting virtue in it, to feed their souls, and nourish them up to everlasting life. Josephus [12] says of the *manna*, which was a type of this bread, that there was such a divine quality in it, that whoever tasted of it needed nothing else: and the Jews also say [13] that,

"In the manna were all kinds of tastes, and every one of the Israelites tasted all that he desired; for so it is written in *Deut. 2:7, These forty years the Lord thy God hath been with thee, thou hast lacked nothing*, or *not wanted any thing*; what is any thing? When he desired to eat any thing, and said with his mouth, O that I had fat to eat, immediately there was in his mouth the taste of fat.—Young men tasted the taste of bread, old men the taste of honey, and children the taste of oil."

Yea, they say, [14]

"Whoever desired flesh, he tasted it; and whoever desired fish, he tasted it; and whoever desired fowl, chicken, pheasant, or peahen, so he tasted whatever he desired."

And to this agrees what is said in the apocryphal book of Wisdom, chapter 16:20-21:

---

[12] Antiqu. l. 3. c. 1. sect. 6.

[13] Shemot Rabba, sect. 25. fol. 108. 4.

[14] Bemidbar Rabba, sect. 7. fol. 188. 1.

"Thou feddest thine own people with angels' food, and didst send them from heaven bread prepared without their labor, able to content every man's delight, and agreeing to every taste; for thy sustenance (or manna) declared thy sweetness unto thy children, and serving to the appetite of the eater, tempered itself to every man's liking."

All which must be understood of that pleasure, satisfaction, and contentment which they had in it; for it was a very uncommon case to eat it, and live upon it as their common food for forty years together: and no doubt but that there was something remarkable in suiting it to their appetites, or giving them appetites suitable to that, to feed upon it, and relish it for so long a time. Twice indeed in that length of time we read they complained of it, saying, that they had nothing but this manna before their eyes, and their souls loathed it as *light bread, Num. 11:6* and *21:5*, and lusted after the flesh and the fish they had eaten in Egypt. And so it is with some professors of Christ and His Gospel; for there is a mixed multitude among them, as there was among the Israelites, who disrelish the preaching of Christ, and the truths of the Gospel, respecting His person, blood, and righteousness, and salvation by Him; they cannot bear to have these things frequently inculcated and insisted upon; their souls are ready to loathe them as light bread, and want to have something else set before them, more suitable to their carnal appetites: but to such who are true believers in Christ, who *have tasted that the Lord is gracious* [*1 Pet. 2:3*], Christ, the true manna, and bread of God, is all things to them; nor do they desire any other: they taste everything that is delightful, and find everything that is nourishing in Him.

Verse 35. **And Jesus said unto them, I am the bread of life**, &c. Christ is called *the bread of life*, because He gives life to dead sinners: men in a state of nature are dead in trespasses and sins; and whatever they feed upon tends to death; Christ, the true bread, only gives life, which is conveyed by the Word, and made effectual by the Spirit; and because He supports and maintains the life He gives: it is not in the power of a believer to support the spiritual life he has; nor can he live on any thing short of Christ; and there is enough in Christ for him to live upon: and because He quickens, and makes the saints lively in the exercise of grace, and discharge of duty, and renews their spiritual strength, and secures for them eternal life;

He that cometh to me shall never hunger; not corporeally, to hear Him preach, or preached, or merely to His ordinances—to baptism, or the Lord's table; but so as to believe in Him, feed, and live upon Him, as the next clause explains it:

and he that believeth on me shall never thirst. And which is owing, not to the power and will of man, but to divine teachings, and the powerful drawings of the efficacious grace of God; see *verses 44-45*. Now of such it is said, that they shall never hunger and thirst; which is true of them in this life, though not to be understood as if there were no sinful desires in them; much less, that there are no spiritual hungerings and thirstings after they are come to Christ; but that they shall not desire any other food but Christ; they shall be satisfied with Him; nor shall they hereafter be in a starving and famishing condition, or want any good thing: and in the other world there will be no desires after that which is sinful, nor indeed after outward ordinances, in order to enjoy communion with God in them, as now, for they will then be needless; nor shall they have any uneasy desires after Christ and His grace, and the enjoyment of Him, since He will be all in all to them.

Verse 36. **But I said unto you,** &c. The substance of what follows in *verse 26*, though the Persic and Ethiopic versions render it, *I say unto you*; and so refers not to any thing before said, but to what He was about to say:

That ye also have seen me, and believe not. That is, they had not only seen Him in person, which many kings, prophets, and righteous men had desired, but not enjoyed, yet nevertheless believed; but they had seen His miracles, and had shared in the advantages of them, being healed, and fed corporeally by Him, and yet believed not in Him as the spiritual Savior and Redeemer of their souls; nor did they come to Him in a spiritual way, for eternal life and salvation.

Verse 37. **All that the Father giveth me**, &c. The *all* design not the apostles only, who were given to Christ as such; for these did not all, in a spiritual manner, come to Him, and believe in Him; one of them was a devil, and the son of perdition; much less every individual of mankind: these are, in some sense, given to Christ to subserve some ends of His mediatorial kingdom, and are subject to His power and control, but do not come to Him, and believe in Him: but the whole body of the elect are here meant, who, when they were chosen by God the Father, were given and put into the hands of Christ, as His seed, His spouse, His sheep, His portion, and inheritance, and to be saved by Him with an everlasting salvation; which is an instance of love and care on the Father's part, to give them to Christ; and of grace and condescension in Him to receive them, and take the care of them; and of distinguishing goodness to them: and though Christ here expresses this act of His Father's in the present tense, *giveth*, perhaps to signify the continuance and unchangeableness of it; yet He delivers it in the past tense, in *verse 39*, *hath given*; and so all the Oriental versions render it here. And it certainly respects an act of God antecedent to coming to Christ, and believing in Him, which is a fruit and effect of electing love, as is clear from what follows:

203

shall come unto me; such who are given to Christ in eternal election, and in the everlasting covenant of grace, shall, and do, in time, come to Christ, and believe in Him to the saving of their souls; which is not to be ascribed to any power and will in them, but to the power and grace of God. It is not here said, that such who are given to Christ have a *power* to come to Him, or *may* come if they will, but they *shall* come; efficacious grace will bring them to Christ, as poor perishing sinners, to venture on Him for life and salvation:

and him that cometh to me I will in no wise cast out. Such who come to Christ in a spiritual manner, and are brought to believe in Him truly and really, He not only receives kindly, but keeps and preserves them by His power, and will not cast them out, or thrust them from Him into perdition: the words are very strongly and emphatically expressed in the original, *I will not, not,* or *never, never, cast out without*; or cast out of doors. Christ will never cast them out of His affections; nor out of His arms; nor out of that family that is named of Him; nor out of, and from His church, which is His body, and of which they are members; nor out of a state of justification and salvation; and therefore they shall never perish, but have everlasting life. The three glorious doctrines of grace, of eternal election, efficacious grace in conversion, and the final perseverance of the saints, are clearly contained in these words.

Verse 38. **For I came down from heaven,** &c. Not by change of place, or local motion; for Christ is the immense, infinite, and omnipresent God, and cannot be said properly to move from place to place; for He fills all places, even heaven and earth, with His presence, and was in heaven as the Son of God, at the same time He was here on earth as the Son of man: wherefore this must be understood in a manner becoming His proper Deity, His divine Sonship, and personality: this descent was by the assumption of the human nature into union with His divine person, which was an instance of amazing grace and condescension. The Jew[15] objects to this, and says,

> "If this respects the descent of the soul, the soul of every man descended from thence; but if it respects the body, the rest of the evangelists contradict his words, particularly Luke, when he says, *chapter 2:7*, that his mother brought him forth at Bethlehem."

But this descent regards neither His soul nor body, but His divine person, which always was in heaven, and not any local descent of that; but, as before observed, an assumption of human nature, which He took of the virgin on earth; and so there is no contradiction between the evangelists; nor is descent from heaven unsuitable to Christ as a divine person, since it is ascribed to God, *Gen. 11:7* and *18:21*; and if God may be said to *go down* from heaven by

---

[15] R. Isaac Chizzuk Emuna, par. 2. c. 44. p. 434.

some display of His power, and intimation of His presence, Christ may be said to *descend* from heaven by that marvelous work of His, taking upon Him our nature, and walking up and down on earth in the form of a servant; and which was done with this view, as He says,

not to do mine own will, but the will of him that sent me. That is, not to do His own will, as separate from His Father's, and much less as contrary to it; otherwise He did come to do His own will, which, as God, was the same with His Father's, He being one with Him in nature, and so in power and will; and though His will, as man, was distinct from His Father's, yet not repugnant, but resigned unto it: and this will He came to do, was to preach the Gospel, fulfil the law, work miracles, and obtain the eternal redemption and salvation of His people. What the above Jewish writer[16] objects to this part of the text is of very little moment: whose words are:

"Moreover, what he says, *not to do mine own will, but the will of him that sent me*, shows, that he that sent, is not one and the same with him that is sent, seeing the will of him that is sent, is not as the will of him that sends."

It is readily granted that they are not one and the same person; they are two distinct persons, which sending, and being sent, do clearly show; but then they are one in nature, though distinct in person, and they agree in will and work. Christ came not to do any will of His own, different from that of His Father's; nor do these words imply a difference of wills in them, much less a contrariety in them, but rather the sameness of them.

Verse 39. **And this is the Father's will which hath sent me**, &c. This explains both who He was that sent Him; the Father of Him, and of His people; whose sending of Him does not suppose any change of place, or inequality between them, or disrespect unto Him, or compulsion of Him, but agreement between them, and love to the persons on whose account He was sent; and also what is the will He came to do, and is what was declared by Him to Christ, when He gave the elect to Him: for this expresses His secret will in the council and covenant of grace,

that of all which he hath given me, I should lose nothing; that is, that of all the elect which were given to Christ by His Father, in eternal election, He should not lose any one of them, not the meanest [*or* lowliest] among them, nor any thing of theirs, their grace, or glory, or any thing belonging to them, either to their souls or bodies, and particularly the latter;

---

[16] Ibid.

but should raise it up again at the last day. Even every part of their bodies, and every dust belonging to them; their bodies being given to Christ, and redeemed by His blood, as well as their souls: so the Jews,[17] speaking of the resurrection, and making mention of that passage in *Num. 23:10, Who shall count the dust of Jacob?* add,

"and he (that is, God) shall order it all, ולא יתאביד כלום, *and not any thing shall be lost*, but all shall rise again; for, lo, it is said, *Dan. 12:2, And many of them that sleep in the dust*, &c."

Verse 40. **And this is the will of him that sent me**, &c. The Vulgate Latin adds, *of my Father*; and all the Oriental versions read only, *and this is the will of my Father*; this is His declared, His revealed will in the Gospel, which the sons of men are made acquainted with, as the other was his secret will, which was only known to the Son till He discovered it:

that every one which seeth the Son, and believeth on him; who so sees Him as to believe in Him; for this is not to be understood of a corporeal sight of Christ, or of a mere speculative knowledge of Him, or historical faith in Him; for it is not to *see* Him, as merely to believe what He is, the Son of God, the Messiah and Savior of the world, or what He says, but to trust in Him for righteousness, life, and happiness. Men are by nature blind, their eyes are shut to all that is spiritually good; it is the Spirit of God that opens blind eyes, and illuminates the understanding: and in His light men see not only themselves, their sin, and want of righteousness, and their lost state and condition, but Christ, and a beauty, glory, and excellency in Him, ability and willingness to save, a suitableness in Him for them, and a fulness of all grace; they see righteousness, peace, pardon, cleansing, wisdom, strength, grace, life, and salvation, and go out of themselves to Him for all: and such a sight, though it may be but glimmering, is saving, and is self-abasing, soul-rejoicing, surprising, and transforming; is attended with certainty, reality, and evidence, and is a foretaste of glory; for it is the will of God, and not man; of a gracious Father, of an unchangeable and eternal being, whose will cannot be resisted, and made void, that such,

may have everlasting life; which will be a life of glory, and will consist in possessing glory both in soul and body; in beholding glory, the glory of one another, the glory of angels, the glory of divine truths, and mysterious providences, the glory of the divine perfections, and of the Lord Jesus Christ; and it will be a life of perfection, of perfect knowledge, holiness, obedience, love, peace, and joy; a life free from all the miseries and inconveniences of this, both in a natural and spiritual sense; a life of pleasure, and which will last for

---

[17] Zohar in Exod. fol. 43. 4.

ever: to which Christ adds,

and I will raise him up at the last day. Christ will be the efficient cause, as well as He is the exemplar, the earnest, and firstfruits of the resurrection of the dead: He will indeed raise all the dead by His power, but the saints particularly, by virtue of union to Him, as the members of His body, and in the first place [see *1 Cor. 15:20-23; 1 Thess. 4:15-16*]; and the very same shall rise, and with the same numerical body, that were given to Him, and believe in Him: and this will be at the last of the last days, at the end of all things; and is mentioned to show, that length of time will not hinder the resurrection of the dead; and in opposition to a Jewish notion, that the resurrection of the dead would be at the Messiah's coming: it will be at His second coming, but was not to be at His first; there was indeed then a resurrection of some particular persons, but not a general one of all the saints. That the Jews expect the resurrection of the dead when the Messiah comes, appears from their Targums, Talmuds, and other writers; so the Targumist on *Hos. 14:8*:

"They shall be gathered from their captivity, they shall sit under the shadow of their Messiah, *and the dead shall live*, and good shall be multiplied in the land."

And in the Talmud[18] it is said,

"The holy, blessed God, will quicken the righteous, and they shall not return to their dust."

The gloss upon it is,

"The holy, blessed God, will quicken them *in the days of* the Messiah." And so the land of the living is said to be,

"the land, whose dead live first in the days of the Messiah"[19]

And hence R. Jeremiah desired to he buried with his clothes and shoes on, and staff in his hand, that when the Messiah came, he might be ready;[20] with which agree others of the more modern writers: so Kimchi on *Isa. 66:5*:

"They shall live at the resurrection of the dead, in the days of the Messiah."

And the same writer on *Jer. 23:20,* observes it is said,

"*ye* shall consider, and not *they* shall consider; which intimates *the resurrection of the dead in the days of the Messiah.*"

And, says Aben Ezra on *Dan. 12:2*:

"The righteous which die in captivity shall live, when the Redeemer comes;"

---

[18] T. Bab. Sanhedrin, fol. 92. 1.

[19] T. Hieros. Kilaim, fol. 32. 3.

[20] Ibid. col. 2.

though some of their writers differ in this point, and will not allow the days of the Messiah, and the resurrection of the dead, to be one and the same.[21]

Verse 41. **The Jews then murmured at him**, &c. When they found that He spoke of Himself as the true bread, the bread of God, and bread of life, and as descending from heaven; and which was to be fed upon in a spiritual manner by faith, which they were ignorant of, and had no desire unto: and thus being disappointed of the delicious corporeal food they expected, they grew uneasy, and displeased,

because he said, I am the bread which came down from heaven. For though, as yet, He had not said this in so many words, and in this direct form, as afterwards, in *verse 51*; yet He had said what amounted to it, and which might be easily gathered from *verses 35* and *38*. The Vulgate Latin reads, *I am the living bread*; and the Persic version, *I am the bread of life*. And this last renders the first clause, *mocked at him*.

Verse 42. **And they said, Is not this Jesus, the son of Joseph?** &c. From murmuring they go to mocking and scoffing at His parentage and descent, and object this to His coming down from heaven; and intend by it to upbraid Him with the meanness [*or* lowliness] of His birth, being the son of Joseph, a poor carpenter; and suggest, that it was great arrogance in Him to claim a heavenly original, and to ascribe such things to Himself, that He was the bread of God, and the bread of life, and came from heaven:

whose father and mother we know? For Capernaum and Nazareth were not at a great distance from each other; so that Joseph and Mary might be personally known by the inhabitants of Capernaum, and they might be intimately acquainted with them.

How is it then that he saith, I came down from heaven? They could not tell how to reconcile these things, not knowing either His miraculous conception and incarnation, nor His divine Sonship; otherwise His being made of a woman, or born of a virgin on earth, is consistent with His being the Lord from heaven.

Verse 43. **Jesus therefore answered and said unto them**, &c. Jesus either overhearing what they said, or knowing, as God, their secret murmurs, and private cavils among themselves, thus addressed them,

murmur not among yourselves. Meaning neither about His descent from heaven, nor about coming to Him, and believing in Him; for it follows,

---

[21] Zohar in Gen. fol. 82. 4.

Verse 44. **No man can come to me,** &c. That is, by faith, as in *verse 35*; for otherwise they could corporeally come to Him, but not spiritually; because they had neither power nor will of themselves; being dead in trespasses and sins, and impotent to every thing that is spiritual: and while men are in a state of unregeneracy, blindness, and darkness, they see no need of coming to Christ, nor any thing in Him worth coming for; they are prejudiced against Him, and their hearts are set on other things; and besides, coming to Christ, and believing in Christ, being the same thing, it is certain faith is not of a man's self, it is the gift of God [*Eph. 2:8; Phil. 1:29*], and the operation of His Spirit; and therefore efficacious grace must be exerted to enable a soul to come to Christ; which is expressed in the following words,

except the Father which hath sent me, draw him: which is not to be understood of moral suasion, or a being persuaded and prevailed upon to come to Christ, by the consideration of the mighty works which God had done to justify that He was the true Messiah, but of the internal and powerful influence of the grace of God; for this act of drawing is something distinct from, and superior to, both doctrine and miracles. The Capernaites had heard the doctrine of Christ, which was taught with authority, and had seen His miracles, which were full proofs of His being the Messiah; and yet believed not, but murmured at His person and parentage. This gave occasion to Christ to observe to them, that something more than these was necessary to their coming to Him, or savingly believing in Him; even the powerful and efficacious grace of the Father in drawing: and if it be considered what men in conversion are drawn off *from* and *to*, from their beloved lusts and darling righteousness, to look unto, and rely upon Christ alone for salvation; from that which was before so very agreeable, to that which, previous to this work, was so very disagreeable; to what else can this be ascribed, but to unfrustrable and insuperable grace? But though this act of drawing is an act of power, yet not of force; God, in drawing of unwilling, makes willing in the day of His power [*Psa. 110:3*]: He enlightens the understanding, bends the will, gives a heart of flesh, sweetly allures by the power of His grace, and engages the soul to come to Christ, and give up itself to Him; He draws with the *bands of love* [*Hos. 11:4*]. Drawing, though it supposes power and influence, yet not always coercion and force: music draws the ear, love the heart, and pleasure the mind. *Trahit sua quemque voluptas*, says the poet. The Jews have a saying,[22]
  "that the proselytes, in the days of the Messiah, shall be all of them, גרים גרורים, *proselytes drawn:*"
that is, such as shall freely and voluntarily become proselytes, as those who are drawn by the Father are.

---

[22] T. Bab. Avoda Zara, fol. 3. 2. & 24. 1.

And I will raise him up at the last day. See the note on *verse 40*; compare with this verse *Judges 4:7*.

Verse 45. **It is written in the prophets**, &c. *In the book of the prophets*, as the Ethiopic version renders it. The Jews divided the books of the Old Testament into three parts, the Law, the Prophets, and the *Hagiographa*; now in that division which was called the Prophets, are the following words: or in one of the prophets, namely, in *Isa. 54:13*; so the Syriac version reads, *in the prophet*; though some think reference is had to more prophets, and more passages than one, as, besides the above mentioned, *Jer. 31:34; Mic. 4:2*;

And they shall be all taught of God. By His Spirit, to know themselves, and Jesus Christ; that is, all that are ordained to eternal life; all that are given to Christ, and are chosen in Him; all the children of Zion, and who are the children of God; these are all, sooner or later, in a special manner, taught of God: and which does not intend mere external instructions, and objective teachings by the ministry of the Word, for many are so taught, who never come to Christ; but special teachings, such as are attended with the energy of divine grace, and the power of the Spirit of God, who guides into all truth, savingly and spiritually: for this is to be understood of their being taught in the Gospel of Christ, and not in the law, as the Targum paraphrases it:
"All thy children shall learn in the law of the Lord."
And that this prophecy refers to Gospel times, is clear from the citation and application of the first verse of it to the church in the times of the apostles, *Gal. 4:27*. The Jews themselves acknowledge the prophecy belongs to the times of the Messiah, to which they expressly apply[23] the words in *Isa. 54:5, thy Maker is thy husband*, &c. And one of their modern commentators allows,[24] that this very passage, *all thy children shall be taught of God*, refers, לעתיד, *to the time to come*; that is, to the times of the Messiah: in this citation, those words, *thy children*, are left out, to show that the words are not to be restrained to the people of the Jews, as they might seem by that clause, and to whom the Jews would limit them: for so they say,[25]
"They are truly taught of God from whom prophecy comes: which comes not to all the world, but to Israel only; of whom it is written, *and all thy children are taught of God*."
But our Lord, by these words, instructs us, and would have us observe, that all that the Father hath given Him, whether Jews or Gentiles, of whom He

---

[23] Shemot Rabba, sect. 15. fol. 102. 4.

[24] Kimchi in loc.

[25] Zohar in Exod. fol. 70. 1.

had been speaking in the preceding verses, should be taught of God; and so taught, as to be drawn and brought to Him, and believe in Him, and have everlasting life: wherefore He infers from hence, that every man, whether a Jew or a Gentile, that is taught of God, will come to Him in a spiritual way, and trust in Him for eternal life and happiness, as follows:

every man therefore that hath heard, and hath learned of the Father, cometh unto me. Every one that has heard the voice of the Father's love, grace, and mercy in the Gospel, and has learned of Him the way of peace, life, and salvation by Christ, under the influence of His grace, comes unto Christ; being encouraged by the declarations and promises of grace he has heard and learned, and ventures his soul on Christ, and commits it to Him; trusting and relying on His person, blood, righteousness, and sacrifice, for justification, pardon, atonement, acceptance with God, and eternal life.

Verse 46. **Not that any man hath seen the Father**, &c. This is said, lest it should be thought from the above words, that our Lord meant that men should be so taught of God, as that they should visibly see the Father, and vocally hear His voice, and be personally instructed by Him; for His voice is not heard, nor His shape seen; see *chapter 1:18* and *5:37*;

save he which is of God; who is begotten of Him, and of the same nature and perfections with Him, though a distinct person from Him, and who was always with Him, and lay in His bosom:

he hath seen the Father. Has perfect knowledge of Him, personal communion with Him; has seen the perfections and glory of His person, and the thoughts, purposes, and counsels of His heart; His whole mind and will, and all the grace, goodness, and mercy which is in Him, and has declared it; see *John 1:18*.

Verse 47. **Verily, verily, I say unto you**, &c. I say, this is a certain truth, and to be depended on:

He that believeth on me hath everlasting life. Not only he may have it, as in *verse 40*, and shall have it, but he has it. He has it in Christ, his head and representative; he has it in the covenant of grace; he has it in faith and hope; he has a right unto it, and a meetness for it; he has the earnest of it, the grace and Spirit of God; and he has the beginning and foretastes of it in his soul, and shall certainly enjoy it.

Verse 48. **I am that bread of life**. See the note on *verse 35*.

Verse 49. **Your fathers did eat manna in the wilderness**, &c. All the while they were in the wilderness, for the space of forty years, till they came to the borders of the land of Canaan; this was their only food on which they lived, during their travels through the wilderness. It is observable, that Christ says, not *our fathers*, but *your fathers*; for though Christ, as concerning the flesh, came of these fathers, yet in every sense they were rather theirs than His; because regard may be had to such of them more especially who ate the manna as common food, and not as spiritual meat, as typical of the Messiah, as others did; and whom, these their offspring, did very much resemble. Though perhaps the reason of the use of this phrase may be, because the Jews themselves had used it in *verse 31*, and Christ takes it up from them;

and are dead. This food, though it supported them in life for a while, could not preserve them from a corporeal death, and still less from an eternal one: for some of them not only died the first, but the second death.

Verse 50. **This is the bread which cometh down from heaven**, &c. Namely, that of which He had spoken, *verses 32,33,35* and *48*, meaning Himself:

that a man may eat thereof, and not die. For this heavenly bread is soul-quickening, soul-strengthening, and soul-satisfying food; nor can there be any want where this is: eating of it is not to be understood corporeally, as these Capernaites took it; nor sacramentally, as if it was confined to the ordinance of the Lord's supper, which was not as yet instituted; but more largely of eating and feeding upon Christ spiritually by faith: He is, by the believer, to be fed upon wholly, and only; all of Him, and none but Him, and that daily; for there is the same need of daily bread for our souls, as for our bodies; and also largely and freely, as such may do; and likewise joyfully, with gladness and singleness of heart: such as are Christ's beloved, and His friends, *may* eat; they have liberty, a hearty welcome to eat; and so has every one that has a will, an inclination, a desire to eat, and all overcomers, whom Christ makes more than conquerors, *Song of Sol. 5:1; Rev. 2:7,17* and *22:17*; which liberty is owing to Christ's gracious invitation, and to His and the Father's free gift; and to the openness and ease of access of all sensible sinners to Him: and the consequence and effect of such eating is, that it secures from dying; not from a corporeal death, to which men are appointed, and saints themselves are subject, though it is indeed abolished by Christ as a penal evil; nor shall His people continue under the power of it, but shall rise again to everlasting life: but then they are, through eating this bread, secured from a spiritual death; for though there may be a decline, as to the exercise of grace, and a want of liveliness, and they may fear they are ready to die, and conclude they are free among the dead, and that their strength and hope are perished; yet he that lives and believes in Christ, the resurrection and the life, shall never die; and such are also secure from an eternal death, on them the second death shall have no power, nor shall they ever be hurt by it.

Verse 51. **I am the living bread which came down from heaven**, &c. This is the same with what is said in *verses 33,35* and *48*, which is true of Christ, as He has life in Him; and is the author and giver of life to others; and is of a heavenly original, and came from heaven to give life to men: and such is the virtue of this living and heavenly bread, that,

if any man eat of this bread he shall live for ever; not a natural, but a spiritual life; a life of sanctification, which is begun here, and will be perfected hereafter; and a life of glory, which will never end:

and the bread that I will give is my flesh; or *body*, as all the Oriental versions render it. Here our Lord explains more clearly and fully what He means, under the notion of bread; and which shows, that by bread He did not design merely His doctrine, but His flesh, His human nature; though not as abstracted from His Deity, but as in union with it:

which I will give for the life of the world. And which He did, by the offering up of His body, and making His soul, or giving Himself an offering, a propitiatory sacrifice for sin; which was done in the most free and voluntary manner, in the room and stead of His people, to procure eternal life for them, even for the whole world of His elect; whether among Jews or Gentiles; particularly the latter are here meant, in opposition to a notion of the Jews, that the world, or the Gentiles, would receive no benefit by the Messiah when He came; see the note on *chapter 3:16*.

Verse 52. **The Jews therefore strove among themselves**, &c. The Jews fell to cavilling and disputing one among another; some understanding Christ, and others not; some being for Him, and vindicated what He said; and others being against Him, and who were the majority, objected,

saying how can this man give us *his* flesh to eat? Which is to be understood, not physically, but as morally impossible and unlawful; since, with the Jews, it was not lawful to eat the flesh of any creature alive, and much less the flesh of man; for the Jews understood Christ of a corporeal eating of His flesh, being strangers to a figurative or spiritual eating of it by faith, in which sense He meant it.

Verse 53. **Then Jesus said unto them**, &c. The Jews, who were litigating this point among themselves:

Verily, verily, I say unto you; or you may assure yourselves of the truth of what follows,

Except ye eat the flesh of the Son of man, and drink his blood, ye have no life in you: by *the Son of man*, Christ means Himself; under which title He often speaks of Himself; because it was a title of the Messiah under the Old Testament; and was expressive of the truth of His human nature, though as attended with weakness and infirmities. The *flesh* and *blood* of Christ do not design those distinct parts of His body; much less as separate from each other; nor the whole body of Christ, but His whole human nature; or Christ, as having united a perfect human nature to Him, in order to shed His blood for the remission of sin, and to offer up His soul and body a sacrifice for it: and the eating of these is not to be understood of a corporeal eating of them, as the Capernaites understood them; and since them the Papists, who affirm, that the bread and wine in the Lord's supper are transubstantiated into the very body and blood of Christ, and so eaten: but this is not to be understood of eating and drinking in the Lord's supper, which, as yet, was not instituted; and some, without participating of this, have spiritual life in them now, and will enjoy eternal life hereafter; and all that partake of that ordinance have not the one, nor shall have the other: and besides, having a principle of spiritual life in the soul, is previously necessary to a right eating of the supper of the Lord. These words, understood in this sense, once introduced infants to the Lord's supper; [just] as a misinterpretation of *John 3:5*, brought in the baptism of them. But the words design a spiritual eating of Christ by faith. To eat the flesh, and drink the blood of Christ, is to believe that Christ is come in the flesh, and is truly and really man; that His flesh is given for the life of His people, and His blood is shed for their sins, and this with some view and application to themselves: it is to partake of, and enjoy the several blessings of grace procured by Him, such as redemption, pardon, peace, justification, &c. and such a feeding upon Him as is attended with growth in grace, and in the knowledge of Him, and is daily to be repeated, as our corporeal food is, otherwise persons have no life in them: without this there is no evidence of life in them; not such live as feed on sinful pleasures, or on their own righteousness; only such that believe in Christ are living souls; and without this there is nothing to support life; every thing else that a man eats tends to death; but this is what will maintain and preserve a spiritual life; and without this there is no just expectation of eternal life; but where there is this, there is good reason to expect it, and such shall enjoy it. Some copies and versions read, *ye shall not have life in you*: eternal life. Now, though the acts of eating and drinking do not give the right to eternal life, but the flesh, blood, and righteousness of Christ, which faith lays hold of, and feeds upon; yet it is by faith the right is claimed; and between these acts of faith, and eternal life, there is an inseparable connection.

Verse 54. **Whoso eateth my flesh, and drinketh my blood**, &c. Eateth and drinketh them spiritually by faith, as explained in the preceding verse:

hath eternal life; the principle of spiritual life, which is evidently implanted in him, as appears from his eating and drinking; and is a durable and lasting principle: grace is an incorruptible seed; every part of it is abiding and permanent; and it is itself the beginning, pledge, and earnest of everlasting life, and is inseparably connected with it. Moreover, such have eternal life itself, not only in Christ their head, but in themselves; they have a right unto it, and a meetness for it: and may be assured of it, as if they were personally possessed of it, from their election to it; the security of it in Christ; from the grace they have received, which is the beginning of glory; and the earnest of it in themselves:

and **I will raise him up at the last day**. To enjoy it in soul and body; see the notes on *verses 39* and *40*.

Verse 55. **For my flesh is meat indeed**, &c. Not in a corporeal, but in a spiritual sense; and the same is said of His blood:

and my blood is drink indeed. That is, they are both *truly* meat and drink, as the Vulgate Latin, Syriac, and Ethiopic versions render it; or are *true* meat and drink, as the Arabic version: in opposition to what was typical meat and drink; as the manna in the wilderness, the water out of the rock, the flesh and wine at the passover, the meat and drink offerings under the law, or any other meats and drinks under that dispensation; and which, though not when Christ said these words, yet now are abolished, being unprofitable, and not to be fed upon. Moreover, these phrases may denote the reality, substance, and solidity of that spiritual food believers have in Christ, in opposition to the imaginary food of sensual sinners, who feed on ashes and bread of deceit; and to that of self-righteous persons, who spend their labor and money for, and live upon that which is not bread, even upon their works of righteousness; and to the superficial tastes of hypocrites and formal professors; and to the charge of enthusiasm; and even to the outward elements of bread and wine in the Lord's supper, since instituted; and as it may be attended upon by persons destitute of the grace of God. And these words may also be expressive of the virtue, efficacy, and excellency of this food, it being soul-quickening, nourishing, strengthening, satisfying, and delightful food, as well as spiritual and savory; not to carnal persons, or outward professors, but to newborn babes, and true believers; and which, by them, may be had, and to the full, and that in due season, even every day, and is what will abide for ever.

Verse 56. **He that eateth my flesh, and drinketh my blood**, &c. In the sense above given; see the note on *verse 53*;

dwelleth in me, and I in him. There is a mutual indwelling of Christ, and believers; Christ is the habitation, or dwelling place of His people: there is a secret dwelling in Christ; so the elect of God dwelt in the heart, and in the hands and arms of Christ from everlasting; and as members in their head in election grace; and representatively in Him, as the Mediator of the covenant; and they secretly and safely dwelt in Him, when all mankind fell in Adam; and when He was on the cross, in the grave, and now He is in heaven; all which is owing to His own love, His Father's gift, and to secret union to Him. But there is an open dwelling in Him in time, which is here meant: God's elect, as in their nature-state, are without Christ, and lie open to the law and justice of God; the Spirit of God convinces them of this state, and directs them to flee to Christ, as a city of refuge; when they find Him a stronghold, a place of defense, and a proper dwelling for them, where they resolve to abide, and do abide; and where they dwell safely, peaceably, comfortably, and pleasantly; and from which dwelling place they will never be turned out. Likewise the saints are the habitation or dwelling place of Christ; He dwells not in their heads and tongues, but in their hearts, and by faith; which is here expressed, by eating His flesh, and drinking His blood; and which, though it is not the cause of Christ's dwelling here, yet is the means or instrument by which men receive Him into their hearts, and retain Him, and have communion with Him; for He dwells in believers, not in such sense as He dwells in the world, by His omnipresence, and power; or as in the human nature, by hypostatical union to it; but by His Spirit, and by faith, which is an instance of wonderful condescending grace, and is owing to union to Him, and is expressive of communion with Him, and is what will continue for ever.

Verse 57. **As the living Father hath sent me**, &c. Sent me into the world, to be the Savior of it; not by local motion, but by assumption of human nature; and not against His will, or as having superiority over Him, but by joint consent and agreement: the first person in the Godhead is here styled, *the living Father*; not because He is the Father of spirits, of angels, and the souls of men; and the Father of all men by creation, and of saints by adoption; and the Father, or author of all mercies, spiritual and temporal; but because He is the Father of our Lord Jesus Christ; and this character is peculiar to Him: He is indeed the living God, and has life in Himself, and is the fountain of life to others; but not in distinction from, and to the exclusion of the Son, or Spirit; but then none but He is the living Father, who ever did, and ever will, live as the Father of Christ:

and I live by the Father; which is to be understood of Christ, not as God, but as Mediator, and as man. As Mediator He was set up by His Father, as the head of life to the elect; and was entrusted by Him with a fulness of life for them; and was sent to open the way of life unto them, and bestow it on them.

As man, He had His human life from God, and was preserved and upheld in it by Him; and he laid it down at His command, and at His death committed His soul or spirit to Him [see note **57** on *Luke 23:46*]; and which was restored unto Him, and is continued with Him. The Vulgate Latin, and all the Oriental versions, read, *for the Father*, or *because of* Him; and may design either that near union and conjunction of Christ with Him, by virtue of which they live the same life; or else His living to the glory and honor of His Father, as He did, and does:

so he that eateth me; in a spiritual sense, by faith. The phrase of eating the Messiah was a familiar one, and well known to the Jews; though these Capernaites cavilled at it, and called it a hard saying.

"Says Rab, the Israelites shall *eat* the years of the Messiah (the gloss on it is, The fulness which the Israelites shall have in those days). Says R. Joseph, It is certainly so; but who shall *eat him*? Shall Chillek and Billek (two judges in Sodom) אכלי לה, *eat him*? Contrary to the words of R. Hillell, who says, Israel shall have no Messiah, for, אכלוהו, *they ate him* in the days of Hezekiah;"[26]

that is, they enjoyed Him then; for he thought that Hezekiah was the Messiah; but that was the doctor's mistake. The Messiah now was, and to be enjoyed and eaten by faith in a spiritual sense, and every one that does so,

even he shall live by me: such have their life from Christ; He is their food, on which they live; and by Him they are continued, upheld, and preserved in their spiritual life, and are by Him brought to the life of glory: or they live *for*, or *because of* Him, as the above versions render it; they derive their life from Him, and because He lives, they live also; and they live to His glory, and will do so to all eternity.

Verse 58. **This is that bread which came down from heaven**, &c. This is that true bread, the bread of God, the bread of life, living bread; meaning Himself, as in *verses 32,33,35,48,50* and *51;*

not as your fathers did eat manna, and are dead: this is bread of a quite different nature from that; that was only typical bread, this true; that was the bread of angels, but this is the bread of God; that came but from the air, this from the third heaven; that men ate of, and died; but whoever eats of this, lives for ever; see *verse 49*; as follows:

he that eateth of this bread shall live for ever. See the note on *verse 51*.

---

[26] T. Bab. Sanhedrin, fol. 98. 2. & 99. 1.

Verse 59. **These things said he in the synagogue**, &c. Openly and publicly, in the place of divine worship, where the Jews resorted for that purpose:

as he taught in Capernaum. His own city, and where there was a synagogue, into which He often went and taught His doctrines, and wrought miracles; see *Matt. 3:13; 8:5,14; 9:1-2* and *12:9.*

Verse 60. **Many therefore of his disciples**, &c. Not of the twelve, nor of the seventy, but of the multitude of the disciples, who followed Him from place to place, attended on His ministry, and might be baptized in His name; see *chapter 4:1;*

when they had heard *this*; that His flesh and blood were truly and really meat and drink, and that none had life in them, or should have eternal life, but such as eat and drink the same:

said, This is an hard saying; or it is to be objected to; so קשיא, *a hard thing*, the word here used in the Syriac version, and קשה הוא עלי, *it is to me a hard thing*, are phrases used to express an objection in the Talmudic writings, where they are often met with: or it is difficult to be understood and received; so הדבר הקשה, *a hard saying*, or *a hard cause*, is a cause difficult to be tried and determined, *Ex. 18:26*; and is used of that which seems incredible and absurd, and is surprising and unaccountable: so it is said [27] that,

> "It happened to a certain woman, that she came before R. Abika: she said to him, I have seen a spot; he said to her, Perhaps there is a wound in thee; she answered him, Yes, and it is healed; he replied, Perhaps it may be opened, and the blood brought out; she answered him, Yes; and he pronounced her clean. R. Abika saw his disciples look upon one another; and he said unto them, מה הדבר קשה, *is this a hard saying with you?*"

Is it a difficult thing with you? Does it seem absurd to you? or are you surprised at it? Any thing difficult, or which seems irreconcilable, is so called: so the slaying the passover between the two evenings is called by Aben Ezra, in *Ex. 12:6*, מלה קשה, *a hard saying*. In like sense the phrase is used here; and the allusion may be to food that is hard of digestion, since Christ had been speaking of Himself under the metaphors of bread and meat. As some of the doctrines of Christ are comparable to milk, which is easy of digestion; others are like to strong meat, which belongs to those of full age, and cannot be digested by children, by babes in Christ; and much less be received, eaten, and digested, with ease and pleasure, by carnal minds; who therefore say, as these Capernaites did,

---

[27] Mishna Nidda, c. 8. sect. 3.

who can hear it? This saying, or doctrine, concerning eating the flesh, and drinking the blood of Christ; or *him*, Christ, who delivered this doctrine: such preaching, and such a preacher, are intolerable; there is no hearing, nor bearing them: hence we afterwards read, that these withdrew from the ministry of Christ, *verse 66*.

Verse 61. **When Jesus knew in himself**, &c. And of Himself, without any intelligence from others, or hearing what was said, being the omniscient God:

that his disciples murmured at it; at the doctrine He had delivered, looking upon it as absurd, incredible, and contrary to sense and reason:

he said unto them, Does this offend you? Or trouble you? Can you not get over this? Can you not understand it? or account for it? If not, how will ye be able to digest some other things, or reconcile them to your minds, which are less known, and more unexpected, and will appear at first sight more surprising?

Verse 62. **What and if ye shall see the Son of man**, &c. Meaning Himself, then in a state of humiliation, and was taken for a mere man, though the true Messiah, and Son of God:

ascend up where he was before? For Christ *was*, He existed before His incarnation, and He was in heaven before; not in His human nature, but as the Word and Son of God: and He intimates, that when He had done His work, and the will of His Father, for which He came down from heaven, by the assumption of the human nature, He should ascend up thither again; and which would be seen, as it was, by His apostles; and which would prove that He came down from heaven, as He had asserted; see *Eph. 4:9-10*; and that His flesh and blood were not to be eaten in a corporeal sense; in which sense they understood Him: and He hereby suggests, that if it was difficult to receive, and hard to be understood, and was surprising and incredible, that He should come down from heaven, as bread, to be eaten and fed upon; it would be much more so to them to be told, that He, who was in so mean [*or* humble] and lowly a form, should ascend up into heaven.

Verse 63. **It is the spirit that quickeneth**, &c. It is the spirit of man that quickens him; or which being breathed into him, he becomes a living soul; for the body, without the spirit, is dead; it is a lifeless lump: and it is the Spirit of God that quickens dead sinners, by entering into them as the spirit of life, and causing them to live: and it is spiritual eating, or eating the flesh, and drinking the blood of Christ in a spiritual sense, which quickens, refreshes, and comforts the minds of believers; it is that by and on which they live, and by which their spiritual strength is renewed: unless, by *spirit*, is meant the divine nature of Christ, by which He was quickened and raised from the dead, and ascended up into heaven, and was *declared to be the Son of God with power* [*Rom. 1:4*]:

the flesh profiteth nothing; the human nature of Christ, though profitable, as in union with the Son of God, to be given for the life of His people, and to be an offering, and a sacrifice for their sins, yet not as alone, or as abstracted from the divine nature; nor would His flesh and blood, corporeally eaten, could or should it be done, be of any avail to eternal life; nor is any other flesh, literally understood, profitable of itself for life; for man lives not by bread, or meat, or flesh alone, but by the Word and blessing of God upon it, and along with it; nor *flesh*, in a figurative sense, as creature acts and performances, self-righteousness, obedience to the ceremonial law, carnal descent, and birth privileges:

the words that I speak unto you, *they* are spirit, and *they* are life. The doctrines which Christ had then been delivering concerning Himself, His flesh and blood, being spiritually understood, are the means of quickening souls. The Gospel, and the truths of it, which are the wholesome words of our Lord Jesus Christ, are the means of conveying the Spirit of God, as a spirit of illumination and sanctification, into the hearts of men, and of quickening sinners dead in trespasses and sins: the Gospel is the spirit that giveth life, and is the savor of life unto life, when it comes not in word only, or in the bare ministry of it, but with the energy of the Holy Ghost, and the power of divine grace.

Verse 64. **But there are some of you that believe not**, &c. Some believed not, notwithstanding the ministry they sat under, and the words they heard; for though they professed to believe in Jesus as the Messiah, yet they did not truly believe in Him; their faith was not a living faith, or of a spiritual kind, but a mere historical and temporary one, and was feigned and hypocritical:

for Jesus knew from the beginning; of His ministry, and of their profession of Him, being God omniscient, and the searcher of hearts:

who they were that believed not; That is, *believed not in him*, as the Arabic version reads: notwithstanding their following Him, and professing to believe in Him, and the great outward respect and esteem they showed to Him, He could see through all those masks they put on, and knew they had no true faith of Him in them; and the same knowledge He has of every professor of His name: He knows whether their faith is of the right kind or not; whether they have obtained the *like precious faith* with God's elect [*2 Pet. 1:1, 10*]; or whether their profession is only a verbal one. In some copies it is read, *who they were that believed*; who were true believers, as well as who were hypocrites;

and who should betray him. He not only knew how it was with the multitude of the disciples that professed love to Him, and faith in Him; but He also particularly knew the case of the twelve apostles, and that one of them should betray Him, and who he was. This was determined in the decrees of God, and was foretold in the prophecies of the Old Testament, and was predicted by Christ; and the person was pointed at by Him before it was done.

Verse 65. **And he said, Therefore said I unto you**, &c. Referring to *verse 44*, where the substance of what is here said is delivered; though the Ethiopic version reads, *therefore I say unto you*, what follows:

that no man can come unto me, except it were given unto him of my Father. Which is the same, as to be drawn by the Father; for faith in Christ is the gift of God, and coming to Him, is owing to efficacious grace, and is not the produce of man's power and freewill; see the note on *verse 44*.

Verse 66. **From that *time* many of his disciples went back**, &c. Not any of the twelve apostles, for they are distinguished from these in the next verse; nor any of the seventy disciples, for their names were written in heaven, and could not apostatize totally and finally, as these did; but some of the multitude of the disciples, who followed Christ, heard Him, and professed to believe in Him, and were baptized in His name, but were not true disciples, only nominal ones: they had never heard and learned of the Father, otherwise they would have known what it was to come to Christ, as the Father's gift, and under the drawings of His grace; and would not have been offended at the words of our Lord, just now spoken by Him, concerning that sort of coming to Him: but from the time He spoke those words; *because of this word*, as the Syriac, Arabic, and Persic versions render it; they withdrew themselves from His ministry, they dropped their profession of faith in Him, and relinquished Him as a Savior and Redeemer: for finding that He would not be made a king, nor set up for a temporal redeemer; and talking of Himself as *the Bread of life*, and of *coming to Him*, in a sense they did not understand; they turned their backs on Him; and as the words may be literally read, *returned to the things that were behind*; to the world, and to their old companions, to Satan and their own hearts' lusts; like the dog to its vomit, and the swine to its wallowing in the mire [see *2 Pet. 2:22*]: their true picture is drawn, in the parable of the unclean spirit going out of the man, and returning, *Matt. 12:43*. And they returned to their quondam teachers, the Scribes and Pharisees, and to the law of works, and to seek for righteousness by it; setting up their own righteousness, and not submitting to the righteousness of Christ [see *Rom. 10:3*]; and thus to look back and draw back, is a sad case indeed:

and walked no more with him. Never returned to Him more, nor went with Him from place to place as before: never more attended on His ministry, or had any intimacy and fellowship with Him: and so it commonly is with apostates from the profession of Christ; they seldom or ever return, or are recovered; it is difficult, if not impossible, which is sometimes the case, to renew them again to repentance [see *Heb. 6:4-6*].

Verse 67. **Then said Jesus unto the twelve**, &c. *To his own twelve*, as the Persic version reads; that is, to His twelve apostles, whom He had chosen to that office: Christ takes no notice of those that went away from Him, He showed no concern about them; He knew what they were, that the truth of grace was not in them, and that they did not belong to Him, and therefore was not uneasy about their departure; but turns Himself to His apostles, whom He dearly loved, and in a very tender manner thus said to them,

will ye also go away? This He said, not as ignorant of what they were, or of what they would do in this case; He knew full well their faith in Him, their love to Him, and esteem of Him, and close attachment to Him, at least in eleven of them; nor did He say this, as having any fears or jealousies concerning them, by observing any thing in their countenances or gestures, which looked like a departure from Him; but it was said out of a tender regard and strong affection for them: and it is as if He should have said, As for these men that have walked with me for some time, and have now turned their backs upon me, it gives me no concern; but should you, my dear friends and companions, go also, it would give me, as man, real pain and great uneasiness: or He might say this to show, that as they were not pressed into His service, but willingly followed Him, and became His disciples, being made a willing people by Him in the day of His power on them [see *Psa. 110:3*]; so they willingly continued with Him, and abode by Him; as also to strengthen their faith in Him, and cause them the more to cleave to Him, with full purpose of heart, when others left Him; as well as to draw out from them, expressions of their regard for Him, and faith in Him, which end was answered.

Verse 68. **Then Simon Peter answered him**, &c. Who was strong in the faith of Christ, and full of zeal for Him, and love to Him; and who was the mouth of the apostles, and always forward to speak, out of the abundance and sincerity of his heart, in their name; believing, that they all of them, for he had now no suspicion of Judas, no more than of the rest, had the same faith in Christ, love to Him, and esteem of Him, as he himself had; wherefore out of a good opinion of them, and love to Christ, he thus addressed Him:

Lord; or *my Lord*, as the Syriac version renders it; which was either a title of respect, and the same with *Sir* with us; or else, as acknowledging the dominion and authority of Christ, as Lord of all, and especially of the saints, and as claiming his interest in Him; and which carries in it a reason, why he should abide by Him:

to whom shall we go? As a teacher, whose ministry we can attend upon, to greater profit and advantage? Not to the Scribes and Pharisees, whose leaven, or doctrine, Christ had bid them beware of; who taught *for doctrines the commandments of men* [*Matt. 15:9*], and were *blind leaders of the blind* [*Matt. 15:14*]; nor to John the Baptist, who had declared he was not the Messiah; but had pointed Him out to them in His person, as the Son of God; and in His office as the *Lamb of God*, that takes away the sins of men; and perhaps, he might not be now living; and if he was, he would have encouraged them not to follow him, but abide with their Master; so that there was no other, that was *better*, as Nonnus expresses it, that they could go unto; and therefore it would be folly and madness in them to leave Him. And as it was with Peter and the rest of the disciples, so it is with all sensible sinners and true believers, who see there is no other to go to for life and salvation, but Christ; not to the law of Moses, which accuses, curses, and condemns, and by which, there is neither life nor righteousness; nor to any creature, or creature performance, for there is a curse on him that trusts in man, and makes flesh his arm; nor to their own righteousness, which is impure and imperfect, and cannot justify before God, nor answer for them in a time to come; nor to their tears of repentance, which will not satisfy the law, atone for sins, or wash them away; nor to carnal descent, birth privileges, a religious education, sobriety, and civility; to trust to which, is to have confidence in the flesh, which will be of no avail; nor to ceremonial services, nor moral duties, nor even evangelical ordinances, neither of which can take away sin. There is no other Savior but Christ to look to; no other Mediator between God and man, to make use of [see *1 Tim. 2:5*]; no other physician of value, for diseased and sin-sick souls to apply unto; no other fountain but His blood, for polluted souls to wash in, and be cleansed; no other city of refuge, or stronghold, for souls sensible of danger, to flee unto and be safe; no other to come to as the bread of life, where hungry souls may be fed; no other place of rest, for those that are weary and heavy laden; nor is there any other, where there is plenty of all grace, and security from every enemy, as in Him: and therefore, to whom can they have recourse, but unto Him? and that for the following reason:

thou hast the words of eternal life. Meaning, either the promises of eternal life, which were made before the world began, and were put into Christ's hands for His people, and are yea and amen in Him; or the doctrines of eternal life; for so the Gospel, and the truths of it, are called, *Acts 5:20*; and that because the Gospel brings *life and immortality to light* [*2Tim. 1:10*], gives an account of eternal life; of the nature of it, that it is a glorious life, a life free from all the sorrows of the present one; a life of pleasure, and of perfect

223

knowledge and holiness, and which will last for ever: and because it points out the way to it, that it is not by the works of the law, but by the grace of God; that it is His free gift, through Christ; and that Christ is *the way, the truth, and the life* [*John 14:6*], or the true way to eternal life: and because it is a means of quickening dead sinners, and of reviving true believers, and of nourishing them up unto everlasting life: or this phrase may design the power and authority which Christ has, to dispose of and dispense eternal life; for He has the thing itself in His hands, and a power to give it to as many as the Father has given Him; and to them He does give it: and each of these senses carry in them a reason why souls should go to Christ, and to Him only, for life and salvation.

Verse 69. **And we believe and are sure**, &c. Or know of a certainty: they believed upon the first call of them by Christ, and their following of Him, that He was the true Messiah; and they came to an assurance of it, by the miracles He wrought, and by the doctrines which He taught; their faith, how weak soever it might be at first, rose up to a full assurance of faith, and of understanding; there was a reality and a certainty in it, as there is in all true faith, with respect to the object, though not always with respect to interest in it; which former was the case here, as appears by what follows:

that thou art that Christ; or Messiah, that was promised by God of old, spoken of by the prophets, and expected by the Jews; that anointed Prophet Moses had spoken of, that should arise out of Israel, like unto him; that anointed Priest, who, according to the oath of God, was to be *a priest for ever after the order of Melchizedek* [*Heb. 5:6*]; and that anointed King, whom God has *set* [Hebrew: *anointed*] over His *holy hill of Zion* [*Psa. 2:6*]:

the Son of the living God. This they knew, and were sure of, both by John's testimony, and by the Father's voice from heaven; which three of them heard at Christ's transfiguration on the mount. God the Father is called *the living God*; though the Vulgate Latin version leaves out the word *living*; not to distinguish Him from His Son; for He also is the living God, and is so called, *Heb. 3:12*; but to distinguish Him from the idols of the Gentiles, who have no life nor breath in them: and Christ is called the Son of the living God, as He is a divine person, as He is truly God; and to show that He has the same life His Father has; being a partaker of the same nature and divine perfections: and this is another reason why sensible souls will go to Christ, and no other; because He is the Messiah, the Savior, and Redeemer, and an able one; and because He is God, and there is none else.

Verse 70. **Jesus answered them**, &c. The disciples, taking Peter's answer to this question as delivered in the name of them all, and as expressing their mind and sense:

have not I chosen you twelve; not to grace and glory, to holiness and happiness; though this was true of eleven of them, but to be apostles:

and one of you is a devil? Or like to one, is a deceiver, a liar, and a murderer, as the devil is from the beginning; all which Judas was, and appeared to be, in the betraying of his Master. The Syriac, Persic, and Ethiopic versions read, *is Satan*; which name, if given to Peter, as it once was on a certain occasion, *Matt. 16:23*, might very well be given to Judas; who, notwithstanding his profession of faith in Christ, was in the hands and kingdom of Satan, and under his influence and power: and this our Lord said, partly that they might not too much presume upon their faith and love, and steady attachment, and be over confident of their standing; and partly, to prepare them for the apostasy of one from among them.

Verse 71. **He spake of Judas Iscariot,** *the son* **of Simon**, &c. These are the words of the evangelist, pointing out the person Christ intended, lest any other should be suspected:

for he it was that should betray him: as it was determined and foretold, and which Christ knew full well, and therefore said the above words:

being one of the twelve. Apostles, whom Christ had chosen, and which was an aggravation of his crime.

CHAPTER 7

Verse 1. **After these things Jesus walked in Galilee**, &c. That is, after He had fed the five thousand with five loaves and two fishes, near Bethsaida; and had had that long discourse with the Jews at Capernaum, concerning Himself, as the bread of life, and about eating His flesh, and drinking His blood; and had been up to the feast of the passover at Jerusalem, said to be *nigh*, when He went over the sea of Galilee, *chapter 6:4*; otherwise the above places were in Galilee: but the case seems to be this, that after He had been at Capernaum, He went to Jerusalem to keep the passover; and finding that the Jews still sought to take away His life, He returned to Galilee, and *walked* there; He did not sit still, or lie at home, and live an inactive indolent life, but went about from place to place, preaching the Gospel, and healing diseases; He walked, and walked about; but not as the enemy of souls, seeking to do all mischief, but to do all good, to the bodies and souls of men:

for he would not walk in Jewry; in the land of Judea, where He had been, and tarried, and made disciples; but being rejected and ill treated, He left them; which was a prelude of the Gospel being taken from them, and carried to another people; which afterwards took place, in the times of the apostles: His reason for it was,

because the Jews sought to kill him. For healing a man on the sabbath day, and for asserting His equality with God: not that He was afraid to die, but His time was not come; and He had work to do for the glory of God, and the good of men; and therefore it was both just and prudent to withdraw and preserve His life; for like reasons He advised His disciples, when persecuted in one city, to flee to another: and very lawful and advisable it is for good men, when their lives are in danger, to make use of proper means to preserve them, for further usefulness in the cause of God, and for the benefit of men.

Verse 2. **Now the Jews' feast of tabernacles was at hand**. Which feast began on the fifteenth day of the month Tisri, which answers to part of our September; when the Jews erected tents or booths, in which they dwelt, and ate their meals during this festival; and which was done, in commemoration of the Israelites dwelling in booths in the wilderness; and was typical of Christ's tabernacling in human nature; and an emblem of the saints dwelling in the earthly houses and tabernacles of their bodies, in this their wilderness and pilgrimage state. Some assign other reasons of this feast, as that it was appointed in commemoration of the divine command for building the tabernacle; and others, that it was instituted in memory of the protection of the people of Israel under the cloud, as they traveled through the wilderness; by which they were preserved, as in a tent or booth; and to this inclines the Targum of Onkelos, on *Lev. 23:43*, which paraphrases the words thus: *That your generations may know, that in the shadow of the clouds I caused the children of Israel to dwell, when I brought them out of the land of Egypt.* And one of the Jewish commentators[1] suggests, that the reason why the first place the Israelites pitched at, when they came out of Egypt, was called *Succoth*, which signifies *tents*, or *tabernacles*, is because there they were covered with

---

[1] Baal Hatturim in Num. 33:5.

the clouds of glory: but the true reason of this feast is that which is first given, as is clear from *Lev. 23:43*; and because they were obliged to dwell in *tents*, as soon as they came out of Egypt, therefore the first place they encamped at, was called *Succoth*, or *tabernacles, Ex. 12:37; Num. 33:5*. This feast was not kept at the time of year the people came out of Egypt; for that was at the time of the passover; but was put off, as it seems, to a colder season of the year; and which was not so convenient for dwelling in booths; lest it should be thought they observed this feast for the sake of pleasure and recreation, under the shade of these bowers; which, as appears from *Neh. 8:15-16*, were made of olive, pine, myrtle, and palm branches, and branches of thick trees; and were fixed, some on the roofs of their houses, others in their courts, and in the courts of the house of God; and others in the streets: an account of the sacrifices offered at this feast, is given in *Num. 29:13-38*, in which may be observed, that on the first day thirteen young bullocks were offered; on the second, twelve; on the third, eleven; on the fourth, ten; on the fifth, nine; on the sixth, eight; and on the seventh, seven; and on the eighth, but one. The Jews, in their Mishna, have a treatise called *Succa*, or *the Tabernacle*, in which they treat of this feast; and which contains various traditions, concerning their booths, their manner of living in them, and other rites and usages observed by them, during this festival: they are very particular about the measure and form, and covering of their booths; a booth might not be higher than twenty cubits, nor lower than ten hands' breadth; and its breadth might not be less than seven hands' breadth by seven; but it might he carried out as wide as they pleased,[2] provided it had three sides: they might not cover their booths with any thing, but what grew out of the earth, or was rooted up from thence; nor with any thing that received uncleanness, or was of an ill smell, or any thing that was fallen and faded:[3] into these booths they brought their best goods, their best bedding, and all their drinking vessels, &c. and left their houses empty; for here was their fixed dwelling; they only occasionally went into their houses;[4] for here they were obliged to dwell day and night, and eat all their meals, during the seven days of the feast; and however, it was reckoned praiseworthy, and he was accounted the most religious, who ate nothing out of his booth:[5] they were indeed excused when it was rainy

---

[2] Mishna Succa, c. 1. sect. 1. Maimonides Hilchot Succa, c. 4. sect. 1.

[3] Mishna Succa, sect. 4, 5, 6. Maimonides ibid., c. 5. sect. 1, 2, &c.

[4] Maimonides ibid. c. 6. sect. 5.

[5] Mishna ibid., c. 2. sect. 5, 6. Maimonides ibid. sect. 6, 7.

weather, but as soon as the rain was over, they were obliged to return again.[6] And besides their dwelling and sleeping, and eating and drinking, in their booths, there were various other rites which were performed by them; as particularly, the carrying of palm tree branches in their hands, or what they call the *Lulab*; which was made up of branches of palm tree, myrtle, and willow, bound up together in a bundle, which was carried in the right hand, and a pome-citron in the left; and as they carried them, they waved them three times towards the several quarters of the world; and every day they went about the altar once, with these in their hands, saying the words in *Psa. 118:25: Save now, I beseech thee, O Lord; O Lord I beseech thee, send now prosperity*: and on the seventh day, they went about the altar seven times.[7] Also there were great illuminations in the temple; at the going out of the first day of the feast, they went down to the court of the women; they made a great preparation (that is, as Bartenora explains it, they set benches round it, and set the women above, and the men below); and there were golden candlesticks there, and at the head of them four golden basins, and four ladders to every candlestick; and four young priests had four pitchers of oil, that held a hundred and twenty logs, which they put into each basin; and of the old breeches and girdles of the priests, they made wicks, and with them lighted them; and there was not a court in Jerusalem, which was not lighted with that light; and religious men, and men of good works, danced before them, with lighted torches in their hands, singing songs and hymns of praise;[8] and this continued the six nights following.[9] There was also, on every one of these days, another custom observed; which was that of fetching water from the pool of Siloah, and pouring it with wine upon the altar, which was attended with great rejoicing; of which, see the note on *verse 37* of this chapter. To which may be added, the music that was used during the performance of these rites; at the illumination in the court of the women, there were harps, psalteries, cymbals, and other instruments of music, playing all the while; and two priests with trumpets, who sounded, when they had the signal; and on every day, as they brought water from Siloah to the altar, they sounded with trumpets, and shouted; the great *Hallel*, or hymn, was sung all the eight days,

---

[6] Maimonides ibid. sect. 10.

[7] Mishna ibid. c. 4. sect. 1-5. Maimon. Hilch. Lulab, c. 7. sect. 5, 6, 9, 23.

[8] Mishna Succa, c. 5. sect. 2-4.

[9] Maimonides ibid. c. 8. sect. 12.

and the pipe was blown, sometimes five days, and sometimes six;[10] and even on all the eight days; and the whole was a feast of rejoicing, according to *Lev. 23:40.*

Verse 3 **His brethren therefore said unto him**, &c. That is, the brethren of Jesus, as the Syriac and Persic versions express it; who were not James and Joses, and Simon and Judas, the sons of Alphaeus, the brother of Joseph, the husband of Mary, so called, *Matt. 13:55*, for some of these were of the number of the twelve; and all of them believers in Christ; whereas these His brethren were not. The Jew[11] therefore is mistaken, who supposed the above persons are here intended; and objects this their unbelief to Jesus, as if they knew Him too well to give Him any credit; whereas they did believe in Him, and abode by Him to the last; and some of them, if not all, suffered death for His sake. They therefore are here to be understood of some distant relations of Mary or Joseph, that dwelt at Nazareth, or Capernaum, or in some of those parts; and the feast of tabernacles being at hand, they put Him upon going up to it, being willing to be rid of Him: saying,

Depart hence: which is the language of carnal men, who desire not the company of Christ, nor the knowledge of His ways; and, like the Gergesenes, who preferred their swine to Christ, and desired Him to depart out of their coasts:

and go into Judea; among His most inveterate enemies, who sought to take away His life; and which doubtless they knew; which showed a quite different regard to Him, from that of His true disciples, *chapter 11:7-8,* for which they give some plausible reasons:

that thy disciples also may see the works that thou doest. Meaning not His twelve disciples, who were now with Him, but the disciples He had made and baptized in Judea, *chapter 4:1-2.* Or His disciples in the several parts of the land, who would all be at Jerusalem, at the feast of tabernacles; and so, should He go, would have an opportunity of seeing His miracles, and thereby be the more confirmed in the faith of Him.

Verse 4. **For *there* is no man *that* doeth anything in secret**, &c. In *secret*, for so they reckoned His doing miracles in such a corner of the land, and in so obscure a place as Galilee:

---

[10] Mishna ibid. c. 4. sect. 8, 9. & c. 5. 1, 4, 5. & Erachin, c. 2. sect. 3.

[11] R. Isaac Chizzuk Emuna, par. 2. c. 45. p. 434, 435.

and he himself seeketh to be known openly. Suggesting hereby, that Christ was an ambitious person, and sought popular applause, and honor and glory from men, when nothing was more foreign from Him; see *chapter 5:41* and *8:50*.

If thou do these things; for they questioned whether the miracles He wrought were real; and suspected that they were deceptions of the sight, and delusions; or at least they questioned their being done by Him; and rather thought that they were done by diabolical influence, by Beelzebub the prince of devils: but if they were real ones, they advise Him, saying,

shew thyself to the world. Or do these openly, and in the presence of the great men of the world; the princes of it, the rulers of the people, the chief priests and Sanhedrin; and before all the males of Israel; who at this feast would come up from all parts of the land, and are, for their multitude called *the world*. The reason of this their advice was, that if His miracles were real, and He was the person He would be thought to be, the doing of them before such, would gain Him great credit and esteem; and if not, He might be detected by such numbers, and by men of such penetration, as were among them.

Verse 5. **For neither did his brethren believe in him**. At first His brethren might take to Him, and embrace Him as the Messiah, and expect He would set up a temporal kingdom; in which they might hope, on account of their relation to Him according to the flesh, to enjoy great honors and privileges; but finding that He was not inclined to any thing of that nature, and talked in a quite different way, they grew sick of Him, and rejected Him as the Messiah; so, little regard is to be had, or confidence placed, in carnal descent from, or alliance to the best of men; as to Abraham, or any other true believer, if they have not the same grace, or the same faith as such have; and which comes not by blood, or natural generation, but by the free favor of God; for it matters not, if men have known Christ, or have been allied to Him after the flesh, unless they are new creatures in Him; they may be the one, and not the other; even the carnal brethren of Christ, and yet not believers in Him; and it is only such who are so in a spiritual sense, that are regarded by Him, *Matt. 12:49-50*.

Verse 6. **Then Jesus said unto them**, &c. In answer to their solicitations and arguments used with Him, to go up to the feast:

My time is not yet come; meaning, not the time of His death, or of His exaltation and glorification, or of the showing of Himself forth unto the world; though all this was true; but of His going up to this feast, as appears from *verse 8*;

but your time is always ready. Intimating, they might go at any time; their lives were not in any danger, as His was, and had nothing to consult about the preservation of them; it was all one to them when they went up, whether before the feast, that they might be ready for it, or at the beginning, middle, or end of it, as to any notice that would be taken of them, unless they should be guilty of an omission of their duty; but not on any other account; which was not His case.

Verse 7. **The world cannot hate you**, &c. Because they were of the world, and belonged to it; they were like unto it, and every like loves its like; and they were the world's own, and therefore instead of being hated, were loved by it; and they walked according to the course of it; and wicked men not only take pleasure in sin, but in them that do it:

but me it hateth; though without a cause; that is, without a just cause, or reason; a cause there was, and it follows:

because I testify of it, that the works thereof are evil. Even those works of it, which were reckoned good works; Christ bore His testimony of these, that they were evil; being done either not according to the command of God, but the traditions of the elders; or not from a right principle, as of faith and love; nor to a right end, as the glory of God; but only to be seen of men: and very severely did He inveigh against the pride, covetousness, hypocrisy, and uncleanness of the Scribes and Pharisees; and so He continued to do, and this drew upon Him their hatred and ill will.

Verse 8. **Go ye up unto this feast**, &c. Suggesting, that He would not have them stay for Him, or hinder themselves on His account: He encourages them to go up, and observe this festival; for the ceremonial law was not yet abolished; and though they were carnal men, and did not understand what it typified: and so unregenerate persons ought to attend on the outward means, as the hearing of the Word, &c. though they do not understand it; it may be God may make use of it for the enlightening of their minds; and blessed are they that wait at Wisdom's gates [see *Prov. 8:34-35*], and there find Christ, and life and salvation by Him:

I go not up yet unto this feast; this clause in one of Beza's copies is wholly left out; and in some, the word *this* is not read; and in others it is read, *I go not up unto this feast*; leaving out the word *yet*; and so read the Vulgate Latin and Ethiopic versions; and the Persic version only, *I do not go up*; which occasioned Porphyry, that great enemy of Christianity, to reproach Christ, as guilty of inconstancy, or of an untruth, since He afterwards did go up: but in almost all the ancient copies the word is read; and so it is by Chrysostom and Nonnus; and to the same sense the Syriac and Arabic versions render it, *I do* *not go up now to this feast*; that is, just at that very time, that very day or hour: which is entirely consistent with what is afterwards said,

for my time is not yet full come. Not to die, or to be glorified, but to go up to the feast.

Verse 9. **When he had said these words unto them**, &c. When He had exhorted them to go up to the feast, and told them that He should not go yet, and the reason of it:

he abode *still* **in Galilee**. And went not up with His brethren, nor at all at present; showing hereby a firmness and resolution of mind, not using lightness of speech; and His words being not yea and nay, but all of apiece, and by which He abode [see *2 Cor. 1:19-20*].

Verse 10. **But when his brethren were gone up**, &c. But when his brethren were gone up *to the feast*, as all the Oriental versions read, from the next clause:

then went he also up unto the feast; the Ethiopic version reads, *he went up that day*; which is very likely, and no ways contrary to what is said in *verse 14*; for though He did not go up to the temple to teach, till the middle of the feast, He might be up at the feast sooner: and according to the law, it was necessary that He should be there on the first and second days, and keep the *Chagigah*, and make His appearance in the court; though there was a provision made for such that failed, the canon runs thus:[12]
> "He that does not make his festival sacrifice on the first good day of the feast, may make it throughout the whole feast, and on the last good day of the feast; and if the feast passes, and he has not made the festival sacrifice, he is not obliged to a compensation; and of this it is said, *Eccl. 1:15: That which is crooked cannot be made straight*; &c."

But however, whatever day He went on, He went up,

not openly, but as it were in secret. As He was made under the law, and came to fulfil all righteousness, it was necessary that He should observe every precept, and fulfil the whole law: and therefore He went up to this feast; yet in the most private manner, that He might escape those who would lie in wait for Him, and sought to kill Him: and this He did, not through fear of death, but because His hour was *not yet come*; this was not the feast He was to suffer at, but the passover following; which when near at hand, He went up to it, and entered Jerusalem in the most public manner.

---

[12] Mishna Chagiga, c. 1. sect. 6. Maimon. Hilch. Chagiga, c. 2. sect. 4-7.

Verse 11. **Then the Jews sought him at the feast**, &c. The Jews sought Him, some to take Him and kill Him, and others to hear His doctrine, and see His miracles: for all expected Him at the feast, knowing it was always His custom, as it was His duty, as an Israelite, to attend at it:

and said, Where is he? Not naming His name; either through contempt, which might be the case of the far greater part; or through fear of the Jews; or because that He was so well known.

Verse 12. **And there was much murmuring among the people concerning him**, &c. There was a general whisper, and a private controversy and contention among the people about Him, upon inquiry being made after Him:

for some said, He is a good man; a man of a good principle, of a good life and conversation; and who is good, kind, and beneficent, both to the bodies and souls of men; preaches good doctrine, and does many good things:

others said, Nay, or denied Him to be a good man:

but he deceiveth the people. Drawing them off from the law of Moses, teaching them to break the sabbath, setting Himself up for the Messiah, and asserting Himself to be the Son of God.

Verse 13. **Howbeit no man spake openly of him**, &c. No man spoke so loud as to be overheard, at least by many, but in a secret and whispering way; or they did not speak with freedom, or all their mind, what they really thought of Him, nor with courage and boldness:

for fear the Jews. For fear of being mobbed by them, or taken up and prosecuted, or turned out of the synagogue; for a law was made, that whoever confessed Him should be so used; and this deterred persons from expressing the true sentiments of their minds about Him.

Verse 14. **Now about the midst of the feast**, &c. About the fourth day of it, for it lasted eight days; this might be on the sabbath day, which sometimes was בתוך החג, *in the middle of the feast;*[13] and the rather, since it follows,

Jesus went up into the temple; as the Lord and proprietor of it, and as was His usual method; He had for some reasons kept Himself retired till now, and now He appeared publicly,

and taught. The people His doctrine; He expounded the Scriptures, gave the true sense of them, and instructed the people out of them.

---

[13] Mishna Succa, c. 5. sect. 5.

Verse 15. **And the Jews marveled**, &c. Both at the matter, and manner of His doctrine; it was such as *never man spake* [see *verse 46*]; His words were so gracious, and there were such truth and evidence in them, and they were delivered with such power and authority, that they were astonished at them:

saying, How knoweth this man letters: or *the Scriptures*, as the Arabic and Persic versions render it; which are called *holy letters, 2 Tim. 3:15*; according to which, the sense is, that they were surprised at His knowledge of the Scriptures, that He should be conversant with them, and be able to interpret them, and give the sense and meaning of them, in so full and clear a manner, as He did: or else the sense is, How came this man to be such a learned man? Whence has he this wisdom, and all this learning which he shows? as in *Matt. 13:54*. So a learned man is in *Isa. 29:11*, said to be one that יודע הספר, επισταμενος γραμματα, *knows letters*, as the Septuagint there translate the Hebrew text; but how Christ should know them, or be a learned man,

having never learned? This was surprising to them: that is, He had not had a liberal education, but was brought up to a trade; He was not trained up at the feet of any of their Rabbins, in any of their universities, or schools of learning; and in which they were certainly right. Modern Jews pretend to say He had a master, whom they sometimes call Elchanan,[14] but most commonly they make him to be R. Joshua ben Perachiah:[15] with whom they say, He fled into Alexandria in Egypt, for fear of Jannai the king; and one of their writers,[16] on this account, charges the evangelist with a falsehood: but who are we to believe, the Jews who lived at the same time with Jesus, and knew His education and manner of life, or those that have lived ages since?

Verse 16. **Jesus answered them and said**, &c. Having heard them express their surprise, and state their objection:

My doctrine is not mine: it was His, as He was God; as such, He was the author of it, it was from Him, by the revelation of Him; and it was of Him, as He was the subject of it, as Mediator; it respected His person as God-man, His offices, as Prophet, Priest, and King; and His grace, righteousness, and salvation; and it was His, as preached by Him as man; it came by Him, and first began to be spoken by Him; and was so spoken by Him, as it never was

---

[14] Toldos Jesu, p. 5.

[15] Juchasin, fol. 159. 1. Ganz Tzemach David, par. 1, fol. 21. 1. & 24.

[16] R. Isaac Chizzuk Emuna, par. 2. c. 46. p. 435.

before, or since: but it was not human; it was not acquired by Him, as man; He did not learn it of man; He needed no human teachings; He increased in wisdom without them, from His infancy: they said right, in saying He had *never learned*; the spirit of wisdom and knowledge rested on Him, and the treasures of them were hid in Him; nor was it a device or invention of His, as man; it was not from Himself as such, but it was from heaven, from His Father: wherefore He adds,

but his that sent me. Thereby intimating, that it was of God, and was communicated to Him by His Father; from whom He received it, and from whom He had a commission to preach it; so that His doctrine was that wisdom which comes from above, and is pure and peaceable, divine and heavenly, and ought to be received by men.

Verse 17. **If any man will do his will**, &c. Meaning, by *any* man, not one that perfectly fulfils the law, which is the good, and perfect, and acceptable will of God [see *Rom. 12:2*]; for there is no man that does this, or can do it; nor is it so said here, *if any man do his will*, but *if any man will do* it; that is, is desirous of doing it; who has it wrought in Him *both to will and to do*, of the *good pleasure* of God [*Phil. 2:13*], by His grace and Spirit; with whom to will is present, though he has not power to perform [see *Rom. 7:18*], and so is a spiritual man; and who believes in the Lord Jesus Christ, which is one branch of the will of God; and who depends upon the Spirit and grace of God, and acts from a principle of love to God, and in the exercise of faith on Christ:

he shall know of the doctrine, whether it be of God, or *whether* I speak of myself. Not a man of mere natural knowledge and learning, or a man of theory and speculation, is a judge of doctrine; but he that leans not to his own understanding [see *Prov. 3:5*], and implores the assistance of the divine Spirit, and who is for reducing doctrine into practice: he knows by the efficacy of the doctrine upon his heart, and the influence it has on his life and conversation; by its coming not *in word only*, but *in power* [*1 Thess. 1:5*]; and by its working effectually in him, whether it is divine or human, of God or of man.

Verse 18. **He that speaketh of himself**, &c. That speaketh what he himself has devised, and is a scheme of his own; for which he has no divine warrant and commission:

seeketh his own glory; honor and applause from men; as did the Scribes and Pharisees, who taught *for doctrines the commandments of men* [*Matt. 15:9*], the traditions of the elders, their own glosses upon the law, and their own decisions and determinations: and as did the false teachers, who had nothing else in view but themselves, their worldly interest, or vain glory;

these suited their doctrines to the minds and lusts of men, in order to gain their point:

but he that seeketh his glory that sent him; that gave him in commission what he should say and speak, and his only; as did Christ, and so His apostles after Him:

the same is true, and no unrighteousness is in him. He is an upright and faithful man, and what he says is truth; he brings true doctrine along with him, and there is no fraud or imposture in him; nor any *insincerity in his heart*, as the Syriac and Persic versions render it; nor any dishonesty in his conduct; he is no cheat or deceiver; was he, he would seek his own glory and interest; but as he appears to be a man of no ill design, his doctrine is to be depended on and received; and such was Christ.

Verse 19. **Did not Moses give you the law**, &c. After Christ had vindicated Himself and His doctrine, He proceeds to reprove the Jews for their breaking the law of Moses, which contained the will of God; by which it appeared that they were no proper judges of His doctrine, though they cavilled at it: the question He puts could not be denied by them; for though, properly speaking, God was the lawgiver, yet inasmuch as it was delivered by Moses, it is ascribed to him, and said to come by him; and it was put into his hands, to be delivered by him peculiarly to the people of Israel; and being given to the Jewish fathers, not only for themselves, but for their posterity in ages to come, is said to be *given* to the then present generation; and may be understood, either of the whole system of laws—moral, ceremonial, and, judicial, belonging to that people; or else of the particular law concerning the keeping of the sabbath, which was a peculiar law of Moses, and proper to the children of Israel only:

and *yet* none of you keepeth the law? Though they boasted of it as a singular privilege, and rested in it, and their obedience to it, for life and salvation, yet they daily broke it in various instances, in thought, word, or deed; yea, those that sat in Moses's chair, and taught it, did not observe and do what they taught; nor could the most holy and righteous man among them perfectly keep it: and many of them, who were most forward to censure others for the violation of it, paid the least regard to it; and particularly to the law of the sabbath, which both priests and people transgressed, in one point or another, every sabbath day: wherefore our Lord reasons with them,

Why go ye about to kill me? A harmless and innocent man, who never injured you in your persons and properties; and which is a proof of their not keeping that body of laws Moses gave them, since *Thou shalt not kill* is one of them: though rather this may refer to the law of the sabbath, and the sense be, that since Moses had given them the law of the sabbath, and they did not keep it themselves, why should they seek to take away His life, for what they pretended was a breach of it? For our Lord here, as appears by what follows, refers to what they sought to do, above a year and a half ago, and still continued to seek after; namely, to kill Him, because He had healed a man on the sabbath day, *chapter 5:16,18* and *7:1.*

Verse 20. **The people answered and said**, &c. These seem to be the country people, who came from Galilee and other parts, who knew nothing of the designs of the Jerusalem Jews upon Him; nor were they His downright enemies at least, but rather seemed to favor Him, and were on His side, though greatly provoked to hear Him talk after this manner:

Thou hast a devil; or art possessed with one; thou talkest like one of the demoniacs, like a madman, one beside thyself; whom the devil has so much power over, and has so deprived of thy senses, that thou knowest not what thou sayest:

who goeth about to kill thee? No man; for they could not believe that any man, or body of men, would be so wicked, as to attempt to take away the life of so harmless a person, and who did so much good both to the bodies and souls of men.

Verse 21. **Jesus answered and said unto them**, &c. Taking no notice of their passion, reproach, and blasphemy; but proceeding upon the thing He had in view, and which He was determined to reassume, and vindicate Himself in:

I have done one work; that is, on the sabbath day; meaning, His cure of the man that had had a disorder eight and thirty years, who lay at Bethesda's pool; which single action, they charged with being a breach of the sabbath, He mentions with a view to their many, and daily violations of it:

and ye all marvel. At it, as a thing unheard of, as a most shocking piece of iniquity, as an intolerable evil; wondering that any man should have the front, to bid another take up his bed and walk on the sabbath day: they did not marvel at the miracle that was wrought; but were amazed, offended, and disturbed, at its being done on the sabbath day.

Verse 22. **Moses therefore gave unto you circumcision**, &c. Moses gave the command of circumcision, which he renewed and established, *Lev. 12:3;*

(not because it is of Moses; that is, originally, or that he was the first giver of it, for it was enjoined before his time; this is a correction of what is before said, giving a more accurate account of the rise of circumcision:

237

but of the fathers); Abraham, Isaac, and Jacob, to whom it was enjoined by God, and who practiced it before the times of Moses; so that this command was in force before him, and obligatory upon the descendants of Abraham, before he delivered it; and would have been, if he had never mentioned it; though the Jews say,[17]

> "We do not circumcise because Abraham our father, on whom be peace, circumcised himself and his household, but because the holy blessed God commanded us by Moses, that we should be circumcised, as Abraham our father was circumcised."

But no doubt it would have been binding on them, if Moses had said nothing about it; the command to Abraham is so express, for the circumcision of his male offspring, *Gen. 17:10-12*; however, it being both of Moses and of the fathers, laid a very great obligation on the Jews to observe it:

and ye on the sabbath day, circumcise a man. A male child, as they did, when the eighth day fell on a sabbath day; for the law of circumcision was before the law of the sabbath, and therefore was not to be made void by it, nor was it made void by it; and so much is intimated by our Lord's observing, that it was not *of Moses, but of the fathers*; and this is the reason which the Karaite Jews give for circumcision on the sabbath day: for,[18]

> "Say they, because it is a former command, from the time of Abraham our father, on whom be peace, before the giving of the law of the sabbath, היו מלים בשבת, *they circumcise on the sabbath day*; and when the command of the sabbath afterwards took place, it was not possible it should disannul circumcision on the sabbath day; and for the same reason, they also allow the sacrifice of the passover to be done on the sabbath day, because it is a command which went before the command of the sabbath."

And this was also the sense and practice of the other Jews: thus citing the law of Moses in *Lev. 12:3*: *And in the eighth day, the flesh of his foreskin shall be circumcised*, by way of gloss upon it add, ואפילו בשבת, *and even on the sabbath day*;[19] and on the same text another writer observes,[20] that by gematry, every day is fit for circumcision. R. Jose says,[21]

---

[17] Maimonides in Mishna Cholin, c. 7. sect. 6.

[18] R. Eliaha in Adderet apud Trigland. de Sect. Karaeorum, c. 9. p. 134.

[19] T. Bab. Sabbat, fol. 132. 1. Mitzvot Tora, pr. Affirm. 28.

[20] Baal Hatturim in Lev. 12:3.

[21] Mishna Sabbat, c. 18. sect. 3.

"they do all things necessary to circumcision, on the sabbath day."
R. Abika says,[22]

"All work that can be done on the evening of the sabbath, does not drive away the sabbath; but circumcision, which cannot be done on the evening of the sabbath, drives away the sabbath: they do all things necessary to circumcision; they circumcise, and make bare, and suck, and put (on the wound) a plaster and cummin; and which, if not bruised on the evening of the sabbath, they may chew with their teeth."

Also it is allowed of [23] to,

"wash the infant on the third day of circumcision, which happens to be on the sabbath."

Moreover, a case is put after this manner:[24]

"If a man has two infants, one to be circumcised *after* the sabbath, and the other to be circumcised *on* the sabbath, and forgets, and circumcises that, that was to be after the sabbath, on the sabbath, he is guilty of sin; if one is to be circumcised in the evening of the sabbath, and the other on the sabbath, and he forgets, and circumcises that which should be on the evening of the sabbath, on the sabbath, R. Eliezer pronounces him guilty, but R. Joshua absolves him."

And we have an instance[25] of,

"R. Sheshana, the son of R. Samuel bar Abdimo, that when he was to be circumcised, it was the sabbath day, and they forgot the razor; and they inquired of R. Meni and R. Isaac ben Eleazar, and it was driven off to another day."

From all which it appears, that circumcision on the sabbath day was a common practice, and which confirms the assertion of Christ.

Verse 23. **If a man on the sabbath day receive circumcision**, &c. As it was certain in many instances he did:

that the law of Moses might not be broken; either the law concerning circumcision, which confirmed the law given to Abraham, and required it should be on the eighth day, let it fall when it would, even on a sabbath day;

---

[22] Mishna Sabbat, c. 19. sect. 1, 2. T. Bab. Pesachim, fol. 69. 2. Maimon. Hilchot Milah, c. 2. sect. 6, 7.

[23] Ibid. sect. 3. Bereshit Rabba, sect. 8. fol. 70. 3. Maimon. ibid., sect. 8.

[24] Ibid. sect. 4. T. Bab. Ceritot, fol. 19. 2.

[25] Juchasin, fol. 105. 2.

and therefore on that day, male children received circumcision, that that law might be kept, and not be broken: or else the law concerning the sabbath; and the sense be, if circumcision was administered on the sabbath day, *without breaking the law of Moses*, as some render the words, which commanded the observation of the sabbath,

are ye angry at me; and pursue me with so much wrath and bitterness,

because I have made a man every whit whole on the sabbath day? Or *a man that was whole, sound on the sabbath day*; who was wholly, or all over disordered, every limb of whom shook with the palsy: or, as some think the sense is, he was made every whit whole, both in soul and body; and then the argument is, if it was no breach of the sabbath to make a wound, and lay a plaster on it, as in circumcision; it would be no violation of it, nor ought any to be offended with it, that Christ should heal a diseased man, who was so in every part of his body, and restore health to his soul likewise: and nothing is more common with the Jews than to say,

> "the danger of life, and פיקוח נפש, *the preservation of the soul*, or life, drive away the sabbath."[26]

Verse 24. **Judge not according to the appearance**, &c. Judge not through respect of persons, and so as to please men, the Scribes and Pharisees; who had condemned the action of Christ, in curing the diseased man on the sabbath day, and sought to kill Him for it:

but judge righteous judgment. Give your sense and judgment of things, according to the truth and evidence of them; and do not find fault with that which you yourselves allow of, and which Moses and his law, and your own practices, justify.

Verse 25. **Then said some of them of Jerusalem**, &c. Some who were inhabitants of Jerusalem, and so are distinguished from the people, *verse 20*, who came up out of the country to the feast; so Jose ben Jochanan is called איש ירושלים, *a man of Jerusalem*;[27] that is, an inhabitant of it: now these men living in the city, knew more of the temper and disposition, the designs and attempts, of the chief priests, Scribes, and elders, to take away the life of Christ; and therefore say,

is not this he whom they seek to kill? They knew that they had formed a design to kill Him, ever since the passover before the last; when He wrought

---

[26] T. Bab. Sabbat, fol. 132. 1.

[27] Pirke Abot, c. 1. sect. 4, 5.

the miracle referred to in the text, and that they had been ever since plotting against His life, and were now at this feast seeking an opportunity to lay hold on Him and kill Him.

Verse 26. **But lo, he speaketh boldly**, &c. And with great freedom, and openly and publicly in the temple, as if He had a license from the chief priests for so doing:

and they say nothing unto him. They do not contradict Him, or forbid Him speaking; He goes on without control; though He takes great liberty in charging the Jews with an intention to kill Him, in arguing from their practices in vindication of Himself, and in suggesting that they judged in favor of men, and not according to the truth of things.

Do the rulers know indeed that this is the very Christ? Have they changed their minds concerning Him, and so their conduct towards Him? Are they convinced, and do they know by plain demonstrations, and full proof, that He is really the Messiah that has been promised of old, and long expected?

Verse 27. **Howbeit, we know this man whence he is**, &c. They signify, that if the rulers had altered their minds, and had gone into the belief of Jesus of Nazareth being the Messiah, they should not follow them in it, for this reason; because they knew from whence He came; meaning not so much the place of His birth, which they supposed was Galilee, and Nazareth in Galilee, in which they were mistaken, as the manner of His birth, which they could account for: they pretended to know His extract, that He was the son of Joseph and Mary, that He was begotten in wedlock, and was born as other persons are; there was no difficulty with them in accounting for His coming into the world, no more than any other ordinary person; His descent from Joseph and Mary was well known to them, and to be accounted for in a rational way, and therefore concluded he could not be the Messiah:

but when Christ cometh, no man knoweth whence he is. They knew the place from whence He was to come; so the chief priests and Scribes did, *Matt. 2:4-5*; and so did these Jews, *verse 42*. They knew He would come from Bethlehem, and they knew that He would come out of the seed of David; but then He was to be born of a virgin, according to *Isa. 7:14*; and such a coming into the world was not to be known, reasoned upon, and accounted for: wherefore since Jesus, according to the notion of these men, came into the world in the common and ordinary way, they thought they had an invincible argument against His being the Messiah; and therefore, let the rulers do what they would, for their parts, they were determined to reject Him: and because it could not be known from whence the Messiah should come; hence the ancient Jews used to call Him *the seed which comes from another place*; not from the place from whence seed ordinarily comes, from the loins of men, but from some other place they knew not where: their words are very remarkable on that passage in *Gen. 4:25*: *and she* [that is, Eve] *called his name Seth, for God hath appointed me another seed*, &c. This observation is made by R. Tanchuma, in the name of R. Samuel;[28] says he,

> "She has respect to that seed, which is he that comes, ממקום אחר, *from another place*. And what is this? This is the King Messiah."

And elsewhere,[29] the same Rabbi observes on those words in *Gen. 19:32*: *that we may preserve seed of our father*:

> "it is not written, *that we may preserve a son of our father*, but *that we may preserve seed of our father*; that seed which is He that comes from *another place*; and what is this? This is the King Messiah."

The modern Jews[30] endeavor to explain away the sense of this phrase, *another seed*, as if it regarded strange seed; and that the sense of the expression is only, that the Messiah should spring from the family of Moab, and from Ruth the Moabitess: nor is their sense what Aquinas[31] attributes to the Jewish Rabbins,

> "that the more noble part of that mass, of which Adam was made, remained untouched (by sin), and was afterwards transfused into Seth; and so through all descending from him, unto Joakim, or Eliakim, or Heli, the father of the virgin, out of which the body of the blessed Virgin was made:"

which is no other than a Popish device, fathered upon the Jews, and made for the sake of the Virgin Mary, rather than for the sake of Christ. But their meaning is, that Christ should not be begotten of man, or come into the world in the ordinary way of generation, but should be born of a virgin; and so could not be known, and accounted for from whence He was, or from whence that seed was of which He was made. The angel gives the best account of this in *Luke 1:35*: a body was prepared for Christ by the Lord; it was conceived by the power of the Holy Ghost; His birth of a virgin was miraculous; it is beyond the comprehension of men, and cannot be explained by any mortal; from whence He is it cannot be said; no man can be pointed to as His father; all that can be said is, *He was made of a woman* [*Gal. 4:4*], *a virgin* [*Matt. 1:23-25*].

---

[28] Bereshit Rabba, sect. 23. fol. 20. 4. Midrash Ruth, fol. 36. 1.

[29] Bereshit Rabba, sect. 51. fol. 46. 1. Midrash Ruth, fol. 35. 4.

[30] Mattanot Cehunah & Jade Moseh in ibid.

[31] In 3 sent. distinct. 3. art. 2.

Verse 28. **Then cried Jesus in the temple as he taught**, &c. Overhearing the reasonings of these men, or however, knowing what they said; so the Persic version adds, *having secretly known this*; exalted His voice as He was teaching in the temple, and in the midst of His discourse, publicly before all the people, in the temple, spoke out with a loud voice, that all might hear:

saying, Ye both know me, and ye know whence I am; some, as the Ethiopic version, read these words by way of interrogation, *Do ye both know me, and do ye know from whence I am?* No; you do not. Or they may be considered as an ironical concession; Yes, you know me, and you know whence I am; you know me to be Jesus of Nazareth, but you are wrong, I am not of Nazareth; you suppose I come from Galilee, but that is your ignorance; you take me to be the real son of Joseph, to be begotten by him of Mary, but that is your mistake: such is your knowledge of me; you know me indeed who I am, and from whence I come:

and I am not come of myself; into this world, by incarnation, or the assumption of human nature, to work out the salvation of men: the Father called Him to it, and He agreeing to do it, was in the fulness of time sent about it; this was not a device of His own, or an honor He took to Himself; He was not alone in it; it was a mutual agreement between Him and His Father, in consequence of which He was sent and came;

but he that sent me is true; to the covenant He made with Christ, and to the promises He made to the fathers of the Old Testament, concerning the mission of His Son; and He is true to be believed, in the testimonies He gave of Him, particularly by a voice from heaven, declaring Him His beloved Son;

whom ye know not. So that notwithstanding all their boasted knowledge of Him, they knew not His Father, from whence He came, and by whom He was sent; and notwithstanding also their boasted knowledge of the one, only, true, and living God, see *Rom. 2:17*, yet they knew Him not in a spiritual sense; they knew Him not in Christ, nor as the Father of Christ; they knew neither the Father nor the Son: and this their ignorance of both was the reason of their hatred of Christ, and of His followers, *John 15:21* and *16:3*.

Verse 29. **But I know him**, &c. His nature and perfections, His purposes and promises, His council and covenant, His mind and will; and indeed none knows Him but He, and those to whom He pleases to reveal Him [see *Luke 10:22*]; and there is good reason why He should have intimate and perfect knowledge of Him:

for I am from him; being the only begotten of Him, and as such lay in His bosom, and knew Him, and His whole heart, and was privy to all of Him, and that that is within Him;

243

and he hath sent me. In an office capacity to redeem His people. This is the original descent of Christ, which the Jews knew not, though they pretended to know Him, and whence He was.

Verse 30. **Then they sought to take him**, &c. By force, and carry Him before the Sanhedrin, in order to be tried and condemned as a blasphemer; being enraged to hear Him claim a descent from God, whom they took to be a mere man, the son of Joseph the carpenter:

but no man laid hands on him; though they had a good will [*or* earnest intention] to do it, they had no power to do it, being restrained by the secret providence of God from it, and awed by the majesty of Christ, which showed itself in His looks and words; and perhaps also they might be afraid of the people, lest they should rise in His favor; and so every man being fearful of being the first that should seize Him, no man did: however, so it was ordered by divine providence, that He should not be apprehended at this time,

because his hour was not yet come. To suffer and die, to depart out of this world, and go to the Father: there was a precise time fixed for this in the council and covenant of God, by mutual compact, called *due time*; as His coming into the world is called *the fulness of time*; nor could He die before that time, and therefore no man was suffered to lay hands on Him, whatever good will he had to do it. And there is a time for every man's death, nor can any man die before that time, or live beyond it; see *Eccl. 3:2; Job 14:5*; and this is the sense of the ancient Jews; for they say,[32]

"A man before his years, or his time, does not die;"

that is, before he comes to the years appointed for him: and they ask,[33]

"Who is there that goes before his time? that is, dies before his time?"

And it is said[34] of a certain person who was in his house,

"and מטא זמניה, *his time was come*; and he died without sickness:"

though it must be owned some of them were otherwise minded, and say,[35] that death, by the hand of heaven, or God, shortens a man's years; and that there are some reasons for which righteous men depart out of this world before their

---

[32] T. Bab. Yebamot, fol. 114. 2. & Sanhedrin, fol. 29. 1. & Bava Metzia, fol. 85. 1.

[33] T. Bab. Chagiga, fol. 4. 2.

[34] Zohar in Exod. fol. 71. 4.

[35] Piske Tosephot. Sabbat, art. 113.

time is come; and particularly of Enoch they say, *God took him before his time was come.*[36]

Verse 31. **And many of the people believed on him**, &c. While some were displeased at His doctrine, others were induced by His miracles to believe on Him, as an extraordinary person, if not the Messiah; and these were the common people, especially those that came out of the country; for the city Jews, and above all the rulers, were very averse to Him: and it is easy to observe, that faith in Christ, and true religion, spread and flourish most among the meaner sort of people [that is, those lacking in social distinction];

and said, When Christ cometh, will he do more miracles than these which this *man* hath done? Referring not so much to the miracles many of them might have seen done by Him in other parts of Judea, and in Galilee; nor only to those He had done in the preceding feasts at Jerusalem, but to those that were done by Him now, though not recorded by the evangelist. The Jews expected many miracles to be wrought by the Messiah when He came, and they had good reason for it from *Isa. 35:5-6*. To these Christ sends John the Baptist, and the Jews, for proofs of His being the Messiah, *Matt. 11:4; John 10:37-38*; and by these He was approved of God as such, *Acts 2:23*. And it is certain that the Jews expected miracles in the days of the Messiah.

"Says R. Simeon to Eleazar his son, Eleazar, at the time that the King Messiah is raised up, how many *signs and other wonders* will be done in the world? A little after, from that day all the *signs*, and *wonders*, and *mighty works*, which the holy blessed God did in Egypt, He will do to the Israelites, as it is said, *Mic. 7:15, According to the days of thy coming out of the land of Egypt, will I show unto him marvelous things.*"[37]

So the Targumist on *Isa. 53:8* paraphrases thus:

"From afflictions and punishment he will deliver our captivity, and *the wonderful things* which shall be done for us in his days, who can tell?"

It is true indeed that the modern Jews have laid aside such expectations, and pretend they were not looked for formerly. Maimonides says,[38]

"Let it not enter into thy heart, that the King Messiah hath need to do signs and wonders (as that he shall renew things in the world, or raise

---

[36] Zohar in Exod. fol. 4. 4.

[37] Zohar in Exod. fol. 3. 4. & 4. 2.

[38] Hilchot Melakim, c. 11. sect. 3.

the dead, and the like; these are things which fools speak of); the thing is not so."

And he instances in Ben Coziba, who set up for the Messiah, of whom R. Akiba, and the rest of the wise men of that age, did not require a sign or miracle: yet this same writer elsewhere says[39] that,

"all nations shall make peace with the Messiah, and serve him, because of his great righteousness, and the *miracles* which shall be done by him."

Verse 32. **The Pharisees heard that the people murmured**, &c. Or whispered, privately talked among themselves:

such things concerning him; as that surely He must be the Messiah, since such wonderful things were done by Him, and might also express some uneasiness and surprise, that the rulers did not receive Him as such:

and the Pharisees and the chief priests sent officers to take him. And bring Him before the Sanhedrin, by them to be condemned, and so a stop be put to the people's receiving Him, and believing in Him as the Messiah; fearing, that should things go on at this rate, their principles and practices would be rejected, and their persons and authority be brought into contempt.

Verse 33. **Then said Jesus unto them**, &c. To the officers that were sent to take Him, and other unbelieving Jews that were about Him:

yet a little while am I with you; no longer than till the next passover, which was but about half a year at most: this He might say, partly to quicken the attention of the people to Him, to make the best use and improvement of His ministry while they had it, since in a little time He would be removed from them; and partly to suggest to the officers that were sent to take Him, that they, and their masters, need not have given themselves that trouble, for in a short time He should be gone from them, and till that time He should continue in spite of them.

And *then* I go unto him that sent me. Still confirming His mission from God, expressing His death by going, and as being voluntary, and signifying His glory and happiness after it.

Verse 34. **Ye shall seek me**, &c. That is, the Messiah, who He was; meaning, that after His departure they should be in great distress, and be very much on the inquiry after, and solicitous for the coming of the Messiah, to be a redeemer and deliverer of them out of their troubles:

---

[39] In Mishna Sanhedrin, c. 11. sect. 1.

and shall not find *me*; no Messiah will appear, no Savior will be sent, no Redeemer will come to relieve them; they shall inquire, and look for one in vain, as they did;

and where I am, *thither* **ye cannot come**. Intimating hereby, that not only their temporal estate and condition would be very distressed and miserable, but also their eternal estate; since they should not be able to come where He would be in His human nature, and where He now was, as a divine person, namely, in heaven.

Verse 35. **Then said the Jews among themselves**, &c. That is, the unbelieving, scoffing Jews; it may be the officers, at least some of them, that were sent to take Him:

whither will he go that we shall not find him? What distant, or obscure part of the world will He betake Himself to, and there hide Himself, that so He cannot be found?

will he go unto the dispersed among the Gentiles: or Greeks; and so may design the Jews, who were scattered abroad in the times of the Grecian monarchy, under the successors of Alexander, and particularly Antiochus, in distinction from the Babylonish dispersion; or *the strangers scattered through Pontus, Galatia*, &c. to whom Peter writes, *1 Pet. 1:1.* The Arabic version renders it, *the sect of the Greeks* by which the Hellenistic Jews seem to be meant: or the Jews in general, wherever, and by whomsoever scattered; who might be thought to be more ignorant than the Jews in Judea, and therefore more easily to be imposed upon: hence, in a flouting manner, they inquire whether He will go to those, when He is rejected by them. The Syriac and Ethiopic versions read, *will he go into the countries, or country of the Gentiles?* into heathen countries, not to the Jews there, but to the Gentiles themselves:

and teach the Gentiles? Suggesting, that He was more fit to be a teacher of them than of the Jews, and might meet with more encouragement and success among them, who would not be able to detect Him.

Verse 36. **What** *manner* **of saying is this that he said**, &c. It is not easy to be understood; and if that is not meant, which is suggested, what should He mean by saying,

Ye shall seek me, and shall not find *me*, **and where I am,** *thither* **ye cannot come?** Repeating the words of Christ just now expressed by Him.

Verse 37. **In the last day, that great day of the feast**, &c. That is, of the feast of tabernacles, as appears from *verse 2,* which was usually called גֹח, *the*

feast, in distinction from the passover and Pentecost;[40] and the eighth day of it was called הרגל האחרון, *the last day of the feast*,[41] as here: and it was a *great day*, being, as is said in *Lev. 23:36, a holy convocation, a solemn assembly*, in which no servile work was done, and in which an offering was made by fire unto the Lord. According to the traditions of the Jews, fewer sacrifices were offered on this day than on the rest; for on the first day they offered thirteen bullocks, and lessened one every day; so that on the seventh day, there was but seven offered, and on the eighth day but one, when the priests returned to their lots, as at other feasts:[42] but notwithstanding the Jews make out this to be the greater day for them, since the seventy bullocks offered on the other seven days, were for the seventy nations of the world; but the one bullock, on the eighth day, was peculiarly for the people of Israel:[43] and besides, they observe, that there were several things peculiar on this day, as different from the rest; as the casting of lots, the benediction by itself, a feast by itself, an offering by itself, a song by itself, and a blessing by itself:[44] and on this day they had also the ceremony of drawing and pouring water, attended with the usual rejoicings as on other days; the account of which is this:[45]

> "The pouring out of water was after this manner; a golden pot, which held three logs, was filled out of Siloah, and when they came to the water gate, they blew (their trumpets) and shouted, and blew; (then a priest) went up by the ascent of the altar, and turned to the left hand, (where) were two silver basins—that on the west side was filled with water, and that on the east with wine; he poured the basin of water into that of wine, and that of wine into that of water."

At which time there were great rejoicing, piping, and dancing, by the most religious and sober people among the Jews; insomuch that it is said[46] that,

> "He that never saw the rejoicing of the place of drawing of water, never

---

[40] Shirhashirim Rabba, fol. 5. 3. & 7. 3.

[41] Mishna Bava Metzia, c. 7. sect. 6. & Maimonides in ibid.

[42] Bartenora in Mishna Succa, c. 5. sect. 6.

[43] T. Bab. Succa, fol. 55. 2. Bemidbar Rabba, sect. 21. fol. 231. 1.

[44] T. Bab. Succa, fol. 48. 1.

[45] Mishna Succa, c. 4. sect. 9.

[46] Mishna Succa, c. 5. sect. 1, 4.

saw any rejoicing in his life."
And this ceremony, they say,[47] is a tradition of Moses from Mount Sinai, and refers to some secret and mysterious things; yea, they plainly say, that it has respect to the pouring forth of the Holy Ghost.[48]

"Says R. Joshua ben Levi, why is its name called the place of drawing water? Because, from thence שואבים רוח הקודש, *they draw the Holy Ghost*, as it is said, *and ye shall draw water with joy out of the wells of salvation, Isa. 12:3.*"

Moreover, it was on this day they prayed for the rains for the year ensuing: it is asked,[49]

"From what time do they make mention of the powers of the rains (which descend by the power of God)? R. Eliezer says, From the first good day of the feast (of tabernacles); R. Joshua says, From the last good day of the feast.—They do not pray for the rains, but near the rains;"

that is, the time of rains; and which, one of their commentators says,[50] is the eighth day of the feast of tabernacles; for from the feast of tabernacles, thenceforward is the time of rains. The Jews have a notion, that at this feast the rains of the ensuing year were fixed: hence they say[51] that,

"At the feast of tabernacles judgment is made concerning the waters;"
or a decree or determination is made concerning them by God. Upon which the Gemara[52] has these words,

"Wherefore does the law say pour out water on the feast of tabernacles? Says the holy blessed God, Pour out water before me, that the rains of the year may be blessed unto you."

Now when all these things are considered, it will easily be seen with what pertinency our Lord expresses Himself on this day, with respect to the effusion of the gifts and graces of the Spirit of God, as follows:

---

[47] T. Zebachim, fol. 110. 2. Maimon. in Mishna Succa, c. 4. sect. 9. & Hilchot Tamidin, c. 10. sect. 6.

[48] T. Hieros. Succa, fol. 55. 1. Bereshit Rabba, sect. 70. fol. 62. 3. & Midrash Ruth, fol. 32. 2. Caphtor, fol. 52. 1.

[49] Mishna Taanith, c. 1. sect. 1, 2.

[50] Bartenora, in ibid.

[51] Mishna Roshhashana, c. 1. sect. 2.

[52] T. Bab. Roshhashana, fol. 16. 1.

Jesus stood and cried; He now stood up, whereas at other times He used to sit, and spoke with a loud voice, both to show His fervor and earnestness, and that all might hear:

saying, If any man thirst, let him come unto me and drink. This is to be understood, not of a natural thirst, though the allusion is to it, which is very painful and distressing; as the instances of the Israelites in the wilderness, Samson after he had slain the Philistines, and our Lord upon the cross, show; much less a sinful thirst, a thirst after the riches, honors, and pleasures of this life; but a spiritual thirst, or a thirst after spiritual things, after salvation by Christ, and a view of interest in it, free and full pardon of sin through Him, justification by His righteousness, a greater degree of knowledge of Him, more communion with Him, and conformity to Him, and after the sincere milk of the Word, and the breasts of Gospel ordinances: and such that thirst after these things, and eagerly desire them, and are in pain and uneasiness without them, as a man is who has a violent thirst upon him, are such as are regenerated and quickened by the Spirit of God, and are made sensible of themselves, and of their state and condition by nature. Now these Christ invites to *come* unto Him; not to Moses and his law, moral or ceremonial, and to obedience to them, and works of righteousness done by them, nor to any creature, or creature acts; for these are cisterns without water, where no true peace, joy, righteousness, and salvation are to be had; but to Himself, who is the fountain of gardens, the well of living waters, and who is as rivers of water in a dry land, to thirsty souls: and when come to Him, which is by believing in Him, they are encouraged to *drink*; that is, to take of the water of life freely, or to take of His grace freely; salvation by Him is of free grace, and the pardon of sin is according to the riches of grace, and justification is freely by His grace, and so all other blessings; and of this they may drink abundantly, or they may partake of it largely: there is a fulness of grace in Christ, and there is an abundance of it communicated to His people; it is exceeding abundant; it flows, and overflows, and may be drank of to satisfaction, till their souls are as a watered garden, and they are satisfied with the goodness of the Lord.

Verse 38. **He that believeth on me**, &c. Which explains what is meant by coming to Christ, and drinking; for these acts are no other than for a man to go out of himself to Christ, and live by faith on Him, and His grace. To which what follows is a great encouragement;

as the Scripture hath said: some refer these words to the preceding clause concerning believing in Christ, which the writings of the Old Testament speak of, as in *Deut. 18:15; Isa. 28:16; Hab. 2:4*; and the sense is, that he that believes on Christ, the object of faith the Scripture points at, and in Him, as that directs and requires; that believes in Him as the mighty God, and as the

Prophet, Priest, and King, and as the only foundation of the church, and lives by faith upon Him, as just men do, then,

out of his belly shall flow rivers of living water. Though rather they belong to what follows; and do not design any particular place of Scripture; for no such one is to be found, where the following passage is expressed in so many words; but all those Scriptures which speak of grace, under the metaphors of water, and abundance of water, as rivers and floods of water, and of the effusion of the Holy Spirit, under such figurative expressions, such as *Isa. 41:17-18; 43:20; 44:3* and *58:11; Joel 2:28*. Hence the Syriac version reads in the plural number, *as the Scriptures hath said*; referring to more than one: *out of his belly shall flow rivers of living water*; the grace of the Spirit of God is signified by *water*, because it is of a cleansing and purifying nature, as faith and hope are, having to do with the blood of Christ, which cleanses from all sin; and because it fructifies and causes the saints, as trees of righteousness, to grow, and bring forth fruit; and especially because it is cooling to those who are scorched with the heat of a fiery law, and very refreshing to thirsty souls: and it is called *living* water, because by it dead sinners are quickened, drooping saints are revived and comforted; spiritual life in them is maintained and supported, and it springs up to, and issues in eternal life: and it is expressed by *rivers of living water*, because of the abundance of it in regeneration, justification, and pardon; it is grace for grace, abundance of grace believers receive from Christ; and from Him, in whom those large measures of grace are, they *flow out* again, even *out of his belly*: from within him, out of his heart, the seat of it, by his lips, both in prayer to God, and in conversation with the saints, to whom he communicates his rich experiences of grace, to their comfort, and the glory of God: for grace is of a diffusive and communicative nature; out of the abundance of the heart, the mouth speaketh: and also it flows out by his life and conversation, which is sober, righteous, and godly; and this the grace of God teaches and influences: and this grace, as it is permanent and lasting itself, even perpetual, and always abiding; so it continues to flow, and to show itself in its acts and effects, in one way or another. The Jews ought not to find fault with Christ's using such expressions, mystically understood, since they, comparing Moses and the Messiah together, say,

"As the first redeemer caused a well to spring up, so the last Redeemer shall cause waters to spring up, according to *Joel 3:18*." [53]

Verse 39. (**But this spake he of the Spirit**, &c. These are the words of the evangelist, explaining the figurative expressions of Christ; showing, that by

---

[53] Midrash Kohelet, fol. 63. 2.

rivers of living water, He meant the Spirit in His gifts and graces; and which is the plain sense of the passages referred to by Him, particularly *Isa. 44:3; Joel 2:28*; and which, as before observed, the Jews supposed were intimated by their drawing and pouring water at the feast of tabernacles;

which they that believe on him should receive; the apostles, and others, that had believed on Christ, and had received the Spirit, as a spirit of regeneration and sanctification; as a spirit of illumination and conversion; as a spirit of faith and adoption; but on the day of Pentecost they were to receive a larger, even an extraordinary measure of His gifts and grace, to qualify them for greater work and service:

for the Holy Ghost was not yet *given*; the word *given* is not in the original text; but is very properly supplied, as it is in the Vulgate Latin, Syriac, and Persic versions. The Arabic version renders it, *for the Holy Ghost was not yet come*; He was; He was in being as a divine person, equal with the Father and Son, so He was from everlasting; and He had been bestowed in His grace upon the Old Testament saints, and rested in His gifts upon the prophets of that dispensation; but, as the Jews themselves confess,[54]

> "After the death of the latter prophets, Haggai, Zachariah, and Malachi, the Holy Ghost removed from Israel."

And they expressly say, He was not there in the time of the second temple. Maimonides says,[55]

> "They made the Urim and Thummim in the second temple, to complete the eight garments (of the priests) though they did not inquire by them. And why did they not inquire by them? *Because the Holy Ghost was not there*; and every priest that does not speak by the Holy Ghost, and the Shekinah, does not dwell upon him, they do not inquire by him."

They observe[56] there were five things in the first temple which were not in the second, and they are these:

> "the ark with the mercy seat, and cherubim; the fire (from heaven); and the Shekinah, ורוח הקודש, *and the Holy Ghost*, and the Urim and Thummim."

Now, though He had removed, He was to return again; but as yet the time was not come, at least for the more plentiful donation of Him: the reason of which was,

---

[54] T. Bab. Yoma, fol. 9. 2. Sota, fol. 48. 2. & Sanhedrin, fol. 11. 1.

[55] Hilchot Cele Hamikdash, c. 10. sect. 10. Vid. T. Bab. Yoma, fol. 73. 2.

[56] T. Bab. Yoma, fol. 21. 2. Vid. Jarchi & Kimchi in Hagg. 1:8.

because that Jesus was not yet glorified). He had not as yet gone through His state of humiliation; He had not yet suffered, and died, and rose again, and ascended, and sat down at the right hand of God; for the Holy Spirit was to come upon His departure, and in consequence of His sufferings and death, and being made sin, and a curse for His people; and through His mediation and intercession, and upon His exaltation at the Father's right hand; when being made, and declared Lord and Christ, this should be notified by the effusion of His Spirit; see *Acts 2:33,36*.

Verse 40. **Many of the people therefore**, &c. Of the common people, and it may be chiefly those that came out of the country:

when they heard this saying; or discourse of Christ, on the last and great day of the feast, relating to the large measure of grace, and the effusion of the Spirit on him, that believed:

said, Of a truth this is the Prophet. Spoken of in *Deut. 18:15*, which some understood not of the Messiah, but of some extraordinary prophet distinct from Him, who should come before Him, or about the same time; or they imagined He was one of the old prophets raised from the dead, whom they also expected about the times of the Messiah: or their sense might only be, that He was *a prophet*, which was true, though not all the truth; they had some knowledge, though but small; and they spake of Him, though but as children in understanding.

Verse 41. **Others said, This is the Christ**, &c. The true Messiah, which they concluded, not only from the miracles, *verse 31*, but from His speaking of rivers of living water flowing from him that believes in Him; for the same prophecy that speaks of miracles to be performed in the times of the Messiah, speaks also of waters breaking out in the wilderness, and streams in the desert; of the parched ground becoming a pool, and the thirsty land springs of water, *Isa. 35:5-7*.

But some said, Shall Christ come out of Galilee? As they supposed Jesus did; and because He was educated at Nazareth, and Capernaum was His city, and He chiefly conversed, preached, and wrought His miracles in these parts, they concluded that He was born there; and therefore object this to His being the true Messiah. For if they did not mean this, according to their own accounts, the Messiah was to be in Galilee, and to be first revealed there; for they affirm[57] this in so many words, that ית×'לי מלכא משיחא בארעא דגליל, *the King Messiah shall be revealed in the land of Galilee*; accordingly Jesus, the

---

[57] Zohar in Gen. fol. 74. 3. & in Exod. fol. 3. 3. & 4. 1.

true Messiah, as He was brought up in Galilee, though not born there, so He first preached there, and there wrought His first miracle; here He chiefly was, unless at the public feasts; and here He manifested Himself to His disciples after His resurrection.

Verse 42. **Hath not the Scripture said**, &c. These objectors were those who were accounted the more wise and knowing; who were conversant with the Scriptures, and pretended at least to a large knowledge of them:

That Christ cometh out of the seed of David; that He should be *a rod out of the stem of Jesse*, and a Branch *out of his roots*; that He should be one out of David's loins, and of the *fruit* of his body, referring to *Isa. 11:1; Psa. 132:11,17*; which was very true, and what was commonly known, and expected among the Jews, that the Messiah should be David's son, as Jesus of Nazareth was, *Acts 13:23;*

and out of the town of Bethlehem, where David was? Where His parents lived, and He was born; and, according to Jerome,[58] He was buried here. The account he gives of this city, where he himself for some time lived, is:

"Bethlehem, the city of David, in the lot of the tribe of Judah, in which our Lord and Savior was born, is six miles from Ælia (that is, Jerusalem), to the south, by the way which leads to Hebron, where also is shown the sepulcher of Jesse and David."

In which may be observed likewise the exact distance of this place from Jerusalem; which, according to Josephus,[59] at least as he is generally understood, was but twenty furlongs; and, according to Justin,[60] thirty-five: but that this is the true distance, is clear from the old Jerusalem Itinerary,[61] and which agrees with Jerome about the sepulcher of David; for not far from it is the monument of Ezekiel, Asaph, Job, Jesse, David, and Solomon. However, it is certain that David was born here, and therefore it is called *his* city; and from hence the Messiah was to come; and here Jesus, the true Messiah, was born, and which the Jews themselves own; see the notes on *Matt. 2:1* **[1]** and *Luke 2:4* **[46]**. And in vain it is for them to expect the Messiah from thence, where none of their nation live, nor have lived, for many hundreds of years; being

---

[58] De locis Hebraicis, fol. 89. E.

[59] Antiqu. l. 7. c. 12. sect. 4.

[60] Apolog. 2. p. 75.

[61] In Reland. Palestina illustrata, l. 2. c. 4. p. 416. Vid. c. 9. p. 445. & l. 3. p. 645.

particularly forbid by Adrian, after he had subdued them, living in or near Jerusalem, and also Bethlehem. Tertullian[62] refers to this when he thus argues with them, and very justly, and strongly:

"If he is not yet born, who, it is said, shall come forth a Ruler out of Bethlehem, of the tribe of Judah, he must come (says he) out of the tribe of Judah, and from Bethlehem; but we now observe, that no one of the stock of Israel remains in Bethlehem, because it is forbidden that any one of the Jews should continue on the border of that country—how shall the Governor be born in Judea, come forth from Bethlehem, as the divine books of the Prophets declare, when there is none of Israel left there at this day, of whose lineage Christ can be born? How shall he come out of Bethlehem, when there is none in Bethlehem of the stock of Israel?"

And the passage they had in view, is *Mic. 5:2*. Now those very things they object to Jesus' being the Messiah, were what were fulfilled in Him, and proved Him to be the person; for His supposed father, and real mother Mary, were of the house and lineage of David; and though He was conceived at Nazareth, and brought up there, yet, by a remarkable providence, which brought Joseph and Mary to Bethlehem, He was born there, *Luke 2:4-7*.

Verse 43. **So there was a division among the people concerning him**. Some, though they did not go so far as to believe Him to be the Messiah, yet took Him to be a prophet, and a very extraordinary one; others made no difficulty to assert Him to be the Christ; and others objected to it on account of the country from whence He came, and so fulfilled the words of Christ, *Luke 12:51*.

Verse 44. **And some of them would have taken him**, &c. Some of the latter sort, who did not believe He was the Messiah; who were the most averse to Him, and hot and furious against Him; these were for seizing Him at once in a violent manner, and for carrying Him before the Sanhedrin, as an impostor and blasphemer to be examined, and tried, and judged by them, to whom it belonged to judge and determine concerning such persons:

but no man laid hands on him. Though they had a good will to do it, no man had power to do it; they were held back and restrained by the providence of God; and were diverted from it upon one consideration or another; either fearing the people, or being awed by the majesty of Christ's countenance, or words; the true reason of which was, that which is before given, that His hour was not yet come.

---

[62] Adv. Judaeos, c. 13. p. 224, 225.

Verse 45. **Then came the officers to the chief priests and Pharisees**, &c. Who were assembled together in council, as the great Sanhedrin of the nation; who were sitting and expecting Jesus to be brought before them. The same officers they sent to take Him, *verse 32*, returned to them without Him; for though they were sent on that errand which they intended to have performed, yet they were not on the side of those who were for seizing Him by force, nor of those who objected to His being the Messiah; but rather took part with those who affirmed He was the Messiah; or at least looked upon Him to be some extraordinary prophet:

and they said unto them; that is, the chief priests and Pharisees said to the officers; the Syriac version reads, *the priests said unto them*:

Why have ye not brought him? They mention not the name of Jesus, by way of contempt, and knowing that the officers would easily understand them; though the Persic version expresses it, reading the words thus, *Why have ye not brought Jesus?* Seeing them returned without Him, they were transported with rage and fury, and fell upon them in a fierce and furious manner, for disobeying their orders, who had sat there waiting some time: and hoping, and not doubting, but they should have Him in their hands, whose blood they were thirsting after: wherefore it was a great disappointment to them, and much enraged them to see the officers come without Him.

Verse 46. **The officers answered**, &c. Very honestly and uprightly, making use of no shifts and excuses; as that they could not find Him, or could not come at Him, because of the multitude about Him, or that they were afraid of the people, lest they should rise upon them, and stone them, and rescue Jesus; which would have carried a show of probability, and have brought them off; but they tell the naked truth, saying,

never man spake like this man. Not Moses, the spokesman of the people of Israel; nor David, the anointed of the God of Jacob, the sweet Psalmist of Israel; nor Solomon, the wisest of men; nor that sublime and evangelical prophet Isaiah; nor any of the other prophets; nor John [the] Baptist, His forerunner, *the voice of one crying in the wilderness*: never man spoke words for matter like Him; such gracious words, or words and doctrines of grace, which so fully express the grace of God, and are so grateful to men; such as free justification by His righteousness, full pardon by His blood, peace and reconciliation by His sacrifice, the liberty of captives from the bondage of sin, Satan, and the law, and spiritual and eternal salvation by Him: never man spoke such words of truth, as He who is full of truth, and truth itself did: or such words of wisdom, who is the wisdom of God, on whom the spirit of wisdom rested, and *in whom are hid all the treasures of wisdom and knowledge* [*Col. 2:3*]; nor such wholesome and salutary words, which nourish up unto eternal life. Nor did ever any speak words for form and manner, as He did; words so apt and pertinent, with such propriety, beauty, and gracefulness, with such majesty and authority, and with such power and efficacy; which at once charmed the ear, affected the heart, carried evidence and conviction with them, enlightened the understanding, and fastened attention to them; which was the case with these men, so that they had not power to execute their commission. He delivered such excellent things, and in such a charming manner, they could not find in their hearts to use any violence towards Him; or be the means of bringing Him into any trouble or danger. The Syriac, Arabic, and Persic versions read, *never man spake as this man speaks.*

Verse 47. Then answered them the Pharisees, Are ye also deceived? As well as the common people; you that have been so long in our service, and should know better; or who, at least, should have taken the sense of your superiors, and should have waited to have had their opinion and judgment of Him, and been determined by that, and not so hastily have joined with a deluded set of people. It was the common character of Christ, and His apostles, and so of all His faithful ministers in all succeeding ages, that they were deceivers, and the people that followed them deceived, a parcel of poor deluded creatures, carried aside by their teachers; when, on the other hand, they are the deceived ones, who live in sin, and indulge themselves in it; or who trust in themselves that they are righteous; who think they are something, when they are nothing; who imagine, that touching the righteousness of the law, they are blameless, are free from sin, and need no repentance; who follow the traditions and commandments of men: whereas those cannot be deceived, who follow Christ, the way, the truth, and the life, and His faithful ministers, who show unto men the way of salvation.

Verse 48. Have any of the rulers, &c. In the Sanhedrin, or of the synagogues; or the civil magistrates, the noble, rich, and wealthy:

or of the Pharisees, believed on him? Men famous for wisdom, learning, and holiness. It must be owned, there were but very few of this sort, and perhaps not an instance of this kind had as yet occurred to them; there was Nicodemus, who is mentioned in the context, who was both a ruler and a Pharisee; and Joseph of Arimathea, a rich counselor; but they neither of them openly showed themselves to be the disciples of Christ till His death: and besides these, there were some women, as Joanna, the wife of Chuza, Herod's steward, Susanna, and some other women, who ministered to Him of their substance; but the far greater part of His followers were poor and illiterate: and this has been the common case of those that have believed in Jesus, for the most part, ever since, and therefore should not be a stumbling to any. God is pleased to hide the great things of the Gospel from the wise and prudent, the rich and noble, and preach and reveal them to the poor and foolish: nor is a doctrine a whit the truer for being espoused by the rich, and wise men of this world, but rather to be suspected on that account [see *1 Cor. 1:26-31*].

Verse 49. **But this people, &c.** With great contempt they style the followers of Jesus *this people*; the common people, the dregs of them, the refuse of the earth; and whom they call, עַם הָאָרֶץ, *the people of the earth*, in distinction from the wise men, and their disciples: and when they speak the best of them, their account is this;[63]

> "One of the people of the earth is one that has moral excellencies, but not intellectual ones; that is, there is in him common civility, but the law is not in him;"

as here,

who knoweth not the law is cursed. They always reckon them very ignorant. Says one[64] of their writers,

> "They that are without knowledge are the multitude."

And elsewhere it is said,[65]

> "The old men of the people of the earth, when they grow old, their knowledge is disturbed (or is lost), as it is said, *Job 12:20*; but so it is not with the old men of the law, when they grow old, their knowledge rests upon them, as it is said, *Job 12:12, with the ancient is wisdom."*

Upon which one of the commentators[66] has this gloss:

> "these are the disciples of the wise men; for the people of the earth, what wisdom is there in them?"

By the *law* here, is meant either the written law of Moses, which the Pharisees boasted of, and of their knowledge of it, as having the key of knowledge to open it; as understanding the true sense, and capable of giving a right interpretation of it to the people; though they themselves were wretchedly ignorant of it, as appears by their false glosses on it, refuted by our Lord in *Matt. 5:17-48*; or else the oral law is here intended, which they pretended was given by word of mouth to Moses, and handed down to posterity from one to another; and this lay among the doctors: they tell us,[67]

---

[63] Maimonides in Pirke Abot, c. 2. sect. 5. & c. 5. sect. 7.

[64] Abarbinel in proph. post. fol. 473.

[65] Mishna Kenim, c. 3. sect. 6. Vid. T. Bab. Sabbat, fol. 152. 1.

[66] Bartenora in Mishna ib.

[67] Pirke Abot, c. 1. sect. 1-12.

that Moses received it at Sinai, and delivered it to Joshua, and Joshua to the elders, and the elders to the prophets, and the prophets to the men of the great synagogue (Ezra's), the last of which was Simeon the just: Antigonus, a man of Socho, received it from him; and Jose ben Joezer, and Jose ben Jochanan, received it from him; and Joshua ben Perachia (whom they sometimes say was the master of Jesus of Nazareth), and Nittai the Arbelite, received it from them; by whom it was delivered to Judah ben Tabia, and Simeon ben Shetach; and from them it was received by Shemaiah, and Abtalion, who delivered it to Hillell, and Shammai; who, or whose scholars, were at this time, when these words were spoken, the present possessors of it, and taught it their disciples in their schools: and thus it was handed down from one to another, until the times of R. Judah, who collected the whole of the traditions of the elders together, and published it under the title of the *Mishna*; and then, as Maimonides says,[68] it was revealed to all Israel; whereas before it was but in a few hands, who instructed others in it; but as for the common people, they knew little of it, especially of the nice distinctions and decisions of it; and these people were always had in great contempt by the wise men: they would not receive a testimony from them, nor give one for them, nor deliver a secret to them, nor proclaim any thing of theirs that was lost, nor walk with them in the way, nor make a guardian of any of them.[69] The people of the earth were not reckoned holy or religious,[70] but generally profane and wicked; that they were abandoned to sin, rejected of God, and to be cast off by men; yea, they will not allow that they shall rise again at the last day, unless it be for the sake of some wise men they are allied unto, or have done some service for. They say,[71]

> "Whoever ministers in the light of the law, the light of the law will quicken him; but whoever does not minister in the light of the law, the light of the law will not quicken him—though it is possible for such a one to cleave to the Shekinah—for every one that marries his daughter to a scholar of a wise man, or makes merchandise for the disciples of the wise men, and they receive any advantage from his goods, this brings on him what is written, as if he cleaved to the Shekinah."

Thus we see in what contempt the common people were with the learned doctors, and what an opinion these men had of the followers of Christ; though,

---

[68] Praefat. ad Yad. Hazaka.

[69] Buxtorf. Lex. Talmud. col. 1626.

[70] Ibid. Florileg. Heb. p. 276.

[71] T. Bab. Cetubot, fol. 111. 2.

in truth, they were not so ignorant of the law as themselves: they knew the spirituality of it: that it reached to the thoughts of the heart, as well as to external actions; they knew what it required, and their own impotence to answer its demands; they knew the wrath, terror, and curses of it, and that Christ only was the fulfilling end of it, for righteousness to those that believed in Him: and they were far from being *cursed* persons: they were blessed with all spiritual blessings: with the pardon of their sins, and the justification of their persons; with grace and peace in their souls, and would be introduced as the blessed of the Father into His kingdom and glory.

Verse 50. **Nicodemus saith unto them**, &c. To the Jewish Sanhedrin, who were running down Christ, and His followers, in great wrath and fury:

(he that came to Jesus by night; see *John 3:1-2;*

being one of them); a member of the Sanhedrin:

Verse 51. **Doth our law judge *any* man**, &c. Or condemn any man; or can any man be lawfully condemned:

before it hear him: what he has to say for himself? Is this the usual process in our courts? or is this a legal one to condemn a man unheard?

and know what he doeth? What his crimes are? This he said, having a secret respect for Christ, though he had not courage enough openly to appear for Him.

Verse 52. **They answered and said unto him**, &c. Being displeased with him, and as reproaching him, though they could not deny, or refute what he said:

Art thou also of Galilee? A follower of Jesus of Galilee, whom, by way of contempt, they called *the Galilean*, and His followers *Galileans*, as Julian the apostate after them did; for otherwise they knew that Nicodemus was not of the country of Galilee.

Search and look; into the histories of former times, and especially the Scriptures:

for out of Galilee ariseth no prophet. But this is false, for Jonah the prophet was of Gath hepher, which was in the tribe of Zebulun, which tribe was in Galilee; see *2 Kings 14:25; Josh. 19:10,13,16.* And the Jews[72]

---

[72]   T. Hieros. Succa, fol. 55. 1.

themselves say, that Jonah, the son of Amittai, was, מזבולון, *of Zebulun*, and that his father was of Zebulun, and his mother was of Asher;[73] both which tribes were in Galilee: and if no prophet had, as yet, arose from thence, it did not follow that no one ever should arise: besides, there is a prophecy in which it was foretold, that a prophet, and even the Messiah, the great Light, should arise in Galilee; see *Isa. 9:1-2*; and they themselves say, that the Messiah should be revealed in Galilee; see the note on *verse 41*.

Verse 53. **And every man went unto his own house**. The officers not bringing Jesus with them, and the Sanhedrin being posed [*or* baffled] by Nicodemus, broke up without doing any business, and every member of it went home. This we may suppose was about the time of the evening sacrifice: for,

"The great Sanhedrin sat from the time of the morning daily sacrifice, to the time of the evening daily sacrifice."[74]

And it is said[75] that,

"After the evening daily sacrifice, the Sanhedrin went, לביתם, *to their own houses;*"

as they now did, and not to their booths, the feast of tabernacles being now over.

CHAPTER 8

Verse 1. **Jesus went unto the Mount of Olives**. This mount lay eastward of Jerusalem, about a mile from it; hither Christ went on the evening of the last day of the feast of tabernacles; partly to decline the danger, and avoid the snares the Jews might lay for Him in the night season, having been disappointed and confounded in the daytime; and it may be for the sake of recreation and diversion, to sup with His dear friends Lazarus, Martha, and

---

[73] Bereshit Rabba, sect. 98. fol. 85. 4.

[74] Maimon. Hilchot Sanhedrin, c. 3. sect. 1.

[75] Piske Tosephot Sanhedrin, art. 35.

Mary, who lived at Bethany, not far from this mount; and chiefly for private prayer to God, on account of Himself as man, and for His disciples, and for the spread of His Gospel, and for the enlargement of His interest; this being His common and usual method, *Luke 21:37.*

Verse 2. **And early in the morning he came again into the temple**, &c. Early, which shows His diligence, constancy, and assiduity in His ministerial work, as well as His courage and intrepidity; being fearless of His enemies, though careful to give them no advantage against Him, before His time:

and all the people came unto him; which also commends the industry and diligence of His hearers, who were forward to hear Him, and were early at the temple for that purpose, and that in great numbers:

and he sat down and taught them. He sat, as His manner was; see the note on *Matt. 5:1* [**7**]; and *taught them as one having authority* [*Matt. 7:29*], and such doctrine, and in such a manner, as never man did; with all plainness, boldness, and freedom.

Verse 3. **And the Scribes and Pharisees**, &c. The members of the Sanhedrin, who had been so miserably disappointed the day before, were no less diligent and industrious in their wicked way, seeking all opportunities, and taking all advantages against Christ; and fancying they had gotten something whereby to ensnare Him, and bring Him into disgrace or danger, they pursue it; and,

brought unto him a woman taken in adultery; who, as some conjecture, might have been taken in it the day before, in one of their booths; being drawn into it through intemperance and carnal mirth, which at this feast they greatly indulged themselves in; which shows, that they were far from drawing the Holy Ghost at this time upon them, that, on the contrary, they fell into the hands, and under the power of the unclean spirit. Who this woman was, is not material to know; what is pretended to be taken out of the annals of the Spanish Jews, is no doubt a fable; that she was the wife of one Manasseh of Jerusalem, an old man, whose name was Susanna:[1]

and when they had set her in the midst; of the company, as the Persic version reads, to be seen by all the people. This history of the woman taken in adultery, is wanting in the Alexandrian copy, and in other ancient copies; nor is it in Nonnus, Chrysostom, and Theophylact; nor in any of the editions of the Syriac version, until it was restored by De Dieu, from a copy of Archbishop Ussher's; but was in the Arabic and Ethiopic versions, and in the

---

[1] Vid. Selden. Uxor. Hebr. l. 3. c. 11. p. 377.

Harmonies of Tatian and Ammonius; the former of which lived about the year 160, and so within 60 years, or thereabouts, of the death of the Evangelist John, and the other about the year 230; it was also in Stephens's sixteen ancient Greek copies, and in all Beza's seventeen, excepting one; nor need the authenticness of it be doubted of; Eusebius[2] says, it is in the Gospel according to the Hebrews; nor should its authority be called in question.

Verse 4. **They say unto him, Master**, &c. They applied to Him in a handsome and respectful manner, the better to cover their ill design:

this woman was taken in adultery; by two persons at least, who could be witnesses of it; otherwise the accusation was not legal; see *Deut. 19:15*; though in the case of a wife suspected of adultery, they admitted a single witness as valid:[3]

in the very act; or *in the theft itself*, for adultery is a theft; it is an unlawful use of another's property; see this word used in the same sense, in *Heliodor,* l. 1. sect. 11.

Verse 5. **Now Moses in the law commanded us, that such should be stoned**, &c. Not in *Lev. 20:10*; for though according to the law there, an adulteress, one that was a married woman, and so an adulterer, that was a married man, were to be put to death; yet the death was not stoning, but strangling; for it is a rule with the Jews,[4] that where death is simply mentioned (without restraining it to any particular kind) strangling is intended, and which rule they apply to this law: and accordingly in their Mishna, or oral law, one that lies with another man's wife, is reckoned among those that are to be strangled.[5] Kimchi indeed says,[6] that adulteresses, according to the law, are to be stoned with stones; but then this must be understood of such as are betrothed, but not married; and such a person,

---

[2] Hist. Eccles. l. 3. c. 39.

[3] Maimon. Hilchot Eduth, c. 5. sect. 2.

[4] Maimon. Hilchot Issure Bia, c. 1. sect. 6.

[5] Mishna Sanhedrin, c. 10. sect. 1.

[6] In Ezek. 16:40.

Moses has commanded in the law, to be stoned, *Deut. 22:23-24*. And with this agree the traditions of the Jews:[7]

"A daughter of Israel must be stoned, who is, ארוסה ולא נשואה, *betrothed, but not married*."

And such a one we must believe this woman was; she was betrothed to a man, but not married to him, and therefore to be stoned: the Jews[8] have also a saying, that,

"If all adulterers were punished with stoning, according to the law, the stones would be consumed; but they would not be consumed;"

adultery was so common with that people:

but what sayest thou? Dost thou agree with Moses, or not?

Verse 6. **This they said, tempting him**, &c. For they brought this woman, and exposed her in this manner, not because of their abhorrence and detestation of the sin; nor did they put the above question to Christ, out of their great respect to the law of Moses; which in many instances, and so in this, they in a great measure made void, by their traditions; for they say, that for such an offense as adultery, they did not put to death, nor beat, unless there was a previous admonition; the use of which was, to distinguish between presumptuous sins, and wilful ones;[9] but if there was no admonition, and the woman, even a married woman, if she confessed the crime, all her punishment was to have her dowry taken from her, or to go away without it.[10] Now these masters say nothing about the admonition, nor do they put the question, whether this woman was to be dealt with according to their traditions, or according to the law of Moses? But what was the sense of Christ, whether Moses's law was to be attended to, or whether He would propose another rule to go by? And their view in this was,

that they might have to accuse him. That should He agree with Moses, then they would accuse Him to the Roman governor, for taking upon Him to condemn a person to death, which belonged to him to do; or they would charge Him with severity, and acting inconsistently with Himself, who received such sort of sinners, and ate with them; and had declared, that publicans and harlots would enter into the kingdom of heaven, when the Scribes and

---

[7] T. Bab. Sanhedrin, fol. 51. 2.

[8] Apud Castell. Lex. Polyglott, col. 2180.

[9] Maimon. ibid. sect. 3.

[10] Mishna Sota, c. 1. sect. 5.

Pharisees would not; and if He should disagree with Moses, then they would traduce Him among the people, as an enemy to Moses and his law, and as a patron of the most scandalous enormities:

But Jesus stooped down, and with *his* finger wrote on the ground; some think[11] He wrote in legible characters the sins of the woman's accusers; and the learned Wagenseil[12] makes mention of an ancient Greek manuscript he had seen, in which were the following words, *the sins of every one of them*: Dr. Lightfoot is of opinion, that this action of Christ tallies with, and has some reference to, the action of the priest at the trial of the suspected wife; who took of the dust of the floor of the tabernacle, and infused it in the bitter waters for her to drink; but it is most likely, that Christ on purpose put Himself into this posture, as if He was busy about something else, and did not attend to what they said; and hereby cast some contempt upon them, as if they and their question were unworthy of His notice: and this sense is confirmed by what follows,

as though he heard them not. Though this clause is not in many copies, nor in the Vulgate Latin, nor in any of the Oriental versions, but is in five of Beza's copies, and in the Complutensian edition.

Verse 7. **So when they continued asking him**, &c. For observing that He put Himself in such a posture, they concluded that they had puzzled and perplexed Him, and that He knew not what to say; and therefore they were more urgent for a speedy answer, hoping they should get an advantage of Him; and that they should be able to expose Him, and that His confusion would appear to all the people:

he lifted up himself, and said unto them; having raised up Himself, He looked wistfully at them, and returned them this wise answer, to their confusion:

He that is without sin among you; meaning, not that was entirely free from sin, in heart, in lip, and life; for there is no such person; the most holy man in life, is not in such sense free from sin; but that was without any notorious sin, or was not guilty of some scandalous sin, and particularly this of adultery; which was in this age a prevailing sin, and even among their doctors; hence our Lord calls that generation an *adulterous* one, *Matt. 12:39*; and which was literally true of them; with this compare *Rom. 2:22*. Adultery increased to such a degree in this age, that they were obliged to leave off the

---

[11]   Hieron. adv. Pelagianos, l. 2. fol. 96. H. tom. II.

[12]   In Mishna Sota, c. 1. sect. 5.

trial of suspected wives, because their husbands were generally guilty this way; and the waters would have no effect, if the husband was criminal also: so the Jews say,[13]

"When adulterers increased, the bitter waters ceased; and Rabban Jochanan ben Zaccai (who was now living) caused them to cease."

In vindication of which, he cited the passage in *Hos. 4:14*; and this agrees with their own account of the times of the Messiah, and the signs thereof, among which stands this:[14]

"In the age in which the Son of David comes, the house of assembly (the gloss interprets it the place where the disciples of the wise men meet to learn the law) shall become, לזנות, *a brothel house.*"

And that this sin so greatly prevailed, our Lord well knew; and perhaps none of those Scribes and Pharisees were free from it, in one shape or another; and therefore bids him that was,

let him first cast a stone at her. Alluding to the law in *Deut. 17:7*, which required the hands of the witnesses to be upon a person first, to put him to death; and as Dr. Lightfoot thinks, referring to their own sense and opinion, in trying a wife suspected of adultery; that if the husband was guilty the same way, the waters would have no effect. By this answer of our Lord, He at once wrought Himself out of the dilemma they thought to distress Him with; for though He passed no sentence upon the woman, and so took not upon Him the judiciary power, with which they could accuse Him to the Roman governor, yet He manifestly appeared to agree with Moses, that such a one deserved to be stoned; wherefore they could not charge Him with being contrary to Moses; and by putting him that was *without sin*, to cast the first stone at her, He showed Himself merciful to the woman, and proved Himself to them to be the searcher of hearts [see *Jer. 17:10*].

Verse 8. **And again he stooped down, and wrote on the ground**. As before, having said enough to confound them; and yet unwilling to pursue the matter any further, or publicly expose them in any other way; and that they might have an opportunity of withdrawing themselves without any further notice of His, He took this method.

Verse 9. **And they which heard *it***, &c. Not all, not the disciples of Christ, nor the multitude, but they of the Scribes and Pharisees:

being convicted by *their own* conscience; that they were not *without sin*,

---

[13] Mishna Sota, c. 9. sect. 9.

[14] Mishna ibid. c. 9. sect. 15. T. Bab. Sanhedrin, fol. 97. 1.

nor free from this; they had a beam in their own eye, who were so forward to observe the mote in another's; and oftentimes so it is, that those who are most forward to reprove, and bear hardest on others for their sins, are as culpable in another way, if not in the same; when sin lies at the door, and conscience is awakened and open, it is as good as a thousand witnesses; and lets in, and owns the sin which lies heavy, and makes sad work; and fills with anguish, confusion, and shame, as it did these men, who,

went out one by one; from the temple, in as private a manner, and as unobserved as they could:

beginning at the eldest: who might have been most culpable, or however soonest took the hint; being more wise and sagacious:

even **unto the last**; this is wanting in the Vulgate Latin, Syriac, and Persic versions, and in two of Beza's copies, and the Basil edition:

and Jesus was left alone; not by His disciples, nor the multitude, but by His antagonists, who came to tempt and ensnare Him: for it follows,

and the woman standing in the midst. That is, of the company, as before.

Verse 10. **When Jesus had lifted up himself**, &c. Lifted up Himself from the earth, towards which He stooped, and on which He had been writing:

and saw none but the woman; that is, none of those that had brought her there, and had accused her to Him:

he said unto her, Woman, where are those thine accusers? The Syriac and Arabic versions read only, *where are these?* these men, that brought thee here, and charged thee with this crime:

hath no man condemned thee? Has no one offered to do unto thee what I proposed? What, not one that could take up a stone, and cast at thee? Was there not one of them free from this sin? Could no man take upon him to execute this sentence?

Verse 11. **She said, No man, Lord**, &c. No man said a word to me, or lift up his hand against me, or moved a stone at me:

and Jesus said unto her, Neither do I condemn thee; Christ came not into the world to act the part of a civil magistrate, and therefore refused to arbitrate a case, or be concerned in dividing an inheritance between two brethren, *Luke 12:13-14*. Nor did He come into the world to condemn it, *but that the world through him might be saved, chapter 3:17*; nor would He pass any other sentence on this woman than what He had done; nor would He inflict any punishment on her Himself; but suitably and agreeably to His

THE GOSPEL OF JOHN

office as a Prophet, He declares against her sin, calls her to repentance, and bids her,

go and sin no more. *Lest,* as He said to the man He cured at Bethesda's pool, *a worse thing* should come unto her. Wherefore the Jew[15] has no reason to object to this conduct of Christ, as if He acted contrary to the law in *Deut. 13:5: Thou shalt put the evil away from the midst of thee*; and also to the sanctions of all civil laws among men, which order the removal of evil, by putting delinquents to death; and He observes, that those that believe in Him, do not follow Him in this, but put adulterers and adulteresses to death; and that indeed, should His example and instructions take place, all courts of judicature must cease, and order be subverted among men: but it should be observed, that our Lord manifested a regard, even to the law of Moses, when He bid this woman's accusers that were without sin, to cast the first stone at her; though as for the law in *Deut. 13:5*, that respects a false prophet, and not an adulterer or an adulteress; nor do the civil laws of all nations require death in the case of adultery; and did they, Christ here, neither by His words nor actions, contradicts and sets aside any such laws of God or man; He left this fact to be inquired into, examined, and judged, and sentence passed by proper persons, whose business it was. As for Himself, His office was not that of a civil magistrate, but of a Savior and Redeemer; and suitably to that He acted in this case; He did not connive at the sin, He reproved for it; nor did He deny that she ought to suffer according to the law of Moses, but rather suggests she ought; but as this was not His province, He did not take upon Him to pronounce any sentence of condemnation on her; but called her to repentance, and as the merciful and compassionate Savior, gave her reason to hope for pardon and eternal life.

Verse 12. **Then spake Jesus again unto them**, &c. The Syriac fragment of Bishop Ussher's, published by De Dieu, prefaces this verse thus, *When they were gathered together, Jesus said*, &c. that is, the Scribes and Pharisees, who went out and returned again; or some others of them, who came after this, to whom Christ addressed Himself thus:

saying, I am the light of the world; which He might say, on occasion of the rising sun, which was now up, and might shine brightly in their faces, see *verse 2*; which is, אור העולם, *the light of the world*, as Aben Ezra in *Psa. 19:8* rightly calls it. Thus on occasion of the water in Jacob's well, He discoursed of *living water*; and upon the Jews at Capernaum mentioning the manna, He treated at large concerning Himself as *the bread of life*: and He might also make use of this character, and apply it to Himself, with a view to some

---

[15] R. Isaac Chizzuk Emuna, par. 2. c. 47. p. 435, 436.

passages in the Old Testament, which speak of Him under the metaphor of *the sun*, as *Psa. 84:11; Mal. 4:2*, and represent Him as *the light*; and the Jews[16] themselves say, that *light* is one of the names of the Messiah; and God Himself is called by them, *the light of the world*:[17] and likewise He may have regard to those pompous titles and characters, which the Jewish doctors assumed arrogantly to themselves, and oppose himself to them; for they not only called Moses their master, **אור העולם**, *the light of the world*,[18] and also the law of Moses,[19] but their Rabbins and doctors; see the note on *Matt. 5:14*

[8]. By *the world* here is meant, not the whole world, and all the individuals of it; for though Christ, as the Creator of all things, is the light of men, and does lighten every individual man with the light of nature and reason, yet not in a spiritual and saving manner, as is here intended; nor the whole body of the elect of God, though they are sometimes called *the world*, being the better part of it, and are made *light in the Lord* [*Eph. 5:8*], in a special sense; nor the Jews only, and the chosen of God among them, though Christ was a great *light* to many of them, that sat *in darkness, and in the shadow of death* [*Luke 1:79*]; but the Gentiles are here designed, who were usually called by the Jews, *the world*; see the note on *chapter 3:16*. And these were in gross darkness before the coming of Christ, about the Divine Being, concerning the object, nature, and manner of worship; the Scriptures, the Law, and Gospel; the Messiah, and His office and work; the Spirit of God, and His operations of grace; the resurrection of the dead, and a future state. Now Christ came to be *a light of the Gentiles*, as well as the *glory of* His people Israel [*Luke 2:32*]. Our Lord seems to have respect to the prophecy of Him, in *Isa. 42:6*, as well as alludes to the sun in the firmament; whose light is diffused to all the nations of the earth, and not confined to one spot of land only. But since Christ was the minister of the circumcision, and was sent only to *the lost sheep of the house of Israel* [*Matt. 15:24*], it may be asked, how could He be the *light of the Gentiles*? To which it may be replied, That He was so by His apostles, who were sent by Him with the light of the Gospel into all the world; and by His Spirit, who enlightens the minds of men, who were darkness itself, with the light of Christ: for He is not only the author and giver of the light of nature to all men, but also of the light of grace to all His chosen ones, Gentiles as well as Jews; who in His light see light; see themselves lost and undone, and Him

---

[16] Bereshit Rabba, fol. 1. 3. Echa Rabbati, fol. 50. 2. & Jarchi in Psa. 43:3.

[17] Bemidbar Rabba, sect. 15. fol. 217. 2.

[18] Tzeror Hammor, fol. 114. 3.

[19] T. Bab. Bava Bathra, fol. 4. 1.

to be the only willing, able, suitable, and complete Savior; and behold wondrous things in the doctrines of the Gospel, and have some glimpse of glory: and He is likewise the author of all the light of glory the saints enjoy in the other world; *the Lamb is the light* of that state [*Rev. 21:23*]; He is their everlasting light, and their glory; and happy are they who are His followers now:

he that followeth me; not corporeally, but spiritually, by faith; for as believing is expressed by coming to Christ, so by following after Him: compare with this, *chapter 12:46*; and with love and affection to Him, the desires of the soul being unto Him, and to the remembrance of Him; and in the exercise of every grace, and discharge of every duty, in imitation of Him; and through a variety of sufferings and tribulations, pressing after Him as the guide, captain, and forerunner: and such,

shall not walk in darkness; in the darkness of unregeneracy, not knowing what they are, and where they are, and whither they are going; for such know they are in the light; and though they were blind, now they see; they know in whom they have believed, and that they are in Christ, in the covenant of grace, and in the love of God, and are going to heaven and eternal happiness; such shall not walk in the darkness of unbelief; but walk by faith on Christ; nor in the darkness of error, but in the truth of the Gospel, and as becomes it; and though they may sometimes walk without the light of God's countenance, yet light shall arise to them; and such *shall not go into darkness*, as the Ethiopic version renders the words, into outer darkness, or the darkness of eternal death:

but shall have the light of life. The grace of God abiding in them now; which as it is a well of living water, springing up to eternal life, so it is a shining light, which increases to the perfect day: as darkness and death, so light and life go together; grace, which is enlightening, is also quickening and comforting, and issues in eternal light and life; a light that will never be extinguished, and a life that will continue for ever, with never fading joys and pleasures; see *Job 33:30*.

Verse 13. **The Pharisees therefore said unto him**, &c. They said this on account of His declaring Himself *the light of the world*: these were either the same who went out of the temple, filled with remorse of conscience, and were now returned, and, bearing Him a grudge, came to take some advantage against him, if they could; or they were others of the same complexion, sent by them, to make their observations on him:

Thou bearest record of thyself; the Ethiopic version renders it, *Dost thou praise thyself?* which does not seem so decent and comely; see *Prov. 27:2*;

270

though it does not follow, that what a man says of himself is not truth, as these suggest:

thy record is not true. For John testified of himself, that he was not the Christ, nor Elias, nor that prophet; but *the voice of one crying in the wilderness*; and this testimony he bore of himself, at the importunity of the Jews themselves, *chapter 1:19-23*; and his testimony was true; so was that which Christ bore of Himself; but their sense rather seems to be, that it was not firm and authentic, and would not pass in any court of judicature, since no man can be a witness in his own cause.

Verse 14. **Jesus answered and said unto them**, &c. In vindication of Himself, and His testimony:

though I bear record of myself, *yet* my record is true; which seems contradictory to what He says, in *chapter 5:31*, and may be reconciled thus: there He speaks of Himself as man, and in the opinion of the Jews, who took Him to be a mere man; and also as alone, and separate from His Father, as the context shows; therefore His single testimony, and especially concerning Himself, could not be admitted as authentic among men; but here He speaks of Himself as a divine person, and in conjunction with His Father, with whom He was equal; and therefore His testimony ought to be looked upon, and received as firm and good, giving this as a reason for it:

for I know whence I came, and whither I go; that He was truly the Son of God, the only begotten of the Father, and had His mission and commission from Him into this world; and which, as He knew Himself, He was able to make known, and make appear to others, by His credentials, the doctrines taught, and the miracles wrought by Him; which proved Him to be what He said He was, *the light of the world*; and He knew that when He had done His work He came about, He should go to His God and Father, and take His place at His right hand:

but ye cannot tell whence I come, and whither I go. They took Him to be the son of Joseph, and that He came out of Galilee; in which they were mistaken; and when He talked of going away, they did not understand Him, nor know whither He was going; they ask if He was going to the dispersed among the Gentiles, to teach them? and at another time, whether He would kill Himself? They knew not, that through a train of sufferings and death, He must, and would enter into His glory. The Persic version inserts another clause without any foundation; *but ye know not from whence ye come, and whither ye go*, and then follows the former; there might be a truth in this, they did not know their true original, that they were *from beneath* [*verse 23*]; nor whither they were going, to what dismal abode, when they expected to enter, and enjoy the kingdom of heaven.

Verse 15. **Ye judge after the flesh**, &c. They judged according to their carnal affections and prejudices; taking the Messiah to be a temporal prince, and His kingdom to be of this world, they judged that Jesus could not be He; they looked upon Him as a mere man, and seeing Him in much outward meanness [*or* lowliness], in His human nature [see *Isa. 53:1-3*], they judged of Him according to this outward appearance: or *ye that are after the flesh judge*; to which sense the Persic version agrees, *for ye are carnal*; and so judged as carnal men, who are very improper persons to judge of spiritual things:

I judge no man. In the same way, after the flesh, or in a carnal manner, nor according to outward appearances, according to the sight of the eyes, or the hearing of the ears: Christ did not take upon Him to judge and determine in civil affairs, or in things pertaining to a court of judicature among men; this was not His province; an instance of this there is in the context, in not condemning the woman brought to Him; nor did He judge the persons and states of men, or proceed to pass any sentence of condemnation on them; He came not to condemn, but save the world; this was not His business now; otherwise, all judgment is committed to Him, and which He will exercise another day.

Verse 16. **And yet if I judge, my judgment is true**, &c. True, because He saw not as man did, nor looked unto, and judged according to the outward appearance of things; but looked into the heart, and knew what was in it, being the searcher and trier of it; to whom all things are naked and open, and therefore cannot be deceived or imposed upon; His judgment must be sure and infallible:

for I am not alone, but I and the Father that sent me; He was not separate from the Father, or at a distance from Him, when He was here on earth; He was in His bosom, and in heaven, as the Son of God, when, as the Son of man, He was below; nor was He alone in His testimony and judgment, the Father joined with Him therein: and which is a further proof of the truth of His testimony, and the certainty of His judgment.

Verse 17. **It is also written in your law**, &c. Written in the law of Moses, which was given unto them, and they boasted of; the passage referred to is in *Deut. 19:15*; see also *Deut. 17:6*; where, though what follows is not to be found in so many words, yet the sense is there expressed:

that the testimony of two men is true. Concerning which the Jewish writers say,[20]

> "They used not to determine any judiciary matter by the mouth of one witness, neither pecuniary causes, nor causes of life and death, as it is said, *Deut. 17:6*. It is asked[21] in their oral law, *if the testimony of two men stand*, why does the Scripture particularly mention three? (For no other reason) but to compare or equal three with two, that as three convict two of a falsehood, two may also convict three."

On which one of their commentators[22] has this observation, taking notice of *Deut. 19:18*, which speaks of a single witness:

> "Mar (a doctor) says, Wherever it is said *a witness*, it is to be understood of two, unless the Scripture particularly specifies one."

In the case of a wife suspected of adultery, and in the business of striking off the neck of the heifer in case of murder, they admitted of one witness.[23]

Verse 18. **I am one that bear witness of myself**, &c. As He bears witness of His Sonship, in *1 John 5:7*:

and the Father that sent me, beareth witness of me. As He did, by the descent of the Spirit upon Him at His baptism, and by a voice from heaven, both at that time, and at His transfiguration; and by the miracles which He wrought; and particularly He bore testimony of Him long before in prophecy, that He was *the light of the world* He now said He was, *Isa. 42:6*; so that here were two testifiers, His Father and Himself; which show them to be two distinct divine persons, and equal to each other: and now if the testimony of two men is true, firm, and authentic, and to be depended upon and received, then much more the testimony of two divine persons; see *1 John 5:9*.

Verse 19. **Then said they unto him, Where is thy Father?** &c. The Persic version adds, *show* him *unto us*: produce this witness boasted of, let us see him; this they said in a sneering, taunting, and insulting manner; Where is thy Father? What! he is in Galilee; fetch him from thence; it is Joseph the carpenter you mean; a goodly witness indeed!

---

[20] Maimon. Hilchot Eduth, c. 5. sect. 1.

[21] Mishna Maccot. c. 1. sect. 7.

[22] Bartenora in ibid.

[23] Maimon. Hilchot Eduth, ibid. sect. 2.

Jesus answered, Ye neither know me, nor my Father; if ye had known me, ye should have known my Father also. They did not know the divine original of Christ, that He was the Son of God, and that God was His Father; they greatly boasted of their knowledge of God, but they knew Him not; their ignorance of Christ showed it: the knowledge of both go together, and which is life eternal [see *1 John 5:20*]; nor can any truly know the one, without the other: and where the one is known, the other will be also; Christ is *the brightness of His Father's glory, and the express image of His person* [*Heb. 1:3*]: so that He that has seen the one, must know the other; and indeed, no one can know the Father, but he to whom the Son reveals Him [see *Matt. 11:27*]: this was a severe mortification to these men of knowledge.

Verse 20. **These words spake Jesus in the treasury**, &c. The treasury, the place where the thirteen chests stood, into which the people put their voluntary contributions for the sacrifices, and service of the temple: the Ethiopic version renders it, *at the alms chest*; see the note on *Mark 12:41* **[43]**. The design of this observation of the evangelist, is to suggest to us, that it was in a very public place, in the temple, openly, that Christ delivered the above words:

as he taught in the temple; where the Jews resorted, where His ministry was public, and He spake freely, and without reserve; in a very bold manner, with intrepidity, and without fear of man:

and no man laid hands on him; though they had sought to do it the day before; had sent officers to take Him; and they themselves had a good will to it; and yet they were so awed and overruled by one means, or on one account or another, that no man did it; the reason was,

for his hour was not yet come. The time appointed for His sufferings and death.

Verse 21. **Then said Jesus again unto them**, &c. It may be immediately after He had said the above words; or rather, some time after, perhaps on the same day:

I go my way; meaning, the way of all flesh, or that He should die: this way of speaking shows, that His death was certain, a determined thing; which must be, and yet was voluntary: He was not driven, nor forced, but went freely; this being the path, the way, through which He must enter into His kingdom and glory:

and ye shall seek me; that is, shall seek the Messiah, as their Deliverer and Savior, when in distress; and whom He calls Himself, because He was the true

Messiah, and the only Savior and Redeemer of His people, in a spiritual sense; otherwise they would not, nor did they seek Jesus of Nazareth:

and shall die in your sins; or *in your sin*; so it is in the Greek text, and in the Vulgate Latin, and Persic versions: meaning, in their sin of unbelief, and rejection of Him the true Messiah: the sense is, that in the midst of their calamities, which should come upon them for their sin against Him, they should in vain seek for the Messiah, as a temporal deliverer of them; for their nation, city, and temple, and they therein should utterly perish, for their iniquity; and their ruin would not only be temporal, but eternal: since it follows,

whither I, go ye cannot come. Signifying, that whereas He was going to His Father, to heaven and glory; to enjoy eternal happiness at His Father's right hand, in the human nature; they should never come there, but while many sat down in the kingdom of heaven, with their fathers Abraham, Isaac, and Jacob, who should come from afar, they would be shut out, and not suffered to enter in [see *Matt. 13:27-30*].

Verse 22. **Then said the Jews, Will he kill himself?** &c. Which was not only a wicked, but a foolish consequence, drawn from His words: for it by no means followed, because He was going away, and whither they could not come, that therefore He must destroy Himself; this seems to be what they would have been glad He would have done, and suggested the thought that He might do it: in which they imitated Satan, *Matt. 4:6*, under whose influence they now apparently were, and hoped that He would, which would at once extricate them out of their difficulties on His account:

because he sayeth, Whither I go ye cannot come. This is no reason at all; for had Christ's meaning been, as they blasphemously intimate, they might have destroyed themselves too, and have gone after Him.

Verse 23. **And he said unto them**, &c. He said, upon this wicked remark of theirs, and query on His words:

Ye are from beneath: not only of the earth, earthy, and so spoke of the earth, and as carnal men; but even of hell, they were the children of the devil; they breathed his spirit, spoke his language, and did his lusts, as in *verse 44*.

I am from above; not with respect to His human body, which He did not bring with Him from heaven, that was formed below, in the virgin's womb; otherwise He would not have been the seed of the woman, the son of Abraham, David, and Mary: but either with regard to His divine nature and person, He was of God, the Son of God, the only begotten of the Father, who then lay in

His bosom, and was in heaven above at that time; or to His mission, which was from heaven;

ye are of this world; they were, as they were born into the world, sinful, carnal, and corrupt; they were in it, and belonged to it, had never been *chosen*, or *called* out of it; they had their conversation according to the course of it, and conformed to its evil customs and manners; they were under the influence of the god of the world, and were taken with the sinful and sensual lusts thereof; they were men of worldly spirits; they minded earth, and earthly things, and had their portion in this world, and might be truly called the men of it.

I am not of this world. He was in it, but not *of* it; He was come into it to save the chief of sinners, but He did not belong to it, nor did He conform to it; for though He conversed with sinners, ate with them, and received them, being called to repentance by Him; yet He was separate from them [see *Heb. 7:26*], and did not as they did: nor did He pursue the pleasures, honors, and riches of this world, being all His days a man of sorrows, and despised of men; and though Lord of all, *had not where to lay his head [Matt. 8:20]*.

Verse 24. **I said therefore unto you**, &c. He so said, because they were from beneath, and of the world, and discovered an earthly, worldly, carnal, yea, devilish disposition, in their conduct towards Him:

that ye shall die in your sins; this He had said in *verse 21*, and now repeats it, and confirms it by the following reason:

for if ye believe not that I am *he*; the everlasting and unchangeable I AM, the true God, God *over all, blessed for ever* [Rom. 9:5]; the eternal Son of God, God manifest in the flesh, really made flesh, and become incarnate; the true Messiah, the only Savior of sinners; the one and only Mediator between God and man; the Head of the church, Prophet, Priest, and King, and the Judge of quick [*or* living] and dead; as also *the Light of the world* He had declared Himself to be: these are things that are necessary to be believed concerning Christ; indeed, carnal and unregenerate men may believe all these things; the devils themselves do, and tremble at them; but then they, and so unconverted men, have no faith in them, with an application thereof to themselves. True faith in Christ deals not with Him in a general way, but in a special regard to a man's self; it is a seeing of Christ for a man's self; it is not an implicit faith, or a believing Him to be what He is, merely upon report, but upon sight; it is a going out of the soul to Christ, a renouncing its own righteousness, and a trusting in Him alone for life and salvation; it is with the heart, and from it, and is unfeigned; it works by love to Christ, and His people, and is attended with the fruits of righteousness, and a cheerful obedience to the commands and ordinances of Christ. Though perhaps no more than a general faith is here intended, for want [or lack] of which, and their rejection of Jesus as the Messiah, the Jews suffered temporal ruin; and had they but believed that Jesus was the Son of God, and true Messiah, they had been saved from that temporal destruction which came upon their nation, city, and temple; but not believing this in a general and national way, they perished, as is here threatened:

ye shall die in your sins. In which they were, being defiled with them, guilty before God for them, under the power of them, and liable to punishment for them; and so they remained, and did remain, and were yet in their sins, even until death, when they died in them, and for them, not only a corporeal, but an eternal death: for dying in their sins, these would be found upon them, and they would be charged with them, and must be answerable for them, and consequently endure the punishment of them, which is the second death. Dying in sin, and dying in Christ, are two things widely different. They that die in faith, die in Christ: they that die in unbelief, die in sin; and this is a dreadful dying; see *Josh. 22:20*, where the Targum paraphrases it, *and he, one man* (or alone), לא מות בחוביה, *did not die in his sins*.

Verse 25. **Then said they unto him, Who art thou?** &c. Who art thou, that talkest at this rate, and threatenest us with death, in case of unbelief; this they said with a haughty air, and in a scornful manner.

And Jesus saith unto them, Even *the same* **that I said unto you from the beginning**. Meaning, either of this discourse, as that He was *the Light of the world*, and which He continued to assert; or of His being had before the Sanhedrin, when He affirmed that God was His Father, and by many strong arguments proved His divine Sonship; or of His ministry, when by miracles, as well as doctrines, He made it to appear that He was He that was *to come*, the true Messiah; or who spake from the beginning to Moses, saying, I AM *that* I AM, hath sent thee [see *Ex. 3:14*], and to the church, and Jewish fathers in the wilderness; and who is that Word that was from the beginning with God; and who is called the Beginning, the first Cause of all things, and of the creation of God; and some think this is intended here.

Verse 26. **I have many things to say and to judge of you**, &c. Being God omniscient, He knew their persons and actions, their lives and conversations, and all their sins and transgressions, which He could justly have complained of, and charged them with, and proved against them, and judged and condemned them for; but this was not His present business, He came not now to judge and condemn, but to *save*: wherefore He waved these things, and took no notice of them, leaving them to His Father, who would call them to an account, and punish them for them:

but he that sent me is true; as to His promises concerning the mission of His Son, to be the Savior of sinners; so to His threatenings, to bring down vengeance on those that disbelieve Him, and reject Him:

and I speak to the world, or *in the world*,

those things which I have heard of him. As concerning His love, grace, and mercy to those that should believe in Him, so of the destruction of the despisers and rejecters of Him; which things He spoke not in secret, in a corner, but publicly and openly, before all the world, to Jews and Gentiles, and to as many as were in the treasury in the temple at this time; see *chapter 18:20.*

Verse 27. **They understood not that he spake to them of the Father**. Of the Father that sent Him, and who was true and faithful to all He had said, whether in a way of promise, or threatening; such was their stupidity, that they did not know that He meant God the Father by Him that sent Him, so deriving His mission and doctrine from Him; their hearts were made fat, and hardened, and their eyes were blinded. The Vulgate Latin version reads, *they did not know that he said, God was his Father*; and so Beza's most ancient copy, and another exemplar of his.

Verse 28. **Then said Jesus unto them**, &c. Upbraiding them with their ignorance, and giving them a sign, as well as pointing out the time when they, either by good or sad experience, should have knowledge of Him:

When ye have lifted up the Son of man; meaning Himself, who was to be lifted up upon the cross, as the serpent was upon the pole in the wilderness; and which signified the manner of death He should die, the death of the cross; and suggested, that what the Jews designed for His reproach, shame, and abasement, would be the way and means of His rise and exaltation; and this lifting Him up, or crucifying Him, He ascribes to them, because they would deliver Him to Pontius Pilate to be condemned, and stir up the people to ask, and be importunate themselves for His crucifixion:

then shall ye know that I am *he*; the Son of God, and true Messiah, as the centurion, and those that were with him did, when they observed the earthquake, and the things that were done at His death; and after the death, resurrection, and ascension of Christ, and the pouring forth of His Spirit, many of the Jews had not only a notional, but a true and spiritual knowledge of Jesus, as the Messiah; and upon the destruction of their temple, city, and nation, and their disappointment by false Christs, they, doubtless many of them, must and did know, that the true Messiah was come, and that Jesus of Nazareth was He:

and *that* I do nothing of myself; see the note on *chapter 5:19*;

but as my Father hath taught me, I speak these things. This He says, not as lessening Himself, or making Himself inferior to the Father, but to show the excellency of His doctrine, and to assert the original [*or* source], authority, and divinity of it; suggesting, that it was not a human doctrine, or a device of man's, or His own, as man, but was divine, and from God; see *chapter 7:16*.

Verse 29. **And he that sent me is with me**, &c. By virtue of that near union there is between them, they being one in nature, essence, power, and glory, and by the gracious, powerful, comfortable, assisting, and strengthening presence of His Father, which He vouchsafed to Him as man, and Mediator;

the Father hath not left me alone; Christ, as the Word, was with the Father from all eternity, and, as the Son of God, was in heaven, and in the bosom of the Father, when He, as the Son of man, was here on earth; for though He came forth from the Father into this world, by assumption of the human nature, yet the Father was always with Him, and He with the Father, through the unity of the divine nature; nor did He withhold His supporting and assisting presence from Him as man; nor did He withdraw, at least He had not yet withdrawn His gracious and comfortable presence from Him, though He afterwards did, when upon the cross: compare with this *chapter 16:32*;

for I do always those things that please him; by submitting to Gospel ordinances, as to baptism, at which the Father declared His well-pleasedness in Him; and by complying with the ordinances of the ceremonial law which were typical of Him; and by perfectly obeying the precepts of the moral law, and bearing the penalty of it; or by suffering and dying in the room and stead of His people; all which were the will of God, and well-pleasing to Him.

Verse 30. **As he spake these words**, &c. Concerning His being lifted up, or His crucifixion, and the knowledge the Jews should then have of Him; of the excellency and divinity of His doctrine, of His mission from the Father, and of the Father's presence with Him, and of His always doing the things that are pleasing in His sight; which were spoken by Him with majesty and authority, and came with power:

many believed on him. As the Son of God, and true Messiah: faith came by hearing. Christ's hearers were of different sorts; some understood Him not, and disbelieved, and rejected Him; others had their eyes and their hearts opened, and received Him and His words.

Verse 31. Then said Jesus to those Jews which believed on him, &c. For He knew instantly who they were, and when they believed on Him; and therefore He immediately turned Himself to them, and thus addressed them;

If ye continue in my word; meaning the Gospel, called His, because He was both the author, and preacher, and sum, and substance of it: and to continue in it, is having cordially received it, to abide by it, and hold it fast, and not to be moved from it, by the temptations of Satan; the cunning of those that lie in wait to deceive; nor by the revilings and persecutions, the frowns and flatteries of men: and when men continue thus steadfast in it, and faithful to it, it is an evidence that it has come with power, and has a place in their hearts, and that they are the true followers of Christ:

then are ye my disciples indeed; there are two sorts of disciples of Christ; some are only nominal, and merely in profession such; and these sometimes draw back from Him, discontinue in His Word, and go out from among His people; which shows that they never were of them, nor are the true disciples of Jesus [see *1 John 2:19*]; for the genuine disciples of Christ continue in His Gospel, hold fast to Him, the head, and remain with His people; which to do to the end, is an evidence of their being disciples indeed.

Verse 32. And ye shall know the truth, &c. Shall know either the truth of the Gospel, the truth as it is in Jesus; meaning, that they should have a larger knowledge of it, while others are *ever learning*, and *never come to the knowledge of the truth* [*2 Tim. 3:7*]; but the Spirit of truth should lead them into all truth, and cause them to grow and increase in Gospel light and knowledge [see *John 16:13*]; or Jesus Himself, who is *the way, the truth, and the life* [*John 14:6*]; and the sense is, that they should know more of Him, of the dignity of His person, of the nature and usefulness of His offices; of the efficacy of His blood, the excellency of His righteousness, and the fulness of His grace, and that for themselves:

and the truth shall make you free. From ignorance and error, and the prejudices of education, under which the whole nation labored, and from the thraldom of the law.

Verse 33. They answered him, &c. Not the believing Jews, whom He peculiarly addressed, but the unbelieving Jews, who were present, and heard these things:

We be Abraham's seed; this the Jews always valued themselves upon, and reckoned themselves, on this account, upon a level with the nobles and the princes of the earth.

"Says R. Akiba,[24] even the poor of Israel are to be considered as if they were בני חורין, *noblemen*, that are fallen from their substance, because they are *the children of Abraham, Isaac, and Jacob;*"

and were never in bondage to any man; which is a very great falsehood, for it was declared to Abraham himself, that his seed should serve in a land not theirs, and be afflicted four hundred years [see *Gen. 15:13*], as they were; and as the preface to the law which the Jews gloried in, shows, which says, that the Lord their God brought them out of Egypt, *out of the house of bondage* [*Exod. 20:2*]; and they were frequently overcome by their neighbors, the Moabites, Ammonites, and Philistines, and reduced to servitude under them, until delivered by one judge, or another: and not to take notice of their seventy-years' captivity in Babylon, they were at this very time under the Roman yoke, and paid tribute to Caesar; and yet such was the pride of their hearts, they would not be thought to be in bondage; and therefore, with an haughty air, add,

how sayest thou, Ye shall be made free? When they thought themselves, and would fain have been thought by others, to have been free already, and so to stand in no need of being made free.

Verse 34. **Jesus answered them, Verily verily I say unto you**, &c. Taking no notice of their civil liberty, to which He could easily have replied to their confusion and silence, He observes to them their moral servitude and bondage, and in the strongest manner affirms that,

Whosoever committeth sin, is the servant of sin. Which must be understood, not of one that commits a single act of sin, though ever so gross, as did Noah, Lot, David, Peter, and others, who yet were not the servants of sin; nor of such who sin through ignorance, weakness of the flesh, and the power of Satan's temptations; and especially who commit sin with reluctance, the spirit lusting against it; nor indeed of any regenerate persons, though they are not without sin; nor do they live without the commission of it, in thought, word, or deed; and though they fall into it, they do not continue and live in it, but rise up out of it, through the grace of God, and by true repentance; and so are not to be reckoned the servants of sin, or to be of the devil. But this is to be understood of such whose bias and bent of their minds are to sin; who give up themselves unto it, and sell themselves to work wickedness; who make sin

---

[24] Mishna Bava Kama, c. 8. sect. 6. & T. Bab. Bava Kama, fol. 86. 1. & 91. 1.

their trade, business, and employment, and are properly workers of it, and take delight and pleasure in it: these, whatever liberty they promise themselves, are the servants of corruption; they are under the government of sin, that has dominion over them; and they obey it in the lusts thereof, and are drudges and slaves unto it, and will have no other wages at last but death, even eternal death, if grace prevent not; see *Rom. 6:16; 2 Pet. 2:19.*

Verse 35. **And the servant abideth not in the house for ever**, &c. The servant of God, and of Christ, does, but not the servant of sin: there may be servants of sin in the house or church of God here below; and such were these Jews Christ is speaking to; but such shall not abide there for ever: some that get into this house are quickly discerned, as Simon Magus was, and are soon removed; and others that may stay longer, are sometimes suffered to fall into some foul sin, or into some gross error and heresy, for which they are cast out of the house or church of God, according to the rules of God's Word; others make parties, draw disciples after them, and separate themselves, and go out of their own accord, to serve their own purposes; and others, when persecution and tribulation arise because of the Word, they are offended and gone [see *Matt. 13:21*]; this is the fan with which Christ sometimes winnows His floor, and removes the chaff; and those that continue longest, even to the end of their days, or of the world, or the second coming of Christ, as the foolish virgins, will then be discerned and separated; *for the ungodly shall not stand in judgment, nor sinners in the congregation of the righteous* [*Psa. 1:5*]; they shall not enter into the house above, into the *house not made with hands, eternal in the heavens* [*2 Cor. 5:1*], which is Christ's Father's house: none but sons are brought to glory; these are the only heirs of salvation; others will be bid to depart, as workers of iniquity, as the servants of sin; even such who have made a profession of religion, and have been, and have had a standing in the house of God below. The allusion is to the case of servants in common; and, in a literal sense, it is true both of good and bad servants: good servants do not always continue in their master's house; even a Hebrew servant, that loved his master, and would not go out free at the end of his servitude; and who, after having his ear bored, is said to serve him for ever, *Ex. 21:6*; yet that *for ever* was but until the year of jubilee, whether near or remote, as the Jewish commentators[25] in general explain it; nay, if his master died before that time, he went out free: he was not obliged to serve his son or heirs; and so say the Mishnaic doctors:[26]

"One that is bored is obtained by boring, and he possesses himself (or

---

[25] Jarchi, Aben Ezra, & ben Gersom in Ex. 21:6.

[26] Mishna Kiddushin, c. 1. sect. 1.

becomes free) by the year of jubilee, and by the death of his master."
And to this agrees what Maimonides[27] says:

"He that has served six years, and will not go out, lo, this is bored, and
he serves until the year of jubilee, or until his master dies; and
although he leaves a son, he that is bored does not serve the son; which
may be learned from the letter of the words, *he shall serve him*, not his
son, *for ever*; for his ever of the jubilee: from whence it appears, that he
that is bored does not possess himself (or is free), but by the jubilee,
and by the death of his master."

And one of their writers[28] observes, that the word rendered, *shall serve him*,
is by gematry, and not his son. And among the Romans, good servants were
oftentimes made free, and bad ones were turned out, and put into a work-
house, to grind corn in mills, a sort of bridewell*; and such evil servants may
more especially be respected, since Christ is speaking of servants of sin:

but the Son abideth ever. The Son of God, the only begotten Son of God,
the Lord Jesus Christ, will always continue as a Son in His own house, as the
Lord and proprietor of it; and as a high priest over it, having *an unchangeable
priesthood* [*Heb. 7:24*]; and as He that takes care of it, provides for it, and
manages all the affairs thereof, the family in heaven and in earth being
named of Him. And as He, so all the adopted sons of God shall continue, being
pillars in this house, that shall never go out: such are no more servants, nor
foreigners, *but fellow citizens with the saints, and of the household of God*
[*Eph. 2:19*]; and being sons, are heirs and shall never be cast out, as the
bondwoman and her son have been: but these being the children of the free,
shall for ever enjoy the inheritance they are adopted to; once sons, always so;
the relation ever continues; they will ever remain in the family, and being
entitled to the heavenly estate, shall ever possess it.

Verse 36. **If the Son therefore shall make you free**, &c. Alluding to the
custom of adoption by the sons or brethren in the family, which obtained in
Greece, called αδελφοθεσια, *the adoption of brethren*, as Grotius, and others
have observed; or rather to a custom among the Romans, of a son's making
free, after his Father's death, such as were born slaves in his house. Such a
case as this is supposed:[29]

"A man having a son or a daughter by his maidservant, that which is

---

[27] Hilchot Abadim, c. 3. sect. 6, 7.

[28] Baal Hatturim in Ex. 21:6.   *or prison; from Bridewell, a London jail - *Editor*

[29] Theophili Antecensor. Institut. Imperat. Justinian. l. 1. tit. 6. sect. 5. p. 38.

born of her, since of a servant, is without doubt a servant: wherefore if he (the son) should say, This is my natural brother or my natural sister; for since my father had children by his maidservant, *whom he did not make free*; and he dying, the law has made me lord of these, εγω τουτους ελευθερωσα, *I have made these free*, because of their natural kindred."

This is allowed to be a just and good reason of manumission. Now this answers very much to the case in hand. Men are home-born slaves; the chosen people of God are such by nature; they are born in sin, and are the servants of it; Christ the Son makes them free; and then they are no more foreigners and strangers, *but fellow citizens with the saints, and of the household of God* [*Eph. 2:19*]. This suggests, that true freedom is by Jesus Christ, the Son of God; see *Gal. 5:1*. He it is that makes the saints free from sin; not from the being of it in this life, but from the bondage and servitude of it, from its power and dominion; and from its guilt and liableness to punishment for it; by procuring the pardon of their sins through His blood, and justifying their persons by His righteousness. He also makes them free, or delivers them from the captivity of Satan, by ransoming them out of his hands, taking the prey from the mighty, binding the strong man armed, and delivering them from him, and from the power of darkness, and putting them into His own kingdom: He does not indeed free them altogether from his temptations, but He preserves them by His power from being hurt and destroyed by him. He likewise makes His people free from the law, not only the ceremonial law, which is abolished by Him, but from the moral law; not from obedience to it, as it is in His hands, and a rule of walk and conversation to them, but as in the hands of Moses, and as a covenant of works, and from the rigorous exaction of it, and from seeking justification and life by it, and from its curse and condemnation. And He gives them freedom of access to God, as their Father, through His blood, and by His Spirit; and admits them to all the privileges and immunities of the church below; and gives them a right to, faith in, and an expectation of, the glorious liberty of the children of God hereafter; and such are truly Christ's freemen:

ye shall be free indeed. This is true freedom; what the Jews boasted of, supposing what they said was right, was but a shadow of freedom in comparison of this; and that liberty which sinful men promise themselves in sin, is all deceit; there is no true, solid, substantial freedom but what is by Christ, the Son of God. Even that freedom which the children of God had under the legal dispensation, was a servitude, in comparison of that which the saints enjoy by Christ under the Gospel dispensation; though they were sons and heirs, yet being in nonage [*or* not of maturity], differed nothing from servants, *being under tutors and governors, in bondage under the elements of the world*, and under the influence of a *spirit of bondage* unto fear; see *Gal.*

284

4:1-3; Rom. 8:15; but such that have received *the Spirit of adoption* from Christ, they are really free: they have not only the name of *children*, and of *freemen*, but they are truly such, and wholly so. Perhaps there may be some reference had to such sort of persons among the Jews, who were partly servants, and partly free: so it is said,[30]

"מי שחציו עבד, *he who is half a servant*, or partly a servant, and partly free, shall serve his master one day, and himself another."

And such a one, as the commentators[31] say, is one who is a servant of two partners, and is made free by one of them; or who has paid half his price to his master (for his freedom), but the other half is still due: and of one in such circumstances it is said[32] that,

"He that is partly a servant, and partly free, may not eat of his master's (lamb at the passover)."

But now those who are made free by Christ the Son of God, they are not in part only, but are wholly free, and have a right to all the privileges of His house, to the supper of the Lord, and to every other immunity.

Verse 37. **I know that ye are Abraham's seed**, &c. In answer to the other part of the Jews' objection to Christ, and in favor of themselves, Christ owns that they were the natural seed of Abraham; for truth must be allowed to an adversary. But then this hindered not but they might be, as they were, in moral bondage to sin, and *a generation of vipers*, as those of them who came to John's baptism were [*Matt. 3:7*]; and might not be the sons of God, for not because they were the natural seed of Abraham, were they all the adopted sons of God; and might be cast out of the house of God, as Ishmael was cast out of Abraham's, though he was his natural seed. And what follows proves them to be under the power, and in the servitude of sin, and that they were the seed of the serpent that was to bruise the heel of the woman's seed, or put the Messiah to death, though they were the natural seed of Abraham:

but ye seek to kill me; which none but such who are under the governing power of sin, are slaves unto it, and the vassals of the devil, would ever do: the reason of which is,

because my word hath no place in you. Their hearts were barred and bolted against it, with ignorance, enmity, and unbelief; it had no entrance into them; it did not come with power to their hearts, nor work effectually in them;

---

[30] Mishna Gittin, c. 4. sect. 5. & Ediot, c. 1. sect. 13.

[31] Maimonides, Jarchi, & Bartenora in ibid.

[32] Mishna Pesachim, c. 8. sect. 1.

it had no place at all in them, much less a dwelling; had it had one, it would have produced another effect in them, even love to Christ; which the doctrine of Christ, wherever it comes with power, and takes place in the soul, brings along with it; but where it does not, as here, hatred and indignation, envy and malice, more or less, show themselves. This clause is differently rendered, and so admits of different senses. The Vulgate Latin renders it, *my word does not take in you*; it did not take place in them, nor did it take with them; they could not receive it; in which sense the word is used in *Matt. 19:11*; for the natural man cannot receive the doctrines of Christ; they are not suited to his taste: they are disagreeable to him. The Syriac version renders it, *ye are not sufficient for my word*, to take it in; they were not capable of it; they could not understand it; it requires divine illumination, and a spiritual discerning, which they had not: the Persic version is, *ye are not worthy of my words*; of having the Gospel preached to them, and continued with them; they contradicting and blaspheming it, and rejecting the author of it; see *Acts 13:45-46*. The Ethiopic version renders it, *my word does not remain with you*; and to the same purpose the Arabic version, *my word is not firm in you*; as soon as it was heard by them, it was caught away from them by Satan, whose children they were; it made no lasting impressions on them, but was like water spilt upon the ground: it may be rendered, *my word does not enter into you*; it did not make its way and penetrate into their hearts; for though, when attended with the demonstration of the Spirit, and of power, it is *quick and powerful, and sharper than a twoedged sword*, and enters into the conscience, and penetrates *to the dividing asunder of soul and spirit*, and lays open the secret *thoughts and intents of the heart* [*Heb. 4:12*]; yet of itself is an insufficient means of conversion; it cannot make its own way; there must be an exertion of powerful and efficacious grace; which shows the hardness and obstinacy of the heart of man.

Verse 38. **I speak that which I have seen with my Father**, &c. This is an aggravation of the sin of the Jews, in seeking to kill Christ on account of His doctrine, since it was not His own, but His Father's; was not merely human, but divine; was what He, the only begotten Son that lay in the bosom of His Father, had seen in His heart, in His purposes, and decrees, in His council, and covenant; and so was clear, complete, certain, and to be depended on:

and ye do that which ye have seen with your father. Meaning the devil, whom, though they had not seen with their eyes, nor any of his personal actions; yet acted so much under his influence, and according to his will, as if they had close and intimate consultation with him, and took their plan of operation from him, and had him continually before them, as their example and pattern, to copy after. The Ethiopic version reads, *what ye have heard*; and so it is read in three of Beza's copies, and in three of Stephens's.

Verse 39. **They answered and said unto him**, &c. On account of His making mention of a father, whose works they did, and whom they imitated:

Abraham is our father; meaning their only one, nor had they any other:

Jesus saith unto them, If ye were Abraham's children, ye would do the works of Abraham. For who should children imitate but their parents? Abraham was a merciful, charitable, and hospitable man, as well as a man of strict justice and integrity; he feared God, believed in Him, and was ready to receive every message and revelation which came from Him; and they are His genuine children and offspring, who walk in the steps of His faith, charity, justice, and piety: and this is a rule which the Jews themselves give,[33] whereby the seed of Abraham may be known:

"Whoever is merciful to the creature (man), it is evident that he is of the seed of Abraham our father; but whoever has not mercy on the creature, it is a clear case that he is not of the seed of Abraham our father."

And if this is a sure rule of judging, these men could not be the seed of Abraham, who were a merciless, barbarous, and cruel generation. Another of their writers[34] has this observation, agreeable to the way of reasoning Christ uses:

"A disciple is to be judged of according to his manners; he that walks in the ways of the Lord, he is of the *disciples of Abraham* our father, seeing he is used to his manners, and learns of his works; but the disciple who is corrupt in his manners, though he is of the children of Israel, lo, he is not of the disciples of Abraham, seeing he is not accustomed to his manners."

Whence it appears, that they say these things, not to distinguish themselves from other people who claimed a descent from Abraham, as the Ishmaelites or Saracens did; as did also the Spartans or Lacedemonians; for so writes Areus their king, to Onias the high priest of the Jews,

"It is found in writing, that the Lacedemonians and Jews are brethren, and that they are of the stock of Abraham," (1 Maccab. 12:20-21).

But to distinguish those who were religious and virtuous among the Jews themselves, from those that were not; and so, our Lord means not to deny that the Jews, though they were evil men, were the seed of Abraham according to the flesh; but that they were not so in a spiritual sense, they did not tread in his steps, or do the works he did. The Persic version reads in the singular number, *ye would do the work of Abraham*; and if any particular work is

---

[33] T. Bab. Betza, fol. 32. 2.

[34] Abarbinel Nachaleth Abot, fol. 183. 1.

designed, it is most likely to be the work of faith, since it was that which Abraham was famous for; and the doing of which denominated men, even Gentiles, the children of Abraham, and which the Jews were wanting [*or* lacking] in, they disbelieving and rejecting the Messiah.

Verse 40. **But now ye seek to kill me**, &c. A temper and disposition very foreign from that of Abraham's:

a man that hath told you the truth, which I have heard of God; to seek to kill a man is a very great crime, and punishable with death; to kill an innocent one, that had done no sin, who was pure, holy, harmless, and inoffensive to God and man, was an aggravation of the iniquity; and to kill a prophet, and one more than a prophet, who brought a revelation from God Himself, and declared the whole truth of the Gospel, and particularly that of His divine, eternal Sonship, which incensed them against Him, and put them upon seeking to take away His life, still increased the sin.

This did not Abraham. The sense is not, that Abraham did not tell the truth he had heard of God; for he did instruct, and command his children after him, to walk in the ways of the Lord, which he had learned from Him; but that Abraham did not reject any truth that was revealed unto him, and much less seek to take away the life of any person that brought it to him; and indeed not the life of any man that deserved not to die: and our Lord suggests, that if he had been on the spot now, he would not have done as these his posterity did, since he saw His day by faith, and rejoiced in the foresight of it, *verse 56*. The Jew[35] makes an objection from these words against the Deity of Christ:

"You see (says he) that Jesus declares concerning himself, that he is not God, but man; and so says Paul concerning him, *Rom. 5:15*; and so Jesus, in many places, calls himself *the son of man*: nor do we find in any place that he calls himself God, as the Nazarenes believe."

To which may be replied, That Jesus does not declare in these words, nor in any other place, that He is not God; He says no such thing; He only observes, that He was a man, as He really was: nor is His being man any contradiction to His being God; for He is both God and man; and so those that believe in Him affirm: and though Christ does not in express terms call Himself God, yet He owned Himself to be *the Son of God, Mark 14:61*; and said such things of Himself, as manifestly declared Him to be God; and upon account of which the Jews concluded, that He not only made Himself equal with God, but that He made Himself God, *John 5:17-18* and *10:33*. Besides, He suffered Himself to be called God by a disciple of His, which He would never have done, had he

---

[35] R. Isaac Chizzuk Emuna, par. 2. c. 48. p. 436. & par. 1. c. 10. p. 118.

not been really and truly God, *chapter 20:28*; yea, He seems to call Himself so, when being tempted by Satan, He observed to him what is written, *Thou shalt not tempt the Lord thy God, Matt. 4:7.* The reason why He so often calls Himself the Son of man is, because it was more suitable to Him in His state of humiliation; and indeed, there was no need for Him to assert His Deity in express words, since His works and miracles most clearly proved that He was God. And as for the Apostle Paul, though he sometimes speaks of Him as a man, he also says of Him, that He is *God over all, blessed for ever*; and calls Him *the great God, and our Savior*, and *God manifest in the flesh, Rom. 9:5; Titus 2:13; 1 Tim. 3:16.*

Verse 41. **Ye do the deeds of your father**, &c. Not Abraham, but the devil.

Then said they unto him, We be not born of fornication: meaning either literally, that they were not a brood of bastards, children of whoredom, illegitimately begotten in unlawful copulation, or wedlock; or figuratively, that they were not the children of idolaters, idolatry being called fornication in Scripture; but that they were the holy seed of Israel, and children of the prophets, who had retained the pure Word, and the true worship of God: though in all this they might have been contradicted and refuted; to which they add,

we have one Father, *even* God. Israel being called by God *His son*, and *firstborn*, to them belonged the adoption, in a national sense; and of this they boasted; though few of them were the children of God by special adoption, or God their Father by regenerating grace.

Verse 42. **Jesus said unto them, If God were your Father**, &c. If ye were God's children by adoption, or discovered by the grace of regeneration that ye were born of God,

ye would love me; for in regeneration love to Christ is always implanted: it is a fruit of the Spirit, which always comes along with the superabounding grace of God in conversion; whoever are begotten again, according to abundant mercy, love an unseen Jesus; and where there is no love to Christ, there can be no regeneration: such persons are not born again; nor is God their Father, at least manifestatively:

for I proceeded forth, and came from God; the former of these phrases is observed by many learned men to be used by the Septuagint, of a proper natural birth, as in *Gen. 15:4* and *35:11*; and here designs the eternal genera-tion of Christ, as the Son of God, being the only begotten of the Father, and the Son of the Father in truth and love: and the other is to be understood of His mission from Him, as Mediator:

neither came I of myself; or did not take the office to Himself, without being called unto it, and invested with it, by His Father:

but he sent me. Not by force, or against the will of Christ, or by change of place, but by assumption of nature; He sent Him at the time agreed upon, in human nature, to obtain eternal redemption for His people: and upon both these accounts Christ is to be loved by all regenerate persons, or who have God for their Father; both on account of His being the Son of God, of the same nature and essence with Him, see *1 John 5:1*; and on account of His mission into this world, as Mediator, since He was sent, and came to be the Savior of lost sinners.

Verse 43. **Why do ye not understand my speech?** &c. My language, idiom, dialect, and form of speaking, in a figurative way; for they did not know what He meant by liberty, and bondage; and by having another father than Abraham; or by His own procession and coming forth from God:

even **because ye cannot hear my word.** As they had no spiritual discerning and understanding of the doctrine of Christ, which showed them to be carnal, and natural men, and not regenerate ones, and the children of God; so they had an aversion to it, and could not bear to hear it.

Verse 44. **Ye are of *your* father the devil**, &c. Not of his substance, but by imitation and example; and as being under his authority and influence, his instructions and directions, and ready to follow after him, and obey his commands; the word *your* is rightly supplied, and is in some copies:

and the lusts of your father ye will do. The Syriac and Persic versions read in the singular number, *the lust*, or *desire of your father*; by which may be particularly meant, his eager desire after the death of Christ, which he showed at different times: he instigated Herod to seek to destroy His life in His infancy, and when He was just entering on His public ministry, he tempted Him to destroy Himself; and often stirred up the Scribes and Pharisees to stone Him, or kill Him some other way; and at last put it into the heart of one of His disciples, Judas Iscariot, to betray Him. This looks as if, though the devil had a notion of the salvation of men by Christ, yet that he thought, as some erroneous men have also done, that it was only by His doctrine and example, and therefore he was in haste to get Him out of the world, that He might not be useful, or any more so that way; and not by the shedding of His blood, the sacrifice of Himself, or by His sufferings and death, in the room of sinners; or otherwise it is scarcely credible, that he would have sought His death so earnestly: now this selfsame lust and insatiable desire after the death of Christ prevailed in the Jews; and they were resolute and bent upon fulfilling it at any rate, nor could any thing divert them from it; this is the thing Christ is speaking of in the context, and is what fully proved the devil to be their father, and them to be his children:

He was a murderer from the beginning; he was not only spoken of from the beginning as he that should bruise the Messiah's heel, or should compass His death, but he was actually a murderer of Adam and Eve, and of all their posterity, by tempting them to sin, which brought death and ruin upon them; and who, quickly after that, instigated Cain to slay his brother; and has had, more or less, a concern in all murders committed since; and has been in all ages, and still is, a murderer of the souls of men; and therefore is rightly called *Abaddon*, and *Apollyon*, which signify *the destroyer*. The phrase, *from the beginning*, does not intend the beginning of his own creation; for he was created a holy creature, was in the truth, though he abode not in it; and was in a happy state, though he lost it: nor strictly the beginning of time, or of the creation of the world, which were some days at least before the fall of man, when the devil commenced a murderer; but it being very near it, therefore this phrase is made use of. The Syriac version renders it, *from Bereshith*, which is the first word in the Hebrew Bible, and is frequently used by the Jewish Rabbins for the six days of the creation; and if Adam fell, as some think, the same day he was created, it might be properly said that the devil was a murderer from thence. Philo[36] speaks of Eve's serpent, as ανθρωπου φονωντα, *a murderer of man*; applying to this purpose the text before referred to, *Gen. 3:15;*

and abode not in the truth; neither in the integrity, innocence, and holiness, in which he was created; nor in veracity, or as a creature of veracity, but spake lies, and formed one, by which he deceived Eve, saying, *Ye shall not surely die* [*Gen. 3:4*], when God had said they should [*Gen. 2:17*]; nor in the truth of the Gospel, which was, at least in part, made known unto him; particularly that the Son of God should become man, and in that nature be the head of angels and men: this he and his associates, in the pride of their hearts, not bearing that the human nature should be exalted above that of theirs, left their first estate, broke off their allegiance to God, and turned rebels against Him:

because there is no truth in him. Not that this is a reason why he continued not in the truth, for there was originally truth in him, though he abode not in it; but a reason, showing there was none in him now, since he was fallen from it, and abode not in it; there is no truth in him, that is natural and genuine, and essential to him; and if at any time he speaks it, it is not from his heart, but because he is forced to it, or has an evil design in it:

---

[36] De Agricultura, p. 203.

When he speaketh a lie, he speaketh of his own; that is genuine and natural, of his own devising, willing, and approving:

for he is a liar, and the father of it. He was a liar, as early as he was a murderer, or rather earlier; it was with a lie he deceived, and so murdered our first parents, and he has continued so ever since; he was the first author of a lie; the first lie that ever was told, was told by him; he was the first inventor of one; he was the first of that trade; in this sense the word *father* is used, *Gen. 4:20-21*; so the serpent is by the Cabalistic Jews[37] called, *the lip of a lie*, or *the lying lip*.

Verse 45. **And because I tell *you* the truth**, &c. And no lie, the whole truth of the Gospel, and particularly the truth of His divine Sonship:

ye believe me not. To such an infatuation and judicial blindness were they given up, to disbelieve Him, because He told the truth, and to believe a lie, that they might be damned; which showed them to be the children of the devil, and under his power and influence [see *2 Thess. 2:7-12*].

Verse 46. **Which of you convinceth me of sin?** &c. Of any immorality in life, or of any imposture, corruption, or deceit in doctrine. There were many of them that were forward enough to charge Him with both scandalous sins, and false doctrines; but none of them all could prove any thing against Him, so as to convict Him according to law: they called Him a wine bibber, and a glutton; gave out they knew He was a sinner; charged Him with blasphemy and sedition; sought to bring proof of it, but failed in their attempt:

And if I say the truth, why do ye not believe me? Since as no sin in life, so no corruption in doctrine, could be proved against Him, what He said must be truth; and therefore it was a most unreasonable thing in them, and showed invincible obstinacy, not to believe Him.

Verse 47. **He that is of God**, &c. Who is born, not of blood, by carnal descent from any person, or of the carnal will, or by the power of freewill, or of the will of the best man in the world [see *John 1:12-13*]; but of God, *according to his abundant mercy* [*1 Pet. 1:3*], *of His own will*, by the power of His grace [see *James 1:18*]; and so has God to be His Father: such a one,

heareth God's words; the doctrines of the Gospel, which have God for their author, being of His ordaining, sending, and publishing; and His grace for the matter of them, displayed in election, redemption, justification, pardon, adoption, and eternal salvation, and His glory for the end: now a regenerate

---

[37] Lex. Cabalist. p. 724.

man has eyes to see into the glory, loveliness, excellency, suitableness, and usefulness of these things; and He has ears to hear, and a heart to understand them, which others have not; and therefore hears them with pleasure, receives them in the love of them, cordially embraces them by faith, and distinguishes them from the words of man; and puts such of them in practice, as requires it:

ye therefore hear *them* not, because ye are not of God. Because God was not their Father, or they were not born of Him, as they boasted; therefore they had not eyes to see, nor ears to hear, nor hearts to understand: and it may as fairly be inferred, that because they did not hear the words of God, therefore they were not of God; for these two necessarily imply each other; it looks very dark on such persons, who neither hear the doctrines of the Gospel, externally nor internally.

Verse 48. **Then answered the Jews, and said unto him**, &c. Being incensed to the last degree, that He should say they were of their father the devil, and not of God; and that He spoke the truth, and no one could convince Him of sin:

Say we not well, that thou art a Samaritan; it seems they had said so before, though it is not recorded; and now they thought themselves justified in it, since He treated them, the true sons of Abraham, in such a manner; and the rather, since He had been lately among the Samaritans, and had in a parable spoken in favor of a Samaritan. They meant by this expression, that He was an irreligious man, and one that had no regard to the law of Moses; or at least played fast and loose with religion and the law, and was for any thing, as times served: the Jews had a very ill opinion of the Samaritans on these accounts; and to call a man a Samaritan, was all one as to call Him a heretic, a idolater, or an excommunicated person; for such were the Samaritans with the Jews; they charged them with corrupting the Scriptures, and with worshiping idols, which were hid in Mount Gerizim; and they give us a dreadful account of their being anathematized by Ezra, Zorobabel, and Joshua; who, they say,[38]

> "gathered the whole congregation into the temple, and brought in three hundred priests, and three hundred children, and three hundred trumpets, and three hundred books of the law, in their hands; they blew the trumpets, and the Levites sung, and they anathematized the Samaritans, by the inexplicable name of God, and by the writing on tables, and with the anathema of the house of judgment, above and below; (saying,) let not any Israelite for ever eat of the fruit, or of the least morsel of a Samaritan; hence they say, whoso eateth the flesh of

---

[38] Pirke Eliezer, c. 38.

a Samaritan, it is all one as if he ate swine's flesh; also let not a Samaritan be made a proselyte, nor have a part in the resurrection of the dead; as it is said, *You have nothing to do with to build an house unto our God, Ezra 4:3*, neither in this world, nor in the world to come: moreover, also let him have no part in Jerusalem; as it is said, *But you have no portion, nor right, nor memorial in Jerusalem, Neh. 2:20*; and they sent this anathema to the Israelites that were in Babylon, and they added thereunto, curse upon curse; moreover, king Cyrus added an everlasting anathema to it, as it is said, *And the God that hath caused his name to dwell there, destroy, &c. Ezra 6:12.*"

And hence, because the Samaritans were had in such abhorrence by the Jews, they would not ask a blessing over food in company with them,[39] nor say *Amen* after they had asked one;[40] nor indeed, after the better sort of them had asked, unless the whole blessing was distinctly heard,[41] that so they might be sure there was no heresy in it: by all which it appears, how opprobrious this name was, and what a sad character was fixed upon a man that bore it; see the note on *chapter 4:9*; and as Christ was called by the Jews *a Samaritan*, they having no name more hateful and reproachful to call Him by, so the Christians are still in their writings called *Cuthites*, or *Samaritans*; and it is indeed with them a general name for all Gentiles and idolaters, or whom they esteem such:

and hast a devil? Familiarity and converse with one; by which means they imagined He knew their thoughts, and their actions, and by his assistance performed His miracles; or they took Him for a lunatic, or a madman; whose lunacy and madness proceeded from the devil, with whom He was possessed: and this rather seems to be the sense, since in *verse 52* the Jews say they knew He had a devil, which they concluded from His saying, that such that observed His words and kept them, should never die; which they considered as the words of a man out of his senses, seeing all men, even the best of men die, they not understanding His meaning; whereas they could not gather from hence, that He dealt with familiar spirits; and what still confirms this sense is, that these two are joined together in *chapter 10:20, he hath a devil, and is mad*, and such as were demoniacs, men possessed with devils, were either mad, or lunatic, and melancholy; see *Matt. 8:28; Mark 5:2-5; Matt. 17:15*, compared with *Mark 9:17,25*. To which may be added, that it was a prevailing

---

[39] Bartenora in Mishna Beracot, c. 7. sect. 1.

[40] Elias in Tishbi in voce כות.

[41] Mishna Beracot, c. 8. sect. 8. & Maimon. & Bartenora in ibid.

notion with the Jews, that madness and melancholy were owing to evil spirits, which had the predominancy over men: and seeing Christ was thought to be beside Himself by His friends and relations, *Mark 3:21*, it need not be wondered at, that His enemies should fix such a character on Him; nor was this an unusual one to be given to good men; the prophets and spiritual men of the Old Testament were accounted madmen, *2 Kings 9:11; Hos. 9:7.* And since our Lord was used in this abusive manner, it need not seem strange, that His followers should be treated in the same way; as the Apostle Paul and his companions in the ministry were, *Acts 26:24; 2 Cor. 5:13*; see *chapter 10:20.*

Verse 49. **Jesus answered, I have not a devil,** &c. He takes no notice of the first charge, and scandalous character, that He was a Samaritan; it being so notorious to all the Jews, that He was not; but was, as they supposed, a Galilean, and of Nazareth; and besides, this was a term of reproach, which they gave to any man, that they had no good opinion of; just as we call [42] a man a Turk, or a Jew; not meaning that he is in fact such à one, but behaves like one. To the other Christ replies, that He had not a devil, had no conversation with one, nor was He possessed or assisted by him, nor was mad, nor acted the part of a madman: in proof of which He observes,

but I honor my Father; by ascribing His doctrine and miracles to Him, by doing His will, seeking His glory, and speaking well of Him; all which He would not do, had He been in confederacy with the devil; for no man can be familiar with him, or be assisted by him, and honor God; nor could a man out of his senses do all this:

and ye do dishonor me. By such wicked charges, and scandalous imputations: and the Jews, who deny Jesus to be the Messiah, and treat Him in this opprobrious manner, are not the only persons that dishonor Christ; there are many that are called by His name who greatly dishonor Him; some by their bad principles, and others by their evil practices: such highly reflect upon Him, who deny His proper Deity, and eternal Sonship; who assert, that He is only God by office, and did not exist before His incarnation; who despise and reject His righteousness, submit not to it, but establish their own; who account His blood as common and useless, and speak disrespectfully of His sacrifice and satisfaction; and who consider His sufferings and death only as an example to men, and for the confirmation of His doctrine, but not as in the room and stead of His people, to answer and satisfy divine justice for them [see *Matt. 1:21*]: and others, they dishonor Him, though they talk much of Him, and pretend to faith in Him, and love to Him, and hope of eternal life by

---

[42] In the eighteenth century cultural context - *Editor.*

Him, through their scandalous lives and conversations; dishonor His name and Gospel; give the enemy an occasion to reproach and blaspheme, and by reason of them, the ways and truths of Christ are evil spoken of.

Verse 50. **I seek not mine own glory**, &c. In His doctrine, or in His miracles; which showed that He was no impostor, but a true, faithful, and upright person; and though He was so very much reproached and abused, He was not over-solicitous of His own character, and of retrieving His honor, and of securing glory from man; He knew that Wisdom was justified of her children [*Matt. 11:19*], and He committed Himself to God that judgeth righteously, who would take care of His glory, and vindicate Him from all the unjust charges and insults of men:

there is one that seeketh and judgeth. Meaning God His Father, who had His glory at heart; who had glorified Him on the mount, and would glorify Him again, when He should raise Him from the dead, and spread His Gospel in all the world; and when He would judge the nation of the Jews, and bring wrath upon them, upon their nation, city and temple, for their contempt and rejection of Him.

Verse 51. **Verily, verily, I say unto you**, &c. This is truth, and may be depended upon, as coming from the *Amen*, and faithful witness:

If a man keep my saying; or doctrine, receives the Gospel in the love of it, obeys it from his heart, and cordially embraces and firmly believes it; and retains and holds it fast, having a spiritual and comfortable experience of the doctrines of Christ, and yielding a cheerful and ready obedience to His commands and ordinances, in faith and love:

he shall never see death. The second death, eternal death, which is an everlasting separation of a man, body and soul, from God: this death shall have no power on such a person, he shall never be hurt by it; and though he dies a corporeal death, that shall not be a curse, a penal evil to him; nor shall he always lie under the power of it, but shall rise again, and live in soul and body, for ever with the Lord: seeing and tasting death, as in *verse 52*, are Hebraisms expressive of dying.

Verse 52. **Then said the Jews unto him**, &c. Upon these last words that He spake, giving assurance, that whoever kept His saying, should not die:

Now we know that thou hast a devil. They thought and said so before, but now they were assured, that He must be under diabolical influence, must be possessed with the devil, and mad, and out of His senses; for they thought no man in his senses would ever talk at this rate:

Abraham is dead, and the prophets; that is, *they are dead also*, as the Ethiopic version adds; see *Zech. 1:5*;

and thou sayest, If a man keep my saying, he shall never taste of death. Abraham and the prophets were so far from pretending by their doctrine to communicate life and secure men from death, that they could not keep themselves from dying; and therefore it must be diabolical madness and frenzy to assert any thing of this kind.

Verse 53. **Art thou greater than our father Abraham**, &c. So the woman of Samaria said, concerning Jacob, *chapter 4:12*. The Jews had a mighty opinion of their ancestors, especially of Abraham; and yet they allow the Messiah to be greater than he, as Jesus truly was: so one of their ancient commentators[43] on those words of *Isa. 52:13,* thus paraphrases them:

> *"Behold my servant shall deal prudently*, this is the King Messiah; *he shall be exalted* above Abraham, as it is written, *Gen. 14:22; and extolled* above Moses, as it is written, *Num. 11:12*; and he shall be higher than the ministering angels, as it is written, *Ezek. 1:26; Zech. 4:7*; for he shall be גדול מן אבות, *greater than the fathers."*

They add here, of *Abraham*,

which is dead? he was a great and good man, and yet dead:

and the prophets are dead; though they truly kept, and faithfully delivered the Word of God:

whom makest thou thyself? Who art a poor carpenter's son, a Galilean, a Nazarene, and yet makest thyself greater than Abraham, or any of the prophets; yea, makest thyself to be God, to promise security from death, and an everlasting continuance of life, upon keeping thy Word.

Verse 54. **Jesus answered, If I honor myself, my honor is nothing**, &c. It is empty and vain, and will not continue; see *2 Cor. 10:18*;

it is my Father that honoreth me: by a voice from heaven, both at His baptism, and transfiguration, declaring Him to be His beloved Son, and by the works and miracles He did by Him; as He afterwards also honored Him by raising Him from the dead, and setting Him at His own right hand, by pouring forth His Spirit on His disciples, and succeeding His Gospel in every place:

of whom ye say, that he is your God. Your covenant God and Father, being *the God of Abraham, Isaac, and Jacob*; of this the Jews boasted. The

---

[43] Tanchuma apud Huls. p. 321.

Alexandrian copy, and some others, and all the Oriental versions read, *our God*.

Verse 55. **Yet ye have not known him**, &c. Not as the Father of Christ, nor as in Christ, whom to know is life eternal [see *1 John 5:20*]: they had no spiritual knowledge of Him, nor communion with Him; nor did they know truly His mind and will, nor how to worship and serve Him as they ought:

but I know him; His nature and perfections, being of the same nature, and having the same perfections with Him; and His whole mind and will, lying in His bosom: nor did, or does any know the Father but the Son, and he to whom He is pleased to reveal Him:

and if I should say, I know him not, I shall be a liar like unto you; our Lord still intimates, that they were of their father the devil, and imitated him not only as a murderer, but as a liar: this is quite contrary to the character they give of themselves, for they say,[44] that *an Israelite will not tell a lie*.

but I know him, and keep his saying. Do His will, and always the things that please Him; observe His law, preach His Gospel, fulfil all righteousness, and work out the salvation of men, which were the will and work of His Father He came to do.

Verse 56. **Your father Abraham rejoiced to see my day**, &c. Or *he was desirous to see my day*, as the Syriac and Arabic versions rightly render the word; or *very desirous*, as the Persic version: and indeed, this was what many kings and prophets, and righteous men, were desirous of, even of seeing the Messiah and His day. We often read of, ימות המשיח, *the days of the Messiah*: and the Jews in their Talmud,[45] dispute much about them, how long they will be; one says forty years, another seventy, another three ages: it is the opinion of some, that they shall be according to the number of the days of the year, three hundred and sixty-five years; some say seven thousand years, and others as many as have been from the beginning of the world; and others, as many as from Noah; but we know the day of Christ better, and how long He was here on earth; and whose whole time here is called His day; this Abraham had a very great desire to see:

and he saw *it*, and was glad. He saw it with an eye of faith, he saw it in the promise, that in his seed all the nations of the earth should be blessed; and when it was promised him he should have a son, which was the beginning of

---

[44] Maimon. in Mishna Pesachim, c. 8. sect. 6.

[45] T. Bab. Sanhedrin, fol. 99. 1.

the fulfilment of the other, he laughed, and therefore his son was called Isaac, to which some reference is here made; He saw Him in the birth of his son Isaac and rejoiced, and therefore called his name Isaac, that is, *laughter*: He saw also Christ and His day, His sufferings, death, and resurrection from the dead, in a figure; in the binding of Isaac, in the sacrifice of the ram, and in the receiving of Isaac, as from the dead; and he not only saw the Messiah in His type Melchizedek, and who some think was the Son of God Himself, but he saw the second person, the promised Messiah, in a human form, *Gen. 18:2*; and all this was matter of joy and gladness to him. This brings to mind what the Jews say at the rejoicing at the law, when the book of the law is brought out:[46]

"Abraham rejoiced with the rejoicing of the law, he that cometh shall come, the Branch with the joy of the law; Isaac, Jacob, Moses, Aaron, Joshua, Samuel, David, Solomon, rejoiced with the joy of the law; he that cometh shall come, the Branch with the joy of the law."

Verse 57. **Then said the Jews unto him, Thou art not yet fifty years old**, &c. One copy reads *forty*, but He was not that; no, not much more than thirty; not above two or three and thirty years old. The reason of their fixing on this age of fifty might be, because Christ might look like such a one, being *a man of sorrows and acquainted with grief* [*Isa. 53:3*], as well as of great gravity; or they might be free in allowing Him as many years, as could be thought He should be of, and gain their point; for what were fifty years, when Abraham had been dead above two thousand? And therefore He could never see Abraham, nor Abraham see Him; moreover, this age of fifty, is often spoken of by the Jews, and much observed; at the age of fifty, a man is fit to give counsel, they say;[47] hence the Levites were dismissed from service at that age, it being more proper for them then to give advice, than to bear burdens. A *Methurgeman*, or an interpreter in a congregation, was not chosen under fifty years of age;[48] and if a man died before he was fifty, this was called *the death of cutting off*;[49] a violent death, a death inflicted by God, as a punishment; Christ lived not to that age, He was now many years short of it:

---

[46] Seder Tephillot, fol. 309. 1. Ed. Basil.

[47] Pirke Abot, c. 5. sect. 21.

[48] T. Bab. Chagiga, fol. 14. 1. Juchasin, fol. 44. 2.

[49] T. Hieros. Biccurim, fol. 64. 3. T. Bab. Moed Katon, fol. 28. 1. Massecheth Semachot, c. 3. sect. 9. Kimchi in Isa. 38:10.

and hast thou seen Abraham? If He had not, Abraham had seen Him, in the sense before given, and in which Christ asserted it, and it is to be understood.

Verse 58. **Jesus said unto them, Verily, verily, I say unto you,** &c. Whether it will be believed or not, it is certainly fact:

Before Abraham was, I am. Which is to be understood, not of His being in the purpose and decree of God foreordained to sufferings, and to glory; for so all the elect of God may be said to be before Abraham, being chosen in Christ *before the foundation of the world* [*Eph. 1:4*]: or that Christ was man, before Abraham became the father of many nations; that is, before the calling of the Gentiles; for nothing is said in the text about His being the father of many nations; it is a bold and impudent addition to it: and besides, Abraham was made the father of many nations, as Ishmaelites, Israelites, Hagarenes, &c. long before the incarnation of Christ; yea, he was so from the very promise in *Gen. 17:5*, which so runs, *a father of many nations have I made thee*; so that this appears a false sense of the text, which is to be understood of the Deity, eternity, and immutability of Christ, and refers to the passage in *Ex. 3:14: I AM that I AM—I AM hath sent me unto you*, the true *Jehovah*; and so Christ was before Abraham was in being, the everlasting I AM, *the eternal God* [*Deut. 33:27*], which is, and was, and is to come: He appeared in a human form to our first parents before Abraham was, and was manifested as the Mediator, Savior, and living Redeemer, to whom all the patriarchs before Abraham looked, and by whom they were saved: He was concerned in the creation of all things out of nothing, as the efficient cause thereof; He was set up from everlasting as Mediator; and the covenant of grace was made with Him, and the blessings and promises of it were put into His hands before the world began; the eternal election of men to everlasting life was made in Him before the foundation of the world; and He had a glory with His Father before the world was; yea, from all eternity He was the Son of God, of the same nature with Him, and equal to Him; and His being of the same nature proves His eternity, as well as Deity, that He is from everlasting to everlasting God; and is what He ever was, and will be what He now is: He is immutable, the same today, yesterday, and for ever; in His nature, love, grace, and fulness, He is the invariable and unchangeable I AM.

Verse 59. **Then they took up stones to cast at him**, &c. Supposing that He had spoken blasphemy; for they well understood that He, by so saying, made Himself to be the eternal God, the unchangeable Jehovah. Should it be asked how they came by their stones in the temple? It may be replied, The temple was still building, *chapter 2:20*, and stones, or pieces of stones, might lie about, with which they furnished themselves, in order to have destroyed

Christ: and this they attempted, though it was on the sabbath day, as appears from *chapter 9:1,14*; and with them, סקילה בשבת, *stoning on the sabbath day*,[50] was allowed in some cases:

but Jesus hid himself, not in any corner of the temple, or behind a pillar; but He withdrew Himself from them directly, and made Himself invisible to them, by holding their eyes, or casting a mist before them, that they could not see Him:

and went out of the temple; by one of the gates of it:

going through the midst of them; not of the persons that took up stones to stone Him; but the rest of the people, who were there in great multitudes to hear His doctrine, and see His miracles:

and so passed by. And escaped out of their hands; the last words, *going through the midst of them, and so passed by*, are not in Beza's most ancient copy, and in the Vulgate Latin version.

CHAPTER 9

Verse 1. **And as *Jesus* passed by**, &c. The word *Jesus* is not in the Greek text, but is rightly supplied by us, as it is in the Vulgate Latin, and as the word *Christ* is in the Persic version; for of His passing from the temple, and by the multitude that were there, and on His way to the place He designed to make to, is this said, as appears from the close of the preceding chapter; though some think this is to be understood of His passing by at another time and place, since the preceding fact of the woman's being taken in adultery, and the discourse of our Lord with the Jews, were quickly after the feast of tabernacles; whereas the following ones, both in this, and the next chapter, seem to be at the feast of dedication, *chapter 10:22*, which was some months after: but it may be, that the parable of the sheep, though it runs in connection with what is said in this chapter, might be delivered then; or what follows, *chapter 10:22*, might be said at the feast of dedication, when the parable, and what is related here, might be delivered before, seeing there is

---

[50] T. Hieros. Yom Tob, fol. 63. 2.

so very strict a connection between this, and the preceding chapter; and the Ethiopic version is very express, rendering it, *and departing from thence*; that is, from the temple, at that time when the Jews took up stones to stone Him:

he saw a man which was blind from *his* birth. Which man was an emblem of God's elect in a state of nature, who being conceived in sin, are transgressors from the womb, and so are alienated from the life of God through their ignorance and blindness: they are blind as to any true and spiritual knowledge of God in Christ; as to any true sight of sin, or sense of their own estate and condition; and with respect to Christ, and the way of peace, righteousness, and salvation by Him; and as to the Spirit, and the operations of His grace, and with regard to the Scriptures, and the doctrines of the Gospel: and as Christ saw this man first, and not the man Him, for he was blind, so Christ first looks upon His chosen ones with an eye of love and mercy, as He passes by them, and both enlightens and quickens them, *Ezek. 16:6,8*. He saw Matthew the publican first, as He passed along, and called Him from the receipt of custom to be a follower of Him, *Matt. 9:10*.

Verse 2. **And his disciples asked him**, &c. It may be that some of the twelve apostles, or others of His disciples, might put the following question to Him on sight of this blind man, who by some means or another knew was born blind:

saying, Master, who did sin, this man, or his parents, that he was born blind? The first of these questions, whether the man himself had sinned before he was born, which might be the occasion of his blindness, proceeds not upon the doctrine of original sin, though the Jews then believed that; see the note on *Rom. 5:12* **[60]**; since that was common to all men, and therefore could not admit of such a question; but either upon the notion of the transmigration of souls into other bodies; and so the disciples might ask whether this man had sinned in a preexistent state when in another body, which was the reason of this blindness, or of his being put into a blind body. This notion, Josephus says,[1] was embraced by the Pharisees; though, according to him, it seems, that they only understood it of the souls of good men; and if so, this could lay no foundation for such a question, unless these disciples had given into the Pythagorean notion of a transmigration of all souls, which was to be known by defects, as blindness, &c.;[2] or else this question proceeded upon a principle received by the Jews, that an infant might do that which was faulty and criminal, and actually sin in the womb; of which Dr. Lightfoot has given

---

[1] De Bello Jud. l. 2. c. 8. sect. 14.

[2] Sallust. de Diis, c. 20.

instances. The second question proceeds upon the methods which sometimes God has taken with men, by visiting the iniquities of the fathers upon the children; or, as the above learned writer observes, upon a notion the Jews had, that a child might suffer for what the mother did while it was in the womb; or on another, which prevailed among them, that there should be neither merit nor demerit in the days of the Messiah; that is, that neither the good deeds, nor bad deeds of their parents, should be imputed to their children, neither the one to their advantage, nor the other to their disadvantage: and therefore since He the Messiah was come, they ask, how this blindness should come to pass? what should be the reason of it?

Verse 3. **Jesus answered, Neither hath this man sinned, nor his parents**, &c. Not but that both were guilty of original sin, and had committed actual transgressions; but Christ's answer is to be considered agreeable to the design of the question; and the sense is, that it was not any sin that either of them had committed, while he was in the womb, or previous to his birth, that was the cause of this blindness; otherwise, all such irregularities and afflictions arise from sin, and the fall of man, as does that spiritual blindness with which all mankind are attended:

but that the works of God should be manifest in him. That is, that Christ might have an opportunity of working a miracle in the cure of him, whereby it might appear that He is truly and properly God, the Son of God, and the Messiah. And so spiritual blindness, which has followed the fall of man, takes place in the elect of God in common with others, that the power of divine grace might be displayed in bringing them *out of darkness into marvelous light* [*1 Pet. 2:9*].

Verse 4. **I must work the works of him that sent me**, &c. This shows, that the works of God, that were to be manifest, were to be done by Christ: many were the works which the Father gave Him to do, and which He undertook to perform; and therefore there was a necessity of doing them, as principally the work of redemption, by fulfilling the law, and satisfying justice: and besides this, there were the preaching of the Gospel, and doing of miracles, and among these was this of giving sight to the blind, see *Isa. 35:5*, both in a natural and spiritual sense: and with a view to this He speaks of the works He must do,

while it is day; while the day of life lasts, for in the grave there is no work nor device:

the night cometh, when no man can work. Meaning the night of death, and of the grave, and suggesting His own death hereby, that He had but a little time to be in this world, and therefore would make the best use of it, to do the will and work of His Father that sent Him; and which should be a pattern to us. This life is but short, it is but as the length of a day; a great deal of business is to be done; and death is hastening on, which will put a period to all working.

Verse 5. **As long as I am in the world**, &c. Which had been now two or three and thirty years; but was not to be much longer.

I am the light of the world; see the note on *chapter 8:12*. Though doubtless He said this with some view to the cure He was about to perform, it being agreeable to His character and work, while He was in the world.

Verse 6. **And when he had thus spoken**, &c. In answer to the disciples' question, and declaring His own work and office in the world, and the necessity He was under of performing it:

he spat on the ground, and made clay of the spittle; the Mishnaic doctors speak[3] of טיט נרוק, *clay that is spitted*, or *spittle clay*, which their commentators say[4] was a weak, thin clay, like spittle or water; but this here was properly spittle clay, or clay made of spittle, for want of water; or it may be rather, through choice Christ spat upon the dust of the earth, and worked it together into a consistency, like clay:

and he anointed the eyes of the blind man with the clay; however, spittle, especially fasting spittle, might be thought proper in some disorders of the eyes to be used, as it was by the Jews; see the note on *verse 16;* yet clay was a most unlikely means of restoring sight to a man that was born blind, which might be thought rather a means of making a man blind that could see. This may be an emblem of the Word of God, the eye salve of the Gospel; which is a very unlikely means in the opinion of a natural man, who counts it foolishness, of enlightening and saving sinners; and yet by this foolishness of preaching God does save those that believe.

Verse 7. **And said unto him, Go, wash in the Pool of Siloam**, &c. A fountain of this name is called *Siloah, Isa. 8:6*, and according to the Jewish writers, sometimes *Gihon;*[5] and this, they say,[6] was without Jerusalem,

---

[3]   Mishna Mikvaot, c. 7. sect. 1.

[4]   Jarchi, Maimon. & Bartenora in ibid.

[5]   Targum, Jarchi, Kimchi, & Solomon ben Melech in 1 Kings 1:33.

[6]   Jarchi & Bartenora in Mishna Succa, c. 4. sect. 9.

though near unto it: hither the Jews went at the feast of tabernacles,[7] and drew water with great rejoicing, and brought it, and poured it on the altar; the waters thereof also the priests drank for digestion, when they had eaten too much flesh;[8] and this was likewise made use of to wash in, in case of uncleanness. It is said[9] of Benaiah, one of David's worthies, that,

> "one day he set his foot upon a dead toad, and he went down to Siloah, and broke the pieces of hail (or ice congealed together), and dipped himself."

This fountain was to the southwest of Jerusalem; and was, as Josephus says, sweet and large;[10] and from it were two watercourses, upper and lower, *2 Chron. 32:30*, which ran into two pools; the one was called the pool of *Siloam*, which may be the same that Josephus[11] calls the pool of *Solomon*, and is here meant, and which was situated on the south of the wall of Sion, towards the east; and the other was called the pool of *Shelah*, and which, in *Neh. 3:15*, is called in our translation, and in some others, the pool of *Siloah*. Now both the fountain, and the pool, were without the city; and yet we read of a *Siloah* in the midst of the city.[12] This blind man was sent, not to wash himself all over, but only his face or eyes; and so the Arabic and Persic versions read, *wash thy face*, the clay from it. This may be emblematical of the grace of the Spirit, sometimes signified by water and washing, which accompanying the Word, makes it effectual to the salvation of souls:

(which is by interpretation, Sent). This interpretation of the word *Siloam* does not determine which of the pools is meant, the upper or lower, *Siloah* or *Shelah*, since they both come from the word שלח, which signifies to *send*; but by the flexion of the word, the upper pool *Siloah* seems plainly intended, which was not so forenamed, as Nonnus suggests, from the sending this man thither, but rather from the sending forth its waters, which flowed softly and gently for the supply of the city of Jerusalem. Some think Christ gave this interpretation of it with a view to Himself, as the *sent* of God, the true Messiah: but the words seem not to be the words of Christ, but of the

---

[7] Mishna Succa, c. 4. sect. 9.

[8] Abot R. Nathan, c. 35. fol. 8. 3.

[9] Targum in 1 Chron. 11:22.

[10] De Bello Jud. l. 5. c. 4. sect. 1.

[11] Ibid. l. 6. c. 6. vel. l. 5. c. 4. sect. 2.

[12] T. Hieros. Chagigah, fol. 76. 1.

evangelist, who interprets this word; wherefore they are left out in the Syriac and Persic versions, where such an interpretation was needless.

He went his way therefore, and washed, and came seeing. He did as he was commanded; he was obedient to the directions and orders of Christ, though they seemed so unlikely to answer the end; and yet that was brought about through the divine power of Christ, which appeared the more in making use of such unlikely means.

Verse 8. **The neighbors therefore, and they which before had seen him**, &c. For it seems the blind man was not a stranger, one that came out of the country to the city to beg; but a native of Jerusalem, that had long lived in a certain neighborhood in it, and was well known to be what he was;

that he was blind; the Alexandrian copy, and one of Beza's exemplars, and the Vulgate Latin version read, *that he was a beggar*; to which agree the Syriac, Arabic, and Ethiopic versions: wherefore they,

said, Is not this he that sat and begged? They particularly remark his begging posture; he was not laid all along, as the lame man in *Acts 3:2*; nor did he go from door to door, as others were used to do, but he sat in some certain place, as blind men generally did; see *Matt. 20:30*.

Verse 9. **Some said, This is he**, &c. It is the same man that was blind, and begged:

others *said*; in one of Beza's copies it is added *no*, and so read the Vulgate Latin, and all the Oriental versions; though they owned and said,

He is like him. This discourse of the neighbors concerning the blind man restored to sight, resembles the talk that generally is among relations, acquaintance, and neighbors, when anyone belonging to them is called by grace, and converted, saying, What is come to such a one? Is he mad or melancholy? He is not the man he was: he is scarcely the same; is it he, or another? What is the matter with him?

but **he said, I am** *he*. And so put an end to the dispute between them, by his frank acknowledgment that he was the blind man, and the beggar they before knew as such. So persons enlightened by the Spirit of God, and effectually called by His grace, are very free and ready to acknowledge what they were before conversion: what poor, blind, and miserable, and contemptible creatures they were: Matthew owns himself to have been a publican; and Paul confesses he was a blasphemer, a persecutor, an injurious person, and the chief of sinners.

Verse 10. **Therefore said they unto him,** &c. When the case was clear, and it was out of question that he was the man:

How were thine eyes opened? Or made to see? They might well ask this question, since such a thing was never known before, that one born blind received his sight; and as great a miracle it is in grace, and as great a mystery to a natural man, how one should be born again, or be spiritually enlightened.

Verse 11. **He answered and said, A man that is called Jesus,** &c. Whom he had as yet little knowledge of, only by some means or another he had learned His name;

made clay, and anointed mine eyes, &c. See the notes on *verses 6 and 7.*

Verse 12. **Then said they unto him, Where is he?** &c. For Christ had withdrawn Himself and was gone; whether on account of the Jews, who He knew would be irritated by this miracle, or whether to avoid all popular applause and glory, which He sought not, is not certain; it may be on both accounts. This question, however, was put, not out of good will to Christ, but that they might apprehend Him, and bring Him before the Sanhedrin, for doing work on the sabbath day; and such enmity there is in carnal men, at the conversion of sinners, their acquaintance, instead of rejoicing at it:

He said, I know not. For when he returned from the pool, Jesus was gone. And so it sometimes is, that when Christ has wrought a good work of grace upon the heart, He withdraws Himself for a while, and the converted sinner knows not where He is.

Verse 13. **They brought to the Pharisees,** &c. That is, to the Sanhedrin, which chiefly consisted of Pharisees; and so Nonnus calls them the priests and chief priests:

him that was aforetime blind. To be examined by them. And something like this is the method used by carnal relations and friends, who when they have any belonging to them under a work of grace, have [*or* take] them to their learned doctors of a different religion, to talk to them, and dissuade them from the ways of truth and godliness.

Verse 14. **And it was the sabbath day when Jesus made the clay,** &c. Which was reckoned a violation of the sabbath, *verse 16,* and was one reason why they had [*or* took] the man to the Pharisees to be examined, and why they were desirous of knowing where Jesus was:

and opened his eyes. By putting on the clay, and sending him to wash in the pool of Siloam: nor did the miracle, nor the good done to the man, excuse with them what they thought a breach of the sabbath.

Verse 15. **Then again the Pharisees asked him**, &c. Not that they had put any question of this kind to him before; but they also, as well as the neighbors, inquired of him,

how he had received his sight. From whom, and by what means:

He said unto them, He put clay upon mine eyes, and I washed, and do see. This account agrees with the matter of fact, and with that he gave to his neighbors: he did not vary as to the truth of the relation, but this is somewhat more concise and short; and it is reasonable to suppose, that the Pharisees had talked much with him before, which made it less necessary to be more particular; for he makes no mention of the name of Jesus, nor of His making the clay, and the manner of it, nor of the Pool of Siloam, or of His orders to go there and wash; see the notes on *verses 6 and 7.*

Verse 16. **Therefore said some of the Pharisees**, &c. Or Sanhedrin, for they were not all of one mind, as appears by what follows:

This man is not of God; meaning not the blind man, but Jesus; and their sense is, He is not *sent* of God, He does not come from Him to do His will and work, nor does He seek His glory, nor is He on His side, or for His interest;

because he keepeth not the sabbath day. This they concluded from His making clay of spittle, and spreading it on the blind man's eyes, which was contrary to the traditions of their elders: one of whose rules and canons is [13] that,
"It is forbidden to put fasting spittle even on the eyelid on a sabbath day."
An eye salve, or a plaster for the eye, if it was put on for pleasure, was lawful, but not for healing:[14] but if it was put on on the evening of the sabbath, it might continue on the sabbath day.[15]

Others said, How can a man that is a sinner, or a sabbath breaker,

do such miracles? As curing a man born blind, the like of which was never heard: those that reasoned after this manner may be supposed to be

---

[13]   T. Hieros. Sabbat, fol. 14. 4. & Avoda Zara, fol. 40. 4. & T. Bab. Sabbat, fol 108. 2. & Maimon. Hilchot Sabbat, c. 21. sect. 25.

[14]   Piske Tosephot Sabbat, art. 67.

[15]   T. Hieros. Sabbat, fol. 3, 4. Maimon. ibid.

Nicodemus and Joseph of Arimathea.

And there was a division among them. Even in the Sanhedrin, they could not agree about the character of the person that had done this miracle.

Verse 17. **They say unto the blind man again**, &c. After they had discoursed among themselves, and could not agree about the author of the miracle, they turn to him that had been blind, who is called *the blind man*, because he had been so, and ask him his sentiments of Him:

What sayest thou of him, that he hath opened thine eyes? The question seems, at first sight, as if it was, whether Jesus had opened his eyes or not; but by the answer it appears, that it required his thoughts of Him, *who hath opened thine eyes*, as the Vulgate Latin and Persic versions read; or *seeing*, or *because he hath opened thine eyes*, as the Arabic and Ethiopic versions:

He said, He is a prophet. The Syriac and Persic versions read, *I say, He is a prophet*; or, *He is certainly a prophet*, as the Arabic version. The Jews were wont to conclude a man's being a prophet from miracles wrought by him; see *chapter 6:14* and *7:31*; though it does not appear that he believed Him, as yet, to be *that prophet*, or the Messiah, that was to come; see *verse 36*.

Verse 18. **But the Jews did not believe concerning him**, &c. Not Jesus, but the blind man;

that he had been blind, and received his sight; they imagined there was a fraud in the case, that it was a juggle [that is, a deceit] between Jesus and this man; that he was a man who had never been blind, but only had given out that he was, and pretended he had now received his sight from Jesus, on purpose to spread His fame, and induce people to believe He was the Messiah; and in this imagination they endeavored to strengthen themselves and others:

until they called the parents of him that had received his sight. They sent messengers to them, and summoned them before them, that they might examine them about this matter, hoping, they might get something out of them, which might detect the supposed fraud, and bring Jesus under disgrace.

Verse 19. **And they asked them, saying, Is this your son**, &c. The first question they put was, whether the man that stood before them, pointing to him, was their son or not; whether they knew him by any marks to be their son, and would own him as such: had they answered to this in the negative, they would have gotten an advantage against him, and would have convicted him of a lie, since he had given out that he was the son of such parents; and proving such a lie upon him, would at once have brought the whole affair into suspicion at least: they add,

who ye say was born blind? This contains a second question, whether, if this was their son, he was born blind or not; and if he was not born blind, though he had been blind, it would have greatly lessened the miracle: and besides, they would have put other questions upon this, whether his blindness was real, and by what means it came. Next follows a third question,

how then doth he now see? By what means has he received his sight? They might hope, that if he was their son, and was really born blind, that he had his sight some other way than by Jesus; or they might object this to his being born blind, as being a thing impossible, or at least not credible, that he should ever see, was that the case.

Verse 20. **His parents answered them and said**, &c. What follows, which contains distinct answers to the several questions: and to the first they reply very freely, and with great confidence,

We know that this is our son; for though his receiving his sight made a considerable alteration in him, yet his features were the same; and there might be some marks in his body, which they were acquainted with, by which they knew assuredly he was their son: and if even the neighbors, though they disagreed about him, yet some of them knew him to be the same person that had been blind and begged, then much more his parents; and even those who said it was not he, yet they owned he was like him: and with respect to the second question they answer,

and that he was born blind: this they were ready to attest, and did attest.

Verse 21. **But by what means he now seeth, we know not**, &c. As to the third question they could say nothing to it, they were not present when the cure was wrought, and knew nothing of the matter, but what they had heard from their son, or from others, or both:

or who hath opened his eyes, we know not; they had heard it was Jesus, and their son had doubtless told them it was He; but since they could say nothing of their own personal knowledge, they choose not to say any thing of Him:

he is of age; at man's estate, as with the Jews, one was who was at the age of thirteen years, if he could produce the signs of puberty: and such a one was allowed a witness in any case, but not under this age; nor if he was arrived to it, if the above signs could not be produced.[16] This man very likely was much older, as may be thought from the whole of his conduct, his pertinent answers,

---

[16]   Maimon. Hilchot Eduth, c. 9. sect. 7.

and just reasoning: wherefore his parents direct the Sanhedrin to him for an answer to their third question:

ask him: he shall speak for himself. Or *of himself*, as the Vulgate Latin and Ethiopic versions render it: their sense is, he is capable of giving an account of himself in this matter, and he will do it, and let him do it; put the question to him, and a proper answer will be returned; and so they left the affair to be issued in this way.

Verse 22. **These *words* spake his parents**, &c. These were the answers they returned to the three questions put to them: and the reason why they answered in the manner they did to the third, was,

because they feared the Jews; the Jewish Sanhedrin, otherwise they were Jews themselves:

for the Jews had agreed already; the Sanhedrin had made a decree, either at this time, upon this account, or some time before,

that if any man did confess that he was Christ; that Jesus of Nazareth was the Messiah,

he should be put out of the synagogue. Which was not that sort of excommunication which they called נדוי, *Niddui*, a separation from civil society for the space of four cubits, and which held but thirty days, if the person repented; if he did not, it was continued to sixty days; and after that, in case of non-repentance, to ninety days; and if no amendment, then they proceeded to another excommunication called חרם, *Cherem*, or שמתא, *Shammatha*, whereby such were anathematized, and cut off from the whole body of the Jewish church and people, called sometimes *the synagogue and congregation of Israel*;[17] and this struck great terror in the minds of the people; and this was what intimidated the parents of the blind man, being what is intended here. Though these are sometimes put one for another, and signify the same thing; and he that was under the former of those censures, is said to be מובדל מן ציבור, *separated from the congregation*,[18] a phrase by which the word here used may be very well rendered: but in some things there was a difference between them; the one was without cursing, the other with; he that was under *Niddui*, might teach others the traditions, and they might teach him; he might hire workmen, and be hired himself: but he that was

---

[17] Vid. Maimon. Talmud Tora, c. 7. sect. 6. Buxtorf. Lex. Rab. col. 1303. & Epist. Heb. Institut. p. 57.

[18] Maimon. Hilchot Talmud Tora, c. 7. sect. 4.

under *Cherem* might neither teach others, nor they teach him; but he might teach himself, that he might not forget his learning; and he might neither hire, nor be hired; and they did not trade with him, nor did they employ him in any business, unless in very little, just to keep him alive;[19] yea, the goods which he was possessed of, were confiscated, and which they conclude should be done from[20] *Ezra 10:8*, which may be compared with this passage; so that this greatly and chiefly affected them in the affairs of civil life, and which made it so terrible: for I do not find that they were obliged to abstain from the temple, or temple worship, or from the synagogue, and the worship of it, and which is the mistake of some learned men. It is certain, they might go into places of worship, though with some difference from others; for it is said[21] that,

"All that go into the temple, go in, in the right hand way, and go round, and come out in the left, except such a one to whom any thing has befallen him, and he goes about to the left; (and when asked,) Why dost thou go to the left? (he answers,) Because I am a mourner; (to whom it is replied,) He that dwells in this house comfort thee: (or) שאני מנודה, *because I am excommunicated*; (to whom they say,) He that dwells in this house put it into thy heart (that thou mayest hearken to the words of thy friends, as it is afterwards explained), and they may receive thee."

And it is elsewhere said[22] that,

"Solomon, when he built the temple, made two gates, the one for bridegrooms, and the other for mourners and excommunicated persons; and the Israelites, when they went in on sabbath days, or feast days, sat between these two gates; and when any one came in by the gate of the bridegrooms, they knew he was a bridegroom, and said unto him, he that dwells in this house make thee cheerful with sons and daughters: and when any one came in at the gate of mourners, and his upper lip covered, they knew that he was a mourner, and said unto him, He that dwells in this house comfort thee: and when any one came in at the gate of mourners, and his upper lip was not covered, they knew שהיה מנודה, *that he was excommunicated*; and said unto him, He that dwells in this house comfort thee, and put it into thy heart to

---

[19] Ibid. sect. 5.

[20] T. Bab. Moed Katon, fol. 16. 1.

[21] Mishna Middot, c. 2. sect. 2.

[22] Pirke Eliezer, c. 17.

hearken to thy friends."
And it is afterwards also said in the same place, that when the temple was destroyed, it was decreed that such persons should come into synagogues and schools; but then they were not reckoned as members of the Jewish church, but as persons cut off from the people of Israel, and scarce allowed to be of their commonwealth. And it may be further observed, that excommunication with the Jews was not only on religious accounts, but on civil accounts; on account of money, or when a man would not pay his debts, according to the decree of the Sanhedrin.[23] The twenty-four reasons of excommunication, given by Maimonides,[24] chiefly respect contempt of the Sanhedrin, and of the wise men, and breach of the traditions of the elders; sometimes they excommunicated for immorality, particularly the Essenes, as Josephus relates, who says,[25]

> "that such who are taken in grievous sins, they cast them out of their order; and he that is so dealt with commonly dies a miserable death; for being bound by oaths and customs, he cannot eat the food of others, and so starves."

The same is reported[26] by R. Abraham Zachuth: and sometimes excommunication was for Epicurism, or heresy, and such they reckoned the belief of Jesus of Nazareth, as the Messiah; on account of which this decree was made, and which continued with them; for not only this blind man was cast out of the synagogue by virtue of it, but our Lord tells His disciples, that they should be so treated by the Jews after His death; and we find it remained in force and practice many hundreds of years afterwards. Athanasius[27] relates of a Jew, that lived in Berytus, a city in Syria, between Tyre and Sidon, that an image of Christ being found in his house by another Jew, though unknown to him; and this being discovered to the chief priests and elders of the Jews, they cast him out of the synagogue. Sometimes this sentence was pronounced by word of mouth, and sometimes it was delivered in writing: the form of one is given us by Buxtorf,[28] out of an ancient Hebrew manuscript; and a dreadful shock-

---

[23] T. Bab. Moed Katon, fol. 16. 1. & Gloss in ibid.

[24] Hilchot Talmud Tora, c. 6. sect. 14.

[25] De Bello Jud. l. 2. c. 8. sect. 8.

[26] Juchasin, fol. 139. 2.

[27] Oper. ejus, Tom. 2. p. 12, 17. Ed. Commelin.

[28] Lex Rab. col. 828.

ing one it is; and is as follows:

"according to the mind of the Lord of lords, let such a one, the son of such a one, be in *Cherem*, or anathematized, in both houses of judgment, of those above, and those below; and with the anathema of the saints on high, with the anathema of the *Seraphim* and *Ophanim*, and with the anathema of the whole congregation, great and small; let great and real stripes be upon him, and many and violent diseases; and let his house be a habitation of dragons; and let his star be dark in the clouds; and let him be for indignation, wrath, and anger; and let his carcass be for beasts and serpents; and let those that rise up against him, and his enemies, rejoice over him; and let his silver and his gold be given to others; and let all his children be exposed at the gate of his enemies, and at his day may others be amazed; and let him be cursed from the mouth of Addiriron and Actariel (names of angels, as are those that follow), and from the mouth of Sandalphon and Hadraniel, and from the mouth of Ansisiel and Pathchiel, and from the mouth of Seraphiel and Zaganzael, and from the mouth of Michael and Gabriel, and from the mouth of Raphael and Meshartiel; and let him be anathematized from the mouth of Tzabtzabib, and from the mouth of Habhabib, he is Jehovah the Great, and from the mouth of the seventy names of the great king, and from the side of Tzortak the great chancellor; and let him be swallowed up as Korah and his company, with terror, and with trembling; let his soul go out; let the reproof of the Lord kill him; and let him be strangled as Ahithophel in his counsel; and let his leprosy be as the leprosy of Gehazi; and let there be no raising him up from his fall; and in the sepulchers of Israel let not his grave be; and let his wife be given to another; and let others bow upon her at his death: in this anathema, let such a one, the son of such a one be, and let this be his inheritance; but upon me, and upon all Israel, may God extend his peace and his blessing. Amen."

And if he would, he might add these verses in *Deut. 29:19-21: And it come to pass, when he heareth the words of this curse, that he bless himself in his heart, saying, I shall have peace, though I walk in the imagination of mine heart, to add drunkenness to thirst: the Lord will not spare him, but then the anger of the Lord and his jealousy shall smoke against that man, and all the curses that are written in this book shall lie upon him, and the Lord shall blot out his name from under heaven. And the Lord shall separate him unto evil out of all the tribes of Israel, according to all the curses of the covenant that are written in this book of the law.* There were many rites and ceremonies, which in process of time were used, when such a sentence was pronounced, as blowing of horns and trumpets, and lighting candles, and putting them out:

hence, trumpets are reckoned[29] among the instruments of judges. It is said[30] of R. Judah, that being affronted by a certain person, he resented the injury, and brought out the trumpets and excommunicated him: and they tell us,[31] that Barak anathematized Meroz, whom they take to be some great person, with four hundred trumpets. And they also say,[32] that four hundred trumpets were brought out, and they excommunicated Jesus of Nazareth; though these words are left out in some editions of the Talmud. Now this was done in order to inject terror both into those that were guilty, and also into the whole congregation of the people, that they might hear and fear; for the *Cherem*, or that sort of excommunication which goes by that name, was done publicly before the whole synagogue, all the heads and elders of the church being gathered together; and then candles were lighted, and as soon as the form of the curse was finished, they were put out, as a sign that the excommunicated person was unworthy of the heavenly light.[33] Very likely the Papists took their horrible custom from hence of cursing with bell, book, and candle.

Verse 23. **Therefore said his parents, He is of age**, &c. See the note on *verse 21.*

Verse 24. **Then again called they the man that was blind**, &c. That had been blind. After they had examined his parents, and could get nothing from them for their purpose, they try a second time what they could do with the son:

and said unto him, Give God the praise; a phrase used when confession of sin was required; see *Josh. 7:19*; and this may be the meaning of it here; confess this fraud and imposture before the omniscient God, the searcher of hearts, and in so doing glorify that perfection of His. One and the same word, ידה, signifies both to *confess* the truth of any thing, as a sinful action, *Prov. 28:13*, and to *give thanks* and praise to God for any mercy and blessing, *Psa. 45:17; Dan. 2:23*. Some take this to be the form of an oath, and that the Pharisees adjured the man by the living God, that he would tell the truth, and discover the cheat and collusion used in this affair of receiving his sight; and

---

[29] T. Bab. Sanhedrin, fol 7. 2.

[30] T. Bab. Kiddushin, c. 4. in Beth Israel, fol. 57. 1.

[31] T. Bab. Moed Katon, fol. 16. 1. & Shebuot, fol. 36. 1.

[32] T. Bab. Sanhedrin, fol. 107. 2. Ed. Venet.

[33] Buxtorf. Epist. Heb. Institut. c. 6. p. 56.

thought hereby to have deterred him from speaking of this benefit he had received from Christ, especially in such a manner as to reflect any honor upon the author of it. Or the sense may be, if this really is matter of fact, that thou wast born blind, and hast received thy sight by the means of this man, give all the glory of it to God, to whom alone it is due, and not to Him. God sometimes works by wicked instruments, when the glory of what is done ought not to be ascribed to them, but to Him.

We know that this man is a sinner. This they concluded from His breaking the sabbath, as they supposed; though they also aspersed His character, and accused Him of other things, yet falsely; see *Matt. 11:19*; *Luke 23:2*; nor could they prove one single instance of sin in Him, though they express themselves here with so much assurance.

Verse 25. **He answered and said**, &c. That is, the man who had been blind, who takes no notice of the confession they pressed him to, which is what he could not do; there being no collusion in this case, he only replies to the reproachful character they had given of his benefactor.

Whether he be a sinner *or no*, **I know not**: or *if he is a sinner I know not*, as the Vulgate Latin version renders it, suggesting, that he did not know He was a sinner; he could not charge Him with being one; nor could he join with them in saying He was a sinner; nor did he think and believe He was. However, he was sure He had done a good thing to him, and in that He was no sinner; and what proof they had of His being one he could not tell: and be that as it will, adds he,

one thing I know, that whereas I was blind, now I see. As if he should say, Whatever charges you bring against the person that has done me this favor, which I am not able to answer to, you cannot reason me out of this; this I am sure of, that once I had no eyes to see with, and now I have, and that by the means of this man you reproach. And so it is with persons enlightened in a spiritual sense, whatever things they may be ignorant of, though they may not know the exact time of their conversion, nor have so much Gospel light and knowledge as others, or be so capable of expressing themselves, or giving such a distinct and orderly account of the work of God upon them as some can, nor dispute with an adversary for the truths of the Gospel, nor have that faith of assurance, and discoveries of God's love, and the application of such great and precious promises as others have; yet this they know, that they were once *blind*, as to the knowledge of spiritual things, as to a saving knowledge of God in Christ, as to a true sight and sense of themselves, their sins and lost estate, as to the way of righteousness and salvation by Christ, or the work of the Spirit of God upon their souls, or as to any true and spiritual discerning of the Scriptures, and the doctrines of grace in them: but now they are comfortably assured, they *see* the exceeding sinfulness of sin, the plague of their own hearts, the insufficiency of their righteousness to justify them before God, and the beauty, fulness, suitableness, and ability of Christ as a Savior; and that their salvation is, and must be of free grace; and that they see the truths of the Gospel in another light than they did before, and have some glimpse of eternal glory and happiness, in the hope of which they rejoice.

Verse 26. **Then said they to him again**, &c. Finding they could not bring him to deny the fact, nor cause him to entertain an ill opinion of Him that did it, they examine him again about the manner of it:

What did he to thee? how opened he thine eyes? These questions they had put before, *verse 15*, and proposed them again, in hope he would vary in the account, which they would not fail of improving against him; or that it would appear that he had not been really blind, at least from his birth; or that Christ made use of some unlawful means, as magic art, which they were always ready to charge Him with, and to impute His miracles to a diabolical familiarity and influence; and they would have been glad to have had something to support such a calumny.

Verse 27. **He answered them, I have told you already**, &c. As he had, *verse 15*,

and ye did not hear; the Vulgate Latin version reads, *and ye have heard*; and so some copies of Stephens's; that is, an account had been given of the manner how his eyes were opened, and they had heard the account with their bodily ears, though not with the ears of their minds; and therefore, according to most copies and versions, it is read, *ye did not hear*; did not regard it, or give credit to it; and so the Persic version renders it, *and ye have not believed*; they would not believe the man had been blind, until they sent for his parents; much less would they believe the account of his cure:

wherefore would ye hear it again? Once is sufficient, especially since the former account has been disregarded and discredited: their view could not be their own information, but to baffle and confound the man, if they could. The Syriac, Arabic, and Ethiopic versions leave out the word *again*, and only read, *wherefore would ye hear?* What end can you have in it? Of what avail would it be? or what purpose can be answered by it?

will ye also be his disciples? As many whom you call ignorant and accursed people are, and as I myself desire to be. This he might say either in an ironical and sarcastic way; or else seriously, suggesting, that if they were willing to examine into this fact, with upright views and sincere intentions, that should it appear to be a true miracle, they would become the disciples

317

and followers of Jesus, then he would, with all his heart, relate the account to them over and over again, or as often as they pleased.

Verse 28. **Then they reviled him**, &c. Called him an impertinent, saucy, impudent fellow, for talking in this pert manner to them, the great Sanhedrin of the nation; or, as the Vulgate Latin version reads, *they cursed him*; they thundered out their anathemas against him, and pronounced him an execrable and an accursed fellow:

and said, Thou art his disciple; for they looked upon it a reproach and scandal to be called a disciple of Jesus of Nazareth; though there is nothing more honorable than to be a follower of Him, the Lamb, whithersoever He goes: wherefore these Jews threw off what they thought a term of reproach from themselves to the blind man; and perhaps they might say this to ensnare him, hoping that he would own himself to be a disciple of Jesus, and profess Him to be the Christ, that they might, according to their own act, excommunicate him. The Vulgate Latin, Persic, and Ethiopic versions read, *be thou his disciple*, if thou wilt, we despise the character; far be it from us that we should be followers of Him:

but we are Moses's disciples. Thus they preferred Moses to Christ, and chose to be the disciples of Moses the servant, rather than of Christ the Son; though indeed they were not the genuine disciples of Moses; for if they had, they would have been the disciples of Christ, and believers in Him, since Moses wrote and testified of Him: they might indeed be so far the disciples of Moses, or of his law, since they sought for righteousness and justification by obedience to his law. This was a phrase in use among the Jews: so the Targumist[34] on *Num. 3:2* says,

"These are the names of the sons of Aaron, the priests, תלמידיא דמשה, *the disciples of Moses,* the master of the Israelites;"

particularly the Pharisees, as here, claimed this title to themselves: for it is said,[35]

"All the seven days (before the day of atonement) they delivered to him (the high priest) two of the disciples of the wise men, to instruct him in the service (of that day), who were, מתלמידיו של משה, *of the disciples of Moses*, in opposition to the Sadducees."

From whence it appears, that these disciples of Moses were of the sect of the Pharisees, who assumed this character as peculiar to themselves. Sometimes they call themselves the disciples of Abraham, though the description they

---

[34]   Jonathan ben Uzziel in ibid.

[35]   T. Bab. Yoma, fol. 4. 1.

give of such, by no means belongs to them; see the note on *chapter 8:39*. They say,[36]

> "Whoever has three things in him, is מתלמידיו של אברהם, *of the disciples of Abraham* our father, and who has three other things is of the disciples of Balaam the wicked: he that has a good eye (beneficence, or temperance, or contentment), a lowly spirit, and a humble soul, he is of *the disciples of Abraham* our father; but he that has an evil eye, and a proud spirit, and a large soul (lustful or covetous), is of the disciples of Balaam."

This last character best agrees with those very persons, who would be thought to be the disciples of Abraham and of Moses.

Verse 29. **We know that God spake unto Moses**, &c. Out of the bush, and told him who He was, and sent him to deliver the children of Israel out of Egyptian bondage, and spoke the ten words, or Law unto him, and by him delivered them to the children of Israel; and to whom He spake *face to face*, as a man does to his friend [*Ex. 33:11*], and *mouth to mouth*, and not in dark sayings [*Num. 12:8*]. They mean, they knew that Moses had his mission, commission, and credentials from God: but,

as for this **fellow**; so they contemptuously called the Lord Jesus Christ,

we know not from whence he is. Contradicting what others of them had said, *chapter 7:27*. They imagined they knew the country from whence He came, which they supposed to be Galilee, and the place where He was born, which they concluded was Nazareth; though in both they were in the wrong; and they knew His parents, Joseph and Mary, and His brethren and sisters; but as to His divine filiation, they knew nothing of it; nor would they own His mission, commission, and credentials to be from heaven; and pretended they had no reason to conclude they were.

Verse 30. **The man answered and said unto them**, &c. Very appositely and pertinently,

Why herein is a marvelous thing; strange and unaccountable,

that ye know not from whence he is; that you learned doctors, men of sagacity and penetration, should not be able to discern that this man is of God, is a prophet sent by Him, and that there should be any doubt from whence He comes, or from whom He has His commission:

and *yet* he hath opened mine eyes. Which was so clearly and plainly the

---

[36] Pirke Abot, c. 5. sect. 19.

work of the Messiah, and to be done by Him when He came, *Isa. 35:4-5* and *42:7*.

Verse 31. **Now we know that God heareth not sinners**, &c. All mankind are sinners, even God's elect; yea, such who are truly gracious and righteous persons; for there is no man without sin; and God hears such who cry unto Him day and night; such Christ came to save; for such He died; and these He calls to repentance; and every penitent sinner God hears: but by *sinners* are here meant notorious sinners, such in whom sin reigns, who live in sin, and particularly impostors. The man takes up the word the Jews had made use of, and applied to Christ, *verse 24*, and suggests, that had Jesus been a *sinner*, that is, an impostor, God would not have heard him, or have assisted him in doing a miracle, to support an imposture, or cover and encourage a fraud; but that He was heard and assisted, was a plain case: whereas not only they, the learned doctors of the nation, but such an illiterate man as himself knew, that notoriously wicked men, cheats, and deceivers, were not heard of God; and this was known from the Scripture, and all experience; see *Psa. 66:18; Isa. 1:15*. The Persic and Ethiopic versions read, *I know that God*, &c.

but if any man be a worshiper of God; fears the Lord, and worships Him *in spirit and in truth* [*John 4:23-24*], both with internal and external worship:

and doeth his will; for it is not every one that says Lord, Lord, or draws nigh to God with his mouth, and honors Him with his lips, that is a true and sincere worshiper of Him; but he that does His will in faith, from a principle of love, and with a view to His glory: and,

him he heareth. For He is nigh to all that call upon Him in truth; and such a one the man intimates Jesus must be, since it was out of all dispute that God had heard Him, and had borne a testimony to Him.

Verse 32. **Since the world began**, &c. εκ του αιωνος, *from eternity*, or *never*: the phrase answers to מעולם, frequently used by the Jews,[37] for never; and so the Arabic version renders it, *it was never heard*, &c. since time was:

was it not heard that any man opened the eyes of one that was born blind. As not any physician by any natural means, or art, so not any prophet in a miraculous way, no not Moses himself; among all the miracles he wrought, which the Jews say[38] were seventy-six, and which were two more

---

[37] Abot R. Nathan, c. 35. fol. 8. 2. Maimon. Mechira, c. 20. sect. 8. & Shelchim & Shotaphim, c. 10. sect. 1, 2, 3, 4. & passim.

[38] Menasseh ben lsrael, Conciliat. in Deut. Quaest. 11. p. 240.

than were wrought by all the prophets put together, this is not to be found in the list of them, nor in the catalog of miracles done by others. Elisha indeed prayed to God to restore sight to an army smitten with blindness; but then they were persons who saw before, and were not blind from their birth. Wherefore it must follow, that Jesus, the author of this miracle, must be greater than any of the prophets, even than Moses himself, and has a greater confirmation of His mission from God, than either he or they had: and as this was a miracle in nature, it is no less a miracle in grace, that one born in the blindness and darkness of sin, ignorance, and infidelity, should have the eyes of his understanding opened, to behold divine and spiritual things.

Verse 33. **If this man were not of God**, &c. If He had not His mission, commission, and credentials from God; if He had not been sent by Him, and had not authority from Him, and was not assisted by Him, as man, or God was not with Him,

he could do nothing. Or *not do these things*, as the Syriac version reads; that is, such miraculous works; or, as the Persic version, *he could not do this miracle*: open the eyes of a man born blind. His doing this is a full proof that He is of God, and comes from Him.

Verse 34. **They answered and said unto him**, &c. Being nettled, and stung at what he said, and not able to confute his reasoning; and it is amazing that a man that could never read the Scriptures, who had had no education, was not only blind, but a beggar from his youth, should be able to reason in so strong and nervous a manner, and should have that boldness and presence of mind, and freedom of speech before the whole Sanhedrin. Certainly it was God that gave him *a mouth and wisdom [Luke 21:15]* which these learned doctors could not resist, and therefore they reply in the following manner,

Thou wast altogether born in sins; meaning not in original sin, as all mankind are, for this might have been retorted on themselves; but having imbibed the Pythagorean notion of a transmigration of souls into other bodies, and of sinning in a preexistent state, or a notion of infants sinning actually in the womb, and so punished with blindness, lameness, or some deformity or another for it, they reproach this man, calling him a vile miscreant [*or* unbeliever], saying, Thou vile, sinful creature, who came into the world covered with sin, with the visible marks of having sinned, either in another body, or in the womb before birth, and therefore wast born blind:

and dost thou teach us? Us holy, wise, and learned men! Which breathes out the true pharisaical spirit they were possessed of, and which appeared in their ancestors before them; see *Isa. 65:5; Luke 18:9.*

321

And they cast him out. Not merely out of the place where the Sanhedrin sat, or out of the temple; this would have been no great matter, nor have made any great noise in the city, or have been taken notice of by Christ, or moved His compassion towards him; nor merely out of any particular synagogue, nor was the excommunication called *Niddui*, which was a separation for thirty days, and for the space of four cubits only; but was what they call *Cherem*, which was a cutting him off from the whole congregation of Israel [see the note on *verse 22*]; an anathematizing him, and a devoting him to ruin and destruction: and now in part was fulfilled *Isa. 66:5*, for this was done in pretense of zeal, for the honor and glory of God; and Christ appeared to the joy and comfort of this man, and to the shame and confusion of those that cast him out, as the following verses show.

Verse 35. **Jesus heard that they had cast him out**, &c. For this being perhaps the first instance, of putting in execution the act they had made, *verse 22*, and was a stretching of that act; which only threatened with an ejection, in case any should confess Jesus to be the Messiah; which this man had not done as yet, only had said He was a prophet, and that He was *of God*; it made a very great noise in the city, and the report of it was soon spread over it; and it became the talk of every one, and so Jesus, as man, came to hear of it; though He, as God, knew it the very instant it was done, and needed not any to make report of it to Him:

and when he had found him: not by chance, or meeting him unawares, but seeking him; and knowing where he was, went to the very place, and found him in this piteous condition, abandoned by all mankind. This is an emblem of Christ's seeking after His chosen ones, both in redemption and in effectual vocation [*or* calling], who are like sheep going astray, and never come to, and lay hold on Christ, till He comes first, seeks after, and apprehends them. He sends His ministers and His Gospel after them, where they are, and His Spirit into their hearts; yea, He comes Himself, and enters there, and dwells in them by faith. He knows where they are, as He did Matthew the publican, Zacchaeus, and the woman of Samaria; and even though they are at the ends of the earth; and He goes and looks them up, and finds them; and He finds them in a deplorable condition, *in a desert*, in a *waste howling wilderness* [*Deut. 32:10*], hopeless and helpless, poor and miserable, and blind and naked; in a pit wherein is no water; in the mire and clay of sin; in the paw of Satan, and under the power of darkness.

He said unto him, Dost thou believe on the Son of God? The Persic version adds, *who hath healed thee*: this supposes that there was a Son of God, or a divine person known by the Jews under this character, and that the expected Messiah would appear as such; and that, as such, He is the object of faith, and therefore, as such, must be God; since a creature, though ever so much dignified, or with whatsoever office invested, is not the object of faith, trust, and confidence, with respect to everlasting life and happiness. And it may be observed, that whenever Christ finds any of His people, He brings them to believe in Him, as the Son of God, for righteousness and life: He Himself is the author of faith in them, as well as the object of it; and no doubt power went along with these words, creating faith in this man. This was a most proper and pertinent question put to him in his present case, and suggests, that if he believed in the Son of God, it was no matter in what situation he was among men; since he would then appear to be a son of God himself by adopting grace, and so an heir of God, and a joint heir with Christ [see *Rom. 8:17*]; would receive the remission of his sins, be openly justified in the court of conscience, as well as of God, and be everlastingly saved. And this question is put by Christ, not as though He was ignorant whether he believed in Him or not; for He knew from the beginning who would, and who would not believe in Him: He that knew whether Peter loved Him or not, knew whether this man believed in Him or not; but this He said to draw forth the principle of faith, which was wrought in him, into act and exercise, and to direct it to its proper object. And this effect it had, as appears by what follows.

Verse 36. **He answered and said**, &c. That is, *he that was healed*, as the Syriac version reads:

Who is the Lord, that I might believe in him? Which shows, that though he knew there was a Messiah expected, and he believed in Him as to come, yet he knew not that He was already come, nor the particular person in human nature who was the Messiah, and the Son of God; even though he had been cured of his blindness by Him, and had vindicated Him, and pleaded for Him before the Sanhedrin, and had also suffered for Him; which makes it appear, that Christ does many and great things for His people before they know Him: nor does their interest in Him, in His favor, and in the blessings of His grace, depend upon their knowledge of Him, and faith in Him; as likewise, that a man may plead for Christ, and suffer much for Him, and yet be ignorant of Him: however, there were in this man desires of knowing Christ; he was not like those in *Job 21:14*; and there was a readiness in him to believe on Him, as soon as He was pointed out to him; not that there is any natural disposition in men to believe, or any readiness in themselves to it, or that it is of themselves; nothing of this nature was in this man; but he having, by the power and grace of Christ, the principle of faith implanted in his heart, what he wanted was to be directed to the proper object of it, as he is in the next verse.

Verse 37. **And Jesus said unto him**, &c. Giving him the tokens by which he might know Him:

Thou hast both seen Him; not that he had seen Him before now, with his bodily eyes; for he was blind when Christ anointed him, and sent him to Siloam to wash; nor when he came back, since Jesus was gone, and he knew not where He was; but he had seen Him, that is, he had perceived and felt the power of Him in restoring him to sight; and now he had seen Him bodily, and did at this present time. But as this was not sufficient to distinguish Him from other persons in company, He adds,

and it is he that talketh with thee. In like manner He made Himself known to the woman of Samaria, *chapter 4:26.*

Verse 38. **And he said, Lord, I believe**, &c. He immediately found faith in his soul, and that in exercise, moving towards, and acting upon Christ, as the Son of God, and true Messiah, for everlasting life and salvation; and as soon as he did perceive it, he made an open and hearty profession of it:

and he worshiped him. As God, with religious worship and adoration, not only trusting in Him, but ascribing honor, glory, and blessing to Him, which are due to God only, and not a creature.

Verse 39. **And Jesus said, For judgment I am come into this world**, &c. The Syriac version reads, *for the judgment of this world I am come*; and with which agrees the Ethiopic version, *for the judgment of the world, I am come into the world*; and the Arabic and Persic versions still more expressly, *to judge this world*, or *the world, am I come*; which seems contrary to what Christ elsewhere says, *chapter 3:17* and *12:47*. Nor is the sense of the words that Christ came by the judgment of God, or the order of divine providence, or to administer justice in the government of the world, in a providential way, or to distinguish His own people from others, though all these are true; but either to fulfil the purpose and decree of God in revealing truth to some, and hiding it from others; or in a way of judgment to inflict judicial blindness on some, while in a way of mercy He illuminated others. So Nonnus interprets it of κριμα θισσον, *a twofold judgment*, which is different the one from the other;

that they which see not, might see; meaning, not so much corporeally as spiritually, since in the opposite clause corporeal blindness can have no place; for though Christ restored bodily sight to many, He never took it away from any person. The sense is, that Christ came as a light into the world, that those who are in the darkness of sin, ignorance, and unbelief, and who are sensible of the same, and desire spiritual illumination, as this man did, might see what they are by nature, what need they stand in of Him, and what fulness of grace, life, righteousness, and salvation there is in Him for them:

and that they which see might be made blind. That such who are wise and knowing in their own conceit, who fancy themselves to have great light and knowledge, to have the key of knowledge, and to have the true understanding of divine things, and to be guides of the blind, such as the Scribes and Pharisees, might be given up to judicial blindness and hardness of heart, so as to shut their eyes, and harden their hearts against the Gospel, and the truths of it, and which was in judgment to them. Such different effects Christ and His Gospel have, as to illuminate and soften some, and blind and harden others; just as some creatures, as bats and owls, are blinded by the sun, while others see clearly by the light of it; and as that also has these different effects to soften the wax, and harden the clay; see *Isa. 6:9.*

Verse 40. **And *some* of the Pharisees which were with him**, &c. Who had followed Him, and were watching Him, and observing what He said and did, in order to take all advantages, and every opportunity against Him, they could,

heard these words, and said unto him, Are we blind also? They perceived He pointed at them, and therefore with indignation ask this question, taking it as a great affront unto them, to put such wise, learned, and knowing men as they in company with the ignorant and unlearned common people; see *Isa. 42:19.*

Verse 41. **Jesus said unto them, If ye were blind**, &c. And sensible of it, and knew yourselves to be blind, and were desirous of light and knowledge,

ye would have no sin: or your sin would not be so aggravated; it would not be imputed to you; it would be pardoned and taken away from you: for the sense cannot be, that their blindness would not have been criminal, or they should have had no sin in them, or any done by them; only, that had this been barely their case, there would have been some hope of them, that their sin might be forgiven, and put away, and be no more; see *1 Tim. 1:13*;

but now ye say, We see; they thought themselves to be wise and knowing, and stood in no need of any illumination from Him, but were obstinate and hardened in their infidelity, and wilfully opposed and shut their eyes against all the light and evidence of truth:

therefore your sin remaineth. Untaken away, yea, immoveable, or unpardonable; the guilt of it abode upon them; nor was there any hope of its being removed from them; owning that they saw, and yet believed not: sinning wilfully against light and knowledge in rejecting Jesus, as the Messiah, they sinned the sin against the Holy Ghost, which is never forgiven. And so the Ethiopic version renders it, *your error shall not be forgiven you*; see *Matt. 12:32.*

CHAPTER 10

Verse 1. **Verily, verily, I say unto you**, &c. To the Scribes and Pharisees, who had taken it ill that they should be thought to be blind; and who had cast out the man that Christ had cured of blindness, for speaking in favor of Him; and who had traduced Christ as an impostor, and a deceiver, and set up themselves to be the shepherds of the flock, and the guides and rulers of the people; all which occasion the following parable; the design of which is to show, that Christ is the true and only Shepherd, who was appointed, called, and sent of God, whose the sheep are, whose voice they hear, and know, and whom they follow; and that they, the Scribes and Pharisees, were thieves and robbers, and not shepherds of the flock; who were not sent of God, nor did they come in at the right door, but in another way, and usurped a domination which did not belong to them.

He that entereth not by the door into the sheepfold: the sheepfold, with the Jews, was called דיר; and this, as their writers say,[1] was an enclosure sometimes in the manner of a building, and made of stone, and sometimes was fenced with reeds, and in it was a large door, at which the shepherd went in and out, when he led in, or brought out the sheep. At tithing, which was done in the sheepfold, they made a little door, so that two lambs could not come out together; and to this enclosure is the allusion here; and by the *sheepfold* is meant the church of God; see *verse 16*; and a good fold it is, *Ezek. 34:14.* The church may be compared to a sheepfold, because it is separated from the world: it is where the people of God, and sheep of Christ are gathered together; where there is a strict union between them; have society with each other; keep one another warm and comfortable; and where they are fed and nourished, and are preserved; and where they lie down and have rest; and

[1] Maimonides & Bartenora in Mishna Becorot, c. 9. sect. 7.

which, like a sheepfold, will be taken down, and not always continue in the form it now is. And by *the door* into it, is meant Christ Himself, as appears from *verses 7 & 9*; faith in Him, a profession of Him, and authority from Him. Now he that does not come into the church of God, whether as a member of it, or officer in it, at this door,

but climbeth up some other way; by hypocrisy and deceit; or, like the prophets of old, who *ran* and were not *sent*; prophesied when they were not spoken to, but took their place and post by usurpation:

the same is a thief and a robber. Steals into the church, or into an office in it, and robs God or Christ of their power and authority; and such were the Scribes and Pharisees. The Persic version renders the words, *Whoever does not introduce the sheep through the door of the sheepfold, know that that man is a thief and a robber*; which these men were so far from doing, that they would not suffer those that were entering to go in, *Matt. 23:13*. The difference between a thief and a robber, with the Jews, was, that the former took away a man's property privately, and the latter openly.[2]

Verse 2. **But he that entereth in by the door**, &c. With a divine commission, and by a divine authority, who comes not of himself, but is sent; does not take the honor to himself, or thrust in himself, and assume an office to himself, but is called unto it, and invested in it, he,

is the shepherd of the sheep. By whom Christ means Himself, as is evident from *verses 11 & 14*; whose the sheep are, and who takes care of them, and feeds them, as a shepherd does his flock; and which holds true of any under shepherd, having his mission and commission, and deriving his authority from Christ.

Verse 3. **To him the porter openeth**, &c. There is nothing in the explanation of this parable given by Christ, that directs to the sense of this clause; the allusion cannot be, as some have thought, to great men, who have porters at their gates, to open them, and let in persons that come and knock; since the parable is concerning the sheepfold, and the shepherd, and the sheep that go into it; and therefore must refer to one that at least, at certain times, stood by the door of the sheepfold, and had the care of it, and opened it upon proper occasions: by whom is designed not Michael the Archangel, nor the virgin Mary, nor Peter, the supposed doorkeeper of heaven, as say the Papists, nor Moses, as others, who wrote of Christ; nor does it seem so well to understand it of the ministers of the Gospel, who preach Jesus Christ, and open the door

---

[2] Maimon. Hilchot Genuba, c. 1. sect. 3.

of faith, or set open the door of the Gospel, whereby Christ comes into the souls of men, and they come to Him; though this is a sense not to be despised; but rather this intends God the Father, from whom Christ, as man and Mediator, derives His authority, and by whom He is let into, and invested with His office, as the Shepherd of the sheep; or else the Holy Spirit, who opens the everlasting doors of the hearts of men, of Christ's sheep, and lets Him in unto them.

And the sheep hear his voice; not the porter's; though they do hear the voice of Christ's ministers, and of God the Father, and of the Holy Ghost; but the Shepherd's, even the voice of Christ; and which is no other than the Gospel, which is a voice of love, grace, and mercy; which proclaims peace, pardon, liberty, life, righteousness, and salvation; and which is a soul-quickening, alluring, delighting, refreshing, and comforting voice: this the people of Christ are made to hear, not only externally, but internally; so as to understand it, delight in it, and distinguish it from another. And these are called *sheep*, and that before conversion; not because they have the agreeable properties of sheep; nor because predisposed unto, and unprejudiced against the Gospel of Christ, for they are the reverse of these; nor can some things be said of them before, as after conversion, as that they hear the voice of Christ, and follow Him; nor merely by anticipation, but by reason of electing grace, and because given to Christ the great Shepherd, under this character, to be kept and fed by Him. And they are so called after conversion, because they are harmless and inoffensive in their lives and conversations; and yet are exposed to the malice, cruelty, and butchery of men; and are meek and patient under sufferings; and are clean, social, and profitable;

and he calleth his own sheep by name; the Ethiopic version adds, *and loves them*. These are Christ's own, by the Father's gift of them to Him, by the purchase of His own blood, and by the power of His grace upon them; who looks them up, and finds them out, and brings them home, and takes care of them as His own, and feeds them as a shepherd his flock: these He may be said to *call by name*, in allusion to the eastern shepherds, who gave names to their sheep, as the Europeans do to their horses and other creatures, and who could sit and call them by their names: this is expressive not only of Christ's call of His people by powerful and special grace, but of the exact and distinct knowledge He has of them, and the notice He takes of them, as well as of the affection He has for them; see *Isa. 43:1; 2 Tim. 2:19*.

And leadeth them out. From the world's goats, among whom they lay, and from the folds of sin, and the barren pastures of Mount Sinai, and their own righteousness, on which they were feeding, and out of themselves, and from off all dependence on any thing of their own; and He leads unto Himself, and the fulness of His grace, and to His blood and righteousness, and into His

Father's presence and communion with Him; and in the way of righteousness and truth, and into the green pastures of the Word and ordinances, beside the still waters of His sovereign love and grace.

Verse 4. **And when he putteth forth his own sheep**, &c. The Ethiopic version reads, *When he leads them all out*; in order to bring them into proper pastures:

he goeth before them; in allusion to the eastern shepherds, who when they put out their flocks, did not, as ours do, drive them before them, and follow after them, at least not always, but went before them: so Christ, the great Shepherd, goes before His flock, not only to provide for them, but by way of example to them; in many instances He is an example to the flock, as under shepherds, according to the measure of grace received, should be. He has left them an example in many respects, that they should tread in His steps:

and the sheep follow him; in the exercise of the graces of humility, love, patience, self-denial, and resignation of will to the will of God; and in the discharge of duty, walking, in some measure, as He walked:

for they know his voice. In the Gospel, which directs and encourages them to exercise grace in Him, and to walk in the path of duty: this they know by the majesty and authority of it; and by the power with which it comes to their souls; and by its speaking of Him, and leading to Him; and by the evenness, harmony, and consistency of it. The Persic version renders the whole thus; *When he calls and leads out the sheep, they go before him, and their lambs after them, for they know his voice.*

Verse 5. **And a stranger will they not follow**, &c. One that knows not Christ, is not sent by Him, and who does not preach Him:

but will flee from him; shun Him and His ministry, as not only disagreeable, but dangerous:

for they know not the voice of strangers. They do not approve of their doctrine, nor take any delight in it, or receive any profit from it. The Persic version, as before, reads, *Neither will the lambs ever go after strange sheep, and if they see* them, *they will flee* from them.

Verse 6. **This parable spake Jesus unto them**, &c. To the Pharisees, who were with him, *chapter 9:40*;

but they understood not what things they were which he spake unto them. The things spoken by Him being delivered in a parabolical way, though in lively figures, and in terms plain and easy to be understood; yet, what through the blindness of their minds, and the hardness of their hearts, and their prejudices in favor of themselves, and against Christ, they did not understand what were meant by them; see *Matt. 13:13-15.*

Verse 7. **Then said Jesus unto them again**, &c. By way of explanation of the above parable, since they did not understand it:

Verily, verily, I say unto you; this is certainly truth, and what may be depended on as such, whether it will be believed or not:

I am the door of the sheep. And of none but them; not of goats, dogs, or swine; none but sheep enter at this door; and all the sheep do sooner or later: Christ is the *door* to them, by which they enter into a visible church state, and are let into a participation of the ordinances of it, as baptism and the Lord's supper. No man comes into a church, at the right door, or in a right way, or has a right to partake of Gospel ordinances, but he that truly believes in Christ, and makes a profession of faith in Him. Christ is the door of the under shepherds of the sheep; none are fit to be pastors of churches, but who first enter into a Gospel church at this door, and are qualified, and called, and sent forth by Christ: He is the door of the sheep, by which they are let into the presence of His Father, and have communion with Him, and partake of all the blessings of grace; it is through Him that sanctifying, justifying, pardoning, and adopting grace, are conveyed unto them, and they brought into the enjoyment of them; it is through Him they have all their peace, joy, and comfort, and deliverance from, and victory over all their enemies; through Him they have heirship, and a right unto eternal life, and that itself; for He is the door into heaven itself, through which they shall have an abundant entrance into it: and He is the only door into each of these; there is no coming to God the Father but by, and through Him; nor to a participation of the blessings of the covenant, nor rightly into a Gospel church state, and to the ordinances of it, nor into heaven at last, but in at this door. And this is a door of faith and hope, and an open one, for all sensible sinners, for all the sheep of Christ, to enter in at; though it is a strait gate, the number being few that enter in at it; and those that do, though they are certainly, yet but scarcely saved; for it is through many tribulations and afflictions that they enter.

Verse 8. **All that ever came before me are thieves and robbers**, &c. This must be understood with some restrictions, not of every individual person, nor of every individual prophet or shepherd; not of Moses, nor of the prophets of the Lord, nor of John the Baptist, who came immediately before Christ, was His harbinger, and prepared His way; but of those prophets who came, and were not sent of God, and so did not come in by the door; of the shepherds of Israel, who fed themselves, and not the flock, but lorded it over God's heritage; and of such, as Theudas, and Judas the Galilean, who boasted that they were some great persons, but were only *thieves and robbers*; and particularly of the *three shepherds* cut off in one month, *Zech. 11:8*, supposed to be the three sects among the Jews, and the leaders of them, the Pharisees, Sadducees, and Essenes, especially the former; who were wolves in sheep's clothing, usurped a power that did not belong to them, robbed God of His authority and glory; and, in a literal sense, plundered men of their substance, and devoured widows' houses, as well as destroyed their souls. The phrase, *before me*, is wanting in seven of Beza's exemplars, and in several others; and in the Vulgate Latin, Syriac, and Persic versions:

but the sheep did not hear them. The elect of God, some of which there were in all ages, though their number is comparatively few, did not attend to the false prophets, and false teachers, and idol shepherds; did not receive their doctrines, nor follow their practices; for it is not possible that these should be finally and totally deceived, or carried away with the error of the wicked.

Verse 9. **I am the door**, &c. Of the sheep, as before, see *verse 7*. The Ethiopic version reads, *I am the true door of the sheep*; which is repeated for further confirmation, and for the sake of introducing what follows:

by me if any man enter in; into the sheepfold, the church,

he shall be saved; not that being in a church, and having submitted to ordinances, will save any, but entering into these, at the right door, or through faith in Christ, such will be saved, according to *Mark 16:16*; such shall be saved from sin, the dominion of it, the guilt and condemning power of it, and at last from the being of it; and from the law, its curse and condemnation, and from wrath to come, and from every evil, and every enemy; such are, and for ever shall be, in a safe state, being in Christ, and in His hands, out of which none can pluck them:

and shall go in and out; in allusion to the sheep going in and out of the fold: not that those who come in at the right door, shall go out of the church, or from among the saints again; but this phrase rather denotes the exercises of faith in going unto Christ, and acting upon Him, and in coming forth in the outward confession of Him, and the performance of good works; or in going unto Him, and dealing with His blood, righteousness, and sacrifice, and coming out of themselves, and all dependence on their own righteousness; or it may regard the conversation of the saints in the church, their attendance on ordinances, their safety there, their free and open communion one with another, and with Christ, in whose name and strength they do all they do, coming in and out at this door:

and find pasture. Green and good pasture; pasture for their souls; the words of faith, and good doctrine; the wholesome words of Christ Jesus; the ordinances, *the breasts of consolation* [*Isa. 66:11*]; yea, Christ Himself, whose flesh is meat indeed, and whose blood is drink indeed: the Persic version renders it, *and shall a pastor*, or *shepherd*; see *Jer. 3:15*.

Verse 10. **The thief cometh not, but for to steal**, &c. That is his first and principal view; to steal, is to invade, seize, and carry away another's property. Such teachers that come not in by the right door, or with a divine commission, seek to deceive, and carry away the sheep of Christ from Him, though they are not able to do it; and to steal away their hearts from Him, as Absalom stole the hearts of the people from their rightful lord and sovereign, David his father; and to subject them to themselves, that they might lord it over them, and make a property of them, as the Pharisees did, who, under a pretense of long prayers, devoured widows' houses;

and to kill and to destroy; either the souls of men by their false doctrines, which eat as doth a canker, and poison the minds of men, and slay the souls that should not die, subverting the faith of nominal professors, though they cannot destroy any of the true sheep of Christ; or the bodies of the saints, by their oppression, tyranny, and persecution, who *are killed all the day long* for the sake of Christ, and *are accounted as sheep for the slaughter* [*Rom. 8:36*], by these men, they thinking that by so doing they do God good service [See *John 16:2*].

I am come that they might have life; that the sheep might have life, or the elect of God might have life, both spiritual and eternal; who, as the rest of mankind, are by nature dead in trespasses and sins, and liable in themselves to an eternal death. Christ came into this world in human nature, to give His flesh, His body, His whole human nature, soul and body, for the life of these persons, or that they might live spiritually here, and eternally hereafter; and so the Arabic version renders it, *that they might have eternal life*; Nonnus calls it, *a life to come*; which is in Christ, and the gift of God through Him; and which He gives to all His sheep, and has a power to give to as many as the Father has given Him:

and that they might have *it* more abundantly. Or, as the Syriac version reads, *something more abundant*; that is, than life; meaning not merely than the life of wicked men, whose blessings are curses to them; or than their own life, only in the present state of things; or than long life, promised under the law to the observers of it; but even than the life Adam had in innocence, which was but a natural and moral, not a spiritual life, or that life which is hid with Christ in God; and also than that which angels live in heaven, which is the life of servants, and not of sons: or else the sense is, that Christ came that His people might have eternal life, with more abundant evidence of it, than was under the former dispensation, and have stronger faith in it, and a more lively hope of it: or, as the words may be rendered, *and that they might have an abundance*: besides life, might have an abundance of grace from Christ, all spiritual blessings in Him now, and all fulness of joy, glory, and happiness hereafter.

Verse 11. **I am the good shepherd**, &c. A shepherd of His Father's appointing, calling, and sending, to whom the care of all His sheep, or chosen ones, was committed; who was set up as a shepherd over them by Him, and was entrusted with them; and who being called, undertook to feed them; and being promised, was sent *unto the lost sheep of the house of Israel* [*Matt. 15:24*]; and under the character of a shepherd, died for them, and rose again, and is accountable to His Father for every one of them; the Shepherd, the great and chief Shepherd, the famous one, so often spoken and prophesied of, *Gen. 49:24; Isa. 40:11; Ezek. 34:23*. And discharging His office aright, He is *the good shepherd*; as appears in His providing good pasture, and a good fold for His sheep; in protecting them from their enemies; in healing all their diseases; in restoring their souls when strayed from Him; in watching over them in the night seasons, lest any hurt them; in searching for them, when they have been driven, or scattered in the dark and cloudy day [see *Ezek. 34:12*]; in caring for them, so that He lose none of them; and in nothing more than in what follows,

the good shepherd giveth his life for the sheep. Not only exposes it to danger, as David did his for the sake of his father's flock, but gives it away freely and voluntarily, for the sake of the sheep; in their room and stead, as a ransom for them, that they may be delivered from death, and might have eternal life. The Ethiopic version renders it, *the good shepherd gives his life for the redemption of his sheep*; so Nonnus paraphrases it, the *ransom price of his own sheep*: this belongs to Christ's priestly office, and with the Jews, priests were sometimes shepherds: hence we read[3] of, רועים כהנים, *shepherds that were priests*. Philo the Jew, speaks[4] of God as a shepherd and king; and of His setting His Word, His firstborn Son, over the holy flock, to take care of it: and a good shepherd is thus described by the[5] Jews,

> "as רועה טוב, *a good shepherd*, delivers the flock from the wolf, and from the lions (see *verse 12*), so he that leads Israel, if he is good, delivers them from the idolatrous nations, and from judgment below and above, and leads them to the life of the world to come, or eternal

---

[3] Mishna Becorot, c. 5. sect. 4.

[4] De Agricultura, p. 195. & de nom. mutat. p. 1062.

[5] Zohar in Exod. fol. 9. 3.

life; (see *verse 10*)."

Which description agrees with Christ, the Good Shepherd; and so the Lord is said to be רועה טוב, *the good shepherd*, and merciful, and there is none like Him.[6]

Verse 12. **But he that is an hireling, and not the shepherd**, &c. That is, who is not the owner of the sheep, though he keeps them, yet only for reward: by whom are meant, not the faithful ministers of the Word, who live upon the Gospel, as Christ has ordained, and who are worthy of their reward, and are not to be called hirelings by way of reproach; since they teach not for hire and reward, but for the good of souls, and the interest of the Redeemer; but such who seek only their gain from their quarter, and mind their own things, and not the things of Jesus Christ:

whose own the sheep are not; who have neither a propriety in them, nor a hearty affection for them, and so care not what becomes of them: such a one,

seeth the wolf coming; by whom may be meant, either Satan; so the Jews compare Israel to a flock of sheep, and *Satan*, they say, הוא הזאב, *he is the wolf*;[7] or any false prophet, or teacher, who are ravenous wolves; though sometimes in sheep's clothing; or any tyrant, oppressor, or persecutor of the saints:

and leaveth the sheep; as *the idol shepherd*, against whom a woe is pronounced, *Zech. 11:17*;

and fleeth; not being willing to bear any reproach or persecution, for the sake of Christ; not such a keeper of the flock as David, who went after the lion and the bear, and when they rose up against him, did not flee, but caught them by the beard and slew them; nor like the Apostle Paul, who fought with beasts at Ephesus, and would turn his back on none, nor give place, no, not for an hour, that truth might continue;

and the wolf catcheth them; some of them:

and scattereth the sheep. The rest; so are the sheep of Christ and His churches sometimes scattered, by persecution raised against them; see *Acts 8:1,4*. The Jews have a rule concerning such a hireling shepherd,[8] which is this:

---

[6] Aben Ezra in Psal. 23:3. & Kimchi in Psa. 23:2.

[7] Caphtor, fol. 58. 1.

[8] T. Bab. Bava Metzia, fol. 41. 1. & 93. 2. & 106. 1.

"A shepherd that feeds his flock, and leaves it, and goes to the city, and a wolf comes and ravens, and the lion comes and tears in pieces, he is free; but if he leaves by it his staff and his scrip, he is guilty."
Which Maimonides thus[9] expresses and explains:
"A shepherd who can deliver that which is torn, and that which is carried captive, with other shepherds, and with staves, and does not call the other shepherds, nor bring the staves to deliver them, he is guilty: one that keeps freely, and one that keeps for hire; he that keeps freely, calls the shepherds, and brings the staves freely; and if he does not find them, he is not guilty; but he that keeps for hire, is obliged to hire shepherds and staves, in order to deliver them."

Verse 13. **The hireling fleeth, because he is an hireling**, &c. And has no propriety in the sheep; had he, he would abide by them, and defend them; but because he has not, he will not expose himself to any danger, but leaves them:

and careth not for the sheep. What becomes of them, providing only for his own safety. Abarbinel[10] has a note on *Isa. 40:11* which may serve to illustrate this passage:
"*He shall feed his flock like a shepherd*; not as he that feeds the flock of others, for the hire they give him, but as a shepherd that feeds his own flock; who has compassion more abundantly on it, because it is his own flock; and therefore he saith, *behold his reward is with him*, for he does not seek a reward from another; *and his work is before him*; for he feeds what is his own, and therefore his eyes and his heart are there."
Which is not the case of the hireling; he does not care for them, he has not their good at heart; but *the good shepherd* has, such a one as Christ is.

Verse 14. **I am the good shepherd**, &c. See the note on *verse 11*;

and know my *sheep*; so as to call them all by their names: Christ has an universal, special, distinct, and exact knowledge of all His sheep, as they are the choice of His Father, as His Father's gift to Him; and as His own purchase; He bears an affectionate love to them, and takes special care of them; indulges them with intimate communion with Himself; and owns and acknowledges them as His, both here and hereafter:

and I am known of mine. Not in a general way, as devils and external professors may know Him, but with a special, spiritual, and saving knowl-

---

[9] Hilchot Shechirut, c. 3. sect. 6.

[10] Mashmai Jeshua, fol. 20. 4.

edge: Christ's own approve of Him, as their Shepherd and their Savior, and desire no other; they love Him above all, in the sincerity of their souls, and with a love as strong as death; they trust in Him as their Shepherd, believing they shall not want; and appropriate Him to themselves, as their own; and care for Him, His cause and interest, His Gospel, ordinances, and ministers; and are not ashamed to own Him as theirs, in the most public manner.

Verse 15. **As the Father knoweth me**, &c. These words, with what follow, are in connection with the preceding verse; and the sense is, that the mutual knowledge of Christ and His sheep, is like that which His Father and He have of each other. The Father knows Christ as His own Son, and loves Him as such, in the most strong and affectionate manner; and has entrusted Him with the persons, grace, and glory, of all His people:

even so know I the Father; or rather, *and I know the Father*; as He needs must, since He lay in His bosom [*John 1:18*], and still does, and knows His nature, perfections, purposes, and His whole mind and will; and loves Him most ardently, which He has shown by His coming down from heaven to do His will; and trusts in Him for the accomplishment of every thing He promised unto Him:

and I lay down my life for the sheep. Which proves Him to be *the good shepherd*, *verse 11*. The Vulgate Latin version reads, *for my sheep*; which were His by the Father's gift, and for no other has He laid down His life. The Ethiopic version, as before, renders it, or rather explains it, *I lay down my life for the redemption of my sheep.*

Verse 16. **And other sheep I have**, &c. Not distinct from those for whom He laid down His life, but from those who were under the Old Testament dispensation, and who heard not the thieves and robbers that were before Christ, *verse 8*; others besides *the lost sheep of the house of Israel*, or the elect among the Jews, to whom Christ was sent [*Matt. 15:24*]; and by whom are meant the chosen of God among the Gentiles, who were sheep, though not called and folded, for the reasons given in the note on *verse 3*. These, though uncalled, belonged to Christ; He had an interest in them, they were given Him by His Father [*John 6:37; 17:6,9*]; He had them in His hands, and upon His heart; His eye was upon them, and they were under His notice, inspection, and care:

which are not of this fold, of the Jewish nation and church, *being aliens from the commonwealth of Israel, and strangers to the covenants of promise* [*Eph. 2:12*]; *were as sheep going astray* [*1 Pet. 2:25*], and were scattered about in the several parts of the world; and were to be redeemed out of every kindred, tongue, people, and nation:

them also I must bring; out of the wilderness of the world, from among the men of it, their former sinful companions, from the folds of sin and Satan, and the pastures of their own righteousness; to Himself, and into His Father's presence, to His house and ordinances, to a good fold and green pastures; and at last to His heavenly kingdom and glory: and there was a necessity of doing all this, partly on account of His Father's will and pleasure, His purposes and decrees, who had resolved upon it; and partly on account of His own engagements, who had obliged Himself to do it; as well as because of the case and condition of these sheep, who otherwise must have eternally perished:

and they shall hear my voice; in the Gospel, not only externally, but internally; which is owing to His powerful and efficacious grace, who quickens them, and causes them to hear and live; unstops their deaf ears, and gives them ears to hear; and opens their hearts to attend to His Word [see *Acts 16:14*], and gives them an understanding of it. The Arabic version reads this in connection with the preceding clause, thus, *and I must bring them also to hear my voice*; as well as the rest of the sheep among the Jews, and therefore the Gospel was sent among them:

and there shall be one fold, *and* one shepherd. One church state, consisting both of Jews and Gentiles; the middle wall of partition being broken down, these two coalesce in one, become one new man, and members of one and the same body [see *Eph. 2:13-16*]; for though there may be several visible Gospel churches, yet there is but one kind of church state, and one *general assembly and church of the firstborn* [*Heb. 12:23*], one family to which they all belong; for what reasons a church is comparable to a fold, see the note on *verse 1*. And over this fold, or flock, there is but one shepherd, Jesus Christ; who is the rightful proprietor, and whose own the sheep are; and who knows how to feed them, and does take care of them; though there are many under shepherds, whom He employs in feeding them; in the original text the copulative *and* is wanting, and the words stand thus, *one fold, one shepherd*; which not only expresses a peculiar elegance, but answers the proverb delivered in the same form; and to which agree the Arabic and Ethiopic versions, which render them, *and there*, or *they shall be one fold of one shepherd*; or one flock which belongs to one shepherd only; see *Ezek. 34:23* and *37:24*.

Verse 17. **Therefore doth my Father love me**, &c. Christ was the object of His Father's love from all eternity, and was loved by Him on various accounts; first and chiefly, as His own Son, of the same nature with Him, and equal to Him; and also as Mediator, engaging for, and on the behalf of His chosen people; and likewise as He was clothed with their nature, and even in His state of humiliation; and not only as subject to His ordinances, and obedient to His will, and doing what was pleasing in His sight, but likewise as suffering in their room and stead, and He loved Him on this account; the bruising of Him was a pleasure to Him, not for the sake of that itself, but because hereby His counsels and decrees were accomplished, His covenant fulfilled, and the salvation of His people obtained: hence it follows here,

because I lay down my life; that is, *for the sheep*; to ransom them from sin and Satan, the law, its curse and condemnation, and from death and hell, wrath, ruin and destruction: and the laying down His life on this account, was not only well-pleasing to His Father, but likewise was done, with the following view; or at least this was the event of it,

that I might take it again. As He did, by raising Himself from the dead, by which He was declared to be the Son of God; and to have made full satisfaction to divine justice for the sins of His people, and therefore rose again for their justification; and to be the victorious conqueror over death, having now abolished it, and having in His hands the keys of it, the power over that and the grave: and which life He took up again, by His divine power, and as the surety of His people, to use it for their good; by ascending to His God and theirs, entering into heaven as their forerunner, appearing in the presence of God for them, as their advocate, and ever living to make intercession for them.

Verse 18. **No man taketh it from me**, &c. It was indeed taken away at the instigation of the Jews, and by the order of Pilate, and by means of the Roman soldiers, who crucified Him; and the former of these are often charged with slaying Him, and killing Him, the Prince of life; and it is expressly said, *his life is taken from the earth*, Acts 8:33; and yet no man could, nor did take it away, without His Father's will, and determinate counsel and knowledge, by which He was delivered up into the hands of the above persons, and by which they did to Him what they did, or otherwise they could have had no power over Him [see *Acts 2:23*]; nor could any man, nor did any man, take away His life from Him, without His own consent; He voluntarily surrendered Himself, or He could never have been taken; He went freely to the cross, or He could never have been led there; He suffered Himself to be nailed to the accursed tree, and when He hung on it, He could easily have disengaged Himself, and come down; and when they had Him there, they could not have taken away His life, had He not of Himself given up the ghost, and breathed out His life and soul:

but I lay it down of myself; *of my own will*, or *of my own accord*, as the Syriac, Arabic, and Persic versions render it; which was done with the greatest patience and meekness, resolution, courage and magnanimity; and with a full will, and with the greatest cheerfulness and alacrity; and that as a ransom for His people, and that they might live through Him:

338

I have power to lay it down; this was not His life as God, but as man; and was so His own, as it was not His Father's, and was entirely at His own disposal; for it was the life of that individual human nature, which was united to His divine person; and so in a sense *His*, as it was not either the Father's or the Spirit's; and was so His *own*, as our's are not, which are from God, and dependent on Him, and entirely to be disposed of by Him, and not by ourselves: but Christ, the Prince of life, had a power of laying down His life of His own accord, as a ransom price for His sheep:

and I have power to take it again. As He was the Son of God, and truly God, and as the surety of His people; having satisfied law and justice by His obedience, sufferings, and death, and for the ends mentioned in the note on the preceding verse:

This commandment have I received of my Father; which may respect both branches of His power, but is not the foundation of it, but the reason of His exercising it; because it was so agreeable to His Father's will, which is the same with His own, as He is the Son of God, and one with His Father, and equal to Him; and what He delights in as Mediator, in which capacity He is considered as a servant; and in which He cheerfully became obedient, even unto death, to His Father's command, or in compliance with His will. The Syriac, Arabic, and Persic versions read, *because this commandment have I received of my Father*: this is a reason why He so readily exerted His power, both in laying down His life, and taking it again, because it was His Father's command and will, and which He received from Him with the utmost pleasure; His and His Father's love, goodwill, gracious ends and views towards the elect, herein being the same.

Verse 19. **There was a division therefore again among the Jews**, &c. As there had been before; see *chapter 7:12* and *9:16;*

for these sayings; concerning His being the Good Shepherd, and laying down His life for the sheep, and having both a power to lay it down, and take it up again.

Verse 20. **And many of them said, He hath a devil, and is mad**, &c. It was a notion of the Jews, that madness or distraction was from the devil, and therefore these two are here joined together: having a devil, and being mad. There is a spirit which they call *Tazazith*, and which, they say,[11]
      "is an evil spirit that takes away the understanding of men;"
and under the influence of such a *demon*, the Jews thought Christ to be: and

---

[11]   R. David Kimchi, Sepher Shorash rad. חזן.

therefore say,

why hear ye him? He is a lunatic, He is distracted, He is a madman; how can you bear to hear such ranting blasphemous stuff, which no man in his senses would ever utter? Nor is any thing He says to be regarded, since He is not in His right mind; but is under the power and influence of some evil spirit, which instills these wild and frantic notions into Him, and puts Him upon venting them; but surely no sober man will ever heed to them.

Verse 21. **Others said, These are not the words of him that hath a devil**, &c. No madman or demoniac, one possessed of a devil, and under the influence of Satan, would ever talk in so divine a manner, and speak such words of truth and soberness: these were some of the wiser sort, and were well disposed to Christ, who reasoned thus, and they were but few: whereas those that charged Him with madness and distraction, were many, as in the preceding verse;

Can a devil open the eyes of the blind? Referring to the late instance of Christ's curing a man that was blind from his birth; if it was in the power of a devil to do such an action, which it is not, yet it is not in his nature, it is not usual with him to do any good; but to do all the hurt he can, both to the bodies and souls of men. In one of Beza's copies it is read, *Can one that has a devil, open the eyes of the blind?* So the Persic version, *Can a demoniac*, &c.? which reading suits best with what is before said; and then the sense is, Can a madman, one that is a lunatic, one possessed with the devil, either talk in the manner this man does, or do such wonderful actions as He has done, particularly cure a man that was born blind?

Verse 22. **And it was at Jerusalem the feast of the dedication**, &c. That is, of the temple; not as built by Solomon, as Nonnus in his paraphrase suggests; or as rebuilt by Zerubbabel, for there were no annual feasts appointed in commemoration of either of these; and besides, they were neither of them in the winter time; the dedication of Solomon's temple was in autumn, at the feast of tabernacles, about our September, *1 Kings 8:2, 65, 66*; and the dedication of the house in Zeroubbabel's time, was in the spring, about our February, *Ezra 6:15-16*; but this was the feast of dedication, appointed by Judas Maccabaeus and his brethren, on account of the purging the temple, and renewing the altar, after the profanation of them by Antiochus; which feast lasted eight days, and began on the twenty-fifth of the month Chisleu [or Kislev], which answers to part of our December; see [the Apocrypha] 1 Maccabees 4:52, 56, 59:

> "*52* Now on the five and twentieth day of the ninth month, which is called the month Chisleu, in the hundred forty and eighth year, they rose up betimes in the morning; *56* And so they kept the dedication of

the altar eight days and offered burnt offerings with gladness, and sacrificed the sacrifice of deliverance and praise; *59* Moreover Judas and his brethren with the whole congregation of Israel ordained, that the days of the dedication of the altar should be kept in their season from year to year by the space of eight days, from the five and twentieth day of the month Chisleu, with mirth and gladness;"
and in 2 Maccabees 10:5,8:

"*5* Now upon the same day that the strangers profaned the temple, on the very same day it was cleansed again, even the five and twentieth day of the same month, which is Chisleu; *8* They ordained also by a common statute and decree, That every year those days should be kept of the whole nation of the Jews;"

and with which the Jewish writers agree.[12] The account Maimonides gives[13] of it is this:

"When the Israelites prevailed over their enemies and destroyed them, it was on the twenty-fifth of the month Chisleu; and they went into the temple, and could not find any pure oil in the sanctuary, but one vial; and it was not enough to light but one day only, and they lighted lamps of it for eight days, until the olives were squeezed, and they brought forth pure oil. Wherefore the wise men of that generation ordered, that those eight days beginning at the twenty-fifth of Chisleu, should be days of rejoicing and praise, and they lighted lamps at the doors of their houses; every night of these eight nights, to show and make known the miracle; and these days are called חנוכה, *the dedication*; and they are forbidden mourning and fasting, as the days of *Purim*; and the lighting of the lamps on them, is a commandment from the Scribes, as is the reading of the book of Esther.—How many lamps do they light at the feast of the dedication? The order is, that every house should light one lamp, whether the men of the house be many, or whether there is but one man in it; but he that honors the command, lights up lamps according to the number of the men of the house, a lamp for every one, whether men or women; and he that honors it more, lights up a lamp for every man the first night, and adds, as he goes, every night a lamp; for instance, if there be ten men in the house, the first night he lights up ten lamps, and on the second night twenty,

---

[12] Ganz Tzemach David, par. 1. fol. 22. 1. Tzeror Hammor, fol. 137. 2.

[13] Hilchot Megilla Uchanucha, c. 3. sect. 2, 3. & 4. 1, 2. Vid. T. Bab. Sabbat, fol. 21. 2.

[14] Antiqu. l. 12. c. 7. sect. 7.

and on the third night thirty; until he comes to the eighth night, when
he lights up fourscore lamps."

Wherefore, as Josephus says,[14] this feast was called φωτα, *lights*; though he
seems to assign another reason of its name, because that prosperity and
happiness appeared to them beyond hope, and unexpected: and though this
was only an order of Judas and his brethren, and the congregation of Israel,
yet the Jews observe it as religiously as if it was the appointment of God
Himself, and they do not spare to call it so; for in the service of this feast, they
have these words:[15]

"Blessed art thou, O Lord our God, the King of the world, who hath
sanctified us by his commandments, and hath *commanded* us to light
the lamp of the dedication; blessed art thou, O Lord our God, the King
of the world, who did wonders for our fathers on those days, at this
time; blessed art thou, O Lord our God, the King of the world, who has
kept us alive, and preserved us, and brought us to this time; these
lamps we light, because of the wonders and marvelous things, and
salvations, and wars, thou hast wrought for our fathers on those days
at this time, by the hand of thine holy priests.—These lamps are holy,
we have no power to use them, but only to behold them, so as to confess
and praise thy great name, for thy miracles, and for thy wonders, and
for thy salvations."

And though this feast is said to be at Jerusalem, yet it was not confined there,
as were the other feasts, of the passover, pentecost, and tabernacles, for this
might be kept in any part of the land: mention is made of the feast of
dedication at Lydda,[16] and in other countries; Maimonides[17] says,

"It is a common custom in all our cities in Spain, that all the men of the
house light up a lamp the first night, and add as they go along, a lamp
every night, till he lights up on the eighth night eight lamps, whether
the men of the house be many, or there be but one man."

Some have been of opinion, that this feast of dedication was on the account of
the victory Judith gained over Holophernes, by cutting off his head; or
however, that the commemoration of that victory was a part of this festival.
In the Vulgate Latin edition of Judith 16:31, it is said,

---

[15] Seder Tephillot, fol. 234. 1, 2. Ed. Amsterd.

[16] T. Bab. Roshhashana, fol. 18. 2.

[17] Hilchot Chanuca, c. 4. sect. 3.

"The day of the festivity of this victory is received by the Hebrews into the number of holy days; and is kept by the Jews from that time, to the present day."

And Sigonius[18] asserts, that it is celebrated by the Jews on the twenty-fifth day of the month Chisleu; which is the same day the feast began, that was instituted by Judas Maccabaeus, on the above account; and certain it is, that the Jews do make mention of that fact of hers, in the service for the first sabbath of this feast;[19] and some of their writers would have this fact to be in the times of the Maccabees, though as one of their chronologers[20] observes, it appears from the history of Judith, to have been in the times of Nebuchadnezzar; and there are some that say it was in the times of Cambyses, son of Cyrus, king of Persia, and was two or three hundred years before the miracle of the dedication: but he observes, that the wise men of that age agreed to comprehend the memorial of that wonderful event, with the miracle of the dedication: and so R. Leo Modena[21] says,

"They have a tradition, that in ordaining this feast to be kept, they had an eye also upon that famous exploit performed by Judith upon Holophernes; although many are of opinion, that this happened not at this time of the year; and that they make a commemoration of that piece of gallantry of hers now, because she was of the stock of the Maccabees."

But that cannot be, since she must be some hundreds of years before them; wherefore others make mention of another Judith, a daughter of one of the Maccabees, who performed a like exploit upon Nicanor, a general of Demetrius's army: to which R. Gedaliah has respect, when he says,[22]

"The wise men agreed to comprehend together in the joy of the feast of dedication, the affair of Judith, seeing there was another Judith, from her that killed Holophernes, a daughter of the Maccabees."

But it is not clear that there was any such woman, nor that Nicanor was slain by one; and besides, he was killed on the thirteenth of Adar, and that day was ordained to be kept yearly on that account, [in the Apocrypha] 1 Maccabees 7:43, 49:

---

[18]   De Repub. Heb. l. 3. c. 17.

[19]   Seder Tephillot, fol. 133. 2.

[20]   Ganz Tzemach David, par. 1. fol. 22. 1.

[21]   History of the Rites, &c. of the Jews, c. 9.

[22]   Shalshelet Hakabala, fol. 17. 2.

"43 So the thirteenth day of the month Adar the hosts joined battle: but Nicanor's host was discomfited, and he himself was first slain in the battle; *49* Moreover they ordained to keep yearly this day, being the thirteenth of Adar."

and 2 Maccabees 15:36:

"And they ordained all with a common decree in no case to let that day pass without solemnity, but to celebrate the thirtieth day of the twelfth month, which in the Syrian tongue is called Adar, the day before Mardocheus' day;"

and the month of Adar answers to part of February:

and it was winter; for the month Chisleu answers to our November and December; so that the twenty-fifth of that month might be about the tenth of December, and the Jews reckon part of that month winter, and it must be the part in which this feast was; they say,[23]

"half Chisleu, Tebeth, and half Shebet, are, חורף, *winter:*"

so that the evangelist might with propriety say, according to the sense of the Jewish nation, that it was winter; though it was but just entered, even not more than ten days: the reason why this is observed, may be for what follows.

Verse 23. **And Jesus walked in the temple**, &c. To keep Himself warm, and to secure Him the better from the inclemency of the weather:

in Solomon's porch. Which was covered over, and the outside of it was enclosed with a wall, which made it very convenient for such a purpose: this was on the outside of the temple eastward, and was a very magnificent structure. The account Josephus[24] gives of it is this:

"There was a porch without the temple, overlooking a deep valley, supported by walls of four hundred cubits, made of four-square stone, very white; the length of each stone was twenty cubits, and the breadth six; the work of king Solomon, who first founded the whole temple."

Now, though this was not the porch that was built by Solomon, yet as it was built on the same spot, and in imitation of it, it bore his name; mention is made of it in *Acts 3:11* and *5:12*.

Verse 24. **Then came the Jews round about him**, &c. Who might be walking there on the same account, and seeing Jesus, took this opportunity, and got about Him in great numbers, and hemmed Him in; having a design upon Him to ensnare Him, if possible:

---

[23] Bereshit Rabba, sect. 34. fol. 30. 2. T. Bab. Bava Metzia, fol. 106. 2.

[24] Antiqu. l. 20. c. 8. sect. 7.

and said unto him, How long dost thou make us doubt? Or, as the Vulgate Latin, Syriac, Persic, and Ethiopic versions literally render it, *How long dost thou take away our soul?* that is, deprive us of the knowledge of thee; Nonnus renders it, *Wherefore dost thou steal away our minds with words?* So Jacob when he went away privately, without the knowledge of Laban, is said to steal away the heart of Laban, as it is in the Hebrew text, in *Gen. 31:20, 26.*[25] In like manner the Jews charge Christ with taking away their soul, or stealing away their heart, or hiding Himself from them; not telling them plainly, who He was: therefore say they,

If thou be the Christ, tell us plainly. Freely, boldly, openly, in express words; this they said, not as desirous of knowing who He was, or for the sake of information, but in order to ensnare Him; that should He say He was not the Christ, as they might hope He would, for fear of them, now they had gotten Him by Himself, and hemmed Him in, it would then lessen His credit among the people; and should He say He was the Messiah, they would have whereof to accuse Him to the Roman governor, as an enemy to Caesar, as one that set Himself up for king of the Jews.

Verse 25. **Jesus answered them, I told you, and ye believed not**, &c. He had often said what amounted to it, in His ministry and doctrine; as that God was His Father, and He was the Light of the world, and the Good Shepherd, and the like; but they gave no heed nor credit to His words, even though He told them, that unless they believed He was such a person, they should die in their sins:

the works that I do in my Father's name, they bear witness of me. Such as healing the sick, dispossessing devils, cleansing lepers, giving sight to the blind, causing the deaf to hear, the dumb to speak, and the lame to walk, and raising the dead to life [see *Matt. 11:5; Mark 7:37*]; suggesting, that besides His words, His doctrine and ministry, they had His miracles before them, which plainly showed who He was; so that they need not have been in any doubt of mind, or suspense about Him; nor had they any reason to complain of His hiding Himself from them, or depriving them of the knowledge of Him.

Verse 26. **But ye believe not**, &c. In me, as the Messiah:

because ye are not of my sheep; they were not among the sheep given Him by His Father, were they, they would have come to Him; that is, have believed in Him, according to *John 6:37*; they were not the chosen of God, pre-

---

[25] See De Dieu in loc.

destinated unto eternal life; for as many as are ordained of God to eternal happiness, do believe in God's own time, *Acts 13:48*; but these not being the elect of God, had not *the faith of God's elect* [*Titus 1:1*]. Christ, as the omniscient God, knew this, that they were not the chosen of God; for He was present, when the names of God's elect were written in the book of life [see *Rev. 13:8* and *17:8*]; had they been His sheep, He must have known them, for He knows all the sheep, and calls them by name; had they been given Him by the Father, He must have known it, and would have owned them as such; but so it was not, and therefore they were left to hardness and unbelief:

as I said unto you. Which seems to refer to what follows, since He had said before, that the sheep hear the voice of the Shepherd, and follow Him, and that He knows them, *verses 4* and *14*. This clause is omitted in the Vulgate Latin version, and in Nonnus, but is in the Greek copies, and Oriental versions.

Verse 27. **My sheep hear my voice**, &c. The voice of Christ in His Gospel, both externally and internally; see the notes on *verses 4* and *16;* and since therefore these Jews did not, it was a plain case they were not of His sheep:

and I know them; see the note on *verse 14*; but Christ knew not these as the elect of God, or as the Father's gift to Him, and therefore they could not be His sheep:

and they follow me; both in the exercise of grace, and in the discharge of duty, and whithersoever He the Good Shepherd leads them; see the notes on *verses 3* and *4*. But now, whereas these Jews did not follow Christ, but turned their backs on Him, and rejected Him, it was notorious that they were none of His sheep; but both happy and safe are those persons that are the sheep of Christ, as appears from what is next said of them.

Verse 28. **And I give unto them eternal life**, &c. Christ gives eternal life to His sheep, or people now; He gives them a spiritual life, or a life of grace, which issues in eternal life; He gives them Himself, who is the true God and eternal life, and whoever has Him, has life; He gives them the knowledge of Himself, which is life eternal [see *1 John 5:20*]; and He gives them His righteousness, which is their justification of life, or what entitles them to eternal life; and He gives them the foretastes of it, in faith and hope, in the enjoyment of Himself, and the discoveries of His love; He gives them the earnest and pledge of it, His own Spirit; and they have this life in Him as their representative, and it is hid with Him in God, and is safe and secure for them; and He will actually give it to them in their own persons, to be for ever enjoyed by them; and because of the certainty of it, He is said to do it now: this is a pure gift, it is of grace, and not of works; and it is in the gift of Christ as Mediator, who has power to give it to as many as the Father has given Him:

and they shall never perish; though they were lost in Adam, and in a perishing condition in themselves, during their state of unregeneracy; in which condition they see themselves to be, when convinced by the Spirit of God; and come to Christ as persons ready to perish, as a Savior, resolving, that if they perish, they will perish at His feet: and though after conversion, they are subject to many falls and spiritual declensions, and lose their peace, joy, and comfort, and imagine their strength and hope are perished, or at least fear they shall one day perish through one sin, or snare, or temptation or another, yet they shall never perish in such sense as the wicked will; they will not be punished with everlasting destruction from the presence of the Lord, and the glory of His power:

neither shall any pluck them out of my hand. Christ's sheep are in His hand, being put there by God the Father, both as an instance of His love to Christ, and them; and this was done from all eternity, even when they were chosen in Him [see *Eph. 1:4-6*]; so that they were in the hand of Christ before they were in the loins of Adam; and were preserved in Him, notwithstanding Adam's fall, and through the ruins of it. To be in the hand of Christ, is to be high in His esteem and favor; the saints are a crown of glory in the hand of the Lord, and a royal diadem in the hand of their God; they are a signet on His right hand that shall never be plucked off; they are engraven on the palms of His hands: to be in the hand of Christ, is to be in His possession, and at His disposal, as all the elect of God are; and to be under His guidance, care, and protection, as they be; they are fed according to the integrity of His heart, and guided by the skilfulness of His hands; they are always under His care and watchful eye, who protects them from all their enemies, and hides them in the hollow of His hand: hence, because they are so, they are called *the sheep of his hand, Psa. 95:7*. And none shall ever pluck them from thence; no man can do it, not any false teacher can remove them from Christ, by all the art and cunning he is master of; nor any violent persecutor, by all the force and power he can use; nor can any sin, or snare, or temptation, draw them out of Christ's hands; nor any adversity whatever separate them from Him: they must be safe, and always abide there, who are in the hand of Christ; for His hands have laid the foundations of the heavens and the earth, they grasp the whole universe, and hold all things together; and who then can pluck any out of these hands? Moreover, Christ, as Mediator, has all power in heaven and earth [see *Matt. 28:18*]; and even as man, He is the man of God's right hand, made strong for Himself [see *Psa. 80:17*].

Verse 29. **My Father which gave *them* me**, &c. So the sheep came to be Christ's, and to be in His hand; the Father gave them to Him, put them into His hand, and made them His care and charge:

is greater than all; than all gods [see *1 Cor. 8:1-6* and *10:19-20*], than all beings, than all creatures, angels and men, and than all the enemies of His people; this must be allowed: the Vulgate Latin version, and so some of the ancients read, *what my Father gave to me, is greater than all*; meaning, that the church given to Him, and built on Him, is stronger than all its enemies:

and none is able to pluck *them* out of my Father's hand. So that these sheep have a double security; they are in the hand of Christ, and they are in the hand of the Father of Christ; wherefore could it be thought, which ought not to be, that they could be plucked out of Christ's hand, yet it can never be imagined, that any can pluck them out of the hand of God the Father; and there is no more reason to think that they can be plucked out of the hand of the one, than there is that they can be plucked out of the hand of the other, as is clear from what follows in the next verse; see [the Apocrypha] Wisdom 3:1:

> "But the souls of the righteous are in the hand of God, and there shall no torment touch them."

Verse 30. **I and *my* Father are one**. Not in person, for the Father must be a distinct person from the Son, and the Son a distinct person from the Father; and which is further manifest, from the use of the verb plural, *I and* my *Father*, εσμεν, *we are one*; that is, in nature and essence, and perfections, particularly in power; since Christ is speaking of the impossibility of plucking any of the sheep, out of His own and His Father's hands; giving this as a reason for it, their unity of nature, and equality of power; so that it must be as impracticable to pluck them out of His hand, as out of His Father's, because He is equal with God the Father, and the one God with Him. The Jew[26] objects that,

> "if the sense of this expression is, that the Father and the Son are one, as the Nazarenes understand and believe it, it will be found that Jesus himself destroys this saying, as it is written in *Mark 13:32*, for saith Jesus, *that day and that hour, there is none [that] knoweth, not the angels, nor the Son, but the Father only*; lo, these words show, that the Father and the Son are not one, since the Son does not know what the Father knows."

But it should be observed, that Christ is both the Son of God, and the Son of man, as the Christians believe; as He is the Son of God, He lay in the bosom of His Father [see *John 1:18*], and was privy to all His secrets, to all His

---

[26] R. Isaac Chizzuk Emuna, par. 2. c. 50. p. 438, 439.

thoughts, purposes, and designs; and as such, He knew the day and hour of judgment, being God omniscient; and in this respect is one with the Father, having the same perfections of power, knowledge, &c. But then as the Son of man, He is not of the same nature, and has not the same knowledge; His knowledge of things was derived, communicated, and not infinite; and did not reach to all things at once, but was capable of being increased, as it was: and it is with regard to Him as the Son of man, that Jesus speaks of Himself in *Mark 13:32*; whereas He is here treating of His divine Sonship, and almighty power; wherefore considered in the relation of the Son of God, and as possessed of the same perfections with God, He and His Father are one; though as man, He is different from Him, and knew not some things He did: so that there is no contradiction between the words of Christ in one place, and in the other; nor is He chargeable with any blasphemy against God, or any arrogance in Himself, by assuming Deity to Himself; nor deserving of punishment, even to be deprived of human life, as the Jew suggests; nor is what He produces from a Socinian writer, of any moment, that these words do not necessarily suppose, that the Father and the Son are of the same essence; since it may be said of two men, that they are one, and yet are not the same man, but one is one man, and the other another; for we do not say they are one and the same person, which does not follow from their being of one and the same nature, but that they are one God, and two distinct persons.

Verse 31. **Then the Jews took up stones again to stone him**. As they had done before, *chapter 8:59*; see the note there.

Verse 32. **Jesus answered them, Many good works**, &c. Such as healing the sick, and all manner of diseases; dispossessing devils, cleansing lepers, giving sight to the blind, causing the dumb to speak, the deaf to hear, and the lame to walk; which were not only works of power, but of mercy and beneficence; and therefore are called good works, as well as they were great and miraculous ones:

have I showed you from my Father; which Christ did in the name, and by the command and authority of the Father; who gave Him them to do, and did them by Him; and which were evident and notorious, and were done so openly and publicly, that they could not be denied:

for which of these works do ye stone me? Suggesting, that His public life had been a continued series of such kind actions to the sons of men, and it could be for nothing else, surely, that they took up stones to stone Him; wherefore the part they acted, was a most ungrateful, cruel, and barbarous one.

Verse 33. **The Jews answered him, saying,** &c. As follows:

For a good work we stone thee not: they could not deny that He had done many good works; this was too barefaced to be contradicted; yet they cared not to own them; and though they industriously concealed their resentment at them, yet they were very much graveled and made uneasy by them, but chose to give another reason for their stoning Him:

but for blasphemy; which required death by stoning, according to *Lev. 24:16*, and according to the Jews' oral law:[27]

and because that thou, being a man, makest thyself God. Which they concluded very rightly, from His saying, *verse 30*, that God was His Father, and that He and His Father were one; that is, in nature and essence, and therefore He must be God; but then this was no blasphemy, but a real truth, as is hereafter made to appear; nor is there any contradiction between His being man, and being God; He is truly and really man, but then He is not a mere man, as the Jews suggested; but is truly God, as well as man, and is both God and man in one person, the divine and human nature being united in Him, of which they were ignorant. Two mistakes they seem to be guilty of in this account; one, that Christ was a mere man, the other, that He made Himself God, or assumed Deity to Himself, which did not belong to Him, and therefore must be guilty of blasphemy; neither of which were true: the phrase is used by the Jews of others who have taken upon them the name and title of God; as of Hiram king of Tyre, of whom they say, שעשה עצמו אלוה, *that he made himself God*;[28] the same they say of Nebuchadnezzar; and the modern Jews still continue the same charge against Jesus, as their ancestors did, and express it in the same language, and say of Him, that He was a man, and set Himself up for God.[29]

Verse 34. **Jesus answered them, Is it not written in your law**, &c. In the law which was given unto them, of which they boasted, and pretended to understand and interpret, even in *Psa. 82:6*; for the law includes not only the Pentateuch, but all the books of the Old Testament. It is an observation of one

---

[27] Mishna Sanhedrin, c. 7. sect. 4.

[28] Bereshit Rabba, sect. 96. fol. 83. 4. & Tzeror Hammor, fol. 134. 4.

[29] Aben Ezra in Gen. 27:39. & Abarbinel Mashmai Jeshua, fol. 5. 1.

[30] R. Azarias in Meor Enayim, c. 7. fol. 47. 1.

of the Jewish doctors[30] that,

> "With the wise men of blessed memory, it is found in many places that
> the word *law*, comprehends the Prophets and the Hagiographa."

Among which last stands the book of Psalms; and this may be confirmed by
a passage out of the Talmud;[31] it is asked,

> "From whence does the resurrection of the dead appear, מן התורה, *out*
> *of the law?*"

It is answered,

> "As it is said in *Psa. 84:4*: *Blessed are they that dwell in thy house, they*
> *will still praise thee, Selah; they do praise thee*, it is not said, but *they*
> *will praise thee*; from hence is a proof of the resurrection of the dead,
> *out of the law.*"

The same question is again put, and then *Isa. 52:8* is cited, and the like
observation made upon it. Moreover, this is a way of speaking used by the
Jews, when they introduce another citing a passage of Scripture thus,[32]
הלא כתיב בתורתכם, *is it not written in your law, Deut. 4:9, only take heed to*
thyself, &c. So here the Scripture follows,

I said, Ye are gods? Which is spoken to civil magistrates, so called, because
of their authority and power; and because they do, in some sort, represent the
divine majesty, in the government of nations and kingdoms. Many of the
Jewish writers, by *gods*, understand *the angels*. The Targum paraphrases the
words thus:

> "I said ye are accounted as angels, as the angels on high, all of you;"

and to this sense some of their commentators interpret it. Jarchi's gloss is,

> "*ye are gods*; that is, *angels*; for when I gave the law to you, it was on
> this account, that the angel of death might not any more rule over you."

The note of Aben Ezra is, *and the children of the Most High*: as angels; and the
sense is, your soul is as the soul of angels: hence the[33] Jew charges Christ with
seeking refuge in words that will not profit, or be any help to Him, when He
cites these words, showing that magistrates are called gods; when the sense
is only, that they are like to the angels in respect of their souls. But let it be
observed, that it is not said, *ye are as gods*, as in *Gen. 3:5*, but *ye are gods*; not
like unto them only, but *are* in some sense gods; and besides, to say that they
are *like* to angels, with respect to their souls, which come from above, is to say

---

[31] T. Bab. Sanhedrin, fol. 91. 2.

[32] T. Bab. Beracot, fol. 32. 2.

[33] R. Isaac Chizzuk Emuna, par. 2. c. 51. p. 440, 441.

no more of the judges of the earth, than what may be said of every man: to which may be added, that this objector himself owns, that judges are called אלהים, *gods*, as in *Ex. 22:9: the cause of both parties shall come before* אלהים, *the judges*; and that even the word is used in this sense in this very psalm, from whence these words are cited, *Psa. 82:1, he judgeth among* אלהים, *the gods*; and both Kimchi and Ben Melech interpret this text itself in the same way, and observe, that judges are called gods, when they judge truly and aright: all which is sufficient to justify our Lord in the citation of this passage, and the use He makes of it.

Verse 35. **If he called them gods, unto whom the word of God came**, &c. The Syriac version reads, *because the word of God came to them*; either the divine *Logos*, the essential Word, the Son of God, who appeared to Moses, and made him *a god to Pharaoh* [*Ex. 7:1*], and who appointed rulers and magistrates among the Jews; and who is the King of kings, and Lord of lords, from whom all receive their power and dominion. This sense is favored by the Ethiopic version, which renders it, *if he called them gods to whom God appeared, the word of God was with them*: or else the commission from God, authorizing them to act in the capacity of rulers and governors, is here meant; or rather, the Word of God, which, in the passage of Scripture cited, calls them so, as it certainly does:

and the Scripture cannot be broken; or be made null and void; whatever that says is true, there is no contradicting it, or objecting to it: it is a Jewish way of speaking, much used in the Talmud;[34] when one doctor has produced an argument, or instance, in any point of debate, another says, איכא למיפרך, *it may be broken*; or objected to, in such and such a manner, and be refuted: but the Scripture cannot be broken, that is not to be objected to, there can be no confutation of that.

Verse 36. **Say ye of him, whom the Father hath sanctified**, &c. Not by making His human nature pure and holy, and free from all sin, and by bestowing the Holy Spirit on Him without measure, though both true; but these were upon, or after His mission into the world; whereas sanctification here, designs something previous to that, and respects the eternal separation of Him to His office, as Mediator, in the counsel, purposes, and decrees of God, and in the covenant of His grace, being preordained thereunto, before the foundation of the world [see *Eph. 1:3-12; Heb. 4:3; Rev. 13:8*]; which supposes His eternal existence as a divine person, and tacitly proves His true and proper Deity:

---

34 T. Bab. Zebachim, fol. 4. 1. & Becorot, fol. 32. 1. & passim.

and sent into the world; in human nature, to obtain eternal redemption and salvation for His people [see *Matt. 1:21*]: to save them from sin, Satan, the world, law, hell and death, which none but God could do:

Thou blasphemest, because I said, I am the Son of God; for what He had said in *verse 30,* is equivalent to it; and in it He was rightly understood by the Jews, and what He here and afterwards says confirms it. The argument is what the Jews call קל וחומר, *from the lesser to the greater*, and stands thus: that if mere frail mortal men, and some of them wicked men, being made rulers and judges in the earth are called *gods*, by God Himself, to whom the Word of God came in time, and constituted them gods, or governors, but for a time; and this is a fact [that] stands recorded in Scripture, which cannot be denied or disproved; then surely it cannot be blasphemy in Christ, to assert Himself to be the Son of God, who existed as a divine person from all eternity; and was so early set apart to the office of Prophet, Priest, and King; and in *the fulness of time*, was sent into this world, to be *the author of eternal salvation to the sons of men* [*Gal. 4:4-5; Heb. 5:9*].

Verse 37. **If I do not the works of my Father**, &c. Not only what the Father had given Him to finish, and which He wrought by Him as man, but such as were as great as the Father had done, and were equal to them; and which could not be done by any, but by the Father, or by one that is equal with Him:

believe me not. Christ appeals to His miracles as proofs of His Deity, Sonship, and Messiahship, and desires no other credit than what they demand; see *Matt. 11:3-5; John 5:36.*

Verse 38. **But if I do**, &c. Works, which none but God can do:

though ye believe not me; what Christ said in His doctrine and ministry, though they paid no regard to that, and did not receive His testimony, on the credit of Him the testifier, as they ought to have done:

believe the works; not only that they are true and real, and not imaginary and delusory; but for the sake of them believe the above assertion, that Christ is the Son of God, He and His Father being one; or take such notice of these works and miracles, consider the nature, evidence, and importance of them, and the divine power that attends them,

that ye may know, and believe, that the Father is in me, and I in him; or *in the Father*, as one of Beza's exemplars, the Vulgate Latin, Persic, and Ethiopic versions read; or *in my Father*, as read the Syriac and Arabic versions; that they are one in nature, distinct in person, equal in power, and have a mutual inhabitation and communion in the divine essence; all which is manifest, by doing the same works, and which are out of the reach and power of any mere creature.

Verse 39. **Therefore they sought again to take him**, &c. Not to take away His life by stoning Him, as before, in the manner the furious zealots did, and was the part they were about to act just now; but to lay hold upon Him, and bring Him before the Sanhedrin, as they had done in *chapter 5:18*: He being so far from clearing Himself from the charge of blasphemy, they had brought against Him, that in their opinion He had greatly strengthened it; and they thought they had now sufficient proof and evidence to convict Him as a blasphemer, in their high court of judicature; and therefore attempted to lay hands on Him, and bring Him thither:

but he escaped out of their hands. Either by withdrawing from them in some private way; or by open force, exerting His power, and obliging them on every side to fall back, and give way to Him; or by rendering Himself invisible to them; and this He did, not through fear of death, but because His time was not yet come, and He had other work to do, before He suffered and died.

Verse 40. **And went away again beyond Jordan**, &c. Where He had been before; and whither He went, not merely for the security of His person, much less to indulge Himself in ease; but to preach the Gospel, work miracles, and bring many souls to believe on Him, as did: and He went

into the place where John at first baptized; that is, Bethabara, where he baptized before he was at Ænon, *near Salim, chapter 1:28* and *3:23*, and was the place where Christ Himself was baptized, and where John bore such a testimony of Him:

and there he abode. How long is not certain, perhaps till He went to Bethany, on account of raising Lazarus from the dead.

Verse 41. **And many resorted unto him**, &c. From all the parts adjacent, having heard of His being there, and of the fame of Him; and many of them doubtless personally knew Him; these came to Him, some very likely to be healed by Him, others to see His person and miracles, and others to hear Him preach:

and said, John did no miracle; though it was now three years ago, yet the name, ministry, and baptism of John, were fresh in the memory of men in those parts; and what they say one to another, was not to lessen the character of John, but to exalt Jesus Christ, and to give a reason why they should receive and embrace Him; for if John, who did no miracle, who only taught and baptized, and directed men to the Messiah, was justly reckoned a very great person, and his doctrine was received, and his baptism was submitted to; then much more should this illustrious person be attended to, who besides His divine doctrine, did such great and amazing miracles; to which they add, though John did no miracle to confirm his mission, ministry, and baptism,

but all things that John spake of this man, were true; as that He was greater than he, was the Lamb of God, yea, the Son of God, the Savior of the world, and true Messiah, who should baptize men with the Holy Ghost and with fire.

Verse 42. **And many believed on him there**. Through the doctrine He preached, the miracles He wrought, and through comparing these things with what John had said of Him. This shows the reason of Christ's leaving Jerusalem, and coming into these parts: there were others that were to believe in His name. The word *there*, is left out in the Vulgate Latin, Syriac, and Persic versions.

CHAPTER 11

Verse 1. **Now a certain man was sick**, &c. Very likely of a fever; Nonnus calls it a morbid fire, a hot and burning disease:

***named* Lazarus, of Bethany**; for his name, which the Ethiopic version reads *Eleazar*, and the Persic version *Gazarus*, see the notes on *Luke 16:24* **[54]**; and for the place Bethany, see the notes on *Matt. 21:1* and *17* **[26, 30]**.

the town of Mary and her sister Martha. Where they were both born, as well as Lazarus, or at least where they dwelt; of the former, some account is given in the next verse, and of the latter, see the note on *Luke 10:38* **[51]**.

Verse 2. (**It was *that* Mary which anointed the Lord with ointment**, &c. Not the woman in *Luke 7:37*, as some have thought, whose name is not mentioned, and which history is not related by John at all: but Mary in *John 12:3*, who is both mentioned by name, and along with Lazarus her brother, and with whom all the circumstances of the affair suit; and though the fact

355

was not yet done, yet John writing many years after it was done, and when it was well known, proleptically, and in a parenthesis, takes notice of it here:

and wiped his feet with her hair; instead of a napkin, after she had anointed them with oil; see the notes on *Luke 7:37* **[49]** and on *John 12:3*;

whose brother Lazarus was sick). This is observed, to show how well they were all acquainted with Christ, and affected to Him.

Verse 3. **Therefore his sisters sent unto him**, &c. Both the sisters of Lazarus, Mary and Martha, sent to Jesus; they did not go themselves, being women, and the place where Jesus was, was at some distance; and besides, it was necessary they should abide at home, to attend their brother in his sickness, and therefore they sent a messenger, or messengers to Christ,

saying, Lord, behold, he whom thou lovest is sick. For it seems that Lazarus was in a very singular manner loved by Christ, as man, as John the beloved disciple was; and this is the rather put into the message by the sisters, to engage Jesus to come to his assistance; and they were very right in applying to Christ in this time of need, who is the physician, both of the bodies and souls of men; and are greatly to be commended both for their modesty and piety, in not prescribing to Christ what should be done in this case. And it may be further observed, that such who are the peculiar objects of Christ's love, are attended in this life with bodily sickness, disorders, and diseases, which are sent unto them, not in a way of vindictive wrath, but in love, and as fatherly chastisements; which, as they are designed, so they are overruled for their good; and are to be considered, not as instances of wrath, but as tokens of love.

Verse 4. **When Jesus heard *that***, &c. That His friend Lazarus was sick,

he said; either to His disciples, or to the messenger or messengers that brought the account to Him, and that on purpose to yield some relief to the afflicted family when it should be reported to them:

This sickness is not unto death; it was to issue in death, but not in death which was to continue, or under which Lazarus was to continue till the general resurrection; for though he should die, yet he should be so quickly restored again to life, that it scarcely deserved the name of death. The Jews distinguish between sickness and sickness; there are some that are *sick*, the greater part of whom are, לחיים, *for life*; and there are others that are *sick*, the greater part of whom are, למיתה, *for death*,[1] or are sick unto death, whose

---

[1]   T. Bab. Kiddushin, fol. 71. 2.

sickness issues in death; but this of Lazarus's was not to be unto death, at least not finally:

but for the glory of God; of His power and goodness in raising him again:

that the Son of God might be glorified thereby. That is, that His glory, as the Son of God, might be made manifest in the resurrection of him from the dead; see *chapter 2:11*.

Verse 5. **Now Jesus loved Martha, and her sister, and Lazarus**. Not only with an everlasting love, a love of complacency and delight, an unchangeable one, and which never varies, nor will ever end, with which He loves all His people alike; but with a very great human affection, and which was very singular and peculiar to them: these were the intimate friends, and familiar acquaintance of Christ, whom He often visited, at whose house He frequently was when in those parts; they were very hospitable to Him; they kindly received Him into their houses, and generously entertained Him, and which He returned in love to them: hence Nonnus paraphrases the words,
  "Jesus loved the women, φιλοξεινους, *who were lovers of hospitality*, by the law of kindness."

Verse 6. **When he had heard therefore that he was sick**, &c. Though Christ had heard that Lazarus was sick, and by such good hands, a message being sent Him by his sisters, to acquaint Him with it; and though He had such a very great love for him, and the whole family, yet He did not go directly to him, and to his assistance: but,

he abode two days still in the same place where he was. At Bethabara, beyond Jordan; this He did to try the faith and patience of the sisters of Lazarus, and that the miracle of raising him from the dead might be the more manifest, and His own glory might be the more illustrious, and yet equal, if not greater tenderness and love, be shown to His friends.

Verse 7. **Then after that**, &c. The next day, the third day after He had heard of Lazarus's sickness:

saith he to *his* disciples, Let us go into Judea again. For the country beyond Jordan was distinguished from Judea; see *Matt. 4:25*, and the note there **[6]**.

Verse 8. ***His* disciples say unto him, Master**, &c. Addressing Him very reverently, and with great concern for His safety, as well as their own:

the Jews of late, or but now,

sought to stone thee; as they had attempted to do twice in a very little time; see *chapter 8:59* and *10:31*;

and goest thou thither again? Where there are so many enemies, and so much danger, and but little hope of doing much good; whereas here He was among His friends, and in safety, and very useful.

Verse 9. **Jesus answered, Are there not twelve hours in the day?** &c. So the Jews reckoned, and so they commonly say,[2] שתים עשרה שעות הוי היום, *twelve hours are a day*, or a day consists of twelve hours, which they divided into four parts, each part consisting of three hours. This was a matter well known, and Christ puts the question as such, it being what might be easily answered, and at once assented to:

if any man walk in the day: within any of the twelve hours, even in the last of them,

he stumbleth not, at any stone or stumbling block in the way,

because he seeth the light of this world; the sun in the horizon not being as yet set, by the light of which he sees what is before him, and avoids it; see the note on *chapter 8:12*. So our Lord intimates, that as yet it was day with Him, His time of life was not expired; and so, as yet, it was a time of walking and working; nor did He fear any danger He was exposed to, or any snares that were laid for Him, since He could not be hurt by any, nor His life taken from Him before His time.

Verse 10. **But if a man walk in the night**, &c. After the sun is set, and there is no light in the air and heavens to direct him:

he stumbleth; at every thing that lies in the way,

because there is no light in him. There being none from above communicated to him. So our Lord suggests, that when the time of His death was come, He should then fall a prey into the hands of His enemies, but till then He should walk safe and secure; nor had He any thing to fear from them, and therefore could go into Judea again, with intrepidity and unconcern.

Verse 11. **These things said he**, &c. In answer to His disciples, and made a pause:

and after that he saith unto them, Our friend Lazarus sleepeth; meaning, that he was dead; in which sense the word is often used in the Old

---

[2] T. Bab Sanhedrin, fol. 38. 2. Avoda Zara, fol. 3. 2. Vid. Philo. de Somniis, p. 1143.

Testament, and in the common dialect of the Jews, and frequently in their writings; and especially it is so used of good men. And it is an observation of theirs[3] that,

"It is usual to say of the righteous, that there is no death in them, שׁינה אלא, *but sleep;*"

see the notes on *Matt. 9:24* **[10]**; *1 Cor. 15:18, 20* **[61]**; *1 Thess. 4:13-14* **[63]**;

but I go, that I may awake him out of sleep. That is, to raise him from the dead, for, the resurrection of the dead is expressed by awaking; see *Psa. 17:15; Isa. 26:19; Dan. 12:2*; which for Christ to do, was as easy as to awake a man out of natural sleep. These words respecting Lazarus's sleeping and awaking, express both the omniscience and omnipotence of Christ: His omniscience, that He should know that Lazarus was dead, when at such a distance from Him; and His omnipotence, that He could raise him from the dead; and yet His great modesty to signify it in such covert language, though not difficult to be understood.

Verse 12. **Then said his disciples, Lord, if he sleep**, &c. Soundly, quietly, and comfortably, and takes rest in it:

he shall do well. Or *be saved* from the disease; he will be delivered from it; he will recover out of it; it is a sign the distemper is leaving him, and he is growing better, and will be restored to his health again. The Ethiopic version renders it by many words, *he will be well*, and *will awake*, and *will live*. Sound sleep is a sign of health. This they said to put off their Master from going into Judea, fearing the danger He would be exposed unto.

Verse 13. **Howbeit Jesus spake of his death**, &c. Under the figurative phrase of sleeping:

but they thought that he had spoken of taking of rest in sleep. In a literal and natural sense.

Verse 14. **Then said Jesus unto them plainly**, &c. Without a figure, when He perceived they did not understand Him, and yet it was a very easy and usual metaphor which He had made use of; but such was the present stupidity of their minds, that they did not take in His meaning: wherefore, without reproaching them with it, He said to them in so many words,

Lazarus is dead. The Persic version reads, *Lazarus is dead indeed*, as he really was.

---

[3]   Gloss in T. Hieros. Celaim in En Yaacob, fol. 4. 4.

Verse 15. **And I am glad for your sakes that I was not there**, &c. At Bethany, before he died, or when he died; because He might have been prevailed upon through the solicitations of His dear friends, Mary and Martha, and through tender affection to Lazarus, to have prevented his death, by rebuking the distemper, and restoring him to health, or to have raised him immediately as soon as he was dead; and in either case the miracle would not have been so illustrious, nor have been such a means of confirming the faith of His disciples, as now it would be:

to the intent ye may believe; more strongly, that He was the Son of God, and true Messiah:

nevertheless, let us go unto him. To Lazarus, to the grave where he lies: the Syriac version reads, *let us go there*; to Bethany, where he lived, and died, and now lay interred.

Verse 16. **Then said Thomas, which is called Didymus**, &c. The former was his Hebrew name, and the latter his Greek name, and both signify *a twin*; and perhaps he may be so called because he was one: the same said,

unto his fellow disciples; the other eleven; though the Ethiopic version reads, *to the next of the disciples*; as if he addressed himself only to one of them, to him that was nearest him:

Let us also go, that we may die with him. Either with Lazarus, as some think, or rather with Christ; for he, and the rest of the disciples, imagined that Christ, by returning to Judea, would be in great danger of losing His life; yea, by this expression they seem to be positive of it, that it was a matter out of question with them, that He would die, should He venture there again: and therefore Thomas stirs up his fellow disciples to go along with Him, and die all together; signifying, that they should have but little comfort when He was taken from them. But both Thomas, and the rest, were differently minded, when Christ was apprehended, for they all forsook Him and fled, and provided for their own safety, and left Him to die alone, *Matt. 26:56*.

Verse 17. **Then when Jesus came**, &c. The Alexandrian copy, and all the Oriental versions add, *to Bethany*; though it seems by what follows, that He was not come to the town itself, but near it; and it looks as if it was not far from Lazarus's grave; and it was usual to bury without the city; and here He had intelligence of his, Lazarus's, death, and how long he had been dead: for,

he found he had *lain* in the grave four days already. It is very likely that he died the same day that Mary and Martha sent to Christ to acquaint Him with his sickness, and the same day he was buried; for the Jews used to bury the same day a person died, and so they do now: and after Christ had this account, He stayed two days where He was, and on the third day, He proposed to His disciples to go into Judea; and very probably on that, or on the next day, which was the fourth, they set out and came to Bethany; see the note on *verse 39*.

Verse 18. **Now Bethany was nigh unto Jerusalem**, &c. Which was a reason why there were so many of the Jews come there to condole the two sisters upon the death of their brother; and by this means the following miracle became more known there: it was,

about fifteen furlongs off; that is, about two miles, for seven furlongs and a half made a Jewish mile, as appears from one of their canons,[4] which runs thus:

"They do not spread nets for doves, except it be distant from an habitable place, שלשים ריס, *thirty furlongs*;"

which the commentators say[5] are *four miles*: and still more expressly it is said[6] that,

"Between Jerusalem and Zuck (the place where the scape goat was had [*or* taken]), there were ten tents, and ninety furlongs, ומחצה לכל מיל שבעה, *seven and a half to every mile*."

Hence a furlong was called one-seventh and a half of a mile,[7] which was 266 cubits, and two thirds of one.

Verse 19. **And many of the Jews came to Martha and Mary**, &c. Or *to those that were about Martha and Mary*; in order to have access to them, they came to them, and to the rest of the family; though the phrase may design them only, as the Vulgate Latin, and all the Oriental versions read. These Jews, as appears from the context, *verses 18, 45, 46*, came from Jerusalem, and might be some of the principal inhabitants; and it may be concluded, that these persons—Lazarus, Martha, and Mary, were people of note and figure; and indeed all the accounts of them here, and elsewhere, show the same; see *Luke 10:38; John 12:1-3*. The end of their coming to them was,

to comfort them concerning their brother. By reason of his death, as was

---

[4] Mishna Bava Kama, c. 7. sect. 7.

[5] Maimonides Jarchi, & Bartenora in ibid.

[6] Mishna Yoma, c. 6. sect. 4.

[7] T. Bab. Bava Metzia, fol. 33. 1. Maimon. Hilch. Rotzeach, c. 13. sect. 6.

usual with the Jews to do, after the dead was buried; for they did not allow of it before. Hence that saying[8] of R. Simeon ben Eleazar,

"Do not comfort him (thy friend) in the time his dead lies before him."

The first office of this kind was done when they returned from the grave; for it is said,[9]

"When they return from the grave they make rows round about the mourner, לנחמו, *to comfort him*; and they make him to sit, and they stand, and there never were less than ten in a row."

It was an ancient custom for the mourners to stand in their place in a row, and all the people passed by, and every man as he came to the mourner *comforted him*, and passed on.[10] But besides these consolations, there were others administered at their own houses, which were usually done the first week, for it is said,[11]

"The mourner the first week does not go out of the door of his house; the second he goes out, but does not sit, or continue in his place; the third he continues in his place, but does not speak; the fourth, lo, he is as every other man. R. Judah says, There is no need to say, the first week he does not go out of the door of his house, for behold, all come to his house, לנחמו, *to comfort him*."

And is was on the third day, more particularly, on which these consolatory visits were paid:[12]

"on the first day he (the mourner) did not wear his phylacteries; on the second, he put them on; on the third day, others come *to comfort him*."

This rule the Jews here seem to have observed, since Lazarus had been dead four days; and they were come from Jerusalem hither to comfort his sisters on account of his death. The whole of this ceremony is thus related by Maimonides:[13]

"How do they comfort mourners? After they have buried the dead, the mourners gather together, and stand on the side of the grave; and all that accompany the dead stand round about them, one row within

---

[8] Pirke Abot, c. 4. sect. 18.

[9] Gloss in Cetubot, fol. 8. 2. & in Beracot, fol. 16. 2.

[10] Gloss in T. Bab. Sanhedrin, fol. 19. 1.

[11] T. Bab. Moed Katon, fol. 23. 1.

[12] Massech. Semachot, c. 6. fol. 14. 3.

[13] Hilch. Ebel, c. 13. sect. 1-4.

another: and there is no row less than ten; and the mourners are not of the number; the mourners stand on the left hand of the comforters; and all the comforters go to the mourners, one by one, and say to them, תנוחמו מן השמים, *may ye be comforted from heaven*: after that the mourner goes to his house, and every day of the seven days of mourning, men come *to comfort him*; whether new faces come, or do not, the mourner sits down at the head (or in the chief place), and no comforters may sit but upon the floor, as it is said, *Job 2:13, and they sat with him on the ground*: nor may they say any thing until the mourner has opened his mouth first, as it is said, *Job 2:13, and none spake a word unto him*: and it is written afterwards, *Job 3:1, so opened Job his mouth*, &c. and *Eliphaz answered, Job 4:1*, and when he nods with his head, the comforters may not sit with him any longer, that they may not trouble him more than is necessary. If a man dies, and there are no mourners to be comforted, ten worthy men go and sit in his place all the seven days of mourning; and the rest of the people gather to them; and if there are not ten fixed every day, ten of the rest of the people gather together, and sit in his place."

This business of comforting mourners was reckoned an act of great piety and mercy;[14] and these Jews here might come, not so much out of respect to the dead, or to his sisters, as because it was thought to be a meritorious act.

Verse 20. **Then Martha, as soon as she heard that Jesus was coming**, &c. Which she might hear of, either by a messenger sent by Christ to her, to acquaint her of it; or rather by some of the people of the town, who knew Him, and ran and told her of it; and she being an active person, and stirring about house, might receive the report unknown to her sister, as it seems she did; and as soon as she had the hint, without staying to communicate it to her sister,

went and met him; either through her great affection to Him, and eager desire of seeing Him; or to consult His safety, and let Him know what number of Jews were in their house, that He might consider whether it would be safe for Him to be at their house or not;

but Mary sat *still* in the house. Not out of disrespect to Jesus, or through want [*or* lack] of affection to Him, or through any indifference and sloth, but because she knew not that Jesus was coming; see *verses 28, 29*.

Verse 21. **Then said Martha unto Jesus**, &c. When she was come to Him,

---

[14] Maimonides in Mishna Peah, c. 1. sect. 1.

Lord, if thou hadst been here, my brother had not died. This speech expresses much faith, but with a mixture of weakness, as if the presence of Christ was necessary for the working a cure; whereas He could as well have restored her brother to health absent, as present, had it been His will, as He did the centurion's servant, and the nobleman's son of Capernaum.

Verse 22. **But I know, that even now**, &c. At this distance of time, though her brother had been in the grave four days:

whatsoever thou wilt ask of God, God will give *it* **thee**. Whether Martha had such a clear notion of the Deity of Christ, as yet, as she afterwards had, is not so certain: however, she was persuaded that He had great interest with God, and that whatever He desired of Him was granted to Him; and though she does not mention the resurrection of her brother, yet it seems to be what she had in view.

Verse 23. **Jesus saith unto her, Thy brother shall rise again**. Christ knew what she meant, and accordingly gave her an answer, and yet in such general terms, that she could not tell whether His meaning was, that he should rise now, or at the general resurrection.

Verse 24. **Martha saith unto him**, &c. Being desirous of knowing the sense and meaning of Christ, as well as to express her own faith;

I know that he shall rise again in the resurrection, at the last day. The Jews were divided about the doctrine of the resurrection: the Sadducees denied it, the Pharisees asserted it; and on this latter side was Martha: she believed there would be a resurrection of the dead; that this would be at the last day, or at the end of the world; and that her brother would rise at that general resurrection: wherefore, if Christ meant no more than that, this was what she always believed. The Syriac version renders it, *in the consolation* at *the last day*; and so the time of the resurrection is by the Jews called, *the days of consolation*.[15] And good reason there is for it in those who shall have part in the first resurrection, or come forth to the resurrection of life; their bodies will rise glorious, powerful, spiritual, and incorruptible, fashioned like to the glorious body of Christ; they will no more be attended with infirmities, disorders, and diseases; they will feel no more pain, nor die any more; being reunited to their souls, they will meet the Lord in the air, and in the judgment they will stand at His right hand; they will enter into His joy, and be for ever with Him; with their bodily eyes they will behold Christ, and see Him for themselves, and not another; they will meet their spiritual friends and

---

[15] Targum Jon. in Gen 1:21. & in Hos. 6:2.

acquaintance, and enjoy their company for ever; they will have uninterrupted communion with angels and saints, and with God—Father, Son, and Spirit; their consolation will be inconceivable and inexpressible.

Verse 25. **Jesus said unto her, I am the resurrection and the life**, &c. Signifying, that He was able of Himself to raise men from death to life, without asking it of His Father; and that He could do it now, as well as at the general resurrection; at which time Christ will be the efficient cause of it; and which will display both His omniscience and His omnipotence; as His resurrection is the earnest and pledge, and will be the model and exemplar of it. This is true of Christ, with regard to a spiritual resurrection from a death of sin to a life of grace; He is concerned both in the life itself, and in the resurrection to it: He is the meritorious and procuring cause of it; He died for His people, that they, being dead to sin, might live unto God, and unto righteousness. He is the author of it; He says unto them, when dead in sin, *live*; He speaks life into them: He commands it in them, and by His Spirit breathes into them the breath of spiritual life, and implants the principle of it in their souls; and He supports and maintains it by giving Himself to them as the bread of life to feed upon, and by supplying them with grace continually; yea, He Himself is their life; He lives in them, and their life is hid with Him. It is owing to His resurrection, that they are begotten again to a lively hope, or are quickened; that has a virtual influence upon it; and it is not only the cause, but the exemplar of it. Saints, as they are *planted together in the likeness of his death*, so *in the likeness of his resurrection* [*Rom. 6:5*]: to which may be added, that it is His voice in the Gospel, attended with an almighty power, which is the means of quickening them, which they hear, and so live; and it is His image that is enstamped upon them; and by His Spirit they are made to live, and to walk in newness of life;

he that believeth in me, though he were dead, yet shall he live: believers in Christ die as well as others, though death is not a penal evil to them; its curse is removed, its sting is taken away, being satisfied for by Christ, and so becomes a blessing and privilege to them, and is desirable by them; but though they die, they shall live again; their dust is under the peculiar care of Christ; and they shall rise by virtue of union to Him, and shall rise first, in the morning of the resurrection, and with peculiar privileges, or to the resurrection of life, and with the peculiar properties of incorruption— power, glory, and spirituality. So likewise such that have been dead in sin, and dead in law, under a sentence of condemnation, as all mankind are in Adam, and being in a natural and sinful estate, and as the chosen of God themselves are; yet being brought to believe in Christ, that is, to see the excellency and suitableness of Him as a Savior, and the necessity of salvation by Him; to go out of themselves to Him, disclaiming their own righteousness;

venture their souls upon Him, give up themselves to Him, trust in Him, and depend upon Him for eternal life and salvation; these live spiritually: they appear to have a principle of life in them; they breathe after spiritual things; they see the Son of God, and behold His glory; they handle the Word of life; they speak the language of Canaan, and walk by faith on Christ, as they have received Him; they live a life of sanctification and justification; they are manifestly in Christ, and have Him, an interest in Him, and so must have life; they live comfortably; they live by faith on Christ and His righteousness, and have communion with Him here, and expect to have, and shall have eternal life hereafter.

Verse 26. **And whosoever liveth and believeth in me**, &c.. Whoever will be found alive at Christ's second coming, and is a believer in Him,

shall never die. But shall be changed, and shall be for ever with Christ; and such as shall be raised to life by Him, shall never die any more, not even a bodily death, and much less an eternal one, or the second death: and though believers die a corporeal death as others do, yet their souls live, and live in happiness, while their bodies are under the power of death; nor shall they always continue so, but being raised, shall become immortal, and die no more. So living believers in Christ shall never die more a spiritual death; they are passed from death to life, and shall never return to death more; their spiritual life cannot be lost; grace in them is an immortal seed, a well of living water springing up into everlasting life: grace may be very low in its exercise, and may seem to be ready to die; they may be in lifeless frames, and without the comforts of a spiritual life, and be under the hidings of God's face, which is as death unto them, and may reckon themselves as free among the dead; yet the principle of life will never be extinct in them; nor shall they die the second death, which lies in an eternal separation from God, and in an everlasting sense of His wrath; that shall have no power on them, nor shall they be in the least hurt by it; for they are *ordained to eternal life [Acts 13:48]*, and have the promise of it; they are united to Christ, and their life is secured in Him; and He has redeemed them from death; and they have the *Spirit of life [Rom. 8:2]* dwelling in them, as the pledge and earnest of eternal glory [see *Eph. 1:13-14*].

Believest thou this? The whole of this concerning the power of Christ, and privilege of believers; every tittle of it is to be believed. And as with respect to a corporeal resurrection, so with regard to a spiritual one; that men by nature are dead in sins; that Christ is the author of the resurrection from such a state, to a spiritual life; that this life is only by Christ, and can never be lost: this is a doctrine to be believed; it is the doctrine of the Scriptures; it *is according to godliness [2 Tim. 6:3]*; it makes for the comfort of the people of God, and glorifies the divine perfections.

Verse 27. **She saith unto him, Yea, Lord**, &c. That is, she firmly believed all that He said concerning Himself, and the happiness of those that believed in Him: and for the confirmation of it adds,

I believe: or, *I have believed*, as the Vulgate Latin version renders it; that is, long ago, ever since she knew Him:

that thou art the Christ, the Son of God, which should come into the world. That He was the true Messiah, and the proper and natural Son of God, of the same nature with God, equal to Him, having the same perfections with Him; and who was long promised, much prophesied of, and greatly expected to come into the world; and was now come into the world by the assumption of human nature, to work out salvation for His people; and therefore, since she believed all this of Him, she must believe that He was able to raise the dead to life, and to secure those that believe in Him from dying eternally.

Verse 28. **And when she had so said**, &c. When she had expressed her faith in Christ in such terms, as the apostles themselves did, *Matt. 16:16; John 1:49* and *6:69*;

she went her way; from Christ, being ordered by Him to go to her sister Mary, and fetch her to Him:

and called Mary her sister secretly; either beckoned her to come to her, or whispered her in the ear privately, as Nonnus paraphrases it, that the Jews, who were enemies to Christ, might not hear:

saying, The Master is come; near the town; is not a great way off. She might use the phrase, *the master*, for greater privacy, that should she be overheard, it would not be known who she meant; and because it was a usual appellation by which Christ was called in that family, and by which He was well known; and was expressive of honor to Him, and subjection in them as His disciples:

and calleth for thee. To come to Him: Christ asked after her, desired to see her, and ordered her to come to Him; which was an instance of His respect for her.

Verse 29. **As soon as she heard *that***, &c. When she heard that Christ was come, and inquired for her, and wanted to see her:

she arose quickly, and came unto him. She having an equal affection for Him as her sister Martha, showed it by leaving her comforters at once, and by making the haste she did, to another and better comforter: both Martha and Mary, out of their great love to Christ, break through the rule for mourners mentioned in *verse 19*, of not going out of the door of the house the first week of mourning.

Verse 30. **Now Jesus was not yet come into the town**, &c. Of Bethany, but stayed without, being nearer to Lazarus's grave, which He intended to go to, in order to raise him to life, it being usual to bury the dead without the towns and cities; see the notes on *Matt. 8:28* **[9]**, and *Luke 7:12* **[48]**.

but was in that place where Martha met him. Here He stopped, and here He continued: the Persic version reads, *but was sitting in the same place*, &c. waiting for the coming of Mary along with Martha; judging this to be a more suitable place to converse together in, than their own house, which was thronged with Jews; and especially He chose it for the reason above given.

Verse 31. **The Jews then which were with her in the house**, &c. Who came from Jerusalem to visit this afflicted family, and continued in the house with them:

and comforted her; which was the end of their coming, *verse 19*. This they endeavored to do, though they did not succeed:

when they saw Mary, that she rose up hastily, and went out, followed her; they did not know what Martha whispered to her, but observed that she rose off her seat in great haste, and went out of the house at once; and therefore they went after to see where she went, and to persuade her to return;

saying, within themselves; *thinking*, as all the Oriental versions seem to read,

she goeth unto the grave to weep there. The Jews were wont to go to the graves on different accounts; one was to see whether the persons were dead or not: for so it is said,[16]
    "They go to the graves and visit until three days."
It happened that they visited one, and he lived five and twenty years, and after that died; and another was on a religious account: such went to the graves of the prophets, wise men, and righteous, and prostrated themselves upon them, to pray with weeping and supplication, and seek mercy for themselves, and for their brethren, expressing their faith in the resurrection.[17]

---

[16] Massech. Semachot, c. 8. fol. 15. 1.

[17] Cippi Heb. p. 3, 4.

Dr. Pocock[18] has given a large form of prayer used by them at such times, from Solomon bar Nathan, and is as follows:

"Let it be the will of the Lord our God, our Creator, our Holy One, the Holy One of Jacob, who hath created all the children of his covenant in judgment, and causes them to die in judgment, and will raise them again to the life of the world to come, who knows the number of them all; that he would hasten to awake our master and doctor, (such a one) that holy (or that righteous, or that wise doctor), whose body dwells in this sepulcher, whose bones rest in the midst of these stones; and that he would quicken him with that eternal life which no death follows; with that life which swallows up all death, and which wipes away all tears, and takes away all reproach; together with all those who are written unto life in Jerusalem; with the seven shepherds, and eight principal men, who are spoken of in *Mic. 5:5,* and give him a part with them that understand, and with them that justify many, who will be like the stars for ever and ever; and the whole residue of the people of the Lord, the house of Israel, who keep the covenant of our God, and do his pleasure, may the Lord our God shake all these out of their dust, and let their lot, and our lot, be in life, in everlasting life, that in it he may establish all, both great and small, according to what is written, *Psa. 72:16: there shall be an handful of corn,* &c. and confirm the assurance he gave by Isaiah the prophet, the son of Amos, *Isa. 26:19: thy dead men shall live,* &c. and as he promised to Daniel, a man of desires, *Dan. 12:13: but go thou thy way till the end be,* &c. and as he promised to all the congregations of Israel, by his servant Ezekiel, the son of Buzi the priest, *Ezek. 37:12: therefore prophesy and say to them,* &c. that the saints may rejoice with glory, and sing upon their beds, and that the righteous may rejoice, and exult before God, and be glad in his salvation, and say in that day, *behold this is our God, we have waited for him,* &c. *Isa. 25:9*; and we will bless the Lord from this time forth, and for ever, Hallelujah."

A shorter one, which is in their liturgies, and is used as they pass by the sepulchers of the Israelites, is this:

"Blessed art thou, O Lord our God, who has formed you in judgment, and has quickened you in judgment, and has fed you in judgment, and knows the number of all of you, and he will quicken you, and restore you; blessed art thou, O Lord, that quickens the dead."

But sometimes they went only to vent their grief, and lament the loss of their deceased friends, which the Jews imagined was the case of Mary. And such a custom as this is used by the Turks, whose women on Friday, which is their

---

[18] Misc. not. in port. Maimon. p. 224.

day of worship, go before sun rising to the graves of the deceased, which are without the city, where they mourn over the death of their friends, and sprinkle their monuments with water and flowers; and even such as are not at the funeral or interment of the dead, after some days, will go to the graves, and make their lamentations there, and inquire of the dead the reason of their departure; and, as it were, expostulate with them, and to their lamentations add oblations of loaves, cheeses, eggs, and flesh.[19] The Persians also visit the sepulchers of their principal *Imams*, or prelates;[20] and the Jews were wont to visit the graves of their great men, in honor to them; yea, the disciples of the wise men used to meet there to study the law, thereby showing respect, and doing honor to the deceased. It is said of Hezekiah, *2 Chron. 32:33: that all Judah, and the inhabitants of Jerusalem, did him honor at his death*; from whence say the Talmudists,[21] we learn, that they fixed a sitting or a school at his grave; the gloss is, a session (or school) of the wise men to study in the law there. So says Maimonides,[22] when a king dies they make a sitting at his grave seven days, as it is said, *2 Chron. 32:33*, they *did him honor at his death*; that is, they made a sitting at his grave.

Verse 32. **Then when Mary was come where Jesus was**, &c. Where Martha met Him, and where she left Him. Travelers tell us, that close by a well, about a stone's cast out of the town of Bethany, is shown the place where Martha met our Lord when He came to raise Lazarus, and where Mary, being called also, met Him; but this is not to be depended on, nor is it of any moment to know it. It is blessed meeting Christ any where: and where He is preached, and His ordinances administered, let it be in what place it will, there may the presence of Christ be expected; and it is an encouragement to go there where others have met with Him. Martha had been here before, and had had some conversation with Christ to her great satisfaction, and she goes and calls her sister, that she might enjoy the same: so souls that have met with Jesus under such a ministry, in such a place, invite others to go thither also; and often it is that this is a means, in providence, of finding Christ, and enjoying communion with Him;

and saw him, she fell down at his feet; in great respect to Him, and reverence of Him, worshiping Him as her Lord and God:

---

[19] Gejer. de Ebraeor. Luctu, c. 6. sect. 26.

[20] Reland. de Relig. Mohammed. l. 1. p. 72.

[21] T. Bab. Bava Kama, fol. 16. 2.

[22] Hilchot Ebel. c. 14. sect. 25.

saying unto him, Lord, if thou hadst been here, my brother had not died. Which were the same words Martha uttered upon her first meeting Jesus, *verse 21*; and it is very likely that they had often expressed themselves in such language one to another, saying to each other, if our Lord Jesus had been but here, our dear brother Lazarus would not have died.

Verse 33. **When Jesus therefore saw her weeping, &c.** At His feet, who, for sorrow and grief of heart, could say no more to Him; but having expressed these words, burst out into floods of tears:

and the Jews also weeping which came with her; either through sympathy with her, or hypocritically:

he groaned in the spirit; in His human soul; and which shows, that He had a real human soul, subject to passions, though sinless ones. The word signifies an inward motion of the mind, through indignation and anger; and it may be partly at the weakness of Mary's faith, and at her immoderate sorrow; and partly at the hypocrisy of the Jews: or else this inward groaning was through grief, sympathizing with Mary, and her friends, His human soul being touched with a fellow-feeling of their griefs and sorrows:

and was troubled; or *troubled Himself*; threw Himself into some forms and gestures of sorrow and mourning, as lifting up His eyes, wringing His hands, and changing the form of His countenance.

Verse 34. **And said, Where have ye laid him?** &c. This He might say as man, though He, as the omniscient God, knew where He was laid; and that it might appear there was no juggle [*or* deception] and contrivance between Him, and the relations of the deceased; and to raise some expectation of what He intended to do; and to draw the Jews thither, that they might be witnesses of the miracle he was about to work.

They say unto him; That is, Martha and Mary,

Lord, come and see. It being but a little way off.

Verse 35. **Jesus wept**. As He was going along to the grave, see *verse 28*; as He was meditating upon the state of His friend Lazarus, the distress his two sisters were in, and the greater damnation that would befall the Jews then present, who, notwithstanding the miracle, would not believe in Him. This shows Him to be truly and really man, subject to like passions, only without sin.

Verse 36. **Then said the Jews, Behold, how he loved him!** That is, Lazarus; for they supposed that these tears were shed purely on his account;

and by all circumstances they could not but judge, that they proceeded from a hearty and sincere affection to him; and it was amazing to them, that His love to him should be so strong, when He was no relation, only, as they imagined, a common friend. Christ's love to all His people, even when they are dead in trespasses and sins, is wonderful, and passes knowledge. And it is amazing indeed, if it be considered who the lover is, the eternal Son of God, who is God over all, blessed for ever, the Creator of all things, the King of kings, and Lord of lords: and also, who they are that are loved by Him; not only creatures, but sinful ones, exceeding mean and abject; the base things of this world, bankrupts, beggars, yea, comparable to the beasts that perish; who had nothing external, nor internal, to recommend them to Him, and engage His affections; yea, every thing to give Him an aversion to them, and render them odious in His sight, being enemies in their minds by wicked works, and children of wrath, as others. And likewise, if it be considered what He has done for these, in which His love appears to them: as before time, in espousing their persons, becoming their surety, engaging in covenant with His Father for them, agreeing to all He proposed, taking the care of their persons, and of all blessings and promises, grace and glory for them; and in time here on earth, by assuming their nature, fulfilling the law for them, dying in their room and stead, paying their debts, procuring all blessings for them—peace, pardon, righteousness, and eternal redemption; and now in heaven, by preparing a place for them, being their intercessor and advocate there, supplying their wants, frequently visiting them, and indulging them with communion with Himself, preserving them safe to His kingdom and glory, into which He will introduce them, presenting them to His Father with exceeding joy; all which are marvelous acts of love and grace: to which may be added, the consideration of the nature of His love, that it should be from everlasting, before these persons were born; that it should be a love of complacency and delight in them; that it should be free, and unmerited, without any reason, or motive on their part; that it should be distinguishing—that they, and not others, should be the objects of it; and that it should continue unchangeably the same, notwithstanding their manifold transgressions, and provocations; wherefore it may be justly said, *Behold, how He loved them!*

Verse 37. **And some of them said**, &c. Who were averse to Him, and bore Him a secret grudge, and were willing to put the worst construction on every action of His:

Could not this man, which opened the eyes of the blind; as it is said, at least pretended, that He did, *chapter 9:6-7*; for this must be understood as calling the miracle into question, and as a sneer upon it, and not as taking it for granted that so it was; and even supposing that, it is mentioned to His reproach, since if so, He might,

have caused that even this man should not have died? For either the above cure was a sham, or, if it was a real thing, He who did that could have prevented Lazarus's death; and if He could, and would not, where is His friendship? And what must be thought of all this show of affection to him? And what are these tears, but crocodile ones? But this reasoning, as specious as it may seem, was very fallacious; for He that cured the man born blind, could raise Lazarus from the dead, which He intended; and therefore did not prevent his death, that He might still give more joy to the family, bring more glory to God and Himself, and more shame and confusion to His enemies.

Verse 38. **Jesus therefore again groaning in himself**, &c. Not only through grief, just coming up to the grave where His dear friend lay, but through a holy anger and indignation at the malice and wickedness of the Jews;

cometh to the grave: of Lazarus.

It was a cave; either a natural one, such as were in rocks and mountains, of which sort there were many in Judea, and near Jerusalem, being a rocky and mountainous country; of which Josephus[23] makes mention; where thieves and robbers sheltered themselves, and could not easily be come at, and where persons in danger fled to for safety, and hid themselves; and the reason why such places were chosen to bury in, was because here the bodies were safe from beasts of prey: or this was an artificial cave made out of a rock, in [the] form of one, as was the tomb of Joseph of Arimathea; and it was the common custom of the Jews to make caves and bury in; yea, they were obliged to it by their traditions: thus says Maimonides,[24]

> "He that sells a place to his friend to make in it a grave, or that receives from his friend a place to make in it a grave, עושה מערה, *must make a cave*, and open in it eight graves, three on one side and three on another, and two over against the entrance *into the cave*: the measure of *the cave* is four cubits by six, and every grave is four cubits long, and six hands broad, and seven high; and there is a space between every grave, on the sides a cubit and a half, and between the two in the middle two cubits."

And elsewhere[25] he observes that,

> "they dig מערות, *caves* in the earth, and make a grave in the side *of the*

---

[23] Antiqu. l. 14. c. 15. sect. 5.

[24] Hilchot Mecira, c. 21. sect. 6.

[25] Hilchot Ebel, c. 4. sect. 4.

cave, and bury him (the dead) in it."

And such caves for burying the dead, were at and near the Mount of Olives; and near the same must be this cave where Lazarus was buried; for Bethany was not far from thence: so in the *Cippi Hebraici* we read,[26] that at the bottom of the Mount (of Olives) is a very great *cave*, said to be Haggai the prophet's; and in it are many caves.—And near it is the grave of Zachariah the prophet, in a *cave* shut up; and frequent mention is made there of caves in which persons were buried; see the note on *Matt. 23:29* **[34]**; perhaps the custom of burying in them might take its rise from the cave of Machpelah, which Abraham, their father, bought for a burying place for his dead. The sepulcher of Lazarus is pretended[27] to be shown to travelers to this day, over which is built a chapel of marble, very decent, and comely, and stands close by a church built in honor of Martha and Mary, the two sisters of Lazarus, in the place where their house stood; but certain it is, that the grave of Lazarus was out of the town:

and a stone lay upon it. Our version is not so accurate, nor so agreeable to the form of graves with the Jews, nor to this of Lazarus's; their graves were not as ours, dug in the earth and open above, so as to have a stone laid over them; for they often were, as this, caves in rocks, either natural, or hewn out of them by art; and there was a door at the side of them, by which there was an entrance into them; and at this door a stone was laid: it would be better rendered here, and *a stone was laid to it*; not *upon it*, for it had no opening above, but *to it*, at the side of it; and accordingly the Syriac and Persic versions read, *a stone was laid at the door of it*; and the Arabic version, *and there was a great stone at the door of it*, as there was at the door of Christ's sepulcher. In the Jewish sepulchers there was חצר, a *court*,[28] which was before the entrance into the cave; this was foursquare; it was six cubits long, and six broad; and here the bearers put down the corpse, and from hence it was carried into the cave, at which there was an entrance, sometimes called פי המערה, *the mouth of the cave*;[29] and sometimes, פתח הקבר, the *door of the grave*;[30] of its form, measure, and place, there is no express mention in the Jewish writings: it is thought to be about a cubit's breadth, and was on the

---

[26] Pg. 27, 29. Ed. Hottinger.

[27] Itinerar. Bunting. p. 364.

[28] Mishna Bava Bathra, c. 6. sect. 8.

[29] Mishna, ibid.

[30] Maimon. R. Samson, & Bartenora in Mishna Ohalot, c. 15. sect. 8.

side thereof, so that at it, the cave might be looked into; and at the mouth of it there was a stone put to stop it up, which was called גולל, from its being rolled there; though that with which the mouth of the cave was shut up, was not always a stone, nor made of stone; Maimonides[31] says, it was made of stone, or wood, or the like matter; and so in the Mishna[32] it is said,

"גולל לקבר, *the covering for a grave* (or that with which it is stopped up), if it be made of a piece of timber, whether it stands, or whether it inclines to the side, does not defile, but over against the door only;"
see the note on *Matt. 27:60* [40].

Verse 39. **Jesus said, Take ye away the stone**, &c. This was said either to the Jews, or rather to the servants that came along with Martha and Mary; and this He ordered, not to facilitate the resurrection, or merely in order to make way for Lazarus: He that could command Him to come forth, could have commanded away the stone; but He chose to have it removed this way, that the corpse might be seen, and even smelt; and that it might be manifest, there was no fallacy, nor any intrigue between Him and the sisters of the deceased in this matter. This order was contrary to a rule of the Jews, which forbid the opening of a grave after it was stopped up;[33] but a greater than the fathers of the traditions was here, even He who has the keys of hell, or the grave, and can open, or order it to be opened, when He pleases:

Martha, the sister of him that was dead: that is, of Lazarus, as the Persic version expresses it, calling him, *Gazarus,*

saith unto him, Lord, by this time he stinketh; or smells; not that she perceived this upon their moving the stone, but she concluded it from the time he had been dead, and had lain in the grave, in which dead bodies usually putrefy and smell. Whether she said this out of respect to her brother, being unwilling he should be exposed to the view of persons in such a state of corruption, she knew he must now be; or whether out of respect to Christ, lest He should be disordered with the offensive smell, is not certain. However, it seems as if she had no notion that Christ was about to raise her brother from the dead; and that the stone was commanded to be removed for that purpose, not merely for a sight of the dead, but that the dead might be seen to come forth alive: she imagined that Christ only wanted to have the stone removed, that He might have a sight of His deceased friend, which she thought would

---

[31] In Mishna Ohalot, c. 2. sect. 4.

[32] Ibid. c. 15, sect. 8.

[33] Apud Buxtorf Lex. Rab. col. 437.

be very disagreeable and nauseous; so soon had she forgot what Christ had said to her, and lost that little exercise she had of faith and hope, with respect to the resurrection of her brother. Frames of soul, and acts of grace, are very changeable, and uncertain things; and especially when carnal reasoning is indulged;

for he hath been *dead* four days. He had been so long in the grave, *verse 17*. The word *dead* is not in the text; he might have been dead longer; though the Jews usually buried on the same day a person died: however, the sense is here, he had been so long in the grave; and so the Persic version renders it, *for it is the fourth day that he has been in the grave*; in the original text it is, *he is one of four days*; so many days he had been in the house appointed for all living; so long he had been removed from the sight of men, and had been in another world, and had begun another era, and four days had passed in it; he was so many days old according to that: so that his countenance was changed, he was not fit to be seen, nor approached unto; nor was there any hope of his returning to life. The Jews[34] say that,

> "for three days the soul goes to the grave, thinking the body may return; but when it sees the figure of the face changed, it goes away, and leaves it, as it is said, *Job 14:22*."

So of Jonah's being three days and three nights in the whale's belly, they say,[35]

> "these are the three days a man is in the grave, and his bowels burst; and after three days that defilement is turned upon his face."

Hence, they do not allow any one to bear witness of one that is dead or killed, that he is such a one, after three days, because then his countenance is changed,[36] and he cannot be well known.

Verse 40. **Jesus saith unto her, Said I not unto thee**, &c. Not in so many words, but what might be concluded from what He said; yea, the following express words might be delivered by Christ, in His conversation with Martha, though they are not before recorded by the evangelist:

that, if thou wouldest believe, thou shouldest see the glory of God? A glorious work of God, wherein the glory of His power and goodness would be displayed, and the Son of God be glorified; or she should see such a miracle

---

[34] Bereshit Rabba, sect. 100. fol. 88. 2. & T. Hieros. Moed Katon, fol. 82. 2.

[35] Zohar in Exod. fol. 78. 2.

[36] Mishna Yebamot, c. 16. sect. 3. & Maimonides Jarchi, & Bartenora in ibid. & Maimon. Hilchot Gerushim, c. 13. sect. 21. T. Bab. Yebamot, fol. 120. 1. & Gloss. in ibid.

wrought, which should engage her to glorify God; and on account of which, she would see just reason to do it, and would be concerned in it: and when it would appear that the sickness and death of her brother, which had given her and her sister so much distress and uneasiness, were for the glory of God, and the honor of Christ; see *verse 4*. Moreover, to *see the glory of God*, is to see Christ, who is the brightness of His Father's glory [see *Heb. 1:3*]; and though she had a sight of Him now, and before this time, with her bodily eyes, and also with the eyes of her understanding, and knew that He was the Son of God, and the true Messiah; yet it is suggested, that upon a fresh and strong exercise of faith on Christ, with respect to the resurrection of her brother, and by means of that, she should have a clearer view of His glory, as the only begotten of the Father; for as He was declared to be the Son of God, by His own resurrection from the dead afterwards, so He was more fully manifested to be that glorious and divine person, by His raising others from the dead, than by any other miracle; and to be indulged with such a sight of Him, is a very high favor; see *Psa. 63:2*; and such who have their faith most in exercise, see much of the glory of God, both in the face of Christ, and in His providences, and the performance of His promises.

Verse 41. **Then they took away the stone**, &c. *From the door of the sepulcher*, as the Arabic version adds;

from the place **where the dead was laid**. This clause is left out in the Alexandrian copy, and in the Vulgate Latin, and all the Oriental versions:

And Jesus lifted up his eyes; to heaven; this is a praying gesture, as in *chapter 17:1*,

and said, Father, I thank thee that thou hast heard me. Which cannot refer to the resurrection of Lazarus from the dead, or to any assistance given Him in performing that miracle, because that as yet was not done; and when it was done, was done by His own power, as all the circumstances of it show; but it relates to every thing in which He had before heard Him, and was a foundation for Him, as man, to believe He still would, in whatever was to come; and particularly to the present opportunity of showing His power in so remarkable a manner, and before so many witnesses.

Verse 42. **And I knew that thou hearest me always**, &c. Which was not only a support to the faith of Christ, as man, but is also to His people, whose advocate, intercessor, and mediator He is:

but because of the people which stand by, I said *it*; that He was heard, and always heard by God; and, therefore must have great interest in His affection, and knowledge of His will; yea, their wills must be the same:

377

that they may believe that thou hast sent me. For if He had not sent Him, He would never have heard Him in any thing, and much less in every thing; wherefore this was a full proof, and clear evidence of His divine mission.

Verse 43. **And when he had thus spoken**, &c. To God His Father, in the presence and hearing of the people;

he cried with a loud voice; not on account of the dead, but for the sake of those around Him, that all might hear and observe; and chiefly to show His majesty, power and authority, and that what He did was open and above board, and not done by any secret, superstitious, and magical whisper; and as an emblem of the voice and power of His Gospel in quickening dead sinners, and of the voice of the archangel and trumpet of God, at the general resurrection;

Lazarus come forth. He calls him by his name, not only as being His friend, and known by Him, but to distinguish him from any other corpse that might lie interred in the same cave; and He bids him come forth out of the cave, he being quickened and raised immediately by the power which went forth from Christ as soon as ever He lifted up His voice; which showed Him to be truly and properly God, and to have an absolute dominion over death and the grave.

Verse 44. **And he that was dead came forth**, &c. That is, he who had been dead, being now made alive, and raised up, and set on his feet, came out of the cave:

bound hand and foot with grave clothes; not that his hands were bound together, and much less his hands and feet together, with any bands or lists of cloth; but his whole body, as Nonnus expresses it, was bound with grave clothes from head to foot, according to the manner of the eastern countries— Jews, Egyptians, and others, who used to wrap up their dead in many folds of linen cloth, as infants are wrapped in swaddling bands: and their manner was to let down their arms and hands close by their sides, and wind up all together from head to foot: so that there was another miracle besides that of raising him from the dead; that in such a situation, in which he could have no natural use of his hands and feet, he should rise up, stand on his feet, walk, and come forth thus bound, out of the cave:

and his face was bound about with a napkin. The use of which was not only to tie up the chin and jaws, but to hide the grim and ghastly looks of a dead corpse; and one of the same price and value was used by rich and poor: for it is said,[37]

> "The wise men introduced a custom of using סודר, *a napkin* (the very word here used, which Nonnus says is Syriac), of the same value, not exceeding a penny, that he might not be ashamed who had not one so good as another; and they cover the faces of the dead, that they might not shame the poor, whose faces were black with famine."

For it seems,[38]

> "formerly they used to uncover the faces of the rich, and cover the faces of the poor, because their faces were black through want, and the poor were ashamed; wherefore they ordered, that they should cover the faces of all, for the honor of the poor."

Jesus saith unto them; to the servants that stood by:

Loose him, and let him go. Unwind the linen rolls about him, and set his hands and feet at liberty, and let him go to his own house.

Verse 45. **Then many of the Jews which came to Mary**, &c. To her house, to comfort her, and that came along with her to the grave:

and had seen the things which Jesus did; in raising the dead body of Lazarus, and causing him to walk, though bound in grave clothes:

believed on him. That He was the true Messiah: such an effect the miracle had on them; so that it was a happy day for them, that they came from Jerusalem to Bethany to pay this visit.

Verse 46. **But some of them went their ways to the Pharisees**, &c. At Jerusalem, who were members of the Sanhedrin; so far were some of them from receiving any advantage by this miracle, that they were the more hardened, and filled with malice and envy to Christ, and made the best of their way to acquaint His most inveterate enemies:

and told them what things Jesus had done. At Bethany; not to soften their minds, and bring them to entertain a good opinion of Him, but to irritate them, and put them upon schemes to destroy Him; thus even miracles, as well as the doctrines of the Gospel, are to some *the savor of death unto death*, while to others *the savor of life unto life* [*2 Cor. 2:16*].

---

[37] Maimon. Hilchot Ebel, c. 4. sect. 1.

[38] T. Bab. Moed Katon, fol. 27. 1.

Verse 47. **Then gathered the chief priests and the Pharisees a council**, &c. They convened the Sanhedrin, the great council of the nation together, of which they were some of the principal members:

and said, What do we? that is, Why is nothing done? Why are we so dilatory? Why do we sit still, and do nothing? or what is to be done? This now lies before us, this is to be considered and deliberated on:

for this man doeth many miracles. This is owned, and could not be denied by them; and should have been a reason why they should have acknowledged Him to have been the Messiah, and embraced Him; whereas they used it as a reason, why they should think of, and concert some measures, to hinder and put a stop to the belief of Him as such.

Verse 48. **If we let him thus alone**, &c. Going about from place to place, teaching the people, and doing such miracles:

all *men* will believe on him; the whole nation will receive Him as the Messiah, and proclaim Him their king, and yield a cheerful obedience to all His commands:

and the Romans shall come; against us, with their powerful armies; interpreting the setting Him up as Messiah, to be an instance of rebellion against Caesar, and his government:

and take away both our place and nation. That is, will destroy the temple, their holy place, the place of their religion and worship; and their city, the place of their habitation, and lay waste their country; and take away from them that little share of power and government they had, and strip them both of their civil and religious privileges. The Persic version renders it, *they will take away our place, and make a decree against our religion.*

Verse 49. **And one of them, *named* Caiaphas**, &c. See the notes on *Matt. 26:3* **[35]**; *Luke 3:2* **[47]**; *John 18:13.*

being the high priest that same year; the high priesthood originally was not annual, but for life; but towards the close of the second temple, it came into the hands of the king, to appoint who would to be high priest;[39] and it became venal; it was purchased with money; insomuch that they changed the priesthood once a twelvemonth, and every year a new high priest was made.[40] Now this man being in such a high office, and a man of no conscience, and of

---

[39] Mishna Yebamot, c. 6. sect. 4.

[40] T. Bab. Yoma, fol. 8. 2. Juchasin, fol. 139. 1.

bad principles, being a Sadducee, as seems from *Acts 4:6* and *5:17*, who denied the resurrection of the dead, and was unconcerned about a future state; and having no restraint upon him, in a bold, haughty, and blustering manner,

said unto them, Ye know nothing at all; ye are a parcel of ignorant and stupid creatures, mere fools and idiots, to sit disputing and arguing, *pro* and *con*, about such a fellow as this; what is to be done is obvious enough, and that is, to take away this man's life, without any more ado; it matters not what He is, nor what He does; these are things that are not to be considered, they are out of the question: would you save the nation, destroy the man; things are come to this crisis, that either His life must go, or the nation perish; and which is most expedient, requires no time to debate about.

Verse 50. **Nor consider that it is expedient for us**, &c. Priests, Levites, Pharisees, the Sanhedrin, and ecclesiastical rulers of the people; who, as Caiaphas apprehended, must suffer in their characters and revenues, must quit their honorable and gainful posts and places, if Jesus went on and succeeded at this rate: wherefore it was most expedient and advantageous for them, which was the main thing to be considered in such a council, so he thought it was,

that one man should die for the people, and that the whole nation perish not. He proceeded entirely upon this political principle, that a public good ought to be preferred to a private one; that it was no matter what the man was, whether innocent or not; common prudence, and the public safety of the nation, required Him to fall a sacrifice, rather than that the Romans should be exasperated and provoked to such a degree, as to threaten the utter ruin and destruction of the whole nation.

Verse 51. **And this spake he not of himself**, &c. Not of his own devising and dictating, but by the Spirit of God; as a wicked man sometimes may, and as Balaam did; the Spirit of God dictated the words unto him, and put them into his mouth; nor did he use them in the sense, in which the Holy Ghost designed them:

but being high priest that year; by his office he was the oracle of God, and was so esteemed by the people, and therefore a proper person to be made use of in this way; and especially being high priest *that year*, in which the priesthood was to be changed, and vision and prophecy to be sealed up:

he prophesied; though he did not know he did, as did Pharaoh, *Ex. 10:28*, and the people of the Jews, *Matt. 27:25*;

that Jesus should die for that nation; these words, with what follows in the next verse, are the words of the evangelist, interpreting the prophecy of

Caiaphas, according to the sense of the Holy Ghost, that Jesus should die, which was contrary to a notion the Jews had imbibed, concerning the Messiah; see *chapter 12:34*. But Jesus the true Messiah must die; this was determined in the counsel of God, agreed to by Christ in the covenant of grace, foretold by the prophets from the beginning of the world, typified by sacrifices and other things under the former dispensation, predicted by Christ Himself, and accordingly came to pass; and upon the above accounts was necessary, as well as for the salvation of His people, who otherwise must have perished; and yet was free and voluntary in Him, and a strong expression, and a demonstrative proof of His love to them. And not only this prophecy declared that Jesus should die, but that He should die for that nation, for the nation of the Jews: not for every individual in it, for all of them were not saved by Him; some received Him not; they rejected Him as the Messiah, Savior, and Redeemer, and died in their sins; but for all the elect of God among them, the sheep of the house of Israel, to whom He was sent, and whom He came to seek and save; and whom He blessed, by turning them away from their iniquities, and by taking away their iniquities from them. And moreover, this prophecy suggests, that Jesus was to die, not merely as a martyr, to confirm with His blood the doctrine He preached, nor only as an example of courage, meekness, patience, and love; but for, or in the room and stead of His people, as their surety; giving His life a ransom, and Himself a sacrifice to the justice of God for them; thereby fulfilling the law and satisfying it, and appeasing the wrath of God on their account.

Verse 52. **And not for that nation only**, &c. For though Christ, as prophet, was sent to the Jews only, and was the minister of the circumcision, yet as a priest He did not die for them only, but for the Gentiles also; even for the whole mystical Israel of God, all the world over, whether among Jews or Gentiles; see *1 John 2:2*;

but that also he should gather together in one the children of God that were scattered abroad. By which may be meant, not only the elect of God among the Jews, who were scattered amidst the nations of the world, for whom Christ died, and to whom the Gospel was in the first place sent, and who were gathered together into a Gospel church state; see *John 7:35; 1 Pet. 1:1-2; James 1:1*; but rather, the elect of God among the Gentiles, called *the children of God*, in opposition to a notion of the Jews, who took this character to themselves, on account of their national adoption, and denied it to the Gentiles, reckoning them no other than as dogs; and because they were the children of God by special adoption, in divine predestination, and in the covenant of grace; and were so considered, when given to Christ, who looked upon them as in this relation, when He assumed their nature, and died in their room and stead; and not merely because they would hereafter appear to be the children of God in regeneration, and by faith in Christ Jesus, and have the witnessings of the Spirit that they were so; and much less because they had a fitness and disposition to be the children of God, since they were by nature as others, *children of wrath* [*Eph. 2:3*]. And these are said to be *scattered abroad*, both from God, as they were by the fall, and by their own transgressions; which separated between God and them, and set them at a distance from Him; for in their nature head, and nature state, they are afar off from Him, and from one another; which may regard not only distance of place, being scattered about in the several parts of the world, but their disagreement in mind and judgment, in religion and manners; every one pursuing his own way, going astray like lost sheep: now Christ died for them, in order to bring them nigh to God, to the one true and living God; and to gather them together under one head, Himself, their common head; by whom they were represented in His crucifixion, burial, and resurrection; and to make them one body, and bring them into one fold, into one church state here, and at last to one place, to heaven, there to be for ever with Him; and so the Persic version renders it, *that he might gather them into one place*: and in this, the red heifer was a type of Christ; whose blood was sprinkled directly before the tabernacle of the congregation, and without the camp; and which was done, as a Jewish writer says,[41]

> "to call to mind the design of the heifer, which was to bring המרוחקים, *those that were afar off*, from the camp of the Shekinah, to be near unto it."

Verse 53. **Then from that day forth**, &c. Caiaphas's reasoning appeared so good, and his advice so agreeable, that it was at once, and generally assented to, except by one or two, as Nicodemus, and Joseph of Arimathea; that ever after this,

they took counsel together; at certain times, and that very often, and agreed in their counsel,

for to put him to death. This they resolved upon, before there was any legal process, before any crime was charged upon Him, or any proof given, or He was heard what He had to say for Himself; so highly approved of was Caiaphas's motion, to put Him to death, right or wrong, whether He was innocent or not; that they had nothing to do, but to consult of ways and means of getting Him into their hands, and of taking away His life in a manner, as would be most for their own credit among the people, and to His shame and disgrace, and at the most proper and suitable time.

---

[41] Abarbinel in Lev. 19:3, 4.

Verse 54. **Jesus therefore**, &c. Knowing the resolution the Sanhedrin had taken to put Him to death, and the schemes they were forming to apprehend Him:

walked no more openly among the Jews; at, or near Jerusalem; He did not teach in their streets, nor work miracles, nor appear in public company:

but went thence, from Bethany:

unto a country near to the wilderness: whether this was the wilderness of Judea, where John came preaching, and near to which our Lord was before He came to Bethany, or the wilderness of Bethaven, *Josh. 18:12*, is not certain:

into a city called Ephraim; the Vulgate Latin, Syriac, Arabic, and Persic versions, call it Ephrem, and so some copies; it seems to be the same with the Ephraim of the Mishnaic and Talmudic doctors; concerning which they say,[42]

> "Micmas and Mezonicha are the first for fine flour, and the next to them is Ephraim in the valley."

For it seems there were two Ephraims, one in the valley, and another in the mount.[43] It was a place very fruitful for wheat; hence that saying of Jannes and Jambres, the magicians of Egypt, to Moses:[44]

> "Do you bring straw to Ephraim?"

which was a proverbial expression, the same with ours of carrying coals to Newcastle: they seeing Moses do signs and wonders, supposed he did them by enchantment; and the sense of their proverb is, Do you bring enchantments into Egypt, where there are so many already? This Ephraim, the Jews say,[45] is the same with that in *2 Chron. 13:19*; and as there Bethel is mentioned with it, it seems to have been in the tribe of Benjamin: and it may be observed, that Josephus[46] speaks of an Ephraim, along with Bethel likewise; so that they all seem to mean the same place; and according to the same writer, it was but a little city, and it may be an obscure one, for which reason Christ withdrew to

---

[42] Mishna Menachot, c. 8. sect. 1.

[43] Bartenora in ibid.

[44] T. Bab. Menachot, fol. 85. 1. Gloss. in ibid. Tzeror Hammor, fol. 170. 2. Bereshit Rabba, sect. 86. fol. 75. 4.

[45] Yom. Tob. in Mishna Menachot, c. 8. sect. 1. & Gloss. in T. Bab. Menachot, fol. 83. 2.

[46] De Bello Jud. l. 4. c. 9. sect. 9.

it. Epiphanius[47] makes mention of the wilderness of Bethel and Ephraim, through which he traveled, accompanied by a Jew, as he came up from Jericho to the hill country; and is very likely the same wilderness which is here spoken of; and by some called *Quarentana*, and placed by the river Chereth, in the tribe of Benjamin, northeast of Jerusalem; and the same writer elsewhere calls[48] Ephraim, the city of the wilderness. According to Jerome,[49] it was twenty miles from Ælia, or Jerusalem; though according to Eusebius, it was but eight miles, which is thought to be the truest account; and by them both is said to be a very large village, and in which they may not differ from Josephus; for it might be a large village, and yet a little city. Jerome[50] takes notice of a place called Aphra, in the tribe of Benjamin, which he says at that time was called the village Effrem, and was five miles from Bethel eastward; and of another called Aphraim, a city in the tribe of Issachar, which in his time went by the name of the village Affarea, six miles from the legion, northward; the former agrees best with this Ephraim:

and there continued with his disciples. Spending His time in private conversation with them, teaching and instructing them in things concerning the kingdom of God, His time with them being now but short.

Verse 55. **And the Jews' passover was nigh at hand**, &c. Which was the fourth passover from Christ's entrance on His public ministry, and the last He ate with His disciples; when He, by being sacrificed for His people, put an end to that, and all other ceremonial observances:

and many went out of the country up to Jerusalem before the passover: not only from the country where Ephraim was, but from all other countries in Judea and Galilee: all the males were obliged to go up to Jerusalem at the time of the passover, where it was only kept; but many went before that time, for the reason following:

to purify themselves. We read in *2 Chron. 30:18*, of many that had not cleansed themselves, and yet ate the passover; for whom Hezekiah prayed, that they might be pardoned, which shows that they had done amiss: upon which place, Jarchi has this observation, that,

"Judah (the men of Judah) were all clean, because they were near to

---

[47] Adv. Haeres. l. 1. Tom. II. Haeres. 30.

[48] Ibid. Haeres. 29.

[49] De locis Hebraicis, fol. 91. A.

[50] Ibid. fol. 88. H. I.

Jerusalem, and could purify and sanctify themselves, and return to Jerusalem; but many of Ephraim, and Manasseh, and Issachar, and Zebulon, could not do so."

And this seems to be the case of these people, they were country people, that lived at a distance, and not having purified themselves from several uncleannesses, came up before the time, that they might cleanse themselves, and be ready at the time. In several cases purification was required; as in women after lying-in [that is, after giving birth], menstruous and profluvious persons, and such that had touched a dead body, or any creeping thing, and in other cases; and which by reason of distance, might be neglected; wherefore it was necessary they should come up before the time of the passover, to fit themselves for it. The rule about defiled persons eating the passover, is this:[51]

"If the congregation is polluted, or the greatest part of it, or the priests are unclean, and the congregation pure, it is kept in uncleanness; but if the lesser part of the congregation is defiled, the pure keep the first passover, and the unclean the second."

This, their commentators say,[52] is to be understood of uncleanness by touching the dead, which required seven days of purification; and it is very probable that this was the case of these persons, since it was about so many days before the passover, that they came up; see *chapter 12:1*. The account Maimonides[53] gives of this matter, is this:

"Who is a defiled person, that is put off to the second passover? Every one who cannot eat the passover on the night of the fifteenth of Nisan, because of his uncleanness; as profluvious men and women, menstruous and lying-in women [that is, new mothers], and the husbands of menstruous women; but he that toucheth the dead carcass of a beast, or a creeping thing, and the like, on the fourteenth, lo, he dips, and they slay for him (the passover) after he has dipped; and in the evening, when his sun is set, he eats the passover; he that is defiled by touching the dead, whose seventh day happens to be on the fourteenth, though he dips and is sprinkled on, and lo, he is fit to eat the holy things at evening, yet they do not kill for him, but he is put off to the second passover; as it is said, *Num. 9:6*: *And there were certain men who were defiled by the dead body of a man, that they could not keep the passover on that day*; by tradition it is learned, that it was their

---

[51] Mishna Pesachim, c. 7. sect. 6. Vid. Maimon. Korban Pesach. c. 7. sect. 1-6. & Biah Hamikdash, c. 4. sect. 10-18.

[52] Maimon. & Bartenora in Mishna, ibid.

[53] Hilchot Korban Pesach. c. 6. sect. 1-3.

seventh day, and therefore they asked if it should be killed for them, and they should eat at evening? And it was declared to them, that they should not kill for them: of what is this to be understood? When he is polluted with a defilement by the dead, which Nazarites shave for; but if he is polluted with other defilements by the dead, which the Nazarites do not shave for, they kill for him on his seventh day, after he has dipped, and is sprinkled upon; and when his sun is set, he eats his passover; a profluvious person, who sees two appearances, and reckons seven days, and dips on the seventh, they kill for him, and he eats at evening.—They do not kill for a menstruous woman on her seventh day, for lo, she does not dip till the eighth night, and she is not fit to eat holy things until the ninth night."

These, with many other cases there instanced, may serve to illustrate this passage.

Verse 56. **Then sought they for Jesus**, &c. That is, the country people; some on one account, and some on another; some out of curiosity to see His person, others to see His miracles, and others to hear His doctrine; and some, it may be, to take Him, and deliver Him up to the Sanhedrin, who had issued out a proclamation to that purpose, and doubtless offered a reward:

and spake among themselves, as they stood in the temple; whither they came to purify themselves, according to the law of the sanctuary:

What think ye, that he will not come to the feast? It was a matter of dispute with them, whether Christ would come or not, to the feast; some might be of opinion that He would not, at least they very much questioned it, since the Sanhedrin had published such an order for the discovery of Him; and since upon it He was gone from Bethany, farther into the country; though others might be differently minded, and believe He would come, since all the males of Israel were obliged to appear at that feast, and it was His duty; and they could not persuade themselves that He would neglect His duty, for fear of the Jews.

Verse 57. **Now both the chief priests and the Pharisees**, &c. Who were of the Sanhedrin:

had given a commandment; or published an edict, a decree of the senate:

that, if any man knew where he were, he should show *it*, **that they might take him**. And this made it a doubtful point with some, whether He would come to the feast or not; and was the reason why others sought for Him, and inquired after Him, that they might discover Him to the chief priests and Pharisees, and have the promised reward.

CHAPTER 12

Verse 1. **Then Jesus, six days before the passover**, &c. Or *before the six days of the passover*; not as designing the days of that feast, for they were seven; but as reckoning so many days back from it, that is, before the sixth day from the ensuing passover: if there were six complete days between this and the passover, as this way of speaking seems to imply, then this must be the day before the Jewish sabbath; and this is more likely, than that Christ should travel on the sabbath day. But if this was the sixth day before it, it was their sabbath day, and so at the going out of it in the evening, a supper was made for Him, which with the Jews on that night, was a plentiful one; for they remembered the sabbath in its going out, as well as in its coming in,[1] and this was to prevent grief at the going out of it. So some days before the passover, the lamb was separated from the flock, and kept up till the fourteenth day, *Ex. 12:3, 6;* particularly it may be observed, that seven days before the day of atonement, the high priest was separated from his own house, and had [*or* taken] to the chamber Palhedrin;[2] and much such a space of time there was, between the day of the great atonement by Christ, and His unction by Mary; which is said to be against [*or* in preparation of] the day of His burial, which being the same day with His sufferings, was the great day of atonement: at this time Jesus,

came to Bethany, where Lazarus was which had been dead; the last clause is left out in the Syriac, Persic, and Ethiopic versions:

whom he raised from the dead. That is, *Jesus*, as the Alexandrian copy, the Vulgate Latin, and all the Oriental versions express; and the Ethiopic version adds, *in Bethany*. This was the town of Lazarus; here he lived, and here he died, and here he was raised from the dead; and here he continued and dwelt, after his resurrection; and hither Christ came to see him, and the rest of the family, though He knew He exposed Himself to danger in so doing.

---

[1] Maimon. Hilchot Sabbat. c. 29. sect. 1. 11, 12, 29.

[2] Mishna Yoma, c. 1. sect. 1.

Verse 2. **There they made him a supper**, &c. At Bethany, in the house of Lazarus, Martha, and Mary; by whose order, and at whose charge it was prepared for Him; and not in the house of Simon the leper, which was four days after this, *Matt. 26:2,6*;

and Martha served; who was always a busy, active, and stirring woman; and this she did, to testify her love to Christ, and great respect for Him; otherwise, as she was a person of substance, she had servants enough to wait at table:

but Lazarus was one of them that sat at the table with him. And ate, and drank, and conversed; by which it appeared, that he was really risen from the dead, and was in a good state of health.

Verse 3. **Then took Mary a pound of ointment of spikenard, very costly**, &c. Worth three hundred pence, according to Judas's estimation of it. This Mary, was the other sister of Lazarus; see the notes on *Matt. 26:7* **[36]** and *Mark 14:3* **[44]**, concerning the nature and value of this ointment:

and anointed the feet of Jesus; as He lay upon the bed or couch, at supper:

and wiped his feet with her hair; see the note on *Luke 7:38* **[50]**.

And the house was filled with the odor of the ointment. See *Song of Sol. 1:3,12*. Ointment of spikenard was very odoriferous: this may be an emblem of the sweet savor of Christ, in the ministration of the Gospel throughout the whole world.

Verse 4. **Then saith one of his disciples**, &c. Who had no true love for his master, was a hypocrite, and a covetous person:

Judas Iscariot; so called, to distinguish him from another Judas, an apostle; see the note on *Matt.10:4* **[13]**.

Simon's *son*; this is omitted in the Vulgate Latin, Syriac, Persic, and Ethiopic versions; see the note on *chapter 13:2*;

which should betray him; and so he did; this was predetermined by God, foretold in prophecy, and foreknown by Christ; and is observed here, to show the temper and character of the man.

Verse 5. **Why was not this ointment sold for three hundred pence**, &c. Meaning Roman pence, one of which is, of the value of our money, seven-pence halfpenny; so that three hundred pence amount to nine pounds seven shillings and six-pence:

and given to the poor? This was his pretense, and with which he covered himself; his uneasiness was, because it was not sold, and the money put into his hands, as appears by what follows.

Verse 6. **This he said, not that he cared for the poor**, &c. He had no affection for them, and was unconcerned about them, and took no care of them to feed and clothe them; he was no ways solicitous for their support, refreshment, and more comfortable living:

but because he was a thief; to his master, and purloined the money he was intrusted with by Him, and put it to his own use:

and had the bag, and bare what was put therein. The word rendered a *bag*, is adopted by the Rabbinical Jews into their language; and is sometimes read *gloskema*, and at other times *dloskema*, and is used by them for different things; sometimes[3] for a bier, or coffin, in which the dead was buried, which sense can have no place here; sometimes for a chest, or coffer;[4] and so the Septuagint use the Greek word in *2 Chron. 24:8,10,11*, for the chest into which the people put their collection; and it may be so interpreted here, and so Nonnus renders it; it may signify the chest or coffer which Judas had the care of, the keys of which were in his hands, and whatever was to be put into it, he bore, or carried thither: and it is also used by the Jewish writers, for a purse;[5] it is asked,

"what is *dloskema?* Says Rabbah bar Samuel, טליקא דסבי, *the purse of old men*;"

or such as ancient men use; and this is the signification of it here. It may be the same with the *Loculi* of the Romans, and so the Vulgate Latin renders it here; which were different from a chest, or coffer, being moveable, and to be carried about, and which were carried by servants, as well as the purse.[6] Judas had the purse, into which was put whatsoever was ministered to Christ, for the common supply of Him and His disciples, and for the relief of the poor.

---

[3] Targum Jon. & Jerus. in Gen. l. 26. T. Bab. Moed Katon, fol. 24. 2. & Massech. Samacot, c. 3. sect. 2.

[4] Mishna Meila, c. 6. sect. 1. T. Bab. Megilla, fol. 26. 2.

[5] T. Bab. Gittin, fol. 28. 1. & Bava Metzia, fol. 20. 2.

[6] Vid. Pignorium de Servis, p. 327, 328.

Verse 7. **Then said Jesus, Let her alone**, &c. Do not disturb her in what she does, or hinder her, or blame her for it:

against the day of my burial hath she kept this. This ointment, which she now poured on Christ. It was usual to embalm the dead with ointments and spices: Christ suggests, that the time of His death and burial were nigh, and that this woman had kept this ointment till now, for such a purpose; and whereas she would not be able to make use of it at the time of His interment, she had embalmed His body with it now, beforehand; though without any knowledge of His death, or any such intention and design in her, but the Holy Ghost so directing her: for this is not to be understood of her keeping any part of it till that time, which it does not appear she did.

Verse 8. **For the poor always ye have with you**, &c. And so would not want [*or* lack] opportunities of showing a regard to them, which Christ always recommended; nor does He here in the least discourage an ingenuous [*or* honorable] and affectionate concern for them: the words seem to be a sort of prophecy, that there would be always poor persons in the churches of Christ, to be taken care of and provided for; see the note on *Matt. 26:11* **[37]**; and yet the Jews suppose cases, in which the collectors of alms may have no poor to distribute to, and direct what they shall do in such cases:[7]

but me ye have not always. Meaning, with respect to His corporeal presence, which would be quickly withdrawn from them, when there would be no more an opportunity of showing Him personal respect, in such a way.

Verse 9. **Much people of the Jews therefore knew that he was there**, &c. That is, many of the Jews that dwelt at Jerusalem, knew that Jesus was at Bethany; for it being but two miles from Jerusalem, the report of His being come soon reached thither:

and they came, from Jerusalem to Bethany,

not for Jesus' sake only; to see Him, and hear Him, and observe what He said and did:

but that they might see Lazarus also, whom he had raised from the dead. That is, whom Jesus had raised from the dead, as the Alexandrian copy, and the Ethiopic version express it; for it equally excited their curiosity, to see the person that had been dead, and was raised from the dead, as to see Him who raised him: and it is very likely before they had no opportunity of seeing him; it may be he did not appear publicly before, but kept himself

---

[7] T. Bab. Pesachim, fol. 13. 1. & Bava Metzia, fol. 38. 1. & Bava Bathra, fol. 8. 2.

retired; but now Jesus being come, he showed himself openly; which the Jerusalem Jews being informed of, induced them to come to see both the one and the other.

Verse 10. **But the chief priests**, &c. With the rest of the Sanhedrin:

consulted that they might put Lazarus also to death; as well as Jesus, and that for no other crime, but because he was raised from the dead by Him; which shows, what consciences these men had, and how horribly wicked they were; that they stuck [*or* stopped] at nothing, whereby they might satisfy their malice and envy, and secure their worldly interests and advantages.

Verse 11. **Because that by reason of him**, &c. Of the miracle which was wrought upon him, in raising him from the dead, of which he was a living and an abiding witness:

many of the Jews went away; not from Jerusalem only, but from the chief priests and Pharisees, and the rest of the Jews, that combined against Christ; they withdrew themselves from their party, and deserted them:

and believed on Jesus. As the Messiah; so that they found their interest was decreasing and weakening every day, and that those on the side of Christ were increasing; and this they could not bear, and therefore consulted to take away the life of Lazarus, as well as that of Jesus; who they imagined, as long as he lived, would be a means of inducing persons to believe in Jesus as the Messiah; whereas if he was dead, the fact would be forgotten, or be more easily denied.

Verse 12. **On the next day much people that were come to the feast**, &c. Of the passover; and they were *much people* indeed, that came yearly to this feast, from all parts of the nation; for all the males in Israel, were obliged to appear at this time; and though the women were not obliged, yet multitudes of them came, and the fame of Jesus might bring the more; add to which, that there was now a general expectation of the Messiah's coming, which brought the Jews from all parts of the world to Jerusalem; so that this might be called indeed, פסח מעובין, *a crowded passover*: and though the following account is a stretching it too far, yet it may serve to illustrate this matter:

> "Would you desire to know what multitudes were at Jerusalem of the priests, you may know, as it is written, *1 Kings 8:63*, and the tradition is, that an ox was offered for twenty-four, and a sheep for eleven.—King Agrippa sought to know what was the number of the multitude, which were in Jerusalem; he said to the priests, lay by for me one kidney of every passover lamb; they laid by for him six hundred thousand pair of kidneys, double the number of those that came out of

Egypt: and there is never a passover lamb, but there are more than ten numbered for it,[8] &c."

Now the day following the supper at Bethany, and which seems to be the first day of the week, this multitude of people,

when they heard that Jesus was coming to Jerusalem; from Bethany, which was soon known, it being so near.

Verse 13. **Took branches of palm trees**, &c. The Ethiopic version adds, *and young shoots from Jerusalem*; these grew in great plenty on one part of the Mount of Olives, that next to Bethany, from whence that town had its name; for it signifies *the house of dates*, the fruit of the palm tree; see the note on *Matt. 21:17* **[30]**. And as that tree was a sign of joy and victory, they carried branches of it in their hands, as they met the King Messiah, who was about to make His public entrance into Jerusalem, in triumph; and where by His sufferings and death He should gain the victory over sin, Satan, the world, and death; and lay a solid foundation for joy and peace, to all that believe in Him: the Jews say,[9]

"If a man takes באיין (the very Greek word here used), palm tree branches in his hands, we know that he is victorious."

The Persic version reads, *branches of olives*;

and went forth to meet him, and cried; when they came up to Him, and as He passed by them:

Hosanna, blessed *is* the King of Israel, that cometh in the name of the Lord. See the note on *Matt. 21:9* **[28]**.

Verse 14. **And Jesus, when he had found a young ass**, &c. Which He sent His disciples for to a neighboring village, and they brought to Him:

sat thereon, as it is written; in *Zech. 9:9*; though some part of the words seems to be taken out of *Isa. 62:11*; see the note on *Matt. 21:5* **[27]**; and so Nonnus paraphrases it here, *that it might be fulfilled which Esaias said*.

Verse 15. **Fear not, daughter of Sion**, &c. But rejoice; see *Zech. 9:9*, and see the note on *Matt. 21:5* **[27]**.

Verse 16. **These things understood not his disciples at the first**, &c. Or *at that time*, as the Syriac and Persic versions render it; or *on that day*, as the

---

8   Echa Rabbati, fol. 42. 3, 4.

9   Vajikra Rabba, sect. 30. fol. 170. 3.

Ethiopic version; they did not then know the sense of that prophecy, nor that the things which were now doing, were a fulfilling of it:

but when Jesus was glorified; was raised from the dead, and ascended to heaven, and was set down at the right hand of God, crowned with glory and honor; and when having received the promise of the Father, the Holy Ghost, and His gifts, He poured them forth in a very plenteous and extraordinary manner upon them; whereby their minds were greatly illuminated, and they had a very distinct knowledge of the Scriptures of the Old Testament; and saw clearly, how they severally had their accomplishment in Christ:

then remembered they that these things were written of him; in the prophecies of the Old Testament;

and *that* they had done these things unto him. Both the disciples and the multitude, or that these things were done to Him; such as bringing the ass to Him, laying their clothes on it, and setting Him upon it, attending Him with shoutings and hosannas to the city of Jerusalem, &c.

Verse 17. **The people therefore that was with him**, &c. The Jews, that came from Jerusalem to Bethany, to comfort the two sisters of Lazarus upon his death, who believed in Christ; and others of the town of Bethany, who with them were along with Christ:

when he called Lazarus out of his grave; saying, *Lazarus, come forth*:

and raised him from the dead; to life:

bare record. To the Jews at Jerusalem, and to the people that came out of the several countries, of the truth of that fact; declaring, that they were eye and ear witnesses of the whole, and that it was a truth that might be depended on.

Verse 18. **For this cause the people also met him**, &c. This was a principal reason, among others, which induced them to set out in the manner they did, with palm tree branches in their hands, and accost Him as the king of Israel, when they met Him, and hosanna'd Him into the city:

for that they heard that he had done this miracle. The witnesses were so many, and the proofs they gave so strong, that they firmly believed it: and this being a most amazing miracle, and which exceeded even any of the same kind; Jairus's daughter was but just dead, and the widow of Nain's son was not buried, when they were raised, but Lazarus had been dead and buried four days; it made a very strong impression upon the minds of the people, and engaged their attention to Him, and belief in Him.

Verse 19. **The Pharisees therefore said among themselves**, &c. Either when assembled in their own private houses, or in the Sanhedrin; or as they stood together in the streets, seeing Jesus pass by in such pomp, and such a multitude with Him:

Perceive ye how ye prevail nothing? The Vulgate Latin and Arabic versions read, *we prevail nothing*, so Nonnus; the sense is the same; suggesting, that all their wise schemes and crafty councils, signified nothing; the commands they enjoined the people not to follow Him, or to apprehend Him, or to show them where He was, were disregarded; their threatenings to put out of the synagogue such as should confess Him, were taken no notice of; their promises of reward were slighted; their examples were not followed; and all their artifice and cunning, backed with power and authority, did not succeed:

behold, the world is gone after him. The Vulgate Latin, Syriac, Arabic, and Ethiopic versions read, *the whole world*, and so Nonnus; the Persic version, *all the people*; that is, a very great number of people; for they could not mean, that all the inhabitants of the world, or every individual of mankind were followers of Him, and became His disciples, nor even all in their own land; they themselves, with multitudes more of the same complexion, were an exception to this: but they speak in the common dialect of that nation; of which take two or three instances:

"It happened to a certain high priest, that he went out of the sanctuary, וְהֲווֹ אַזְלֵי כּוּלֵי עַלְמָא בַּתְרֵיהּ, *and the whole world went after him*; and when they saw Shemaiah and Abtalion, they left him, and went after them."[10]

And again,[11]

"R. Aba proclaimed, Whoever seeks riches, and whoever seeks the way of life in the world to come, let him come and study in the law, and כּוּלֵי עַלְמָא, *the whole world* will gather together to him."

Once more,[12]

"Jonathan said to David, *1 Sam. 23:17*: *Thou shall be king over Israel, and I will be next to thee*; What is the meaning of this? Perhaps Jonathan the son of Saul saw עַלְמָא, *the world* draw after David."

---

[10] T. Bab. Yoma, fol. 71. 2.

[11] Zohar in Gen. fol. 60. 4.

[12] T. Bab. Bava Metzia, fol. 85. 1.

This shows the sense of those phrases, *the world*, and *the whole world*, when used in the article of redemption by Jesus Christ; see the note on *1 John 2:2* [64].

Verse 20. **And there were certain Greeks**, &c. *Hellenes*, so called, from Hellen, a king of that name, as Pliny says.[13] These were not Graecizing Jews, or Jews that dwelt in Greece, and spoke the Greek language; for they were called not *Hellenes*, but *Hellenists*; but these were, as the Vulgate Latin and Syriac versions render it, *Gentiles*; and were either mere Gentiles, and yet devout and religious men, who were allowed to offer sacrifice, and to worship in the court of the Gentiles; or they were proselytes, either of *righteousness*, and so were circumcised, and had a right to eat of the passover, as well as to worship at it; or of *the gate*, and so being uncircumcised, might not eat of the passover, yet might worship at it; which latter seems to be the case, by what follows: for these were,

among them, that came up to worship at the feast; of the passover, which was near at hand: these were among those that went forth to meet Jesus, and that attended Him to Jerusalem, who were come up out of the country to this feast; and these came along with them to worship at it, to offer their sacrifices, and join in prayer, though they might not eat of the passover.

Verse 21. **The same came therefore to Philip**, &c. Who might know him; they might have been some of his neighbors formerly, for that Philip's parents, though Jews, dwelt among Greeks, seems probable, from the name given to him, which is a Greek one; some have thought, that these Greeks were Syrophoenicians, who dwelt upon the borders of Tyre and Sidon, and were not far off from Galilee, and from Bethsaida, the native place of Philip, and is therefore mentioned as follows:

which was of Bethsaida of Galilee; as in *John 1:44*; see the note there. This place may be interpreted, *the house of hunting*, or *of fishing*; for it is not easy to say which it has its name from, since צידא, *saida*, signifies both hunting and fishing. And seeing it was in or near the tribe of Naphtali, where was plenty of deer, and a wilderness was near it, where might be wild beasts, it might be so called from hunting: and as it was situated near the lake of Gennesaret, it might have its name from the fishing trade used in it; for Peter and Andrew, who were of it, were both fishermen. But it is yet more difficult to determine, whether this is the same with, or different from the Bethsaida

[13] Nat. Hist. l. 4. c. 7.

Josephus[14] speaks of, as rebuilt by Philip, and called by him *Julias*, after the name of Caesar's daughter, as I have observed in the notes on *Luke 9:10* and *John 1:44*; since this was in Galilee, of which Herod Antipas was tetrarch, and where Philip could have no power to rebuild places, and change their names; and besides, the city, which he repaired, and called Julias, according to Josephus[15] was in lower Gaulonitis, and therefore must be different, unless that, or any part of it, can be thought to be the same with Galilee: wherefore the learned Reland[16] thinks, that there were two Bethsaidas, and which seems very probable; and it is likely, that this is here purposely called Bethsaida of Galilee, to distinguish it from the other, which, by some persons, might still be called Bethsaida, though it had gotten a new name. Moreover, this Bethsaida is mentioned in other places along with Capernaum and Chorazin, *Matt. 11:21,23*, which were in Galilee. And Epiphanius says,[17] that Bethsaida and Capernaum were not far distant one from another: and according to Jerome,[18] Chorazin was but two miles from Capernaum; and who elsewhere says,[19] that Capernaum, Tiberias, Bethsaida, and Chorazin, were situated on the shore of the lake of Gennesaret. It is said to be fifty-six miles from Jerusalem:

and desired him, saying, Sir, we would see Jesus. That is, they entreated him, that he would introduce them into the company of Jesus; they wanted to be admitted into His presence, to have some discourse and conversation with Him; and what might make them the more desirous of it, was the miracle He had lately wrought in raising Lazarus from the dead; as also the uncommon manner of His entering into Jerusalem, which they saw; and which shows, that it was not a bare sight of His person they meant, but the enjoyment of His company for a while; and this favor they ask of Philip, with great respect to Him, and in a very polite way, and yet with great sincerity, and strong affection, and earnest importunity; and was a pledge and presage of the future conversion of the Gentiles, when the Jews would be rejected. And it may be observed, that sensible sinners are very desirous of

---

[14] Antiqu. l. 18. c. 2. sect. 1. Ed. Hudson.

[15] De Bello. Jud. l. 2. c. 9. sect. 1.

[16] Palestina Illustrata, l. 3. p. 654, 655.

[17] Contra Haeres. l. 2. Haeres. 51.

[18] De locis Hebraicis, fol. 90. 6.

[19] Comment. in Esaiam, c. 9. 1.

having a spiritual sight of Christ, of the glories of His person, and the fulness of His grace, and to see their interest in Him, and to have communion and fellowship with Him: He is all in all to them; no object so delightful, and satisfying to them as He is; and they never see Him, but they receive something from Him, and are made more like unto Him.

Verse 22. **Philip cometh and telleth Andrew**, &c. The request the Greeks made to him, and this he did, that he might have his advice in this matter; and that not only because he might be a senior man as well as apostle, but because he was of the same town, and might know these men as well as Philip:

and again Andrew and Philip told Jesus. After they had consulted together, whether it was proper or not to move this thing to their Master; since He had forbid them going in the way of the Gentiles, they agreed to acquaint Him with it, that He might do His pleasure.

Verse 23. **And Jesus answered them**, &c. Not directly and particularly; He did not in plain terms signify what was His will, whether these Greeks should be admitted or not; and yet expressed Himself in such a manner as shows He was not averse to it, but was pleased with it, and takes notice of it, as an evidence of the near approach of His glorification:

saying, The hour is come, that the Son of man should be glorified. By rising from the dead, ascending to heaven, sitting at the right hand of God, and from thence pouring forth the Spirit upon His disciples, who should go and preach the Gospel to the Gentiles, as well as Jews; and which would issue in the conversion of many of them, and so in His glory, of which the coming of these Greeks was an earnest. But He intimates, in the next verse, that He must first die.

Verse 24. **Verily, verily, I say unto you**, &c. This is a certain truth in nature, Christ was about to assert; and what He signifies by it would be a certain fact, and which He mentions, that His death might not be a stumbling block to His disciples, or any objection to His glorification; but was rather to be considered as a means of it, and necessary in order to it:

Except a corn of wheat fall into the ground; or is sown in the earth; for sowing with the Jews is expressed by the falling of the seed into the earth; see the note on *Matt. 13:4* **[17]**; and is a very fit phrase to set forth the death of Christ by, who fell a sacrifice to justice by the hands of men:

and die; or is corrupted, and putrefies; and which is done in three days time in moist land, but is longer in dry ground ere it perishes:[20] and a corn of wheat is almost the only seed, that being cast into the earth, does die; and therefore is very aptly used by Christ:

it abideth alone; a mere single corn as it is:

but if it die; if it wastes, consumes, and rots, as it does, being cast into the earth, in the time before mentioned:

it bringeth forth much fruit. It shoots out, and rises above ground, and appears in blade, and stalk, and ear, and produces many corns or grains of wheat; all which our Lord intends should be accommodated to Himself, and to His death, and the fruits of it. He compares Himself to a corn of wheat; to *wheat*, for the choiceness and excellency of it above all other grain, He being the chiefest among ten thousand, angels or men; and for the purity and cleanness of it, He being, even in His human nature, pure, and free from sin; and for its fruitfulness, He being fruitful in Himself, and the cause of all fruitfulness in His people; and for its usefulness for food, He being the bread of life, and the finest of the wheat. And whereas the wheat must be threshed, and ground, and sifted, and kneaded, and baked, before it is fit for food, all this may express the sufferings and death of Christ, in order to be proper food for the faith of His people: and Christ here compares Himself to a single corn of wheat, because He was of little account among men, and but little or nothing was expected by them from Him; and chiefly because He was alone in the salvation of His people. The death of Christ is signified by the falling of the corn of wheat into the ground, and dying, and shows that Christ's death was not accidental, but designed; it was determined in the counsels and purposes of God, and intended for His glory and the redemption of men; even as wheat falls out of the hands of the sower, not casually, but on purpose, that it may die and spring up again, and produce an increase: and also, that the death of Christ was voluntary, both on His Father's part, and on His own; and was real, and not in appearance only, and yet was but for a short time; as the corn of wheat that dies, soon revives again, and is quickly above ground, so Christ, though He really died, did not long continue under the power of death, but rose again the third day, and now lives for ever. Moreover, Christ intimates by this simile, that if He had not died, He should have been alone; not without His Father, and the blessed Spirit; nor without the holy and elect angels, but without any of the sons of men, who all fell and died in Adam; and had not Christ died, none of them would have lived; none of them could have been justified; nor could their sins have been expiated; nor would any of them

---

[20] Rabbenu Samson & Bartenora in Mishna Celaim, c. 2. sect. 3.

have been regenerated: Christ must have been without them in heaven; wherefore He chose rather to die for them, that they might be for ever with Him, than be alone in the human nature. And He further observes hereby, that His death would be productive of much fruit; which may be understood both of a large harvest of souls, that should be saved, among Jews and Gentiles, and especially the latter; and of the blessings of grace, as redemption, justification, peace, pardon, and eternal life, that should follow upon it.

Verse 25. **He that loveth his life shall lose it**, &c. The sense is, that whoever is so in love with this present temporal life, as to be anxiously careful of it, and takes all precautions to secure it; and rather than to expose it to any danger, chooses to deny the faith of Christ, and desert His cause and interest; as such a one shall not long enjoy this life, so he shall come short of an eternal one:

and he that hateth his life in this world: on the other hand, whoever seems careless about it, and not to consult the safety of it, but is unconcerned about it; yea, as if he was throwing it away, as of no great moment and significancy, rather than do any thing to preserve it, which would be scandalous to himself, and be dishonorable to his Lord and Master; he,

shall keep it unto life eternal. He shall be preserved in his temporal life, in a remarkable manner, until he has done the will and work of God, notwithstanding all attempts upon it; and he shall appear to have that spiritual life, which is the beginning and pledge of, and which springs up unto, and issues in eternal life; and that he shall enjoy in the world to come. This Christ said to let His disciples and followers know, that they must suffer and die, as well as He, though not on the same account, and for the selfsame reasons; and that their sufferings and death in His cause, and for His Gospel, would turn to their advantage.

Verse 26. **If any man serve me**, &c. Or is willing to be a servant of Christ, and to be esteemed as such;

let him follow me; as in the exercise of the graces of love, humility, patience, self-denial, and resignation of will to the will of God, and in the discharge of every duty, walking as He walked, so in a way of suffering; for as the Master, so the servants, as the Head, so the members, through many tribulations must enter the kingdom; to which He encourages by the following things:

and where I am; in heaven, as He now was, as the Son of God; or *where I shall be*, as the Syriac and Persic versions render it, even as man, in the human nature, when raised from the dead:

400

there shall also my servant be; when he has done his work, and the place is prepared for him, and he for that, and where he shall ever abide; and as a further encouragement, He adds,

if any man serve me, him will *my* Father honor. By accepting his service, affording him His gracious presence here, and by giving him eternal glory hereafter, to which He has called him.

Verse 27. **Now is my soul troubled**, &c. At the hardness and unbelief of the Jews, and the rejection of them, when the Gentiles would be called, and converted, by which He would be glorified; and at the conduct and carriage of His disciples to Him, He had a foreknowledge of: at the betraying of Him by one, and the denial of Him by another, and the flight of them all from Him; and at the devil, and the furious and violent attack He knew he would make upon Him, though He had obliged him to leave Him, when he assaulted Him before, and knew he could find nothing in Him now, and that as God, He was able to destroy him; but this was to be done by Him, as man, and by dying too. He was in His human soul troubled at the thoughts of His death, though it was His Father's will, and He had agreed to it, and was for the salvation of His people, His heart was so much set upon; yet it was terrible to the human nature, and especially as attended with the wrath of God; at the apprehensions of which, His soul was exceedingly troubled; not as about to fall on Him on His own personal account, but as being the surety of His people, and as having their sins upon Him to satisfy angry and injured justice for:

and what shall I say? This question He puts, as being in the utmost distress, and difficulty, as if He knew not what to say; and yet not as advising with His disciples, what was to be said or done in His case; but is rather used to introduce another question, as the following words may be formed: shall I say,

Father, save me from this hour? as requesting His Father, that He might be strengthened under His sufferings and death, and carried through them, and out of them; or rather as deprecating them, desiring the cup might pass from Him, as He afterwards did; and then the sense is, Shall I put up such a petition to my Father, to save me from sorrows, sufferings, and death? No, I will not: the human nature through frailty might prompt Him to it, and He be just going to do it, when He corrects Himself, saying:

but for this cause came I unto this hour. This hour or time of sorrow and suffering was appointed for Him; it was fixed in the covenant of grace, and Christ had agreed to it; He was sent into this world, and He came into it, on account of this hour; and was preserved hitherto for this purpose; and was now come to Jerusalem, and was there at this instant, for that very reason, namely, to suffer and die. And since this was the case, He would not put up such a petition to His Father, but the following one.

Ver 28. **Father, glorify thy name**, &c. The perfections of His nature, particularly His justice and holiness, meaning in Himself, by His sufferings and death; intimating hereby, that His Father's glory was what He had in view, and that the securing of that would give Him an infinite pleasure amidst all His sorrows. The Arabic version, and Nonnus, read *glorify thy Son*, as in *chapter 17:1*, and the Ethiopic version takes in both, *glorify thy name, and thy Son*: and indeed, what glorifies the one, glorifies the other; see *chapter 13:31-32*.

Then came there a voice from heaven; as at His baptism and transfiguration, and which came from the Father, and was an articulate one, and what the Jews call *Bath Kol*, or *the daughter of the voice*:

saying, **I have both glorified** *it*; meaning in the incarnation, ministry, obedience and miracles of Christ; and particularly in that late one in raising Lazarus from the dead:

and will glorify *it* **again**. By supporting Him under, and carrying Him through His sufferings and death, and by raising Him from the dead, and setting Him at His own right hand.

Verse 29. **The people therefore, that stood by, and heard** *it*, &c. Some more confusedly, who were farthest off; others more distinctly, who were nearer: the first of these,

said that it thundered; as it used to do when *Bath Kol* was heard, which, as the Jews say,[21]
"is a voice that comes out of heaven proceeding from the midst of another voice,"
as thunder; wherefore some took this for thunder, and others for the voice of an angel out of the thunder:

others said, An angel spake to him. These being nearer, perceived it was an articulate voice, which expressed certain distinct words, which they thought were delivered by an angel; for the Jews had a mighty notion of the discourse and conversation of angels with men, which their doctors pretended

---

[21] Piske Tosephot in T. Bab. Sanhedrin, art. 30.

to understand; particularly R. Jochanan ben Zaccai, a Rabbi, who was living at this time, had learned their speech, and was well versed in it.[22]

Verse 30. **Jesus answered and said**, &c. To the people that stood by, and were disputing among themselves about what they heard, whether it was thunder, or the voice of an angel:

This voice came not because of me; at least not only and chiefly; it was not so much in answer to His prayer, or in order to comfort Him under the apprehensions He had of His sufferings and death, or to assure Him of His future glorification, though all this was true:

but for your sakes. To convince them that He was the Messiah, and engage them to believe in Him, or to leave them without excuse; since not only miracles were wrought before their eyes, but with their ears they heard God speaking to Him, and which is the rule that they themselves prescribe; for according to them, no man is to be hearkened to, though he should do as many signs and wonders as Moses, the son of Amram, unless they hear with their ears, that the Lord speaks to him as He did to Moses.[23]

Verse 31. **Now is the judgment of this world**, &c. That is, in a very short time will be the judgment either of the Jewish world, when that shall be reproved, convinced, and condemned for their sin of rejecting Christ, and crucifying Him, by the Spirit, in the ministration of the Gospel; and they still continuing in their impenitence and unbelief, in process of time wrath will come upon them, upon their nation, city, and temple, to the uttermost; or of the Gentile world, when there shall be a discrimination, and separation made in it, of the chosen of God, who shall be called by special grace, and with the converted and believing Jews, shall form a Gospel church state, separate from the world of the ungodly; or of the world of God's elect among Jews and Gentiles, whose cause, being undertaken by Christ, He will now vindicate it, and redeem them from sin and Satan, who have usurped a power and dominion over them: hence it follows,

now shall the prince of this world be cast out. The phrase, שר העולם, *the prince of the world*, is much used by Jewish writers,[24] by whom an angel is meant; and they seem to design the angel of death, which is the devil: and it

---

[22] T. Bab. Succa, fol. 28. 1. & Bava Bathra, fol. 134. 1.

[23] R. Moses Kotsensis praefat. ad Mitzvot Tora, pr. Affirm.

[24] T. Bab. Yebamot, fol. 16. 2. & Sanhedrin, fol. 94. 1. & Cholin, fol. 60. 1.

is certain, that he is here intended, and is so called, not because he has any legal power and authority over the world; but because he has usurped a dominion over it, and has great power and efficacy in the hearts of the children of disobedience, who yield a voluntary subjection to him, as if he was their proper lord and sovereign: now the time was at hand, when he should be cast out of the empire of the world he had assumed, and out of the temples of the Gentiles, and out of the hearts of God's elect among them.

Verse 32. **And I, if I be lifted up from the earth**, &c. The death of Christ is here signified by His being *lifted up from the earth*, in allusion to the lifting up of the brazen serpent on the pole; and shows, that His death would not be natural, but violent, and would be public, and not private; and fitly expresses His mediation between God, and men, being lifted up between the heavens and the earth; and points out the death of the cross, as is intimated in the next verse: and the *if* here does not suppose that His death, and the manner of it, were uncertain, for it was determined by God, agreed to by Himself, predicted in the Scriptures, signified by types, and foretold by Himself, and was necessary for the salvation of His people; but it designs the time of His drawing persons to Himself, which is afterwards expressed, and may be rendered, *when I am lifted up*, as it is by the Syriac, Arabic, and Persic versions: now when this will be, Christ says, I,

will draw all *men* to me; which is not to be understood of the concourse of people about Him, when on the cross—some for Him, and others against Him, some to bewail Him, and others to reproach Him; but rather, of the gathering of the elect to Him, and in Him, as their head and representative, when He was crucified for them; or of the collection of them, through the ministry of the apostles, and of their being brought to believe on Him for eternal life and salvation: and this drawing of them to Him, in consequence of His death, supposes distance from Him, want [*or* lack] of power and will to come to Him, and the efficacious grace of God to bring them, though without any force and com-pulsion; and this is to be understood not of every individual of human nature; for all are not drawn to Christ, or enabled to come to Him [see *John 6:44*], and believe in Him. There were many of the Jews who would not, and did not come to Him for life; and who, instead of being drawn to Him in this sense, when lifted up on the cross, vilified and reproached Him; moreover, in the preceding verse, a *world* is spoken of, whose judgment, or condemnation, was now come; and besides, there was at this time a multitude of souls in hell, who could not, nor never will be, drawn to Christ; and a greater number still there will be at the last day, who, instead of drawing to Him in this gracious way and manner, will be bid to depart from Him, as having been workers of iniquity. Christ died indeed for all men who are drawn unto Him; but this is not true of all men, that are, were, or shall be in the world. Add to this, that the word *men* is not in the text, it is only παντας, *all*: Beza's most ancient copy, and some others, and the Vulgate Latin version read παντα, *all things*; and by *all* are meant, all the elect of God, all the children of God, *that were scattered abroad*; the Persic version reads, *I will draw my friends to me*; it designs some of all sorts of men, of every state, condition, age, sex, and nation, Gentiles as well as Jews, and especially the former; which agrees with the ancient prophecy, *Gen. 49:10*, and with the context, and the occasion of the words, which was the desire of the Greeks, that were come to the feast, to see Jesus; and which was a specimen of the large numbers of them, that should be drawn to Christ, through the preaching of the Gospel, after His death. The Jews say,

"that in the time to come, or in the days of the Messiah, all the proselytes shall be גרורים, *drawn*, shall freely become proselytes."[25]

The allusion here, is to the setting up of a standard or ensign, to gather persons together. Christ's cross is the standard, His love is the banner, and He Himself is the ensign, which draw souls to Himself, and engage them to enlist themselves under Him, and become His volunteers in the day of His power; see *Isa. 11:10*.

Verse 33. **This he said**, &c. These are the words of the evangelist, interpreting the design of Christ in the above words, thereby,

signifying what death he should die. The phrase of being *lifted up from the earth*, not only signified His death, but the kind, or manner of it, that it should be by crucifixion; a person crucified being stretched forth upon a cross, and that erected, was lifted up between earth and heaven.

Verse 34. **The people answered him**, &c. Not the Greeks, but the Jews, and these not such as were friends to Christ, but cavilers at Him:

We have heard out of the law; not the five books of Moses, but the Prophets, and Hagiographa; even all the books of the Old Testament are called *the law*; see the note on *chapter 10:34*;

that Christ abideth for ever; referring to those places which speak of the perpetuity of His priesthood, and the everlasting duration of His kingdom, *Psa. 110:4; 45:6; 72:17* and *89:36-37; Dan. 2:44* and *7:13-14*; in which last text express mention is made of the Son of man, and that and the first may be more especially respected; from whence it appears, that these passages were understood of the Messiah by the ancient Jews: they knew He was designed in *Psa. 110:4*. He is David's Lord that was bid to sit at the right hand of

---

[25] T. Bab. Avoda Zara, fol. 24. 1. & Gloss. in ibid.

Jehovah, after He was raised from the dead, and had ascended on high [see *Acts 2:29-36*]; whose Gospel went forth with power, and whose people, by it, were made willing to submit to Him, to His righteousness, and the scepter of His kingdom; and who also is a priest for ever; and which is appealed to as a proof of the nature, kind, and duration of Christ's priesthood, *Heb. 5:6* and *7:17*; and so it may be observed it is expressly applied to Him by Jewish writers: in *Zech. 4:14* it is said, *These are the two anointed ones, that stand by the Lord of the whole earth*; of which this interpretation is given:[26]

"These are Aaron and the Messiah; and it would not be known which of them is (most) beloved, but that he says, *Psa. 110:4, the Lord hath sworn, and will not repent, thou art a priest for ever*; from whence it is manifest that the Messiah is more beloved than Aaron the righteous priest."

And so another of them,[27] speaking of Melchizedek, says,

"this is that which is written, *Psa. 110:4, the Lord hath sworn*, &c. Who is this? This is he that is just, and having salvation, the King Messiah, as it is said, *Zech. 9:9*."

So the 45th Psalm is understood by them of the Messiah; the King, in *verse 1*, is by Ben Melech, said to be the King Messiah; *verse 2* is thus paraphrased by the Targum,

"Thy beauty, O King Messiah, is more excellent than the children of men."

And Aben Ezra observes, that this Psalm is either concerning David, or the Messiah his son, whose name is David, *Ezek. 37:25*;[28] and the passage in *Psa. 72:17* is frequently interpreted of the Messiah and His name, and is brought as a proof of the antiquity of it;[29] and *Psa. 89:36* is also applied to Him; and as for *Dan. 7:13*, that is by many, both ancient and modern Jews, explained of the Messiah:[30] and since then they understood these passages of Him, it is easy to observe from whence they took this notion that the Messiah should abide for ever. But then they should have observed out of the same law, or

---

[26] Abot R. Nathan, c. 34.

[27] R. Moses Hadarsan in Galatin. de cath. Verse l. 10. c. 6.

[28] Vid. Tzeror Hammor, fol. 49. 2.

[29] T. Bab. Pesachim, fol. 54. 1. Nedarim, fol. 39. 2. Bereshit Rabba, fol. 1, 2. Echa Rabbati, fol. 50. 2. Pirke Eliezer, c. 32.

[30] Zohar in Gen. fol. 85. 4. Bemidbar Rabba, sect. 13. fol. 209. 4. Jarchi & Saadiah Gaon in Dan. 7:13. & R. Jeshua in Aben Ezra in ibid.

Holy Scriptures, that the Messiah was to be stricken and cut off, was to be brought to the dust of death, and to pour out His soul unto death; all which is consistent with His abiding for ever, in His person and office; for though according to the said writings, He was to die and be buried, yet He was not to see corruption; He was to rise again, ascend on high, sit at the right hand of God, and rule till all His enemies became His footstool; His sufferings were to be in the way, and in order to His entrance into the glory that should always abide. The Jews have entertained a notion that Messiah the son of David shall not die; and they lay down this as a rule, that if any one sets up for a Messiah, and does not prosper, but is *slain*, it is a plain case He is not the Messiah. So all the wise men at first thought that Ben Coziba was the Messiah, but when he was slain it was known to them that he was not.[31] And upon this principle these Jews confront the Messiahship of Jesus, saying,

and how sayest thou, The Son of man must be lifted up? for it seems Christ used the phrase the Son of man in His discourse, though John has not recorded it; he attending to His sense, and not to His express words. The Jews rightly understood Him, that by the Son of man He meant the Messiah, and by His being lifted up, His death; but they did not understand, how the Messiah could die, and yet abide for ever; and therefore since He intended Himself by the Son of man, they concluded He talked very inconsistent with the Scriptures, and with the character He assumed, and ask very pertly,

who is this Son of man? Is there any other son of man besides the Messiah? And can the Son of man, that is the Messiah, be lifted up, or die, who is to abide for ever? And if thou art to be lifted up, or die, thou art not the Messiah or Daniel's Son of man, whose kingdom is everlasting. But how come the Jews themselves to say, that the days of the Messiah, according to some, are but forty years, according to others seventy, according to others, three hundred and sixty-five?[32] Yea, they say, He shall be as other men, marry, have children, and then die.[33] And how comes it to pass that Messiah ben Joseph shall be slain?[34] The truth of the matter is this, they having lost the true sense of the prophecies concerning the Messiah, and observing some that seem to differ, and which they knew not how to reconcile, have fancied two

---

[31] Maimon Hilchot Melacim, c. 11. sect. 3, 4. Vid. Bereshit Rabba, sect. 98. fol. 86. 2.

[32] T. Bab. Sanhedrin, fol. 99. 1.

[33] Maimonides in Mishna Sanhedrin, c. 11. sect. 1.

[34] T. Bab. Succa, fol. 52. 1.

Messiahs, the one that will be much distressed and be overcome and be slain; the other, who will be potent and victorious.

Verse 35. **Then Jesus said unto them**, &c. Not directly answering to their questions, but suggests to them their ignorance and stupidity, amidst so much light that was about them:

yet a little while is the light with you. Meaning either Himself, the Light of the world, *chapter 8:12* and *12:46*, who was to be but a very little while longer with them, a few days more, and He was to go away from them by death, and be seen and heard no more by them: or the Gospel, which, though that was to continue somewhat longer, it being after Christ's death, resurrection, and ascension, to be preached to the Jews, both in Judea, and in other parts of the world; yet that would be but for a little while, as the event has shown; for the Jews rejecting the Gospel, and putting it away from them, the apostles, as they were ordered, turned to the Gentiles, *Acts 13:46-47*.

Walk while ye have the light: that is, as it is explained in the following verse, *believe ye in the light*: which the Persic version adds here, and leaves out there: and the sense is, believe in the Messiah, and in His Gospel; embrace Him and that, and walk on in Him, and worthy of Him and of His Gospel, as children of the light:

lest darkness come upon you; suddenly, at an unawares; either a greater degree of the darkness of ignorance and unbelief; even a judicial blindness and stupidity, which did seize on that people, and continues upon them to this day; or the darkness of afflictions, calamities, and distress, and which have come upon them to the uttermost, to the destruction of their temple, city, and nation; or else a worse darkness, even blackness of darkness, outer darkness in hell, where are weeping, wailing, and gnashing of teeth;

for he that walketh in darkness, knoweth not whither he goeth. He cannot see his way, nor the stumbling blocks that lie in it, and the dangers he is exposed unto; nor does he know where it leads, and what is the end of it; and just so it is with a man in a state of unregeneracy, and more especially under judicial blindness: he is not aware of the pits and snares that lie in his way, or of the dark mountains on which he stumbles; and though destruction and misery are in his ways, he knows not that he is going thereunto.

Verse 36. **While ye have light, believe in the light**, &c. Receive the Messiah, and credit the Gospel revelation; this is an explanation of the exhortation in the preceding verse:

that ye may be the children of the light. That is, that they might appear to be such who are enlightened persons; and such are truly so, who are made light in the Lord, or who are enlightened by the Spirit of God to see their own sinfulness, impotency, and unrighteousness, and their need of Christ, and His righteousness and strength, and of salvation by Him; and who are made meet, by the grace of God, to be partakers of the inheritance of the saints in light; and which is made manifest by believing in Christ, and walking on in Him, as they have received Him, and by walking honestly, as in the daytime, and circumspectly, not as fools, but as wise, for such walk as children of the light.

These things spake Jesus, and departed; from those Jews, as being unworthy of any further conversation with Him; and from Jerusalem, very likely to Bethany, whither He frequently retired, especially at night, during the few days before the passover:

and did hide himself from them. For His safety, for He knew that they were irritated by what He said, and would seek to lay hold upon Him, and deliver Him to the Sanhedrin; and whereas His hour was not yet fully come, there were a few more sands in the glass to run, He provided for His security, by absconding from them; and this was an emblem of His wholly removing from them, and leaving them, and their house, desolate [see *Matt. 23:38*]; and it is very likely that from this time forward, they saw Him no more as ministering the Word unto them; and also of His taking His Gospel from them in a little time, and of His hiding the things of it from them, which respected Himself, and salvation by Him.

Verse 37. **But though he had done so many miracles before them**, &c. Openly, and in the presence of them; meaning those miracles which were done at Jerusalem, as those which brought Nicodemus to Him, and to an acknowledgment of Him as a teacher sent from God; and particularly the cure of the lame man at Bethesda's pool, the giving sight to the man that was born blind, by anointing his eyes with clay, and sending him to wash in the Pool of Siloam, and the raising Lazarus from the dead at Bethany, which was within two miles of Jerusalem, in the presence of many of them who were come there to comfort Martha and Mary:

yet they believed not on him; the miracles done by Christ before their eyes, which they could not deny, nor disprove, and were so many, and so great, were aggravations of their unbelief; and such indeed is the nature of that sin, and so deeply rooted is it, that the most powerful means, and mighty works, will not bring a person to believe in Christ, without the powerful and efficacious grace of God.

Verse 38. **That the saying of Esaias the prophet might be fulfilled**, &c. For though this was not the end of these men in disbelieving Christ, that the words of Isaiah might be fulfilled, yet hereby they were eventually fulfilled;

and though the predictions of the prophet had no such influence on the wills of these men, as to lay upon them a coercive necessity, or force them to do, or to answer to the things foretold; yet they were to have, and had an infallible event or completion, otherwise the foreknowledge of God, and the authority of the prophetic writings, could not be maintained:

which he spake in *Isa. 53:1*:

Lord, who hath believed our report? Which words the prophet delivered by way of complaint to God the Father; not so much with respect to his own time, and the men of it, as to the times of Christ, and His apostles, whom he personates [that is, represents]; for the whole chapter is a prophecy of the Messiah, and suggests, that in those times there would be but few that would believe the report made in the ministry of the Gospel concerning the Messiah, His person, office, and grace, though so true in itself, and so much confirmed by miracles, and mighty deeds; the reason of which, He intimates, would be His outward mean [*or* lowly and humble] appearance in the world; and which, it is certain, was the true reason, God denying the influence of His powerful and special grace, as follows:

and to whom hath the arm of the Lord been revealed? Meaning either the Gospel, which is *the power of God unto salvation* [*Rom. 1:16*], and which was bid from the wise and prudent; or the Lord Jesus Christ Himself, who is the power of God, by whom He made the heavens and the earth, and upholds them in their being, and by whom He has redeemed and saved His people; and who was not revealed, neither to them in the ministry of the Word, nor in them the hope of glory: or the Holy Spirit is meant, the finger of God, by whom these surprising miracles were done; and yet He did not exert Himself in these persons, in the special operations of His grace; or the powerful and efficacious grace of God itself is designed, which was not put forth, and did not attend the report of the Gospel, and therefore it was not believed.

Verse 39. **Therefore they could not believe**, &c. God had determined to leave them to the blindness and hardness of their hearts, and to deny them His grace, which only could cure them of it, and enable them to believe: He had foretold this in prophecy, and they were manifestly the persons spoken of; and therefore considering the decrees of God, the predictions of the prophet, and the hardness of their hearts they were left unto, it was morally impossible they should believe,

because that Esaias said again, in *Isa. 6:9-10*:

Verse 40. **He hath blinded their eyes, and hardened their heart**, &c. It is of no great moment, whether the *He*, who is said to blind and harden, be

God or Christ, or whether the words be rendered, *it hath blinded*, &c. that is, malice or wickedness; or whether they be read impersonally, *their eyes are blinded*, &c. since God or Christ blind and harden not by any positive act, but by leaving and giving men up to the blindness and hardness of their hearts, and denying them the grace which could only cure them, and which they are not obliged to give; and which was the case of these Jews, so as never to be converted, or be turned even by external repentance and reformation, that they might be healed in a national way, and be preserved from national ruin, as it follows,

that they should not see with *their* eyes, &c. see the notes on *Matt. 13:14-15* **[18]**. The Syriac and Persic versions read, *they have blinded their eyes*, &c.

Verse 41. **These things said Esaias**, &c. Concerning the blinding and hardening of the Jews:

when he saw his glory, and spake of him. When he saw, in a visionary way, the glory of the Messiah in the temple, and the angels covering their faces with their wings at the sight of Him; and when he spake of Him as the King, the Lord of hosts, whom he had seen, *Isa. 6:1-10*; from whence it is clear that he had respect to the Jews in the times of the Messiah. The prophet says in *Isa. 6:1*, that he *saw the Lord*: the Targumist renders it, *I saw*, את יקרא דיי, *the glory of Jehovah*; and in *Isa. 6:5* he says, *mine eyes have seen the King*, Jehovah, Zebaot, the Lord of hosts; which the Chaldee paraphrase renders, *mine eyes have seen*, את יקר, *the glory* of the Shekinah, the King of the world, the Lord of hosts. Agreeably to which our Lord says here, that he saw His glory, the glory of His majesty, the glory of His divine nature, the train of His divine perfections, filling the temple of the human nature; and he spoke of Him as the true Jehovah, the Lord of hosts; and which therefore is a very clear and strong proof of the proper divinity of Christ. And it may be observed from hence, that such persons who have a true, spiritual, and saving sight of Christ, of the glory of His person, and the fulness of His grace, cannot but be speaking of Him to others, either in private, or in public, as Isaiah here did, and as the church in *Song of Sol. 5:10-16*; and as the apostles of Christ, *John 1:14; 1 John 1:1-2*; and indeed, should they hold their peace, the stones would cry out; such must, and will speak of His glory in His temple, *Psa. 29:9* and *145:4-7,11,12*.

Verse 42. **Nevertheless among the chief rulers also**, &c. These were the members of the Jewish Sanhedrin, as Nicodemus, Joseph of Arimathea, and others:

many believed on him; that He was the Messiah, though they did not believe in Him in a spiritual and saving manner, as their Redeemer and

Savior, only in their minds, being convicted by His miracles, gave an assent unto Him, as the promised Messiah. The two persons just mentioned may be thought truly to have believed in Christ; but the *many* here spoken of seem to have had only a historical faith in Him, as appears by what follows:

but because of the Pharisees they did not confess *him*; as they ought to have done, and as they would have done, if their faith had been right; for where with the heart men believe in Christ to righteousness, there, with the mouth, confession is made to salvation; and between a nonconfession of Christ, and a denying Him, is no medium; and Christ interprets the one to be the same with the other; see *Rom. 10:9-10; Matt. 10:32-33*; and this they did not do, because of the Pharisees, who were the inveterate and implacable enemies of Christ, and were the prevailing party in the Sanhedrin: wherefore these chief rulers, though many, were afraid of them,

lest they should be put out of the synagogue; for they had made a decree in the Sanhedrin, that whoever confessed that Jesus was the Messiah, should be cast out; and they had put it into execution upon the man born blind, whose eyes Christ opened, for speaking in favor of his benefactor; and this had struck terror in the minds, not only of the common people; but of the chief rulers themselves; for it was looked upon as a very dreadful thing to be put out of the synagogue; see the note on *chapter 9:22*.

Verse 43. **For they loved the praise of men**, &c. To be esteemed of men, to have their applause, and receive honor from them:

more than the praise of God. Than either to receive honor from Him, and be praised by Him, or to praise and glorify Him. By confessing Christ they knew they should run the risk of losing their places of honor and profit, and of falling under the disgrace and contempt of men; and therefore they chose rather not to confess Christ, than by so doing to glorify God, and please Him, and be praised by Him, as all the faithful professors of Christ will be at the last day; for then every such a one will have praise of God, and it will be said, *Well done good and faithful servant, enter into the joy of thy Lord* [*Matt. 25:23*].

Verse 44. **Jesus cried and said**, &c. Upon this occasion, on account of the prevailing hardness and unbelief of the Jewish nation, and the nonconfession of Him by those who did believe Him to be the Messiah. He *cried* with a loud voice, that He might be heard, and His audience left inexcusable; it denotes the concern of His mind, the vehemency of His spirit, and that openness and freedom in which He discharged His ministry, by showing the nature, excellency, and usefulness of believing in Him, and the dangerous consequences of unbelief:

He that believeth on me, believeth not on me; which is not to be understood simply and absolutely, for this would be a contradiction in terms. They that believe in Christ, do believe in Him, and they do right to believe in Him; Christ is the object of faith; He is proposed as such in the Gospel; and it is His Father's will, and His own advice, that His people should believe in Him. But then those that truly believe in Him, do not believe in Him as a mere man, but as God, as the Son of God; and not as separate from, or to the exclusion of His Father: nor do they believe in Him as a new, or another god, but as the one God with the Father, and the Spirit; for He and His Father are one: nor do they believe in Him *only*; and so the Arabic version reads; but in God the Father also: nor does their faith rest in Him, but it proceeds through Him, as the Mediator unto God; see *1 Pet. 1:21*. Besides, He is here to be considered in His office capacity, as being sent of God; and he that believes on Him as the sent of God, does not so much believe on Him, as on the sender of Him, as follows:

but on him that sent me. Just as whatever honor or dishonor are done to an ambassador, sent by an earthly king to a foreign court, are not so much done to the ambassador that is sent, as to the king that sends him; for what is done to him, is all one as if it was personally done to his prince: so he that despises Christ, despises Him that sent Him; and he that receives Christ, receives Him that sent Him; and he that believes on Christ, believes on Him that sent Him; see *Luke 10:16; Matt. 10:40*.

Verse 45. **And he that seeth me, seeth him that sent me.** Not with bodily eyes, for there were many that saw Christ, who never saw the Father: they saw Christ as a mere man, and were offended at the meanness [*or* lowliness] of His outward appearance; they saw nothing divine in Him, nor the glory of the Father through Him; but with the eyes of the understanding, whoever saw or perceived the glory of Christ in His miracles, saw the glory of God in them also, for the Father that dwelt in Him did the works, *John 2:11; 11:40* and *14:10*; and whoever truly sees Christ with an eye of faith, sees His glory, as the glory of the only begotten of the Father, as *the brightness* of His Father's glory [*Heb. 1:3*], as having *the fulness of the Godhead* dwelling in Him [*Col. 2:9*], the same perfections as in the Father; so that he that hath seen the one, hath seen the other also, *John 14:9*.

Verse 46. **I am come a light into the world**, &c. And even as the light of it, being the sun of righteousness, that was to arise, and now was risen, to enlighten men with the light of the living; see *chapter 3:19* and *8:12*;

that whosoever believeth on me should not abide in darkness. God's elect themselves, while in a state of unregeneracy and unbelief, are in darkness; when Christ shines in upon them, and infuses the light of faith into them, they are no longer in darkness; the darkness is past, at least in a great measure, and the true light shines; in which they see light, see the glory and grace of Christ, and the invisible realities of another world: nor do they continue in the darkness of sin, ignorance, and unbelief; but walk in the light of truth, faith, and holiness, until the perfect day comes, when all the shadows of remaining darkness will flee away.

Verse 47. **And if any man hear my words and believe not**, &c. Men may hear the Gospel of Christ, and not understand it; and they may understand it literally and grammatically, though not spiritually and experimentally, and not believe it; not so much as give credit or an assent to the truth of it, but reject and deny it; for though faith comes by hearing to some, it does not come to all: some receive no profit by hearing it, because it is not mixed with faith by them [see *Heb. 4:2*]. The Alexandrian copy, and all the Oriental versions, and also Nonnus, read the last clause thus, *and keep* them *not*; or does not observe them, is negligent of them, and shows no regard, and yields not *the obedience of faith* to them [*Rom. 16:26*]; the sense is the same.

I judge him not; I do not accuse him to the Father, nor do I condemn him, nor shall I take vengeance on him for so doing; meaning, that He should do none of these things now, though hereafter He will be a swift witness against him, and will convict and condemn him, and pass sentence on him, and execute it:

for I came not to judge the world, but to save the world. Christ, at His first coming, came not under the character of a judge, but a Savior; wherefore, suitable to His character, and the end of His coming, He would not accuse, condemn, or judge any man, even the greatest unbelievers in Him, and despisers of Him, but would leave them to another day, when righteous judgment shall take place.

Verse 48. **He that rejecteth me**, &c. As the Messiah, with abhorrence and contempt, as many among the Jews did, who would not have Him to reign over them, but sought to put Him to death:

and receiveth not my words; the doctrines of the Gospel, but disbelieves them, and denies them to be true, looking upon them as the doctrines of a mere man, and an impostor:

hath one that judgeth him; let not such a one think that he shall escape righteous judgment; though Christ does not judge him now, there is one that judges him, yea, even now; and declares, that *he that believeth not shall be damned* [*Mark 16:16*], and that he is condemned already:

414

the word that I have spoken unto you, the same shall judge him in the last day. According to the different dispensations wicked men are under in this world, will be the rule of their judgment hereafter: such who are only under the law of nature, will be judged according to that, that will accuse them, convict them, and condemn them; such who have been under the law of Moses, or the written law, will be arraigned, proved, and pronounced guilty, and punished by, and according to that law; and such who have been under the Gospel dispensation, and have been favored with the revelation of the Gospel, but have contemned [that is, shown contempt for] and denied it, that will judge them at the last day. The judge will act by its present declaration, and according to that proceed, as it stands in *Mark 16:16*. It will rise up in judgment against such persons, and be an aggravation of their condemnation.

Verse 49. **For I have not spoken of myself**, &c. As man, or as separate from His Father; His doctrine was not human, but divine, and therefore a rejection of it cannot escape notice at the future judgment:

but the Father which sent me, he gave me a commandment what I should say, and what I should speak. Christ, as man, had His mission, and commission, and His instructions from His Father to preach the Gospel unto men; He was anointed for it by the Holy Ghost; He was enjoined the preaching of it by His Father, and the several doctrines He published were delivered Him by Him; see *chapter 8:28* and *17:8*.

Verse 50. **And I know that his commandment is life everlasting**, &c. By *his commandment* is not meant the law; that indeed is often styled the commandment; and it is the commandment of God; and many excellent things are said of it; and among the rest it is called *life*, *Deut. 30:15*, but not everlasting life: it only promised a continuation of natural life to man, on condition of obedience to it; more than this it did not promise to Adam, in innocence; and what it promised to the obedient Israelites, was only a prolongation of natural life in the land which God gave unto them: but it neither promises, nor gives spiritual life to the fallen sons of Adam. It leaves men as it finds them, dead in trespasses and sins; and cannot communicate either a life of sanctification, or of justification to them; nor does it so much as give them any hopes of life, or show where it is to be had; nor is everlasting life to be obtained by the works of it: justification is not by the works of the law; nor salvation by works of righteousness done by men; and consequently eternal life is never to be attained unto by obedience to the commands of the law: it is so far from being in this sense life everlasting, that it is the ministration of condemnation and death [see *2 Cor. 3:7-9*]. But the Gospel is here meant, and is called a commandment; not that it has the nature of a law, or consists of precepts, as the law does; but because it is by the commandment of the everlasting God published by Christ, and His apostles. Christ, as appears from the preceding verse, had a commandment from His Father, what He should say and speak; now, not the doctrine He delivered was the commandment itself, but it was a commandment of the Father that He should deliver that doctrine; besides, the word *commandment* sometimes signifies no other than a doctrine, as in *Psa. 19:8; 1 John 2:7*; and the sense is, that the doctrine of the Gospel, which Christ had in commission from the Father to preach, is life everlasting; and is so called, because it is a means of quickening sinners with a spiritual life, which issues in an eternal one; it is *the savor of life unto life*, and the Spirit which giveth life, and is the ministration of it; and it is a means of implanting the graces of the Spirit of God in the heart, which spring up unto everlasting life; and of bringing souls to the knowledge of Christ, which is the beginning, pledge, and earnest of eternal life. And besides all this, it gives an account of the nature of eternal life; it directs the way unto it, which is by Christ, and describes the persons who shall enjoy it; showing, that their title to it is the righteousness of Christ, and their meetness for it the regenerating grace of the Spirit; and that all that believe in Christ shall have it:

whatsoever I speak therefore, even as the Father said unto me, so I speak. And not otherwise, and therefore ought to be received, and not rejected. This is to be understood not of what Christ spoke in common conversation, but in the ministry of the Word, even of the doctrines of the Gospel, which were given Him by His Father, and which He knew were agreeable to His mind and will, and to His council and covenant, and to every thing done and agreed therein, to which He was privy. These He delivered as He received them, and both as to matter and manner, as it was His Father's will and pleasure He should: He preached the righteousness of God, and hid it not; He declared His faithfulness, and His salvation, and concealed not His lovingkindness and truth, *Psa. 40:9-10*. Now, though it is a sufficient ground of faith to receive and believe the doctrines of the Gospel, because Christ has spoken them, who is truth itself; yet it is a further confirmation of them, that they are what His Father, the God of truth, said unto Him: and His delivering them as He had them from Him, is an instance of His faithfulness to Him that sent Him; and should be imitated by His ministers, who ought to declare the whole counsel of God, and keep back nothing they have received from Christ, and which may be profitable to the souls of men.

CHAPTER 13

Verse 1. **Now before the feast of the passover**, &c. This feast was instituted as a memorial of the deliverance of the children of Israel out of Egypt, and was an eminent type of Christ; and this passover was what Christ had greatly desired, it being His last, and when He was to express His great love to His people, mentioned here, by dying for them. It was two days before this feast, so the Persic version reads this text, at Bethany, in the house of Simon the leper, that the things recorded in this chapter were transacted; see *Matt. 26:2,6*;

when Jesus knew that his hour was come that he should depart out of this world unto the Father. The death of Christ is here signified by a departing out of this world, a way of speaking frequently used by the Jews as expressive of death; see the note on *Phil. 1:23* **[62]**. Much such a phrase is made use of concerning Moses, of whom it is said,[1] that the fourth song that was sung in the world, was sung by him,

"when *his time was come,* למפטר מן עלמא, *to depart out of the world*;"
an easy and familiar form of speech to express death by, as if it was only a removing from one place to another. The place from whence Christ was about to remove is called *this world*: this present world, into which He was come to save sinners, and in which He then was, and where He had already met with very ill usage, and barbarous treatment, and was to meet with more: where He was going is said to be *to the Father*, in whose bosom He lay, by whom He was sent, from whom He came; to His God and Father, and the God and Father of all His people, to take His place in their nature at His right hand. A time or hour was fixed for this; for as there was a set time, called *the fulness of time*, agreed upon for His coming into the world, so there was for His going out of it: and now this *his hour was come*; the time was now up, or at least very near at hand; and He *knew* it, being God omniscient, which gave Him no uneasiness: nor did it in the least alienate His affections from His people: for,

having loved his own which were in the world, he loved them to the end. The objects of His love are described by His property in them, *his own*; by whom are meant, not all mankind, who are His by creation; nor the Jews,

---

[1]   Targum in Cant. [Song of Sol.] 1:1, 7. Vid. Bereshit Rabba, sect. 96. fol. 84. 1. & Debarim Rabba, sect. 11. fol. 245. 2.

who were of His nation and countrymen according to the flesh; nor the twelve apostles only, whom He had chosen; but all the elect of God, who are His own, by His choice of them, by the Father's gift of them to Him, by the purchase He made of them with His blood, and by His effectual call of them by His grace. These are also described by their condition and situation, *which were in the world*; which is not said to distinguish them from the saints that were in heaven, or to express their former state of unregeneracy, but their present situation in this vain and evil world, which is no objection to Christ's love to them; for though while in this world they carry about with them a body of sin and death, are liable to many snares and temptations, and are involved in the troubles, and exposed to the hatred of the world, yet are, and always will be, the objects of the love and care of Christ. The acts of His love to them are expressed both in time past, and to come: *having loved* them; so He did from everlasting, with a love of complacency and delight, which He showed as early by espousing their persons to Himself, by undertaking their cause, by taking the charge of their persons, and the care of both their grace and glory, and in time by assuming their nature; and having done all this, *he loved them to the end*: and which He showed by dying for them; and continues to show by interceding for them in heaven, by supplying them with all grace, and by preserving them from a final and total falling away; and He will at last introduce them into His kingdom and glory, when they shall be for ever with Him; and so that love to them continues not only to the end of His own life, nor barely to the end of theirs, but to the end of the world, and for ever; and so εις τελος, signifies, and is rendered *continually*, *Luke 18:5*, and in the Septuagint on *Psa. 9:6,18* and *44:23*, answers to לנצח, which signifies *for ever*; and is so translated here by the Ethiopic version.

Verse 2. **And supper being ended**, &c. Or rather *supper being*, or *it being supper time*, for it was not ended; not the paschal supper, nor the Lord's supper, but the supper in Simon's house at Bethany, two days before the passover. There is no mention made in this whole chapter of the passover supper, or of any of its rites: the washing of the disciples' feet was a peculiar action of our Lord's, and had no manner of regard to any usage among the Jews at such a time; nor was it ever usual with them, at the passover, to wash the feet of those that ate of it; there is not the least trace of any such custom in any of their writings. Besides, it is said in so many words, in *verse 1*, that this was *before the feast of the passover*; and by comparing it with *Matt. 26:2, 6*, it appears to be two days before it; and so much time seems necessary to be allowed, for Judas to do what he did after this supper, in which he was first instigated to it: and that the feast of the passover was yet to come, when this supper was ended, and Judas had taken the sop, and was bid to do quickly what he did, is manifest from the sense the disciples put upon those words of Christ, who thought He ordered him to get the necessaries for the feast, *verse*

29; which can be understood of no other than the feast of the passover, which was at hand, and for which many things were to be gotten ready; to which may be added, that Satan's entering into Judas, and putting it into his heart to betray his master, and his covenanting with the high priests to do it for such a sum, were before the passover supper, as is clear from *Luke 22:1,3,4,7.* Nor is it reasonable to suppose that Judas could meet that night, after the supper, with the chief priests, captains, and all the council, the great Sanhedrin, who could not be together; since by the law of the passover, every head of a family was to be with his respective family: and if this could be supposed, yet there seems to be some time between this agreement, and the execution of it, in which he sought for a proper opportunity, *Matt. 26:16.* Nor can it be thought there was time enough to do all he did, as to covenant with the chief priests, form his scheme for apprehending Christ, and get such a number of men together for that purpose, between the supper, and the time of night in which Christ was betrayed. Besides, certain it is, that Christ and His disciples arose from the place where He ate His supper, and went from thence elsewhere, *John 14:31,* which cannot be understood very well of any other departure than His going from Bethany to Jerusalem, and not of His going from Jerusalem to the garden, which is afterwards spoken of as a distinct thing, *John 18:1.* And to say no more, there is not in this chapter the least hint of the institution of the Lord's supper, which all the other evangelists make mention of, when they relate the last passover of our Lord. The reader may be more fully satisfied of the truth of this by consulting Dr. Lightfoot on *Matt. 26:6.*

the devil having now put it into the heart of Judas Iscariot, Simon's son, to betray him; the person Satan influenced and acted upon, for his purpose, was *Judas Iscariot, Simon's son*: whether this was Simon the Pharisee, or Simon the leper, in whose house Christ and His disciples were, or who he was, is not certain; was there any reason to think it might be Simon the tanner that was the father of Judas, or that either he or his father were tanners, I would venture to add one conjecture more to what has been made on *Matt. 10:4* and *27:5*, concerning Judas's surname, Iscariot, as that it may come from *Iscortia*, which signifies a tanner's coat: for so it is said in the[2] Talmud,

"What is איסקורטיא, *Iscortia*? Says Rabba bar Chanah, it is דצלא כיתונא, *a tanner's coat*:"

a sort of a leathern garment, as the gloss says, which tanners put over their clothes. However, this man was an apostle of Christ's whom Satan tempted

---

[2] T. Bab. Nedarim, fol. 55. 2. Vid. Maimon. & Bartenora in Mishna Celim. c. 16. sect. 4. & Oholot, c. 8. sect. 1.

to betray Him; so that we see that the highest office, and greatest gifts, cannot secure men from the temptations of Satan. The manner in which he tempted him was, he *put*, or *cast* it *into his heart*; it was a dart, and a fiery one, he threw into him, into his very heart; which shows the access Satan has into, and the influence he has upon the minds of men. His end in this temptation was to work upon him *to betray* Christ, his Lord and Master, who had chosen him to be an apostle of His, and had invested him with this high office, into the hands of His enemies, in order to be put to death. This was an affair determined by God, known by Christ, and which He foretold to His disciples; yet all this did not in the least excuse the malice of Satan, and the wickedness of Judas. It was an action devilish indeed, and which, one would think, could never have entered into his heart, had not the devil put it there; and this was at supper time, while they were at table together, that this thought was darted into his mind; which is mentioned to show, that no place and company can preserve persons from the evil suggestions of the devil, and to aggravate the sin of Judas, who when, and while he was eating bread with Christ, first thought of, and determined to lift up his heel against Him. Moreover, it was when the ointment was poured on the head of Christ, and while Judas was fretting at it, that Satan took the opportunity of his choler [*or* irritation] and wrath, to stir him up to so vile an action. This account is prefaced to Christ's washing the feet of His disciples, to show the great composure of mind Christ was in, though He knew what was doing; and His wonderful condescension in washing the feet of so vile a creature, into whose heart Satan had already put it to betray Him; and also His care of, and love to the rest of the disciples, when Satan had gotten possession of one of them.

Verse 3. **Jesus knowing that the Father**, &c. These words express the sense Christ had of His own greatness and dignity as Mediator:

had given all things into his hands; all the persons of the elect, all blessings both of grace and glory for them, and power and authority over all other persons and things, to make them subservient to His purposes:

and that he was come from God; had His mission and commission, as man, from God; did not come of Himself, but He sent Him:

and went to God; or was going to Him in a very little time, to sit at His right hand, to have a name above every name, and to have angels, authorities, and powers subject to Him; which, as it shows His high esteem with His Father, and His exalted character as Mediator, so it greatly illustrates His wonderful humility, that in the view, and under a sense and consideration of all this, He should condescend to wash the feet of His disciples; of which an account is given in the following verses.

Verse 4. **He riseth from supper**, &c. In the midst of the entertainment, and which no doubt was considerable, His mind being intent on something else; and it being His meat and drink to do His Father's will, He rises and leaves His disciples sitting to finish their meal; and while they were murmuring at the waste of the ointment poured on His head, and were filled with indignation at it, as they all of them were, see *Matt. 26:8*, He rises up to wash their feet; amazing patience and humility!

and laid aside his garments; not all His garments, only His upper ones, that He might better dispatch the business He was going about; and which was an emblem of His laying aside, as it were for a while, His glory and dignity as the Son of God, and of His appearing in the form of a servant.

And took a towel; or *linen cloth*, λεντιον, the same with לונטית, in the Jerusalem Talmud:[3]

and girded himself. With the towel, or linen cloth, which served both for a girdle, and after He had washed His disciples' feet, to wipe them with. This was a servile habit; so servants used to stand at the feet of their masters, girt about with a linen cloth;[4] and shows, that *the Son of man came not to be ministered unto, but to minister* [Mark 10:45].

Verse 5. **After that be poureth water into a bason**, &c. This also was a servile work, and what properly belonged to servants to do; see *chapter 2:5-7*. The bason to wash the feet in, called by the Jews עריבת רגלים, was fixed by their doctors to hold, *from two logs to nine kabs*;[5] not *from two logs to ten*, as Dr. Lightfoot has rendered the passage referred to. A *kab* held about a quart of our measure, and a *log* was the fourth part of a *kab*.

and began to wash the disciples feet: this custom of washing the feet was not used by the Jews at their passover, nor at their private entertainments, or common meals, but at the reception of strangers or travelers, which were just come off of a journey, whereby they had contracted dirt and filth, and was a servile work, never performed by superiors to their inferiors, but by inferiors to superiors; as by the wife to the husband, by the son to the father, and by the servant to his master; and was an instance of great humility in any others, as in Abigail, who said to David, *let thine handmaid be a servant to wash the feet*

---

[3] Sabbat, fol. 3. 1. & 12. 1.

[4] Suetonius in Caligula, c. 26.

[5] Mishna Yadaim, c. 4. sect. 1. Vid. Mishna Celim, c. 20. sect. 2.

of the servants of my lord, 1 Sam. 25:41: upon which place some Jewish Rabbins[6] have this note:

> "This she said, על צד הענוה, *by way of humility*, to show, that it would have been sufficient to her, if she became a wife to one of the servants of David, and washed his feet, as was the custom of a wife to her husband."

But what a surprising instance of humility and condescension is this, that Christ, the Lord and Master, should wash the feet of His disciples, when it was their proper work and business to have washed His? Though Dr. Lightfoot says, he does not remember that this was expected from the disciple toward his master, unless included in that rule, *That the disciple is to honor his master, more than his father*; whereas it was a fixed point[7] with the Jews,

> "that all works which a servant does to his master, a disciple does to his master, except unloosing his shoe."

Since therefore it was the work of a servant to wash his master's feet, a disciple was obliged to do this to his master likewise:

and to wipe them with the towel wherewith he was girded. As He began He went through with His work; and having washed their feet, He wipes them clean; which may design the purity of the lives and conversations of the saints in general, and of the ministers of the Gospel in particular, whose feet are beautiful when shod with the preparation of the Gospel of peace, and their conversations are as become the Gospel they preach; both which they have from Christ.

Verse 6. **Then cometh he to Simon Peter**, &c. After having washed the feet of some of the disciples, as is thought by some interpreters, and particularly the feet of Judas, without any repulse; though others are of opinion that He began with Peter, who modestly, and out of reverence to Him, refuses to be washed by Him:

and Peter saith unto him, Lord, dost thou wash my feet! He speaks as one surprised and astonished that Christ should offer to do any such thing to him; that He, who was the Son of the living God, should wash the feet of such a sinful man as he was; that those hands, with which He had wrought such miracles, as the opening the eyes of the blind, cleansing lepers, and raising the dead, should be employed in washing his defiled feet, the meaner and inferior

---

[6] R. Levi ben Gersom & R. Samuel Laniado in I Sam. 25:41. Vid. T. Bab. Cetubot, fol. 96. 1. & Maimon. Hilch. Ishot, c. 21. sect. 7.

[7] T. Bab. Cetubot, fol. 96. 1.

parts of his body; this he thought was greatly below His dignity and character, and too much to be done by Him to such a worthless creature as he was.

Verse 7. **Jesus answered and said unto him**, &c. Christ replies,

What I do, thou knowest not now: Peter knew that He was about to wash his feet, and the rest of His disciples, but he did not know the meaning and mystery of it, what Christ designed by it, and what instruction they were to receive from it,

but thou shalt know hereafter. As he did, when He had performed this service, and explained it to him. This may teach us, under dark providences, the meaning of which is not yet known by us, to wait the Lord's own time to make things clear and plain to us, and in the mean time patiently submit to the divine will.

Verse 8. **Peter saith unto him, Thou shalt never wash my feet**, &c. Before he had behaved with modesty, but now with obstinacy and perverseness; and though these expressions might arise from great reverence to Christ, yet they were wrong and rashly spoken. Peter ought to have been satisfied with Christ's reply, and have submitted, since though he then did not know the reason of such a surprising conduct, he should hereafter. In order therefore to bring him to a compliance,

Jesus answered him, If I wash thee not, thou hast no part with me. He does not say, if I wash not thy feet, but *thee*, meaning not with water, but with His blood, and by His Spirit; for Christ uses the word *wash* here, not literally, but in a mystical and figurative sense, and takes an occasion, as He sometimes does, from things natural, to discourse of things spiritual. Moreover, He does not say, thou hast no part *in* me, but thou hast no part *with* me, that is, no fellowship and communion with me; see *2 Cor. 6:14-15*; and it is as if He should say, Peter, if I had not washed thee with the washing of regeneration by my Spirit, and if I should not shed my blood for thee, and wash thee in it from thy sins, sad would be thy case; thou couldest have no communion with me in this world, nor any part and portion with me in the heavenly inheritance hereafter. Hence it may be observed, that unless a man is washed by Christ, he can have no part with Him in this, or the other world. God's elect have a part, an interest in Christ through eternal, electing, and covenant grace; and in consequence of this are washed by Christ, both with His blood, and with the washing of regeneration: and this is done in order that they may have a part with Christ, spiritual fellowship with Him now, and possess with Him the undefiled inheritance, when time shall be no more.

Verse 9. **Simon Peter saith unto him**, &c. Being convinced of his mistake in not submitting to Christ, fearing he should be deprived of communion with Him, than which nothing was more desirable to him, or more highly esteemed of by him, says,

Lord, not my feet only, but also *my* **hands and** *my* **head**. Which shows the sense he had of the general pollution of his nature, and the need he stood in particularly of having his feet, hands, and head washed, both as a minister, and a believer. By his *feet* may be meant, either the grace of faith, which is the foot of the soul, by which it goes to Christ, and walks on in Him, and was not without its imperfections; or the affections of the mind, which are that to the soul, as the feet are to the body; and when they move right, move Heavenward, Godward, and Christward; but sometimes they are inordinate, and cleave to the things of this world: or the outward life and conversation is meant, which is attended with daily infirmities; and each of these need washing in the blood of Christ. His *hands* may design all his actions, works, services, duties, and performances, the hand being the instrument of action; and not only the hands of wicked men, but even of saints, need washing, their best righteousnesses being *as filthy rags* [see *Isa. 64:6*]. By his *head* may be meant doctrines and principles imbibed in the mind, and expressed by the lips, which were not free from mistake and pollution, and needed purging and cleansing; for the disciples were not as yet clear from the prejudices of the Jewish nation, especially relating to the nature of the Messiah's kingdom.

Verse 10. **Jesus saith to him, He that is washed**, &c. Not he that is baptized; for every such person is not wholly clean, but he who is regenerated by the Spirit of God, or rather, who is washed in the blood of Christ: such a one *is clean every whit*; is all over clean; not that he has no sin in him, nor commits any; but as he is washed in the blood of Christ, and justified by His righteousness, he is wholly and entirely clean in the sight of God; for he is justified from all things he could not be justified from by the law of Moses; all his sins are pardoned, and he is perfectly righteous before God; and so is perfectly clean through the word or sentence of justification and absolution pronounced on him, which must be understood in a forensic or law sense. And such a one,

needeth not save to wash his feet, but is clean every whit; the feet of his life and conversation, which are continually gathering dirt, and need daily washing in the blood of Christ; and therefore recourse must be constantly had to that *fountain* to wash in, *for sin and for uncleanness* [*Zech. 13:1*]. The allusion is either to persons washed all over in a bath, who have no need to wash again, unless their feet, which may contract some soil in coming out of it; or to travelers, who have often need to wash their feet, though no other part, and such is the case of the children of God in this life; or rather to the priests, who having bathed themselves in the morning, needed not to wash again all the day, except their hands and feet, on certain occasions.[8]

And ye are clean, but not all. Which shows, that justifying and regenerating grace are common to all the true disciples of Christ; they are equally born again, alike justified, and are as clean one as another in the sight of God; not only Peter, but all the apostles, were clean, excepting one; there was one of them, Judas, who was not clean; and therefore He says, *but not all*: whence it may be observed, that among the purest societies, there are some unclean persons; there was a Judas, an unclean person among the pure disciples of Christ; there are chaff and tares among His wheat, goats among his sheep, and foolish virgins along with the wise ones.

Verse 11. **For he knew who should betray him**, &c. That is, *Jesus*, as Beza's ancient copy, and the Syriac and Persic versions read. This He knew from the beginning; not only from the beginning of His ministry, when He chose His twelve apostles, but from the beginning of time, yea, from everlasting; this being fixed by the determinate counsel of God, which He, as the omniscient God, was privy to: He knew what preparations were making, and how things were then working, in order to bring it about; He knew that Satan had already put it into Judas's heart, and that he had consented to it;

therefore, said he, Ye are not all clean. He does not mention his name, though He could have done so, it not being as yet proper to make so full a discovery of him before the matter was ripe for execution; and also to put all the disciples upon examination of themselves.

Verse 12. **So after he had washed their feet**, &c. Not Peter's only, but the rest of the disciples also: some have thought, that He washed only the feet of some of them, and not all; but it seems, by this expression, that He performed this service to each of them. And when He had gone through it with every one of them:

and had taken his garments, and put them on,

and was sat down again; at the table with His disciples, supper not being yet ended; when having done His work as a servant, He reassumes the air and authority of Lord and Master, and begins to teach and instruct, into the design and use of what He had been doing, which He introduces by putting this question:

---

[8]   Mishna Yoma, c. 3. sect. 3.

he said unto them, Know ye what I have done to you? They knew the outward action He had done to them, that He had washed their feet; but, as yet, they did not know the mystery of it, Christ's design in it, and what He would have them learn from it.

Verse 13. **Ye call me Master and Lord**, &c. רבי, and מר, *Master* and *Lord*, were dignified titles among the Jews, which they frequently[9] gave to their doctors and men of learning, and are often to be met with in their writings: hence the disciples called Christ by these names, not out of flattery, but reverence of Him, and esteem for Him; nor are they blamed, but commended for it:

and ye say well, for so I am. Though He had acted the part of a servant in such a surprising manner, by washing their feet; yet He had not dropped and lost, but still maintains His place and authority as a *Master*, to teach and instruct them, and as a *Lord*, to rule and govern them.

Verse 14. **If I then, *your* Lord and Master**, &c. Christ argues from these titles and characters, which His disciples rightly gave Him, and from what He had done to them, though He stood in such a superior relation to them, to their duty one towards another; that since, says he, I,

have washed your feet, ye also ought to wash one another's feet. By which He does not mean barely, that they should perform this single action; but as this was an instance of humility and condescension, and doing a good office to strangers and travelers, and was afterwards an expression of love to the saints, see *1 Tim. 5:10*, so He would teach them hereby to behave in a spirit of humility and condescension to one another, to do every kind and good office, and by love to serve one another in all things.

Verse 15. **For I have given you an example**, &c. Christ is an example to His people, in many things; not in His miraculous performances and mediatorial work, but in the exercise of grace, of meekness, humility, love, patience, and the like; and in the discharge of duty, in submission to ordinances, and in attending on them; and in the several duties, both to them that are without, and to them that are within; and also in His sufferings and death; not that He died merely as an example, but likewise in the room and stead of His people; but here He is spoken of as an example, in a particular instance:

that ye should do as I have done to you. Wash one another's feet, as He had washed theirs; which is not to be understood literally and singly of this

---

[9]   Vid. T. Bab. Beracot, fol. 3. 1. Derech Erets, c. 6. fol. 18. 2.

action, as though this was an ordinance binding upon all persons, in all places, and to be attended to at certain stated times, as has been the practice of some: it was so understood by the church at Milan, and there practiced; and this custom was continued and defended by St. Ambrose, even though not received by the church of Rome; in some places the bishop used to wash the feet of those that were baptized, which in process of time being thought sufficient, instead of baptism, was forbidden by the council at Eliberis. In imitation of this, the pope every year, on Thursday in the passion week, washes the feet of twelve men; and it is an anniversary ceremony performed by the kings of England and France, to wash the feet of twelve poor people, in com-memoration of this action of Christ's: but our Lord is not to be understood literally, nor of any thing that was to be done once a year, but of what was daily and constantly to be practiced; and which was to be done not by one only to all the rest, but what they were mutually to do; what they were to do to one another; for the thing signified, reaches to, and is obligatory upon all Christians. Our Lord's meaning is, that as He had by this action given them an example of humility, condescension, and love; so they should exercise these graces, and perform such kind offices to one another, and to all their fellow Christians.

Verse 16. **Verily, verily, I say unto you**, &c. This is a strong way of asseveration, and is used when any thing of moment and importance, and worthy of attention and observation, is delivered.

The servant is not greater than his lord; it is enough that he be as his Lord, which was a common phrase among the Jews; see the notes on *Matt. 10:24-25* **[14]**; and as it is there made use of, to inform the disciples they must expect persecution, and to encourage them to bear it with patience; here it is designed to engage them to humility; for if a master condescends to perform such an action, much more may a servant:

neither he that is sent is greater than he that sent him. This is also a way of speaking in use among the Jews;

"R. Meir says,[10] Who is greatest, he that keeps, or he that is kept? From what is written in *Psa. 91:11*, he that is kept, is greater than he that keeps. Says R. Judah, Which is greatest, he that carries, or he that is carried? From what is written in *Psa. 91:12*, he that is carried, is greater than he that carries. Says R. Simeon, from what is written, in *Isa. 6:8*, הוי המשלח גדול מן המשתלח, *he that sends is greater than he that is sent.*"

---

[10] Bereshit Rabba, fol. 68. 1.

Which is the very phrase here used by Christ; and His meaning is this, that if it was not below Him, who had chosen and called, and sent them forth as His apostles, to wash their feet, they who were sent by Him, should not disdain to wash one another's.

Verse 17. **If ye know these things**, &c. The duties they owed to Him, and one another; those kind offices of love and respect to each other; the humility, condescension, and brotherly love, which ought to be in them, and of which He had given them an example:

happy are ye if ye do them. For the bare theory, or a mere speculative knowledge of these things, is not sufficient; not he that knows and *does not*, but he that knows and *does* his Master's will, is blessed; he is blessed with communion with his Lord, and shall hereafter enter into His joy, with *Well done, good and faithful servant* [*Matt. 25:23*]. There is a happiness *in* doing well, and which follows *on* it, though not *for* it, in a way of merit; on the other hand, persons who *know* and *do not*, are very unhappy; the Jews have a saying,[11]

"שהלמד שלא לעשות, *he that learns but not to do*, it would have been better for him, if he had never been created. And, says R. Jochanan, He that learns, but not to do, it would have been better for him if his secundine had been turned upon his face, and he had never come into the world."

Verse 18. **I speak not of you all**. What He had before said on the one hand, *Ye are not all clean, verse 11*, for one of them was not; and on the other hand, when He put an *if* upon, or seemed to doubt of their knowing and doing these things [*verse 17*]; or what He was about to say concerning His being betrayed, this He did not speak of them all:

I know whom I have chosen; not to apostleship, for they were all chosen to that, Judas as well as the rest, but to grace and glory, to everlasting salvation and happiness; of these He was well assured that they were all clean, pure, and spotless, in the sight of God; were truly regenerated by the Spirit of God, and had an experimental and practical knowledge of the things He recommended by His example, and would be the happy persons He spake of;

but, He observes, so it is, and will come to pass, that there is one of you which will betray me:

---

[11] Hieros. Beracot, fol. 3. 2.

that the Scripture may be fulfilled: *Psa. 41:9*, as it literally[12] was in Judas's betraying Christ. The passage is by many interpreted either of Ahithophel, or of some other counselor of Absalom's, or of Absalom himself; and is applied to their conduct, with respect to David, at the time of their rebellion against him; and which is thought to be typical of the treatment Christ met with from an apostle of His. But we do not find that, at the time of that rebellion, David was sick, or had any disease upon him, from whence they might hope for his death; it does not seem, as though it could be literally understood of David at all, and of the behavior of any of his servants; but most properly of David's son, the Messiah, Jesus, with whom every thing in the Psalm agrees; and particularly this verse, which so plainly describes Judas, and expresses his base ingratitude, hypocrisy, and malice. The former part of the text is not cited, *yea, mine own familiar friend*, or *the man of my peace, in whom I trusted*; though it fully agrees with him, he being admitted to great familiarity with Christ, and lived peaceably with Him; and who was intrusted by Him with the bag, into which the money was put, which was ministered either for the sustenance of Him and His apostles, or for the use of the poor: but our Lord thought fit to cite no more of it than what follows, that being sufficiently descriptive of him; and especially at this present time, when he was at table with his Lord.

He that eateth bread with me, hath lifted up his heel against me. He sat down with Him at table frequently, and ate bread with Him; and was doing so when Satan put it into his heart to betray Him; which is strongly expressed, by *lifting up* his *heel against* Him; and sets forth the ingratitude, wickedness, and cruelty of him; who, like an unruly horse that has thrown his rider, spurns at him to destroy him; and also the insidious manner in which he did it; he supplanted, he tripped Him, as wrestlers do, in order to cast Him down to the ground, and then trample upon Him, and triumph over Him: he first מארב, *laid snares for him*, as Jarchi explains the phrase used in the *psalm*, and then הגדיל, *he magnified his heel*, he behaved proudly and haughtily to Him.

Verse 19. **Now I tell you before it come**, &c. That is, gave them notice of this beforehand, that one of them should betray Him:

that, when it is come to pass; and they had seen it fulfilled exactly to a tittle, and according to this Scripture:

ye may believe that I am *he*. The Lord God omniscient, who knows and declares things before they come to pass, just as they do come to pass; which

---

[12] See my Book of the Prophecies of the Messiah, &c. p. 168, &c.

THE GOSPEL OF JOHN

none but the eternal God can do; and that He was the Savior and Redeemer, the Messiah spoken of and promised, the very person prophesied of in *Psalm 41*. For that whole psalm is applicable to Jesus Christ, the true Messiah. In *verses 1-3*, the happiness of such is declared, who *consider the poor*; the Messiah, in His low estate of humiliation, who became poor for the sake of His people; in *verse 5*, His enemies are represented as wishing for His death; their hypocrisy, perfidy, and vile designs upon His life, are aptly described in *verses 6-7*, which they executed by suborning false witnesses, bringing a wrong charge, דבר בליעל, *a wicked accusation against him, verse 8*, which succeeded, to the taking away of His life; and then they are introduced as triumphing over Him, lying dead in the grave, whom they believed would never rise more; but in this they were mistaken, for He was raised up again; for which He prays, *verse 10*, that He might requite them, as He did, by destroying their city, temple, and nation; and the whole is concluded with thankfulness to God, for raising and exalting Him, and setting him before His face for ever, *verses 11-13*. There is but one passage in it, which has any difficulty in applying it to Christ, and that is, *verse 4*, where He is spoken of as having sinned against the Lord; but the words may be rendered thus, *heal my soul*, that is, deliver me out of my sorrows and afflictions, כי הטאתי לך, *because I have made an offering for sin unto thee*; and well agrees with Christ, who was to make, and has made His soul an offering for sin.

Verse 20. **Verily, verily, I say unto you**, &c. You may assure yourselves of the truth of what I am going to say, and which I say for your comfort and encouragement:

He that receiveth whomsoever I send receiveth me; and he that receiveth me receiveth him that sent me. I have sent you in my name to preach the Gospel; you are my ambassadors, and you will be honorably received by many; and which I shall regard and take notice of, and esteem, as though they had received me; even as my Father has sent me into this world, as a Savior and Redeemer, a prophet, priest, and King; and as many as have received me, are looked upon by my Father, as having received Him. In short, such as cordially receive and embrace the ministers of the Gospel, receive Christ, in whose name they come, and whom they preach; and such who receive Christ, as preached and held forth in the everlasting Gospel, receive the Father of Christ; and partake of His love, grace, and kindness, shown forth in the mission and gift of Christ to them: Christ, as Mediator, personated [or represented] His Father that sent Him; and the ministers of Christ personate Him; so that what is done to them, either in a way of reception or rejection, He takes as done to Himself: it is a common saying among the Jews,[13] שלוחו של אדם כמותו, *that the messenger of a man is as himself.*

Verse 21. **When Jesus had thus said**, &c. Having spoken of the mission of His disciples by Him, of their reception among men, and the notice that would be taken of it by Him:

he was troubled in spirit; in His soul, which shows Him to be truly and really man, and to have a human soul, which some have denied; and that to be of like passions with ours, only without sin: He was troubled, not at what He had said, but at what He was about to say concerning the betrayer; and that not so much on His own account, because of the danger, the sorrows, and sufferings He should be exposed to, as on account of the horrible blackness of the crime, and the vengeance that would fall upon the criminal; and being thus inwardly distressed at this affair, he,

testified, and said: He spake out openly and plainly, what He had before secretly intimated, and that with the greatest certainty:

Verily, verily, I say unto you; it is truth, it may be believed, however unexpected and strange it may seem to be:

that one of you shall betray me. To the chief priests and elders, in order to be put to death.

Verse 22. **Then the disciples looked one on another**, &c. As persons surprised and astonished, and as scarce crediting what was said; not having had the least suspicion of any one among them that could be guilty of such an action; and expressing by their looks their detestation of, and indignation at so horrible an iniquity; or they looked one to another, to observe if they could, whether the countenance of any one would discover who the person was:

doubting of whom he spake. Not being able to conceive and imagine, who the person was He had in view; from whence it appears, that Judas, to this time, had behaved outwardly as well as any of the other disciples; he had given no occasion by his conduct to suspect him more than any other: upon this broad intimation, or rather strong protestation which Christ made, that one of them should betray Him, their eyes were not turned to him directly and particularly, but to one another.

---

[13] T Bab. Beracot, fol. 34. 2. Kiddushin, fol. 41. 2. & 42. 1. & 43. 1. Bava Metzia, fol. 96. 1.

Verse 23. **Now there was leaning on Jesus' bosom**, &c. Not pressing upon that part of Christ's body, which would have been irreverent in John, and troublesome to Christ; but leaning at table upon his bed or couch, on which he lay; and which was next to, and just before Christ; so that he was very near unto, and seemed to lie in the bosom of Christ; as such are said to do who sit next to another at table. The posture of the Jews at table, was either *sitting* or *lying*, and a difference they make between these two;

"If, (say they,[14]) היו יושבין, *they sat* to eat, every one asked a blessing for himself; but if הסיבו, *they lay down*, one asked a blessing for them all."

This lying down was not on their backs, nor on their right side, but on their left; for they say[15] that,

"lying down on the back, is not called הסיבה, *lying down*; and lying on the right side, is not called lying down."

And the reason given is,[16] because they have need of the right hand to eat with; but as they elsewhere[17] observe,

"they used to eat lying along, leaning on the left side, their feet to the ground, and every man on a single couch."

Would you know the order in which they lay, take the account as they have given it:[18]

"When there were but two couches, the principal person lay first, and the second to him above him; and when there were three, the principal person lay in the middle, the second to him above him, and the third below him; and if he would talk with him, he raised himself upright, and sitting upright he talked with him; that is, as the gloss explains it, if the principal person was desirous to talk with him that was second to him, he must raise himself up from his lying down, and sit upright; for all the while he is leaning, he cannot talk with him, because he that is second to him, is behind the head of the principal person, and the face of the principal person is turned to the other side; and it is better for the second to sit below him, that he may hear his words, while he is leaning."

---

[14] Mishna Beracot, c. 6. sect. 6.

[15] T. Bab. Pesachim, fol. 108. 1.

[16] Gloss in ibid.

[17] Gloss in T. Bab. Beracot, fol. 46. 2. & Bartenora in Mishna Beracot, c. 6. sect. 6.

[18] T. Bab. Beracot, fol. 46. 2.

The form in which Christ and his disciples sat or lay at table, we may conceive was this:[19] a table was placed in the middle and as many beds or couches round it, as there were persons; Christ, the principal and most worthy person, lay first, with His head toward the table, His face somewhat turned from it, leaning on His left elbow upon the couch; in this posture lay Jesus, upon the first couch; in the same posture lay John, in the next to Him, and just before him; the hinder part of his head being towards, and near the breast and bosom of Jesus; whence he is said to lean upon it: now to lie next to the principal person, was a very great honor, as well as a mark of great affection; and for John to lie next to Jesus, and as it were to lean on His bosom, showed how much he was respected and honored by Him; and therefore John modestly conceals his name, and only says,

one of his disciples, whom Jesus loved. Christ, as the Son of God, and surety of His people, loved His true disciples, as He does all His elect, alike; not one more than the other; but as man, He had a particular affection for this disciple, and therefore admitted him nearest His person, and was very familiar with him.

Verse 24. **Simon Peter therefore beckoned to him**, &c. Peter perhaps lay at a distance from Christ, or in some such position, that he could not whisper to Him himself; and besides, he knew that John might use more freedom, as he was admitted to more familiarity with Him; and being at some distance also from him, he *beckoned* to him; which was usually done at meals, when they could not, by reason of their posture, discourse together: this being the case, מחוי ליה במחוג, *they made signs*, by nodding to one another;[20] that is, as the gloss explains it, they pointed with their hands and fingers, and by nodding or beckoning; such a method Peter took, signifying his desire,

that he should ask who it should be of whom he spake. Which he did not out of mere curiosity, but from an honest intention and pure zeal, that he, with the rest, might show their abhorrence of such a person, and avoid him; and do all that lay in their power to hinder him from putting his wicked designs into execution, and that the innocent might be free from all suspicion.

Verse 25. **He then lying on Jesus' breast**, &c. Being on the couch just before Jesus, with his back to Him, he bends backwards, and falling on Jesus' breast, whispers in His ear: and,

---

[19] Vid. Alstorphium de lectis veterum, p. 109, 110.

[20] T. Bab. Beracot, ibid.

saith unto him, Lord, who is it? Using his interest in Christ, and making thus free with Him, in compliance with Peter's request; and was no doubt desirous himself of knowing who the person was.

Verse 26. **Jesus answered, He it is,** &c. Jesus replied, by whispering; for had He spoken out, the rest could not have been so ignorant, as they still continued, after the sign was given: Christ, I say, whispered to John, and told him by what sign he might know the person, and that it was he,

to whom, says He,

I shall give a sop, when I have dipped *it*. This was not the passover sop, which was dipped into a sauce made of various things, called by the Jews חרוסת; for this was not the *paschal* supper, but a common supper at a private house, two days before the feast of the passover; but this sop, or rather crust of bread, which whether dipped into a liquid, or only a piece of dry bread, which Christ dipped His hand into the dish for, and took, as some think, is not very material, was a piece of common bread, which Christ took up, without regard to any custom, or ceremony used at any feasts, and gave it to the betrayer, as a sign by which John might know him:

and when he had dipped the sop; either into some sort of broth, or any other liquid, or had dipped His hand into the dish for it:

he gave it to Judas Iscariot, *the son* **of Simon.** So called, to distinguish him from another apostle, whose name was Judas, and was then present.

Verse 27. **And after the sop,** &c. After he had taken and eaten the sop, or crust of bread, by which he was pointed out to be the betrayer,

Satan entered into him; possessed his body, and filled his mind, and stirred him up more eagerly to pursue with vigor his wicked design. The Jews have a saying[21] that,

> "no man commits a transgression, until, נכנס בו רוח שטות, *a spirit of madness enters into him.*"

Such an evil spirit entered into Judas, which pushed him on to commit this horrid iniquity.

Then said Jesus unto him, That thou doest, do quickly. This He said, not as approving his wicked design, and exhorting him to it as a laudable action, but rather as deriding him, having nothing to care about, or fear from him; or as upbraiding him with his perfidy and wickedness, and signifying that He should take no methods to prevent him, though He fully knew what

---

[21] T. Bab. Sota, fol. 3. 1. Tzeror Hammor, fol. 112. 1. & 117. 3.

was in his heart to do; and it seems also to express the willingness of Christ, and His eager and hearty desire to suffer and die for His people, in order to obtain salvation for them.

Verse 28. **Now no man at the table**, &c. Not one of those who lay upon the couches at the table, excepting John, to whom the signal was given:

knew for what intent he spake this unto him. And perhaps John might not know the meaning of His last words, that He spoke concerning the act of betraying Him; or did not imagine that the thing was so near and so speedily to be done as it was.

Verse 29. **For some of *them* thought**, &c. This was the thought of some of the disciples, it may be of all of them but John;

because Judas had the bag: which was for the common supply of Christ and His disciples, and for the relief of the poor; see the note on *chapter 12:6;*

that Jesus had said unto him, Buy those things that we have need of against the feast; the feast of the passover, which was to be two days after; and shows, that this was not the passover which Christ now ate with His disciples:

or, that he should give something to the poor. For whom Christ cared, and had a hearty concern, and for whom Judas had very little, notwithstanding his high pretensions.

Verse 30. **He then having received the sop**, &c. As soon as ever he received it, he,

went immediately out; fearing lest an entire discovery should be made, and he be prevented accomplishing his design; or being more violently stirred up to it by Satan, who after the sop entered into him, he directly went from Bethany to Jerusalem, to the chief priests there, in order to consult and agree upon the delivery of Him into their hands:

and it was night. This circumstance is added, to show how eagerly he was bent upon it; that though it was night, it did not hinder or discourage him from setting out on his journey to Jerusalem; and as this was a work of darkness, the night was the fittest time for it, and was a proper emblem of the blackness of the crime he was going to perpetrate.

Verse 31. **Therefore, when he was gone out, Jesus said**, &c. Christ and His true disciples being together alone, He used a greater freedom of conversation with them, and entered into some discourse about His sufferings and death; with a view to give them some instructions about their future conduct and behavior, and in order to support them under the loss of His presence; and tells them in the first place, that,

Now is the Son of man glorified: by *the Son of man*, He means Himself; a phrase He often uses when speaking of Himself; this was a title the Messiah went by in prophecy; was true in fact of Jesus, who was the son of Abraham, and the son of David, and expresses the truth of His humanity; and He the rather chooses to use it now, because He is speaking of a glorification, which He in His divine nature was incapable of, and which regards either time past, present, or to come: the meaning may be, either that He had been already glorified by His doctrines and miracles; or that He was now glorified, by discovering the traitor, before he made one single overt act towards betraying Him; or that in a very short time He should be glorified, meaning at His death; see *chapter 17:1*. But how was He then glorified, when it was an accursed one, and attended with so much ignominy and reproach? He was then glorified by His Father, who supported Him in it, and carried Him through it; so as that He conquered all His enemies, and obtained eternal salvation for His people. Moreover, the death of Christ was not only His way to glory, but was attended with many wonderful and surprising events; as the darkness, the earthquakes, the rending of the rocks, and veil of the temple, and the like; and it was also glorious in the eyes of His Father, because hereby His purposes were accomplished, His covenant transactions brought about, His law and justice were satisfied, and the salvation of His people finished:

and God is glorified in him. The glory of God was great, in the salvation of His elect by the death of Christ; for hereby His wisdom and power, His truth and faithfulness, His justice and holiness, as well as His love, grace, and mercy, were glorified.

Verse 32. **If God be glorified in him**, &c. Seeing this is a certain truth, is indisputably matter of fact, that all the perfections of God are glorified in Christ, by His sufferings and death:

God shall also glorify him in himself; either *with himself*, with His own glory, which was promised to Christ, and which He had before the world was, and for which He prays, *chapter 17:5*; or *by himself*: by His own power, in raising Him from the dead, setting Him at His own right hand, and crowning Him with glory and honor:

and shall straightway glorify him. This He will do very quickly, He will not leave Him in the grave, nor suffer Him to see corruption; He will raise Him again the third day, and give Him glory.

Verse 33. **Little children, yet a little while I am with you**, &c. Christ having removed the scandal of His death, by observing, that both He and His Father would be glorified by it, begins more freely to open His mind to His disciples, and acquaint them with it; whom He addresses in the most kind, tender, and affectionate manner, *little children*, expressing the relation which subsisted between them, of which He was not unmindful; His great affection for them, His consideration of their weakness, and sympathy with them on that account; who were very ill able to bear His departure, which He now thought high time to acquaint them with, that it would be very shortly: it was but a little while He was to be with them, a few days more; the time of His departure was at hand, His hour was as it were come, and the last sands were dropping:

Ye shall seek me; as persons in distress, under great concern, not knowing what to do, or where to go:

and as I said unto the Jews, *chapter 7:33-34*;

Whither I go, ye cannot come; so now I say to you. But with this difference, whereas the unbelieving Jews, who died in their sins, could never come whither He went, these His disciples, though they could not come now, yet they should hereafter, all of them, as well as Peter, *verse 36*.

Verse 34. **A new commandment I give unto you**, &c. As parents, when they take their leave of their children, in their dying moments, give them proper instructions and orders, and lay their dying injunctions on them, so Christ, taking His leave of His disciples, gives them His; which were,

That ye love one another: as brethren in the same family, children of the same Father, and fellow disciples with each other; by keeping and agreeing together, praying one for another, bearing one another's burdens, forbearing and forgiving one another, admonishing each other, and building up one another in faith and holiness: and this He calls *a new commandment*; that is, a very excellent one; as a *new name*, and a *new song*, denote excellent ones; or it is so called, because it is set forth by Christ, in a new edition of it, and newly and more clearly explained than before; and being enforced with a new argument and pattern, never used before,

as I have loved you; and to be observed in a new manner, not *in the oldness of the letter, but in the newness of the spirit* [see *Rom. 7:6*]: besides, though this commandment, as to the matter of it, is the same with that of Moses, *Lev. 19:18*; yet it takes in more, and *new* objects; since by *neighbor* there, seems to be meant *the children of their people*, the Jews; and so they understood it only of their countrymen, and of proselytes at farthest, whereas this reaches to any *other* person; see *Rom. 13:8*; and as the measure, as well as the motive is new, for it is not now *as thy self*, but *as I have loved you*; the Jew has no reason to object as he does,[22] to its being called a *new commandment*: and its being *new*, carries in it a reason or argument, why it should be observed, as does also the following clause;

that ye also love one another. Than which, nothing can, or should, more strongly engage to it: as Christ has loved His people freely, notwithstanding all their unworthiness and ungratefulness, so should they love one another, though there may be many things in them observable, which are disagreeable; as Christ loves all His children without any distinction, so should they love one another, whether poor or rich, weaker or stronger, lesser or greater believers; and as Christ loves them not in word only, but in deed and in truth, so should they love one another with a pure heart fervently, and by love serve one another.

Verse 35. **By this shall all *men* know**, &c. Not only by this you yourselves will know that ye have passed from death to life, that the true work of grace is begun upon your hearts; nor only by this will you know one another to be Christians; but by this all men, even the men of the world will know,

that ye are my disciples, if ye have love one to another. And own and acknowledge it, as Tertullian[23] says the very heathens did in his time; who would say when they saw the Christians pass along the streets, and meet and express their affection to each other, *See how they love one another!*: would to God the same was as observable now. The distinguishing badge and character of a disciple of Christ, is not any outward garb, or any austerities of life, by which the disciples of John and of the Pharisees were known; nor were the ordinary nor extraordinary gifts of the Spirit, bestowed upon the disciples of Christ, what distinguished them as such; since those who were not truly His disciples, had these bestowed on them; but love to one another, brotherly love was the distinguishing character, and this is another reason or argument enforcing a regard unto it.

Verse 36. **Simon Peter said unto him**, &c. One might have expected that Peter would have taken some notice of what Christ said last, about love to one another; but he passes over it, and takes no manner of notice of it; which did not arise from inattention to it, or from any dislike of it, or disaffection to it; for it appears from his whole conduct and writings, that he had the utmost regard for it; he very frequently presses it, and most fervently practiced it; but

---

[22] R. Isaac Chizzuk Emuna, l. 2. c. 54. p. 444.

[23] Apolog. c. 39.

having observed some words which dropped from Christ's lips, *whither I go ye cannot come, verse 33*, his mind was intent upon them, was uneasy about them, and very much wanted to know the meaning of them; and as soon as Christ had done speaking, took the opportunity to put the question:

Lord, whither goest thou? imagining He was going to some distant place in the country, and which was difficult of access; whereby he betrayed his weakness and ignorance, as the Jews did, *chapter 7:35.*

Jesus answered him, Whither I go, thou canst not follow me now; which words imply, that Christ was going somewhere in a little time; He was going to the garden to surrender Himself up into the hands of His enemies, and hither Peter could, and did follow Him, and therefore that is not here meant; He was going to die for His people, in order to take away the sting of death and the curse of the law, and work out salvation for them; He was going to His Father in heaven, to receive gifts for men, and to send the Comforter; to open the way to heaven, take possession of it, and prepare it for His saints; to plead the cause, and transact the business of His dear children; and to receive a kingdom for Himself, and return. Now hither, as yet, Peter could not follow Him; for His time of suffering death was not yet come; Christ had some other work for him to do first; he must open the door of faith to the Gentiles, and preach the Gospel to them:

but thou shalt follow me afterwards. When thy time is come, and thou hast done the work allotted for thee, thou shalt follow me by dying for me; and thou shalt follow me into my kingdom and glory, and be for ever with me: all the saints shall follow Christ to heaven, who is their forerunner for them entered; and as sure as He is there, so sure shall they be also. The counsels of God are unalterable, the covenant of grace is firm and sure, the blood of Christ can never be spilled in vain, His prayers and preparations cannot be fruitless, nor the work of the Spirit be ever lost; wherefore not one of those who are given to Christ, and come to Him, and follow Him here, but shall follow Him hereafter.

Verse 37. **Peter said unto him**, &c. Not understanding Christ's answer, and being dissatisfied with it, he inquires:

Lord, why cannot I follow thee now? Is the place inaccessible? Are the difficulties in the way to it insuperable? The roughness of the road, or the dangers of it, will not discourage me; I am ready to go through the greatest dangers and difficulties, to follow thee: yea,

I will lay down my life for thy sake. Whatever enemies I should meet with in following thee, would not dismay me; I would readily hazard my life, and cheerfully lay it down in defense of thee.

Verse 38. **Jesus answered him, Wilt thou lay down thy life for my sake**?
&c. Christ speaks these words as questioning, not Peter's sincerity, but his
strength; or as deriding him, or rather pitying him; as if He should say, Thou
poor vain self-sufficient man, thou dost not know what thou talkest of:

**Verily, verily, I say unto thee, The cock shall not crow, till thou hast
denied me thrice**. Not that Peter should deny Him three times, before the
cock crowed once; for certain it is, that Peter denied Christ but once, before
the cock crew, *Mark 14:68*; but the meaning is, that before the cock had done
crowing, or within the time of cock crowing, he should deny Him thrice.
Whence it follows, that there is no necessity of concluding from hence, that
this night was the passover night, and the night in which Judas betrayed
Christ, and Peter denied Him, but was two nights before; and therefore it is
not said here, as by the other evangelists, *this day*, or *this night*, or *this day,
even this night thou shalt deny me*; only in general *before the cock crows*, or
within the time of cock crowing: so that it appears, that Peter twice expressed
his confidence, in laying down his life for Christ; once at the supper in Simon's
house at Bethany, two days before the passover, and again at the passover
supper in Jerusalem; and as often Christ rebuked his confidence by this
expression, only varying it as the different times required, and therein gave
a full proof of His omniscience.

CHAPTER 14

Verse 1. **Let not your heart be troubled**, &c. In some copies this verse
begins thus, *and He said to His disciples*; and certain it is, that these words
are addressed to them in general, Peter being the only person our Lord was
discoursing with in the latter part of the preceding chapter; but turning, as it
were, from him, He directs His speech to them all. There were many things
which must needs lie heavy upon, and greatly depress the minds of the

disciples; most of all the loss of Christ's bodily presence, His speedy departure from them, of which He had given them notice in the preceding chapter; also the manner in which He should be removed from them, and the circumstances that should attend the same, as that He should be betrayed by one of them, and denied by another; likewise the poor and uncomfortable situation they were likely to be left in, without any sight or hope of that temporal kingdom being erected, which they had been in expectation of; and also the issue and consequence of all this, that they would be exposed to the hatred and persecutions of men. Now in the multitude of these thoughts within them, Christ comforts them, bids them be of good heart, and exhorts them to an exercise of faith on God, and on Himself, as the best way to be rid of heart troubles, and to have peace:

ye believe in God, believe also in me. Which words may be read and interpreted different ways: either thus, *ye believe in God, and ye believe in me*; and so are both propositions alike, and express God and Christ to be equally the object of their faith; and since therefore they had so good a foundation for their faith and confidence, they had no reason to be uneasy: or thus, *believe in God, and believe in me*; and so both are exhortations to exercise faith alike on them both, as being the best antidote they could make use of against heart troubles: or thus, *believe in God, and ye believe in me*; and so the former is an exhortation, the latter a proposition: and the sense is, put your trust in God, and you will also trust in me, for I am of the same nature and essence with Him; *I and my Father are one*; so that if you believe in one, you must believe in the other: or thus, and so our translators render them, *ye believe in God, believe also in me*; and so the former is a proposition, or an assertion, and the latter is an exhortation grounded upon it: you have believed in God as faithful and true in all His promises, though you have not seen Him; believe in me also, though I am going from you, and shall be absent for a while; this you may be assured of, that whatever I have said shall be accomplished. The words considered either way are a full proof of the true Deity of Christ, since He is represented as equally the object of faith with God the Father, and lay a foundation for solid peace and comfort in a view of afflictions and persecutions in the world.

Verse 2. **In my Father's house are many mansions**, &c. This He says to draw off their minds from an earthly kingdom to a heavenly one; to point out the place to them whither He was going, and to support them with the views and hopes of glory under all their troubles. By His *Father's house* is meant heaven; see *2 Cor. 5:1*; which is of His Father's building, where He has, and will have all His family. This Christ says, partly to reconcile the minds of His disciples to His departure from them, and partly to strengthen their hope of following Him thither; since it was His Father's, and their Father's house

441

whither He was going, and in which *are many mansions*; abiding or dwelling places; mansions of love, peace, joy, and rest, which always remain: and there are *many* of them, which does not design different degrees of glory; for since the saints are all loved with the same love, bought with the same price, justified with the same righteousness, and are equally the sons of God, their glory will be the same. But, it denotes fulness and sufficiency of room for all His people; for the many *ordained to eternal life* [*Acts 13:48*], for whom Christ gave His life *a ransom* [see *Matt. 20:28*], and whose blood is shed for the remission of their sins, whose sins He bore, and whom He justifies by His knowledge; who receive Him by faith, and are the many sons He will bring to glory. And this is said for the comfort of the disciples, who might be assured from hence, that there would be room not only for Himself and Peter, whom He had promised should follow Him hereafter, but for them all. Very agreeable to this way of speaking are many things in the Jewish writings:

"says R. Isaac,[1] How many מדורין על מדורין, *mansions upon mansions*, are there for the righteous in that world? And the uppermost mansion of them all is the love of their Lord."

Moreover, they say[2] that,

"in the world to come every righteous man shall have מדור, *a mansion*, to himself."

Sometimes they[3] speak of *seven* mansions (a number of perfection) being prepared for the righteous in the other world, though entirely ignorant of the person by whom these mansions are prepared: who here says,

if *it were* not *so*, I, would have told you; this expresses the certainty of it, that His Father had a house, and in it were many mansions, room enough for all His people, or He would have informed them otherwise, who must needs know the truth of these things, since He came from thence; and who never deceives with vain hopes of glory; and whatever He says is truth, and to be depended on; every thing He here delivers; both what He said before, and also what follows:

I go to prepare a place for you. Heaven is a kingdom prepared by the Father for His saints, from the foundation of the world; and again, by the presence and intercession of Christ, who is gone before, and is as a forerunner entered into it, and has taken possession of it in the name of His people; and

---

[1]   Zohar in Deut. fol. 113. 1.

[2]   Praefat ad Sepher Raziel, fol. 2. 1. Nishmat Chayim, fol. 26. 2. & 27. 1.

[3]   T. Bab. Bava Bathra, fol. 75. 1. Nishmat Chayim, fol. 32. 2. Midrash Tillim in Galatin. l. 12. c. 6.

by His own appearance there for them with His blood, righteousness, and sacrifice, He is, as it were, fitting up these mansions for their reception, while they are by His Spirit and grace fitting and preparing for the enjoyment of them.

Verse 3. **And if I go and prepare a place for you**, &c. Seeing I am going to prepare, and will prepare a place for you, of the truth of which you may be fully assured:

I will come again; either by death, or in person, a second time, here on earth:

and receive you unto myself; I will take you up with me to heaven; I will receive you into glory;

that where I am, *there* **ye may be also**. And behold my glory, and be for ever with me, and never part more.

Verse 4. **And whither I go ye know**, &c. They might have known, at least, whither He was going, since He had spoken of His Father's house, and of His going to prepare a place for them there, and doubtless had some knowledge thereof, though very confused and imperfect:

and the way ye know. This also they might have known from some expressions of His, that the way to His Father's house lay through sufferings and death, in which way they also were to follow Him to His kingdom and glory. Though these words may be read with an interrogation, *And whither I go do ye know? and the way do ye know?* which best agrees with Thomas's answer, and removes all appearance of contradiction between Christ's words and his.

Verse 5. **Thomas saith unto him, Lord**, &c. Who was one of His apostles, and here betrays his ignorance, as elsewhere his unbelief; and not only speaks for himself, but for the rest of the apostles, of whom he judged by himself; and who, it may be, might understand things better than himself, though their knowledge at present was but small:

we know not whither thou goest; though He had but just told them of His Father's house, and of His going to prepare a place for them:

and how can we know the way? For if we do not know the place, it is not reasonable to think we should know the way to it. Thomas seemed to have no other notion than that Christ was talking of some particular place in Judea, whither He was going, and of the road to it.

Verse 6. **Jesus saith unto him, I am the way**, &c. Our Lord takes the opportunity of this discourse about the place He was going to, and the way unto it, more fully to instruct His disciples concerning Himself, saying, *I am the way*; Christ is not merely the way, as He goes before His people as an example; or merely as a prophet, pointing out unto them, by His doctrine, the way of salvation; but He is the way of salvation itself, by His obedience and sacrifice; nor is there any other; He is the way of His Father's appointing, and which is entirely agreeable to the perfections of God, and suitable to the case and condition of sinners; He is the way to all the blessings of the covenant of grace; and He is the right way into a Gospel church state here; no one comes rightly into a church of Christ but by faith in Him; and He is the way to heaven: He is entered into it Himself by His own blood, and has opened the way to it through Himself for His people: He adds, and,

the truth; He is not only true, but truth itself: this may regard His person and character; He is the true God, and eternal life; truly and really man; as a Prophet He taught the way of God in truth; as a Priest, He is a faithful, as well as a merciful one, true and faithful to Him that appointed Him; and as a King, just and true are all His ways and administrations. He is the sum and substance of all the truths of the Gospel: they are all full of Him, and center in Him; and He is the truth of all the types and shadows, promises and prophecies of the Old Testament; they have all their accomplishment in Him; and He is the true way, in opposition to all false ones of man's devising. And this phrase seems to be opposed to a notion of the Jews, that the law was the true way of life, and who confined truth to the law. They have a saying,[4] that משה ותורתו אמת, *Moses and his law are the truth*; this they make Korah and his company say in hell. That the law of Moses was truth, is certain; but it is too strong an expression to say of Moses himself, that he was truth; but well agrees with Christ, by whom grace and truth came, in opposition to Moses, by whom came the law: but when they say,[5] אין אמת אלא תורה, *there is no truth but the law*, they do not speak truth. More truly do they speak, when, in answer to that question, מה אמת, *What is truth?* it is said, That He is the living God, and King of the world,[6] characters that well agree with Christ;

---

[4] T. Bab. Bava Bathra. fol. 74. 1. Bemidbar Rabba, fol. 223. 2.

[5] T. Hieros. Roshhashanah, fol. 59. 1. Praefat. Echa Rabbati, fol. 36. 2.

[6] Ibid. Sanhedrin, fol. 18. 1.

and the life: Christ is the author and giver of life—natural, spiritual, and eternal; or He is the way of life, or *the living way*; in opposition to the law, which was so far from being the way of life, that it was the ministration of condemnation and death [see *2 Cor. 3:7-9*]: He always, and ever will be *the way*; all in this way live, none ever die; and it is a way that leads to eternal life: and to conclude all the epithets in one sentence, Christ is the true way to eternal life. It is added by way of explanation of Him, as the way,

no man cometh unto the Father but by me. Christ is the only way of access unto the Father; there is no coming to God as an absolute God, nor upon the foot [or basis] of the covenant of works, nor without a Mediator; and the only Mediator between God and man is Christ [see *1 Tim. 2:5*]: He introduces and presents the persons and services of His people to His Father, and gives them acceptance with Him.

Verse 7. **If ye had known me**, &c. Christ having made mention of His Father's house, and of Himself as the way thither, and the way of access to the Father, was willing to inform His disciples better concerning Him before His departure from them, which He introduces, saying. *If ye had known me*; that is, more fully and perfectly; for that they knew Christ to be the Son of God, the Savior of the world, and true Messiah, is certain, though they were not so thoroughly acquainted, as afterwards, with His person, power, and office:

ye should have known my Father also; for the knowledge of the Father, and of Christ, go together; he that sees the one, sees the other; he that believes in the one, believes in the other; and the knowledge of both is necessary to eternal life; and as a person increases in the knowledge of the one, so of the other. The disciples had some knowledge of them both, but what was very small and obscure, in comparison of what they afterwards had:

and from henceforth ye know him, and have seen him. Some read these words, *henceforwards ye shall know him, and see him*; that is, in a very short time, when the Spirit is poured down from on high upon you, and you have received the gifts of the Holy Ghost, you shall then have an enlarged knowledge both of me and my Father. Others render them, as an exhortation, *henceforward know ye him*; acknowledge the Father in all that I have done, believing that you see the Father in me, and in all my works; though they are rather to be considered as an assertion, declaring, that they then had some knowledge of the Father; *and now ye know him, and*, or *because ye have seen him*; in me, who am *the brightness of his glory, and the express image of his person* [*Heb. 1:3*].

Verse 8. **Philip saith unto him, Lord**, &c. Another of His disciples addresses Him in a reverend and becoming manner, as Thomas before had done, calling

Him *Lord*, and saying to Him, *show us the Father, and it sufficeth us*: he speaks in the name of them all, seems to own their ignorance of the Father, and expresses their desire of seeing Him:

show us the Father; it was a corporeal sight of Him he asked for; such a sight of the glory of God as Moses desired, and the elders of Israel had at Mount Sinai; and signifies, that if this could be obtained, it would give them full satisfaction:

and it sufficeth us. We shall be no more uneasy at thy departure from us; we shall have no doubt about thy Father's house, and the many mansions in it; or of thyself, as the way unto it, and of our everlasting abode with thee in it; we shall sit down easy and contented, and trouble thee no more with questions about this matter.

Verse 9. **Jesus saith unto him, Have I been so long time with you**, &c. Conversing familiarly with you, instructing you by my ministry, and performing so many miraculous works among you, for so long a time; see *Heb. 5:11-12;*

and yet hast thou not known me, Philip? Surely you cannot be so ignorant as this comes to; as you have seen me with your bodily eyes, as a man, you must know that I am God by the doctrines I have taught you, and the miracles I have wrought among you: and,

he that hath seen me; not with the eyes of his body, but with the eyes of his understanding; he that has beheld the perfections of the Godhead in me:

hath seen the Father; the perfections which are in Him also; for the same that are in me are in Him, and the same that are in Him are in me: I am the very image of Him, and am possessed of the same nature, attributes, and glory, that He is; so that He that sees the one, sees the other:

and how sayest thou *then*, **Show us the Father**? Such a request is a needless one, and betrays great weakness and ignorance.

Verse 10. **Believest thou not that I am in the Father?** &c. This surely is, as it must needs be, and ought to be, an article of your faith, *that I am in the Father,*

and the Father in me; phrases which are expressive of the sameness of nature in the Father and the Son; of the Son's perfect equality with the Father, since the Son is as much in the Father, as the Father is in the Son; and also of the personal distinction there is between them; for nothing with propriety can be said to be in itself. The Father must be distinct from the Son who is in Him, and the Son must be distinct from the Father, in whom He is;

the Father and Son, though of one and the same nature, cannot be one, and the same person:

the words that I speak unto you I speak not of myself: the doctrines which I preach among you are a proof of what I assert, and to them I appeal; for these are not of myself, as man,

but the Father that dwelleth in me; and so prove that I am truly God, of the same nature with my Father; that He is in me, and I in Him; since they are such as none but the only begotten, who is in the bosom of the Father, could ever have declared and made known unto you; Likewise, the works which I do, as man, I do not of myself; but,

he doeth the works. For so this passage must be understood and supplied, in which Christ proceeds to another argument, taken from His works, proving the Father to be in Him, and that He is in the Father, which is enlarged on in the next verse.

Verse 11. **Believe me that I *am* in the Father, and the Father in me**, &c. Take my word for the truth of this; you may assure yourselves that nothing is more certain; but if you will not believe upon my saying so, either believe for the sake of the doctrines I have preached unto you, which are such as never any mere man spoke, and which have been delivered in such a manner, and with such authority, as never were by man. Some copies read, by way of interrogation, and so the Ethiopic version; and the Vulgate Latin version reads, *believe ye not?*

or else believe me for the very works' sake. Meaning His miraculous works, such as raising the dead, cleansing the lepers, causing the deaf to hear, and giving sight to the blind; and which were such as none but a divine person could ever perform.

Verse 12. **Verily, verily, I say unto you, He that believeth on me**, &c. Having mentioned His miracles as proofs of His Deity, He assures His disciples, in order to comfort them under the loss of His bodily presence, that they should do the same, and greater works; for we are not to understand these words of every one that believes in Christ, of every private believer in Him, but only of the apostles, and each of them, that were true believers in Him: to whom He says,

the works that I do shall he do also; he shall raise the dead, heal all manner of diseases, and cast out devils; things which Christ gave His apostles power to do, when He first gave them a commission to preach the Gospel, and when He renewed and enlarged it: and which they did perform, not in their own name, and by their own power, but in the name, and by the power of Christ:

and greater *works* than these shall he do; meaning, not greater in nature and kind, but more in number; for the apostles, in a long series of time, and course of years, went about preaching the Gospel, not in Judea only, but in all the world, *God also bearing them witness with signs and wonders, and divers miracles and gifts of the Holy Ghost*, [*Heb. 2:4*], wherever they went. Though perhaps by these *greater works* may be meant the many instances of conversion, which the apostles were instrumental in, and which were more in number than those which were under our Lord's personal ministry. Besides, the conversion of a sinner is a greater work than any of the miracles of raising the dead, &c. for this includes in it all miracles: here we may see a sinner, dead in trespasses and sins, quickened; one born blind, made to see; one who was deaf to the threatenings of the law, and to the charming voice of the Gospel, made to hear, so as to live; and one that had the spreading leprosy of sin all over him, cleansed from it by the blood of the Lamb. Yea, though a *miracle in nature* is an instance and proof of divine power, yet the conversion of a sinner, which is a *miracle in grace*, is not only an instance of the power of God, and of the greatness of it, but of the exceeding greatness of it: and the rather one may be induced to give into this sense of the passage, since it is added, as a reason,

because I go unto my Father. And upon my ascension the Spirit will be given to you, which shall not only enable you to perform miracles, as proofs of your apostleship, and the doctrine you preach, but which shall powerfully attend the Gospel to the conversion of multitudes of souls.

Verse 13. **And whatsoever ye shall ask in my name**, &c. Whether it be for assistance in preaching of the Gospel; or for the performance of miraculous operations in confirmation of it; or for success to attend it; or for any blessings whatsoever, whether for themselves or others:

that will I do; He does not say, that He would be a Mediator between God and them, an advocate with the Father for them, and would intercede, and use His interest with Him that it might be done, which would have been saying much, and all which He does; but He declares He will do it Himself, which is a proof of His Deity, and an instance of His omnipotence:

that the Father may be glorified in the Son. This may be referred either to the petition, which must be made with this view, that the Father may be glorified by, or in the Son, in whose name it is put up, and for whose sake it is made; or to Christ's promise to do it; who in doing it, seeks not His own glory, at least not singly; but, as the good of His people, so the glory of His heavenly Father.

Verse 14. **If ye shall ask any thing**, &c. These words are much the same with the former, and have been thought, by some, to have crept into the text from the margin; though they seem rather to be repeated by Christ, the more to strengthen and confirm the faith of His disciples in this matter; that whatsoever they asked, says He,

in my name, either calling upon it, He being equally the object of prayer with the Father, or making mention of it, pleading the merits of His blood, righteousness, and sacrifice:

I will do *it*. Whatever was according to the will of God, was for His glory, and their real good, He would do it for them, as well when absent from them, as present with them.

Verse 15. **If ye love me**, &c. Not that Christ doubted of the love of His disciples to Him; but He argues from it to their observance of His precepts, seeing ye do love me; as all do who are born again, who have had any spiritual sight of Him, of His glory, suitableness, and fulness; who believe in Him, and have received from Him; who have had His love shed abroad in their hearts, having enjoyed communion with Him, and know the relation He stands in to them: these love Him above all others, and all of Him, and that belong to Him, unfeignedly, and in the sincerity of their souls, as did the disciples; and since they professed to love, and did love Him, as they ought to do, He exhorts them, saying,

keep my commandments. Christ is Lord over His people, as He is the Creator and Redeemer of them, and as He is a head and husband to them; and as such He has a right to issue out His commands, and enjoin a regard unto them; and these are peculiarly *His*, as distinct from, though not in opposition to, or to the exclusion of, His Father's commands; such as the new commandment of loving one another, and the ordinances of baptism, and the Lord's supper, which are to be observed and kept as Christ has ordered them—constantly, in faith, and with a view to His glory.

Verse 16. **And I will pray the Father**, &c., Here Christ speaks as Mediator, and promises His disciples that He would intercede for them with the Father; which is designed as an encouragement to them to ask for what they want in His name, and to comfort their hearts, which were troubled at the news of His departure from them;

and he shall give you another Comforter. This is no inconsiderable proof of a trinity of persons in the Godhead: here is the Father prayed unto, the Son in human nature praying, and the Holy Ghost the Comforter prayed for; who is the gift of the Father, through the prevalent mediation of the Son, and is *another Comforter*; distinct from the Messiah, to whom reference is here had. One of the names of the Messiah, with the Jews, is מנחם,[7] *a Comforter*; such a one Jesus had been to His disciples; and now He was about to leave them, and for their support under their sorrows, He promises to use His interest with His Father, that He would give them *another Comforter*, meaning the Spirit, who performs this His work and office, by taking of the things of Christ, and showing them to His people; by shedding abroad the love of the Father, and of the Son, into their hearts; by opening and applying the precious promises of the Gospel to them; by being a Spirit of adoption in them; and by abiding with them as the seal, earnest, and pledge of their future glory [see *Eph. 1:13-14*]; and with this view Christ promises to pray for Him,

that he may abide with you for ever; not a few years only, as I have done, but as long as you live; and with all those that shall succeed you in the work of the ministry, and with the church, and all true believers unto the end of the world: this is a proof of the saints' final perseverance. When we consider these words, in connection with the preceding exhortation, to keep the commands of Christ, and as an encouragement so to do, it brings to mind a saying of R. Eliezer ben Jacob:[8]

"He that does one commandment gets for himself פרקליט אחד (ενα παρακλητον, the very word here used), *one advocate*, or *comforter*; and he that transgresses one command, gets for himself one accuser."

But though the word signifies both an advocate and a comforter, the latter seems to be the meaning of it here, as being more suited to the disconsolate condition of the disciples.

*Verse 17. **Even** the Spirit of truth; whom the world cannot receive*, &c. These words explain who is meant by the Comforter, *even the Spirit of truth*; the true Spirit of God, the dictator of the Scriptures of truth, who leads men into the truths of the Gospel, confirms them in them, and gives boldness and freedom to own, and confess them before men:

whom the world cannot receive; the men of the world, who are as they came into the world, carnal and natural men, can neither receive the Spirit nor the things of the Spirit, the truths and doctrines of the Gospel [see *1 Cor.*

---

[7] T. Hieros. Beracot, fol. 5. 1. T. Bab. Sanhedrin, fol. 98. 2. Echa Rabbati, fol. 50. 2.

[8] Pirke Abot, c. 4. sect. 11.

2:14]; they can neither receive them into their understandings, nor into their affections; and indeed, because they cannot understand them, therefore they do not love them, but despise and hate them:

because it seeth him not, neither knoweth him; the world, and the men of it, can neither see Him with their bodily eyes, because He is a *spirit*; nor know Him with their understandings, because He is the *Spirit of truth*, which they are ignorant of, for want of a spiritual discerning;

but ye know him; as a spirit of illumination, regeneration, and conversion:

for he dwelleth with you; He is an inhabitant in your hearts, He has taken up His residence in you as His temples [see *1 Cor. 6:19-20*]:

and shall be in you. As a Comforter, when I am gone from you; and as a Spirit of truth to *guide you into all truth* [*John 16:13*], to stand by you, and assist you in preaching it, and to enable you to bear a faithful and glorious testimony for it.

Verse 18. **I will not leave you comfortless**, &c. Greek: *orphans*, or *fatherless*. Christ stands in the relation of a Father to His people, and they are His children, His spiritual seed and offspring; and so the disciples might fear, that as Christ was going from them, they should be left as children without a father, in a very desolate and comfortless, condition: to support them against these fears, Christ promises that He would not leave them thus, at least not long:

I will come to you. In a very short time, as He did; for on the third day He rose again from the dead, and appeared to them, which filled them with great joy. So among the Jews, disciples, and the world too, are represented as fatherless, when their doctors and wise men are removed by death. Says R. Aba,[9] and so sometimes others, concerning R. Simeon ben Jochai,

"Woe to the world when thou shalt go out of it, woe to the generation that shall be in the world when thou shalt remove from them, יתמין וישתארון, *and they shall be left fatherless by thee.*"

And in another place:[10]

"Afterwards R. Akiba went out and cried, and his eyes flowed with water, and he said, Woe Rabbi, woe Rabbi, for the world is left, יתום, *fatherless* by thee."

---

[9]   Zohar in Num. fol. 96. 3. & in Lev. fol. 42. 3. & in Exod. fol. 10. 3. & 28. 3.

[10]   Midrash Hannealam in Zohar in Gen. fol. 65. 4.

Verse 19. **Yet a little while, and the world seeth me no more**, &c. The men of the world now see me with their bodily eyes, which is all the sight they have of me; and this they will be deprived of in a very little time; they will see me no more until the time that I shall come in the clouds of heaven to judge the world; and then every eye shall see me:

but ye see me; ye see me now, and shall see me after my resurrection, as they did; for then He appeared alive, and conversed with them for forty days; and when He ascended into heaven, and sat down at the right hand of God, they saw Him by faith crowned with glory and honor; and will see Him as He is when He comes a second time to take them to Himself in glory;

because I live, ye shall live also. Christ lives as God, as man, and as Mediator: as God, He lives the same life His Father does, partaking of the same nature, and possessing the same perfections; so He lived from everlasting, and will live to everlasting. As man, He lived first a private, and then a public life, attended with meanness [*or* lowliness], reproaches, sorrows, and sufferings; a life which was filled up with acts of devotion and piety to God, and with doing good to the bodies and souls of men; He lived in all obedience to the law of God, and at last endured the penalty of that law, in the room and stead of His people; when His life was taken away for a while, and then taken up by Him again; and now, as man, He lives, and lives for evermore. As Mediator, He has His life from the Father, which is dependent upon Him, by whom He was set up in an office capacity from everlasting; and as such will live to everlasting, to see the travail of His soul, the fruit of His sufferings, to make intercession for His people, and to rule until all enemies are made His footstool. And His people *live also*; which is to be understood, not of the preservation of His disciples from dying with Him, when He died; for then it should rather have been said, *because I die, ye shall live*: nor of the continuance of their natural life in this world; for the saints are not to live always here; nor do they desire it, nor is it proper they should; death is for their advantage; it is a blessing to them. Though these words may be understood of a corporeal life, which they shall live after the resurrection; for though they die, they shall live again, and never die more; they shall not only live and reign with Christ a thousand years, but to all eternity. They also live a spiritual life now; a life of grace and holiness from Christ; a life of faith on Him, and sometimes of communion with Him, and desire to live to His honor and glory; and shall hereafter live an eternal life of perfection and pleasure, with Father, Son, and Spirit, for evermore. Now between these two lives, the life of Christ, and of His people, there is a close connection; the one is dependent on the other, and secured by the other: *because I live, ye shall live also*; the spiritual life of a believer is from Christ, and is maintained by Him; the same which is in the head, is in the members; yea, it is not so much they that live, as Christ that lives in them [see *Gal. 2:20*], and therefore their life can never be lost; it is bound up in the bundle of life with Christ, and is hid safe and secure with Him in God, and so out of the reach both of men and devils. The corporeal life of the saints after death, in the resurrection morn, springs from, and is secured by the life of Christ: His resurrection from the dead is the pattern and pledge of theirs; He undertook to raise them from the dead, and will do it; as sure as His dead body is raised and lives, so sure shall theirs; their bodies, as well as their souls, are united to Christ; and by virtue of this union, which death does not, and cannot dissolve, they shall be raised and live again. They are in Christ while they are dead; and because they are *the dead in Christ*, they shall *rise first* [*1 Thess. 4:16*]. Their eternal life is in the hands of Christ, and when He, who is the true God, and their eternal life, shall appear, they shall appear with Him in glory.

Verse 20. **At that day ye shall know**, &c. The things they should know, or the objects of knowledge are,

that I *am* in my Father; in His bosom, in union with Him, partaker of the same nature, perfections, and glory with Him, and equal to Him:

and ye in me: that they were in union with Him as the branches in the vine, and as the members are in the head, and how they were loved in Him, chosen in Him, righteous in Him, risen with Him, and made to sit together in heavenly places in Him:

and I in you. Formed in their hearts, living in them, dwelling in them, as in His temples, and filling them with grace and glory. The knowledge of these things promised, designs a more clear and distinct knowledge of them; something of them was known already, but not so perfectly as should be hereafter: and this does not suppose that these unions between the Father and Christ, and between Christ and His people, shall then begin to be; for as the union between the Father and the Son is as eternal as themselves; so the union between Christ and His people, as He is the head and representative of them, is as early as His investiture with the office of a Mediator, and His suretyship engagements for them, which were from eternity; and are the ground, and foundation of His being in them, and they in Him in effectual vocation [*or* calling]; nor does it suggest that they shall begin to be known; only that they shall be known in a more perfect manner: the time when this will be, is *at that day*: meaning either when He should *live* in the body again, be raised from the dead, when He should be *declared to be the Son of God with power* [*Rom. 1:4*], when it would appear that He had the same power with the Father, by raising Himself from the dead, and when He would rise as a public head representing them, for their justification, and they should see themselves justified and discharged in Him; or the day of *Pentecost*, when *the*

Spirit of truth, He promises to pray for, should come to them in an extraordinary manner, and lead them into the knowledge of these things; or the last day, the resurrection morn, when, by virtue of union to Christ, the saints shall rise and *live* with Him for ever, and shall have a perfect knowledge of these several unions; see *chapter 17:21,23,24.*

Verse 21. **He that hath my commandments, and keepeth them**, &c. He that has not merely the external revelation of them in the Bible; but has them written on his heart, by the finger of the Spirit of God, and keeps them under the influence of grace and strength received from Him:

he it is that loveth me: others may talk of loving Christ, but this is the man that truly does love Him; for his observance of Christ's commands is a proof and evidence that he loves Him not in word only, but in deed and in truth: and to encourage souls to love and obedience, Christ adds,

and he that loveth me shall be loved of my Father; not that love to Christ is the cause, condition, or motive of the Father's love to His people; nor does His love to them begin when they begin to love Christ; but this expression denotes some further and greater manifestation of the Father's love to such persons, and shows how grateful to the Father are love and obedience to the Son:

and I will love him; which must be understood in the same manner; Christ does not begin to love His people when they begin to love and obey Him; their love and obedience to Him, spring from His love to them; which love of His towards them was from everlasting: but this phrase designs a clearer discovery of His love to them, *which passeth knowledge [Eph. 3:19]*; and some fresh mark and token of His affection for them; and which is explained in the next clause:

and will manifest myself to him. Not in a visible way, or in a corporeal form, as He did to His disciples after His resurrection; but in a spiritual manner, as when He makes Himself known to His people in ordinances, and favors them with communion with Him, and they see His beauty, His fulness, His grace and righteousness, His power, and His glory.

Verse 22. **Judas saith unto him, not Iscariot**, &c. This was Judas Lebbeus, whose surname was Thaddeus, the same with Jude the apostle, the author of the epistle which bears his name; and is said to be *not Iscariot*, to distinguish him from the betrayer. The question put by him,

Lord, how is it, τι γεγονεν, which answers to מאי דאר, or מאי האי, or מהו, with the Talmudists, *What is this thou sayest?* What is the meaning of it? How can it be? or, What is the reason of it,

that thou wilt manifest thyself to us, and not unto the world? arises either from ignorance of what Christ was speaking, imagining He meant a specter, or some apparition of Himself after His death, which should be visible to His disciples, and not to others; and how this could be, he wanted to know; or from that national prejudice which Judas and the rest of the apostles had given into, of a temporal kingdom of the Messiah, the glory of which should be visible to all the world; and therefore he wonders that He should talk of the manifestation of Himself only to some; or from an honest hearty desire that the glory of Christ might not be confined to a few only; but that the whole world might see it, and be filled with it: or rather from His modesty, and the sense He had of his own unworthiness, and of the rest of the apostles, to have such a peculiar manifestation of Christ to them, when they were no more deserving of it than others. The question is put by him with admiration and astonishment; and as not being able to give, or think of any other reason of such a procedure, but the amazing grace of Christ, His free favor and sovereign will and pleasure.

Verse 23. **Jesus answered and said unto him**, &c. This answer is returned, and these words are spoken, for the further confirmation and explanation of what was before said:

If a man love me, he will keep my words; by His *words* are meant not His doctrines, but His ordinances; the same with His commandments, *verse 21*; which He has said, ordered, and commanded to be observed, and which are observed by such who truly love Him, and that from a principle of love to Him, and with a view to His glory. And for the encouragement of such persons as before, He says,

and my Father will love him: which is to be understood not of the love of the Father, as in His own heart, which is not taken up in time, but was in Him from all eternity; nor of the first discovery of it to His people, but of greater manifestations of it to them, and a quicker sense of it in their hearts, and also of some other effects of it, to be enjoyed by them in a higher manner; such as larger measures of grace, more communion with Him here, and eternal honor and glory hereafter:

and we will come unto him: I, who am now going away, and my Father to whom I am going, and the Holy Spirit, the Comforter, I have promised to pray for: hence a proof of a plurality of persons in the Godhead, of a trinity of persons, of there being neither more nor fewer than three; since neither more nor less can be collected from the context; and of their distinct personality, or it could not be said with any propriety, *we* each of us *will come unto him*; not locally and visibly, but spiritually, by affording our gracious and comfortable presence, the continuance of which is promised next:

and make our abode with him. Which denotes habitation; for the saints are the dwelling places or temples of the living God—Father, Son, and Spirit; and the constancy and perpetuity of their residence in them, not as a wayfaring man, but always, though this may not be always discerned by believers; and is a wonderful instance of the grace and condescension of God to dwell on earth with sinful men; and a far greater one it is, than if the most mighty potentate on earth should take up His abode in a poor despicable cottage with the meanest [*or* lowliest] of His subjects.

Verse 24. **He that loveth me not, keepeth not my sayings**, &c. These words may have respect both to external professors of religion, who being destitute of true love to Christ, though they outwardly observe His ordinances and commands; yet inasmuch as this does not spring from a principle of love to Him, and is done only to be seen of men, or to obtain life for themselves, may be said, not to keep His words or commands, because they do not keep them aright; and to the profane world, who, as they have no affection to Christ, pay no regard to any orders or ordinances of His: and they may be considered as having in them a reason or argument, justifying the conduct of Christ, in manifesting Himself to His disciples, and not unto the world; as the following words give a reason why the Father takes so much notice of, comes and makes His abode with such as keep the words of Christ:

and, or *for*,

the word which ye hear is not mine, but the Father's which sent me. That is, it is not only mine, but my Father's also: it is not mine as man; it is not a scheme of things of my own devising; it is not from earth, but from heaven; my Father has a concern in it, and therefore regards such who hear, receive, and keep it. And this is said by Him partly to engage a greater regard and attention to His Word, His truths, and ordinances, by His disciples; and to expose and aggravate the sin of those who despised and rejected them; since it was not barely casting contempt on Him, but on His Father likewise.

Verse 25. **These things have I spoken unto you**, &c. Concerning His Father, and His Father's house, and the way to both; concerning His being in the Father, and the Father in Him; concerning keeping His commandments, and the advantages and benefits following upon it:

being, says He,

yet **present with you**. Which is a strong intimation that in a little time He should not be present with them; and that while He was present with them, He was desirous of saying such things to them, in a brief compendious manner, as they were able to bear; which might be of future use and instruction to them.

Verse 26. **But the Comforter, *which is* the Holy Ghost**, &c. Before spoken of, *verse 16*, for whom Christ promised to pray the Father that He might be given to them. The word used there, as here, signifies an *Advocate,* and is so rendered, *1 John 2:1*; a patron, one that pleads and defends the cause of another, before kings and princes; so the Jewish writers[11] use the word פרקליט, the same with παρακλητος, here, and give this as the sense of it: and which agrees well enough with the work and office of the Spirit of God, who has promised to the apostles to speak in them and for them, when they should be brought before kings and governors for Christ's sake; and would so thoroughly plead His cause and theirs, as to convince the world of sin, righteousness and judgment; and who acts the part of an intercessor, or advocate, for private believers, in prayer to the King of kings: but inasmuch as it also signifies a *Comforter,* and this being agreeable to the present condition of the apostles, as before observed, it may be most proper to retain that sense of it here, who is explained to be *the Holy Ghost*; which is a more clear and explicit account of Him than before, and very distinctly points out the third person in the Trinity, who is in His nature holy, equally with the Father and Son, and the author of holiness in all the saints;

whom the Father will send in my name: the mission of the Spirit is here ascribed to the Father, but not to the exclusion of the Son, who is also said to send Him, *chapter 15:26* and *16:7*; which was not so proper to be mentioned here, because He speaks of His being sent, *in His name*; that is, at His request, through His mediation and intercession, in His room and stead, acting the same part, and bearing the same name of an Advocate or Comforter, and for the glory and honor of His name: which act of sending does not suppose any local motion, which cannot agree with an infinite and immense Spirit; nor inferiority in Him to the other two persons, since He who is *sent* by Christ, and in His name, is also the *sender* of Christ; but it denotes the joint consent and agreement of Father, Son, and Spirit, in this affair:

he shall teach you all things: this is the proper work and business of the Spirit, to teach, interpret, and explain all things which Christ had said to them; to make them more plain and easy to their understandings; to instruct them in all things necessary to salvation, and to be known by them, that they might teach them to others:

---

[11] Maimonides & Bartenora in Pirke Abot, c. 4. sect. 11.

and bring all things to your remembrance, whatsoever I have said unto you. Which through inattention, or want of understanding in them, had slipped their minds, and were forgotten by them. This accounts for it, how the evangelists, some years after the death of Christ, at different times and places, and without consulting each other, could commit to writing the life, actions, sayings, and sermons of Christ, with all the minute circumstances attending them.

Verse 27. **Peace I leave with you**, &c. Christ being about to die and leave His disciples, makes His last will and testament, and as the best legacy He could leave them, bequeaths peace unto them;

my peace I give unto you: He left the Gospel of peace with them, to be preached by them to all the world; which is a declaration and publication of peace made by His blood; is a means of reconciling the minds of men to God and Christ, to the truths, ordinances, and people of Christ; of relieving and giving peace to distressed minds; and which shows the way to eternal peace: and as Christ had kept His disciples in peace one with another, so He left them in peace; and left orders with them to maintain it, one among another. But what seems chiefly designed here, is peace with God, which Christ is the sole author of; He was appointed in the council and covenant of peace to effect it; He became incarnate with that view, and did procure it by His sufferings and death; and as it was published by angels, when He came into the world, He left it, and gave it to His disciples when He was going out of it: or else that peace of conscience is meant, which follows upon the former, which arises from the sprinklings of the blood of Christ, and from a comfortable view, by faith, of an interest in His justifying righteousness, and is enjoyed in a way of believing, and commonly in the use of ordinances: *leaving* it supposes that Christ was about to leave His disciples, but would not leave them comfortless; He leaves a Comforter with them, and bequeaths peace unto them as His last legacy: *giving* it, shows that it is not to be acquired by any thing that man can do, but is a pure free grace gift of Christ; and which being given as His legacy, is irrevocable; for the allusion is to the making of a will or testament when persons are about to die: though some have thought it refers to the custom of wishing peace, health, and prosperity, among the Jews; but Christ does not say, *Peace be to you*; which was the more usual form of salutation among them, and which was used by them when they met, and not at parting; especially we have no instance of such a form as here used, by dying persons taking their leaves of their relations and friends. It must indeed be owned that the phrase, *to give peace*, is with them the same as to salute, or wish health and prosperity. Take two or three of their rules as instances of it:

"Whoever knows his friend, that he is used, ליתן לו שלום,[12] *to give him peace*; he shall prevent him with peace (that is, salute him first), as it is said, *Seek peace and pursue it*; but if he *gives* it to him, and he does not return it, he shall be called a robber."

Again,[13]

"A man may not go into the house of a stranger, on his feast day, שלום ליתן לו, *to give peace unto him* (or salute him); if he finds him in the street, he may *give* it to him with a low voice, and his head hanging down;"

once more,[14]

"A man לא יתן שלום, *may not give peace to*, or salute his master, nor return peace to him in the way that they *give* it to friends, and they return it to one another."

Likewise it must be owned, that when they saluted persons of distinction, such as princes, nobles, and doctors, they repeated the word *peace*,[15] though never to any strangers; however, certain it is, that it was another sort of peace which Christ left, and gave to His disciples, than what the Jews were wont to give, or wish to one another;

not as the world giveth, give I unto you. The peace Christ gives is true, solid, and substantial; the peace the world, the men, and things of it give, is a false one; and while they cry, *Peace, peace, sudden destruction is at hand* [see *1 Thess. 5:3*]: the peace of the world is at best but an external one, but the peace Christ is the giver of, is internal; the peace the world affords is a very transient, unstable, and short-lived one, but the peace of Christ is lasting and durable; the peace of the world will not support under the troubles of it, but the peace which Christ gives, cheerfully carries His people through all the difficulties and exercises of this life. And as these differ in kind, so likewise in the manner of giving, and in the persons to whom they are given; the world gives peace in words only, Christ in deed; the world gives feignedly, Christ heartily; the world gives it for its own advantage, Christ for His people's sake; the world gives its peace to the men of it, to the ungodly, none to the godly, whom it hates; Christ gives His; not *to the wicked*, for *there is no peace* to them [*Isa. 57:21*], but to the saints, the excellent in the earth. Wherefore says Christ,

---

[12] T. Bab. Beracot, fol. 6. 2.

[13] T. Bab. Gittin, fol. 62. 1. Maimon. Obede Cochabim, c. 10. sect. 5.

[14] Maimon. Talmud Tora, c. 5. sect. 5.

[15] T. Bab. Gittin, fol. 62. 1. Maimon. Hilch. Melacim, c. 10. sect. 12.

Let not your heart be troubled; at my departure from you, since I leave such a peace with you:

neither let it be afraid. At the dangers you may be exposed unto, and the troubles you may be exercised with; for in the midst of them all, *in me ye shall have peace* [*John 16:33*].

Verse 28. **Ye have heard how I said unto you**, &c. Christ had not only told His disciples that He should depart from them in a little time, but also that He should return again to them, and comfort them with His presence, and receive them to Himself, to be with Him in His Father's house for ever: and this He again suggests,

I go away, and come *again* unto you. So that they had not so much reason to be troubled and afraid, as they were: had He only said to them that He should go away, without giving any hint of His coming again, they might well have been uneasy; what made the friends of the Apostle Paul so sorrowful at his departure, was most of all, because he had signified to them they should see his face no more [see *Acts 20:25,38*]; but Christ assured His disciples that in a little time they should see Him again, to their unspeakable joy and comfort:

If ye loved me, adds He,

ye would rejoice; not but that the disciples did truly love Christ, and their concern for the loss of His bodily presence is a proof of it; nor was their love unknown to Him, nor does He call it in question, only corrects it, or rather uses means to increase it, to draw it forth aright, that it might move and run in a proper channel; they loved Him, and therefore were unwilling to part with Him: but this was not a pure expression of love to Him, it showed too much a regard to themselves, than to the object loved; whereas had they considered things aright, since it was to His greater advantage to remove, they should rather have discovered a willingness to it, and have rejoiced at it; this would have shown pure love and unbiased affection to Him. Two reasons our Lord gives why they should have rejoiced at His removing; one is, says He,

because I said, I go unto the Father; who was not only His, but their Father also; at whose right hand He was to sit, an honor which no mere creature ever had; where He was to be glorified and exalted above all created beings: and besides, His glorification would secure and bring on theirs; as sure as He lived in glory, so sure should they; yea, they should immediately sit down in heavenly places in Him, as their head and representative, and therefore had good reason to rejoice at His going away: the other is,

for my Father is greater than I. Not with respect to the divine nature, which is common to them both, and in which they are both one; and the Son is equal to the Father, having the selfsame essence, perfections, and glory: nor with respect to personality, the Son is equally a divine person, as the Father is, though the one is usually called the first, the other the second person; yet this priority is not of nature, which is the same in both; nor of time, for the one did not exist before the other; nor of causality, for the Father is not the cause of the Son's existence; nor of dignity, for the one has not any excellency which is wanting in the other; but of order and manner of operation. These words are to be understood, either with regard to the human nature, in which He was going to the Father, this was prepared for Him by the Father, and strengthened and supported by Him, and in which He was made a *little lower than the angels* [*Heb. 2:7*], and consequently must be in it inferior to His Father; or with regard to His office as Mediator, in which He was the Father's servant, was set up and sent forth by Him, acted under Him, and in obedience to Him, and was now returning to give an account of His work and service. Or rather with regard to His present state, which was a state of humiliation: He was attended with many griefs and sorrows, and exposed to many enemies, and about to undergo an accursed death; whereas His Father was in the most perfect happiness and glory, and so in this sense *greater*, that is, more blessed and glorious than He; for this is not a comparison of natures, or of persons, but of states and conditions: now He was going to the Father to partake of the same happiness and glory with Him, to be glorified with Himself, with the same glory He had with Him before the foundation of the world; wherefore on this account, His disciples ought to have rejoiced, and not have mourned.

Verse 29. **And now I have told you before it came to pass**, &c. This is a strong proof of His true and proper Deity, for none but the omniscient God can tell of things before they come to pass; this is peculiar to Him, and distinguishes Him from the gods of the Gentiles; see *Isa. 41:22-23; 45:21* and *46:9-10;*

that, when it is come to pass, ye might believe. That is, that when He was removed from them, and gone to His Father, they might then believe that He was truly God, the Son of God, the promised Messiah; and that He was then in glory, and at the right hand of God.

Verse 30. **Hereafter I will not talk much with you**, &c. Meaning before His death; for after His resurrection He talked much with them, about the things pertaining to the kingdom of God; being seen of them and conversing with them, for the space of forty days; *not much*, He says, chiefly what is delivered in the two next chapters: the design of this was, to observe to them that His time of departure was near at hand, and to quicken their attention to what He did say to them; since they could not expect to hear Him long, or much more from Him; He would be otherwise engaged;

for the prince of this world cometh: by *the prince of this world*, is meant the devil; why he is so called, see the note on *chapter 12:31*; the reason why Christ chooses to use this circumlocution, rather than to say Satan or the devil cometh, is partly to point out what a powerful adversary He had, and was about to engage with, and partly to observe to His disciples, what they must expect from the world, even hatred and persecution; since Satan was the prince of it, and had such powerful influence over the minds of the men of it. When it is said that he *cometh*, it is to be understood of his coming to Christ, though it is not expressed, and that with an intent agreeable to his character, as a thief, to kill and to destroy; and not of his coming merely by Judas, into whom he had already entered, and had put it into his heart to betray Him; and by the armed soldiers, who would accompany him to apprehend Him; and by the chief priests, rulers, and people of the Jews, who with united voices would cry, *Crucify him, crucify him*; nor only invisibly by his angels, his principalities and powers, he was now employing in different ways, to bring about his purposes; but of his coming himself personally, and visibly: as he visibly appeared to Christ in the wilderness, tempting Him, where he left Him for a season; so this season or opportunity being come, he takes it, and visibly appears to Him in the garden, where a sharp agony and combat was between them; what success he had in this conflict, is next mentioned;

and hath nothing in me. Or as some copies read it, *shall find nothing in me*; or as others, *hath nothing to find in me*; Christ had no sin in Him, which can be said of none but Him. The Jews say,[16] that Samuel, by whom they mean the devil, when he wrestled with Jacob, שלא מצא בו עון, *could not find any iniquity in him*, he had committed; but this is only true of Jacob's antitype: for though His emissaries sought diligently for it, they could find none in Him; though He had sin upon Him, He had none in Him; the sins of His people were imputed to Him, but He had no sin inherent in Him; hence, though He the Messiah was *cut off*, according to *Dan. 9:26*, *but not for himself*; which by the Septuagint is rendered και κριμα ουκ εστιν εν αυτω, *but there is no judgment* or *condemnation in him*, that is, no cause of condemnation; which agrees with what is here said: though the accuser of men sought to have something against Him, to accuse Him of, he could find none; some pretenses indeed were made, and charges brought, but could not be made good, insomuch that the judge himself said, *I find in him no fault at all* [*John 18:38*]: so that the devil had no power over Him, no rightful power, nor any but what he had by permission, nor indeed did he prevail over Him; for though

---

[16] Tzeror Hammor, fol. 44. 2.

according to the first prophecy of the Messiah, Satan bruised the heel of Christ; yet Christ bruised his head, destroyed him and his works, spoiled him, and his principalities and powers; whence it appears that the death of Christ was not owing to any sin of His own, for He had none, nor could any be found in Him; nor to the superior power of the devil over Him; He submitted to death, not through the power of Satan over Him, and complied with all the circumstances leading to it, not out of fear of him, but in love to His Father, and obedience to His command; as is clear from the following verse.

Verse 31. **But that the world may know**, &c. Not the wicked and unbelieving world, but the world of God's elect, such as are brought to believe in Christ:

that I love the Father; Christ must needs love the Father, as being of the same nature and essence with Him, and as standing in the relation of a Son to Him; He loved all that the Father loves, and approved of all His purposes, counsels, and determinations, concerning Himself and the salvation of His people; and therefore He voluntarily laid down His life for them:

and as the Father gave me commandment, even so I do. As a son is obedient to a father, so was Christ in all things obedient to the commands of His heavenly Father, in preaching the Gospel, obeying the law, and suffering death; all which He did and suffered, as the Father gave commandment to Him, as man and Mediator: and that it might fully appear how much He loved His Father, and agreed with Him in all His designs of grace; how much His will was resigned to His, and what respect He paid to whatever He said or ordered; He said to His disciples,

Arise, let us go hence. Not from the passover, or the supper, for the passover was not as yet, and the Lord's supper was not instituted; nor in order to go to Mount Olivet, or to the garden, where Judas and his armed men would be to meet Him, and lay hold on Him, as is generally thought; but from Bethany, where He and His disciples now were, in order to go to Jerusalem and keep the passover, institute the supper, and then surrender Himself into the hands of His enemies, and die for the sins of His people: for between this and the sermon in the following chapters, was the Lord's supper celebrated; when Christ having mentioned the *fruit of the vine*, He should drink new with His disciples in His Father's kingdom, He very pertinently enters upon the discourse concerning the *vine* and *branches*, with which the next chapter begins: the phrase is Jewish; so R. Jose and R. Chiyah say to one another as they sat, קום וניזיל, *Arise, and let us go hence*.[17]

---

[17] Zohar in Exod. fol. 74. 1.

CHAPTER 15

Verse 1. **I am the true vine**, &c. The fruit of which He had been just speaking
of at supper with His disciples; and then informs them, that He Himself is the
vine from whence that fruit must be expected, which should be partaken of by
them in His Father's kingdom; for though Christ may be compared to a vine
for its tenderness, weakness, and being subject to cuttings and prunings; all
which may express His outward meanness [*or* lowliness] in His birth,
parentage, and education, which exposed Him to the contempt of men; the
weakness of the human nature in itself, His being encompassed with the
infirmities of His people, and His sufferings and death for their sakes; yet He
is rather called so with respect to His fruitfulness: for as the vine is a fruitful
tree, brings forth and bears fruit in clusters, so Christ, as man and Mediator,
is *full of grace and truth*, of all spiritual blessings, and exceeding great and
precious promises; from Him comes the wine of divine love, of Gospel truths
and Gospel ordinances, the various blessings of grace, and the joys of heaven,
which are the *best wine* reserved by Him till last: Christ is *the true vine*; not
that He is really and literally so, without a figure; but He is, as the Syriac
renders it, נפתא דשררא, *the vine of truth*. Just as Israel is called *a noble vine,*
wholly a right seed, זרע אמת, *a seed of truth, Jer. 2:21*; right genuine seed; or,
as the Septuagint render it, *a vine*, bringing forth fruit, πασαν αληθινην,
wholly true; to which the allusion may be here. Christ is the noble vine, the
most excellent of vines, wholly a right seed, in opposition to, and distinction
from, the wild and unfruitful, or degenerate plant of a strange vine: to Him
agree all the properties of a right and real vine; He really and truly
communicates life, sap, juice, nourishment, and fruitfulness to the several
branches which are in Him. The metaphor Christ makes use of was well
known to the Jews; for not only the Jewish church is often compared to a vine,
but the Messiah too, according to them: thus the Targumist explains the
phrase in *Psa. 80:15, the branch thou madest strong for thyself*, of the King
Messiah: and indeed, by comparing it with *Psa. 80:17,* it seems to be the true
sense of the passage.[1] The Cabalistic doctors say,[2] that the Shekinah is called,

---

[1] Vid. R. Mosem Hadersan in Galatin. de Arcan. Cathol. verit, l. 8. c. 4.

[2] Zohar in Exod. fol. 70. 2. & Cabala denudata, par. 1. p. 241.

גֶּפֶן, *a vine*; see *Gen. 49:11*, where the Jews observe,[3] the King Messiah is so called. The Jews[4] say, there was a golden vine that stood over the gate of the temple, and it was set upon props; and whoever offered a leaf, or a grape, or a cluster (that is, a piece of gold to the temple, in the form of either of these), brought it, and hung it upon it. And of this vine also Josephus[5] makes mention, as being in Herod's temple; of which he says, that it was over the doors (of the temple), under the edges of the wall, having clusters hanging down from it on high, which filled spectators with wonder as for the largeness of it, so for the art with which it was made. And elsewhere he says,[6] the inward door in the porch was all covered with gold, and the whole wall about it; and it had over it golden vines, from whence hung clusters as big as the stature of a man: now whether our Lord may refer to this, being near the temple, and in view of it, and point to it, and call Himself *the true vine*, in distinction from it, which was only the representation of one; or whether He might take occasion, from the sight of a real vine, to compare Himself to one, may be considered; since it was usual with Christ, upon sight or mention of natural things, to take the opportunity of treating of spiritual ones: though it may be rather this discourse of the vine and branches might be occasioned by His speaking of the fruit of the vine, at the time He ate the passover, and instituted the ordinance of the supper:

and my Father is the husbandman. Or vinedresser. So God is called by Philo the Jew,[7] γεωργος αγαθος, *a good husbandman*; and the same the Targumist says of the Word of the Lord,[8]

"and my Word shall be unto them, כאכרא טבא, *as a good husbandman*."

Now Christ says this of His Father, both with respect to Himself, the vine, and with respect to the branches that were in Him: He was the husbandman to Him; He planted the vine of His human nature, and filled it with all the graces of the Spirit; He supported it, upheld it, and made it strong for Himself, for the purposes of His grace, and for His own glory; and took infinite delight

---

[3] Zohar in Gen fol. 127. 3.

[4] Mishna Middot, c. 3. sect. 8. T. Bab. Cholin, fol. 90. 2. & Tamid, fol. 29. 1, 2.

[5] Antiqu. l. 15. c. 11. sect. 3.

[6] De Bello Jud. l. 5. c. 5. sect. 4.

[7] Leg. Allegor. l. 1. p. 48.

[8] Targum in Hos. 11:4.

in it, being to Him a pleasant plant, a plant of renown. The concern this husbandman has with the branches, is expressed in the following verse.

Verse 2. **Every branch in me that beareth not fruit**, &c. There are two sorts of branches in Christ the vine; the one sort are such who have only a historical faith in Him, believe but for a time, and are removed; they are such who only profess to believe in Him, as Simon Magus did; are in Him by profession only; they submit to outward ordinances, become church members, and so are reckoned to be in Christ, being in a church state, as the churches of Judea and Thessalonica, and others, are said, in general, to be in Christ; though it is not to be thought that every individual person in these churches were truly and savingly in Him. These branches are unfruitful ones; what fruit they seemed to have, withers away, and proves not to be genuine fruit; what fruit they bring forth is to themselves, and not to the glory of God, being none of the fruits of His Spirit and grace: and such branches the husbandman,

taketh away; removes them from that sort of being which they had in Christ. By some means or another He discovers them to the saints to be what they are; sometimes he suffers persecution to arise because of the Word, and these men are quickly offended, and depart of their own accord; or they fall into erroneous principles, and set up for themselves, and separate from the churches of Christ; or they become guilty of scandalous enormities, and so are removed from their fellowship by excommunication; or if neither of these should be the case, but these tares should grow together with the wheat till the harvest, the angels will be sent forth, who will gather out of the kingdom of God all that offend and do iniquity, and cast them into a furnace of fire, as branches withered, and fit to be burned [see *Matt. 13:37-42*];

and every *branch* that beareth fruit, he purgeth it, that it may bring forth more fruit. These are the other sort of branches, who are truly and savingly in Christ; such as are rooted in Him; to whom He is the green fir tree, from whom all their fruit is found; who are filled by Him with all the fruits of His Spirit, grace, and righteousness. These are purged or pruned, chiefly by afflictions and temptations, which are as needful for their growth and fruitfulness, as the pruning and cutting of the vines are for theirs; and though these are sometimes sharp, and never joyous, but grievous, yet they are attended with the peaceable fruits of righteousness, and so the end of bringing forth more fruit is answered [see *Heb. 12:11*]; for it is not enough that a believer exercise grace, and perform good works for the present, but these must remain; or he must be constant herein, and still bring forth fruit, and add one virtue to another, that it may appear he is not barren and unfruitful in the knowledge of Christ, in whom he is implanted [see *2 Pet. 1:5-8*]. These different acts of the vinedresser *taking away* some branches, and *purging* others, are expressed by the Mishnaic doctors[9] by פיסולה, and זירודה. The former, the commentators[10] say, signifies to cut off the branches that are withered and perished, and are good for nothing; and the latter signifies the pruning of the vine when it has a superfluity of branches, or these extend themselves too far; when some are left, and others are taken off.

Verse 3. **Now ye are clean through the word which I have spoken unto you**. These words being inserted in the discourse concerning the vine and branches, and the pruning and purging them to make them fruitful, are thought, by the learned Dr. Lightfoot, to be an allusion to the law in *Lev. 19:23*; by which the fruit of trees, for the first three years, were accounted uncircumcised or unclean, and in the fourth year fit for use; concerning which the Talmudists have a whole tract, called ערלה, *Orla*; the apostles having enjoyed the ministry of Christ, and been His disciples about such a time. Though the *now* seems to refer to the removal and taking away of that withered and unfruitful branch, Judas. Christ, in a former chapter [*13:10*], had told His disciples, that they were *clean, but not all*, because the betrayer was among them; but he being discovered by Christ, and ordered by Him to be gone, went out from among them about his wicked design; and now Christ could say of them all, that they were *clean*: which may be understood of their regeneration and sanctification, in which their hearts were sprinkled with clean water [see *Ezek. 36:25*]; were washed with *the washing of regeneration* [*Titus 3:5*]; had their hearts purified by faith in the blood of Christ, and had pure principles of grace formed in their souls; of all which the Gospel of Christ was the instrumental means: or of their justification by the righteousness of Christ, by which they were justified from all sin; and were all fair, and without spot; which was through the Gospel of Christ revealing His righteousness to them, or through the sentence of justification He, by His Spirit, passed upon their consciences.

Verse 4. **Abide in me, and I in you**, &c. The former of these is an exhortation to continue in the exercise of faith and love upon Christ, holding to Him the head, cleaving to Him with full purpose of heart, and so deriving life, grace, strength, and nourishment from Him; the latter is a promise encouraging to the former; for as Christ is formed in the hearts of His people, He continues there as the living principle of all grace. And so,

---

[9]   Mishna Sheviith, c, 2. sect. 3.

[10]   Maimonides & Bartenora in ibid.

As the branch cannot bear fruit of itself, except it abide in the vine, no more can ye, except ye abide in me. Which strongly expresses the necessity of abiding in Christ by fresh repeated acts of faith: and it is easy to observe, that when believers depart from Christ, though it be but partially, and for a time, for they cannot finally and totally depart from Him, in what a poor, withered, fruitless condition they are, both in their frames [*or* dispositions] and duties.

Verse 5. **I am the vine, ye** *are* **the branches**, &c. Christ here repeats what He said of Himself, *the vine*, for the sake of the application of *the branches* to His disciples: which expresses their sameness of nature with Christ; their strict and close union to Him; and the communication of life and grace, holiness and fruitfulness, of support and strength, and of perseverance in grace and holiness to the end from Him:

he that abideth in me, and I in him; which is the case of all that are once in Christ, and He in them:

the same bringeth forth much fruit; in the exercise of grace, and performance of good works; and continues to do so as long as he lives, not by virtue of his own free will, power, and strength, but by grace continually received from Christ:

for without me ye can do nothing. Nothing that is spiritually good; no, not any thing at all, be it little or great, easy or difficult to be performed; cannot think a good thought, speak a good word, or do a good action; can neither begin one, nor, when it is begun, perfect it. Nothing is to be done *without Christ*; without His Spirit, grace, strength, and presence; or as *separate* from Him. Were it possible for the branches that are truly in Him, to be removed from Him, they could bring forth no fruits of good works, any more than a branch separated from the vine can bring forth grapes; so that all the fruitfulness of a believer is to be ascribed to Christ, and His grace, and not to the free will and power of man.

Verse 6. **If a man abide not in me**, &c. Christ does not say, *if ye abide not in me*; He would not suppose this of His true disciples; Judas now being removed, to whom He may have some respect in this verse; though it may be applied to any one who has made a profession of Christ, and denies the truths of the Gospel, neglects the ordinances of it, or walks unworthy of his profession: of whom the following things may be truly said,

he is cast forth as a branch; that is unfruitful, and is therefore taken away from the vine, and cast forth out of the vineyard. This signifies the ejection of worthless and fruitless professors out of the churches; for such who are either unsound in their principles, or are remiss and negligent in their attendance on the worship of God, with the church, or are loose and vain in their lives and conversations, are to be removed from communion with the people of God;

and is withered; some versions, as the Arabic, Syriac, and Persic, read this as an epithet of the word *branch*, thus: *the branch that is withered*; expressing the condition the branch is in before it is cast forth out of the vineyard, and the reason of its being cast forth. But others read it as a new and distinct predicate of the branch, showing the case it is in, immediately upon its being cast forth: it may be cut off, and cast out with its leaves upon it, though without fruit; but as soon as ever it is ejected, it withers away. So mere external professors of religion, when they are cast out of the communion of the church, presently the leaf of profession, which once seemed green, decays, loses its verdure, and that seeming fruit which grew upon them, shrinks to nothing, and they become *trees whose fruit withereth, without fruit* [*Jude 12*]: their show of life, zeal, religion, and holiness disappears, and all their external gifts, light, knowledge, and understanding, even in a speculative way, vanish:

and men gather them; or, as some copies have it, αυτο, *it*, which best agrees with the word *branch*. This was a common thing, when branches were thrown out of a vineyard, for men to come and gather them up for a use hereafter mentioned. So when unworthy members are put out of a church of Christ, the men of the world gather them into their society: or they are taken into the congregations of false teachers, who being sensual, and without the Spirit, separate themselves; or it may be read impersonally, *they are gathered*, or *it is gathered*: so wicked men, and Christless professors, will be gathered by the angels at the last day, and severed by them from the righteous, whom they will place at Christ's left hand to receive their awful doom:

and cast *them*, or *it*,

into the fire, and they are burned. Or *it is burned*; for nothing else is such a branch good for; see *Ezek. 15:2-5*. This may respect either the gnawings of conscience, that distress of mind, if not despair, that *fearful looking for of judgment, and fiery indignation* [*Heb. 10:27*], which attend apostates in this life; or their being cast into the everlasting burnings of hellfire by angels at the last day, as will be the case of every unfruitful tree, of the chaff and tares.

Verse 7. **If ye abide in me, and my words abide in you**, &c. Abiding in Christ is here explained by His words or doctrines abiding in His disciples; by which are meant His Gospel, and the truths of it. This abides when it comes in power, and becomes the engrafted Word; and may be said to do so, when such, in whose hearts it has a place, and has taken deep root, continue to have a relish and savor of it, a true and hearty affection for it, esteeming it above

469

their necessary food; when they hold fast the profession of it, stand fast in it, steadfastly abide by it, and constantly attend on it; all which is a considerable evidence that they do, yea, there is a promise that they *shall continue in the Son and in the Father, 1 John 2:24.* The blessing and privilege that such shall enjoy is,

ye shall ask what ye will, and it shall be done unto you. Or, as some copies read it, *it shall be given you*: but this must be understood not of temporal things, as riches, honors, profits, pleasures, or whatever even the carnal mind of a believer himself may sometimes desire; but of things spiritual, and with such limitations and restrictions as these; whatever is according to the will of God, for the Spirit of God Himself asks for no other for the saints [see *1 John 5:14*]; whatever is for the glory of God, and for their own spiritual profit and edification; and whatever is agreeable to the words and doctrines of Christ, which abide in them. Every thing of this kind they ask in faith, and with a submission to the divine will, they may expect to receive.

Verse 8. **Herein is my Father glorified**, &c. This does not so much refer to what goes before, concerning the disciples abiding in Christ, and He and His words abiding in them, and doing for them whatever they ask, though by all this God is glorified; as to what follows, the fruitfulness of the disciples:

that ye bear much fruit; of doctrine, grace, and good works, which show them to be *trees of righteousness, the planting of the Lord [Isa. 61:3]*, and the work of His hands; wherein the glory of His power, grace, and mercy, is greatly displayed. All the fruits of righteousness, with which they were filled by Christ, were by Him to the praise and glory of God; yea, by the fruitfulness of grace, and of life and conversation, by the lively exercise of grace, and conscientious discharge of duty, as well by light of doctrine, and usefulness in the ministration of the Gospel, the disciples and servants of Christ not only glorify God themselves, but are the means of others glorifying Him. It follows,

so shall ye be my disciples. Or *disciples to me*; to my honor and glory also, as well as to my Father's; not that their fruitfulness made them the disciples of Christ, but made them appear to be so, or made them honorable ones. Just as good fruit does not make the tree good; the tree is first good, and therefore it brings forth good fruit; but shows it to be good: as by continuing in His Word, abiding by His Gospel they appeared to be *disciples indeed [John 8:31]*, really and truly such; and as by loving one another, so by other fruits of righteousness, other men, all men know that they are the disciples of Christ.

Verse 9. **As the Father hath loved me**, &c. As His own Son, and as Mediator, from everlasting; and in time, in His state of humiliation, throughout the course of His obedience, and under all His sufferings; which

470

He testified more than once by a voice from heaven; which He showed by concealing nothing from Him as Mediator, by giving all things into His hands, by showing Him all that He Himself did, by appointing Him the Savior of the body, and making Him the head of the church, by exalting Him at His right hand, and ordaining Him to be judge of quick and dead;

so have I loved you: Christ loves His as His spouse and bride, as His dear children, as members of His body, as branches in Him the vine, as believers in Him, and followers of Him; which He has shown by espousing both their persons and cause, by assuming their nature, by suffering and dying in their room and stead, and making all suitable provision for them, both for time and eternity. And there is a likeness between the Father's love to Him, and His love to His disciples and followers: as His Father loved Him from everlasting, so did He love them; as His Father loved Him with a love of complacency and delight, so did He, and so does He love them; and as His Father loved Him with a special and peculiar affection, with an unchangeable, invariable, constant love, which will last for ever, in like manner does Christ love His people; and with this He enforces the following exhortation:

continue ye in my love. Meaning either in His love to them, which, as He always continues in it without any variableness or shadow of turning, so He would have them continue in believing their interest in it, prizing and valuing it, in imitating, and remembering it; or else in their love to Him, to His person, to His people, to His Gospel, to His ordinances, ways, and worship, which He knew was liable to wax cold, though it could not be lost.

Verse 10. **If ye keep my commandments, ye shall abide in my love**, &c. Not that their continuance in the heart's love and affection of Christ depended upon their observation of His commands; for as the keeping of them is not the cause or reason of the saints having an interest in the love of Christ, so it is not the cause or reason of their abiding in it; but to such that observe the commandments of Christ He will continue to make further discoveries of His love, and let them see more clearly and largely what a value He has for them, and how much He loves them: or the sense is, that by keeping the commandments of Christ, His disciples and followers show that they love Him, and continue in their affection to Him:

even as I have kept my Father's commandments, and abide in his love. The commandments of the Father kept by Christ were not only the precepts of the moral law, and the rites of the ceremonial one, which He strictly observed; but the preaching of the Gospel, and submitting to the ordinances of it, doing of miracles, and laying down His life for His people; in performing which, as His Father testified His approbation of them, and how strongly He was affected to Him, what an abiding He had in His love; so

Christ hereby showed His constant and continued love to His Father; and which was done by Him, that the world, as well as His disciples, might know how much He loved Him; see *chapter 14:31*.

Verse 11. These things have I spoken unto you, &c. Concerning the vine and branches, His abiding in them, and they in Him, their fruitfulness from Him, and perseverance in Him, His love to them, and theirs to Him:

that my joy might remain in you; meaning either that joy with which He joyed in and over them, as united to Him, and which is of the same nature as the joy of the bridegroom over the bride, and which will always remain and continue the same; or rather that joy which He is the author, object, ground, and matter of; for there is always reason to rejoice in Him, even in the most afflictive circumstances of life:

and *that* your joy might be full. That grace of joy which is implanted in the soul, by the Spirit of God in regeneration, and arises from, and is increased by discoveries of the person, grace, blood, righteousness, and sacrifice of Christ; and is *full of glory* [*1 Peter 1:8*], upon a clear sight of Him in this life, and will be entirely full, completely perfected in the other world, when He will be seen as He is,

Verse 12. This is my commandment, That ye love one another, &c. Christ had been before speaking of His commandments; and He mentions this as the principal one, and to which all the rest may be reduced; for as the precepts of the second table of the moral law may be briefly comprehended in this one duty, love to our neighbor, so all the duties of Christianity, relative to one another, are reducible to this, by love to serve each other. This was the commandment which lay uppermost on Christ's heart, and which He knew, if attended to, the rest could not fail of being observed. The argument by which, and the manner in which He presses it, is as before:

as I have loved you. Than which nothing can be more strong and forcible; see *John 13:34*.

Verse 13. Greater love hath no man than this, &c. By these words our Lord shows, how far love to another should extend, even to the laying down of our lives for the brethren; which is the highest instance of love among men;

that a man lay down his life for his friends. And in which believers should not come short of them; and also His great love to His people, and explains what He had just said, *as I have loved you* [*verse 12*]; which in a little time would be seen, by His laying down His life for them: for He not only came down from heaven, and laid aside His glory and royal majesty, but He laid down His life; not His gold and silver, and the riches of this world, which were all His, but His life; than which, nothing is dearer to a man, is himself, his all: and besides, Christ's life was not a common one, it was not the life of an innocent person only, or the life of a mere man, but of a man in union with the Son of God; it was the Lord of glory and Prince of life, who was crucified, and slain; a life that was entirely at His own disposal; it had never been forfeited by sin, nor could it have been forced away from Him by men or devils; it was laid down of and by Himself, freely and voluntarily; and that *for*, in the room, and instead of His people, as a ransom for them; He being their surety and substitute, and standing in their Law place and stead, He took their sins upon Him, bore the curse of the Law, sustained His Father's wrath, and all the punishment due to sin; and so suffered death, the death of the cross; the just, in the room and stead of the unjust. The persons for whom He laid down His life, are described as *his friends*; not that they were originally so; being enemies and enmity itself to God, when He laid down His life for them, and reconciled them [see *Rom. 5:8-10*]; they were not such as had carried themselves friendly, or had shown any love and affection to Him, but all the reverse: but they are so called, because He had chosen them for His friends; He had pitched upon them, and resolved to make them so; and by dying for them, reconciled them who were enemies; and in consequence of this, by His Spirit and grace, of enemies makes them friends; so that His love in dying for His people, is greater than any instance of love among men: He laid down His life for His enemies, without any sinister selfish views, and that freely and voluntarily; whereas among men, when one man has laid down his life for others, either they have been very deserving, or he has been forced to it, or it has been done with the view of popular applause and vainglory.

Verse 14. **Ye are my friends,** &c. This is an application of the foregoing passage, and more clearly explains it. The character of *friends*, is applied to the disciples of Christ; and belongs not only to His apostles, but to all that love Him, believe in Him, and obey Him; to whom He has shown Himself friendly, by laying down His life for them: for this clearly shows, that Christ had respect in the former words, to His own laying down His life for His people, in consequence of His great love to them; whereby He has made them friends, and who appear to be so by their cheerful obedience to Him:

if ye do whatsoever I command you. Not that their doing of the commandments of Christ interested them in His favor; or made them His friends; or was the reason and motive of His laying down His life for them, and showing Himself in such a friendly manner to them: but the sense is, that by observing His commands, from a principle of love, they would make it appear that they were His friends, being influenced by His grace, and constrained by a sense of His love in dying for them, to act such a part.

Verse 15. **Henceforth I call you not servants**, &c. As they and the rest of the people of God had been, under the legal dispensation; for though they were children, yet differed nothing from servants; and were very much influenced and impressed with a servile spirit, a spirit of bondage unto fear, being kept under tutors and governors by a severe discipline; but now Christ being come in the flesh, and being about to lay down His life, and make reconciliation for them, henceforward He would not use, treat, or account them as servants:

for the servant knoweth not what his lord doeth; designs to do, or is about to do; he is not made privy to all his counsels and purposes; these are only opened to him as necessity requires; which was pretty much the case of the Old Testament church, who, comparatively speaking, were used as servants; and had not the knowledge of the mysteries of grace, and of the counsels of God, as they are now laid open under the Gospel dispensation:

but I have called you friends; that is, accounted, reckoned of them, used them as His friends and familiar acquaintance; whom He told all His mind unto, and would go on to treat them as such; by leading them more and more, as they were able to bear it, into the designs of His grace, and the doctrines of His Gospel: just as Abraham was called *the friend of God* [*James 2:23*], and proved to be so, by His not concealing from him the thing He was about to do:

for all things that I have heard of my Father, I have made known unto you. Not all that He knew as the omniscient God, for there was no necessity that all such things should be made known to them; but all things which He had delivered to Him as man and Mediator, by His Father, respecting the salvation of men; all things which He Himself was to do and suffer, in order to obtain eternal redemption; and the whole of the Gospel, as to the essential and substantial parts of it, they were to preach; for otherwise, there were some things which as yet they were not able to bear, and were reserved to another time, to be made known unto them by His Spirit.

Verse 16. **Ye have not chosen me, but I have chosen you**, &c. Not but that they had made choice of Him as their Lord and Master, Savior and Redeemer; but not first, He was beforehand with them; He chose them, before they chose Him; so that His choice of them was entirely free, did not arise from any character, motive, or condition in them: the allusion is to a custom of the Jews, the reverse of which Christ acted; with whom it was usual for disciples to choose their own masters, and not masters their disciples: hence that advice of R. Joshuah ben Perachiah, said[11] to be the master of Jesus of Nazareth,

---

[11] Ganz Tzemach David, fol. 24. 2.

"עשה לך רב,"[12] *make*, provide, or chose *thyself a master*, and get thyself a companion."

Those words in *Song of Sol. 2:16*; *My beloved is mine, and I am his*, are thus paraphrased by the Jews:[13]

"He hath chosen me, and I have chosen him:" which is not amiss, provided the latter choice is thought to be by virtue, and in consequence of the former; if not, our Lord directly opposes the words and sense. This may be understood both of election to salvation, and of choice to the office of apostleship; in both which Christ was first, or chose them before they chose Him, that good part, which shall never be taken away; for as they were chosen in Him, so by Him, before the foundation of the world; being as early loved by Him, as by His Father; and in consequence thereof, were chosen by Him, for His people and peculiar treasure; He first chose and called them to be His disciples and apostles, to follow Him, preach His Gospel, and become fishers of men; and clothed them with full power and authority to exercise their high office:

and ordained you; which may design either ordination to eternal life, or apostleship, before the world began; as Jeremiah was ordained to be a prophet, before He was born; or else the investiture of them with that office, and with all gifts and graces necessary for the discharge of it; for when He called and sent forth His disciples to preach the Gospel, He is said to *ordain* them, *Mark 3:14*; and the rather this may be meant here, because the former is designed by His choosing them; or He *set* them, or planted them in Himself, a fruitful soil, that they might shoot up and bear much fruit, as it follows:

that ye should go and bring forth fruit; go first into Judea, and then into all the world; and brings forth the fruits of righteousness and holiness in themselves, and be the happy means of the conversion, and so of bringing in a large harvest of souls to Jesus Christ:

and *that* your fruit should remain; as it has done; for they not only persevered themselves in faith and holiness, in preaching the Gospel, and living according to it, but the persons, whose conversion they were instruments of, continued steadfastly in their doctrine, and in the fellowship of the saints; and the Gospel which was preached by them, has remained, though not always in the same place, yet in the world ever since:

that whatsoever ye shall ask of the Father in my name, he may give it you. This is added, to encourage their perseverance in the work he chose

---

[12] Pirke Abot, c. 1. sect. 6.

[13] Zohar in Exod. fol. 9. 1.

and called them to, which would be attended with many difficulties and discouragements; wherefore as they would stand in need of divine assistance, they might assure themselves of it; for be it what it would they should ask of His Father, making mention of His name and righteousness; whether for a sufficiency of gifts and grace in the discharge of their duty; or for success in it; or for the confirmation of the truths delivered by them; or for liberty and boldness to speak in vindication of themselves, when called to it before kings and governors, it should be given them.

Verse 17. **These things I command you**, &c. The doctrines which Christ spake, as one having authority, concerning the vine and branches; His love to His disciples, in laying down His life for them, and in accounting and using them as friends, and not servants; in choosing, ordaining, and sending them forth, for the ends above mentioned; these were delivered by Him with this view, to promote brotherly love among them:

that ye love one another. This lay much upon His heart, He often mentions it; this is the third time it is expressed by Him, in these His last discourses; and indeed, since He had declared such strong love and affection for them, it was but right and proper they should love one another; nor does any thing more tend to increase mutual love among the saints, than the consideration of their common interest in the unchangeable love of their Lord.

Verse 18. **If the world hate you**, &c. After our Lord had signified how much He loved His disciples, and what great things He had done for them, He faithfully acquaints them with the world's hatred of them, and what they must expect to meet with from that quarter, and says many things to fortify their minds against it; His words do not imply any doubt about it, but He rather takes it for granted, as a thing out of question; *if*, or *seeing the world hate you*; they had had some experience of it already, and might look for more, when their master was gone from them: wherefore, He, in order to engage their patience under it, says,

ye know that it hated me before it *hated* you. Which words are an appeal of Christ to His apostles, for the usage He had met with from the wicked and unbelieving world of the Jews; how they had expressed their hatred, not only by words, calling Him a gluttonous man, and a winebibber, a sinner, a Samaritan, a madman, one that had a devil, yea, Beelzebub himself, but by deeds: taking up stones to stone Him more than once, leading Him to the brow of a hill, in order to cast Him down headlong, consulting by various means to take away His life, as Herod did in His very infancy; which was done before they showed so much hatred to His disciples; and perhaps reference may be had to the original enmity between the seed of the woman, and the seed of the serpent, mentioned *Gen. 3:15*, as well as to these instances. Moreover, the words πρωτον υμων, rendered *before you*, may be translated *the first* or *chief of you*, your Lord and head; and denotes the dignity, excellency, and superiority of Christ; wherefore it is suggested, that if He, who was so much before them in personal worth and greatness, was hated by the world, they should not think it hard, or any strange thing, that this should be their case.

Verse 19. **If ye were of the world**, &c. Belonged to the world, were of the same spirit and principles with it, and pursued the same practices:

the world would love its own; for every like loves its like; the men of the world love each other's persons, company, and conversation:

but because ye are not of the world; once they were, being born into it, brought up in it, had their conversation among the men of it, were themselves men of carnal, worldly, principles and practices; but being called by Christ, and becoming His disciples, they were no more of it; and as He was not of the world, so they were not of it, though they were in it. The Jews distinguish the disciples of the wise men, from אינשי דעלמא, *the men of the world*,[14] pretending that they were not; but this is a character that only belongs to the disciples of Christ, in consequence of their being called by Him out of it:

but I have chosen you out of the world: which designs not the eternal election of them, but the separation of them from the rest of the world in effectual vocation [*or* calling], and the designation of them to His work and service:

therefore the world hateth you. And since it was upon that account, they had no reason to be uneasy, but rather to rejoice; seeing this was an evidence of their not belonging to the world, and of being chosen and called by Christ out of it.

Verse 20. **Remember the word that I said unto you**, &c. For their further consolation under the hatred of the world, He puts them in mind of a saying of His, which He had lately used, *chapter 13:16*; to teach them humility, self-denial, and brotherly love, and elsewhere, as in *Matt. 10:24*, for the same purpose as here; namely, to engage them patiently to bear the hatred of men, and all indignities and insults from them, for His name's sake:

The servant is not greater than his lord. Nor so great, and consequently not more, nor so much deserving of respect, or to be treated in a better

---

[14] T. Bab. Kiddushin, fol. 80. 2.

manner: suggesting, that Christ was their Lord and Master, as He was, and they were His servants; and therefore were not greater than Him, but much inferior to Him, and could not expect better usage from men than He had.

If they have persecuted me; as they did, both by words and deeds, as before observed:

they also will persecute you; and so they did in like manner, and from place to place:

if they have kept my saying; which is either ironically spoken, or designs that insidious malicious observation of Christ's words, made by the Jews, with an intent to catch and lay hold on something to improve against Him:

they will keep yours also. That is, either they will attend to your doctrines, or they will make the same spiteful remarks, and put the same evil constructions on your words as on mine.

Verse 21. **But all these things will they do unto you**, &c. Christ here signifies, that all the hatred and persecutions raised against His people by the world, would not be on their own account, for any evil actions done by them; they would not suffer as thieves, murderers, and evildoers, but as Christians; or as He says,

for my name's sake: because they were called by His name, and called upon His name; because they professed His name, and confessed Him to be the Messiah and Redeemer; because they loved His name Jesus, a Savior, believed in His name, and hoped in Him for eternal life; and also preached Him, and in His name salvation, and encouraged others to believe in Him; and therefore they had no reason to be ashamed, but rather to rejoice; as they afterwards did, that they were counted worthy to suffer shame for His name. Besides, this malice and hatred of theirs arose from ignorance of the Father of Christ:

because they know not him that sent me. They did not know that Jesus was the *Christ*, and *sent* of God; they did not acknowledge Him to be so, or the Father to be the sender of Him; and because Christ and His disciples asserted this, therefore they were the objects of their hatred.

Verse 22. **If I had not come and spoken unto them**, &c. The ignorance of the Jews is represented as inexcusable, since Christ was come, and had preached unto them; if He had not come and told them that He was the Messiah, they might have pleaded an excuse for their ignorance of Him and His mission, and of the Father that sent Him: but inasmuch as He was come in the flesh, and came to them His own; and came also a *light* into the world, carrying along with Him evidence, conviction, and demonstration, of His being the Messiah; speaking such words as never man did; preaching with such authority as the Scribes and Pharisees did not; declaring in plain terms He was the Christ of God, and that if they did not believe Him to be so, they would die in their sins; they could have no pretext to make for their ignorance and disbelief: if all this had not been done,

they had not had sin; or been guilty of the sin of unbelief, in the rejection of the Messiah; not that they would have been without sin in any sense, or without any kind of sin, but without this particular sin; at least they would have excused and wiped themselves clean, and would have looked like innocent and sinless persons, under all their ignorance and unbelief:

but now they have no cloak for their sin. They could not say, had He come to us, and told us that He was the Messiah, and given evidence of His being sent by the Father, we would have believed Him, and received Him as the Messiah; for He did do this, and so cut off all excuses and pretenses from them.

Verse 23. **He that hateth me, hateth my Father also**. The hatred the world bears to the followers of Christ, is interpretatively hatred to Christ Himself; and hatred to Christ Himself, is no other than hatred to His Father; and indeed, all the hatred that is shown by the men of the world to Christ, to His Gospel, and to His faithful ministers and followers, originally arises from that enmity, that is naturally in the heart of every unregenerate man against God: now since not only Christ, but the Father also, is hated by the world, the children of God and disciples of Christ may sit easier under all the resentment, frowns, and malice of the world.

Verse 24. **If I had not done among them the works**, &c. This is another, and a new argument, evincing the inexcusableness of their ignorance, and infidelity, and sin, taken from the works that Christ did; such as healing the sick, raising the dead, giving sight to the blind, causing the dumb to speak, the deaf to hear, and the lame to walk, cleansing lepers, and casting out devils; which were clear proofs, and full demonstrations of His Deity, and of His being the true Messiah: and,

which none other man did; in His own name, and by His own power; and which none of the men of God ever did; as Moses, Elijah, Elisha, or others; and particularly that of giving sight to one that was born blind: now if these works had not been done *among them*, openly, visibly, and publicly,

they had not had sin; or so much sin; or their sin of unbelief would not have been so great, or attended with such aggravating circumstances; or they would not have been guilty of the sin against the Holy Ghost, as many of them were;

479

who saw His works and miracles, and were convicted in their own consciences that He was the Messiah, and yet rejected Him, against all the light and evidence which the Spirit of God gave by them, and by whom Christ wrought His miracles:

but now have they both seen; the works which were done, and the Messiah, whose mission from the Father they proved;

and hated both me and my Father. For their rejection of Him as the Messiah, notwithstanding the doctrines He taught, and the miracles He wrought, plainly arose from obstinacy, malice, and inveterate hatred against Christ, and against the Father that sent Him.

Verse 25. **But *this cometh to pass***, &c. This hatred against Christ, and which is pointed at His people for His sake, and reaches to the Father also on His account, is suffered to be, and therefore should be patiently borne:

that the word might be fulfilled which is written in their law: either in *Psa. 35:19*, or rather in *Psa. 69:4*; which is a psalm of Christ, as appears by citations out of it in the New Testament, or references to it; see *John 2:17* and *19:28; Matt. 27:48*. The whole Scripture is sometimes called *the law*, as here; for not the law of Moses is meant, or the five books of Moses, but the writings of the Old Testament; which the Jews had in their hands, to them being committed the oracles of God; and sometimes are so called, when the book of Psalms is particularly referred to as now; see *John 10:34* and *12:34*; the words cited are,

They hated me without a cause; without any reason for it, Christ having given them no provocation, or just cause of offense, anger, or hatred. This sin of hating without a cause, is represented by the Jews as a very heinous one, and as the reason of the destruction of the second temple; under which they observe, that men studied in the law, and in the commandments, and in doing of good; and therefore ask, Why it was destroyed? The answer is, Because there was under it, שנאת חנם, *hatred without a cause:* to teach us, that hatred without a cause is equal to the three (capital) transgressions—idolatry, adultery, and murder, for which they say the first temple was destroyed. [15] This is a tacit acknowledgment that the sin here mentioned was a reigning one, or that it much abounded in the time of Christ.

Verse 26. **But when the Comforter is come**, &c. Or *Advocate*, the Spirit of God; who was to be, and has been an advocate for Christ, against the world, and for His people, against all their enemies; and who as He was to reprove,

---

[15] T. Bab. Yoma, fol. 9. 2. Hieros. Yoma, fol. 38. 3.

and did *reprove the world of sin, righteousness, and judgment* [*John 16:8*], in favor of Christ, so He was to assist His people, and plead their cause, and help them, in vindication of themselves, before the princes of the earth, as He did: and who also was to act, and has acted the part of a *comforter* to them, under all the hatred and violence they have met with from the world; by taking and applying the things of Christ to them; by shedding the love of God in them; by applying the promises of the Gospel to them; by witnessing their adoption, and sealing them up to the day of redemption:

whom I will send unto you from the Father; visibly, as on the day of Pentecost, in cloven tongues as of fire; and invisibly into their hearts, by the secret influence of His light and grace; which mission, as it suggests no inferiority in the Spirit, either to the Father or the Son; since the same Spirit with the Father, was the sender of Christ; so it is expressive of the equal Deity of Christ, and His joint power and authority with the Father:

even **the Spirit of truth**; who is the true Spirit, truth itself; yea, the true God, with the Father and Son; the Spirit of Him who is truth; the dictator of the Scriptures of truth; who leads His people into all truth; and is the Spirit of truth, as He is a witness or testifier of Christ, hereafter promised:

which proceedeth from the Father; Christ is not content to describe Him by His work and office, as an Advocate and Comforter, and as the Spirit of truth; and from His mission by Him from the Father; all which shows His usefulness and authority: but also from His nature and essence, which is the same with the Father's; and from His peculiar personal and distinctive character, expressed by His proceeding from the Father; and which is mentioned, as what is distinct from His mission by Christ, from the Father before spoken of; and designs no other, than the eternal, ineffable, and continued act of His procession from the Father and the Son; in which He partakes of the same nature with them, and which personally distinguishes Him from them. The ancient Jews[16] spoke of Him just in the same language; *the Spirit of God*, in *Gen. 1:2*, they say is the Holy Spirit, דנפיק מאלהים, *which proceedeth from God*: very pertinently does Christ take notice of this His character here, when He was about to speak of Him as His testifier:

he shall testify of me: of His Deity and Sonship, of His incarnation, of His being the Messiah, of His sufferings and death, of His resurrection and ascension, of His exaltation at the right hand of God, and of His ordination to be the Judge of quick and dead; all which He bore testimony to, by the gifts bestowed upon the apostles, and the great grace that was upon them all; by the signs, wonders, and divers miracles, by which the Gospel of Christ was

---

[16] Zohar in Gen. fol. 1. 4.

confirmed; and by the power, influence, and success, which attended the preaching of it every where. Thus He testified of Christ, against the blaspheming Jews, and persecuting Gentiles, to the reproof and confusion of them; and He testified of Him to the apostles, and all true believers, to their great joy and comfort, and to the support of them, under all the malice and hatred of the world.

Verse 27. **And ye shall also bear witness**, &c. That is, of Christ; of all the things He did in Jerusalem, and in the land of the Jews; being eyewitnesses, and ministers, or servants of the Word, who constantly attended upon Him; of all the good He did to the bodies and souls of men; of the various miracles He wrought, and of the several doctrines which were taught by Him: what they saw with their eyes, heard with their ears, and with their hands handled of the Word of life [see *1 John 1:1-3*], that they could declare, and did declare, and bore a faithful testimony to; they were to be, and were witnesses of His sufferings and death, of His resurrection from the dead, and ascension to heaven; they were a company of select men, chosen before of God, for this purpose; they were the most proper to be concerned herein, having been for a considerable time His intimates and associates:

because ye have been with me from the beginning. From the beginning of His ministry; for as soon as He entered on His public work, He called them to be followers of Him; and who continued with Him to the end, and therefore were the most capable of bearing a testimony concerning His person, doctrines, and works; of all He did and suffered, from first to last.

CHAPTER 16

Verse 1. **These things have I spoken unto you**, &c. Concerning the world's hatred and persecution of them, and the little regard they would show to their doctrine: these things Christ thought proper to give them notice of beforehand, that expecting them, they might be prepared for them, and be fortified against them;

that ye should not be offended. His view in speaking of them, was not to discourage them, but to prevent their stumbling at them, and falling by them. Hardships coming upon persons at unawares, bear the harder upon their spirits, and they are more apt to take offense at them and be impatient under them, which is prevented by previous intimation: had Christ said nothing of these things that should befall His disciples, they might have surprised them, and have been a stumbling to them; and might have tempted them to have relinquished their profession of Him, and dropped their ministerial work; whereas being apprised of them beforehand, they were not so shocking to them. This shows the tender concern of Christ for His disciples, how careful He was to remove every occasion of stumbling, or what might be matter of offense to them; and may teach us to act in such like manner towards one another, in this, or any other case.

Verse 2. **They shall put you out of the synagogues**, &c. The Jews had made a law already, that he who confessed that Jesus was the Messiah, should be cast out of their synagogues; and they had put it in execution upon the blind man Christ restored to sight, for his profession of faith in Him; which struck such a terror upon the people, that even many of the chief rulers who believed that Jesus was the true Messiah, durst not confess Him, because of this law; for it was what they could not bear the thoughts of, to be deemed and treated as heretics and apostates, and the vilest of wretches: for this putting out of the synagogue, was not the lesser excommunication, which was called, נידוי, *Niddui*, and was a *separation* from a particular synagogue for a while; but the greater excommunication, either by חרם, *Cherem*, or שמתא, *Shammatha*; when a person was cut out from the whole body of the Jewish church, called often the *synagogue*, or *congregation* of the people; and was devoted and consigned to utter destruction, which was the height of their ecclesiastical power, their rage and malice could carry them to: and this the apostles were to expect; nay, not only this, but to have their lives taken away by ruffians, under a pretense of zeal for the service of God, and interest of religion:

yea, the time cometh, that whosoever killeth you will think that he doeth God service. For this is not to be understood of their being delivered up into the hands of civil magistrates, and of their being tried, judged, condemned, and put to death by their orders, but of their being murdered by a set of men called *zealots*; who, in imitation of Phinehas, as they pretended [see *Num. 25:7-13*], took upon them, whenever they found any person guilty of a capital crime, as idolatry, blasphemy, &c. or what they judged so, to fall upon him at once, and without any more ado kill him; nor were they accountable to any court of judicature for such an action, and which was reckoned laudable and praiseworthy: in this way, and by the hands of such miscreants, Stephen the protomartyr lost his life [see *Acts 6:8-7:60*]; for though they had him before a council, and suborned witnesses against him, yet, when in his own defense he said what these *zealots* interpreted blasphemy, they ran upon him at once, and cast him out of the city, and stoned him to death; and without any leave or authority from the Sanhedrin, as appears: and these men were accounted good men, zealous, קנאתו של מקום,[1] *with a zeal for God*, His honor and glory; and valued themselves much upon such butcheries and inhumanity, and thought, as our Lord here says, that they *did God service*; or as the Syriac renders it, דקורבנא מקרב, *offered a sacrifice to God*, and so the Arabic and Ethiopic versions: and indeed this is a rule with the Jews,[2] and which they form upon the instance and example of Phinehas:

> "that whoever sheds the blood of wicked men (and such they reckoned the apostles and followers of Christ to be), כאלו הקריב קרבן, *it is all one as if he offered a sacrifice;*"

they looked upon this to be a sacrifice acceptable and well pleasing to God: so the Apostle Paul, in his unregenerate state, thought he ought to do many things contrary to the name of Christ; and that he was doing God service, when he prosecuted the church, and gave his voice with these ruffians, to put the saints to death.

Verse 3. **And these things will they do unto you**, &c. Christ here opens the true spring and source of the furious zeal of the Jews against the apostles, in putting them out of their synagogues, and taking away their lives; it was pure wilful ignorance of the Father and Himself:

because they have not known the Father, nor me. Though they boasted of their knowledge of God, yet they knew Him not as the Father and sender of Christ, at least they would not own Him as such: nor Jesus as the true Messiah, and sent of the Father, to redeem and save His people from their sins. And since they neither knew the Father, nor Christ, it is no wonder they did not know, own, and acknowledge, the disciples of Christ, but used them in the ill manner they did; their zeal was *not according to knowledge* [*Rom. 10:2*], it was a blind and misguided one: and this is mentioned, not to extenuate or excuse their sin, though it shows, they were not out of the reach of mercy, because they, as the apostle says of himself, *did it ignorantly in unbelief* [*1 Tim. 1:13*]; but as an argument with the disciples to bear their ill usage with patience, and to pity them and pray for them.

---

[1] Jarchi & Bartenora in Mishna Sanhedrin, c. 9. sect. 6.

[2] Bemidbar Rabba, Parash, 21. fol. 229. 3.

Verse 4. **But these things have I told you**, &c. Christ enlarged on this disagreeable subject, and was the more particular in enumerating the evils His apostles were to endure for His name's sake:

that when the time shall come; some copies read it, *their time*; so the Vulgate Latin, Syriac, and Arabic render it; that is, the time when wicked men will be suffered to vent all their rage and malice:

ye may remember that I told you of them. Which might serve greatly to confirm them in the faith of Him as the omniscient God, and the true Messiah, and encourage them to depend on His veracity and faithfulness in His promises; that since the evil things which He spoke of came upon them, so they might hope, believe, and expect, that all the good things He had assured them of, should be accomplished; and also to engage them to bear their sufferings with the greater patience, since they were appointed by God, and foretold by their Lord and master.

And these things, adds Christ,

I said not unto you at the beginning; when He first called them to be followers of Him; for though when He ordained them, and sent them forth to preach the Gospel in the cities of Judea, which was some time after He had called them by His grace, He did acquaint them with some of the troubles and exercises they should meet with; as that they should be hated by all men, persecuted from city to city, beat in the synagogues, delivered up to councils, and brought before kings and governors; see *Matt. 10:17-19*; yet He did not so fully and distinctly speak of these things, as here and at this time: His reason for such a conduct was this,

because, says He,

I was with you. Wherefore He never spoke so fully and distinctly of their troubles, because He was with them, and took them upon Himself: and indeed, while He was with them, the rage and malice of the Jews were not so much against His disciples, as Himself; nor did He for the same reason speak so largely of the Comforter, and of the comforts they should receive from Him, because as they had not the exercises they should afterwards have, so they then had Christ for their comforter.

Verse 5. **But now I go my way to him that sent me**, &c. These words seem to belong to the preceding verse, and to contain a reason why Christ spoke of the trials and afflictions of His disciples now, because He was going away from them to His Father; when, as they would be at the head of His affairs in this world, so they would the more become the butt of the rage of men:

485

and none of you asketh me, Whither goest thou? Peter indeed asked the question, *chapter 13:36*; but his meaning was, What part of the country He was going to? What private and inaccessible place He was about to betake Himself to? He had no notion of His going out of the world, or to heaven to His Father, and therefore inquired nothing about it; and when Christ had suggested to His disciples, that He was going to His Father's house, to prepare mansions for them, they did not seem to understand Him, *chapter 14:2,3,5*. Nor did they ask what He meant by His *Father's house*, or what those *mansions* were He was going to prepare; and what the glory was, He was going to possess for Himself and them; they ask neither about the place He was going to, nor the way to it, nor the happiness to be enjoyed there.

Verse 6. **But because I have said these things unto you**, &c. Of being hated and persecuted by the Jews, of being put out of their synagogues, and of losing of their lives; and particularly of His departure from them, or the loss of His bodily presence:

sorrow hath filled your heart. Sorrow for His absence so possessed their minds, seized on all the powers and faculties of their souls, and engrossed all their thoughts, that it never entered into the heart of any of them to inquire about the place He was going to, or the state He should enter upon; which had they had any right notions of, would have greatly contributed to have abated their sorrow, quieted their minds, made them easy under, and reconciled them unto, His departure from them.

Verse 7. **Nevertheless I tell you the truth**, &c. Christ was truth itself, and could say nothing else; but He makes use of this way of speaking, to raise the attention of His disciples, and to engage their belief of what He was about to say, and of which they were not easily persuaded; which was, that however overwhelmed they were with grief and sorrow, because of His going away from them, a greater truth He could not tell them, than that this would be to their real good and advantage:

it is expedient for you that I go away; Christ's death here, as in many other places in these discourses of His, is signified by *going away*, a *departure*, taking a sort of a *journey*, such a one as indeed is common to all mankind; death is *the way of all the earth* [*Josh. 23:14*], and which Christ took by agreement with His Father; a *dark* way is the valley of the shadow of death, and so it was to Christ, who went away in the dark, under the hidings of His Father's face. It is a man's going to his long home, and a long journey it is, till he returns in the resurrection morn; though it was a short one to Christ, who rose again the third day. The phrase supposes the place and persons He went from, this world and His disciples; and the place and persons He went unto, the grave, heaven, His Father, the blessed Spirit, angels, and glorified saints; and is expressive of the voluntariness of His death; He was not fetched, or thrust and forced away, but He went away of Himself; and is a very easy and familiar way of expressing death by, and greatly takes off the dread and terror of it: it is only moving from one place to another, as from one house, city, or country, to another; and shows, that it is not an annihilation of a man, either in body or soul, only a translating of him from one place and state to another. Now the death of Christ was expedient, not only for Himself, which He does not mention; He being concerned more for the happiness of His people than for Himself; but for His disciples and all believers; for hereby a great many evils were prevented falling upon them, which otherwise would; as the heavy strokes of divine justice, the curses and condemnation of the law, the wrath and vengeance of God, and eternal death, ruin, and destruction: as well as many good things were hereby obtained for them; as the redemption of their souls from sin, law, hell, and death; peace, reconciliation, and atonement; the full and free forgiveness of all their sins, an everlasting righteousness, and eternal life. Moreover, Christ's going away was expedient for His people; since He went to open the way for them into the holiest of all, by His blood [see *Heb. 10:19*]; to take possession of heaven in their name and stead; to prepare mansions of glory for them; to appear in the presence of God for them; to be their advocate, and make intercession for all good things for them; to transact all their business between God and them; to take care of their affairs; to present their petitions; to remove all charges and accusations; and to ask for, and see applied every blessing of grace unto them. The particular instanced in, in the text, of the expediency of it, is the mission and coming of the Spirit:

for if I go not away, the Comforter will not come unto you; but if I depart, I will send him unto you. The Spirit of God in some sense had come, before the death of Christ; He had appeared in the creation of all things out of nothing, as a joint Creator with the Father and Son; He was come as a spirit of prophecy upon the inspired writers, and others; the Old Testament saints had received Him as a spirit of faith; He had been given to Christ as man, without measure, and the disciples had been partakers of His gifts and graces: but He was not come in so peculiar a manner, as He afterwards did; as the promise of the Father, the glorifier of Christ, the comforter of His people, the *Spirit of truth* [see *verse 13*], and the reprover of the world. There are reasons to be given, why the Spirit of God should not come in such a manner before, as after the death of Christ. The order of the three divine persons in the Trinity, and in the economy of man's salvation, required such a method to be observed; that the Father should first, and for a while, be more especially manifested; next the Son, and then the Spirit: besides, our Lord has given a reason Himself, why the Spirit *was not yet given, because Jesus was not yet glorified, chapter 7:39*. And the coming of the Spirit as a comforter, and the *Spirit of truth*, was to be through the intercession, and by the mission of Christ; and therefore it was proper He should go away first, in order to send Him: add to all this, that if Christ had not gone away or died, there would have been nothing for the Spirit to have done; no blood to sprinkle; no righteousness to reveal and bring near; no salvation to apply; or any of the things of Christ, and blessings of grace, to have taken and shown; all which are owing to the death of Christ, and which show the expediency of it. The expediency of Christ's death for the mission of the Spirit to His disciples, is very conspicuous; for hereby they were comforted and supported under a variety of troubles; were led into all truth, and so furnished for their ministerial work; and were made abundantly successful in it, that being attended with the *demonstration of the Spirit and of power* [*1 Cor. 2:4*].

Verse 8. **And when he is come**, &c. The coming of the Spirit here, chiefly designs His descent upon the apostles at the day of Pentecost: as the things ascribed to Him, and which were then done by Him, clearly show; though it may also include His coming along with, and by the ministration of the Gospel, into the hearts of His people at conversion, in all after ages of time:

he will reprove the world of sin, and of righteousness, and of judgment: by *the world* is principally meant, the Jews; the world among whom Christ personally was, who knew Him not, disbelieved Him, rejected Him as the Messiah, hated and persecuted Him, even unto death; though not to the exclusion of the Gentiles, the whole world that lies in wickedness [see *1 John 5:19*]; since both joined, and were concerned in these things, and reproved of them; which *reproving*, as it may respect different persons, may intend both such reproofs and convictions, as are not attended with conversion, and issue in salvation; and such as are powerful, spiritual, and to saving purposes: the several things the Spirit of God is said to reprove of, being repeated in the following verses, with reasons or specifications annexed to them, will be there considered.

Verse 9. **Of sin, because they believe not on me**; the *sin* here primarily intended, is that of the Jews, in disbelieving, rejecting, and crucifying Christ; and which the Spirit of God, by Peter, charged upon them on the day of Pentecost, and fully proved against them; gave such clear evidence, and wrought such strong convictions of in their minds and consciences, that being pricked to the heart, they cried out, *What shall we do? Acts 2:23,36,37*; though as this passage may be applied to the ordinary work of the Spirit of God upon the souls of men, through the ministry of the Word; so it may take in convictions of sin of all sorts, as of original and actual sins, and particularly the sin of unbelief: for the Spirit of God convinces of the sinfulness and corruption of nature, the wickedness and plague of a man's heart, the sin that dwells in him; how that has overspread all the powers and faculties of his soul, rendered both him and his services unacceptable to God, loathsome in His sight, and himself hopeless and helpless, and deserving of His wrath and displeasure. He also convinces of actual sins and transgressions, showing that they are breaches of the law of God, and are committed against God Himself; that they are deserving of death, even eternal death; that the wrath of God is revealed against them, and for them comes upon the children of disobedience; and that there is no atonement for them, or cleansing from them, but by the blood of Christ. He likewise convinces of the sin of unbelief, here particularly mentioned: showing the evil nature and consequences of it, to persons enjoying a Gospel revelation; that such who disbelieve the Messiah, shall die in their sins; that whoever believes not in Him shall be damned; and that faith in Christ is necessary to salvation, and that without it there is none.

Verse 10. **Of righteousness, because I go to my Father**, &c. The *righteousness* here spoken of, does, in the first sense of the word, design the personal righteousness of Christ. The Jews had traduced Him as a wicked man, said He was a sinner Himself, and a friend of publicans and sinners; that He was guilty of blasphemy and sedition, maintained a familiarity with Satan, yea, that He had a devil. Now the Spirit of God, by the mouth of Peter on the day of Pentecost, proved, to the conviction of the Jews, that all this was slander; that Christ was an innocent, holy, and righteous person, and *a man approved of God* among them, as they themselves must be conscious of, *Acts 2:22*; of all which, His going to the Father, and being received by Him, were a full proof and demonstration. The effusion of the Spirit in that extraordinary manner upon the disciples, showed that He was gone to the Father, and had received from Him the promise of the Holy Ghost, which He then shed abroad; and His going to the Father, and being set down by Him at His right hand, made it clear that He came from Him, and was no impostor; that He had acted the faithful and upright part, and was free from all the charges the Jews had laid against Him. Moreover, this may also be very well understood of the mediatorial righteousness of Christ, which He, as the surety and Savior of His people, was to work out and bring in for them, in obedience to the law of God; which required holiness of nature, perfection of obedience, and bearing its penalty, death; all which were complied with by Christ, and so the whole righteousness of the law was fulfilled by Him; and which is imputed by God as the justifying righteousness of all that believe in Jesus; and the proof of His having wrought out this, lies in His going to the Father; for as this was the work He came about, the will of His Father He came to do, had He not done it, it is reasonable to think He would never have met with such a welcome from Him. Besides, the donation of the Spirit, in consequence of its being wrought out, most clearly demonstrates it: likewise in the ordinary work of the Spirit of God upon the souls of His people, He always convinces them of the necessity of a righteousness to justify them before God, to render them acceptable in His sight, and to give them a right to the heavenly glory; for to admit them without a righteousness, or any unrighteous persons there, would be contrary to the justice of God, disagreeable to His pure and holy nature, and destructive of the comfort and happiness of the saints. He, the Spirit of God, convinces men of the insufficiency of their own righteousness for such purposes; that they have no righteousness that deserves the name of one, and that what they have will not justify them before God, and entitle them to heaven: and this He does, by showing them the corruption of their nature, their daily sins and infirmities, in thought, word, and deed; the purity of the divine perfections, and the spirituality and extensiveness of the law of God; which when a man is thoroughly apprised of, he can never hope for and expect justification before God by his own righteousness. Hence the Spirit of God proceeds to convince men of the glory, excellency, fulness, and suitableness of the righteousness of Christ; which He does, by revealing it to them in the Gospel, setting it before them, and working faith in them to lay hold upon it; when they desire to be found in Christ, not having on their own, but His righteousness; which convictions appear by the mean [or lowly] thoughts they have of their own righteousness, by hungering after Christ's, by disclaiming all but His, by their constant mention of it, dependence on it, and satisfaction in it; and thus to convince of it, is the peculiar work of the Spirit, since naturally men are fond of their own righteousness, are ignorant of Christ's, and set against it. It is added,

and ye see me no more; not but that the disciples were to see Christ, and did see Him after His resurrection, and will with the rest of the saints see Him at His second coming: but the meaning is, that they should see Him no more, in a mean [or lowly] and despicable condition on earth, in a state of humiliation, in the form of a servant; He having faithfully performed the whole work He came about, and particularly that of righteousness, He came to bring in.

Verse 11. **Of judgment, because the prince of this world is judged**. This is to be understood of the judiciary power and authority of Christ, who has *all judgment* committed to Him by the Father, as Mediator; has all power in heaven and in earth; and as He is appointed, so He is a very fit person to judge the world at the last day. Now this being disputed and disbelieved by the Jews, the Holy Ghost, in the ministry of Peter, most clearly demonstrated to their full conviction, that He was raised from the dead, set upon His throne, and was made, or declared, Lord and Christ, *Acts 2:24,34-36*; of which the pouring forth of the Holy Ghost was an evidence; and the instance in the text proving it, and which is a very considerable one, is the judgment, or condemnation and destruction of Satan, the prince of the world; for Christ, by His death, has destroyed him and his works; has spoiled his principalities and powers [see *Col. 2:15*]; and by His resurrection from the dead, and ascension to heaven, has carried him and them captive, triumphing over them; and, through the effusion of the Holy Spirit upon the apostles, and the power of it attending their ministry, Satan was judged, condemned, and cast out of the heathen world, their temples, and the souls of men; the prey was taken from the mighty, and the lawful captive delivered. But as this may refer to the ordinary work of the Spirit in conviction and conversion, it may be differently applied; for He convinces of various things, which come under this name: He convinces of the wrong judgment which men in a state of nature form of God, whom they take to be such a one as themselves; of a crucified Christ, whom they esteem foolishness; of the doctrines of Christ, which they judge to be absurd and irrational; of the people of Christ, whom they reckon *the filth of the world*, and *the offscouring of all things* [*1 Cor. 4:13*]; of the ways and ordinances of Christ, which are thought to be grievous, unpleasant, and unprofitable; and of themselves, and their own state and condition, which they fancy to be good, and they in a fair way for heaven. He also convinces them of the excellency, truth, power, and usefulness of the Gospel, which is called *judgment, Isa. 42:1,4* and *51:4*, so as to understand it truly, believe it cordially, receive it in the love of it, and feel the power of it: He convinces them of a future judgment; of the reality and certainty of it; that it will be universal, reach to all persons and things; that it will be carried on in the most righteous manner, and there will be no escaping it, of which the judgment and condemnation of Satan is a standing proof: and He moreover convinces of judgment or damnation; that men are under a sentence of condemnation in Adam; that they are liable to eternal damnation in themselves; that except they believe in Christ they will be damned, as sure as the prince of this world is.

Verse 12. **I have yet many things to say unto you**, &c. Not with respect to the main doctrines of the Gospel, for every thing of this kind He had made known unto them, *chapter 15:15*; but what regarded the rejection of the Jews, and the calling of the Gentiles, the abrogation of the Mosaic economy, and settling the Gospel church state, which were to come to pass after the death and resurrection of Christ, and the sending of the Spirit:

but ye cannot bear them now. Because of their prejudices in favor of their own nation, the law of Moses, and the ceremonies of it, and the setting up of a temporal kingdom.

Verse 13. **Howbeit, when he, the Spirit of truth, is come**, &c. Of this character of the Spirit, see *chapter 14:17*. His coming, as before, intends more especially His descent on the apostles at Pentecost; though what is here said of Him is true of His office, and of His operations on other per ⌐ns, and at other times:

he will guide you into all truth; necessary to be known, useful to men, profitable to the churches, even the whole counsel of God; what relates to worship, the nature, form, and spirituality of it, as well as doctrine. He is as a guide, He goes before, leads the way, removes obstructions, opens the understanding, makes things plain and clear, teaches to profit, and leads in the way men should go, without turning to the right hand or left, which, without such a guide, they would be apt to do. The Jews[3] have a notion of the Holy Ghost being a guide into all wisdom and knowledge:

"R. Phinehas says, the Holy Spirit rested upon Joseph from his youth to the day of his death, and *guided him into all wisdom*, as a shepherd leads his flock, according to *Psa. 80:1*;"

for he shall not speak of himself: as Christ, the Son, spoke not of Himself in opposition to the Father, so the Spirit speaks not of Himself in opposition either to the Father or the Son, but in perfect agreement with both; being, as of the same nature and essence, power and glory, so of the same mind, understanding, and will; and as they agreed and wrought jointly and harmoniously, in the works of nature and providence, so in the economy of grace and salvation;

but whatsoever he shall hear, *that* shall he speak; as Christ Himself did, *chapter 15:15*; and they are such things as ear has not heard besides; what were secretly transacted in the council and covenant of peace, and agreed upon by all the three persons; things which concern the salvation of men, the Gospel church state, another world, and the glory of all the divine persons:

and he will show you things to come. Which would come to pass after the death, resurrection, and ascension of Christ; things relating to the state and settlement of the Gospel church, the partition wall being broken down, the law of commandments contained in ordinances abolished [see *Eph. 2:14-15*], and a new face of things appearing in the kingdom and interest of Christ, in consequence of the Spirit being sent forth, and poured down: or this may respect the spirit of prophecy in the apostles, who showed to them many things to come in after ages; as the rise of the man of sin, the great departure from the faith, and decline of the power of godliness in the last days, the calling of the Jews, the destruction of antichrist, the burning of the world, and the making of new heavens and new earth; and, in short, what would be the state of the church of Christ, and religion, in all the several periods of time,

---

[3] Pirke Eliezer, c. 39.

quite down to the coming of Christ, when dead saints shall be raised, and living ones changed, as is declared throughout the book of the Revelation.

Verse 14. **He shall glorify me**, &c. In the ministration of the Gospel, which is *the ministration of the Spirit* [*2 Cor. 3:8*]; and asserts Christ to be God over all, to have all that the Father hath, to be possessed of all divine perfections, to have the fulness of the Godhead dwelling in Him [see *Col. 2:9*]; ascribes the same works and worship to Him as to the Father; and, as in a glass, holds Him forth to be beheld as the brightness of His glory, and His glory to be seen in it, as the glory of *the only begotten of the Father, full of grace and truth* [*John 1:14*]: it declares Him to be the only Savior and Redeemer of lost sinners, that justification is solely by His righteousness, pardon by His blood, and atonement by His sacrifice; and which ministration the Spirit makes effectual to the bringing of many souls to Christ to believe in Him, profess His name, and expect life and salvation from Him, by all which He is glorified. Moreover, the Spirit of God glorifies Christ in the experience of the saints, by leading them to Him for righteousness, peace, and pardon, for grace, and fresh supplies of it, for wisdom and strength, for food and rest, for life and happiness; and by enabling them to live by faith on Him, on whom He has encouraged them to venture, and to whom they have committed their all; and by instructing them to glory in Him, as their wisdom, righteousness, sanctification, and redemption [see *1 Cor. 1:30*]; and by ascribing the glory of their salvation to Him, and by making continual application to Him, under His direction and influence; by leaning on Him, and expecting every good thing from Him both for time and eternity. The particular instance in which He glorifies Christ, follows,

for he shall receive of mine, and shall show *it* unto you. Which is to be understood, not of gifts Christ received from His Father, and which He gives to men by His Spirit; nor of internal grace, as faith, love, &c. which the Spirit from Christ works in the hearts of men; but either of the doctrines of the Gospel, the deep things of God and Christ, which the Spirit searches, and reveals in the ministration of the Word. The Gospel is a sort of a *Kabala*, though of a different kind from the oral law of the Jews. Christ received it from the Father, the Spirit received it from Christ, the apostles received it from the Spirit, and the churches of Christ from them in succeeding generations: or this may be understood of the blessings of grace held forth in the Gospel, such as justification, pardon, adoption, &c. which are in Christ; and which the Spirit from Christ takes and shows to the saints, and witnesses their special and particular interest in, and so comforts them, and glorifies Christ.

Verse 15. **All things that the Father hath are mine**, &c. Though it is true that the same divine nature the Father is possessed of, the Son is; and the same divine perfections belong to the one, as to the other; and the Son shares in the same glory and felicity the Father does; so that in the utmost extent of the phrase, all that the Father hath are His; yet since Christ is speaking of things received of Him by the Spirit, and shown unto His people, it rather seems that the blessings of grace, which the Father has in store for His chosen ones, and the doctrines of grace, those deep things of His, are here more especially meant; which to reveal and apply, is the peculiar work of the Spirit; and in these Christ is equally concerned with the Father:

therefore said I, he shall take of mine, and shall show *it* unto you. He does not mention the things of the Father, only His own; nor was there any necessity for it, because whatever is His, is the Father's, and whatever the Father has is His: they are jointly concerned in every thing relating to the salvation, benefit, comfort, and happiness of the saints; so that when the Spirit of God takes of the things of the one, He takes of the things of the other, and discovers, and applies them.

Verse 16. **A little while, and ye shall not see me**, &c. Meaning, that He should be quickly taken from them by death. And in a very little time after this, having put up a prayer for them, recorded in the next chapter, He went into the garden, where He was met by Judas with his band of men, who laid hold on Him, bound Him, and led Him first to Annas, then to Caiaphas, and from him to Pilate, when all the disciples forsook Him and fled, and saw Him no more in this mortal state, except Peter and John. He took His trial, was soon condemned, and crucified, and laid in the dark tomb, and silent grave, where for awhile He was out of sight:

and again, a little while, and ye shall see me; referring either to His rising again the third day from His death, as was prophesied of, *Hos. 6:2*; and was typified by Jonah's lying three days and three nights in the whale's belly, when He appeared to, and was seen by His disciples, to their great joy; or else to the short time in which He was to be, and was seen by them; namely, forty days between His resurrection and ascension; a longer stay it was not necessary He should make, for He had other work to do, for Himself and them:

because I go to the Father. To give an account of the work He had finished on earth; to carry in His blood, righteousness, and sacrifice; to present Himself to His Father on behalf of His people; to appear in the presence of God for them; to be their advocate, plead their cause, and make intercession for them, and take possession of heaven in their name; to take His place at the right hand of God in their nature; to receive a kingdom for Himself, and then return.

Verse 17. **Then said *some* of his disciples among themselves**, &c. It may be, some of them might better understand the meaning of Christ than others, or they might all be ignorant of it; for before the effusion of the Spirit on them, they were attended with a great deal of ignorance; and what through their being overwhelmed at this time with sorrow, and what with their national sentiments they retained about a temporal kingdom, they understood very little of what Christ said to them concerning His death the nature, use, and end of it. Wherefore some might make the motion first, and inquire,

What is this that he saith unto us, A little while and ye shall not see me? They knew not what He meant by it, though He had so often, and so clearly spoken of His death unto them: and as ignorant were they what He should design by saying,

and again, a little while, and ye shall see me; though He had expressly told them in so many words, some time ago, that whereas He should die, He should rise again the third day: and as much at a loss were they to guess what He should intend by the reason He gives,

and, Because I go to the Father? Though He had often mentioned it already, and as what might be [a] matter of joy unto them.

Verse 18. **They said therefore**, &c. One, and all of them; the inquiry became universal;

What is this that he saith, A little while? It seems as if this phrase was the most intricate and perplexing to them; for whatever conceptions they might have of not seeing, and seeing Him again, as expressive of His going from them, and returning to them, yet had no notion at all what He should mean by *a little while*: and therefore add,

we cannot tell what he saith. They knew His words, but not His meaning.

Verse 19. **Now Jesus knew that they were desirous to ask him**, &c. This is a proof of Christ's Deity, that He is the omniscient God who knows all things, what is in man, even the secrets of the heart; for He not only knew the whisperings of the disciples, and their inquiries among themselves about the sense of His words, but also their secret desires to ask Him concerning it:

and said unto them, Do ye inquire among yourselves of that I said, A little while and ye shall not see me: and again, a little while and ye shall see me? Which He said before they could put the question to Him, they being bashful, and backward through fear or shame; and which not only confirms what is before observed of His omniscience, but also shows His readiness to open His mind and meaning, and explain Himself to His disciples, as He does in the following words.

Verse 20. **Verily, verily, I say unto you**, &c. A strong asseveration, a way of speaking often used by Him, when He solemnly affirms any thing, and would assure of the truth of it, as here:

That ye shall weep and lament; meaning at His death, when He should be removed from them, so that they should not see Him; when they should be filled with inward grief on account thereof, and express it by mournful gestures, and a doleful voice; and which was fulfilled in them, *Mark 16:10*; and how pensive the two disciples were that were going to Emmaus, it is easy to observe from the account given of them [see *Luke 24:13-32*];

but the world shall rejoice; the unbelieving Jews; and not only the common people, but the chief priests, with the Scribes and elders, mocked at Him, insulted Him, and triumphed over Him when on the cross, being glad at heart they had gotten Him there; imagining now, that it was all over, the day was their own, and they should be no more disturbed by Christ and His followers:

and ye shall be sorrowful; Christ repeats it again, and uses a variety of words to express the greatness of their sorrow, and the many ways in which they would signify it:

but your sorrow shall be turned into joy. As it was, when He was raised from the dead, which was so wonderful and surprising to them, that for joy they could scarce believe their own eyes; it being a mercy unexpected, though they had been told of it, and too great for them to enjoy; yea, that very thing which was the occasion of their sorrow, became the foundation of their joy; namely, the death of Christ, salvation, and all the benefits and blessings of grace coming to them in this way.

Verse 21. **A woman when she is in travail hath sorrow**, &c. As was said she should have, *Gen. 3:16*; This is God's ordination and appointment for sin:

because her hour is come; is at hand; the fixed time in nature is up, and there is no avoiding it:

but as soon as she is delivered of the child; for though the sorrow is great, yet there is a deliverance, and she is saved in child bearing: when,

she remembereth no more the anguish; the sharp pains she has endured in her travail;

for joy that a man is born into the world. Much such a way of speaking is used by the Jews,[4] who observe,

"If a woman brings forth a male child, all is forgot, and she repents (that is, of her impatience, or any unbecoming expression in the time of labor), בשמחת הזכר, *for the joy of a man child*."

And our Lord seems to have respect to a prevailing notion among them, as well as many others, of the felicity of male children: it is a common saying with them,[5]

"Blessed is he whose children are males, and woe to him whose children are females:"

for they say,[6]

"when שבא זכר בעולם, *that a man child comes into the world*, peace comes into the world."

Now our Lord, by this instance, illustrates the sorrow His disciples should have by His departure, and the joy that they should be possessed of upon His return to them; that as the pains of a woman in travail are very sharp and severe, and the distress of her mind, about the issue of things respecting herself and offspring, is very great, so would be the grief and trouble of the disciples on account of the death of their Lord and Master: but as when a woman is safely delivered of a man child, she is so filled with joy, that her sorrow is remembered no more, so should it be with them, when Christ should appear to them; all their trouble, concern, anxiety of mind, and fears that attended them, would all vanish away, and they be distressed with them no more.

Verse 22. **And ye now therefore have sorrow**, &c. This is the application of the preceding case. As it is with a woman in travail, when her hour is come, so it was now with them, and would be when Christ was removed from them; and as it is with every believer, when Christ is absent: for though there are many things that cause sorrow now, as sin, Satan, and afflictive dispensations of providence, yet nothing more sensibly touches believers to the quick, and gives them more uneasiness, than when Christ is out of sight: the reasons are, because He is so nearly related to them, being their everlasting Father, kind husband, loving brother, and faithful friend; and because they are so strongly affected to Him, there is none like Him in their esteem in heaven and in earth:

---

[4] Tzeror Hammor, fol. 98. 2.

[5] T. Bab. Pesachim, fol. 65. 1. Kiddushin, fol. 82. 2. Bava Bathra, fol. 16. 2. Sanhedrin, fol. 100. 2.

[6] T. Bab. Nidda, fol. 31. 2.

He is the person whom their souls love; He is the very life of their souls; His favor, His gracious presence is life to them, and His absence is as death; nor can they be easy, but are restless, and upon the inquiry after Him, until He returns to them, which He does in His own time; and therefore this sorrow is but *now*, for the present, it is not perpetual.

But I will see you again; as He did see His disciples upon His resurrection once and again, for the space of forty days, at certain times, by intervals: and so, in a spiritual sense, He comes and sees His people, makes them a visit, manifests Himself unto them, and abides with them: they are always under His omniscient eye; He always sees them as God; and they are always under His eye of love, grace, and mercy, as Mediator: but this means such a seeing of them, as that they see Him as well as He sees them; and is expressive of a delightful intercourse between Christ and them, than which nothing is more desirable:

and your heart shall rejoice: as did the hearts of the disciples, when they saw Christ risen from the dead; and as the hearts of believers do, when Christ so looks upon them that they can view Him with an eye of faith; such a sight is a heart-rejoicing one. To see the glory and beauty of Christ's person, the fulness and suitableness of Him as a Savior; to have an appropriating view of Him as such; or to see Him so as to have sensible communion with Him, must needs fill the heart of a believer with *joy unspeakable, and full of glory* [*1 Pet. 1:18*]: such a sight of Christ will rejoice the heart under a sense of sin, the pollution and guilt of it, when tempted by Satan, or under God's afflicting hand, and even in the view of death and eternity:

and your joy no man taketh from you. The joy of the hypocrite is *but for a moment* [*Job 20:5*], and the joy of the chief priests, Scribes, and Pharisees, was a short-lived one, on account of Christ's death; for Jesus was soon raised from the dead, and the apostles were filled with the Spirit, and went forth boldly preaching in the name of Christ, to the great grief of these men. But the joy of the disciples was durable; their risen Lord would never die more; the blessings of grace, such as redemption, pardon, righteousness, and atonement, would, and do ever remain as the foundation of solid joy: nor could a stranger intermeddle with it; ουδεις, *not one*, either man or devil, could take it away, not by all the reproaches they could cast upon them, or persecutions they could follow them with. And so, though a believer's joy may be damped by sin, and Satan, and the world, it may not be always in lively exercise; yet the matter of it always remains in Christ, and the principle of it in themselves can never be destroyed, but will issue in everlasting joy in another world.

Verse 23. **And in that day ye shall ask me nothing**, &c. Meaning, not the whole Gospel dispensation, so often called in prophetic language, *that day;*

and is, in the New Testament, opposed to the *night* of Jewish and Gentile darkness; and, in comparison of the former dispensation, is a time of great spiritual light and knowledge: nor the latter part of that day, when there will be no night of darkness and desertion, of error and severity, of affliction and persecution, with the church; when the earth shall be filled with the knowledge of the Lord; when all the children of God shall be taught of Him, and there will be no need to say, Know the Lord, for all shall know Him, from the least to the greatest [see *Heb. 8:10-11*]: nor the day of judgment, which, by way of emphasis, is so frequently called *that day*: nor the state of ultimate happiness, the everlasting day of glory; when all imperfections shall be done away, when saints will know, as they are known [see *1 Cor. 13:12*], and see Jesus as He is [see *1 John 3:2*], and need not ask any questions about Him: but the time when Christ and His apostles should meet again, and see each other's faces with joy and pleasure, is meant; and the time following thereon, especially the day of Pentecost, when the Spirit was poured down upon them, and, according to His promise, came to them, taught them all things, and led them into all truth. This asking is not to be understood of asking in prayer; for it appears, by what follows, that they should ask in His name then, and He encourages to it; but of asking Him questions, and that not of any sort; for it is certain, that, within this time, they did ask many things. Peter asked what John, the beloved disciple, should do; and they all asked Him, a little before His ascension, whether He would at that time restore again the kingdom to Israel; but it is to be restrained to such things as they had been, or were, desirous of asking Him; such as, Whither goest thou? Show us the Father? How is it that thou wilt manifest thyself unto us, and not unto the world? And more especially these last questions, they greatly desired to put to Him, What is this, *a little while and ye shall not see me?* And what is this, *a little while and ye shall see me?* And what is the meaning of these words, *because I go to the Father?* [*verse 17*]. Now our Lord intimates, that at this time all these things would be so clear and evident to them, that they should ask Him no questions about them. But He adds,

Verily, verily, I say unto you, Whatsoever ye shall ask the Father in my name, he will give *it* you. Asking here signifies *prayer*, and a different word is here used than before. The object of prayer is the Father, though not to the exclusion of the Son and Spirit, who were both separately, or in conjunction with the Father, prayed unto after this; see *Acts 7:59* and *22:16; 2 Thess. 3:5; Rom. 1:7; 1 Cor. 1:2-3; Rev. 1:4-5.* The medium of access to the Father is the name of Christ; He is the Mediator between God and man, the way of access unto Him; whatever is asked, is to be asked on account of His blood, righteousness, and sacrifice, and then there is no doubt of success; whatever is asked will be given; His blood within the veil speaks loud for every blessing; His righteousness, God is always pleased with; His sacrifice is a sweet smelling savor; His mediation is powerful; and His name is always prevalent.

Verse 24. **Hitherto have ye asked nothing in my name**, &c. Not that they had never prayed as yet; for they had desired Him to teach them to pray, which He did: they had prayed to Him particularly for an increase of faith, and for many other things; but either they had only asked Him, He being present with them, and not the Father; or if they had asked the Father any thing, yet not in the name of Christ: they had made no mention of His blood, righteousness, and sacrifice, nor any use of His mediation; things they had not as yet such clear knowledge of; or they had not asked as yet any extraordinary thing, as they afterwards did; see *Acts 4:29-30*;

ask, and ye shall receive; that is, in my name, and whatever ye ask for, ye shall have it, to fit you for your work, to carry you through it, and to give you success in it: see *Matt. 7:7*;

that your joy may be full. Go cheerfully through your work, find much pleasure in it, and with great satisfaction see the Gospel spread, souls converted, Satan's kingdom weakened, and the interest of your Redeemer thrive and flourish; than which nothing can more contribute to complete the joy of the ministers of Christ.

Verse 25. **These things have I spoken unto you in proverbs**, &c. Concerning His Father, and His Father's house, and the many mansions in it, of His going to prepare a place for them there, and of the way unto it, all which they seemed not to understand; of the nature of communion with Him and His Father, and of the manifestation of them to them, so as not unto the world, which they could not account for; of their union to Him under the simile of the vine and its branches; and of His departure from them, and return unto them; and of the sorrow that should follow upon the one, and the joy that should attend the other, set forth in the case of a woman in travail, having sorrow, and being joyful when delivered. All which, one would think, were plain and easy to be understood; but such was the then present state and case of the disciples, that these all seemed as proverbs, parables, and dark sayings, which they did not clearly understand: wherefore our Lord says,

but the time cometh; meaning either the time of His appearing unto them after His resurrection, or the day of Pentecost:

when I shall no more speak unto you in proverbs, but I shall show you plainly of the Father. By pouring forth His Spirit upon them, who should not only take of His things, but of His Father's also, and show them unto them clearly and plainly; so as that they should have a clear understanding of them, as they were capable of; of the perfections of His nature, His distinct personality, His being the Father of Christ, and of all the elect in Him; of His everlasting love to their persons; of His choice of them in Christ; of His covenant with them in Him; of His mind and will concerning them, and His gracious designs towards them; of His Father's house, and the way to it; and of the nature, design, and usefulness of His going to Him; of the distinction between speaking in parables and dark sayings, and speaking plainly, openly, and apparently; see *Num. 12:8.*

Verse 26. **At that day ye shall ask in my name**, &c. For when the Spirit was poured upon them, they not only received His extraordinary gifts, and had a larger measure of His grace bestowed upon them; but were also blessed with Him, as a spirit of grace and supplication, in a more remarkable manner than ever they had been before: they then better understood the throne of grace, and the advantages of it; had greater enlargements and assistances at it; and were better acquainted with the mediation of Christ, and the necessity of making use of His name, blood, and righteousness, in all their petitions and requests;

and I say not unto you, that I will pray the Father for you: this Christ had promised before, *John 14:16*; nor was there any occasion to repeat it now, of which they might be strongly assured: besides, at that day the Spirit would be given to them by virtue of His intercession; so that there would be no need of praying to the Father for them on that account. This is said, not as if the intercession of Christ for His people would then cease; for He is always their advocate with the Father, and ever lives to make intercession for them [see *Heb. 7:25*]; though it may not be carried on in the same manner, by prayer, as when He was here on earth, His personal appearance, and the presentation of His blood, sacrifice, and righteousness, being sufficient; but to declare the disposition and readiness of His Father to hear them, and grant unto them whatsoever they should ask of Him in His name.

Verse 27. **For the Father himself loveth you**, &c. The Father loved them as well, and as much as the Son did, and of Himself too, without any merit or motive in them: He loved them from everlasting, and had given proofs of it in time, in the gift of His Son to them, and for them, and in calling them by His grace; and therefore being thus strongly affected to them, they might depend upon a ready and speedy answer from Him, as might be best for His glory, and their good;

because ye have loved me; not that their love to Christ was the cause of the Father's love to them; but, on the contrary, the Father's love to them was the cause of their love to Christ; and therefore as the cause is known by its effect, they might be assured of the Father's love to them by their love to Christ; for if the Father had not loved them, they had never loved God, nor Christ; but since they did love Christ, it was a clear case the Father loved them; and this their love is joined with faith:

and have believed that I came out from God. Being sent by Him, and am no impostor, but the true Messiah that was to come: faith in Christ, and love to Him, go together; where the one is, there is the other; faith works by love; they are both the gifts of God's grace, and the fruits and effects of His everlasting love; and those who are possessed of them may be firmly persuaded of their interest therein.

Verse 28. **I came forth from the Father**, &c. This is the sum of what the apostles believed, and Christ, in these discourses of His, had been speaking of. This His coming forth from the Father is to be understood, not of His eternal filiation; nor of His coming forth in a way of grace towards His own people in the council and covenant of grace and peace; nor of His constitution, as Mediator, from everlasting; but of His coming in the flesh in the fulness of time: which supposes that He was, that He existed as a divine person before; that He was with the Father before; that He came forth from Him with His knowledge, mind, and will; He came not of Himself, but He sent Him; and yet He came willingly, was not forced, or did not come against His will: and this does not suppose any local motion, or change of place, but only intends an assumption of the human nature into unity with His divine person, who fills heaven and earth with His presence; nor any separation from His Father, with whom He was, and in whose bosom He lay when He was made flesh, and dwelt among men; nor any absence from heaven, for He was there when on earth;

and am come into the world; where He was before, as the Creator and upholder of it, by His immensity and powerful presence; this designs His coming and manifestation in the flesh, which in general was to do the whole will of God, which He in council and covenant agreed to do, and for which He came down from heaven; and in particular to preach the Gospel, call sinners to repentance, give life and light to many; and to fulfil the law, by obeying its precepts, and bearing its penalty, and both to do and suffer in the room and stead of His people, and to save lost sinners, even the chief of them;

again, I leave the world; not that He relinquished the sustentation and government of it, as God, nor the care of His people in it, as Mediator, for whom He retains the same love as ever, and will not leave them fatherless and comfortless; nor was He leaving it as never to return more; for He will descend in like manner as He ascended, and will come a second time and judge the world in righteousness: but He was about to depart from it by death, having done the work and business for which He came about:

and go to the Father. To give an account of His work unto Him, as His righteous servant, being faithful to Him that had appointed Him; and to transact the affairs of His people; to appear in the presence of God for them; to present their petitions, be their advocate, make intercession for them, take possession of heaven in their name, and prepare it for them; to take His place at the right hand of God in human nature, and to be glorified with the glory promised Him before the world was.

Verse 29. **His disciples said unto him**, &c. Upon the above discourse of Christ, such rays and beams of light darted into the minds of the apostles, and things stood so clear in their view, and they so well understood what Christ had said, that they declare,

Lo, now speakest thou plainly, and speakest no proverb. What He had said before, were to them like proverbial, or parabolical expressions, not easy to be understood; they were like enigmas, riddles, and dark sayings, the meaning of which they could not apprehend; but now they observe, with admiration, that what He delivered was plain, and intelligible; which was not so much owing to Christ's different way of speaking now, from what it was before, as to their former dulness of hearing, and now having some further degree of light given unto them.

Verse 30. **Now are we sure that thou knowest all things**, &c. Not only all men, but all things, even the secrets of men's hearts, of which the apostles had now a convincing proof; for whereas Christ had delivered some expressions, *verse 16*, which they did not understand, and were desirous to ask Him the meaning of, *verse 19*; which He knowing, being God omniscient, prevents their putting the question to Him, and enters upon a discourse, in which He so clearly explained what they wanted to be informed of, without their asking Him, that they were fully assured that He must know all things;

and, as they add,

needest not that any man should ask thee: the meaning is, that should Christ deliver any thing not so intelligible to any of His audience, and they were desirous of knowing the sense of it, there would be no need of putting the question in form to Him, since He is privy to the first motion of desire rising up in the mind; and can, and will, if He thinks fit, explain Himself on such a head [*or* subject], to the satisfaction of the person, without ever asking Him; at least there is no need of putting the question to make Him acquainted with his desire, this being before known unto Him:

by this we believe that thou camest forth from God. Was the true Messiah, and had His mission and commission from God, as such; doubtless they believed this before, but this instance of Christ's omniscience was a strengthening proof of it. So Nathanael, by Christ's saying to him, that before Philip called him, and when he was under the fig tree, He saw him when he thought no eye did but an omniscient one; it laid him under such full convictions of Him, as at once to acknowledge Him the Son of God, the King of Israel [see *John 1:43-51*]. This is one of the signs and characters of the Messiah with the Jews, that He should have a discerning spirit of men and things, according to *Isa. 11:3*.[7]

Verse 31. **Jesus answered them, Do ye now believe?** Not as calling their faith in question; or as denying they had any; or as despising it for the smallness of it; but as reproving them for their security, vain confidence and boasting, as if their faith was so very strong that it would never be moved; and perhaps for the lateness of it too: the words may be read affirmatively, without an interrogation, *Ye do believe now*; they are in the Syriac and Arabic versions read imperatively, *believe ye now*? though the *now* is left out by the former, which is not to be spared, for the emphasis lies on it; and a regard seems to be had both to time past and to come. The words carry in them a tacit reproof, that they believed no sooner, or were not before this time more established in their faith, when He had been so long with them, and they had heard so many discourses from Him, and had seen so many miracles wrought by Him. However, it was not too late, and they would do well to go on believing; but it is suggested to them they would meet with something that would try their faith: and it is as if Christ had said, Ye believe in me now, while I am with you, and all things go according to your mind; but what will you do anon, when I shall be taken from you, be apprehended by mine enemies, be delivered into the hands of the Gentiles, be crucified, die, and be laid in the grave? Will ye believe then? One of you will betray me, another deny me, and all will forsake me, and some express their doubts about me.

Verse 32. **Behold the hour cometh, yea, is now come**, &c. The time is at hand, yea, it may, in a sense, be said to be already come, it was within an hour: and indeed the following prayer might be delivered in less than an hour's time; when He went immediately into the garden, and was apprehended; or at least in a very little while it would come to pass,

that ye shall be scattered, every man to his own; to his own friends, relations, and acquaintance; to his own house and home; to his own country,

---

[7] T. Bab. Sanhedrin, fol. 93. 2.

Galilee, whither they all went, and to their trade of fishing again; see *chapter 21:3*; and so was fulfilled the prophecy in *Zech. 13:7*;

and shall leave me alone; as they did in the hands of His enemies; for they all forsook Him and fled, some one way, some another; though one or two of them, Peter and John, followed Him at a distance; and all came together again, but not to Christ, until His resurrection from the dead;

and yet I am not alone; He was not alone at this time; and His meaning is, that He should not be alone then when they should be scattered from Him:

because the Father is with me. Not only as the Son of God, by virtue of union to Him, and as one with Him; but as Mediator, in consequence of His promise to uphold Him, and assist Him in His human nature; and though He withdrew His gracious and comforting presence from Him, He bearing the sins, and standing in the room and stead of His people, yet not His powerful and supporting presence.

Verse 33. **These things I have spoken unto you**, &c. As this is the conclusion of our Lord's sermon to His disciples, these words may well enough be thought to have regard to all that He had said in general; as concerning His departure from them; His going to prepare a place for them; His union to them, and their communion with Him; and the various persecutions and afflictions they should endure for His sake; and the many blessings both of grace and glory they should enjoy; and particularly what He had said in the context, concerning their forsaking Him, which supposed tribulation, and would be a prelude of what they were afterwards to have in the world; and concerning the presence of His Father with Him, and which they might also expect to have:

that in me ye might have peace. Not in the world, in which they were to have tribulation: there is no true, solid peace to be enjoyed in the world, and the things of it; the world can neither give it, nor take it away; nor have the men of it any knowledge and understanding of it; and much less enjoy it: nor in themselves; spiritual peace does not arise from any duties, services, and performances of men; no, not from an attendance on the Gospel, and the ordinances of it; nor even from the graces of the Spirit; for though peace may be enjoyed herein, and hereby, and through these, as means; yet does it not come from them, but from Christ, in whose strength alone all duties are performed aright; who is the sum and substance of the Gospel, and the ordinances of it, and the object of all grace: it is in Him, and in Him only, in His person, blood, righteousness, and sacrifice, which speak peace, pardon, and atonement, that a soul finds any true, solid peace, rest, comfort, and joy; and here he may, and does find it, in opposition to the cry of sin, law, and justice, for wrath, ruin, hell, and damnation. There is a peace by Christ, which He has made for His people by the blood of His cross; and there is a peace in Him, which is enjoyed through faith's looking to His blood for pardon, to His righteousness for justification, to His sacrifice for atonement and satisfaction; and by having communion with Him, and discoveries of His love, and by seeing safety and security in Him.

In the world ye shall have tribulation; this is certain from this declaration of Christ, who is the omniscient God, and truth itself; from the instance and example of Christ, who was all His life *a man of sorrows* [*Isa. 53:3*]; from the conformity of the members to the head; from the divine appointment that has so determined it; from the natural enmity of the world to the saints; from the experience of the people of God in all ages; from the usefulness of tribulation to try the graces, and bring about the temporal, spiritual, and eternal good of believers: and though they have tribulation in the world, yet not by way of punishment for sin, but as fatherly corrections and chastenings for their good, that they may not be condemned with the world [see *Acts 14:22; Rom. 5:3-5; 2 Cor. 1:3-4; Heb. 12:2-11*]; and it is only in this present world they have it; as soon as they have done with the world, they will have done with tribulation:

but be of good cheer; I have overcome the world. It is very observable how the phrase, *in the world ye shall have tribulation*, stands, and is encompassed, before, with these words, *that in me ye might have peace*, and behind, with these, *be of good cheer*, &c. Believers, of all men, notwithstanding their tribulations, have reason to be of good cheer, since their sins are forgiven, the love of God is shed abroad in their hearts, their redemption draws nigh, and they have hopes of glory; and particularly, because as Christ here says, for their encouragement under all their tribulations in the world, *I have overcome the world*: Satan, the god and prince of the world, with all his principalities and powers, which Christ has led captive, ransomed His people from, and delivers them from the power of; and all that is in the world, the lusts and sins of it; their damning power, by the sacrifice of Himself, and their governing power, by His Spirit and grace; and the men of the world, with all their rage and fury, whom He has trodden down in His anger, restrains by His power, and causes the remainder of their wrath to praise Him; in all which conquests He makes His people share, and even makes them more than conquerors, through Himself: so that they have nothing to fear from the world; nor any reason to be cast down by the tribulation they meet with in it.

CHAPTER 17

Verse 1. **These words spake Jesus**, &c. Referring to His sermons and discourses, His words of comfort, advice, direction, and instruction, delivered in the three preceding chapters:

and lifted up his eyes to heaven; the seat of the divine majesty, the throne of His Father. This is a prayer gesture. It is said [1] of R. Tanchuma,
    "that הגביה פניו לשמים, *he lifted up his face to heaven*, and said before
    the holy blessed God, Lord of the world, &c."
And this is expressive of the ardency and affection of the mind of Christ, and of His confidence of the divine favor: it shows that His mind was filled with devotion and faith, and was devoid of shame and fear, and was possessed of great freedom, boldness, and intrepidity:

and said, Father; or *my Father*, as the Syriac, Arabic and Persic versions read; and no doubt but He used the word *Abba*, which signifies *my Father*, thereby claiming His interest in Him, and relation to Him:

the hour is come; to depart out of the world, to suffer and die for His people, which was agreed upon between Him and His Father from all eternity; and it was welcome to Him, on account of the salvation of His people, and therefore He spoke with an air of pleasure and satisfaction; and it would be quickly over, was but an hour, as it were, though a time of great trouble, distress and darkness, and so a fit time for prayer:

glorify thy Son; as man and Mediator; for as God, He needed no glory, nor could any be added to Him: but it designs some breakings forth of glory upon Him at His death; by supporting Him under all the sorrows and sufferings of it; and in carrying Him through it; so that He conquered all His people's enemies, and His own—sin, Satan, the world, and death, and obtained eternal redemption for them: and at His resurrection; by not suffering Him to remain so long in the grave, as to see corruption; and by raising Him at the exact time that was foretold by the prophets and Himself; and by sending an angel to roll away the stone; and by raising some of the saints along with Him; and by putting such a glory on His body, as that it is the pattern and exemplar of the

---

[1] Vajikra Rabba, sect. 34. fol. 174. 4.

saints' resurrection: and at His ascension to heaven, when He led captivity captive; and at His session at the right hand of God, above all principalities and powers; and through the effusion of the Spirit upon His disciples, and the divine power that attended His Gospel, to make it effectual to great multitudes, both to Jews and Gentiles; by all which He was glorified, pursuant to this petition of His; in which His end is,

that thy Son also may glorify thee; as He had done throughout the whole of His life and conversation, and by His ministry and miracles; so now at His sufferings and death, through the salvation of His chosen ones, in which the wisdom, grace, justice, holiness, power, and faithfulness of God are greatly glorified; and in the after discharge of other branches of His mediatorial office, in making intercession for His people, in the ministry of His Word and ordinances by His servants, attended with His holy Spirit, and by the administration of His kingly office.

Verse 2. **As thou hast given him power over all flesh**, &c. All men, in distinction from angels; and these as fallen, as weak, frail, sinful, and mortal creatures; men of every nation, Jew or Gentile, and of every character, elect or non-elect. Not but that He has also a power over angels; nor is His power over men limited to their *flesh* or bodies, but reaches to their spirits or souls also: which power is a governing, disposing, and judicial one; He rules them with a scepter of righteousness, He disposes of them in providence as He pleases, and will judge them at the last day. And this is a power that is *given* Him by His Father, and is not that original power over all things He has as God, and the Creator of them, which is natural, essential, and underived; but is a derived and delegated power, which He has as Mediator, as subservient to the ends and designs of His office: and as God glorified Him as such, by giving Him this power; so He glorifies Him again, by acknowledging it, and by using it for the end for which it is given:

that he should give eternal life to as many as thou hast given him. Eternal life is a gift, and not owing to the merits of men; indeed there is no merit in men's works, no, not in the best; for these are previously due to God, cannot be profitable to him, if done aright; are not done in the creature's strength, but through the grace of God, and bear no proportion to eternal life; which is in Christ's gift: not only the promise of it is in Him, but that itself; it is put into His hands, and He came into this world, that His people might have it; He has procured it, and has removed what lay in the way of their enjoyment of it; He has a right to bestow it, and their right unto it comes by Him, through His blood and righteousness: the persons on whom He confers this gift, are not all men, but such as the Father in the everlasting covenant has given to Him, as His people and portion, His spouse and children, His jewels and His treasure, to be saved and enjoyed by Him [see also *John 6:37-*

40]; whom He has chosen and preserved in Him, and made His care and charge; to these, and every one of these, Christ gives this great blessing; nor shall any of them come short of it; and it is for the sake of this, that all creatures and things, all power in heaven and in earth, are given to Him.

Verse 3. **And this is life eternal**, &c. That is, the beginning and pledge of it, the way unto it, and means of it, and what will certainly issue in it:

that they might know thee the only true God, and Jesus Christ, whom thou hast sent. The knowledge of God, here spoken of, is not the knowledge of Him by the light of nature, and works of creation; for a man may know God in this sense, and not know Him in Christ, nor any thing of Christ; yea, may know God and profess Him in words, and in works deny Him, as the heathens did; nor is eternal life known hereby, nor connected with it: nor is it such a knowledge of God as is to be obtained by the law of Moses, in which God is represented as a righteous and incensed Being; nor is there in it any discovery of God, as a God of love, grace, and mercy in Christ; nor any revelation of a Mediator, Savior and Redeemer; nor can it either show, or give to persons eternal life; and yet what is here said of the knowledge of God and Christ, the Jews say of the law:[2]

"One man said to his friend, let us dash them against that wall and kill them, because they have left חיי עולם הבא, *eternal life* (the gloss upon it is, תורה, *the law*), and employ themselves in a temporary life (the gloss says of this world), which is merchandise."

More truly does Philo the Jew say[3] that,

"Fleeing to the Divine Being, *is eternal life*; and running from him is death."

But this is to be understood of an evangelical knowledge of God, as the God and Father of Christ, as the God of all grace, pardoning iniquity, transgression and sin [see *Jer. 33:8; Micah 7:18-19*], and of Christ the Mediator; not a general, notional, and speculative knowledge; but a practical and experimental one; a knowledge of approbation and appropriation; a fiducial one, whereby a soul believes in Christ, and trusts in His blood, righteousness, and sacrifice for salvation; and which, though imperfect, is progressive. The Arians and Unitarians urge this text, against the true and proper Deity of our Lord Jesus, and His equality with the Father, but without success; since the Father is called the only true God, in opposition to the many false gods of the heathens, but not to the exclusion of the Son or Spirit; for Christ is also styled

---

[2] T. Bab. Taanith, fol. 21. 1.

[3] De profugis, p. 461.

the one Lord, and *only Lord God* [*Jude 4*], but not to the exclusion of the Father; yea *the true God and eternal life* [*1 John 5:20*]; was He not, He would never, as here, join Himself with the only true God; and besides, eternal life is made to depend as much upon the knowledge of Him, as of the Father. The reason of this different mode of expression, is owing to the character of Christ as Mediator, who is said to be sent by the only true God, about the business of man's salvation. Nor is it of any moment what the Jew[4] objects, that Jesus here confesses, that the true God is only one God; nor does He call Himself God, only the Messiah sent by God; and that the Apostle Paul also asserts the unity of God, *1 Tim. 1:17*; and therefore Jesus cannot be God: for Christ and His Father, the only true God, are one; and that He is the one true God with His Father, He tacitly suggests here by joining Himself with Him; and what the Apostle Paul says of the one and only wise God, may as well be understood of Christ, the Son of God, as of the Father; since all the characters in the text agree with Him, and of Him he had been speaking in the context.

Verse 4. **I have glorified thee on the earth**, &c. This is made use of as a reason and argument, why the Father should glorify Him: Christ glorified His Father personally, as He held forth and expressed the glory of His person; and verbally, by ascribing, on all occasions, praise and glory to Him; and really, or by deeds, and that by various ways: as in and by His ministry; by asserting He had His mission, qualifications, and doctrine, from Him as a prophet; His principal work was to declare His Father's mind and will, His love and grace; nor did He seek His own, but His Father's glory: and by His miracles; for though these were proofs of His Deity and Messiahship, and displays of His own glory; yet the glory of His Father, especially of His power, was eminently seen in them, for He referred them to Him; and these were often the means of men's glorifying the God of Israel: and by His whole life and conversation, which was entirely according to the will of God; and every action of it was directed to His glory; particularly He glorified Him by His early regard to His will, and the business He sent Him about; by His zeal for His Father's house; and by the exercise of the various graces of faith, hope, and love upon Him: and as by His life, so at His death, even all the while He was *on the earth*; where God had been dishonored by the sin of men; where Christ now was debased in human nature, and even that was for the glory of God; and this is said in distinction from heaven, where God is glorified by the angels, and where Christ would shortly be glorified in His human nature:

I have finished the work which thou gavest me to do. By *the work* is meant obedience to the will of God; the destruction of all spiritual enemies, as

---

[4]   R. Isaac Chizzuk Emuna, par. 2. c. 55. p. 445.

sin, Satan, the world, and death; and the redemption and salvation of His people, which was *given* Him to do: He did not take it upon Himself, but being called to it He readily accepted of it; it was appointed, and cut out for Him, in the council and covenant of grace; He was thoroughly acquainted with it; and though it was difficult, it was pleasant and delightful to Him; nor did He leave it till He could say, *It is finished* [*John 19:30*]; as it was, by Himself alone, without the help of man; and is so complete that nothing can be added to it; and so firmly done, that it cannot be unraveled by men or devils: He speaks of it as done, because the time was come to finish it, and He was sure of the accomplishment of it.

Verse 5. **And now, O Father, glorify thou me with thine own self**, &c. Not with His perfections, these He had, they dwelt bodily in Him; nor with His nature, in which He was one with Him; but, as Mediator, with His glorious presence in heaven, by setting Him at His right hand, and crowning Him with glory and honor. The Jews have a notion that God will give to the King Messiah, מן הכבוד של מעלה, *of the supreme glory:*[5] the glory Christ prays for is, He says,

the glory which I had with thee before the world was. The same phrase with לעולם, or קודם העולם, used by the Jews.[6] This is not to be understood of the glory of the human nature of Christ, abstractly considered; for that is no person of itself, but what is taken up into personal union with the Son of God; and therefore cannot be intended by this personal character, *I*; nor did it exist from eternity; it was indeed written in God's book of predestination, even all its members, when as yet there were none of them in actual being [see *Psa. 139:16*]; it was set up in God's thoughts and counsel, as the pattern and exemplar of human nature; it had a federal union with the Son of God, or a covenant subsistence with Him; and in the Old Testament Christ was often spoken of as man, because of His frequent appearances in a human form, and because of the certainty of His incarnation; but He did not really and actually exist as man, until He took flesh of the virgin; for Christ, as man, is the seed of the woman, the son of David, Abraham, and Adam; He is called the *last* and *second Adam*, and was not, as man, before the first: the Old Testament speaks of His incarnation as future; nor is it possible that a creature can exist before time; for as soon as a creature exists, time begins, which is nothing else than the measure of a creature's duration; nor was the human nature of Christ with the Father from eternity; nor had it a glory before the world began,

---

[5] Midrash Tillim in Psal. 20. apud Galatin. de Arcan. Cathol. Verse l. 3. c. 9.

[6] Gloss in T. Bab. Pesachim, fol. 54. 1.

neither in whole, nor in part: nor is the glory of the divine nature abstractly considered, here meant; this glory indeed Christ had from everlasting; He had it with His Father, in common with Him, being in union to Him; and it is true that it was in some measure veiled and covered in His state of humiliation; for though there were some breakings forth of it in that state, these were seen but by a few; wherefore He is thought by some to pray here for the manifestation of this glory; but this glory was essential to Him, was His natural right, and not to be prayed for, and which He then had as much as ever, and of which there could be no suspension: but this designs the glory of Him as God-man, and Mediator; He was not only predestinated to be a Mediator, but was really set up as such from everlasting, and had a mediatorial fulness of grace put into His hands, and had the honor and glory of that office given unto Him by the other two Persons: and now that He might appear to be what He was, to be made, that is, made manifest that He was both Lord and Christ, He here prays; which was to be done upon His ascension to heaven, and session at the right hand of God, by the pouring down of the Holy Ghost.

Verse 6. **I have manifested thy name**, &c. Not the *Nomen Tetragrammaton*, the name of four letters [that is, YHWH], the name *Jehovah*, and which the Jews call *Shemhamphorash*, and say is ineffable, and to be pronounced by Adonai; who also speak of other names, and say,[7]

"truly the former wise men had holy names, which they received from the prophets, as the name of *seventy-two* letters, and the name of *forty-two* letters, and the name of *twelve* letters, and many other holy names; and by which they could do new signs and wonders in the world; but they did not make use of them, only in case of necessity, as in a time of persecution and distress."

The name of twelve letters, Galatinus[8] pretends, is Father, Son, and Holy Ghost, the words for which in the Hebrew language consist of twelve letters; and that of forty-two letters he makes to be this, the Father God, the Son God, the Holy Ghost God, yet there are not three Gods, but one God; or thus, the Father God, the Son God, the Holy Ghost God, three in one, one in three; the Hebrew words for which contain forty-two letters; but the authorities by which he would support all this are insufficient. However, it is none of these names, nor any other Scriptural ones, that are here meant; but either God Himself, or the perfections of His nature, or His will of command, or rather His Gospel; unless Christ Himself, or His name *Jesus*, God by the angel gave Him, and in whose name there is salvation, and no other can be thought to be meant; and

---

[7] Shaare ora, fol. 1. 3.

[8] De Arcan. Cathol. Verse l. 2. c. 11, 12.

which, as it was manifested to His disciples, so it is to all whom God has chosen and given to Christ:

unto the men which thou gavest me out of the world; which is to be understood, not merely of their being given to Him as apostles, nor of their being given and brought to Him in effectual vocation [*or* calling] only, but of an eternal act of God's in election, and in the covenant of grace; when these persons were given to Christ as His spouse, His spiritual seed and offspring, the sheep of His pasture, and His portion and inheritance, to be saved and preserved by Him; which, as it is an instance of love and care on God's part to give, and of grace and condescension on Christ's to receive, so of distinguishing goodness, to the persons given; since not all the world, but some of it, share in this favor:

thine they were, and thou gavest them me; the persons given were not the Father's merely by creation; for so others are His also; nor would they be peculiarly His, for they are the Son's likewise in this sense; but they are His by electing grace, which is the peculiar act of the Father in Christ, and is unto salvation by Him, through the *sanctification of the Spirit* [*2 Thess. 2:13*]; these are chosen to be His peculiar people, and given to Christ as such:

and they have kept thy word. The Gospel, not only in their memories, but in their hearts; and having publicly professed it, they defended it valiantly against the enemies of it, and kept it pure and incorrupt; this shows that the Gospel is meant by the name of God manifested to these persons.

Verse 7. **Now they have known**, &c. The Syriac version reads it, ידעת, *I have known*; and so the Persic and Gothic versions, contrary to most copies and other versions, which read, as we render, *they have known*, that is, the disciples and apostles of Christ:

that all things whatsoever thou hast given me; all temporal things, the world and the fulness of it; all power in heaven and in earth, or a power of disposing of all things for His own service, as Mediator; all spiritual things, the covenant of grace, with all its blessings and promises, the Spirit of God, with all His gifts and graces, a fulness of all grace for His people, yea, eternal life and glory; and every thing relating to His mediatorial office and character, power to perform miracles, knowledge and wisdom to preach the Gospel, strength to procure the salvation of His people; every thing to qualify Him for the government of the church and the judgment of the world:

are of thee. Owing to His good will and pleasure, by His appointment and constitution, as an instance of love to Him, and that He might, as man, and Mediator, be honored, and in all things have the preeminence, and all for the good of His chosen ones. Now the knowledge of this by His disciples, must

513

greatly confirm the mission of Christ, render Him very suitable to them, cause them to entertain a greater esteem for Him, lead them into some admiring views of the grace of God, in giving so much into Christ's hands for them, and engage them the more cheerfully to obey His commands.

Verse 8. **For I have given unto them the words**, &c. Not commands, but doctrines; and these not the doctrines of men; nor any of the divers and strange doctrines; but what are called in Scripture the doctrine of God, of Christ, of the apostles, are agreeable to the Scriptures, and according to godliness; and are styled the word of truth, of faith, of righteousness, of peace and reconciliation, of life and salvation, and of the Gospel; and which Christ gave to His disciples, and gifts along with them to preach them, and abilities to defend them:

which thou gavest me; for the words and doctrines which Christ, as the great prophet in Israel spoke, were not His own, but His Father's; and these were given Him to speak and deliver to others, and in which He was faithful. So Jonathan ben Uzziel[9] paraphrases the text in *Deut. 18:18*; concerning that prophet, the Messiah, God would raise up, after this manner:

"A prophet will I raise up unto them from among their brethren, in whom the Holy Spirit shall be, like unto thee; ואיתן פתגמי, *and I will give the words*, of my prophecy into his mouth, and he shall speak with them all that I have commanded."

And so the Messiah Jesus did:

and they have received *them*; willingly and gladly, with reverence and meekness, with love and thankfulness; so as to understand them, and believe them, and so as to be affectionately and closely attached to them:

and have known surely that I came out from thee; which is meant, not of His eternal filiation, but of His constitution and commission, as Mediator, by His Father: of which they had certain knowledge, full assurance of faith, and sincerely owned and confessed, being fully persuaded He was the true Messiah, and no impostor:

and they have believed that thou didst send me. Into this world, to seek and to save lost sinners, to redeem all the chosen ones, and perform every thing necessary to their salvation.

Verse 9. **I pray for them**, &c. This is to be understood of Christ, not as God; for as such He is the object of prayer; nor need He pray to any other; nor is there any superior to Him, under that consideration, to pray unto; but as man

---

[9]   Targum Jon. in Deut. 18:18.

and Mediator: nor is His praying any argument against His Deity; nor proof of inferiority to His Father with respect to His divine nature; since it is not in that, but in His human nature, that He prayed; though this may be ascribed to His whole person as God-man; hence He had the greatest qualifications and abilities for this work, and His prayers were always heard. Praying, as attributed to Christ, must be restrained to His state of humiliation; prayer is never spoken of Christ but while He was here on earth; His intercession in heaven is never expressed by prayer; and the saints when they come thither, will have done praying. Christ while on earth, was an excellent pattern of prayer; of private and solitary prayer; of social prayer, for and with His disciples; of frequent and fervent prayer; of submission to the will of God in prayer; and of praying even for enemies: the persons He is here said to pray for are His apostles; which shows their danger and their wants, His care over them, and concern for them, and His love unto them:

I pray not for the world; the inhabitants of it, the carnal unbelieving part of the world, which lie in sin, and will be condemned; as He died not for them, so He prayed not for them; for whom He is the propitiation, He is an advocate; and for whom He died, He makes intercession; and for no other in a spiritual saving way:

but for them which thou hast given me; out of the world, as distinct from them, to be saved with an everlasting salvation by Him; and to be preserved safe to His kingdom and glory; for these He prays, for the conversion of them, the application of pardon to them, their final perseverance and eternal glory:

for they are thine. Not merely by creation, and as the care of His providence, but by eternal election, and special grace in vocation [*or* calling]; which is a reason why Christ prayed for them, and an argument why the Father should, and would regard His prayers.

Verse 10. **And all mine are thine, and thine are mine**, &c. Christ is speaking not of things, but of persons; otherwise all the perfections of His nature as God, and all the works He did, and doctrines He taught as man, were of His Father; as all the perfections of His Father—His nature, His names, His works, His worship, were His; the same that belongs to the one belongs to the other: but persons are here meant, and these the elect of God, particularly the apostles, who were His and His Father's; belonged to them both by election, covenant transactions, redemption, and efficacious grace in conversion; which mutual interest arises from a union in nature, an agreement in covenant, and a conjunction in operation:

and I am glorified in them. Or by them, they ascribing all divine perfections, works and worship to Him; attributing the whole of their salvation to

515

Him, and giving Him all the glory of it; believing in Him; walking worthy of Him, in their lives and conversations; suffering patiently and cheerfully for His sake; and abiding by His Gospel and ordinances; and He will be glorified by them, and in them hereafter, and that to all eternity.

Verse 11. **And now I am no more in the world**, &c. In the earth; which is no contradiction to His resurrection from the dead, and stay with His disciples for a while; nor to His return to judge the world at the last day; nor to His reigning on earth with His saints a thousand years; since it will not be the world as it now is, but it will be a new earth, renewed, purified and refined, and clear of the wicked inhabitants of it; and in which will only dwell righteous persons. Besides, Christ was to be, and will be no more in the world, in such circumstances, and doing such work as He then was: the meaning is, that whereas He had been in the world, and had done, or as good as done the work He came about, He was now just going out of it; it was but a very little while He had to stay in it; nor should He continue long with His disciples when He rose from the dead; and whereas His bodily presence had been a guard unto them, a protection of them, and He had borne the heat and burden of the day for them, and had taken all reproaches and persecutions upon Himself, now He was going from them:

but these are in the world; and will continue for some time, they having much work to do, and be exposed to the evils, snares and temptations of it; where they were hated, and were liable to great hardships, afflictions and persecutions; which shows that Christ was not so intent on His own glory, as to neglect the good of His people, and to be unconcerned for them:

and I come to thee. Signifying His death; the deposition of His soul into His Father's hands; His ascension in soul and body to Him; His entrance into heaven, and session at the right hand of God; and therefore had nothing to ask for on His own account: but His disciples He was parting with lay near His heart, and therefore He prays:

Holy Father, keep through thine own name, those whom thou hast given me; the person prayed unto is God the Father, the Father of Christ, and of His people; a very proper relation to consider God in and under in prayer to Him: since it must give freedom, boldness, and hope of success. The epithet *holy* is exceeding suitable, as it perfectly agrees with Him who is essentially so; and since it was holiness, and an increase of it, Christ prays for; and that these His disciples might be kept from the evil of sin. The persons prayed for are those that were given to Christ in election, and in the covenant, to be kept by Him, and therefore He is the more solicitous for their preservation: His request is, that His Father would keep them from the evil of the world; from sinking under temptations and afflictions; faithful to Him

516

and to His Gospel, and in unity among themselves; and that *through* or *in* His own name; *in* it, in the doctrine of the Gospel, and in the worship of God, and profession of Him; *through* it, through Himself, as *a wall of fire* about them [*Zech. 2:5*], and by His power through faith unto salvation:

that they may be one as we *are*. In nature, will, affection and understanding; which must be understood not of equality, but of likeness; and designs not their union to Christ, but to one another; abiding together, cleaving to each other, standing fast in one Spirit, having the same designs, and the interest of a Redeemer in view, and at heart.

Verse 12. **While I was with them in the world**, &c. This does not imply that Christ was not in the world now, for He was; but signifies that He was just going out of it; and that His continuance in it was very short: nor that He was, and would be no longer with His disciples; for this is to be understood of His bodily, not of His spiritual presence; in which respect Christ is with His people while they are on earth, and they are with Him when He is in heaven:

I kept them in thy name; by His Father's authority and power, in His doctrine:

those that thou gavest me I have kept; that is, those that were given Him to be His apostles;

and none of them is lost; these He kept close to Himself, and from the evil of the world, and from temporal and eternal ruin:

but the son of perdition; Judas, a child of Satan, whose name is Apollyon the destroyer, who was now about to betray his Lord and Master; and was one that was appointed to eternal ruin and destruction, of which he was justly deserving [see *Acts 1:25; Rom. 9:21-23; 1 Pet. 2:7-8; Jude 4*]; and which is no instance of the apostasy of saints, since though he was given to Christ as an apostle, yet not in eternal election, to be saved by Him:

that the Scripture might be fulfilled. This respects either Christ's keeping of His people, and their final perseverance, whereby the Scriptures that speak of it are fulfilled; or rather the destruction of Judas, whereby such passages as speak of that, have their accomplishment, particularly *Psa. 109:8*. Some have thought that this only refers to the general sense of the Scriptures, both the law and prophets; that some are chosen to everlasting life, and others are appointed to wrath [see *1 Thess. 5:9*]; that some are saved, and others lost; some sons of God, and others sons of perdition; but it rather seems to regard some particular passage or passages of Scripture relating to Judas, his character, condition and end, and which are very manifestly pointed at, in the Psalm referred to; see [the Apocrypha] 2 Esdras 2:26:

"As for the servants whom I have given thee, there shall not one of them perish; for I will require them from among thy number."

Verse 13. **And now come I to thee**, &c. As in *verse 11*, which He repeats as a very great happiness to Himself, and with much pleasure and joy, but not without concern for those He was parting from:

and these things I speak in the world; which He had expressed in this prayer concerning the nature of eternal life, and His power to give it to all the Father had given Him; concerning the work of redemption finished by Him, and the glory due unto Him on that account; concerning His chosen ones, particularly the apostles, and the mutual interest He and His Father had in them; and what He had done for them, in revealing the Gospel to them, keeping them by the powerful influence of His grace, and the great concern He had for their future preservation: and these things He took notice of in His prayer, while He was in the world, before He took His leave of them; and adds,

that they may have my joy fulfilled in themselves. Either the joy which Christ had in them, which was of an early date, is still continued towards them, and will be more fully expressed, when they shall all be brought safe home to glory, and be for ever with Him; or else the joy of which Christ is the author and object, which comes from Him, and centers in Him. Saints rejoice in the person of Christ; in the greatness and dignity of His person, as God *over all* [*Rom. 9:5*]; hence they know that what He did and suffered answered the purpose; that He must have great interest in heaven, and they must be safe in His hands; and in the fitness of it, to be a Mediator, He being God and man in one person; and in the fulness of it, which is all theirs: it is with delight they view it, with joy they receive from it, and believe they shall not want; and in the beauty of it, He being *fairer than the children of men* [*Psa. 45:2*]. The offices Christ bears as Prophet, Priest, and King, the relations He stands in as father, husband, brother and friend; His Gospel and communion with Him, the blessings of grace in Him, as peace, pardon, righteousness and salvation, lay a foundation for solid joy in them that believe; as do also His death, resurrection, exaltation and intercession. This joy in Him is a grace of the Spirit, and is attended with faith in Christ; it should be constant, but is frequently interrupted; though the ground and foundation of it is always the same; it is therefore at present imperfect, but may be increased; it is unknown to the world, and inexpressible by the saints; and may be said to be *fulfilled in them*, when it abounds in them more and more; when they are full of it, and that is full of glory, and which will be fulfilled in glory.

Verse 14. **I have given them thy word**, &c. The Gospel, and a commission and abilities to preach it, and which is a reason of what follows, namely, the world's hatred of them; because this Word is not of men, nor agreeable to carnal reason; it magnifies the grace of God, and destroys boasting in men; it is against the carnal interest, worldly views and lusts of men:

and the world hath hated them; the inhabitants of the world, worldly men, such as are what they were when they first came into the world; are under the influence of *the god of the world* [2 Cor. 4:4], and led by the spirit of it, and are wholly taken up with the things thereof. The unbelieving Jews are chiefly designed, who bore an implacable hatred to Christ and His apostles; and the same fate do the faithful ministers of Christ and His members share, in all ages and places, more or less: the men of the world gnash their teeth at them, secretly plot against them, and inwardly curse them; rejoice at any evil that befalls them; greedily catch at any thing to reproach them; stick [*or* hesitate] not to say all manner of evil of them, and to do all manner of evil to them:

because they are not of the world; they were of the world by their natural birth, and had their conversation with the men of it, while in a state of unregeneracy; but now they were called out of it, and were guided and led by another spirit; and were separate from the world in their lives and conversations, and which brought the hatred of the world upon them; inasmuch as they had been of them, but now had left them, and professed they did not belong to them; and because their religious lives put a distinguishing mark on them, and reproved and condemned them:

even as I am not of the world. Not that Christ and His people are alike in their original; they are of the earth earthly, He is the Lord from heaven; nor are they so perfect in their walk and conversation in the world, and separation from it, as He; yet there is some likeness between Him and them, and some conformity in them to Him, which makes the world hate them.

Verse 15. **I pray not that thou shouldest take them out of the world**, &c. Either in an unusual manner, by a translation, as Enoch and Elijah were; or by death in its common form, before their time, and purely to be rid of afflictions: this He prayed not for; for He had much work for them to do, by preaching the Gospel, for the conversion of sinners and comfort of saints; and it was for His interest they should live longer; and it would make most for His glory, and be best for His chosen people and churches:

but that thou shouldest keep them from the evil. Either of sin, which is an evil and bitter thing, being committed against a good God, and a righteous law, and brings ruin and destruction upon men; from this the apostles were kept, and all the saints are; not from indwelling sin, nor from the commission of sin, but from the dominion of it, and from falling into it and by it, so as to perish eternally: or from the evil of the world; not from afflictions in it; nor from the reproach and persecution of it; but from its wickedness and lusts, and from the evil men of it: or from Satan the evil one, who is eminently, originally, and immutably so; not from being tempted by him, but from sinking under his temptations, and from being devoured by him [see *1 Cor. 10:13*]. Christ's praying for this, after this manner, shows that evil is very abhorrent, pernicious and powerful; the danger saints are in by it; their incapacity to keep themselves from it; and that the Lord alone is the keeper of His people; but does not suggest that Christ has dropped the charge of them, or is unequal to it; but by so doing He expresses His great love to them, how dear they are to Him, and what care He takes of them, and what concern He has for them.

Verse 16. **They are not of the world, even as I am not of the world**. These words are repeated from *verse 14*, where they are given as a reason of the world's hatred to them; and here, as showing that they are exposed to the evil of it; and in both are used as an argument with His Father, that He would take notice of them, and preserve them.

Verse 17. **Sanctify them through thy truth**, &c. The Syriac version introduces this petition, with the appellation אבא, *Abba,* Father: and the sanctification prayed for regards the apostles, either as ministers of the Word, and may intend their separation for their work and office; for which, though they were sanctified or separated from their mother's womb, and by Christ when He sent them forth, yet they were to have a fresh commission and unction after our Lord's resurrection, and upon His ascension to heaven; and also their qualification for it, with the truth of grace and doctrine, with holiness of heart and life, and with a preservation in the truth, by being kept faithful to it: or it may also regard them as Christians and believers, and intend a greater degree of the sanctification of the Spirit, which is imperfect in this life; for though sanctification in Christ is perfect, and so it is in the saints, as to parts, yet not as to degrees; which appears from the imperfection of faith, hope, love, and knowledge, from indwelling sin being in the best of saints, from their necessities, from their disclaiming perfection, and their desires after it. Sanctification is a progressive work, which is carried on gradually; as is clear from the characters of regenerate ones, who are first newborn babes, then young men, and afterwards fathers in Christ; from the similes, by which it is expressed: as seed, which opens and grows up by degrees, and light, which shines more and more unto the perfect day [see *Prov. 4:18*]; from exhortations to a concern for the growth of it, and prayers for it. And it is indeed continually carrying on, as may be concluded from the hand in which it is; and the progress and finishing of this work, as well as the beginning of it, are entirely the Lord's; and the way and means in which this is done, are by or through the truth of the Gospel:

thy word is truth. It is *peculiarly* so, as the Arabic version reads it. The Gospel is here meant, and is so called on account of its original, it comes from the God of truth; and because of the concern which Christ, who is the truth, has in it, He being the author, preacher, and sum and substance of it; and because the Spirit of truth has dictated it, leads into it, qualifies men to preach it, and makes it effectual; and because it contains all truth necessary to salvation, and nothing but truth, and particularly that eminent truth, salvation alone by Christ; and because it is opposed to the law, which is but a shadow, of which the good things in the Gospel are the substance: now this is the means both of the beginning, and increasing, and carrying on the work of sanctification in the hearts of God's people, as well as of an experimental knowledge of it; and an increase of that knowledge does more and more qualify the ministers of it for their ministerial work and service, which seems here chiefly designed.

Verse 18. **As thou hast sent me into the world**, &c. Which does not suppose inequality of nature, nor change of place, nor any force upon Him, nor disrespect unto Him, nor a state of separation from His Father; but that He *was* before He was sent; that He was a person, a divine distinct person from His Father; and designs the manifestation of Him in human nature; and shows, that as Mediator, He had a divine warrant and authority, and was no impostor: what He was *sent* into the world to do, was in general the will of God; particularly to preach the Gospel, and chiefly and more especially to work out the salvation of His people:

even so have I also sent them into the world. To preach the Gospel likewise: He had already sent them forth on this errand, and in a little time they were to receive a new and enlarged commission for this service; which mission of them to such work, implies great honor put upon them, authority in them, and qualifications with them; and hence success attended them. The place into which they were sent is, *the world*; first the Jewish, and then the Gentile world, and every part of it; out of which He would not have them taken; and where they were sure to meet with reproach and persecution; and where God's elect lay, who were to be converted through their ministry; for the work they were sent thither for, was to open blind eyes, turn men from darkness to light, from the power of Satan unto God, that they might receive forgiveness of sin, and an inheritance among them that are sanctified. Now though there is not an equality between the mission of Christ by His Father, and of the apostles by Him, yet there is a likeness; there is an agreement in their original, both are divine and of authority, in the place they were sent, the world; and in their work, to declare the mind and will of God: all which carries in it a strong argument with His Father to regard these persons; for inasmuch as they were in a world that hated them, they needed divine power and protection; and being in a wicked world, they needed sanctification and preservation; and having such work to do, they therefore needed divine assistance, and fresh supplies of grace.

Verse 19. **And for their sakes I sanctify myself**, &c. Which is to be understood, not of His making Himself holy; for He never was a sinner, and so stood in no need of sanctification: He was made like unto us, yet without sin; He looked like a sinner, but was not one; He was traduced, charged, and treated as such, but was perfectly holy, and free from all sin; He was essentially and infinitely holy as God; and as man, He was holy in His conception and birth; He was filled with the Holy Ghost, and was holy in His life and in His death: rather this may be meant of His being separated, and set apart for His office as Mediator, which, though done by the Father, and is ascribed unto Him, *chapter 10:36*, yet may also be attributed to Himself; since He voluntarily devoted Himself to this work, and cheerfully accepted of it: though it seems best to understand it of His offering Himself a sacrifice for, and in the room and stead of His people, in allusion to the offerings under the law, the sacrificing of which is expressed by sanctifying, *Ex. 13:2,14-15*; and because His sacrifice was a holy one: what He sanctified or offered was *Himself*: not His divine, but human nature, His body and His soul; and these as in union with His divine person: which gives His sacrifice the preference to all others, and is the true reason of its virtue and efficacy; and this is expressive of His great love. He Himself is also the sanctifier or offerer, which shows Him to be a priest, and that He had a power over His own life, and that He sacrificed it voluntarily [see *John 10:18*]; and this He is said to do at that present time, because the time was very near that He was to be offered up, and His present prayer and intercession were a part of His priestly office. This He did not for His own sake, nor for the sake of angels, nor for all men, but for His disciples, as distinct from the world; and not for the apostles only, but for all that the Father had given to Him; and that as their substitute and surety, in their room and stead:

that they also might be sanctified through the truth. That is, have all their sins expiated, and they be cleansed from all the guilt and filth of them, through Christ Himself and His sacrifice, who is the truth; or *in truth*; as it may be rendered, really and truly, in opposition to the legal sacrifices which atoned for sin, not really, only typically; or through the Gospel of truth, bringing the good news of atonement by the blood and sacrifice of Christ, and which the Spirit of God seals to the conscience with comfort and joy.

Verse 20. **Neither pray I for these alone**, &c. Meaning His immediate apostles and disciples, for whose preservation and sanctification He had been particularly praying in the preceding verses; and now, that it might not be thought that these were His only favorites, and the only persons He had a regard for, and to whom His intercession and sacrifice were confined, He adds,

but for them also which shall believe in me through their word; Christ is the object of true faith; which faith is not a mere assent of the mind to any truth concerning Christ, as that He is the Son of God, the Messiah and Savior of the world; but it is a spiritual sight of Him, of the necessity, fitness, and suitableness of Him as a Savior; a going forth unto Him, laying hold on Him, and depending upon Him for life and salvation; of which the preaching of the Gospel is the instrumental means: it is indeed a gift of God, and a fruit of electing grace, and which is secured by it; hence our Lord knew that there would be a number in all successive generations, that would believe in Him through the ministry of the Word; and for these persons, and their conversion, and the success of the Gospel to the good of their souls, He prays.

Verse 21. **That they all may be one**, &c. Among themselves. This may regard their unity in faith, and in the knowledge of Christ; for there is but one faith which all truly experienced souls agree in: they are converted by the same Spirit, and have the same work of grace wrought in them; and though they have not the same degree of light, and measure of spiritual knowledge, yet they agree in the main point of the Gospel, salvation alone by the Lord Jesus Christ; and such an agreement in the doctrine of faith, and the grand articles of it, respecting the person and offices of Christ, is absolutely necessary to their comfortably walking together in church fellowship, and the more honorable carrying on the worship of God together; and which will be more manifest in the latter day, when saints shall see eye to eye: likewise a unity in affection may be here designed, a *being knit together in love* to each other [*Col. 2:2*]; which is the *bond of perfectness* [*Col. 3:14*], the evidence of regeneration, the badge of the Christian profession, the beauty of church communion, and the barrier and security from the common enemy; and without which, social worship and mutual service will be either neglected or coldly performed. Moreover, this petition may have respect to the gathering together all the saints at the last day, as one body united together in faith and love; as one *general assembly and church of the firstborn* [*Heb. 12:23*]; as one fold of which Christ is the Head, Savior, and Shepherd:

as thou, Father, *art* **in me, and I in thee**; there is a mutual inbeing of the Father and the Son, who are one in nature and essence, in power and will, and in understanding and affection; which union, though it infinitely transcends any kind of union among men, or that can be conceived of by men, yet is the exemplar of the saints' union one with another, and to the divine persons; and which must be understood not of an equality, but a likeness:

that they also may be one in us: there is a union of all the elect to God and Christ, which is already complete, and not to be prayed for; they are all loved by God with an everlasting love, by which they are inseparably one with Him; they are all chosen in Christ [see *Eph. 1:4; 2 Thess. 2:13; 1 Pet. 2:4*], as members in their Head, and are federally united to Him, as their Mediator, surety, and representative; in consequence of which He has assumed their nature, stood in their place and stead, and brought them nigh to God [see *Eph. 2:13*]. There is a manifestation of union in conversion, when persons openly appear to be in Christ; and as a fruit and effect of everlasting love, are with loving kindness drawn unto Him; and which will be more gloriously seen, when all the elect shall be brought in, and God shall be all in all, and is what Christ here prays for:

that the world may believe that thou hast sent me. Either the rest of God's chosen people in the world, not yet called; or rather the wicked and reprobate part of the world, particularly Jews and Deists: they shall see the concord and agreement of the saints in doctrine, worship, and affection in the latter day; and when all the elect shall be gathered together, and not only their union to each other, but to the divine persons, shall clearly appear; they will then believe, and be obliged to own, that Jesus is the true Messiah, was sent of God, and is no imposter.

Verse 22. **And the glory which thou gavest me**, &c. Not the glory of His Deity; this is the same with His Father, what He has in right of nature, and not by gift; nor can it be communicated to creatures; this would be to make them one in the Godhead, as the three are one, which is not the design of the expression in the close of the verse: nor His mediatorial glory, which He had with the Father before the world began; this indeed was given Him by the Father, but is not given to the saints: nor the glory of working miracles; which glory Christ had, and which, as man, He had from the Father, and in which His own glory was manifested; this He gave to His disciples; but all that are His have not had it, and some have had it who are none of His: rather the Gospel is meant, which is glorious in its author, matter and subject, in its doctrines, in the blessings of grace it reveals, and promises it contains, and in the efficacy and usefulness of it to the souls of men. This was given to Christ, and He gave it to His disciples:

I have given them; as He did the words that were given to Him, *verse 8*,

that they may be one, even as we are one; for the Gospel was given to the apostles, and still is to the ministers of it, to bring men to *the unity of the faith*, for *the perfecting of the saints*, and *the edifying of the body of Christ* [*Eph. 3:12-13*]: or else the fulness both of grace and glory, which is in Christ's hands for His people, is here designed. This is one considerable branch of the glory of Christ, as Mediator, to be *full of grace and truth* [*John 1:14*]; this was given Him by the Father, and is what He communicates to His; even the Spirit, and all sorts of grace, and every supply of it; and which greatly contributes to the union of the saints among themselves: yea, eternal happiness is often signified by *glory*; and this is given to Christ; He has it in His hands to give to others; and He does give it, a view of it, a right unto it, a meetness for it, a pledge of it, some foretastes of it, and a kind of a possession of it; for the saints have it already, at least in Him; and He will give them the actual enjoyment of it, and this in order to their consummate and perfect union together, as *a glorious church* without *spot or wrinkle, or any such thing* [*Eph. 5:27*].

Verse 23. **I in them**, &c. Christ is in His saints; not as He is in all the world, being the omnipresent God; or as He is in every man, communicating the light of nature as Creator [see *John 1:1-4,9*]; or as He is in the human nature, which is united to His divine person; or circumscriptively to the exclusion of Him elsewhere; for He is in heaven, His blood is within the veil, and His righteousness without [*or* outside of] us: but He is in them, in a gracious manner, in regeneration; when He is revealed to them, formed in them, enters into them, takes possession of them, communicates His grace, grants fellowship with Himself, and dwells in them; not only by His Spirit and grace, but in person, as the Head in the members, as the Master of the house, and the King of them; which is an instance of condescending grace, and is peculiar to God's elect: hence all their holiness and fruitfulness; nor shall they ever perish; their bodies shall rise from the dead, and being reunited to their souls, Christ will be in them in a glorious manner to all eternity:

and thou in me; the Father is in Christ, not only by union of nature, nor merely in Him, as Mediator, in a way of grace; but as He will show Himself in and through Him in glory for evermore, and is what is here prayed for:

that they may be made perfect in one; this regards not their justification, which is already perfect; nor their sanctification, which will be; but either perfection in glory, when they will be perfect in knowledge, in holiness, in peace, joy and love: or rather the perfection of their numbers is meant, when the whole election of grace will be completed in regeneration, sanctification, and glorification:

and that the world may know that thou hast sent me: as before, *verse 21*; see the note there;

and hast loved them, as thou hast loved me. The Oriental versions, the Syriac, Arabic, Persic, and Ethiopic, all read the words thus, *and I have loved them, as thou hast loved me*; contrary to all the Greek copies, and other versions, which read as we do. The Father loved Christ as His own Son, and as Mediator; so He loved Him when He assumed human nature, and became obedient to His will both in doing and suffering; when His Father left Him, and poured out His wrath upon Him, and when He laid down His life for the sheep [see *John 10:11*]. The instances of His love to Him as Mediator are, His putting all things into His hands, showing Him all that He does, and concealing nothing from Him, and appointing Him the only Savior, the Head of the church, and Judge of the world. The nature of this love is, that it is from eternity; is a love of complacency and delight; it is special and peculiar, unchangeable and inseparable, and will last for ever: now God has loved His people, as He has loved His Son; He loves them not merely as creatures, as the descendants of Adam, or as considered in themselves, but as in Christ. The instances of His love to them are, His choosing them in Christ; making a covenant with them in Him; the mission of Him into this world, to obtain salvation for them; the quickening and calling of them by His grace; the care He takes of them afterwards in supplying their wants, supporting them under temptations, delivering them out of afflictions, and causing all things to work together for their good [see *Rom. 8:28*]; to all which add the provisions He makes for them, both for time and eternity. The nature of this love is such as that He bears to Christ; it is from everlasting; a love of the utmost delight and pleasure; it is special and peculiar, unchangeable, and will continue for ever: there is not the same reason for His loving them as His Son; and this *as* must not be thought to denote equality, but similitude and order.

Verse 24. **Father, I will that they also, whom thou hast given me**, &c. Not all the world, but a select number; not apostles only, nor as such; nor believers, or as such, for as such they were not given to Christ; nor as considered in effectual vocation [*or* calling]; but as the elect of God, and by that eternal act of His grace; when they were given to Christ as His children, as His spouse, as His church, as the sheep of His hand, as His portion, and to be preserved by Him; which is known by their calling and conversion. The form in which these words are delivered, is not so much by way of entreaty, as demand; they are a declaration of Christ's will, in which He insists on it as His right, upon the foot [*or* basis] of His purchase, and those covenant transactions which passed between Him and His Father, on the behalf of those that were given to Him: that they,

be with me where I am; not where He was then, unless it may be meant of Him as the omnipresent God, and as such then in heaven; though He rather designs where He should be as man, after His resurrection, and where the souls of saints are after death; and where they will be, soul and body, when raised again; and which is desirable both to Christ, and to His people; this was *the joy that was set before Him* [*Heb. 12:2*], and what they comfort one another with, that they shall be for ever with Him:

that they may behold my glory which thou hast given me; not the simple abstract glory of His Deity; which, as it was not given to Him, is not to be seen by them; but His glory as Mediator: this was seen, though imperfectly by some, *in the days of his flesh* [*Heb. 5:7*]; and in the glass of the Gospel, a believer now has some views of it, and by faith sees, knows, and is assured that Christ is glorified in heaven; but hereafter the saints in their own persons, and with their own eyes, shall *see him as he is* [*1 John 3:2*], and appear in glory with Him; which sight of His glory will be near, and not at a distance, appropriating and assimilating, rejoicing, satisfying, and for ever:

for thou lovedst me before the foundation of the world. This is mentioned both as a reason why such a glory was given Him, because of His Father's early love to Him as Mediator; and as an argument why He might expect to be heard and answered, because of the interest He had in His affections, which had been strongly towards Him, even from everlasting; and because the persons He asks, or rather demands these things for, shared in the same ancient love.

Verse 25. **O righteous Father**, &c. God is righteous in all the divine persons: the Father is righteous, the Son is righteous, and the Holy Spirit is righteous; He is so in His nature: righteousness is a perfection of it; He is so in all His purposes and promises; in all His ways and works of providence and grace; in predestination, redemption, justification, pardon of sin, and eternal glory. Christ makes use of this epithet, as containing a reason why He might justly expect that all His petitions and claims, on behalf of Himself and people, would be regarded:

the world hath not known thee; the unbelieving Jews, and idolatrous Gentiles, wicked men, one or another, know not God: as not the Father, so neither the Son, nor Spirit; though Deity may be known by them, or that there is a God, yet they know not God in Christ, nor as the Father of Christ, or as their Father in Him, nor what it is to have communion with Him; nor do they know any of the things of God in a spiritual way; which shows the darkness and blindness of men by nature, the necessity of a divine illumination, and the miserable state of men without one:

but I have known thee; His nature, perfections and glory, His secret thoughts, purposes and designs, His covenant, promises and blessings, His love, grace and good will to His people, His whole mind and will; as He needs must, since He was one with Him, and lay in His bosom;

and these have known that thou hast sent me. Meaning His disciples and apostles, whom He distinguishes from the world; these knew the Father that sent Him, and that He was sent by the Father; they knew the love of the Father in sending of Him, the manner in which He was sent, and the end, man's redemption, for which He was sent; and acknowledged all this, and which laid them under an obligation to trust in Him, love Him, and magnify His grace; and is used by Christ as an argument with the Father to be concerned for them.

Verse 26. **And I have declared unto them thy name**, &c. Himself, His nature, His perfections, especially of grace and mercy, His mind and will, His Gospel; see the note on *verse 6.* A very fit person Christ was to make this declaration, since He was with Him from all eternity, and was in His bosom; the Father did all in Him, and His name is in Him; and He is *the faithful witness [Rev. 1:5]*; nor is any thing of God to be known savingly, but in and through Christ; the apostles are here particularly meant, though the same is true with respect to all that are given to Christ, who are His children and brethren, to whom He also declares the name of God:

and will declare it; more fully to them after His resurrection, during His forty-days' stay with them, and upon His ascension, when He poured down His Spirit in such a plentiful and extraordinary manner upon them; and will declare it to others besides them in the Gentile world; and still more in the latter-day glory, and to all believers more and more:

that the love wherewith thou hast loved me may be in them; that is, that a sense of that love with which God loves His Son, as Mediator, might be in them, and abide in them; and which is the rather mentioned, because they are loved by the Father with the same love, and share all the blessed consequences of it, the knowledge and sense of which they come at, through Christ's declaring His Father's name unto them; and which they will have a greater sense of, and will be swallowed up in it in heaven to all eternity:

and I in them; dwelling in them, taking up His residence in them; not only by His Spirit and grace here, but by His glorious presence with them hereafter; when they shall be brought to His Father's house, behold His glory, and be for ever with Him.

CHAPTER 18

Verse 1. **When Jesus had spoken these words**, &c. Referring either to His discourses in *chapters 14,15 and 16*, in which He acquaints His disciples with His approaching death; comforts them under the sorrowful apprehension of His departure from them; gives them many excellent promises for their relief, and very wholesome advice how to conduct themselves; lets them know what should befall them, and that things, however distressing for the present, would have a joyful issue: or else to His prayer in the preceding chapter, in which He had been very importunate with His Father, both for Himself and His disciples; or to both of these, which is highly probable:

he went forth with his disciples over the brook Cedron; the same with *Kidron* in *2 Sam. 15:23*, and elsewhere: it had its name, not from cedars, for not cedars but olives chiefly grew upon the mount, which was near it; and besides the name is not Greek, but Hebrew, from קֶדֶר, which signifies *black*, though the Arabic version renders it, *the brook* אל אֶדֶר, *of Cedar*: it had its name either from the darkness of the valley in which it ran, being between high mountains, and having gardens in it, and set with trees; or from the blackness of the water through the soil that ran into it, being a kind of a common sewer, into which the Jews cast every thing that was unclean and defiling; see *2 Chron. 29:16* and *30:14*. Particularly there was a canal which led from the altar in the temple to it, by which the blood and soil of the sacrifices were carried into it.[1] This brook was but about three feet over from bank to bank, and in the summer time was quite dry, and might be walked over dry shod; and is therefore by Josephus sometimes called the brook of Kedron,[2] and sometimes the valley of Kedron:[3] in this valley were corn fields; for hither the Sanhedrin sent their messengers to reap the sheaf of the

---

[1] Mishna Middot, c. 3. sect. 2. Meila, c. 3. sect. 3. & Bartenora in ibid. Maimon. & Bartenora in Mishna Zebachim, c. 8. sect. 7. & Temura, c. 7. sect. 6.

[2] Antiqu. l. 8. c. 1. sect. 5.

[3] Ibid. l. 9. c. 7. sect. 3. & de Bello Jud. l. 5. c. 4. sect. 2. & c. 6. sect. 1.

firstfruits, which always was to be brought from a place near to Jerusalem;[4] and it is very likely that willows grew by the brook, from whence they might fetch their willow branches at the feast of tabernacles; for the Jews say,[5] there is a place below Jerusalem called *Motza* (in the Gemara it is said to be *Klamia* or *Colonia*), whither they went down and gathered willow branches; it seems to be the valley of Kidron, which lay on the east of Jerusalem, between that and the Mount of Olives;[6] it had fields and gardens adjoining to it; see *2 Kings 23:4*. So we read of a garden here, into which Christ immediately went, when He passed over this brook. The blood, the filth and soil of it, which so discolored the water, as to give it the name of the *Black Brook*, used to be sold to the gardeners to dung their gardens with.[7] It was an emblem of this world, and the darkness and filthiness of it, and of the exercises and troubles of the people of God in it, which lie in the way to the heavenly paradise and Mount of Zion, through which Christ Himself went, drinking *of the brook in the way* [*Psa. 110:7*]; and through which also all His disciples and followers enter into the kingdom of heaven. It may also be a figure of the dark valley of the shadow of death, through which Christ and all His members pass to the heavenly glory. And I see not why this black and unclean brook may not be a representation of the pollutions and defilements of sin; which being laid on Christ when He passed over it, made Him so heavy and sore amazed in the human nature, as to desire the cup might pass from Him. Once more let it be observed, that it was the brook David passed over when he fled from his son Absalom; in this David was a type of Christ, as in other things: Absalom represented the people of the Jews, who rejected the Messiah, and rebelled against Him; Ahithophel, Judas, who betrayed Him; and the people that went with David over it, the disciples of our Lord; only there was this difference; there was a father fleeing from a son, here a Son going to meet His Father's wrath; David and his people wept when they went over this brook, but so did not Christ and His disciples; the sorrowful scene to them both began afterwards in the garden. This *black* brook and *dark* valley, and it being very late at night when it was passed over, all added to that dark dispensation, that hour of darkness, which now came upon our Lord; yet He went forth over it of His own accord, willingly and cheerfully; not being forced or compelled by any; and His disciples with Him, not to be partners of His sufferings, but to

---

[4] Mishna Menachot, c. 10. sect. 2, 3.

[5] Mishna Succa, c. 4. sect. 5.

[6] Jerome de locis Hebraicis, fol. 92. C.

[7] Mishna Yoma, c. 5. sect. 6. Maimon. Meila, c. 2. sect. 11.

be witnesses of them, and to receive some knowledge and instruction from what they should see and hear:

where was a garden, into the which he entered, and his disciples. There were no orchards nor gardens within the city of Jerusalem, but rose gardens, which were from the times of the prophets;[8] all others were without; and this was a very proper place for gardens, where so much dung was near at hand. Whether this garden belonged to one of Christ's friends, is not certain; but since He often resorted hither, no doubt it was with the leave, and by the consent of the proprietor of it. However, so it was, that as the first Adam's disobedience was committed in a garden, the second Adam's obedience to death for sin, began here [see *1 Cor. 15:45-47*]; and as the sentence of death, on account of sin, was passed in a garden, it began to be executed in one.

Verse 2. **And Judas also, which betrayed him, knew the place**, &c. This character is given of Judas, to distinguish him from another disciple of the same name; and though as yet he had not betrayed Him, yet it was determined he should, and Christ knew it, and he was now about to do it: and it is observed, that Judas was as well acquainted with the place of Christ's resort, and knew the garden He frequently retired to, as the rest of the disciples; to show that Christ did not go there to hide and secure Himself from him, but to meet him, and that he might have an opportunity of finding Him with the greater ease:

for Jesus ofttimes resorted thither with his disciples. When at Jerusalem at any of the feasts, and at this festival; partly for refreshment and rest after He had been preaching in the temple, and partly for prayer, and also for private conversation with His disciples.

Verse 3. **Judas then, having received a band** *of men*, &c. From the captain of this band, who in *verse 12* is called a *Chiliarch*, that is, a commander of a thousand men, one might conclude there were so many in this band; but it seems, that such an officer might have two bands under his command; and if this was the case, there were at least five hundred men in this company; a large number indeed, to take an unarmed person; and yet, as if this was not sufficient, it is added,

and officers from the chief priests and Pharisees; servants that belonged to each of these, and who seem to be a considerable number also; for these are said to be *a great multitude*; *Matt. 26:47*; nay, not only so, but the chief

---

[8] T. Bab. Bava Kama, fol. 82. 2. Abot. R. Nathan, c. 35. Maimon. Beth Habbechira, c. 7. sect. 14. Moses Kotsensis Mitzvot Tora praecept. Aff. 164.

priests, captains of the temple, and elders of the people, were themselves among them, *Luke 22:52*, to see that the men did their work, and did not return without Him; as these officers, when sent by them once before, did:

cometh thither with lanterns and torches and weapons. פנס, which is no other than the Greek word here used for *a lantern*, the Jews tell us,[9] was an earthen vessel, in which a candle was put and covered, that the wind might not put it out, and it had holes in the sides of it, through which light was let out; their לפיד, or *lamp*, here rendered *torch*, they say,[10] was also an earthen vessel in the form of a reed, at the top of which was a proper receptacle, in which they burnt old rags dipped in oil: now though it was full moon, being the time of the passover, they brought these along with them to discover Him by the light of, and find Him out with them, if He should hide Himself among the trees, or in any of the more shady places in the garden; and they took warlike instruments, as swords, spears, and staves, as if they had a thief or a murderer to apprehend, or a little army of men to encounter with; whereas there were only Christ, and His eleven disciples; and these in no condition, nor had any design, to defend themselves in a hostile manner.

Verse 4. **Jesus therefore, knowing all things**, &c. As being the omniscient God, so His knowledge reaches to all persons and things, without any limitation and restriction; though here it has a regard to the all things,

that should come upon him; even all the sufferings He should endure, which were all determined by God; agreed to by Him, in the covenant of grace; predicted in the Old Testament, and foretold by Himself: He knew all the circumstances that would attend His sufferings, as that He should be betrayed by Judas; be forsaken by the rest of His disciples; that the Jews would give Him gall and vinegar in His thirst; and the soldiers part His garments among them. He knew the time of His sufferings; and that it was now at hand; and that Judas and his company were not far off: and therefore,

went forth; out of the garden, or at least from that part of it where He was, and His disciples with Him: this was done to show His willingness to suffer; He went forth of His own accord; He did not hide Himself in the garden, as the first Adam did; He did not stay till those that sought His life came up to Him: He went forth, not to make His escape from them, but to meet them, and make Himself known unto them;

---

[9] Maimonides & Bartenora in Mishna Celim, c. 2. sect. 4.

[10] Ibid. in sect. 8.

and said unto them; Whom seek ye? This question was put, not out of ignorance; for He knew full well who they were seeking after: nor with a design to deceive them, and make His escape; but to show that He was not afraid of them, and that they could not have known Him, nor have taken Him, had He not made Himself known, and offered Himself to them; and which makes it appear, that He was willingly apprehended by them, and voluntarily suffered.

Verse 5. **They answered him, Jesus of Nazareth**, &c. Their answer is not, *thee*; for they knew Him not, their eyes were holden, or struck with dimness, or blindness, as the men of Sodom were [see *Gen. 19:11*]; or they that answered might be such who never personally knew Him: nor do they say *Christ*, for they rejected and denied Him as the Messiah; nor do they call Him that deceiver, or seditious person, as they sometimes did, being willing to cover their malicious views and intentions; but *Jesus of Nazareth*, a name by which He was commonly known, being taken from His education and conversation [*or* abiding] in that place; though this was sometimes given Him in a contemptuous way:

Jesus saith unto them, I am *he*. Or *I AM*, respecting His name Jehovah, averring Himself to be the Christ, and owning Himself under the name they were pleased to call Him by; which shows how willing He was to be taken by them, and may teach us not to be ashamed of Him, or of any nickname we may bear for His sake.

And Judas also, which betrayed him, stood with them. This circumstance is recorded, to show that Judas at first did not know Him any more than the rest; so that He might easily have passed them if He had pleased; and that Judas did not stand with them as an idle spectator; he came with them to betray Him, and was looking out for Him; though when He spake he knew Him not. It also expresses the different company Judas was in; a little while ago, he was at supper with Christ, and the other disciples, and now he is at the head of a band of soldiers, and others, to betray Him: and also his continuance in his iniquity, and wicked resolutions and agreement; as yet he had no remorse of conscience, or sense of his sin. And it seems to be mentioned also with this view, to inform us, that he fell to the ground with the rest; which is related in the next verse. The Jew[11] asserts, that there is a disagreement between the Evangelist John and the rest of the evangelists in this account: he observes, that when Judas came with his armed men to take Jesus, Jesus went out to meet them, and asked them, saying, *Whom seek ye?* They say, *Jesus of Nazareth*; to whom He replies, *I am he*; and then Judas,

---

[11] R. Isaac Chizzuk Emuna, par. 2. c. 56. p. 445, 446.

that betrayed Him, stood with them: but Matthew, in his Gospel, *Matt. 26:47*, and Mark, *Mark 14:43*, and Luke, *Luke 22:47*, relate, that Judas gave a sign to the soldiers, when they came to take Jesus, saying, him whom I shall kiss, lay hold on; and they did so. But here is no contradiction, John does not deny that Judas gave a sign to the soldiers; though he omits it, it being so particularly observed by the other evangelists; and only relates what is not taken notice of by them, and which no ways contradicts what they have asserted. The force of the objection seems to lie here: that, according to the other evangelists, Judas, as soon as he came into the garden, made [*or* went] up to Christ, and gave the signal by which He might be known, whereas he is here said to stand with the soldiers and officers; and that seeing such a signal was given, Jesus must be, and was known by it, whereas He is here represented as if He was not known by them, until He had made Himself known to them; and that as soon as Judas had given the sign, they immediately seized Him; whereas, according to this account, they did not, until some words had passed between Christ and them, and they first fell to the ground. In answer to which, it may be said, that admitting that Judas did make [*or* go] up to Christ as soon as he entered the garden, and gave the signal to the soldiers, he might upon that immediately retire, and place himself among the multitude; either to give further directions and instructions to them, or that they might defend him from Jesus, should there be any occasion for it: and though it should be allowed that the signal was given by Judas before this, it might not be discerned by the soldiers, either not being near enough to observe it; or, as some think, being stricken with blindness, for a time, as the Sodomites were [*Gen. 19:11*]; or even supposing it was seen, and they knew by it which was Jesus, it is still a fuller proof of the courage and intrepidity of Christ to go forth, and present Himself to them, and put the questions He did, and confirm unto them the truth of it, that He was Jesus whom they sought. To which may be added, that it does not appear that Christ was immediately seized by the soldiers, upon the signal given them by Judas, without some intervening words and actions; for though the signal and the seizure lie very near together in the accounts of Matthew and Mark, yet Luke relates many things between them, as the question of the disciples, whether they should smite with the sword; Peter's cutting off the ear of the high priest's servant; Christ's rebuking him, and touching the servant's ear, and healing it; and some discourse which passed between Him, and the chief priests, captains, and elders. All which agree with the account the Evangelist John here gives.

Verse 6. **As soon then as he had said unto them, I am *he***, &c. Immediately upon His speaking these words, which were delivered with so much majesty and authority, and were attended with such a divine power:

they went backward, and fell to the ground. They were confounded, surprised, and intimidated, and seemed as if they would have chosen rather to have fled from Him, than to have apprehended Him; and as they retired and went backward, they fainted away, as it were, either at the majesty of His looks, or at the power of His words, or both, so that they became like dead men, falling to the ground. Sometimes the majesty of a man's person, or his fame for some remarkable things done by him, or the innocence and uprightness of his cause, have had such an influence upon his enemies, that they have not been able to execute upon him what they intended. It is reported of Caius Marius, that being reduced to the utmost misery, and shut up in a private house at Minturnae (a town in Italy), an executioner was sent to kill him; and though he was an old man, and unarmed, and in the most miserable condition, yet the executioner having drawn his sword, could not attempt to use it; but, as the historian[12] says, being struck with blindness at the glory of the man, ran away astonished and trembling. Now, besides the above things, in their highest perfection, there was in our Lord something more than human; He was God as well as man, and He displayed His divine majesty, glory, and power. This was done, not to make His escape from them; but to give proof of His Deity, and a specimen of His power at the great day; and to let them know, that if He had not thought fit to have surrendered Himself voluntarily to them, though He was an unarmed person, they with all their men and arms, could never have laid hold on Him; and to show them, that He could as easily have struck them dead, as to cause them to fall to the ground. And sometimes striking a person dead immediately, is expressed by this phrase of striking to the ground; and is ascribed to God, who does it by the ministry of angels: says R. Simeon ben Shetach,[13] to some persons at variance,

"Let the master of thoughts come (that is, the blessed God), and take vengeance on you. Immediately Gabriel came, והבטן בקרקע, *and smote them to the ground*; and they died immediately."

The like is elsewhere said,[14]

"If thou transgresseth thy Father's command, immediately comes Gabriel, and *smites to the ground*."

Verse 7. **Then asked he them again, Whom seek ye**? &c. This supposes them to be risen up again, and on their feet; no hurt being done to them; for Christ always did good, and not hurt, to the bodies of men; He never disabled

---

[12] Valerius Maxim. l. 2. c. 5.

[13] T. Bab. Sanhedrin, fol. 19. 2.

[14] Shemot Rabba, sect. 1. fol. 91. 2.

any, nor took away life, or limb: He only did this to show His power, and not to do them any real damage; and the same divine person that struck them down, suffered them to rise, and gave them power and strength to get up; which showed His great clemency and goodness. But they, on the contrary, persisted in their wicked intentions, and were still seeking after Him: a plain proof of that judicial hardness of heart, under which they were; and that even miracles wrought will not bring hardened sinners to repentance without powerful and efficacious grace. When Christ, as fearless of them, and to show that by this action He had no design to make His escape from them, though He could easily have done it, and that He was willing to be apprehended by them, puts the question a second time, and asks them who they were seeking for. Something like this Josephus[15] reports concerning Elisha the prophet, though not repeated as here, nor attended with the like effect: he relates, that Elisha having requested of God that He would smite his enemies with blindness, and that being granted, he went into the midst of them, and asked them, τινα επιζητουντες ηλθον, *Whom do ye come to seek?* They say, *Elisha the prophet*: he promised them to deliver him to them, if they would follow him into the city, where he was; and so they, being blinded by God, both in their sight and in their mind, followed the prophet [see also *2 Kings 6:18-23*].

And they said, Jesus of Nazareth. Having recovered their spirits, and being hardened in desperate malice and wickedness, impudently make this reply to Him; nor would they, notwithstanding this instance of His power, own Him to be the Messiah; but still contemptuously style Him *Jesus of Nazareth*.

Verse 8. **Jesus answered, I have told you that I am *he***, &c. This He said, upbraiding them with their stupidity; signifying He was ready to deliver Himself up into their hands; and which He did with intrepidity and calmness, only on this condition, with this proviso for His disciples:

if therefore ye seek me, let these go their way: Christ was about to suffer for them, and therefore it was not just that they should suffer too; nor was it proper that they should suffer with Him, lest their sufferings should be thought to be a part of the price of redemption. Besides, their suffering time was not come, and they had other work to do: this shows the love of Christ to His disciples, and His care of them, and also His power, and that He could have saved Himself as well as them. Moreover, these words may be considered as an emblem and pledge of the acquittance and discharge of God's elect, through the suretyship engagements, and performances of Christ, who drew near to God on their account, substituted Himself in their room, and undertook for them in the counsel [*or* purpose] and covenant of peace, and laid

---

[15] Antiqu. l. 9. c. 4. sect. 3.

Himself under obligation to pay their debts, to satisfy for their sins, to bring in an everlasting righteousness, to keep and preserve them in this world, and to make them happy in another. Accordingly, in the fulness of time He was made under the law, and stood in their place and stead, and was taken, suffered, died, and rose again. Now, as there was a discharge and acquittance of them from eternity, a non-imputation of sin to them, and a secret letting of them go upon the suretyship engagements of Christ, and in virtue thereof, a passing by, and over, the sins of the Old Testament saints; so there was an open acquittance and discharge of them all upon the apprehension, sufferings, death, and resurrection of Christ; complete deliverance from wrath and condemnation being obtained, and a full title to eternal glory made. Moreover, these words may be considered not only and merely as spoken to the Jews, but as addressed to the law and justice of God; or however, as having some respect to them, while directed to the others; for justice finding the sins of all the elect upon Christ, on whom the Father had laid them, and Christ having taken them upon Himself, was seeking for, and about to demand satisfaction of Him for them; and He being under the law, and coming into the world to fulfil it, in the room and stead of His people, was about to bear the curse of it; wherefore seeing this was the case, He insists upon it, that they who were convicted of the law as transgressors, and held under it as condemned criminals and malefactors, and who were liable, as considered in themselves, to be seized upon by the justice of God, and to have the sentence of condemnation and death executed upon them, might be discharged and let go; and accordingly, upon the satisfaction made by Christ, this is the case: Christ's people are no longer under the law, as a ministration of condemnation and death, nor liable to suffer the vindictive wrath of God; they are become free from the curses of a righteous law, and are let go by divine justice, and will never suffer the strokes of it, neither in this world nor in that to come; there is no demand to be made upon them, either by the law or justice of God; there is no wrath or punishment [that] will be inflicted on them, either here or hereafter; and they may, and shall go their way into everlasting life, when time shall be no more with them, neither law nor justice having anything to say to the contrary.

Verse 9. **That the saying might be fulfilled, which he spake**, &c. See *chapter 17:12;*

Of them which thou gavest me have I lost none. Which saying, though it has a peculiar respect to the apostles, is true of all the elect of God; who are given to Christ, and shall none of them be lost, neither their souls nor bodies; for Christ's charge of them reaches to both; both were given to Him, both are redeemed by Him, and both shall be saved in Him with an everlasting salvation: He saves their souls from an eternal death, and will raise their bodies from a corporeal one; wherefore that His care of His disciples, with respect to their bodies as well as souls, with respect to their temporal lives as well as eternal happiness, might be seen, He made this agreement with the Jews that came to take Him, or rather laid this injunction on them, to dismiss them; and which, it is very remarkable they did; they laid hands on none of them, even though Peter drew his sword and struck off the ear of one of them: and which is a very considerable instance of the power which Christ had over the spirits of these men, to restrain them; and so a proof of His proper Deity, as well as of the care of Christ for the preservation of His apostles, while He was here on earth; for to that time only the words cited have a respect; in which Christ speaks of His keeping them while He was with them, and uses this as an argument with His Father to keep them, now [that] He was removing from them. Wherefore their losing their lives afterwards for His sake, as they all did excepting the Apostle John, is no contradiction to this expression of His; and besides, they were preserved by the power of God so long, until they had done the work which was appointed them to do, and for which they were given Him, and chosen by Him to be His apostles, and for which they were better furnished after His resurrection and ascension; for had they been apprehended by the Jews at this time, in all probability, according to a human view of things, such was their weakness, they would have fallen most foully and shamefully, as the instance of Peter, the strongest of them, shows; and therefore to prevent such a temptation, and to preserve them, our Lord took this method to deliver them out of the hands of the Jews; the saving clause, *but the son of perdition*, is here left out, because Judas, who is designed by that character, was now openly declared to be what he was; he was no longer among the disciples; he was separated from them, and had betrayed his master, and was not of the number of those Christ insisted upon might be let go.

Verse 10. **Then Simon Peter having a sword**, &c. Girt about him, which he either wore in common; or particularly at the feast, as the Galilaeans are said to do, to preserve them from thieves and wild beasts by the way; or was one of the two the disciples had with them in the garden; or what Peter purposely furnished himself with to defend his master, taking a hint from what was said by Him, *Luke 22:36*:

drew it; before Christ could give an answer to the question put by His disciples, whether they should smite or not, *Luke 22:49*; being encouraged thereunto either by what Christ said, *Luke 22:38*; or by what He had just done in striking the men to the ground; and being provoked by that servant's going to lay hold on Christ, and who it is probable was more forward and busy than any of the rest; for it appears from the other evangelists, that Peter did this, though he is not mentioned by name by any of the rest, just as they were seizing and apprehending Christ:

and smote the high priest's servant, and cut off his right ear. He doubtless struck at his head, and intended to have cleaved him down, but missed his aim, and took off his ear: the person is particularly described that he was a servant, and the servant of the high priest, and he is mentioned also by name:

The servant's name was Malchus. That if the truth of this relation was called in question, it might easily be looked into and examined, when it would appear that it was perfectly right. All the evangelists give an account of this action of Peter's, but none of them mention his name but this evangelist; perhaps the reason might be, that Peter was alive when the other evangelists wrote, and therefore it was not safe to say who it was that did it, lest he, who was the minister of the circumcision [see *Gal. 2:7-9*], and dwelt among the Jews, should be prosecuted for it, or their minds should be prejudiced against him on that account; but John writing his Gospel many years after his death, the reason for the concealment of his name no longer subsisted: nor indeed is the name of the high priest's servant mentioned by any other of the evangelists: John had, or however he writes, a more exact and particular account of this matter. This was a name frequent with the Syrians, Phoenicians, and Hebrews. Jerome[16] wrote the life of one Malchus, a monk or Eremite, who was by nation a Syrian; and Porphyry, that great enemy of Christianity, who was by birth a Tyrian, his original name was Malchus, as was his father's; and which, in the Syrian, and his country dialect, as he himself[17] and others[18] say, signifies a *king*. Josephus[19] speaks of one Cleodemus, whose name was Malchus, that wrote a history of the Hebrews. And some Jewish Rabbins were of this name; hence we read of רב מלוך, *R. Maluc*,[20] and of רב מלכיו, *R. Malcio*;[21] the name is the same with Malluch, *Neh. 10:4*.

---

[16] Tom. I. fol. 87.

[17] Porphyr. vita in Plotin. c. 17.

[18] Eunapius in vita Porphyr. p. 16.

[19] Antiqu. l. 1. c. 15.

[20] T. Hieros. Succa, fol. 53. 3. & Bava Bathra, fol. 16. 1.

[21] T. Bab. Nidda, fol. 52. 1.

Verse 11. **Then said Jesus unto Peter**, &c. By way of rebuke, and to prevent his repeating the blow, and that further mischief might not ensue; for such a bold imprudent action risked the lives of all the disciples, who, in all probability, would have fallen a sacrifice to the fury and resentment of these men, had not Christ interposed in this prudent manner; who also, Luke says, touched the servant's ear and healed him, *Luke 22:51*, which no doubt tended greatly to conciliate their minds, and make them easy:

Put up thy sword into the sheath: Peter was not a proper person to bear the sword, and use it; it was a very daring attack, and a dangerous one, and was very unnecessary; since Christ could have defended Himself, had He thought fit, without Peter's drawing his sword; and besides, for a word speaking, He could have had of His Father more than twelve legions of angels; and it was also contrary to the nature of His kingdom, which was not of this world, nor to be supported and defended in any such manner; and was, moreover, as much as in Peter lay, a hindrance of His sufferings, and of the execution of His Father's will and decree; wherefore He adds,

the cup which my Father hath given me: by the cup is meant, the wrath of God, and punishment due to sin, endured by Christ in His sufferings: and is said to be *given* Him by His Father; because He called Him to these sufferings, they were appointed and determined by Him; yea, He was even ordered, and commanded by His Father to drink of this cup; justice mixed it up, and put it into His hands; and He took it as coming from His Father, who delighted in seeing Him drink it up, as the surety of His people; and a dreadful one it was, a cup of trembling and astonishment, of curse, and not of blessing, of wrath and fury. The allusion seems to be to the master of the family, who appointed, and gave to every one their cup:

shall I not drink it? Which expresses His willingness to do it, His eager desire after it, His delight in it, and displeasure at Peter's attempt to hinder Him; He being now perfectly reconciled in His human nature to drink it, though it was so bitter a potion: He found it was impossible, considering the decree of God, His own agreement, and the salvation of His people, that it should be otherwise; and besides, it was His Father's will and pleasure, He considered it as coming from Him; and therefore cheerfully accepted it, and was resolved to drink it up, and that nothing should hinder Him. The Persic version reads it, *I will not give it to another to drink*; Peter, by this rash action, seeming as if he would have the cup out of Christ's hands, and have drank it himself; which, as it could not be, nor would Christ suffer it, so if He had, it would have been of no advantage to the salvation of His people.

Verse 12 **Then the band and the captain and the officers of the Jews**, &c. Which Judas received, and which came along with him, *verse 3*. When

Jesus had rebuked Peter, and healed the servant's ear, and showed such a willingness to surrender Himself to them, they,

took Jesus, and bound him. This they did, partly for safety and security, He having several times escaped from them; and partly for contempt, and by way of reproach, using Him as they would do the vilest of malefactors: and this was submitted to by Christ, that His people might be loosed from the cords of sin, be delivered from the captivity of Satan, and be freed from the bondage of the law; hereby the types of Him were fulfilled, as the binding of Isaac, when his father was going to offer him up, and the binding of the sacrifice with cords to the horns of the altar. Who that has read the ceremonies of the sheaf of the firstfruits, but must call them to mind, upon reading this account of the apprehension and binding of Christ, and leading Him to the high priest. This sheaf was fetched from places the nearest to Jerusalem, particularly from the fields of Kidron: the manner was this: [22]

"The messengers of the Sanhedrin went out (from Jerusalem) on the evening of the feast day (the sixteenth of Nisan, and over the brook Kidron to the adjacent fields), and bound the standing corn in bundles, that it might be the easier reaped; and all the neighboring cities gathered together there, that it might be reaped in great pomp; and when it was dark, one (of the reapers) says to them, Is the sun set? They say, Yes; and again, Is the sun set? They say, Yes: With this sickle (shall I reap?) They say, Yes; again, With this sickle (shall I reap?) They say, Yes; In this basket (shall I put it?) They say, Yes; again, In this basket (shall I put it?) They say, Yes; If on the sabbath day he says to them, Is this sabbath day? They say, Yes; again, Is this sabbath day? They say, Yes (it was sabbath day this year); Shall I reap? They say to him, Reap; Shall I reap? They say to him, Reap; three times upon every thing; then they reap it, and put it into the baskets, and, bring it to the court, where they dry it at the fire."

Whoever reads this, will easily observe a likeness: the messengers of the great Sanhedrin go to the fields of Kidron in the evening, with their sickles and baskets; bind the standing corn; questions and answers pass between them and the people before they reap; and when they have done, they bring the sheaf in their basket to the court, to be dried at the fire. So the officers of the high priest, with others, pass over the brook Kidron, with lanterns, torches, and weapons; in the night go into a garden; there apprehend Jesus; questions and answers pass between them there; then they lay hold on Him, bind Him, and bring Him to the high priest.

---

[22] Mishna Menachot, c. 10. sect. 2-4.

Verse 13. **And led him away to Annas first**, &c. Who is elsewhere mentioned with Caiaphas as a high priest also, *Luke 3:2; Acts 4:6*; or was the *sagan* of the high priest; he and Caiaphas seem to have had the high priesthood alternately; and either now, because his house lay first in the way, or rather, because he was a man of age, learning, and experience, as these men usually were, that they might supply the deficiencies of the high priests, who were sometimes very weak and unlearned men;[23] therefore they first lead Christ to him, to have his advice how to proceed, and to take him along with them to his son-in-law, where the great council was convened, and that he might use his interest and authority, in taking proper measures, in order to put Jesus to death; and especially they led Him to him, for the reason here assigned;

for he was father-in-law to Caiaphas; so that he was, it is very probable, the older man: and being related to him, had an interest in him; and to whom such a sight was equally pleasing as to the high priest himself, or any of the council:

which was the high priest that same year. For the high priesthood was not for life, but was often changed, being bought and sold for money; see the note on *Luke 3:2* **[47]**; so that this clause is very properly added, though Caiaphas held it longer, or, at least, had it more years than one; for Caiaphas was high priest when John began to preach, *Luke 3:2*; but he now succeeded Simeon ben Camhith, who was priest the year before; as was Eleazar the son of Ananus, the year before that; and before him Ishmael ben Phabi, who were all three successively put into the priesthood by Valerius Gratus, the Roman governor; as was also Caiaphas this year, and whose name was Joseph.

Verse 14. **Now Caiaphas was he which gave counsel to the Jews**, &c. The chief priests and Pharisees, who met in council about Jesus, *chapter 11:47* &c. The counsel he gave was,

that it was expedient that one man should die for the people. And which advice was given out of ill will and malice to Christ, and to prevent, as he thought, the people of the Jews being destroyed by the Romans; though the words have a very good sense, which he did not understand. The people Christ was to die for, was not all the people of the world, nor only the people of the Jews, nor all of them; but all the elect of God, whom God has chosen for His special and peculiar people, and has given to Christ as such [compare *John 10:11* with *10:26-28*]: these Christ were to die for, and did; not merely as a martyr, to confirm His doctrine to them, or as an example to teach them

---

[23] Mishna Yoma, c. 1. sect. 3, 6.

542

meekness, patience, and courage, but in the room and stead of them, as a surety for them; and it was expedient that He should, in such sense, die for them, because of His suretyship engagements, that He might make satisfaction to the law and justice of God, and procure the salvation of His people, and send forth the Spirit, to make application of it to them.

Verse 15. **And Simon Peter followed Jesus**, &c. It is certain he first fled with the rest, and forsook Him, as they all did, notwithstanding his resolution to abide by Him; however, he was very desirous to know what would become of Jesus, and what would be the issue of things; with this view he followed Him, and not to deny Him; though that was the consequence. Other evangelists say he followed Him *afar off*, at a distance [*Matt. 26:58; Mark 14:54; Luke 22:54*]; which showed some fear; and yet to follow Him at all discovered love and zeal. To follow Christ is a property of His sheep, and is highly commendable, especially to follow Him in sufferings; a greater character a person cannot well have, than to be a follower of Jesus, in the exercise of grace, in the discharge of duty, and in bearing the cross. And yet it does not appear that Peter did well in following Christ now; for Christ had cautioned him of his overconfidence, had hinted to him that he should deny Him, and had dismissed him, and took his leave of him, and the rest, on whose discharge He insisted, when He was apprehended, *verse 8*;

And *so did* another disciple, and that disciple was known unto the high priest: this is thought to be the Apostle John, because he frequently speaks of himself, without mentioning his name; and these two, Peter and John, were generally together; and certain it is, that John was present at the cross at the time of Christ's crucifixion; and who is supposed to be known to the high priest, by carrying fish to his house, and selling it to him; so Nonnus says, he was known from his fishing trade: but it is not probable that he was known, or could be known by the high priest, so as to have any intimacy with him; nor is it likely that he, being a Galilean, would venture in; he was discoverable by his speech, and would have been in equal danger with Peter: rather it was some one of the disciples of Christ, who had not openly professed Him; one of the *chief rulers* that believed in Him, but, for fear of the Pharisees, had not confessed Him; it may be Nicodemus, or Joseph of Arimathea, or the man at whose house Christ had eaten the passover. In the Syriac version he is called *one of the other disciples*; not of the twelve, but others. However, through his knowledge of the high priest, he,

went in with Jesus into the palace of the high priest. Not Annas, but Caiaphas; for Christ was now brought from Annas's house to Caiaphas's, where the Scribes and elders were assembled together.

Verse 16. **But Peter stood at the door without,** &c. It being difficult to get in; and perhaps he might be fearful too of going in, lest he should be known; however, he waited, if he could hear or see any thing, and for a proper opportunity of entrance: it would have been well if he had taken the hint of providence, access not being easy, and have gone his way; for he was now at the door of temptation. It would have been best for him, if he had kept without; and indeed at a greater distance; but his curiosity had led him thus far, and he hoped for an opportunity of getting nearer, which offered in the following manner:

Then went out that other disciple, which was known unto the high priest; seeing Peter through the window, by the light of the moon, for it was full moon; and knowing him, who he was, concluded he had a mind to come in, and hear and see what he could, steps out,

and spake unto her that kept the door; which might be thought more properly the business of menservants; but these being employed in apprehending and guarding Jesus, the maidservants might be obliged to take this post. The Ethiopic version, in the next verse, calls her *the doorkeeper's daughter*; her father might be the porter, and he being busy, she supplied his place. Though there is no need of these conjectures, since it was usual with other nations, and it might be with the Jews, for women to be doorkeepers, as Pignorius[24] has shown out of Plautus, Petronius, Pausanias, and others. However, the other disciple, who was a man of figure and authority, and was known by the servants of the family, ordered her to open the door, and let Peter in; who accordingly did:

and brought in Peter. Into the hall, where Jesus was, under the examination of the high priest.

Verse 17. **Then saith the damsel that kept the door unto Peter,** &c. She being relieved, either by her father, if porter, or by a fellow servant, had the opportunity of coming into the hall, where Peter was, and was curious to observe him, who he should be, that that person of note should order him to be admitted, when an affair of so much privacy and importance was transacting; and either by Peter's language, or the trouble that appeared in his countenance, or fancying she had seen him in the temple, or in some part of the city in company with Jesus, addresses him after this manner:

Art not thou also *one* of this man's disciples? She speaks of Christ in the vulgar dialect of the Jews, calling Him *this man*; not only esteeming Him a mere man, but a worthless man; and knowing He had disciples, challenges

---

[24] De Servis, p. 454, 455.

him as one of them; when he, all in a fright and surprise, not expecting such a question to be put to him, without any further thought, rashly and suddenly,

he saith, I am not: he never denied that Christ was God, or the Son of God, or that He was come in the flesh, or that He was the Messiah and Savior of sinners; but either, that he did not know what the maid said, or the person she spoke of; or, as here, he denied that he was one of His disciples; which was a very great untruth: and many are the aggravations of his fall; which came to pass as soon as ever he was entered almost; and that by the means of a maid, a servant maid, a very inferior one; and at first perhaps they were alone; and the question put to him might not be in a virulent way, nor proceed from malice, but commiseration of him; and yet he had not resolution enough to own himself a disciple of Jesus; which he might have done, and in all likelihood might have gone safe off directly: but he that had so much confidence as to say, *though all men deny thee, yet will not I*; and had so much courage, as, in the face of a band of soldiers, to draw his sword, and smite one of the high priest's servants, but a few hours before, has not spirit enough in him to own his master before a servant maid!

Verse 18. **And the servants and officers stood there**, &c. In a certain part of the hall, the middle of it; the Vulgate Latin reads, *by the coals*: it follows,

who had made a fire of coals; for it was cold; though it was the passover, and harvest near. Dr. Lightfoot has observed from our countryman Biddulph, who was at Jerusalem at this time of the year, that though in the daytime it was as hot as with us at midsummer, yet such very great dews fell as made it very cold, especially in the night; and from one of the Jewish canons,[25] that the year was not intercalated (which when done was chiefly on account of the passover), neither for snow nor frost; which, as he justly remarks, supposes there might be frost and snow at the time of the passover. The same is observed in the Talmud,[26] where the gloss upon it is,

"that they might not desist, on that account, from coming to the passover."

The sense is, that whereas sometimes snow fell about the time of the passover; which might be thought to be a hindrance to some from coming to it; this never was a reason that came into consideration with the Sanhedrin, or prevailed upon them to intercalate a month, that so the passover might not fall at a time of year when there was usually snow. The passover was always in the spring of the year, when nights are commonly cold, as they are gen-

---

[25] Maimon. Hilch. Kiddush Chodesh, c. 4. sect. 6.

[26] T. Bab. Sanhedrin, fol. 11. 1.

erally observed to be at the vernal equinox: this night might be remarkably cold; which seems to be suggested by the Persic version, which reads, *for it was cold that night*; and the Ethiopic version, *for the cold of that night was great*; and adds, what is neither in the text, nor true, *for the country was cold*. The Arabic version, as it should seem, very wrongly renders it, *for it was winter*; since the passover was never kept in the winter season, but always in the spring, in the month Nisan: the winter season, with the Jews, were half the month of Chisleu, all Tebeth, and half Shebet;[27] though this is to be observed in favor of that version, that the Jews distinguish their winter into two parts; the one they call חורף, which, as the gloss says, is the strength of winter, the coldest part of it, and which lasts the time before mentioned; and the other they call קור, which is the end of winter, and when the cold is not so strong; and half Nisan is taken into this; for they say that half Shebet, all Adar, and half Nisan, are reckoned to this part of winter: so that, according to this account, the fourteenth of Nisan, which was the day on which the passover was killed; or at least the fifteenth, which was now begun, was the last day of winter, and so just secures the credit of the above version:

and they warmed themselves, and Peter stood with them, and warmed himself. He was cold both inwardly and outwardly; and being so, he gets into bad company; and it may be with a view that he might not be suspected, but be taken for one of their own sort, as one who had the same ill opinion of Jesus they had; and by the light of the fire he is again discovered and challenged, which makes way for a second denial.

Verse 19. **The high priest then asked Jesus**, &c. Being now brought from Annas to Caiaphas, who was the high priest and mouth of the Sanhedrin, and to whom it appertained to hear and try a cause relating to doctrine. And what he did was by putting questions to Him, instead of opening the charge against Him, and calling for witnesses to support it. The person he interrogated was a greater high priest than himself; was that *Prophet* Moses spoke of, to whom the Jews were to hearken [see *Deut. 18:15-18*], and no other than the Son of God, and King of Israel; who, when at twelve years of age, asked the doctors questions, and answered theirs, to their great astonishment [see *Luke 2:40,47*]. He first inquires,

of his disciples, not so much who they were, and what they were, and how many they were, and where they were now, as for what purpose He gathered them together; whether it was not with some seditious views to overturn the present government, and set up Himself as a temporal prince; and this he did, that he might be able to send Him, with a charge against Him, to the Roman

---

[27] T. Bab. Bava Metzia, fol. 106. 2.

governor. He did not ask for His disciples to come and speak on His behalf, if they had any thing to say for Him, which, by their canons,[28] was allowed and encouraged:

> "If any of the disciples (of the person accused) says, I have a crime to lay to his charge, they silence him; but if one of the disciples says, I have something to say in his favor, they bring him up, and place him between them; nor does he go down from thence all the day; and if there is any thing in what he says, שומעין לו, *they hearken to him*."

The Jews indeed pretend,[29] that after Jesus was found guilty, a herald went before Him forty days declaring His crime, and signifying, that if any one knew any thing worthy in Him, to come and declare it; but none were found: but this is all lies and falsehood, to cover their wickedness; no disciple of His was allowed to speak for Him. The high priest next asked Jesus,

of his doctrine. Not for the sake of information and instruction, nor to see whether it was according to the Scriptures; but if it was a new doctrine, and His own, and whether it tended to idolatry or blasphemy, and whether it was factious and seditious, that so they might have wherewith to accuse Him; for though they had gotten His person, they were at a loss for an accusation; and yet this selfsame man that put these questions, and was fishing for something against Him, had before given counsel to put Him to death, right or wrong: all this was doing, and these questions were put to Jesus, while Peter was denying Him.

Verse 20. **Jesus answered him**, &c. Not to the first of these questions, concerning His disciples; not because they had all now forsaken Him, and one was denying Him; nor because He would not betray them; nor because He would suffer alone; but because if His doctrine was good, it could not be blameworthy to have disciples, and to teach them: and the charge of sedition, blasphemy, and idolatry they wanted to fasten on Him, would sufficiently appear to be groundless by the doctrine He preached; and as to that He answers not directly what He taught, but declares the manner in which He delivered it, and which was such, that they that heard Him could not be strangers to it.

I spake openly to the world; with all plainness, freedom, and boldness, without any reserve or ambiguity; and that not to a few persons only, to His own particular disciples, but to all the people of the Jews, who crowded in

---

[28] T. Bab. Sanhedrin, fol. 40. 1. Maimon. Hilch. Sanhedrin, c. 10. sect. 8.

[29] T. Bab. Sanhedrin, fol. 43. 1.

great numbers to hear Him; insomuch that it was said by His enemies, that the world was gone after Him.

I ever taught in the synagogue; the Arabic, *the synagogues*; the places of public worship in all parts of the nation, where the Jews met to pray, and read, and hear the Word:

and in the temple; at Jerusalem, whenever He was in that city;

whither the Jews always resort; for prayer, and to offer sacrifice, and particularly at the three grand festivals of the year—the passover, Pentecost, and feast of tabernacles, when all the males from all parts appeared before the Lord. Accordingly, the Alexandrian copy, and some others, read, *whither all the Jews resort*; and so read the Vulgate Latin, Syriac, Persic, and Ethiopic versions.

And in secret have I said nothing. Not but that our Lord taught in other places than what are here mentioned, as on mountains, in deserts, by the sea-shore, and in private houses, yet generally to great multitudes; and though He sometimes conversed alone, and in secret with His disciples, yet what He taught them was either an explanation of what He had said in public, or was perfectly agreeable to it.

Verse 21. **Why askest thou me?** &c. He seems surprised at the high priest's conduct, that he should put such questions to Him, who stood bound before him; was brought there as a criminal, and was the defendant, and not obliged to accuse Himself; nor could it be thought that whatever evidence or testimony He should give, would have much weight with the persons before whom He stood.

Ask them which heard me, what I said unto them; He appeals to His hearers, many of whom were then present; and these His enemies, even His worst enemies: so clear was His case, so free was His doctrine from sedition and blasphemy, so innocent was He in the whole of His deportment and conduct, that He even submits to have His case issued and determined by what His hearers should say of Him; and these not His friends, but His enemies; see *Isa. 50:8*;

behold, they, or these,

know what I have said. Pointing at some persons present, perhaps the very officers who had been sent to take Him before, but returned without Him, declaring that never man spake like Him [see *John 7:46*].

Verse 22. **And when he had thus spoken**, &c. What was so right and reasonable, in so becoming a manner, without heat or passion:

one of the officers which stood by; it may be one of those who had been sent to Him, and had been a hearer of Him, whom Jesus might look wistfully at, or point unto, when He said the above words, at which he might be provoked: and therefore,

struck Jesus with the palm of his hand; or gave him a rap with a rod, or smote Him with a staff, as some think, is the sense of the phrase; though the Syriac, agreeable to our version, reads it, he smote Him, על לועוהי, *upon his cheek*; gave Him, what we commonly call, *a slap on the face*; and which is always esteemed a very great affront, and was a piece of rudeness and insolence to the last degree in this man:

saying, Answerest thou the high priest so? This he said, as well as gave the blow, either out of flattery to the high priest, or to clear himself from being a favorer of Christ; which, by what had been said, he might think would be suspected: some have thought this was Malchus, whose ear Christ had healed; if so, he was guilty of great ingratitude.

Verse 23. **Jesus answered him**, &c. For the high priest took no notice of him, nor any of the Sanhedrin, though the action was so insolent and indecent, both as to the manner in which it was done, and the person, an officer, by whom it was done; and considering the circumstances of it, in the palace of the high priest, in his presence, and before so grand a council, and while a cause was trying; and it was a barbarous, as well as an impious action, considering the Person to whom it was done. Wherefore Jesus replies to him, without making use of His divine power as the Son of God, or discovering any warmth of spirit, and heat of passion, as a man, mildly and rationally argues with him;

If I have spoken evil, bear witness of the evil: meaning, either if He had, to his knowledge, delivered any wicked doctrine in the course of His ministry, or had at that time said any evil thing of the high priest, or any other person, He desires that he would make it to appear, and give proper proof and evidence of it:

but if well, why smitest thou me? If He had said nothing contrary to truth, reason, and good manners, then He ought not to be used and treated in such an injurious way. And moreover, the officer ought to have been corrected by the Council, and have been made to pay the two hundred *zuzim*, or pence, the fine for such an affront, according to the Jewish canon, or more, according to the dignity of the person abused.[30]

---

[30] Mishna Bava Kama, c. 8. sect. 6.

Verse 24. **Now Annas had sent him bound**, &c. As he found Him, when the captain, band, and officers brought Jesus to him; who having pleased himself with so agreeable a sight, and had asked Him some few questions, and perhaps insulted Him, sent Him away in this manner,

unto Caiaphas the high priest. His son-in-law, as the more proper person to be examined before; and especially as the grand council was sitting at his house. This was done before Peter's first denial of Christ; which, it is plain, was in the palace of the high priest, and not in Annas's house; though there seems no reason on this account to place these words at the end of the *13th verse*, as they are by some, since they manifestly refer to time past, and do not at all obscure or hinder the true order of the history, as standing here.

Verse 25. **And Simon Peter stood and warmed himself**, &c. This is repeated from *verse 18* to connect the history, and carry on the thread of the account of Peter's denial of Christ, which is interrupted by inserting the examination of Christ before the high priest, which was made at the same time. Peter stood among, and continued with the servants and officers of the high priest, warming himself by a fire they had made, it being a cold night; and this proved of bad consequence to him. The company and conversation of wicked men should be abstained from; no good is gotten thereby; continuance among such is very dangerous; men are too often more concerned for their bodies than their souls; Satan baits his temptations for the fleshly and sensitive part; and that which is thought to be for good, is the occasion of hurt.

They said therefore unto him; the servants and officers, among whom he stood warming himself, having observed what the maid had said to him:

Art thou not also *one* of his disciples? Suspecting that he was, though he had denied it, and therefore press him to give a direct answer: they might observe his countenance to fall, when the maid put the question to him; there might be something in his dress, and especially in his speech, which increased the suspicion: but,

He denied *it*, and said, I am not. A second time. This denial of his being a disciple of Christ, as before, did not arise from a sense of his unworthiness to be one; nor from diffidence and distrust of a right to such a character; but from the fear of men; and being ashamed of Christ, he denies that which was his great mercy, privilege, and glory.

Verse 26. **One of the servants of the high priest**, &c. Hearing him so stiffly deny that he was a disciple of Jesus, when he had great reason to believe he was:

being *his* **kinsman, whose ear Peter cut off**; a near relation of Malchus, to whom Peter had done this injury; and who was present at the same time, and no doubt took particular notice of him; and the more, because of what he had done to his kinsman:

saith unto him,

Did not I see thee in the garden with him? As if he should have said, I saw thee with my own eyes along with Jesus, this very night in the garden, beyond Kidron, where He was apprehended, how canst thou deny it? And wilt thou stand in it so confidently, that thou art not one of His disciples?

Verse 27. **Peter then denied again**, &c. *A third time*, as the Ethiopic version renders it; and that, according to other evangelists, with cursing and swearing [see *Matt. 26:74; Mark 14:71*]; for now he was more affrighted than before, lest should he be taken up, and it be proved upon him, that he was the person that cut off Malchus's ear, he should be sentenced to a fine, or it may be some capital punishment. The fine for plucking a man's ears, and which some understand of plucking them off, was four hundred *zuzim*,[31] or, pence; which, as they answer to Roman pence, amount to twelve pounds ten shillings; a sum of money Peter perhaps could not have raised, without great difficulty: and therefore, that it might be believed he was not a disciple of Christ, so not the man; he swears in a profane manner, and imprecates the judgments of God upon him:

and immediately the cock crew. The second time; which was a signal by which he might call to remembrance what Christ had said to him; that before the cock crowed twice, he should deny Him thrice, *Mark 14:72*. It was now early in the morning, about three o'clock, or somewhat after.

Verse 28. **Then led they Jesus from Caiaphas**, &c. When Peter had denied Him, one of the officers had smote Him, the high priest had examined Him, and they thought they had enough out of His own mouth to condemn Him; they, the chief priests, elders, Scribes, and the whole multitude, led Him, bound as He was, from Caiaphas's house,

unto the hall of judgment; or the *praetorium*; the place where the Roman governor, who was now Pontius Pilate, used to hear and try causes in; the Romans now having matters and causes relating to life and death, in their hands:

---

[31] Mishna Bava Kama, c. 8, sect. 6. Vid. L'Empereur in ibid.

and it was early; the morning indeed was come; but it was as soon as it was day; they had been all night in taking and examining Jesus, and consulting what to do with Him; and as soon as they could expect the governor to be up, they hurry Him away to him, eagerly thirsting after His blood, and fearing lest He should be rescued out of their hands:

and they themselves went not into the judgment hall, lest they should be defiled; that is, the Jews, only the band of Roman soldiers went in; the reason of this was, because it was the house of a Gentile, and with them, מדורות העכ"ום טמאים, *the dwelling houses of Gentiles*, or idolaters, *are unclean*;[32] yea, if they were the houses of Israelites, and Gentiles were admitted to dwell in them, they were defiled, and all that were in them; for so they say,[33]

"If the collectors for the government enter into a house to dwell in, all in the house are defiled."

They did not think it lawful to let [*or* rent] out a house in Judea to a heathen,[34] or to assist in building a *Basilica* for them; which they explain to be a palace, in which judges sit to judge men.[35] Hence the reason of their caution, and which they were the more observant of,

that they might eat the passover. Pure and undefiled; not the passover lamb, for that they had eaten the night before; but the *Chagigah*, or feast on the fifteenth day of the month. Many Christian writers, both ancient and modern, have concluded from hence, that Christ did not keep His last passover, at the same time the Jews did; and many things are said to illustrate this matter, and justify our Lord in it. Some observe the distinction of a sacrificial, and commemorative passover; the sacrificial passover is that, in which the lamb was slain, and was fixed to a certain time and place, and there was no altering it; the commemorative passover is that, in which no lamb is slain and eaten, only a commemoration made of the deliverance of the people of Israel out of Egypt; such as is now kept by the Jews, being out of their own land, where sacrifice with them is not lawful; and this it is supposed our Lord kept, and not the former: but it does not appear that there was such a commemorative passover kept by the Jews, in our Lord's time, and while the temple stood. And supposing there was such a one allowed, and appointed for

---

[32] Mishna Oholot, c. 18. sect. 7.

[33] Maimon. Mishcab & Mosheb, c. 12. sect. 12.

[34] Mishna Avoda Zara, c. 1. sect. 8.

[35] Jarchi & Bartenora in ibid. sect. 7.

those that were at a distance from Jerusalem, and could not come up thither (which was not the case of Christ and His disciples), it is reasonable to conclude, that it was to be kept, and was kept at the time the sacrificial passover was, in the room of which it was substituted, as it is by the Jews to this day; so that this will by no means clear the matter, nor solve the difficulty; besides it is very manifest, that the passover our Lord kept was sacrificial; and such a one the disciples proposed to get ready for Him, and did, of which He and they are said to eat: *and the first day of unleavened bread, when they KILLED the passover, his disciples said to him, Where wilt thou that we go and prepare, that thou mayest EAT the passover? Mark 14:12; and again, then came the day of unleavened bread, when the passover MUST be KILLED, Luke 22:7; they made ready the passover, verse 13, and he sat down, and the twelve apostles with him, verse 14, and he said unto them, With desire I have desired to eat this passover, verse 15.* Others suggest, that this difference of observing the passover by Christ and the Jews, arose from fixing the beginning of the month, and so accordingly the feasts in it, by the φασις, or appearance of the moon; and that our Lord went according to the true appearance of it, and the Jews according to a false account: but of this, as a fact, there is no proof; besides, though the feasts were regulated and fixed according to the appearance of the moon, yet this was not left to the arbitrary will, pleasure, and judgment of particular persons, to determine as they should think proper; but the Sanhedrin, or chief council of the nation sat, at a proper time, to hear and examine witnesses about the appearance of the moon; and accordingly determined, and none might fix it but them;[36] and as this was doubtless the case at this time, it is not very reasonable to think, that Christ would differ from them: besides, it was either a clear case, or a doubtful one; if the former, then there would be no room nor reason to keep another day; and if it was the latter, then two days were observed, that they might be sure they were right;[37] but then both were kept by all the Jews. And that the time of this passover was well known, is clear from various circumstances; such and such facts were done, so many days before it; six days before it, Jesus came to Bethany, *John 12:1;* and two days before it, He was in the same place, *Matt. 26:2,6,* and says to His disciples, *Ye know that after two days is the feast of the passover,* &c. Others taking it for granted, that Christ kept the passover a day before the usual and precise time, defend it, by observing the despotic and legislative power of Christ, who had a right to dispense with the time of this feast, and could at His pleasure anticipate it, because the betraying of Him and His death were so near at hand: that He had such a power will not

---

[36] Maimon. Kiddush Hachodesh, c. 2. sect. 7, 8.

[37] Ibid. c. 5. sect. 6, 7, 8.

be disputed; but that He should use it in this way, does not seem necessary, on account of His death, seeing none but the living were obliged to it; nor so consistent with His wisdom, since hereby the mouths of His enemies would be opened against Him, for acting not agreeably to the law of God. Moreover, when it is considered that the passover, according to the Jews, was always kept במועדו, *in its set time*,[38] and was not put off on the account of the sabbath, or any thing else, to another day; and that though when it was put off for particular persons, on account of uncleanness, to another month, yet still it was to be kept on the fourteenth day at even, in that month, *Num. 9:10-11;* it will not easily be received that Christ observed it a day before the time: besides, the passover lamb was not killed in a private house, but in the temple, in the court of it, and that always on the fourteenth of Nisan, after noon: so says Maimonides,[39]

"It is an affirmative command, to slay the passover on the fourteenth of the month Nisan, after the middle of the day...The passover is not slain but in the court, as the rest of the holy things; even in the time that altars were lawful, they did not offer the passover on a private altar; and whoever offers the passover on a private altar, is to be beaten; as it is said, *Thou mayest not sacrifice the passover within any of thy gates, which the Lord thy God giveth thee, Deut. 16:5.*"

And seeing therefore a passover lamb was not to be killed at home, but in the court of the priests, in the temple, it does not seem probable, that a single lamb should be suffered to be killed there, for Christ and His disciples, on a day not observed by the Jews, contrary to the sense of the Sanhedrin, and of the whole nation. Add to this, that the sacred text is express for it, that it was at the exact time of this feast, when it was come according to general computation, that the disciples moved to Christ to prepare the passover for Him, and did, and they with Him kept it. The account Matthew gives is very full: *Now the first day of the feast of unleavened bread*; that is, when that was come in its proper time and course, *the disciples came to Jesus*; saying unto Him, *Where wilt thou that we prepare for thee to eat the passover?* He bids them go to the city to such a man, and say, *I will keep the passover at thy house with my disciples. And the disciples did as Jesus had appointed, and they made ready the passover. Now when the even was come*, the time of eating the passover, according to the law of God, *he sat down with the twelve, and as they did eat*, &c. *Matt. 26:17-20;* and Mark is still more particular, who says, *And the first day of unleavened bread, when they killed the passover;* that is, when the Jews killed the passover, on the very day the lamb was slain and

---

[38] Maimon. in Mishna Pesachim, c. 7. sect. 4. & Bartenora in ibid. c. 5. sect. 4.

[39] Hilchot Korban Pesach. c. 1. sect. 1, 3.

eaten by them; and then follows much the same account as before, *Mark 14:12-18*. And Luke yet more clearly expresses it, *Then came the day of unleavened bread, when the passover must be killed*; according to the law of God, and the common usage of the people of the Jews; yea, he not only observes, that Christ kept the usual day, but the very hour, the precise time of eating it; for he says, *And when the hour was come, he sat down, and the twelve apostles with him, Luke 22:7-14*. Nor is there any thing in this text, that is an objection to Christ and the Jews keeping the passover at the same time; since by the passover here is meant, the *Chagigah*, or feast kept on the fifteenth day of the month, as it is sometimes called. In *Deut. 16:2*, it is said, *Thou shalt therefore sacrifice the passover unto the Lord thy God, of the flock and the herd*: now the passover of the herd, can never mean the passover lamb, but the passover *Chagigah*; and so the Jewish commentators explain it; *of the herd*, says Jarchi, thou shalt sacrifice for the *Chagigah*; and says Aben Ezra, for the peace offerings: so Josiah the king is said to give for the passovers, three thousand bullocks, and the priests three hundred oxen, and the Levites five hundred oxen, *2 Chron. 35:7-9*; which Jarchi interprets of the peace offerings of the *Chagigah*, there called *passovers*; and so in [the Apocrypha] 1 Esdras 1:7-9, mention is made of three thousand calves, besides lambs, that Josias gave for the passover; and three hundred by some other persons, and seven hundred by others. The passage in Deuteronomy, is explained of the *Chagigah*, in both Talmuds,[40] and in other writings;[41] so besides the passover lamb, we read of sacrifices slain, פסח לשום, *in the name of* the passover, or *on account of* it;[42] and particularly of the calf and the young bullock, slain for the sake of the passover.[43] And now this is the passover which these men were to eat that day, and therefore were careful not to defile themselves, that so they might not be unfit for it; otherwise had it been the passover lamb in the evening, they might have washed themselves in the evening, according to the rules of, יום טבול, or *the daily washing*, and been clean enough to have eaten it: besides, it may be observed, that all the seven days were called *the passover*; and he that ate the unleavened bread, is said by eating that, to eat the passover; and thus they invite their guests daily to

---

[40] T. Hieros. Pesach. fol. 33. 1. T. Bab. Pesachim, fol. 70. 2.

[41] Maimon. Korban Pesach. c. 10. sect. 12. Moses Kotsensis Mitzvot Tora, pr. neg. 349.

[42] Mishna Pesachim, c. 6. sect. 5.

[43] T. Bab. Menachot, fol. 3. 1

eat the bread, saying,[44]

"Every one that is hungry, let him come and eat all that he needs, וֹפֶּסַח, *and keep the passover*."

It is easy to observe the consciences of these men, who were always wont to *strain at a gnat and swallow a camel* [*Matt. 23:24*]; they scruple going into the judgment hall, which belonged to a heathen governor, and where was a large number of heathen soldiers; but they could go along with these into the garden to apprehend Christ, and spend a whole night in consulting to shed innocent blood. No wonder that God should be weary of their sacrifices and ceremonious performances, when, trusting to these, they had no regard to moral precepts. However, this may be teaching to us, in what manner we should *keep the feast*, and eat of the true passover, *Christ*; not with *malice and wickedness*, as these Jews ate theirs, but with *sincerity and truth* [*1 Cor. 5:7-8*]: besides, a Sanhedrin, when they had adjudged [*or* sentenced] any one to death, were forbidden to eat any thing all that day;[45] and so while scrupling one thing, they broke through another.

Verse 29. **Pilate then went out unto them**, &c. Either into the street, or rather into the place called *the pavement*, and in Hebrew *Gabbatha*; see *chapter 19:13;* the place where the Jewish Sanhedrin used to sit; wherefore, in complaisance to them, since they would not come into his court of judicature, he condescends to go into one of theirs, which showed great civility and humanity in him:

and said, What accusation bring ye against this man? Meaning, what offense had He committed? What crime had they to charge Him with? What did they accuse Him of? And what proof had they to support their charge? His view was, to have the matter stated, the cause opened, and evidence given; that the accused being face to face with the accusers, might answer for Himself; and he, as a judge, be capable of judging between them: all which were very commendable in him, and agreeable to the Roman laws; and have an appearance of equity, justice, and impartiality.

Verse 30. **They answered and said unto him**, &c. Offended at the question put to them, and filled with indignation that they should be so interrogated, with an air of haughtiness and insolence reply to him:

If he were not a malefactor, we would not have delivered him up unto thee. Insinuating, that He was guilty of some very wicked action; not merely

---

[44]   Haggadah Shel Pesach. p. 4. Ed. Rittangel.

[45]   T. Bab. Sanhedrin, fol. 63. 1. Maimon. Hilch. Sanhedrin, c. 13. sect. 4.

of a breach of some of their laws peculiar to them; for then they would have tried and judged Him according to them, and not have brought Him before Pilate; but they suggest, that He was guilty of some malpractices cognizable by Caesar's court; and which they did not care to mention expressly, lest they should not succeed, not having, it may be, as yet their witnesses ready; and hoped he would have taken their own word for it, without any further proof, they being men of such rank and dignity, and of so much knowledge, learning, and religion; and therefore took it ill of him, that he should ask such persons as they were, so famous for their prudence, integrity, and sanctity, such a question: however, they own themselves to be the betrayers and deliverers up of our Lord, which Christ had before foretold, and which Stephen afterwards charged them with.

Verse 31. **Then said Pilate unto them**, &c. Either ironically, knowing that they did not, or it was not in their power, to judge in capital causes; or seriously, and with some indignation, abhorring such a method of procedure they would have had him gone into, to condemn a man without knowing his crime, and having evidence of it:

Take ye him, and judge him according to your law. This he said, as choosing to understand them in no other sense, than that He had broken some peculiar law of theirs, though they had otherwise suggested; and as giving them liberty to take Him away to one of their courts, and proceed against Him as their law directed, and inflict some lesser punishment on Him than death, such as scourging, &c. which they still had a power to do, and did make use of:

The Jews therefore said unto him, It is not lawful for us to put any man to death; thereby insinuating, that He was guilty of a crime which deserved death, and which they could not inflict; not that they were of such tender consciences, that they could not put Him to death, or that they had no law to punish Him with death, provided He was guilty; but because judgments in capital cases had ceased among them; nor did they try causes relating to life and death, the date of which they often make to be forty years before the destruction of the temple;[46] and which was much about, or a little before the time these words were spoken: not that this power was taken away wholly from them by the Romans; though since their subjection to the empire, they had not that full and free exercise of it as before; but through the great increase of iniquity, particularly murder, which caused such frequent

---

[46] T. Bab. Sabbat, fol. 15. 1. Sanhedrin, fol. 41. 1. T. Hieros. Sanhedrin, fol. 18. 1. & 24. 2. Juchasin, fol. 51. 1. Moses Kotsensis pr. affirm. 99.

executions, that they were weary of them;[47] and through the negligence and indolence of the Jewish Sanhedrin, and their removal from the room *Gazith*, where they only judged capital causes:[48] as for the stoning of Stephen, and the putting of some to death against whom Saul gave his voice [see *Acts 22:4*], these were the outrages of the zealots, and were not according to a formal process in any court of judicature. Two executions are mentioned in their Talmud; the one is of a priest's daughter that was burnt for a harlot,[49] and the other of the stoning of Ben Stada in Lydda;[50] the one, according to them, seems to be before, the other after the destruction of the temple; but these dates are not certain, nor to be depended upon: for since the destruction of their city and temple, and their being carried captive into other lands, it is certain that the power of life and death has been wholly taken from them; by which it appears, that the scepter is removed from Judah, and a lawgiver from between his feet [see *Gen. 49:10*]; and this they own almost in the same words as here expressed; for they say[51] of a certain man worthy of death,

"Why dost thou scourge him? He replies, Because he lay with a beast. They say to him, Hast thou any witnesses? He answers, Yes; Elijah came in the form of a man, and witnessed. They say, If it be so, he deserves to die. To which he answers, *From the day we have been carried captive out of our land,* לית לן רשותא למקטל, *we have no power to put to death.*"

But at this time, their power was not entirely gone; but the true reason of their saying these words is, that they might wholly give up Christ to the Roman power, and throw off the reproach of His death from themselves; and particularly they were desirous He should die the reproachful and painful death of the cross, which was a Roman punishment: had they taken Him and judged Him according to their law, which must have been as a false prophet, or for blasphemy or idolatry, the death they must have adjudged Him to, would have been stoning; but it was crucifixion they were set upon; and therefore deliver Him up as a traitor, and a seditious person, in order thereunto.

---

[47] T. Bab. Avoda Zara fol. 8. 2. Juchasin, fol. 21. 1.

[48] Gloss. in T. Bab. Avoda Zara, fol. 8. 2.

[49] T. Hieros. Sanhedrin, fol. 24. 2.

[50] Ibid. fol. 25. 4.

[51] T. Bab. Beracot, fol. 58. 1.

Verse 32. **That the saying of Jesus might be fulfilled**, &c. That He should be delivered by the Jews to the Gentiles, to crucify Him; and that He should be lifted up from the earth, and as the serpent upon the pole:

which he spake, signifying what death he should die. *Matt. 20:19; John 12:32-33* and *3:14;* and which was brought about this way, by the providence of God conducting this whole affair; and was cheerfully submitted to by Christ, in great love to His people, to redeem them from the curse of the law, being hereby made a curse for them.

Verse 33. **Then Pilate entered into the judgment hall again**, &c. Where he went at first, but the Jews refusing to come in thither to him, he came out to them; and now they speaking out more plainly, that He was guilty of a crime deserving of death; as that He set up Himself as a king, in opposition to Caesar, and taught the people not to pay tribute to him; he goes into the *praetorium* again,

and called Jesus; beckoned, or sent for Him; or ordered Him to come in thither to him, that he might alone, and the more freely, converse with Him; which Jesus did, paying no regard to the superstitious observances of the Jews:

and said unto him, Art thou the king of the Jews? This he might say, from a rumor that was generally spread, that there was such a person to come, and was born; and by many it was thought, that Jesus was he; and particularly from the charge of the Jews against Him, which though not here expressed, is elsewhere; see *Luke 23:2.* Wherefore Pilate was the more solicitous about the matter, on account of Caesar, and lest he should be charged with dilatoriness and negligence in this affair: some read these words not by way of question, but affirmation, *Thou art the king of the Jews*; which method he might make use of, the more easily to get it out of Him, whether He was or not: and to this reading, Christ's answer in the next verse seems best to agree.

Verse 34. **Jesus answered him, Sayest thou this thing of thyself**, &c. That He was the king of the Jews: Christ's meaning is, whether he asserted this from the sentiments of his own mind; or moved the question from any thing he himself had observed, which might give him just ground to suspect that He had, or intended to set up Himself as the king of that nation:

or did others tell it thee of me? Whether the Jews had not intimated some such thing to him, out of malice and ill will? Not but that Christ full well knew, where the truth of this lay; but He was desirous of convincing Pilate of his weakness, if he so judged of himself, and of his imprudence and hastiness, if he took up this from others; and also to expose the baseness and wickedness of the Jews, to charge Him with this, when they themselves would have made Him a temporal king, and He refused; and when He had not only paid tribute Himself to Caesar, but had exhorted them to do the like.

Verse 35. **Pilate answered, Am I a Jew**? &c. This he said, in a sort of derision and contempt; who was not a Jew, neither by birth, nor by religion, and so had never imbibed any notions of their King Messiah, nor read any thing about Him; and knew nothing of His distinguishing characters and properties, by which He was described, and might be known; and therefore it remained, that what he had said, though not expressed, was not of himself, of his own knowledge or observation, but arose from some intimations and suggestions the Jews had given him:

Thine own nation and the chief priests have delivered thee unto me; that is, the men of His nation, His countrymen the Jews, who best understood their own laws and books of prophecy; and what expectations they had formed from thence, concerning their king, and His kingdom; and the principal of the priesthood, who were accounted men of the greatest learning, piety, and integrity, they had brought Him bound before him; they had entered a charge against Him, and had delivered Him up into his hands, as an enemy to Caesar, and a traitor to his government:

what hast thou done? As an occasion of such treatment, and as the foundation of such a charge; surely there must be something in it, or men of such character would never impeach a man altogether innocent, and one of their own country too!

Verse 36. **Jesus answered, My kingdom is not of this world**, &c. By saying which, He tacitly owned He was a king: as such He was set up, and anointed by His Father from everlasting; was prophesied of in the Old Testament; declared by the angel, both when He brought the news of His conception, and of His birth; was owned by many, who knew Him to be so *in the days of his flesh* [*Heb. 5:7*]; and since His resurrection, ascension, and session at God's right hand, more manifestly appears to be one: He also hereby declares, that He had a kingdom; by which He means, not His natural and universal kingdom, as God, and the Creator and Governor of all things; but His mediatorial kingdom, administered both in the days of His flesh, and after His resurrection; which includes the whole Gospel dispensation, Christ's visible church state on earth, and the whole election of grace; it takes in that which will be at the close of time, in the latter day, which will be more spiritual, and in which Christ will reign before His ancients gloriously; and also the kingdom of God, or of heaven, even the ultimate glory: the whole of which is not of this world; the subjects of Christ's kingdom are not of the world, they are chosen and called out of it; the kingdom itself does not appear in worldly pomp and splendor, nor is it supported by worldly force, nor administered by worldly laws; nor does it so much regard the outward, as the inward estates of men; it promises no worldly emoluments, or temporal rewards. Christ does not say it is not *in* this world, but it is not *of* it; and therefore will not fail, when this world does, and the kingdoms thereof. Every thing that is carnal, sensual, and worldly, must be removed from our conceptions of Christ's kingdom, here or hereafter: and to this agrees what some Jewish writers say of the Messiah, and His affairs:

> "The Messiah (they say,[52]) is separated from the world, because he is absolutely intellectual; but the world is corporeal; how then should the Messiah be in this world, when the world is corporeal, and, לא גשמי עניין המשיח הוא אלהי, *the business of the Messiah is divine, and not corporeal?*"

And since this was the case, Caesar's, or any civil government, had no reason to be uneasy on account of His being a king, and having a kingdom; since His kingdom and interests did not in the least break in upon, or injure any others: and that this was the nature of His kingdom, He proves by the following reason;

if my kingdom were of this world, then would my servants fight, that I should not be delivered to the Jews: if Christ's kingdom had been a worldly one, set up on worldly views, and governed with worldly policy, and was to answer some worldly ends, Christ would have had servants enough among the Jews, who would have declared for Him, and taken up arms in His favor against the Romans; His own disciples would not have suffered Him to have been betrayed into the hands of the Jews by Judas; nor would He have hindered them from attempting His rescue, as He did Peter; nor would they suffer Him now to be delivered by Pilate into their hands, to put Him to death; since they had such a Prince at the head of them, who, was He to make use of His power, was able to drive all the Roman forces before them out of the nation, and oblige a general submission among the Jews, to the scepter of His kingdom:

but now is my kingdom not from hence. It does not rise out of, nor proceed upon, nor is it supported by worldly principles, wherefore none of the above methods are made use of.

---

[52] R. Juda Bezaleel Nizeach Israel, fol. 48.

Verse 37. **Pilate therefore said unto him**, &c. Upon this free and full declaration of Christ, concerning His kingly office, and the nature of His kingdom:

Art thou a king then? Or *Thou art a king then*: for, from His having a kingdom, it might be very justly inferred that He was a king:

Jesus answered, Thou sayest that I am a king. And which was very rightly said; and Christ by these words owns and confesses that He was one: adding,

To this end was I born, and for this cause came I into the world, that I should bear witness unto the truth. The end of Christ's being born, which was of a virgin, in a very miraculous manner, and of His coming into the world, which was by the assumption of human nature, among many other things, was to bear testimony to truth in general; to the whole Gospel, the Word of truth, and every branch of it, which He brought with Him, constantly preached in His life, and confirmed by His death; and particularly to this truth, that He was a King, and had a Kingdom in a spiritual sense:

Every one that is of the truth; that is of God, belongs to the sheep of Christ, knows the truth as it is in Jesus, and is on the side of truth, and stands by it:

heareth my voice. The voice of His Gospel; and that not only externally, but internally; so as to approve of it, rejoice at it, and distinguish it; and the voice of His commands, so as cheerfully to obey them from a principle of love to Him.

Verse 38. **Pilate saith unto him, What is truth?** &c. That is, in general, or that which Christ then particularly spoke of. Many things might be observed in answer to this question, as that there is the truth and faithfulness of God in His Word and promises; the truth of grace in the hearts of His people; Jesus Christ Himself is truth, He is true God, and true man; the truth of all covenant transactions, of all types, promises, and prophecies; whatever He said and taught, was truth, and the truth of all doctrine comes from Him. The Gospel is truth in general; it comes from the God of truth; lies in the Scriptures of truth; Christ, who is truth itself, is the substance of it; the Spirit of truth has a hand in it, leads into it, and makes it effectual; the whole of it is true, and every particular doctrine of it; as the manifestation of the Son of God in human nature, His coming into the world to save the chief of sinners, justification by His righteousness, pardon by His blood, atonement by His sacrifice, the resurrection of the dead, &c. The same question is put in the

Talmud,[53] מה אמת, *What is truth?* And it is answered, That He is the living God, and the King of the world: we do not find that our Lord gave any answer to this question, which might be put in a scornful, jeering way; nor did Pilate wait for one; for,

when he had said this, he went out again unto the Jews: as soon as he had put the question about truth, having no great inclination to hear what Christ would say to it; nor did he put it for information sake, or as having any opinion of Christ, and that He was able to answer it; he directly goes out of the judgment hall, taking Jesus along with him, and addresses the Jews after this manner:

and saith unto them, I find in him no fault *at all*. And indeed how should he? There was no sin in His nature, nor guile in His lips, nor any iniquity in His life; the devil himself could find none in Him. This confession is both to the shame of Pilate and the Jews; to the reproach of Pilate, that after this he should condemn Him; and of the Jews, that after such a fair and full declaration from the judge, they should insist upon His crucifixion; it shows, however, that He died not for any sin of His own, but for the sins of others.

Verse 39. **But ye have a custom**, &c. Not a law, either of God or man's, but a custom; and which was not originally observed at the feast of the passover, and perhaps was not of any long standing; but what the Roman governors, by the order of Caesar, or of their own pleasure, had introduced to ingratiate themselves into the affections of the people; and being repeated once and again, was now looked for:

that I should release unto you one at the passover; which was at this time; and more than one it seems it was not customary to release:

will ye therefore that I release unto you the King of the Jews? Who they had said called Himself so, and was so accounted by others, and which Pilate says, in a sneering, sarcastic way; though he was heartily willing to release Him, and was in hopes they would have agreed to it, since nothing could be proved against Him; however, he proposes it to them, and leaves it to their option.

Verse 40. **Then cried they all again**, &c. For it seems that Pilate had made this proposal once before, and that this was the second time, though not mentioned; yet some copies, and the Syriac, Arabic, Persic, and Ethiopic

---

[53] T. Hieros. Sanhedrin, fol. 18. 1.

versions, leave out the word *again*: they all, priests and people, in a very clamorous manner, cried out as one man, with one united voice, all at once;

saying, Not this man, but Barabbas. Now Barabbas was a robber. Who was an emblem of God's elect in a state of nature, released and set free when Christ was condemned. These, as he, many of them at least, are notorious sinners, the chief of sinners, robbers and murderers; who have robbed God of His glory, and destroyed themselves; are prisoners, concluded in sin and unbelief [see *Gal. 3:22; Rom. 11:32*], and shut up in the law [see *Gal. 3:23*], and in a *pit wherein is no water* [*Zech. 9:11*], in their nature-state; and were, as this man, worthy of death, and by nature *children of wrath* [*Eph. 2:3*]; and yet children of God by adopting grace, as his name *Bar Abba* signifies, *the son of the father*: these, though such criminals, and so deserving of punishment, were let go free, when Christ was taken, condemned, and died; and which was according to the wise and secret counsel of *Jehovah*, and is a large discovery of divine grace; and what lays those who are released, under the greatest obligations to live to Him who suffered for them, in their room and stead.

CHAPTER 19

Verse 1. **Then Pilate therefore took Jesus**, &c. Finding that the Jews would not agree to His release, but that Barabbas was the person they chose, and being very desirous, if possible, to save His life, thought of this method: he ordered Jesus to be taken by the proper officers,

and scourged *him*. That is, commanded Him to be scourged by them; which was done by having [*or* taking] Him to a certain place, where being stripped naked, and fastened to a pillar, He was severely whipped: and this he did, hoping the Jews would be satisfied therewith, and agree to His dismission; but though he did this with such a view, yet it was a very unjust action in him to scourge a man that he himself could find no fault in. However, it was what was foretold by Christ Himself, and was an emblem of those strokes and scourges of divine justice He endured, as the surety of His people, in His soul, in their stead; and His being scourged, though innocent, shows, that it was not for His own, but the sins of others; and expresses the vile nature of sin, the strictness of justice, and the grace, condescension, and patience of Christ: and this may teach us not to think it strange that any of the saints should endure

564

scourgings, in a literal sense; and to bear patiently the scourgings and chastisements of our heavenly Father, and not to fear the overflowing scourge or wrath of God, since Christ has borne this in our room.

Verse 2. **And the soldiers platted a crown of thorns**, &c. This was an emblem of His being surrounded by wicked men, *sons of Belial* [see *2 Sam. 23:6*], comparable to *thorns*, while He hung suffering on the cross; and of the sins of His people compassing Him about, which were as thorns, very grievous to Him; and of His various troubles in life, and of His being made a curse for us at death; thorns being the produce of the curse upon the earth [see *Gen. 3:17-18*]:

and put *it* on his head: not only by way of derision, as mocking at His character, the King of the Jews, but in order to afflict and distress Him:

and they put on him a purple robe; Matthew calls it *a scarlet robe* [*Matt. 27:28*]; and the Arabic and Persic versions here, *a red* one. It very probably was one of the soldiers' coats, which are usually red: this was still in derision of Him as a king, and was an emblem of His being clothed with our purple and scarlet sins [see *Isa. 1:18*], and of the bloody sufferings of His human nature for them, and through which we come to have a purple covering, or to be justified by His blood, and even to be made truly kings, as well as priests, unto God [*e.g. Rev. 1:6* and *5:10*].

Verse 3. **And said, Hail, King of the Jews!** &c. Some copies before this clause read, *and they came unto him*; and so read the Vulgate Latin, Arabic, Coptic, and Ethiopic versions; that is, they came and prostrated themselves before Him; bowed the knee unto Him, and addressed Him in a mock way, as if He was an earthly monarch just come to His crown, and whom they wished long to live; thus mocking at His kingly office, and despising Him under that character, as many do now: some will not have Him to reign over them, but reject Him as King; and others, though in words they own Him to be King, yet disregard His commands, and act no better part than these scoffing soldiers did:

and they smote him with their hands. *Upon His cheeks*, as the Syriac version reads it. These, and many other affronts they gave Him; in all which they were indulged by Pilate, and was a pleasing scene to the wicked Jews, whose relentless hearts were not in the least moved hereby, though Pilate hoped they would; and which was his view in allowing the soldiers to use such incivilities and indecencies to Him.

Verse 4. **Pilate therefore went forth again**, &c. When all this was done to Jesus, Pilate went again out of the judgment hall, or however from the place where Jesus had been scourged, and ill used in the manner He was: he went a little before Him unto the Jews that stood without,

and saith unto them, Behold I bring him forth unto you; that is, he had ordered Him to be brought forth by the soldiers, and they were just bringing Him in the sad miserable condition in which He was, that the Jews might see with their own eyes how He had been used:

that ye may know that I find no fault in him. For by seeing what was done to Him, how severely He had been scourged, and in what derision and contempt He had been had, and what barbarity had been exercised on Him, they might know and believe, that if Pilate did all this, or allowed of it to be done to a man whom he judged innocent, purely to gratify the Jews; that had he found any thing in Him worthy of death, he would not have stopped here, but would have ordered the execution of Him; of this they might assure themselves by his present conduct. Pilate, by his own confession, in treating, or suffering to be treated in so cruel and ignominious a manner, one that he himself could find no fault in, or cause of accusation against, was guilty of great injustice.

Verse 5. **Then came Jesus forth**, &c. Out of the judgment hall, or place where He had been scourged, as soon as Pilate had said these words:

wearing the crown of thorns, and the purple robe. With His temples scratched and torn with the thorny crown, and the blood running down from thence, and His face and eyes swollen with the blows He had received from their closed fists, and all besmeared with His own blood, and the soldiers' spittle; His body appearing to be almost of the same color with the purple or scarlet robe, through the stripes and lashes He had received, when that was thrown back.

And *Pilate* saith unto them, Behold the man! Not their king, that would have provoked them; though he did say so afterwards, when he found he could not prevail upon them to agree to His release; but *the man*, to move their compassion; signifying, that He was a man as they were, and that they ought to use Him as such, and treat Him with humanity and pity; and that He was a poor despicable man, as the condition He was in showed; and that it was a weak thing in them to fear any thing with respect to any change of, or influence in, civil government from one that made such a figure; and therefore should be satisfied with what had been done to Him, and dismiss Him.

Verse 6. **When the chief priests therefore and officers saw him**, &c. In this piteous condition, in His mock dress, and having on Him all the marks of cruel usage, enough to have moved a heart of stone: and though they were the principal men of the priesthood, and who made great pretensions to religion and piety, and the officers were their servants and attendants, and all of them used to sacred employments; which might have been thought would have at least influenced them to the exercise of humanity and compassion to fellow creatures; yet instead of being affected with this sight, and wrought upon by it, to have agreed to His release, as Pilate hoped,

they cried out, saying, Crucify *him*, crucify *him*. Which was done in a very noisy and clamorous way; and the repetition of their request shows their malignity, vehemence, and impatience; and remarkable it is, that they should call for, and desire that kind of death the Scriptures had pointed out that the Messiah should die, and which was predicted by Christ Himself.

Pilate saith unto them, Take ye him, and crucify *him*: for I find no fault in him. This was not leave to do it, as appears from the reason he gives, in which the innocence of Christ is again asserted; nor did the Jews take it in this light, as is evident from their reply; and it is clear, that after this Pilate thought he had a power either to release or crucify Him; and he did afterwards seek to release Him; and the Jews made a fresh request to crucify Him; upon which He was delivered to be crucified: but this was said in a way of indignation, and as abhorring the action; and is an ironical concession, and a bitter sarcasm upon them, that men that professed so much religion and sanctity, could be guilty of such iniquity, as to desire the death of one that no fault could be found in; and therefore, if such were their consciences, for his part, he desired to have no concern in so unrighteous an action; but if they would, they must even do it themselves.

Verse 7. **The Jews answered him,** &c. Finding they could make nothing of the charge of sedition against Him, and that Pilate could not be prevailed upon to adjudge Him to death upon that score, they try another method, and charge Him with blasphemy; which, if the other had succeeded, they would have concealed; because this, if proved, according to their law, would not have brought on Him the kind of death they were desirous of:

We have a law; meaning the law of Moses, which they had received by his hands from God:

and by our law he ought to die; referring either to the law concerning blasphemy in general, or concerning the false prophet, or to the having and asserting of other gods, and enticing to the worship of them; in either of which cases death by stoning was enjoined:

because he made himself the Son of God. The natural and essential Son of God; not by adoption, or on account of His incarnation and mediatorial office; but as being one with the Father, of the same nature with Him, and equal to Him in all His perfections and glory. This He had often asserted in His ministry, or what was equivalent to it, and which they so understood; and indeed had said that very morning, before the high priest in his palace, what amounted thereunto, and which he so interpreted; upon which he rent his garments, and charged Him with blasphemy: for that God has a Son, is denied by the Jews, since Jesus asserted Himself to be so, though formerly believed by them; nor was it now denied that there was a Son of God, or that He was expected; but the blasphemy with them was, that Jesus set up Himself to be He. But now it is vehemently opposed by them, that God has a Son; so from *Eccl. 4:8,* they endeavor to prove,[1] that God has neither a brother, וֹלֹא בֵן, *nor a son;* but, *hear, O Israel,* they observe, *the Lord our God is one Lord.* And elsewhere:[2]

> *"there is one;* this is the holy blessed God; *and not a second;* for he has
> no partner or equal in his world; *yea, he hath neither child nor brother;*
> he hath no brother, nor hath he a son; but the holy blessed God loves
> Israel, and calls them his children, and his brethren."

All which is opposed to the Christian doctrine relating to the Sonship of Christ. The conduct of these men, at this time, deserves notice, as their craft in imposing on Pilate's ignorance of their laws; and the little regard that they themselves had to them, in calling for crucifixion instead of stoning; and their inconsistency with themselves, pretending before, it was not lawful for them to put any man to death; and now they *have a law,* and *by that law,* in their judgment, *he ought to die.*

Verse 8. **When Pilate therefore heard that saying**, &c. That Jesus had asserted Himself to be the Son of God, and that the Jews had a law to put such a person to death that was guilty of such blasphemy:

he was the more afraid; he was afraid to put Him to death, or to consent to it before; partly on account of his wife's message to him [see *Matt. 27:19*], and partly upon a conviction of the innocence of Christ in his own conscience: and now he was more afraid, since here was a charge brought against Him he did not well understand the meaning of; and a law of theirs pretended to be violated hereby, which should he pay no regard to, might occasion a tumult, since they were already become very clamorous and noisy; and he might be the more uneasy, lest the thing they charged Him with asserting, should be really fact; that He was one of the gods come down in the likeness of man; or that He was some demigod at least, or so nearly related to deity, that it might

---

[1]   Debarim Rabba, sect. 2. fol. 237. 3.

[2]   Midrash Kohelet, fol. 70. 1.

be dangerous for him to have any thing to do with Him this way: and in this suspicion he might be strengthened, partly from the writings of the heathens, which speak of such sort of beings; and partly from the miracles he might have heard were performed by Jesus; and also by calling to mind what He had lately said to him, that His kingdom was not of this world, and that He was come into it to bear witness to the truth.

Verse 9. **And went again into the judgment hall**, &c. From whence he came out, taking Jesus along with him, in order to interrogate Him alone upon this head:

and saith unto Jesus, Whence art thou? Meaning, not of what country He was, for he knew He was of the nation of the Jews; nor in what place He was born, whether at Bethlehem, or at Nazareth, for this was no concern of his; but from whence He sprung, who were His ancestors, and whether His descent was from the gods, or from men; and if from the former, from which of them; for as Pilate was a heathen, he must be supposed to speak as such:

But Jesus gave him no answer. For his question was frivolous, and deserved none; and besides, He was not worthy of one, who had used Him so ill, when he knew in his own conscience that He was innocent; nor was he capable of taking in an answer, or able to judge whether it was right or wrong; and since Christ was come to die for the salvation of His people, it was not proper He should say any thing that might be a means of hindering it.

Verse 10. **Then saith Pilate unto him**, &c. Being angry with Him, resenting His silence, and looking upon it as a contempt of him;

Speakest thou not unto me? He wondered that He stood in no fear of him, who was the Roman governor, His judge; who had the power of life and death; and that He should make no answer to him, who was in so much dignity, and in so high and exalted a station:

knowest thou not that I have power to crucify thee, and have power to release thee? Proudly boasting of his authority to do one or the other. The sudden change of the man from fear, to vain and proud boasting, is to be observed; just now he was afraid of the divine power of Christ, lest He should have any divinity in Him; and now he boasts and brags of his own power, and menaces and threatens with his authority to punish with death, even the death of the cross; in which he discovers his wickedness, as a magistrate, to endeavor to terrify one that he himself believed to be innocent. And besides, his assertion is false; for he had no power, neither from God nor man, to crucify innocent men, and release criminals: and moreover, he himself must be self-condemned, who had a power, as he says, of releasing Him, and yet did not do it, though he had once and again declared he found no fault in Him.

Verse 11. **Jesus answered**, &c. With great intrepidity and courage, with freedom and boldness, as being not at all dismayed with his threatenings, or affected with his proud boasts, and in order to expose the vanity of them:

Thou couldst have no power at all against me, except it were given thee from above: meaning, not from the Jewish Sanhedrin, whose court of judicature was in the temple, which was higher than the other part of the city; nor from the Roman emperor, or senate of Rome, the higher powers; by whom Pilate was made governor of Judea, and a judge in all causes relating to life and death; but reference is had to the place from whence He came, and to the decree and council of God above, and the agreement between the eternal three in heaven. Christ speaks of a power he had against Him, that is, of taking away His life; he had no lawful power to do it at all; nor any power, right or wrong, had it not been given him by God: and which is to be ascribed, not merely to the general providence of God, without which nothing is done in this world; but to the *determinate counsel* of God, relating to this particular action of the crucifying of Christ [see *Acts 2:22-23*]; otherwise Christ, as God, could have struck Pilate His judge with death immediately, and without so doing could as easily have escaped out of his hands, as He had sometimes done out of the hands of the Jews; and, as man and Mediator, He could have prayed to His Father for, and have had, more than twelve legions of angels, which would soon have rescued Him. But this was not to be; power was given to Pilate from heaven against Him; not for any evil He Himself had committed, or merely to gratify the envy and malice of the Jews, but for the salvation of God's elect, and for the glorifying of the divine perfections: and to this the Jews themselves agree in general,

> "that all the things of this world depend on above; and when they agree above first (they say[3]), they agree below; and that there is no power below, until that דאתייהיב שולטנותא לעילא, *power is given from above*; and the whole of that depends on this:"

therefore he that delivered me unto thee, hath the greater sin. דילך מן, *than thine*, as the Syriac version adds; and to the same purpose the Persic. Pilate had been guilty of sin already in scourging Christ, and suffering the Roman soldiers to abuse Him; and would be guilty of a greater in delivering Him up to be crucified, who he knew was innocent: but the sin of Judas in delivering Him into the hands of the chief priests and elders, and of the chief priest and elders and people of the Jews, in delivering Him to Pilate to crucify

---

[3] Zohar in Gen. fol. 99. 1.

Him, according to the Roman manner, were greater, inasmuch as theirs proceeded from malice and envy, and was done against greater light and knowledge; for by His works, miracles, and ministry, as well as by their own prophecies, they might, or must have known, that He was the Messiah, and Son of God. And it is to be observed, that as there is a difference in sin, and that all sins are not equal, the circumstances of things making an alteration; so that God's decree concerning the delivery of His Son into the hands of sinful men, does not excuse the sin of the betrayers of Him.

Verse 12. **And from thenceforth Pilate sought to release him**, &c. From the time that Christ spoke the above words; or, as the Syriac version renders it, מטול הדא, *because of this*, or on account of the words He had spoken; to which agree the Arabic and Ethiopic versions: he sought by all means, and studied every way to bring the Jews to agree to His release. His reasons were, because of the consciousness of guilt, and the danger of contracting more; the sense he might have of a Divine Being, to whom he was accountable for the exercise of his power; his suspicion that Jesus was the Son of God, or that He was more than a man; for he perceived that power went along with His words, by the effect they had on him: but though he sought to release Him, he did not do it, nor use the power he boasted he had; the reason in himself was, he was desirous, that the Jews would concur with him; the secret one in providence was, God would not have it so; and yet things must be carried to this pitch, that it might appear that Christ suffered not for His own sins, but ours, and that He suffered willingly:

but the Jews cried out, saying, If thou let this man go, thou art not Caesar's friend: these were the chief priests, Scribes, and elders of the people, more especially, and by whom the common people were stirred up to request His crucifixion: these still made a greater outcry, and in a more clamorous way urged, that should He be released, Pilate would show but little regard to Caesar, by whom he was raised to this dignity; who had put him into this trust; whom he represented, and in whose name he acted. This was a piece of craftiness in them, for nothing could more nearly affect Pilate, than an insinuation of want of friendship and fidelity to Tiberius, who was then Caesar, or emperor; and also, it was an instance of great hypocrisy in them, to pretend a regard to Caesar, when they scrupled paying tribute to him, and would have been glad, at any rate, to have been free from his yoke and government; and is a very spiteful hint, and carries in it a sort of threatening to Pilate, as if they would bring a charge against him to Caesar, should he let Jesus go with His life, whom they in a contemptuous manner call *this man*: adding,

whosoever maketh himself a king, speaketh against Caesar. Returning to their former charge of sedition, finding that that of blasphemy had not its effect. Their reasoning is very fallacious, and mere sophistry; for though it might be allowed that whoever set up himself as a temporal king in any of Caesar's dominions, must be an enemy of his, a rebel against him; and such a declaration might be truly interpreted as high treason; yet Christ did not give out that He was such a king, but, on the contrary, that His kingdom was not of this world, and therefore did not assume to Himself any part of Caesar's dominions and government; and though the Jews would have taken Him by force, and made Him a king, He refused it, and got out of their hands.

Verse 13. **When Pilate therefore heard that saying**, &c. Of the Jews, that a dismission of Jesus would show an unfriendliness to Caesar; and gave very broad hints, that they would accuse him to Caesar of treachery and unfaithfulness, in letting go a man, that made pretensions to be a king in his territories; and knowing well the jealousies and suspicions of Tiberius, and fearing lest it would turn to his own disrepute and disadvantage, immediately,

he brought Jesus forth, out of the judgment hall, the place where He had been examined in; not to declare His innocence, nor to move their pity, nor to release Him, but to pass sentence on Him;

and he,

sat down in the judgment seat: for that purpose. He had sat but little all this while, but was continually going in and out to examine Jesus, and converse with the Jews; but he now takes his place, and sits down as a judge, in order to give the finishing stroke to this affair; and where he sat down, was,

in the place that is called the Pavement, but in the Hebrew, Gabbatha. This place, in the Greek tongue, was called *Lithostrotos*; or *the pavement of stones*, as the Syriac version renders it: it is thought to be the room *Gazith*, in which the Sanhedrin sat in the temple when they tried capital causes;[4] and it was so called, because it was paved with smooth, square, hewn stones:

> "it was in the north part; half of it was holy, and half of it common; and it had two doors, one for that part which was holy, and another for that which was common; and in that half which was common the Sanhedrin sat."[5]

---

[4] Gloss. in T. Bab. Avoda Zara, fol. 8. 2.

[5] T. Bab. Yoma, fol. 25. 1. Maimon. Hilch. Beth Habbechira, c. 5. sect. 17. Bartenora in Mishna Middot, c. 5. sect. 3.

So that into this part of it, and by this door, Pilate, though a Gentile, might enter. This place, in the language of the Jews, who at this time spoke Syriac, was *Gabbatha*, from its height, as it should seem; though the Syriac and Persic versions read *Gaphiphtha*, which signifies a fence, or an enclosure. Mention is made in the Talmud[6] of the upper *Gab* in the mountain of the house; but whether the same with this *Gabbatha*, and whether this is the same with the chamber *Gazith*, is not certain. The Septuagint use the same word as John here does, and call by the same name the pavement of the temple on which the Israelites fell and worshiped God, *2 Chron. 7:3*.

Verse 14. **And it was the preparation of the passover**, &c. So the Jews[7] say, that Jesus suffered on the eve of the passover; and the author of the blasphemous account of His life says,[8] it was the eve both of the passover and the sabbath; which account so far agrees with the evangelic history; but then this preparation of the passover was not of the passover lamb, for that had been prepared and eaten the night before. Nor do I find that there was any particular day which was called *the preparation of the passover* in such sense, and much less that this day was the day before the eating of the passover. According to the law in *Ex. 12:3-6*, the lamb for the passover was to be separated from the rest of the flock on the *tenth* day of the month, and to be kept up till the *fourteenth*; but this is never called the *preparation* of the passover; and was it so called, it cannot be intended here; the preparing and making ready the passover the evangelists speak of, were on the same day it was eaten, and design the getting ready a place to eat it in, and things convenient for that purpose, and the killing the lamb, and dressing it, and the like, *Matt. 26:17,19; Mark 14:12,15,16; Luke 22:8,9,12,13*. There is what the Jews call, פורס הפסח, which was a space of fifteen days before the passover, and began at the middle of the thirty days before the feast, in which they used to ask questions, and explain the traditions concerning the passover:[9] but this is never called the preparation of the passover; and on the night of the fourteenth month they sought diligently, in every hole and corner of their houses, for leavened bread, in order to remove it;[10] but this also never went by

---

[6] T. Bab. Sabbat, fol. 115. 1.

[7] T. Bab. Sanhedrin, fol. 43. 1. & 67. 1.

[8] Toldos Jesu, p. 18.

[9] Mishna Shekalim, c. 3. sect. 1. & Bartenora in ibid. T. Bab. Pesachim, fol. 6. 1.

[10] Mishna Pesachim, c. 1. sect. 1-3.

any such name. Wherefore, if any respect is had to the preparation for the passover, it must either design the preparation of the *Chagigah*, which was a grand festival, commonly kept on the fifteenth day, and which was sometimes called the passover; or else the preparation for the whole feast all the remaining days of it; see the note on *chapter 18:28*; but it seems best of all to understand it only of the preparation for the sabbath, which, because it was in the passover week, is called the passover preparation day. And it may be observed, that it is sometimes only called *the day of the preparation*, and *the preparation*, Matt. 27:62; Luke 23:54; John 19:31; and sometimes the *Jews' preparation day, John 19:42*; and it is explained by the Evangelist Mark, *chapter 15:42: It was the preparation, that is, the day before the sabbath*; on which they both prepared themselves for the sabbath, and food to eat on that day; and this being the time of the passover likewise, the preparation was the greater: and therefore to distinguish this preparation day for the sabbath, from others, it is called the *passover preparation*; nor have I observed that any other day is called the preparation but that before the sabbath. The Jews dispute about preparing food for the sabbath on a feast day, as this was; they seem to forbid it, but afterwards soften their words, and allow it with some provisos: their canon runs thus:[11]

> "A feast day which falls on the eve of the sabbath, a man may not boil (any thing) at the beginning of the feast day for the sabbath, but he may boil for the feast day; and if there is any left, it may be left for the sabbath; and he may make a boiling on the eve of a feast day, and depend on it for the sabbath: the house of Shammai say, two boilings; and the house of Hillel say, one boiling."

Bartenora, on the passage, observes, that some say the reason of this boiling on the evening of a feast day, is for the honor of the sabbath; for because from the evening of the feast day, the sabbath is remembered, that which is best is chosen for the sabbath, that the sabbath may not be forgotten through the business of the feast day. The account Maimonides[12] gives of this matter is:

> "On a common day they *prepare* for the sabbath, and on a common day they prepare for a feast day; but they do not prepare on a feast day for the sabbath, nor is the sabbath, מכינה, *a preparation* for a feast day."

This seems to be contrary to the practice of the Jews in the time of Christ, as related by the evangelists, understanding by the preparation they speak of, a preparation of food for the sabbath; but what he afterwards says[13] makes

---

[11] Mishna Betza, c. 2. sect. 1.

[12] Hilchot Yom Tob. c. 1. sect. 19.

[13] Ibid. c. 6. sect. 1.

some allowance for it:

> "A feast day, which happens to be on the eve of the sabbath (Friday), they neither bake nor boil, on a feast day what is eaten on the morrow, on the sabbath; and this prohibition is from the words of the Scribes (not from the word of God), that a man should not boil any thing on a feast day for a common day, and much less for the sabbath; but if he makes a boiling (or prepares food) on the evening of a feast day on which he depends, and boils and bakes on a feast day for the sabbath, lo, this is lawful; and that on which he depends is called the *mingling of food*."

And this food, so called, was a small portion of food prepared on a feast for the sabbath, though not less than the quantity of an olive, whether for one man or a thousand;[14] by virtue of which, they depending on it for the sabbath, they might prepare whatever they would, after having asked a blessing over it, and saying,[15]

> "By this mixture it is free for me to bake and boil on a feast day what is for the morrow, the sabbath; and if a man prepares for others, he must say, For me, and for such a one, and such a one; or, For the men of the city; and then all of them may bake and boil on a feast day for the sabbath."

And about the sixth hour; to which agrees the account in *Matt. 27:45* and *Luke 23:44,* but Mark says, *chapter 15:25*, that *it was the third hour, and they crucified him*; and Beza says he found it so written in one copy; and so read Peter of Alexandria, Beza's ancient copy, and some others, and Nonnus: but the copies in general agree in, and confirm the common reading, and which is differently accounted for; some by the different computations of the Jews and Romans; others by observing that the Jewish day was divided into four parts, each part containing three hours, and were called the *third*, the *sixth*, the *ninth*, and the *twelfth* hours; and not only that time, when one of these hours came, was called by that name, but also from that all the space of the three hours, till the next came, was called by the name of the former: for instance, all the space from nine o'clock till twelve was called *the third hour*; and all from twelve till three in the afternoon *the sixth hour*: hence the time of Christ's crucifixion being supposed to be somewhat before, but yet near our twelve of the clock, it may be truly here said that it was *about the sixth hour*; and as truly by Mark the *third hour*; that space, which was called by the name of the third hour, being not yet passed, though it drew toward an end. This

---

[14] Maimon. & Bartenora in Mishna Betza, c. 2. sect. 1.

[15] Maimon. Hilchot Yom Tob, c. 6. sect. 8.

way go Godwin and Hammond, whose words I have expressed, and bids fair for the true solution of the difficulty: though it should be observed, that Mark agrees with the other evangelists about the darkness which was at the *sixth hour*, the time of Christ's crucifixion, *Mark 15:33-34;* and it is to be remarked, that he does not say that it was the third hour *when* they crucified Him, or that they crucified Him at the third hour; but it was the third hour, *and* they crucified Him, as Dr. Lightfoot observes. It was the time of day when they should have been at the daily sacrifice, and preparing for the solemnity of that day particularly, which was their *Chagigah*, or grand feast; but instead of this they were prosecuting His crucifixion, which they brought *about* by the *sixth hour*. And about this time Pilate said, and did the following things:

and he saith unto the Jews, Behold your king! Whom some of your people, it seems, have owned for their king, and you charge with setting up Himself as one; see what a figure He makes; does He look like a king? This he said, in order to move upon their affections, that, if possible, they might agree to release Him, and to shame them out of putting such a poor despicable creature to death; and as upbraiding them for their folly, in fearing any thing from so mean [*or* lowly] and contemptible a man.

Verse 15. **But they cried out, Away with *him*,** &c. As a person hateful and loathsome to them, the sight of whom they could not bear; and this they said with great indignation and wrath, and with great vehemency, earnestness and importunacy, in a very clamorous way; repeating the words,

away with *him*: they were impatient until He was ordered away for execution; and nothing would satisfy them but the crucifixion of Him; and therefore they say,

crucify him. Which is also repeated in the Syriac version; for this was what they thirsted after, and were so intent upon; this cry was made by the chief priests:

Pilate saith unto them, Shall I crucify your King? This he said either seriously or jeeringly, and it may be with a view to draw out of them their sentiments concerning Caesar, as well as Him; however it had this effect:

The chief priests answered, We have no king but Caesar. Whereby they denied God to be their king, though they used to say, and still say in their prayers; *we have no king but God:*[16] they rejected the government of the King Messiah, and tacitly confessed that the scepter was departed from Judah [see

---

[16] T. Bab. Taanith, fol. 25. 2. Seder Tephillot, fol. 46. 2. Ed. Basil. fol. 71. 2. Ed. Amsterd.

Gen. 49:10]; and what they now said, came quickly upon them, and still continues; for according to prophecy, *Hos. 3:4*, they have been many days and years *without a king*: and this they said in spite to Jesus, and not in respect to Caesar, whose government they would have been glad to have had an opportunity to shake off. They could name no one as king but Jesus, or Caesar; the former they rejected, and were obliged to own the latter: it is a poor observation of the Jew[17] upon this passage, that it,

> "shows that before the crucifixion of Jesus, the Roman Caesars ruled over Israel; and that this Caesar was Tiberius, who had set Pilate over Jerusalem, as is clear from *Luke 3:1*. Wherefore here is an answer to the objection of the Nazarenes, who say that the Jews, for the sin of crucifying Jesus, lost their kingdom."

To which may be replied, that this is not said by any of the writers of the New Testament, that the kingdom of the Jews was taken away from them for their sin of crucifying Jesus;[18] and therefore this is no contradiction to any thing said by them; this is only the assertion of some private persons, upon whom it lies to defend themselves; and what is asserted, is defensible, nor do the words of the text militate against it: for though before the crucifixion of Christ the Jews were tributary to the Roman Caesars, and Roman governors were sent to preside among them; yet the government was not utterly taken from them, or their kingdom lost; they indeed feared this would be the case, should Jesus succeed and prosper, as He did, saying, *the Romans shall come and take away both our place and nation, John 11:48*, which shows, that as yet this was not done; though for their disbelief and rejection of the Messiah, their destruction was hastening on apace; and after the crucifixion of Him, all power was taken from them; the government was seized upon by the Romans entirely, and at last utterly destroyed; besides, the Jews did not own Caesar to be their king, though they said this now to serve a turn; and after this they had kings of the race of Herod over them, though placed there by the Roman emperor or senate.

Verse 16. **Then delivered he him therefore**, &c. Perceiving he could not by any means work upon them, and that nothing would satisfy them but His death; he therefore passed sentence on Him, and gave Him up to their will,

---

[17] R. Isaac Chizzuk Emuna, par. 2. c. 57. p. 446.

[18] The reader is referred to Gill's comments on the parable of the wicked husbandmen in *Matt. 21:33-45*, compared with those on *1 Pet. 2:3-10*, concerning the removal of the *spiritual* kingdom from the Jews - *Editor*.

unto them to be crucified. As they requested, and which was done in a judicial way, and all by divine appointment, according to the counsel and foreknowledge of God [see *Acts 2:23*]:

And they took Jesus and led *him* away. Directly from the judgment hall, out of the city to the place of execution, whither He was led as a lamb to the slaughter, without opening His mouth against God or man; but behaved with the utmost patience, meekness, and resignation.

Verse 17. **And he bearing his cross**, &c. Which was usual for malefactors to do, as Lipsius[19] shows out of Artemidorus, and Plutarch; the former says,
"the cross is like to death, and he that is to be fixed to it, *first bears it;*"
and the latter says,
"and every one of the malefactors that are punished in body, *carries out his own cross.*"
So Christ, when He first went out to be crucified, carried His cross Himself, until the Jews, meeting with Simon the Cyrenian, obliged him to bear it after Him; that is, one part of it; for still Christ continued to bear a part Himself: of this Isaac was a type, in carrying the wood on his shoulders for the burnt offering; and this showed that Christ was made sin, and a curse for us, and that our sins, and the punishment which belonged to us, were laid on Him, and borne by Him; and in this He has left us an example to go forth without the camp, bearing His reproach:

went forth in a place called *the place* of a skull, which is called in the Hebrew, Golgotha: and signifies a man's *skull*. It seems, that as they executed malefactors here, so they buried them here; and in process of time, their bones being dug up to make room for others, their skulls, with other bones, lay up and down in this place; from whence it had its name in the Syriac dialect, which the Jews then usually spake. Here some say Adam's skull was found, and that it had its name from thence. This was an ancient tradition, as has been observed in the notes on *Matt. 27:33*, and *Luke 23:33* [*q.v.* **38, 56**]. The Syriac writers have it,[20] who say,
"When Noah went out of the ark there was made a distribution of the bones of Adam; to Shem, his head was given, and the place in which he was buried is called *Karkaphta*: where likewise Christ was crucified;"
which word signifies a *skull*, as Golgotha does: and so likewise the Arabic

---

[19] De Cruce, l. 2. c. 5. p. 76.

[20] Bar Bahluli apud Castel. Lexic. Polyglot. col. 3466.

writers;[21] who affirm that Shem said these words to Melchizedek:
"Noah commanded that thou shouldst take the body of Adam, and bury
it in the middle of the earth; therefore let us go, I and thou, and bury
it. Wherefore Shem and Melchizedek went to take the body of Adam,
and the angel of the Lord appeared to them and went before them, till
they came to the place Calvary, where they buried him, as the angel of
the Lord commanded them."
The same also had the ancient fathers of the Christian church: Cyprian[22] says,
that it is a tradition of the ancients, that Adam was buried in Calvary under
the place where the cross of Christ was fixed; and Jerome makes mention of
it more than once; so Paula and Eustochium, in an epistle supposed to be
dictated by him, or in which he was assisting, say,[23] in this city, meaning
Jerusalem, yea in this place, Adam is said to dwell, and to die; from whence
the place where our Lord was crucified is called *Calvary*, because there the
skull of the ancient man was buried. And in another place he himself says,[24]
that he heard one disputing in the church and explaining, *Eph. 5:14,* of Adam
buried in Calvary, where the Lord was crucified, and therefore was so called.
Ambrose[25] also takes notice of it; the place of the cross, says he, is either in the
midst of the land, that it might be conspicuous to all, or over the grave of
Adam, as the Hebrews dispute. Others say that the hill itself was in the form
of a man's skull, and therefore was so called; it was situated, as Jerome says,[26]
on the north of Mount Zion, and is thought by some to be the same with the
hill Gareb, in *Jer. 31:39.* It was usual to crucify on high hills, so Polycrates
was crucified upon the highest top of Mount Mycale.[27]

Verse 18. **Where they crucified him**, &c. Namely, at Golgotha, the same
with *Calvary*; and so had what they were so desirous of:

---

[21] Elmacinus, p. 13. Patricides, p. 12. apud Hottinger. Smegma Oriental. l. 1. c. 8. p. 257.

[22] De Resurrectione Christi, p. 479.

[23] Epist. Marcellae, fol. 42. L. Tom. I.

[24] Comment. in Eph. 5:14.

[25] Comment. in Luc. 20:33.

[26] De locis Hebraicis, fol. 92. F.

[27] Valer. Maxim. l. 6. c. ult.

and two other with him, on either side one, and Jesus in the midst. These other two men were thieves, as the other evangelists declare; among whom Christ was placed, being numbered and reckoned among transgressors [see *Isa. 53:12*]: He was no transgressor of the law of God Himself, but He was accounted as such by men, and was treated as if He had been one by the justice of God; He, as a surety, standing in the law-place, and stead of His people; hence He died in their room, and for their sins: this shows the low estate of Christ, the strictness of justice, the wisdom of God in salvation, and the grace and love of the Redeemer; who condescended to every thing, and every circumstance, though ever so reproachful, which was necessary for the redemption of His people, and the glory of the divine perfections, and for the fulfilment of purposes, promises, and predictions.

Verse 19. **And Pilate wrote a title**, &c. *Luke* calls it *a superscription* [*23:38*], *Mark, the superscription of his accusation* [*15:26*]; and *Matthew*, the *accusation* itself [*27:37*]; it contained the substance of the charge against Him, and was written upon a table or board, and nailed to the cross, as Nonnus suggests; to this is the allusion, *Col. 2:14*. The form of it was drawn up by Pilate, His judge, who ordered it to be transcribed upon a proper instrument, and placed over Him:

and put *it* on the cross. Not with his own hands, but by his servants, who did it at his command; for others are said to do it, *Matt. 27:37*. It was put upon *the top of the cross*, as the Persic version reads it; *over him*, or *over his head*, as the other evangelists say; and may denote the rise of His kingdom, which is from above, the visibility of it, and the enlargement of it, through the cross:

And the writing was; the words written in the title were,

JESUS OF NAZARETH THE KING OF THE JEWS. Jesus was His name, by which He was commonly called and known, and signifies a Savior, as He is of all the elect of God; whom He saves from all their sins, by bearing them in His own body on the cross, and of whom He is the able and willing, the perfect and complete, the only and everlasting Savior. He is said to be *of Nazareth*; this was the place of which He was an inhabitant; here Joseph and Mary lived before His conception; here He was conceived, though born in Bethlehem; where He did not abide long, but constantly in this place, till He was about thirty years of age; this title was sometimes given Him as a term of reproach, though not always: *the King of the Jews*; which both expresses His accusation, and asserts Him to be so.

Verse 20. **This title then read many of the Jews**, &c. Who were in great numbers, at the place of execution, rejoicing at His crucifixion, and insulting Him as He hung on the cross:

for the place where Jesus was crucified was nigh unto the city;
Golgotha, the place of Christ's crucifixion, was not more than two furlongs, or
a quarter of a mile from the city of Jerusalem: so that multitudes were
continually going from thence to see this sight; the city also being then very
full of people, by reason of the feast of the passover; to which may be added,
that the cross stood by the wayside, where persons were continually passing
to and fro, as appears from *Matt. 27:39; Mark 15:29*; and where it was usual
to erect crosses to make public examples of malefactors, and to deter others
from committing the like crimes: so Alexander, the emperor, ordered a eunuch
to be crucified by the wayside, in which his servants used commonly to go to
his suburb[28] or country house. Cicero says,[29]

"The Mamertines, according to their own usage and custom, crucified
behind the city, in the Pompeian way;"

and Quinctilian observes,[30]

"as often as we crucify criminals, the most noted ways are chosen,
where most may behold, and most may be moved with fear."

And now Christ being crucified by a public road side, the inscription on the
cross was doubtless read by more than otherwise it would:

and it was written in Hebrew, *and* Greek, *and* Latin. That it might be
read by all, Jews, Greeks, and Romans; and to show that He is the Savior of
some of all nations; and that He is King over all. These words were written in
Hebrew letters in the Syriac dialect, which was used by the Jews, and is called
the Hebrew language, *verses 13 and 17;* and in which it is most likely Pilate
should write these words, or order them to be written; and which, according
to the Syriac version we now have, were thus put, ישוע נצריא מלכא דיהודיא;
in Greek the words stood as in the original text, thus, Ιησους ο Ναζωραιος ο
βασιλευς των Ιουδαιων: and in the Latin tongue, as may be supposed, after
this manner, *Jesus Nazarenus Rex Judaeorum*. These three languages may
be very well thought to be understood by Pilate; at least so much of them as
to qualify him to write such an inscription as this. The Latin tongue was his
mother tongue, which he must be supposed well to understand; and the Greek
tongue was very much used by the Romans, since their conquest of the
Grecian monarchy; and the emperors' edicts were generally published in
Greek, which it was therefore necessary for Pilate to understand; and as he
was a governor of Judea, and had been so for some time, he must have

---

[28] Lipsius de Cruce, l. 3. c. 13. p. 158.

[29] Orat. 10. in Veriem. l. 5. p. 604.

[30] Declamat. 275.

acquired some knowledge of the Hebrew language; and these being the principal languages in the world, he chose to write this title in them, that persons coming from all quarters might be able to read it, and understand it in some one of them.

Verse 21. **Then said the chief priests of the Jews to Pilate**, &c. Who were not only informed of this inscription, but might read it themselves, for they were present at the crucifying of Christ, and mocked at Him as He hung on the tree; these, when they read the title, were greatly offended at it, partly because it was doing too great an honor to Jesus to call Him *The King of the Jews*: and partly because it fixed a public brand of infamy upon their nation, that a king of theirs should be crucified: wherefore they went to Pilate and addressed him, saying,

Write not, The King of the Jews: because they did not own Him for their king, which this title seemed to suggest, nor had He in their opinion any right to such a character; wherefore they desired that in the room of these words he would be pleased to put the following,

but that he said, I am King of the Jews. That so He might be thought to be a seditious person and a traitor; one that laid claim to the temporal crown and kingdom of Israel, and one that suffered justly for attempts of that kind.

Verse 22. **Pilate answered, What I have written I have written**, &c. He seems to say this, as one angry and displeased with them; either because they would not consent to release Jesus, which he was desirous of, but pressed him so very hard to crucify Him; or at their insolence, in directing him in what form to put the superscription, which he determines shall stand unaltered, as he had written it. This he said, either because he could not alter it after it was written, for it is said[31] that,

> "A proconsul's table is his sentence, which being once read, not one letter can either be increased or diminished; but as it is recited, so it is related in the instrument of the province."

Or if he could have altered it, he was not suffered by God to do it; but was so directed, and overruled by divine providence, as to write, so to persist in, and abide by what he had written inviolably; which is the sense of his words. Dr. Lightfoot has given several instances out of the Talmud, showing that this is a common way of speaking with the Rabbins; and that words thus doubled signify that what is spoken of stands good, and is irrevocable: so a widow taking any of the moveable goods of her husband deceased for her

---

[31] Apulei Florid. c. 9.

maintenance, it is said,[32] מה שתפסה תפסה, *what she takes, she takes*; that is, she may lawfully do it, and retain it: it continues in her hands, and cannot be taken away from her; and so the gloss explains it, *they do not take it from her*; and in the same way Maimonides[33] interprets it. So of a man that binds himself to offer an oblation one way, and he offers it another way, שהביא הביא מה, *what he has offered, he has offered*;[34] what he has offered is right, it stands good, and is not to be rejected. And again, among the rites used by a deceased brother's wife, towards him that refuses to marry her, if one thing is done before the other, it matters not, מה שעשוי עשוי, *what is done, is done*;[35] and is not to be undone, or done over again in another way; it stands firm and good, and not to be objected to. And the same writer observes, that this is a sort of prophecy of Pilate, and which should continue, and for ever obtain, that the Jews should have no other King Messiah than *Jesus of Nazareth*; nor have they had any other; all that have risen up have proved false Messiahs; nor will they have any other; nor indeed any king, until they *seek the Lord their God, and David their king, Hos. 3:5;* that is, the Son of David, as they will do in the latter day; when they shall be converted, and when they shall own Him as their king, whom their ancestors at this time were ashamed of.

Verse 23. **Then the soldiers, when they had crucified Jesus**, &c. The crucifixion of Christ was at the request and solicitation of the Jews, was ordered by the Roman governor, and performed by the Roman soldiers; the sinful men into whose hands Christ was to be delivered:

took his garments; which they had stripped His body of, crucifying Him naked; as what properly belonged to them, it being usual then, as now, for executioners to have the clothes of the persons they put to death; these were His inner garments:

and made four parts, to every soldier a part; for it seems there were four of them concerned in His execution, and who were set to watch Him:

and also *his* coat; or upper garment;

---

[32] T. Bab. Cetubot, fol. 96. 1.

[33] Hilchot Ishot, c. 18. sect. 10.

[34] T. Bab. Menachot, fol. 3. 1.

[35] T. Bab. Yebamot, fol. 106. 2.

now the coat was without seam, woven from the top throughout. In such a one the Jews say,[36] Moses ministered: and of this sort and make was the robe of the high priest, said to be of *woven work*, *Ex. 28:32;* upon which Jarchi remarks, ולא במחט, *and not with a needle*; it was all woven, and without any seam: and so the Jews say[37] in general of the garments of the priests:

"The garments of the priests are not made of needlework, but of woven work; as it is said, *Ex. 28:32*. Abai says, it is not necessary (that is, the use of the needle) but for their sleeves; according to the tradition, the sleeve of the garments of the priests is woven by itself, and is joined to the garment, and reaches to the palm of the hand."

So that this was an entire woven garment from top to bottom, excepting the sleeves, which were woven separately and sewed to it; but the coat of the high priest, which Jacob Iehudah Leon says,[38]

"was a stately woollen coat of a sky color, wholly woven, all of one piece, without seam, without sleeves;"

such a garment Christ our great High Priest wore, which had no seam in it, but was a curious piece of texture from top to bottom. The very learned Braunius[39] says, he has seen such garments in Holland, and has given very fine cuts of them, and also of the frame in which they are wrought. What authority Nonnus had to call this coat a *black* one, or others for saying it was the work of the Virgin Mary, I know not.

Verse 24. **They said therefore among themselves**, &c. When they saw what a curious piece of work it was, and that it was pity to divide it into parts: and besides, that it would have been rendered entirely useless thereby: they moved it to each other, saying,

Let us not rend it, but cast lots for it, whose it shall be: that the Scripture might be fulfilled: not that they knew any thing of the Scripture, or had any intention of fulfilling it hereby, but they were so directed by the providence of God, to take such a step; whereby was literally accomplished the passage in *Psa. 22:18*:

which saith, They parted my raiment among them, and for my vesture they did cast lots. The whole Psalm is to be understood of the Messiah, not

---

[36] T. Bab. Taanith, fol. 11. 2. Gloss in ibid.

[37] T. Bab. Yoma, c. 7. fol. 72. 2. Maimon. Hilch. Cele Hamikdash, c. 8. sect. 16.

[38] Relation of Memorable Things in the Tabernacle, &c. c. 5. p. 23.

[39] De vestitu Sacerdot. Heb. l. 1. c. 16. p. 346, 360, 361.

of David, as some do;[40] many passages in it cannot be applied to him, such as speak of the dislocation of His bones, the piercing of His hands and feet, and this of parting His garments, and casting lots for His vesture: all which had their literal accomplishment in Jesus: nor can it be understood of Esther, as it is by some Jewish[41] interpreters; there is not one word in it that agrees with her, and particularly, not the clause here cited; and there are some things in it which are manifestly spoken of a man, and not of a woman, as *verses 22:8, 24;* nor can the whole body of the Jewish nation, or the congregation of Israel be intended, as others say;[42] since it is clear, that a single person is spoken of throughout the Psalm, and who is distinguished from others, from his brethren, from the congregation, from the seed of Jacob and Israel, *verses 22:22, 23,* and indeed, no other than the Messiah can be meant; He is pointed at in the very title of it, *Aijeleth Shahar,* which words, in what way soever they are rendered, agree with Him: if by *the morning daily sacrifice,* as they are by the Targum; He is *the Lamb of God,* who continually *takes away the sins of the world* [*John 1:29*]; and very fitly is He so called in the title of a psalm [*Psa. 22*], which speaks so much of His sufferings and death, which were a propitiatory sacrifice for the sins of His people: or by *the morning star,* as others[43] interpret them; Christ is *the bright and morning star* [*Rev. 22:16*], *the dayspring from on high* [*Luke 1:78*], the *Sun of righteousness* [*Mal. 4:2*], and *light of the world* [*John 8:12*]: or by *the morning help,* as in the Septuagint; Christ had early help from God in the morning of His infancy, when Herod sought His life, and in the day of salvation of His people; and early in the morning was He raised from the dead, and had glory given Him: or by *the morning hind,* which seems best of all, to which He may be compared, as to a *roe* or *hart,* in *Song of Sol. 2:9, 17* and *8:14,* for His love and loveliness, and for His swiftness and readiness in appearing for the salvation of His people; and for His being hunted by Herod in the morning of His days; and being encompassed by those *dogs,* the Scribes and Pharisees, Judas and the band of soldiers; see *Psa. 22:16.* The first words of the Psalm were spoken by Jesus the true Messiah, when He hung upon the cross, and are truly applied to Himself; His reproaches and sufferings endured by Him there, are particularly and exactly described in it, and agree with no other; the benefits which the people of God were to enjoy, in consequence of His sufferings, and

---

[40] R. R. in Kimchi in Psalm 22.

[41] R. R. in Jarchi in Psalm 22.

[42] Kimchi & Ben Melech in ibid.

[43] Vid. Kimchi & Abendana in ibid.

the conversion of the Gentiles spoken of in it, which is peculiar to the days of the Messiah, show to whom it belongs. The Jews *themselves* are obliged to interpret some parts of it concerning Him; they sometimes say,[44] that by *Aijeleth Shahar* is meant the Shekinah, a name that well suits with the Messiah Jesus, who tabernacled in our nature; the 26*th verse* is applied by Jarchi to the time of the redemption, and the days of the Messiah; so that upon the whole, this passage is rightly cited with respect to the Messiah, and is truly said to be fulfilled by this circumstance, of the soldiers doing with His garments as they did:

These things therefore the soldiers did. Because they were before determined and predicted that they should be done: and therefore they were disposed and directed by a superior influence, in perfect agreement with the freedom of their wills to do these things. The whole of this account may be spiritually applied. The Scriptures are the garments of Christ; or, as a prince of Anhalt said, the swaddling clothes in which the infant of Bethlehem was wrapped; these exhibit and show forth Christ in His glory, and by which He is known and bear witness to, and are pure and incorrupt, fragrant and savory. Heretics are the soldiers that rend and tear the Scriptures in pieces, part them, add unto them, or detract from them; who corrupt, pervert, wrest, and misapply them; but truth is the seamless coat; it is all of a piece, is of God, there is nothing human in it; though it may be played with, betrayed, sold, or denied, it cannot be destroyed; but is, and will be preserved by divine providence: or the human nature of Christ is the vesture, with which His divine person was as it were covered, was put on and off, and on again as a garment; is of God, and not man; is pure and spotless; and though His soul and body were parted asunder for a while, this could never be parted from His divine person: or else the righteousness of Christ may be signified by this robe, which is often compared to one, because it is put on the saints, and they are clothed with it [*e.g. Rev. 9:9,13-14*]: it covers, keeps warm, protects, beautifies, and adorns them; this is seamless, and all of a piece, and has nothing of men's works and services tacked unto it; is enjoyed by a divine lot by some men, and not all, and even such as have been sinful and ungodly; it is pure, perfect and will last for ever.

Verse 25. **Now there stood by the cross of Jesus**, &c. So near as not only to see Him, but to hear Him speak:

his mother; the mother of Jesus, Mary; which showed her affection to Christ, and her constancy in abiding by Him to the last; though it must be a cutting sight: and now was fulfilled Simeon's prophecy, *Luke 2:35*, to see her son in

---

[44] Zohar in Lev. fol. 5. 4. & Imre Bina in ibid.

such agonies and sorrow, and jeered and insulted by the worst of men; and though she herself was exposed to danger, and liable to be abused by the outrageous multitude; and it also showed that she stood in need, as others, of a crucified Savior; so far was she from being a co-partner with Him in making satisfaction for sin, as the Papists wickedly say:

and his mother's sister, Mary the *wife* of Cleophas. The Syriac, Persic, and Ethiopic versions distinguish *Mary the wife of Cleophas* from His mother's sister, by placing the copulative *and* between them, and so make two persons; whereas one and the same is intended, and who was the sister of Mary, the mother of Christ; not her own sister, for it is not likely that two sisters should be of the same name; but her husband Joseph's sister, and so her's; or else Cleophas was Joseph's brother, as Eusebius from Hegesippus says:[45] and who was also not the daughter of Cleophas, as the Arabic version has here supplied it; much less the mother of him; but his wife, as is rightly put in our translation: for, according to the other evangelists, she was the mother of James and Joses, and who were the sons of Cleophas, or Alphaeus; which are not the names of two persons, nor two names of one and the same person, but one and the same name differently pronounced; his true name in Hebrew was, חלפי, or חלפאי, or חילפי, *Chelphi*, or *Chelphai*, or *Chilphi*, a name frequently to be met with in Talmudic and Rabbinic writings; and so a Jewish writer[46] observes, that חילפא והוא אילפא, *Chilpha is the same as Ilpha*; and in Greek may be pronounced either *Cleophas*, or *Alphaeus*, as it is both ways: ignorance of this has led interpreters to form different conjectures, as that either the husband of this Mary had two names; or that she was twice married to two different persons, once to Alphaeus, and after his death to Cleophas; or that Cleophas was her father, and Alphaeus her husband; for neither of which is there any foundation. She was no doubt a believer in Christ, and came and stood by His cross; not merely to keep her sister company, but out of affection to Jesus, and to testify her faith in Him:

and Mary Magdalene. Out of whom He had cast seven devils, and who had been a true penitent, a real believer in Him, a hearty lover of Him, was zealously attached to Him, and followed Him to the last. Three Marys are here mentioned as together; and it is observable, that the greater part of those that are taken notice of, as following Christ to the cross, and standing by it, were women, the weaker, and timorous sex, when all His disciples forsook Him and fled; and none of them attended at the cross, as we read of, excepting John; no, not even Peter, who boasted so much of his attachment to Him. These good

---

[45] Euseb. Eccl. Hist. l. 3. c. 11.

[46] Juchasin, fol. 92. 1.

women standing by the cross of Christ, may teach us to do, as they did, look upon a crucified Christ, view His sorrows, and His sufferings, and our sins laid upon Him, and borne and taken away by Him; we should look unto Him for pardon, cleansing, and justification, and, in short, for the whole of salvation: we should also weep, as they did, while we look on Him; shed even tears of affection for, and sympathy with Him; of humiliation for sin, and of joy for a Savior: and likewise should abide by Him as they did, by His person, offices, and grace; by the doctrine of the cross, continuing steadfastly in it; and by the ordinances of Christ, constantly attending on them, and that notwithstanding all the reproaches and sufferings we may undergo.

Verse 26. **When Jesus therefore saw his mother**, &c. Standing near Him, within the reach of His voice, as well as sight, He took notice of her, and showed a concern for her temporal, as well as for her eternal good:

and the disciple standing by; either by His cross, or by His mother, or both:

whom he loved: meaning John, the writer of this Gospel, who for modesty's sake often describes himself in this manner; he being distinguished by Christ from the rest, by some peculiar marks of affection as man; though as God, and as the Redeemer, He loved His disciples alike, as He does all His true and faithful followers:

he saith unto his mother, Woman, behold thy son! Meaning not Himself, but the disciple, who was her son, not by nature, nor adoption; but who would show himself as a son, by his filial affection for, care of, honor and respect unto her. Christ calls her not *mother*, but *woman*; not out of disrespect to her, or as ashamed of her; but partly that He might not raise, or add strength to her passions, by a tenderness of speaking; and partly to conceal her from the mob, and lest she should be exposed to their rude insults; as also to let her know that all natural relation was now ceasing between them; though this is a title He sometimes used to give her before [see the note on *John 2:4*].

Verse 27. **Then saith he to the disciple**, &c. The same disciple, John:

Behold thy mother! Take care of her, and provide for her, as if she was thine own mother: this shows the meanness [*or* humble state] of Christ, who had nothing to leave her, though Lord of all; it is very probable that Joseph was dead, and Mary now a widow; and whereas Christ had taken care of her, and maintained her hitherto, He now, in His dying moments, commits her to the care of this disciple; which is an instance of His humanity, and of His regard to every duty; and this in particular, of honoring parents, and providing for them in distress, and old age:

And from that hour that disciple took her to his own *home*. Or *house*; so the Septuagint render ביתו, *to his house*, by εις τα ιδια, in *Esther 6:12*, the phrase here used, and in *John 16:32*. Some say she lived with John at Jerusalem, and there died; and others say, that she died in the twelfth year after the resurrection of Christ, being 59 years of age, and was buried by John in the garden of Gethsemane. Where his house was is not certain, whether at Jerusalem or in Galilee, nor how long she lived with him; but this is not to be doubted, that he took care of her, and provided for her as if she was his own mother; and his doing this forthwith, shows his great regard to Christ, his readiness and cheerfulness to comply with His orders and directions, and his unfeigned love unto Him.

Verse 28. **After this**, &c. After He had committed His mother to the care of John, which was about the sixth hour, before the darkness came over the land: and three hours after this was the following circumstance, which was not without the previous knowledge of Christ:

Jesus knowing that all things were now accomplished; or just upon being accomplished, were as good as finished; and as they were to be, would be in a very short time; even all things relating to His sufferings, and the circumstances of them, which were afore appointed by God, and foretold in prophecy, and of which He had perfect knowledge:

that the Scripture might be fulfilled: might appear to have its accomplishment, which predicted the great drought and thirst that should be on Him, *Psa. 22:15*, and that His enemies at such a time would give Him vinegar to drink, *Psa. 69:21*:

saith, I thirst. Which was literally true of Him, and may be also understood spiritually of His great thirst and eager desire after the salvation of His people.

Verse 29. **Now there was set a vessel full of vinegar**, &c. In a place near at hand, as Nonnus observes; not on purpose, for the sake of them that were crucified, either to refresh their spirits, or stop a too great effusion of blood, that they might continue the longer in their misery; but for the use of the soldiers who crucified Christ, vinegar being part of the allowance of Roman soldiers,[47] and what they used to drink: sometimes it was mixed with water; which mixed liquor they called *Posca*,[48] and was what even their generals

---

[47] Julian. Imperator. Epist. 27. p. 161. Vid. Lydium de re militari, l. 6. c. 7. p. 245.

[48] Salmuth. in Panciroll. rerum memorab. par. 1. Tit. 53. p. 274.

sometimes used; as Scipio, Metellus, Trajan, Adrian, and others; vinegar was also used by the Jews for drink, as appears from *Ruth 2:14: and dip thy morsel in the vinegar*, which Boaz's reapers had with them in the field; *because of heat*, as the commentators say;[49] that being good to cool, and to extinguish thirst; for which reason the soldiers here offer it to Christ; though the Chaldee paraphrase of the above place, makes it to be a kind of sauce or pap boiled in vinegar; and such an *Embamma* made of vinegar the Romans had, in which they dipped their food;[50] but this here seems to be pure vinegar, and to be different from that which the other evangelists speak of, which was mingled with gall, or was sour wine with myrrh, *Matt. 27:34; Mark 15:23.* Vinegar indeed is good to revive the spirits, and *hyssop*, which is after mentioned, is an herb of a sweet smell; and if the reed, which the other evangelists make mention of, was the *sweet calamus*, as some have thought, they were all of them things of a refreshing nature: vinegar was also used for stopping blood,[51] when it flowed from wounds in a large quantity; and of the same use were sponges; hence Tertullian[52] mentions "spongias retiariorum," *the sponges of the fencers*, which they had with them to stop any effusion of blood that should be made in their exercises: but then it can hardly be thought that these things should be in common prepared at crucifixions for such ends, on purpose to linger out a miserable life a little longer, which would be shocking barbarity; and especially that such a provision would ever be made at this time, on such an account, since the Jew's sabbath drew nigh, and they were in haste to have the executions over before that came on, that the bodies might not remain on the cross on that day; for which reason they would do nothing at this time, however, to prolong the lives of the malefactors: wherefore it is most reasonable to think, that this vessel of vinegar was not set for any such purpose, but was for the use of the soldiers; and therefore this being at hand when Christ signified His *thirst*, they offered some of it in the following manner:

and they filled a sponge with vinegar; it being the nature of a sponge (which Nonnus here calls, βλαστημα θλασσης, *a branch of the sea*, because it grows there) to swallow up any thing that is liquid, and which may be again

---

[49] Jarchi & Aben Ezra in loc.

[50] Salmuth. ibid. par. 2. Tit. 2. p. 83.

[51] Pliny Nat. Hist. l. 31. c. 11.

[52] De Spectaculis, c. 25.

squeezed and sucked out of it; hence the Jews say[53] of it, ספוג שבלע משקין, *the sponge which swallows up liquids*; and used it for such a purpose;

and put it upon hyssop; meaning not the juice of hyssop, into which some have thought the sponge with vinegar was put, but the herb, and a stalk of it: the other evangelists say, it was put *upon a reed*; meaning either that the sponge with the hyssop were put about a reed, and so given Him; or rather it was a stalk of hyssop, which was like a reed or cane; and in this country of Judea grew very large, sufficient for such a purpose. The hyssop with the Jews was not reckoned among herbs, but trees; see *1 Kings 4:33;* and they speak[54] of hyssop which they gather, לעצים, *for wood*; the stalks of which therefore must be of some bigness; yea, they call[55] a stalk which has a top to it, קנה, *a reed*, or cane; which observation seems to reconcile the other evangelists with this: and they distinguish their hyssop which was right for use, from that which had an epithet joined to it; as, Roman hyssop, Grecian hyssop, wild and bastard hyssop:[56] and some writers[57] observe, even of our common hyssop, that it has sometimes stalks of nine inches long, or longer, and hard and woody, nay, even a foot and a half; with one of which a man with his arms stretched out might possibly reach the mouth of a person on a cross: how high crosses usually were, is not certain, nor was there any fixed measure for them; sometimes they were higher, and sometimes lower; the cross or gallows made by Haman for Mordecai was very high indeed, and the mouth of a person could not have been reached with an hyssop stalk; but such a one might, as was erected for Saul's sons, whose bodies on it could be reached by the beasts of the field, *2 Sam. 21:10;* and so low was the cross on which Blandina the martyr suffered, as the church at Lyons relates,[58] when on the cross she was exposed to beasts of prey, and became food for them: so that there is no need to suppose any fault in the text, and that instead of *hyssop* it should be read *hyssos*; which was a kind of javelin the Romans call *pilum*, about five or six

---

[53] Maimon. in Mishna Sabbat, c. 21. sect. 3. Misn. Celim, c. 9. sect. 4.

[54] Mishna Parah, c. 11. sect. 8. Maimon. Hilch. Parah Adumah, c. 11. sect. 7.

[55] Gloss. in T. Bab. Succa, fol. 13. 1.

[56] Mishna Parah, c. 11. sect. 7. Negaim, c. 14. 6. T. Bab. Succa, fol. 13. 1. & Cholin, fol. 62. 2.

[57] Dodonaeus, l. 4. c. 19.

[58] Apud Euseb. Eccl. Hist. l. 5. c. 1. p. 161. Vid. Lipsium de Cruce, l. 3. c. 11.

feet long, which, it is supposed, one of the soldiers might have, and on it put the hyssop with the sponge and vinegar; but this conjecture is not supported by any copy, or ancient version; the Syriac version, which is a very ancient one, reads *hyssop*. The Arabic and Persic versions render it, *a reed*, as in the other evangelists; and the Ethiopic version has both, *they filled a sponge with vinegar, and it was set round with hyssop, and they bound it upon a reed*; and so some have thought that a bunch of hyssop was stuck round about the sponge of vinegar, which was fastened to the top of a reed; and the words will bear to be rendered, *setting it about with hyssop*: this they might have out of the gardens, which were near this place, or it might grow upon the mountain itself; for we are told,[59] it grew in great plenty upon the mountains about Jerusalem, and that its branches were almost a cubit long. Josephus[60] makes mention of a village beyond Jordan called *Bethezob*, which, as he says, signifies the *house of hyssop*; perhaps so called from the large quantity of hyssop that grew near it:

and put it to his mouth. Whether Christ drank of it or not is not certain; it seems by what follows as if He did; at least He took it, being offered to Him: the Jews themselves say,[61] that Jesus said, give me a little water to drink, and they gave Him, חומץ חזק, *sharp vinegar*; which so far confirms the evangelic history.

Verse 30. **When Jesus therefore had received the vinegar**, &c. Of the Roman soldiers, who offered it to Him, either by way of reproach, or to quench His thirst; and He drank of it, as is very likely:

he said, It is finished; that is, the whole will of God; as that He should be incarnate, be exposed to shame and reproach, and suffer much, and die; the whole work His Father gave Him to do, which was to preach the Gospel, work miracles, and obtain eternal salvation for His people, all which were now done, or as good as done; the whole righteousness of the law was fulfilled, a holy nature assumed, perfect obedience yielded to it, and the penalty of death endured; hence a perfect righteousness was finished, agreeable to the law, which was magnified and made honorable by it, and redemption from its curse and condemnation secured; sin was made an end of, full atonement and satisfaction for it were given; complete pardon procured, peace made, and redemption from all iniquity obtained; all enemies were conquered; all types,

---

[59] Arabes Lexicograph. apud de Dieu in loc.

[60] De Bello Jud. l. 6. c. 3. sect. 4.

[61] Toldos Jesu, p. 17.

promises, and prophecies were fulfilled, and His own course of life ended: the reason of His saying so was, because all this was near being done, just upon finishing, and was as good as done; and was sure and certain, and so complete, that nothing need, or could be added to it; and it was done entirely without the help of man, and cannot be undone; all which since has more clearly appeared by Christ's resurrection from the dead, His entrance into heaven, His session at God's right hand, the declaration of the Gospel, and the application of salvation to particular persons:

and he bowed his head; as one dying, and freely submitting to His Father's will, and the stroke of death:

and gave up the ghost. His spirit or soul into the hands of His Father [see the note on *Luke 23:46* **(57)**]; freely laying down that precious life of His which no man could take away from Him.

Verse 31. **The Jews therefore, because it was the preparation**, &c. That is, either of the passover, as in *verse 14;* which was the *Chagigah* or grand festival in which they offered their peace offerings, and slew their oxen, and feasted together in great mirth and jollity; or of the sabbath, the evening of it, or the day before it, as in *Mark 15:42;*

that the bodies should not remain upon the cross on the sabbath day; which was now drawing near: according to the Jewish law, *Deut. 21:22-23*, the body of one that was hanged on a tree was not to remain all night, but to be taken down that day and buried; though this was not always observed; see *2 Sam. 21:9-10*. What was the usage of the Jews at this time is not certain; according to the Roman laws, such bodies hung until they were putrefied, or eaten by birds of prey; wherefore that their land might not be defiled, and especially their sabbath, by their remaining on the cross, they desire to have them taken down:

(for that sabbath day was an high day); it was not only a sabbath, and a sabbath in the passover week, but it was the day in which all the people appeared and presented themselves before the Lord in the temple, and the sheaf of the first fruits was offered up; all which solemnities meeting together made it a very celebrated day: it is in the original text, *it was the great day of the sabbath*; which is the language of the Talmudists, and who say,[62]

"נקרא שבת הגדול, *is called the great sabbath*, on account of the miracle or sign of the passover;"

---

[62] Piske Tosephot Sabbat, art. 314.

and in the Jewish Liturgy[63] there is a collect for the *great sabbath*: hence the Jews pretending a great concern lest that day should be polluted, though they made no conscience of shedding innocent blood,

besought Pilate that their legs might be broken; which was the manner of the Jews,[64] partly to hasten death, since, according to their law, the body was to be taken down before night; and partly that it might be a clear point that the person was rightly executed; for this was not the Roman custom, with whom breaking of the legs, or rather thighs, was a distinct punishment, and was done by laying a man's legs or thighs upon an anvil, and striking them with an hammer;[65] which could not be the case here; this seems to have been done by striking the legs of those that were crucified, which were fastened to the cross, with a bar of iron, or some such instrument. Nonnus suggests that their legs were cut off with a saw or sword; but the former seems more reasonable:

and *that* they might be taken away. Which it seems the Jews had not power to do, but must be done by the Roman soldiers, or by leave at least from the Roman governor; and therefore they make their request to him.

Verse 32. **Then came the soldiers**, &c. Pilate having granted the Jews what they desired; either the soldiers that crucified Christ, and the others with Him, and watched their bodies, being ordered by Pilate, went from the place where they sat; or a fresh company, which were sent for this purpose, came from the city:

and brake the legs of the first; they came unto, which whether it was he that was crucified on His right hand, and was the penitent believer in Him, as some have thought, is not certain:

and of the other which was crucified with him. Who, if the former is true, must be he that reviled Him; and was this their position, it was a lively emblem of the last day, when the sheep shall stand at the right, and the goats on the left hand of Christ.

Verse 33. **But when they came to Jesus**, &c. Whom they passed by before, and now returned to; this they did not out of tenderness to Him, but that He

---

[63] Seder Tephillot, fol. 183. 2. &c. Ed. Basil.

[64] Lactantii Divin. Institut. l. 4. c. 26.

[65] Lipsius de Cruce, l. 2. c. 14. p. 110, 114.

might be the longer in His torture, and whom they reserved till last, that they might use Him with the greater cruelty and barbarity:

and saw that he was dead already; as they might, from the bowing down of His head, the ghastliness of His countenance, the falling of His jaws, and other signs:

they brake not his legs; there being no occasion for it, nor would it have answered any end, were they ever so spiteful and malicious against Him; though the true reason was, and which restrained them from it, divine providence would not suffer them to do it.

Verse 34. **But one of the soldiers**, &c. Whose name some pretend to say was *Longinus*, and so called from the spear with which he pierced Christ:

with a spear pierced his side; His left side, where the heart lies; though the painters make this wound on the right, and the Arabic version of Erpenius, as cited by Dr. Lightfoot, adds the word *right* to make the miracle the greater: this the soldier did, partly out of spite to Christ, and partly to know whether He was really dead; and which was so ordered by divine providence, that it might beyond all doubt appear that He really died, and was not taken down alive from the cross; so that there might be no room to call in question the truth of His resurrection, when He should appear alive again:

and forthwith came there out blood and water. This is accounted for in a natural way by the piercing of the *pericardium*, which contains a small quantity of water about the heart, and which being pierced, a person, if alive, must inevitably die; but it seems rather to be something supernatural, from the asseverations the evangelist makes. This water and blood some make to signify baptism and the Lord's supper, which are both of Christ's appointing, and spring from Him, and refer to His sufferings and death; rather they signify the blessings of sanctification and justification, the grace of the one being represented by water, as it frequently is in the Old and New Testament, and the other by blood, and both from Christ: that Christ was the antitype of the rock in the wilderness, the apostle assures us, in *1 Cor. 10:4;* and, if the Jews are to be believed, He was so in this instance; Jonathan ben Uzziel, in his Targum on *Num. 20:11*, says that,

"Moses smote the rock twice, at the first time, אטיפת אדמא, *blood dropped out*: and at the second time *abundance of waters flowed out*."

The same is affirmed by others[66] elsewhere, in much the same words and order.

---

[66] Shemot Rabba, sect. 3. fol. 94. 1. Zohar in Num. fol. 102. 4.

Verse 35. **And he that saw** *it* **bare record,** &c. Meaning himself, John the evangelist, the writer of this Gospel, who, in his great modesty, frequently conceals himself, under one circumlocution or another; he was an eyewitness of this fact, not only of the piercing of Christ's side with a spear, but of the blood and water flowing out of it; which he saw with his eyes, and bore record of to others, and by this writing; and was ready to attest it in any form it should be desired:

and his record is true; though it is not mentioned by any of the other evangelists, none of them but himself being present at that time:

and he knoweth that he saith true; meaning either God or Christ, who knew all things; and so it is a sort of appeal to God or Christ, for the truth of what he affirmed, as some think; or rather himself, who was fully assured that he was under no deception, and was far from telling an untruth; having seen the thing done with his eyes, and being led into the mystery of it by the Divine Spirit; see *1 John 5:6,8;* wherefore he could, and did declare it with the strongest asseverations:

that ye might believe. The truth of the fact, and in Christ, both for the expiation of the guilt of sin, and cleansing from the filth of it; both for sanctifying and justifying grace, which the water and the blood were an emblem of.

Verse 36. **For these things were done,** &c. The not breaking His bones and piercing His side, and that not by chance, and without design; but,

that the Scripture should be fulfilled, A bone of him shall not be broken. Referring either to *Psa. 34:20, He keepeth all his bones, not one of them is broken;* which, if to be understood of the righteous in general, had a very particular and remarkable accomplishment in Christ; though a certain single person seems to be designed; nor is it true in fact of every righteous man, some of whom have had their bones broken; and such a sense would lead to despair in case of broken bones; for whereas such a calamity befalls them, as well as wicked men, under such an affliction, they might be greatly distressed, and from hence be ready to conclude, that they are not righteous persons, and are not under the care and protection of God, or otherwise this promise would be made good: nor have the words any respect to the resurrection of the dead, as if the sense of it was, that none of the bones of the righteous shall be finally broken; and though they may be broken by men, and in their sight, yet the Lord will raise them again, and restore them whole and perfect at the general resurrection; for this will be true of the wicked, as well as of the righteous: and much less is the meaning of the words, one of His bones shall not be broken, namely, the bone *luz,* the Jews speak of; which, they say,[67] remains uncorrupted in the grave, and is so hard that it cannot be softened by water, nor burnt in the fire, nor ground in the mill, nor broken with a hammer; by and from which God will raise the whole body at the last day: but the words are to be understood of Christ, He is the *poor man* that is particularly pointed at in *Psa. 34:6;* who was poor in His state of humiliation, and who cried unto the Lord, and He heard Him, and saved Him; and He is the *righteous* one, whose afflictions were many, and out of which the Lord delivered Him, *Psa. 34:19;* whose providential care of Him was very particular and remarkable; He kept His bones from being broken, when others were; and by this incident this passage had its literal fulfilment in Him: or else it may refer to the passover lamb, a type of Christ, *1 Cor. 5:7;* a bone of which was not to be broken, *Ex. 12:46; Num. 9:12.* The former of these passages is a command, in the second person, to the Israelites concerning the paschal lamb, *neither shall ye break a bone thereof*; and the latter is delivered in the third person, *nor shall they break any bone of it*; which may be rendered impersonally, *a bone of it, or of him, shall not be broken; or a bone shall not be broken in him*; and so the Syriac and Persic versions read the words here; and in some copies it is, *A bone shall not be broken from him*; and so read the Vulgate Latin and Ethiopic versions; and he that violated this precept, according to the traditions of the Jews, was to be beaten. Maimonides[68] says,

"He that breaks a bone in a pure passover, lo, he is to be beaten, as it is said, *and a bone ye shall not break in it*: and so it is said of the second passover, *and a bone ye shall not break in it*; but a passover which comes with uncleanness, if a man breaks a bone in it, he is not to be beaten: from the literal sense it may be learned, that a bone is not to be broken, whether in a pure or defiled passover: one that breaks a bone on the night of the fifteenth, or that breaks a bone in it within the day, or that breaks one after many days, lo, he is to be beaten; wherefore they burn the bones of the passover in general, with what is left of its flesh, that they may not come to damage: none are guilty but for the breaking of a bone on which there is flesh of the quantity of an olive, or in which there is marrow; but a bone in which there is no marrow, and on which there is no flesh of the quantity of an olive, a man is not guilty for breaking it; and if there is flesh upon it of such a quantity, and he breaks the bone in the place where there is no flesh, he is guilty, although the place which he breaks is quite bare of its flesh: he that breaks after (another) has broken, is to be beaten."

---

[67] Bereshit Rabba, sect. 28. fol. 23. 3. Vajikra Rabba, sect. 18. fol. 159. 3. Zohar in Gen. fol. 51. 1. & 82. 1.

[68] Hilchot Korban Pesach. c. 10. sect. 1-4.

And with these rules agree the following canons:[69]
> "the bones and sinews, and what is left, they burn on the sixteenth
> day, but if that falls on the sabbath, they burn them on the
> seventeenth, because these do not drive away the sabbath or a feast
> day."

And so it fell out this year in which Christ suffered, for the sixteenth was the sabbath day: again,

> "he that breaks a bone in a pure passover, lo, he is to be beaten with
> forty stripes; but he that leaves any thing in a pure one, and breaks in
> an impure one, is not to be beaten with forty stripes;"

yea, they say,[70] though,

> "it was a little kid and tender, and whose bones are tender, they may
> not eat them; for this is breaking of the bone, and if he eats he is to be
> beaten, for it is the same thing whether a hard or a tender bone be
> broken."

Now in this, as in many other respects the paschal lamb was a type of Christ, whose bones were none of them to be broken, to show that His life was not taken away by men, but was laid down freely by Himself: and also the unbroken strength of Christ under the weight of sin, the curse of the law, and wrath of God, and conflict with Satan, when He obtained eternal redemption for us: and also this was on account of His resurrection from the dead, which was to be in a few days; though had His bones been broken He could easily have restored them, but it was the will of God it should be otherwise. Moreover, as none of the bones of His natural body were to be broken, so none that are members of Him in a spiritual sense, who are bone of His bone and flesh of His flesh, shall ever be lost.

Verse 37. **And again another Scripture saith**, &c. *Zech. 12:10;* which, as the former, is referred to on account of the not breaking of His bones, this is cited as fulfilled by the piercing of His side:

They shall look on him whom they pierced. In the Hebrew text it is, *upon me whom they have pierced*; the reason of this difference is, because Christ, who is Jehovah, is there speaking prophetically of Himself; here the evangelist cites it as fulfilled in Him, that is, that part of it which regards the piercing of Him; for that of the Jews looking upon Him and *mourning* is yet to be fulfilled, and will be at the time of their conversion in the latter day, and at the day of judgment. And as the piercing of the Messiah has been literally

---

[69] Mishna Pesachim, c. 7. sect. 10, 11.

[70] Maimon. Korban Pesach. c. 10. sect. 9.

fulfilled in Jesus, there is reason to believe, though the Jews are to this day hardened against Him, that that part of the prophecy which concerns their looking to Him, and mourning for Him on account of His being pierced by them, will also, in God's own time, be fulfilled. Nor is it any objection to the application of this prophecy to our Lord Jesus, that not the Jews, but the Roman soldiers pierced Him, since what one does by another, he may be said to do himself: though it was a Roman soldier that pierced the side of Christ, the Jews might desire and urge him to do it; and however, they agreed to it, and were well pleased with it; and just so Christ is said to be crucified and slain by them; though this was done by the above soldiers, because they prevailed upon Pilate to pass the sentence of death upon Him, and to deliver Him to the soldiers to be crucified. From the citation of this passage it appears, that the writers of the New Testament did not always follow the Greek version of the Old Testament, which here renders the words very differently, and very wrongly; but John cites them according to the Hebrew text, even which we now have, and which is an instance of the truth, purity, and integrity of the present Hebrew books of the Old Testament. The Jewish doctors[71] themselves own that these words respect the Messiah, though they pretend that Messiah ben Joseph is meant, who shall be slain in the wars of Gog and Magog; for since their disappointment, and the blindness and hardness of heart which have followed it, they feign two Messiahs as expected by them; one Messiah ben David, who they suppose will be prosperous and victorious; and the other Messiah ben Joseph, who will suffer much, and at last be killed.

Verse 38. **And after this**, &c. That is, after Jesus had given up the ghost, when it was a clear case that He was dead; as it was before the soldiers came to break the legs of the crucified, and before one of them pierced the side of Jesus with his spear, though that confirmed it: but it seems to be before these last things were done, and yet after the death of Christ, that,

Joseph of Arimathea, went to Pilate, and desired leave to take down the body of Jesus. This Joseph was a counselor, one of the Jewish Sanhedrin; though he did not give his consent to the counsel of the court concerning Jesus: he is here described by the place of his birth, Arimathea. This place has been generally thought to be the same with Ramah or Ramathaim Zophim, the birthplace of Samuel the prophet; and so I have taken it to be in the note on *Matt. 27:57* [*q.v.* **39**]; but there seems to be some reason to doubt about it, since Ramathaim Zophim was in Mount Ephraim, or in the mountainous parts

---

[71] T. Bab. Succa, fol. 52. 1. & ex eodem R. Sol. Jarchi, R. David Kimchi, R. Aben Ezra, & R. Sol. ben Melech. in Zech. 12:10.

of that tribe, *1 Sam. 1:1;* whereas Arimathea is called a city of the Jews, *Luke 23:51.* But if it was in the tribe of Ephraim, it would rather, as Reland[72] observes, be called a city of the Samaritans, to whom that part of the country belonged; besides, as the same learned writer shows from *Judges 4:5; 2 Chron. 19:4,* the mountainous parts of Ephraim were about Bethel, to the north of Jerusalem; whereas Arimathea is mentioned along with Lydda, which lay to the west of it, as it is by Jerome, and others: that ancient writer says,[73] that not far from Lydda, now called *Diospolis,* famous for the raising of Dorcas from the dead, and the healing of Æneas, is Arimathia, the little village of Joseph, who buried the Lord; though he makes this elsewhere[74] to be the same with Ramathaim Zophim: his words are, Armatha Zophim, the city of Elkanah and Samuel, is in the region of Thamna by Diospolis (or Lydda), from whence was Joseph, who, in the Gospels, is said to be of Arimathia; and so in Josephus,[75] and in [the Apocrypha] 1 Maccabees 11:34:

> "Wherefore we have ratified unto them the borders of Judea, with the three governments of Apherema and Lydda and Ramathem, that are added unto Judea from the country of Samaria, and all things appertaining unto them, for all such as do sacrifice in Jerusalem, instead of the payments which the king received of them yearly aforetime out of the fruits of the earth and of trees."

Lydda and Ramatha, or, as in the latter, Ramathem, are mentioned together, as *added unto Judea from the country of Samaria;* which last clause, *from the country of Samaria,* seems to bid fair for a reconciliation of this matter, that those two are one and the same place: and as the birth place of Samuel the prophet is called, by the Septuagint, Armathaim, as has been observed on the note on *Matt. 27:57* [*q.v.* **39**]; so it is likewise called, רמתא, *Ramatha,* by the Targumist on *Hos. 5:8,* as it is also by Josephus.[76] The city of this name, near Lydda, is now called Ramola, and is about thirty-six or thirty-seven miles from Jerusalem. The Syriac, Arabic, and Persic versions render it, *who was of Rama.* Some take this Joseph to be the same with Joseph ben Gorion, the brother of Nicodemus ben Gorion, and who is supposed to be the same

---

[72] Palestina Illustrata, l. 3. p. 581.

[73] Epitaph. Paulae, fol. 59. A.

[74] De locis Hebraicis, fol. 88. K.

[75] Antiqu. l. 13. c. 4. sect. 9.

[76] Ibid. l. 5. c. 10. sect. 2.

Nicodemus mentioned in the next verse. The character the Jews[77] give of Joseph ben Gorion is, that he was a priest, and of the richest and most noble of the priests in Jerusalem; that he was a very wise, just, and upright man; and that three or four years before the destruction of Jerusalem, he was about sixty-seven years of age:

being a disciple of Jesus, but secretly, for fear of the Jews; not one of the twelve, but a private hearer, who had sometimes secretly attended on the ministry of Christ, loved Him, and believed in Him as the Messiah; but had not courage enough to confess Him, and declare for Him, for fear of being put out of the synagogue and Sanhedrin: but now being inspired with zeal and courage, *went in boldly*, as Mark says, and,

besought Pilate that he might take away the body of Jesus: from off the cross, that it might not be any more insulted by His enemies, and might not be thrown with the other bodies into the place where the bodies of malefactors were cast, but that it might be decently interred. This Pilate, the Roman governor, had the disposal of, and to him Joseph applies for it; which was a great instance of his affection for Christ, and was a declaring openly for Him, and must unavoidably expose him to the malice and resentment of the Jews:

and Pilate gave him leave. Having first inquired of the centurion whether He was dead; of which being satisfied, he readily granted it; not only in complaisance to Joseph, who was a man of note and figure, but on account of the innocence of Jesus, of which he was convinced, and therefore was very willing He should have an honorable burial:

He came therefore; to the cross, with proper servants with him,

and took the body of Jesus. Down from the cross, and carried it away. The Alexandrian copy, different from all others, and in language uncommon, reads, *the body of God*.

Verse 39. **And there came also Nicodemus**, &c. To the cross, at the same time as Joseph did; who, whether they were brethren, as some conjecture, and met here by consent, since one prepared one thing, and another another, for the interment of Christ, is not certain. This Nicodemus is thought to be the same with Nicodemus ben Gorion, the Talmudists speak of, who, they say,[78] was one of the three rich men in Jerusalem; as this appears to be a rich man, from the large quantity of myrrh and aloes he brought with him, and which

---

[77] Ganz. Tzemach David, par. 1. fol 25. 1. & 27. 1.

[78] T. Bab. Gittin, fol. 56. 1.

must be very costly. Moreover, they say,[79] that he had another name, which was *Boni*; and they themselves observe,[80] that Boni was one of the disciples of Jesus, as this Nicodemus was, though a secret one, as Joseph: this is he,

which at the first came to Jesus by night; who, when Christ first entered on His ministry, or when he first came unto Him, came to Him by night to discourse with Him about His Messiahship, doctrine, and miracles, *John 3:1-2;* for being one of the Pharisees, a ruler of the Jews, and a Rabbi or master in Israel, he was ashamed, or afraid to converse publicly with Him; however, he went away a disciple; and though he did not openly profess Him, he loved Him, and believed in Him, and now being dead showed his respect to Him:

and brought a mixture of myrrh and aloes, about an hundred pound weight. Not himself, but by his servants. This mixture of myrrh and aloes together, and which was a very large quantity, and exceeding costly, was not designed for the embalming of His body, and preserving it from putrefaction; for He was not embalmed, though myrrh and cassia and other odors were used in embalming;[81] but for perfuming it, and in honor and respect unto Him: it was sweet smelling myrrh, and an aromatic spice called *aloe*, he brought, and not the common aloe. Nonnus calls it the *Indian aloe*, which was of a sweet odor; for which reason it was brought. These are both reckoned with the chief spices, *Song of Sol. 4:14*. *Myrrh* was one of the principal spices in the anointing oil and holy perfume, *Ex. 30:23, 34*. It is a kind of gum or resin called *stacte*, that issues either by incision, or of its own accord, out of the body or branches of a tree of this name, which grows in Arabia and Egypt; and being of an agreeable smell, was used at funerals: hence those words of Martial[82]— & *olentem funera myrrham*; and so Nazianzen, speaking of his brother Caesarius, says,[83]

"He lies dead, friendless, desolate, miserable, σμυρνης ολιγης ηξιωμενος, *favored with a little myrrh*."

And so the aloe was used to perfume, and to give a good scent, *Prov. 7:17*; and Christ's garments are said to smell of *myrrh, aloes, and cassia, Psa. 45:8*. Some have thought, that this was a mixture of the juice of myrrh, and of the

---

[79] T. Bab. Taanith, fol. 20. 1.

[80] T. Bab. Sanhedrin, fol. 43. 1.

[81] Herodotus in Euterpe, c. 86.

[82] L. 11. Epigr. 35.

[83] Epist. 18. p. 781. tom. I.

juice of the aloe plant, and was a liquid into which the body of Christ was put: but this will not so well agree with the winding of the body in linen, with these in the next verse, where they are called spices. A Jew[84] objects to this relation of the evangelist as unworthy of belief: he affirms, that this was enough for two hundred dead bodies, and that it could not be carried with less than the strength of a mule, and therefore not by Nicodemus. In answer to which, it is observed by Bishop Kidder,[85] that we having nothing but the Jew's own word for it, that this was enough for two hundred bodies, and a load for a mule; and that it should be told what was the weight of the λιτρα, or pound, mentioned by the evangelist, ere the force of the objection can be seen; and that it is a thing well known, that among the Jews the bodies of great men were buried with a great quantity of spices: it is said of Asa, that *they buried him in his own sepulcher which he had made for himself, in the city of David, and laid him in the bed which was filled with sweet odors, and divers kinds of spices, 2 Chron. 16:14*. To which may be added, what is before observed, that this was not brought by Nicodemus himself, but by his servants; and what they did by his orders, and he coming along with them, he may be said to do. Just as Joseph is said to take down the body of Jesus from the cross, wind it in linen, and carry it to his sepulcher, and there bury it; this being done by his servants, at his orders, or they at least assisting in it; and as Pilate is said to put the title he wrote upon the cross, though it was done by others, at his command.

Verse 40. **Then took they the body of Jesus**, &c. It being taken down from the cross, and carried to the designed place of interment; they, Joseph and Nicodemus, either themselves, or by their servants, took the body;

and wound it in linen clothes; or *swathed*, or *wrapped it in linen*; rolled it about the body many times, as was the custom of the eastern nations to do; this was what Joseph prepared:

with the spices; which they either wrapped up with the linen, or strew over the body when it was wound up; these Nicodemus brought;

as the manner of the Jews is to bury. Both were usual with them; both to wind up the dead in linen; hence R. Jonathan, alluding to this custom, when R. Isai was taken, and others would have delivered him, said, בסדינו

---

[84] Jacob Aben Amram, porta veritatis No. 1040. apud Kidder, Demonstration of the Messiah, part 3. p. 65, 66. Ed. fol.

[85] Ibid.

יכרך המת, *let the dead be wrapped in his own linen;*[86] and also to bury them with spices; hence we read of *the spices of the dead* in a Jewish canon:[87]

"they do not say a blessing over a lamp, nor over the spices of idolaters; nor over a lamp, nor over הבשמים של מתים, *the spices of the dead:*"
the use of which, Bartenora on the place says, was to drive away an ungrateful smell. The wrapping up the body of Christ in a fine linen cloth, was a token of His purity and innocence; and significative of that pure and spotless righteousness He had now brought in: the strewing it with spices, may denote the fragrancy of Christ's death to Jehovah the Father, in whose sight it was precious, and whose sacrifice to Him is of a sweet smelling savor; and also to all sensible sinners, to whom a crucified Christ is precious; since by His death sin is expiated, the law fulfilled, justice satisfied, reconciliation made, security from condemnation obtained, and death is abolished.

Verse 41. **Now in the place where he was crucified**, &c. Which takes in all that spot of ground that lay on that side of the city where He was crucified; or near to the place of His crucifixion, for it was not a garden in which He was crucified:

there was a garden; all gardens, except rose gardens, were without [*or* outside of] the city, as has been observed on *chapter 18:1*. This, it seems, belonged to Joseph: rich men used to have their gardens without the city for their convenience and pleasure:

and in the garden a new sepulcher; they might not bury within the city. Some chose to make their sepulchers in their gardens, to put them in mind of their mortality, when they took their walks there; so R. Dustai, R. Jannai, and R. Nehurai, were buried, בפרדס, *in a garden*, or orchard;[88] and so were Manasseh and Amon, kings of Judah, *2 Kings 21:18,26*. Here Joseph had a sepulcher, hewn out in a rock, for himself and family, and was newly made. The Jews distinguish between an old, and a new sepulcher; they say,[89]

"קבר חדש, *a new sepulchre* may be measured and sold, and divided, but an old one might not be measured, nor sold, nor divided."

Wherein was never man yet laid. This is not improperly, nor impertinently added, though the evangelist had before said, that it was a *new*

---

[86] T. Hieros. Terumot, fol. 46. 2.

[87] Mishna Beracot. c. 8. sect. 6.

[88] Jechus haabot, p. 43. Ed. Hottinger.

[89] Massech. Sernacot, c. 24. fol. 16. 3.

sepulcher; for that it might be, and yet bodies have been lain in it; for according to the Jewish canons,[90]

> "there is as a new sepulcher, which is an old one; and there is an old one, which is as a new one; an old sepulcher, in which lie ten dead bodies, which are not in the power of the owners, הריזה כקבר חדש, *lo, this is as a new sepulcher.*"

See the note on *Matt. 27:60* **[40]**. Now Christ was laid in a new sepulcher, where no man had been laid, that it might appear certainly that it was He, and not another, that was risen from the dead.

Verse 42. **There laid they Jesus therefore**, &c. Because it was a new sepulcher, and no man had been ever laid there before; and some other reasons are added:

because of the Jews' preparation day; either for the *Chagigah*, or the sabbath, which was just at hand; the Persic version reads, *the night of the sabbath*: for this reason, they could not dig a grave purposely for Him; for it was forbidden on feast days; and therefore they put Him into a tomb ready made: the canon runs,[91]

> "They may not dig pits, וקברות, *nor graves,* on a solemn feast day."

The former of these, the commentators say,[92] are graves dug in the earth, and the latter, edifices built over graves; and for the same reason, because it was such a day, they did not take His body to any of their houses, and embalm and anoint it, as they otherwise would have done; but this being a solemn day, and the sabbath drawing on apace, they hastened the interment, and took the most opportune place that offered:

for the sepulcher was nigh at hand. Some say about a hundred and eight feet from the cross, and others a hundred and thirty feet, though some say but fifty or sixty; at furthest, it was not far off.

---

[90] Ibid.

[91] Mishna Moed Katon, c. 1. sect. 6.

[92] Maimon. & Bartenora in ibid.

CHAPTER 20

Verse 1. **The first *day* of the week**, &c. On the sixth day of the week, towards the close of it, Christ was interred; He lay in the grave all the seventh day, and on the first day of the week, rose from the dead: so the women, after they had observed where the body was laid, went home and prepared spices and ointments, to anoint it; but the sabbath coming on, they were prevented; on which they rested, according to the Jewish law: but as soon as it was over,

cometh Mary Magdalene; not alone, but other women with her; who had attended Christ at the cross, observed where He was buried, and had prepared spices to anoint Him, and now came for that purpose; for not merely to see the sepulcher, and weep at the grave, did she with the rest come, but to perform this piece of funeral service:

early, when it was yet dark; as it was when she set out, the day just began to dawn; though by that time she got to the sepulcher, the sun was rising:

unto the sepulcher; where she saw the body of Jesus laid by Joseph, in a tomb of his, and in his garden; by whose leave, it is probable, being asked over night, she with her companions were admitted:

and seeth the stone taken away from the sepulcher. Which Joseph rolled there, and the Pharisees sealed, and set a watch to observe it. This was removed by an angel; for though Christ Himself could easily have done it, it was proper it should be done by a messenger from heaven, by the order of divine justice, who had laid Him as a prisoner there. Mary's coming so early to the grave, shows her great love and affection to Christ, her zeal, courage, and diligence, in manifesting her respect unto Him: and oftentimes so it is, that the greatest sinners, when converted, are most eminent for grace, particularly faith, love, and humility; and are most diligent in the discharge of duty.

Verse 2. **Then she runneth, and cometh to Simon Peter**, &c. That is, after she had not only seen that the stone was taken away, but had looked into the sepulcher, and saw that the body of Christ was removed; for otherwise she could not have said, that it was taken away out of it: upon which she made all the haste she could to Peter; who, where he was she knew; and she was particularly bid by the angel she saw in the sepulcher to go to him:

and to the other disciple, whom Jesus loved; That is, John, the writer of this Gospel; for these two were together, as they usually were; nor were they alone, for the rest of the disciples were with them:

and saith unto them, They have taken away the Lord out of the sepulcher, and we know not where they have laid him. The Oriental versions, the Syriac, Arabic, Persic, and Ethiopic, read, *I know not where they have laid him*; who they were that had taken the body of Christ away, whether friends or enemies, she could not say; nor did she, or any of the women that were with her, know where it was put; whether in some other grave, or was exposed to the insults of men, or to birds and beasts of prey; whether it was laid in a more suitable and convenient place, or in a scandalous one; and whether this removal was for His greater honor, or reproach; to know this, gave her great concern and uneasiness, as she knew it must the disciples also: so Christ, in a spiritual sense, may be removed from His people for a time, and they know not where He is; sometimes He removes Himself, to chastise them for their former carriage, to try and exercise their grace, to inflame their love to Him, and sharpen their desires after Him, and to endear His presence to them the more, when they enjoy it again; sometimes He is taken away from them by preachers, when they leave Him out of their discourses; and by their own sins and transgressions, which separate between Him and them, with respect to communion; and who, for a time, may not know where to find Him: and for the direction of such, it may be observed, that He is to be found in the ministration of His Word and ordinances, in His churches.

Verse 3. **Peter therefore went forth**, &c. Out of the house where he was, upon hearing the account Mary gave:

and that other disciple; John, the Evangelist and Apostle; the rest of the disciples staying at home and continuing together, waiting to hear what account these two would bring:

and came to the sepulcher. To see with their own eyes what was done, and whether things were as Mary had related; and to make a more particular inquiry into, and examination of them.

Verse 4. **So they ran both together**, &c. At first setting out, and for a while; not content to walk, they ran, being eagerly desirous to know the truth of things:

and that other disciple did outrun Peter, and came first to the sepulcher; John was a younger man than Peter, and so more nimble and swift of foot, and got to the sepulcher before him; and besides, had not that concern of mind to retard him, Peter might have; as, supposing Christ was risen, and he should see Him, how he should be able to look Him in the face, whom he had so shamefully denied.

Verse 5. **And he stooping down, *and looking in*,** &c. That is, John; when he came to the sepulcher, stooped down to look into it, and see what he could see; he only went into the court, or stood upon the floor, where the bearers used to set down the bier, before they put the corpse into one of the graves in the sepulcher, which were four cubits lower; See the note on *Mark 16:5* **[45]**. Hence he was obliged to stoop down, ere he could see any thing within: when he,

saw the linen clothes lying; in which the body had been wrapped, but that itself not there:

yet went he not in. To the sepulcher itself, but waited in the court or porch, till Peter came; and perhaps might be timorous and fearful of going into such a place alone; the Arabic version reads it, *he dared not go in.*

Verse 6. **Then cometh Simon Peter following him,** &c. In a very little time after him:

and went into the sepulcher; itself, though not without first stooping down, as John did; see *Luke 24:12*;

and seeth the linen clothes lie; as John did; and as by the mouth of two or three witnesses every thing is confirmed, so was this [see *Matt. 18:16*]; both saw the linen in which the body was wrapped, but the body was gone; and which was a sign that it was not stolen away, otherwise the linen would not have been left; and besides, it would have taken up some time, and given a good deal of trouble to have unwrapped the body, when it is considered how many foldings the Jews used to wind up their corpse in.

Verse 7. **And the napkin, that was about his head,** &c. The word σουδαριον, rendered *napkin*, is thought to be originally Latin, and signifies an handkerchief, with which the sweat is wiped off the face, and so it is used in *Acts 19:12*, but Nonnus says it is a common word with the Syrians, and the word, סודרא, is used in the Syriac version; and which he renders, κεφαλης ζωστηρα, *the girdle,* or *binding of the head,* for with this the head and face of the dead person were bound; see *John 11:44*. Now Peter, by going into the sepulcher, and looking about him, and examining things more strictly and narrowly, observed that which neither he nor John had taken notice of, when only stooping they looked in: and that is, that this head binder, or napkin, was,

not lying with the linen clothes, but wrapped together in a place by itself. And was plainly the effect of thought, care, and composure; and clearly showed, that the body was not taken away in a hurry, or by thieves, since every thing lay in such order and decency; and which was done, either by our Lord Himself, or by the angels.

Verse 8. **Then went in also that other disciple**, &c. John, being animated by the example of Peter, went down into the sepulcher likewise; whither Peter also might beckon, or call him to be witness with him, of the order and situation in which things lay:

which came first to the sepulcher; yet went last into it; so it was, that the first was last, and the last first:

and he saw; the linen clothes lie in one place, and the napkin folded up in order, lying by itself in another:

and believed. That the body was not there, but either was taken away, or was raised from the dead; but whether as yet he believed the latter is doubtful, by what follows; unless what follows is considered as an illustration, especially of the faith of John, that he should believe the resurrection of Christ, though till now he did not know nor understand the Scriptures that spake of it.

Verse 9. **For as yet they knew not the Scripture**, &c. Meaning, not some particular passage of Scripture, but the writings of the Old Testament in general, and the various places in it which spoke of the resurrection of Christ, either in a way of type, or prophecy; such as *Gen. 22:3-4* and *10:13; Jonah 2:1-7; Psa. 16:10; Hos. 6:2; Isa. 26:19;* and though our Lord had often referred to some of them, at least as in *Matt. 12:40; 16:21* and *20:18-19,* yet such was the dulness of the disciples, or such their prejudices in favor of the Messiah being to continue, and set up a temporal kingdom, that even John, who leaned on His breast, and Peter, who was so inquisitive and desirous of knowing our Lord's meaning in every thing, did not understand the sense of His words, nor of those places of Scripture He had reference to:

that he must rise again from the dead. So it was determined, thus it was predicted, and the justification and salvation of God's elect required it; and yet they knew not the thing, nor the necessity and importance of it.

Verse 10. **Then the disciples**, &c. Peter and John, after they had seen and examined things, and satisfied themselves as much as they could:

went away again unto their own home. Or *to themselves*, as in the original text, and so the Vulgate Latin reads it; not that the meaning is, that they had been out of their minds, and proper exercise of them, and now came to themselves; but they returned to their own company, to the rest of the disciples they left at home, who were as themselves. The Syriac renders it,

לדוכתהון, *to their own place*, and so the Arabic and Persic versions; the place from whence they came, and where the rest were assembled together, to pray, converse, and consult together what was to be done at this juncture.

Verse 11. **But Mary stood without at the sepulcher**, &c. She returned from the city to the sepulcher again, following Peter and John thither, who continued here when they departed, being willing to get some tidings of her Lord, if possible. The word *without*, is omitted by the Syriac, Arabic, and Persic versions, but is in the Greek copies; and is properly put by the evangelist, when rightly understood; for the meaning is not, that she stood without [or outside] the sepulcher, taken in its full extent; for she stood, בחצר, *in the court*, where the bearers set down the corpse, in order to carry it into the cave, or vault; she stood without the innermost part of the sepulcher, but not withoutside the sepulcher itself; as appears from her stooping and looking into it:

weeping; that the body of her dear Lord was taken away, and she prevented of showing that respect unto it she designed; and not knowing in whose hands it was, but fearing it would be insulted and abused by wicked men, her heart was ready to break with sorrow:

and as she wept, she stooped down, *and looked* into the sepulcher; to see if she could see Him, if she and the disciples were not mistaken, being loath to go without finding Him: so it is in a spiritual sense, the absence of Christ is cause of great distress and sorrow to gracious souls; because of the excellency of His person, the near and dear relations He stands in to them; and on account of the nature of His presence and company, which is preferable to every thing in this world; nor can such souls, when they have lost sight of Christ, sit down contented; but will seek after Him in the Scriptures, under the ministry of the Word, and at the ordinances of the Gospel, where a crucified, buried, risen Jesus is exhibited.

Verse 12. **And seeth two angels in white**, &c. Matthew and Mark speak but of one, but Luke of two, as here; whom he calls *men*, because they appeared in a human form, and in shining garments, or white apparel; and which appearance is entirely agreeable to the received notion of the Jews, that as evil angels or devils, are clothed in black, so good angels, or ministering spirits, לבושי לבנים, *are clothed in white*,[1] expressive of their spotless purity and innocence:

---

[1] Gloss. in T. Bab. Kiddushin, fol. 72. 1.

sitting, the one at the head, and the other at the feet, where the body of Jesus had lain. In what position the body of Christ was laid, whether from west to east, as some, or from north to south, as others, is not certain; since the Jews observed no rule in this matter, as appears from the form of their sepulchers, and the disposition of the graves in them; some lying one way, and some another, in the same vault; see the note on *Luke 24:12* **[58]**.

Verse 13. **And they say unto her, Woman, why weepest thou?** &c. Signifying, that she had no reason to weep, but to rejoice and be glad; since, though the body of her Lord was not there, yet He was risen from the dead, and was alive. This they said, partly to rebuke her for her grief, and to comfort her under it: Beza's ancient copy adds here, as in *verse 15, whom seekest thou?* and so does the Ethiopic version:

She saith unto them; without any concern of mind about what they were, and as if they had been of the human kind; for her grief made her fearless, and she cared not who she opened the case to, so that she could get any relief, and any tidings of her Lord:

Because they have taken away my Lord, and I know not where they have laid him. And which she thought was reason sufficient for her weeping; could she but have known that if He was taken away, it was by His friends, and was well used, and she could have had the opportunity of paying her last respects to Him, it would have been a satisfaction; but nothing short of this could dry up her tears.

Verse 14. **And when she had thus said**, &c. As soon as the words were out of her mouth, before she could have an answer from the angels:

she turned herself back; perceiving, either by the looks and gesture of one of the angels, or by hearing a noise, that somebody was behind her:

and saw Jesus standing, and knew not that it was Jesus. She saw a person, but did not know who He was, by reason of the form of His appearance, the difference of His clothes, and not expecting to see Him alive; or through modesty, she might not look wistfully at Him; and besides, her eyes were filled with tears, and swollen with weeping; so that she could not see clearly; and her eyes might be holden also, as the disciples were, that as yet she might not know Him: so sometimes, in a spiritual sense, Christ is with, and near His people, and they know it not: Christ, as God, is omnipresent; He is every where, and in all places; the spiritual presence of Christ is, more or less, in some way or another, always in all His churches, and among His dear people; but the sight of Him is not always alike to them, nor does He appear to them always in the same form; sometimes against them, at least in their apprehensions, nor always in a manner agreeable to their expectations; nor is His grace always discovered in the same way, nor has it the same effect.

Verse 15. **Jesus saith unto her, Woman, why weepest thou**, &c. The same question He puts to her, as was put by the angels: adding,

whom seekest thou? for she was not only weeping for the loss of Him, but was inquiring after Him, if any one saw Him removed from thence, and where He was carried:

She, supposing him to be the gardener; who had the care of the garden, in which the sepulcher was; for not the owner of the garden, who was Joseph, but the keeper of it is meant; she could not imagine that Joseph should be there so early in the morning, but might reasonably think the gardener was:

saith unto him, Sir, if thou have borne him hence, tell me where thou hast laid him, and I will take him away. She addresses Him, though she took Him to be but the gardener, in a very civil and courteous manner; which was rightly judged, especially since she had a favor to ask of Him: she does not mention the name of her Lord, but imagined He knew who she meant, being so lately buried there; and suggests, that perhaps it might not have been so agreeable to the gardener to have His body lie there, and therefore had removed it; and would He but be so kind as to let her know where He was put, she, with the assistance of her friends close by, would take Him away with them. So, in a spiritual sense, a truly gracious soul is willing to do any thing, and to be at any trouble, so that it may but enjoy Christ; it dearly loves Him, as this good woman did; it early, and earnestly, and with its whole heart, seeks after Him, as she did; and absence of Him, or loss of His presence for a while, sharpens the desire after Him, and makes His presence the more welcome.

Verse 16. **Jesus saith unto her, Mary**, &c. He might alter the tone of His voice, and speak unto her as He used to do, calling her by her name in His usual manner: so Christ has personal knowledge of all His people, and can call them by name; He knows them, and makes Himself known to them, before they can know Him; and though He may absent Himself from them for a while, yet not always:

She turned herself, and saith unto him, Rabboni, which is to say, Master. It seems, as if she had dropped her conversation with the supposed gardener at once, and scarce waited for an answer from Him, but turns herself to the angels again, if she could hear any tidings from them; acting like a person in the utmost distress, hurry and confusion; looking this way and that way, to this or the other person: and now upon Christ's speaking to her, in this plain, familiar manner, she turns herself again; when fully knowing Him, she addresses Him with the greatest faith and affection, reverence and humility; calling Him her Lord and Master, and throws herself at His feet. Thus when Christ is pleased to manifest Himself to His people, there goes a power along with His Word, making Himself known; and a word from Christ, attended with divine power, will give a soul a turn to Him from the most excellent creatures, even angels; and when Christ is known, He will be acknowledged with all love, humility, and obedience. The word Rabboni, is of the Chaldee and Syriac form, and signifies *my Lord,* or *Master*; and is commonly applied to one that has a despotic power over another; though all the Oriental versions say, that she spoke to Him in Hebrew. The Syriac and Ethiopic, *Rabboni*, but the Arabic and Persic, *Rabbi*. The titles of *Rab*, *Rabbi*, and *Rabban*, are frequent with the Jewish doctors; who say,[2] that *Rabbi* is greater than *Rab*, and *Rabban* is greater than *Rabbi*; and a man's own name, greater than *Rabban*: but the word in the form here used *Rabbon*, I do not remember ever to have observed applied to any of the doctors; but is frequently used of the Divine Being, who, in their prayers, is often addressed in this manner, עולם רבונו של, *Lord of the world*.[3] I conjecture therefore, that Mary used this word, as expressive of her faith in His power and Godhead, seeing Him alive from the dead; though it might be a name she was used to call Him by before, being convinced from what He had done to her, and by the miracles she had observed performed by Him on others, of His proper Deity; as the poor blind man expresses His faith in the power of Christ to cure Him, by addressing Him in the same language, using the same word, *Mark 10:51.*

Verse 17. **Jesus saith unto her, Touch me not**, &c. Not that His body was an aerial one, or a mere phantom, which could not be touched; the prohibition itself shows the contrary; and besides, Christ's body was afterwards presented to Thomas, to be touched by him, and to be handled by all the disciples; and His feet were held by the women, which is what Mary would have now done: upon the discovery of Him, she threw herself at His feet, and was going to embrace and kiss them, to testify her affection and joy, when she is forbid; not as unworthy of the favor, because she sought Him among the dead, for which the angels reproved her and the rest; but either because He was not to be conversed with, as before His death, His body being raised immortal and glorious; or rather, because He had an errand to send her on to His disciples, which required haste; nor need she stay now to show her respect to Him, since

---

[2] Halichot Olam Tract. 1. c. 3. p. 25.

[3] T. Bab. Taanith, fol. 20. 1. Sanhedrin, fol. 94. 1. Abot R. Nathan, c. 9. Bereshit Rabba, sect. 8. fol. 6. 4.

she would have opportunity enough to do that before His ascension; which though it was to be quickly, yet not directly and immediately; and this seems to be the sense of our Lord's reason:

for I am not yet ascended to my Father; nor shall I immediately go to Him; I shall make some stay upon earth; as He did, forty days before His ascension; when He intimates, she might see Him again, and familiarly converse with Him; at present He would have her stay no longer with Him:

but go to my brethren; this He says, to show that their carriage to Him, being denied by one of them, and forsaken by them all, and the glory He was raised unto, as all this made no alteration in their relation to Him, so neither in His affection to them: Mary was a very proper person to be sent unto them, since she had lately been with them, and knew where they were all assembled together:

and say unto them; as from Himself, personating [*or* representing] Him as it were:

I ascend unto my Father, and your Father, and to my God, and your God. God was His Father, not by creation, as He is to angels and the souls of men, and therefore is called *the Father of spirits* [*Heb. 12:9*]; nor by adoption, as He is to the saints; nor with respect to the incarnation of Christ, for, as man, He had no father; or with regard to His office as Mediator, for as such He was a servant, and not a Son: but He was His Father by nature, or with regard to His divine person, being begotten of Him, and so His own proper Son, and He His own proper Father; which hold forth the natural and eternal Sonship of Christ, His equality with Him, and distinction from Him: and God was the Father of His disciples by adopting grace, in virtue of the covenant of grace made with Christ, and through their spiritual relation to Him, as the natural and eternal Son of God. God the Father, is the God of Christ as man, who prepared, formed, anointed, supported, and glorified His human nature; and in which nature, He prayed to Him as His God, believed in Him, loved and obeyed Him as such; wherefore the Jew[4] very wrongly infers from hence, that He is not God, because the God of Israel was His God; since this is spoken of Him as He is man: and He was the God of His disciples, in and by the covenant of grace made with Christ, as their head and representative; so that their interest in God, as their covenant God and Father, was founded upon His being the God and Father of Christ, and their relation to, and concern with Him; and which therefore must be firm and lasting, and will hold as long as God is the God and Father of Christ. This was good news to be brought to His disciples; which, as it carried the strongest marks of affection, and

---

[4]   R. Isaac Chizzuk Emuna, par. 2. c. 58. p. 446.

expressions of nearness of relation; and implied, that He was now risen from the dead; so it signified, that He should ascend to God, who stood in the same relation to them, as to Him; when He should use all His interest and influence on their behalf, while they were on earth; and when the proper time was come for a removal, that they might be with Him, and with His God and Father and theirs, where they would be to all eternity.

Verse 18. **Mary Magdalene came,** &c. Directly and immediately, being ready and willing to obey the commands of her Lord, with the utmost cheerfulness; and glad to go on such an errand, and carry such news to His disciples, even though her private interest and personal affection might have inclined her to desire to stay with Christ:

and told the disciples that she had seen the Lord; not only that He was risen from the dead, and she had been told so by the angels, but she had seen Him herself, and was an eyewitness of His resurrection, and which she firmly believed; this she said, not only with all the marks of pleasure, joy and transport, but with an air of assurance and confidence:

and *that* he had spoken these things unto her. As that He called them brethren, and bid her go unto them, and acquaint them, that as He was risen, He should in a short time ascend to His Father and theirs, to His God and theirs; all which she faithfully related to them.

Verse 19. **Then the same day at evening**, &c. The same day Christ rose from the dead, and appeared to Mary; at the evening of that day, after He had been with the two disciples to Emmaus, about eight miles from Jerusalem, and they had returned again to the rest [see *Luke 24:13-53*]; and after there had been such a bustle all day in Jerusalem, about the body of Jesus; the soldiers that watched the sepulcher giving out, by the direction of the elders, that the disciples of Christ had stolen away the body, while they slept:

being the first *day* of the week; as is said in *verse 1,* and here repeated, to prevent any mistake; and that it might be clear what day it was the disciples were assembled together, and Christ appeared to them:

when the doors were shut; the doors of the house where they were, which it is plain was in Jerusalem, *Luke 24:33;* but whether it was the house where Christ and His disciples ate the passover together, or whether it was John's home or house, to which he took the mother of Christ, since he and Peter, and the rest, seem to be afterwards together in one place, is not certain: however, the doors were shut; which is not merely expressive of the time of night, when this was usually done; but signifies, that they were really locked and bolted, and barred, for which a reason is given as follows:

where the disciples were assembled for fear of the Jews; after their scattering abroad upon the taking of Christ, and after His crucifixion was over; and especially after the report of His body being taken away, they gathered together, and made fast the doors of the place, lest the Jews should come in upon them, and surprise them; for they might fear, that since they had taken away their master's life, theirs must go next; and especially since it was rumored abroad that they had stolen away His body, they might be under the greater fear that search would be made after them, and they be apprehended and brought into trouble on that account:

came Jesus and stood in the midst; on a sudden, at once, and when they had no thought or fear of any one's coming upon them, without some previous notice; but He being the Almighty God, did, by His omnipotent power, cause the bars and bolts, and doors, in the most secret and unobserved manner, to give way to Him, and let Him in at once among them: when, as a presage and pledge of the accomplishment of His promise to be with, and in the midst of His, when met together, either in private or public [see *Matt. 18:20*], He stood and presented Himself in the midst of them: and to let them know at once He was no enemy, He,

saith unto them, Peace *be* unto you. שלום לכם, *Peace be unto you*, is a usual form of salutation among the Jews; see *Gen. 43:23;* expressive of all prosperity in soul and body, inward and outward, spiritual and temporal; and here may have a special regard to that peace He said He gave unto them, and left with them, upon His departure from them [see *John 14:27*]; and which He had obtained by the blood of His cross, and now preached unto them.

Verse 20. **And when he had so said**, &c. The above salutation, in the most kind, tender and affectionate manner: and to put them out of all pain, and that they might know certainly who He was,

he showed them *his* hands and his side. His hands, which had been pierced with the nails, the marks of which were then to be seen; and which they all knew must be the case, since He was crucified; and His side, which was pierced with a spear, and which left a wide open wound, and which John, who was among them, was an eyewitness of. These He showed, partly to convince them that He was not a spirit, or an apparition, which at first sight they took Him to be, from His sudden appearance among them, the doors being locked and barred; and partly to assure them of the truth of His resurrection, and in the same body, as well as to lead them into a view of His great love in suffering the death of the cross for them; and also to observe to them, from whence that peace and happiness sprung, He had just now saluted them with. It is needless to inquire, whether these marks in His hands, feet, and side, still continue; He was raised with them, that He might show them, for the reasons above given; and should they be thought to continue till all the effects of His death are wrought, since He appears in the midst of the throne and elders, *a Lamb, as it had been slain* [*Rev. 5:6*], and till His second coming, when they that pierced His hands and feet, and side, shall look and mourn [see *Rev. 1:7*], it is not very unreasonable:

Then were the disciples glad when they saw the Lord. For by these marks in His hands, and feet, and side, they were fully convinced, and entirely satisfied that it was He; and that He was risen from the dead; and who now appeared to them: than which a more delightful sight could not be enjoyed by them; whereby was fulfilled, what He had foretold and promised, *chapter 16:22*. So a spiritual sight of Christ, is always rejoicing to a disciple of His; that is, one that has learned of Christ, and *learned Christ* [*Eph. 4:20*], who has believed in Him, and is enabled to deny sinful, righteous, civil, worldly, and natural self, for Christ; and is made willing to take up the cross, bear it, and follow after Him: a sight of Christ as God and man, of His personal beauties and excellencies, of His fulness and suitableness, as a Savior and Redeemer, and so as to have sensible communion with Him, is exceeding delightful to such a one; especially when under a sense of sin, when accused or tempted by Satan, or when Christ has been long absent, or when under affliction, and on a death bed; for Christ is a believer's all; He stands in all relations to Him; and such a soul never sees Christ aright, but it receives something from Him.

Verse 21. **Then said Jesus to them again**, &c. The words He said before:

Peace *be* unto you; which He repeated, to put them out of their fright, by reason of which they returned Him no answer; and to raise and engage their attention to what He was about to say; and to pacify their consciences, distressed with a sense of their conduct towards Him; and with a view to *the gospel of peace* [*Rom. 10:15*], He was now going to send them to preach:

as *my* Father hath sent me, even so send I you. Christ's mission of His disciples, supposes power in Him, honor done to them, authority put upon them, qualifications given them, and hence success attended them; what they were sent to do, was to preach the Gospel, convert sinners, build up saints, plant churches, and administer ordinances. The pattern of their mission, is the mission of Christ by His Father, which was into this world, to do His will, preach the Gospel, work miracles, and obtain eternal redemption for His people; and which mission does not suppose inferiority in His divine person, nor change of place, but harmony and agreement between the Father and Son; the likeness of these missions, lies in these things: their authority is both divine; they are both sent into the same place, the world; and in much the same condition, mean, despicable, hated and persecuted; and in part for the same end, to preach the Gospel, and work miracles for the confirmation of it;

but not to obtain redemption, that being a work done solely by Christ; in which He has no partner, and to whom the glory must be only ascribed.

Verse 22. **And when he had said this**, &c. That is, declared He sent them forth in like manner as His Father sent Him:

he breathed on *them*; in allusion to God's breathing the breath of life into man at His creation; or rather, to the Spirit Himself, who is the breath of God, and proceeds from Him, as from the Father; and who breathes both upon persons in regeneration, and in qualifying for ministerial service, at the instance and influence of Christ: and such an opinion the Jews have of the Spirit of the Messiah, who say[5] that,

"the Spirit went from between the wings of the cherubim, ונשביה, *and breathed upon him* (Menasseh) by the decree, or order of the word of the Lord;"

and saith unto them, Receive ye the Holy Ghost; meaning not the grace of the Holy Ghost in regeneration, which they had received already; but the gifts of the Spirit, to qualify them for the work He now sent them to do, and which were not now actually bestowed; but this breathing on them, and the words that attended it, were a symbol, pledge, and confirmation, of what they were to receive on the day of Pentecost: hence it appears, that it is the Spirit of God, who by His gifts and grace, makes and qualifies men to be ministers of the Gospel; and our Lord by this action, and these words, gives a very considerable proof of His Deity: the Papists show their impudence and wickedness, in imitating Christ by their insufflations, or breathing on men; pretending thereby to convey the Holy Spirit to them.

Verse 23. **Whose soever sins ye remit**, &c. God only can forgive sins, and Christ being God, has a power to do so likewise; but He never communicated any such power to His apostles; nor did they ever assume any such power to themselves, or pretend to exercise it; it is the mark of antichrist, to attempt any thing of the kind; who, in so doing, usurps the divine prerogative, places himself in His seat, and shows himself as if he was God: but this is to be understood only in a doctrinal, or ministerial way, by preaching the full and free remission of sins, through the blood of Christ, according to the riches of God's grace, to such as repent of their sins, and believe in Christ; declaring, that all such persons as do so repent and believe, all their sins are forgiven for Christ's sake: and accordingly,

---

5 Targum in 2 Chron. 33:13.

THE GOSPEL OF JOHN

they are remitted unto them; in agreement with Christ's own words, in His declaration and commission to His disciples; see *Mark 16:16; Luke 24:47*. On the other hand He signifies, that,

whose soever *sins* ye retain, they are retained. That is, that whatsoever sins ye declare are not forgiven, they are not forgiven; which is the case of all final unbelievers, and impenitent sinners; who dying without repentance towards God, and faith in the Lord Jesus Christ [see *Acts 20:21*], according to the Gospel declaration, *shall be damned* [*Mark 16:16*], and are damned; for God stands by, and will stand by and confirm the Gospel of His Son, faithfully preached by His ministering servants; and all the world will sooner or later be convinced of the validity, truth, and certainty, of the declarations on each of these heads, made by them.

Verse 24. **But Thomas, one of the twelve, called Didymus**, &c. The person here spoken of, is described by his Hebrew name *Thomas*, and his Greek one *Didymus*, which both signify a twin; and perhaps he was one. It was common with the Jews to have two names, a Jewish and a Gentile one; by the one they went in the land of Israel, and by the other when out of that land;[6] nay, they often went by one name in Judea, and by another in Galilee;[7] where Thomas might go by the name of *Didymus* with the Greeks, that might live with the Jews in some of those parts: he is also said to be *one of the twelve* apostles, which was their number at first, though Judas now was gone off from them, and therefore are sometimes only called the *eleven*; but this having been their complement, it is still retained; but what is observed of him to his disadvantage and discredit is, that he,

was not with them when Jesus came. Beza's ancient copy reads, *he was not there with them*; and so read the Syriac, Arabic, and Persic versions; he either had not returned to the rest, after their scattering one from another upon the apprehending of Christ; or did not choose to assemble with the rest, for fear of the Jews; or was taken up with some business and affair of life; however, he was not with the rest of the disciples, when they were assembled together, and Jesus appeared among them. As it is of good consequence to attend the assemblies of Christ's disciples and followers, so it is of bad consequence to neglect or forsake them: it is frequently to good purpose that persons attend them [see *Heb. 10:23-25*]; here God comes and blesses His people; Jesus grants His presence, the graces of the Spirit are increased, and drawn forth into exercise; souls that have lost sight of Christ find Him,

---

6 T. Hieros. Gittin, fol. 43. 2.

7 Ibid. fol. 45. 3.

disconsolate ones are comforted, weak ones strengthened, and hungry ones fed: on the other hand, not to attend is of bad consequence; neglect of assembling together, exposes to many snares and temptations; brings on a spiritual leanness; leads to an indifference and lukewarmness; issues in a low degree of grace, and a non-exercise of it, and in a loss of Christ's presence.

Verse 25. **The other disciples therefore said unto him**, &c. Some time in the same week, as they had opportunity of seeing him, with great joy, and full assurance of faith in Christ's resurrection:

We have seen the Lord. They had not only the testimony of the women, and the declaration of the angels, but they saw Him with their own eyes, and beheld even the very prints of the nails in His hands and feet, and of the spear in His side, and therefore could not be mistaken and imposed upon: a spiritual sight of Christ is a blessing often enjoyed by attending the assembly of the saints; to see Christ, is the desire of every gracious soul; this is the end of their meeting together for social worship; the Word and ordinances have a tendency in them to lead souls to a sight of Him; and it may be expected, because it is promised; and whenever it is enjoyed, it is very delightful; and a soul that meets with Christ in an ordinance, cannot but speak of it to others; and which He does with joy and pleasure, in an exulting, and even in a kind of a boasting manner; and that for the encouragement of others to attend likewise:

But he said unto them, Except I shall see in his hands the print of the nails, and put my finger into the print of the nails, and thrust my hand into his side, I will not believe. That nails were used in the crucifixion of Christ, is certain from this place, though nowhere else mentioned; whereby the prophecy of Him in *Psa. 22:16* was fulfilled; for these were not always used in this kind of death. The bodies of men were sometimes fastened to the cross with cords, and not nails.[8] How many were used, whether three, as some, or four, as others, or more, as were sometimes used,[9] is not certain, nor material to know. The Alexandrian copy, and some others, and the Vulgate Latin, Syriac, and Persic versions read, *the place of the nails*; that is, the place where the nails were driven. Thomas knew that Christ was fastened to the cross with nails, and that His side was pierced with a spear; which he, though not present, might have had from John, who was an eyewitness thereof; but though they had all seen Him alive, he will not trust to their testimony; nay, he was determined not to believe his own eyes; unless

---

[8] Vid. Lipsium de Cruce, l. 2. c. 8. p. 87.

[9] Ibid. c. 9. p. 91.

he put his finger into, as well as saw, the print of the nails, and thrust his hand into His side, as well as beheld the wound made by the spear, he is resolved not to believe. And his sin of unbelief is the more aggravated, inasmuch as this disciple was present at the raising of Lazarus from the dead by Christ, and had heard Christ Himself say, that He should rise from the dead the third day. We may learn from hence how great is the sin of unbelief; that the best of men are subject to it; and that though this was overruled by divine providence to bring out another proof Christ's resurrection, yet this did not excuse the sin of Thomas: and it may be observed, that as Thomas would not believe without seeing the marks of the nails and spear in Christ's flesh; so many will not believe, unless they find such and such marks in themselves, which often prove very ensnaring and distressing. Just such an unbeliever as Thomas was, the Jews make Moses to be, when Israel sinned: they say,

"He did not believe that Israel had sinned, but said, איני רואה איני מאמין אם, *if I do not see, I will not believe.*"[10]

Verse 26. **And after eight days**, &c. That is, after another week, the same day a week later, which, taking in the day in which Christ rose and appeared to Mary Magdalene, and His disciples, and the day in which He now appeared to the disciples with Thomas, made eight days; a like way of speaking see in *Luke 9:28,* compared with *Matt. 17:1.* And Dr. Hammond has proven from Josephus,[11] that the Jews used to express a week by eight days.

again his disciples were within; within doors, in some private house; probably the same as before, in some part of the city of Jerusalem:

and Thomas with them: which shows their harmony and agreement, their frequency and constancy in meeting together, and their Christian forbearance with Thomas, notwithstanding his unbelief; whom they looked upon as a good man, and retained in their company, hoping by one means or other he would be convinced: and it also shows Thomas's regard to them, and affection for them, by meeting with them, though he had not the same faith in the resurrection of Christ:

then **came Jesus**; when the disciples, with Thomas, were together; so making good His promise to meet with His people when they meet; and thereby putting an honor upon, and giving encouragement to attendance with the saints: If it should be asked, Why did not Christ come sooner? It may be replied, That the reason, on His part, was, it was His will and pleasure to

---

[10] Shemot Rabba, sect. 46. fol. 142. 2.

[11] Antiqu. l. 7. c. 9.

come at this time, and not before; Christ has His set times to Himself, when He will appear and manifest Himself to His people: on Thomas's part the reasons might be, partly to rebuke him for his sin, and that the strength of his unbelief might appear the more, and that some desire might be stirred up in him to see Christ, if He was risen. And on the part of the disciples, because they did not meet together sooner; and for the further trial of their faith, whether it would continue or not, Thomas obstinately persisting in his unbelief:

the doors being shut; as before, and for the same reason, *for fear of the Jews*, as well as for the privacy of their devotion and conversation:

and stood in the midst; having in the same powerful manner as before caused the doors, locks, and bars to give way, when at once He appeared in the midst of them all, not to Thomas alone, but to all the eleven; and this the rather, because the disciples had borne a testimony to Christ's resurrection, and which He meant now to confirm; and to rebuke Thomas publicly, who had sinned before them all:

and said, Peace *be* **unto you**. Which He had said before, and now, saluting Thomas in like manner as He did the rest, notwithstanding his unbelief.

Verse 27. **Then saith he to Thomas**, &c. For whose sake He chiefly came, and whom He at once singled out from the rest, and called by name in the most friendly manner, without upbraiding or reproaching him for not believing the testimony that had been given him:

Reach hither thy finger, and behold my hands, and reach hither thine hand and thrust *it* **into my side**; that is, make use of every way by seeing, feeling, and examining the scars in my hands, and the hole in my side, and satisfy thyself in the manner thou hast desired; which shows the omniscience of Christ, who knew what had passed between him and the other disciples, and the very words Thomas had expressed himself in; also His great humility and condescension in submitting Himself to be examined in the very manner he had fixed; and likewise the reality of His resurrection:

and be not faithless, but believing. In which words Christ dissuades him from unbelief, which is very evil in its own nature, and in its effects; it is the root of all evil; it unfits for duty, and renders the word unprofitable, and leads men off from Christ; and is the more aggravated in the people of God, by the instances, declarations, and promises of grace, and discoveries of love made unto them: and He also encourages him to believe. The exercise of the grace of faith is well pleasing to Christ; it gives glory to Him, and makes for the soul's comfort; and a word from Christ, His power going along with it, will enable men to believe, as it did Thomas; which appears by what follows.

Verse 28. **And Thomas answered and said unto him**, &c. Without examining His hands and side, and as astonished at His condescension and grace, and ashamed of his unbelief:

My Lord and my God. He owns Him to be *Lord*, as He was both by creation and redemption; and *God*, of which he was fully assured from His omniscience, which He had given a full proof of, and from the power that went along with His words to his heart, and from a full conviction he now had of His resurrection from the dead. He asserts his interest in Him as *his* Lord and *his* God; which denotes his subjection to Him, his affection for Him, and faith in Him; so the divine Word is called in Philo the Jew, κυριος μου, *my Lord*.[12]

Verse 29. **Jesus saith unto him, Thomas**, &c. The word *Thomas* is omitted in the Alexandrian copy, and in Beza's ancient copy, and in some others, and in the Syriac, Arabic, and Ethiopic versions;

because thou hast seen me, thou hast believed; which carries in it a tacit and gentle reproof for his unbelief, and suggests, that if he had not seen, he would not have believed; but is not so harsh as if that had been expressed; and which the Jews were wont to do in a severe manner:[13]

> "One said to R. Jochanan, Expound *Rabbi*; for it is beautiful for thee to expound: for as thou sayest, so I see. He replied to him, Raka, האמנת אלמלא לא ראית לא, *if thou seest not, thou wilt not believe*."

Christ here allows that Thomas had believed that He was risen from the dead, and that He was his Lord and God; and though his faith was late and slow, it was sure and certain, and was appropriating; it was a faith of interest, though upon sight, and not on hearing, or the report of the other disciples: now faith on sight may be in persons who have no true spiritual faith; as in some that saw both the person and miracles of Christ on earth, and in others who will see Him come in the clouds of heaven; and it has been in others who have truly believed in Christ, as the apostles of the Lamb: but yet, though it may be, as in many it has been, right, yet not so commendable as that without it. From hence may be observed, that Christ allows of the epithets and titles given Him by Thomas, and therefore must be Lord and God; and approves of Thomas's faith, and therefore that must be right; though He prefers faith without personal sight of Him to it, in the next clause:

blessed *are* they that have not seen, and *yet* have believed. The author of the apocryphal book of 2 Esdras 1:37, says of,

---

[12] Lib. Allegor. l. 2. p. 101.

[13] T. Bab. Bava Bathra, fol. 75. 1. & Sanhedrin, fol. 100. 1.

"the people to come, whose little ones rejoice in gladness, in the person of the Almighty Lord, *though they have not seen me with bodily eyes, yet in spirit they believe the thing that I say.*"

It seems as if there were some at this time in the city of Jerusalem, who firmly believed that Christ was risen from the dead, upon the testimony of others, though they had not seen Him themselves. Faith without sight, in other respects, may be considered as opposed to the beatific vision in heaven; and as destitute of sensible communion with God; and as giving credit to doctrines and things above carnal sense and reason; such as the doctrines of the Trinity, the Sonship of Christ, His incarnation, and the union of the two natures in Him, and the resurrection of the dead; and as believing whatever is said in the Word of God, upon the credit of His testimony; and which has for its objects things past, as what were done in eternity, in the council and covenant of grace; the works of creation and providence in time, the birth, sufferings, death, and resurrection of Christ; and also things present, Christ, and the blessings of grace; and things to come, the invisible glories of the other world. Now such are happy that have true faith in these things, for they enjoy many blessings now, as a justifying righteousness, pardon of sin, adoption, freedom of access to God, and security from condemnation; they have spiritual peace, joy, and comfort in their souls, and shall at last be saved with an everlasting salvation.

Verse 30. **And many other signs truly did Jesus**, &c. Besides these wonderful appearances to His disciples once and again, when the doors were shut about them: and which signs refer not to what was done before, but after His resurrection; and which He did,

in the presence of his disciples; for He appeared to, and conversed with no other but them after His resurrection:

which are not written in this book; of John's Gospel; though they may be elsewhere; such as His appearing to the two disciples going to Emmaus [*Luke 24:13-22*], and to the eleven on a mountain in Galilee [*Matt. 28:16*], and to five hundred brethren at once [*1 Cor. 15:6*], which other inspired writers speak of: and many there are which He did, which are not particularly written in this, nor in any other book; for He was seen of His disciples forty days, and showed Himself alive, *by many infallible proofs* [*Acts 1:3*]; all of which are not recorded.

Verse 31. **But these are written**, &c.. The several ends of recording what is written in this book, in proof of Christ's resurrection, are as follow: one is,

that ye might believe that Jesus is the Christ, the Son of God; that Jesus, who was diminutively called Jesus the son of Mary, the son of Joseph, the carpenter's son, Jesus of Nazareth, and of Galilee, was the *Christ*, or true Messiah; which signifies *Anointed*, and takes in all His offices of Prophet, Priest, and King, to which He was anointed; and is an article of faith of the greatest importance; and is to be believed through the signs proving His resurrection, who, according to the Scriptures, was to rise again; and which, by the signs here recorded, it appears He is risen indeed, and therefore must be the true Messiah of the prophets, and also *the Son of God*; which was a known title of the Messiah among the Jews; and is not a name of office, but of nature and relation to God, and designs Christ in His divine nature, or as a divine person; and is an article of great moment, and well attested, by God, by angels, and men; and receives a further confirmation by the resurrection of Christ, who is thereby declared to be the Son of God with power; and with this view did this evangelist write the signs proving it, herein to be found. And his other end in recording them is,

and that believing ye might have life through his name. Believers have their spiritual and eternal life through Christ; their life of grace, of justification on Him, of sanctification from Him, and communion with Him; the support and maintenance of their spiritual life, and all the comforts of it: and also their life of glory, or eternal life, they have *through* or *in* His name; it lies in His person, it comes to them through Him as the procuring cause of it; it is for His sake bestowed upon them, yea, it is in His hands to give it, and who does give it to all that believe: not that believing is the cause of their enjoyment of this life, or is their title to it, which is the name, person, blood, and righteousness of Christ; but faith is the way and means in which they enjoy it; and therefore these signs are written by the evangelist for the encouragement of this faith in Christ, which is of such use in the enjoyment of life, in, through, and from Him. Beza's ancient copy, two of Stephens's, the Coptic, Syriac, Arabic, Persic, and Ethiopic versions read, *eternal life*.

CHAPTER 21

Verse 1. **After these things**, &c. The resurrection of Christ from the dead, His appearance to Mary Magdalene, and twice to His disciples; once when Thomas was absent, and at another time when he was present:

Jesus showed himself again to the disciples, a third time, as in *verse 14*, though not to them all; seven are only mentioned, as together, when He appeared to them:

at the sea of Tiberias; the same with the sea of Galilee; of this sea frequent mention is made in Jewish writings;[1] see *John 6:1*; for after the second appearance of Christ to His disciples, they went from Jerusalem to Galilee, by the order of Christ, who appointed to meet them there, *Matt. 28:10,16*.

and on this wise showed he *himself*. The manner in which He made His appearance, and the persons to whom, are as follow.

Verse 2. **There were together**, &c. In one place, in one house, in some town, or city of Galilee, not far from the sea of Tiberias; nor, as very likely, far from the mountain where Christ had promised to meet them;

Simon Peter, who though he had denied his Lord, dearly loved Him, and truly believed in Him, kept with the rest of His disciples, and was waiting for another interview with Him:

and Thomas, called Didymus; who, though for a while an unbeliever with respect to the resurrection of Christ, was now fully assured of it, and, for the future, was unwilling to lose any opportunity of meeting with his risen Lord.;

and Nathanael of Cana in Galilee; *an Israelite indeed*, in whom there was no guile. Dr. Lightfoot thinks he is the same with Bartholomew, and so one of the eleven. The Syriac version reads it, *Cotne*, and the Persic, *Catneh* of Galilee; no doubt the same place is meant, where Jesus turned water into wine, of which Nathanael was an inhabitant:

and the *sons* of Zebedee; who were James, whom Herod killed *with the sword* [*Acts 12:2*], and John, the writer of this Gospel:

and two other of his disciples. Who are thought to be Andrew and Philip; which is very likely, since they were both of Bethsaida, *John 1:44*, a city in Galilee, and not far from the sea of Tiberias. Andrew is particularly mentioned by Nonnus: so that here were seven of them in all; four of them, according to this account, being wanting; who must be James the less, the brother of our Lord, Judas called Lebbeus, and surnamed Thaddaeus, Simon the Canaanite, or Zealot, and Matthew the publican.

Verse 3. **Simon Peter saith unto them, I go a fishing**, &c. Which was his business before his conversion; and now having nothing to do, and his Lord and Master having, as yet, no service for him in the ministry of the Word, until the Spirit was poured down in an extraordinary manner, which was given to be expected, in the mean while he was inclined to, and resolved upon taking up his former employment; partly that he might not live an idle life,

---

[1] See Yalkut, par. 2. fol. 74.1 & 98.3. T. Bab. Bathra, fol. 74.2.

and partly to obtain a livelihood, which was now to be sought after in another manner, since the death of Christ; and these inclinations and resolutions of his he signifies to the rest of the disciples, who agreed with him:

They say unto him, We also go with thee. That is, a fishing; for it seems to have been the business and employment of them all formerly: the place they went to was the sea of Tiberias, as appears from *verse 1*, a place free for any to fish at. This is said to be one of the ten traditions which Joshua delivered to the children of Israel, when he divided the land among them:[2]
"that any man should be free to catch fish in the waters (or sea) of Tiberias; and he might fish with a hook only; but he might not spread a net, or place a ship there, except the children of the tribe to whom that sea belonged in their division."
But now these disciples, or the greater part of them at least, belonging to the tribe and division in which this sea was, had a right to carry a ship or boat thither, and make use of a net, as they did. Besides, there was another reason for fishing here, because there were no unclean fish; for the Jews say[3] that,
"In a place of running water no clean fish goes along with unclean fish, and lo, the sea of Tiberias is כגון המים מהלכין הן, *as running waters*."

They went forth: from the house, town, or city where they were, whether Capernaum, or Bethsaida, or Tiberias itself:

and entered into a ship immediately; which was either one of their own, that belonged to some one of them before their call; which though they had left, had reserved their right and claim unto; see *Luke 5:3;* or which they hired for their present purpose: the word *immediately* is not in the Vulgate Latin, nor in the Syriac, Arabic, Persic, and Ethiopic versions, nor in Beza's ancient copy:

and that night they caught nothing. They went out in the evening of the day, and fished all night, that being a proper time for such business, and the most likely to succeed in, but caught no fish, or very little: and so it is sometimes with Gospel ministers, who are fishers of men, though they take every opportunity, and the most proper methods to gain souls to Christ, yet sometimes do not succeed; which makes things look dark and gloomy in their apprehensions.

---

[2] Maimon. Hilch. Nezike Mammon, c. 5. sect. 3. Vid. T. Bab. Bava Kama, fol. 81.1.

[3] T. Hieros. Avoda Zara, fol. 42. 1.

Verse 4. **But when the morning was now come**, &c. The day began to dawn, and light to appear, very early in the morning; for Christ visits His right early, and is a present help to them in their time of trouble.

Jesus stood on the shore: on firm ground, while His disciples were beating about in the waves, and toiling to no purpose. So Christ, risen from the dead, is glorified, is in heaven; but not unmindful of His people amidst all their afflictions in this world:

but the disciples knew not that it was Jesus. Though He was so near them that they could hear what He said; but it not being broad daylight they could not distinctly discern Him, or their eyes might be held that they could not know Him. So Christ is sometimes near His people, and they know it not.

Verse 5. **Then Jesus saith unto them, Children**, &c. And still they knew Him not, though He used this endearing and familiar appellation, and which they had been wont to hear from Him; and He had called them by a little before His departure from them, *John 13:33*; and which He uses here as expressive of His tender affection for them, their relation to Him, and that He might be known by them:

have ye any meat? That is, as the Syriac renders it, מדם למלעס, *anything to eat*; meaning fish that they had caught; and whether they had gotten a sufficient quantity to make a meal of for Him and them.

They answered him, No. They had gotten nothing at all; or at least what they had, was far from being enough to make a breakfast of; for so a meal early in a morning may be most properly called, though it was afterwards called dining. Christ's children, true believers, are sometimes without spiritual food; there is always indeed enough in Christ, and He has a heart to give it; but either through prevailing iniquity they feed on something else, or do not go to Him for food, or go elsewhere; but He will not suffer them to starve; for as He has made provision for them in the ministry of the Word and ordinances; and He Himself is the bread of life; if they do not ask Him for food, He will ask them whether they have any; will kindly invite them to the provision He Himself makes; will bid them welcome, and bless them to them.

Verse 6. **And he said unto them**, &c. Willing to make Himself known by a miracle, since they knew Him not by His person, nor voice:

Cast the net on the right side of the ship, and ye shall find. That is, a large multitude of fish, as they did. The ship was an emblem of the church in its present afflicted state; the right side of it points to the elect, and where they are to be found in this world; the casting of the net signifies the preaching of the Gospel; the promise of finding fish, the assurance Christ

628

gives of the success of His Word, which He owns and blesses for the conversion of elect sinners:

They cast therefore; the net, willing to try what success they might have at the instance of this person, whom they knew not. The Ethiopic version reads the passage thus, *And they said unto him, We have labored all night, and have found nothing, but at thy word we will let down*; which seems to be taken out of *Luke 5:5*. However, they obeyed His orders and directions, as the faithful ministers of the Gospel do, and should, and succeeded:

and now they were not able to draw it for the multitude of fishes. The Syriac adds, *which it held*; being in number, as in *verse 11, an hundred and fifty and three* great fishes; which was an emblem and presage of that large number of souls, both among the Jews and Gentiles, which they should be instrumental in bringing to Christ, through the preaching of the Gospel.

Verse 7. **Therefore that disciple whom Jesus loved**, &c. Which was John the Evangelist and Apostle, the writer of this Gospel:

saith unto Peter, It is the Lord. Which two disciples were very intimate with each other, and communicated their thoughts freely to one another. John knew that it was the Lord, either by some special revelation, or from the multitude of fishes which were taken, and which showed a divine hand and power to be concerned. So faithful ministers of the Gospel know when Christ is with them, by His power attending their ministrations to the conversion of souls. The Cambridge copy of Beza's reads, *our Lord*; as do the Syriac, Persic, and Ethiopic versions; and it is reasonable to think, John speaking to a fellow disciple, who had equal interest in Him with himself, might so say.

Now when Simon heard that it was the Lord; faith came by hearing [as in *Rom. 10:17*], he was immediately convinced, and thoroughly satisfied, having received the hint upon a reflection on the surprising capture of the fishes, that it must be the Lord:

he girt *his* fisher's coat *unto him*; the Greek word, επενδυτης, here used, is manifestly the אפונדת of the Hebrews; and which, the Jewish writers say,[4] was a strait garment, which a man put on next [to] his flesh to dry up the sweat; and a very proper one for Peter, who had been toiling all night, and very fit for him to swim in; and, by what follows, appears to be put on him next [to] his flesh:

---

[4] Maimonides & Bartenora in Mishna Sabbat, c. 10. sect. 3.

(for he was naked); for to suppose him entirely naked, while fishing, being only in company with men, and those parts of nature having a covering, which always require one, was not at all indecent and unbecoming:

and did cast himself into the sea. The Syriac adds, *that he might come to Christ*; and the Persic, *and he came to Christ*; showing his great love and eagerness to be with Him; and, as fearless of danger, risks all to be with Christ; his love being such, that many waters could not quench, nor floods drown.

Verse 8. **And the other disciples came in a little ship**, &c. The same that they were fishing in, in which they came to Christ as soon as they could, not choosing to expose themselves, as Peter did; nor was it proper that they should leave the ship, and, as it was, might have hands few enough to bring both ship and net, so full of fish, safe to shore; and the rather, they did not think fit to do as he did,

(for they were not far from land, but as it were two hundred cubits); which was about a hundred yards:

dragging the net with fishes. Towing the net full of fishes all along in the water, till they came to land; an emblem of laborious Gospel ministers, who being once embarked in the work of the ministry, continue in it to the end, notwithstanding all toil, labor, and difficulties that attend them; and will at last bring the souls with them they have been made useful to, with great satisfaction and joy, to their dear Lord and Master.

Verse 9. **As soon then as they were come to land**, &c. As soon as they were come out of the ship, and safe on shore, not only Peter, but all the rest of the disciples:

they saw a fire of coals there: on the shore, to their great surprise:

and fish laid thereon; which could not be any that they had taken, for, as yet, the net was not drawn up, and the fish taken out:

and bread. Not upon the coals baking, but hard [*or* close] by, being ready prepared to eat with the fish, when sufficiently broiled. This was all of Christ's preparing, and a considerable proof of His Deity; and a confirmation of that provision He will make for His ministering servants, while they are about His work, and in this world; and a representation of that spiritual and eternal refreshment they shall have with Him in heaven to all eternity, when they have done their work.

Verse 10. **Jesus saith unto them**, &c. The disciples:

Bring of the fish which ye have now caught. For they might have caught some before, though so few and small, as scarcely to be reckoned any; nor were they bid to bring all they had taken, only some of them, to add to these Christ had prepared for them on land; they being both indeed of a miraculous production, and the effects of His divine power. Christ's view in ordering to bring some of them, and put to those that lay upon the coals, was partly that they might have enough to make a meal of for them all; and also, that they might have a more perfect knowledge of the miracle wrought, by seeing the number and largeness of the fishes, and by bringing the net full of them to shore unbroken; and may be an emblem of the bringing of souls to Christ by the ministry of the word, thereby adding to those that are already gathered.

Verse 11. **Simon Peter went up,** &c. Either to the sea, that being higher than the land, or to the ship which lay by the shore: he went aboard it,

and drew the net to land full of great fishes; not alone, but others of the disciples with him; though he only is mentioned, being the leading person in this affair; an emblem of the whole number of God's elect being brought safe to shore, to Christ, and to heaven, through various tribulations and afflictions in the world, fitly signified by the *waves* of the sea;

an hundred and fifty and three; what mystery there may be in the number, I know not. The conjecture of Grotius, that it is a figure of the proselytes in the days of David and Solomon, seems to be without foundation; since they were not only so many thousands, but six hundred over. And as little to be regarded is the thought of others, that the larger number, one hundred, regards the converted among the Gentiles, and the lesser those among the Jews; much better is the observation of others, that it may design a collection, out of all sorts of people, to Christ, and His church [see the note on *verse 6*];

and for all there were so many; in number, and these so large and big, and the weight of them so great. The Syriac reads, בהנא כלה יוקרא, *with all this weight*, or *burden*, and so the Persic; but the Arabic, *with such a number*; both ideas of number and weight are to be preserved, to make what follows the more observable:

yet was not the net broken. Which must be ascribed to the divine power of Christ; and is an emblem of the power of God attending the Gospel, to the regeneration, conversion, and salvation of His people, and of the great usefulness of it, however mean [*or* lowly] and despicable it may be in the eyes of men, and of its permanence and duration, until all the elect of God are gathered in by it.

Verse 12. **Jesus saith unto them, Come and dine**, &c. One would think it should rather have been said, Come and take a breakfast, than a dinner, since it was so early in the morning: but Grotius has observed, out of Homer, that αριστον, is used for food taken in a morning; so that it may signify here, not what we properly call dining, but eating a morning's meal; and may be an emblem of that spiritual refreshment believers enjoy with Christ in His house and ordinances now, and of those everlasting pleasures they will partake with Him in the resurrection morn: and it is to be observed, that He does not say, *Go and dine*, but *Come and dine*; that is, along with Himself. He does not send His disciples elsewhere for food, but invites them to come to Him, to hear His Word, which is food for faith, to wait in His house, where plenty of provision is made, and to attend on His ordinances, and in all to feed upon Himself, and to feed with Him; to all which they are heartily welcome.

And none of the disciples durst ask him, Who art thou? knowing that it was the Lord. To ask such a question was altogether unnecessary, and would have been impertinent, and they might justly have been upbraided and rebuked for it: it would have looked like insolence, or unbelief, or both, and that greatly aggravated, when it was so clear a case that it was the Lord; who might be known by His voice and person, especially when they came near to Him, and also by the miracles which He wrought: so at the last day, when every eye shall see Him coming in the clouds of heaven, none will ask who He is; all will know Him.

Verse 13. **Jesus then cometh, and taketh bread**, &c. After they had taken the fish out of the net, and all was prepared for the meal, and the disciples were set down to eat, Christ came and took His place as the Master of the feast, and Head of the family; and taking up the bread, as was His usual method, He asked a blessing over it, and gave thanks for it. Beza's ancient copy, and one of Stephens's read, *and having given thanks, he gave*, &c. which is agreeable to His usual practice at meals:

and giveth them, and fish likewise. He distributed both bread and fish to His disciples. So, in a spiritual sense, He provides plentifully for His people; gives them to eat of the hidden manna, and tree of life, and leads to fountains of living waters; encourages them to eat and drink freely, what is of His own preparing, and at His own expense provided for them.

Verse 14. **This is now the third time**, &c. Or day of Christ's appearance to His disciples: He appeared to them first on the same day He rose, and then a second time eight days after, or that day se'nnight [*or* seven nights and days: a week later], and now at the sea of Tiberias; for within this compass of time

He had made more appearances than three, though to particular persons, and not to such a number of the disciples as at these three times:

that Jesus showed himself to his disciples, after that he was risen from the dead. And thus, as by *the mouth of two or three witnesses*, every thing is established [*Matt. 18:16*]; so by these three principal appearances of Christ to His disciples, His resurrection from the dead was confirmed.

Verse 15. **So when they had dined**, &c. The Persic version adds, *Jesus turned his face to Simon Peter*; He did not interrupt them while they were eating; but when they had comfortably refreshed themselves, He looked at Peter, and singled him out from the rest, and directed His discourse to him;

Jesus saith to Simon Peter, Simon, *son* of Jonas; not *John*, as the Vulgate Latin, and Nonnus, and some copies read; for this answers not to the Hebrew word *Jochanan*, but *Jonah*, the same name with the prophet. Some have observed, that Christ spoke to him particularly by his original name, and not by that which He Himself had given him, with a view to his strong faith, as Cephas, or Peter; but it should be known that Christ calls him by this name of *Simon bar Jonah*, when he made the most ample profession of his faith in Him, and was pronounced blessed by Him, *Matt. 16:16-17*,

lovest thou me more than these? Meaning, not than the fishes he had caught, nor the net and boat, or any worldly enjoyment, nor than he loved the disciples; but the question is, whether he loved Christ more than the rest of the disciples loved Him: the reason of which was, because he had some time ago declared, though all the disciples were offended at Christ, and should deny Him, he would not; and had just now thrown himself into the sea to come to Him first, as if he loved Him more than they did: which question is put, not out of ignorance, or as if Christ knew not whether he loved Him or not, and what was the degree of his affection to Him; but because the exercise of this grace, and the expressions of it, are very grateful to Him; and that Peter also might have an opportunity of expressing it before others, who had so publicly denied Him:

He saith unto him, Yea, Lord; thou knowest that I love thee. Not in word and tongue, but in deed and in truth; in sincerity, and without dissimulation, fervently and superlatively: for the truth of which he appeals to Christ Himself; for he was so conscious to himself of the reality of his love, and the sincerity of his affection, that he chooses to make Christ Himself judge of it, rather than say any more of it himself; though he modestly declines saying that he loved Him more than the rest of the disciples did, having had an experience of his vanity and self-confidence. He was sure he loved Christ heartily; but whether he loved Him *more* than the rest did, he chose not to say:

He saith unto him, Feed my lambs. The younger and more tender part of the flock, weak believers, Christ's little children, newborn babes, the day of small things, which are not to be despised [see *Zech. 4:10*], the bruised reed that is not to be broken, and the smoking flax that is not to be quenched [see *Isa. 42:3*]; but who are to be nourished, comforted, and strengthened, by feeding them with the milk of the Gospel, and by administering to them the ordinances and *breasts of consolation* [*Isa. 66:10-11*]. These Christ has an interest in, and therefore calls them *my lambs*, being given Him by the Father, and purchased by His blood, and for whom He has a tender concern and affection; and nothing He looks upon as a firmer and clearer proof and evidence of love to Him, than to feed these lambs of His, and take care of them.

Verse 16. **He saith unto him again the second time**, &c. Willing to have the expressions of his love repeated and confirmed;

Simon, *son* of Jonas, lovest thou me? He leaves out the words, *more than these*, though Nonnus expresses them; He saw Peter's heart, and observed the modesty of his answer, and would not urge him any more in that comparative way, only required a repetition of his sincere and hearty love to Him:

he saith unto him, Yea, Lord; thou knowest that I love thee. Expressing himself in the same language as before; and it is, as if he should say, Lord, what can I say more? I can say no more than I have done, and by that I abide:

He saith unto him, Feed my sheep. Both *the lost sheep of the house of Israel*, and His *other sheep* among the Gentiles, whom the Father had given Him, and He had paid a price for, and must be brought in [see *Matt. 15:24; John 10:16*]; these being called, He would have fed with the Word and ordinances, with the bread of life, and water of life, not lorded over, and fleeced, and much less worried and destroyed; every instance of care and love shown to these, He takes as a mark of affection and respect to Himself.

Verse 17. **He saith unto him the third time**, &c. That by these three testimonies, out of his mouth, the thing might be established, and be out of all doubt:

Simon, *son* of Jonas, lovest thou me? Is it so indeed that thou lovest me? Is thy love really so hearty and sincere as thou sayest? May it be depended upon?

Peter was grieved because he said unto him the third time, Lovest thou me? Because it put him in mind of his having denied his Lord three times; the remembrance of which cut him to the heart; and it added to his grief, that his love, which he knew was unfeigned, notwithstanding his conduct, should seem to be suspected:

And he said unto him, Lord, thou knowest all things; thou knowest that I love thee. He appeals with great warmth and earnestness to Him, as the omniscient God, and the searcher of all hearts, who knows all persons and things, and the secret thoughts, dispositions, and affections of men's minds, for the truth of his love to Him; for though he knew the treachery of his own heart, and durst not trust to it, and therefore chose not to be determined by his own assertions, and was well aware that the sincerity of his love might be called in question by fellow Christians, because of his late conduct; but as every thing was naked and open to his Lord, with whom he had to do [see *Heb. 4:13*], he lodges and leaves the appeal with Him: so every soul that truly loves Christ, whatever Satan, the world, professors, or their own hearts under unbelieving frames, may suggest to the contrary, can appeal to Christ, as the trier of the reins of the children of men, that He it is whom their souls love; and though their love may be greatly tried, and they themselves be sorely tempted by Satan, and suffered to fall greatly; yet their love to Christ can never be lost; the fervency of it may be abated, the exercise of it may be very languid, but the principle itself always remains, as it did in Peter:

Jesus saith unto him, Feed my sheep. It may be observed from the repetition of this phrase following upon Peter's declaration of his love to Christ, that such only are proper persons to feed the lambs and sheep of Christ, who truly and sincerely love Him; and in doing which they show their love to Him: and who indeed would be concerned in this service, but such? Since the work is so laborious, the conduct of those to whom they minister oftentimes is so disagreeable, the reproach they meet with from the world, and the opposition made unto them by Satan, and all the powers of darkness: it is true indeed, there are some that take upon them this work, and pretend to do it, who do not love Christ; but then they are such who feed themselves, and not the flock; and who feed the world's goats, and not Christ's lambs and sheep, and in time of danger leave the flock; only the true lovers of Christ faithfully perform this service, and abide in it by preaching the pure Gospel of Christ, by administering His ordinances, in their right manner,[5] and by directing souls in all to Christ, the heavenly manna, and bread of life. Dr.

---

[5] On the authority of Christ delivering His ordinances of believer's baptism and the Lord's supper to His Gospel ministers, see *Luke 22:19* with *Acts 2:41-42* and *1 Cor. 11:2, 23 - Editor*.

Lightfoot thinks that by the threefold repetition of the order to feed Christ's lambs and sheep, is meant the threefold object of Peter's ministry; the Jews in their own land, the Gentiles, and the Israelites of the ten tribes, that were in Babylon.

Verse 18. **Verily, verily, I say unto thee**, &c. A way of speaking often used by Christ, when about to deliver any thing of considerable moment, partly to raise the attention, and partly for the more strong asseveration of what is spoken; and may have reference both to what went before, confirming Peter's declaration of his love, which would be demonstrated by dying for Him, and the testimony of His omniscience, by foretelling his death, and the kind of it; and to what follows after, which contains an account of Peter in his younger years, and a prophecy of what should befall him in old age:

When thou wast young; not that he was old now, and capable he was of doing, and he did do but just now, what our Lord ascribes to his younger years:

thou girdest thyself, and walkest whither thou wouldest; that is, he could put on his clothes himself, and girded them about him with a girdle, as was the custom of the eastern nations, who usually wore long garments; and as he, a little before, had girt his fisher's coat about him, and walked where he pleased; denoting the liberty of his will in things natural and civil, which every man is possessed of, though not in things spiritual without the grace of God; and also his power of doing what was most grateful to him, without being hindered by, or obliged to ask the leave of others:

but when thou shalt be old; implying, that he should live to a good old age, and be continued to be useful and serviceable in the cause of Christ, in preaching His Gospel, and feeding His lambs and sheep, as he did; for he lived to the times of Nero,[6] under whom he suffered, about forty years after this:

thou shalt stretch forth thy hands, and another shall gird thee; this refers not so much to an inability through old age to gird himself, and therefore should stretch forth his hands, that another might with more ease do it for him, and which would be the reverse of his former and present case; for the word *gird* is used in another sense than before, and signifies the binding of him as a prisoner with cords, or chains; so *girding*, with the Jews, is the same as הקשירה והאסירה, *tying and binding*:[7] but either to the stretching out of his hands upon the cross, when he should be girt and bound

---

[6] Euseb. Eccl. Hist. l. 2. c. 23.

[7] R. David Kimchi, Sepher Shorash. rad. חגר.

to that; for persons were sometimes fastened to the cross with cords, and not always with nails:[8] or, as others think, to his carrying of his cross on his shoulders, with his hands stretched out and bound to the piece of wood which went across; though his being girded or bound may as well be thought to follow the former, as this: indeed, what is added best suits with the latter,

and carry *thee* whither thou wouldest not. To a painful, cruel, shameful, and accursed death, the death of the cross; not that Peter in spirit would be unwilling to die for Christ, nor was he; but it signifies, that he should die a death disagreeable to the flesh.

Verse 19. **This spake he**, &c. These are the words of the evangelist, explaining the meaning of Christ in like manner as in *chapter 12:33*:

signifying by what death he should glorify God. For by the above words Christ not only intimated that Peter should die, not a natural, but a violent death, or that he should die a martyr in His cause, but the very kind of death he should die, namely by crucifixion; and that Peter was crucified at Rome, ecclesiastical history confirms,[9] when Christ was magnified, and God was glorified by His zeal and courage, faith and patience, constancy and perseverance to the end:

And when he had spoken this: concerning the usage and treatment he should meet with, the sufferings he should undergo, and death he should die for His sake, for the present trial of him, and to see how these things would be relished by him:

he saith unto him, Follow me. Which may be understood literally, Jesus now rising up, and ordering him to come after Him; and yet as a sign of his following Him in a spiritual sense, exercising every grace upon Him, discharging every duty towards Him, faithfully and constantly performing his work and office, as an apostle and preacher of the Gospel, in which He had now reinstated and confirmed him, and patiently bearing and suffering all kind of reproach, persecution, and death, for His name's sake.

Verse 20. **Then Peter, turning about**, &c. After He was risen, and was following Christ:

seeth the disciple whom Jesus loved following also; by whom is designed John the Evangelist, and writer of this Gospel; who hearing Christ bid Peter

---

[8]   Lipsius de Cruce, l. 2. c. 8. Bartholinus de Cruce, p. 57. 112.

[9]   Euseb. Eccl. Hist. l. 2. c 23.

follow Him, rose up likewise, and went after Him, in token of his willingness to serve Him, and suffer for Him too:

which also leaned on his breast at supper; at the *paschal supper*, as the Persic version here reads it:

and said, Lord, which is he that betrayeth thee? This disciple had a peculiar share in the love of Christ, as man, and was admitted to great nearness and freedom with Him, signified by his leaning on His breast; and who being so near His person, and allowed to use a liberty with Him every one did not take, at the motion of Peter, asked our Lord at supper, who the person was He meant that should betray Him; all this is said as descriptive of the disciple here spoken of, which leaves it without any doubt that it was the Apostle John; and who, from *verse 2*, appears to be one of this company, and is further confirmed at *verse 24*.

Verse 21. **Peter seeing him saith to Jesus**, &c. Peter took a great deal of notice of John, and very likely understood, that he meant by his rising up and following Christ, to signify his readiness for service and suffering in the cause of Christ: and therefore says,

Lord, and what *shall* this man *do*? The phrase in the original is very short and concise, *Lord, and this what?* The Arabic version renders it, *And this, of what mind is he?* It looks as if he was of the same mind with me to follow thee; but it is better rendered by us, *What shall this man do?* In what work and service shall he be employed, who seems as willing as I am to serve thee? Or it may be rendered thus, *And what shall this man suffer?* Shall he suffer at all? And if he shall, what kind of death shall he undergo? What will become of him? What will be his end? How will it fare with him? This he said, partly out of curiosity, and partly out of concern for him, they two being associates and intimates, who had a strong affection for each other.

Verse 22. **Jesus saith unto him**, &c. Christ vouchsafes an answer to Peter, but not a very clear one, nor such a one as he wished for, and not without a rebuke to him:

If I will that he tarry till I come, what is *that* to thee? Meaning, that if it was His pleasure that he should live, not till His second coming to judge the quick and dead at the last day, but till He should come in His power and take vengeance on the Jewish nation, in the destruction of their city and temple by the Romans, and in dispersing them through the nations of the world; till which time John did live, and many years after; and was the only one of the disciples that lived till that time, and who did not die a violent death; what was that to Peter? it was no concern of his. The question was too curious, improper, and impertinent; it became him to attend only to what concerned himself, and he was bid to do:

follow thou me. Whence it may be observed, that it becomes the saints to mind their duty in following Christ, and not concern themselves in things that do not belong to them. Christ is to be followed by His people as their leader and commander; as the Shepherd of the flock; as a guide in the way, and the forerunner that is gone before; as the Light of the world; as the pattern and example of the saints, and as their Lord and Master; and that in the exercise of every grace, as humility and meekness, love, zeal, patience, and resignation to the will of God; and also in the discharge of duty, both with respect to moral life and conversation, and instituted worship, as attendance on public service, and submission to ordinances; and likewise in enduring sufferings patiently and cheerfully for His sake. Saints are under obligation to follow Christ; it is their interest so to do; it is honorable, safe, comfortable, and pleasant, and ends in happiness here and hereafter.

Verse 23. **Then went this saying abroad among the brethren**, &c. It not being rightly understood by some one or more of the disciples present: it was divulged with a wrong sense annexed to it among other persons; who, though not of the eleven, yet were followers of Christ, children of God, that belonged to the same family, and were, in a spiritual relation, brethren to each other, and to the apostles:

that that disciple should not die; but should remain till the second coming of Christ, and be found among them that shall be then alive, and be changed. And such a notion not only was among the ancients; but Beza, in his notes on this text, tells us of a strolling wicked fellow, that gave out that he was the Apostle John; and was encouraged by some, particularly Postellus, a Sorbonic doctor, but was afterwards burnt at Tholouse [that is, Toulouse, France];

yet Jesus said not unto him, He shall not die, but, If I will that he tarry till I come, what is *that* to thee? These are the words of John himself, the disciple spoken of, who gives a true and just account of Christ's words, freeing them from the false sense that was put upon them; which shows his ingenuous disposition, his integrity and love of truth; being unwilling that such an error should obtain among the disciples, and pass in the world for truth.

Verse 24. **This is the disciple which testifieth of these things**, &c. Recorded in this chapter concerning the appearance of Christ to His disciples at the sea of Tiberias, and what were done by Him in their presence, what passed between them; particularly the conversation He had with Peter, both concerning himself, and the disciple John: and also, of all things that are written in this whole Gospel. These are testified to be true by this very disciple John, concerning whom the above report went, upon a mistaken sense of Christ's words,

and who himself,

wrote these things; all that is contained in this book, as well as the particulars relating to this conversation of Christ with Peter:

and we know that his testimony is true. The testimony of one that was an eye and ear witness, as John was, of all that he testified and wrote, must be known, owned, and allowed by all to be true, firm, and unquestionable; and therefore the apostle speaks in the plural number, as being not only his own sense, but the sense of all men. Though some take this to be the attestation of the Ephesian church, or of the bishops of the Asiatic churches, who put John upon writing this Gospel; of which they give their judgment and testimony, as believing it to be a true and faithful narrative.

Verse 25. **And there are also many other things which Jesus did**, &c. Which refer not to His doctrines and discourses, His sermons and prayers, and the conversation He had with His disciples, and others, on different accounts; but to the signs, and wonders, and miraculous operations, which were done by Him, that are neither recorded in this, nor in any of the evangelists:

the which, if they should be written every one; with all the particular circumstances relating to them:

I suppose that even the world itself could not contain the books that should be written. The Arabic version renders it, *the things written in the books*; and the Syriac, *that the world would not be sufficient for the books that should be written*; and so the Persic, which adds, *and the Scribes of the world would fail,* or *be deficient*; there would not be Scribes enough in the world to write them; nor could they be read by men, if they were written; the world would be overloaded with them; and therefore the Holy Ghost has not thought fit to lay such a burden on men they could not bear, as to read such numbers of volumes; but has reduced them into a brief compendium, which may be read with ease, delight, and pleasure; and which is abundantly sufficient to attest the truth of Christ's incarnation, miracles, doctrines, obedience, sufferings, death, resurrection, ascension, session at God's right hand, &c. and of the whole of Christianity, and all that appertains to it, or whatever is necessary to be known for the salvation of men: for this cannot be understood of the carnal and unbelieving part of the world, not receiving and bearing what would be contained in such volumes, were they written; for they are not able to receive and bear what is now written, but reject and despise it as foolishness [see *1 Cor. 1:21-25* and *2:14*]. Some understand this as a hyperbolical expression; but the sense above given may be admitted without a hyperbole; though a hyperbole may very well be allowed of; nor, taken literally, will it appear greater than some others used in Scripture; as when the posterity of Abraham are said to be as numerous as the stars of the sky; and especially when said to be as the sand by the seashore, innumerable, *Heb. 11:12; Hos. 1:10;* and when Capernaum is said to be exalted unto heaven, or to reach unto it, *Matt. 11:23;* see *Gen. 11:4;* and particularly the Jews have no reason to object, as one of them does,[10] to such a way of speaking, whose writings abound in hyperbolical expressions, and in some like to this; as when one of their Rabbins says,[11]

> "If all the seas were ink, and the bulrushes pens, and the heavens and the earth volumes, and all the children of men Scribes, לכתוב תורה אין מספיקין, *they would not be sufficient to write the law,* which I have learned, &c."

And it is commonly said[12] by them, if this, or that, or the other thing was done, לא יכיל עלמא למסבל, *the world would not be able to bear them.* And a later writer[13] of theirs, speaking of the different interpretations given by some of their Rabbins of a certain passage, says,

> "They are so many, that an ass is not able to carry their books."

And the intention of this expression, supposing it hyperbolical, is to show, that but a few of the wonderful things done by Christ were recorded by the evangelist, in comparison of the many which He every day did, in all places where He came; for He was continually going about doing good, and healing all manner of diseases; but these that were written are sufficient to prove Him to be the true Messiah, and to require faith in Him as such. To all which the evangelist sets his,

Amen. As attesting and confirming the truth of all he had written; and which may be depended upon, and assented to, as truth, by all that read this Gospel. The Alexandrian copy, and Beza's Cambridge copy, have not the word *Amen*; nor have the Vulgate Latin, Syriac, Arabic, and Persic versions. In some copies the following words are added,

> "the Gospel according to John was given out thirty-two years after the

---

[10] Jacob Aben ben Amram, porta veritatis, No. 1094. apud Kidder, Demonstration of the Messiah, par. 3. p. 67. Ed. fol.

[11] Shirhashirim Rabba, fol. 4. 2.

[12] Zohar in Exod. fol. 106. 4. & in Lev. fol. 26. 2. & 49. 3. & in Num. fol. 52. 2. & 59. 3. & 63. 3. & 64. 4. & 82. 3, 4.

[13] R. Abraham Seba in Tzeror Hammor, fol. 79. 1.

ascension of Christ;"
which would fall on the year of Christ 66, and so before the destruction of
Jerusalem; which is contrary to the common opinion of learned men, some
placing it in the year 97, others in the year 99.

Pulpit used by John Gill at the Carter Lane Baptist Chapel. "He
came into his *pulpit*, at times," wrote John Rippon, "with an heavenly
lustre on his countenance, *in the fulness of the blessing of the Gospel
of Christ*; enriched, and generally enriching." *A Brief Memoir of the
Life and Writings of the Late Rev. John Gill, D. D.* (London: J.
Bennett, 1838), 122.

ENDNOTES

ENDNOTES ON THE GOSPEL OF MATTHEW

[1] Matt. 2:1

Verse 1. **Now when Jesus was born**, &c. Several things are here related respecting the birth of Christ, as the place where He was born,

in Bethlehem of Judea; so called to distinguish it from another Bethlehem in the tribe of Zebulon, *Josh. 19:15.* Here Christ was to be born according to a prophecy hereafter mentioned, and accordingly the Jews expected He would be born here, *Matt. 2:4,* and so Jesus was born here, *Luke 2:4-6; John 7:41-42;* and this the Jews themselves acknowledge;

> Such a year (says a noted[1] chronologer of theirs), Jesus of Nazareth was born in Bethlehem Juda, which is a *parsa* and a half (that is, six miles), from Jerusalem.

Benjamin Tudelensis[2] says, it is two parsas, that is, eight miles, from it; and according to Justin Martyr[3] it was thirty-five furlongs distant from it. Yea even they own this, that Jesus was born there, in that vile and blasphemous book[4] of theirs, written on purpose to defame Him; nay, even the ancient Jews have owned that the Messiah is already born, and that He was born at Bethlehem; as appears from their Talmud,[5] where we meet with such a passage.

> It happened to a certain Jew, that as he was plowing, one of his oxen bellowed; a certain Arabian passed by and heard it, who said, O Jew, Jew, loose thy oxen, and loose thy plowshare, for lo, the house of the sanctuary is destroyed: it bellowed a second time; he said unto him, O Jew, Jew, bind thy oxen, and bind thy plowshare, for lo, יליד מלכא משיחא *the king Messiah is born*. He said to him, What is his name? Menachem (the comforter); he asked again, What is his father's name? Hezekiah; once more he says, From whence is he? He replies, בירת מלכא ביתלחם יהודה מן *From the palace of the king of Bethlehem Judah*; he went and sold his oxen and his plowshares, and became a seller of swaddling clothes for infants; and he went from city to city till

---

1 R. David Ganz. Zemach David, pars 2. fol. 14.2.

2 Itinerarium, p. 48.

3 Apolog. 2. p. 75.

4 Toldos, p. 7.

5 Hieros. Beracot. fol. 5. 1.

he came to that city, (Bethlehem,) and all the women bought of
him, but the mother of Menachem bought nothing."

Afterwards they tell you, he was snatched away by winds and tempests. This
story is told in much the same manner in another[6] of their writings. Bethlehem
signifies *the house of bread*, and in it was born, as an ancient writer[7] observes,
the bread which comes down from heaven: and it may also signify *the house of
flesh*, and to it the allusion may be in *1 Tim. 3:16, God manifest in the flesh*. The
time of Christ's birth is here expressed,

in the days of Herod the king. This was Herod the great, the first of that
name. The Jewish chronologer[8] gives an account of him in the following
manner:

"Herod the first, called Herod the Ascalonite, was the son of
Antipater, a friend of king Hyrcanus, and his deputy; him the
senate of Rome made king in the room of Hyrcanus his master.
This Herod, while he was a servant of king Hyrcanus (so in the
Talmud[9] Herod is said to be עבדא דבית חשמונא *a servant of the
family of the Asmonaeans*) king Hyrcanus saved from death, to
which he was sentenced by the Sanhedrin of Shammai; that
they might not slay him for the murder of one Hezekiah, as is
related by Josephus, l. 6. c. 44; and Herod took to him for wife
Miriam, the daughter of Alexander the son of Aristobulus, who
was the daughter's daughter of king Hyrcanus."

This writer tacitly owns afterwards,[10] that Jesus was born in the days of this
king; for he says, that in the days of Hillell and Shammai (who lived in those
times) there was one of their disciples, who was called R. Joshua ben Perachiah,
and he was, adds he, רבו הנוצרי, *the master of the Nazarene*, or of Jesus of
Nazareth. Herod reigned, as this same author observes, thirty-seven years; and
according to Dr. Lightfoot's calculation, Christ was born in the thirty-fifth year
of his reign, and in the thirty-first of Augustus Caesar, and in the year of the
world *three thousand nine hundred and twenty-eight*, and in the month Tisri,
which answers to part of our September, about the feast of tabernacles; which
indeed was typical of Christ's incarnation, and then it may reasonably be

---

[6] Echa Rabbati, fol. 50. 1.

[7] Hieron. Epitaph. Paulae. fol. 59. E. tom. 1.

[8] R. David Ganz. Zemach David, pars 1. fol. 24. 1.

[9] T. Bab. Bava Bathra, fol. 3. 2. Juchasin. fol. 17. 1. & 18. 1. & Seder Olam Zuta, p. 111.

[10] R. David Ganz. Zemach David, pars 1. fol. 24.2.

thought that *the word was made flesh*, and εσκηνωσεν, *tabernacled among us, John 1:14.*

[2] Matt.3:3

Verse 3. **For this is he that was spoken of by the prophet Esaias**, &c. These are not the words of the Baptist himself, as in *John 1:23*, but of the evangelist, who cites and applies to John a passage in the prophet Isaiah, in *chapter 40:3;* and that very pertinently, since that chapter is a prophecy of the Messiah. The consolations spoken of in *Isa. 40:1-2*, were to be in the days of the king Messiah, as a writer of note[11] among the Jews observes. The Messiah is more expressly prophesied of in *Isa. 40:9-11*, as one that should appear to the joy of His people, and *come with a strong hand*, vigorously prosecute His designs, faithfully perform His work, and then receive His reward. He is spoken of under the character of a *shepherd*, who would tenderly discharge the several parts of His office as such; which character is frequently given to the Messiah in the Old Testament. Now the person spoken of in *Isa. 40:3* was to be His harbinger to go before Him, proclaim and make ready for His coming; and what is said of him agrees entirely with John the Baptist, as the character given of him, *the voice of one crying*, Βοωντος, *lowing like an ox*; which expresses the austerity of the man, the roughness of his voice, the severity of his language: that he called aloud and spoke out, openly, publicly, and freely; and that he delivered himself in preaching with a great deal of zeal and fervency. The place where he preached was,

in the wilderness, that is, of Judea, where he is said before, in *Matt. 3:1,* to come preaching. The doctrine he preached was,

saying, prepare ye the way of the Lord, make his paths straight. Which is best explained by what is said before, in *Matt. 3:2, Repent ye, for the kingdom of heaven is at hand.* The Lord whom ye have sought, the Messiah whom ye have expected, is just coming, He will quickly appear; prepare to meet Him by repentance, and receive Him by faith: relinquish your former notions and principles, correct your errors, and amend your lives; remove all out of the way which may be offensive to Him. The allusion is to a great personage being about to make his public appearance or entrance; when a harbinger goes before him, orders the way to be cleared, all impediments to be removed, and every thing gotten ready for the reception of him.

---

[11] R. David Kimchi in Isa. 40:1.

[3] Matt.3:7

Verse 7. **But when he saw many of the Pharisees and Sadducees**, &c. This being the first place in which mention is made of *the Pharisees and Sadducees*, it may not be amiss to give some account of them once for all: and to begin with the *Pharisees*, and first with their name. Some derive this word from פרץ *pharatz*, to *divide*, to *make a breach*, from whence Phares had his name *Gen. 38:29;* so Jerome,[12] who observes that,

> "The Pharisees, who separated themselves from the people as righteous persons, were called "divisi," *the divided*."

And in[13] another place,

> "Because the Pharisees were *divided* from the Jews on account of some superfluous observations, they also took their name from their disagreement."

Origen[14] seems to refer to this etymology of the word, when he says,

> "the Pharisees, according to their name, were διηρημενοι τινες και στασιωδεις, *certain divided and seditious persons*."

And true it is, that this sect often meddled with the affairs of the government, and were very ambitious of being concerned therein. Josephus[15] observes of queen Alexandra, that *she governed others, and the Pharisees governed her*; hence, though they were in great esteem with the people, they were rather dreaded than loved by the government. Others derive this name from פרש, *Pharas*, to *expand*, or *stretch out*; either because they made broad their phylacteries, and enlarged the borders of their garments [see *Matt. 23:5*]; or because they exposed themselves to public notice; did all they could to be seen of men; prayed in the corners of the streets; had a trumpet blown before them when they gave alms; chose the uppermost rooms at feasts, and the chief seats in the synagogues; greetings in the markets; and to be called of men *Rabbi*: all which to be sure are their just characters. Others derive it from the same word, as signifying to *explain* or *expound*; because it was one part of their work, and in which they excelled, to expound the law: but this cannot be the reason of their general name, because there were women Pharisees as well as men, who cannot be thought to be employed in that work. The more generally received opinion is, that this name is taken from the above word, as signifying to *separate*; because they separated themselves from the men and manners of the world, to the study

---

[12] Trad. Heb. in Gen. fol. 72. D. tom. 3.

[13] Adv. Luciferian. fol. 49. K. tom. 2. so Tertullian. praescript. Haeret. c. 45.

[14] Comment. in Joan. p. 115. Ed. Huet.

[15] De Bello Jud. [The Jewish War] l. 1. c. 5. sect. 2.

of the law, and to a greater degree of holiness, at least in pretense, than other persons. They were strict observers of the traditions of the elders; are said to hold both fate and free will[16]; they owned the resurrection of the dead, and that there were angels and spirits, in which they differed from the Sadducees. Or rather they have their name from פרס, which signifies *a reward*; they being stiff defenders of the doctrine of rewards and punishments in a future state, which the Sadducees denied. The Talmudic writers[17] say, there were seven sorts of them, and if it would not be too tedious to the reader, I would give the names of them; and the rather, because some of them seem to tally with the complexion and conduct of the Pharisees mentioned in the Scriptures. There were then,

1. פרוש שיכמי, *the Shechemite Pharisee*, who does as Shechem did; is circumcised, not on God's account, or for His glory, or because circumcision is a command of His, but for his own profit and advantage, and that he may get honor from men.

2. פרוש ניקפי, *the dashing Pharisee*; who walks gently, the heel of one foot touching the great toe of the other; and scarce lifts up his feet from the earth, so that he dashes them against the stones, and would be thought hereby to be in deep meditation.

3. פרוש קיזאי, *the Pharisee letting blood*; who makes as if he shut his eyes, that he may not look upon women, and so runs and dashes his head against the wall, till the blood gushes out, as though a vein was opened.

4. פרוש מדוכיא, *the depressed Pharisee*; who went double, or bowed down, or as others render the phrase, *the mortar Pharisee*; either because he wore a garment like a mortar, with the mouth turned downwards; or a hat resembling such a vessel; so that he could not look upward, nor on either side, only downward, or right forward.

5. פרוש מה חובתי ואעשנה, *the Pharisee, that said, What is my duty and I will do it*? The gloss upon it is, *Teach me what is my duty, and I will do it*: Lo! this is his excellency, if he is not expert in the prohibitions and niceties of the commands, and comes to learn; or thus, *What is more to be done and I have not done it*? So that he shows himself, or would appear as if he had performed all.

6. פרוש יראה, *the Pharisee of fear*; who does what he does from fear of

---

[16] So Josephus, Antiq. 1. 13. c. 5. f. 9.

[17] T. Hieros. Beracot, fol. 14. 2. & Sota, fol. 20. 3. Bab. Sota, fol. 22. 2. Eight sorts are reckoned in Abot R. Nathan. c. 37. fol. 8. 4.

punishment.

7. ‏פרוש אהבה‎ *the Pharisee of love*; who does what he does from love; which the gloss explains thus: *For the love of the reward of the commandment, and not for the love of the commandment of his Creator*; though they say of all these there is none to be beloved, but the Pharisee of love.

When this sect first began, and who was the first author of it, is not easy to say; it is certain there were great numbers of them in the times of John the Baptist, and of Christ, and for some time after. The Jews say,[18] that when the temple was destroyed the second time, the Pharisees increased in Israel.

Next let us consider the Sadducees, who they were, and from whence they sprung. These have their name not from ‏צדיק‎, *Saddik, righteous*,[19] or ‏צדק‎, *Sedek, righteousness*, being self justitiaries; for though they were, yet this would not have distinguished them from the Pharisees, who were likewise such; but from ‏צדוק‎, *Sadok* or *Saduk*, a disciple of Antigonus, a man of Socho.[20] The occasion of this new sect was this: Antigonus, among the instructions he gave to his scholars, had this saying,

> "Be not as servants who serve their master for the sake of reward; but be ye as servants that serve their master not for the sake of reward, and let the fear of God be upon you."

Which, when Sadok and a fellow scholar, whose name was *Baithos*, or *Baithus*, heard, not rightly understanding him, concluded that there was no future state of rewards and punishments; which notion they broached, and had their followers, who from the one were called *Sadducees*, and sometimes from the other *Baithuseans*: these men held the Scriptures only, rejecting the traditions of the elders. According to Josephus, they denied fate, and ascribed all to free will; they affirmed that there is no resurrection of the dead; that the soul dies with the body; that there is no future state after this life; and that there are neither angels nor spirits. Now when *John saw* or observed *many* of both these sects,

come to his baptism; not merely to see it administered, led thither by the novelty of the thing; but to submit to it; to which they might be induced by that

---

[18] T. Bab. Bava Bathra, fol. 60. 2.

[19] So Epiphanius contr. Haeres. l. 1. Haeres. 14. Hieron. Comment. in Matt. c. 22. l. 3. fol. 30. M. tom. 9.

[20] Abot R. Nathan c. 5. fol. 3. 1. Sepher Cosri orat. 3. fol. 187. 2. & R. Juda Muscatus in ibid. Maimon. in Pirk. Abot. c. 1. sect. 3. Juchasin. fol. 15. 2. Ganz. Tzemach David. par. 1. fol. 20. 2. & Bartenora in Mishna Judaim, c. 4. sect. 6.

very great character of a very holy good man, which John had gotten among the people; and they were desirous of being thought so too, and therefore desired to be baptized by him; but he knowing the men and their manners,

said unto them; addressed them in a very severe style, quite contrary to their expectation, and the opinion the people had of them,

O generation of vipers! It seems their parents before them were vipers, and they their offspring were like them, in hypocrisy and malice. The viper appears very beautiful outwardly, but is full of poison; it looks harmless and innocent, as if it neither could nor would do any hurt, its teeth being hid, but is a most deadly and hurtful creature: so these men, though they made specious pretenses to religion and holiness, yet were full of the deadly poison of hypocrisy, malice, and error. A very disagreeable salutation this must be to men, who were desirous of being reckoned very religious, and who boasted of, and trusted in, their being the seed of Abraham; when they were the children of the devil, the seed of the old serpent, and the offspring of the worst of men, and in whom was verified the proverb, "Like father like son." John proceeds and asks, saying,

Who hath warned you to flee from the wrath to come? Who has suggested this to you? From whom have ye received this hint? Who has pointed out the way to you to escape divine vengeance, or the ruin which will quickly come upon you? For by *wrath to come* is not meant hellfire, everlasting destruction, from which baptism could not save them; but temporal calamity and destruction; the wrath which in a little time came upon that nation to the uttermost, for rejecting the Messiah, and the Gospel dispensation: from which they might have been saved, had they given credit to Jesus as the Messiah, though only with a bare assent; and had they entered into the kingdom of heaven, or Messiah, the Gospel dispensation, by receiving its doctrines, and submitting to its ordinances, though only externally.

[4] Matt. 3:11

Verse 11. **I indeed baptize you with water**, &c. These words, at first view, look as if they were a continuation of John's discourse with the Pharisees and Sadducees, and as though he had baptized them; whereas by comparing them with what the other evangelists relate, see *Mark 1:5,8; Luke 3:10,15,16;* they are spoken to the people, who, confessing their sins, had been baptized by him; to whom he gives an account of the ordinance of water baptism, of which he was the administrator, in what manner, and on what account he performed it: *I indeed baptize you*; or, as Mark says, *I have baptized you*; I have authority from God so to do; my commission reaches thus far, and no farther; I can administer, and have administered the outward ordinance to you; but the inward grace and increase of it, together with the ordinary and extraordinary gifts of the Spirit, I cannot confer. I can, and do baptize, upon a profession of repentance, and I can threaten impenitent sinners with divine vengeance; but I cannot bestow the grace of repentance on any, nor punish for impenitence, either here or hereafter; these things are out of my power, and belong to another person hereafter named: all that I do, and pretend to do, is to baptize *with water*, or rather *in water*, as, εν υδατι should be rendered. Our version seems to be calculated in favor of pouring, or sprinkling water upon, or application of it to the person baptized, in opposition to immersion in it; whereas the *preposition* is not instrumental, but local, and denotes the place, the *river Jordan*, and the element of water there, in which John was baptizing: and this he did,

unto repentance, or *at*, or *upon repentance*: for so εις may be rendered, as it is in *Matt. 12:41*. For the meaning is not that John baptized them, in order to bring them to repentance; since he required repentance and fruits *meet* for it, previous to baptism; but that he had baptized them upon the foot [*or* basis] of their repentance. And so the learned Grotius observes, that the phrase may be very aptly explained thus: *I baptize you upon the profession of repentance which ye make*. John gives a hint of the person whose forerunner he was, and of His superior excellency to him: he indeed first speaks of Him as one behind him, not in nature or dignity, but in order of time as man;

but he that comes after me; John was born before Jesus, and began his ministry before He did; he was His harbinger; Jesus was now coming after him to Jordan from Galilee, to be baptized by him, and then enter on His public ministry: but though He came *after* him in this sense, He was not beneath, but *above* him in character; which he freely declares, saying,

is mightier than I; not only as He is the mighty God, and so infinitely mightier than he; but in His office and ministry, which was exercised with greater power and authority, and attended with mighty works and miracles, and was followed with the extraordinary gifts of the Spirit. Not to mention the mighty work of redemption performed by Him; the resurrection of His own body from the dead; and His exaltation in human nature, above all power, might, and dominion. The Baptist was so sensible of the inequality between them, and of his unworthiness to be mentioned with Him, that he seems at a loss almost to express his distance from Him; and therefore signifies it by his being unfit to perform one of the most servile offices to Him,

whose shoes I am not worthy to bear; or as the other evangelists relate it, *whose shoelatchet I am not worthy to unloose*; which amounts to the same sense, since shoes are unloosed in order to be taken from, or carried before, or after a person; which to do was the work of servants among the Jews. In the Talmud[21] it is asked,

> "What is the manner of possessing of servants? or what is their service? He buckles his (master's) shoes; he *unlooses his shoes, and carries them before him to the bath*."

Or, as is elsewhere[22] said,

> "*he unlooses his shoes*, or *carries after him* his vessels (whatever he wants) to the bath; he unclothes him, he washes him, he anoints him, he rubs him, he clothes him, he buckles his shoes, and lifts him up."

This was such a servile work, that it was thought too mean [*or* lowly] for a scholar or a disciple to do; for it is[23] said,

> "All services which a servant does for his master, a disciple does for his master, חוץ מהתרת לו מנעל, *except unloosing his shoes*."

The gloss on it says,

> "he that sees it, will say, he is a *Canaanitish servant*,"

for only a Canaanitish, not a Hebrew servant,[24] might be employed in, or obliged to such work; for it was reckoned not only mean and servile, but even base and reproachful. It is one of their[25] canons:

> "If thy brother is become poor, and is sold unto thee, thou shalt not make him do the work of a servant; that is, עבורת של נגאי, *any reproachful work*; such as to buckle his shoes, or unloose them, or carry his instruments (or necessaries) after him to the bath."

Now John thought himself unworthy; it was too great an honor for him to do that for Christ, which was thought too mean [*or* lowly] for a disciple to do for a wise man, and too scandalous for a Hebrew servant to do for his master, to whom he was sold; which shows the great humility of John, and the high opinion he had of Christ. It has been controverted whether Christ wore shoes or not; Jerome affirmed that He did not: but it seems from hence that He did; nor were the Jews used to walking barefoot, but on certain occasions. The Baptist points at the peculiar work of this great person, in which He greatly exceeds any thing done by him;

---

[21] T. Hieros. Kiddushin, fol. 59. 4. Maimon. & T. Bartenora in Mishna Kiddushin, c. 1. sect. 3.

[22] T. Bab. Kiddushin, fol. 22. 2. Maimon. Hilch. Mechirah, c. 2. sect. 2.

[23] T. Bab. Cetubot, fol. 96. 1. Maimon. Talmud Tora, c. 5. sect. 8.

[24] Maimon. Hilch. Abadim, c. 1. sect. 7.

[25] Moses Kotzensis Mitzvot Torah, precept. neg. 176.

He shall baptize you with the Holy Ghost, and with fire; referring, either to the extraordinary gifts of the Spirit, to be bestowed on the disciples on the day of Pentecost, of which the *cloven tongues, like as of fire*, which *appeared unto them*, and *sat upon them*, were the symbols [*Acts 2:3*]; which was an instance of the great power and grace of Christ, and of His exaltation at the Father's right hand. Or rather, this phrase is expressive of the awful judgments which should be inflicted by Him on the Jewish nation; when He by His Spirit should *reprove* them for the sin of rejecting Him; and when He should appear as a *refiner's fire*, and as *fuller's soap* [*Mal. 3:2*]; when *the day of the Lord* should *burn as an oven* [*Mal. 4:1*]; when He should *purge the blood of Jerusalem*, His own blood, and the blood of the Apostles and Prophets shed in it, *from the midst thereof, by the spirit of judgment, and by the spirit of burning* [*Isa. 4:4*]; the same with *the Holy Ghost and fire* here, or the fire of the Holy Ghost, or the Holy Spirit of fire; and is the same with *the wrath to come*, and with what is threatened in the context: the unfruitful trees shall be *cut down, and cast into the fire*, and the *chaff* shall be burnt *with unquenchable fire*. And as this sense best agrees with the context, it may the rather be thought to be genuine; since John is speaking, not to the disciples of Christ, who were not yet called, and who only on the day of Pentecost were baptized *with the Holy Ghost and fire*, in the other sense of this phrase; but to the people of the Jews, some of whom had been baptized by him; and others were asking him questions, others gazing upon him, and wondering what manner of person he was; and multitudes of them continued obdurate and impenitent under his ministry, whom he threatens severely in the context. Add to all this, that the phrase of *dipping* or *baptizing* in *fire* seems to be used in this sense by the Jewish writers. In the Talmud[26] one puts the question, In what does he (God) dip? You will say in water, as it is written, *Who hath measured the waters in the hollow of his hand* [*Isa. 40:12*]? Another replies, בנורא טביל, *he dips in fire*; as it is written, *for behold the Lord will come with fire* [*Isa. 66:15*]. What is the meaning of טבילותא בנורא, *baptism in fire?* He answers, according to the mind of Rabbah, the root of *dipping in the fire*, is what is written; *All that abideth not the fire, ye shall make go* through the water. Dipping in the fire of the law, is a phrase used by the Jews.[27] The phrases of *dipping, and washing in fire*, are also used by Greek[28] authors.

---

[26] T. Bab. Sanhedrin, fol. 39. 1.

[27] Tzeror Hammor. fol. 104. 4. & 142. 3. & 170. 1.

[28] Moschi Idyll. 1. Philostrat, Vit. Apollon, l. 3. c. 5.

[5] Matt. 3:16

Verse 16. **And Jesus, when he was baptized**, &c. Christ, when He was baptized by John in the river Jordan, the place where he was baptizing,

went up straightway out of the water. One would be at a loss at first sight for a reason why the evangelist should relate this circumstance; for after the ordinance was administered, why should He stay in the water? What should He do there? Every one would naturally and reasonably conclude, without the mention of such a circumstance, that as soon as His baptism was over, He would immediately come up out of the water. However, we learn this from it, that since it is said, that He came *up out of the water*, He must first have gone down into it; must have been in it, and was baptized in it; a circumstance strongly in favor of baptism by immersion: for that Christ should go down into the river, more or less deep to the ankles, or up to the knees, in order that John should sprinkle water on His face, or pour it on His head, as is ridiculously represented in the prints, can hardly obtain any credit with persons of thought and sense. But the chief view of the evangelist in relating this circumstance, is with respect to what follows; and to show, what happened as soon as Christ was baptized, and before He had well gotten out of the water,

and, lo, the heavens were opened unto him: and some indeed read the word *straightway*, in connection with this phrase, and not with the words *went up*: but there is no need of supposing such a trajection, for the whole may be rendered thus: *And Jesus, when he was baptized, was scarcely come up out of the water, but lo*, immediately, directly, as soon as He was out, or rather before, *the heavens were opened to him*; the airy heaven was materially and really opened, parted, rent, or cloven asunder, as in *Mark 1:10,* which made way for the visible descent of the Holy Ghost in a bodily shape. A difficulty arises here, whether the words, *to him*, are to be referred to Christ, or to John; no doubt but the opening of the heavens was seen by them both: but to me it seems that John is particularly designed, since this vision was upon his account, and for his sake, and to him the following words belong;

and he saw the Spirit of God descending like a dove, and lighting upon him: That is, John saw this; for this is what was promised to John, as a sign, which should confirm his faith in Jesus, as the true Messiah; and which he himself says he saw; and upon which he based the record and testimony he bore to Christ, as the Son of God; see *John 1:32-34;* not but that the descent of the Holy Ghost in this manner might be seen by Christ, as well as John, according to *Mark 1:10. The Spirit of God*, here said to descend and light on Christ, is the same which, in the first creation, *moved upon the face of the waters* [*Gen. 1:2*]; and now comes down on Christ, just as He was coming up out of the waters of

Jordan, where He had been baptized; and which the Jews[29] so often call רוח של מלד המשיח, *the spirit of the king Messiah, and the spirit of the Messiah.* The descent of Him was in *a bodily shape,* as Luke says, *chapter 3:22;* either in the shape of a dove, which is a very fit emblem of the Spirit of God who descended, and the fruits thereof, such as simplicity, meekness, love, &c. and also of the dovelike innocence, humility, and affection of Christ, on whom He lighted; or it was in some other visible form, not expressed, which pretty much resembled the hovering and lighting of a dove upon any thing: for it does not necessarily follow from any of the accounts the evangelists give of this matter, that the Holy Spirit assumed, or appeared in, the form of a dove; only that His visible descent and lighting on Christ was ωσει περιστερα, *as a dove descends, hovers and lights;* which does not necessarily design the form of the creature, but the manner of its motion. However, who can read this account without thinking of Noah's dove, which brought in its mouth the olive leaf, a token of peace and reconciliation, when the waters were abated from off the earth? Give me leave to transcribe a passage I have met with in the book of Zohar:[30]

> "a door shall be opened, and out of it shall come forth the dove which Noah sent out in the days of the flood, as it is written, *and he sent forth the dove,* that famous dove; but the ancients speak not of it, for they knew not what it was, only from whence it came, and did its message; as it is written, *it returned not again unto him any more:* no man knows whither it went, but it returned to its place, and was hid within this door; and it shall take a *crown* in its mouth, and put it upon *the head* of the king Messiah."

And a little after, the dove is said to abide upon his head, and he to receive glory from it. Whether this is the remains of some ancient tradition, these men studiously conceal, concerning the opening of the heavens, and the descent of the Spirit of God, as a dove, upon the Messiah; or whether it is hammered out of the evangelic history, let the reader judge.

[6] Matt. 4:25

Verse 25. **And there followed him great multitudes of people,** &c.***The places from whence they came are particularly mentioned, as,

from Galilee; where He had called His disciples, had been *preaching the*

---

[29] Bereshit Rabba, fol. 2. 4. & 6. 3. Vajikra Rabba, fol. 156. 4. Zohar in Gen. fol. 107. 3. & 128. 3. Baal Hatturim in Gen. 1:2. Caphtor Uperah, fol. 113. 2.

[30] In Num. fol. 68. 3, 4.

Gospel, and healing all manner of diseases; and therefore it is not to be wondered at that He should have a large number of followers from hence. This country was divided into[31] three parts:

> "There was *upper* Galilee, and *nether* Galilee, and the *valley* from Capharhananiah and upwards: all that part which did not bring forth sycamine trees was upper Galilee, and from Capharhananiah downwards: all that part which did bring forth sycamine trees was nether Galilee; and the coast of Tiberias was the valley."

Frequent mention is made in the Talmudic[32] writings of *upper* Galilee, as distinct from the other.

and *from* Decapolis; a tract of land so called, from the *ten cities* that were in it; and which, according to Pliny,[33] were these following: Damascus, Opoton, Philadelphia, Raphana, Scythopolis, Gadara, Hippondion, Pella, Galasa, and Canatha; see *Mark 5:20,* and *Matt. 7:21.*

and *from* Jerusalem; the metropolis of the whole land; for His fame had reached that great city, and there were some there, curious and desirous to see Him, and hear Him; though He was in those distant and obscure parts.

and *from* Judea; from the other parts of it:

and *from* beyond Jordan. Which was a distinct country of itself, known by the name of *Peraea*; so called, perhaps, from περαν, the word here translated, *from beyond*. It is to be observed, that here are three countries distinctly mentioned, *Galilee, Judea,* and *beyond Jordan*; which was the division of the land of Israel; of these three lands the Talmudists often speak:

> "It is a tradition of the Rabbins,[34] that in three countries they intercalate the year; Judea, and beyond Jordan, and Galilee."

Again,[35]

> "There are three lands, that are obliged to the removing of fruits; Judea, and beyond Jordan, and Galilee."

---

[31]   Mishna Sheviith. c. 9. sect. 2.

[32]   T. Bab. Bava Kama, fol. 80. 1. Cetubot, fol. 67. 2. & Succa, fol. 27. 2. & 28. 1. Zohar in Gen. fol. 129. 3.

[33]   Nat. Hist. l. 5. c. 18.

[34]   T. Bab. Sanhedrin, fol. 11. 2.

[35]   Mishna Sheviith. c. 9. sect. 2.

Once more,[36]

> "There are three countries for celebration of marriages, Judea, and beyond Jordan, and Galilee."

The account which Maimonides gives[37] of these three countries, is this:

> "The land of Judea, all of it, the mountain, the plain, and the valley, are one country: beyond Jordan, all of it, the plain of Lydda, and the mountain of the plain of Lydda, and from Bethoron to the sea, are one country: Galilee, all of it, the upper and nether, and the coast of Tiberias, are one country.

The country *beyond Jordan* was not so much esteemed, as what was properly the land of Canaan, or Israel; for the Jews[38] say,

> "the land of Israel is holier than all lands; because they bring out of it the sheaf, the firstfruits, and the showbread, which they do not bring from other lands: the land of Canaan is holier than beyond Jordan; the land of Canaan is fit to be the habitation of the Shekinah; beyond Jordan is not."

This, they say,[39] was not the land flowing with milk and honey.

[7] Matt. 5:1

Verse 1. **And seeing the multitudes**, The great concourse of people that followed Him from the places before mentioned,

he went up into a mountain; either to pray alone, which was sometimes His custom to do, or to shun the multitude; or rather, because it was a commodious place for teaching the people:

and when he was set: not for rest, but in order to teach; for *sitting* was the posture of masters, or teachers, see *Matt. 13:2; Luke 4:20 and 5:3; John 8:2.* The form in which the master and his disciples sat, is thus described by Maimonides:[40]

> "The master sits at the head, or in the chief place, and the disciples before him in a circuit, like a crown; so that they all

---

[36] Mishna Cetubot, c. 13. sect. 10.

[37] Hilch. Shemittah, c. 7. sect. 9.

[38] Bemidbar Rabba, sect. 7. fol. 188. 3. Maimon. Beth Habechira, c. 7. sect. 12.

[39] Mishna Biccurim, c. 1. sect. 10.

[40] Hilch. Talmud Torah, c. 4. sect. 2.

see the master, and hear his words; and the master may not sit upon a seat, and the scholars upon the ground; but either all upon the earth, or upon seats: indeed from the beginning, or formerly, היה הרב יושב, *the master used to sit*, and the disciples *stand*; but before the destruction of the second temple, all used to teach their disciples as they were *sitting*."

With respect to this latter custom, the Talmudists say[41] that,

"from the days of Moses, to Rabban Gamaliel (the master of the Apostle Paul), they did not learn the law, unless standing; after Rabban Gamaliel died, sickness came into the world, and they learnt the law sitting: hence it is a tradition, that after Rabban Gamaliel died, the glory of the law ceased."

His disciples came unto him; not only the twelve, but the company, or *multitude of his disciples, Luke 6:17,* which He made in the several places, where He had been preaching; for the number of His disciples was larger than John's.

[8]   Matt. 5:14

Verse 14. **Ye are the light of the world**, &c. What the luminaries, the sun and moon, are in the heavens, with respect to corporal light, that the apostles were in the world, with regard to spiritual light; carrying and spreading the light of the Gospel, not only in Judea, but all over the world, which was in great darkness of ignorance and error; and, through a divine blessing attending their ministry, many were turned from the darkness of Judaism and Gentilism, of sin and infidelity, to the marvelous light of divine grace. The Jews were wont to say, that of the Israelites in general, and particularly of their Sanhedrin, and of their learned doctors, what Christ more truly applies here to His apostles; they observe[42] that,

"On the fourth day it was said, *Let there be light*: which was done with respect to the Israelites, because they are they, לעולם מאירים, *which give light to the world*, as it is written, *Dan. 12:3.*

And in another place,[43] say they,

"How beautiful are the great ones of the congregation, and the

---

[41]   T. Bab. Megilla, fol. 21. 1. Vid. Mishna Sota, c. 9. sect. 15. & Jarchi, Maimonides, & Bartenora in ibid.

[42]   Tzeror Hammor, fol. 1. 3.

[43]   Targum in Canticles [Song of Solomon] 4:1.

wise men, who sit in the Sanhedrin! for they are they לעלמא מנהרין, *that enlighten the world*, the people of the house of Israel."

So R. Meir, R. Akiba his disciple, and R. Judah the prince, are each of them called[44] אור העולם, *the light of the world*; as R. Jochanan ben Zaccai is by his disciples, נר עולם, *the lamp of the world*:[45] and it was usual for the head of a school, or of an university, to be styled[46] נהורא דעלמא, *the light of the world*; but this title much better agrees and suits with the persons Christ gives it to; who, no question, had a view to those exalted characters the Jews gave to their celebrated Rabbins.

A city that is set on an hill cannot be hid. Alluding either to Nazareth, where He was educated, and had lately preached, which was built on a hill, from the brow of which the inhabitants sought to have cast Him headlong, *Luke 4:29;* or to Capernaum, which, on account of its height, is said to be *exalted unto heaven, Matt. 11:23;* or to the city of Jerusalem, which was situated on a very considerable eminence. The land of Israel, the Jews say,[47] was higher than all other lands; and the temple at Jerusalem was higher than any other part of the land of Israel. And as a city cannot be hid which is built on a high place, so neither could, nor ought the doctrines which the apostles were commissioned to preach, be hid, or concealed from men: they were not to shun *to declare* the whole *counsel of God* [*Acts 20:27*], nor study to avoid the reproaches and persecutions of men; for they were to be *made a spectacle* [*1 Cor. 4:9*]; to be set as in a public theater, to be seen by *the world, angels, and men.*

[9] Matt. 8:28b

Verse 28b. **There met him two possessed with devils, coming out of the tombs,** &c. Their cemeteria, or burying places, were at some distance from towns or cities; wherefore Luke says, the possessed met him *out of the city*, a good way off from it; for the Jews[48] say, שלא היו בתי הקברות סמוכין לעיר, *that the sepulchers were not near a city*; see *Luke 7:12;* and these tombs were built so large, that persons might go into them, and sit and dwell in them, as these

---

44   Juchasin, fol. 63. 2.

45   Abot R. Nathan. c. 25. fol. 6. 3.

46   Juchasin. fol. 121. 1.

47   T. Bab. Kiddushin, fol. 69. 1. Sanhedrin, fol. 87. 1. Zebachim, fol. 54. 2.

48   T. Bab. Kiddushin. fol. 80. 2. Gloss.

demoniacs did, and therefore are said to come out of them. The rules for making them are[49] these:

> "He that sells ground to his neighbor to make a burying place, or that receives of his neighbor, to make him a burying place, must make the inside of the cave four cubits by six, and open in it eight graves; three here and three there, and two over against them; and the graves must be four cubits long, and seven high, and six broad. R. Simeon says, he must make the inside of the cave six cubits by eight, and open within thirteen graves, four here, and four there, and three over against them; and one on the right hand of the door, and one on the left: and he must make חצר, *a court*, at the mouth of the cave, six by six, according to the measure of the bier, and those that bury; and he must open in it two caves, one here and another there: R. Simeon says, four at the four sides. R. Simeon ben Gamaliel says, all is according to the nature of the rock."

Now in the *court*, at the mouth, or entrance of the cave, which was made for the bearers to put down the bier or coffin upon, before the interment, there was room for persons to enter and lodge, as these possessed with devils did: which places were chosen by the devils, either because of the solitude, gloominess, and filthiness of them; or, as some think, to confirm that persuasion some men had, that the souls of men after death, are changed into devils; or rather, to establish a notion which prevailed among the Jews, that the souls of the deceased continue for a while to be about their bodies; which drew persons to necromancy, or consulting with the dead. It is a notion that obtains among the Jews,[50] that the soul for twelve months after its separation from the body, is more or less with it, hovering about it; and hence, some have been induced to go and dwell among the tombs, and inquire of spirits: they tell us,[51]

> "it happened to a certain holy man, that he gave a penny to a poor man, on the *eve* of the new year; and his wife provoked him, and he went ולן בבית הקברות, *and lodged among the tombs*, and heard two spirits talking with one another."

[10] Matt. 9:24

Verse 24. **He said unto them, give place**, &c. Depart, be gone; for He put them

---

[49] Mishna Bava Bathra, c. 6. sect. 8.

[50] Nishmat Chayim, par. 2. c. 22. p. 81. 2. c. 24. p. 85. 1. & c. 29. p. 93. 1. p. 94. 1, 2.

[51] T. Bab. Beracot, fol. 18. 2.

out of the room, and suffered none to be with Him, when He raised her from the dead, but Peter, James, and John, and the father and mother of the child, who were witnesses enough of this miracle.

for the maid is not dead, but sleepeth. Not but that she was really dead; and Christ signifies as much, when He says, she *sleepeth*; a phrase that is often used in Talmudic writings,[52] for one that is dead: but Christ's meaning is, that she was not so dead as the company thought; as always to remain in the state of the dead, and not to be restored to life again: whereas our Lord signifies, it would be seen in a very little time, that she should be raised again, just as a person is awakened out of sleep; so that there was no occasion to make such funeral preparations as they did. The Jews say[53] of some of their dead, that they are asleep, and not dead: it is said, *Isa. 26:19, Awake and sing, ye that dwell in the dust*.

> "These (say they), are they that sleep and die not; and such are they that sleep in Hebron, for they לאו מתין אלא דמיכין, *do not die, but sleep*,—the four couples in Hebron (Adam and Eve, &c.) they *sleep, but are not dead*."

And they laughed him to scorn; they mocked at His words, and had Him in the utmost contempt, as a very weak silly man; taking Him either to be a madman, or a fool; knowing that she was really dead, of which they had all the evidence they could have; and having no faith at all in Him, and in His power to raise her from the dead.

[11] Matt. 10:2-4

Verse 2. **Now the names of the twelve apostles are these**, &c. This is the first time these disciples are called *apostles*, they were learners before; now, being instructed, they are *sent* forth to preach publicly, and therefore are called apostles, or messengers—persons that were *sent*: so the elders of the priesthood are called שלוחי בית דין, *the apostles*, or messengers *of the Sanhedrin*,[54] to whom the high priest was delivered, before the day of atonement. So six months in the year, שלוחים, *apostles*, or messengers, were sent by the[55] Sanhedrin, throughout

---

[52] T. Hieros. Beracot, fol. 6. 1. Avoda Zara, fol. 42. 3. Bereshit Rabba Parash. 91. fol. 79. 3.

[53] Zohar in Exod. fol. 62. 4.

[54] Mishna Yoma, c. 1. sect. 5.

[55] Mishna Roshhashana, c. 1. sect. 3. & Maimon. & Bartenora in ibid.

all the land of Israel, and to the captive Jews in other parts, to give notice of the new moon: in allusion to which, the disciples might be so called. It was proper to give the names of them, for the truth of the history, and confirmation of it; for the sake of the persons themselves, and the honor done them; and for the exclusion and detection of false apostles.

The first, Simon, who is called Peter; his pure Hebrew name was שמעון, *Simeon*, as he is called, *Acts 15:14*; but in the then Jerusalem dialect, and in Rabbinical language, this name is frequently read and pronounced סימון, *Simon*, as here: we often read of R. Simon, and of R. Juda bar Simon, in both Talmuds.[56] This apostle is also called Peter, to distinguish him from Simon the Canaanite, and which signifies a stone, or rock, in allusion to the object of his faith, and the steadiness of it. He is said to be *the first*; not that he was the head of the rest of the apostles, or had any primacy, dominion, and authority over them; but because he was first called, and was the first that was to open the door of faith to the Gentiles: but chiefly he is said to be so for order's sake; for, some one in the account must be named first, and he as proper as any:

and Andrew his brother; who was called at the same time with him, and therefore are put together. This name is also to be met with in the Talmudic writings; see the note on *Matt. 4:18.*

James the son of Zebedee, and John his brother; these two were called next and together, and therefore are placed in this order: the former is so called, to distinguish him from another *James, the son of Alphaeus*, after mentioned; and the latter is the beloved disciple; these were surnamed *Boanerges*, that is, *sons of thunder*.

[12] Matthew 10:3

Verse 3. **Philip and Bartholomew**; the first of these was called next; his name is a Greek one, which his parents, though Jews, might take from the Greeks that dwelt among them, see *John 12:20-21;* mention is made of one R. Phelipi, and Phulipa, in the Jewish writings.[57] The latter of these, *Bartholomew*, is conjectured, by Dr. Lightfoot, to be the same with *Nathanael*, he being called next in order after *Philip*; and that his name was *Nathanael*, בר תלמי, *Bar Talmai*, or *the son of Talmai*, or *Ptolomy*: a name once common to the kings of Egypt: so Talmai, king of Geshur, is by the Septuagint, in *2 Sam. 3:3* and *13:37*,

---

[56] T. Hieros. Shekalim, fol. 46. 4. Bab. Sabbath, fol. 55. 1. & Bava Kama, fol. 47. 2.

[57] Massechet Sopherim, c. 21. sect. 7. Bereshit Rabba, sect. 71. fol. 63. 4.

called *Tholmi*, and in *1 Chron. 3:2, Tholmai*: hence it appears, that Bartholomew is no other than *Bartholmi*, or *the son of Tholmi*. We read of one R. Jonathan, בן אבטולמוס, *ben Abtolemus*, in the Talmud,[58] whether the same name with this, may be considered;

Thomas, and Matthew the publican: by the other evangelists *Matthew* is mentioned first; but he being the writer of this Gospel, puts *Thomas* first, which is an instance of his modesty; and also calls himself *the publican*, which the others do not: this he mentions, to magnify the grace of God in his vocation [*or* calling]. The Jews[59] speak of מתאי, *Matthai*, or *Matthew*, as a disciple of Jesus. *Thomas* was sometimes called *Didymus*; the one was his Hebrew, the other his Greek name, and both signify a *twin*, as it is very likely he was: mention is made of R. Thoma, or Thomas bar Papias, in a Jewish writer.[60] Next follow,

James the son of Alphaeus, and Lebbaeus, whose surname was Thaddaeus: the former of these is so called, to distinguish him from James, the son of Zebedee. This is the James, who was the brother of our Lord, *Gal. 1:19*, and is called *James the less, Mark 15:40*. Alphaeus his father, is the same with *Cleopas, Luke 24:18*, or *Cleophas, John 19:25*. The Hebrew name, חלפי, which often occurs among the Jews,[61] may be pronounced either *Chlophi*, or *Alphi*, or with the Greek termination *Cleopas*, or *Alphaeus*. The latter of this pair of apostles is the same person with Jude, the writer of the epistle, which bears that name, and was the brother of James, with whom he is coupled: he was called *Lebbaeus*, either from the town of Lebba, a sea coast town of Galilee, as Dr. Lightfoot thinks; or from the Hebrew word לבי, *my heart*, as others, either for his prudence, or through the affections of his parents to him; as the Latins call one they love, "meum corculum," *my little heart*; or from לביא, *a lion*, that being the motto of the tribe of Judah. His surname *Thaddaeus*, is thought by some to be a deflexion of *Jude*; or *Judas*, and as coming from the same root, ידה, which signifies *to praise*, or *give thanks*; or from the Syriac word, תד, *a breast*, and may be so called for the same reason as he was *Lebbaeus*. Frequent mention is made of this name, תדיא, *Thaddai*, or *Thaddaeus*, among the Talmudic[62] doctors. The

---

[58] T. Bab. Nidda, fol. 19. 1.

[59] T. Bab. Sanhedrin, fol. 43. 1.

[60] Juchasin, fol. 105. 2.

[61] Echa Rabbati, fol. 58. 4. Midrash Kohelet, fol. 60. 4. Juchasin, fol. 92. 1.

[62] T. Hieros. Celaim, fol. 27. 2. Sabbat, fol. 6. 1. Erubim, fol. 23. 3. Bab. Sabbat, fol. 123. 1. & Erubim, fol. 71. 2. Juchasin, fol. 81. 1. & 105. 2. & 108. 1.

Jews themselves speak[63] of one תודה, *Thodah*, as a disciple of Jesus, by whom, no doubt they mean this same disciple. Eusebius[64] mentions one *Thaddaeus*, as one of the seventy disciples, who was sent to Agbarus, king of Edessa, who was healed and converted by him. This Agbarus is reported to have written a letter to Jesus Christ, desiring Him to come and cure him of his disease; to which Christ is said to return an answer, promising to send one of His disciples, who should do it; and that accordingly, after Christ's death, Thomas sent this Thaddaeus to him.

[13] Matt. 10:4

Verse 4. **Simon the Canaanite, and Judas Iscariot**: this is the last couple, for they are all mentioned by pairs, because they were sent forth *by two and two*, as the Evangelist Mark says, *chapter 6:7*. The former of these is called *Simon the Canaanite*, to distinguish him from Simon Peter, before mentioned; not that he was a Canaanite, that is, an inhabitant of the land of Canaan, a man of Canaan, as a certain woman is called *a woman of Canaan, Matt. 15:22*; for all the disciples of Christ were Jews; though in Munster's Hebrew Gospel he is called שמעון הכנעני, *Simeon the Canaanite*, or of *Canaan*, as if he belonged to that country; nor is he so called from Cana of Galilee, as Jerome and others have thought; but he was one of the קנאים, *Kanaim*, or *Zealots*; and therefore Luke styles him, *Simon called Zelotes, chapter 6:15*. The *Kanaites*, or *Zelotes*, were a set of men, who, in imitation of Phinehas, who slew Zimri and Cozbi in the very act of uncleanness, when they found any persons in the act of adultery, idolatry, blasphemy, or theft, would immediately kill them without any more ado: this they did, from a pretended zeal for the honor and glory of God: nor were they accountable to any court of judicature for it; yea, such an action was highly applauded, as a very laudable one:[65] under this specious name of Zealots, innumerable murders, and most horrible wickedness, were committed, both before, and during the siege of Jerusalem, as Josephus[66] relates. Now Simon was one of this sect before his conversion, and still retained the name afterwards.

---

[63] T. Bab. Sanhedrin, fol. 43. 1.

[64] Eccl. Hist. l. 1. c. 12, 13.

[65] Mishna Sanhedrin, c. 9. sect. 6. & Bartenora, in ibid. T. Avoda Zara, fol. 36. 2. Maimon. Issure Bia, c. 12. sect. 4, 5, 6, 14. & Sanhedrin, c. 18. sect. 6. & Obede Cochabim, c. 2. sect. 9. Philo de Monarchia, l. 1. p. 818.

[66] De Bello Jud. l. 5. c. 1, 2. & 6. 1. Vid. Abot R. Nathan, c. 6. fol. 3. 2.

Judas, the last of the twelve, is called *Iscariot*; concerning which name, the notation of it, and the reason of his being so called, many are the conjectures of learned men: some think that he belonged to the tribe of Issachar, and that he is called from thence, יששכר איש, *a man of Issachar*, as a certain man is, in *Judges 10:1;* others, that he takes his name from the place he belonged to, and that he was called, קריות איש, *a man of Kerioth*. A place of this name is mentioned, *Josh. 15:25;* and some manuscripts and copies in some places read *Judas* απο Καρυωτου, of *Caryot*. Caryota is said[67] to be a plain of the city of Jericho, about eighteen miles from Jerusalem, which abounded in palm trees, called, קורייטי, *Caryotae*, of which mention is made in the[68] Talmud, and other writers.[69] Others think he is so called, from the Syriac word, סכריוטא, *secariota*, which signifies a *purse*, or *bag*, because he carried the bag. Some copies read it, σκαριωτες, *scariotes*: others are of opinion, that he is so called, from the manner of death he died, which was strangling: for אסכרא, *ascara*, a word often used in the[70] Talmudic writings, signifies *strangling*; and is accounted by the Jews the hardest of deaths, and an evil one; and which seems to bid fair for the true reason of his name: however, it is mentioned here, as elsewhere, to distinguish him from Jude, or Judas, the true and faithful apostle of Christ; for this was he,

who also betrayed him. That is, Christ, as the Persic version reads it; and which is mentioned, not only for further distinction's sake, but to his great reproach. We learn from hence, that in the purest society on earth there has been an impure person; nor can it therefore be expected it should be otherwise in the best of churches, in the present state of imperfection; yea, that a man may have the highest gifts and attainments, as Judas had, ministerial gifts, and power of performing miracles, and yet be a vile person.

[14] Matt.10:24-25

Verse 24. **The disciple is not above *his* master**, &c. So far from it, that he is inferior to him; as in knowledge, so in reputation and character; and cannot expect the same honor to be given him, and the same respect shown to him, as to his master; and therefore if his master is not used with that decency, and in

---

[67] Vid. Wolfii Heb. Bibl. p. 410.

[68] T. Bab. Beracot, fol. 50. 2. & Avoda Zara, fol. 14. 2.

[69] Pliny, Nat. Hist. l. 13. c. 4.

[70] T. Bab. Beracot, fol. 8. 1. & Sabbat, fol. 33. 1. Sota, fol. 35. 1. Pesachim, fol. 105. 1. Taanith, fol. 19. 2. & 27. 2. Yebamot, fol. 62. 2.

that becoming manner he ought to be, he must not think it any hardship if he is treated in the same way. Our Lord hereby intends to fortify the minds of His disciples against all the reproach and persecution they were to meet with from the world, by observing to them the treatment He Himself met with; wherefore, if He who was their master, a teacher that came from God, and taught as never man did, and was worthy of the utmost deference that could be paid, was maligned and evilly treated by men, it became them who were His disciples, to look for, and patiently bear such indignities; since they could expect no better usage than He Himself had: the same doctrine is suggested in the next clause,

nor the servant above his lord. And both seem to be proverbial expressions. The Jews have a saying[71] much like unto them, אין העבד זכה מרבו, *no servant is worthier than his master*; and Christ might make use of such common, well known expressions, that He might be the more easily understood, and in the most familiar manner convey what He intended, into the minds of His disciples; as, that since He was their Lord, and they were His servants, if His superior character and dignity did not secure Him from the obloquy and insults of men, it could not be thought by them, who were inferior to Him, that they should escape them.

Verse 25. **It is enough for the disciple that he be as his master**, &c. A disciple should think himself very well off, be entirely satisfied, yea, abundantly thankful, if he meets with no worse treatment than his master; if he has the same honor done him his master has, this is more than could be expected by him; and if he has the same ill usage with his master, he need not wonder at it, but should solace himself with this consideration, that it is no other, nor worse than his master had before him: and the same is equally true in the other case,

and the servant as his lord: these expressions, as before, were proverbs, or common sayings among the Jews, which our Lord chose to make use of, and adapt to His present purpose; להיות כרבו, *vel* דיו לעבד שיהא, *it is enough for the servant, that he be as his master*, is a saying often to be met with in their writings;[72] which our Lord applies, and reasons upon, in the following manner:

if they have called the master of the house Beelzebub, how much more shall they call them of the household? By *the master of the household*; He means Himself, who is master of the family both in heaven and in earth; who

---

71 T. Hieros. Maaser Sheni, fol. 55. 1.

72 T. Bab. Beracot, fol. 58. 2. Bereshit Rabba, fol. 43. 3. Juchasin, fol. 93. 1. Tzeror Hammor, fol. 64. 2. Aben Ezra in Hos. 1:2.

is Son over His own house, the high priest over the house of God, the Lord and governor of all the household of faith; who takes care of, provides for, and protects all that are of God's household: and yet, though in such a high office, and of such great usefulness, He did not escape the severest lashes of the tongues of the wicked Jews; who called Him by the most opprobrious names they could think of, and among the rest *Beelzebub*; see *Matt. 12:24; Luke 11:15*. This was the god of the Ekronites, *2 Kings 1:2*. The word signifies *a masterfly* or the *lord of a fly*: and so the Septuagint there calls him βααλ μυιαν, *Baal the fly*, the god of the Ekronites. And this idol was so called, either because it was in the form of a fly: or else from the abundance of flies about it, by reason of the sacrifices, which it was not able to drive away; and therefore the Jews contemptuously gave it this name. They observe,[73] that in the temple, notwithstanding the multitude of sacrifices offered up there, there never was seen a fly in the slaughter house: or else this deity was so called from its being invoked to drive away flies, and the same with *Myiodes*, the god of flies, mentioned by Pliny,[74] or *Myagros*, which the same author[75] speaks of; so Jupiter was called απομυιος, *a driver away of flies*; as was also Hercules;[76] and were worshiped by some nations on this account. In most copies, and so in the Arabic version, it is read *Beelzebul*; that is, as it is commonly rendered, the *lord of dung*, or *a dunghill god*; and it is generally thought the Jews called the god of the Ekronites so, by way of contempt; as it was usual with them to call an idol's temple, זבול, *zebul*, *dung*, and worshiping of idols מזבל, *dunging*;[77] but I must own, that I should rather think, that as *Beelsamin*, the god of the Phoenicians, is the same with *Beelzebul*, the god of the Ekronites, so it signifies the same thing: now בעל שמין, *Beelsamin*, is *the lord of the heavens*, and so is *Beelzebul*; for, זבול, *Zebul*, signifies *heaven*; so the word is used in *Hab. 3:11, the sun and the moon stood still*, זבלה, *in their habitation*; by which, as a Jewish[78] writer observes, הרצון בו השמים, *is meant the heavens*; for they are the habitation of the sun and moon: see also *Isa. 63:15*. And so among the seven names of the heavens, reckoned up by them, this is accounted one.[79] Now as the Jews looked upon all the deities of the Gentiles as demons, or devils; and since Beelzebub

---

[73] Pirke Abot, c. 5. sect. 5.

[74] Nat. Hist. 1. 29. c. 6.

[75] Ibid. 1. 10. c. 28.

[76] Pausanias, 1. 5. p. 313. & 1. 8. p. 497. Clement. Alex. ad Gentes, p. 24.

[77] T. Hieros. Beracot, fol. 13. 2.

[78] R. Sol. Urbinas in Ohel Moed, fol. 100. 1.

[79] T. Bab. Chagiga, fol. 12. 2.

was the chief of them, they thought they could not fix upon a more reproachful name, to give to Christ, than this: and our Lord suggests, that since the great master of the family was called in such an abusive manner, it should be no cause of stumbling and offense, if those of a lower class in the family should be so stigmatized; if Christians are called by ever such hard names, even devils, they should not be disturbed at it; since their Lord and Master was called the prince of them.

[15] Matt. 10:40

Verse 40. **He that receiveth you, receiveth me**, &c. This is said to comfort the disciples, lest they should conclude from this account of the sorrows, afflictions, and persecutions they were to meet with, that there would be none that would receive them and their message; Christ therefore suggests, that there would be some that would embrace the Gospel preached by them, and receive them kindly into their houses, and entertain them in a very hospitable manner: and, for the encouragement of such persons, who would risk their own goods and lives by so doing, He lets them know, that receiving of His disciples, was interpreted by Him, a receiving of Himself; and what they did to them, would be taken as kindly, as if done to Him personally; and, in like manner, would it be understood and accepted by His Father:

and he that receiveth me, receiveth him that sent me. To which agrees, what the Jews say[80] of the angel, in *Ex. 23:22, If thou shalt indeed obey his voice, and do all that I shall speak*: who observe, that it is not written, *that he shall speak*, but *that I shall speak*; intimating, that אתם הימנו כאלו לי אתם מקבלים אם מקבלין, *if ye receive him, it is all one as if you received me*: and the whole of this accords with a common saying among[81] them, ששלוחו של אדם כמותו, *that a man's messenger is as himself*. The Jew[82] therefore, has no reason to reproach Christ and His followers as he does, as if it was the sense of these words of Christ, and which the Christians give of them, that Christ and His twelve apostles were but one person.

---

[80] Shemot Rabba Parash. 32. fol. 135. 3.

[81] T. Bab. Baracot, fol. 34. 2. Kiddushin, fol. 41. 2. 42. 1. & 43. 1. Bava Metzia, fol. 96. 1.

[82] R. Isaac Chizzuk Emuna, par 2. sect. 14. p. 404.

[16] Matt. 11:14

Verse 14. **And if ye will receive** *it*, &c. The words carry in them some suspicion of unbelief and hardness of heart, as though they would not receive it: however, whether they would or not, it was a certain truth, that,

this same person, *John the Baptist,*

is Elias, which was for to come; who was appointed by God to come, and was prophesied of, *Mal. 4:5,* that he should come; and even according to the doctrine of the Scribes and Rabbins, he was expected to come *before* the Messiah; only they in general thought, that Elijah the Tishbite, in person, was meant; though some, as before observed,[83] were of opinion, that some *great prophet* equal to Elijah, and endued with the same spirit, is intended; and which is true of John the Baptist, who came *in the spirit* and *power* of Elias, *Luke 1:17.* And, as it was usual with the Jews,[84] to call Phinehas by the name of Elias, and Elias, *Phinehas*, because of his zeal for the Lord of hosts; for the same reason may John be called by the same name, there being a great resemblance between Elias and him; in their temper and disposition; in their manner of clothing, and austere way of living; in their very great piety and holiness; in their courage and integrity, in reproving vice; and in their zeal and usefulness in the cause of God, and true religion: in respect to which, Christ must be here understood, when He affirms John to be *Elias*; not Elias in person, but he that was intended by Elias, that was said should come: hence here is no contradiction to the words of the Baptist, in *John 1:21,* when he says, that he *was not Elias*; for the Jews, who put the question to him, whether he was Elias, or not? meant whether he was Elias in person, Elias the Tishbite, or not; and so John understood them, and very honestly and sincerely replies, he was *not*: but he does not deny that he was intended by this *Elias*, that was prophesied should come; yea, he says such things as might induce them to believe he was that person; hence, Christ, and he, say nothing contrary to, and irreconcilable, as the Jew[85] suggests, with each other.

---

[83] Vid. Pocock. not. in porta Mosis, p. 219.

[84] Baal Hatturim in Num. 25:12. Kimchi in 1 Chron. 9:20. Targum Jon. in Ex. 6:18.

[85] R. Isaac Chizzuk Emuna, par. 1. c. 39. & par. 2. c. 15.

[17] Matt. 13:4

Verse 4. **And when he sowed**, &c. Or, *as he sowed*, as the other evangelists; that is, *while he was sowing,*

some seeds fell; either out of his hand, or out of the cart drawn by oxen; hence the Talmudists[86] distinguish between מפולת יד, *the falling of the hand*, or what falls out of the hand; and מפולת שוורים, *the falling of the oxen*, or what falls from them; where the gloss is,

> "In some places they sow the grain with the hand; and in other places they put the seed on a cart full of holes, and oxen draw the cart on the plowed land, and it falls upon it."

[18] Matt. 13:14-15

Verse 14. **And in them is fulfilled the prophecy of Esaias**, &c. In *Isa. 6:9-10,*

which saith, which runs, or may be read thus,

By hearing ye shall hear, and shall not understand, and seeing ye shall see, and not perceive. The words are a prophecy concerning the people of the Jews, which began to be accomplished in the times of Isaiah; and were again fulfilled in the times of some after prophets; and had been in part fulfilled under the more plain and easy ministry of Christ; and was to have a further accomplishment under this parabolical way of preaching; as it also was to have, and had, a yet further completion under the ministry of the apostles; see *Acts 28:26-27; Rom.11:8*; and the judicial blindness here predicted, was to go on among them, until the land of Judea was utterly destroyed by the Romans, and the cities and houses thereof left without any inhabitants. All which accordingly came to pass: for that this prophecy refers to the times of the Messiah, and to the people of the Jews, is clear from this one observation made by Christ Himself, that Esaias foretold those things when he saw the glory of the Messiah, and spake of Him, *John 12:40-41;* and because it was to have, and had, its accomplishment over and over again in that people, therefore the word αναπληρουται, which may be rendered *is fulfilled again*, is made use of. The sense of the prophecy is, with respect to the times of the Messiah, that the Jews, while hearing the sermons preached by Him, whether with, or without parables,

---

[86] T. Bab. Bava Metzia, fol. 105.2.

should hear His voice, and the sound of it, but not understand His words internally, spiritually, and experimentally; and while they saw, with the eyes of their bodies, the miracles He wrought, they should see the facts done, which could not be denied and gainsayed by them, but should not take in the clear evidence, full proof, and certain demonstration given thereby, of His Messiahship. In the prophecy of Isaiah, the words run in the imperative, *hear ye, see ye*, &c. but are here rendered in the future, *shall hear, shall see*, &c. which rendering of the words is supported and established by the version of the Septuagint, by the Chaldee paraphrase, and by many Jewish commentators;[87] who allow, that the words in Isaiah may be so understood; which is sufficient to vindicate the citation of them, by the evangelist, in this form of them.

Verse 15. **For this people's heart is waxed gross,** &c. Or *fat*, become stupid and sottish, and without understanding; and so incapable of taking in the true sense and meaning of what they saw with their eyes, and heard with their ears; for they had their outward senses of hearing and seeing, and yet their intellectual powers were stupefied.

And *their* ears are dull of hearing, and their eyes they have closed; which is expressive of the blindness and hardness, which were partly brought upon themselves by their own wilfulness and obstinacy, against such clear evidence as arose from the doctrine and miracles of Christ; and partly from the righteous judgment of God, giving them up, for their perverseness, to judicial blindness and obduracy; see *John 12:40;* and are in the prophet ascribed to the ministry of the Word; that being despised, was, in righteous judgment, the *savor of death unto death*, unto them [*2 Cor. 2:16*]; and they under it, as clay under the influence of the sun, grew harder and harder by it, stopping their ears, and shutting their eyes against it:

lest at any time they should see with *their* eyes, and hear with *their* ears, and should understand with *their* heart: which may be understood either of God's intention, and view, in giving them up to judicial blindness, and hardness of heart, under such miracles, and such a ministry, as a punishment for their wilful contempt of them; that so they might never have any true sight, hearing, and understanding of these things, and be turned from the evil of their ways, have repentance unto life, and remission of sins; which seems to be the sense of the other evangelists, *Mark 4:12; Luke 8:10; John 12:40;* or, as if these people purposely stupefied themselves, stopped their ears, and pulled away the shoulder, and wilfully shut their eyes; fearing they should receive some conviction, light, and knowledge,

---

[87] In R. David Kimchi in Isa. 6:9.

and should be converted, by the power and grace of God:

and I should heal them. Or, as in Mark, *and their sins should be forgiven them*; for healing of diseases, and forgiveness of sins, are, in Scripture language, one and the same thing; and this sense of the phrase here, is justified by the Chaldee paraphrase, which renders it, וישתבק להון, *and they be forgiven*, or *it be forgiven them*, and by the Jewish commentator on the place; who interprets *healing*, of the healing of the soul, and adds והיא הסליחה, *and this is pardon*.[88]

[19] Matt. 13:57

Verse 57. **And they were offended in him**, &c. It was a stumbling to them, how He came by His wisdom and power; since He had not these things from men of learning, and could not have them from His relatives: and therefore, rather than believe He had them of Himself, or from God, they chose to indulge at least a suspicion, that He had them from the devil, and so *were offended in him*: or this offense was taken at the meanness [*or* lowliness] of His birth, parentage, and education, though without reason; for if without the advantage of an education, without human literature, and the instructions of men, He was able to expound the Scriptures, preach such doctrine, and deliver such words of wisdom, and confirm all this by miracles, and mighty works, they ought to have considered Him as a divine person, and all this, as a demonstration of it, and of His having a divine mission at least, and of His being raised up by God for extraordinary purposes.

But Jesus said unto them; being unmoved at their offense in Him, and contempt of Him, which was no other than what He expected:

A prophet is not without honor, save in his own country, and in his own house. Which seems to be a proverbial speech in common use, though I have not met with it in Jewish writings; showing, that a prophet, or any teacher, or preacher, generally speaking, is more esteemed among strangers, who have no personal pique, nor prejudices against him, and who judge of him, not by what he has been, but by his present abilities, doctrine, and conduct, than among his countrymen; who are apt to think meanly [*or* lowly] of him, because familiarly acquainted with him, and knew, if not his vices, yet his infirmities; and envy him any superior degree of honor to them, he has attained unto. I say, generally speaking, for this is not always the case on either side; sometimes a prophet is

---

[88] R. David Kimchi in loc.

affronted and abused in strange places, as Christ Himself was: and sometimes is received with esteem and applause among his countrymen, relations, and acquaintance; but this is rare and uncommon; the proverb respects what is usually and ordinarily done, and the truth of it is easy to be observed.

[20] Matt.14:22

Verse 22. **And straightway Jesus constrained his disciples**, &c. As soon as ever He had wrought the above miracle, and perceived that the people were so convinced by it, of His being the Messiah, that they were determined, whether He would or not, to set Him up for a temporal king, to deliver them from the Roman yoke; which they doubted not He was able to do, who could feed so large a number, with such a small quantity of provision; see *John 6:14-15;* and knowing also, that His disciples had imbibed the same notion of a temporal kingdom, were very fond of it, and big with expectation thereof; and would have readily encouraged the populace, and joined with them in such an action: wherefore, in all haste, He hurried them away, obliged them to depart, lest any step should be taken, which might be of dangerous consequence to them, and the people: it looks as if the disciples were bent upon the same thing, and that it was with much difficulty and reluctance, they were brought off of it. Christ was forced to use His power and authority; and order them directly,

to get into a ship; very likely, the same they came over in;

and to go before him unto the other side, of the lake of Tiberias, or sea of Galilee, over against Bethsaida, to Capernaum, or the land of Gennesaret;

while he sent the multitudes away. Who would not so easily have been prevailed upon to have departed, if Christ had not first shipped off His disciples; for had He withdrawn Himself, and left His disciples with them, they would have been in hopes of His return, and would have continued in a body with them, in expectation of it; and therefore, the better to disperse them, and prevent their designs, He sends away His disciples before Him.

[21] Matt. 14:25-26

Verse 25. **And in the fourth watch of the night**, &c. This is said, according

to the division of the night into *four* watches, by the Jews; who[89] say that,
> "there are four watches in the night, and four watches in the
> day."

It is true indeed, that it is disputed among them, whether there were four watches, or only three in the night: some say there were four, others say there were but three;[90] not but that these made a division of the night into four parts, the three first of which, they thought were properly the watches of the night, and the fourth was the morning. The first watch began at six o'clock in the evening, and lasted till nine; the second began at nine, and ended at twelve, which was midnight; the third began at twelve, and closed at three; the fourth began at three, and ended at six in the morning. But since some[91] Jewish writers are so positive for the division of the night into *three* watches only, and a watch is with them called[92] the third part of the night; and it is dubious with some, whether the Jewish division is here referred to; and since it is so clear a point, that the Romans[93] divided their night into four watches, and their writers speak not only of the first, second, and third watches, but also of the fourth watch;[94] it is thought by some, that the evangelist speaks after the Roman manner: but however, certain it is, that within this period, probably at the beginning of it, after three o'clock in the morning, Christ came to his disciples, when they had been almost all the night at sea, tossed with waves, and in great danger.

Jesus went unto them; from the mountain where he had been praying the greatest part of the night, to the seaside, and so upon the waters to them; for it follows,

walking upon the sea. As on dry land: though it was so stormy and boisterous, that the disciples, though in a ship, were in the utmost danger, yet He upon the waves, was in none at all; by which action He showed Himself to be the Lord of the sea, and to be truly and properly God; whose character is, that he *treadeth upon the waves of the sea, Job 9:8.*

Verse 26. **And when the disciples saw him walking on the sea**, &c. It being

---

[89]   T. Hieros. Beracot, fol. 2. 4. Echa Rabbati, fol. 54. 4.

[90]   T. Bab. Beracot, fol. 3. 1, 2.

[91]   Jarchi & Kimchi in Judges 7:19. & in Psa. 119:147.

[92]   Gloss. in T. Bab. Beracot, fol. 2. 1.

[93]   Alex. ab Alex. Genial. Dier. 1. 4. c. 20.

[94]   Livy, Hist. 1. 36, c. 24.

now morning, and perhaps might have moonlight; and besides, there is always more light upon the water than land; they were able to discern something like a man, walking upon the surface of the sea, but had not light enough to distinguish what, or who it was; and, moreover, had no thought of Christ, or expectation of seeing Him; and the appearance of a man walking upon the waters being so unusual, and astonishing,

they were troubled, saying, It is a spirit: a nocturnal apparition, a demon in human form. The Jews, especially the sect of the Pharisees, had a notion, from whom the disciples might have their's, of spirits, apparitions, and demons, being to be seen in the night; hence that rule,[95]

"It is forbidden a man to salute his friend in the night, for we are careful, lest שׁד הוא, *it should be a demon*."

They say a great many things of one לילית, *Lilith*, that has its name from hlyl, *the night*, a she demon, that used to appear in the night, with a human face, and carry off young children, and kill them. Some such frightful notions had possessed the minds of the disciples:

and they cried out for fear. As persons in the utmost consternation, in the greatest danger, and in want of help. The fear of spirits, arises from the uncommonness of their appearance; from their superiority to men in power and strength; from the enmity there is between men and evil spirits; and from a general notion of their doing hurt and mischief: hence, demons are, by the Jews, called, מזיקין, *hurtful*, or *hurting*, all their study being to do hurt to men; and the same word is here used in Munster's Hebrew Gospel: add to all this, that the fear of the disciples might be increased, through a vulgar notion among seafaring men, that such sights are ominous, and portend evil to sailors; and they might the more easily be induced to give credit to this, and fear, since they were already in such imminent danger.

[22]   Matt. 14:27

Verse 27. **But straightway Jesus spake unto them**, &c. Directly, the very moment, as soon as ever they cried out, and He perceived the consternation they were in, as one truly affected towards them, and concerned for their welfare; He called out aloud unto them, not coming with any intention to fright them, but to save them;

---

[95]   T. Bab. Megilla, fol. 3. 1. Sanhedrin, fol. 44. 1.

saying, Be of good cheer, it is I, be not afraid. Take heart, be of good courage, do not be affrighted at my appearance, from whom you have nothing to fear; nor be afraid of the storm and tempest in which you are, I will deliver you; for it is I, your Master, Savior, and Redeemer, and not any hurtful spirit; who am able to save you, and am come for that purpose. Christ may be sometimes near His people, and they not know Him; as the Lord was in the place where Jacob was, and he knew it not, *Gen. 28:16;* and as Christ was standing by Mary Magdalene at the sepulcher, and she took Him to be the gardener: and for want of a distinct knowledge of Christ in His person, offices, and grace, persons have wrong apprehensions of Him, and are filled with dread and fears, concluding they have no interest in Him; that He is a Savior, but not of them; that their sins are so many, and of such a dye, and attended with such aggravating circumstances, that though He is able to save them, He never can be willing to receive such vile sinners as they are: but when Christ makes Himself known unto them, as the able and willing Savior, and their Savior and Redeemer, then, instead of dreading Him as a judge, their fears vanish, their faith increases, and they are ready to do any thing He shall order them; as Peter says in the next verse, who was willing to come to Christ on the water, when he knew who He was, if He was but pleased to bid him come.

[23]   Matt.14:29

Verse 29. **And he said, Come**, &c. This He said, partly to assure them who He was; for had He denied him, he and the rest might have concluded, it was none of Jesus; and partly to commend his love, and confirm his faith, by giving a further instance of His power, in enabling him to walk upon the water, as he did:

And when Peter was come down out of the ship; as he immediately did, having orders from Christ; and being by this second speech fully convinced it was He,

he walked on the water; a little way, being supported and enabled by the power of Christ; for this was an extraordinary and miraculous action; for if it was so in Christ, it was much more so in Peter: Christ walked upon the water by His own power, as God; Peter walked upon the water, being held up by the power of Christ. The Jews[96] indeed, call swimming השיטה על פני המים, *walking upon the face of the waters*: hence we read of a swimmer's vessel, which is

---

[96]   R. David Kimchi, Sepher Shorash. rad. שחה.

675

explained to be what men make to learn in it, how לשוט על פני המים, *to go* or *walk upon the face of the waters*;[97] but then this is not going upon them upright, but prone, or lying along upon the surface of the waters, which was not Peter's case; he did not, as at another time, cast himself into the sea, and swim to Christ; see *John 21:7*; but as soon as he came down from the ship, standing upright, he walked upon the waters,

to go to Jesus. Not merely for walking's sake, but for the sake of Christ, he dearly loved; that he might be with Him, and be still more confirmed of the truth of its being He, and not a spirit.

[24] Matt.16:17

Verse 17. **And Jesus answered and said unto him**, &c. Not waiting for any other declaration from them; but taking this to be the sense of them all, He said,

Blessed art thou Simon Bar-jona, or *son of Jona*, or *Jonas*, as in *John 1:42* and *21:15*. His father's name was *Jonah*, whence he was so called: so we read[98] of R. Bo bar Jonah; and of a Rabbi of this very name,[99] ר שמעון בר יונא, *Rabbi Simeon bar Jona*; for *Simon* and *Simeon* are one and the same name. Some read it *Bar Joanna*, the same with *John*; but the common reading is best. *Bar Jona* signifies *the son of a dove*, and *Bar Joanna* signifies *the son of one that is gracious*. Our Lord, by this appellation, puts Peter in mind of his birth and parentage; but does not pronounce him blessed on that account: no true blessedness comes by natural descent; men are by nature *children of wrath* [*Eph. 2:3*], being conceived in sin, and *shapen in iniquity* [*Psa. 51:5*]: though he was Bar Jona, *the son of a dove*, and his father might be a good man, and answer to his name, and be of a dovelike spirit; yet such a spirit was not conveyed from him to Peter by natural generation: and though he might be, according to the other reading, Bar Joanna, or *the son of a gracious man*, yet grace was not communicated to him thereby; for he was not *born of blood, nor of the will of the flesh, nor of the will of man, but of God, John 1:13*. He was a blessed man, not by his *first*, but by his *second* birth: and the reason why our Lord makes mention of his father, is to observe to him, that he was the son of a mean [*or* lowly] man, and had had, but a mean education, and therefore his blessedness in general

---

[97] R. Sol. Urbin. Ohel moed, fol. 78. 1.

[98] Juchasin, fol. 85. 1.

[99] Ibid. fol. 105. 1.

was not of nature, but of grace; and this branch of it in particular: the knowledge he had of the Messiah, was not owing to his earthly father, or to the advantage of an education, but to the revelation he had from Christ's Father which is in heaven, as is hereafter affirmed. He is pronounced *blessed*, as having a true knowledge of God, and of His Son Jesus Christ, whom to know is life eternal [see *1 John 5:20*]; and all such as he are so, appear to be the favorites of God, to have an interest in Christ and in all the blessings of His grace; are justified by His righteousness, pardoned through His blood, are accepted in Him, have communion with Father, Son, and Spirit, and shall live eternally with them hereafter.

For flesh and blood hath not revealed *it* unto thee: nothing is more frequent to be met with in Jewish writings, than the phrase of *flesh and blood*, as designing *men* in distinction from *God*: so the first man is said[100] to be,

"the workmanship of the blessed God, and not the workmanship רבשר ודם, *of flesh and blood*."

Again,[101]

"בשר ודם, *flesh and blood*, who knows not the times and seasons, &c. but the holy, blessed God, who knows the times and seasons, &c."

Instances of this way of speaking are almost without number: accordingly, the sense here is, that this excellent confession of faith, which Peter had delivered, was not revealed unto him, nor taught him by any mere man; he had not it from his immediate parents, nor from any of his relations, or countrymen; nor did he attain to the knowledge of what is expressed in it, by the dint of nature, by the strength of carnal reason, or the force of his own capacity and abilities:

but my Father which is in heaven. From whom both the external and internal revelation of such truths come; though not to the exclusion of the Son, by whose revelation the Gospel is taught, and received [see *Gal. 1:11-12*]; nor of the Holy Ghost, who is a *spirit of wisdom and revelation* [*Eph. 1:17*, with *1 Cor. 2:7-13*], but in opposition to, and distinction from any mere creature whatever. Neither the Gospel, nor any part of it, is a human device or discovery; it is not *after* man, nor according to the carnal reason *of* man; it is above the most exalted and refined reason of men; it has in it what *eye has not seen, nor ear heard*, nor has it *entered into the heart of man* to conceive of: its truths are *the deep things of God*, which the Spirit of God searches and reveals: and which men, left to the light of nature, and force of reason, must have been for ever ignorant of, and could never have discovered [see *1 Cor. 2:9-16*]. The Gospel is

---

[100]   Zohar in Gen. fol. 43. 3.

[101]   R. Simeon in Jarchi in Gen. 2:2.

a revelation, it consists of revealed truths; and which are to be received and believed upon the testimony and credit of the revealer, without entering into carnal reasonings, and disputes about them: and it is the highest reason, and the most noble use of reason, to embrace it at once, as coming from God; for this revelation is from heaven, and from Christ's Father; particularly the Deity, Sonship, and Messiahship of Christ, are doctrines of pure revelation. That there is *a God*, is discoverable by the light of nature; and that He is the living God, and gives being, and life, and breath, and all things, to His creatures; but that He has *a Son* of the same nature with Him, and equal to Him, who is the Messiah, and the Savior of lost sinners, this could never have been found out by *flesh and blood: no man knows the Son, but the Father*, and He to whom He reveals Him [see *Matt. 11:27; Luke 10:22*]; He bears witness of Him, and declares Him to be His *Son*, in whom He is *well pleased* [*Matt. 3:17*]; and happy are those who are blessed with the outward revelation of Jesus Christ in the Gospel, but more especially such to whom the Father reveals Christ in them the hope of glory!

[25]   Matt. 17:10

Verse 10. **And his disciples asked him, saying**, &c. That is, these three, Peter, James, and John, before they came to the rest; while they were going down the mountain, or from it, to the place where the others were; for the rest knew nothing of the appearance of Elias, and so cannot be thought to join in a question concerning him.

Why then say the Scribes, that Elias must first come? That is, come before the Messiah comes; for certain it is, that this was the sense of the Scribes, as it was of the ancient Jews, and is still the opinion of the modern ones. They say, [102]
> "That in the second year of Ahaziah, Elias was hid; nor will he appear, till the Messiah comes; then he will appear, and will be hid a second time; and then will not appear, till Gog and Magog come."

And they expressly affirm [103] that,
> "before the coming of the son of David, יבא אליהו לבשר, *Elias will come to bring the good news* of it."

---

[102]   Seder Olam Rabba, p. 45, 46.

[103]   Gloss. in T. Bab. Erubin, fol. 43. 2.

And this, they say,[104] will be one day before the coming of the Messiah. And Maimonides[105] observes,

> "That there are of their wise men that say, המשיח יבא אליהו שקודם ביאת, *that before the coming of the Messiah, Elias shall come.*"

So Trypho the Jew, the same with R. Tarphon, so often mentioned in Talmudic writings, disputing with Justin Martyr, tells him[106] that the Messiah,

> "shall not know himself, nor have any power, μεχρι αν ελθων Ηλιας, *till Elias comes*, and anoints him, and makes him known to all."

And hence the Targumist[107] often speaks of Messiah and Elias as together, and of things done by them; and in their prayers, petitions are put for them, as to come together:[108] this is founded upon a mistaken sense of *Mal. 4:5,* and which is the general sense of their commentators.[109] Now the Scribes made use of this popular sense, to disprove Jesus being the Messiah: they argued, that if He was the Messiah, Elias would be come; but whereas he was not come, therefore He could not be the Messiah. The disciples having just now seen Elias, are put in mind of this tenet of the Scribes, and of their use of it; and inquire of Christ, not so much about the truth of it, and the reason of their imbibing it, as why they were suffered to make use of it, to His disadvantage; and especially why they, the disciples, should be forbid publishing what they had seen; whereas, were they allowed to divulge this vision, and bear their testimony to this truth, that Elias had appeared, and they had seen him, it might be a means of stopping the mouths of these Scribes; and of convicting men of the truth of the Messiahship of Jesus, upon their own principles, and of confirming them that believed it. Or else the sense is, whereas they had seen Elias, and he was gone again, without making any public appearance in the nation, their question is, How came the Scribes to say, that he should *come first*? And if there was any truth in this, how came it to pass, that he did not come sooner, even before Christ came in the flesh. And inasmuch as he did now appear, why he did not appear more publicly, as the person that was to come, at least, before the setting up of the kingdom and glory of the Messiah; which they might hope were at hand, and

---

[104] R. Abraham ben David in Mishna Ediot, c. 8. sect. 7.

[105] Hilch. Melacim, c. 12. sect. 2.

[106] Dialog. cum Tryph. p. 226.

[107] In Ex. 40:10; Deut. 30:4. & Lam. 4:22.

[108] Seder Tephillot, fol. 56. 2. & 128. 2.

[109] Aben Ezra, Kimchi, & Abarbinel in loc.

that Elias was come to usher it in: but that he did not appear publicly, and they were not allowed to speak of it, they wanted to know Christ's sense of these things; and took this opportunity as they came from the mountain, to converse with Him about it.

[26]   Matt. 21:1

Verse 1. **And when they drew nigh unto Jerusalem**, &c. The Syriac, Persic, and Ethiopic versions read, *when he drew nigh, or was near*; but not alone, His disciples were with Him, and a multitude of people also; as is evident from the following account. They might well be said to be near to Jerusalem, since it is added,

and were come to Bethphage; which the Jews say[110] was within the walls of the city of Jerusalem, and was in all respects as the city itself, and was the outermost part of it;[111] and that all within the outward circumference of the city of Jerusalem was called Bethphage:[112] it seems to me to be part of it within the city, and part of it without, in the suburbs of it, which reached to Bethany, and that to the Mount of Olives. Various are the derivations and etymologies of this place: some say it signifies *the house*, or *place of a fountain*, from a fountain that was in it; as if it was a compound of *Beth*, a house, and πηγη, *pege*, a fountain: others, *the house of the mouth of a valley*; as if it was made up of those three words, בית פי גיא, because the outward boundary of it was at the foot of the Mount of Olives, at the entrance of *the valley of Jehoshaphat*: others say, that the ancient reading was *Bethphage, the house of slaughter*; and Jerome says,[113] it was a village of the priests, and he renders it, *the house of jaw bones*: here indeed they might bake the showbread, and eat the holy things, as in Jerusalem;[114] but the true reading and signification of it is, בית פאגי, *the house of figs*; so called from the fig trees which grew in the outward limits of it, near

---

[110]   Gloss. in T. Bab. Sanhedrin, fol. 14. 2. & Pesach. fol. 91. 1.

[111]   Gloss. in T. Bab. Pesach. fol. 63. 2. & 91. 1.

[112]   Gloss. in T. Bab. Sota, fol. 45. 1. & Bava Metzia fol. 90. 1.

[113]   In loc. & ad Eustoch, fol. 59. 3. tom. 1.

[114]   Mishna Menachot, c. 11. sect. 2. T. Bab. Menachot, fol. 63. 1. & 78. 2. Maimon. Hilch. Pesul. Hamukdash, c. 12. sect. 16. Gloss. in Pesach. fol. 63. 2.

Bethany, and the Mount of Olives; hence we read of[115] פגי בית היני, *the figs of Bethany*; which place is mentioned along with Bethphage, both by Mark and Luke, where Christ, and those with Him, were now come: the latter says, they were come *nigh* to these places, for they were come,

unto the Mount of Olives; near to which were the furthermost limits of Bethany, and Bethphage, from Jerusalem. This mount was so called from the abundance of olive trees which grew upon it, and was on the east side of Jerusalem;[116] and it was distant from it a sabbath day's journey, *Acts 1:12*, which was two thousand cubits, or eight furlongs, and which made one mile:

then sent Jesus two disciples; who they were is not certain, perhaps Peter and John, who were afterwards sent by Him to prepare the passover, *Luke 22:8*.

[27]   Matt.21:5

Verse 5. **Tell ye the daughter of Zion**, &c. These words seem to be taken out of *Isa. 62:11*, where it is said, *Say ye to the daughter of Zion, Behold thy salvation cometh*, or *thy Savior cometh*; meaning, without doubt, the Messiah: by *the daughter of Zion* is meant, not the city of Jerusalem, but the inhabitants thereof, the Jewish synagogue; or, as the Targum renders it, כנישתא דציון, *the congregation of Zion*, the people of the Jews; particularly the elect of God among them, those that embraced the true Messiah, and believed in Him:

Behold, thy king cometh unto thee: this, and what follows, are cited from *Zech 9:9;* and to be understood of the king Messiah, who, in a little time after this prophecy was given out, was to come to Zion, and redeem Jacob *from all his iniquities* [*Psa. 130:8*], and was now come. One of the Jewish commentators says,[117] that interpreters are divided about the sense of this prophecy; but observes, that there are some that say this is the Messiah: and another[118] of them affirms, that it is impossible to explain it of any other than the king Messiah; and that it can be understood of no other, I have elsewhere[119] shown;

---

[115]   T. Bab. Pesach. fol. 53. 1. & Erubin, fol. 28. 2.

[116]   Zech. 14:4. Targum in Ezek. 11:23. & Bartenora in Mishna Middot, c. 1. sect. 3.

[117]   Aben Ezra in Zech. 9:9.

[118]   Jarchi in ibid.

[119]   Prophecies of the Messiah literally fulfilled in Jesus, c. 9. p. 151, &c.

meek; in the prophecy of Zechariah it is, עָנִי, *poor*, as the Messiah Jesus was, in a temporal sense; but the word, both by the Septuagint, and our evangelist, is rendered, *meek*; as it is by the Targum, Jarchi, and Kimchi, who all explain it by עֲנוּתָן, *lowly, humble, or meek*: and a character it is, that well agrees with Jesus, who, in the whole of His deportment, both in life, and in death, was a pattern of meekness, and lowliness of mind:

and sitting upon an ass, and a colt the foal of an ass; This is applied to the Messiah by the Jews, both ancient[120] and modern,[121] who consider this as an instance and evidence of his humility: they suppose, this ass to be a very uncommon one, *having a hundred spots on it*; and say, that it was *the foal of that which was created on the eve of the sabbath*;[122] and is the same that Abraham and Moses rode upon: and they own, as before observed, that Jesus of Nazareth rode on one to Jerusalem, as is here related. Their ancient governors, patriarchs, princes, and judges, used to ride on asses, before the introduction and multiplication of horses in Solomon's time, forbidden by the law of God: wherefore, though this might seem mean and despicable at this present time, yet was suitable enough to Christ's character as a King, and as the Son of David, and King of Israel; strictly observing the law given to the kings of Israel, and riding in such manner as they formerly did.

[28] Matt. 21:9

Verse 9. **And the multitudes that went before**, &c. That is, *that went before Christ*; accordingly the Syriac, Arabic, Persic, and Ethiopic versions, and Munster's Hebrew Gospel, read, *that went before him*: these seem to be the *much people* that met Him from Jerusalem,

and that followed; which were perhaps those that came from Jericho, and other parts;

cried, saying, Hosanna to the Son of David: by calling Jesus the *Son of*

---

[120] T. Bab. Sanhedrin, fol. 98. 1. & 99. 1. Bereshit Rabba, fol. 66. 2. & 85. 3. Midrash Kohelet, fol. 63. 2. Zohar in Gen. fol. 127. 3. & in Num. fol. 83. 4. & in Deut. fol. 117. 1. & 118. 3. Raya Mehimna in Zohar. in Lev. fol. 38. 3. & in Num. fol. 97. 2.

[121] Jarchi in Isa. 26:6. Baal Hatturim in Exod. fol. 88. 2. Abarbimel, Mashmia Jeshua, fol. 15. 4.

[122] Pirke Eliezer, c. 31. Caphtor, fol. 81. 2.

David, they owned and proclaimed him to be the Messiah; this being the usual title by which the Messiah was known among the Jews; see the note on *Matt. 1:1;* and by *crying* and *saying Hosanna* to Him, which was done with loud acclamations, and the united shouts of both companies, before and behind; they ascribe all praise, honor, glory, and blessing to Him, and wish Him all prosperity, happiness, and safety. The word is a Hebrew word, and is compounded of נא and הושיעה, which signifies, *save I beseech*; and which words stand in *Psa. 118:25;* to which the multitude had reference, as appears from what follows; and are formed into one word, הושענא, *Hosana*, or *Hosanna*, in which form it frequently appears in the Jewish writings; and because of the often use of it at the feast of tabernacles, that feast was called *Hosanna*; and the seventh day of it was called הושענא רבה, *the great Hosanna.*[123] Moreover, the *Lulabs*, or the bundles made of branches of palm trees, and boughs of willow and myrtle, which they carried in their hands at the feast of tabernacles, often go by this name: it is said,[124]

"The Egyptian myrtle is right or fit להושענא, *for the Hosanna.*"

That is, to be put into the *Lulab*, or bundle of boughs and branches, which was carried about, and shaken at the above feast. Again,[125]

> "It is a tradition of R. Meir, that it was the practice of the honorable men of Jerusalem, to bind their *Lulabs* with golden threads—says Rabbah, These are they, מגדלי הושענא, *that bind the Hosanna.* The gloss on it is, *that bind the Lulabs*, of the house of the head of the captivity; for in binding the Hosanna of the house of the head of the captivity, they leave in it a hand's breadth and, says the same Rabbah, A man may not hold an Hosanna in a linen cloth."

Once more,[126]

> "Says R. Zera, A man may not prepare הושענא, *a Hosanna* for a child, on a good day."

Sometimes the Hosanna seems to be distinguished from the *Lulab*, and then by the *Lulab* is meant, only the branches of palm tree; and by the Hosanna, the

---

[123] Seder Tephillot. fol. 298. 2.

[124] T. Bab. Succa, fol. 33. 1.

[125] Ibid. fol. 37. 1.

[126] Ibid. fol. 46. 2. Vid. Maimon. Hilch. Lulab, c. 8. sect. 10.

boughs of willow and myrtle; as when,[127]

> "Rabbah says, A man may not fix the *Lulab*, בהושענא, *in the Hosanna.*"

And a little after says the same,

> "A man may not bind the *Lulab* with the *Hosanna.*"

Now these bundles might be so called, because they were lifted up and shaken, when the above words out of *Psa. 118:25* were recited: for thus it is said,[128]

> "When do they shake, that is, their *Lulabs*, or *Hosannas*? At those words, *O give thanks unto the Lord*, *Psa. 118:1*, the beginning and end; and at those words, *Save now I beseech thee*, *Psa. 118:25*. The house of Hillell, and the house of Shammai say also at those words, *O Lord I beseech thee, send now prosperity*: says R. Akiba, I have observed Rabban Gamaliel and Rabbi Joshua, that all the people shook their Lulabs, but they did not shake, only at those words, *Save now I beseech thee, O Lord.*"

Hence some have thought, that *these* are meant by the Hosanna in this text; and that the sense is, that the multitude cried, saying, These branches of palm trees we carry in our hands, and strow by the wayside, are in honor to the Son of David, the true Messiah, Jesus of Nazareth: but then this sense will not agree with the following clause, *Hosanna in the highest*: it may therefore be further observed, that certain prayers and songs of praise, were called *Hosannas*: hence we read[129] of, הושענות של שבת, *the Hosannas of the sabbath*; which consisted of various sentences in praise of the sabbath, and thanksgivings to God for it, and are concluded with this word *Hosanna*; and of various petitions that God would save them, as He had done others; and at the end of each petition, is this word. As also of,[130] הושענות של הושענא רבה, *the Hosannas of the great Hosanna*; which are certain words of prayer and praise, used on the seventh day of the feast of tabernacles. And whereas at that feast the *Hallell*, or hymn, was sung, which concluded with the *118th Psalm,* where the words, *Save now I beseech thee, O Lord*, stand; from whence this word is formed; the true sense and meaning of it here appears to be this: that the multitude that attended Christ to Jerusalem, as they went along, sung songs of praise to Him, as the true Messiah; particularly, applying the above passage to Him, and earnestly wished Him all

---

[127] T. Bab. Succa, fol. 37. 2.

[128] Mishna Succa, c. 3. sect. 9.

[129] Seder Tephillot, fol. 297. 1.

[130] Ibid. fol. 298. 2.

ENDNOTES

success and prosperity; and importunately prayed for salvation by Him; adding,

Blessed *is* he that cometh in the name of the Lord: which words are taken also out of *Psa. 118:26;* and is an ascription of blessing and praise to Jesus, the Messiah; who being sent by God, came from Him with His authority, as His apostle, and as representing Him; and contains another petition for Him, that He might be crowned with the blessings of divine goodness, for His people; and be blessed and praised by them, for all the spiritual blessings they are blessed with in Him. And very properly and pertinently were those words used and applied to Christ, since the Psalm from whence they are taken belongs to Him: the whole of it is, by some Jewish interpreters,[131] said to be spoken concerning Him; and particularly, He is designed in *Psa. 118:22,* by *the stone the builders refused*, as is clear from *verse 42* of this chapter, and from *Acts 4:11* and *1 Pet. 2:7;* and which is allowed by some Jewish writers, ancient and modern;[132] and *Psa. 118:27,* the words following these, are by them interpreted of the days of the Messiah, the times of Gog and Magog, and the future age.[133] And others of them said, as *Mark* observes, *chapter 11:10, Blessed be the kingdom of our father David, that cometh in the name of the Lord*; see the note there. Moreover, as it may be thought others of the people said, as *Luke* relates, *chapter 19:38, Blessed be the king that cometh in the name of the Lord*; see the note there. To which is added,

Hosanna in the highest. That is, *Let songs of praise be sung to God, who is in the highest heavens, for all His grace and goodness vouchsafed to the sons of men, through Christ His beloved Son; or Let not only all salvation, happiness, and prosperity attend the Messiah, David's Son, here on earth, but all glory and felicity in the highest heavens, above which He will be exalted.*

[29]   Matt. 21:12

Verse 12. **And Jesus went into the temple of God**, &c. At Jerusalem, which was built by His order, and dedicated to His worship, and where the Shekinah, or the divine presence was. Christ went not to the tower of David, the strong hold of Zion, the palace of His father David; for He entered not as a temporal king; but He went to the house of His heavenly Father, as the Lord and

---

[131]   Vid. Kimchi in Psa. 118:1.

[132]   Zohar in Exod. fol. 93. 3. Jarchi in Mic. 5:2.

[133]   T. Hieros. Megilla, fol. 73. 1.

proprietor of it, to preach in it, and purge it; whereby the glory of the latter house became greater than that of the former; and so several prophecies had their accomplishment, particularly *Hag. 2:7,9; Mal. 3:1;* though this was not the first time by many, of Christ's being in the temple; yet this His entrance was the most public and magnificent of any: after, He had alighted from the colt, and sent back that and the ass to their proper owners, as is very probable, He went by the eastern gate, called the king's gate, *1 Chron. 9:18,* into the temple;

and cast out all them that sold and bought in the temple: not in the holy of holies, nor in the holy place, nor in the court of the priests, nor in the court of the Israelites, but in the court of the Gentiles, and in the mountain of the house, in which were shops, where various things were sold, relating to sacrifices. What these persons bought and sold, whom Christ cast out, is not said, but may be collected from *John 2:14,* where besides *doves,* of which hereafter, mention is made of *sheep* and *oxen*; which were brought to be sold, on account of the passover, for it was then near their time of passover, as now; for besides the lambs and kids, which were here also sold and bought for the passover supper, sheep and oxen were here also killed and sold for the *Chagiga*, or feast,[134] which was the day following: here likewise the drink offerings were bought and sold, of which take the following account.

> "There were fifteen presidents במקדש, *in the sanctuary*: Jochanan ben Phinehas was over the tickets, and Ahijah over the drink offerings, &c.—He that inquired for drink offerings, went to Jochanan, who was appointed over the tickets: he gave him the money, and took a ticket; he then went to Ahijah, that was appointed over the drink offerings, and gave him the ticket, and received from him the drink offerings; and in the evening they came together, and Ahijah produced the tickets, and took for them the money."[135]

This was one way of buying and selling in the temple;

and overthrew the tables of the money changers; of which sort were they, who sat in the temple at certain times, to receive the half shekel, and change the money of such who wanted one, by which they gained something to themselves. It was a custom in our Lord's time, for every Israelite, once a year, to pay half a shekel towards the temple charge and service; which was founded upon the orders given by God to Moses in the wilderness: that upon his numbering the people, to take of every one that was twenty years of age and upwards, rich or

---

[134] Vid. R. Sol. Jarchi, in Deut. 16:2.

[135] Mishna Shekalim, c. 5. sect. 4. Maimon. Cele Hamikdash, c. 7. sect. 10-12.

poor, half a shekel, *Ex. 30:13;* though this does not seem to be designed as a perpetual rule. However, it now obtained, and was annually paid:

> "On the first day of Adar (which answers to our February) they proclaimed concerning the shekels."[136]

That is, they gave public notice, in all the cities in Israel, that the time of paying the half shekel was near at hand, that they might get their money ready, for every one was obliged to pay it: the Jews[137] say,

> "It is an affirmative command of the law, that every man in Israel should pay the half shekel every year; even though a poor man that is maintained by alms, he is obliged to it, and must beg it of others, or sell his coat upon his back and pay it, as it is said, *Ex. 30:15.* The rich shall not give more, &c.—All are bound to give it, priests, Levites, and Israelites, and strangers, and servants, that are made free; but not women, nor servants, nor children."

Notice being thus given,[138]

> "on the fifteenth day (of the same month), שולחנות, *tables* were placed in the province, or city (which Bartenora[139] interprets of Jerusalem; but Maimonides[140] says, the word used is the name of all the cities in the land of Israel, excepting Jerusalem), and on the twenty-fifth they sit, במקדש, *in the sanctuary.*"

The same is related by Maimonides,[141] after this manner:

> "On the first of Adar they proclaim concerning the shekels, that every man may prepare his half shekel, and be ready to give it on the fifteenth; השולחנים, *the exchangers* sit in every province or city, and mildly ask it; every one that gives them it, they take it of them; and he that does not give, they do not compel him to give: on the twenty-fifth, they sit *in the sanctuary* to collect it; and henceforward they urge him that does not give, until he

---

[136] Mishna Shekalim, c. 1. sect. 1.

[137] Maimon. Hilch. Shekalim, c. 1. sect. 1. 7.

[138] Mishna Shekalim, c. 1. sect. 3.

[139] In ibid.

[140] In ibid.

[141] Hilch. Shekalim, c, 1. sect. 9.

gives; and every one that does not give, they oblige him to give a pledge, and they take his pledge, whether he will [*or is willing*] or not, and even his coat."

This gives us a plain account of these money changers; of their tables, and of their sitting at them in the temple, and on what account. Now these exchangers had a profit in every shekel they changed.[142]

"When a man went to an exchanger, and changed a shekel for two half shekels, he gave him an addition to the shekel; and the addition is called קלבון, *Kolbon*; wherefore, when two men gave a shekel for them both, they were both obliged to pay the *Kolbon*."

Would you know what this *Kolbon* is, whence these exchangers are called, κολλυβισται, *Collybistae*, in this text, or the gain which these men had? Take this question and answer in their own words.[143]

"How much is the *Kolbon*? A silver *meah*, according to. R. Meir; but the wise men say, half a one."

Or as it is elsewhere expressed,[144]

"what is the value of the *Kolbon*? At that time they gave two pence for the half shekel, the *Kolbon* was half a *meah*, which is the twelfth part of a penny; and since, *Kolbon* less than that is not given."

Now a *meah* was the half of a sixth part of the half shekel, and the twenty-fourth part of a shekel, and weighed sixteen barley corns: half a *meah* was the forty-eighth part of a shekel, and weighed eight barley[145] corns; a *meah* was, of our money, the value of somewhat more than a penny, and half a one more than a halfpenny. This was their gain, which in so large a number that paid, must amount to a great deal of money. There seems to be nothing lie against these men being the very persons, whose tables Christ overturned, unless it should be objected, that this was not the time of their sitting; for it was now within a few days of the passover, which was in the month Nisan; whereas it was in the month Adar, that the half shekel was paid. But it should be observed, according to the above account, that they did not begin to sit in the temple to receive this money, until the twenty-fifth of Adar; and it was now but the tenth of Nisan,

---

[142] Ibid. c. 3. sect. 1.

[143] Mishna Shekalim, c. 1. sect. 7.

[144] Maimon. Hilch. Shekalim, c. 3. sect. 7.

[145] Maimonides & Bartenora in Mishna Shekalim, c. 1, sect. 7. & Cholin, c. 1. sect. 7.

when Christ entered the temple and found them there: so that there was but fifteen days: between the one and the other; and considering the large numbers that were obliged to pay, and the backwardness and poverty of many, they may reasonably be thought to be still sitting on that account. And what Maimonides before relates, deserves notice, and will strengthen this supposition; that on the twenty-fifth: of Adar, they sat in the temple to collect this money; and that henceforward they urged and compelled persons to pay it. Moreover, these men had other business, in a way of exchange, than this to do; and especially at such a time as the passover, when persons came from different parts to attend it; and who, might want to have their foreign money changed for current coin; or bills of return, to be changed for money. Add to all this the following account, which will show the large and perpetual business of these men:[146]

> "In the sanctuary there were before them, תמיד, *continually*, or *daily*, thirteen chests (and there were as many tables[147]); every chest was in the form of a trumpet: the first was for the shekels of the present year, the second for the shekels of the year past; the third for every one that had a *Korban*, or vow upon him, to offer two turtledoves, or two young pigeons; the one a burnt offering, the other a sin offering: their price was cast into this chest: the fourth for every one that had the burnt offering of a fowl only on him, the price of that was cast into this chest. The fifth was for him, who freely gave money to buy wood, to be laid in order on the altar; the sixth, for him that freely gave money for the incense; the seventh, for him that freely gave gold for the mercy seat; the eighth, for the remainder of the sin offering; as when he separated the money for his sin offering, and took the sin offering, and there remained of the money, the rest he cast into this chest; the ninth, for the remainder of the trespass offering; the tenth, for the remainder of the doves for men and women in fluxes, and women after childbirth; the eleventh, for the remainder of the offerings of the Nazarite; the twelfth, for the remainder of the trespass offering of the leper: the thirteenth, for him that freely gave money for the burnt offering of a beast."

and the seats of them that sold doves, which were the offerings of the poorer sort after childbearing, and on account of running issues: which cases were very frequent, and sometimes raised the price of doves very high, of which what

---

[146] Maimon. Hilch. Shckalim, c. 2. sect. 2.

[147] Mishna Shekalim, c. 6. sect 1.

follows is an instance:[148]

> "It happened at a certain time, that doves were sold in Jerusalem for a golden penny each; said Rabban ben Simeon Gamaliel, by this habitation (or temple which he swore by) I will not lodge (or lie down) this night, until they are sold for a silver penny each: he went into the council house and taught, that if a woman had five certain births, or five certain issues, she should bring one offering, and eat of the sacrifices, nor should there remain any debt upon her; and doves were sold that day for two fourths."

That is, for a silver penny; now a golden penny was the value of twenty-five silver pence;[149] so that the price, by this means, was sunk very much: but not only doves were sold in the markets in Jerusalem, but in the temple itself.[150]

> "There was a president over the doves, which was he with whom they agreed, who sold doves for the offerings, so and so by the shekel; and every one that was obliged to bring a pair of turtle doves, or two young pigeons, brought the price of them, למקדש, *to the sanctuary*; and the president gave the doves to the masters of the offerings, and made up the account with the treasurers."

Now at a feast time, as this was, there was a greater demand for doves than usual; for women who had lain in [that is, had lately given birth], and such as had fluxes, whether men or women, who lived in distant parts, reserved their offerings till they came up to the feast;[151] and which in consequence must occasion a greater call for these birds, and furnishes out a reason, why there should be so many sitting at this time in the temple to sell doves. Some have thought, that those persons are here meant, which are often mentioned by the Jewish doctors,[152] as an infamous sort of men, who are not admitted as witnesses in any case; and are reckoned among thieves, robbers, usurers, and players at dice; who מפריחי יונים, *teach doves to fly*, either to decoy other doves

---

[148] Mishna Cerithot, c. 1. sect. 7.

[149] Maimon. & Bartenora in ibid.

[150] Maimon. Hilch. Cele Hamikdash, c. 7. sect. 9.

[151] Gloss. in T. Bab. Sanhedrin, fol. 11. 1.

[152] T. Bab. Erubin, fol. 82. 1. T. Sanhedrin, fol. 25. 2. & Gloss. in ibid. Mishna Sanhedrin. c. 3. sect. 3. Maimon. Bartenora, & Ez. Chayim in ibid. & Edayot, c. 2. 7. & Bartenora in ibid. Maimon. Hilch. Gazela veabada, c. 6. sect. 7. Toen unitan, c. 2. sect. 2. & Eduth, c. 10. sect. 4.

from their dove houses, or to outfly others for money, or to fight one against another; and these sat in the temple to sell this sort of doves, which was still more heinous; but the other sense is more agreeable.

[30] Matt. 21:17

Verse 17. **And he left them, and went out of the city into Bethany** &c.*** which was about fifteen furlongs from Jerusalem, or almost two miles, *John 11:18*. Hither He went to converse with His dear friends, Lazarus, and Martha, and Mary, who were all of this place, and where He could lodge and rest quietly. The name of the town is variously interpreted: according to some ancient writers,[153] it signifies *the house of obedience*; so Christ went from the disobedient and faithless city, to a place of obedience, where He had some faithful and obedient disciples. Others read it, and so Munster's Hebrew Gospel, בית עניה, *the house of affliction*; a suitable place for Christ to go to, who was about to suffer for the sins of His people. The Syriac version renders it בית עניא, and which is interpreted *a house*, or *place of business*, as this town of Bethany was. We read[154] of חנויות של בית היני, *the shops of Bethany*, which were destroyed three years before Jerusalem, because they made their affairs to stand upon the words of the law; that is, as the gloss explains it, they found that what was forbidden by the wise men, was free by the law: a great trade might be driven here for olives, dates, and figs, which grew hereabout in great plenty. Mention is made in the Talmud of[155] פגי בית היני, *the figs of Bethany*: hence, as Christ departed from this place, the next morning He saw a fig tree. But the true etymology and signification of the name is בית אהיני, *the house*, or *place of dates*, the fruit of the palm tree: hence they that came from Jerusalem to meet Christ, might have their palm tree branches. One part of Mount Olivet abounded with olives, from whence it had its name; another part bore palm trees, and that was called *Bethany*, from whence this town over against it had its name; and another part had great plenty of fig trees growing on it, and this called *Bethphage*; and that part of Jerusalem which was nearest to it went by the same name. We read[156] also of מרחץ של בית היני, *the washing place of Bethany*; which seems to

---

[153] Jerome in loc. Origen in Joan p. 131. T. 2. & in Matt. p. 435, 446, 447. T. 1. Ed. Huet.

[154] T. Bab. Bava Metzia, fol. 88. 1.

[155] T. Bab. Pesachim, fol. 53. 1. & Erubin, fol. 28.

[156] T. Bab. Cholin, fol. 53. 1.

me to be not a place for the washing and purification of unclean men and women, as Dr. Lightfoot thinks, but for washing of sheep; for the story is, that,

> "a fox tore a sheep in pieces at the washing place of Bethany,
> and the affair came before the wise men;"

that is, at Jerusalem, to know whether that sheep might be eaten or not, since that which was torn was forbidden [see *Exod. 22:31*]. And some have interpreted *Bethany, a house*, or *place of sheep*: but so much for this town, and what account is given of it.

and he lodged there. Either in the house of Lazarus, and his two sisters, or in that of Simon the leper; for it was eventide when He went out of Jerusalem, as Mark observes. The Ethiopic version adds, *and rested there*; and so Origen[157] reads it; and, according to Harpocratian,[158] the word used by the evangelist signifies to *lie down*, and *sleep*, and take one's *rest*. Christ lodged here all night.

[31]   Matt. 21:25

Verse 25. **The baptism of John, whence was it**? &c. By *the baptism of John*, is meant the ordinance of water baptism, which was first administered by him; from whence he took the name of *John the Baptist*: and the doctrine which he preached concerning it, and previous to it, and even the whole of his ministry; which is denominated from a principal part of it, and which greatly distinguished his ministry from all others: and the question put by Christ concerning it is, *whence it was*? By what authority did John administer the ordinance of water baptism, which had never been administered before by any? Who sent him to *preach the baptism of repentance for the remission of sins* [*Mark 1:4*], a doctrine the world had never heard of before? Who gave him a commission to discharge the several parts of his ministry, which he performed in such a wonderful and powerful manner? Did he receive his authority,

from heaven, or of men? That is, from God or man? as the opposition requires; and as it was usual for the Jews to call God by the name of *heaven*: in this sense it is used by them, when they say,[159] that such have no part in the world to come, who affirm, that the law is not מן השמים, *from heaven*, that is, from God;

---

[157] In Matt. p. 447.

[158] Lexic. Decem Orator. p. 55.

[159] T. Hieros. Sanhedrin, fol. 27. 3. Vid. ibid. fol. 19. 3. T. Bab. Sanhedrin, fol. 99. 1.

which is exactly the phrase here: and when they observe,[160] that care should be taken that a man does not pronounce שֵׁם שָׁמַיִם, *the name of heaven*, that is, God, in vain: and when they tell[161] us of,

> "a certain man that built large buildings by the way side, and put food and drink there, so that everyone that came went in and eat, and drank, וּבֵרֵךְ לַשָּׁמַיִם, *and blessed heaven;*"

that is blessed, or gave thanks to God; and when they speak of[162] מִיתָה לַשָּׁמַיִם, *death by heaven;* that is, death which is immediately inflicted by God. So when Christ here asks, whether John's baptism was *from heaven*, or *of men*, His meaning is, whether it was of divine institution, and that John acted by divine authority, and commission; or whether it was a human device of his own, or of other men; and that he took the office of preaching and baptizing upon himself of his own head, or by some human appointment? To this He requires a direct answer, as is said in Mark, *answer me;* whether it was from the one, or from the other;

and they reasoned with themselves; either *within themselves*, as the Arabic version renders it, *in their own minds*, as the Syriac; or they took some little time and privately conferred together, what answer they should return; when they argued the point among themselves,

saying, If we shall say, From heaven; if we shall return for answer, that the baptism and ministry of John were of divine appointment, and that he acted by a divine authority,

he will say unto us, Why did ye not believe him? Why did not ye believe the doctrine that he preached? and receive the testimony that he gave concerning the Messiah? And why were ye not baptized by him? Why did ye reject the counsel of God against yourselves? They saw plainly, that if they owned the divine authority of John's baptism and ministry, they must allow Jesus to be the true Messiah, John bore witness to; and consequently, that it was by a divine authority he did what he did; and then there was an end of their question, and is the very thing that Christ had in view.

---

[160] T. Bab. Megilla, fol. 3. 1.

[161] Abot. R. Nathan, c. 7. fol. 3. 2.

[162] Ibid. c. 11. fol. 4. 1. Vid. ibid. c. 14. fol. 4. 4. & 5. 1. & c. 27. fol. 7. 1.

[32] Matt. 23:7

Verse 7. **And greetings in the markets**, &c. They [the Scribes and the Pharisees] used to stroll about the markets, being public places, where there was a great concourse of people, on purpose to be taken notice of before multitudes, with singular marks of respect; as stretching out the hand, uncovering the head, and bowing the knee:

and to be called of men Rabbi, Rabbi. Because of their great authority, and largeness of their knowledge: the repetition of the word *Rabbi*, is not made in the Vulgate Latin, nor in the Syriac, Arabic, Persic, and Ethiopic versions, nor in Munster's Hebrew Gospel, but is in all the Greek copies, and very justly; since it was usual in the salutations of them, to double the word. It is reported[163] of R. Eleazar ben Simeon, of Migdal Gedur, that having reproached a deformed man he met in the road; when he came to the city where the man lived,

> "the citizens came out to meet him, and said to him, Peace be upon thee, רבי רבי מורי מורי, *Rabbi, Rabbi, Master, Master*; he (Eleazar) said to them, Who do you call *Rabbi, Rabbi*? They replied to him, He who followed thee. He said unto them, If this be a Rabbi, let there not be many such in Israel."

The Jews pretend, that king Jehoshaphat used to salute the doctors with these titles; though they forget that they were not in use in his time, as will be hereafter observed: they say,[164]

> "whenever he saw a disciple of the wise men, he rose from his throne, and embraced and kissed him, and called him, מרי מרי אבי אבי רבי רבי, *Father, Father, Rabbi, Rabbi, Master, Master*."

Where you have the three different words used by our Lord in this and the following verses, by which these men loved to be called, and he inveighed against; nay, they not only suggest, that kings gave them these honorable titles, and they expected them from them, but even they liked to be called kings themselves. It is said[165] of R. Hona and R. Chasda, that as they were sitting together,

> "one passed by them, and said to them, *Peace be to you kings*, עליכו מלכי amlv, *peace be to you kings*: they said to him, From

---

[163] T. Bab. Taanith, fol. 20. 2.

[164] T. Bab. Maccot, fol. 24. 1. & Cetubot, fol. 103. 2.

[165] T. Bab. Gittin, fol. 62. 1.

whence does it appear to thee, that the Rabbins are called kings? He replied to them, From what is written, *by me kings reign*, &c. They said to him, From whence hast thou it, that we are to double or repeat peace, or salutation to kings? He answered them, That R. Judah said, that Rab said from hence, 1 Chron. 12:18. *Then the spirit came upon Amasai, &c.*"

This title began but to be in use in the times of our Lord, or a very little while before: none of the prophets had it, nor Ezra the Scribe, nor the men of the great synagogue, nor Simeon the Just, the last of them; nor Antigonus, a man of Socho, a disciple of his: and it is observed by the Jews themselves,[166] that,

> "*the five couple* are never called by the name of *Rabban*, nor by the name of *Rabbi*, only by their own name."

By whom are meant, Joseph ben Joezer, and Joseph ben Jochanan; Joshua ben Perachia, said to be the master of Jesus of Nazareth, and Nittai the Arbelite; Judah ben Tabai, and Simeon ben Shetach; Shemaiah and Abtalion; Hillell and Shammai. The sons, or disciples of the two last, first took these titles. Rabban Simeon, the son of Hillell, thought by some to be the same Simeon that had Christ in his arms, is[167] said to be the first that was called by this name. And it is also observed by them,[168] that *Rabban* was a name of greater honor than *Rabbi*, or *Rab*, and that *Rabbi* was more honorable than *Rab*; and to be called by a man's own name, was more honorable than any of them. The Karaite Jews make much the same complaint, and give much the same account of the pride and vanity of the Rabbinical doctors, as Christ here does; for so one of them says:[169]

> "The Karaites do not use to act according to the custom of the wise men among the Rabbans, to make to themselves gods of silver, and guides of gold, with this view, להקרא רב, *to be called Rab*; and also to gather wealth and food to fulness, &c."

---

[166] Ganz. Tzemach David, par. 1. fol. 21. 1.

[167] Ganz. Tzemach David, par. 1. fol. 25. 1.

[168] Ibid.

[169] Eliahu Adderet, c. 6. apud Trigland. de. Sect. Kar. c. 10. p. 164.

[33] Matt. 23:8

Verse 8. **But be not ye called Rabbi**, &c. Do not be ambitious of any such title, fond of it, or affect it, or be elated with it, should it be given you; nor look upon yourselves as men of power and authority over others; as having the dominion over men's faith, a power to make laws for others, impose them in a magisterial way, and bind and loose men's consciences at pleasure, as these men do:

for one is your Master, *even* **Christ**; meaning Himself, the true *Messiah*, the Head of the church, King of saints, and Lord of all; who had all power in heaven and in earth, to make laws, appoint ordinances, and oblige men to receive His doctrines, and obey His commands: the word *Christ*, is left out in the Vulgate Latin, the Syriac, Persic, and Ethiopic versions; but is in the Arabic version, and Munster's Hebrew Gospel, and in all the ancient Greek copies Beza consulted, excepting two: no other indeed can be meant; He is the great Rabbi, and doctor, that is to be hearkened to, and the Master we are all to obey:

and all ye are brethren. Not merely as the descendants of Adam, but as being, in a spiritual relation, the children of God, and disciples of Christ, and so have no superiority one over another. This may regard the disciples, both as believers and Christians, partakers of the same grace, and standing in the same relation to God, Christ, and one another, and having an equal right to the same privileges: and as apostles and ministers, one as such, no, not Peter, having no preeminence over the other, having the same commission, doctrine, and authority, one as the other.

[34] Matt. 23:29

Verse 29. **Woe unto you Scribes and Pharisees, hypocrites**! &c. This is the seventh and last time, in which these words are delivered in this exact form by our Lord, in this chapter; and expresses the certainty, both of their sin and punishment: and the instance annexed to it, no less discovers the hypocrisy of these persons, and supports the character given of them; as also furnishes out a sufficient reason why a woe is denounced upon them;

because ye build the tombs of the prophets, and garnish the sepulchers of the righteous; meaning by the *prophets* and *righteous* men, the same persons—the prophets, who were righteous men; or else the prophets, and also other righteous men besides them. Rightly is the word *build*, used of tombs and sepulchers: the Jews have a canon, which runs thus:[170]

"They do not dig graves nor sepulchers, on a feast day."

The commentators[171] on it say that,

"the graves are the holes which they dig in the earth, and the sepulchers are the buildings over the graves."

In the Gemara it is asked,[172]

"What are the graves? and what are the sepulchers? Says R. Judah, The graves are made by digging and the sepulchers or tombs בבנין, *by building;*"

and these edifices which they built over the graves of some of their prophets, and righteous men, were very grand and beautiful. The *Cippi Hebraici* furnish us with many instances of this kind: in Hebron, in the land of Canaan, which is *Kirjath Arba*, is the cave of Machpelah; in which were buried the fathers of the world, Adam and Eve, Abraham and Sarah, Isaac and Rebekah, Jacob and Leah; and over it is a wonderful, ונאה, *and beautiful* building, and it is the building of David the king; and over against the city, in the mountain, is a *beautiful* building, and there was buried Jesse, the father of David the king: in the way from Hebron to Jerusalem, is Chalchul, where Gad, David's seer, was buried; and Tekoah, where Isaiah the prophet was buried, and over him a *beautiful* structure: at the Mount of Olives is a beautiful fabric, which they say is the sepulcher of Huldah, the prophetess; at the bottom of the mount is a very great cave, attributed to Haggai the prophet, and in the middle of it are many caves; near it, is the sepulcher of Zechariah the prophet, in a cave shut up, and over it is כיפה נאה, *a beautiful arch,* or vault of one stone: between Rama and Jerusalem are caves ascribed to Simeon the just, and the seventy (elders of the) Sanhedrin: at Rama, Samuel was buried, also his father Elkanah, and Hannah his mother, and in a cave shut up, and over the cave buildings: at Cheres, which is Timnath Cheres, in Mount Ephraim, are buried Joshua the son of Nun, and Nun his father, and Caleb the son of Jephunneh, and over them are trees. At Avarta is the school of Phinehas, the son of Eleazar the priest, and Eleazar is buried upon the mountain; and below the village, between the olive trees, Ithamar, and over him a large monument: at the barns is a temple of the Gentiles, with a vault and a cave, where they say are buried seventy elders. At Belata, a village about a sabbath day's journey from Shechem, Joseph the righteous was buried: at Mount Carmel, is the cave of Elijah the prophet, and

---

[170] Mishna Moed Katon, c. 1. sect. 6.

[171] Maimon. & Bartenora in ibid.

[172] T. Bab. Moed Katon, fol. 8. 2.

there was buried Elisha, the son of Shaphat the prophet: at Jordan was buried Iddo the prophet, and over it is a great elm tree, and it is in the form of a lion; and there was buried Shebuel, the son of Gershom, the son of Moses, over whom is a great oak tree: at Geba, in Mount Lebanon, is buried Zephaniah the prophet, in the middle of a cave shut up. On a mountain, a sabbath day's journey from Zidon, Zebulun was buried, in a beautiful vault; at Cephar Noah, was buried Noah the just; and at Kadesh Nephtalim, Barak the son of Abinoam, and Deborah his wife, and Jael; and at Timnath, Shamgar the son of Anath, over whom are two marble pillars. At Cephar Cana, is buried Jonah, the son of Amittai, on the top of a mountain, in a temple of the Gentiles, in a *beautiful* vault: at Jakuk, was buried in the way, Habakkuk the prophet; and at the north of the village of Raam, was buried Obadiah the prophet: at Shushan the palace, was buried Mordecai the Jew, and over him a beautiful stone statue; and on it written, this is the sepulcher of Mordecai, the son of Jair, the son of Shimei, the son of Kish, a man of Jemini; and near the river Hiddekel, Ezekiel the prophet was buried. In this account, many things may be observed, which confirm and illustrate the words of the text. And certain it is, that it was accounted very honorable and laudable in persons, to beautify the sepulchers of the patriarchs and prophets. Among the excellent characters given of Benaah, R. Jochanan's master, it is said,[173]

> "that he was a very wise man, and a judge, and understood mysteries and parables; וציין מערת, *and painted the cave* of Adam the first, and the cave of Abraham."

Though perhaps this is to be understood of him in a figurative sense, but yet must allude to a literal one: the sepulchers of the prophets, were especially very sacred:

> "All sepulchers (they say,[174]) might be removed, but the sepulchers of a king, and the *sepulchers of a prophet.* They say unto him, Were not the sepulchers of the sons of David removed? And the sepulchers of the sons of Huldah, were in Jerusalem, and a man might not touch them, to remove them for ever. R. Akiba replied to them, Because of decency it was forgiven (or allowed) there, and from thence the uncleanness being channeled, went out to the brook Kidron."

Now our Lord must not be understood as blaming them for barely building *the tombs of the prophets*, and garnishing the sepulchers of *the righteous*, which they might have done without blame: but because they did all this, that they might

---

[173] Juchasin, fol. 86. 1.

[174] T. Hieros. Nazir, fol. 57. 4.

be thought to be very innocent and holy men, and far from being guilty of the crimes their forefathers were; when they were of the very selfsame bloodthirsty, persecuting spirit; and did, and would do the same things to the prophets and apostles of the New Testament, their fathers had done to the prophets of the Old. They have a saying,[175] that,

> "they do not erect monuments *for the righteous*; for their words are their memorial."

But this can only mean, that there is no need of monuments for them; since their sayings are sufficient to keep up the memory of them. Hence Dr. Lightfoot thinks, that our Lord reproves them out of their own mouths, for despising the words of the prophets; imagining they performed piety enough, by bestowing cost in adorning their sepulchers; when they themselves own, their sayings are the best remembrances of them, and therefore ought to be regarded more than their tombs.

[35] Matt. 26:3

Verse 3. **Then assembled together the chief priests**, &c. About the same time, two days before the passover, that Jesus said these things to His disciples, as is plain from *Mark 14:1*. By *the chief priests* are meant, either such who had been high priests, or such as were the heads of the twenty-four courses of the priests; or rather, the principal men of the priesthood, who were chosen out of the rest, to be members of the great Sanhedrin:

and the Scribes; the doctors of the law, who wrote out copies of the law for the people, and interpreted it to them in a literal way: this clause is left out in the Vulgate Latin, and in Munster's Hebrew Gospel, and in the Arabic and Ethiopic versions, and in the Alexandrian copy, and some others; but is retained in the Syriac version; and no doubt but these men had a place in this grand council:

and the elders of the people; these were the civil magistrates; so that this assembly consisted both of ecclesiastics and laymen, as the Sanhedrin did, of priests, Levites, and Israelites:[176] these came,

unto the palace of the high priest, who was called Caiaphas; his name

---

175 T. Hieros. Shekalim, fol. 47. 1.

176 Maimon. Hilch. Sanhedrin, c. 2. sect. 1.

was Joseph, but his surname Caiaphas; a word not of the same original with Cephas, as Camero thought; for these two words begin with different letters, nor are the rest the same. Now, though a king of Israel might not sit in the Sanhedrin, yet a high priest might, provided he was sufficiently qualified with wisdom.[177] The president of this grand council at this time, should be Rabban Gamaliel, Paul's master; unless it was Caiaphas, at whose house they were: how they came to meet at the high priest's palace, deserves inquiry; since their proper and usual place of meeting, was a chamber in the temple, called Gazith,[178] or the paved chamber: now let it be observed, that according to the accounts the Jews themselves give, the Sanhedrin removed from this chamber, forty years before the destruction of the temple;[179] and which, as Dr. Lightfoot conjectures, was about a year and a half before the death of Christ; and as others say,[180] four years; at least three years and a half before that time: but then, though the Sanhedrin removed from *the paved chamber*, they met at "Chanoth," *the sheds*, which was a place within the bounds of the temple, in the mountain of the house; and the question still returns, How came it to pass they did not meet there? To me the reason seems to be, that they chose not to meet there, but at the high priest's palace, because of privacy, that it might not be known they were together, and about any affair of moment; and particularly this: the high priest's house was always in Jerusalem, and he never removed from thence; nor did he go from the temple thither only in the night, or an hour or two in the day; for he had an apartment in the temple, which was called the chamber of the high priest, where he was the whole day.[181]

[36] Matt. 26:7

Verse 7. **There came unto him a woman**, By some thought to be the same that is spoken of in *Luke 7:37*; and by most, to be Mary, the sister of Lazarus, *John 12:3*, which may be true; for it is possible that one and the same woman might perform a like action at different times; for to neither of the above, at the same time, will the following agree. Not to the former, for though that was done

---

[177] Ibid. sect. 4.

[178] Mishna Middot c. 5. sect. 3.

[179] T. Bab. Sabbat, fol. 15. 1. Avoda Zara, fol. 8. 2. Sanhedrin, fol. 41. 1. Maimon. Hilch. Sanhedrin, c. 14. sect. 13. Juchasin, fol. 21. 1.

[180] Edzard. not. in Avoda Zara, c. 1. p. 236.

[181] Maimon. Cele Hamikdash, c. 5. sect. 7.

in the house of one Simon, yet not Simon the leper, but Simon the Pharisee; who though he had a particular respect for Christ, which few of that sect had, yet appeared to be then of a Pharisaical spirit; that was done in Galilee, this near Jerusalem in Bethany; the woman there anointed the feet of Christ, but this woman poured the ointment on His head; nor did any such conversation as here follow upon it, between Christ and His disciples; but what discourse was had on that occasion, was between Simon and Christ. Not to the latter, for that does not appear to be done in Simon's house, but rather in the house of Lazarus; no mention is made of the alabaster box, nor was the ointment poured on His head, but on His feet; besides, that was done six days before the passover, whereas this was but two; moreover, Judas only objected to that, but the disciples in general had indignation at this; and though the objections to it, and Christ's defense of it, are much in the same language, in one place as in the other, yet it was no unusual thing with Christ, to make use of the same words on a like incident, or when the same objections were made. The fact here recorded, is the same as in *Mark 14:3*, where it stands in the same order as here, and seems to have been done at the supper, of which mention is made, *John 13:2*, when Satan entered into Judas, and put it into his heart to betray his master, the account of which follows this here:

having an alabaster box of very precious ointment; Mark calls it, *ointment of spikenard, Mark 14:3*, which was very odorous, and of a very fragrant smell; see *Song of Sol. 1:12*. Some there render it, *pure nard*; unadulterated, unmixed, sincere and genuine; others, *liquid nard*, which was drinkable, and easy to be poured out; and some *Pistic* nard, so called, either from *Pista*, the name of a place in India, from whence it was brought, as some think; or as Dr. Lightfoot, from פיסתקא, *Pistaca*, which is the maste of a tree,[182] and of which, among other things, Pliny says,[183] the ointment of nard was made. The Persic version in both places read it, *ointment of Gallia*; and the just now mentioned writer,[184] speaks of *nardum Gallicum, Gallic nard*, which is what may be meant by that interpreter. But be it what ointment it will, it was ointment, *very precious*, very costly, and of a very great price; for the disciples observe, it might have been sold for more than three hundred pence: and for the better preserving of such ointments incorrupt, they used to be put into vessels made of *alabaster*,[185] though some think not the matter, but the form of these vessels is referred to; and observe, that vessels of gold, silver, and glass, for this use, being made in

---

[182] T. Bab. Gittin, fol. 69. 1. Gloss. in ibid.

[183] Nat. Hist. l. 13. c. 1.

[184] Ibid. c. 2. & l. 12. c. 12.

[185] Pliny, Nat. Hist. l. 13. 2. & 36. 8.

the form of *alabasters*, were called by that name; and that this might be made of the latter, since Mark says, that *she brake the box*; not into pieces, for then she could not be said to pour it out; but either the top, or side of it: though some critics observe, that the word signifies no more, than that she shook it, that the thicker parts of the ointment might liquify, and be the more easily poured out. The Arabic version has omitted that clause, and the Syriac, Persic, and Ethiopic read it, *she opened it*; that is, as the Persic adds, *the top of the vessel*: she took off the covering of the box, or took out the stopple,

and poured it on his head, as he sat *at meat*. Which was usually done at festivals, or at any considerable entertainments, as at weddings particularly:

> "Says Rab, they *pour ointment on the heads of the doctors*; (the gloss is, the women put ointment on the heads of the scholars). Says R. Papa to Abai, does the doctor speak of the ointment of the bridechamber? He replies, Thou orphan, did not thy mother cause for thee, that *they poured out ointment on the heads of the doctors*, at thy wedding? For lo! one of the Rabbins got a wife for his son, in the house of R. Bar Ula; and they say, that R. Bar Ula got a wife for his son in the house of one of the Rabbins, ודרדיג מישחא ארישא דרבנן, *and poured ointment on the head of the doctors;*"[186]

to this custom are the allusions in *Psa. 23:5*; *Eccl. 9:8*. The pouring of this ointment on the head of Christ was emblematical of His being anointed *with the oil of gladness* above His fellows [*Psa. 45:7*]; of His having the Holy Spirit, and His gifts and graces without measure; which, like the ointment poured on Aaron's head, that ran down to his beard, and the skirts of his garments, descends to all the members of His mystical body: and was a symbol of the Gospel, which is like ointment poured forth; and of the sweet savor of the knowledge of Christ, which was to be diffused, throughout all the world, by the preaching of it; and was done by this woman in the faith of Him, as the true Messiah, the Lord's anointed, as the Prophet, Priest, and King of His church.

[37] Matt. 26:11

Verse 11. **For ye have the poor always with you**, &c. This is said in answer to the objection of the disciples, that the ointment might have been sold, and the money given to the poor. Christ seems to have respect to *Deut. 15:11*, and which,

---

[186] T. Bab. Cetubot, fol. 17. 2.

agreeable to the sense of the Jews, refers to the times of the Messiah: for they say,[187]

> "There is no difference between this world (this present time) and the times of the Messiah, but the subduing of kingdoms only; as it is said, *Deut. 15:11, for the poor shall never cease out of the land*: the gloss on it is, From hence it may be concluded, that therefore, לעולם יש עניות, *for ever there will be poverty, and riches*."

Our Lord's words also show, that there will be always poor persons in the world; that there will be always such with His people, and in His churches; for God has chosen, and He calls such by His grace; so that men may always have opportunities of showing kindness and respect to such objects: in Mark it is added, *and whensoever ye will ye may do them good, Mark 14:7*; by relieving their wants, and distributing to their necessities:

but me ye have not always. Referring not to His divine and spiritual presence, which He has promised to His people, churches, and ministers, to the end of the world, but to His corporeal presence; for He was to be but a little while with them, and then go to the Father; be taken up to heaven, where He now is, and will be until the restitution of all things; so that the time was very short in which any outward respect could be shown to Him in person, as man.

[38] Matt. 27:33

Verse 33. **And when they were come to a place called Golgotha**, &c. The true pronunciation is *Golgoltha*, and so it is read in Munster's Hebrew Gospel. It is a Syriac word, in which language letters are often left out: in the Syriac version of this place, the first *l* is left out, and the latter retained, and it is read *Gogoltha*: and so, in the Persic, *Gagulta*; and in the Arabic, *Gagalut*. The Ethiopic version reads it, *Golgotha*; and so, Dr. Lightfoot observes, it is read by the Samaritan interpreter of the first chapter of Numbers:

that is to say, a place of a skull: some say Adam's skull was found here, and from thence the place had its name; this is an ancient tradition, but without foundation:[188] it seems to be so called, because it was the place where malefactors were executed, and afterwards buried; whose bones and skulls in

---

[187] T. Bab. Sabbat, fol. 63. 1.

[188] Mishna Sanhedrin, c. 6. sect. 4. 5.

process of time might be dug up, and some of them might lie scattered about in this place: for, one that was executed as a malefactor,[189]

> "they did not bury him in the sepulchers of his ancestors; but there were two places of burial appointed by the Sanhedrin; one for those that were stoned, and for those that were burnt; and another for those that were killed with the sword, and for those that were strangled; and when their flesh was consumed, they gathered the bones, and buried them in their place;"

that is, in the sepulchers of their ancestors. This place was as infamous as our Tyburn, and to be crucified at *Golgotha*, was as ignominious as to be hanged at Tyburn; which shows to what shame and disgrace our Lord was brought, and what He condescended to bear on our account.

[39] Matt. 27:57

Verse 57. **When the even was come**, &c. The second evening, when it was just on sunsetting; at which time the Jewish sabbath began, and when the bodies of those that were crucified, must be taken down; and if not dead, their bones must be broken, and they dispatched, in order to be interred in the common burying place of malefactors:

there came a rich man of Arimathea: not from thence now, for he lived at Jerusalem; but this was the place of his nativity, or former abode, and from whence he originally came; and is the same with Ramathaim Zophim, and Ramah, and was the birthplace of Samuel the prophet, *1 Sam. 1:1,19*, and is by the Septuagint called Armathaim, in *1 Sam. 1:1,3,19; 8:4; 15:34; 16:13; and 28:3*. His character, as *a rich man*, is particularly mentioned, not merely to show that such men may be, and sometimes are, instances of the grace of God; much less in a way of boasting, that such a man was attached to Jesus; but rather to point out the reason, how he came to have such easy access to Pilate, and to succeed in his business with him; as well as to observe the accomplishment of a prophecy, in *Isa. 53:9*;

named Joseph; the same name with one of the patriarchs, the sons of Jacob; between whom there was a resemblance, not only as good men, but in their observance of funeral rites and obsequies; the one in those of his father, the

---

[189] T. Bab. Sanhedrin, fol. 43. 1. Maimon. Hilch. Sanhedrin, c. 13. sect. 2, 3.

other in those of his dear Lord and Master. Some think[190] he is the same with *Joseph ben Gorion*, the brother of Nicodemus ben Gorion, often spoken of as a priest, and one of the richest of them in Jerusalem:

who also himself was Jesus' disciple. Though he was only a secret one, as Nicodemus was: he had not as yet, or till now, publicly professed Him, for fear of the Jews, who had made a law, that whoever did, should be cast out of the synagogue; see *Luke 19:38.*

[40] Matt. 27:60

Verse 60. **And laid it in his own new tomb**, &c. Christ was laid not in His own, but in another's tomb; for as in His lifetime He had not *where to lay his head* [*Matt. 8:20*]; so when He was dead, He had no sepulcher of His own to put His body in: and moreover, this shows that as He was born for others, and suffered and died not for Himself, but them; so He was buried for them, as well as rose again for their justification [see *Rom. 4:25*]: and it was a *new* tomb in which He was laid, in which none had been laid before; and was so ordered by providence, for the confirmation of the truth of His resurrection; for had another body been laid there, it might have been said that it was that, and not His that was raised. The Jews distinguish between a new grave, and an old grave:[191]

> "A new grave may be measured, and sold, and divided; an old one may not be measured, nor sold, nor divided: there is a new grave, which is as an old one; and an old one, which is as a new one; an old grave, in which are ten dead bodies, which is not in the power of the owners, lo! this is as a new grave;"

which he had hewn out in the rock; it was usual with the Jews to make their sepulchers in rocks:

> "In the midst (of the court of the sepulcher, they say[192]) two caves are opened, one on one side, and the other on the other; R. Simeon says, four on the four sides; Rabban Simeon ben Gamaliel says, all are לפי הסלע, *according to the rock;*"

---

[190] Alting. Shilo, p. 309.

[191] Massech. Semachto, c. 14. fol. 16. 3.

[192] Mishna Bava Bathra, c. 6. sect. 8.

that is, according to the nature of the rock, out of which the sepulcher is hewn; see *Isa. 22:16*;

and he rolled a great stone to the door of the sepulcher; for the sepulchers were made with doors to go in and out at: hence we often read[193] of הפתח הקבר, *the door of the sepulcher*; and this was not only the custom of the Jews, but of other nations also:[194] the stone rolled to the door, was what the Jews call, גולל, from its being *rolled to, and from* the door of the sepulcher; and which, they say,[195] was a large and broad stone, with which the mouth of the sepulcher was stopped above: and it was at the shutting up of the sepulcher with this stone, that mourning began;[196] and after it was shut with this sepulchral stone, it was not lawful to open it:[197] now this was done by Joseph, to preserve the body from any injury, either from beasts, or from the Jews:

and when he had so done, he,

departed. To his own house; for the sabbath drew on, and there was no more time to do any thing more in this affair. The Syriac version reads these last clauses in the plural number; *they rolled a great stone, and they put it*, &c. and *they* went away; intimating, that Joseph did not do this himself; the stone was too great; but by others, or with their assistance. It may be observed, that all this was done on a feast day; on one of the days of the feast of the passover, when no servile work was to be done; and yet this was agreeable to the Jewish canons, which say,[198]

> "They do all things needful for the dead on a feast day; they shave his head, and wash his clothes, and make him a coffin; and if they have no boards, they bring timber and saw boards of it, silently within doors; and if the person is a man of note, they do it even in the street; but they do not cut wood out of the forest, to saw planks of it for the coffin; nor do they hew stones, to build a tomb with them."

In this case, there was no need for the latter, because the sepulcher in which the

---

[193] Mishna ibid. & Bartenora in Mishna Ohalot, c. 15. sect. 8.

[194] Vid. Kirchman de Funer. Roman. l. 3. c. 15. p. 438.

[195] Bartenora & Yom. Tob. in Mishna Ohalot, c. 2. sect. 4.

[196] T. Bab. Sanhedrin, fol. 47. 2. Maimon. Hilchot Ebel, c. 1. sect. 2. & c. 2. sect. 8.

[197] Vid. Buxtorf. Lex. Rab. p. 437.

[198] Maimon. Hilchot Yom. Tob. c. 7. sect. 15.

body of Christ was laid, had been hewn out of a rock before; but the body was wrapped in a clean linen cloth, and wound up in it with myrrh and aloes to preserve it, and was interred; and so the women on this day, prepared spices and ointments, to anoint it with; though they rested on the sabbath day according to the commandment; but then as soon as that was over, though it was a feast day, they came to the sepulcher with their spices and ointments, *Luke 23:56* and *24:1*.

ENDNOTES ON THE GOSPEL OF MARK

[41]　Mark 6:37

Verse 37. **He answered and said unto them, give ye them to eat**, &c. This He said to try their faith, and make way for the following miracle:

and they say unto him, Shall we go and buy two hundred pennyworth of bread, and give them to eat? This might be just the sum of money they now had in the bag, as Grotius, and others conjecture; and the sense be, shall we lay out the two hundred pence, which is all we have in hand, to buy bread for this multitude? Is it proper we should? Is it thy will that so it should be? And if we should do so, as Philip suggests, *John 6:7*, it would not be enough to give every one a little: wherefore they say this, as amazed that He should propose such a thing unto them: or the reason of mentioning such a sum, as Dr. Lightfoot observes, might be, because that this was a noted and celebrated sum among the Jews, and frequently mentioned by them. A virgin's dowry, upon marriage, was *two hundred pence*;[1] and so was a widow's; and one that was divorced,[2] if she insisted on it, and could make good her claim; this was the fine of an adult man, that lay with one under age; and of a male under age, that lay with a female adult;[3] and of one man that gave another a slap of the face.[4] This sum answered to six pounds and five shillings of our money.

[42]　Mark 6:45

Verse 45. **And straightway he constrained his disciples**, &c. The reasons of this is see in the notes on *Matt. 14:22,*

to get into the ship; in which they came to this place, and which was waiting for them:

and to go to the other side before unto Bethsaida; or rather, *to go to the other side over against Bethsaida*; for they were now in a desert belonging to that city, wherefore they were ordered to go, and did go to the other side of the sea of Tiberias, or Galilee, even to Capernaum, as appears from *John 6:17, 24, 25*;

while he sent away the people. See the note on *Matt. 14:22.*

[43]　Mark 12:41

Verse 41. **And Jesus sat over against the treasury**, &c. The Arabic version reads, *at the door of the treasury*; the place where the chests stood, into which money was put for various uses: there were thirteen chests in the temple;[5] six of them were, לנדבה, *for voluntary oblations*, or *freewill offerings*; for what remained of the sin offering, and of the trespass offering, and of the turtles; for those that had fluxes, and for lying-in women [that is, those who had lately given birth]; and of the sacrifices of the Nazarite, and of the trespass offering for

---

1　Mishna Cetubot, c. 1. sect. 2. & 4. 7. & 5. 1.

2　Ibid. c. 2. sect. 1. & 11. 4.

3　Ibid. c. 1. sect. 3.

4　Mishna Bava Kama, c. 6. sect. 8.

5　Mishna Shekalim, c. 6. sect. 5. & Maimon. & Bartenora in ibid. & Moses Kotsensis, Mitzvot Tora, pr. affirm. 44. & Maimon. Hilch. Shekalim, c. 2. sect. 2, 3.

the leper; and the last was for a freewill offering in general; and into one of these chests, or all them, was the money cast, afterwards spoken of. The Ethiopic version renders it, *over against the alms chest*; but this contribution in the temple, was not for the maintenance of the poor, but for the supply of sacrifices, and other things, as mentioned. Jesus having done preaching, and the Scribes and Pharisees having left Him, and the multitude being dismissed, He sat down, being weary, and rested Himself in this place:

and beheld; with pleasure.

how the people, of all sorts, rich and poor,

cast money into the treasury; into one or other of the above chests: the word rendered *money*, signifies *brass*, which the Jews call, מעות; for they had shekels of brass, as well as silver; and brazen pence, as well as silver pence;[6] and also *prutas*, or mites of brass;[7] and such, the poor woman cast in:

and many that were rich cast in much: they gave very liberally and largely, as they were possessed with much worldly substance; for though religion was at a low ebb with them, yet they took care to support the external and ritual part of it.

[44] Mark 14:3

Verse 3. **And being in Bethany**, &c. Being at a place about two miles from Jerusalem, whither He retired after He had taken His leave of the temple, and had predicted its destruction; a place He often went to, and from, the last week of His life; having some dear friends, and familiar acquaintance there, as Lazarus, and his two sisters, Martha and Mary, and the person next mentioned:

in the house of Simon the leper; so called because he had been one, and to distinguish him from Simon the Pharisee, and Simon Peter the apostle, and others; see the note on *Matt. 26:6*;

as he sat at meat there came a woman; generally thought to be Mary Magdalene, or Mary the sister of Lazarus:

having an alabaster box of ointment of spikenard; or *pure nard*, unmixed

---

[6] Mishna Maaser Sheni, c. 2. sect. 8, 9. & Ediot, c. 1. sect. 9, 10.

[7] Vid. Hottinger de Nummis Heb. p. 118.

and genuine; or *liquid nard*, which was drinkable, and so easy to be poured out; or *Pistic nard*, called so, either from *Pista*, the name of a place from whence it was brought, or from *Pistaca*, which, with the Rabbins, signifies *maste*; of which, among other things, this ointment was made. Moreover, ointment of nard was made both of the leaves of nard, and called *foliate nard*, and of the spikes of it, and called, as here, *spikenard*. Now ointment made of nard was, as Pliny says,[8] the principal among ointments. The Syriac is, by him, said to be the best; this here is said to be,

very precious, costly, and valuable:

and she brake the box. The Syriac and Ethiopic versions render it, *she opened it*; and the Persic version, *she opened the head*, or *top of the bottle*, or *vial*:

and poured it on his head; on the head of Christ, as the same version presses it; see the note on *Matt. 26:7*.

[45] Mark 16:5

Verse 5. **And entering into the sepulcher**, &c. For the sepulchers of the Jews were made so large, that persons might go into them: the rule for making them is this;[9]

> "He that sells ground to his neighbor to make a burying place, or that receives of his neighbor to make a burying place, must make the inside of the cave four cubits by six, and open in it eight graves; three here, and three there, and two over against them: and the graves must be four cubits long, and seven high, and six broad. R. Simeon says, he must take the inside of the cave six cubits by eight, and open within thirteen graves: four here, and four there, and three over against them; and one on the right hand of the door, and one on the left; and he must make, חצר, *a court*, at the mouth of the cave, six by six, according to the bier, and those that bury; and he must open in the midst of it two caves, one here and another there. R. Simeon says, four at the four sides; R. Simeon ben Gamaliel says, all is according to the nature of the rock."

---

[8] Nat. Hist. l. 12. c. 12.

[9] Mishna Bava Bathra, c. 6. sect. 8.

Now it was in the court that the women entered, where the bier was to be put down by the bearers; and where they could look into the sepulcher, and the several caves and graves in it, and what were in them. So Maimonides says,[10]

> "They dig caves in the earth, and make a grave on the side of the cave, and bury in it."

And there being a door into one of these caves, persons might enter in, and see where the graves were, and the bodies lay;

they saw a young man; an angel; as angels used to appear in the form of men: nor is this any contradiction to John's account, who says there were two angels, one at the head, and another at the feet, *John 20:12*; since Mark does not say there was no more than one; besides, John relates what Mary Magdalene saw, when alone, and Mark what all the women saw:

sitting on the right side; from whence we learn, on what side of the door of the sepulcher Christ was laid, according to the above description of one:

clothed in a long white garment: see the note on *Matt. 28:3*; which was as white as snow:

and they were affrighted, At the sight of him; not expecting such a vision, but to have seen the body of their Lord.

---

[10] Maimon. Hilch. Ebel, c. 4. sect. 4.

ENDNOTES ON THE GOSPEL OF LUKE

[46] Luke 2:4

Verse 4. **And Joseph also went up from Galilee**, &c. Where he now lived, and worked at the trade of a carpenter; having for some reasons, and by one providence or another, removed hither from his native place:

out of the city of Nazareth; which was in Galilee, where he and Mary lived; and where he had espoused her, and she had conceived of the Holy Ghost:

into Judea; which lay higher than Galilee, and therefore he is said to go up to it:

unto the city of David; not what was built by him, but where he was born and lived; see *1 Sam. 17:12.*

which is called Bethlehem: the place where, according to *Mic. 5:2*, the Messiah was to be born, and was born; and which signifies *the house of bread*: a very fit place for Christ, the bread which came down from heaven, and gives life to the world, to appear first in. This place was, as a Jewish chronologer says,[11] a *parsa* and half, or six miles from Jerusalem; though another of their writers, a historian and traveler,[12] says, it was two *parsas*, or eight miles; but Justin Martyr[13] says, it was but thirty-five furlongs distant from it, which is not five miles; hither Joseph came from Galilee,

because he was of the house and lineage of David. He was of his family, and lineally descended from him, though he was so poor and mean [*or* lowly]; and this is the reason of his coming to Bethlehem, David's city.

---

[11] Ganz. Tzemach David, par. 2. fol. 14. 2.

[12] R. Benjamin Itin. p. 47.

[13] Apolog. 2. p. 75.

[47] Luke 3:2

Verse 2. **Annas and Caiaphas being the high priests**, &c. Some difficulty here arises, how these two could be both high priests; when, according to the law of God, and the usages of the Jewish nation, there was to be, and was but one high priest at a time: many things are observed by writers, to solve this difficulty. Some go this way: that though according to the divine institution, and the practice of former times, there was but one high priest at a time; yet now, through the corruption of the present age, there were two high priests; or at least, which officiated alternately in the same year: but of such a corruption, no instance can be given, even in those corrupt times; and as Maimonides says, [14] there can be but *one high priest* בכל העולם, *in all the world*; and besides, is contrary to their canons, which were then in being, and still remain; one [15] of which runs thus, אין ממנין שני כהנים גדולים כאחת, *they do not appoint two high priests at once*. Others suppose, that these two annually performed the office of high priest by turns; that Caiaphas was high priest one year, and Annas another: it is true indeed, that through the corruption of those times, this office became venal, hence it is said in the Talmud, [16]

> "Because they gave money for the priesthood, they changed it every twelve months."

And which is more largely expressed by one of their commentators: [17]

> "Because the high priests, who were under the second temple, after Simeon the just, gave money to minister in the high priest's office, and because they were wicked, they did not fill up their years, therefore they changed every year."

But though it is certain, that there were frequent, and sometimes annual changes in the priesthood, hence it is said of Caiaphas, *John 11:49* and *18:13*, that he was *high priest the same year*, yet it does not appear that he and Annas took it yearly by turns: for Caiaphas continued in that office some years, even till after the death of Christ: and besides, had this been the case, as one of them could be but high priest for the year being, both in one year, as here, could not with propriety be said to be high priests. Others take another method, and suppose Caiaphas to be properly the high priest, as he certainly was; and Annas

---

[14] In Mishna Menachot, c. 13. sect. 10.

[15] T. Hieros. Sanhedrin, fol. 29. 1. Maimon. Hilch. Cele Hamikdash, c. 4. sect. 15.

[16] T. Bab. Yoma, fol. 8. 2.

[17] Bartenora in Mishna Yoma, c 1. sect. 1.

so called, because he had been one formerly, the same with *Ananus*, the son of Seth; who was put into the priesthood by Quirinius, in the room of Joazar, and was deposed by Valerius Gratus, and Ishmael ben Phabi was put into his room: but though there may be instances of persons being called high priests, who had been in that office, after they were removed from it, yet no reason can be given, why Annas should be peculiarly called so, when there were in all probability, several alive who had been in that office as well as he; as Joazar his predecessor, and Ishmael ben Phabi, who succeeded Joazar, and after him Eleazar, the son of Annas, and then Simeon ben Camhith; nor why he should be put in the annals of the high priests, in a year in which he was not one. It seems most likely therefore, that he was the *Sagan* of the priests, of which office mention is frequently made in the Jewish writings;[18] yea, we often read of *Chanina*, or *Chananiah*, or *Ananias*, perhaps the same with this *Annas*, who is called, כהנים סגן, *the Sagan of the priests*.[19] This officer was not a deputy high priest, or one that was substituted to officiate occasionally, in the room of the high priest, when any thing hindered him, or rendered him unfit for his office; as on the day of atonement, if the high priest contracted any pollution, they substituted another to minister;[20] which was not the Sagan, but another priest; and even such a one was called an high priest, as appears from the following story.[21]

> "It happened to Simeon ben Camhith (a predecessor of Caiaphas), that he went out to speak with the king, on the evening of the day of atonement, and the spittle was scattered from his mouth, upon his garments, and he was unclean; and his brother Judah went in, and ministered in his stead in the high priesthood; and their mother saw her *two sons*, ביום אחד שני כהנים גדולים *high priests in one day*."

But the Sagan was not an officer *pro tempore*, or so much under the high priest, and one in his stead, as a ruler and governor over other priests. Maimonides says of him thus;[22]

> "they appoint one priest, who is to the high priest as a second to the king, and he is called *Sagan*; and he is called a ruler: and he stands at the right hand of the high priest continually; and this

---

[18] Targum in 2 Kings 23:4; 25:18, and in Jer. 20:1, 3; 29:26, and 52:24.

[19] Mishna Shekalim, c. 6. sect. 1. T. Bab. Yoma, fol. 8. 1. Juchasin, fol. 57. 1.

[20] Mishna Yoma, c. 1. sect. 1.

[21] T. Hieros. Yoma, fol. 38. 4. Megilla, fol. 72. 1. Horavot, fol. 47. 4. T. Bab. Yoma, fol. 47. 1. Bemidbar Rabba, sect. 2. fol. 180. 3.

[22] Hilch. Cele Hamikdash, c. 4. sect. 16.

is an honor to him, and all the priests are under the hand of the Sagan."

The account given of him in the Talmud[23] is this:

"In five things the Sagan ministers; the Sagan says to him, My lord, high priest, lift up thy right hand (that is, when he took the lots out of the vessel for the goats, on the day of atonement,[24] which should be slain); the Sagan is on his right hand, and the father of the Sanhedrin on his left (that is, when he went to the east of the court and the north of the altar,[25] where were the two goats, and the vessel in which were the lots); the Sagan waved with the veils, or linen clothes; the Sagan held him by his right hand, and caused him to ascend (by the steps to the altar); and no man was appointed a high priest, before he was a Sagan."

Now these might be as Seraiah and Zephaniah, the one chief priest, and the other second priest, *Jer. 52:24*, where the Targum and Jarchi interpret the text, the *Sagan* of the priests. And this being an office of such dignity and authority, supposing Annas in it, though he was not *the* high priest, yet being the head of the other priests, he might be called one, and be joined with Caiaphas, and set before him; not only because he had been a high priest, but because he was his father-in-law:

the word of God came to John the son of Zachariah: a priest of the order of *Abia*; and son of Elisabeth, a daughter of Aaron, and cousin of Mary, the mother of Jesus; as it had come formerly to the prophets, and particularly to Jeremiah, who was sanctified from the womb, as the Baptist was: he was blessed with a prophetic spirit, and with the extraordinary gifts of the Holy Ghost, and with a wonderful revelation of the Messiah, and of the Gospel dispensation; and was abundantly qualified for the work he was called to, and sent to perform: and this befell him,

in the wilderness; that is, of Judea, where he had been brought up and lived, and from whence and where he came, preaching: he had lived a solitary life, and had not learned his doctrine from men, but had his mission, ministry, and baptism, from heaven.

---

[23] T. Hieros. Yoma, fol. 41. 1.

[24] Mishna Yoma, c. 4. sect. 1.

[25] Ibid. c. 3. sect. 9.

[48] Luke 7:12

Verse 12. **Now when he came nigh to the gate of the city,** &c. The city of Nain:

behold: there was a dead man carried out; of the city; for they used not to bury in cities, but in places without, and at some distance: the burying places of the Jews were not near their cities;[26] and they had different ways of carrying them out to be buried, according to their different ages: a child under a month old, was carried out in the bosom of a person; if a full month old, in a little coffin, which they carried in their arms; one of a twelvemonth old was carried in a little coffin on the shoulder; and one of three years old on a bier or bed,[27] and so upwards; and in this manner was this corpse carried out: who was,

the only son of his mother; hence the sorrow and mourning were the greater; see *Zech. 12:10*;

and she was a widow; and if she had been supported by her son, her loss was very considerable; and having neither husband, nor son, to do for her, her case was very affecting:

and much people of the city was with her; according to the age of persons, was the company that attended them to the grave: if it was an infant, not a month old, it was buried by one woman, and two men, but not by one man, and two women; if a month old, by men and women; and whoever was carried out on a bier or bed, many mourned for him; and whoever was known to many, many accompanied him;[28] and which was the case of this dead man: he seems to have been well known and respected by the company that attended him to his grave; of these some were bearers, and these had their deputies, and these again theirs; for as they carried their dead a great way, they were obliged often to change their bearers; and of the company, some went before the bier, and others went after it:[29] besides, what served to increase company at a funeral was, that it was looked upon as an act of kindness and mercy to follow a corpse to the grave;[30] to which may be added, and what must always tend to increase the

---

[26] T. Bab. Kiddushin, fol. 80. 2. Gloss.

[27] T. Moed Katon, fol. 24. 1, 2. & Kiddashin, fol. 80. 2. Massech. Semachot, c. 3. sect. 2, 3. Maimon. Hilch. Ebel, c. 12. sect. 10, 11.

[28] Ut in locis supra citatis.

[29] Vid. Mishna Beracot, c. 3. sect. 1.

[30] Maimon. in Mishna Peah, c. 1. sect. 1.

number at such a time, that, according to the Jewish canons:[31]

> "It was forbidden to do any work at the time a dead man was buried, even one of the common people."

[49]   Luke 7:37

Verse 37. **And behold, a woman in the city**, &c. Not Mary Magdalene, spoken of in the next chapter, [*Luke 8*] *verse 2,* under another character; and is a different person, who had not been taken notice of by the evangelist before; nor Mary the sister of Lazarus, who is said to anoint the feet of Christ, and wipe them with her hair, *John 12:3.* The character given of this woman, does not seem so well to agree with her; at least, the fact here recorded, cannot be the same with that; for this was in Galilee, and that in Bethany; this in the house of Simon the Pharisee, that in the house of Lazarus; this was some time before Christ's death, for after this He went a circuit through every city and village; that was but six days before His death, and after which He never went from those parts; nor is this account the same with the history recorded in *Matt. 26:6,* for that fact was done in Bethany also, this in Galilee; that in the house of Simon the leper, this in the house of Simon the Pharisee; that was but two days before the death of Christ, this a considerable time before; the ointment that woman poured, was poured upon His head, this upon His feet: who this woman was, is not certain, nor in what city she dwelt; it seems to be the same in which the Pharisee's house was; and was no doubt one of the cities of Galilee, as Nain, Capernaum, or some other at no great distance from these:

which was a sinner; a notorious sinner, one that was known by all to have been a person of a wicked, life and conversation; a lewd woman, a vile prostitute, a harlot, commonly reputed so: the Arabic word here used, signifies both a sinner and a whore;[32] and so the word *sinners*, seems to be used elsewhere by Luke; see *chapter 15:1-2*, compared with *Matt. 21:31-32.* Some think she was a Gentile, Gentiles being reckoned by the Jews sinners, and the worst of sinners; but this does not appear:

when she knew that *Jesus* sat at meat in the Pharisee's house; having observed it herself, that He was invited by him, and went with him, or being informed of it by others,

---

[31]   Piske Tosaphot Megilla, art. 106. T. Bab. Moed Katon, fol. 27. 2.

[32]   Vid. Castell. Lex. Heptaglott. col. 1195.

brought an alabaster box of ointment: ointment was used to be put in vessels made of *alabaster*, which kept it pure and incorrupt; and this stone was found about Damascus,[33] so that there might be plenty of it in Judea; at least it might be easily had, and such boxes might be common; and as this woman appears to have been a lewd person, she might have this box of ointment by her to anoint herself with, that she might recommend herself to her gallants. The historian[34] reports that,

> "Venus gave to Phaon an alabaster box with ointment, with
> which Phaon, being anointed, became the most beautiful of men,
> and the women of Mitylene were taken with the love of him."

If this box had been provided with such a view, it was now used to another and quite different purpose.

[50] Luke 7:38

Verse 38. **And stood at his feet behind *him*,** &c. Christ lay upon a bed, or couch, as was the custom of the ancients, both Jews and others, at meals, with His feet put out behind; and between the couches and the walls of the room, there was a space for servants to wait and serve, and such are therefore said to *stand at the feet*; and the phrase is used, as descriptive of servants in waiting;[35] and in such a situation this woman put herself, as being also ashamed and afraid to come before Christ, and look Him in the face; and here she stood weeping for her sins, and melted down with the love of Christ to her soul, and at His discourse:

and began to wash his feet with tears: which fell from her eyes in such abundance upon His feet, as she stood by Him that they were like a shower of *rain*, as the word signifies, with which His feet were as it were bathed and washed; His shoes or sandals being off, as was the custom at eating so to do, lest they should daub the couch or bed, on which they lay.[36] Her tears she used instead of water; for it was the custom first to wash the feet before they were anointed with oil, which she intended to do; and for which purpose she had

---

[33] Pliny, Nat. Hist. l. 36. c. 8.

[34] Ælian. var. Hist. l. 12. c. 8.

[35] Vid Alstorphium de lectis veterum, p. 106, 107.

[36] Ibid. p. 123, 124.

brought with her an alabaster box of ointment: it is said[37] of one,

> "when he came home, that his maid brought him a pot of hot water, and he washed his hands and his feet in it; then she brought him a golden basin full of oil, and he dipped his hands and his feet in it, to fulfil what is said, *Deut. 33:24*; and after they had eaten and drank, he measured out oil, &c."

And it is a general rule with the Jews,[38]

> "that whoever anoints his feet, is obliged to washing or dipping."

And did wipe *them* with the hairs of her head; which were long, and hung loose about her shoulders, it being usual and comely for women to wear long hair, *1 Cor. 11:15*. That which was her ornament and pride, and which she took great care of to nourish and put in proper form, to render her desirable, she uses instead of a towel to wipe her Lord's feet, and her tears off of them. A like phrase is used of one by Apuleius,

> *"His verbis & amplexibus mollibus decantatus maritus, lachrymasque ejus suis crinibus detergens, &c.:"*[39]

and kissed his feet. This was no unusual practice with the Jews; we often read of it:[40]

> "R. Jonathan and R. Jannai were sitting together, there came a certain man, ונשק רגלוי, *and kissed the feet* of R. Jonathan."

Again,[41]

> "R. Meir stood up, and Bar Chama, נשקיה אכרעיה, *kissed his knees*, or *feet*."

This custom was also used by the Greeks and Romans among their civilities,

---

[37] T. Bab. Menachot, fol. 85. 2.

[38] T. Bab. Zebachim, fol. 26. 2. Maimon. Hilchot Biath Hamikdash, c. 5. sect. 5.

[39] Metamorph. l. 5.

[40] T. Hieros. Peah, fol. 15. 4. & Kiddushin, fol. 61. 3. T. Bab. Cetubot, fol. 49. 2. Vid. ibid. fol. 63. 1.

[41] T. Bab. Sanhedrin, fol 27. 2.

and in their salutations:[42]

and anointed *them* with the ointment. Which she brought with her.

[51] Luke 10:38

Verse 38. **Now it came to pass, as they went**, &c. As Christ and His disciples went from Jerusalem, having been at the feast of tabernacles, *John 7:2,10,* or at the feast of dedication, *John 10:22,* to some other parts of Judea:

that he entered into a certain village; called Bethany, which was about fifteen furlongs, or two miles from Jerusalem, *John 11:1,18*;

and a certain woman, named Martha: this is a common name with the Jews; hence we read of Samuel bar Martha,[43] and of Abba bar Martha,[44] and of Isaac bar Martha;[45] and of Martha, the daughter of Baithus,[46] who is said to be a rich widow; and this Martha here, is thought by Grotius to be a widow also, with whom her brother Lazarus, and sister Mary lived: though sometimes, this name was given to men; so we read of Martha,[47] the uncle of Rab, who had five brethren; and the same writer observes,[48] that it is not known whether Martha is a man or a woman, but this is determined here:

received him into her house. In a very kind and courteous manner, she being mistress of it; and having known Christ before, or at least had heard much of Him, and believed in Him, as the true Messiah.

---

[42] Vid. Aristophanem in vespis, p. 473. Arian Epictet. l. 3. c. 26. & Alex. ab. Alex. Gen. Dier. l. 2. c. 19.

[43] T. Bab. Beracot, fol. 13. 2. & 25. 2. & Pesachim, fol. 106. 2. Yoma, fol. 19. 2. Juchasin, fol. 76. 2.

[44] T. Bab. Sabbat, fol. 121. 2. Juchasin, fol. 72. 2.

[45] T. Bab. Pesachim, fol. 33. 2. Juchasin, fol. 91. 1.

[46] Mishna Yebamot, c. 6. sect. 4. T. Bob. Yoma, fol. 18. 1. Succa, fol. 52. 2. Cetubot, fol. 104. 1. Gittin, fol. 56. 1. Juchasin, fol. 57. 1.

[47] Juchasin, fol. 99. 1.

[48] Ibid. fol. 105. 1.

[52] Luke 14:15

Verse 15. **And when one of them that sat at meat with him**, &c. One of the Scribes, lawyers, or Pharisees, that were guests at this feast:

heard these things: which were spoken by Christ, and was pleased and affected with them, though he was ignorant:

he said unto him, Blessed *is* **he that shall eat bread in the kingdom of God**. In the world to come, in the kingdom of the Messiah; concerning feasting in which, the Jews had entertained very gross notions; and which this man was reminded of by Christ's making mention of the resurrection of the just, and of recompense at that time, which the Jews expected at the Messiah's coming. They suppose, that God will make a splendid feast, a sumptuous entertainment; in which, besides *bread*, which they call, לחמה של מלכות, *the bread of the kingdom*, and *the bread of the world to come*,[49] there will be great variety of flesh, fish, and fowl, plenty of generous wine, and all sorts of delicious fruit: particularly they speak of a large ox, which they suppose to be the Behemoth in Job, that will then be prepared; and of Leviathan and his mate, which will then be dressed; and of a large fowl, called *Ziz*, of a monstrous bigness; and of old wine kept in the grape from the creation of the world, which will then be drank; and of the rich fruits of the garden of Eden, that will then be served up:[50] such gross and carnal notions have they entertained of the world to come; and which this man seemed to have imbibed, and placed his happiness in.

[53] Luke 16:6

Verse 6. **And he said an hundred measures of oil**, &c. Or, *a hundred baths of oil*, the same quantity as in *Ezra 7:22*, where Aben Ezra[51] calls them, מדות, *measures*, as we do here; and Jarchi[52] observes, that they were, לבלול מנחות, *to mingle with the meal*, or *flour offerings*; which illustrates the above observation, that they were for the temple service; and the bath was the measure of oil, as

---

[49] Midrash Ruth, fol. 33. 2. Bereshit Rabba, sect. 82. fol. 72. 4.

[50] See my Notes on the Targum in Canticles [Song of Solomon] 8:2.

[51] In Ezra 7:22.

[52] In ibid.

the ephah was of wheat;[53] and they were both of the same quantity, *Ezek. 45:11*. According to Godwin[54] it held four gallons and a half; so that a hundred of them contained four hundred and fifty gallons; though some make the measure much larger. Some say the *bath* held six gallons, one pottle, and half a pint; and others, seven gallons, two quarts, and half a pint; and others, nine gallons, and three quarts.

And he said unto him, Take thy bill, or *writing*; which showed the bargain made for so many measures; and which acknowledged the receipt of them, and promised payment:

and sit down quickly; for his case required haste;

and write fifty. Just half; that it might appear he had bought but fifty, and was accountable for no more.

[54] Luke 16:24

Verse 24. **And he cried and said, Father Abraham**, &c. The Jews used to call Abraham their father, and were proud of their descent from him, *Matt. 3:9*; *John 8:33,39*; and so persons are after death represented by them, as speaking to, and discoursing with him; as in the passage cited in the note on [*Luke 16*] *verse 22*; to which the following may be added:[55]

> "Says R. Jonathan, From whence does it appear that the dead discourse with each other? It is said, *Deut. 34:4, And the Lord said unto him, This is the land which I sware unto Abraham, unto Isaac, and unto Jacob, saying*," &c. What is the meaning of the word *saying*? The holy blessed God said to Moses, *Go say to Abraham*, &c."

And here the Jews, in their distress, are represented as applying to him, saying,

have mercy on me, and send Lazarus; which seems to have respect to the

---

[53] Kimchi in Ezek. 45:14.

[54] Moses & Aaron, l. 6. c. 9.

[55] T. Bab. Beracot, fol. 18. 2.

mercy promised to Abraham, the covenant made with him, and the oath swore unto him, to send the Messiah, *Luke 1:72-73;* and which now, too late, these wretched Jews plead, the Messiah being sent already:

that he may dip the tip of his finger in water; in allusion to the washings and purifications among the Jews, and the sprinkling of blood by the finger of the high priest; which were typical of cleansing, pardon, comfort, and refreshment, by the grace and blood of Christ:

and cool my tongue; which had spoken so many scurrilous and blasphemous things of Christ; saying that He was a sinner, a glutton, and a winebibber, a Samaritan, and had a devil; that He cast out devils by Beelzebub, the prince of devils; and that He was a seditious person, and guilty of blasphemy. So the Jews represent persons in hell, desirous of cooling water, and as sometimes favored with it, and sometimes not. They say[56] he that reads *Keriat Shema* (that is, *Hear, O Israel*, &c.), and very accurately examines the letters of it, מצנין, *they cool hell for him*, as it is said, *Psa. 68:14*. And elsewhere,[57] they speak of a disciple, or good man, that was seen after death amidst gardens, and orchards, and fountains of water; and of a publican, or wicked man, seen standing by the bank of a river, seeking ממטי מיא ולא מטי, *to come to the water, but could not come at it*. So Mahomet[58] has a passage that is somewhat like to this text;

> "The inhabitants of hellfire, shall call to the inhabitants of paradise, saying, Pour upon us some water, or of those refreshments God hath bestowed on you."

This man could not so much as get a drop of water to cool his tongue, not the least refreshment, nor mitigation of the anguish of his conscience, for the sins of his tongue:

for I am tormented in this flame. In the destruction of Jerusalem, and calamities at Bither, and other afflictions; together with the wrath of God poured into the conscience, and the bitter remorses of that, for speaking against the Messiah; and which are still greater in hell, where the *worm dies not, and the fire is not quenched* [*Mark 9:48*].

---

[56] Ibid. fol. 15. 2.

[57] T. Hieros. Sanhedrin, fol. 23. 3. & Chagiga, fol. 77. 4.

[58] Koran, c. 7. p. 121. [sura 7:50].

[55] Luke 19:10

Verse 10. **For the Son of man**, &c. Meaning Himself, who was truly man, and the Messiah, and which was one of His names in the Old Testament:

is come: from heaven, into this world, being sent by the Father, and with the full consent and good will of His own:

to seek and to save that which was lost. As all His elect were in Adam, and by their own actual transgressions; and are considered as such, while in a state of unregeneracy: and particularly the lost sheep of the house of Israel are meant, one of which Zacchaeus was; and so the words are a reason of Christ's looking him up, and calling him by His grace, and making a discovery of Himself, and an application of salvation to Him; see *Matt. 18:11*.

[56] Luke 23:33

Verse 33. **And when they were come to the place which was called Calvary**, &c. Called Calvary, or Cranion, which signifies *a skull*; so called from the skulls of persons that lay about, who were executed. It is a tradition of the ancients,[59] that Adam was buried in this place where Christ was crucified, and that his skull lay here. It was usual to crucify on high places, and on mountains, such a one as this was:[60]

there they crucified him, and the malefactors; the two thieves;

one on the right hand, and the other on the left. And so fulfilled the prophecy in *Isa. 53:12*.

[57] Luke 23:46

Verse 46. **And when Jesus had cried with a loud voice**, &c. He cried aloud a second time; for at the first loud cry, he uttered these words, *Eli, Eli, lama,*

---

[59] Cyprian de Resurrectione Christi, p. 479. Hieron. tom. 1. fol. 42. Bar Bahluli apud Castell. Lex. Polyglott. col. 3466.

[60] Lipsius de Cruce, l. 3. c. 13.

sabachthani; and at the second what follows; see *Matt. 27:46,50*, and the notes there;

he said, Father, into thy hands I commend my spirit; not the Holy Spirit, nor His divine nature, but His human soul: for that He had a reasonable soul, as well as a true body, is certain; from His having a human understanding, will, and affections, ascribed to Him; and indeed, without this He would not have been a perfect man, nor like unto us; and could not have been tempted, bore sorrows and griefs, and endured the wrath of God; nor could He have been a Savior of souls: now just as He was expiring, as He made His *soul an offering for sin [Isa. 53:10]*, and which He offered unto God [see *Heb. 9:14*], He committed it to His divine care and protection; and to enjoy His presence, during its separation from His body, using the words of the Psalmist in *chapter 31:5;* and this shows, that His spirit, or soul, belonged to God, the Father of spirits, and now returned to Him that gave it [see *Eccl. 12:7*]; that it was immortal, and died not with the body, and was capable of existing in a separate state from it, and went immediately to heaven; all which is true of the souls of all believers in Christ; and what the dying Head did, dying members may, and should, even commit their souls into the same hands:

and having said thus, he gave up the ghost; breathed out His soul, dismissed His spirit, laid down His life, freely and voluntarily; and which no man, or devil, otherwise could have taken away from Him.

[58] Luke 24:12

Verse 12. **Then arose Peter**, &c. Who, though he did not believe the report made, yet listened to it, and was alarmed and aroused by it, and was willing to know the truth of it:

and ran unto the sepulcher; not alone, but with John, being in haste to be satisfied how things were:

and stooping down; see the notes on *Mark 16:5* and *John 20:5*.

he beheld the linen clothes laid by themselves; in which the body of Jesus was wrapped; these lay by themselves, without the body, in one place; and the napkin about His head was wrapped together, and lay in another place by itself: so that it was a plain case the body was not stolen, nor taken away; for neither friends, nor foes, would have taken the pains, or have lost so much time, as to

725

have stripped the body, but would rather have carried off the clothes along with it. The Alexandrian copy leaves out the word μονα, *alone*, or *by themselves*:

and departed; from the sepulcher to Jerusalem, to John's house there:

wondering in himself at that which was come to pass. That the body should not be there, and yet the clothes should remain; he could not tell what to make of it. As for a resurrection, he had no notion of that, and yet could not account for the removal of the body, either by friends or foes, and the clothes left behind.

ENDNOTES ON ACTS

[59] Acts 3:22

Verse 22. **For Moses truly said unto the fathers**, &c. The Jewish fathers, the Israelites in the times of Moses. The Ethiopic version reads, *our fathers*. This phrase, *unto the fathers*, is left out in the Vulgate Latin and Syriac versions, and in the Alexandrian copy: the passages referred to are in *Deut. 18:15, 19*;

A prophet shall the Lord your God raise up unto you: which is not to be understood of a succession of prophets, as some of the Jewish writers[61] think; for the Jews never had a constant succession of prophets, and those they had, were not like to Moses: but of a single prophet, and so the Targums or Onkelos and Jonathan understood it; but not to be applied to Joshua, as some,[62] or to

---

[61] Jarchi in Deut. 18:15.

[62] Aben Ezra in loc.

Jeremiah,[63] as others, or to David;[64] but to the Messiah, and which is the Lord Jesus Christ, who answers to all the characters: He was a prophet in every sense, who brought a revelation of the divine will, taught the way, and explained the Scriptures of truth perfectly, and foretold things to come; He was raised up by the Lord God of Israel, and was anointed by His Spirit, and sent by Him, and that to the people of the Jews, *to the lost sheep of the house of Israel* [*Matt. 15:24*]; He was the minister of the circumcision:

of your brethren; in the Hebrew text in *Deut. 18:15*, it is also said, *out of the midst of thee*; but as these phrases are synonymous, the apostle here only retains one of them, which suggests that this prophet, the Messiah, should be of Jewish extract; as Jesus was, of the seed of David, and a son of Abraham:

like unto me; that is, to Moses, who is the person speaking, between whom and Christ there is an agreement; the law was given by Moses, and the Gospel came by Christ; Moses was a mediator between God and the people of Israel, and Christ is the *mediator between God and men* [*1 Tim. 2:5*]; Moses, under God, was an instrument of redeeming the people of Israel out of Egypt; and Christ, He is the Redeemer of His people from sin, Satan, and the law, and all their enemies: the Jews[65] have a common saying,

"As was the first redeemer, so shall be the last redeemer;"

and they moreover observe,[66] that,

"As Israel was redeemed in the month Nisan, so they shall be redeemed in the month Nisan;"

in the future redemption by the Messiah. Let the Jews abide by this; the Messiah Jesus suffered in the month Nisan, and obtained eternal redemption for His people. One of their[67] writers has a notion, that when the Messiah comes, there will be the same disposition of the constellations as when Moses brought the people out of Egypt, and gave them the law; and that the conjunction will be of Jupiter and Saturn, in the constellation Pisces. There was likewise between Moses and Christ, an agreement in the miracles they wrought,

---

[63] R. Abraham Seba in Tzeror Hammor, fol. 127. 4. & 143. 4. Baal Hatturim in Deut. 18:15.

[64] Herban. disp. cum Gregent. p. 13.

[65] Bemidbar Rabba, fol. 202. 2. Midrash Ruth, fol. 33. 2. Midrash Kohelet, fol. 63. 2.

[66] T. Bab. Roshhashana, fol. 11, 1. 2.

[67] R. Abraham ben R. Chiia apud Wolfii Hebr. Bibliothec. p. 51.

and in other things:

him shall ye hear in all things, whatsoever he shall say unto you. All His doctrines are to be believed, embraced, and professed; and all His commands are to be obeyed, and all His ordinances submitted to; and this is hearing, or hearkening, to Him in all things, delivered or enjoined by Him.

ENDNOTES ON ROMANS

[60] Romans 5:12

Verse 12. **Wherefore as by one man sin entered into the world**, &c. The design of these words, and of the following, is to show how men came to be in the condition before described, as *ungodly* [*verse 6*], *sinners* [*verse 8*], and *enemies* [*verse 10*]; and to express the love of Christ in the redemption of them; and the largeness of God's grace to all sorts of men: the connection of them is with the forgoing *verse* [*11*], by which it appears that the saints have not only an expiation of sin by the blood of Christ, but a perfect righteousness, by which they are justified in the sight of God; and the manner how they came at it, or this becomes theirs, together with the necessity of their having such a one, are here declared: by the *one man,* is meant Adam the first man, and parent of mankind, who is mentioned by name in *verse 14*; sin which came by him, designs a single sin, and not many, even the first sin of Adam, which goes by different names, as *sin* here, *transgression, verse 14*, the *offense* or *fall, verses 15,17,18, disobedience, verse 19*, and whatever was the first step or motive to it, which led to it, whether pride, unbelief, or concupiscence, it was finished by eating the forbidden fruit; and is called *sin* emphatically, because it contained all sin in it, was attended with aggravating circumstances, and followed with dismal consequences. Hence may be learned the origin of moral evil among men, which comes not from God, but man; of this it is said, that it *entered into the world*; not the world above, there sin entered by the devil; but the world below, and it first entered into paradise, and then passed through the whole world; it entered into men by the snares of Satan, and by him it enters into all the inhabitants of the world; into all men that descend from Adam by ordinary generation, and that so powerfully that there is no stopping of it. It has entered by him, not by imitation, for it has entered into such as never sinned after the similitude of his transgression, infants, or otherwise death could not have entered into them, and into such who never heard of it, as the heathens; besides, sin entered as death did, which was not by imitation but imputation, for all men are reckoned dead in Adam, being accounted sinners in him; add to this, that in the same way Christ's righteousness comes upon us, which is by imputation, Adam's sin enters into us, or becomes ours; upon which death follows,

and death by sin; that is, death has entered into the world of men by sin, by the first sin of the first man; not only corporeal death, but a spiritual or moral one, man in consequence of this, becoming *dead in sin*, deprived of righteousness, and averse, and impotent to all that is good; and also an eternal death, to which he is liable; for *the wages of sin is death* [*chapter 6:23*]; even eternal death: all mankind are in a law [*or* legal] sense dead, the sentence of condemnation and death immediately passed on Adam as soon as he had sinned, and upon all his posterity;

and so death passed upon all men; the reason of which was,

for that, or because *in him*,

all have sinned. All men were naturally and seminally in him; as he was the common parent of mankind, he had all human nature in him, and was also the covenant head, and representative of all his posterity; so that they were in him both naturally and federally, and so *sinned in him*; and fell with him by his first transgression into condemnation and death. The ancient Jews, and some of the modern ones, have said many things agreeable to the apostle's doctrine of original sin; they own the imputation of the guilt of Adam's sin to his posterity to condemnation and death:

> "through the sin of the first man (say they[68]) אתה מת, *thou art dead*; for he brought death into the world:"

nothing is more frequently said by them than that Adam and Eve, through the evil counsel of the serpent, גרימו מותא לון ולכל עלמא, *were the cause of death to themselves and to all the world*;[69] and that through their eating of the fruit of the

---

[68] Debarim Rabba, sect. 9. fol. 244. 2.

[69] Zohar in Gen. fol. 27. 1-4. & 36. 3. 4. & 37. 2. & 46. 4. & 54. 3. & 67. 3. & 86. 1. & 98. 1. in Exod. fol. 106. 1. & 127. 2. in Lev. fol. 46. 2. 3. Bemidbar Rabba, fol. 225. 3. Caphtor, fol. 37. 2.

tree, אתחייבו מותא כל דיירי ארעא, *all the inhabitants of the earth became guilty of death:*[70] and that this was not merely a corporeal death, they gather from the doubling of the word in the threatening, *in dying thou shalt die*, Gen. 2:17 [margin];

> "this doubled death, (say they,[71]) without doubt is the punishment of the body by itself, ולנפש בפני עצמה, and also of the *soul by itself.*"

They speak of some righteous persons who died, not for any sin of their own, but purely on the account of Adam's sin; as Benjamin the son of Jacob, Amram the father of Moses, and Jesse the father of David, and Chileab the son of David;[72] to these may be added Joshua the son of Nun, and Zelophehad and Levi. The corruption and pollution of human nature through the sin of Adam is clearly expressed by them:

> "when Adam sinned, (say they,[73]) he *drew upon him a defiled power*, וסאיב ליה ולכל בני עלמא, and defiled himself and all the people of the *world.*"

Again,[74]

> "this vitiosity which comes from the sin and infection of our first parents, has invaded both faculties of the rational soul, the *understanding* by which we apprehend, and the *will* by which we desire."

This corruption of nature they call יצר הרע, *the evil imagination*, which, they say,[75] is planted in a man's heart at the time of his birth; and others say,[76] that it is in him before he is born: hence Philo the Jew says,[77] that συμφυες το αμαρτανον εστι, *to sin is connatural*, to every man that is born, even though a

---

[70] Targum in Ruth 4:22. & in Eccl. 7:29.

[71] R. Joseph Albo in Sepher Ikkarim, l. 4. c. 41.

[72] T. Bab. Sabbat, fol. 55. 2. Bava Bathra, fol. 17. 1. Zohar in Gen. fol. 36. 4. & Imre Binah in ibid. & 44. 4. & lmre Binah in ibid. & Numb. fol. 83. 2.

[73] Zohar in Gen. fol. 37. 1.

[74] Menasseh ben Israel Praefat. ad lib. de Fragilitate Humana.

[75] Aben Ezra in Psa. 51:5. Abraham Seba in Tzeror Hammor, fol. 14, 3. 4.

[76] T. Bab. Sanhedrin, fol. 91. 2. Bereshit Rabba, fol. 30. 1.

[77] De Vita Mosis, p. 675.

good man; and talks[78] of συγγεγηνηνον κουκον, *evil that is born with us*, and of[79] συγγενεις κηρες, *spots that are of necessity born with* every mortal man. And so his countrymen[80] often speak of it as natural and inseparable to men; yea, they represent Adam as the root and head of mankind, in whom the whole world and all human nature sinned. Descanting on those words, *as one that lieth upon the top of a mast, Prov. 23:34*:

> "This (say they,[81]) is the first man who was ראש לכל בני אדם, *a head to all the children of men*: for by means of wine death was inflicted on him, and he was the cause of bringing the sorrows of death into the world."

And in another place, speaking of Adam, they say[82] that,

> "he was עיקר בריאה של עולם, *the root of the creation*, or *of the men of the world*; and death was inflicted upon him and on his seed, because he sinned one sin in eating of the tree."

And it is observed,

> "that הא הידיעה, the *He* demonstrative is not prefixed in Scripture to proper names, which yet is to the word *Adam*; the reason is, (say they,[83]) because in Adam all his posterity are pointed at, and the whole human species designed."

Again, they observe,[84] that,

> "the end of man is to die, of which this is the reason, because מין האדם, *mankind* has sinned; that is, the nature of which he is composed, or in other words, Adam and Eve have sinned."

One more,[85]

---

[78] De Praemiis, p. 920.

[79] De Nomin. Mutat. p. 1051.

[80] Kimchi in Psa. 51:5. Menasseh ben Israel de Fragilitate, par. 1. p. 2.

[81] Bemidhar Rabba, fol. 198. 3.

[82] Caphtor, fol. 102. 1.

[83] Menasseh ben Israel de termino Vitae, c. 3. sect. 8. p. 198.

[84] En Jaacob, par. 1. fol. 19. 4.

[85] Zohar in Lev fol. 46. 2. R. Menachem Rakanati apud Voisin. Obs. in Pugionem Fidei, p. 590.

"when he (Adam) sinned, כל העולם כלו חטא, *all the whole world sinned*, and his sin we bear;"

and[86] that,

"the whole congregation of Israel have need of atonement for the sin of the first Adam, for he was חשוב ככל העדה, reckoned as the whole congregation;"

which exactly tallies with the apostle's assertion in this text.

ENDNOTES ON 1 CORINTHIANS

[61] 1 Cor. 15:18, 20

Verse 18. **Then they also which are fallen asleep in Christ**, &c. That is, who are dead, and have died in Christ: death is often represented by a sleep, and that more than once in this chapter; and doubtless with a view to the resurrection, which will be an awaking out of it, since it will not be perpetual: some understand this of such only who were fallen asleep, or died martyrs for the sake of Christ and His Gospel; as Stephen, James the brother of John, and others; but rather it designs all such as die in Christ, in union with Him, whether in the lively exercise of faith, or not; of whom it must be said, if Christ is not risen, that they,

are perished. Soul and body; for if there is no reason to believe the resurrection of the dead, there is no reason to believe the immortality of the soul, or a future state; but rather, that the soul perishes with the body, and that there is no existence after death: though should it be insisted on that the soul survives, and shall live without the body to all eternity, it must be in a state of misery, if Christ is not risen, because it must be in its sins; and neither sanctified nor justified, and consequently cannot be glorified, so that the whole

---

[86] Zohar in Gen. fol. 76. 3. & 36. 3.

may be said to be perished; the body perishes in the grave, the soul in hell; but God forbid that this should be said of those, who have either died for Christ, or in Him: can it be that any that are in Christ, that are united to Him, one body and spirit with Him, should ever perish? or those that are asleep in Him be lost? No, those that sleep in Jesus, will God bring with Him at the last day, who shall be for ever with Him, and for ever happy.

Verse 20. **But now is Christ risen from the dead**, As was before proven by ocular [*or* eyewitness] testimonies, and before preached and asserted; and now reassumed and concluded, from the glaring contradictions, and dreadful absurdities that follow the denial of it:

and became the firstfruits of them that slept. Who were already fallen asleep; respecting chiefly the saints that died before the resurrection of Christ; and if Christ was the firstfruit of them, there is no difficulty of conceiving how He is the firstfruits of those that die since. The allusion is to the firstfruits of the earth, which were offered to the Lord: and especially to the sheaf of the firstfruits, which was waved by the priest before Him, *Deut. 26:2;* and to which Christ, in His resurrection from the dead, is here compared. The firstfruits were what first sprung out of the earth, were soonest ripe, and were first reaped and gathered in, and then offered unto the Lord; so Christ first rose from the dead, and ascended to heaven, and presented Himself to God, as the representative of His people; for though there were others that were raised before Him, as the widow of Sarepta's son by Elijah, the Shunammite's son by Elisha, and the man that touched the prophet's bones when put into his grave, and Jairus's daughter, the widow of Nain's son, and Lazarus by Christ; yet as these did not rise by their own power, so only to a mortal life: but Christ, as He raised Himself by His own power, so He rose again to an immortal life, and was the first that ever did so; He was the first to whom God showed, and who first trod this path of life. The firstfruits were the best, what was then ripest, and so most valuable; Christ is the first, and rose the first in dignity, as well as in time; He rose as the head of the body, as the firstborn, the beginning, *that in all things he might have*, and appear to have, as He ought to have, *the preeminence [Col. 1:18]*. The firstfruits sanctified the rest of the harvest, represented the whole, gave right to the ingathering of it, and ensured it; Christ by lying in the grave, and rising out of it, sanctified it for His people, and in His resurrection represented them; they rose with Him, and in Him; and their resurrection is secured by His: because He lives, they shall live also. The firstfruits were only such, and all this to the fruits of the earth, that were of the same kind with them, not to tares and chaff, to briers and thorns; so Christ, in rising from the dead, is only the firstfruits of the saints; of such as are the fruits of His death and of His grace, who have the fruits of His Spirit in them, and are filled with the fruits of righteousness by Him; just as He is the firstborn from the dead, with respect to the many

733

brethren, to whom He stands in the relation of a firstborn: once more, as the allusion is particularly to the sheaf of the firstfruits, it is to be observed, that that was waved before the Lord, the morrow after the sabbath, *Lev. 23:11;* which, as the Jews[87] interpret, was the morrow after the first good day, or festival of the passover; the passover was on the fourteenth day of the month; the festival, or Chagiga, on the fifteenth, and which, in the year that Christ suffered, was a sabbath day also; and the morrow after that, the sheaf of the firstfruits was waved; now Christ suffered on the passover, rested in the grave on the seventh day sabbath, and on the morrow after that rose from the dead, the very day that the first fruits were offered to the Lord: so that the allusion and phrase are very appropriately used by the apostle.

ENDNOTES ON PHILIPPIANS

[62] Phil. 1:23

Verse 23. **For I am in a strait betwixt two**, &c. Life and death; or *between these two counsels*, as the Arabic version reads; two thoughts and desires of the mind; a desire to live, for the reasons above, and a desire to die, for a reason following. The apostle was pressed with a difficulty in his mind about this, as David was when he was bid to choose, either seven years' famine, or three months' flight before his enemies, or three days' pestilence; upon which he said, *I am in a great strait, 2 Sam. 24:14*; to which passage it is thought the apostle alludes; the same word as here is used by Christ, *Luke 12:50*;

having a desire to depart; to die, a way of speaking much in use with the Jews, as expressive of death; thus Abraham is represented by them speaking after this manner, on account of his two sons Isaac and Ishmael, the one being righteous and the other wicked:[88]

> "Says he, If I bless Isaac, lo, Ishmael will seek to be blessed, and he is wicked; but a servant am I, flesh and blood am I, and

---

[87] Targum & Jarchi in Lev. 23:11.

[88] Bemidbar Rabba, sect. 11. fol. 202. 3.

tomorrow אכתר מן העולם, *I shall depart out of the world*, or *die*; and what pleases the holy blessed God himself in his own world, let him do: כשנפטר, *when Abraham was dismissed* or *departed*, the holy blessed God appeared to Isaac and blessed him."

And again it is said,[89]

"Iniquities are not atoned for, until דאתפטר מעלמא, a *man is dismissed*, or *departs out of the world*."

And once more,[90]

"When a man נפטר מזח העולם, *departs out of this world*, according to his merit he ascends above;"

See the note on *John 13:1*. The same word is used in the Syriac version here; death is a *departing* out of this life, a going out of the body, a removal out of this world; it is like moving from one place to another, from the world below to the world above; with the saints it is no other than a removing from one house to another, from the *earthly house* of their *tabernacle*, the body [2 *Cor.* 5:1], to their Father's house, and the mansions of glory in it, preparing for them. Death is not an annihilation of men, neither of soul nor body; it is a separation of them, but not a destruction of either; it is a dissolution of the union between them for a while, when both remain in a separate state till the resurrection. Now this the apostle had a desire unto, which was not a new and sudden motion of mind; it was a thought that had long dwelt with him, and still continued; and this desire after death was not for the sake of death, for death in itself is a king of terrors, very formidable and terrible, and not desirable; it is an enemy, the last enemy that shall be destroyed; it is contrary to nature, and to desire it is contrary to a first principle in nature, self-preservation; but death is desired for some other end: wicked men desire it, and desire others to put an end to their lives, or do it themselves to free them from some trouble they are in; or because they are not able to support themselves under a disappointment of what their ambition or lust have prompted them to: good men desire death, though always when right, with a submission to the will of God, that they may be rid of sin, which so much dishonors God as well as distresses themselves; and that they may be clothed upon with the shining robes of immortality and glory;

and, as the apostle here,

to be with Christ: for the former clause is to be strictly connected with this; he did not desire merely to depart this life, but chiefly to be with Christ, and the former only in order to the latter; the saints are in Christ now, chosen in Him,

---

[89] Zohar in Numb. fol. 51. 3.

[90] Tzeror Hammor, fol. 2. 1.

set upon His heart, and put into His hands; are created in Him, and brought to believe in Him, and are in Him as branches in the vine; and He is in them, formed in their hearts, lives and dwells in them by faith, and they have sometimes communion with Him in private duties, and public worship; He comes in to them and sups with them, and they with Him: but this is only at times, He is as a wayfaring man that continues but for a night; hence the present state of the saints is a state of absence from Christ; while they are at home in the body, they are absent from the Lord, especially as to His bodily presence; but after death they are immediately with Him, where He is in His human nature; and their souls in their separate state continue with Him till the resurrection morn, when their bodies will be raised and reunited to their souls, and be both for ever with Him, beholding His glory, and enjoying uninterrupted communion with Him; which will be the completion and full end of Christ's preparations and prayers: hence it appears that there is a future being and state after death: the apostle desires to depart this life, and *be*, exist, be somewhere, *with Christ*; for the only happy being after death is with Him; if souls are not with Him, they are with devils and damned spirits, in the lake which burns with fire and brimstone: and it is also manifest that souls do not sleep with the body in the grave until the resurrection; the souls of the saints are immediately with Christ, in the enjoyment of His presence, in happiness and glory, hoping, believing, and waiting for the resurrection of their bodies. Had the apostle known that he must have remained after death in a state of inactivity and uselessness, deprived of the communion of Christ and of His church, it would have been no difficulty with him to determine which was most eligible, to live or die; and it would have been much better for him, and more to the advantage of the churches, if he had continued upon earth to this day, than to be sleeping in his grave, senseless and inactive; whereas he adds,

which is far better: to depart and be with Christ is better than to live in the flesh in this sinful world, in the midst of a variety of sorrows and troubles, and in which communion with Christ is but now and then enjoyed, though such a life is better than sleeping in the grave; but upon a soul's departure and being with Christ, it is free from sin and sorrow, and in the utmost pleasure, enjoying communion with Him without interruption; and this is better than laboring in the ministry: for though no man took more pleasure in the work of the ministry than the apostle did, and no man's ministry was more profitable and useful; yet it was toilsome, laborious, and wearisome to the flesh; wherefore dying and being with Jesus could not but be desirable, since he should then rest from his labors, and his works would follow him; at least, it was better for him, and so the Syriac version adds, לי, *to me*, far better for me; and so the Arabic: to live longer might be better and more to the advantage of Christ, the glory of His name, the good of His churches, it might be better for others; but leaving the world, and being with Christ, were better for him; and this was an argument swaying on the side of death, and inclining him to desire that, and made it so difficult with him what to choose.

ENDNOTES ON 1 THESSALONIANS

[63] 1 Thess. 4:13-14

Verse 13. **But I would not have you to be ignorant, brethren,** &c. As they seem to have been, about the state of the pious dead, the rule and measure of mourning for them, the doctrine of the resurrection of the dead, the second coming of Christ, and the future happiness of the saints; wherefore the apostle judged it necessary to write to them upon these subjects: the Alexandrian copy and others, the Complutensian edition, the Vulgate Latin, Arabic, and Ethiopic versions read, *we would not have you to be ignorant*, &c.

concerning them which are asleep; that is, dead: it was in common use among the Eastern nations, when they spoke of their dead, to say they were *asleep*. This way of speaking is used frequently, both in the Old and the New Testament; see *1 Kings 2:10* and *11:43; Dan. 12:2; John 11:11; 1 Cor. 15:20*; and very often with the Targumists; so the Targum on *Eccl. 3:4, a time to weep*, paraphrases it,

"a time to weep על שכיבא, *over them that are asleep*:"

and in *Eccl. 4:2*:

"I praised ית שכיבא, *those that are asleep*,"

the dead: the reason of this way of speaking was, because there is a likeness between sleep and death; in both there is no exercise of the senses, and persons are at rest, and both rise again; and they are common to all men, and proper and peculiar to the body only. The apostle designs such persons among the Thessalonians, who either died a natural death, or were removed by violence, through the rage and fury of their persecutors, for whom their surviving friends were pressed with overmuch sorrow, which is here cautioned against:

that ye sorrow not, even as others that have no hope. The apostle's view is not to encourage and establish a stoical apathy, a stupid indolence, and a brutal insensibility, which are contrary to the make of human nature, to the

737

practice of the saints, and even of Christ and His apostles, and our apostle himself; but to forbid excessive and immoderate sorrow, and all the extravagant forms of it the Gentiles ran into; who having no notion of the doctrine of the resurrection of the dead, had no hope of ever seeing their friends more, but looked upon them as entirely lost, as no longer in being, and never more to be met with, seen, and enjoyed; this drove them to extravagant actions, furious transports, and downright madness; as to throw off their clothes, pluck off their hair, tear their flesh, cut themselves, and make baldness between their eyes for the dead; see *Deut. 14:1;* practices forbidden the Jews, and which very ill become Christians, that believe the doctrine of the resurrection of the dead: the words are to be understood not of other Christians, who have no hope of the eternal welfare of their deceased friends; not but that the sorrow of those who have a good hope of the future well-being of their dear relatives, must and ought to be greatly different from that of others, who have no hope at all: it is observed by the Jews[91] on those words in *Gen. 23:2, and Abraham came to mourn for Sarah,* &c. that,

> "it is not said to weep for Sarah, but to mourn for her; *for such a woman as this, it is not fit to weep*, after her soul is joined in the bundle of life, but to mourn for her, and do her great honor at her funeral; though because it is not possible that a man should not weep for his dead, it is said at the end, *and to weep for her:*"

but here the words are to be understood of the other Gentiles that were in a state of nature and unregeneracy, who had no knowledge of the resurrection of the dead, or and hope of a future state, and of enjoying their friends in it: they are called οι λοιποι, *the rest*; and the Syriac version renders it, *other men.*

Verse 14. For if we believe that Jesus died, and rose again, &c. As every Christian does, for both the death and resurrection of Christ, are fundamental articles of faith; nothing is more certain or more comfortable, and more firmly to be believed, than that Christ died for the sins of His people [see *Matt. 1:21*], and rose again for their justification; on these depend the present peace, joy, and comfort of the saints, and their everlasting salvation and happiness: and no less certain and comfortable, and as surely to be believed, is what follows,

even so them also which sleep in Jesus will God bring with him. The saints that are dead, are not only represented as asleep, as before, but as *asleep in Jesus*; to distinguish them from the other dead, the wicked; for the phrase of sleeping in death, is promiscuously used of good and bad, though most

---

[91] Tzeror Hammor, fol. 23. 4.

commonly applied to good men: and so say the Jews,[92]

> "we used to speak of just men, not as dead, but as sleeping; saying, afterwards such a one fell asleep, signifying that the death of the righteous is nothing else than a *sleep*."

To represent death as a *sleep* makes it very easy and familiar; but it is more so, when it is considered as sleeping *in Jesus*, in the arms of Jesus; and such as are asleep in Him must needs be at rest, and in safety: some join the phrase *in*, or *by Jesus*, with the word *bring*, and read the passage thus, *them that are asleep, by Jesus will God bring with him*; intimating, that God will raise up the dead bodies of the saints by Christ, as God-man and Mediator; and through Him will bring them to eternal glory, and save them by Him, as He has determined: others render the words, *them which sleep through*, or *by Jesus*; or die for His sake, and so restrain them to the martyrs; who they suppose only will have part in the first resurrection, and whom God will bring with Jesus at His second coming; but the coming of Christ will be *with all his saints*; see *1 Thess. 3:13*; wherefore they are best rendered, *them that sleep in Jesus*; that is, *in the faith of Jesus*, as the Arabic version renders it: not in the lively exercise of faith on Christ, for this is not the case of all the saints at death; some of them are in the dark, and go from hence under a cloud, and yet go safe, and may be said to die, or sleep, in Jesus, and will be brought with Him; but who have the principle, and hold the doctrine of faith, are, and live and die, true believers; who die interested in Christ, in union with Him, being chosen and blessed, and preserved in Him from everlasting, and effectually called by His grace in time, and brought to believe in Him; these, both their souls and bodies, are united to Christ, and are His care and charge; and which union remains in death, and by virtue of it the bodies of the saints will be raised at the last day: so that there may be the strongest assurance, that such will God bring with Him; either God the Father will bring them with His Son, or Jehovah the Son will bring them with Himself; He will raise them from the dead, and unite them to their souls, or spirits, He will bring with Him; the consideration of which may serve greatly to mitigate and abate sorrow for deceased friends.

---

[92] Shebet Juda, p. 294. Ed. Gent.

ENDNOTES ON 1 JOHN

[64]   1 John 2:2

Verse 2. **And he is the propitiation for our sins**, &c. For the sins of us who now believe, and are Jews:

and not for ours only; but for the sins of Old Testament saints, and of those who shall hereafter believe in Christ, and of the Gentiles also, signified in the next clause:

but also for *the sins of* the whole world. The Syriac version renders it, *not for us only, but also for the whole world*; that is, not for the Jews only, for John was a Jew, and so were those he wrote unto, but for the Gentiles also. Nothing is more common in Jewish writings than to call the Gentiles עלמא, *the world*; and כל העולם, *the whole world*; and אומות העולם, *the nations of the world*;[93] see the note on *John 12:19*; and the word *world* is so used in Scripture; see *John 3:16*; and stands opposed to a notion the Jews have of the Gentiles, that כפרה אין להן, *there is no propitiation for them*:[94] and it is easy to observe, that when this phrase is not used of the Gentiles, it is to be understood in a limited and restrained sense; as when they say,[95]

> "it happened to a certain high priest, that when he went out of the sanctuary, כולי עלמא, *the whole world* went after him;"

which could only design the people in the temple. And elsewhere[96] it is said,

> "כולי עלמא, *the whole world* has left the Mishna, and gone after the Gemara;

which at most can only intend the Jews; and indeed only a majority of their doctors who were conversant with these writings: and in another place,[97]

> "כולי עלמא, *the whole world,* fell on their faces, but Raf did not fall on his face;"

---

[93]   Jarchi in Isa. 53:5.

[94]   T. Hieros. Nazir, fol. 57. 3. Vid. T. Bab. Succa, fol. 55. 2.

[95]   T. Bab. Yoma, fol. 71. 2.

[96]   T. Bab. Bava Metzia, fol. 33. 2.

[97]   T. Bab. Megilla, fol. 22. 2.

where it means no more than the congregation. Once more, it is said,[98] when

> "R. Simeon ben Gamaliel entered (the synagogue), כולי עלמא,
> *the whole world* stood up before him;"

that is, the people in the synagogue: to which may be added,[99]

> "when a great man makes a mourning, כולי עלמא, *the whole
> world* come to honor him;"

that is, a great number of persons attend the funeral pomp: and so these phrases, כולי עלמא לא פליגי, *the whole world* is not divided, or does not dissent;[100] כולי עלמא סברי, *the whole world* are of opinion,[101] are frequently met with in the Talmud, by which, an agreement among the Rabbins, in certain points, is designed; yea, sometimes the phrase, *all the men of the world*,[102] only intend the inhabitants of a city where a synagogue was, and, at most, only the Jews: and so this phrase, *all the world*, or *the whole world*, in Scripture, unless when it signifies the whole universe, or the habitable earth, is always used in a limited sense, either for the Roman empire, or the churches of Christ in the world, or believers, or the present inhabitants of the world, or a part of them only, *Luke 2:1; Rom. 1:8* and *3:19; Col. 1:6; Rev. 3:10, 12:9* and *13:3*; and so it is in this epistle, *1 John 5:19*; where the whole world lying in wickedness is manifestly distinguished from the saints, who are of God, and belong not to the world; and therefore cannot be understood of all the individuals in the world; and the like distinction is in this text itself, for *the sins of the whole world* are opposed to *our sins*, the sins of the apostle and others to whom he joins himself; who therefore belonged not to, nor were a part of the whole world, for whose sins Christ is a propitiation, as for theirs: so that this passage cannot furnish out any argument for universal redemption; for besides these things, it may be further observed, that for whose sins Christ is a propitiation, their sins are atoned for and pardoned, and their persons justified from all sin, and so shall certainly be glorified, which is not true of the whole world, and every man and woman in it; moreover, Christ is a propitiation through faith in His blood, the benefit of His propitiatory sacrifice is only received and enjoyed through faith; so that in the event it appears that Christ is a propitiation only for believers, a character

---

[98] T. Bab. Horayot, fol. 13. 2.

[99] Piske Toseph. Megilla, art. 104.

[100] T. Bab. Cetubot, fol. 90. 2. & Kiddushin, fol. 47. 2. & 49. 1. & 65. 2. & Gittin, fol. 8. 1. & 60. 2.

[101] T. Bab. Kiddushin, fol. 48. 1.

[102] Maimon. Hilch. Tephilla, c. 11. sect. 16.

which does not agree with all mankind; add to this, that for whom Christ is a propitiation He is also an advocate, *1 John 2:1*; but He is not an advocate for every individual person in the world; yea, there is a world, He will not pray for [*John 17:9*], and consequently is not a propitiation for them. Once more, the design of the apostle in these words is to comfort his *little children* with the advocacy and propitiatory sacrifice of Christ, who might fall into sin through weakness and inadvertency; but what comfort would it yield to a distressed mind, to be told that Christ was a propitiation not only for the sins of the apostles and other saints, but for the sins of every individual in the world, even of these that are in hell? Would it not be natural for persons in such circumstances to argue rather against, than for themselves, and conclude that seeing persons might be damned notwithstanding the propitiatory sacrifice of Christ, that this might, and would be their case. In what sense Christ is a propitiation, see the note on *Rom. 3:25*. The Jews have no notion of the Messiah as a propitiation or atonement: sometimes they say,[103] repentance atones for all sin; sometimes the death of the righteous;[104] sometimes incense;[105] sometimes the priests' garments;[106] sometimes it is the day of atonement;[107] and indeed they are in the utmost puzzle about atonement; and they even confess in their prayers,[108] that they have now neither altar, nor priest to atone for them.

---

[103] Zohar in Lev. fol. 29. 1.

[104] Ibid. fol. 24. 1. T. Hieros. Yoma, fol. 38. 2.

[105] T. Bab. Zebachim, fol. 88. 2. & Erachin, fol. 16. 1.

[106] T. Bab. Zebachim, ibid. T. Hieros. Yoma, fol. 44. 2.

[107] T. Bab. Yoma, fol. 87. 1. & T. Hieros. Yoma, fol. 45. 2, 3.

[108] Seder Tephillot, fol. 41. 1. Ed. Amsterd.

EXPOSITION OF ROMANS

By John Gill

This excellent commentary on the Book of Romans is here published for the first time as a separate volume, complete and unabridged, from Dr. Gill's larger work, *An Exposition of the New Testament*, published by Mathews & Leigh, 1810. Our edition has been completely retypeset in a large, easy to read print, while retaining the wording of Dr. Gill's original text.

John Gill (1697-1771) was by any measure a most exceptional and gifted man of God. His enduring influence justifies the claim that he is one of the greatest theologians to appear in the annals of Christian history. In his *Exposition of Romans*, readers will profit from Gill's industry and patient labor in presenting a sound exegesis of the Word of God. Gill was an eminent Biblical and Rabbinical scholar, and there is no sterile detachment from the precious realities of the Divine life evident here. On the contrary, when Gill writes of Christ and His finished work on the cross and the benefits conveyed to the believer by virtue of being united to Him by grace, his depictions are quite moving and eloquent. Gill neither lived in an ivory tower nor shrank from a loving pastoral care for his hearers. The gospel minister, he wrote, "can not but wish that all that hear him might be converted and saved." His *Exposition of Romans* was written during the course of his regular ministry at the Goat Yard Chapel, Horselydown, from 1720 until 1757, when both he and his devoted hearers moved to their new chapel at Carter Lane. Comprehensive, authoritative and judiciously written, this exposition on Romans will prove to be an invaluable aid in understanding "the way of God more perfectly." (Acts 18:26).

First in the Newport Commentary Series, this 635 page volume is hardbound in Grade B black cloth vellum with gold stamping on the front cover and spine, with a nice two color dust jacket, and is $28.00 plus shipping.

Particular Baptist Press
2766 W. FR 178
Springfield, MO   65810

EXPOSITION OF HEBREWS

by James A. Haldane

This heretofore scarce volume by the esteemed Scottish Baptist James Alexander Haldane (1768-1851) deserves a place among the finest commentaries on this New Testament epistle. Haldane had originally penned this work with a view towards writing a fuller exposition, but died before he could complete the task. Nonetheless these "notes of an intended exposition" alone comprise a full and rich mine of Biblical instruction.

Haldane's correspondence from his latter years revealed "how much his mind was interested in the work" and "had cost him so much thought and pleasant labour." In the book of Hebrews, Haldane reminds us, "the consideration of the surpassing dignity of the Son of God, by whom God had spoken in these last days" (p. 44), is the focal point of this entire epistle. "Believers ought diligently to attend to whatever the Lord Jesus has said in His Word. The Gospel itself is the great truth, the belief of which is salvation, however great men's ignorance in other respects may be; yet nothing which God has said is to be over-looked, but everything is to be attended to as far as it is understood" (p. 45). Haldane, in faithfulness to the text, sets forth Christ as the one true Deliverer from sin as the Savior of His People.

C. H. Spurgeon's classic *Commenting and Commentaries* was originally "compiled for the use of ministers" as an aid in guiding his pastoral students in purchasing the best Bible commentaries for their libraries. Spurgeon was very well-read and well-qualified for such an appraisal. In his introductory "Remarks Upon the Catalog of Commentaries," Spurgeon noted that the books *most heartily recommended* are listed with *** after the book. In this select category was James A. Haldane's *Exposition of the Epistle to the Hebrews* (1860), to which Spurgeon appended the following comments: "a posthumous work issued not as a finished exposition, but as 'notes of an intended exposition.' Very valuable for all that."

Out of print since the first edition of 1860, this quality facsimile reprint is produced from Spurgeon's own personal copy, to which is added Haldane's work on "The Duty of Self-Examination." Black cloth with gold stamping on front cover and spine in a color dust jacket. 424 pages - $26 plus shipping.

Our second volume in the Newport Commentary Series.

EXPOSITION OF GALATIANS

James A. Haldane

James A. Haldane was in the last few years of his life when he penned this excellent Exposition of the Epistle to the Galatians. His stated desire in writing this commentary on Paul's epistle was that it might "prove useful in leading any of the Lord's people to a more diligent study of the Scriptures, and to a clearer understanding of the relation of the old and new covenants." What makes Haldane's *Exposition of Galatians* unique among all others is his handling of its major premise - that in confusing and even mixing the Old Covenant with the New, many Christians have been led astray not only on Law and Grace, but in the very nature of the New Testament church and her ordinances. "This epistle," wrote Haldane, "and that to the Hebrews, contain a full exposition of the Mosaic dispensation, and its relation to the kingdom of Christ. Had these epistles been understood, the corruption of the Gospel, and the ordinances of Christ, would not have taken place; but in them and the rest of the New Testament, a highway is prepared for the followers of Jesus to retrace their steps, and to be guided by "the pattern showed to them in the mount," where the voice from the excellent glory proclaimed, "This is my beloved Son, *Hear Him!*"

This fine exposition is appended with other good works by Haldane, including *Judaism and Christianity* and *Reasons for a Change in Sentiments Regarding Baptism*, directly relating to these important subjects, and that which relates his own spiritual journey to a solid New Testament foundation.

This is the third volume in the *Newport Commentary Series*. 480 pages, cloth vellum with dust jacket. $27.00 plus shipping

MINUTES OF THE PHILADELPHIA BAPTIST ASSOCIATION 1707 - 1807

Edited by A. D. Gillette

NEWLY EXPANDED & ILLUSTRATED EDITON

Altogether the membership of the five constituting churches of the Philadelphia Association in 1707 would probably not have exceeded 300 persons. But taking the Biblical admonition not to despise the day of small things, this "feeble band," in forming the Philadelphia Baptist Association, set themselves on a course of growth and influence the full scope of which they could not have foreseen at the time. The Association became a pattern in the development of other early associations, and as an advisory body its influence extended throughout the whole of the incipient United States - in doctrine, polity, education and missions. Historian Henry C. Vedder has well stated that, "From 1741 the influence of the Philadelphia Association was paramount," to which he also added, "Its missionary zeal was great; men closely connected with this body, and fully believing its Confession, became preachers of the gospel in New England, New York, and the Carolinas. By the close of the century, the Calvinistic party was in the ascendency everywhere."

It is mainly due to the diligent labors of Abram Dunn Gillette (1807-1882) that this valuable book has come down to us as part of the legacy of our Regular Baptist history. As pastor of the Eleventh Baptist Church of Philadelphia, Gillette was chairman of a six-member committee appointed in 1843 by the association to collect its early minutes for publication. He was also selected as editor for the project. The Baptist Encyclopedia characterized this book as "a work of great labor and of unusual value."

What makes this edition so collectible? To enhance the usefulness of this book we have enlarged the text by 15%, set in a 7 X 10 format to aid readability. We have also replaced the original 8 page index with a new greatly expanded and comprehensive 75 page index including a complete index of persons (with over 1,100 entries), a complete index of churches, a subject index and a scripture index. In addition we have included 25 illustrations of early pastors and meeting-houses of the Association during this period, and two maps, showing member churches. It is hard bound in a grade B cloth vellum, acid free paper, marble end sheets and individually shrink wrapped. This valuable volume is $38 plus shipping.

THE THREE MRS. JUDSONS

by Arabella Stuart

Particular Baptist Press has completely retypeset this excellent inspiring missionary story from the 1875 edition. We have added 24 pictures and documents, plus two important historical appendices. Appendix A is the sermon that was preached at the ordination of Adoniram Judson, Luther Rice and other missionaries in February 1812. Appendix B is the *Sermon on Baptism* by Adoniram Judson, after he had become a Baptist. 375 pages, 6 X 9 in grade B vellum hard bound on acid free paper. $24 plus shipping.

THE LIFE & WORKS OF JOSEPH KINGHORN

Volume I

Edited by Terry Wolever

This excellent work is a reprint of the mid nineteenth century edition of Martin Wilkin's biography of Kinghorn. Kinghorn was an early supporter of William Carey and the modern missions movement, as well as a notable scholar. His ability in the Word was much in demand by his peers and much respected by those with whom he differed. He was considered second only to John Gill in his rabbinical learning and was one of the godliest of pastors.

When complete this will be a four volume set. Volumes 3 and 4 will contain the complete debate between Kinghorn and his good friend Robert Hall over the communion issue. Mr. Kinghorn took issue with Hall's *open communion* position and a congenial, thorough debate followed. Both sides will be presented, so that any interested person will get the best arguments of each position from these two scholars.

Vol I is a hard bound, grade B cloth vellum work on acid free paper. 530 pages. $24.50 plus shipping.

THE ANNUAL REGISTER OF INDIAN AFFAIRS
1835-1838

Isaac McCoy

For the first time these four Annual Registers are made available in one volume.

Those who are familiar with early American Baptist history, especially the history of missions, will recognize the name of Isaac McCoy as one of the most important in our American heritage.

These registers are a treasure of first hand accounts of everything that relates to the Indians of the Midwest. McCoy started the first Baptist church in the Indian Territory and his work is timeless and extremely valuable, though almost unknown today.

The material contained in these rare volumes, predates most of what is available today on Indians. The registers were privately printed, so that very few originals exist. We are honored to make them known. They are essential for any school, college or library whose curriculum requires information of early Indian affairs or mission work among the Indians.

Particular Baptist Press of Springfield, Missouri, has made clean facsimile copies and have had them hard bound in green grade B cloth vellum, printed on acid free paper, and completely indexed. They are $55.00 each plus shipping.

HISTORY OF BAPTIST INDIAN MISSIONS

by Isaac McCoy

Completed in 1839 and published the following year, Isaac McCoy's *History of Baptist Indian Missions* constitutes one of the most original and valuable contributions ever made to the literature of the American Indian or to the annals of missionary endeavor.

"The author resided more than twenty years among the Ottawas, Pottawatomies, and Miamis as a missionary. During this period, he kept a journal of events and incidents of Indian life, which with his letters and reports, formed a great mass of material from which to form his history. It is largely composed of the records of personal experience; but is far from being a mere missionary report of religious progress. It is in fact the work of a highly intelligent man, who recorded with the judgment of a historian, while he labored with the zeal of an ecclesiastic; and the result of his early philosophical observations has been, to give us a very valuable record of the characteristic traits of the Indian tribes he lived among. The first forty pages are occupied with remarks on the origin of the Indian tribes. The awfully rapid destruction of the aboriginal race, by contact with the whites; the murders, the debauchery, and the superstition of the Indians, as well as the nobler traits, receive a large share of the author's attention."

Thomas W. Field

An Essay Towards An Indian Bibliography, Being a Catalogue of Books Relating to the History, Antiquities, Languages, Customs, Religion, Wars, Literature, and Origin of the American Indians (New York: Scribner, Armstrong, and Co., 1873), p. 255

Reading the story of Isaac and Christiana McCoy and of their compassionate and heroic labors in the face of such tremendous adversity is an unforgettable experience.

Particular Baptist Press has expanded McCoy's work by adding to this new edition a Biographical Introduction and Epilogue, a complete index of persons and subjects, a genealogy of Isaac and Christiana, as well as a number of black and white and color illustrations, all making this the most useful and collectable edition of this enduring work now available.

Grade C cloth bound vellum, with attractive dust jacket, 690 pages, acid free paper, $37 plus shipping